D0341483

Sinclair Lewis: An American Life

Books by Mark Schorer

SINCLAIR LEWIS: AN AMERICAN LIFE

THE WARS OF LOVE

WILLIAM BLAKE: THE POLITICS OF VISION

THE STATE OF MIND

THE HERMIT PLACE

A HOUSE TOO OLD

McGraw-Hill Book Company Inc.

Sinclair Lewis

AN AMERICAN LIFE

BY Mark Schorer

New York, Toronto, London

SINCLAIR LEWIS: AN AMERICAN LIFE

COPYRIGHT © 1961 BY MARK SCHORER

PRINTED IN THE UNITED STATES OF AMERICA.

ALL RIGHTS RESERVED. THIS BOOK OR PARTS

THEREOF MAY NOT BE REPRODUCED IN ANY FORM

WITHOUT PERMISSION OF THE PUBLISHERS.

LIBRARY OF CONGRESS

CATALOG CARD NUMBER: 61-12961

FIRST EDITION

55549

This book is for my children,

Page and Suki,

who in the long course of its

composition became a man

and woman

Permissions

I AM GRATEFUL to the following publishers, authors, and authors' representatives for permission to quote from the works named below:

A Peculiar Treasure, copyright 1938, 1939 by Edna Ferber. Copyright © 1960 by Morris L. Ernst, et al., Trustees. All rights reserved.

Across the River and Into the Trees, Ernest Hemingway, by permission of Jonathan Cape, Ltd.

American Memoir, Henry S. Canby, by permission of Houghton Mifflin Company.

"America's Nobel-Man," Ernest Boyd, *Vanity Fair,* May 1931; copyright © 1931 by The Condé Nast Publications, Inc.; reprinted by permission of The Condé Nast Publications, Inc.

Ann Vickers, Sinclair Lewis, by permission of Michael Lewis and Jonathan Cape, Ltd.

Arena, copyright 1940 by Hallie Flanagan, by permission of Duell, Sloan & Pearce, Inc.

Arnold Bennett, Reginald Pound, by permission of William Heinemann, Ltd., and Harcourt, Brace & World, Inc.

Arrowsmith, Sinclair Lewis, copyright 1924, 1925 by The Designer Publishing Company, copyright 1925 by Harcourt, Brace & World, Inc., copyright 1952, 1953 by Michael Lewis, by permission of Jonathan Cape, Ltd.

As I Remember It, James Branch Cabell, by permission of Archer House, Inc.

Babbitt, Sinclair Lewis, copyright 1922 by Harcourt, Brace & World, Inc., copyright 1950 by Sinclair Lewis, by permission of Jonathan Cape, Ltd.

Before I Forget, Burton Rascoe, copyright 1937 by Burton Rascoe; reprinted by permission of Doubleday & Company, Inc.

Bethel Merriday, Sinclair Lewis, by permission of Doubleday & Company, Inc., and Jonathan Cape, Ltd.

Cass Timberlane, Sinclair Lewis, by permission of Random House, Inc. and Jonathan Cape, Ltd.

Chronicles of Barabbas, George H. Doran, by permission of Holt, Rinehart & Winston.

Civilization in the United States, Harold Stearns, by permission of Harcourt, Brace & World, Inc.

"Dickens at Work," C. P. Snow, *New Statesman,* July 27, 1957, by permission of *New Statesman* and the author.

Disturber of the Peace, William Manchester, by permission of Harold Matson Company.

Dodsworth, Sinclair Lewis, copyright 1929 by Harcourt, Brace & World, Inc., copyright 1956 by Michael Lewis, by permission of Jonathan Cape, Ltd.

Elmer Gantry, Sinclair Lewis, copyright 1927 by Harcourt, Brace & World, Inc., copyright 1954 by Michael Lewis, by permission of Jonathan Cape, Ltd.

"*Elmer Gantry:* A Reassessment," Mark Schorer, *New Republic,* October 31, 1955, by permission of the *New Republic.*

Exile's Return, Malcolm Cowley, rev. ed., by permission of The Viking Press, Inc.

Free Air, Sinclair Lewis, copyright 1919 by Harcourt, Brace & World, Inc., copyright 1947 by Sinclair Lewis.

From Main Street to Stockholm, Letters of Sinclair Lewis, 1919-1930, ed. Harrison Smith, copyright 1952 by Melville H. Cane and Pincus Berner, Harcourt, Brace & World, Inc.

Garrets and Pretenders, Albert Parry, by permission of Dover Publications, Inc.

Gideon Planish, Sinclair Lewis, by permission of Random House, Inc. and Jonathan Cape, Ltd.

Gift of Life, William E. Woodward, by permission of E. P. Dutton & Co., Inc.

Green Hills of Africa, Ernest Hemingway, by permission of Jonathan Cape, Ltd.

Half a Loaf, Grace Hegger Lewis, by permission of the author.

Hudson River Bracketted, © 1929 Edith Wharton; renewed 1957; by permission of A. Watkins, Inc.

"I'm an Old Newspaper Man Myself," Sinclair Lewis, *Cosmopolitan,* April and May 1947, by permission of *Cosmopolitan.*

Intellectual Vagabondage, Floyd Dell, copyright 1926 by George H. Doran Company; by permission of Doubleday & Company, Inc.

It Can't Happen Here, Sinclair Lewis, by permission of Doubleday & Company, Inc. and Jonathan Cape, Ltd.

Journalist's Wife, Lilian T. Mowrer, William Morrow & Company, Inc., 1937; copyright 1937 by Lilian T. Mowrer; by permission of William Morrow & Company, Inc. and the author.

Kingsblood Royal, Sinclair Lewis, by permission of Random House, Inc. and Jonathan Cape, Ltd.

Laughter in the Next Room, Sir Osbert Sitwell, Atlantic Monthly Press, by permission of Little, Brown & Company.

Letters of Ellen Glasgow, ed. Blair Rouse, by permission of Harcourt, Brace & World, Inc.

Letters of Sherwood Anderson, ed. Howard Mumford Jones and Walter Rideout, by permission of Little, Brown & Company, Mrs. Sherwood Anderson, and Harold Ober Associates.

Letters of Theodore Dreiser, Volume III, ed. Robert H. Elias, by permission of the University of Pennsylvania Press.

Low Man on a Totem Pole, H. Allen Smith, copyright 1941 by H. Allen Smith;

by permission of Doubleday & Company, Inc., and Harold Matson Company.

Main Street, Sinclair Lewis, copyright 1920 by Harcourt, Brace & World, Inc., copyright 1948 by Sinclair Lewis, by permission of Jonathan Cape, Ltd.

"Main Streets and Babbitts of Britain," Sinclair Lewis, syndicated by the United Press International, 1928, by permission of the United Press International.

Mantrap, Sinclair Lewis, copyright 1926 by Harcourt, Brace & World, Inc., copyright 1954 by Michael Lewis, by permission of Jonathan Cape, Ltd.

Memoirs of a Superfluous Man, Albert J. Nock, by permission of Harper & Brothers.

Memories: An Autobiography, Ethel Barrymore, by permission of Harper & Brothers.

More Miles, Harry Kemp, by permission of Sunny Tasha.

My America, Louis Adamic, by permission of Harper & Brothers.

My Lifetime in Letters, Upton Sinclair, by permission of the University of Missouri Press.

Off with Their Heads, Peggy Bacon, by permission of the author.

On Native Grounds, Alfred Kazin, by permission of Harcourt, Brace & World, Inc., and the author.

One American, copyright 1938 by Frazier Hunt, by permission of Simon and Schuster, Inc.

Our Mr. Wrenn, Sinclair Lewis, by permission of Michael Lewis and Jonathan Cape, Ltd.

Paint and Prejudice, C. R. W. Nevinson, by permission of Harcourt, Brace & World, Inc., and Methuen & Co., Ltd.

Paris Salons, Cafes, Studios, Sisley Huddleston, by permission of J. B. Lippincott Company.

Paris Was Our Mistress, Samuel Putnam, by permission of The Viking Press, Inc.

Party of One, Clifton Fadiman, by permission of The World Publishing Company, Fadiman Associates, Ltd., and the author.

Personal History, Vincent Sheean, Doubleday & Company, Inc., 1935; copyright 1935 by Vincent Sheean; reprinted by permission of the author and A. D. Peters.

Preface to the Past, James Branch Cabell, by permission of Archer House, Inc.

Prejudices, Fifth Series, H. L. Mencken, by permission of Alfred A. Knopf, Inc.

Samuel Clemens of Hannibal, Dixon Wecter, by permission of Houghton Mifflin Company.

Selected Letters of Stephen Vincent Benét, Charles Fenton, by permission of Yale University Press.

Selected Short Stories, Sinclair Lewis, by permission of Doubleday & Company, Inc., and Jonathan Cape, Ltd.

Semi-Centennial, Leonard Bacon, by permission of Harper & Brothers.

"Sinclair Lewis and the 'Labor Novel,'" Ramon Guthrie, *Proceedings of the American Academy of Arts and Letters and the National Institute of Arts and Letters,* Second Series, Number Two, 1952; by permission of the American Academy of Arts and Letters and the author.

"Sinclair Lewis and the Method of Half Truths," *Society and Self in the Novel,* ed. Mark Schorer, by permission of Columbia University Press.

"Sinclair Lewis at 17," John G. Olmstead, Oberlin *Alumni Magazine,* October 1954; by permission of the Oberlin *Alumni Magazine.*

"Sinclair Lewis Conducts Unusual Sunday School Class," Samuel Harkness, *The Christian Century,* August 5, 1926; copyright 1926 by the Christian Century Foundation; reprinted by permission.

Sinclair Lewis's Dodsworth, dramatized by Sydney Howard, by permission of Harcourt, Brace & World, Inc., and A. Watkins, Inc.

Sinclair Lewis's undergraduate contributions to the *Yale Literary Magazine,* reprinted by permission of the *Yale Literary Magazine.*

Some Experiences, Alfred Harcourt, by permission of Mrs. Ellen Knowles Harcourt.

Stephen Vincent Benét: The Life and Times of an American Man of Letters, 1898–1943, Charles Fenton, by permission of the Yale University Press.

Textual and Literary Criticism, Fredson Bowers, by permission of Cambridge University Press.

The American Adam, R. W. B. Lewis, copyright by The University of Chicago; reprinted by permission of The University of Chicago Press.

The American Novel, Carl Van Doren, by permission of The Macmillan Company.

The Dust Which Is God, William R. Benét, by permission of Alfred A. Knopf, Inc.

"The Emergence, Rise and Decline of the Reputation of Sinclair Lewis," unpublished Ph.D. dissertation by William Couch, Jr., University of Chicago, 1954; by permission of William Couch, Jr.

The End of American Innocence, Henry May, by permission of Alfred A. Knopf, Inc.

The God-Seeker, Sinclair Lewis, by permission of Random House, Inc., and William Heinemann, Ltd.

The Innocents, Sinclair Lewis, by permission of Harper & Brothers.

The Irreverent Mr. Mencken, Edgar Kemler.

The Job, Sinclair Lewis, copyright 1917 by Harcourt, Brace & World, Inc., copyright 1945 by Sinclair Lewis, by permission of Jonathan Cape, Ltd.

The Journals of Arnold Bennett, 1932, 1933, by permission of The Viking Press, Inc., and A. P. Watt & Son.

The Letters of George Santayana, ed. Daniel Cory, by permission of Charles Scribner's Sons.

The Man From Main Street, ed. Harry E. Maule and Melville H. Cane, Random House, Inc.

The Man in the Street, Meredith Nicholson, by permission of Charles Scribner's Sons.

The Man Who Knew Coolidge, Sinclair Lewis, copyright 1928 by Harcourt, Brace & World, Inc.; copyright 1955 by Michael Lewis; by permission of Jonathan Cape, Ltd.

The Prodigal Parents, Sinclair Lewis, by permission of Doubleday & Company, Inc., and Jonathan Cape, Ltd.

The Radical Novel in the United States, 1900–1954, Walter Rideout, by permission of the Harvard University Press.

"The 'Sauk Centricities' of Sinclair Lewis," Charles Breasted, *Saturday Review,* August 14, 1954; by permission of *Saturday Review* and the author.

The Trail of the Hawk, Sinclair Lewis, copyright 1915 by Harcourt, Brace & World, Inc., copyright 1943 by Sinclair Lewis, by permission of Jonathan Cape, Ltd.

The Tumult and the Shouting, George Slocombe, by permission of the author.

The Twenties: American Writing in the Postwar Decade, Frederick J. Hoffman, by permission of The Viking Press, Inc.

The Way It Was, Harold Loeb, copyright 1959, by permission of Criterion Books, Inc.

The World of George Jean Nathan, George Jean Nathan, by permission of Alfred A. Knopf, Inc.

"The World of Sinclair Lewis," Mark Schorer, *New Republic,* April 6, 1953, by permission of the *New Republic.*

Three Worlds, Carl Van Doren, by permission of The Viking Press, Inc.

Time and the Town, Mary Heaton Vorse, by permission of A. Watkins, Inc.

To the Best of My Memory, Albert P. Terhune, by permission of Harper & Brothers.

"To Thersites" by Henry van Dyke from *Henry van Dyke* by Tertius van Dyke, copyright 1935 by Tertius van Dyke, by permission of Harper & Brothers.

Troubadour, Alfred Kreymborg, by permission of the author.

"Two Houses, Two Ways," Mark Schorer, *New World Writing,* Number 4, by permission of The New American Library of World Literature, Inc.

With Love from Gracie, Grace Hegger Lewis, by permission of Harcourt, Brace & World, Inc.

Work of Art, Sinclair Lewis, by permission of Doubleday & Company, Inc. and Jonathan Cape, Ltd.

World So Wide, Sinclair Lewis, by permission of Random House, Inc. and William Heinemann, Ltd.

Yankee Priest, Edward F. Murphy, copyright 1935 by Edward F. Murphy; reprinted by permission of Doubleday & Company, Inc.

You Can't Go Home Again, Thomas Wolfe, by permission of Harper & Brothers.

Foreword

THIS BOOK BEGAN IN 1951, I later discovered—began in Berkeley, California, in the house of Mr. and Mrs. Joseph Henry Jackson, who had invited me to dine with Edward C. Aswell, then the Editor-in-Chief of the Trade Department of the McGraw-Hill Book Company. The book, or at least the idea that I could write such a book, began with him, and not many months later he wrote to ask whether I could come to New York to meet Melville H. Cane and Pincus Berner, the executors of the Sinclair Lewis Estate, who would have to be persuaded that I could write a book not unworthy of the potentialities of the Sinclair Lewis papers, which they controlled and which Lewis had willed to Yale University. I, too, had to be persuaded. At an amiable luncheon we discussed the nature of the Lewis papers no less than the nature of the possible biographer, and all parties were persuaded. For the contractual arrangements that followed, I am indebted to Bernice Baumgarten, that most intelligent and effective of literary agents whose loss to domesticity from publishing circles is every day lamented in New York and in the hearts of many more than a score of writers throughout the United States. But my first debt (if debt it is; at that luncheon I said to myself that I could write this book in about two years; it took, all details of an author's part in bookmaking considered, over nine) is to Melville H. Cane and Pincus Berner, not only for their interest and cooperation, but for the right to use any and all unpublished material by Sinclair Lewis that appears in this book, and all other literary properties of the Lewis Estate.

My next debt is to Edward C. Aswell, who is now dead. Many other people who kindly helped me, through reminiscence or through the loan of documents, are also dead now, beyond my gratitude. These include Joseph Warren Beach, Bernard Berenson, Donald Brace, Jonathan Cape, Charles Fenton, Alfred Harcourt, John G. Olmstead, Laurel Kells, Sonya Levien, Claude B. Lewis, Arturo Loria, John Marquand, H. L. Mencken, Douglas M. Moffat, Elizabeth Nowell, and Katherine Powers.

I have omitted the name of that one among the dead who is the most important of all: Dorothy Thompson Kopf, Sinclair Lewis's second wife, who died in Lisbon on January 30, 1961. I did not meet Dorothy Thompson until I was writing about her, when she graciously received me. The experience was extraordinary. I think that I have known no other woman who was so completely without vanity. I have known no other woman who could speak of her past as though it were the past of someone else. That she opened all her papers to me and gave me permission to use anything in them that I pleased is a measure of her detachment. That in the course of our many meetings we became true friends is a measure of my blessings. In October of 1960 she finished reading an uncorrected copy of the typescript of this book; if she read it with approval and finished it in tears, may I, at least, regard this as some measure of its success?

The materials that Dorothy Thompson made available to me make of her a collaborator; but a book such as this is by its nature a collaboration with many others. I want next to thank the two other women who were closest to Sinclair Lewis: his first wife, Mrs. Telesforo Casanova, who also most kindly let me examine her Lewis materials (which she has since deposited in the Humanities Research Center of the University of Texas as The Grace Hegger Lewis-Sinclair Lewis Collection), was more than tolerant in answering my many questions, and has permitted me to quote from unpublished materials as well as from her novel of 1931, *Half a Loaf;* and Marcella Powers, Lewis's younger friend in his late years, who, again, was candid beyond any expectations that a biographer might have, and gracious in letting me read and use all of Lewis's letters to her over the period of about ten years that marked their association. These women, too, I hope, are now my friends.

Others who kindly let me use unpublished letters or other manuscript materials are Mrs. Sherwood Anderson and Harold Ober Associates (her late husband's letters to Lewis and Lewis's in reply); Sir Norman Angell (his letter to Lewis); C. Waller Barrett (Lewis's letters to Clara Carpenter, the Lewis materials in his William E. Woodward papers, and Lewis's letter to Guy Holt); Mrs. Stephen Vincent Benét and Brandt and Brandt (Stephen Vincent Benét materials); Mrs. J. D. Beresford (letters to Lewis from her late husband); Van Wyck Brooks (his letter to Lewis); The City Bank of Portage, Wisconsin, Trustee of the Estate of Zona Gale Breese (letters from Zona Gale to Lewis); Janice Biala Brustlein (a letter from Ford Madox Ford to Lewis, and Lewis's reply); Kenneth Cant (his Lewis correspondence); General John E. Dahlquist (his letter to Lewis); Floyd Dell (his letters to Lewis); Edna Ferber and Morris L. Ernst, Trustee, (her letter to Lewis); Norman Foerster (his Lewis correspondence and recollections); E. M. Forster (his letter of congratulation to Lewis); Waldo Frank (his letter to Lewis and his recollections to me); A. S. Frere (his Lewis correspondence); Ruth Goodman Goetz (letters from her father, Philip Goodman, to H. L. Mencken); Carl Haessler (Lewis's letter to him, and his correspondence with me); Edith Haggard (her letter to Lewis and her recollections to me); Halsey, Lightly & Hemsley for the John Galsworthy Estate (letter from John Galsworthy to Lewis); Mrs. Alfred Harcourt, Hastings Harcourt, and Holt, Rinehart & Winston (Lewis's early letters to Mrs. Harcourt when she was Ellen Eayrs, Lewis's letters written to Alfred Harcourt before the founding of Harcourt, Brace and Howe, Inc., and Harcourt's letters to Lewis); William W. Howells, on behalf of the William Dean Howells Estate (Howell's letter to Lewis); the Rupert Hughes Estate (Hughes's letter to Lewis); Margot Johnson (letter from Lewis to her); Mildred Y. Johnson (the letter to Stephen Vincent Benét from her late husband, Malcolm Johnson); Clyde F. Kelley (a letter from Edith Summers Kelley to Louis Adamic); Freeman and Virginia Lewis (an enormous collection of letters from Lewis to his parents); Michael Lewis (a letter to his mother and certain of his father's works now in copyright to him); Nicholas C. Lindsay (the letter to Lewis from his late father, Vachel Lindsay); Frederick F. Manfred (an unpublished anecdote); W. Somerset Maugham (his letters to Lewis); Gene Baker McComas (her extensive Lewis correspondence); August Mencken and the Mercantile–Safe Deposit and Trust Co., Baltimore (the letters of H. L. Mencken); Mrs. Douglas M. Moffat (the note to Lewis written by her late husband); Julia Haydon Nathan (Lewis's letters to George Jean Nathan); Harold Ober Associates on behalf of the F. Scott Fitzgerald Estate (Fitzgerald's letter to Lewis); Mrs. Celeste Phelps Osgood on behalf of the Estate of her uncle, William Lyon Phelps (Phelps's letters to Lewis); James Roers (his letter to a friend, Lewis's letters to him, and his recollections to me); Katherine Cook Ryan (her mother's diary); James Schevill (a letter in French to his father, Rudolph Schevill, and one from his father to Brush); Irving Shephard (the Jack London part of the exchange with Lewis); Upton Sinclair (his letters to Lewis); Eva Holmquist Smith (her diary); Mrs. Loring E. Staples (Lewis's many letters to her when she was Mary Baxter); Mark Sullivan, Jr. (letter from his father to Lewis); the Estate of Booth Tarkington (letters from Tarkington to Lewis); Allan Updegraff (his letters to Lewis and his recollections to me); Mark Van Doren (his brother Carl's letters to Lewis, and his own recollection to me); A. Watkins, Inc., New York, on behalf of the heirs of the Edith Wharton Estate (Edith Wharton's letters to Lewis); and again, Armitage Watkins (Lewis's letters to Ann Watkins); Marjorie Wells and A. P. Watt and Son, on behalf of the executors of the H. G. Wells Estate (Wells's letter to Lewis). All these documents continue, of course, to be the possessions of their owners and cannot be published without their permission.

Some older friends than the new associates for which this book is responsible cannot be thanked warmly enough for their encouragement and assistance: Bessie Z. Jones, Ruth Newhall, Daniel Aaron, that master of historical fact, B. H. Lehman, that master of prose, and above all, my best friend in this world and out, David Park, now dead, too.

Writing such a book as this is often a dogged process, full of ennui and pain; but it has this saving element of pleasure, the making of new friends. There are few names on the following long list of people whom I wish to thank for helping me who have not also made my life brighter and sometimes more exciting because I had the privilege of coming to know them. For the time they gave me out of their lives, either in oral reminiscence or in written recollection or in the kind of personal interest that persuades one to go on and to go on as well as one can, I am indebted to John Aaker, Harold Acton, Stella Adamic, Samuel E. Allen, Elsa Anneke, Newton Arvin, Allen Austin, Frank Babcock, Mrs. Leonard Bacon, Peggy Bacon Brook, Commendatore Enrico Barfucci, Nellie Barnes, Hamilton Basso, Dagmar Beach, S. N. Behrman, Reverend Mr. George E. Beilby, Laura Benét, Primrose Billwiller, Dorothy Walton Binder, Agnes S. Birkhead, Kenneth M. Birkhead, Reverend Mr. Earl Blackman, Phyllis Bottome, Ernest Brace, Charles Breasted, Joseph Brewer, Mrs. C. A. Broaddus, Robert M. Buck, George W. Bunn, Jr., Roger Burlingame, Fanny Butcher, James M. Cain, Dr. Benjamin Camp, Robert Cantwell, Hodding Carter, Horace R. Cayton, Bennett Cerf, Herbert Cerwin, C. C. Champine, Mitchell V. Charnley, Clara Claasen, James Mitchell Clarke, Alan C. Collins, William E. Collins, Ida Kay Compton, Marc Connelly, Barnaby Conrad, Thomas Costain, William Couch, Malcolm Cowley, George Cukor, Edna Larson Cunningham, Mrs. Herbert Dancer, Virginia Dean, Clarence R. and Mary Decker, June Oppen Degnan, Elizabeth Deegan, Paul de Kruif, August Derleth, John Dos Passos, William Dozier, Ben DuBois, Robert H. Elias, Ernestine Evans, Helen Everitt, William T. Evjue, Clifton Fadiman, H. A. Farr, Herbert Feinstein, Dr. Morris Fishbein, Don Martinelli Fosco, Lewis Galantière, Lewis Gannett, Felicia Geffen, Brendan Gill, Arnold Gingrich, Dorothy Gish, Lillian Gish, Brigadier General John N. Greeley, Horace Gregory, Dr. Paul Gross, Ramon Guthrie, Emily Walker Haberman, Markham Harris, Stuart Harris, Edward H. Hart, James D. Hart, Rupert Hart-Davis, Molly Costain Haycraft, Elizabeth E. Heffelfinger, Anthony Henderson, Malcolm C. Henderson, Irma H. Herron, John Hersey, B. W. Huebsch, Granville Hicks, Serrell Hillman, Arthur Sullivant Hoffman, Lyne S. S. Hoffman, Arthur Hornblow, Jr., Mrs. Sydney Howard, James H. Hull, Frazier Hunt, Virginia Radcliffe Hurst, Robert M. Hutchins, Inez Hayes Irwin, Mrs. Katherine Gauss Jackson, Gunnar Johansen, Lawrence C. Jones, Hannah Josephson, Norman Katkov, Robert Knittel, Blanche W. Knopf, Frederick Kuh, Lawrence Langner, Asher and Barbara Lans, Prof. Dr. Vincenzo Lapiccirella, William C. Lengel, Catharyn Lewis, "William Lindholm," Louis Lochner,

Stephen Longstreet, Dan Longwell, Leonard Lyons, John B. McConaughy. Ken McCormick, A. D. MacGibbon, J. R. M. MacGibbon, Miriam McGrail, St. Clair McKelway, William McNally, Luther Mansfield, Signora Elizabetta Mariano, Herbert R. Mayes, Gorham Munson, Edward F. Murphy, S.S.J., Ruth Cole Nash, Clara Nelson, Sir Harold Nicolson, Judge Mark Nolan, Frances O'Brien Garfield, John O'Hara, Irving S. Olds, Theodore O'Leary, George Oppenheimer, Mary F. Parton, Frances Perkins, Robert E. Pfeiffer, Samson Raphaelson, Daniel Reed, Charles Rembar, Ferdinand Reyher, Reverend Mr. and Mrs. Sturges Riddle, Meta Ries, Samuel Rogers, William A. and Louise Rosenthal, Dr. and Mrs. Peyton Rous, Dore Schary, Margaret Culkin Banning Salsich, Calvin E. Schorer, Emilio Segrè, George Seldes, Gilbert Seldes, Robert Shaplen, Diana Sheean, Dr. Walter M. Simpson, Henry Nash Smith, Paul C. Smith, William Jay Smith, Sterling Sorenson, George Soule, Mils Ståhle, Betty Stevens, Anna Louise Strong, Newton Taylor, James Thurber, Chauncey B. Tinker, Dr. Cornelius H. Traeger, Lady Una Troubridge, Louise Untermeyer, Irita Van Doren, Carl Van Vechten, Mary Heaton Vorse, Dale Warren, Morris R. Werner, Rebecca West, Poppy Cannon White, Ronald J. Williams, Peter Wolfe, Fay Wray

Libraries, too, become "friends," in a curious way, when one is plugging away at a long job. My most obvious debt here is to the Sterling Library at Yale University, to James T. Babb, the librarian, and to the American Literature Collection and its kindly and highly educated and interested curator, Dr. Donald C. Gallup. To the Yale University Library I am indebted for permission to use in this book not only all the unpublished Lewis material that the Library contains, but also for manuscript materials, which I use as well, from Sherwood Anderson, Sir Norman Angell, F. Scott Fitzgerald, Ford Madox Ford, Van Wyck Brooks, William Rose and Stephen Benét, J. D. Beresford, Floyd Dell, A. S. Frere, Waldo Frank, Norman Foerster, Edna Ferber, E. M. Forster, Zona Gale, John Galsworthy, William Dean Howells, Rupert Hughes, Vachel Lindsay, Jack London, Douglas M. Moffat, W. Somerset Maugham, William Lyon Phelps, Upton Sinclair, Mark Sullivan, Booth Tarkington, Allan Updegraff, Arthur Vandenberg, and Carl Van Doren.

At the University of California, I am especially indebted to the patient people at the General Reference Desk in the Doe Library—and particularly to Allen Covici, Geraldine Clayton, Margaret Kahn, Audrey Phillips, Virginia Pratt, Myra Kolitsch, and Priscilla Yu—and to the very helpful people in the Inter-Library Borrowing Service—Jeannot Myles and Mrs. M. D. Uridge.

To the Bancroft Library of the University of California I am indebted for permission to quote from Lewis's letter to Tom Mooney; to the Cornell University Library for the letters of George Jean Nathan; to the Baker Library, Dartmouth College, for Ramon Guthrie's collection of Lewis "labor novel" material; to the Houghton Library, Harvard, for Eldon

James material; to the Huntington Library, San Marino, California, for the already mentioned London-Lewis material and for the Gene Baker McComas collection of Lewis letters; to the University of Indiana Library for Lewis letters to Edith Summers, Upton Sinclair, and Mrs. Upton Sinclair; to the University of Illinois Library for Lewis's letters to H. G. Wells; to the University of Kansas Library for inscriptions to Wells in gift copies of *It Can't Happen Here* and *Arrowsmith;* to the Newberry Library, Chicago (and Mr. Stanley Pargellis), for Lewis's letters to Sherwood Anderson, Floyd Dell, and Harry T. Webster; to the library of the New York Academy of Medicine for the key to the characters in *Arrowsmith;* to the Berg Collection in the New York Public Library (and John Gordon) for Lewis's letters to Hugh Walpole, F. L. Lucas, and David Karsner, and to the Manuscript Division, for Lewis's letters to Harriet Ford; to the University of Minnesota Library for Lewis's inscriptions in copies of seven of his novels; to the University of Pennsylvania Library for material in the Theodore Dreiser papers; to the Firestone Library of Princeton University for early Lewis-Harcourt exchanges, for Lewis and Dorothy Thompson letters to Christian Gauss, for Lewis's letter to the unidentified "Hans," for Lewis's letters to Carl Van Doren, Eleanor Wylie, and Booth Tarkington, and for Lewis's "reader's report" on Benét's *The Dust Which Is God;* to the William Allen Neilson Library of Smith College for Lewis's letter to Margot Johnson; to the Library of the University of Southern California (and especially to its curator of rare books and manuscripts, Lloyd A. Arvidson) for Lewis's letters to Hamlin Garland and to Gordon R. Young, and for the privilege of borrowing a collection of Lewis short stories in tear sheets; to the Humanities Research Center of the Library of the University of Texas for Lewis inscriptions in novels that he gave to Grace Hegger Lewis, and for the Lewis-Hergesheimer correspondence; and finally to the Library of Congress for Lewis's letter to Groff Conklin and for the inscription to Jean Hersholt in a copy of *Cass Timberlane* and in a copy of the privately printed "Launcelot."

Elsewhere I acknowledge publishers, authors, and authors' representatives for permission to quote from published works. My great debt to publishers is to those firms that published Sinclair Lewis: Harper and Brothers; Harcourt, Brace and World, Inc.; Doubleday and Company, Inc.; Random House, Inc.; Jonathan Cape, Ltd.; and William Heinemann, Ltd. They have all permitted me to quote as I needed from the Lewis titles that they published, and their editors have been kind beyond measure in their personal interest. I wish to say that I am especially indebted to Miss Catherine McCarthy, the delightful and unrecorded historian of Harcourt, Brace and World.

The fact that one mentions money only toward the end of one's list of indebtedness does not mean that one is least grateful for it. I must begin with my gratitude for the Fulbright Award that sent me to Italy in 1952–

1953 and enabled me to follow Lewis's fleeing steps through southern Europe in his last years; then thanks to the Regents of the University of California for a sabbatical leave of half a year in 1955, when I was enabled to begin the actual writing of this book; then—most magnificently! —to the Center for Advanced Study in the Behavioral Sciences, where I was a Fellow during 1958–1959, the greatest year of my life from the point of view of stimulation and the wish to work, with every possible implement conducive to activating that wish arranged for (thank you, Ralph Tyler, Preston Cutler, Jane Kielsmeyer, and all the other "guardians" in that fair place); to the American Philosophical Society for a grant that made possible some of my many necessary excursions to the scattered seats of information; to the Bollingen Foundation for a fellowship in 1960 to assist me in the completion of this book while I remained on leave from the University of California after my year at the Center; and to the American Council of Learned Societies for a grant that helped me defray the expenses of preparing the manuscript.

The individuals who worked most intimately with me as research assistants, informed secretaries, and willing helpers of one sort or another, I have not yet mentioned. Their aid was indispensable. They are: Ann W. Barnard, Olga Champlin, Carol Hart Field, Miriam Gallaher, Marian Grodzins, Kathryn Montgomery, Carol Nathan, Claire Rosenfield, Marcia Rothenberg, and cheerfully industrious Robert Hogan.

I want to thank, too, my friend and agent, Carol Brandt; my sympathetic young editor at McGraw-Hill, Robert Gutwillig; his superb copy editor, checker, and indexer, Edward Schneider; and Man Ray, for permitting the use of his photograph of Sinclair Lewis on the dust jacket.

Finally, a book such as this almost always involves a few people whose faithful efforts put them somewhere beyond the proprieties of gratitude; for better or worse for them, they become, if they have not already been, part of oneself. I name three: Ann Goolsby, Joan Warmbrunn, and Ruth Page Schorer, the last of whom, in the long course of it, took a degree in what is called "library science," the more effectively to help me. W. B. Yeats wrote:

> Though Pedantry denies,
> It's plain the Bible means
> That Solomon grew wise
> While talking with his queens.

Charming Yeats! If I had more such women as have helped me with this book or more time than the time that I will have with one of them, even I might hope to become moderately wise.

8 June 1961 *Mark Schorer*
Berkeley, California

"People especially reporters are always asking me this question, do aviators have imagination? I'm not sure I know what imagination is. It's like this stuff about 'sense of humor.' Both phrases are pretty bankrupt now. A few years ago when I was running a car I would make believe I was different people, like a king driving through his kingdom, but when I'm warping and banking I don't have time to think about making believe. Of course I do notice sunsets and so on a good deal but that is not imagination. And I do like to go different places; possibly I take the imagination out that way—I guess imagination is partly wanting to be places where you aren't—well, I go when I want to, and I like that better."

—Carl Ericson's "Diary,"
The Trail of the Hawk, 1915.

"Now begins the journey!"

ONE

Small Town

I

HE WAS A QUEER BOY, always an outsider, lonely. Once he had become famous, he began to promulgate an official view of his youth that represents perhaps an adult wish for an inoffensive life that never was, a mild and happy fantasy of a "totally normal boyhood—dull school routine, skating, sliding, skiing, swimming, duck-hunting." But could a "totally normal boyhood" have produced such a wild man, at once so mad and so unhappy? He was a queer boy with only one real friend in a town full of boys, laughed at by girls and particularly by that one of them toward whom his puppy love groped out through all his adolescence.

He was nearly six feet tall before he was sixteen, with a short torso set on very long and spindly legs, and weighed only a hundred and twenty pounds; lank and lean, but with a puffy, acne-ridden face ("pimples," they said), big feet and hands, badly coordinated in his movements, everything about his body hanging and dangling and swinging and lunging and stumbling, and ice-blue eyes (astigmatic) rather protruding, all of this thatched with a carrot-colored wig. Or perhaps his own phrase, from an early story, is more exact: "hair like a new copper cent." Nicknames pursued him: Harry to his family and Hal to his few friends, he was first Doodle, then Mink or Minnie, then Ginger, then Bonfire, finally Red. He was the original reuben of the joke books and the itinerant vaudeville troupe of that time, and the butt of every crude piece of horseplay. He, whose work was one day to illustrate Constance Rourke's conception of American humor, was himself, first of all, an illustration of it. He was lonely. He became Sinclair Lewis.

No figure in American letters of the past fifty years is more familiar than that of the Moon-Calf, the sensitive and misunderstood adolescent who is driven into his brooding, introspective life by the bleak, inapposite realities of the life around him. Our literature nearly persuades us that this is the first agony of American life—the second agony may well be the learning to live with fantastic success. Since the literary account derives immediately from the biographical experience, one has in mind not only a familiar novelistic type but the authors of many novels, Sherwood Anderson and George Willard, Thomas Wolfe and the nearly indistinguishable Eugene Gant, Floyd Dell and Felix Fay at once. But Sinclair Lewis was to write no *Moon-Calf,* was almost never to write subjective autobiography; as a boy, he was expelled from rather than repelled by his environment, ejected rather than rejecting. In him we have the doubly pathetic sight of a youth who is driven into an inner world even more bleak and barren than the exterior world that expelled him, who would gladly have chosen that world. And this difference from the novelistic pattern was to make for the real enigma of his novels, a persistent conflict of values that clashed no less within him.

He was born in Sauk Centre, Minnesota, at the end of an unseasonable thaw and the beginning of a long and bitter cold spell: February 7, 1885. Thirty years before, there was nothing here but native earth, rolling prairie, roving Indians, a crossing of stagecoach trails. Then, in 1857, at the point where the Sauk River widens into the nine or ten miles of Big Sauk Lake, the first settlers came—seven New Englanders who called themselves the Sauk Centre Townsite Company. On a bluff rising above the reedy swamplands and the sand flats of the river's swell they established the first residence in this place, an excavation lined with poles. In July of 1857 a first general meeting of settlers organized the Sauk Valley Claim Association, and before the rigor of Minnesota winter locked them in, they had begun the construction of a dam and had built a log house on the river bank. When the ice broke up in the spring of 1858 it swept away the partially constructed dam, but a post office was established in that year, the first frame residence went up in the next, and in 1860 a new dam was finished, a small sawmill was put into operation, and the first blacksmith shop. In 1861 one Joseph Casper built the first general store, and Nellie Pendergast, the first white child, was born.

All over the Midwest such Gopher Prairies as this were then coming into being in this fashion, and once begun, their growth, up to a certain point, was rapid. Sometimes there was a last frightened skirmish with an earlier history, as when, in Sauk Centre in 1862, an Indian outbreak brought the settlers in the vicinity scurrying into the village and a stockade was built around the general store, with several houses and a small military post within the enclosure. Generally, however, things moved on. In 1863 the townsite of Sauk Centre was laid out and plotted, and in that year, too, a small gristmill was built to accommodate the wheat fields that were fanning out on all sides of the town. German immigrants arrived in 1863, and in 1865, with the cessation of the Civil and the Indian wars, immigrants of other nationalities. A first school meeting had been held in 1861 (a Minneapolis girl became the first teacher, boarded by the lowest bidder at ninety cents a week), in 1869 the School District of the Town of Sauk

Centre was organized and chartered by the state, in 1870 the first school building was erected under the new charter, and in 1881 the first class was graduated from the high school. In 1869 a group of villagers formed the Bryant Library Association, membership fees being a dollar a year for men, fifty cents for ladies. Named after William Cullen Bryant, the library had as its first book an autographed copy of the poems of that worthy—which later was stolen. The name remained; bylaws were drawn up in 1879, and in 1880 the Bryant Public Library was organized and a tax of one mill per citizen was voted to support it. The prevalence of piety in this village, which was incorporated only in 1876 and had held no elections before then, is evidenced in the fact that by 1890 it contained eight churches. With tidy if accidental symmetry, eight liquor licenses had been granted immediately upon the organization of the Village Council.

Until 1878, communication with the outside world was by stagecoach to St. Cloud and Melrose, and by Red River carts to the north; but in that year these were largely abandoned when an extension of the St. Paul, Minneapolis and Manitoba Railroad thrust through the town. In 1882, the Sauk Centre Northern came in, the two to be merged presently in the Great Northern, and still in 1882, a third line, the Little Falls and Dakota, a branch of the Northern Pacific, cut through the town from the northeast. In 1884, with power supplied by the mill, a system of waterworks was laid, and in 1889 a system of public sewerage, at first limited to the business district but extended to the whole village in 1903, the year that Harry S. Lewis, eighteen years old, went off to New Haven. In 1905 the Lewis residence achieved a bathroom.

The countryside was beautiful and generous, the once-hard prairie converted now into oceans of waving wheat that held over thirty lakes, like blue islands, within a ten-mile radius of the village. In the winter the land was transformed into quiet, undulating snow fields broken only by an occasional farm house and the stark, tangled branches of a grove. In the summers the deep-blue skies were tumultuous with great white clouds, and the sunsets in the haze of dust were spectacular, the summer moonrise no less so. In the autumn, the golden stubble fields were alive with quail and prairie hens and rabbits, the stands of oak and elm with squirrels, the reedy edges of the lakes full of ducks, and the lakes, of fish. It was a country boy's paradise, this landscape—if he had a country boy's passions and his skills; and if he had them, it was almost impossible not to lead a totally normal boyhood: skating, sliding, skiing, swimming, duck-hunting. . . .

But the village, which was the heart of the land, was ugly—raw and bare and gawky. In the year of Sinclair Lewis's birth the combined population of the village and its township was 2,807, and in 1889 the village was divided into two wards and thus officially became a city. But it was still only a new and ugly village—bleached and parched and sweltering in summer, the temperature mounting sometimes to 110 degrees; gaunt and rutted and cruelly frozen in winter, the temperature falling sometimes to 40 degrees below zero. It had besides its public school, an "academy" and a business college and presently a state school for delinquent and homeless girls. It had its library, its lodge halls, its newspapers, its hotel and its opera house. It had its railroad station, or depot, and its trains, shuttling freight cars, passenger cars that swept to the distant cities and awakened yearnings. It had a small boy named Harry who felt them, and of whom we read in the Sauk Centre *Herald* of April 28, 1898, this account of an early attempt to fulfill them:

> Harry Lewis, the thirteen year old son of the doctor, felt that the United States needs his services in the present Spanish unpleasantness. On Tuesday evening he left a note stating that he had gone to enlist as a drummer boy. He walked down to Melrose and was awaiting an eastward train when his father walked in and dampened his patriotic zeal. . . . The lad had about fifty cents with which to reach the seat of the war.*

When they trotted back into the village, the angry father and the intimidated boy in the buggy, they were greeted by a group of loafing youths who were waiting for them and who now burst into "Yankee Doodle" in derisive unison. And Doodle the boy became.

It is not the first mention of him in the local newspapers. On August 1, 1895, the *Avalanche* (another, sporadically published and short-lived journal) records this:

> What might have been a fatal accident to Master Harry Lewis last Friday was narrowly averted by the prompt action of his brother Claude. It was while they were swimming with several other boys. . . . The bottom shelves off very suddenly at this place and Harry had been warned not to venture beyond his depth, as he could not swim, but he accidentally stepped off into deep water and went down. His disappearance was not at once observed by the boys, but Mr. Al Pendergast, who was watching the bathers, noticed that he did not come to the surface after going down, and, convinced that something was wrong, he spoke to the other boys. Claude was on a springboard and with one quick plunge succeeded in finding the lad and bringing him to the surface, still conscious but dazed and gasping for breath. Harry was a pretty thoroughly scared lad, but as he was otherwise none the worse for the accident it is perhaps not to be much regretted as it taught him a lesson he will not soon forget.

The village had other lessons to teach him than the difficulties of pursuing a totally normal boyhood, and lessons perhaps more incisive. "Is

* Lewis's recollection of the episode in "This Golden Half-Century, 1885–1935" (*The Man from Main Street,* pp. 260–61) is somewhat inaccurate in its details, as his autobiographical remarks frequently are.

it not a fact," ruminates Van Wyck Brooks's Oliver Allston, "that novelists usually thrive best on their irritations?"—and he thinks of Sinclair Lewis as one of his half-dozen exemplars of this axiom in the form of a question. The village taught the young Harry Lewis the lesson of its Main Street, the lesson that Gopher Prairie is indeed not Friendship Village, nor a genteel tradition in American literature the equivalent of American life. Main Street was not paved until 1924; until then it was muddy in the spring and autumn, dusty in the summer, frozen into the ruts of wagon wheels in the winter. It had wooden sidewalks and hitching posts and the continuous twang of the cracker barrel, the splatter of tobacco juice as it hit the cuspidor. It had five or six blocks of false fronts, and that was it for Harry Lewis.

Main Street had, of course, its "other side," as Henry Johnson published a book in 1943 to demonstrate; and, to those critics of *Main Street* who were to complain that Lewis had missed "the fun" of a small town, he wrote his own answer a number of times, most notably in the reminiscence called "The Long Arm of the Small Town" that he contributed to the fiftieth anniversary issue of the high-school annual, the *O-Sa-Ge,* which concludes as follows:

> If I seem to have criticized prairie villages, I have certainly criticized them no more than I have New York, or Paris, or the great universities. I am quite certain that I could have been born and reared in no place in the world where I would have had more friendliness. Indeed, as I look at these sons of rich men in New England with their motor cars and their travel, it seems to me that they are not having one-tenth the fun which I had as a kid, swimming and fishing in Sauk Lake, or cruising its perilous depths on a raft (probably made of stolen logs), tramping out to Fairy Lake for a picnic, tramping ten miles on end, with a shotgun, in October; sliding on Hoboken Hill, stealing melons, or listening to the wonders of an elocutionist at the G.A.R. Hall. It was a good time, a good place, and a good preparation for life.

And, of course, it was—a good preparation for exactly the kind of life that Sinclair Lewis was to live and for the kind of novelist and social critic that he was to become. But when the editors of the volume in which this little sketch was reprinted preface it with a headnote that declares Sinclair Lewis to have been "one of the least sentimental of men," they could not be more mistaken. He was a profoundly sentimental man, not only in the professed preference for a watered-down, post-Tennysonian medievalism that marked his adolescence and lingered until his death, that colored his relations with women and so readily inverted itself into the bleakest cruelty; not only in the conduct of the plots of his novels, where the values which he opposes to the social follies and vices that are satirized are frequently most grossly sentimental; but more particularly—and for complex reasons that derive directly from his youth—in the human-character evaluation that is shown in his life no less than in his novels. "The Long Arm of the Small Town" is a sound account of the life of the boys who were happy there, but it is a sad sentimentalization of the life of the boy who left it, who made it famous, and who never left it.

He learned to swim after a fashion—a splashing dog paddle that always kept him by the shore. Naturally, he emulated his father and brothers and the boys in the town and tried to fish and hunt; but even though he did now and then catch a fish or hit a rabbit, he was much too impatient to be a good fisherman and much too poor a marksman ever to rival his brothers at shooting, and he did not try for long. In his diary for September 2, 1902, we read:

> Started for hunt at 2 P.M. . . . Pa shot 19 chickens. I shot—! Father did some fine chicken shooting—8 birds in 8 shot. 2 together, then after an interval of 10 minutes 4 in about ½ minute (maybe 1 min.), then 2 more in 5 minutes more. I got out of shells before the last 6 birds. Left 'em at home.

Harry's incompetence has its corollary in a strenuous and touching esteem for those normally athletic boys who do easily what he cannot do at all.

> I went with Jim Hendryx on his "Rural Free (Mail) Delivery" route this morning. Went by Osakis Road. . . . The fields & woods are beautiful now, making the trip delightful. Jim was dressed like a "pony-express-rider"—Broad sombrero, brown flannel shirt, open at neck & arms, & belt. His face & hands are bronzed from exposure (Jim will take law at U. of Minn. next year.) He has always been a great hunter, fisher & trapper. He hunted birds eggs, fished, hunted, trapped, rode box cars many times with Claude. He is bro. of Myra Hendryx, son of Chas. F. Hendryx, prop. of *Herald*. . . .*

It is significant that his youth drops away from him very rapidly. There are few references in his diaries to the fifteen years that preceded their first entry. There is an important passage about "key people," to be quoted presently, and there is a brief mention of Mr. Pendergast—"but for whom I had been drowned"—but very few other passages, even brief, of reminiscence. One of the few is:

> This evening being informed that "an old friend wishes to see you" I went over to Pikes and found Judith Crawford, an old playmate. She attended the 4th grade, used to be a champion of all "spelling-down-matches." Stayed at Pikes. We played house together a thousand times in an old oak blue & red dump cart in Pikes yard. I used to be a doctor with rows of bottles, or

* James B. Hendryx was to grow up to be Sauk Centre's other novelist; more prolific even than Sinclair Lewis, he published novel after novel for boys, in which he pictured just such heroes as he himself seemed to be to young Harry Lewis, nature's bronzed noblemen on plain and prairie.

a minister, delivering wordy sermons. She will be a Senior in "Fargo Christian College" Prep. school next year.

Another—and its associations we can only infer, since it appears in no context at all—is:

> Once when I was in 4 or 5 grade Jacobe Bros. had in their show-window a wax facsimile of an electrocution. I called the placard "facsimile," pronouncing it rightly (as I had been so [told] to pronounce it by Father). Another kid looking on said indignantly, "Why that's 'face smile.' When they turn that current on the fellow smiles." As Rocks Woodkey [answered] him that he was quite right I felt very "cheap" & went into the store and besought the Jacobe's to turn on the current.

As the time of his departure from home in 1902 draws close, the diaries tremble with a special kind of sentiment that has not been observable before, a grasping of the familiar that quite naturally accompanies his excitement and his apprehension; but what was familiar to him in his youth was not, apparently, material over which he later lingered with any pleasure.

One does not, of course, wish to suggest a joyless existence: the boy would hardly have survived his tenth year if that had been the fact. And yet the occasions that Sauk Centre provided Harry Lewis for pleasures unburdened by the sense of not being wanted or by his consequent response in a raucous buffoonery, were chiefly the solitary pleasures, notably of reading. Walking he did enjoy, then and all through his life, and picnics he often did, too, and certain kinds of public entertainment of which, in the years between 1885 and his departure from Sauk Centre, the village offered a good many.

There were frequent dances—an annual fireman's dance, a New Year's Dance, an Easter Monday Ball, school dances, public masquerades, and privately sponsored affairs, as when the Married People's Social Club gave a "shirtwaist and necktie party." But ballroom dancing was not one of Sinclair Lewis's accomplishments, either then or later. ("As I cannot dance I just went along with Ma to look on," we read in his diaries.) One can picture him at county fairs and at circuses—the Gentry's World's Greatest Trained Animal Circus and, later, Ringling Brothers'—and possibly at public athletic events like wrestling matches in the opera house, gun tournaments, contests between the two local ladies' basketball teams, and that occasion when a local pickup nine did not hesitate to trounce the visiting Boston Bloomer Girls, since their shortstop and pitcher were both noticeably in need of a shave.

There were frequent public lectures—the lyceum course, university extension lectures, individual lectures, often illustrated with stereoptican views, on such subjects as "An Evening at the World's Fair." And then there were professional entertainers—Miss Leotta Swanton, the noted elocutionist, and Miss Maude Gilkey, the dramatic reader. Concerts and recitals were not uncommon—military bands, the Ski-U-Mah Quartette, the Ladies Musical Club, the Maharas Minstrels, the Alpine Concert, the Orpheus Jubilee Singers, the Schubert Symphony Club and Lady Quartette of Chicago, the Casgrove Company performing with musical glasses, sleigh bells, Marimbaphone, guitars, mandolins and banjoes, the Jonesville Orchestra "with The Ambitious Swede and Silas Hawkins who 'Kaint Keep Still,' " and Miss Edith Adams, the cellist. Besides frequent home talent productions of plays like *The Heart of Arkansaw,* there was a whole miscellany of professional theatrical entertainment, and this was very probably of greatest interest to Harry Lewis: the Aunt Jerusha Company, *Uncle Tom's Cabin* every few years, *East Lynne, Cinderella, The Merry Minister,* Diamond Brothers Minstrels, the Jolly Della Pringle Company in *The Diamond Breaker* and *The Pulse of New York,* Gideon's Big Minstrel Carnival, D. D. Sutton's Company in *Jesse James and Texas, Peck's Bad Boy,* the Girard Theater Company in *Baxter's Girl, Rip Van Winkle,* and *Man's Enemy,* the "Breezy Time" Company, *A Japanese Wedding,* even *The School for Scandal* and Sandford Dodge "and his talented company" in three nights of Shakespearean tragedy and, in other years, *Quo Vadis* and *Virginius.*

There was much rant and perhaps some eloquence, and a share of it unquestionably fell upon the eager ears of young Harry. And yet one cannot say that Main Street claimed this boy. The man, who knew its every cranny as no other inhabitant of that town knew it, had never possessed it, nor it him; the result was that he could never really leave it. On one corner it had a two-story frame building, and the windows of the second floor were the office windows of Dr. E. J. Lewis. The small boy could look up at those windows; and the man of sixty-two, on his last visit to this place in 1947, could propose that under those windows was the proper place for him to stand when he was photographed for a Chamber of Commerce brochure.

2

BEHIND DR. EDWIN J. LEWIS lay a history of considerable peregrination. Indeed, he held his mother, Emeline Johnson, to be in the direct line of descent from Peregrine White, of the "Mayflower" and Plymouth Plantation. More than that is not known of her except that she lived from 1817 to 1886 and that she was married on November 27, 1836. On his father's side Dr. Lewis did not wish to look back beyond his grandfather; he wrote to Sinclair Lewis in 1921, "Candidly I don't think I would care to go any farther back than my grandfather and some day I will tell you why." But there is no record of his ever having told him. That grandfather (Harry's great-grandfather), one Lemuel Lewis, was born in Binghamton, New York, moved in his youth to Westville in Oxford Township, New Haven County, Connecticut, had five sons and a daughter, of whom John Lewis was the eldest, and died there at the age of seventy-five. According to an unpublished and rather extended autobiographical account that Sinclair Lewis put together in 1932, Lemuel Lewis's ancestors were Welsh miners and Yorkshiremen six or seven generations back, but Dr. Lewis had himself written his son about Lemuel, "He was married to a Hawkins but I don't know her first name and I have no trace of the Lewis' beyond him." *

Of the history of John Lewis, Sinclair Lewis's paternal grandfather, we can be somewhat more certain. Born in 1815, he was a farm boy, presumably his father's helper and then heir to the Westville farm, married Emeline Johnson, had five children by her, and in the year of Edwin's birth, 1848, became a member of the New Haven Company, which purchased the barque *Ann Reynolds* and sailed to California, where they arrived in February, 1849. By Sinclair Lewis's account, "he found a little gold but was robbed by a cousin whom he had nursed in sickness, and came back to Connecticut with nothing." After the birth of a sixth child, the family moved in 1857 to Lisburn, Pennsylvania, near Harrisburg, where John established

* In his diary for February 25, 1905, Sinclair Lewis writes of Woodbridge, a town near New Haven, "from which came Father's Mother's Mother."

a match factory. "Failed," notes the grandson bluntly. "To Southern Minnesota, as farmer. . . ."

If the match factory failed, it did not do so for nine years, since, according to the record in the Lewis family Bible, it was not until 1866 that John Lewis removed his family to a farmstead two and a half miles northwest of Elysian, Minnesota, on the banks of Lake Francis and on a thoroughfare known as Cleveland Road. Edwin J. Lewis was then not quite eighteen years old. Having already taught school in the Pennsylvania hills during the previous year, he continued to do that now in Elysian; and then, on December 28, 1873, he married a fellow schoolteacher, Emma F. Kermott, in Waseca, Minnesota, the nearest county seat and her home.

Emma Kermott was born in London, Ontario, on August 30, 1849, the daughter of a woman of Yorkshire descent named Elisabeth Plews, and of a New Brunswick man named Edward Payson Kermott, whose father had emigrated from the Isle of Man during the Napoleonic Wars. (Dr. E. J. Lewis was apparently mistaken when, in 1921, he wrote his son, Sinclair, that the Kermotts were of French descent and had changed their name from Carmode.) Edward Payson Kermott was a physician and dentist (and "also a veternarian and farmer," said Sinclair Lewis) who may, as the Lewis records have it, have come to the United States as a surgeon in the Union Army during the Civil War, or who may, as the Kermott records claim, have sought out the relatively dry climate of Minnesota because he was suffering from tuberculosis. Emma was educated at a nameless female seminary in New York State and then lived with her parents in Waseca until her marriage.

After his marriage to Emma Kermott, Edwin J. Lewis saw little more of Elysian. He taught school at Redwood Falls, sixty miles away, and began to read medicine with a local physician named W. D. Fluin. After the birth of his first son, Fred, in 1875, he enrolled in the Rush Medical College in Chicago, and took his M.D. in 1877. (Many years later, on May 10, 1942, the famous grandson of John Lewis wandered through the cemetery at Elysian in search of the "graves of my paternal grandfather and grandmother—who had a farm here sixty years ago, on which my father worked—and later paid the mortgage!—and where my mother and Fred took refuge while Father was attending Rush Medical College—these graves are humble and hard to find.") For several years, then, very poor and with a second son born in 1878, E. J. Lewis practiced medicine in Ironton, Wisconsin; much later, his sixteen-year-old third son, Harry, made the following record in his secret diaries and gave us a revelation of a breathless, an extraordinary respect:

> . . . when he went to Ironton with a wife and 2 children, 800 dollars in debt, and with $25 in his pocket . . . the people of Ironton (Wis.) welcomed him with open arms, and were very kind to him. They used to come and

take him out and back in their own buggies and wagons. When they did not do this Father would have to walk no matter how far.... Father made his 1st medicine case by getting a small wooden box and fixing it up; putting in 2 oz bottles.... Mother's 1st dressing table was a wooden packing box modified by Father. Father has since paid the debt and become worth 10 or 15 thousand dollars, raised 3 boys, given Claude a college education, had expenses of 2,000 dollars a year for years, and had many other causes for spending money all through his own efforts. If he had not been such a persistent worker, generous father, and lover of education for himself and his boys, I might be working in some factory all day and loafing in a saloon all night.... I have a huge amount of outside work to do in preparation for Wednesday.

Then, in April of 1883, Dr. Lewis visited Sauk Centre alone, and on June 25 he arrived with his family; and regularly each week thereafter the *Herald* carried this notice among the advertising on its front page:

E. J. Lewis
Physician and Surgeon
Sauk Centre—Minnesota

We would call him a "character." Rather cold, rigid, parsimonious, almost compulsively methodical, absolutely without self-questioning, with a dedicated sense of the value of hard work for hard work's sake, and, with that dubious puritanism, a fine sense of professional responsibility—these are the prominent features of Dr. Lewis. We must see this father as the village saw him if we are to begin to understand why the son could never quite see him at all. A contemporary of Sinclair Lewis who lived on in Sauk Centre wrote in 1953:

His father... hadn't any imagination, little conception of a child's point of view, [was] dictatorial, harsh, and a bit cruel. The doctor took himself seriously and that can be so overdone. From statements made by the old doctor, Harry didn't have a bright future; and I think the doctor's feelings were realized by Harry. Perhaps that was the spur that pushed Harry on.

The considerable solemnity with which he regarded himself is perhaps best illustrated by the rigidity of his personal habits. As with Kant in Königsberg, the villagers set their watches by his comings and goings. One correspondent has written:

...the whole town set its clocks by Dr. Lewis's walk down Main Street to his office. On the dot of seven each morning he appeared. When he had lighted the fires and prepared his office for the day, he reappeared and walked home. It was then exactly 7:15. Year in, year out the timing never varied.

Late risers had another opportunity to set their watches.

> It was his custom to leave his office precisely at 11:30 every morning and go home for [dinner]. He would enter the house, change his hat, and emerge with a pail, which he would fill from the well across the street. Day in and day out for years he never varied. Not once did he fail to change his hat. In the dining room of the Lewis home were three pegs, each for one of the doctor's hats . . . the second Mrs. Lewis, it is said, could see no earthly sense in the system. The pegs, however, remained.

They almost certainly did, and probably until his death. Once established, the most casual matter could become a fixity. On a certain day in early November, it is said, no matter what the prevailing temperature, he and, guided by his example, his sons pulled on their heavy underwoolens for the fierce Minnesota winter; and whether there had been an early blizzard before that day or whether that day was simmering in late Indian Summer, that day remained the same. No tyrant, he was yet possessed of an inflexible sense of what was fit and what was not fit, and this sense he imposed upon his family. The father's word was the sons' law. In one place in his diaries, young Harry Lewis writes, *"Hoc pater meus dixit,"* and the formula of acceptance finds many variations in his various utterances. It underlies, in the most profound ways, Lewis the man and the novelist.

The father's redeeming qualities are clear; and clearest among them was his professional passion (". . . for calls under three miles, he walked; over, he rode horseback," wrote his son of the Ironton period), and it was in this connection that he could provide some companionship for his youngest boy. The other two could hunt and fish with him as peers; Harry could ride along in the buggy or the sleigh on country calls, or to the neighboring town of Melrose which the doctor visited once a week. But there must have been many long silences on those rides. It is difficult to believe that there was much easy communion between them. Harry had an eager, active, speculative and rather fantastical intelligence that appealed to nothing in the down-to-earth, rather dour Dr. Lewis. It is said that for really genial adult discussion, the boy turned to his father's chief competitor, Dr. J. A. DuBois, who was temperamentally Dr. Lewis's opposite. Henry Johnson says of him:

> . . . he had once invaded the home of James Russell Lowell and there recited from memory to Lowell himself "A Fable for Critics." . . . one of his own poems had appeared in the *Century Magazine*. . . . His "I'll be there in half an hour" might mean any time the next day or even the next week. In critical cases he was, however, always on time. He was the special friend of the poor and friendless and held theories about them which made him a hater of the social order as it was.

Such a man not only would have appealed to young Harry but also would have found something considerably appealing in the boy, who was not without a smothered sweetness. Dr. DuBois's son says that he would talk and amiably wrangle with Harry on controversial subjects for hours on end, so the boy began to think of him as in some ways closer to him than his own father; and years later, indeed, Sinclair Lewis approached the old doctor and asked him, "Wasn't there some sinning around here late in the spring of 'eighty-four?"

If friendly and somewhat frivolous conversation was not among Dr. Lewis's virtues, we must say of him that he was not a self-engrossed man, self-important as he may have been. He took a reasonably active interest in civic affairs and was at least respected if not warmly loved by his fellow townsmen. Several times they elected him as health officer in preference to the much more attractive Dr. DuBois. At various times he was elected to the school board (he served on its finance and property committees, not its school committee), becoming its president in 1906. He was also elected to the pension examining board and to the library board, and he was among a group appointed to frame a new city charter in 1900. He was not a gregarious man, but he was a member of at least one lodge and sometimes an officer in it.

He had, finally, a genuine respect for education if none whatever for intellectual refinements. He was distressed by the educational fiasco of his oldest son, Fred, and if he was not equally delighted with the success of his second son, Claude, at the University of Minnesota and at Rush, that was only because he expected success. As a schoolteacher, he had accumulated some books. One may wonder whether there were indeed three or four hundred volumes in the Lewis household, as Sinclair Lewis reports in "A Note on Book Collecting," since in an earlier essay, "Breaking Into Print," where Lewis speculates on the origins of his wish to become a writer, he gives us a picture of an almost resolutely unliterary household. He adds, however, this statement: "And my father, though he never spoke of them, did have books in the house."

Some books there certainly were, probably including sets of Scott, Dickens and Goethe, and certainly a volume of Milton bound together with selections from Beattie, Collins, Gray and Young. It was a book that the father had bought as a very young man in Eberly's Mills, Cumberland County, Pennsylvania, and on the flyleaf he wrote at that time, "Read and profit thereby." This book Sinclair Lewis kept until his death.* If the elder Lewis valued education because he associated it with success, and valued literature because he associated it with improvement, his books nevertheless formed the boy's earliest literary preferences and the subjects for his reverie.

* In one of his last efforts at fiction, a fragment called *The Enchantment of Elaine Kent,* Lewis was to transfer the injunction to read and profit to his heroine's *Anthology of Latin Poetry,* given her by her father.

He soon supplemented his father's library with the Bryant Public Library, and through that collection he read his way voraciously. To his statement about his "totally normal boyhood," Sinclair Lewis added: "except for inordinate (and discoordinated) reading: everything from Grote's *History of Greece,* Max Miller's *Chips from a German Workshop,* Tolstoy's *War and Peace,* to *Frank on the Mississippi* and *The Flamingo Feather,* with *David Copperfield, Nicholas Nickleby, Oliver Twist, Ivanhoe,* and Longfellow as favorites." If "normal" means some general pattern of prevailing behavior, this exception demonstrates the eccentricity of Harry Lewis's boyhood. There is a story that he set up a reading stand next to his father's sawhorse and chopping block, and years later his brother Fred allowed himself to be quoted as follows: "We used to feel sorry for Harry. He never hunted or fished. He'd go out to mow the lawn, cut a couple of strips and then read under a shade tree for half an hour." They thought him queer, and they patronized him when they did not bedevil him. His father shared their opinion.

A schoolmate suggested that of his two parents it was with his stepmother that the boy spent much the greater amount of his time. His own mother died on June 25, 1891, when Harry was six years old, and nothing is known of the Sauk Centre life of this faint figure except for the sparse and yellowing record of her end in the files of the newspaper. Like many another woman in the nineteenth century, she had suffered for some years with tuberculosis, and in the spring of 1888 she was stricken with a "pleuratic attack" that developed into "quick consumption." The winter of 1890 she spent in New Mexico, and the winter of 1891 in California and Texas. It was to El Paso that Dr. Lewis was summoned on May 13 with the news of her sudden decline. On May 23 he brought her back to Sauk Centre, "believing the Minnesota climate would be more beneficial at the present time," but she grew feebler and died in a month. One year and twelve days later, on July 7, 1892, Dr. Lewis married a daughter of the house in which he had roomed as a medical student, Isabel Warner, the new mother for his boys now aged sixteen, fourteen and seven.

The household, so frequently motherless and then for a year totally so, was inevitably a lonely one for a small boy, and we may assume that the arrival of a stepmother was viewed as an unmixed blessing. The new Mrs. Lewis seems to have been well suited to her husband's temperament, a kindly and sensible woman if by no means abundantly open in her affections. She was robust and active, of firm opinion, mildly literate, mildly gifted in the appropriate female accomplishments ("Mrs. Lewis played 'Tarentella' [sic] by Heller, a piano solo, at the Musical Club meeting . . ."; "The entire program was admirably arranged and under the supervision of Mrs. E. J. Lewis . . ."; "Mrs. E. J. Lewis read a story on the program for the special Thank Offering service arranged by the Ladies Missionary

Society of the Congregational Church last Friday"; et cetera). She was, her stepson wrote in his maturity, "pleasantly ambitious," and her ambitions found their expression in a good deal of aggressive club and lodge activity. She was instrumental in founding the local chapter of the Order of the Eastern Star, served as delegate to its state conventions and in 1894 became an officer of the Grand Chapter. She was active in the Congregational Church, and she was one of a voluntary committee established "to inspire better grades by promoting a contest in the lower grades" of the school. Her closest interest seems to have been the Gradatim Club.

Sauk Centre had a considerable club tradition. The original pioneer association had been formed for social as well as economic reasons. In 1865 a few women met together to read, and their books formed the nucleus of what was to become the Bryant Library. A glee club was organized in 1868, and in 1869, the Choral Union. In the '70s, a number of women met regularly and studied in a Chautauqua course under the leadership of a local minister. In the late '80s, a number of men and women met in a hall and church as a discussion group and disbanded in the mid-'90s, when dramatic and social clubs began to flourish.

In 1898 a few women, including Mrs. Lewis, assembled under the name of "The Embroidery Club," and in the next year they organized themselves as the W.N.A. Circle, a group limited to twenty-five women who exchanged wisdom on needlework and performed acts of public good. The Gradatim Club, a study group limited to thirty women, had been organized in 1895, with name and motto deriving from J. G. Holland's poem, "Gradatim":

> Heaven is not reached at a single bound;
> But we build the ladder by which we rise
> From the lowly earth to the vaulted skies,
> And we mount to its summit round by round.

A self-improvement group studying such topics as Foreign Lands and Parliamentary Law, it was also interested in civic improvement. Its first project was the distribution of flower seeds to school children and the award of annual prizes for the most attractive results in gardens and floral displays. In 1898 the club opened a reading room in the City Hall, where the collection of the Bryant Library was then housed. In 1901 it established a public rest room for the benefit of farmers' wives and children who were in town for their marketing. It sponsored an anti-fly campaign in one summer, and the "boys caring for the traps reported over one hundred quarts of flies killed." It was responsible for a curfew law and for a law prohibiting spitting in the streets. It erected a "suitable stone" to mark the site of the old stockade. Thus Mrs. Lewis, always at the center of the club's activities, mounted to the summit. After her death, the membership sponsored the

Isabel Lewis Scholarship Fund "to perpetuate the memory of their leader and inspiration for so many years."

The Gradatim Club was a chapter unit in the Minnesota Federation of Women's Clubs, and Mrs. Lewis was a frequent delegate to its annual conventions. She became a district vice-president, then district president, and ultimately the treasurer of the Federation. This was the crown of her ambitions.

Her affiliations and her interest in her Chicago relatives took her away from Sauk Centre very frequently, and not infrequently Harry, the youngest, went with her. A high-school classmate conjectured that Harry's "early life and mental development was largely under her tutelage," and he pictured the small boy loitering among the women's skirts, "his ear attentive to the topics in those women's club meetings, and to the gossips who were probably present." When in 1902 his mother's picture appeared in the Minneapolis *Journal* together with that of the president of the Sauk Centre Ladies' Musical Club, the young Lewis saved the clipping in his diaries. The adult Sinclair Lewis, who called her "more mother than step-mother" and "psychically my own mother," remembered that she "read to me more than was the village custom." She was, for all that, no softhearted creature. She would not brook his insolence or his tantrums, to which he was early given.

> I was very rude to Mother at supper and tonight she got her satchel and was going to pack up and leave untill I could behave. [I] apologized and she relented.

And is there not some oblique reference to this history of mothers—first an ailing one, then a busy one—in the lonely Brontëlike fantasy-games that Harry played by himself, with keys and screws as characters, in a mythical kingdom located on the workbench of his father's barn?

> *September 4, 1902.* When I was cleaning beneath bench in barn I found several of the old "key-people," i.e. keys which I used as semi-dolls, or, better, as puppets in many a play hour. They lived, died a number of times, fought battles, had houses ect. ect. but for several years they have been in "strict-retirement" as they fell behind bench & were never taken out. Hope to find the old "gold-screw" and "lemon-Screw" which belong to a generation before the "key-people."

When he was speculating on the source of his literary ambitions, Sinclair Lewis wrote:

> A good many psychologists have considered that in such a case [as his], the patient has probably by literary exhibitionism been trying to get even with his schoolmates who could outfight, outswim, out-love, and in general outdo him. Of me that explanation must have been partly true, but only partly, be-

> cause while I was a mediocre sportsman in Boytown, I was neither a cripple nor a Sensitive Soul.

Sensitive soul he certainly was not, but he was a good deal less than a mediocre sportsman and he was living through a crippling process.

His two older brothers, one can be very sure, never played storybook games with discarded keys. Fred, the oldest, was a plodder, without aspirations or abilities. A poor student, he chose briefly to attend a Chicago dental college in 1895. There the work was either without interest or too difficult for him, and he dropped out in mid-course to return to Sauk Centre and work in the flour mill. Village gossip has it that the senior Lewises felt that he married far beneath their station and that as a result they more or less disowned him. The fact seems, rather, that they only lost interest in him, and young Harry's diary account of the wedding does not suggest any ill feeling or wounded pride.

> *October 29, 1901*. Fred was married yesterday to Miss Winnie Hanson. The Hansons live 2 miles from Little Sauk (about 9 miles from Sauk Centre). The 3 seated rig with Pa, Ma, Mr and Mrs Blake, and Mrs. Dunlap and I started at 1 P.M. reaching there at 2:30. The wedding ceremony was at about 3:30. The minister was a jolly-looking nice old Lutheran minister. I think that everybody there except our family, the Blakes, Poms D-, and the Burks were Scandinavians—neighbors of the Hansons. They seemed to be high class Scandinavians, and were all ladies & gentlemen. There were about 50 there. Supper was served in 4 tables. There were some queer delicious cookies which looked like the insides of banana skins. Rain began at about 4:30 but as we had side curtains we did not get wet going home. Home at 9:30.

When nieces and nephews began to appear, Harry wrote of them with a pleasant show of interest; but once Fred was married and had moved away from Sauk Centre to live and die a miller, he seems to have played no role at all in his younger brother's life, and the role had always been small.*

Of Claude the same cannot be said. In 1947 Sinclair Lewis confessed that "for sixty years I have tried to impress my brother Claude," and it is quite true that Claude throws a long if sometimes quite narrow shadow across his younger brother's life. Except for one near-tragedy in his childhood, Claude seems to have lived with the sun of success and approval

* On January 20, 1946, from Duluth, Sinclair Lewis was to write to a friend: "The sad thing was that my older brother, Fred, died suddenly last Tuesday, from a coronary. He was so much older than I and so different in his interests that I did not know him very well and the only really sad thing about it to me was the thought of how many amusing things and pleasant places he has missed in his life. . . . Sauk Centre seemed so small, huddled in the snow; the preacher, at the small Congregational church, kind and good and not mattering; and the final little group in the snow at the graveyard wasn't quite real—so frightened and huddled in the great gray plain with snow flying."

always shining upon him. That early near-tragedy, his skull fractured by a mule's kick, was detailed in the newspaper, and in the following week, his recovery was reported and the editor concluded: "It is a most remarkable case, not one in a thousand of similar injuries but proves fatal." The near-tragedy is converted into a happy augury of fortune's child.

Claude, the constant success, most like his father and most warmly approved by him, his every movement in college and medical school approvingly reported in the local news columns (while Fred is almost never mentioned and Harry very seldom), the example always held up to the others, became a kind of ideal image for the youngest of them. With a difference of six years between them, they shared the same bed except on those occasions when Claude was visited by some college friend; then Harry would betake himself to the parlor sofa, since the spare room was likely to be occupied by his Grandfather Warner.

Claude was in every way what Harry was not: sensible, steady, well-organized, happy, gregarious, good-looking and well-built, gifted at sports and at hunting and fishing, unimaginative, shrewd with money and thrifty, ambitious. At thirteen he was the local agent for out-of-town newspapers. In the summers following his junior and senior years in high school he attended training courses for teachers. At his graduation, the only boy in his class, he delivered the senior address, "Possibilities for American Boys." He taught in country schools for a short time, then gave that up "to devote his attention to Greek, Latin, and German" in preparation for the University of Minnesota, which he entered in 1896. During several of his summers he worked for the telephone company as linesman and installer of new instruments. After taking his B.S. at the University of Minnesota in 1900, he went directly to his father's old medical college. He took his M.D. in 1903, and after a brief internship in Chicago hospitals became a substitute physician in St. Cloud, was immediately successful and stayed there. On March 14, 1907, when Harry, a disgraced renegade from Yale, was living without employment in New York's depressed Lower East Side, Sauk Centre read of Claude's triumphant climax, "St. Cloud's most popular young doctor meets his affinity in Chicago. . . . The lucky young lady is Miss Rosalie W. Freeman of that city, and is a very popular young woman." At eighteen, poor Harry wrote to himself, "Claude is as fine a fellow as I ever met."

Turn, then, Muse of Boytown, to Master Harry. The earliest glimpse of him is provided by a recollection of Mr. Ben DuBois, son of the doctor and slightly younger than Harry, when the new Mrs. Lewis came to call on his mother and brought the boy along. He raced about on the lawn on his hands and knees, his face on the ground, crying, "I eat grass like cows!"—and ate it. He was always, Mr. DuBois remembers, a show-off and something of a bore, and he is supported in this judgment by another contemporary, Mr. Laurel Kells, who told how, when they played make-believe games, like Robin Hood, Harry Lewis would be swept into the fantasy with a kind of mad strenuousness, and he would go on with it for hours, even days, after everyone else was through and on to something else. At the same time, Mr. Kells recalled, Harry had no really sustained interest either in others or in the interests of others. (One cannot be certain with what accuracy Sinclair Lewis himself somewhat formalized this recollection when, in 1931, he told Christian Gauss that he developed the idea of a Robin Hood club and made himself its leader, only to be expelled from the club by the other boys because of the strain on them of his "imaginative exactions.")

Both Mr. DuBois and Mr. Kells remembered him as peculiarly gullible, easy prey to the kind of brutal horseplay that the traits they observed inevitably invited. When Harry was quite small, slightly older boys, including the admirable Claude, would go off into the woods and fields on treasure hunts. One of them would have gone ahead, dug a hole, defecated into it and rejoined the others; when they all came toward the fatal spot, Harry among them, the knowing one would point and shout, "That looks like a good place, let's dig there," and Harry would dash out ahead of the rest and begin to dig, until his hands were in the smelly mess. And this would happen again and again. It was perhaps even earlier that his brother took him into the woods and described rabbit droppings to him as rabbit berries, good to eat—and laughed at the relish with which Harry ate them.

At school, it was always Harry's cap that someone was stealing. In "I'm an Old Newspaper Man Myself," the adult Lewis recorded, with the mellowed tolerance of age, the trials of his boyhood:

> When I was ten or so, Claude's gang, composed of old, seasoned scouts of fifteen, were masters of the woods, the lake, and the swimming-hole in Hoboken Crick (not Creek), up by the Arch. When I tried to swim there, getting no farther than bubbling and choking, Claude's more meticulous vandals tied my clothing in knots and painstakingly soaked it. When I climbed out of the mud and found my knotted costume, I rose to a precocious eloquence which received from Jim Hendryx, Claude's lieutenant, my only compliment: "Gee, Harry musta swallowed the dictionary!" . . . Despite such rebuffs and disasters, I insisted on tagging after the gang, and Claude had to assign none other than his commando-chief, Charley McCadden, expert purloiner of chickens and rutabeggies (sic), to regularly losing me. And he never failed, never.

The details of the all but transparent ruses follow in good-natured anecdotage, but their subject is a continuously humiliated and exasperated boy who was helpless to defend himself and helpless to retaliate except within himself. Among boys of his own age, the situation was not very different. A few, like John MacGibbon, tolerated him but they have professed not to have liked him. He had, in his adolescence, one friend—Irving Fisher, and Irving Fisher only.

There are elements in this early life that suggest the life of Sam Clemens in Hannibal, Missouri. True, young Clemens did not suffer from a lack of friends or from the brutal taunts of boys who were not his friends or from the long stretches of dull monotony that plagued the young Lewis and led him, in later life, to gloss them with factitious recollections of a "normal boyhood." Yet Clemens, in spite of all the nostalgia for the small town that he was to pour into his work, had experienced enough of fear and violence in his youth to struggle with a genuinely tragic animus in his maturity, just as Lewis put a sugar-coating on loneliness, monotony and boorishness.

True, Sam Clemens had an older brother whom he could treat with derision and even contempt, whereas Harry Lewis could only helplessly admire Claude. True, too, Clemens's mother was a good deal more spirited than Lewis's stepmother, less prim and much more tolerant, but her marriage was based on no romantic attachment to the elder Clemens, and we must at least speculate as to whether E. J. Lewis's second marriage was impelled by love or necessity. The elder Clemens, "stern, proud, frugal, . . . almost fanatic in his scruples touching honesty, . . . sternly and irreproachably moral, . . . aloof from churches and creeds . . . yet confounding the Godly with his stern Puritan morality," in the account of Dixon Wecter, is in all these qualities the counterpart of Dr. E. J. Lewis. The elder Clemens, whose inhibitions and austerity encouraged no demonstration of affection in his home, never a kiss, never an embrace except upon the deathbed, a man of stubbornly glacial temper, created an atmosphere of cold inflexibility that was to be duplicated in the household in Sauk Centre.

The results, in at least two ways, became similarly apparent in the two boys: Sam Clemens, like Harry Lewis, "was fitful, idle, erratic, unpredictable," and one can with reason speculate whether Dr. Lewis, like "that arch-Puritan, John Marshall Clemens, put the fear of God and an ironclad moral code into the fiber of his impressionable son," until "a recoil from sex as from something polluting and degrading" became an ambiguous ingredient in young Harry's make-up, as it did in young Sam's.

3

ON NOVEMBER 10, 1900, when he was fifteen and a half years old, Harry Lewis began his retaliation in a diary. At the outset, but less and less as it approaches its petering-out point in 1908, he kept it in a code of his own devising, crabbed but generally easy to decipher.* The mysterious, at first unyielding pages lead one to anticipate, locked within the cryptography, veritable treasures of uncensored subjectivism, of lacerating adolescent confessions and giddy dreams, and of fantasies of gaudy secret sins. One is mistaken. His dreams—or those that he records—are blameless.

> I had beautiful dreams last night. At one time Myra was stroking my hair. Then she and Margaret Norris were members of Chem. class and we had a [jolly] time together. Then at another time Edd Lorass and I were racing them [around] in the woods and at the lake shore.

"Racing around" was an early Lewis habit, whether after the unobtainable Myra Hendryx in dreams, or in the schoolroom where the explosions of his frenetic, undirected energies mitigated what he was later tc call the "dull routine." The school records, the report cards and certain class exercises that Lewis saved from his pre-diary days show us a boy whose grade in deportment was never very high and was sometimes distinctly weak. He was occasionally dismissed from school for his antics; but, for any other reason, he was absent for only a day and a half in eight years. His early grades were uneven. In the sixth grade he failed every period in music and drawing, and he failed all but two periods in writing, or penmanship. His report card for the eighth grade shows that as he

* Both the code and the handwriting present certain difficulties to the reader. There are occasional smudged or simply illegible passages, usually of only a word or two, that cannot be read or can only be guessed at. Sometimes Lewis takes to German script or Greek that cannot always be deciphered. He frequently misspells words, both in code and in handwriting. In quotations from these diaries, illegible portions must remain blank, and if suppositions are made, they will be bracketed; misspellings when easily read will generally be allowed to stand without the usual *sic* (a number of them, notably *prehaps* and *ect.*, are habitual); punctuation will be corrected only for the sake of ready reading.

moved on to high school he stood seventeenth in a class of eighteen. In the first period of his freshman year he seems to have failed in every subject, and so he himself noted on the report card. He was a very poor speller, and his papers are hardly tidy. Not until he is twelve does his handwriting begin to resemble that of his mature years; by thirteen, it is more or less formed; but his signature is still very different and remains so for some years. The final literary signature seems to have been a contrivance cultivated for effect.

His school exercises are his earliest literary effort, but there is nothing in them to suggest another Alexander Pope lisping in numbers. In the fourth grade, when he earned a seventy in numbers of another kind, he wrote, "Addition is Adding two or more numbers togher." In geography in that year he wrote, "The British Empire is England all her positions" (reaching for *possessions*) and "A mountain is some high land. It must be two thousand feet above the sea level to be a mountain. A mountain chain is a few mountains extending in the same direction."

In the spring of 1896, when the household was no doubt buzzing with talk of and preparation for Claude's impending matriculation at Minnesota, and when Harry was in the sixth grade, he wrote this practice letter for his grammar class:

Minneapolis, Minn.,
Apr. 13, 1896.

Dear Mother,—

It is very warm here now. I was over to the U. yesterday. Please send me my summer suit. I saw Claude yesterday. He had a headacke. He had also a letter from Fred. Fred is haveing a big practice now. How are the folks at home?

Your son,
Harry S. Lewis

The literary imagination trembles into life; still in the sixth grade, and again in grammar, Harry developed the following conceit in response to an assignment to make up a sentence and identify all its parts of speech: "He fell on the ground where he had stood and the spider sucked away every drop of blood." In the eighth grade, in a similar assignment, he said: "To write easily is an accomplishment. To write is an infinative the subject of the sentence." As a freshman in high school he was still shaky in the mechanics of composition. A year and a half later, when he was entering his third year in high school, the diaries begin, and details rapidly accrue to the faint outlines of this earlier picture.

Already he has become an omnivorous, unsystematic reader. He opens with a list of about fifty books he had read during the summer just ended, the titles ranging from trash to works by Kipling, Thackeray, George Eliot, Victor Hugo. Such a catalogue of his reading he does not give us again, but he is reading continually and often guiltily ("Wasted a lot of time reading tonight" is a kind of refrain in the diary during the high-school years), and not infrequently he notes a title and sometimes his response to it. In what was often a peculiarly empty life there were many hours that only reading could fill.

> *February 9, 1902.* How I spend Sundays generally. Rise at 7, bring pail of water and armful of wood; then breakfast. Read till between 11 and 12. Then black shoes and take bath. Dinner at 12:30 (generally Chicken or Turkey, or Roast Beef; Potatoes; Bread & Butter; Sauce, Pie or Pudding ect. Some Soup or Nuts (or both). In summer Ice Cream. After Dinner I get the mail. During afternoon I read, walk and fill wood box. Supper at 6. Generally read or study all evening.—sometimes go to church. I almost always go to bed at 10, weekdays or Sunday.

The books that fill his hours show no clearly directed interests: *The Ship of Stars* and *Q* on one weekend, *Tommy and Grizel* and *Sentimental Tommy* on another. If he likes popular adventure like Anthony Hope's *Rupert of Hentzau* and Kirk Monroe's *Under the Dog Star,* he is apparently no less taken by the sentimental solemnities of Hall Cain's *The Christian.* Nor does he limit himself to fiction; he reads in Grote's *History of Greece,* orders a book called *The Story of the Alphabet,* and works toward college examinations in Myers's *Eastern Nations and Greece.*

He is apparently building up a collection of his own; his diary is numbered "1" in the "Private Library" of "Harry Sinclair Lewis," and to this cataloguing is added the enjoinder, "Please Return Promptly." He buys a New Testament to carry in his pocket and obtains a cast-off dictionary "lying about the Chem. lab." His grandfather gives him "a damned Henty book" for Christmas in 1900, and an aunt gives him Mrs. Oliphant's *Makers of Florence,* which becomes "46" in the private library. The last three books that he mentions in these high-school years (*Nicholas Nickleby, Kim* and *Kenilworth*) are by the three writers whom, in his adult life, he named as the favorite novelists of his youth. It is surprising that he never mentions either Thoreau or *Walden,* for in adult life, again, he claimed for *Walden* a strong, formative influence. One must wonder whether, in a statement like the following, he was not imposing on the Minnesota years a maturity of taste and judgment that came only later.

> When I was a boy, in the prairies of Minnesota, there was no book which had for me a more peculiar and literal enchantment than *Walden* of Thoreau. As in the case of most books which exercise an altogether mystical charm, it is difficult to analyze the elements of that charm. It is merely there. . . .
>
> So to this day, dreaming between the wheatfields and the sultry brook, Walden became a Mecca for which he longed more than for any other shrine in all the world—more even than for Kenilworth of Scott.

> Dwelling beside Walden there was, as it came to the boy from the pages of Thoreau, a scholarly simplicity, an authentic American virtue, high song without the silly silken hose of alien troubadours.
>
> The boy dreaming of saving the various nickles which he earned by hours of lawn-mowing that he might visit Walden and there find simple greatness.

On May 5, 1901, he asks himself, "Am wondering why I can't just as well go to Germany this summer. Ride to the Atlantic by wheel and ship for Europe. WHY NOT?" But of Massachusetts there is never a word.

His reading did not seem to interfere seriously with his academic achievement in the last two years of high school. As a junior, he had nineties in all his subjects except Cicero, and only deportment was low. He studied Greek grammar on his own and contemplated dropping chemistry in order to have time to devote to the *Anabasis*. At one point he vowed that he would finish high school in three years and it was only after he studied the catalogue of Harvard College that he abandoned this plan; instead, he determined to master *The Aeneid* by himself, and while he wavered in this project and ultimately took the Vergil course as a senior, he did much of it alone. In his senior year even his grade in deportment became respectable, and as his plans for education beyond Sauk Centre took their final shape, his resolution to do well in his studies grew. ("I made an imitation ΦBK pin from brass today and hung it on my Bertha Calender, to spur my ambition somewhat.")

By his own account, he urged the principal of the school to introduce French into the curriculum, but that gentleman denied the petition and "in assembly hall, explained that to study too many languages was idiotic." He became interested in German, and when, in his senior year, the German teacher proved unable to speak the language, John MacGibbon, Harry's classmate, approached Father Artz, a Catholic priest, for private instruction. The priest agreed on condition that MacGibbon find a few other students, and MacGibbon found his sister and Harry. Mr. MacGibbon later remembered that "in a short while we were speaking the language among ourselves and others, so the classes were called off by that Priest." In his new linguistic enthusiasm, Harry now bought himself a Hebrew grammar, and briefly, at least, he planned to master it.

Only a month after he began his German lessons, he went to another priest, Father O'Conner, to pursue his interests in Greek. This arrangement gave him a language lesson five nights in the week, but he would master the *Anabasis*. "Today I begin the Anabasis with Fr. O'Conner as teacher. I have tried to begin it once or twice before by myself but this time is really the beginning of my study of the Anabasis." The arrangement did not prove entirely successful, and four months later we read the following:

> I really have a Greek teacher again! Fr. O'Conner had forgotten all of his Greek and was untauglich. The new one is Mr. Garland—the new pastor

of the Episcopal Church. He says that he reads some Greek every day. About May 1st he will have time. Meanwhile I am reviewing grammar.

When he found that he would not need physics ("which I hate") for college, he dropped it and returned to the German course where, in a very short time, he completed the work that he had missed. If he did not win one of the four places of honor open to his graduating class of nine at the end of that school year, it was not because of a recent lack of zeal or application. Not now in code but, as if to assure himself that at least he knew a foreign language, in German he lamented, *"Ach dasz ich als* Freshman *und* Sophomore *gearbeitet hätte."*

"In Chemistry," John MacGibbon remembered, "he was always up to pranks. He had high marks but usually had the answers on paper slips in vest pockets and was never caught cribbing by our teachers, either in class or tests." To the second point the diary lends no confirmation, but nearly the first entry confirms the other.

Was making some H[ell] in the chem. lab. tonight after school. Got to "monkeyin." Set some alcohol on fire. Final result—2 rec[ord?]s of H[ell] made. a great amt. of alcohol wasted. 1 al. lamp destroyed. 1 bell glass broken. 1 and ¾ths hours wasted. Last of all I caused myself to think what a fool I am. If I cannot do better than that I had better go and kill myself.

The mood of guilty repentance is not sustained (years later, sometime in his adult life, Sinclair Lewis wrote a memorandum to himself, now yellowing among his papers, that read starkly, "Don't be too brash!"). The very next day he is involved in a scuffle in a classroom and his schoolmate's "algebra and many papers which were in it flew 'all over the room,' " and the day after that, "Prof. made me stay and told me among other things that 'if he couldent trust me at *all* he wouldent allow me to come to school.' Prof. and I have had several talks before. Then I came home and had a 'hell of a scene' with Pa. . . ."

The consistency of what Harry called his "hell making" provides these diaries with one of their few major themes among generally miscellaneous data.

Prof. gave me the deuce for general depravity this morning. . . . I had to clean off a table in German recitation room. . . . Had some fun this noon, in bothering the Freshman girls while they were [practicing] songs. . . . Prof. Stanton told me this afternoon that "the next time" he'd suspend me. . . . We fixed Frank Sneesby's chair in Chem. class so that it collapsed when he sat down. Gee, but it looked funny. . . . I chased around, talked and made a fool of myself generally, but had lots of fun out of it. . . . Had flour thrown all over us . . . but that did not hurt us any. . . . Lathrop gave me hell this noon . . . raised hell in the junior room this afternoon and . . . was sent out of the room. Went out and played hide and go seek with the brats instead of studying as I should have. . . . Got sent out of the room in Ger. class. . . . Got sent home by Lathrop again this afternoon. . . . Got fired from school today.

The extent to which matters of school discipline became problems in home discipline cannot be surmised. Harry's own record seems to suggest that, while his father was concerned about the course of his education and, indeed, determined that course in the choice of institutions, he was less troubled by the boy's antics in school than by the late hours he sometimes kept. The following entries reveal the patience of that rigidly restrained father put to trial and at last snapping:

February 8, 1901. . . . After the lecture tonight I went into O'Gara's [a restaurant] and got home at half after eleven.

February 9, 1901. Pa wasn't going to let me go tonight because got home so late last night. (But I went).

March 14, 1901. . . . When I was coming home I went up to Jim Irsfield's room. Stayed there till eleven o'clock. Pa was hot as hell at me for getting home so late.

March 15, 1901. We lost the debate this evening. . . . When I left the house Pa told me to get home earlier than I did last night. But I did not get home till 11. The door was locked when I got home and I had to ring the door bell. Pa came down and opened the door, and when I was in said, "Before we go any farther, young man, we're going to have a settlement. Are you going to run this house or am I?" He grabbed me by the collar, punched me in the face with his fist, threw me on the floor, bumped my head, and raised hell generally. If Ma hadn't come down there is no telling what he would have done. As it was he did not hurt me a lot. I have a most [secret] belief that if I am not too afraid, I will disappear tomorrow. Make my way to Europe and travel a few years.

March 16, 1901. Had a big fight with myself as to whether I should run away or not. Finally decided not to. . . .

The boy's unpopularity and his buffoonery did not, apparently, prevent his fellows or his teachers from recognizing his merits and permitting him to develop them. The school was divided into two literary societies, the Delphian made up of freshmen and juniors, and the Athenian, of sophomores and seniors. Harry's verbal and forensic gifts seem to have won some recognition for him when he was elected president of the Delphian in the autumn of 1900. Almost at once he seems to have found himself in difficulty, for he wrote at the top of a page, "DAMN DEL. LIT. SOC." The fact that he had been given the topic "Work of Water on Geologic Ages" for a speech at a meeting in the following week might have caused him either to have flung out that curse or to try to erase it, as he did. "Lit. society this evening. They made a lot of motions to bother me, but didn't succeed," he noted, suggesting that the habitual bedevilment followed him to the chair. It was not uncommon to reelect officers in these societies, but when, at the midyear point, elections were coming up, Harry urged that he not be reelected and yet, he rather proudly reports, in spite of his protest, he won fourteen of the fifty votes. What reward was this for one who apparently had worked hard on the Delphian debates? He had contended on the propositions: that Lincoln faced greater difficulties than Washington (Harry led the Affirmative, which lost); and that Indians should have more liberty (Harry led the Negative, which won). He had worked out a speech on the ironical topic of "Some Things We Need to Encourage in Athletics"; and he had had the courage to deliver an oration on a Thanksgiving program on the unpromising subject, "The Puritans Criticized," while his friend Fisher took the more amiable positive, "The Puritans Justified."

He held no class offices, but in the senior play, *Class Day,* he played the lead, Frank Buncombe. He entered the Junior Oratorical Contest with the subject, "Traditional Customs in School," but he left no record of the winner, who clearly was not he. He did not enjoy the meetings of his class, which were usually semi-social affairs held in student homes at night ("Had no fun and recd no profit"), but he made certain creative contributions. It was he who, according to John MacGibbon, "proposed the annual presentation of a loving cup to the winner of the Junior Oratorical Contest. We purchased and presented the Cup to the Board of Education on our graduation night." It was he who thought up the class motto and put it into Latin: *Prorsus non retrorsus.* It was he who was chiefly responsible for the composition of the class yells, a matter of no small importance. Of an early meeting of the junior class, he said, "Got hot and refused to write the class yells," but next day he writes, "Repented a little. Wrote 7 class yell but they will get no more from me," and a few days later, "Damn the class of 1902 (had another time wasting class meeting this noon)"—and here there is no erasure. In his senior year he seems to take some pride in his yells. "We met at the pump house to select yells. Nearly all of mine were selected." Sometimes he was the yell leader ("I'm so hoarse I can't speak without hurting my throat"), and he copied out samples of this American folk art.

Cooma laca, booma laca,
Bow wow wow—
Chingalaca, chingalaca,
Chow chow chow.

Are we in it?
Well, I guess—
Sauk Centre High School,
Yes yes yes.

Was he in it? From his record of outside activities, it would hardly seem so. He avoided dances and parties ("I always wish after a party of this crowd that I had stayed home as I never have any fun at one of them. . . . They say that they had lots of fun at the party last night but all the same I'm glad I didn't go.") There is one exception to his general rule and general fortune:

> *April 11, 1901. . . .* This tonight I went to a hay rack party. Hot time—when I wasn't kissing Clara Carpenter I was kissing Alice Hartley and I was hugging BOTH OF THEM all of the time. However Frank Sneesby and I took Alice home. And that parting—! ?———!!

The exceptions to his practice of avoiding athletic events are hardly more numerous. He lists the events and the winners in the Field Day of 1901 and concludes, "The classes came out in this order in the class relay: seniors, sophs, juniors, freshmen. The only thing I entered was the relay." When we remember that there were only five boys in the junior class and that a relay team requires four, this exception nearly vanishes.* Yet his physical condition troubled him, and he felt obliged to do something about improving it.

> *October 31, 1901.* I begin to believe that it would be wise to wait a year before going to the University of Chicago. Reason. Up to a certain age, the older a person is on entering college the better. 2nd—a year's time to get a little muscle and physical strength.

A few months earlier, he reported that Fisher and he were practicing running the one-hundred- and the two-twenty-yard dashes "a little bit."

> It took me 32 sec. for the 100 and 84 for the 220 yest[erday] (best Kid Thayer ran the 220 was in 25) so that I am a very poor runner but still I need the exercise as I am studying hard this summer. Beside the running I am practicing fencing.

Basketball was a new game and, when it was introduced in the school, Harry tried to play. "We only played a couple of minutes regularly. The rest of the time merely trying to keep the ball away from the other side." That effort ended when he "Had a fall while playing basket ball this morning & hurt my thigh (left). It got so stiff that I had to use a cane to walk with." If he was to develop his muscles, it had to be in noncompetitive exercise, chiefly walking and wheeling, and of the latter there was a good deal in the temperate seasons.

The sedentary pleasures loom larger. He did not read all the time; he played cribbage and he taught chess to Fisher. He conducted a correspond-

* Sinclair Lewis himself dismissed the exception completely when, in an adult reminiscence, he reduced the number of boys in his class from five to four, so that he *had* to run in the relay.

ence with a German boy named Otto Schade. He began a little museum of the natural sciences, with "a few botanical, geological. ect. specimens," but gave it up in two weeks when "Lena (the hired girl) mistook it for my play-house apparently yesterday! Can't stand that." He entertained himself with disguises. "As I amused myself by 'dressing up' (!) last night during the time which I should have been studying, I did not have my Cicero well this morning when I was called on," he wrote, and "Played 'ghost' tonight. To scare the superstitious pedestrian." Masquerading was apparently the earliest form taken by that lifelong propensity for mimicry that was both to make him famous and to bore his friends. "And so behold me a monk—black domino, hood, waist tied with a rope, beads and rosary of cranberries and a huge prayer book."

The religious role was one that, presently, he would attempt with greater seriousness, and even now, in his last years in Sauk Centre, he was developing a considerable interest in religion. He not only attended the Sunday school and the regular services in the Congregational Church, but also developed a habit of visiting other churches—the Episcopalian, the Baptist, the Methodist, the Roman Catholic—and he went to the meetings of the Young People's Society of Christian Endeavor.

It is very probable that one reason he shunned dances and parties is that on those occasions he had to suffer through the agonizing experience of observing the unobtainable Myra Hendryx showering her favors upon other boys. When the diaries begin, she is already "the dearest girl in the world," and he is already reconciled to the impossibility of his love.

> Walked a little way behind MYRA HENDRYX this afternoon, coming home from school. What a waist, what a head, what arms, what shoulders, and what legs! O what a charming girl she is and how I love her. But, alas!, she does not like me.

Every encounter is recorded. When he speaks to her, he notes it. "Myra cast a quick, almost startled, glance at me. WHY?" he writes with sudden hope. He goes to the schoolhouse during the noon hour in the hope of finding a handkerchief with her name on it. He tries to arrange his seat in such a way as to enable him to watch her. She permits him to help her with her Caesar. He learns that she is to be escorted to the New Year's ball, which he had declined, by Earl McNiece. Then he thinks that he may be falling out of love. "Prehaps it is a good thing." But she strokes his hair in dreams, she lets him walk home with her one noon, he meets her at a friend's house and she is not exactly cold, and suddenly she impels him into verse.

> *March 12, 1901.* Can it be that I have said that I love Myra less than everything else which is in terra combined? Can it be that I have ever said that I did not love her. If I have (oh can it be?) I have lied! I love her, I have

ever loved her, and I always will. She is dearer to me even than my books and God knows that they are very dear and near to me.

> Myra when I cease to love thee,
> May this right hand lose its cunning,
> May my life blood cease its flowing,
> May I meet reward in Hades.

Myra wears the blue waist today, the dear blue waist, about which I had my arms last Fri. night, when I tried to take from her (in sport) what she said was the portrait of the "cutest boy on earth." It proved to be a portrait of a baby (James Norris Fuller). My row with Lathrop terminated today by my apology to her. . . .

He persuades himself that he does not love her, and tries to think of other girls. "Is Bertha really the dearest girl on earth, or am I imagining myself in love with her to keep myself from really falling in love again with the lovable but unwinable Myra?" Bertha is a little older than he and writes him now and then from the university, but she is only a friend. A more plausible romantic substitute for Myra is Della Johnson. "Had a lot of fun [with] Della Johnson down at the reading room," it starts. "She is a nice girl and so clever." A rival catalogue of Della's movements begins to accompany that of Myra's. He walks with her, he calls upon her. Then:

I held Della's hand against my breast for a minute, which was most delightful. The way of it, Bertha was sitting on Della's lap and neither could escape. I was sitting by them and made the most of my opportunity.

His affections seem, however, to waver.

Della wore a dressing sack (is that the right name, sure I don't know) which left the neck and arms to the elbow bare. She had such pretty arms and such a pretty neck, dear little girl. I am glad that I am able to like her so well without feeling in love with her.

He spends a Sunday afternoon in May at her house and she plays the piano for him. "Della plays beautifully." He calls on her a second time and, after seeing her at the baccalaureate services, he writes, "Della was there prettiest of all in the church (except Myra) in a dress of soft light yellow. I never realized before how pretty she is." And then abruptly he brings the matter to an end:

June 3, 1901. The G.A.R. encampment is now down. I went down tonight to the grounds. Some guys were making speeches. There was a large tent (yclept "The Bowery") where a dance was going on; stayed and watched the dancers and talked to the kids and girls till 12 o'clock. I was thoroughly disappointed to find that Della Johnson stayed looking at the dance till 12:30. What makes it worse she had been down to the Bowery once or twice before. That ends it. I am not going to chase a girl who hangs around there. A stige id declaro!

Myra victrix!

If the general disesteem in which the young Lewis was held by girls as well as boys closed off the largest areas of what may be regarded as comprising totally normal boyhood on the middle border at the beginning of this century, his father's attitude toward the propriety of work for the young male opened at least one such area to him. He was approaching sixteen when he "commenced," as he says, his "first real 'job' . . . sawing a cord of wood" for some neighbors, who paid him seventy-five cents. This was work to which he was accustomed, since he had been sawing and splitting firewood for his father for some time and continued to do so until he left home. He mowed the family lawn and now and then the lawn of a neighbor; he swept and shoveled the walks; he helped his mother as "chambermaid" on those occasions when the Lewises were without a "hired girl." He seems to have been eager to earn what money he could by odd jobs when they came his way. At least once he set up pins in the local bowling alley—for ten cents; he distributed handbills for fifty cents; he substituted on Fisher's newspaper route for six weeks one summer; he acted as janitor of the school for a day, and he took the regular man's place at the Congregational Church for several weeks; he spent a day in work at a visiting Wild West show in order to earn a pass. For two weeks in the summer of 1902 he served as night clerk in Sauk Centre's new hotel, the Palmer House. He worked from six in the evening until six in the morning and was paid five dollars a week and given his room and board. The wage was somewhat diminished by what is his predictable and almost endearing incompetence.

July 8, 1902. Just been asleep (all day). Broke a show case last night, by leaning on it. Cost me $2. Made a mistake in giving change to amt. of $1.50. Can't afford working at this rate!

He did not enjoy or approve of the commercial activities at the Palmer House, but he liked the Palmers and especially their two children.

. . . his daughter Hazel, a very clever and merry little sprite (though she is only about as big as a mouse she is 12, and will enter the 8th grade this year.) She reads all of the time. Sometimes carries a book to table with her. Yet she is a great girl to have fun when not reading. Doesn't allow the traveling men to be intimate with her, and his son—a rollicking, frolicking lad of 7 or 8.

Thirty-two years later, in a communication to the *Saturday Review of Literature,* Hazel Palmer recalled Harry, the night clerk. The Palmer children were, she said, the eager auditors to long, impromptu narratives that he spun out for them, and while this was to develop into a lifelong habit of Lewis's, and not only with children, the Palmers are the first on record to have been entertained in this fashion. Hazel Palmer recalls, too, his blunders, how, for example, he called a traveling man at half past five one morning to tell him that he had forgotten to call him for the five o'clock train It was generally thought, she adds, "that he would never amount to much," but the children liked him "in spite of the mild contempt with which he was viewed by our elders."

Perhaps the work that he enjoyed most was work for which he was not paid at all. In the summer of 1901 he had his first experience of the world of publishing when for two days he worked in the office of the *Avalanche*. "I will make an attempt to learn the trade of printing. . . . Worked 9 hours in the *Avalanche* office today learning printing. Started type setting." The evidence of the diaries indicates that this much comprised the total experience. Then, at the end of the school year in 1902, he worked again for a few days in the office of the *Herald,* under the eye of Myra's father, C. F. Hendryx. Hendryx suggests a character out of the world of *Winesburg, Ohio* —a man whose gifts are wasted and whose life decays in a drab and rutted environment. A descendant of the Revolutionary patriot Benjamin Harrison and, so, kin of the President, Ben Harrison, he was literate, amiable, and very disorderly in his habits; he was almost always in financial difficulty. He suffered severe headaches, which he cured by crossing the street to the drugstore and inhaling the fumes from a bottle of chloroform. The village regarded him as a drunken failure, but Harry Lewis respected him; and it is perhaps to be regretted that he was not to have a longer exposure to the humanity of C. F. Hendryx. It seems again, in this summer as in the next, to have been a matter of only a few days, and again he worked for nothing. He set up type and he covered the events of his own graduation from high school and he wrote one short column of local news. The rather long graduation story and the news column, too, he pasted into his diaries. The prose is plain, neither distinguished nor undistinguished, and it comprises the first published work of Sinclair Lewis. The pieces appear in the *Herald* for June 5, 1902, and on that date he noted in his diary, "Will work steadily there now if I don't get 'sick of it.' " There is no record of his having done so.*

To what extent this early newspaper experience contributed to his reportorial penchant we can hardly guess, but that he had it early his diaries make clear. He submitted to the necessity of sawing and chopping wood, but he longed for the day when he would have moved beyond that necessity.

* The reader should compare this account with Sinclair Lewis's own in the two essays, "I'm an Old Newspaper Man Myself" and "You Meet Such Interesting People," where he confused his own chronology, gave the impression of a much longer period of work on each of the newspapers, pretended to have written prose near to illiterate, and in general fictionized the facts.

"I finished what may be the last cord of poplar wood that I will ever saw, here at home, today." Yet even the despised wood provides material for the primitive cultural historian:

> Prehaps, as everyone will use coal exclusively, after a while, it would be of interest to tell how wood is bought and prepared for stove. It is bought in "cords," 5 x 4 x 14,* sticks being placed on the "saw-buck." [Here he draws an ink sketch of a sawbuck.] Then each stick is split, by means of the axe. Wood is much used around here. I think that every family uses it in the kitchen range, many use it in other stoves, and some use it in their furnaces. We use it only in the dining room and kitchen, having hot water heating in the rest of the house: (there is a stove in the "spare room" over the dining room, but that is but rarely used).

Although this passage may suggest the methods of the mature novelist, such reportorial prose as this was not the literary kind to which the writer in the young Lewis first aspired.

School yells are, we may suppose, a form of verse, and it is only a step from these to the announcement, on June 26, 1901, of the birth of the writer: "Started to write a ragtime poem." At the end of July he submitted a paper in a weekly contest conducted by "The Junior Journal" supplement of the Minneapolis *Journal*. "The week's general subject is 'The Story the Circus Animals Told.' I took the tiger for my animal, wrote the 'Talk' and sent it in today." This was prose, of course, but on the top of the following page of the diary appears this inscription:

H. Sinclayre Lewys—Poet (?)

The old Harry is going, even though Sinclair Lewis has not quite been achieved.†

Earlier in that year of 1901, he had written "was up on top of school house helping the kids mend the flag pole . . . and I shouted, 'See this in after years.' May it remind me to go up there and look for my initials." What immortality was he dreaming of, he whose sixteen-year-old failure he was all the while so unwittingly recording? It was, first of all, the

* For Harry, the reluctant chore boy, a cord of wood seems to have loomed more than double its actual size.

† The source of the name *Sinclair* has been the subject of much conjecture. It has sometimes been supposed that Lewis himself adopted it, perhaps because of Upton Sinclair. Throughout their lives these two men were confused in all manner of ways, including the receipt by one of mail intended for the other, but the connection of their names was accidental. Minnesotans were much amused by what struck them as its affectation; in an early newspaper story, one native reporter asked, "Who put the Sin in Sinclair?" There is a legend that Dr. Lewis, much impressed with a performance of *Uncle Tom's Cabin* shortly before the boy's birth, wanted to call him St. Clair, and that through the misunderstanding of the recording clerk, it was put in the register as Sinclair. The fact is that Dr. Lewis gave the boy this name to honor an old friend, a Dr. George A. Sinclair, a dentist, of New Lisbon, Wisconsin.

immortality of the poet. He enjoyed Kipling, but for some years his favorite poem was "The Vision of Sir Launfal," and now he began to write imitative verses. In August he records the rejection of three poems by magazines: "Evening Voices" by The Youth's Companion, "Maria Sanctissima" or "Ave Maria"—he refers to it in both ways—by *Outlook,* and "The Fallen Idol" by *Harper's.* In later reminiscences, Lewis said that at fourteen he sent off to *Harper's Magazine* what he believed to be a poem, but in fact, he was sixteen and a half when he wrote of "Evening Voices" that this was "the first M.S. that I ever sent . . . unless one would include that 'Junior Journal Contest Paper.' " He is not without a self-directed irony in his new vocation.

> I am very hopeful about it—that is to say, I am sure that it will be so favorably received that they will not delay more than 2 weeks in sending the refusal. Prehaps this hope is founded upon egotism however.

"I have the poetical fever," he declares, and writes more poems, and then come the first rejections:

> *August 11, 1901.* A great day for throw downs. Found out this morning that my paper wasn't even published in the Junior Journal—let alone a prize or honorable mention. Then this noon I rec'd. a rejection [Here he inked in a tear-shedding profile.] of "Evening Voices" from the *Youths Companion.* (Rec'd. with sack cloth, ashes, and weeping). But then, "Was machs es?" Persistancy is one great element in success. I have 3 other MSS. out and some others shall follow.

Five days later "The Fallen Idol" is returned by *Harper's,* and again: *"Was machs es?"* The rejection of the Maria poem produces no comment, and he even nearly forgets to record the similar fate of "Captain Timothy Lee" at the hands of *The New England Magazine,* although, when he does do so, he adds, "This makes four which I expected."

Momentarily daunted, he soon recovered. On September 13, 1901, he announced the following project:

> I am now writing poetry again! I am going to give Bertha a book of poems written by myself for Christmas. It may be changed before I put it in the book. [This reference is presumably to the opening verse.] Here it is—
>
> A poor thin pamphlet is this book
> Small yet is in its rhymes
> (For they are only poemlets
> Just scribbled at odd times)
>
> Pray do not use them harshly
> For they are dear to me,
> But call them untaught children
> Of the muse of poetry.

I am writing a poem called Pictures in the Fire: which I shall send to the *Youths Companion.*

After the poem has been dispatched, he quotes part of it:

How strange that when I've been reading
Some tale of an ancient knight
I see him in the fire place
Midst the embers, in armor bright—
I see him ride into battle
And charging with gleaming lance
His foemen slain by hundreds
Or flee before his advance.

When this comes back from *The Youth's Companion,* he says, "The aforesaid magazine has become such an expert at declention that I will have to set it at conjugation pretty soon!" and the fever seems to subside while he devotes himself to languages.

A more symptomatic kind of writing appeared simply as a portion of the diary proper. In June of 1902 he went to Minneapolis to take the entrance examinations for Yale, and he began then the practice, which he was to continue whenever he made a journey, of keeping an account of it and of placing some special value on the fact that he was making his notations as he was experiencing them, not as he recollected them afterwards.

Here it is 3:20 A.M. I'm in the G.N. depot waiting to take night train to Mpls. I'll write now & again in this diary as I go along; & in each instance I will really be in the place as I say "I am now in This or That," as I have diary, pen, & ink in satchel.

This is perhaps the real beginning, both chronologically and in point of method, of Sinclair Lewis the novelist.

Making hell, Myra, work, versifying—these are main themes; but there is one other, and that more prominent than any of these—his college ambitions. He begins with thoughts of Harvard in the autumn of 1900, and speckles his pages with the capital letter, *H.* He said later that he had read Charles Flandrau's *Harvard Episodes,* and that this had given him his early vision of the exotic charms of Eastern university life and his determination to go to Harvard.* In the same year, there is a single mention of Yale, for whose catalogue he wrote, and we may speculate whether, as Flandrau had given him his picture of Harvard, Frank Merriwell, the pride of Yale and the scourge of her enemies, may have given him equally fantastic notions about New Haven. His father appeared indisposed to consider Harvard

* Since this book was published in 1897, he might have read it by 1900; if he had, he reread it in New Haven on March 9, 1905, when he called it "disillusioned semi-cynical," and gave no indication at all of ever having heard of it before.

and is not as yet considering Yale, and for six months in 1901 Harry seems willing to consider the University of Minnesota as an alternate to Harvard if his father will not send him there; but the symbol for Harvard continues to appear in his margins, and sometimes little crimson-colored banners. Then, abruptly at the beginning of June, the University of Chicago, for which he develops the unintelligible symbol "lel," appears as an equal contender with Harvard and then slowly pulls ahead of it. During the process, he writes for catalogues from Oxford, Cambridge and Edinburgh. In November he thinks of delaying his entrance into Chicago for a year, and in December he arrives at this wisdom:

> I have decided not to take any undergraduate work at the U. of Chi. as I have found that the undergrad. work there is really not as good as the undergrad work at the U. of Minn. And so I'm to have my undergrad. degree at the U. of Minn., with a year or two of graduate work at the U. of Chi. (as the U. of C's *graduate* work is good) or at Harvard or John Hopkins or some other College as good. Hoc pater meus dixit.

Then he fancies the University of Wisconsin, but in February of 1902 he seems to conclude the endless debate as follows:

> Als Sie vieleicht wissen I have preferred other colleges to U. of Minn. only because many have better teachers in Greek, ect., prehaps, than has Min. But Pa has succeeded in convincing me that Minn is all right and says that he prefers to have me go there therefore to MINNESOTA U. will I, in all probability, go. SKI U MAH! GOPHER!!

It is seeming only. On March 1 he writes:

> I was kicking about Greek at the U. of M. tonight, and Pa said that he'd write to Judge Bishop [a New Haven friend since their Westville boyhood] and find out about board at Yale possibly—Maybe—but I won't say anything. I've changed too often. But I hope that he will let me go to Yale. But wait for Bishop's letter.

In the center of this entry he blocks out a large *Y*, and now *M* and *Y* are intertwined in the margins. It was, presumably, Dr. Lewis's boyhood associations with New Haven County that led him, when he yielded to Harry's Eastern preference, peremptorily to substitute Yale for Harvard. (In later Lewis generations, Harry was to rectify this judgment.) On March 18 Judge Bishop's reply arrived "and showed that a person could live very cheaply at Yale (si!) Pa has been thinking it over and says to work hard and see if I can pass the entrance exam next June 28 '& then decide.' "

> This means that IF I CAN PASS THE YALE ENTRANCE EXAM NEXT JUNE FATHER WILL LET ME GO TO YALE "IN ALL PROBABILITY."

But can I pass!? U. of Minn—Harvard—U. of Chi—U. of Minn—U. of Wis.—U. of Minn—Yale can it be that Yale will end the list. I hope so. Et nunc—to work—YYYYY

In mid-May, apparently moved by some trepidation, Harry wrote to Cyrus Northrop, the president of Minnesota, and a Yale man, describing his preparation and inquiring as to its adequacy. He had already written to Thomas Day Seymour, the professor of Greek at Yale. President Northrop replied at once, firmly insisting on the necessity of another year of preparation.

To this, "Pa said, 'Well, he is an authority & certainly ought to know. If it's necessary, why, of course, you'll have to do it.' " Professor Seymour's advice was identical with President Northrop's. Within a few days Pa was going to the meetings of the American Medical Association in Saratoga Springs, and once there, in spite of the fact that in Chicago Uncle Henry Gates had now recommended Northwestern University as "a good place to prepare for Yale," he decided to go to New Haven to "look up a good Yale Prep. School." Dr. Lewis wrote from New Haven:

Dear Harry:
Have just seen Prof. Hadley, Dean Wright, and Registrar Merritt and they advise you by all means to take the Examination at St Paul even though you fail in every subject and should you pass any it will be a great saving of time and work. Dean Wright and Merritt also Hadley advise the Tambault School highly as you can take there just what you want and need and say that the man who recently went there is strong in Greek. Now you can go down to St. Paul on the 25th in the Flyer and can easily find the Clarendon Hotel which is near the old Capitol High School building where the examinations are held. Go to Bert Hanson and ask him to give you $25.00 which ought to be enough to pay all your expenses. Show him this letter and he will give it to you. By going down on the Flyer you will have plenty of time to find where the Hotel is and get settled before night. Then after your examination if you wish to remain in Minneapolis over Sunday at Johnson's you can do so. A few collars & cuffs [and] your handkerchiefs you can carry in the little black grip in the packing closet in your room.

Now get down and pound some and get through as many examinations as you can.

With our love
Your Father
E. J. Lewis

There followed then the journey to the Twin Cities and the Yale examinations; he passed eleven of the thirteen, failing only in Algebra B and Latin Composition. There was one more step, the selection of the preparatory school. That was taken in late July.

Father has been for some time trying to select a proper preparatory school to Yale for next Year. Shattuck, Carleton, et. al. have been considered. It now seems very probable that I will go to the Academy of Oberlin, at Oberlin Ohio, near Cleveland, still nearer Lake Erie. The College (includ. acad.) numbers now about 1350. . . . OBERLIN Academy seems very sure, as I was talking about Mpls. Academy when Father said, "What's the use of talking about Mpls. Ac. when you're going to Oberlin Academy?"

And Oberlin Academy it was.

What was he like then, this raw and gangling fellow who was about to be plummeted into the world? He had shaved for the first time, but he had not developed his muscles and he had developed a weakness in his vision, probably from his incessant and often furtive reading, that sometimes made it impossible to read at all. He was restless, eager to see the world, and the world beyond Oberlin, but totally ignorant of it and full of fanciful illusions about it. He had a certain humor, sometimes quite lame, sometimes rather whimsical, but often nicely ironical when it turned upon himself. His vices, as far as one can tell, were like his hell making, not very serious and intended chiefly to call attention to himself.

I smoked 2 cigaretts and a cigar. The latter left such a bad taste in my mouth that I got a glass of beer to destroy it (which it did). I do not smoke as an almost invariable rule but I wanted to have fun hearing the Sauk Centre fellows say, "What, do you smoke too?" (lots of 'em said it too.)

He had developed, presumably from his reading, a large vocabulary, and one has the impression that he stopped talking only when he was alone; but he had no notable literary talent, and what facility he had in written expression had shown no marked development in these years. He had stated for himself, however, an adage by which he might, if he chose, live and develop: "Persistancy is one great element in success." As it is in spelling.

Some developments there had been. As his academic ambitions grew and he quieted down in school, so a certain intellectual seriousness, however adolescent it may have been and however much it tended to shade off into mere self-righteousness, had grown in him, and in this again he was marked off from most of his fellows.

Fisher & I rode out as far as cemetery tonight after school. Scrapped over various things. I contended that a belief in a Supreme Being did not necessarily include belief in immortality of the soul. He contested: I contended that nothing can be proven. We agreed that if human beings have souls then the higher animals, prehaps all forms of animal life, must have soul in greater or less degree.

This strain seems to develop with a new strain of piety. He professed to enjoy his work as church janitor. "I believe that I will continue to like the work as I do now, i.e., greatly; for—Famulum in domu Dei et Domini esse jucundum est!" He attends a variety of church services, and of the Roman Catholic he writes: "Seemed to me gorgeous 'and a' that' but not religion." The piety itself seems to have developed not out of any strong background of religious feeling (for there was little of that in the dry Lewis household), but rather, and almost spontaneously, from a form of self-righteousness that is not unusual in a young person who feels both his superior endowments and his social inferiority. Of girls he concluded as follows: "Gott sei dank I am not 'struck on' any one (at present!). Girls take up a part of a fellow's time out of proportion to their value, if he spends any time at all on them. Besides it wastes their time, if that be of importance!" When he was relieved of his work in the Palmer House, pious self-righteousness burst out in a strange "literary" exaltation:

> The regular night clerk arrived last night & I am through, and for the same right thankful. A hotel—uuf!—a comfortless device—for comfort, so modern as to be destitute of that most ancient of things—the divine soul of God and of man. . . . A place where the walls are bare of pictures! Where there are no books! Where the cigar and the newspaper predominates! Where the intellectual life is as nearly nil as can well be in an assorted assemblage of men who can read and write! Who hasten to the cigar stand and to the bar on their arrival instead of to a bookcase. And in this crowd of stupid well-dressed plebians to be a servant—a slave—one expected to be an applauder of lewd and childish stories, a welcomer of fools to fooldom, a quick prompt courteous attendant to those who are as slow, tardy and insolent in mind as in spirit, in fact, to be a hotel clerk! Holy Minerva deliver me! Tibi, oh deae divinissimae, tibi animae mater meae, tibi sanctissimae et doctissimae Minervae oro!
>
> Away with this modern business life of which hotel life is not the worst example. A thinker, who acts, if not always wisely, yet with a divine desire —or not at all—To read books, to gaze on pictures, to wander through green fields and stately woods and by sapphire water, ever ever thinking and progressing ever, though slowly or swiftly, to the divine purity! . . .

More restrained and more characteristic, both, is the entry for the Fourth of July in 1902:

> Fisher and I spent the "4th" at Fairy Lake. We do not approve of such celebrations as those which are held all over the country . . . we took some lunch & some books and went way out on Long Point, on Fairy. . . . After our lunch I read the Declaration of Independence & Fisher the Constitution of the U.S. That was all of our "celebration," yet methinks it was no less acceptable [to] the great Author of Independence than are the fire-works, toy cannons, horse races, potatoe races, fat-mens races; base-ball games; lemonade stands; merry-go-round, ect. ect. of the celebrations of others. Fisher & I have decided to try to read the Bible through . . . saying, "It is ridiculous not to be acquainted thoroughly with the religion of one's ancestors for many generations." We took turns in reading 8 chapters of Genesis. While going & returning we had a wordy-windy-wondrous debate on the question "Does matter exist?" I held the affirmative.

He finished Genesis in that month and Exodus before the end of the next. This piety was to swell. As he was beset by loneliness that he tried to fill with verse, so he was plagued by a gap of value in his inheritance that he was presently to try to fill with religious purpose.

His excitement grew with the summer. Before him lay the whole world; the world held everything. And yet. . . . The narrow world that he was leaving was neither gracious nor adventurous, nor had it been kindly to Harry Lewis; but it was the only world that he had thus far known, and he found himself briefly clinging to it. He had always felt loyalty of a certain kind to Sauk Centre. In the opening pages of his diary he had pasted photographs, clipped from the newspaper, of prominent citizens and of the better residences in the village. He had a habit (and one that, for a time, he was to cultivate) of clipping news items about individual comings and goings and pasting these in his diary. In the spring of 1902 he made an almost uniquely lyrical entry:

> I love to hear all of the church bells ringing together. To ears unaccustomed to them they may, prehaps, sound "jangling," but I have heard them for 17 years and love them. When I hear them in winter I seem to be lying in the hammock under the trees, and listening to them. When I hear them as I do now, in a still evening, they make me feel that the world and its riches are not worth a tithe of home and its surroundings.

Just before his departure, he makes a catalogue of old friends, and the reader of these diaries can only be struck by the irony of the motivating sentiment here, since most of these names have been mentioned only rarely, and then casually, and some have never been mentioned at all. Making lists of "friends" was to become another habit.

Forty years later, when he was living in Minnesota again, he remembered, with only the slightest Proustian overtone, three sparse items from that closing period of his youth:

> Remember from boyhood: streets lighted by arc lights. The tender, John MacGibbon, threw away the used carbon—picked up by boys. In June, bowl of arc light half filled with burned insects. Light associated with pum-pum-pullaway on street corners.
>
> Remember from boyhood: dusty but exciting smell in dark wheat elevator, above bins, and feeling of danger of falling down into that quicksand.

But the third is perhaps the most significant, carrying as it does, however faintly, the buried animus that was to drive him through the world.

> Remember as a boy: eagerness for anything out of Sauk Centre usual, or special in town; the derrick, a stranger in town, house with small tower, odd-shaped window in neighboring town.

Now, in the entries that end his life at Sauk Centre, it was the difference, all that was to be "out of Sauk Centre usual," that he was anticipating. And then, on September 15 and 16, he mingled news of Claude, who was about to come home, with the entries that mark his own departure: "Now begins the journey! . . . My trunk is packed."

He was later to say that his boyish objection to Sauk Centre was only that he could find no ruined castles in the neighborhood; he might more accurately have said that he had found so little human kindness.

"Bluer than waves of the sea in the sun . . ."

TWO

College

I

". . . I AM 17," he wrote on January 1, 1903. "Tall, ugly, thin, red-haired but not, methinks, especially stupid. I am in the academy of Oberlin College."

Oberlin, Ohio, at the beginning of the century was a pleasant residential village that consisted of little more than the college and existed for it. The village and the institution had been founded simultaneously in 1833, and the institution had begun, in fact, with its Preparatory Department, called the Academy after 1892 and abandoned in 1916. Named after an Alsatian pastor and philanthropist, John Frederick Oberlin, it was established by two gifted Congregational clergymen "to train teachers and other Christian leaders for the boundless and most desolate fields of the West." The first coeducational college, it was also the first that permitted no racial barriers and, indeed, it became the center of a famous fugitive-slave episode. When founded, and for some years thereafter, it required that each student do three or four hours of manual labor every day, for reasons of health, economy and morality. It existed within an atmosphere of earnest evangelical liberalism, which still made itself strongly felt at the time that Harry S. Lewis came to it, although by then, of course, it was nonsectarian. Chapel was the fixed point in the fluctuations of daily routine; a special prayer meeting was held on Friday afternoons; classes and all other assemblies were opened with prayer; the college was a training ground for foreign missions, and Harry Lewis witnessed the laying of the cornerstone of a Memorial Arch erected to honor certain missionaries, many Oberlin graduates among them, who had been martyred in the Boxer Rebellion in 1900. He had written that its student population in 1902 was 1,350, but actually it was a good deal smaller; in the year of his attendance there were 578 students in the College, only 330 in the Academy.

The evangelical atmosphere of Oberlin was to give Harry Lewis the first real focus for his interests and provide the first channel for his roving energies. In a lesser way it was to give him for the first time a kind of social function and, through that, although altogether lacking in personal source or warmth, a set of social relationships. He did not become a happier boy or a less lonely one, but for the moment, at least, he ceased merely to flounder, and his life took on the semblance of organized activity. If all this was to prove merely temporary, the Oberlin experience was also to prove of ultimate importance; or so, at any rate, the later Lewis felt. "Very valuable," he was to write—in his unpublished autobiographical account, of 1932—of his six months there; "gave him a notion of such small, highly pious and denominational Midwestern colleges as appear in several of his novels; and a notion of the Eastern Middlewest, in which is situate Zenith." This adult evaluation gives us, to be sure, no notion whatever of what did in fact happen to the boy at Oberlin.

He arrived on September 22 in 1902 after a weekend spent with his mother's family in Chicago, where he bought a new hat—"derby, cost $3.00." With the help of a member of the student reception committee, he found that evening a room in the house of a widow named Brown, a roommate named John G. Olmstead, and a place where he could board for three dollars a week—the German House, managed by a family named Bischof. He enrolled in Algebra 2, Latin Composition, Greek (in which at last he would really read the *Anabasis*), English 4, and Senior Bible. Almost at once he fell into the pattern that was to comprise his nonacademic life and that consisted chiefly of two ingredients—long solitary excursions on foot into the country, and activities associated with the Y.M.C.A., which he joined immediately. During his first weeks he went to a few school parties, but he did not enjoy them and presently began to avoid them almost entirely. At the urging of Edward Increase Bosworth, the professor of New Testament, he considered altering his plans for Yale and continuing college at Oberlin. He apparently proposed the idea to his father, who replied "saying 1st, 'You must prepare for Yale or go to *no* College;' 2nd, 'You must *not* do anything *but* prepare for Yale & take exercise, sleep ect.' " He gives us again a "typical day":

> I will give today as a fair example of my Oberlin days. Rose at 6:10. Breakfast at 6:30. Studied Greek (finished study, rather), 6:55 to 7:25. Greek recitation to 8:30. Returned home & studied English & Latin composition until 10:20. Went to Gym & had gym work for 1 hour. Then usually would have gone to chapel then to Bischof's & studied 5 or 10 minutes till dinner (in reality I "ducked" chapel today, as it was already 23 or 24 min. to 12 when I was dressed after gym work & chapel begins in chapel, a block away, at 25 to 12.) Dinner 12 to 12:20 (I never stay till all are excused. I get excused—which is somewhat impolite but saves much time. I simply *can't* waste so much time in eating. Long enough to eat decently slow is long enough for all purposes). Studied till one. English recitation 1 to 2. Lat. Comp. recitation 2 to 3. Study till 5. (Today I got a shoe from shoemenders, & spent a few minutes in a book store after 3). In evening I study,

ending with reading a chapter of Bible. Then prayers and to bed (to dream of YyYYyYYyYale!)

—where, it would develop, things were not to be different. A clown to the yokels of Sauk Centre, a country boor to the provincials of Oberlin, did he expect to find himself the darling of the senior societies?

For one day on one weekend, he broke his routine by going on a two-dollar student football excursion to Ann Arbor, Michigan. He joined in the processional celebration of the newly elected president of Oberlin, Henry Churchill King. He studied the Yale Phi Beta Kappa lists and chose the name of Hugh Rankin as that of a man suited to advise him about New Haven; Rankin sent him a Yale Y.M.C.A. booklet and, later, copies of *The Yale News* and *The Yale Record* and at least one long letter of advice in which "he spoke of the desirability of doing something—athletics, lit. work, ect., besides digging." He spent more time than is indicated by his "typical day" in browsing in the college library stacks—"nothing I enjoy more"—but he did work at his studies with concentrated energy and almost unremittingly, using even his walking time to review memorized work like Greek verb forms. It was rarely that he fell back into his earlier aimlessness and, for example, pricked himself in order to write his name in his own blood and daub a page of diary with bloody fingerprints. At the close of the first period of the term, as Latin Composition was coming to an end and he was about to substitute Roman History for it, he wondered whether he could not accomplish quite as much at home as at Oberlin, and he dreamed "that I was 'fired' from O. Acad. because I didn't meet the physical requirements & was not attentive enough to religious meetings ect.!"

He remained, of course, and worked even harder in the second period. His eyes began to bother him again and when he went to Chicago for the Christmas holidays, a series of eye examinations showed severe astigmatism and he was fitted with spectacles. When he returned, there was a shift in roommates and he admitted to attacks of acute homesickness, but he was resolved to do well and occasionally reread "a letter of father's in which he gave me a good jacking up for not tending to business (on Nov. 8, '02). Taken once in a while it serves as an excellent tonic to keep me at work." His homesickness led him to hope that he could leave Oberlin when he finished the term that ended with March, and the fact that the Academy could not supply him with a geometry teacher for the final term worked in his favor. "I count as my pleasures in Oberlin eating, sleeping," he wrote, and then, in his lonely life, he added even "gym. work daily" to that sparse catalogue that ended with "walk on Sat. or Mon. and Y.M.C.A. Sun. evening!" Of the gymnasium work he made, a day or two later, the complaint that "I simply *can't* clear the box in vaulting but I *will* before the time to write 'Finis.' "

Whether he cleared the box or not, he did not say, but he finished that term with generally excellent grades and, since a geometry teacher had not been forthcoming, his father permitted him then to return to Sauk Centre early in April and complete his preparation for Yale independently. He took a chair car home to surprise his father by his thrift, and "Mother and Fisher met me at the train. Told Fisher of my missionary ambition."

The last sentence tells us what had been new about that Oberlin experience, which, in its external chronology, was so uneventful. At the very first opportunity he attended a Y.M.C.A. meeting and wrote, "It impressed me very highly as an indication of positive earnest muscular Christianity; so different from the hypocritical watery sort of thing in Sauk Centre's Y.P.S.C.E. . . . Oberlin is, above all else, distinctly Christian and religious." Then follows a very rapid development of zeal. After the meeting of two weeks later, he wrote:

> I professed my self tonight, at the Y.M.C.A. meeting, as one who is trying to be a Christian and asked their help. This means something. It is not cant. I am trying to be a true follower of Jesus Christ. I handed in my name as candidate for membership. . . . This day of my profession of Christ is surely one of the most important in my life.

For four days in the following week, the American Board of Missions was holding meetings in the college. Harry was indefatigable in his attendance, took full notes on sermons and filled his diary with a variety of Biblical injunctions to spread God's word. Suddenly he wrote, "And I will obey the command!" And then: "THE COMMAND TO GO; and, deo volente, et si possum, I WILL OBEY! My action is not temporary emotion, methinks, nor fanaticism. It is well considered, and it is right!" Immediately he became a regular member of Dean King's Training Class ("about the finest Bible class in U.S."); and of the next Y.M.C.A. meeting he wrote:

> . . . tonight I said "Last Sunday I said that I wanted to be a Christian; tonight I say that I am a Christian." I didn't speak thus, twice in two weeks, just to talk, but because I wanted it understood that I *am* a disciple of Christ. Now I can work, without talking much, as I think it is understood that I am a Christian. Had the finest of talks with Ransom [the minister in the First Congregational Church] tonight. He commended highly my choice of life work & gave me advice & encouragement.

One of the functions of the Oberlin Y.M.C.A. was to supply Sunday-school teachers to a small, nearby quarry town named Nickle Plate, and on the day that he became a member of the Y.M.C.A., Harry Lewis taught his first class there.

> Had 8 little girls. I pray to God that I may teach them some of His word, which is but synonimous with eternal right. I try to teach them morals from the lesson not just the History of the lesson. Earl went out with Brown, Hybner & I today.

The young zealots made the trip to Nickle Plate and back by means of a handcar, and except in the severest winter weather, when the railroad tracks were icy or drifted over with snow, some few of them regularly filled their evangelical obligation. When the zeal of the others waned, that of Harry Lewis did not:

> We got out to S.S. this P.M.—Brown & I. . . . I asked for new men tonight in Y.M.C.A. & we got two. One of them I know & I think that he is just the man we want, Earl McCurry. He is good both mentally and physically. . . . The other I don't know. I think I got in my request rather neatly. The fellows tonight, many of them, had expressed a desire for new life, as they had been stirred by the week of prayer meetings. They were telling of intentions to live a more active Christian life ect ect—and I gave 'em a chance to make good their verbal resolve to *do* something! Took 'em "As 'twere by storm" and several men spoke about it to Brown & me.

The flesh of others proved weaker than his.

> There were 5 new fellows 2 weeks ago, where oh where are they now!? McCurry had a cold, Campbell "was busy," where the others were I don't know. Christianity that can't stand the hand car test is rather far from perfect.

He sought for means to put "the fervor of the missionary fire within me" to immediate work.

> Wish I could get hold of Glendenning, whom we call Dinny. He is on the downward road. Doesn't work, spends his evenings with an inferior class of girls, is behind in all studies. Deus me opitulare eum opitulari.

That ambition failing, he continued to fan his own flames. He began to plan on becoming a theological student. To the capital Y he joined the sign of the cross or the capital M. "My old mark Y (equals I *will* go to Yale, if God be willing and it be best) changes to YM (equals Y plus I *will* be a missionary deo volente). YMYM." He joined the Student Volunteers. "Its members pledge is 'It is my purpose, if God permit, to become a foreign missionary.'" He attended not only the regular Friday prayer meeting but an extra one. "Some of us boys meet weekly for 15 minutes before Cad [Academy] Prayer Meet. & hold a little prayer meeting especially praying for a revival here in Oberlin. Such a good devout Cad Prayer Meeting with 'Own experience in Prayer' as subject." Prayer itself he took very seriously, and he questioned the propriety of employing it at secular assemblies:

> Don't like that, & don't like opening classes by prayer. Seems to me that prayer is too precious and sacred a thing to drag into everything we do. Of course an inward mental petition to God for strength and purity is always necessary when starting anything but not verbal, vocal, long prayer.

> Those at a party or Class thus opened who are not Christians both come to have a feeling of weariness at the mere thought of prayer; and spoil the fervency of the prayer for those who are Christians by inattentiveness. So I object *not* because I don't believe prayer an absolutely necessary act, but because I believe it both *sacred* and necessary.

Everything, even football, was colored by his zeal. He said at one point that he did not enjoy watching the game but that he enjoyed participating in the cheering; this too, like hymn singing, was a form of communion. When Oberlin won over Western Reserve in that autumn of 1902, he wrote:

> At last! Rah! Rah! Rickety ax! We've won a victory for which I've prayed—for when Oberlin's proud crimson and Gold are trailed in the dust then is the cause of the Kingdom of God weakened—because Oberlin is one of the most Christian of all colleges.

He indulged in a certain amount of ethico-religious speculation in his diary. The religious element seems sometimes less powerful than the ethical, as, for example, when he becomes indignant over the defense, made by a young woman at the German House, of the custom of decorating hats with feathers. "How remarkable that anyone could grow to young womanhood & not learn that *no one* has a right to do *anything* 'Just because he wants to.' The more civilized we grow the less absolute independence we have. Hideous the custom and childish the reason!" Indeed, the missionary zeal of October and November seems to dim out in the next month before a more general interest in religion. ("It looks as if Minnie were backsliding," his roommate wrote his parents. "He is having a hard fight but I pray God he may be victorious. That is all I can do for if I advised him to do well he would do just the opposite.")

In Chicago during the holidays, he attends a service of the high mass in the Holy Name Cathedral, and he writes, "I like the catholic church better constantly and, at times, I have moments in which I almost resolve to join the grand old church." But he also attends an enormous revivalist meeting conducted by John Alexander Dowie, the founder of Zion City ("D. claims to be a reincarnation of Elija"), a Christian Science service, and a Hebrew service.

When he returned to Oberlin he attended both Anglican and Roman Catholic services, and he began a debate with himself as to which of these had the greater power for him, decided in favor of the Episcopal, was reminded by his father that the traditional Lewis association was Congregational, and presently wrote, "No more Episcopalian Church."

The missionary zeal returned in early 1903. At an open prayer meeting, the Y.M.C.A. secretary "called on men who are making a fight to conquer sin to stand, which I did (solus)." In March he wrote, "For some time my resolve for missionary service has been re-forming (that is forming again) so that now I am as much inclined to foreign missionary service as I was last fall." He listed the countries where he would like to work and gave his preference to Africa. He prayed for strength of purpose. "O God, almighty everlasting omniscient, keep me firm in my missionary resolution."

> Just as the oft repeated Y means "Long Live Yale; for her am I preparing," so henceforth in this diary let the sacred sign [of the cross] be an assurance and a pledge of a firm resolution in me to carry God's word to foreign lands, as a missionary, if, in his great goodness to me, a miserable and indolent wretch, he permit me this most glorious of duties.

And in that mood, he returned to Sauk Centre and to Fisher.

As the aspirant to Yale and the aspirant to Glory were there identified, so the would-be poet and the would-be missionary came together at least once, when he resolved to write "a sacred dialogue, 'The Praise of God,' to be a collection of various poems, hymns, ect. to the glory of God, all to be bound together by poetical dialogue representing these hymns ect. as delivered at the Court of Roderick the Good."

It would seem, however, that verse writing now became a relatively infrequent activity. In the six-month period, he made only three other references to it: once when he said that he hoped to finish a poem called "Tower on Peters Hall" for the *Oberlin Review;* again when by request he sent a poem back to Sauk Centre for a Delphian "newspaper"; and last when he copied out a poem called "Hallowe'en" that he had written in October of 1901 and had rewritten several times since.

His wide and random reading seems likewise to have been curtailed. Pepys' *Diary* he read for pleasure, but most of his reading was in connection with his studies. He read Macaulay's life of Milton, and Johnson's too, in preparation for an English essay on the poet. His reading in the Bible became part of the course in Bible Study. His work on Burke's *Conciliation* was part of his review for the Yale examinations. He bought Catholic and Episcopal prayer books as a part of his piety. Fisher gave him Lowell's poems for Christmas, and he bought a miscellaneous lot of English poets (together with a manual called *What a Young Man Ought to Know,* "a book on personal purity,") from Glendenning when that unfortunate fellow withdrew from the college.

He spent a good deal of time in the library simply looking at books that he was unable to read. This was in connection with a new and rapidly developing interest.

> Spent an hour this morning looking over books of & on Sanskrit, Assyrian, Chaldee, Syriac, Greek, Latin ect. and looked at some Deutsche Handbücher über Deutschen Universitäten. Ah! how I enjoyed it. Such a treat is worth a dozen parties, or banquets, or 2 or 3 theatre goings. Some day I'm going to be able to read them.

In Chicago he did permit himself to attend one theater "and am heartily sorry now that I did. The entertainment was cheap and smutty vaudeville; the air reeked with tobacco smoke. Yet there was a certain fascination in the dancing singing half clad women on the stage and, like a fool, I stayed until the show was over." But he spent a good deal more time in the Chicago museums and universities, and when possible, "in the Egyptian room . . . this interests me most of all—Egyptology." Now and then he wrote the word "Savant" at the top of a diary page, and on one page which is headed "Savant—ego! (futurus)" he made the following statement of an ambition that seemed now to rival his intentions for theology:

> All such work as looking up these references gives me a desire to be a *master* of some subject—say of the Ancient World, or Sanskrit, or Hist[ory] of Rome from 509 B.C. to Birth of Christ; or the History, Literature, & Language of Phoenicia (touching especially or rather studying especially Astarte, a favorite topic of mine). This is certainly a broad range enough to find therein some subject in which to do masterly specializing. Eng[lish], Ger[man], French, Amer[ican], Lat[in], Greek literatures all attract me as does the histories of all the world. Some where I shall find my subject before long. (Bah! what nonsense! A boy—nay, a child of 18 knowing or expecting to know anything. I must wait 50 years to begin to learn).

He had to wait hardly a day to learn that in one way Oberlin was not to prove very different from Sauk Centre, that again he was to be an object of contempt and derision and a social pariah who necessarily lived in an enforced solitude. After Sinclair Lewis's death, his Oberlin roommate, John G. Olmstead, published in the *Alumni Magazine* his recollections of Lewis at Oberlin. He had had his own letters to his parents to draw upon, and he had made inquiries of the surviving members of the German House of 1902–1903 to reinforce his impressions. One of his letters, dated September 23, 1902, reads in part:

> Well, when I returned who should be here but a long, lank, redheaded, freckled face chap from some crossroads up in Minn. and such a fresh youngster you never saw. He was to be my roommate so we took the next hour in discussing each other to see if we would match, and then had to pitch up a coin to see how we would divide the drawers. He is, I believe, a good student. I'm willing to put up with his greenness on that account. Lewis is his name. We already call him Minnie. . . . This roommate is 17. I guess smart enough in books but a little lacking in worldly knowledge although he thinks he knows it all.

At the end of that week, after he had attended a Y.M.C.A. reception, Harry Lewis wrote, "Met several . . . whom I liked *very* much better than my room mate. Hope to get a chance next term & get a room with some one I like." They were off to a bad start and matters rapidly grew worse.

Olmstead was an athlete with many friends, and he liked to have them in his room at night; Lewis had no friends and wanted to study. "He would tell us to 'shut up' and I would threaten to throw him out the window." But by Olmstead's own account, Lewis's trigger temper was so alarming that Olmstead more or less submitted to his tyranny. When Olmstead was invited to move in with a friend named Fulton, he wrote that "Minnie says I can't leave him," and he hoped that Lewis, with his profession of Christianity ("You never saw a fellow take such a flop as Minnie has. He tells me my Christian duty every day.") would become a more congenial roommate. This did not happen.

> I cannot recall anytime when I have had my temper and patience tried as I have since I have been here. To speak frankly, although Minnie is a bright student and smart fellow he is nevertheless not the one I would choose for a roommate. He is 17, just the age when he thinks he knows more than anyone else on earth; he is red-headed which of course means quick tempered; he has never gone with fellows or lived in the city; he has simply read things and knows nothing about the reality of them. . . . He did not know that friendships grew, were not ready made. He knows nothing of men or ways of the world from experience but he thinks he knows it all. Simply he is *fresh.* He talks too much. He is so hot headed that I cannot, and he even told me I should not, crack any jokes. Listen—he told me one night he didn't want me to make any remarks whatever about him unless it was to praise him. He would simply take my head off if he knew I was writing this. When I received that box of fudge from Sis I told him she said to divide up between we four fellows. He took nearly his whole share that first time. Twice afterwards he came over and helped himself to another piece. . . . I cannot reprimand the fellow for he simply goes up in the air. I just merely have to bite my tongue and hang on to my chair. If things only occurred once a month it might be different but when anywhere from once to half a dozen times a day a fellow has to meet such things it certainly is trying.

The German House boarders felt much the same way about him. One of them wrote, "I can't remember ever seeing him laugh, and there was a lot of laughing at mealtimes there. Sometimes he'd come, eat and go with no word to anyone. And if he did speak it was usually some caustic sarcastic remark. I remember him first and last as a sarcastic person." Another said, "To the girls . . . he was very repulsive and when we drew names each week, to change our seats at the table, everyone hoped they would not have to sit beside him." Others thought him "conceited," "aloof and critical, without any friends or intimates," and "a sort of bore." "On any and every occasion he would say 'Where ignorance is bliss, 'tis folly to be wise.' The quotation needed not to be and rarely was in any way apropos."

The other side of the picture is Harry Lewis's and is recorded in his diaries:

November 18, 1902. Am thinking of rooming alone next term.

December 4, 1902. . . . 4 P.M. My room mate & I have just decided that we do not and can not make really congenial companions & that we will separate at end of term. I will probably room alone, next term.

6:30. Since I wrote the last words I have been fighting a hard fight, and have conquered. I almost decided to give up, and go back home & implore Father to let me try it over again, somewhere else. But I have won! I *will* stay here & fight to the end and conquer my studies & my own defects. I will ask Olmstead if he is willing to go on rooming with me rest of year, or for next term at least.

9:00. Have decided to move next term & not ask O. if he will like to have me as mate another term.

When he returned from the Christmas vacation, he found a new roommate waiting for him, one Jess Dellenbaugh, who was "very quiet" and seemed more congenial ("Had good talk with room-mate on literature—the poets especially this evening.") Yet in exactly one week Harry was alone again, and he remained so for the rest of his Oberlin stay.

He left this morning. Said he couldn't stand the smell of Koos' tailoring stove [One of the boys in the house earned money by pressing student clothing.] which the rest of us are used to. He seemed to like me very well & wished me to go along with him to his new room & stay there. In fact he urged me strongly.

But Jess Dellenbaugh is never mentioned again.

One young man Harry Lewis yearned to have as his friend.

To Y.M.C.A. meeting with Carter. After meeting up to Carter's room. For the last few days and especially tonight we have been discovering that almost everyone of our tastes, likes & dislikes, our ambitions, & to a great extent past history corresponds, and that we seem to be intended for the warmest truest of friends. I think that I revealed more of myself to him in a few moments than I ever did to anyone else in months and he remarked the same of himself. Prehaps so rapidly formed a friendship may not prove permanent b[ut] God make it! He seems just the friend for whom I've look[ed] all my life—one who can sympathize with me & *understand* me in every mood. He seemed to regard me in such a light as I him. His name is Holland. "There is a friend that sticketh closer than a brother." (Prov. 18–24).

Holland Carter's name never occurs again, except in the most casual way; and when he called to say goodbye on Harry Lewis's last night at Oberlin, all that Harry wrote was, "Holland Carter was in my room to bid me goodbye, tonight." Never again was he to permit himself to speak even so mutely, even to himself, of his needs, and we begin to see, perhaps, the kind of novelist he was to become: one who would never be able to project in art the forms of his suffering, one who would never wish to allow—if he could—his writing to confront his subjectivity—if it was there.

He tried, at first, to enter the social life of Oberlin, and the evidence he gives us makes it unnecessary for us to guess at what he aspired to in that life. He walked down to the railroad station to watch the arrival of the rooters for a visiting football team. "When they did come, as they alighted—swarmed across the depot yard into a procession, I [k]new that I saw that of which I have so often read—College Life." Even late in his stay, nearly a whole page of the diary is given to drawings of college symbols, many suggesting the world of Frank Merriwell and others suggesting only the private world of Harry Lewis. In the center of the page, written in code, is the name Myra, and below that, "dreamt of her last night." Below this entry is a very large cross with the words "Christo et Ecclesio" written about the top of the cross, and at the very bottom of the page is a small circle within which is what appears to be the insignia of Oberlin College.

He attended a Halloween masquerade at the German House, and he joined an outing of the same group early in the year. The latter occasion suggests poignantly what will follow.

> The whole German house went on an outing; to Cascade Park, Elyria, this afternoon. Elyria is 10 miles from O[berlin]. Delightful ride to & fro, & fine time in the park with its fall & rocks & cliffs. It brought me nearer to God to see the mighty works of His hand, and then think how much greater are such features of Nature as Niagara ect., and I quoted to myself, "The heavens declare the glory of the Lord, and the firmament showeth his handiwork." I liked to stand on one cliff, very high, and look through the trees at a little lake, or at the river tumbling among the rocks; to climb over the rocks & far into little caves; and I sat way up in a big oak tree, far away from all the rest of the party, and sang a song of gladness to God, because he had permitted me to know in some small degree his miracles. I liked the ride home (on electric-car which connects Wellington-Oberlin-Elyria-Cleveland) esp[ecially] as I stood on the step of the car and gazed at the lights of farm houses seen through the dark, which was growing dense, and told myself storiettes about the houses. I think that I liked this melancholy calm happiness of dusk best of all the trip. Fulton was up in room to visit Olmstead in evening.

After that, the refrain reverts to the familiar "I'm not going to class party." Even in Chicago, in the center of what appears to have been the warm family life of his uncle, he withdrew from group festivities.

> In the evening came the party. I was fortunate enough to get out of associating with a lot of strange people for 4 or 5 hours in this manner: there were 2 more boys than girls among those invited, not including Claude and

I. When I saw this I slipped upstairs, after having been introduced to all. Am glad I did as they danced most of the evening & I can't dance.

At Oberlin he ceased to go even to class meetings, and when he amused himself, it was by telling stories to the small Bischof children or by tramping alone over the muddy Ohio fields.

The transparency of his dreams joins with the throbbing delusiveness of his admirations. When his mother sent him a newspaper clipping about the athletic success of a Sauk Centre boy whom Harry knew, he wrote:

> At last! Irsfield has his picture in the paper! Good old Jim. There were but few in S.C.H.S. whom I knew better & none whom I admired more. I met him on the day he became a Freshman (& on which I did the same.) We elected him the pres[ident] of the Freshman class—but he refused the office.—He made the H.S. in 3 y[ea]rs. . . . He rec[eive]d about as good marks as any & yet [rarely?] studied. He was pres[ident] of lit[erary] society, of ath[letic] ass[ociation] & of his class. Capt[ain] of football team & playing the whole game. . . . The time his collar bone was broken he played several minutes (till the end of the half) with the broken bone greatly hurting him. The second half Sauk C[entre] couldn't do anything as he was out of the game. Jim was one of our best singers; a fine debater; by far the best actor in the Senior class play at graduation. He & he alone caused S[auk] Centre to win the Park Region Ath[letic] Ass[ociation] . . . Track Team meet, in 1900 (because he won so many events.) He was the best runner & the best jumper (either high or broad) & next to best shot putter & hammer thrower in school. . . . He was wonderfully well stocked with general information on every subject from evolution to love making [or lawe making?]. He had the blackest hair & the best legs I ever saw. This is a decidedly "hash like" description but all true except that it isn't half good enough. He is now a Soph. in the U. of Minn. Before he graduates he will surely make a great record. I am glad to say that I have several autographs of his & the Latin Gram[mar] he used in S.C.H.S.

The impulse to juxtapose to this paean Harry's account of his own appearance at the Halloween masquerade is irresistible:

> I went in Dinny's football suit with Speiro head gear, half padded pants, cleated shoes, skin guards, big red socks, leather padded red jersey, head gear, rubber nose & mouth guard. All complete just as a player is dressed on the field. Made quite an impression when I entered dining room, as I gave a rousing Hi-O-Hi. (I was late & all were seated so I got to door of room unseen).

As such social participation came to its quick and disappointed end, no intellectual activities, aside from the academic routines, replaced it. There seems to have been no drama and little music. Public lectures were almost invariably on religious themes. Once, it is true, Harry heard Mark Hanna speak at Oberlin, and he made what was for him at this period a rather unusual social criticism: "didn't impress me well—rather [the contrary?] as he often represented [himself?] as the mouthpiece of selfish & dominant capital." If this observation implies a background of a developing social awareness or of any exposure to the discussion of social and economic ideas, his diaries give the implication no support. When he allows his intelligence any speculative rein, it is always in the very generalized moralistic area. Except for the notes on Carter and Irsfield, there is no observation of individual human character, and those passages are not so much observations as private lyrics. He seems to have had no interest in human beings, or perhaps it would be more exact to say that he was mute to them because they had so little interest in him. For the little kindness that was shown him, he was grateful.

> I went over to the train to bid her [Beulah Lewis, a German House boarder] goodbye. She has done many things to make life pleasant for me in the last six months; by her unfailing good nature and cheerfulness; by her wit and repartee.

After the Christmas recess, the aching horrors of homesickness poured over him, and with them, the nagging dreams of Myra, Myra, Myra. "I've been very homesick, ever since I returned from Chi. How much I'd give for an hour at home! But I'll 'stick it out!' . . . have been alone most of the time & so naturally get to thinking more of home." Earlier in the year there had been this pathetic bit: "Father says that he & Mother miss me very much (& so he has said before, as has also Mother)." Now, in January, parental letters meant a great deal to him. "I haven't rec[eive]d a bit of mail since a week from tonight. Something must be wrong." The next day: "A noble sermon by Prof. Bewer—just what I needed, as I had a bad case of blues and, Deo gratius, his sermon dealt with those who feel themselves beaten about by the waves of the sea of life, and despairing, and melancholy." Then there is a lifting of hope when it appears that he may not be able to get the needed instruction in geometry in the final term and he debates "very vigorously the question of Oberlin or Home next term." Common sense tells him that it "would be better for me & please Father better" if he stayed, but he explains the problem to his father and the latter replies that "he WOULD TAKE IT UNDER ADVISEMENT." The capital letters represent the surge of hope. Having considered the matter, his father wrote as follows:

> *Sauk Centre, Minn.*
> *2/23/03*
>
> *Dear Harry:—*
>
> I enclose with this a draft for 20.00 your expenses for March. Put in this month in getting up your references and in having Cairns [an instructor in mathematics] show you about your Geometry & Algebra. And then

should you decide that you can get along just as well at home I will send you a draft for your R.R. transportation last week in March. Probably you can leave there about Mch 29 or 30th.

I am going to trust your judgment for if you fail you will be the one to suffer for it. Not I— In the meantime I will hold the four cords ironwood over to April so you can have something to make muscle should you decide to come home then. This morning is the first one for about 10 days that it has been above zero. Now I repeat dont go thinking and trying to argue what is best to do but put in your best licks and get all you can out of the month. I dont take any stock in what you can get out of Martin and Garland as I imagine that probably you are about as advanced as they and aside from probably a little riper judgment I don't think you will get much help and I look upon it that if you do come home you will simply have to take the chances of preparing yourself by June to pass exams.

Your Father
E. J. Lewis

Even the prospect of the four cords of ironwood—or rather, four and three fourths, as it would develop—could not change his mind now. "I have already long since decided that question; hence—Home next term!"

The rest is work and dreams.

Last night I had a wonderfully constructed dream. I arrived in Sauk Centre only to find that "Wiene" Hedin (who it seems looked exactly like me) had been doing all sorts of things—singing solos, shooting Prof. Stanton with a slingshot, ect.—which everyone supposed I had done, as they believed that I had returned several days earlier!

And again: "The other night I had a dream in which I was on the depot platform in S.C. shaking hands with everyone."

His mother was there with Fisher.

2

THAT SPRING AND SUMMER were a better time for him than perhaps any before and a good many to come. He allowed himself a few days of vacation and then went to work on the ironwood and the *Iliad* at once. The four and three fourths cords of wood he had mastered by April 27. The studying went on until June 24, when he made the trip to St. Paul again for his second experience with Yale examinations. He had been studying on many days for ten to twelve hours, not only his Greek with Reverend Garland, but geometry by himself and the inevitable *Anabasis,* which he was reviewing. In St. Paul he took eight examinations and passed them all, and on July 7 he received notice of his admission to Yale.

This was, of course, the great event of the summer, but the Sauk Centre interlude that he was now experiencing contained a good deal more. He had time for many of the long walks that he enjoyed, often with Irving Fisher. He had time, too, for a good deal of reading, and his reading became more consistently serious than it had yet been. There was the usual proportion of fiction, but it was good fiction: Scott's *The Talisman* and *The Antiquary,* Dickens's *Little Dorrit* and *Martin Chuzzlewit, Adam Bede,* some Kipling (not so much for pleasure as for information about India, a likely location for a missionary), *The Hound of the Baskervilles* and *Pilgrim's Progress.* There was nonfiction as well: Macaulay's *Addison, Sartor Resartus, The Origin of Species,* Washington Irving, and Powell's *Historic Towns,* "preparatory to my eastern trip." There was some poetry: *The Idylls of the King, In Memoriam, Coriolanus.*

He had time, too, for versifying of his own. The three or four pages that he had written on the projected volume, "In Praise of God," he read to Fisher and then, shortly after, without explanation, burned. He translated Homer into rapid iambic pentameter. He addressed a lyric called "Evening" to a sunset over Sauk Lake, and another lyric to the blue of Yale:

> Bluer than waves of the sea in the sun,
> Sparkling, untossed by the gale

(When sea fairies beckon with white glistening arms)
Bluer thy colors, oh Yale.

He copied out half a dozen abortive lyrics on miscellaneous subjects, among them a rather strange one called "Errores in Libris":

Through cloudy rains
And sunny lanes
With Milton's moods I stray
With Spencer oft I hold my breath
And fear to see black armored death
Triumphant in affray.

A judge severe
(Will Shakespeare near)
I look men through & through.
Perchance I hear the deep clear tone
And those rich words which one alone,
Macaulay only, knew.

The notion that he is to become a judge of men—he who had until now seemed so impervious to the variety and complexity of human nature—is interesting in conjunction with a prose project that he was contemplating:

> For some time I have been thinking of making a more or less scientific study of *men* (Homines); of human nature; of mankind; using people as text books. It would be a sort of "practical psychology." Study their mental, moral & physical natures; prevalence & effect of different habits; opinions & knowledge of death, God, the church; politics; ect. ect. and other points ad infinitum. My method of study would be by using ears & eyes; asking things delicately by disguising them in innocent sounding questions ect. ect. My purpose is to learn to know men. How can I do good missionary work unless I know men; all sorts & conditions of them. I shall take some notes on my observations.
>
> Today I made a trial study. I talked with a laborer (John Brown, father of Frank B. an old school mate) getting his opinions on all sorts of subjects. I think that when I learn how to "study" I shall be successful.

Was it to the end of his "practical psychology" that he stopped a small boy and asked him "Who are you?" only to engender this exchange: "He replied, 'Nobody.' 'Where do you live?' 'Nowhere.' What do you do for a living?' 'Nothing.' 'How much wages do you get for it?' 'None!' "?

The diaries do not suggest that the prose he thinks of as "writing" is becoming more scientific. Rather, it becomes more and more "poetical." He notes that he has written "a legendary tale of S. Germany," and he includes a set piece called "On the Road" ("Perchance there stands a goodly manor house; they are returning from the hunt; fair ladies and dashing young maccaronis, gay in red," etc.). More and more he indulges in prose of this sort that is meant to describe his long walks:

> A real summer day.... Bees hasten about the waxen flours of the milk-weed, gay dragon-flies swayed, a-tilt on slender grasses, or floated flowingly through the air. A hawk bounced over the sky line of the trees, and dis-appeared again. Crows talked politics on a shaggy rail fence. Gorgeous the flowers—tall and stately tiger lilies, dainty 'wild geraniums,' wild roses....

In St. Paul, in June, he met his first published writer, who was working in a bookstore: Arthur Wheelock Upson, a poet. Harry Lewis was profoundly impressed. Upson was only eight years older than Harry Lewis and already enjoyed a considerable reputation among the local *cognoscenti.* A frail youth, brought up in a pony cart world, he began writing verse at ten and published his first book of poems in 1900, before he left the university. In spite of continual ill health, he published over half a dozen volumes before his death at thirty-one, published widely in periodicals, won the reputation of being "an aristocrat in verse" and the praise of such arbiters of taste as Aldrich and Stedman—all of which would be of no interest whatever except for the fact that he was writing precisely the sort of thing, both in prose and verse, to which Harry Lewis aspired, and that he served therefore as a living exemplar. The prose:

> Down a green Yew Lane a Sonnet's length, or thereabouts, from the Highway, one discovers the brown, moss-edged gables of the Harp Tavern, whose Rafters have rung with sweetest Music from the days of *Sidney* and *Spenser* to our own. It cannot escape one, for the Lane turns at the Tavern Gate and then, too, there is the Ancient Sign. It is a place of Solace, tidy Hearths and rare Bread and Ale; and so sweet is the Companionship withal, that many a day the present Scribe has overtarried there, to the sad neglect of his proper Duties.

The verse, with its mixture of debased Tennyson and fuzziest Poe:

> Oh, to feel the subtle Spring
> Rouse the fire in everything,
> As she once in Khorassan
> Round the old rose-gardens ran,
> Keeping with the Poet-wooer
> Her sweet tryst at Naishapur!

How long the desire to write such verse kept Sinclair Lewis the nonpoet alive and how long the desire to write such prose kept him from discovering the style that was most appropriate to his own non-pony-cart person, it would be difficult to say, but that he thought he had caught a star, later events would show.

If the poetical and the religious aspirations had separated when "In Praise of God" was thrown into the fire, neither seems to have weakened. On his first Sunday at home, after a meeting of Christian Endeavor, he announced, "It is dead. I must do something to waken it." Then he took it upon himself to solicit new members, revised the membership lists, often led the meetings, was elected vice-president and headed a number of committees. He began to open rather than end his day with his private Bible study, "because I am in the worst of condition for studying just before retiring." He ushered at church, taught Sunday school, attended services in all the churches, memorized the "Sermon on the Mount," read a variety of missionary tracts and nearly succeeded in persuading Fisher that he should become a medical missionary. One day in June he announced his intention to his parents, those practical secularists. "Both disapproved but neither said much. Mother does not think me fitted to be a Missionary; Father does not approve of missionary work in toto, apparently."

Only at the very end of the summer, on a Sunday after he had attended both the Methodist and the Baptist churches, do we hear a single but ominous note of skepticism: "There are many things about the Christian religion which make it almost impossible to believe it."

His Christian zealotry was presently to fade; even sooner was his devotion to Myra. He sought out her father and, because Myra was now helping in the *Herald* office, he worked there for a few days; but he hoped, too, to be paid a wage, and when Mr. Hendryx made no such proposal he stopped working there. He had already written, "Myra is shallow, I fear. Not much to her." Then Mr. Palmer again offered him the position of substitute night clerk in his hotel. He was delighted.

> ... last summer I made a miserable botch of the work. Ever since I have wished to try it over, and see if I couldn't do better work. Hence I was right glad this morning when Mr. Palmer offered me the place ...

On his first night he was not above "a fierce game of poker with Carl (Irish, the bus driver)," but on the next night he was indignant about "some fools" who "played poker till 1:30 in the barroom last night. Of course I don't have anything to do with said barroom, for which I am heartily glad." During this period his diary suffered—many pages are blank—and there is no way of knowing whether he did the job more creditably than in the earlier summer, but in the latter half of August he was taken on by the *Avalanche* for two weeks and did well. He was employed at five dollars a week, but in his second week he was paid six dollars. He gathered news, solicited subscriptions, collected bills, reported on the three nights of performances by the DeRetit Theatrical Company and wrote up the churches and schools of Sauk Centre for a forthcoming special edition. For Harry Lewis, this experience would seem to have been a considerable *coup*.

When he was in St. Paul, he walked up the length of Summit Avenue and was impressed by the "Magnificent residences & a grand view (as the Ave. is on the edge of a high cliff)." As a successful writer, Sinclair Lewis was to inhabit a whole series of "magnificent residences," and the first of them was to be on this street. Was the awkward country boy, shambling along Summit Avenue in his ill-fitting clothes, whose dreams were all of coming triumphs in New Haven, dreaming of this, too? He was entirely a boy still, apparently late in maturing, without (one must infer) any great burden of sexuality or even of sexual anxiety, and still given to idle boyish pursuits. In that summer he entertained himself with a harmonica. On one occasion he entertained himself with the telephone:

> I remember seeing in some comic paper a series of pictures with the title "Gets Busy with the Usual Result." This morning I "got busy" with the usual result. I took the receiver of the telephone apart, broke the connections, and had a dickens of a time getting things straight.

He solemnly studied the Yale Catalogue and chose his courses, but the acne that had plagued him since puberty was more acute than ever. "Father sent me a 'Dietary' (from Chi; where they now are), to aid in clearing my face from pimples." His complexion, like everything else after that summer, would grow worse.

3

AT YALE they called him God-Forbid. It was not long (according to his classmate Allan Updegraff) before the young gentlemen were saying that he was the only man in New Haven who could fart out of his face—an observation intended to comment both on his miserable ugliness and on the quality of his spoken wisdom. It was a brutal shock, although it broke upon him slowly; even for one such as he, accustomed now to the abrupt collapse of anticipatory dreams, it was traumatic, an extended trauma. For Yale was to have been different from everything that had gone before. He would not at once believe that it was not; and, indeed, he tried that whole first year to make something of it that Yale could never be for him.

Simply, he was friendless. In "My First Day in New York," he told how on his journey east he left the train at Albany to take a boat down the Hudson to New York, and how he was overwhelmed with the impression of the savage impersonality of Manhattan's commuting throngs.* In only a few months another traveler, Henry James, was to be impressed with a different savagery when, after years of absence, he returned to New York from the other direction to gather his impressions for *The American Scene*. And how charming it would be if biography permitted one to create those unlikely interviews that would properly mark the modulations in history: the weary old *isolato* coming back and the brash young *isolato*-still-to-be pushing out, the two implausibly meeting in the New York of 1903 and 1904. As the older Harry went on to Boston, the younger rushed pell-mell to New Haven.

New Haven, by comparison with his wild glimpse of New York, was all peace and dreaming antiquity. Yet slowly he was to come to recognize

* In this essay, Lewis gives an account of a trolley ride up and down the length of Manhattan that would have taken hours. Since he disembarked shortly before six in the evening and took a train for New Haven that night at eight, we may assume that the fictional talent is again at work in this apparently factual sketch, as it was in the newspaper sketches. The diary says only, "In New York I landed at Debrosses Pier. Almost bewildered, on E. River, by the endless steamers, docks, buildings on shore. Train at 8 for New Haven."

that, in its more restrained way, the highly selective small society into which he would try intimately to move, was just as closed to him, perhaps more savage.

When he arrived he had already, unknown to himself, transgressed one local custom, and the power of local custom he did not yet suspect.

> From Minnesota to Albany, there was nothing sensational in my journey, though later I found that the youth to whom I had confided, on a station platform, that, proudly, I was a "Yale man," was also going east to enter the business of being a "Yale man." But, having attended a prep school instead of a Western high school, he knew that there was nothing more boorish, nothing that, in the cant of that day, would so thoroughly "queer" you, as to call yourself a Yale man. . . . He let me learn all about it, afterward, in New Haven. . . .

He arrived on September 18, and he had been violating taboos for nearly three weeks with only a vague sense of discomfort, when, finally, he met his correspondent, Hugh Rankin, now a graduate student in economics.

> *October 7, 1903.* I've been doing a lot of things wrong—so Hugh Rankin says and without saying just that. At last I've met Rankin. . . . Tonight he put me next to many things. A feeling which has been growing in me has tonight ripened—I must get a new room & board at commons, in order to get acquainted with my class—which I cannot do at all here. I can see in many ways where I have been fresh—dreadfully so!
>
> I owe Rankin an unbounded debt for what he has told me & what he has suggested tonight. Whether I follow suit let futurus tell.

He corrected the chief blunder and moved from the room he had taken in a boarding house at 124½ Park Street ("It's sort of a post grad. house") into 79 South Middle College, the oldest building then at Yale containing now the rawest youth. Futurus did not do much for him.

In the diary that he kept during his first year at Yale, he lists encounters of one kind or another with some sixty-five students. Of them, forty-three are not mentioned more than twice, most of those not more than once. Only twelve are mentioned more than five times. Only William Everett Fay, who lived across the hall, is mentioned more than fifteen times. The great bulk of these encounters are of the most casual sort—persons he passes on a walk, persons he finds himself involved with in group exercise in the gymnasium, the men at his table in Commons or the men in his South Middle entry. None of these encounters can be described as intimate and only a few as even so modestly personal as that with Hugh Rankin. A few close friends, one or two of the kind of deeply personal associations without which most of us would find life insupportable—this he did not have at all in that year. A whole day can be summed up in a few sentences such as these: "Squirrels very common on campus & Green &

very tame. I can now see one from my window, playing on an elm near by." And we can see him standing at his window, looking out, wondering what more he could put into a diary.

He had associates, of course, and some of them were not above joining him for an occasional beer at the Hofbrau or going with him to a theatrical performance or walking out to East Rock with him; but these associations were so neutral that he could himself almost never discriminate one from another or state a preference. On the last day of November he wrote:

> This—last day in one of the most important year-seasons in my life—was a great one for getting acquainted with the fellows. In P.M. a little Jap [Takagi Senjiro] in our class came up for short visit; following him Breaker —one of my witnesses for tomorrow's mock trial. While he was here Dunaway came in room to borrow knife. Then I went up on East Rock, for a walk, with White. We sat there and watched the lights come out, over New Haven—After supper came Bishop—Dunaway—Parmelee—Steve Thaw!

The man to whose room he himself felt most free to go was Julius Parmelee, son of a medical missionary and an ex-Oberlin graduate student in law, and the man who would seem to have been kindest to him was another graduate student, this one in English, Douglas Moffat, who roomed with Hugh Rankin. Mr. Moffat remembered that to Rankin, whom the young Lewis thought of as his mentor, he proved a considerable embarrassment and that Mr. Moffat relieved his friend of some of the burden that he had so unwittingly acquired. When Lewis's first poem appeared in the *Yale Literary Magazine,* Moffat sent him this post card (which Harry pasted into his diary):

> Great was Launcelot, & great is the writer thereon! Accept my very heartiest congratulations on being the first of your class to get an article in the Lit.
>
> *Douglas M. Moffat*
>
> P.S. Cannot go to *Much Ado* tonight, though I may go this afternoon: I don't know. Are you going then?

There is no indication that Lewis had any other written communication, except for formal notices, from anyone at Yale in that year. Earlier, he had planned to put together a little book of nonsense verses about imaginary animals as a gift to Moffat, and at one point in his diary he made the ambiguous entry, "Such a jolly fellow is Moffat; I know whom I like more than he. He is a post grad. in English." The "he" is Moffat, but who is the other? Hugh Rankin, perhaps? Another Holland Carter? Or did Lewis mean to write: "I *don't* know whom I like more than he. . . ."?

Among the undergraduates, particularly among the men of his own class, where the potentialities of genuine friendship lay, he did not have the grounds to state such preferences. He asked Maude E. Dunaway ("a Senior Academic from Arkansas . . . is an A.B. Hendrix College") to room with him, and for one day the possibility remained open, until Dunaway found that he could not escape earlier commitments. At the end of the year he told himself that in the next year he might room with Howard Bishop of Chicago, but in the next year he roomed alone again. His casual and mechanical associations did not satisfy him, naturally; this was *not* what the college experience was meant to be! On January 2, 1904, during the holiday that he spent in New Haven with a few other strays, he wrote of an evening with John Kitchen:

> Supper and evening's entertainment combined for Kitchen, by a spread—hot dogs, rolls, sugar wafers, nuts, dates, ect. We cooked the dogs, made cocoa. After it we sat and talked almost till nearly eleven. We talked of scholarship, bats, fussing, and a dozen other things. Long discussion—at last.

At last!—and nearly the last.

And what of all that distant glamor that existed but that he had not even seen? In March, when he was writing zealously for the *Literary Magazine,* he said, "The Lit. is secondary—my principal reason in rushing to make it is to be able to associate with such men as Pierce, ect." Frederick Erastus Pierce was a senior, the president of the *Lit* board, the winner of innumerable prizes and awards, the top man in his class, and a member of Phi Beta Kappa, Zeta Psi, and Skull and Bones; and it was his world that Harry Lewis, the freshman, wanted. Allan Updegraff remembered that Lewis tried over and over to gain acceptance from the big men in the college, only to be "kicked in the face over and over again" and to fall back once more among his own kind, the eccentric strays. Notably, these were two, but they did not become Lewis's friends until the next year: Frederick Kinney Noyes, who despised the values of the clubmen and was bored in their company, and Allan Updegraff himself, who was desperately poor. To the others, if he was not beneath notice, he was a gadfly nuisance or an unbelievable naïf. Lewis himself told Christian Gauss that in that first year the New Haven *Journal and Courier,* for which he worked now and then, gave him the assignment of a general piece on Tap Day to precede that occasion—when strong men burst into public tears as the realization slowly floods over them that the long-dreamed-of cachet of Bones or of Wolf's Head is never, after all, to be theirs. Lewis had not heard of Tap Day and therefore went to the office of the *Yale Daily News* where he found an assistant editor whom he asked, "What is this Tap Day anyway?" The assistant editor called in his fellows from nearby rooms and had Lewis repeat the question. The answer was a thunderous guffaw. "Lewis thinks it was this incident," Dean Gauss concluded, "that queered him at Yale." It was this and nearly everything else about him. Yet he was unwilling, for a time, to resign the struggle, and even so late in the year as March he wrote in his diary of a conversation on "Yale snobbishness (of which there is little)."

His professors treated him with both more kindliness and more respect than his peers. Foremost among these was Chauncey B. Tinker, who in 1903–1904 was teaching his first classes at Yale and was Harry's English teacher. The boy was much taken with him. When he first saw him on the campus, he flew up to him and demanded, "Say, are you my prof?" and in November,* just before a lecture was to be delivered by W. B. Yeats, he assailed him in much the same way, crying, "Say, prof, who is this fellow, Yeats?"—pronouncing the name to rhyme with Keats. Professor Tinker found him the most interesting student in the class and was less distressed by his continually waving hand and his irrepressible eagerness to talk all of the time than were Harry's classmates, who found his conduct, quite simply, disgusting. Mr. Tinker enjoyed his enthusiasms, in and out of class.

> *January 28, 1904.* Today has been a great day; not in the spectacular element of life but in the real ones. That is—I had a glorious walk with Dr. Tinker; up Prospect St., to Whitney Ave., to East Rock and back by Orange St. We talked of many things; especially matters literary. He spoke well of my work. We talked of old days at Yale, of such things as the Running the Gauntlet.

The very next day:

> Evening—took some verse, Lit. work, to Dr. Tinker's room for his criticism. He has many books—two large book cases. Floor Turkish rugs. Walls: pictures ect. worth the name; as of cathedrals, ect. Small crucifix on wall. He said to emulate Gray's example and write long on every thing.

They walked again:

> Walk with Dr. Tinker. No less delightful than my former one. He spoke to me in great confidence and with frankness; the class, ect. "I was sorry to see the valedictory abolished," he said. "I had hoped to see you hold it." "You must make the Lit., and let newspaper work alone." We spoke of nature, of Browning, Swinburne, Athletics, what not. A wonderful, a talented man, Dr. Tinker. His name should be Thinker . . .

And there was still another two-hour walk through "orchards & valleys" in May, and the mysterious coded remark, "We spoke of dream town." †

* In his published account of these episodes (*Proceedings,* Second Series, No. 2, American Academy of Arts and Letters, New York, 1952), Professor Tinker telescoped the opening day of the college and the date of the Yeats lecture. Yeats lectured at New Haven on November 16, 1903.

† This may refer to a poem of Harry's that months earlier the *Lit* had rejected because of its subject, Kipling's *Brushwood Boy*. Its second stanza begins,

> I have a dream town of my own,
> Where oft I seem to dwell . . .

Two days after this walk with Tinker, there is a very curious entry: "I went my [way?] to the dream house corner, Sachem and Winchester. Yard smooth, flower bushes, girl—Elaine, dear one, Maud, at the piano, with closed shutters. Up Hill-

Professor Seymour, his Greek teacher, was kind to him, too, and on at least one occasion Harry called at his house. Likewise kind was Robert K. Root, who, like Tinker, was then a young instructor. They walked to the Long Wharf together in the spring rain. He was always buttonholing people for walks, and on one occasion, when young Professor Edward Reed assented, Harry cried, "But I mean a real *long* walk."

There is only one recorded unkindness from a professor, and that was in Harry's second year, in the course on Athenian Drama. Harry was enthusiastic about the *Oedipus Rex,* which he was just discovering, and on one occasion when he was translating before the class, his feeling impelled him into such eloquence that the professor rebuked him. "Lewis, you will please translate like a gentleman, not like a cheap actor." After that, the later Lewis said, he joined the others and used a trot, which until then he had regarded as dishonest.* The anecdote has an analogue in a *Lit* board member's recollection of one criticism meeting, where works under consideration were read aloud by their authors, of Lewis reading his poem "with great gusto and 'elocution,' to the suppressed amusement of his auditors . . . he got some of the rough edges rubbed down, but he remained quite individualistic." Allan Updegraff says that what Lewis's social experience at Yale taught him was the necessity of *learning* charm, social poise as well as purpose. "He was the only man I ever knew who *learned* how to be charming."

The lesson was learned at the cost of much solitary brooding. The long walk alone or the long ride alone on his secondhand bicycle or the aimless rambling alone through slum areas with an occasional visit to a low saloon or the solitary staring out over the harbor from a perch on some wharf as the Connecticut dusk came down over him and the lights went up—these were the occasions for such unrecorded self-assessments as he may have been given to. However naïve he may have been, certain striking differences between his lot and that of others must have forced themselves upon him. He was nineteen now, and all that year, apparently, he did not come near a girl. He dreamed of literary females in the absence of real ones.

---

house Ave. dreaming of männer[?], my Elaine & I (a fairly tale), in the Hillhouse place I sat at the foot of an oak, and saw the fairies dance in a grass. Depressing."

* The recollection is probably inexact. The course was Professor Thomas Goodell's. On October 26, 1905, Lewis wrote: "For the first time I am using a 'trot' (in Gk.) . . . have spent enough time on faithful grind with lexicon and grammar." On November 22 he wrote: "Peace made with Goodell, over use of trot." On February 21: "Good work in Tommy's Greek—flunked 'rough breathing' in reading; & was fined $2 for scratching desk-tablet." If there was any other criticism from Goodell, it was not recorded, and the trot seems to have been in use nearly from the outset. It is possible that the professor made some remark to the effect that Lewis might well pay more attention to his pronunciation and less to dramatic expression, and that out of this, together with the earlier rebuke over the trot, the mangled reminiscence grew. At any rate, the class did not come to *Oedipus* until April.

> Florence! Just as when I read *Dombey and Son* before, I fall in love with her. Gods, what would it not be to know such a pure noble loving girl as she. I know none—I pray that I may some time.

The Prom comes, but it is not, of course, for him. At church on the Sunday of that weekend, however, he had his opportunity to observe "Many swell Queens." Inevitably, he turned back to Myra. He wrote her a long letter on December 27, when the college was deserted, and on February 1 he was still waiting for a reply. "Ye Gods, I wish Myra would write to me. I thought of her in my prayers, last night. Indeed I often do." But no reply ever came. He began then to write to another Sauk Centre girl, Clara Carpenter, whom he had once kissed on a hayrack party. But these are highly unromantic letters on the value of building up one's personal library, the delights of the Egyptian archeological exhibits in the Peabody Museum, the acting of Sir Henry Irving in *Dante,* the interior of the Benedict Arnold house where "Noah Webster began his dict.," and the necessity of reading Tennyson *"carefully."* He wrote her very solemnly, the man of the world informing and advising the country schoolteacher who did not get away from home. ("Better be your own college with such teachers as Milton and Wordsworth; Nature and music; than be one of the many whom one finds at college; lazy, unappreciative of opportunities; stupid. Nicht wahr?")

He wrote to his parents twice every week, eager for news. His diary is cluttered with little news items of the most trivial sort clipped from the *Avalanche,* and never so crowded as during the holiday periods, when they are chiefly about other young people in Sauk Centre who have come home from college for their vacations. On New Year's Eve Harry wrote, "Instead of the theatre I closed the year by quietly reading and by Lit. writing." When a letter came from Fisher, he exclaimed, "Glorious, glorious, tres glorious!"

He was very happy when, at the end of the academic year, his parents, returning home from annual meetings of the Medical Association, arrived in New Haven for a brief visit. Yet, lonely as he had been and much as he had clung to thoughts of Sauk Centre in that loneliness, he did not want now to follow his parents *there.* To Clara Carpenter he had written in January, "You asked me if I ever get homesick. I really do not. . . ." In his diary he wrote:

> Mother and Father seem to want me to come home; but I do not wish to because of the dulness of S.C. Will probably clerk in hotel. Or, as I hope, have Cosgrove's place on the Journal and Cour[ier]. He expects to go away next S[ummer].

Sauk Centre had already taught him that he had explored all the possibilities of personal relationships there, and that they were few.

Yale *promised* so much, the potentialities were so limitless! College life, campus activities, organizations, all those hundreds of young men—surely somewhere.... Out of the traditional group activities some new and intimate relationship must come!

> Tonight college life began with the annual "Soph-Fresh" Wrestling match. We lined up in front of Osborn Hall & marched around [the] Green (torches ahead, classes in line according to seniority, hands in front) yelling & singing, then to Hopkins School lot. Sophs won matches. Afterwards was a rush on York St. which Freshmen won. The two classes form in lines & charge against each other. I was in the thick of it a couple of times & once was down with a lot of fellows on top. After that I didn't get into the rush, as I was to tired to be any good.

College Life! He by no means scorned it in that first year. "On the campus fellows are singing," he wrote. "I wouldn't exchange my room here for a palace on Park St.—not to speak of a 124½!" There is a glowing account of Calcium Night ("A wonderful scene on the campus tonight—the frats paraded the campus in costume, with colored calcium lights, calling on their new members, singing their frat songs as they marched along. It was very brilliant & wierd...") and another of the cheering throngs at the first big football game he had seen, Yale versus Princeton. But if anything was happening within the pageantry, it was happening to others, not to him.

There was the quieter possibility of religious activity—chapel, church, the Student Volunteers (which he investigated but apparently did not join), a Bible class. He resumed his Sunday-school teaching for the Y.M.C.A., first a class of ten- or twelve-year-olds ("Intelligent lads, a trifle disorderly") at Bushnell Hall who proved so refractory that he gave them up, and later in the United Church, where he had a half dozen "Nice lads" for a month at the beginning of 1904, and then a group of "Elm St. orphan asylum boys" ("Never saw such well behaved lads") with whom he met regularly until May, when the ominous note is sounded again: "Have stopped S.S. work, partly because it goes 'gainst the grain to teach about 'manna falling from heaven,' partly because of press of work." If his religious enthusiasm was dying, it may have been in part because church activity at Yale offered even less by way of human communion than it had at Oberlin.

He attempted more secular activities, the first of which was his almost immediate association with the Freshman Union, a debating society, and in October he defended the negative of the proposition that convict labor should not be let out by contract, only to lose. In December he did better when he acted as prosecuting attorney in a mock trial. "My argument received a storm of applause. The jury... found prisoner guilty." "We hear that his pleading at the bar was very well executed, and he was much complimented on it," reported the *Herald* back in Sauk Centre. "We are pleased to hear he won his case." But he was not winning the case that lay nearest his heart, the case of Harry S. Lewis, Yale man. In March, when he tried out for the Freshman-Sophomore debating team, he assumed an air of indifference as to the outcome; he was not chosen. A similar decline in interest seems to have overtaken his November resolution to win the Edward Tompkins McLaughlin Scholarship (he called it the McLaughlin Thompson Prize in his diary) with an essay on "Jonathan Swift & English Politics." He mentioned the project a number of times, then fell silent about it, and in April, when the essays were due, he said nothing at all.

He "heeled" the *Record* and even saw at least one of his jokes in print there, but in November he decided to give his undivided literary attention to the *Lit.* He had already submitted his old poem "Hallowe'en" without success; and the first new one, "Dreamland," like the next, "Spanish Legend," a bloody bit, was rejected because of its subject. He wrote stories, sketches and essays, as well as poems, but it was a poem called "Launcelot," which had been rejected once, that was accepted after some minor revisions and appeared on March 15, 1904, the first publication in the magazine from that freshman class, and the first poem to be published by Harry S. Lewis. He had been reading Tennyson *very* carefully.

LAUNCELOT

"Oft Launcelot grieves that he loveth the Queen
But oftener far that she cruel hath been."

Blow, weary wind,
The golden rod scarce chiding;
Sir Launcelot is riding
By shady wood-paths pleasant
To fields of yellow corn.
He starts a whirring pheasant,
And clearly winds his horn.
The Queen's Tower gleams mid distant hills;
A thought like joyous sunshine thrills,
"My love grows kind."

Blow, weary wind,
O'er lakes, o'er dead swamps crying,
Amid the gray stumps sighing
While slow, and cold, and sullen,
The waves splash on the shore.
O'er wastes of bush and mullen,
Dull crows flap, evermore.
The Autumn day is chill and drear

As yon knight, thinking Guenevere
Proves most unkind.*

He wrote and submitted a good deal more to the *Lit,* and enjoined himself to "write more stories, as a sort of tread mill exercise for Pegasus," but the board accepted no more work from him that academic year. Much of what the *Lit* could not use was favorably received by its younger and livelier sister, the *Courant,* where again he was the first freshman to appear that year, now with his drinking "Song of Prince Hal," on May 21. ("I wrote it the other day in Analyt. Geom. class (afterward polishing it) & dedicated it to Kountze as he sat in front of me.") Two other poems, one of them a student drinking song written in German, were accepted for the June number, and two further contributions, one a "wild story" called "The Coward Minstrel," were accepted for later use. He had, in a small way, made himself known if not liked, and the first review of his work appeared in the Yale *News* for March 17, when Professor Reed wrote generously of his poem, " 'Launcelot' is reminiscent of the Romantic School and yet it is no formal imitation of Morris or Tennyson. The second stanza is the better, both for the music of the verse and effective description."

These were his extracurricular activities. He had several private projects. One was to establish a German *Tisch* in some boarding house or restaurant (he was not studying German now, but French), and for a short time he managed to have several men meet in his room with the freshman from Yokohama, Takagi, where they were instructed in Japanese while attempting to improve his English. Public entertainment consisted of a moderate amount of theatergoing (he frequently attended as drama critic for the *Journal and Courier*) that included some good performances of Shakespeare, Sudermann's *Magda, Everyman,* Shaw's *Candida* (which delighted but bewildered him), as well as a larger proportion of vaudeville. He heard two public lectures, one by William Jennings Bryan, the other by Yeats. The Yeats lecture, he told Professor Tinker later, was responsible for the part that poet plays in the frustrated reveries of Carol Kennicott in *Main Street,* and it was the initiation of Lewis's own lifelong enthusiasm for Yeats, or, at least, for the early Yeats.

As for more frivolous social functions, the diaries would indicate that in the entire year, he attended exactly one, on May 31. "Evening Freshman Union. Banquet. Beside the program were impromptu speeches called for

* In 1947, when Jean Hersholt was president of the Academy of Motion Pictures, Lewis inscribed a privately printed pamphlet version of this poem as follows:

Blow, weary Jean
The Academy scarce chiding
The Oscars all are riding
For films of awful corn

from Lockwood (& others of team), Seymour, myself & others & many stories."

His major energies went into concentrated and enthusiastic study. At the beginning of the year he resolved that he "Must have the valedictory, ΦBK any way. Hence I must work *wie der Teufel.*" He was excited by the intellectual qualities of his instructors and was determined to please them. He read continually in the library, in and around his subjects and on others, including now, with Boccaccio and Daudet, Thoreau's *Cape Cod,* and he built up his private library, especially in the nineteenth-century British poets. He won honors at the end of the first term, and again, at the end of the year—one of sixty-seven in a class of four hundred and thirty-one.

In December his father wrote that "receipts for this year have been $700 less than last year. This looks rather troublesome." He lived very frugally (his expenses for November had been $8.03, including the theater), but he was worried by his father's news and he began to look for work. He canvassed the newspaper offices, but there were no reportorial places to be had at the moment, and he tried to solicit ads and subscriptions on commission for the *Union* and the *Chronicle*. Since he had no success as a salesman, he gave that up after several days. Then, on December 18, when one of the regular men on the *Journal and Courier* was called to New York, Harry was asked to take his place. "I wrote & rewrote some articles, changed headlines of clippings, wrote a long puff on a mark-down sale, and went to different lodges to get the reports of their elections. Worked from 7 till 1:30 A.M." This was the beginning of sporadic but considerable employment. He reported a sermon on the following Sunday and was pleased to see his account in print without any changes. He substituted again later in that month, and in February he was offered a place for a month or six weeks in which he was to work from five to six hours on six nights a week. For about two weeks he did a variety of miscellaneous reporting and then gave up the job; "sleep was suffering, though not lessons." He had obviously been doing competent journalistic work, for in three weeks he was asked to come back as a substitute reporter, but this sporadic work did not enable him to earn enough money to cover even his small expenses. He abandoned Commons, took his noon and evening meals in cheap restaurants and made his own breakfast in his room ("coffee, Uneeda Biscuits, nuts, canned goods, ect."). Then, to save even more, he asked Fay and Smith across the hall from him if they would let him move in with them for the rest of the year. They and the dean agreed, and on April 19 that change was accomplished. On April 20 he became a regular staff member of the *Journal and Courier* when a rather debauched older man was asked to resign; but he worked under this new arrangement for only about a week, when "injury to sleep & lessons" forced him to abandon it until classes were over. He had canvassed the local newspapers for a summer position, and he had taken one day of his spring recess to go to New York (the only day that year that he left New Haven), where he saw the editor of the *Sun* and at least the interiors of the *Times, Tribune* and *Journal-American* buildings, but he found no summer openings. After his examinations, apparently, he worked for the *Journal and Courier* again; but when, on June 23, "Barnes got me to take [his] place as waiter in Randall Hall, at Harvard Summer School," he decided to walk to Cambridge. On June 24 he wrote: "Finished my work on the Courier & broke in E. H. Smith (07) to take my place." He sold his bicycle, sent his suitcase ahead and on June 25 took to the road.

What was he walking to? On New Year's Day, walking alone in the region of Westville, he "Thought over old 'What will I be' question," and ten days later he made a note of having read an article "on the majesty of the scholar's profession." That was a possibility, but the direction is not entirely clear. Did he have a clear sense of himself, or more particularly, of his difference? Early in the year he had said, "It's a trifle startling to learn that many of my class have been to Europe and to hear them talking familiarly and calmly of the Matterhorn and the Rhine." That difference was to be eliminated soon enough, but signs of profounder differences had developed in this first New Haven year. His Christian zeal waned and his missionary ambitions were abandoned. In his diary, the sign of the cross began to appear with a mute question mark standing beside it. In May he wrote, "Who knows but that my old resolves toward this noble work might be renewed, if I could only believe half of Christian theism." A month later, contemplating "the great trio" of Rossetti, Burne-Jones and Morris, he wonders if they "believed in immortality. I scarce believe that many of the 'sapientes' do." In an argument on a Saturday night in spring, he urged the "advisibility of abolishing chapel." And in that same season, in a long argument with Fay and Smith, both of them devout, "on Elbert Hubbard & Willie Hearst with side excursions into the church & Military question," someone held for "socialism ect." Who? It is the first time that we have come upon that word.

Throughout the year, he had been undergoing X-ray treatments for his acne, and late in April he wrote, "X-ray has cured my pimples." He does not mention the pits that remained, or the overexposure that burned his lower right cheek and left him with the permanent scar that almost always caused him, in photographs, to pose with his chin in his hand or with his face averted, and that was to aggravate a precancerous skin condition that would require continuous electric needle treatments which left countless further scars. Nor does he mention any other scars that the year had left.

4

AT ABOUT NOON on June 25 he walked out of New Haven. He had gone about seven miles and was approaching North Haven when a gentleman in "a big Rambler 'touring car' " drew up and stopped "to fix something about the running gear." Harry offered to help him, and the gentleman offered him a ride. They were both going to Boston. This was nearly his first if not indeed his first automobile drive. He wrote his father two days later:

> Except for walking there certainly is nothing like an automobile ride. There is no smell of gasoline to those *in* the car, though there is a goodly whiff left behind. The swift motion makes it very cool; the leather cushions, the springs, and the pneumatic tires make it as easy to ride in as a Pullman. There is as open a view as from an open carriage. We made 15 to 16 miles an hour with fair roads, though we had only an 8 horse power machine. One of these 16 or 18 horse power Winton touring cars would make much better time.

In detail he described the landscape to his father, listed the names of the towns and cities through which they passed, noted their population figures and their chief buildings, and said that Hartford—which he was later to inhabit and loathe—"was the prettiest town we saw." They spent the night in Springfield, where Harry wandered through the streets and visited the editorial and composing rooms of the *Republican.* They drove across Massachusetts next day, and he remarked on the difference between the quiet old colonial towns through which they passed and the raw small towns that he knew best.

He spent the second night in a cheap Boston hotel, crossed the Charles to Cambridge next day, found a furnished room for a dollar a week at 140 Mt. Auburn Street and then betook himself to a desk in Phillips Brooks House to write his father all about it.

He was much impressed with the Harvard Yard. To his father he presented a mild economic argument for preferring Cambridge to New

Haven; in his diary, he based the preference on the richness of historic and literary associations. One can infer that he was contemplating a change. Later in the summer, however, when he wrote his mother about the Cambridge experience, he said only, "I look back to Boston, Harvard & Cambridge with great affection. Someday prehaps, I can have a year or two of graduate work there."

In his short stay he explored the place thoroughly, not only the buildings of Harvard but the Cambridge Public Library, where he obtained borrowing privileges, Mt. Auburn Cemetery, where he lost his way and found that he had to scale a fence to get out, Craigie House, which led him to read Higginson's *Life of Longfellow*, and Elmwood, where he recited scraps of *Sir Launfal* to himself. (He mentioned most of the great New England writers in his diary during these days, and read about a number of them, but again, there is no mention either of Thoreau or of *Walden*, and no thought of a trip to Concord.) He wandered all over Boston, examining every well-known monument, admiring for hours the "deep enchantment" of Abbey's Arthurian murals in the Public Library, and he loitered frequently at the harbor, where the clutter of ships renewed the wish to sail on a cattle boat (during the winter he had written to a steamship company for information) and moved him to write at the top of one page of his diary the word *Wanderlust*.

His work as a waiter in Randall Hall (which served as a commons for students in the summer session, including three hundred American and Spanish teachers from Puerto Rico and one girl from Sauk Centre, Mabel Buchanan) began on June 30 and was to last until mid-August. He received his board and three dollars and fifty cents a week, from which he hoped to save two dollars. Since his room cost him one dollar, this plan would have given him fifty cents a week for private indulgences.

There were other men from New Haven among the waiters at Randall Hall, but Harry only noted the fact of their presence and apparently saw nothing of them. He made one friend, Fritz Düberg, "a young German, graceful, attractive, who is to enter Harvard. We always speak German together." One day they sailed together in a catboat on Boston Harbor, but the day before, July 8, long before his job was finished, Harry had already determined to leave Cambridge. "I went to American Shipping Co., 320 Commercial St., where I took place as cattle feeder on a cattle steamer which leaves a week from tomorrow." In that last week, he tried "to dispose of a story recently written" to Sunday newspaper editors, but he was unable to see any. He read in those last few days chiefly about Portland, from where he would sail, and about Liverpool, to and from which he would sail.

On the evening of July 15 he took a Portland boat, slept uneasily on deck, awoke in the morning in Portland Harbor, and signed on with the

Georgian, a British ship of the Dominion Line, which lifted anchor at noon. The ship carried fifty tons of water and six hundred fifty head of cattle. Before sailing, Harry Lewis helped drive them on board. "Tieing up cattle. Boss—Jack. Cattle forced into pen by 4's; gently caught by rope jerk! Riding the bulls. Pounding, tail twisting." He had embarked upon a most un-Tennysonian experience.

The work was backbreaking, the food was frightful, the living conditions were filthy, and the company was tough. In a long letter to his mother written during the last four days aboard, and less coherently in his diary, Harry recounted the details; this was his first truly "literary" experience, and he was determined to store it for the future. Of the daily routine, he wrote:

> . . . up at 4, water & feed hay (taking till about 6); off till breakfast (at 8); after bxfst, feed grain (½ or 1 pail to each bull); off till dinner (at 12); after dinner water, hoist up grain & hay from lower hatch by steam winch, feed hay. After supper (5 o'clock), sweep alleyway between cattle (taking 20 minutes). Stories & reading on deck or (if cold) in hatchway till 8 or 8:30.

To his mother, he softens and glamorizes the experience, giving much of his attention to the seascape. The diary is franker: "Manure taken out by market gardners at L'pool. . . . Hardest—rolling 225 lb. bales, in narrow aisle; & carrying the sacks of 'mixed grain feed.' " An even more candid account comes from the man who was in command of the portside crews, M. Wayne Womer, a thirty-year-old Methodist minister who, in Harry's diary, "goes incog for material for writing & lectures," and who, after Lewis's death, privately circulated his reminiscence under the title "Sinclair Lewis Was My Sailor." He wrote:

> When we were several days from Liverpool, tons of grain had to be hoisted from the hole and placed on deck so it could be unloaded in a hurry. We only were allowed twenty minutes at that dock. When the 100 pound bags came up, two sailors threw them one by one on the backs of others who stood in line. I was in charge. The first bag landed on Jack the Australian, a short heavy built man; off he went. Lewis was next in line, the bag was on his back and he had not gone a half dozen steps when he fell forward and the bag was on his neck and shoulders. I was frightened, I thought his head hit the deck. Pulling the bag off I yelled, "Red, are you hurt?" "No," he stood up, brushed the dirt off his clothes, turned and looked at me and said, "Doc, I can't do that." . . . It was no easy job, a hundred lbs. on one's back and the ship rolling, only the strongest could keep his feet. I looked at Lewis, I knew he was telling me the truth. He was too tall and he lacked weight. "All right, Red, you rest and take my next shift, I will take your place." The bag was thrown on my back, I staggered but kept going not one, but fo[u]r hours. There were 480 bags and only six men able to carry them.

The food was coarse and minimal.

> Grub on trip was as follows—8 o'clock Bxfst—scouse (a stew, "Soy-vomit!!"); bread & margarine (jam. Some stolen by Bell & Canadians.) & bum tea (or coffee). 12 Noon (which I touched but twice) Salt horse (beans once) & soup. 5 o'clock—supper—Br[ead], margarine & tea . . .

He did not mention here a special delight of this menu, a flour pudding called plum duff. A few of the men found this food and the circumstances of eating it intolerable. Womer wrote, "They ate like hogs, especially the French Canadians. They reached into the big pans which the cook brought with their dirty hands, and we had to be on hand when the food came or go hungry." Several of them who had money and were planning to stay on in Europe, Womer among them, made a special arrangement with the cook and ate different meals apart from the rest; but Harry, who had no money, ate with the others in the foul stench of the forecastle.

He did not, fortunately, have to sleep there. He usually spread his "gunny sack mattress on some fresh shaken hay, under the open hatchway." On two nights he slept on deck ("one night was glorious, the stars filling the sky. It is now too cold for that.") "Only one night did I sleep in the fo'castle; the bunks are most uncomfortable, the air & smell vile, and the language . . . worse." The men, generally, were a depraved lot. Womer described them as "the lowest of human beings, profane, dirty and vile. The cow hands who had come with the cattle from the Far West were French Canadians, others were thieves and criminals and followed the sea to escape the law. Then there were the professional cow hands and cattlemen who made such work their business, a few others who had been shanghaied." He, his friend Phillip Van Kirk (a law student and secretary to the treasurer of Columbia University), a young Southerner named "Reddy" Zimmerman who had been at a military college, and Lewis drew apart from the others in a group of their own. The French Canadians especially were violent, brawling men, and Womer was the object of their wrath in a fist fight that Sinclair Lewis remembered thirty years later, when he received a letter from Womer, who had just learned, from the cover of *Time* magazine, his quondam shipmate's identity.

Womer described their first night out and his first conversation with the "long legged gangling red-headed youth."

> . . . cutting the wire on a bale of hay we made ourselves comfortable. After a moment, I said, "Red, tell me your story." Without hesitation, and in full confidence he began. "I am eighteen years old [he had passed nineteen and a half], a sophomore at Yale. I was born at Sauk Center, Minnesota. My father is a physician; he is an alumnus of Yale, and that is why I went there. It looks as if I have made a mistake, because I do not have a friend in the faculty or student body. Everytime I say anything or do

> anything they ride me. I am tired of it and I am through." He paused and we sat in silence awhile, then he talked a little more. After I had the whole story, I said, "Red. . . . My advice is to go back, you must go back."
>
> Here was a boy who had come to the first great crisis of his life and he was running away and fate had brought him in contact with a man twelve years older than himself, who also had run away. . . . We got up to go to our bunks, it was late, and we stood facing each other. He took my hand and said, "Doc, will you pray for me?" I said, "Now," and together we knelt in the hay while I prayed for both Red and myself. Without a word we went to our bunks.

Are the obvious errors of fact in this account to be attributed to Womer's inexact memory or to Harry's fancy? Womer was never in a position to know Harry's situation at Yale, so that much of the recollection is almost certainly accurate. The older man, whom Harry described in his diary as a "most splendid fellow," unquestionably revived his earlier religious idealism, and it is quite possible that when he went aboard the *Georgian,* Harry had notions of abandoning Yale and somehow managing a *wanderjahr* in Europe. He had had such ideas in the past.

The four congenial spirits formed a group that they called the Liars' Club, and every evening they gathered on the forward deck and told stories. Womer, possibly with the benefit of hindsight, remembered their meetings as follows:

> Each night we met, and one by one, we took our turn. Van Kirk was writing short stories and would read one. Zimmerman could sing like a nightingale and he sang. I usually told of some strange place visited, or described some far off city. The first meeting we had all finished except Lewis. . . . Closing his eyes, he began a story that held us spellbound and every night he came up with a new one. . . .

And Harry himself wrote, "The happiest moments of the trip was the Liars club. . . . One evening we sang a number of old gospel hymns—glorious old songs which can never die—the Doxology, Onward Christian Soldiers, & others."

In other leisure time, he read a guide to London that one of the men had with him and Mérimée's *Colomba,* and he made extensive notes on the voyage itself. He was interested in the vocabulary of the Englishmen aboard. "English vocab—espec. noticeable—oh aye; bloody; bugger (& buggering); vista; sweets; lift; tram; overhead; bloomin' Yankee." For the first time in these diaries, he attempts to characterize his fellows and contemplates their varying histories, and then he organizes his notes in his letter to his mother. Of his own crew, which was less fierce than some others, he wrote:

> There are 5 men & a boss in each of the lower deck crews. . . . The bosses & most of the men curse the animals dreadfully, as an aid to a stick of wood,

> in getting up. "Get oop there, damn yuh, you ——— ect!". . . . In my crew are "Jack" the ultra-Irish boss; the best boss on board, lets us do our work without yelling & swearing, as does "Frenchie," the little Canuck, who is boss in the other lower-deck-alley-way. The men are—"Dad," an English brick layer, 50 or 60 yrs old, returning to England & to his family because he was unable to find much work in the States; "Fred," a hatter by trade, 28 yrs old, nice little fellow, who, like "Shorty" came on the trip to kill a little time before the time to begin work at a job he has secured; Shorty begins work Sept. 1 in Providence R.I. at his trade as meat cutter. "Reddy" Zimmerman is a "Suthenä" from S. Carolina, aged prehaps 21, rather a wanderer who came on the trip to "see what it was like." He is lazy and not pleasant to work with, but outside of working hours tells good stories & shows a good knowledge of operas. He was for 2 or 3 years in a S. Car. Military college.

So, in the diary, he catalogues the rest of the crew, and one can only observe that there had been not even such sparse characterization as this of his fellows at Yale or at Oberlin. He remarks on the changes of the seascape and the weather from day to day, is excited by the sight of Ireland ("the wonderful land of elves & banshees; of Burke & of Yeats; where Carleton's tales were enacted") and the coast of Wales ("land of my forefathers").

Irresistibly one thinks of young Herman Melville, another American innocent making his first sea voyage to Liverpool, as he recounts it in *Redburn.* Sighting Ireland, Redburn thinks of Robert Emmet and Thomas Moore; sighting Wales, of the Prince of Wales. And the disembarkment in Liverpool Harbor was as anticlimactic for him as it was to be for young Harry Lewis. Melville wrote:

> And this is England?
> But where are the old abbeys, and the York Minsters, and the lord mayors, and coronations, and the Maypoles, and fox-hunters, and Derby races, and the dukes and duchesses, and the Count d'Orsays, which, from all my reading, I had been in the habit of associating with England? Not the most distant glimpse of them was to be seen.

Redburn itself, with its disenchanted account of squalor and poverty, brutality and vice, as Melville had discovered them in Liverpool, could have been Harry Lewis's most instructive guidebook, had he but known of it.

When he stepped onto the dock late in the afternoon on July 27, he posted his letter to his mother. In it he had written of his plans in England:

> The ship remains in Liverpool eight days. I have enough money to keep myself while there. I shall stay 3 days in Liverpool; walk to Manchester (32 miles distant, taking 2 days for the walk); stay there a day & return. I shall greatly enjoy the walk thru' the beautiful English country.

In Womer's later account, Harry borrowed some money from him.

> He asked me to make him a small loan. I had promised a paper back home an article, so I paid Red three dollars to write it and sign my name. It was a good article. At that time he had only 15 cents and no job. I made him a small loan, more than I could spare; it was fifteen or twenty dollars. His plan was to make socialistic speeches on the street corners of Liverpool and London and pass the hat for living expenses. He had his passage back to Portland including berth and food.

In his reference to Harry's plan to make socialistic speeches Womer may have been confusing the Lewis of that time with the Lewis of several months later, when Harry visited Womer at Belleville, New Jersey.* At any rate, Harry spoke on no street corners. The first thing he did in Liverpool was to hasten to the Corporation Bathing House. ". . . had warm bath for 2d. I needed it!"

He spent his first night in a cheap lodging house ("near birth place of Felicia Hemans") that cost him four pence and where the "abominable lice" were so troublesome that he vowed henceforth to sleep out of doors in preference to the kind of bed he could afford. All around him slept drunken crewmen off the *Georgian,* but not the other members of the Liars' Club, who had withdrawn to a decent hotel. On Thursday Harry wandered about Liverpool and ended on a country road, chatting with one John Pierson, a farmer, who told him he could sleep in his barn. On Friday he visited museums and in the evening he "wrote article on L'pool for Womer for Amer. Newspaper," thus, presumably, earning his three dollars. Then, on Saturday, he checked his bag at the Y.M.C.A., put on his old clothes ("trousers exceedingly ragged; negligee shirt; out at elbows") and started on foot for Manchester, "hoping to be able to get work along way to earn food." In fifteen miles he had no success, and before he came to Warrington, he turned around.

> Despair at not finding work. Dire hunger. Lovely aspect of loaf of bread. Rest on stone marked "Traveller's Rest. 'For he shall give you rest,' " and resolve to return. Bought bread at country store.

In later reminiscences he said that, at one house at which he stopped to beg, the lady listened to him sweetly and then turned her dog upon him; in his diary he turned upon a dog: "At one house I pursued and kicked

* The details of the Womer account may well be inaccurate here. Lewis's diary says, "All the money I had was $3, borrowed from Womer." There is no evidence that he had more money to spend during his eight days in England. The Womer reminiscence goes on to say that "later in the Fall Lewis came down to New York with the Yale football team. He cut the game and spent most of the afternoon with me at the Belleville Church." Lewis did not go to New York in the autumn; the two exchanged a few letters during those months, but Lewis did not go to New York until March 10–11 in 1905, on a railroad pass offered him by William Fay. He wrote, "Spent night with WAYNE WOMER. . . . Saw Womer's Church . . . and his 'girl' (Miss Gertrude———; a peach)." The Lewis of that spring might very well have been talking socialism.

soundly a fierce yelping cur, tied with a long chain; sign near 'Beware of dog.' " He rode for a while with a sawdust man, watched two cricket matches, made copious observations on local architecture and rural traffic, and ended up reading his Bible in a railroad station. He slept for an hour under a railroad bridge and "started home by glorious flood of moonlight."

> As I swung on at 4½ miles an hour, along the hard road, the crisp night air drove away the lassitude from English climate, & a flood of ambition for next year crowded my mind (track team, dramatic club (pres?), chief editor of Lit. and Courant, debating, first in scholarship in class, with many a prize for exam & essay.

Thus exalted, he walked until two in the morning when he again slept for an hour, now in a roadside grove. He awoke and walked on, saw a "boy tramp asleep in road, another in field," paused to talk to a lad "crouched by warm brazier" but could not understand his Lancashire dialect, slowed down to one or two miles an hour in his weariness, and on Sunday morning sank exhausted in the pew of a Catholic church in Liverpool to observe the early service of the Mass. Then he wrote two letters, one to Judge Bishop in New Haven, asking him to have five dollars at the Portland post office by the day that the *Georgian* came in, and another to his father asking if he could send fifteen dollars to New Haven.

He attended a second church service ("Was just recovering from my semi-annual fit of Catholicism; a form of deliberate self-blinding Episcopaleanism being, prehaps, a stage in the recovery.") and then retrieved his bag from the Y.M.C.A. There he met "Reddy" Zimmerman ("very blue and almost penniless") and they made their way to Pierson's barn, in which they spent their remaining nights together. During the day, they studied the collections in the Walker Art Gallery and the Free Public Museum (especially its Egyptian collection) and read in the railroad station, and in the evening they sat in Septon Park. "Very cheaply we lived—pea soup & bread; 1d meat pies, penny & ha'penny buns and scones. . . . Reddy tramped streets, asking in many shops for chance to earn some food." Three dollars was being stretched very thin indeed when, on their last two mornings, Mrs. Pierson gave them substantial breakfasts. "The Belly Gods are of a surety as strong as the Red Gods of the Wanderlust," the traveler observed.

Getting to their ship on August 3 was a frantic business:

> We were a bit late & had to hurry tremendously with the heavy suit cases, to the dock. Finally I took overhead tram. Just in time, & for an hour almost sick of exhaustion from hauling the cases & running from place to place in the Hoskinson dock. Some one said, "Over there is the Georgian. She's moving." I ran there bawling, "Georgian!" Seeing men with plank. supposed it gang plank; but had lots of time. . . . At last we start for "God's Country" where I am to do good work—great work—again!

In his recovery, his gratitude, his anticipation, he puts a cross in his diary and writes: "This + marks the greatest day this year." And he sinks into reading alternately the Bible and *Childe Harold.*

Except for Womer and Van Kirk and the Englishmen who remained at home, the men on the ship were the same as those who had come over. The Canadians caused Harry some immediate "trouble over mattress," and he "Had to tell [them] that I didn't want anything to do with them." In general, matters were if anything less palatable than they had been on the crossing over. One man, Carpenter, seemed interesting and literate ("Suggested that in a child may lie embryonicly all facts & beliefs of grown mind"), but the Canadians were pugnacious and so were most of the others, notably a circus roustabout named Allert ("God damn it, I'm jest as good a gentleman as any of youse").

There had been no relief of the "Unutterable stench of forecastle," and the food was as bad as before. "Have to be a pig to get enough to live on—Grab." *Childe Harold* did not have the power to take him out of this reality and he dropped it in Canto Three. "Not in it." The Bible was better, and he could put his mind to a review of French grammar. He dreamed of home and his "old call to missions has again been sounded—strange coincidence—George Davitt, whom I told of a half former resolve to enter the ministry, said, 'Why not missionary? You are in a way suited to it.' " He wrote letters to Claude, to Fisher and to Bertha and, four days out of Portland, began a long letter to his mother that, again, he posted upon landing.

In great part this letter is simply an extended account of his eight days in England, with omission of such items as the nights spent in the barn. The more interesting portions of the letter are those that pertain intimately to himself; in these the letter is at once abject ("What would I not give for a chat & a dinner at home!") and boastful (". . . it has proven me no longer a boy. I feel proud . . ."), weary, and full of resolute promises.

> May this year be a better one than last; and my sincerest wish for it is that I may do things in it to make *you* (You plural) proud of me. *What faults & mistakes I have had last year & this summer, forget I pray you,* & I shall start in with renewed energy . . . next year I am to be 1st scholar in my class! Would you not be proud of your western son if he should take 1st place in scholarship? At least, I will keep my place on the "Honor Roll." Then—I must be striding on to the chief editorship of both the Lit & the Courant—either one of which is considered as one of the academic honors. Besides this I hope to take a more active part in YMCA work. Whether I do this or not one thing is certain—I shall endeavor never to use a single "swear word"—not even the convenient damn—or use anything save the purest English. The need of this has [as] never before been enforced on my attention by the foul mouthed cattlemen. . . . Be glad that I have taken

this trip if only for the reason that it has made me see how fortunate I have been to have such parents, home, college & friends. . . . I am learning to get along with men better—to jolly them—or the opposite—an art in which Claude is such an adept—though of course I can never approach to him in it. . . . Though I have saved no money, as yet, however I feel that my vacation has been far from wasted; and that I have taken a good course under that excellent teacher experience.

He had, in fact, no money whatever. They docked on Sunday and the post office was closed. Was Judge Bishop's money inside? Harry panicked, pawned his ring and watch, and wired Dr. Skinner, who had administered the X rays of the year before, for aid. "Blue," he wrote. He attended four church services, napped under a hedge and in the bandstand of a park, and slept until six next morning in Union Station. That Monday morning he had five dollars from Judge Bishop, eight dollars from Dr. Skinner, and one dollar and twenty-five cents from the shipping company. "$ $ to burn!" He took the night boat to Boston and the train from Boston to New Haven next morning. There, he went directly to the office of the *Journal and Courier.*

It is not entirely clear how he filled the month in New Haven before classes began. On his first day back, he made a note of having "Refused Courier Job," of having found a room at 105 Park Street, of buying dishes to prepare his own meals, of availing himself of a typewriter, and of hoping to do some magazine and Sunday newspaper writing. He did some work for the Palladium and he worked a few days for the *Journal and Courier* (and then vowed, "I shall NEVER work [there] again.") On one day he recorded only "All kinds of work sought," and on another, "work sought," and on many days he wrote nothing at all in the diary. He found some employment as a tutor in English and Latin to a classmate, Dwight Meigs, whose "eyes failed at Easter," and there seemed to have been a possibility of his going "to Long Island to tutor our '08 fellow in Latin, but did not materialize."

Soon after his return he encountered another classmate, Charles Hibbard, and only a week after he had taken his room, he moved, either to join Hibbard in his room or at the same address. ". . . trouble in getting things fr[om] 105 [Park] . . ." He walked with Hibbard, and once with Dr. Tinker. He saw Parmelee occasionally. He read Scott. He contemplated his future: "What, collegio finito? Law, writing (& journalism), teaching (English, or history or philosophy or economics)? Which? Now lean to first."

On September 23 he moved his possessions into his new college room, 232 Durfee.

5

NOW BEGAN THE LONG, slow process of conscious disaffection. It began in sporadic lapses into indifference, but it grew into hostility. With it came a degree of self-recognition and, with that, resolution. It is curious that this process should have begun at just the point at which he had made the staunchest vows of earnest effort. It is curious, too, that it should have begun when he had at last made one real friend at Yale and when he seemed to have succeeded in infusing with some intimacy at least a few of those other relationships that until now had been merely mechanical. It is these facts that make this development interesting, just as they make it complex—a zigzag affair, starting slowly, stopping, reversing itself momentarily, starting again, gaining momentum, and reaching its climax in the sudden departure from New Haven in October 1906. If the return, over a year later, seemed like an act of compromise, it was in fact an act of mature judgment and of considered economy. If Yale could be rejected, Yale could also be taken—but now on his more realistic terms. His no longer caring for those things that Yale would not give him demonstrates his maturity; his taking what Yale could give demonstrates his sense.

The new, the first friend, was Allan Updegraff. He was a classmate who, in their freshman year, lived in another building, and whom Harry Lewis never mentioned in his diary of that year. Updegraff remembers that it was Lewis who sought him out on the ground of their common achievement: Lewis was the first freshman to be published in the literary magazines; Updegraff had won the McKenzie Prize for a freshman literary essay. On that first night they walked for a long time through the rain, quoting Kipling, Browning, Keats and Swinburne, one to the other and in unison. They were two literary men together. They were also two awkward squares isolated and uneasy in a social pattern that expected and assimilated smooth rounds. Lewis called Updegraff "Up" or "Updie"; Updegraff called him "Bonfire" or "B.F."

If his second year started off with this promising friendship, it also started off with an overtone of critical lament (that covered the cut of some unrecorded experience, or was it the cut of his general experience of life thus far?) in a quotation from Ella Wheeler Wilcox that stands alone on the diary page for the first Sunday of the term:

> So many Gods, so many creeds
> So many ways which wind, & wind
> When all this sad world really needs
> Is just the art of being kind.

On a Sunday early in the second term, he reverted to the quotation on a page that is headed "My religion." After the lines and after a parenthesis under the author's name ("who is responsible for much sentimental slush, but also for noble lines"), this credo follows:

> "Beauty is truth, truth, beauty, that is all
> Ye know on earth, and all ye need to know." Keats.

> Appreciation of the arts (drama, music, poetry . . .); kindness; minding ones business and broadness enough to let live; sympathy—for "what so ever pertains to men & their minds is of vital interest to me." "Plain living & high thinking." Pure & noble thoughts. This & nothing more. No cant about Sabbath, & priesthoods & gods, & saints, & blasphemy, & such self indulgences as smoking, ect. If there be saints—they are Voltaire—as well as Christ; Shelley as well as St. Paul.

This credo states a clear development; if it proclaims an old need, it also articulates a new commitment—to curiosity, to tolerance, to skepticism. To the old, merely mooning sentimentality, the self-centered "lyricism" of adolescence with its concomitant in self-righteous dogmatism, he wishes now to bring the warmer vein of humanity and doubt. It is not to be thought that with this announcement he achieves maturity, but in it he shows that he is beginning to see where maturity lies. It is to help him, incidentally, to measure Yale.

Allan Updegraff helped him, but very few others. Moffat and Rankin were gone. Parmelee, now an assistant in statistics, was a man several years older who was given to the delivery of stately judgments that the gaping Harry sometimes found worth recording; but they hardly met as equals. Parmelee said to him of the Resurrection: "I cannot see that there is sufficient historical evidence to compel the belief in this solitary perversion of the great natural laws"; and of the Sheffield Scientific School as opposed to Yale College: "Acad[emic] is loath to grant privileges to Shef. today; ten years from now Shef. will be granting privileges to Yale College." Both judgments represent directions in which Harry's mind would move, but there seems to have been none of the give-and-take in his relationship with Parmelee that would suggest that the older man helped push him.

Lewis probably gained more from his occasional arguments with a classmate named Henry Moore, a ritualist and aesthete who dabbled with fine printing and provided a useful vocal opposition to all that Harry Lewis was to become. He occasionally wrangled and debated with others, including the two men Hull and Collins, who, for economic reasons, moved into his room with him after Christmas; but this was definitely a Hull-and-Collins-versus-Lewis situation, and especially on intellectual issues such as religion and politics. A few men there were who almost promised to become friends before Updegraff.

There was Charles Hibbard in the summer ("Hibbard stays with me several days, deo gratias"), but nothing came of this. There was Howard Bishop, also heeling the *Lit,* with whom Harry had hoped to share a room in that year and again in the next; but in the next year, Bishop was rooming with Collins. There was Bishop's roommate of the present year, a freshman named Sydney Frank; "my only worshipper," Harry called him, but later, "Wish Frank would wake up," and finally, Frank "needs . . . a little agreeableness."

These promises of friendship all decayed, as did even the best of them, that with one Philip L. Morrison. They had known each other casually the year before, but in 1904–1905, Morrison lived in Lewis's entry and they began to see each other frequently. Early in the year, Harry wrote, "Have come to know Phil Morrison better . . . clever not deep." Morrison was a good violinist, he had a mandolin, there was music in his rooms, and Harry enjoyed going there; perhaps it was Morrison's influence that led to the unmusical Harry's resolve to study the piano, which he was not to attempt again for forty years. Something unpleasant occurred and Harry wrote in December, "Never go in to Phil Morrison's room now. Each of us is too proud of himself"; but four days later he spent "much of afternoon" there. Morrison gave him rather interesting literary advice: "If you write a novel you ought to use the light, somewhat cynical, style of Trilby, because you notice the peculiarities of folk."

It was Morrison too, who, like only Rankin before him, was candid with Harry about his social manner: "Phil and I had a long & serious talk about my future success in literature; & the need of my being a gentleman (tactful, quiet, ect.)." In this year, Harry affected a cane, worried more about his physique ("I must broaden out my shoulders") and his clothes ("Solomonian glory of white 'veskit,' & new derby. . . . Learning to dress better; shoes, cap, linen, neckties, ect."), and when he acquired new spectacles he wrote, "In my new eye glasses & silk cord I look quite distingue, doncher-know. Almost as good as a monacle." The taste may have been Sauk Centre's, but the influence would seem to have been Morrison's. And again a vague Holland Carter situation developed: "Phil and I are now best of friends, & know some, at least, of each other's inmost secrets, smoke each others cigarettes; I study much in his room." That was in February; after March 1, Morrison vanished forever.

Precisely at that point, Updegraff became important. They had seen each other not infrequently throughout the year, always amiably, one gathers, but in the spring of 1905 the friendship became constant, almost an affair of daily meetings. Updegraff was a Woodstock, New York, boy not in the least overwhelmed by New Haven—poor, to be sure, but with an aggressive independence of mind that young Harry could not at this point in his career lay claim to, and willing, not stumbling into, his difference. Early in the year, he had proposed to Lewis that they publish "a *real* Yale newspaper; to run in opp[osition] to News, which is a mere bulletin," and Lewis would have gone into it "for fair" had he not still been fired by his recent resolves to shine in "scholarly & literary work."

Their friendship developed on literary grounds. They took a walk, "he as Stephen Phillips, myself as Richard Le Gallienne (both of whom he has met)." They called on their professors together, on Root and Goodell ("Do not like to be talked *at,*" said Lewis of the second gentleman), and together they translated eight hundred and fifty lines of the *Medea* one evening, "consuming a glass of claret & a box of Murad cigarettes on the way." They had regularly the "long talks" which Lewis had yearned for and had come by so rarely before—"talk of Haeckel, & the coming school of poets, & the value of marriage, et. mult. al. philosophical questions." Ernst Haeckel was the kind of "advanced thinker" to whom Updegraff was introducing Lewis, who, when he finished reading *Monism,* wrote, "Surely this is nothing but the truth; the whole truth; nothing but the truth. I must study more biology ect."

These young men, reading Ernst Haeckel in 1904 and 1905, were very much in the vanguard of American intellectual fashions, and it is probable that Haeckel came to the attention of young Harry Lewis at precisely the right moment in his own development. Repudiating personal immortality and that "gaseous vertebrate," God, his naturalism was optimistic and not without cloudy pantheistic overtones—a combination that would at once free Lewis from his forced commitments to religion and provide a sanction for his habitual sentimentality. Max Nordau's *Degeneration* was another book that they read and discussed together, agreeing that it was "extreme & too severe, but a good warning."

Updegraff seems to have been the intellectual guide, at least in philosophical reading, but Harry was not above reservations about him. He wrote, "Some of the talk—as on Haeckle—inspiring; but too much smut withal," and he seemed dubious about Updegraff's admiration for and defense of Oscar Wilde. Updegraff shared Harry's new enthusiasm for Whitman ("the only Amer[ican] poet . . . N[ordau] contemnds [him]"), and Harry persuaded him of the beauties of Upson. It was a real relationship. Updegraff had had some poems accepted by commercial magazines, and Harry began to send his own work out. Harry helped Updegraff translate Greek, and Updegraff typed Harry's manuscripts. They drank together ("Happy but straight. Chased cat"), on one occasion picked up two "Stenographers or solch etwas" together, and on Harry's last night in town, after one long walk with Professor Tinker, he and Updegraff had their farewell walk between the hours of eleven and one.

Already at the beginning of the year, Harry's religious views were in jeopardy. The influence of Wayne Womer on the *Georgian* had briefly reconvinced him "of the truth of Christianity & according to my high sworn vow resolved to become missionary at oportet. But again I am 'rational'—'agnostic,' 'unitarian' & what not—a host of hard sounding names. The Bible & Christ are more to me than Mohammed & the Koran only as they are considerably nearer perfection." But miracles, the Resurrection, a personal God—these he was no longer able to accept. He taught Sunday school for a part of that year only because "the boys insist on having one [a teacher]."

He still attended church with reasonable regularity, often approved a sermon for its ethical content, and enjoyed independent preachers ("Liked his 'Grow your own religious tissue. *Of course* you can't think as your grandfather did.' ") But he began to read books in chapel while the "time-honored drool" flowed on, and he argued volubly now with any "aboriginal & orthodox (i.e. childish)" Christian who would listen to him. He debated the problem "as to whether religion & ethics were necessarily joined," and after his close friendship with Updegraff had developed, he concluded that "The Christian Religion is a crutch. Until it is taken away we never can begin to walk well." On Easter Sunday he did not go to church but tried, instead, to convince a freshman of the "wisdom of Socialism." Like Updegraff, he was beginning to take a public position that was opposed to prevailing values in New Haven, and when he was called "Red" now, it was not only because of the color of his hair.

The development shows itself in many ways. At the beginning of the year he still made his occasional attempts to join in the traditional group activities of the college; at the end of the year he hardly noted their occurrence. He tried out unsuccessfully for the dramatic club, but, after considering the possibility, decided not even to try for the debating team or the *News* staff. Attempts at self-improvement (the piano, independent study of Italian) were short-lived. He did compete for the Pundit Prize with an essay on "Bardic Afflatus at Yale, or Could There Be Here a Group Like the Cambridge Apostles?"—but without success. His decision to try for a Rhodes Scholarship led to a brief period of more than the usual physical exercise, since he would have to present himself as some kind of athlete; it was a discouraging experience, of course. "Too tired to run over mile in gym. Legs like sticks. Wish I could jump," he wrote. Later: "Too lame to run much in gym." Finally: "Rhodes Scholarship ambitions gone smash. I am an *American* and I am *not* an Athlete; 2 reasons." His grades declined and the dream of Phi Beta Kappa faded.

It is well known that for many college students, the sophomore year is the academic low point, but the almost immediate slump in the work of the fervently dedicated Harry Lewis of September was astonishing. He fell into a strange, disorganized lassitude. A classmate recalls that he "would sit outside Commons as fellows came from lunch and ask them to toss up—as to whether to go to class that p.m. or to Poli's—the vaudeville theater."

His social experience in the college gave him, of course, small motivation and, more positively, plagued him with moods of loneliness and melancholy that necessarily sapped his energies. "Very 'blue,' " he would write; or, having read, of all books, *Little Women,* "It drives away my gloomy moods . . ."; or, "Humdrum lonely existence of vacation has begun." Usually he said nothing, but in his very muteness lets us picture him, as: "Walk way out Fountain St. (Westville); passed Father's old home; played robber with some small boys. Made me a little verse, as I swung along. . . ." (Something touchingly shamefaced remains in his having put the clause beginning "played robber" in code while the rest of the entry is written out in English.) There is one night scene, when, after a bonfire celebration, he "Couldn't get to sleep. Clad in n[igh]t gown & bath robe I toasted my legs by the remnants of the fire on the campus, at 11:30!"

For a time, before the Updegraff friendship grew close, the lonely walk ("Walk solus," he always wrote) came to be the preferred walk; "Great walk, in the afternoon, Car to lighthouse point; by country roads, & coast (including cliffs) to swamp beyond Monauguin. Built a fire on the edge of woods, dried shoes & stockings, & read WALT WHITMAN, with a pleasant feeling of solitude & freedom."

The feeling of freedom was rare, for his poverty was always a bondage and, like his moods, corrosive of effort. In October he wrote, "Must economize—Father says 'this grind is getting too hard to bear' "; and in November he suggested to his parents that he transfer to a Midwestern university. There was the constant effort to find employment, employment beyond the *Journal and Courier,* which at best could give him small tasks at low fees. (He saw more plays than he would otherwise have managed, because for a time he served the *Courier* as theater critic; but this work was almost certainly done for the pass alone, since he said nothing of being paid.) Occasionally he managed to work as a "super" in an ambitious stage production, and about one of these few occasions, when the management was dishonest, he introduced the usual comic note: "... attempt to get money due. I was one who didn't succeed." He found occasional employment as a tutor to delinquent students.

It is a comment either on his generosity or on his dogged desire to be liked that more often than not he helped other students with their studies for no remuneration at all. "Helped Soandso with French," he would only say in the diary; but Mr. Irving S. Olds, years later, was one who remembered this help gratefully.

> I have always felt a deep debt of gratitude to him for his sympathetic friendship and for the help which he voluntarily gave me at that time—without it, it is conceivable that I might not have survived my second year at Yale.... Sometimes, because of extra-curricular activities, I found it difficult to do my regular home-work as a student. On a number of such occasions, I met "Red" in his room for a few minutes before we went to class and took advantage of his willingness to give me a summary of what I was supposed to have read for that day's lesson.... With this information, I succeeded in writing a daily test which was accurate enough to warrant a passing mark from my instructor.

It is entertaining that it should have been the future chairman of the board of United States Steel, of all that class of 1907, who, while certainly in no real sense a friend, nevertheless penetrated to the true situation of Harry S. Lewis at New Haven.

> It is my belief that "Red" at heart craved popularity, admiration, and social recognition, and that his failure to attain what he desired in these directions explains to a considerable degree his rebelliousness and his apparent hostility to those who should have been close to him as friends and loyal supporters. Lewis's gawkiness and somewhat forbidding facial appearance unquestionably constituted real obstacles in the way of attainment of general social acceptance in his earlier years and may well have colored and distorted his subsequent outlook on life.

It is curious that, in this situation, so little personal venom flowed into Lewis's diaries. In this whole degenerating year, there are no more than five or six inimical remarks about his fellows, and they are as mild as "Sore at the bear Milholland" and "Middlebrook, the accursed, libertine gentleman!" One is perhaps a little stronger: during vacations, it was the college practice to put the men who were staying on the campus in as few rooms as possible, and Harry was moved in with Hibbard and his roommate, Gooden; but Hibbard went home for a few days at Christmas and the relationship of Lewis and Gooden exploded.

> *December 27, 1904.* Evening & P.M. quarelled with Gooden (who has seen fit to practically insult—the pariah pup of a nonentity, as he is—me several times. Left the room.

That is to say, he changed rooms; he moved in with Takagi, another alien.

These were the pressures under which his work decayed. He took to dawdling and wasting his time. Reading became a kind of opiate. (He developed a great enthusiasm for Maeterlinck and Shaw, and in this year read the early work of Edith Wharton and of H. G. Wells.) He cut classes more and more frequently. He felt that he was both smoking and drinking too much. A Miss Minnie Pike of Sauk Centre was enrolled in another New Haven institution, the Anderson Normal School of Gymnastics, and through her he met a number of young women in the school and began to squire them about.

"Fussing" hardly became so frequent that in itself it was a serious threat to study, but it had its distractions. His interest did not settle for long on any one of these young women but moved birdlike among them. There was first a Miss Sooy (whose proximity returned him to thoughts of Myra and set him to writing her a letter, never mailed), and he spent an "evening in the asthetic & spiritual recreation of hugging" her. Miss Pike wrote him a "displeasing note," and Miss Sooy vanished, only to be succeeded by a Miss Bigger. He was attracted by Judge Bishop's oldest daughter, but "Her serene Majesty Cornelia doesn't like me even a little bit." A Miss Miles, Miss Pike's new roommate in January, promised better: *"Met my fate,"* he exclaimed; "oh, she's a peach, a darling. Great dark eyes; smooth dear old fashioned hair; a dainty ankle; a charming virginal manner." And for six weeks he fancied himself in love with her. Then, through her brother, whom he had known at Oberlin, he met an older woman, a Miss Barrows, who was about to take her Ph.D., and he exclaimed again: "God! were I ten years older!" Then he received a letter, in reply to one of his own, from Miss Anna Louise Strong, a senior at Oberlin and "My spiritual affinity, prehaps." But Miss Strong was far away; Miss Miles ceased to occupy herself with him; and he covertly watched and mooned about girls he did not know who were working in the library. "Am much in love with Diana of the Brown; the coldly beautiful."

There was, perhaps, one adventure: with Updegraff, one Wednesday evening in May, he talked to two working girls near the end of Orange Street, and they arranged for a meeting on Friday. Posterity will not know what happened on that occasion; the page for Friday, May 19, is blank; and on Saturday, he was "reading that tragedy—D. G. Rossetti's life." *

From all his distractions he would, every now and then, rouse himself, vow to "stop fooling" and work briefly with a fury. His work for the first

* The encounter with these girls was probably unique in his college experience. At any rate, it impressed him so forcibly that thirty-seven years later, at the Gateway Lodge on Hungry Jack Lake, Minnesota, he recalled it and recorded it in his journal for August 12, 1942. His hostess "actually told the story 'For God's sake' (only she made it 'For pity's sake') 'drop the other shoe' which I remember having first heard told by Allan Updegraff (to me and 2 pick-up phone girls) in 1905."

half of the year gave him honors of the fourth class; his work for the year gave him none. There were no prizes, no awards. There was no glory and there was no God. "Started reviewing 'Medea' for final exam," he wrote. "Probably final w[ith] many senses for me."

Through all this, his attitude toward Yale was changing. The change began as early as October, when he wrote of "Another 'go to other college' fit of Michigan prefered." In the winter he wished that he could accelerate his course; "I often grow weary of wasting so much of my time as I do here." Nothing seemed quite worth the seriousness with which Yale took itself, not even the *Lit,* for which he still worked hard. "These Lit. editors think it a mighty thing, this little periodical of theirs."

Even his favorite professors began to seem less like sages. He had written, when he had read about Abelard in History A1, "He must have been a greater Billy Phelps—or a Phelps combined with Tinker." But on the day that he read Jack London's *Sea Wolf* and walked with Tinker and Root, he speculated about them, "Are they not—am I not—untried Humphrey Van Weydens?"—that is, merely dilettantish critics. And in May, "Verily Tinker hath despised my friendship. He thinketh me too fresh."

In March he wrote to his father that "it seemed to me that I was wasting my time in college." And as far back as December he had written, "In Charley Otis' room told him—truthfully—that I am but drifting; no ambition in regard to anything." Late in May he spent an evening with another casual acquaintance "discussing the advantages of Harvard over Yale." A week later he made this note: "In Tinker's room; speaking of wisdom of going to Harvard next year."

It is not true that he had "no ambition in regard to anything." His literary passion grew and it became clear to him that he was to become a literary man although necessarily something else as well, if not a journalist perhaps a teacher of English. He bombarded both the *Lit* and the *Courant* with contributions, determined as he was to rise to the editorial board of both. In the course of the year, the *Lit* accepted one story and three poems from him; the *Courant,* four stories and seven poems.

The work in the *Lit* consists of an eight-line lyric called "Odysseus at Ogygia" (October), perhaps rather more controlled than most of his verse; a 74-line stretch of blank verse called "The Third Estate" (December), which, using a medieval setting, moralizes on the theme of *"laborare est orare"* (the Jester is named Mink!); a more ambitious, four-page effort called "Behind the Arras: a Christmas Mask" (February), which, utilizing a variety of metrical schemes, is a fantasy of faithless love in a medieval castle, its only suggestive lines being these:

> And weary, weary, never gay
> Is life on Father's wild bleak moors;

and finally, a bit of prose fiction called "The Yellow Streak" (April), little more than an anecdote about a poet whose success has turned him from a healthy, amiable fellow into an affected, mincing snob.

The verse in the *Courant* consists entirely of songs except for one bit that suggests he had been reading *Don Juan,* with lines like

> As they were passing by a harem,
> "I'd like to peak in there, and scare 'em,"
> The caliph said.

The prose is heavy and fanciful: "Father Ambrosial" attempts to reanimate Jack Falstaff in an inn where he is abusing King Henry for his perfidy, when a monk who has wandered in reveals himself to be the king in disguise; "The Royal Glamour" has to do with the rescue of a medieval "princess yclept Selon"; "A Miracle Forsooth" is a bit of nonsense about professors in a German community who are imprisoned by the prince in revenge for his poor grades in the university. Only "Concerning Psychology" has a contemporary subject, although treated no less fantastically: a modernist clergyman wishes to discover the feelings of a criminal and to that end disguises himself as one, is apprehended, and is released through a convenient *deus ex machina.* In this story, the young Lewis thought, he had at last found his proper style and manner in fiction.

He tried out other literary forms. He began a play, *The King is Twins,* but gave it up for another, *A Platonic Friendship,* intended for the Yale dramatic club but ending in his waste basket. He planned a "Boyland Series," stories of his own boyhood, and wrote the first of them, "The Metropolitan Theatre," which was probably a reminiscence of his childhood "key people"; when the *Lit* declined this effort, he apparently did not pursue the plan for the series. He began to send his manuscripts out to commercial periodicals, the first a story about a foreign correspondent, then his verses, then a Japanese prose fantasy called *Matsu-No-Kata* ("plot from Takagi"), and an essay to *The Critic,* a respectable publication of national circulation, which accepted it.

His wide and random reading had brought him his first tangible reward. He had read a best seller called *The Masqueraders,* by the Englishwoman Katherine E. Thurston, and one night in April he "sat up till 3:30 reading Zangwill's 'Premier & Painter,' " convinced that the currently popular book had been plagiarized from the older novel. In one night he wrote out his case, a neat and systematic comparison of the two books that demonstrated their similarity in plot, setting, character conception and formulation, even incidental details. *The Critic,* presenting the matter as a "remarkable coincidence" under the title "Did Mrs. Thurston Get the Idea of 'The Masqueraders' from Mr. Zangwill?", published the article on June 1 and paid its author twenty dollars.* Harry was a published writer, and the name under which he had been published was Sinclair Lewis.

But there were disappointments in the area of literary effort, too. His rhetoric instructor told him, "You ought to write for the waste basket. Having nothing, you can give nothing, yet." (Sinclair Lewis did not forget; in 1937 he wrote of this young man, "There was also a class in short-story writing in which the teacher, later author of a couple of fifth-rate novels, might have been pretty harmful if he had only been brighter.")

Whatever private views he held of the self-importance of the members of the *Lit* board, he showed those gentlemen every deference. A 1905 editor remembers that "when one of us would meet him coming across the campus, [he] would withdraw to the side of the sidewalk and bow most courteously . . . certainly not like other undergraduates." Yet one editor that year told him that a story he had submitted was a painful imitation of a currently popular book, so much like its model that it was without character of its own. His manuscripts were not always very tidy, and when he inquired about the reason for the rejection of another of them, "the editor who had originally disapproved of it said he had not read it through because the ms. was filthy and covered with egg. He then advised Sinclair to get a good stenographer to prepare his stuff. This apparently so disturbed him that he submitted no more stories until that board was out of office." More probably, he only sulked for a time. On February 27, 1905, he wrote in his diary, "May not hand anything more in for Lit, probably not for Courant, for rest of this year." He continued to "hand in" much. While the *Lit* ran his story "The Yellow Streak," it continued to decline many more contributions from him than it accepted, and just before the end of the term, he made an entry that falls into a familiar pattern: "Damn the Lit damn the Courant damn all personal authority." The difference in the pattern now is only that the condition of the handwriting forces the conclusion that the young author was drunk.

Then he returned to Sauk Centre for the summer.

* In the August issue Mrs. Thurston agreed to the similarities, confessed her confusion, called it a "most extraordinary case of dual suggestion," and pleaded that no real theft would be so incredibly obvious. In his contribution to Gelett Burgess' anthology, *My Maiden Effort* (New York, 1921), Lewis gives his account of his "discovery" and the publication that followed, and calls attention to the first occasion on which he became the subject of a newspaper editorial. "The New York *Times Book Review* gave a mildly cynical editorial to it," he wrote. The *Book Review,* which was then called the *Saturday Review of Books,* published this editorial on August 5, 1905, under the title, "Unwisdom of hasty charges of plagiarism." It did not mention Sinclair Lewis by name but implied the presence of a brash young man behind the pen, concluding: "Charges of plagiarism are easy to make. Every newspaper receives many communications embodying such charges from irate, well-meaning persons who cannot be made to understand why the Editor does not immediately lend all his resources to their cause. Frequently men and women of the highest literary standing are thus ruthlessly assailed."

6

THE SUMMER WAS NOT UNPLEASANT, but it was dull and largely unprofitable. It had, to be certain, begun most promisingly with "4 glorious days with Arthur [Upson]" in Minneapolis. Lewis had begun a correspondence with Upson in January, when he had read the complimentary account of Upson in the final pages of Jessie B. Rittenhouse's *Younger American Poets*. "I am walking in nubibus because of receiving an answer from ARTHUR UPSON; 'a consummation devoutly . . . hoped for;' but which I scarce dared expect. He remembers me. . . ." He drew two of Upson's books from the library, spread his fame among his fellows ("I like Upson's rich contemplative verse. He will 'arrive.' "), and argued with one of them that it was not affectation in Upson to use the British spelling of such words as *honour*. They exchanged seven or eight letters in the spring and, after the meeting in Minneapolis, the correspondence was heavy throughout the summer. There were no poets in Sauk Centre with whom he might commune—except himself.

He arrived on June 21, just before his parents departed for a month in the Northwest and Canada, and simultaneously with a friend of Claude's, a young surgeon named Ellison, who was to take over the elder Lewis's practice for that period. Ellison seems to have been a pleasant enough companion and the two of them did a fair amount of squiring among the local belles. Harry himself was now a man who had had a relatively impressive experience of the world, and his diary gives no evidence that the village still hounded him with its bedevilments. Boating, swimming, picnicking, fudge making, band concerts in the park—these were the pleasures of the summer into which Sauk Centre seemed now to have been prepared to admit him. But the tables had been turned; he found Sauk Centre less than tolerable. Even the girls, some of whom let him kiss them now, were poor things. (The Hendryx family had moved, and Myra, alas, was no longer there.) "Made active love to Hildred," he wrote after a boating party, and remarked in her "a vein of coarseness" that he had found in others. The provincial values troubled him, too.

Lily has too little to her. She is a doll with well-molded face, sensuous lips, fairly graceful figure; with a calm expectancy that her court . . . be carefully obedient to her whims. A "jolly"—"nice"—girl—but a typical villager with not three ideas in her pretty little head which are not centered in S.C.—or Alexandria [Minnesota]!

The "smutty stories" of the young men about town and of the "typical drummers," whom he sometimes joined in the park of an evening, were hardly a preferable alternative to the limitations of the young women. The Fishers had moved to Florida.

He wrote a little at first ("Poem on the cynic—'The Vision Passes' " and some nameless "writing for Lit and Courant"), and he read more widely and more variously than ever to fill the long days, read everything from *Bob, Son of Battle* through Garland's *Main-Travelled Roads* to Haeckel's *World Riddle*. But these diversions were insufficient. He drank ("Had enough whiskey to go to sleep at seven thirty") and he lapsed into adolescent japes.

Evening P[aul Hilsdale] & ego, up to woods, viewing. . . . On the way home . . . Wine at "Tom's." Entering school house by third grade window, Paul & I took off our shoes, crept up stairs, & rummaged cupboards till we found the 1902 oratorical cup (for use cup night; will return.)

He even went to work for five days.

During the past week I have worked . . . 50 hours—in helping Nels Orvaar excavate a new cellar for the sewer & water pipes. Dug, loaded wheel barrow, carried armsful of brick, staggered with pails of "Mud" (Mortar). Tried—sans success—to mix a box of the last. Between staggerings with the "mud" I sat on a pile of dirt & read Tolstoi's "War & Peace."

His proposal at the beginning of August that he go back to New Haven early did not please his parents.

After a spat with that illogical & sensible woman, my step mother (in which she ridiculed the idea of early return to New Haven; "I could get no tutoring," etc.); I should go mad; as I nearly did two years ago, from this dull, too-familiar bourgeois life, & mothers sweet self-confident hellishness, were it not for books & things like my calling on Alta Hilsdale, the artist; this afternoon. Paul H[ilsdale] will be Yale freshman this fall.

A few days later he wrote:

This is hell for dullness. Nothing to do but say—"My God—this nothingness for a month & a half more." Poor Father—he says, "I thought you would like this vacation for your writing"—I *can't* write—or study—or read what I ought to in this atmosphere of August heat & lack of sympathy. May be reduced to going out on a farm—tho' I hate manual labor. Today reduced to a solitary swim at Fairy.

This was the actuality of that exasperating and corrosive ennui which the later Lewis forgot in such romanticized recollections of the place of his origin as this of 1944:

> In the lakes, the prairies by moonlight, the wide wheatfields on July afternoons, the hysterical doings of Sunday school picnics and Christmas entertainments, the noble deeds of the high school in athletics . . . , in the amiable mixture of Scandinavians and Bavarians and Yankees, in the shadow of the great North woods that just dimly reached to my town, I found inspiration more than enough.

If it was not precisely inspiration that Sauk Centre gave him toward the end of that summer, matters did improve and, in doing so, gave him at least the germ of an idea. First, his old German teacher, Mr. Gunderson, came back to Sauk Centre on his way to the Harvard Graduate School, and they "had two long talks (& walks) on wisdom of training up present generation of children with evolution; & sans the old ideas of immortality, personal God, etc., i.e. in *rationality*. Need of chloroforming persons (maniacs; helpless & peevish cripples, etc.) injurious to state—etc. etc." Almost simultaneously he met a young lawyer named Dorion who had recently come to Sauk Centre, and with him too he was able to discuss emancipated ideas.

> Darion, Rev. Mr. Adams (of Methodist church) & I rowed up lake. Adams made usual conventional objections to socialism; nicely misunderstanding its principle. "Divide the wealth even & in a few years it would be divided just as it is now"—Probably—*under the competitive system!*

Dorion argued with Harry against the preacher. He was "very well read particularly (being a socialist) in socialistic writers & up to date contemporaries—Jack London, Upton Sinclair, etc. Up on theatre etc.—having ushered in a St. P. theatre." With Dorion, he spent an evening at the home of Mr. Garland, the rector, where they enjoyed "much pipe & talk of music, socialism, Christian Science (which disgusting habit D. has) etc.," for Reverend Garland, unlike Reverend Adams, "highly favors" socialism "tho' not favoring any present soc[ialist] party." With Dorion, he "heard Bro. Adams of the Methodist Ch. preach on 'The Preferability of Superstition to Atheism.' "

> Post hoc Dorion & I had a peripatetic symposium. In the genial warmth of a little flattery on his part, I was quite at my best—sweetly solving deep questions for him.

Today Sauk Centre hardly remembers Dorion. No one remembers his first name or his initials. Even young Harry Lewis was not certain of the spelling of his name. The newspapers do not mention him. No one remembers where he came from, or quite when he was there, or just when he left. They remember that he was "single, eccentric, and something of a misfit in personality," that he was a failure "and could not make a living here," that he had few clients and left in less than a year from the time he came. At least one man, Mr. Laurel Kells, also an attorney, remembered that "a woman had come to Dorion's office and threatened to scream and accuse him of attempted rape unless he gave her money. He was badly frightened and rushed out of the office and down the street. This had been the subject of community gossip for a time." The records of the Law School of the University of Minnesota show that in 1899, when he was twenty years old, Charles Townsend Dorion was enrolled as a student with a deficiency in geometry, but there is no record of his having taken a degree. From those of the Supreme Court of Minnesota one learns only that Charles Townsend Dorion was admitted to practice in June of 1902. And that is all that lingers today.

Did Sinclair Lewis, thirty years later, remember him? In 1937, in his Introduction to the Limited Editions Club *Main Street,* he wrote:

> In 1905 . . . in the third month of vacation, fifteen years before it was published, I began to write *Main Street.* But the title, then, was *The Village Virus,* and the chief character was not Carol Kennicott but Guy Pollock, the lawyer, whom I depicted as a learned, amiable, and ambitious young man (altogether, you see, in the image of Doc Lewis's youngest boy, Harry) who started practice in a prairie village and spiritually starved. I must have written about twenty thousand words of that script, but I remember nothing whatever about the details, and the script is as clean gone and vanished away as the script of my first play. . . .

Charles T. Dorion, not Harry Lewis, was the genesis and prototype of Guy Pollock. That the later Lewis could not remember the details and that the manuscript was "clean gone" is not surprising. There was no manuscript. The very heat and dullness of that third month, he had complained, kept him from writing even his short things, let alone twenty thousand words of sequential prose. Only the animus came into being.

> *September 12, 1905.* In company with Paul Hilsdale,—drank too much port wine. "The village virus"—I shall have to write a book of how it getteth into the veins of a good man & true. "God made the country & man made the town—but the devil made the village." Where in the city one would see a friend or go to the theatre, in Sauk Centre there is nothing to do save drink or play poker (for those who do not read much).

Main Street was not yet even a formulated literary idea. It was only an irritation.

7

HE RETURNED TO NEW HAVEN in September, and at this point he began to lose interest in his diary. The entries for the remaining months of 1905 are few, and there is no diary at all for 1906. Except for the summer of 1906, when his parents preserved some of his correspondence, it is impossible now to reconstruct the details of his daily affairs until November 12, 1907, when he took up his diary again; he maintained it, thereafter, until his graduation from Yale in June 1908. We know exactly, however, the direction in which he was moving, and we know where he arrived. In his third year at Yale he was the outspoken dissident.

Henry Seidel Canby, a young instructor in 1906, living with Tinker, remembered Lewis in *American Memoir* as "a nonconformist, getting what he could—and he got a great deal—from that stronghold of intelligent conformity where radicals, once they are accepted as Yale men, can say or do what they please." * The complacency is perhaps a little excessive, for Lewis had by now given up all hope of being "accepted" as a Yale man. George Soule remembers the patronizing nicknames—"Moon-calf" was now among them—that hounded him, and the general contempt with which he was viewed as a walking caricature of the Yalies' conception of "the artist" as oaf.

A classmate remembered that Lewis "was bitter over the fact that he, a militant atheist, should be obliged to go to compulsory chapel every day. I remember protesting to him on this point that he had come voluntarily to Yale knowing its regulation in advance and I asked him why he did not elect to go to a nice atheists' college where his principles would not be outraged." It was a matter of "principle," certainly, rather than a renewed interest in student activity, that led him in October to debate before the Union against the proposal that an eighteen-dollar "athletic tax" be

* With the same official complacency, the *Yale Alumni Weekly* pontificated in 1929: "The career of Sinclair Lewis, '07, is a striking illustration of the fact that a Yale education may be of service to talent of the vigorous, forthright variety as well as to that of a precious or academic stripe. At least, it proves that it does not place the stamp of learned caution on everything a man may do after graduation."

levied on all students, for, when the advising faculty member praised his performance and urged that his oratorical "talent . . . be cultivated," Lewis wrote, "A fat lot I care!"

His principles were sufficiently aroused by the first American performance of Shaw's *Mrs. Warren's Profession* for him to note that he had seen it, and if there were a diary for January 1906, we would almost certainly find an approving account of the appearance of Jack London in the storied halls of Yale. London was on lecture tour and had been brought to Yale by Dr. Alexander Irvine, a New Haven minister and prominent socialist, who had brought William Jennings Bryan to New Haven in 1904. Lewis on that occasion referred to him as "Rev. Mr. Irvine, whom I know," and recorded that he himself had been "behind scenes" at the Hyperion, where Bryan spoke, and "he was about 2 feet from me." In a reminiscence of 1932, Lewis recalled that "in his Freshman year in Yale . . . [he] had taught Sunday School in Irvine's mission in New Haven."

It was through the assistance of a Yale student with socialist convictions whom he did not name in his autobiography, but who might well have been Lewis, that Irvine arranged with the Yale Union to sponsor the London lecture, although the Union took on the sponsorship only with trepidation. Irvine persuaded a socialist painter to make flamboyant posters, one of which showed London in a red sweater and all of which were printed in red; these caused a great uproar in the Yale community and threatened the whole plan. With the support of young faculty men like William Lyon Phelps, the lecture was permitted to proceed, and London announced the fact of the socialist revolution in America to an audience of twenty-eight hundred people. "The capitalist class has been indicted," London concluded in that speech that was to appear as the title piece, "Revolution," in his collection of essays in 1910. "It has failed in its management and its management is to be taken away from it. . . . The revolution is here, now. Stop it who can."

The Yale students in that audience, in the recollection of George Soule, behaved very badly, laughed and booed and stamped and brayed, and Harry Lewis was wild with outrage. After the lecture London was taken to a student dormitory, where he answered questions for two hours, and surely we must assume that Harry Lewis was volubly present. According to Irving Stone, on evidence that he does not give, Lewis appeared next morning at eight o'clock for an interview. The editors of the newly founded *Monthly Review,* who included Allan Updegraff, persuaded London to contribute an article on the indifference of college men to the universal suffering of mankind.

Little of the active dissident was apparent in the contributions that Harry S. Lewis made in this year to the *Lit.* He was still determined to become an editor, which meant that he had to keep the number of his contributions high, but he sent them to commercial periodicals first. From his records, it would seem that the story which appeared in November, "The Loneliness of Theodore," on which he had been working in the previous spring, had been seen by four editors before it came to the *Lit*. This story, which may have been a fictionized version of the rejected "Boyland" reminiscence, "The Metropolitan Theatre," is a plotless little story of a lonely motherless boy who plays fantasy games with clothespins and nails, imagines that the arrogant little girl next door is a princess or a queen, and finds no companionship in his cold, withdrawn father. His second contribution, which appeared in January, was a brief sketch called "The Heart of Pope Innocent"—an anecdote about a medieval pope who built many churches but was ruthless with the people and who, when he died, was found to be without a heart. These brought his total contributions to seven.

To the *Courant* that year he contributed two drinking songs and a single story, "An Elementary Course in Erotics." This is a satirical absurdity about a professor of English who decides to "take two days off and fall in love." A Vergilian shepherdess being unavailable, a girl who works at a nearby dairy farm seems a likely candidate, but her ignorance of poetry sends the professor back to Miss Sabrina Lorgner, Ph.D., Bonn. In his Yale *News* review, Professor Berdan was not amused; but Harry's *Courant* contributions totaled eighteen.

Election to the editorial board of the *Lit* (and simultaneous membership in Chi Delta Theta), as to the *Courant,* was an almost automatic matter. In the spring of their junior year, the names of contributors and the number of their published contributions were posted and the five men with the highest number were elected, the one with the very highest number becoming the chief editor. The *Lit* had all along been declining many more of Lewis's contributions than it had been accepting, and it came to his ears that the name he was called, "God-Forbid" Lewis, really meant, "God forbid that Lewis should ever make the *Lit*." He went to one of the editors, Mr. J. H. Wallis, disturbed that even this was not to come to him. Mr. Wallis told him the source of his nickname: it went back to his performance as prosecuting attorney in the mock trial of the Yale Union two years before, when, in his impassioned plea for a verdict of guilty, he shouted, "God forbid that this villain should go free!" or some such rhetoric.

The name hung on, and it could have meant many things, including the reluctance of the *Lit* men to take this heeler into the board, but the fact is that when the lists were posted on February 21 Lewis proved to be third in the competition and he became an editor, his specific assignment being the Editor's Table, a regular department of the magazine that appeared on its last page. There was, as usual, an unhappy error to dim his pleasure: not only did the *News* announce this third winner to be one E. H. Lewis of Syracuse, New York, rather than H. S. Lewis of Sauk Centre, Minnesota, but the *Lit* itself, in its formal announcement in the March number, the last under the retiring board, repeated the error. Beginning with the April number, and for a year thereafter, the right name appeared proudly on the masthead, even when Harry Lewis was absent from Yale.

He had other journalistic triumphs. Late in 1905, Updegraff saw his wish for a more mature and more representative university periodical than any then in existence become an actuality. A wealthy young man in the class, Stephen Thaw (a nephew of Harry K. Thaw), founded *The Yale Monthly Magazine,* with W. B. Roulstone and Allan Updegraff as editors. The magazine was to represent the entire university, faculty members as well as students were to contribute, and outsiders when they had something to say that was relevant to the interests of the university community. To the editorial staff of this enterprise, too, Lewis was invited, and while he made one contribution (a rather more substantial story than most of his thus far, called "A Theory of Values," and recounting the decay of a Minnesota country boy's ambition to attend the state university), he declined the office. Similarly, on March 21, he was elected to the editorship of the *Courant,* but again he declined, and the runner-up, William Rose Benét, took the post in his place. Benét was a Sheffield man who had never met Lewis, and while they had a congenial encounter at this time in the offices of the *Lit* and were presently to become close friends, they never met again at Yale.

As soon as Lewis was officially associated with the *Lit* his literary tone and manner changed. He wrote no more poems or stories for it, but each of his three Editor's Table contributions in that spring was, however mildly, polemical and critical of conventional Yale. The first, concerned with "the fallacy of elsewhere," utilizes his endless wanderings in and about New Haven to point out to the settled undergraduate how little he knows of what is immediately about him. The second is a temperate attack on the indifference of Yale men to the pleasures of reading and the treasury of the world's books. The third is a complaint about the stuffiness of most essays and especially of those contributed to the *Lit.* But the most impressive contribution, the most vigorously polemical and the most deeply felt, is a long essay, the lead piece in the June issue, called "Unknown Undergraduates." An attack on the provincialism of collegiate snobbery at New Haven, it was written out of the passion of experience and with something of the passion of prophecy:

> The heretic is more likely to be unknown to you personally, than by fame. You may call him a "cheese with a grouch" and dislike him because he does not think and act as the "typical Yale man," which more or less unconsciously, you have been trying to become. Remember that he may have too

> big and too important a personality to permit it to be crushed in the mold you worship. Incidentally, the heretics of each age, the men with outlandish ideas and customs, have often become the heroes of the next.

James Joyce was about to make the same observation more succinctly: "Civilization may be said indeed to be the creation of its outlaws. . . ."

Lewis's progress toward that splendid, retaliatory fame that he here implied was faltering. With the encouragement of Updegraff, he was now continually striving to see his work published by national periodicals. The influence of another friend, Frederick Kinney Noyes, with whom he had begun to enjoy some intimacy in the spring of 1905, was also strong. Allan Updegraff, in a late reminiscence, claimed that Noyes was the major literary influence on the young Lewis; that "Kin" Noyes not only forced him to write, but taught him what he knew about writing, especially that characteristic combination of the slangy, ordinary vulgar with the "literary" and sophisticated in language; and that Noyes really formed Lewis's literary tastes. The men were close, no doubt, and during the previous summer had conducted a very full correspondence, but it may be questioned whether Noyes exercised any such influence. Lewis's literary tastes were formed largely by his own wide reading and by a temperamental antipathy (which had not yet developed) toward anything that struck him as highfalutin. No such stylistic development as Updegraff indicated had yet taken place. His love poetry is of the same pseudo-Swinburnian variety as before. A manuscript poem of this time, called "In Rose Realm," tells of a peasant and a princess whose "eyes were ever to Bermaut":

> With rose-wreathed viol would I go
> Moon-mad, and sob canzones low
> To you, and feel the veriest boor,
> In old Provence.

For such verse he could find no publisher, but for another kind he did. He began to write what he called "kid verse," and in the autumn of 1905, he sold his first two of these to a magazine called *The Housekeeper* at three dollars each. The subjects of these works included such matters as keeping one's feet warm in bed, the frightening aspect of the gas stove, the "teeter board." Elephantinely kittenish as they are, they are preferable to the sobbing canzones. A representative piece is "The Wash-Tub Sea," which appeared in *Youth* in 1906:

> The pussy and the puppy and my darling doll and me,
> We often go a fishing in the depths of Wash-tub Sea
> It's smaller than the oceans, dolly says that she has heard;
> But where on any ocean, can one hunt the bubble bird?
>
> Around lie Table Country, and the lonely Land of Chair
> The green giraffe and spotted blops hide in the jungle there.

Our slender ship of pasteboard, manned by pirates, fierce and free,
Goes venturing and wandering upon the Wash-tub Sea.

"What ho, she blows, bring out the match harpoon, a rubber whale
Is lying off the larboard," cry the pirates as they sail.
Let Dolly talk of oceans, but, now honest, could there be
A really, truly rubber whale, save on the Wash-tub Sea?

The man was twenty-one, and it was not even a living!

His first commercially published fiction, *Matsu-No-Kata: a Romance of Old Japan,* moved through many editorial offices before it was accepted, in a revised form, by the *Pacific Monthly* in the autumn of 1905. The *Pacific Monthly* was a kind of *Atlantic Monthly* of the West Coast, published in Portland, Oregon; its contributions were from unknown writers except for an occasional item from someone like Elbert Hubbard and a monthly collection of "Impressions" by Charles Erskine Scott Wood. Lewis's story, which was published in December and for which he was paid seven and a half dollars, is a tale of miraculous events in ancient Japan told in that falsely archaic style that he used with equal ease in his treatment of medieval subjects.

He wrote continuously, used much postage, and this was the extent of his success. Small wonder that in April of 1906 he entered these lines in the back of his copy of Stedman's *Victorian Anthology:*

So many poets wept their melancholy hearts away,
So many sang whose songs could not outlive their little day,
We, too, who are 'inglorious' Miltons, tho' we be not mute,
Why should *we* sigh if we find song our singing's only fruit.

In April he had a special reason for lamenting his own small success in the presence of the relatively successful Arthur Upson, with whom (according to a recollection in the diary of 1908) he spent part of his spring vacation in Concord, Massachusetts, and had, then, his first view of Walden Pond. But this would have been a happy event, too, in a generally wearisome year. Then, as that year drew to its end, he faced again the alternative of "the village virus" or "the fallacy of elsewhere." He chose the latter in its only possible form: he signed on with another cattle boat.

This trip was eminently more successful than that of two years before. He joined the crew of the *Philadelphia* in Portland on June 22 with a Yale acquaintance, Robert Pfeiffer, who had lived a few doors down the corridor from him in Berkeley Hall during that year. The food was better than before and the conditions of the ship much better. The work was much the same, but there were no vicious men among the hands and Harry's foreman was a rough but decent fellow. Scotty, he wrote his parents, is "a typical cattle-foreman; strong (he looks like a small miniature of one of the bulls), plucky, quick; cussing the cattle & lazy workers frightfully, but a prince where his friends are concerned." He apparently enjoyed the company of one "Shorty, . . . a typical black-sheep. . . . He has been a butcher, barkeeper, machinist—, been stabbed by a Mexican girl & shot by an English one (if his stories can be *half* believed, as I think they can)." There were six orthodox Jews who made their religious observances in the unlikely atmosphere of the forecastle and whose presence Lewis was later to use when he tried to find a story in this material. The boat docked in Liverpool on July 3, and this time Harry had enough money to stay on in England for most of that month.

He walked to Chester, of which he made a brief but thorough tour and where he sat through a service in the cathedral, and then took a third-class train through Shrewsbury, Birmingham, Kenilworth and Warwick, with pauses at each, to Oxford. There he found a room for eighteen pence a day and managed to live for a dollar a day. He wrote his parents that he was "working on the volume of Prose Fancies [he had read Richard Le Gallienne's work with this title] I hope to have published in the fall of '07; & in London I shall live quietly & write a lot." He stayed in Oxford for a week, enchanted in its "haze of history." He wrote his parents of "the endless & varied beauties of Oxford" and concluded, "I should like to spend a year here, some time, when I have made the requisite cash; if—! The dash expresses some vague doubt as to my financial genius."

He lived in London on five dollars a week for about ten days. Until then, he had apparently been traveling with Pfeiffer, but Pfeiffer was now off "to Switzerland & Paris." Harry, alone in London, was a faithful tourist—St. Paul's, the Houses of Parliament, Kensington Gardens and Albert Hall, the British Museum, the National Gallery and the Tate, Covent Garden, where he stood to hear Caruso sing *Don Giovanni.* At Covent Garden he fell into conversation with a twenty-eight-year-old clerk in a chemical firm who wrote poetry in his leisure time, Ralph Montagu Scott, and after the performance they drove about together in a hansom while Scott pointed out the houses where Keats and Shelley and Johnson had lived.

One can only wonder whether he added a word to his *Prose Fancies* in those crowded, guidebook days. That the book was on his mind is clear from the evidence, among his English notes, of a tentative table of contents for this projected eighty-thousand-word work, now to be called *The Way to Rome: A Book of Prose Fancies and Essays and Tales.* The list consists of twenty-seven little projects, including some already written and published, some projected only—"The Way to Rome," "Richard le Gallienne and the Necessity of Roses," and a variety of sketches, many engendered by the English visit itself.

Of England he observed that "in many forms of enterprise America is ahead of England (where they still use tallow candles o' nights), but the people know how to live fuller, richer, quieter lives," but he also found London "huge, & noisy, & heartless."

On July 19 he wrote to his parents that he was going on a walking trip and that they should not expect another letter for two weeks. But three days later he was writing on board the *Lucania,* homeward bound.

> In my last letter I told you that the next one would take quite a little time arriving—but be a very large one—which was a cryptic way of saying that it would be myself. That is, I had hoped to step in & surprise you—but I find that I shall not have money enough to get to Minn.—tho' I have enough to last me till about August 28th or Sept. 1st, by which time I ought to have sold a story or have a job.
>
> I came home for several reasons. First—I shall have had a 6 weeks interesting and most pleasant jaunt—enough to last for a year. Second—& most important: had I remained in England I should have had to send home for $30 or $35 to complete the summer, & even then run a risk of running short. You see they have made a new ruling, within the past year, whereby one overstaying the cattleship on which he came must pay £2.—Arriving in Liverpool Friday July 20 I found that I should have to hang around till Thursday before getting a cattleboat. This expense, & the £2 & something for a decent & eatable meal once a day on the boat (to be obtained by bribing the cook) would bring the expense up to about $20. So I threw away the scabbard and left yesterday (24 hrs. after booking passage) on the Lucania . . . by 3d class, which is a euphemism for steerage —I shall have $26.50 when I reach New Haven . . . I shall spend the rest of the summer in N.H.—possibly Cambridge, writing industriously. If I had $20 or $25 more I'd have given you a—I hope—pleasant surprise but!

Crowded in among five hundred and fifty steerage passengers of all nationalities, he wrote cheerfully that compared to a "cattleship fo'c'sle . . . it seems 'eavenly." He filled his time by making systematic observations on the variety of national types. Landing in New York on July 28, he proceeded at once to New Haven.

In a kind of summary of his activities in this time when he kept no diary, Sinclair Lewis covered the period between July 28 and "Oct. '06" with the two words, "writing & newsp." It may be assumed that he found work again in the offices of the *Journal and Courier,* at least until college exercises resumed. His manuscript record shows that in August he sold three poems for a total of twenty dollars. He enrolled in the university as a senior in September, "thoroughly bored," he wrote later, "with years of sitting in classrooms sucking in secondhand wisdom." He felt that his experience transcended that of the undergraduate world, and when Allan Updegraff had an opportunity to go to Upton Sinclair's Helicon Hall as one of two janitors, Lewis went with him as the other. He left Yale on October 28, if we can believe a frivolous news story in the New York *Sun.* On his academic transcript, at the bottom of the empty column that should have held his grades for 1906–1907, appears only the cryptic note, "Gone? 'Socialist.' " He did not return to Yale until December of 1907.

His editorial affiliation with the *Lit,* both before his departure and during it, was curious. In the first issue of that autumn, when Lewis was still on the New Haven scene and could quite readily have written the Editor's Table, it appeared over the initials of Howard Bishop. In the second issue, the magazine carried this note: "The *Lit* is greatly indebted to Mr. H. S. Lovejoy for the active assistance he has rendered it during the absence of one of the editors." And the Editor's Table was signed with the initials H.S.L. The initials fit both men, but the writing does not fit Harry S. Lewis, and we may assume it to be that of Lovejoy, runner-up in the competition of the previous spring and brought on to the staff in the present emergency.

But then the surprising thing happened: in the December issue, there was not only an essay by Harry S. Lewis, called "In Praise of South Middle," but the Editor's Table, and every successive one until the next board took over in April, was signed by H. S. Lewis. The December essay might well have been written early in the year and accepted before his departure. Written on the occasion of the refurbishment of South Middle College and the change of its name to Connecticut Hall, this was a nostalgic recollection of its long history. It was a kindly counterpart to that earlier and more acrid farewell, "Unknown Undergraduates," and only at one point did the disenchanted Lewis show himself: "If not in it, then in a sister building near at hand, Calhoun toiled on the foundations of that structure which was portentous in our history. Good deal of a grind, old Calhoun. Not very popular, probably. But big, a mighty big man."

The December, January and February Editor's Tables (on the fascination of fire, on the beauty of the Book and Snake Tomb as viewed through the Egyptian gate in the Grove Street Cemetery in New Haven, and on the charms of romantic verse) did not contain even such a brief glimpse of disaffection, nor did his final contribution, verses called "A Rondeau of Farewell" that conclude the March Editor's Table—a light, formal adieu, "our *Lit.* days done." Where these contributions came from, his adieus having been made in October, is not clear, nor does anyone now remember, but they would suggest that when he left Yale, Harry Lewis was not quite prepared to sever all his ties or to ignore the responsibilities of that one honor for which to the end he strove. That year in the *Courant* (which had assimilated the short-lived *Yale Monthly*) he had only one contribution, a poem. It appeared in November, and it was appropriately entitled "Exit Homo," appropriately signed Sinclair Lewis.

At Helicon Hall his strivings were to be of a different sort. The New York Home Colony Association, under which name the organization was formally incorporated, was one of the shortest-lived of those many experiments in cooperative group living that have lent pathos and comedy to the history of American culture. Upton Sinclair was tired of a more private experiment in a "back-to-nature life" on a farm outside Princeton, and he found to his astonishment that he had thirty thousand dollars in royalties from *The Jungle*. The incorporation of the Home Colony Association was the realization of an old dream for him. In *The Independent* for June 14 he published his prospectus under the title, "A Home Colony." He credited his inspiration to an article of 1904 by Charlotte Perkins Gilman, author of *The Home,* in which she outlined her rather advanced view of municipal housing (views to be reflected fifteen years later in the mooning notions of Carol Kennicott). But Sinclair's immediate motives seem to have been his own: one, the nuisance (and the injustice) of keeping servants, especially for the preparation of meals; and two, the nuisance of having children living with their parents. "I am perfectly and seriously in earnest about the matter," he wrote, "willing to give my time to it, for years, if need be." He expressed the hope that he would hear from one or two hundred people, but he was prepared to proceed with twenty families, including "men and women who are willing to contribute their labor, as waiters, cooks, nurses, teachers or managers" of arts and crafts projects. Furnace tenders were not mentioned, but two had been there from the outset.

On October 4, Upton Sinclair announced the purchase—for $36,000, all but $10,000 of it on mortgage—of Helicon Hall, a former private school near Englewood, New Jersey, on the Palisades, as the establishment in which the Colony would be housed. Helicon Hall, announced the New York *Times,* was "filled with everything that the traditional ascetic does not want" —a swimming pool, a bowling alley, a theater, a pipe organ, a glass-covered court in the central area with a fountain and tropical plants including the "largest [rubber tree] to be found north of Mexico," and an enormous four-sided brazierlike fireplace supported by columns that in turn supported the chimney in the glass ceiling. Balconies around this area led to bedrooms, of which there were nearly fifty. The hall was surrounded by nine and a half acres of woodland.

The establishment was incorporated at $100,000 and shares were put up for sale at $100 each, of which Upton Sinclair held one hundred. Two kinds of people were to be admitted to the Colony: stockholders, and by their vote of admission, "clerks" or "club members," who were to be gifted persons in need of a creative atmosphere. Families were to be admitted—the Sinclairs were themselves a family—but a basic principle of the Colony was the demolition of the idea of the selfish family as a necessary social unit. Children were to sleep in a dormitory, away from their parents, and their supervision was to be budgeted among all mothers. There was to be a common dining room and, to discourage family isolation, meals were to be paid for whether or not they were eaten. Most important, there were to be no servants, ultimately not even a cook; with the work shared by everyone,

everyone's work would be minimal, and the leisure for creative rumination would be large. The *Times,* quoting one of the interested persons, said that "the whole colony will be run simply as one big happy family—an experiment for which the world had long waited." With these assumptions, the Colony got under way on November 1 with forty adults and fourteen children.

The membership implied no central political commitments but represented all varieties of radical opinion and shaded over into lunacy: there were socialists, anarchists, syndicalists, single-taxers, New Thoughtists, spiritualists. In *The Industrial Republic,* Upton Sinclair described the situation with enthusiasm:

> There are so many typewriters in Helicon Hall that as you wander about the galleries in the morning you can fancy you can hear a distant battle with rapid-firing guns; and the products of the industry vary from discussions of Yogi philosophy and modern psychic research to magazine fiction, woman's suffrage debates, and Jungle "muck-raking." And yet all these people share amicably in the ownership of the fireplace and the swimming-pool and the tennis-court; providing thereby a most beautiful illustration of the working out of the formula laid down by Kautsky for the society of the future: "Communism in material production, anarchism in intellectual."

These variously busy spirits included Professor W. P. Montague, of Columbia, and his wife; Professor William Noyes, of Teachers College, and his wife; Edwin Björkman, critic and translator of Strindberg, and his wife, Frances Maule, a suffragette; Alice MacGowan and Grace MacGowan Cooke, free-lance writers; Michael Williams, later the editor of *Commonweal;* Sinclair's secretary, Edith Summers, later the author of *Weeds;* and the literary janitors from New Haven. Visitors were frequent and included John Dewey and William James; Emma Goldman and John Coryell, an anarchist who was also "Bertha M. Clay," novelist; Jo Davidson, the sculptor who was one day to do a head of the sometime furnace-tender and who brought with him Sadakichi Hartman, the art critic and the only visitor whose presence Upton Sinclair, with his detestation of alcohol, deplored. With them was a female remembered only as the "Tramp Madonna." Sadakichi Hartman, arriving in a state of uncontrollable inebriation, "insisted on sleeping on the cushioned seats in front of our fireplace" and had to be turned out in the snow. He wrote an indignant and abusive letter to the press, one more voice in the chorus of newspaper innuendo and vilification. Even the Sauk Centre *Avalanche* had occasion on November 1 to comment:

> A New Haven, Conn. dispatch to the daily press gives the rather sensational news to Sauk Centre people that Harry Lewis, son of Dr. E. J. Lewis of this city, had left Yale College to become a member of Upton Sinclair's Communist colony located in New Jersey.

> This move of the young man was wholly unknown to his parents, and their first intimation of his leaving Yale was had from the daily papers.

Old parental fears and prophecies had been actualized with a vengeance; this settled the matter: Harry was lost.

He was "lost" in Helicon Hall for only a month; and as soon as he had escaped, he sent a rather high-spirited account of the Colony in a diarylike dispatch to the New York *Sun,* which printed it under the head, "Two Yale Men in Utopia." The article appeared on December 16, 1906, and was apparently the work of both Lewis and Updegraff. The banks, or subordinate parts of the headline, read, "Experiences of the Co-Janitors of Helicon Hall. Sinclair Lewis and Allan Updegraff Tell How They Performed Manual Labor and Cultivated the Intellect at Upton Sinclair's Colony Up on the Palisades." In his manuscript accounts for 1906, the final item reads, "Also 1 'Sun' special by Up & myself on Helicon which brought us $23.35."

The article fictionizes matters in that it telescopes the two persons of the authors into one of the janitors and describes "the other janitor" as "a wealthy Providence Wholesaler." Yet perhaps we can assume that the economic arrangement described by the double narrator applied to both of them.

> *Monday, November 5.*—I've been very much on the job all day. I expected to work only seven hours a day, which is to give me an income of $35 a month, with expenses for board and room of about $24, but until things get settled I'll probably have to work nearer seventeen.

If we can take the account seriously, the work was hard, constant and various: furnace man, laundryman, carpenter, ditchdigger, cleaner and general chore boy were among the roles that Lewis played; and, by his own account, he did not do any of them satisfactorily. When he was interviewed by a man from the *Sun* for a story published on October 31, he said, "I'm just having a lazy time. I haven't started on the hot air plant, but have been giving my time to reading. Nothing has happened to me yet worth talking about, but if you want to know my opinions I'll write them, provided your editor orders them from me. That's my business, writing. You just ask your editor if he doesn't want me to write for him."

He was not lazy for long, and presently he developed the feeling that he was being exploited. The rumor reached him that the financial arrangement that had been made with him was regarded as absurd by the management and could not be maintained. His own interest in the colonial experiment was waning. A *Sun* story with the dateline "New Haven, Nov. 19" showed him suddenly to be back in New Haven. "He will spend the next few days at a local sanitarium, getting cured of the jaundice. Then he will take up his studies at Yale. 'Yes, I have come to Yale, and the college looks pretty good to me. I did not come back because I was dissatisfied with the colony, but because of my illness. I intend to go back for two weeks at Christmas, but I shall not go back there permanently.' " Nothing in the Lewis-Updegraff account for the *Sun* indicated this break, and of course, Lewis did not go back to Yale. By Thanksgiving, at any rate, the *Sun,* in another of its facetious accounts, had him back at Helicon Hall, doing a very poor job with the furnace.

By his own account, he at least enjoyed his leisure in the evenings. Upton Sinclair remembered that Lewis and Updegraff and Miss Edith Summers had their meals together at a table for three, where they "doubtless did no end of laughing at the queer assortment of humans about them." Even in the month that Lewis was there, the number of servants was increasing rather than decreasing: the theory of work on which the Colony rested was failing. Yet in some ways the Colony was not a failure. When fire broke out at Helicon Hall (at 4:14 on the morning of Saturday, March 16, 1907, Upton Sinclair's recollection to the contrary), the total number of residents, including workers, was over seventy, and there was a waiting list of three hundred. Nevertheless, on December 2, 1906, the total was reduced by two when Updegraff and Lewis "thankfully departed to New York and an effort to live by free-lancing." He did not regard the month as lost:

> ... Though I can't janit properly, and though I received only $6 wages above my expenses for a month's work, yet a taste for real life has been awakening. Manual work has been hard, yet good for me. It has been a joy to live among real men and women, not schoolboys.
>
> Taking it by and large, where else than at Helicon Hall could I have learned so many new things every minute; or of how little worth I am in manual labor, seen so many novel yet vital things and have met in intimacy and equality so many thoroughly worthwhile people?

His health, if not his spirits, had suffered, and he did not in fact go directly to New York but continued through to New Haven where, for a week, under the care of Dr. Skinner, he was hospitalized for jaundice again.

When he came to New York, he lived for a week in a room on Fifteenth Street and then took a furnished room with Updegraff at 239 Avenue B, between Fourteenth Street and Fifteenth. During the Christmas shopping rush, he was employed as a clerk in the book department of the Siegel-Cooper department store, and Updegraff was similarly employed at Brentano's book store. In his summary of this period, he makes the at first mysterious entry, "Love to chub; Xmas." Chub, it develops, is a contraction of Cherub, and Cherub was his nickname for Edith Summers, who had stayed on at Helicon Hall but with whom he had fallen in love and who was his first fiancée. Upton Sinclair has described her as a "golden-haired and shrewdly observant young person whose gentle voice and unassuming ways gave us no idea of her talent," and, in another place, as "a quiet, unpretentious little woman, red-haired and bespectacled, and glad of a refuge from the maulings of fate. She had been a wage-slave of the Standard dictionary, and her eye-sight was ruined, and her life a torment as a result."

In the Lewis summary, the following notation occurs almost immediately: "Chub Jan first, fire, Cumberland, Point Pleasant." One may translate this to mean that he saw her on January first, that she was in the Helicon fire (as indeed she was; the *Times* reported that she had been hospitalized briefly for shock), and that he saw her in the Hotel Cumberland (where the Sinclairs had taken refuge after the disaster), and that he saw her again at Point Pleasant, New Jersey (where Upton Sinclair then removed his family).* Allan Updegraff remembered that it was through Edith Summers that Lewis obtained his post as assistant editor of *Transatlantic Tales,* that the position had been offered to her and that she managed to get it for him; this is possible if the offer came to Miss Summers while she was still employed by Upton Sinclair; if it did not, the Updegraff recollection is mistaken, since Helicon Hall burned down on March 16 and Sinclair Lewis went to work at *Transatlantic Tales,* by his own record, on March 10.

During the several months before that, both men tried to live by freelancing. Lewis was fairly successful in marketing his "kid verse," and he wrote other things—"squibs" for *Life* and *Puck,* and occasional stories for obscure periodicals. In January of 1907, his sales amounted to $15.34; in February, to $27.75. Updegraff had had no success whatever, and rather than continue to live on Lewis's small income, he found employment as a stock boy with the Western Electric Company. Lewis did their housekeeping. Then, through whatever circumstance, Lewis went to work for *Transatlantic Tales* for twenty dollars a week and they moved to Christopher Street. He read innumerable French and German periodicals and translated both verse and fiction into English. In the spring, Updegraff, who had once suffered from malaria and was now threatened with tuber-

* The clue to the name "Cumberland" appears in a curious context that suggests something about the stability of Upton Sinclair's socialist convictions; it is a squib published in *Life* for June 6, 1907—"A Raking of the Rakers," by S.L., which follows:

"The parody beginning 'They're exposing the exposers' has a certain amount of truth. Helicon Hall burned, and Upton Sinclair has taken luxurious apartments in the Hotel Cumberland. Rexford's verse—

> A socialist, a socialist, that's what I want to be,
> With lodgings in the Waldorf while I set the people free

—is illustrated in his case, as it is in that of Gaylord Wilshire, who edits a magazine devoted to freeing the people and fake medicine ads, and who lives in apartments costing $500 a month. It is whispered that Helicon Hall was a failure, anyway; that the 'workers' had become real servants, and that the colonists were getting tired of a simple life with institutionalized children."

culosis, departed for Idaho and a job in Yellowstone. Lewis was left with the Cherub.

His translations appeared in *Transatlantic Tales* in nearly every issue from June through November, and his other work appeared in a variety of fugitive places. His children's verse made up the bulk of his publication, but now he was also managing to publish some of the high-pitched and highly inept romantic verse, such as his poem "To William Butler Yeats," which appeared in *Book News*. Swinburne and Arthur Upson continue to do their mischief in this poem and in others. "Disillusion" found its way into *Smart Set:*

> Great was the wine of his song, like panting, ineffable seas,
> Moving to passionate tears, and heating my heart with its lies.
> Swayed with oppressive delight, I sought him and looked in his eyes;—
> God! how I shattered the cup of his song, when I tasted those lees!

One could wish that he had turned oftener to the frivolous, as in the poem published by *Century* called "My Lady's Maid," a cavalierish bit in praise of the lady's maid instead of the lady, attempting to combine conventional elegance with the vernacular—"The daintiest of urban fays . . . My lady's really quite the craze," and so on.

But the struggling Sinclair Lewis was not a frivolous young man. George S. Viereck, in a reminiscence published in 1931, gives us a glimpse of a quite dour one:

> I first ran across Sinclair Lewis in a club of magazine editors sometime in 1907 . . . It was known as the Vagabonds, and held forth in the National Arts Club at Gramercy Park. I don't recollect if Lewis was a regular member or if he attended our weekly meetings only occasionally.
>
> Silent, somewhat morose, he did not attract attention. No one would look at him a second time except for his red hair and his lanky figure. No merry twinkle redeemed his freckles. He seemed, in his early twenties, a young man with a chip on his shoulder, at odds with himself and the world.

The two pieces of fiction that he published in 1907 suggest a considerably humorless if not particularly angry young author. One, "A Passage in Isaiah," which appeared in *The Blue Mule* (a five-cent "Western Magazine of Stories" published in San Francisco), is less a story than an expository sketch of Lewis's cattle boat experiences. A character named "Ginger" (which he seems to have been called on the first voyage) roughly resembles Lewis, but the sketch is really about the "Reb," an elderly Rabbi—about his physical sufferings, the jibes at his piety, the insults from "Spuds," the boss, whom he hates and whom he believes God will strike down. In a final melodramatic flourish, after the boat has docked in Liverpool, the drunken "Spuds" is surprised by the sudden presence of the "Reb" at his side and he falls backward to his death through an unfastened gate in the railing of the top deck. The other, called "Art and the Woman," appeared in *The Gray Goose* (a five-cent magazine published by the Outing Press in Deposit, New York). This story concerns a writer with impeccable literary ideals who is blackmailed by a forgotten female out of his past. To meet her demands, he would have to write something frightful for a periodical called *Polloi;* not to meet them would mean his exposure to his lovely wife. He writes a very shabby potboiler about a blackmailed sculptor, in which the wife melodramatically rejects him; and he reads it to his wife. She agrees that some women would act in that fashion, but why doesn't he let the wife already know and let her, uninterested in the indiscretions of his youth, have bought and burned the letters? Exchange of deep glances: she did and had; embraces; pure art is saved.

There is very little in these stories or, for that matter, in most of the fiction that Lewis had so far published that suggests his mature work. "The Yellow Streak," with its exposure of affectation and its preference for the downright, and "A Theory of Values," with its treatment of simple country people and the failure of a dream, are singular in suggesting themes that would later concern him. In the technique of these flimsy, unrealized narratives there is no suggestion of the fullness and the solidity that would finally characterize his structures. His other prose—chiefly a miscellany of brief squibs—shows a certain flair for the topical, a sense of immediate audience interest, and a latent satirical strain. As for his verse, it reveals an ear that is extremely insensitive to poetry as such but that is quick and facile in the imitation of verbal effects. When that ear was to lend itself to other sounds, to those of the speaking local voice, the gift of imitation would find its proper success.

As to his commercial success, "A Passage in Isaiah" and "Art and the Woman" together had brought him $28. By the end of 1907 he had been paid (although sometimes only in copies of the periodical) for fifty-five pieces. His literary income in 1907 totaled $242.69. When Updegraff returned early in October, Lewis decided that he could once more risk free-lancing without other employment. Together they moved to a flat at 576 Fox Street in The Bronx; Lewis got Updegraff his *Transatlantic Tales* job, and at about the same time, Updegraff got the Cherub.

The Updegraff recollection is that Lewis and Miss Summers were affianced and that Lewis "walked out on her." The documentary evidence on the Lewis side proves nothing about the responsibility of either party for the conclusion of their relationship. In the spring of 1907, Edith Summers returned to Point Pleasant for a country rest and to assist the Sinclairs, and she saved certain writings from Lewis—a sheaf of eight unusually clumsy romantic poems typed out on the back of *Smart Set* stationery and one very long letter, written in late May or early June, proposing a

September marriage. After a solid page of rather aimless discussion of *King Lear,* he comes to his extended point:

> You ought to see me, every hour or so, figuring how soon I could save enough to afford a house in the woods, like Upton's, where we could free-lance. Of course, in my estimates, I always forget to allow anything for new shoes, or doctors' bills, or tooth brushes, and assure myself quite confidently that twenty five cents a day is quite enough for tobacco.—But it will come, before so many months. I am sure that I'll get a raise to thirty dollars a week, in (say) September. If I can't persuade the [publishers] to do so, I'm not sure but that I'll threaten to resign—with the chance, of course, that they'll call my bluff by accepting the resignation. However, I'll have enough money by that time to be able to get along for a long time—and perhaps succeed in hacking without another job. If I do get thirty a week, it would be quite enough for the two of us to live on, in a modest way, even supposing that we didn't make anything outside of it. I am certain that we could live on it, sweetheart, from the previous experience I've had in housekeeping. We could get a bully little flat for about twenty six a month; and we'd have enough to furnish it simply. If Upton came back, you could do a little work for him, if you wished to, say three or four hours a day; i.e. the half day regime, which was to have started at Helicon Hall. But it really wouldn't be necessary; for I am quite sure, sweetheart, that you can write and sell without difficulty plenty of stories—and such verse as couldn't be avoided—if you had the leisure time (and the place, and the loved one altogether; really, sweetheart, wouldn't we disprove the "never" in that line of Browning, with such a little home?) Dearheart, I have thought over such a possibility for a long time, and firmly believe that we must be married next fall. We will be sometime, there's no doubt of that, I think; but why wait? . . . And then next spring, when we had both sold a few stories, we'd be off to some hut in the woods—and liberty! . . .
>
> How many times I've thanked God that I left Yale. Think, dear; if I hadn't, I would never have met you, in all probability. And aside from that, the most important factor in my joy over having left, are many other things. Here's one sidelight; last evening, as I was wandering down Broadway, I met two class mates, in whose room I used to sit, boring them and being bored endlessly; yet supposing that I had a hearty liking for them and always would had [*sic*]. Well, when I met them, I chatted for a minute and passed on, quite content with the thought that I probably shall never see them again, as they both go west for business careers, after graduating.—The graduation of my class occurs in two or three weeks, but I don't in the least care to go back for it; and I shan't. Think of having a lot of damned fools asking me endless and rather patronizing questions about my affairs; and probably patronizing Up through me! Good God; I wonder how many of that class realize that some day, if Up makes good the promise he has given they will probably be saying, "Oh yes, I was in his class at Yale; great friend of his!" Liars; half of them don't know him by sight; and of the half that does,

most of them think of him as a rather shabby person who used to earn his living by typewriting—with this same good old machine that I'm pounding now.—Not many weeks ago, I said to myself, "If you want to you can probably jolly your father into sending you back to Yale, this fall; and if you go back you may have some chance of gaining the Oxford scholarship." I thought the whole matter over very thoroughly; and decided that my school boy days were finally and absolutely over.

I wouldn't say so much of this, if it were not with many other things pertaining to the college-days age as it is with college itself. And this fact, carefully considered, makes me sure that my proposal for next fall is not a wild ephemeral notion.

"Dearheart; I love you," he exclaims, and he pleads at length for their simple, literary life together. He abandons these pleas for a page or so while he gives an account of a day on Staten Island, and then he draws the lengthy epistle to a close:

I shall bring down some Browning—no you have Up's. What books shall I bring down, on my vacation, for us to read? If Upton is not going away all summer, I shall probably come down for the last half of July. Do you know yet, for certain, whether he will be away (in Bermuda, or elsewhere), as yet? If so, when? Can have my vacation about any time I wish it; two weeks on pay. Please tell me how much it would cost at the Pine Bluff Inn, or some other convenient place. Wish I might have a tent, on your place. Might rent one, if the idea appealed to H. R. M. Upton, King of the Jungle.

This has been a long letter, sweetheart; rather rambling and confused, no doubt, but with some rather important things in it. Tell me what you really think of my belief regarding next fall.

Good night dear. Think of me often, and take me with you, in spirit, to the gray waves, and the heart of the woods.

H.

If the plans for his vacation as here projected were fulfilled, it is conceivable that the close proximity of two weeks led one or another or even both of them to change their minds about marriage. But, as Upton Sinclair remembers that summer, Lewis did not come to Point Pleasant for his vacation, and it is possible that vacation plans changed when the nuptial fantasy evaporated. At any rate, when Lewis took up his diary again on November 12, one of the first entries—the first coded one—was: "final letter from Cherub." He complained about Updegraff's absence from the flat on an "all evening date daily," and when he returned from Panama in December, his first entry contained the notation, "Evening—must go mad with melancholy. Up having neglected me for Cherub all evening. Hell of a night." On January 1, 1908, once more in New Haven, he wrote, "Cherub's request to burn letters complied w[ith]," and two days later

Edith Summers and Allan Updegraff announced their wedding plans and almost immediately executed them.

If it was indeed Lewis's choice to relinquish Miss Summers, he seems to have suffered no regret; but he could not have settled on a worse time to have made his other choice, the relinquishment of his employment. The panic of 1907 abruptly closed his magazine markets to him. In October he managed to make sales to the amount of thirty-odd dollars for six manuscripts, but in November he made none whatever. He summarized this grim time as follows:

> . . . in flat at 576 Fox St., reading Browning, keeping MS[s]. on road, writing lyrics & working on long poem "In Her Eyes." Little success; both in selling & in writing less than June–Oct—partly because of financial stringency, which resulted in mag[azine] retrenchment.

He had bought a little eleven-volume set of Browning and in the biographical introduction, thinking no doubt of the economic vacuum that Sauk Centre had become for him, he penciled this remark about Browning's father:

> . . . the office he filled in the Bank of England was never close enough to his liking to induce him to rise in it so far as his father had risen; but it enabled him to indulge his tastes for many books and a few pictures and to secure for his son, as that son said shortly before his death, "all the ease and comfort that a literary man needs to do good work."

In January of that year, ten or eleven months earlier, Dr. Lewis had sent him twenty-five dollars, but there had not been, and not until he returned to Yale was there to be, another penny.

November was a wretched month that he spent "intellectually beach combing." The diary echoes with the phrases of discontent: "weary of this solitude . . . devouring opiate novels . . . smoked a box of cigarettes—& that's all! . . . beach-combing continues . . . Bored to death." He was querulous about Updegraff's neglect. "I feel quite the deserted wife," he wrote on one evening, and on another, "In evening had the blues & nearly bit off poor Up's ears." He had ideas for stories that he could not bring himself to execute. He canvassed the editorial offices in search of another position and considered seriously trying to obtain a place that was open at Frederick A. Stokes Company and then decided not to. The only pleasant occasions in that month seem to have been his two excursions to Douglaston, New York, to which Alice MacGowan and Grace MacGowan Cooke had withdrawn from the ruins of Helicon Hall.

These ladies, who were to figure later in Lewis's life, had had a more harrowing time in that holocaust than most of the colonists. Mrs. Cooke had two small daughters, Helen and Katharine. From her upper windows, she dropped them into the arms of Upton Sinclair, on the ground outside.

But when the rather large ladies flung themselves into the taut blanket that he and another colonist held extended for them, the blanket snapped from the gentlemen's hands and both women suffered severe spinal injuries. Thereafter they withdrew to Douglaston to recover before moving on to another colony.

They were moderately successful popular writers and they had taken to Hal Lewis, as they called him. He liked them and he liked their young daughters, especially the twelve-year-old. "Helen's long hair & taper fingers. Of such a soft warmness! I shall fall in love with her or Kit, some day." Since they were mere children, he contented himself at this point by entertaining them with stories. These excursions into the country were pleasant for him but they did nothing to make the dreary Manhattan November any brighter, and they did not help him choose between the alternatives he had set up. On November 22 he wrote, ". . . and *still* I didn't know whether to really try for Stokes job (possible at least), go back to Yale, or go on a jaunt—as to California via Panama." Next day he "decided on last of 3," and on Monday he bought steerage passage on the *Colón,* and a flannel shirt, boots, a pea jacket; on Tuesday, November 26, armed with a Spanish grammar, some Kipling, the Bible, and Henry James's *The Awkward Age,* he set forth once more to test "the fallacy of elsewhere."

8

THE PANAMA CANAL was under construction and it seemed certain that there he could easily find employment and at the same time satisfy his craving for adventure. Crowded in once more with a miscellany of working men—Irish, Scotch, English, Canadian, Norwegian, Venezuelan, French, Texan—he listened to them and made notes on the characteristics of their pronunciation, dialect and manners. "A race of strong, self-reliant men," he wrote his mother, "very intelligent—all of them as regards their own trades, blacksmithing, plumbing, running steam shovels, or what not." He listened to their histories, their wisdom and their prejudices, and he filled his pages with copious, abbreviated notes. When they landed at Colón on December 3, he summarized the advantages to him in the experience of this voyage:

> 1. Personal adv[enture]. 2. The boys. 3. Story plots & hints & descriptions, terms, geog[raphy] etc. Dialects & people (as of Ironbark—*Plans for "The Beachcomber."*)

The motto that he had placed at the head of the diary in which these activities were recorded was *"Nihil humanum mihi alienum est!"* His thirst for experience no less than his poverty led him to take a room in a cheap hotel with one of his steerage mates, the Texan, and to move with him and his companions through the towns of the Isthmus in search of work. Cristobal, he wrote, "struck me in a heap—first really foreign place I've ever seen—china stores, niggers, Spanish signs, palms, balcony & tin roof architecture, little monkey cops in Colon & handsome khaki & riding leggings, cops in Cristobal, diverse costumes & nationality—white duck, khaki, helmets, straw hats, Stetson broad brims; white duck shoes, etc; many English here—"

His diaries degenerate into long catalogues of crammed observation—crammed onto the pages, crammed into seven intense days, as if with a desperate need to pin down everything that was impinging upon him in this new exoticism, not to devour it like a Thomas Wolfe and let it work inside him, not to refine it like an Ernest Hemingway and fix it in its essential externality, not to reflect upon it like a James Joyce until it would transmute itself into a multifaceted symbolism, nor yet to brood upon it like an Edith Wharton or a Scott Fitzgerald until it transcended itself in a pattern; but only to get it down in all its external variety on the external page in order to have it there then for an external use.

He chased frantically across the breadth of the Isthmus and back again in his search for employment, and even the men he interviewed became simply more items in his catalogue. He sought work of any kind, beginning with a supply clerk's examination (he failed seven of the twenty-seven questions) for a construction firm employed by the Isthmian Canal Commission; that possibility lost, he looked for any possibility with the railroads, the wireless station, the newspapers, and he even entertained the idea of tutorial work; finally, he took a stenographer's test, and when he learned that there was "nothing doing," he wrote, "so started for Frisco via Panama, Tex & the Kid helping me off." On his last day, in Panama City, he wrote:

> Phoned to Colon—still *nothing doing on job*—God how hot it was in the central office, over the station—in soft-shirt sleeves I had to sit still—nigger Span[ish]-Eng[lish] operator kept busy lacing filing cards—outside the train blistered in the sun—over green hills & yellow sand & blue lifeless bay whirled a great gyroscope of buzzards. . . . There was still a half hour before going of train on which conductor . . . would take me to Colon free—& in that half hour I tugged—Frisco or Yale—& I started for Yale and Tink!

He did not start, however, without the usual uncalculated crisis. Having sold his "ticket for 'Frisco for $5 gold" when he got back to Colón, he

> hustled over to station to get a steerage ticket on the "Colon" for N.Y. The cranky station agent told me, after I had waited in line for an half hour that there was *no* steerage going up. . . . Me gawd! I certainly had the real story book "sinking at the stomach" and "slowly reiterated, 'Then I—can't get out of this d——d hole?' " Went over to office of Gen'l. Manager of the P[anama] R.R. & he corroborated. Left a complaint against the station agent with chief clerk & hiked down to the "Colon" to see about chief-steward—&—potatoe-peeling job—"He's sick," said me friend Toby. Freight clerk said purser (Brasnahan—formerly of the "Advance") would be back at 5. Meanwhile I sat disconsolately at the "Ironbark" restaurant & went to Royal Mail S.S. office—where I found I couldn't get away for a week & to United Fruit S.S. office where I'd have to pay $40 to New Orleans solum. Might have to do that & telegraph for money from New Orleans—Saw purser—nice chap—He read my letter from Charley [Charles H. Towne, then of *Smart Set,* had given him a letter of recommendation to editors]—took me for forty, practically as a stowaway with connivance, but accommodation only first class. On my honor as a gentleman I wasn't to tell of his little smuggling, but I suppose that if I got caught & jugged for "stowing

> away" I'd have to blow on him—dread & tremor & sweat as I lay in his stateroom at Colon dock, where passengers coming aboard were examined by doctor who checked list—thus preventing both contagion & stowaways—after that I could go any where on the ship—save fear on pulling in to New York harbor—quarantine, customs, etc.—and as I write this I lie on the leather couch in the purser's room damning people who pace by down the deck as tho' they were on guard.

It was an "All's well" ending that Lewis had rarely experienced before.

And it was a very pleasant passage. He traveled, in effect, first class, had first-class food in the same dining room with Colonel Goethals himself and Senator Blackburn, head of the Civil Administration, slept on a comfortable couch in a first-class stateroom, and had leisure not only to study Spanish "for make-up Exam in Yale," but to organize some of his diary notes. The boat came into New York on December 16. He slipped off undetected and later met Brasnahan in an appointed saloon to take his bag. That evening was lonesome and a letdown ("must go mad with melancholy"), but the next day, after packing, he spent with Updegraff and Noyes, and he happily took an early evening train for New Haven. "It actually seemed a home going, as I looked out on bare, wonderful black traceries of boughs against snow in little walled fields." He spent the night in the room of Paul Hilsdale, the junior from Sauk Centre.

If the Panama fiasco was then only the forcing prelude to the return to New Haven, the return was nevertheless a relief to the interested parties. Almost at once a letter came from Sauk Centre:

> You cannot realize how much it means to your Father & I that you have gone back to Yale—and may you pass the examinations & enter the first of the year to finish in June. . . . It was a fine Christmas present. We have great faith in you and your future. Sent a package by mail to you yesterday, which we hope will greet you for Christmas with our love.

Dr. Lewis included a short note in his wife's letter and—almost as if he had smiled—a bank draft for fifty dollars. For Sinclair Lewis himself the return was a pleasant relief from what had proved to be the rather unpleasant pressures of experience in the world beyond ivy, and he was now quite content to relax in books alone. There had, of course, been gains for him. The very ability to relax in an atmosphere that earlier had become so distasteful was a gain, and at some point in the interlude, he had even learned to spell *perhaps* and to abbreviate *et cetera* correctly. He found a room off the campus, bought a two-volume *Anthologie des poètes français contemporains,* and settled down.

His room was at 14 Whalley Avenue, in the house of a ramshackle Irish family named Quinn. The male Quinn kept a saloon, the female, the boarding house. She delighted in gossiping with her roomers, and Sinclair Lewis enjoyed her talk at least to the extent of taking diary notes on much of it.

Surely she is the author of a document that he found worth preserving; written in red crayon in a large freehand, it reads:

> Mr. Lewis I found another large hole burned in the rug by the time Collage closes you will have the rug to pay for and if you burn into the under carpet you will have two to pay for I spoke to you about burning holes but you was not carefull because this one is larger and burned down into the under carpet if you keep on we will be all burned up.

There were a few altercations between them that were more vocal than this admonition (one about heating water more than once a week for a bath), but generally speaking, Lewis enjoyed 14 Whalley Avenue, which had the double advantage of being inexpensive and of giving him his freedom from college routines beyond the classroom.

In his 1932 reminiscence, he spoke of these months as "his best in college; his own class graduated, he . . . was not required to go to chapel, was free equally of class companionships and class ambitions, practically in the status of a graduate student, and enjoyed it." His student associates were almost necessarily younger than he, most of them juniors who were friends of Paul Hilsdale's. He complained of their lack of intellectual interests, but they were, after all, people. In May he encountered a man from his own class, and he noted, "Met Huson '07 at Chat Noir in evening. He's working at a Gas Plant in Derby!! Vague reaching for intimacy; fencing off elements not understood." Not understood by him, even now? He had perhaps one friend, Leonard Bacon, again, of that younger class of '09, and also to become a writer. In Bacon's room,

> I sat before wood fire, drinking tea & eating Butter Thins, while Leonard read me his recent verses, ballades or ballads, strange supple things, deeply dyed with purple & crimson of Byzantium; or while we discussed Swinburne's latest—the Duke of Gandia, or the effects of an accomplished socialism on art—till 2:30 A.M.

In his reminiscence, called "Yale '09," Bacon remembered the significance that Swinburne held for them; he "meant liberty and the casting off of fetters." Again:

> Leonard Bacon & I walked, talking of ballads & such bawdry; then canoed, "gliding over" Lake Whitney. Len knows a world I know little—that of country clubs & golf, & ladies in broughams.

Although Bacon could give him only a conversational glimpse into *that* world, he brought Lewis, for the first time, into the kind of college world that the young freshman had wanted at the outset and had never found. It came too late. Rather ungraciously, Lewis soon found him naïve and imperceptive. His most valued associations were with his professors. But Bacon frequented Tinker's rooms as much as Lewis, and this annoyed him.

> Found Bacon in Tink's room; & he held forth so that T. & I were too afflicted w[ith] mental lassitude even to *try* to "get a word in edgewise." . . . No doubt it's combination of early spoiling & the example of his loquacious & emphatic father. Bacon has read enormously, but is equally shallow in his estimation of either books or men about us.

(One might observe that a taciturn and emphatic father could achieve the identical result.)

On a Friday he wrote, "Tink & I rake Len over coals—'Have you read'—"; but on the very next night, amiability prevailed again as at "Tink's Len and I hour in making portmanteau w[or]ds—Symonstrocity, Mental Tolstoilet, Verlingerie." On the whole, it was a pleasant relationship. An older Leonard Bacon told of his respect for Lewis at this time, especially for his independence of mind, his candor and his curiosity; and that respect, which Lewis had so seldom enjoyed, must have far outweighed the annoyance he sometimes felt with a rival in loquacity. When the term came to an end, it was Bacon who saw him off, "bringing me a train-vol[ume]—Chas. Reade's Peg Woffington."

Toward Yale as an institution he was generally indifferent and only occasionally hostile. He spoke slightingly of "the dread mysteries & whory antiquity of Yale Senior Societies" and loftily of the amateurish *Lit.* "Damn their formalities," he said of traditional occasions. About undergraduates in general he had no complaints and was himself capable of assuming the conventional undergraduate attitude toward graduate students—"typical crude, un-nuanced grad student"! He speaks rather slightingly of one of his teachers, but Tinker was now "Good old Tink"; and Phelps, "St. Billy." Lewis had been readmitted to Yale through a special faculty vote, and the influence of the judgment of these two men upon that vote was considerable. If they could not quite treat him as their peer, they were not above indulging in faculty gossip with him and they even thought of him as the possible successor to an instructor who was resigning his position ("even little I," he wrote, "might be considered").

Lewis's reciprocal influence is apparent in the seriousness with which they took his suggestion that this post should go to Arthur Upson. He talked to a half-dozen influential faculty men and it is almost certain that Upson would have received the appointment if it had not been that, as he explained in reply to an informal inquiry from Phelps, his father's health would prevent him from making any present commitment. Tinker and Phelps provided him with much the same kind of companionship that Upson did, with the kind of random belletristic conversation that he enjoyed. There could, to be sure, have been little agreement on such subjects as socialism and religion, but there was probably no contention.

Nothing in the literary essays that Lewis wrote for Phelps's course on the seventeenth century suggested any of the feeling that shows itself, for example, in this annotation to *Paradise Lost* in his Milton: "Note M's fiendish Xian ingenuousness in devising torment for the 'damned,' i.e., people who do not believe & act like him." As there were subjects on which they could not have met, so there was a whole realm of feeling that they could not share. The diary for these six months, like those of the years before, is not without its notes on moods of "dumpishness," and at least once it breaks out in the old desolate wail of loneliness: "So lonely this evening!—some one to go home to; some one to work *for* & *with*—yet that some one need not *necessarily* be a woman." A friend, *one* true friend!

The continuing necessity of such outbursts forces upon us the conclusion that Yale did not give him, in any real sense, an education; for the word in its full meaning surely implies an organization of the self as well as a consolidation of more abstract interests. When Harry Lewis left Yale his was still a scattered self, as, really, it was always to remain. The complacent gentility that characterized the intellectual life of Yale in the early years of this century could not, on the one hand, assimilate him, and, on the other hand, it gave him no genuine target for rebellion. A Yale man, Charles Fenton, described the Yale of those years as follows:

> The resemblance to a nineteenth-century academy, which it had so recently been, survived at Yale in the paternalistic role of the faculty. Many of them cultivated for themselves personalities appropriate in various ways to such a function. The nature of much of the instruction—drill, lecture, examination—perpetuated adolescence and bestowed gianthood on teachers who were merely adults. Some played a lively and unwholesome part in the senior societies and fraternities. Each of the more luminous had his creatures and his abominations. Faculty feuds were occasionally inherited by and even delegated to suitable undergraduates.

And, writing of the powerful "collegiate" spirit that dominated the university, he quotes William James, who had recently said of Harvard vis-à-vis Yale that "Here we have thought but no school; at Yale a school, but no thought." The undirected dissidence of Harry S. Lewis remained largely the frenetic expression of his personal uneasiness, his psychic restlessness. And one must wonder whether he would not have developed differently if his college education had come in another atmosphere.

It was William James, again, who, at a Harvard commencement dinner in 1903, said, "Our undisciplinable are our proudest products." The Yale undergraduate was conservative, conventional, respectful of accepted upper-middle-class values and contemptuous of others. At Harvard, then, independence and individuality were encouraged. There, Sinclair Lewis would have found what he almost never found in New Haven—an atmosphere in which his own wild eccentricity and his developing political radicalism might well have been assimilated. He would have found many men who would at least have tolerated his difference and some who would have encouraged it. Thus he might have become either a really educated radical, with a genuinely reasoned basis for his dissidence, both personal and intellectual, or, in that more congenial atmosphere, something of a reasoning conformist. Either way, there would almost certainly have been an enormous difference from the product that emerged from Yale in 1908.

Or suppose that he had enrolled at the quite new University of Chicago, where, instead of genteel belletrists, he would have encountered minds of a tougher fiber, like those of Thorstein Veblen and Robert Herrick? Or better yet, suppose it had been one of the great state universities, Minnesota or Wisconsin, with the lingering atmosphere of Populist times moving now towards a new political progressivism. Here the rough exterior like the clumsy manners of the country bumpkin would hardly have been observed, and the raw edges of his mind would not have been subjected to that constant grating which was finally damaging only to himself, and he might well have grown into an easy maturity. Instead, his education left him the nervous tramp who aspired to elegance, the radical who really wished to conform, the puritan from the hinterland who yearned to be the man of the world. "In my new eye glasses & silk cord I look quite distingue, doncherknow. Almost as good as a monacle." All the sadness, somehow, emerges in the spelling.

The heavy demands upon him in study during that last term at New Haven did not permit any frequent indulgence in such moods of fantasy, or in fits of brooding loneliness either. He had taken it upon himself to complete a year's work in half a year. In January he enrolled in a full schedule of new courses, and simultaneously he made up the work of the full schedule that had been offered in the autumn term. In April and May he successfully presented himself for the make-up examinations, and in early June, for the final examinations. Some of his English courses were in writing, to be sure, and that was no task for him; and in others, written exercises were a large part of the work. He preserved none of these, except for the collection of one-page essays on the writers of the seventeenth century to which William Lyon Phelps assigned chiefly the grade of "B" and occasionally that of "A." The grades are just.

These papers are almost always intelligent and never brilliant. They would not, today, lead one to think that the author could become a distinguished professor of literature or even a very good one. They bear the author's mark, however: a strain of priggery (he would have had Suckling expurgated), a certain humorless rigidity (the vanities of Samuel Pepys left him uneasy), a preference for the downright, for "humanity" and "sincerity" as against the merely literary, at the same time that he exercises some insincerity of his own (he abuses the hack writer, while himself hacking away), a practiced contempt for the *Lit,* and a wordy style. Some of this would go; some, grow.

Of work outside the college, there was now almost none. His father sent him about fifty dollars every month (apart from the established expenses of tuition and the cost of a new suit), and, living thriftily, he managed. Soon after he arrived, he took a job as "super" in a production of Oscar Freiburg's *Sunset* and he spent Christmas in Westfield, Massachusetts, with the *Sunset* company. The diaries mention no other work in this time. In 1927, in the New York *Post,* William Lyon Phelps wrote that "Lewis returned to Yale penniless, and made a heroic struggle to work his way through, for which he deserves high admiration. After each college day was over, he went to a newspaper office in New Haven and worked nearly all night." If any such work was done, it is against the whole practice of the diaries that Lewis should not have noted it; indeed, one must conclude that Phelps, twenty years later, has confused the relatively easy months of 1908 with the long but sporadic night work at the *Journal and Courier* in the earlier years. That he made a note of having gone to the office of the *Journal and Courier* to talk about the possibility of a position in the following summer indicates, again, that he held none now.

There is another argument against any such heavy work in the condition of his health. In mid-April he sought out Dr. Skinner with a kidney complaint that was extremely discomforting; Dr. Skinner first diagnosed it as the consequence of an excess of phosphates in the blood, then later as "chronic nephrites," threatening Bright's disease. He ordered "little meat, *no* booze, less smoking," and "resting." His father, concerned, was in correspondence with Dr. Skinner, and his alarm as well as his eagerness to have the boy finish Yale at last no doubt together influenced him in regularly forwarding an adequate if in no sense lavish allowance.*

Whether his poor health was in any way responsible for his physical cowardice, which for the first time in this spring he admits, is conjectural. He was, for whatever reasons, a very apprehensive young man. His room was on the ground floor, with a window on the street. One of the other roomers had imagined a loiterer outside to be a burglar, and not many nights later Fritz Düberg had come tapping at Lewis's window, causing who knows what alarm. A few nights after that, he could not fall asleep and had a "happy little time with hisself imagining burglar alarms & the window." A week later: "Ear toward sudden sound twitches in alarm—Soles of feet flash cold at fear of r.r. wreck."

He was himself in a trolley accident:

> I was up front on running board; gripped tight when I saw what was coming, & wasn't hurt. But, coming back—H[ilsdale] & I sat on rearward-facing seat, and I trembled constantly in the belief a car just behind us was going to collide every time it stopt near us.

* His records show that from November of 1906 through July of 1908, he received a total of $613 from his father.

The fear of robbery lingered into June. "Nearly a hold up in lower Bdwy green as went home at 1 a.m.," he wrote; did he flee? A few nights before:

> Last night I tho't I saw a man lying in grass outside window & roused fellows in next room to see. Consequently, much jollied by Q[uinn] (who handed me a lemon in a napkin) & Marion S., who cried, "O Mr. Lewis, burglars!" outside my window at intervals.

"He would be a Richard Harding Davis hero!" he wrote humorously of himself as he recalled the resolve to go to Panama, but the man quaking in the New Haven boarding house bed hardly suggests a dashing figure in romance. Of romance there was none now; in his private life he returned once more—if he had ever departed from it—to the ascetic state. The Cherub and Updegraff were married and happy for a time. The *Transatlantic Tales* position had evaporated and they lived on the salary that the Cherub earned as a night-school teacher. They "are as happy a 'young married couple' as may be," he wrote, and the example must have left him feeling a little wistful, at the least. Tentatively, they invited him to spend some weeks of the summer with them in a Berkshire cottage that they hoped to rent; and he hoped that he could accept. Nothing came of the plan, and had it, there would still have been nothing but an outsider's visit for him.

He entered briefly into another young marriage when, one night, Fritz Düberg, the German student he had met in Cambridge in 1904, appeared heavily in debt and in flight from his wife and child; Lewis persuaded him, after a few days, to go back. Not many nights later, Fritz appeared again, tapping on Lewis's window and full of more melodrama. Now he had his wife and child with him, and they were in flight from their landlord and the Cambridge police, trying secretly to get out of the country and back to Germany, with Fritz at the same time hoping that there was "an inceptive love affair between his wife & Lincoln Barnes" that would free him. With this suspended detail, Fritz Düberg, like some of Lewis's friends already and scores yet to come, disappears forever.

Lewis developed no new friendships with women. At the time of his kidney infection, he wrote suggestively—and uniquely—"suppose a mediaeval, masturbative monk were afflicted with this infernal, penal (uncouplet) burning—he'd take it to be the punishment from heaven, & try flagellation instead of hair shirts." He made rather leering notes about a young woman who also lived at the Quinns', "Marian Sturdevant of the creamy complexion, tender little form of sixteen, & the bucolic slowness of mind . . . very neat extremidades lajes," but contented himself with chat. He was moved to write his mother with the request that she find Myra Hendryx's address for him, and learned that she was now a governess with a Hubbard Park, Illinois, family. Did he have her in mind when he wrote, "The fancy of ones soul *chaliced* in *her* noble white hands?" Or was it the child, Helen Cooke, whose hands he had always observed and about whom he now let his reverie wander in a maudlin, miasmic haze?

Early photographs of this child (who was to become Mrs. Harry Leon Wilson) show her to have been indeed nothing less than adorable, but she was only thirteen years old and Lewis was twenty-three. His erotic fantasies about a little girl may find some reflexive significance in his derogatory attitude toward mature women. "Women," he wrote after an evening with one of his teachers and his wife, "have a genius for the commonplace—in the liter'y talk as in life (tho' the fact is counterbalanced by the fact that men are often only commonplace emotionally)," and he complains that the lady who had given rise to this generalization is more interested in literary gossip than she is in literature. Immediately after, in code, comes this: "You couldn't keep me from sending picture post cards to Helen C. were you even to lock me up. I'm going to marry that child—but not as a 'Dora'; rather, when she has become the noblehearted woman, destined mother of strong men, that she is to be."

In April he had visited the MacGowan-Cooke home at Douglaston (he was planning a collaboration with them), and afterward wrote, "Love mit Helen," and "reading to Helen & Kit th[e] former with her head against my breast." In May he visited them again.

> Helen, Kit & I went a-questing violets Sat. P.M. Helen had a cold, & became grouchy, whereupon Kit had to act as messenger between our dissevered monarchies. Sat. morning, before any one else was up, a windy tramp. I certainly am in love with that glorious child, Helen. She pretended to be—or was—decidedly bored by me, Sunday, preferring her book; but ruet coelum, for did I not kiss her soft cheek at our season-long parting? God knows the answer, and is very close-lipped; she did not even want me to stroke her hand as I read to them. Will she fall in love with some beast with big muscles? Pray God he be a nice beast. So divine an understanding—in both senses—& for once I speak not erotically, but amourously.

Mrs. Cooke had just obtained a divorce from a deserted husband, and now the sisters and the two little girls moved west, first to Missouri, then on to Carmel in California. Harry, in New Haven, "Dreamed that Helen had written me, beginning, 'My Lover.' " At the same time, he had fantasies of another kind:

> Letter and several verses from Anna Louise Strong. She is going out to Seattle in summer, to live. Wonder if the little girl might not be slightly in love with me [whom she had never seen]. Her verse reads me—egotistically—but in her letter she descants on the impracticability of marriage—for her (bein' quite content alone?) & says the verse is "love pot'ry not written to any one in particular. . . ."

He continued his own verse writing, but he did not return to the undergraduate periodicals. Leonard Bacon remembered that two years earlier, when Lewis was on the board of editors, he was much admired by some of the young heelers and that now "he became once more the delight of the slaves of the *Lit*." If this was true, in the spring of 1908, it was a "delight" wholly apart from the activities of the *Lit* itself and there is no evidence as to whom, beyond Bacon, it extended, unless it was George Soule, who is not mentioned in the diary. Mr. Soule remembered talking with him only once—in 1906—but "the encounter made a deep impression on me. . . . Heelers whose manuscripts had been rejected had the privilege of calling at the office on a certain evening after the contents of the next issue had been announced, and asking criticism from the editors. Usually the critics didn't take the trouble to make more than a few casual observations. Red, on the occasion I remember, was not only warm and friendly, but took the job seriously. I came away feeling that I had really been helped. I don't think I ever received any other criticism as conscientious and discerning as his."

To Bacon he showed a typed volume of his verse that was four inches thick. In that spring, he found commercial acceptances for a half dozen of his poems, and a number of them that had appeared in January in the revived *Overland Monthly* in San Francisco, called forth a letter from William Rose Benét, who was by this time again living with his family in Benicia, California. Three letters from Lewis to Benét are extant; they are interesting because they form the bridge between the casual meeting in New Haven in the spring of 1906 and the close friendship that was to develop in California in 1909; because they are his earliest extant literary exchange and because they reveal Lewis in that mood of aimless and quite irritating japery that is the other side of his discontent, his melancholy, his dourness, they deserve quotation.

i

February 5, 1908

My dear Benét;

I certainly am grateful to you for the "pome," for, to quote you, not infrequently "jections come, the world looks glum (damglum) & I am tired (damtired)." Not often tho'—& surely not ever again, for I shall send your testimonial to the editors of the Atlantic & Young's & the Sunday School Times & say: "Now, damn ye, do you dare to reject my little masterpieces?" . . .

"Up." now has my old job on "Tales," as I'm back here to get my degree (damn & then doubly God damn all minnikin degrees, up the back and down the front, trimming with H_2S—but Father's old and wants—you know how it goes). But it's back to N'Yawk; to editorial work or newspaper making o'days, and o' nights the fee simple of the estates of the gods (I believe in 'em, don't you; Mars & Vishnu & Astarte & all that merry bunch;

a pox on the paler blooded, white corpuscled deities of today; not gods verily, for they take no gin in their tea. All of which means that being a radical, an impressionist, a believer in the new, I have harked back to the fundamental old, & t'ell with the innovaters who go to bed o' nights....

ii

March 20, [*1908*]

Dear Benét;

Gettin' some of my make-up work out of the way, and writing a dramar in verse; nice young pome, with a carefully selected bunch of alliterations, careful mixture of liquid and high-church vowels, and original observations of nature—especially *in re* chrysoprases, silvern, languid lambs and lallygag the lane, and other kindred themes. But taint symbolistic anyway, and hasn't any names highbrower than Ysobel, so that it won't have any worse fate than to land in the jo. Now if this dramar had a surenuff Aglyvaine (hoonell cares how its spelled?) with a few remarks on the "pale green snow, so shillily scented with warm purple and wan patchouli this summer," it might be set to music by Debussy and dragged on-to the Manhattan boards. And wot musick my son! De would etherialize the tom-tom, and with reckless theme and motiff titervate the t-t's effect into an exotic etc etc. (you know the brand, the Melachrino school of criticism, for which see the Times.) [Written in the margin beside this paragraph: "Gawd this sounds nutty to read over. Whats the answer?"] . . .

When I was down in NYawk tother day I found Updegraff quite as much interested in Thompson as you are. He (Up, not Th.) wants to be remembered to you.—"We" might get a very decent bunch of damn, iconoclastic, crazy, irreverent, lazy, adorable Bohs together in the only Paree for us, some day. Hope so. Lord, speaking of Paree, it must be great to be really one of that real Parisian bunch. Apparently there is as much gathering of young and enthusiastic asses today as there was when Gautier wore purple vescit and "charming cubs called Victor, 'Le Maitre.' " Perhaps New York will have an inherent feeling akin to that genuinely metropolitan essence of Paree, some day. SOME DAY! Just as soon as that arrives I shall own evening clothes . . .

iii

May 17 [*1908*]

Dear Bill;

B'old me, drunken with much words, having spent all today on such a story as befits "minstrel's May." . . .

I'm just realizing that with the make-up work and the reading of Meredith, Symons, and Lordnosoo I've been doing, I shall have to get to work like the devil for the next two and a half weeks or else I won't get through. But I will. Then New York, no doubt....

Tink, who's now an assistant prof, and a grreat man as he has always been an adorable one, read me a bunch of De Morgan last evening, and we chortled and giggled together over it like a couple of coyotes. Read any? Called Dickenesque, but it certainly isn't; nor is it Thackeray nor anyone save De Morgan. Evidently that rare beast an individual style. Shall have to get hold of some.

Any chance of seeing you east this summer; of eating a Melton Mowbray with you at the Sign of the Bunch of Grapes, hard by Washington Square?

Affectionately
HSL
variously
Hal,
Red
Sink. Lewis Esq
et al. mult
y generalmente
malos.

Of the "dramar," no vestige remains, or of the unpublished poems, but his vocation was now certain, assumed. Norman Holmes Pearson says that "in his senior year Lewis went to the man who had taught him freshman English, saying that he wanted most of all to be a writer. 'But you will starve,' Tinker said. 'I don't care if I do,' Lewis replied. 'Then you will succeed.' " He wrote prose "drools" for *Puck* and *Life,* but he had in mind a longer prose project, a novel engendered in and by Panama to be called *The Beachcomber,* for which he made one strangely luminous note.

> Woke with a galled kibe of imagination, for I had seen a vision of a Wonder story; how my Panaman beach-comber met w[ith] an enthusiastic young poetic undergrad; how, next morning, half awake & half asleep, he saw the charm of the e.y.p.u. glittering with rain & shower bath, the sunshine thru' his golden sparkling hair & quoting poetry; a vision in that sunshine-in-rain of a Colon morning; how, supposing it had been a vision, he betook him to the poetic refuge of a NY hall bedroom. Well! The Panama glimpse set my mind jaunting; Took out a book on Panama; read there on in the evening; & wrote to I.C.C. & Panama "Star & Herald" *in re* jobs.

It would seem that he finished only one piece of fiction in the spring of 1908, a short story called "The Way to Rome," published three years later in a periodical called *The Bellman* (Minneapolis). A jongleur and a clerk are on a pilgrimage to Rome in the course of which the jongleur decides to become a clerk, and the clerk, to give up orders and become a jongleur. The prose is the now familiar pastiche of archaisms, and the piece reads more like the work of a high-school student than like that of a mature man who has seriously dedicated himself to literature. Yet others took his dedication seriously, among them the ladies Cooke and MacGowan.

When he went to Douglaston in April, he discussed with them their novel in progress, *Strength of the Hills,* and they with him, his projected novel to be called *Ecce Homo*—"on Christ reincarnated as a modern radical." The idea attracted the ladies and it was agreed then that the novel should be a three-way collaboration. After they moved on to Missouri, they wrote him to suggest that he "come out there & work on the Ecce Homo book." That was not feasible, but he kept the project in mind through a half-dozen months, and it was finally to take him to the ladies in California.

His future was naturally much in his mind. A writer, yes; but what would support the writer? He had sometimes thought of emulating his father and brother. In a list of possibilities that he made in 1904, "M.D." stands at the head. In 1905, he wrote,

> The study of "nervous system" which we are taking in psychology is so interesting that it looks as tho' t'would be well to study medicine, like my Father, Brother, Grandfather & Uncle. The priest, & *doctor* & the reporter have of all men the best opportunity of gathering vital 'literary material.'

By 1908, religion and medicine had both fallen from his mind; now it was to be either journalism or the academy. At the same time that he was writing letters of inquiry and application to editors in New York (and on one occasion going down for an interview), he was thinking very seriously of returning to New Haven for graduate study. At the end of the term, he had reached no decision. In 1921 he wrote to Norman Foerster, saying, "thank the Lord I gave up, during the vacation after my senior year at Yale, the plan I'd had thru all that senior year of returning for my Ph.D. in English." It is as well that the restless young man who had found the relatively relaxed routines of undergraduate life restrictive should not have ventured into the captive disciplines of graduate study. It was, after all, only by a narrow margin that he became an alumnus of Yale College at all. With the dean's permission, he was excused from the formalities of commencement exercises, and through special faculty courtesy, his name—still H. S. Lewis—went into the records as that of one who had been graduated with his class, 1907. It was June 11, 1908, when Leonard Bacon put Sinclair Lewis, A.B., on the train for still another and a different kind of voyage. At the front of his last diary he had written, "Humanity outweighs the humanities."

"Persistancy is one great element in success."

THREE

Climb

I

THE YEARS that immediately follow, the remainder of 1908, 1909, 1910, and on, a miscellany of false starts, lost jobs, lost hopes, loose ends, erratic wandering, begin quietly enough with a return to Minnesota that had been decreed for his health. Dr. Skinner had urged Dr. Lewis to bring the young man, now twenty-three years old, home for a time to "rest and get well." In his last letter to New Haven, Dr. Lewis itemized the transportation costs to Sauk Centre and enclosed his check for fifty dollars. He also explained that he and his wife would be away until after the Fourth of July and that for that period Harry was to stay with Claude and his wife, Mary, in St. Cloud.

He paused with his mother's relatives in Chicago long enough to stop in at Hull House to meet Anna Louise Strong, "with whom I've long corresponded." Indeed he had, and Miss Strong was curious. At Yale he had read some articles of hers in the Oberlin College magazine and had opened a correspondence. In a recent letter, Anna Louise Strong recalled the circumstances:

> I was a very prim young miss, a minister's daughter, and was dubious about the propriety of writing to any stranger at all, especially when he almost at once got off on an Abelard-Heloise vein and wrote rapturously about traveling through the beauties of Italy together. I recall that I asked advice from Florence Fitch, dean of women, whom I much admired. She grinned and said it wouldn't hurt me. The correspondence went on for some years, with some reserve on my part and little on his. It is clear now that he got out of it a chance for expression without any responsibility, such as the actual knowing of the person might mean.

He habitually addressed her as Heloise, and when they met he was not disappointed.

> Tall, slender, well-featured, keen sense of humor & of fancy; really delightful. She outlined to me the plot of a play, "Kings' Palaces" *—we, in some sort,

* "I published . . . a rather useless short drama, 'The King's Palace,' describing the shocked idealism of a young girl who sees the world and refuses to enter it—this was after I went back to the university [in 1908]."—Anna Louise Strong, *I Change Worlds* (New York, 1935), p. 28.

went on playing at Kings Palaces. Are they altruists or individualists in the Palace—Does Yeats live there?—On the terrace we sat, in a courtyard as of Le Moyen Age, shut out by irregular lines of buildings from noisome South Halstead Street, talking of ourselves—of how she read my first letter to the Oberlin Women's Dean—how she had "called me down," now & again, & I was charmed by her. She "toted" me, as they say, to see Hull House—far more wonderful than the N.Y. University Settlement.

Miss Strong had thought that this meeting would define their relationship, that it "would either break off all relations or develop them fast. Actually, it left them about as they were. As his other relations developed, our correspondence languished." There was to be at least one interesting consequence many years later, but now, in spite of her seeming attractiveness to him, nothing more developed. They stayed together in Chicago until his train time that evening; then once more he sat up in a day coach through the night "to save $2." In Minneapolis he called on Upson, met the editor of *The Housekeeper,* the first periodical that paid for his verse, and on the same evening arrived in St. Cloud, where he was to stay for nearly three weeks.

It was a happy time—in his words, a "bully time"—that he spent with his brother's family and their friends. Twice he watched Claude in surgery; he learned to play bridge whist and, although he was to say in 1927 that he "has never in his life played bridge," he played it frequently now, and apparently with pleasure. His tennis, he confessed in the same 1927 self-portrait, was like that of "an eight-year-old boy—quite definitely and literally so"; and that too he played for the first time then in St. Cloud. There were outings and picnics and visits to neighboring towns, and only one unpleasantness.

Devil of a row with Claude over his being impossibly autocratic resulted in my spending the night w[ith] the Brighams. Felt very much like pulling out for Kirksville, Mo., & getting to work on the Ecce Homo b[oo]k w[ith] the Cookes.

Instead, he stayed and worked on his independent projects—a story called "The Dawn," of which he had written the first draft in the past autumn, and "an essayic drool" called "Ladies of Shallot." These finished, he mailed them to Flora May Holly, his first literary agent, whom he had met in New York in 1907. He spent part of one day in "arranging story plots, which were on scattered sheets. Have over 100 plots for short stories." He wrote two editorials for the *Outer's Book,* one on "sportsmanship vs sedentariasm," for which he was later paid eleven dollars. Tests administered by Claude indicated that the nephritic condition had been cleared up. He celebrated the Fourth of July in a customary way and went on to Sauk Centre. And here ended his early diaries.

His wish was to leave Sauk Centre as soon as he had something to which he could go. He scanned the Help Wanted sections of the Minneapolis newspapers, came across a request for applications to the editorial offices of the Waterloo (Iowa) *Daily Courier,* made his application and was offered a position at eighteen dollars a week. His father gave him twenty dollars, and on the twenty-eighth of July he was off again.

Attractively bisected by the Cedar River, Waterloo, he found, was a quiet town of nearly twenty thousand inhabitants in east-central Iowa, and the *Courier* was its daily newspaper. Sinclair Lewis recalled in 1932 that he "became combination editorial writer, telegraph editor, proof-reader, and dramatic critic." In an earlier reminiscence written for the *History of the Class of 1907* in 1913, he remembered the *Courier* as having "an office cat, a business manager and one-and-a-half reporters." Much later, in the series on his journalistic experiences, he reported that as drama critic he had had only one assignment, a review of the single musical that came to Waterloo during his stay there. In this recollection he said also that he had been retained on the *Courier* for just ten weeks; in the 1932 piece it was eight weeks, during which he lived on eight dollars a week and saved eighty dollars. He saved a considerable sheaf of his editorials as well; the first of these is dated August 3, and the last, September 14, but a note written on the clipping of August 20 says, "From 8/19/08 on, only *part* of my editorials in Waterloo Courier are kept." Eight weeks would have taken him through September 26; ten weeks, through October 10. Since on October 10 he made a note of having received from his father a check for twenty-five dollars—apparently the last he was ever to receive—a reasonable supposition would be that he was already in New York and that most or all of the eighty dollars he had saved in Waterloo was gone. It is probable, then, that he left Waterloo on about September 26 and for several weeks was without employment in New York.

This was a presidential-campaign year, and the *Courier* was a Republican newspaper. Its editorial writer was expected to defend Taft against Bryan; and whatever Lewis's personal inclination may have been, this he did, but the defense was always made on rather abstract principles and without particular relation to Iowa. He "was expected to deal chiefly with local Iowa politics," and of these he was ignorant. Nor did the more immediately local issues of Waterloo interest him beyond one or two assays into such matters as road improvement and the protection of clams in the Cedar River against the rakes of pearl hunters. He was expected to write from one thousand to fifteen hundred words a day, and he tended to lead off with one or two titled editorials and follow them with brief squibs of one kind or another. The editorials proper, when they did not concern themselves with the Taft and Bryan campaigns, were rather leisurely, essayistic affairs. One of the very first, a defense of critical pessimists, was called "The Needful Knocker" and concluded:

> The booster's enthusiasm is the motive force which builds up our American cities. Granted. But the hated knocker's jibes are the check necessary to guide that force. In summary then, we do not wish to knock the booster, but we certainly do wish to boost the knocker.

Or he would write on American heroism in mass catastrophes, on religious hypocrisy among evangelists, on the cultivation of mustaches, on political slogans and advertising, on card catalogues, on every new development in aeronautics; or appeal for individuality against mass pressure; or defend the nude in art; or mourn the death of Arthur Upson. That unfortunate young man was drowned in August of 1908 when his boat capsized in a Minnesota lake called Bemidji, and to Lewis, this was Chatterton again, this was Keats! "Adonais is dead," he wrote in a column that is sentimental in its judgment and its lack of restraint but that is also felt.

> There was no poet in America whose songs promised a richer harvest to us than did those of Arthur Upson. . . . We wait and wait; the summer days shorten sadly, and never again comes his voice to brighten our heavy dusk.

The trembling feeling is understandable: Upson at first had been kind to him, then had liked and advised him, then had become his friend—and there had been few friends. Respectable authority esteemed his work. But could the citizens of Waterloo, or the editor of the *Courier,* have cared less about any subject than about the death of an effete young poet of whom they had never heard?

Then, too, it was of course impossible for Sinclair Lewis, even in what is plainly a mood of discretion, to suppress his dissidence. A lynching riot in Springfield, Illinois, roused his sense of injustice to protest not once but three or four times. He defended the Christianity of a University of Chicago professor who had publicly disputed the validity of Christian miracles. He cited Upton Sinclair's *The Jungle* in his comments on the vices of the Chicago meat trust. He belabored the national temperance movement even though he took a temperance view. He obliquely defended the socialist position (Eugene Debs was then a presidential candidate):

> . . . if one is merely ignorant of socialism, neither opposed nor favorable, it might be well to learn something of an organization which does not seem entirely fatuous in its claim that this year it will poll a million votes. Such an increase in its vote would call for a percentage of increase considerably less than it displayed during the past few elections. Perhaps socialism is what Carroll D. Wright called it, in mixed metaphors: "A serpent threatening us all with the sword." Perhaps it is an advisable sociological scheme. In neither case is it to be combated by a three line sneer.

In 1932 he said that "his editorials were too radical" and that he soon "suspected that he would be fired."

But the young man was, quite on his own, looking elsewhere. He later described his dull life in Waterloo by writing that sometimes he would walk out of the town to the north—out onto the prairie, and sometimes he would walk out of the town to the south—out onto the prairie; and then he would go back to his furnished room.

It was not all dull.

> Sunday P.M. I went with a "courier" linotype operator to a "Mulligan"—the said M. being a stew of all sorts of meats & vegetables, cooked in a wash-boiler & washed down with *kegs* of beer; boxes of cigars, poker, vile songs, good stories, quoits, cussing, violin music & scrapping being the condiments; all served piping hot to the most wonderful gang of 25 bar tenders, barbers, laundrymen ect. in a rustic grove. Prett' nice, I'd say!

For the first time, he set himself to systematic observation of small-town people. Under the heading "Iowa Talk" he collected a whole sheaf of notes not only on local habits of speech as he heard them in his boarding house, on the street, in the office, but also on dress, amusements, manners, including even a list of Iowa wild flowers and a group of illiterate news items submitted to the *Daily Courier* by a reader ("Mr. and Mrs. Marriale left for Standwood Monday to spend a Weak with there Doter Mrs. Farrington," etc.). Freeing himself of the limited refinements of an Arthur Upson, he was trying to practice his adage of *nihil humanum:*

> *Pianist* in "Jewel" *mov. pict.* show—coat & vest off, suspenders over blue shirt, dirty low collar, small face, short, rather curly light hair, very red, very long cravat, curiously twisted at the knot; high lace shoes. Plays piano during pictures—"sad" music etc—sings brassily for "illustrated songs—don't knock the sailor—playing the song also (In intermission the current is turned on the electric piano plays with expressionless, hard, monotonous brilliancy).

Such material was to be grist for that mill of his which had not yet started to grind; but it was of no use to the editor of the Waterloo *Daily Courier*. That gentleman and his readers could hardly have been expected to interest themselves, for example, in Sinclair Lewis's literary opinions as they crept into his editorials ("Henry James, whose work no man can read") or in an enthusiastic account of the plans for a new national theater in New York, even though the editorialist did his best to point up the relevance of these plans to the lives of the Waterloo citizenry.

> The artist cannot be geographically defined; but this is at least to be believed: The artist capable of the really vital and American play is far more likely to hail from the fresh brightness and unscoured genuineness of the Corn Belt than he is from the New York millions.

It was to New York, however, that he himself was looking.

> On Thursday morning of my tenth week, the Boss came in cheerily with, "Well, he's just wired me—your successor. He'll be on the train in half an hour, so you get through this evening. But," in a debauch of generosity, "I'll pay you right through to Friday evening!"
>
> That was the first I had heard of my successor and of being more succeeded than success, but with the eighty dollars, minus two or three, that I had saved, I was on the train for Chicago on Friday morning. Ahead were New York and glory—quite a way ahead. I had a suitcase containing three extra shirts, the extra pair of trousers, and my Roget's *Thesaurus*.

When his eighty dollars was nearly gone, he found work through Allan Updegraff in the office of a philanthropic organization with the appalling set of initials, J.A.B.C.O.S.A.I.C.P. This was the Joint Application Bureau of the Charity Organization Society and the Association for the Improvement of the Condition of the Poor. Lewis did two jobs at a total salary of seventy-five dollars a month. He served as night clerk, in which capacity he received and interviewed, between early evening and midnight, persons in need of immediate aid. This usually meant giving them a ticket to the Municipal Lodging House and, more frequently than not, a railroad ticket next day that took them out of New York. His second and daytime job consisted chiefly of investigating the cases of applicants for more extensive aid—checking addresses, employment records, character, and then assigning such aid or providing such employment as was possible, or declining both. A modest expense allowance was available to him, and he charged streetcar fares against it, but, by his own account, he always walked, even if his destination was as far away as Brooklyn. "I managed on some days to add as much as thirty beautiful, beautiful cents to my income, and on those days, I had lunch."

He was able to write a little in the evenings, but his total sales since he had left Waterloo brought him only seven dollars and fifty cents until, in December, the miraculous befell him when *Red Book Magazine* bought his story "They That Take the Sword" for seventy-five dollars, minus Miss Holly's ten per cent. A story about railroad men and hoboes that rests on a mechanical reversal of situation and a no less mechanical conversion from evil to good in the central character, it is of interest only because, except for his college effort "A Theory of Values," it is the first of Lewis's stories to attempt to capture the speech of ordinary and even low characters. It is of importance only because it helped to free him from the Charity Organization.

Almost simultaneously with the sale of this story, a telegram from Grace MacGowan Cooke in Carmel, California, invited him to come there as a part-time secretary to the literary ladies, who would send him his railroad fare. All along, he had been thinking of the novel about a modern, radical Christ, *Ecce Homo,* on which they had planned to collaborate. The charity office, grim as it was, had become a probable part of that novel.

> In a better frame of mind, one simply realizes that while the charity here can't do much yet it is doing all that can be expected.
>
> In any case, a lesser man than the Homo must be subjectively injured by his work here. He may come to assume a pedagogical frame of mind, a dinky tin pedestal from which he looks in scorn or pity or impatience or all together on the ignorant and improvident and unfortunate. Like the pedagogue's egoism, his conclusion, from comparison ever with undeveloped minds, that he himself is far wiser than the average; comes the egoism of the little man behind the desk from his position of advising and governing so many. Or he may become cruel, from weariness or from opportunity; or facily sarcastic; or his heart may come to be torn, from sympathy with all these people whom he can help so little, that he becomes melancholy or, by reaction, misanthropic—if he is sensitive. . . .
>
> The Homo might leave his Charities work because he sees that the best worker is one with more mechanical and unimaginative calmness than himself. He would grow too impatient of a state of society which would let its members so suffer, unnecessarily. He would not fear becoming pedagogical; but, being a LEADER, would object to subjecting himself to an unimaginative machine for the relieving of distress, even while admitting that this machine does the work as well as anything that can now be devised.

The *Red Book* sale persuaded him that he could live by the pen; the invitation to Carmel would give him a minimum of work, a good deal of free time, the opportunity to pursue a collaboration on *Ecce Homo,* and ideal physical circumstances, quite opposite from those that prevailed in the gaunt offices of the Application Bureau. It took him, he said, ten hours to decide, resign, pack his few clothes and his copious notes (he had accumulated a considerable sheaf on his charity work alone, chiefly observations on the vagabonds and drifters who came into the place for aid), and, just a day or two before the end of the year, put himself on a train for San Francisco. He had been in New York only a few weeks longer than he had been in Waterloo, and now again he was off to elsewhere. For five days he sat up as he crossed the country to San Francisco and then down to Monterey, "dining on fruit and bread from a pasteboard box all the way, with coffee at station lunch-rooms." He hiked the five miles to Carmel-by-the-Sea, and on January 5, 1909, Grace MacGowan Cooke noted in her diary that "Hal walked in at lunch time." *

Sixty years ago the community of Carmel bore no resemblance whatever to the community of today. Indeed, there was no community. There was

* An unpublished record in possession of Mrs. Cooke's daughter Katherine Cooke Ryan, through whose courtesy it was made available to the present writer.

only the old Mission San Carlos Borromeo, and then, where the fragile clutter of Carmel crowds up and away from the sea today, only the clusters of weirdly gnarled cypresses and the great stands of Monterey pines, the white sand, the indigo sea or, sometimes, in Jack London's words, "the amazing peacock blue" and a mile-long sweep of breaker across the breadth of the bay. After this most beautiful of United States coast lines was discovered by Mary Austin, the San Francisco poet George Sterling built a house there in 1905, and under Sterling's guidance and by his suggestion, other artistic spirits in pursuit of the free and inexpensive life arrived, other redwood cottages went up in random fashion under the pines, upward on the slopes that rise gently from the sea. Michael and Peggy Williams came, and, at their urging, the Cooke ladies with the young daughters, now aged fourteen and seven. There were others, writers and painters, who settled, until the community grew to fifty, and there were still others who came and went as visitors—Anna Strunksy, Jack London, Mary Austin, James Hopper, Arnold Genthe, Harry Leon Wilson. Ambrose Bierce came only once and, declaring that he had found the colony "a nest of anarchists," vowed never to return.

There had been many experiments in communal living in the United States during the past hundred years, but there had not really been any Bohemias of quite the sort that was now beginning in Carmel. Here life was as free as it was easy, and the colonists were determined to keep it that way. On the theory that conveniences are in fact encumbrances, conveniences were to be eschewed. Instead of gas or electricity, the Carmelites would use kerosene lamps or candles. The roads and paths that led through the woods must remain unpaved, and sidewalks were unnecessary. Shops, hotels, restaurants, markets were likewise unnecessary; Monterey had a number of each, and one person could walk there or ride over on a horse or accept the kindness of the single lady who owned an automobile and bring back groceries for many; tradespeople made routine calls on the colony and found orders for supplies and the money to pay for the orders in small wooden stands erected here and there. Communications were made simple by a bulletin board placed before the post office and covered with all manner of messages. Food was simple at best and was eaten chiefly out of doors, beside wood fires. Life was, wasn't it, a picnic?

Almost immediately upon arriving at Carmel, Sinclair Lewis received his first invitation to dine. The invitation, a multigraphed sheet, gives one a quick and clear impression of this Bohemia on the coast of Carmel:

PROGRAMME

Moonlight Picnice (if Luna will kindly oblige), and Camp Fire; Given by Peggy and Mike Williams and Kid MacNichol to the Carmel Bunch, at Smugglers' Cove, Carmel, 7 January, 1909, in order to Celebrate the Opening of the Word Factory of Williams and MacNichol, Perambulating Pen

and Pencil Pushers—"Any Old Literary Thing Tinkered While You Wait"—
if you don't mind waiting!—Oyez, Oyez, Oyez! Whoop-e-e!

SPIRIT OF BOHEMIA (speaks)

(From George Sterling's "The Triumph of Bohemia.")

My worship is a happy one, and hath
Large recompense; and in my temple soon
There shall be gracious spirits that attend
In beauty and in strength . . . O Fire! Come forth!"

* * * * *

The Picnice

All the afternoon. ENJOY yourselves. Everybody keep their razors in their inside pockets—Enjoy YOURSELVES! Walk—read—chat—and loafe.

There follows then the promise of the Mulligan stew with wine and, afterward, "songs, stories, speeches, toasts" around the campfire.

An extended, if fictionalized, account of life in the Carmel colony at this time is to be found in Chapters 6 through 10 of Book Three in Jack London's *The Valley of the Moon.* If London, grinding his own programmatic ax, made the colony sound more like a convention of muscle men than like the assemblage of potboiling dilettantes that it in fact was, he nevertheless included a reasonably accurate record of George Sterling's famous abalone feasts. Sterling had discovered the domestic uses of the abalone and it became the standard culinary fare in the colony. Easily come by among the rocks at the shore, easily prepared and served out of doors, the humble abalone also became the subject of the community poem, "The Abalone Song." All the colonists ate abalone, but Sterling's feasts were noted in California, and the climax to these occasions was the group singing of the song. While Sterling is generally regarded as its author and while he was indeed its inceptor, the poem is a genuinely communal composition. To the basic stanzas by Sterling, others would add stanzas of their own, and if they were satisfactory to the first author and the company, they were assimilated by the poem. William Rose Benét says that "Sinclair Lewis added several stanzas to the original song, one of which runs:

He wanders free beside the sea
Where every crab's a crony
He flaps his wings and madly sings,
The plaintive abalone."

Sinclair Lewis himself remembered Sterling singing another song:

The best night of my six months in Arcady was when in a carryall—yes, with a fringed top—a dozen of us drove miles down the coast and, in the light of a vast bonfire shining out on tides that came straight from China, George Sterling, looking a little like Dante and a good deal like François

Villon, challenged the ocean roar by singing Kipling's "The Last Chantey," and then we all slept on the cliff, among the poppies.

It was a loafing, individualistic, and argumentative life. George Sterling had erected a stone altar to the gods before his house, and Mary Austin wrote in a tree. A few people really did some work. Lewis said, "My job as secretary left me adequate leisure and I kept on writing," and while one has no reason to question him as to his writing, one must wonder whether he performed at all as a secretary. Fred Bechdolt, reminiscing in the Carmel *Pine Cone,* remembered him as "a shabby young enthusiast, whose only claims on fame at the time were an unpredictable disposition, much red hair, and a great many freckles," and he said of Mrs. Cooke, "Among the most lasting of the memories which she left behind her are a gentle voice and gentle ways, and a great patience." Her expectations of Hal Lewis were transformed into a considerable trial of that patience. She found him a little furnished cottage near her house for fifteen dollars a month and waited. Between January 18 and January 23, she wrote in her very sketchy diary,

> Spent in trying Miss Scannell, who proved rather spectacularly incompetent. Alice bought an Underwood at $45.00 for Hal's use. I had supposed that we might get him to do some typing when this second girl proved impossible, but so far he has not come to time with anything.

On January 24 she wrote, "Sent Miss S. away. Hal gone riding to Monterey. . . . Hal still has company at his place and offers no assistance."

The company was William Rose Benét, who had come down to Carmel from Benicia to seek him out. Benét's best friend, Henry Hoyt, had written from New York to say that Lewis, "a great fellow," was out there, and that they must know each other.* Benét remembered:

> He plucked his suitcase off
> the buckboard floor   and looked into the blue
> of piercing eyes   his hand was seized and jerked
> in a nervous grip
> "Welcome to yellow sands!
> Note palatial dwelling!   Us we'll do our own laundry! . . .
> Aint got no liquor   but not so far from here
> Starr Gorham   the great California pote
> has lots of muscadel   and say   can he
> pulverize an abalone!
> Like abalone?"
> And all at once   in a transfixing yowl
> Larry emitted
> "Suh-uh-uh-um
> live on hope and some on dope

* Benét left two recollections of their friendship at Carmel, one in his article called "The Earlier Lewis," the other in his poeticized autobiography called *The Dust Which Is God,* where Harry Lewis appears as Larry Harris.

and some on al-imony—
but our Gib-cat
he likes a fat
and toothsome ab-alone!"

After Lewis cooked their meat ball supper, they tramped the shore and debated on the subject of "that great blind power that moves this world." Larry Harris shouted,

"By God I'll get this world
where I want it before I die they can't down *me*
they've tried it they've got bitten for their pains!"

And they went on then—all through that night, Benét said in his factual reminiscence—arguing about socialism and Christianity.

Benét stayed and shared Lewis's cottage. They cooked, laundered, swept, scrubbed, tramped, swam, argued, and wrote, and Lewis, at least, lived largely on the bounty of Grace MacGowan Cooke, borrowing money when necessary (for a long time his books carry a debit to her of one hundred and fifty-five dollars that he only slowly whittled down to nothing after he departed), while the plans for *Ecce Homo* faded and secretarial assistance remained a hypothesis.

. . . . . rationed their cigarettes
burned flapjacks wolfed mush and bacon wandered over
the cosmos in their eager speculation
moaned and groaned at writing discussed their friends
endlessly cherished the hope that this was love
when some new girl appeared pondered the world
and how to win its huge and stone-deaf ear . . .

To Lewis's literary efforts, the world's ear was indeed deaf during the Carmel period. He said later that in this time he sold exactly one item, a joke, and in one place said that the sale was made to *Puck,* in another, to *Judge*. One may wonder whether it was made to either or to any periodical, since the manuscript account sheets, scrupulously kept, show no such sale. He worked chiefly at short fiction, but without success. Benét remembered that he was writing short stories under the influence of Edith Wharton, "whose work he intensely admired." This influence is not to be detected in the fiction that he had thus far published or that, for some time, he was to publish, and yet it is conceivable that in the present period he tried to emulate her chiseled manner. "He worked for months on a single short story," Lewis himself recalled in 1932, "—never sold!—repolishing every syllable." This was, presumably, the story referred to elsewhere as "Citizen of the Mirage." *

* So Sinclair Lewis named it in "I'm an Old Newspaper Man Myself" (1947); but a story under this title appeared in *Red Book* for May 1921. Whether he merely used the title or whether he had kept the original work for over ten years and then re-

He did, as a matter of fact, sell one story during this period—one of several he never mentioned in his later recollections, and quite understandably. While the story was not to be published until August of 1909, and while he was almost certainly not paid his fifteen dollars until its publication, the sale was accomplished in February through the offices of Mrs. Cooke. Called "The Smile Lady," it appeared in *Nautilus,* a magazine of New Thought edited by Elizabeth and William E. Towne. The editorial notes in the August issue described the Townes' visit to Mrs. Cooke in Carmel early in the year.

> Arrangements had been made for us to sleep at the cottage of Sinclair Lewis . . . a young man six feet tall, slender and very much in earnest, [who] keeps bachelor's hall with the aid of another bright young college man who is also making literature his profession. The boys had quite a time hunting for clean sheets and the other accessories which they thought necessary to our entertainment.

It was not a real kindness to Sinclair Lewis to return his hospitality by publishing "The Smile Lady." This fictional proposal that a happy optimism does indeed pay has as its heroine a cheerful-looking girl who, weary as she may be from standing all day as a clerk at the perfume counter of Wanamacy's (a name that Lewis was to use over and over again, as he was to use certain other words of his invention, notably Hobohemia), still can smile and smile. News has just come that her husband has lost the house he had been purchasing for them in the West because he could not meet the last payment to the owner, an old but now demonstrably perfidious friend. At lunch, the Smile Lady smiles nevertheless, and by her smile causes two strangers to become friends, a lawyer to decide to receipt the last unpaid bill of an old friend, a girl to resist temptation, and a young man to tell the truth. She has been reading an article on a great philanthropist, and wishes that *she* could do something for others. All unknown to her, she *has*—even to the extent of influencing a lawyer to reverse a decision to foreclose a mortgage on the property of her own dear Jim, who had been unable to meet his last payment!

The publication of this story led to a further arrangement with the editors of *Nautilus* whereby Sinclair Lewis was to write a much longer work for them, and the bulk if not all of this story, an eight-part serial, was written in Carmel. Of other writing he left no record beyond the usual notes, now chiefly concerned with the natural beauties of the sunsets and the mountains and of the way that the hills fold into one another, and these notes then arranged under a kind of index, as if he might want quickly to

furbished it is not to be determined. In basic situation, the story of 1921 is like the fanciful stuff that Lewis was chiefly turning out in 1908–1912, but unlike it in the fullness of its development. It bears no resemblance to the stories of Edith Wharton. Later evidence suggests that at about this time he first conceived the novel *Our Mr. Wrenn* and began to write it under, remarkably enough, the influence of Henry James.

refresh himself on "Carmel Sunsets," for example, for a particular project. There are notes, too, on a "Typical Day," in which he visits the various members of the group and carefully records what each is eating. His notes say nothing of his collaborative efforts or of his employment.

Katherine Cooke, the younger of the two girls, remembered Benét at this time as "gentle, retiring; Sinclair Lewis as fresh, gifted, pimpled, and generally disliked." Lewis shone in amateur theatricals, which were frequent, and which were to lead to the formation of the Forest Theatre in 1910, and Lewis, with pillow stuffed into his lean front, masqueraded as a Dutch woman for a market fair that was organized as a community benefit. Both Benét and Lewis, Katherine Cooke thinks, were in love with her sister. In his remembrance of Lewis at Carmel, Arnold Genthe, fifteen years Lewis's senior, did not deny that he himself was.

> . . . a tall, gangling young man. . . . He had a head of unmanageable red hair and a freckled face and a pair of remarkable blue eyes, the pupils of which darted with light. He and I would often walk together through the woods, indulging in philosophical discussions, sometimes lapsing into German, while we both knew that, more than with philosophical problems, our thoughts were concerned with the lovely Helen Cooke to whom we were both devoted.

Benét recalled Lewis's infatuation with her, and her annoyance when Lewis publicly chanted a song that he had written for her, "The Fugitive Queen." Fugitive from him she still was and was presently to vanish entirely into that dream troupe of girls over whom, one by one, he had ineffectually yearned during the past ten years. Katherine Cooke says that the end of his stay in Carmel came when he made a remark about Helen in German that he thought Mrs. Cooke would not understand. Mrs. Cooke herself noted merely, "Hal proved impossible, went his way."

He would have had to go under any circumstances, for he was in debt and had no money with which to stay on in even so simple a life as this. Later he was to say that he regretted having to give up, after only six months, what was "probably the most sensible time of my life." If he was not sensible in working out his economic arrangement with Mrs. Cooke, the fact is that she was yet to find him of use. In March 1911, when she was in trouble with her sister and in difficulty with her own work, she wrote in her diary, "I cannot turn my Pegasus midway the course. If Hal were here. If Carrie [Sterling] was where I could get at her. If any of the Carmel bunch was available for mere consultation and shaping up. But for one reason and another none of them is." And then, in May of that year, "I have six chapters of In A Desert City done, roughly . . . good stuff, I think. . . . Fine letter from Hal. He will read it for me."

That was after he had harnessed himself to routines in New York again. In the meantime, there was more drifting. When they left Carmel, Benét took Lewis home with him to Benicia. It was a very small, nearly a forgotten community on a point of land jutting into Carquinez Strait southeast of Vallejo, suspended between a lost dream in its past of becoming the metropolis of San Francisco Bay and a military boom in the distant future. Its most important establishment was a small Army base and arsenal, instituted in 1849 and dominated by a sandstone edifice with a square clock tower—a social as well as a military center—that suggests still the early life of California towns. Of the small presidio, Colonel James Walker Benét was commanding officer, and he lived a charming life in a Victorian house on the post with his wife and children—the daughter, Laura, the younger son, Steve, or Tibby (who habitually defeated Lewis at tennis), and, when he was at home, the older, Bill. Leonard Bacon, in *Semi-Centennial,* remembered the place and the family as they were at this time:

> It was not like an arsenal. It was like the back-drop of a romantic play, all pepper trees and acacias, and fountains, and pillared porches. Merely to enjoy the hospitality of that family in such a place was more than one deserved, and to know the Colonel, for a man of my tastes, was like a delightful electric shock. The Colonel was a fine soldier, amused at the fact that he commanded forty-five men. But eight years later he ruled forty-five thousand as easily and well. And he differed in one respect from all other soldiers. He knew more about English poetry than most poets and all professors, and he had the Elizabethan lyrics by heart. . . . It was a sight to see him in his white uniform, a mint julep in each hand, as he waited on the leafy porch. . . . And then the talk with him over the cool drink about "Death's Jest Book," and "The Hound of Heaven," or "Farewell, Rewards and Fairies." . . . That place was heaven.

It was June. Laura Benét came down from the Sierra with the ten-year-old Stephen Vincent, and when they arrived Lewis was there, "long and tall and gay," enjoying an easy and familiar rapport with the officers' wives, a part of the family, and liked especially by the Colonel, "a reading man." Both his son and his daughter recalled the endless disputations between Lewis and the older man, long and heated debates on every conceivable subject, an incessant friendly wrangling, with each firm in his opinions, each absolutely outspoken and direct. Lewis was finishing up his twenty-two-thousand-word story for *Nautilus*—the longest work he had yet written—and was, with what degree of seriousness who is to say, necessarily involved in that conglomeration of uplift, mesmerism, and money-making through magnetism that was New Thought, and this topic would come into their arguments. Laura Benét remembers her father telling him that for the whole mess of claptrap, he should substitute the single Browningesque couplet,

> Do the things you cannot do
> So your soul shall grow.

At the other extreme from New Thought, Lewis's interest in aeronautics was stimulated by his meeting with Captain Paul Beck, one of the first Army aviators in the United States, who was to prove of use to him a number of years later. It was here, too, that he first met Kathleen Norris, then a young San Francisco journalist whose name was Thompson. She remembered him as redheaded, of course, and "wild" but likable, deeply involved in the sense of his own destiny, impelled by his sense of his future when he was not more than twenty. He was, in fact, twenty-four.

This summer idyl had to come to an end, and in mid-August young Stephen wrote to his mother, who was away:

> I am having a fine time here. I play tennis every day with Laura. Mrs. Platt, Laura, Billy, Miss Wedgeworth and I went in swimming yesterday. I did not stay in long because of the coldness of the water. Mr. Lewis has gone to the city to get a job. I now have 850 stamps and about 1200 duplicates. Prince has something the matter with his ear & is unhappy at present. My poem which I sent to the Competition got in too late and so did not qualify.

And on August 18, Mr. Lewis wrote back to Benicia:

> *Dear Billy:*
> Already have a room—at 1525 Scott Street (Fifteen Twenty Five). Please send on my mail and, when (really) convenient the box of books—either C.O.D. or paying & letting-me-know-how-much.

To this "shabby semi-genteel private house" Lewis urged his friend to come as often as he could "tho the bed is not *too* big."

He interviewed the editors of a variety of San Francisco newspapers and waited out a month before he was finally employed. Benét came to San Francisco and on at least one weekend Lewis went back to Benicia. It was a demoralizing month. He wrote his friend:

> Read Balzac all yest[erday], except when I wandered out to Golden Gate park; at whose entrance I sat on the porch of a semi-rustic-house-in-the-city, drank beer & listened to the beach leaves a-flutter around me ever the beach leaves old & I wander forth to the infinite beat of—
>
> Getting nutty again. I have powers of becoming that same which even you have not yet entirely fathomed. As proof, I enclose shreds of a letter I wrote you last night. . . .
>
> Let me know if you'll be down Fri. or Sat., (or Thurs.); where & when shall I meet you? Ferry house or here at house, or where. Us for Sanguinetti's eh?

On September 9 his father wrote accurately enough, if not very helpfully, "I had hoped you would find something to do before this as loafing is not good in any way." It was, finally, through the efforts of George Sterling that Lewis found employment. Sterling wrote about Lewis to Joseph Noel, who was on the copy desk of the *Evening Bulletin,* Fremont Older's newspaper, and who presented Lewis's case to the city editor. There were no openings in San Francisco, but when Noel requested that he be shifted to the Alameda County office his copy desk place fell vacant and Lewis fell into it. In his 1947 recollection called "You Get Around So Much," Lewis wrote colorfully of his experience, but as usual, inaccurately. He was employed at thirty dollars a week, beginning on September 20 and continuing until November 27, when he was discharged.

His work, according to the evidence of his letters to Benét, consisted chiefly of rewriting ("Stories & the headlines by me; facts of the stories 'gathered by lower priced men' Oh hit me!"). The news accounts that he saved are human-interest stories with headings like " 'Irish Chink' Frightens Off a Burglar and Saves a Block" and "Transport's Mate Tries to Shoot His Wife." He wrote occasional theatrical and book reviews, and twice he had a by-line, one for a piece of fictionalized humor called "Talks with a Typist" and the other for a poem, written on the occasion of the annual Portola Festival, called "The Masque of Gaspar's Passing." In his own account, Lewis wrote that he was on the "hotel beat" and that he frequently enjoyed a free lunch at one hotel by giving the establishment special notice, and he wrote at length of a hoax about a fictitious bellhop that the hotel manager and he perpetrated on the newspaper. (A search of the newspaper in the months of Lewis's employment reveals no such story or stories as he described.) He attended a Press Club reception where he "met Lord Northcliffe—Alfred Harmsworth—the 'Hearst of England,' " and where he met, as well, the "acting manager of the A.P. . . . May be something doing at *their* shop some day." There was—from December 1, 1909, to February 18, 1910, at twenty-five dollars a week.

His failure is not hard to understand. He began enthusiastically ("Bit large ecstatic chunks outa the job today") but soon wearied of it. Again, to Benét, he wrote: "Gee! This newspaper work is plumb hard. Working most every evening—long hours & no chance to write at stories," and later he was to write his father about the exhaustion to his nervous system that newspaper work involved. He had, curiously, no sharp news sense, and his human-interest stories are rather heavily flippant. He professed in 1947 not to remember the *Bulletin's* position in municipal affairs, and this again is curious, since the *Bulletin* was currently waging a vigorous campaign against corruption in local politics that, one might assume, would have particularly interested Sinclair Lewis. He seems, indeed, to have been politically apathetic except for his theoretical interest in socialism. He attributed his discharge to the specific occasion when he turned in a story about a Telegraph Hill "wine hole" which the editor found pretentiously literary and without any value as news. Never to become associated with the "saloon school" that became so prevalent in later American writing,

Lewis was, in Frank Norris's San Francisco, following in his tradition of slum research.

The recollection to which he attributed his discharge may be accurate, since his research resulted in such a story which does exist in the typescript form that the editor presumably read, as well as in its preliminary form of notes. The notes begin as a letter to Updegraff:

> Wondered what sort of place Frisco is? Quiet, leisurely, ill-built in the un-fire touched section. Going to be handsome.
>
> Tonight I saw some of the whore-house district—from the outside, & amateurishly.—An enormously long dance hall, Thalia[,] with a free vaudeville program; a search-spot-calcium light flashing from the rear thru a dusky 100 feet to fall on the twinkling legs of a soubrette. Orchestra of 10–12 pieces, but cracked plaster on the wall behind the stage. Then the lit[e]s turned on for dancing by the great crowd of muckers, soldiers sailors etc. with whores, who couldn't pass beyond the bar by the rail. Announcers & waiters w[ith] eye shades. Whores leaning over the rail coaxing me "Oh you Ginger—long—thin." Free balcony w[ith] drinks. Long line of gallery booths one side. . . . Reg[ular] vaudeville program.———Another dance hall with small stage; whores leaning over swinging gates only.———

And then, embarking upon his account of a visit to a wine shop, he abandons the letter as he transforms it into a record for his own use even as he seems still to be addressing Updegraff.

> Billy (Benét) & I went again, evening of Sept. 2. Old coat, sweater jacket & Point Pleasant tie & khaki shirt for me—talcum powder on the immaculate —indecently so—polish of my shoes. (Sounds foolish; but makes a good dustiness). For Billy, a soft shirt—but he still looked fearfully respectable. Hat tilted a bit to one side helped that.

The typescript, called "Wrecks of Romance," is about two thousand words long. It opens:

> On a rocky promontory jutting from the "Barbary Coast" is a little dive, the resort of "wine bums;" of hoboes, and of criminals now too "rum dumm" to be formidable. Yet if Robert Louis Stevenson could have seen it, in the days when he alternately shivered and starved here, he would with small effort have found it marvelous, viewing it through his crimson spectacles of romance.
>
> For these ragged men have known strange seas and high adventure. They have known the excitement of fleeing the revenue cutters in sealing waters, and have consorted with maidens of golden-tinted skins on marooners' isies.

Then follows the contrasting catalogue of their present squalor, their lies, their songs, their broken brutality. With every scrap of his notes economically salvaged and amplified, he achieved what might have passed as a competent college essay, and it provided as good occasion as any for the inevitable severance pay check at the *Evening Bulletin.*

He went to the Associated Press as wire editor on the night desk. His father, writing on December 4, 1909, was not pleased:

> Your letter received yesterday was quite a surprise party. I am not sure of the wisdom of your move. It is very seldom that there is any chance to get up in working for the A.P. Alex [Gates, of Chicago] has been working faithfully for years and yet he only gets a nominal sum and there your work is entirely office work which is bad for in the tobacco laden air of an A.P. room it certainly is not a health giver. In your other work you were out in fresh air much more. So I can not see that chances are quite as good as when you were taking all into consideration, and you have practically no chance to make acquaintances or gather any material. It is just a job every day alike and you will soon get into a rut & stay there. It is about the same as a stenographers place. Every day just the same old stunt.

The father, one might suppose, would by this time have known his son better than to fear that he would settle stolidly into a dull routine. Routine it was, to be sure; indeed, some friendly fellow worker typed out Lewis's instructions under the heading, "ROUTINE." Concerned largely with the technicalities of filing wires, this document concludes as follows:

> Don't swear at janitress as is likely to hit you with broom; is very mean lady.
>
> At five o'clock retire, stealing overcoat—you will have none of your own or you wouldn't be doing early A.P.

Routine it may have been, but at least one set of news stories that came over his wire galvanized his attention and probably organized for the first time his old interest in aviation. In the second week of January 1910, the first aviation meet in the United States was held in Los Angeles, and nearly twenty years later, Lewis remembered that, "in charge of the 'early service' (that between one thirty and five in the morning) [he] had to handle the glowing reports of Curtiss's and Paulhan's achievements as they came rattling from the telegraph instrument."

> Outside—all silent, with dawn hinted in the skies; a solitary policeman wandering up gray Market Street. Within the great brilliantly lighted rooms of the Associated Press, a feeling of being in touch, telepathetically as well as telegraphically, with all the world; not forgetting the aviation camp down at Los Angeles.

The event was to lead him to three different attempts to write about aviation in fiction, yet as far as the Associated Press was concerned, he was, he said, "incompetent," and when his immediate superior, Karl Von Wiegand, told him that the superintendent of the bureau intended to dismiss him, Lewis quickly resigned. He had held the *Bulletin* position for only two months and one week; the Associated Press position was, from the point of view of tenure, an improvement: he held it one week longer.

He was adrift again. At the end of February, his assets totaled eighty-two dollars and seventy-four cents. He had managed in the preceding two months to reduce his debt to the Cookes from one hundred and fifty-five dollars to fifty-five dollars. He had lived with great frugality, as his minutely detailed expense accounts show. Sometimes he spent as little as fifty-five cents a day, and the record would read, "Grub .45 Fare .05 Candy 5." The item "Booze" appears fairly regularly and ranges from five cents to as much as fifty. November 8, 1909, is characteristic of his budget: "Short changed .05 Grub .75 Fare .05 Tobac[co] .20 B[ulle]t[in] acc[ount] .15 Candy 05 M[oving] pict[ure] .05." Certain rare extravagances he permitted himself: a Fritz Kreisler concert, a Schumann-Heink recital, the rental of evening clothes for one unknown occasion, a pair of pumps at four dollars, books ("for self & Xmas") at fifteen dollars and fifteen cents.

He knew a few young women in a casual way that would not have required him to lavish entertainment upon them. Among these was Gene Baker (later Gene McComas, the Monterey painter), daughter of the editor of the Oakland *Tribune,* and with her Lewis was to conduct a lifelong, if intermittent, correspondence. In *The Dust Which Is God,* William Rose Benét tells of an evening with Larry Harris when they heard a speech by a labor organizer whom Benét calls Steve Manton (this would seem to have been Tom Mooney) and after which they met Nora Rafferty, who later in the poem becomes the hero's wife. Nora Rafferty's prototype was Miss Theresa Thompson, sister of Kathleen Norris, and on October 13 Lewis wrote in the postscript of a letter to Benét, "Am taking Miss Theresa to the 2nd night of the Passion Play, 's even." For such entertainment, the newspaper provided passes.

The possibility that Lewis heard Mooney in 1909 is an interesting link with his efforts on Mooney's behalf many years later. He developed in San Francisco a practical literary interest in labor organization and, for the purposes of a projected novel, attended a number of meetings of the San Francisco Labor Council. His continued theoretical interest in socialism is indicated by some of the names on a list he wrote inside the back cover of his copy of George Moore's *Evelyn Innes:* "Eliste Reclus, Bakounine, Proudhon, Feuerbach, Max Steiner, G. Etiévant, Jean Grave, Kropotkin, Laurent Tailhade." (The voice of that older Lewis who would have lost interest in socialism may be heard in an annotation to Moore's description of the Mona Lisa smile as "hesitating," where Lewis wrote, "It's not. It's a smug smile. It's a myth. It's a grubby smile.") His socialism was probably given some stimulus by Jack London, who in July of 1909 had returned to California after two years of cruising in the Pacific. Later correspondence suggests that Lewis visited the Londons at Glen Ellen, their establishment in Sonoma.* His most frequent excursions, however, were into the nonpolitical atmosphere of Benicia.

Five years later, in his second novel, *The Trail of the Hawk,* Lewis sends his hero, Carl Ericson, for whom Lewis himself was in some ways the prototype, to an Army post that duplicates the Benicia presidio:

> ... when Colonel Haviland met them at San Spirito station, and Carl heard the kindly salutation ... he knew that he had at last come home to his own people—an impression that was the stronger because the house of Oscar Ericson [Carl's father] had been so much house and so little home.

The gracious way of life at Benicia had its antithesis in Sauk Centre and in Dr. Lewis's persistent concern with money. In December of 1909 he wrote his son:

> I just got a check for 636.00 interest money on some of the mortgages I have and when one gets it you feel just as though you had picked it up some place. Like Cascarets "it works while you sleep," and it's an awfully comfortable thing to have a few thousand in good first class mortgage that is bringing one in 6%. It is not much trouble to get more after you get the first thousand placed as then it begins working for you.

Two weeks later he supplied his son with the identical information and even repeated his poor joke. Early in 1910 he asked, "What are you doing with your savings?" He advises a twenty-payment life insurance policy (like Claude's). "I think by smoking a cigar or two less you could carry 5000. It makes a good 6% investment." He concludes with a discussion of his own financial success in which he says that for the past twenty-five years he has made a net profit of one thousand dollars a year. "So I have no reason to kick on my pill peddling at S.C." Such complacency was hardly calculated to help the twenty-five-year-old son forget the precariousness of his own economic situation as, one can well believe, the life at Benicia could.

To enjoy the affection of a whole family was an unusual experience in the life of Sinclair Lewis, and to find in that family a kind of ideal father would prove to have been an unforgettable experience for the hungry young man. In 1928, when the aged Colonel died, Lewis wrote to his friend William Rose Benét:

> Whatever one may write is so blundering, & I can say only that I authentically loved him—not only for his wit, his learning, his immense kindness to me when I was a youngster & broke (that kindness in which you all shared), & the high standard of honor which he carried so unyieldingly, but most of all for an almost undefinable gracefulness & graciousness & ease

* "My best regards to Mrs. London, and to Unterman if he is still at Glen Ellen." (October 16, 1910)

which has always instructed me, which very much still does, instruct me, that even when mankind seem heavy and commonplace, they can, a few of them, be as beautifully fine as he was. So little I've seen of him, the last twelve years, yet he remains with me more than people I've seen hundreds of times. He does live!

That the Benéts were fond of him is evident from the introduction Lewis wrote for the little booklet of his poems that he typed out and bound with ribbon in a soft-leather cover as their Christmas present in 1909.*

AND LO! IT CAME TO PASS:
It was two when I came home from the Associated Press, *this* Christmas morning; a bit tired from my night's work, but making little of that because I intended to be up at six and catch the seven o'clock train for Benicia, and wish the Benéts a MERRY CHRISTMAS before getting back to work.... And there was a great box waiting for me, and in i[t] the most incredible number of charming things from the Benéts; and I was divided between a great joy in being so richly remembered; and a shame in *seeming* not to remember them better. I'd sent a bloomink pipe to Billy, and that was all. You absolutely wonderful Benéts, how could a newspaperman, used only to his rough sort, whose Christmas gifts are a "Well, how are you! Merry Christmas, old man. Cummon in and I'll buy you a Tom and Jerry. I ain't no tight wad; goin' to make you a Christmas present of that Tom and Jerry. (And then you can recip.)"—how could he . . . ever anticipate such LOTS OF presents.

So there I was. And quoth I, I'll make 'em a book of some of my poems, a book for all of them, the DEARS....

The letter rambles on and on, and at last a variety of verses follow, most of them already published in periodicals. Some of Benét's verse had been finding its way into print, but for more than a year, Lewis had sold none. His single publication since "The Smile Lady" had been in prose, the eight-part serial called *The City Shadow* which was, at the end of 1909 and the beginning of 1910, appearing in *Nautilus*. For this work he had been paid two hundred and twenty-four dollars. It is hard to know whether Lewis wrote out of at least some slight conviction about New Thought or merely for the money. In 1908 he had not been above satirizing this cult of love and success ("I was writing on the New Thot Movement for Puck," he said in his last diary), and yet there were elements in New Thought that would have appealed to his wavering nature ("it exalted the aggressive American spirit on one day and taught ways of escape on another," wrote Gilbert Seldes) and promised remedies for the exact causes of his own suffering—"awkwardness, and lack of confidence, fear, and thwarted

* An account of this and of a similar document prepared for William Rose Benét in the following year may be found in Donald Gallup's "Two Early Manuscripts of Sinclair Lewis" (Yale *Library Gazette,* July 1954).

ambitions, and frustrated lives." A doctrine of unlimited optimism, it preached the reality of universal love and brotherhood, yet it proposed no discipline and no institutional strictures.

> It loved Jesus and Buddha, Tolstoi, and Nietzsche, liberalism and socialism and anarchism, Unitarianism and Ethical Culture and the wisdom of the East, free love and monogamy, wealth and ascetic virtue. It was scientific and poetic and adored nature and exalted man. It was pacifist and admired successful brutality. It was precious and went in for simplicity. It was soft.

A harsh critic of the young uncentered writer could change the impersonal pronoun to *he* in this description by Gilbert Seldes and, with some justice, make its every term apply to Lewis. Whatever his real attitude, the editors of *Nautilus* did not question his sincerity.

> If our new serial is studied, in it will be seen the occult signification . . . as the characters follow the lines of the circle; rising to the top in their love, then on the down curve of the circle as difficulties beset them; then finally rising again with their subconscious mind-entities trained, and circumstances yielding to their conquest.

The story is plain, if feeble, propaganda purveyed through totally unrealized characters; its only possible virtue is a faint evocation of the brutality of city life. Young Ralph Pierson comes to New York from a country town. As a nonsmoker, nondrinker, and vegetarian, he is already on the way to illumination but is still unaware of the deeper complexities of Thought. He falls in love with a nurse, Katherine Brownell, who lives across the areaway from him, and they are married. Together, partly by intuition, partly by exposure to New Thought literature and speakers, they work out the complexities. She revolts against the doctor who employs her and, losing her status as nurse, practices controlled breathing and determined optimism. He loses his job (at Wanamacy's, of course) and falls into depression, but her Thought strengthens him and they win through. They convert an old Irish landlady and in the end, because of Thought, Ralph is made the triumphant manager of a branch of another store in which he had once clerked. And they have a little baby to climax (and begin again) the evolutionary spiral that they have ascended.

Lewis's parents are his only recorded critics of this work. His mother wrote, "I cannot say that I feel proud of your story in The Nautilus & surely do not call peoples attention to it." His father wrote, "The sentiment of the magazine is decidedly bum but it is all right when they pay you good money. They are evidently quite bright people but evidently neurotics chasing off a new or old track"; and again, with finality, "That Nautilus is certainly the greatest amount of dish-water in one package that I have seen for a long time."

His long experience of the harsh absence of sympathy in his parents was the motive behind an ambitious work that Lewis was at this time planning. Called first *The Fathers,* then *Fathers and Sons,* and finally *The Children's Children,* it was to be a novelette of thirty thousand to fifty thousand words. The first notes for it—and they provide a summary of the initial conception—are written in the back of the second volume of his copy of Balzac's *Illusions Perdues.* Whether or not this novel about a beastly father's relationship to his son set in motion Lewis's ideas for *The Children's Children,* there is nevertheless a rather nice irony in the juxtaposition of the Balzac title and what was to be the theme of the Lewis novel—the resolve, in every father, to be more sympathetic to his son's ambitions than his father had been, and the repeated failure of the resolve. The first notes follow:

The Fathers

Novelette in 7 Chapts 30,000 to 35,000 words *
1820 **** 1850 **** 1880 **** 1910
Mar[riage] Rel[igion] Bus[iness] Polit[ics]

Chap 1—1820—Conn[ecticut]. B[,] Son of A[.] N[ew] H[aven] or English importer married to girl beneath him. Goes to Ohio & becomes Meth[odist] exhorter—Stern; indignant man (5000 wds.)

Chap 2—1850—B in Ohio. His son—C—becomes free thinker. Goes out to Iowa—then up to Minn—stern wanderer[,] sternly free tho[ugh]t

Chap 3. 1880—C is now Minn. farmer—wealthy, esteemed. Plans creamery. Son D to college & science, despite C

Chap 4. D now professor in U[niversity of] C[alifornia]. Conventional Son E radical. Struggle w[ith] him, [unreadable word].

5—The shooting

6—Final scene—(Grandfather w[ith] E)

cut down other chaps & have chap 8 on "*comradship* of Father & Son" (D & E or E & F—move dates back if latter)

Have D buck E in *all*[:] rel[igion]—mar[riage]—bus[iness]—pol[itics](?)

These notes Lewis expanded in a separate set of papers. The basic pattern remained the same, but the vow in each generation to do better by the next son is emphasized, a heroine is brought into the last section (called "the Genegirl," she was apparently suggested by his friend, Gene Baker), and the climax comes in a final comradeship. "Don't forget the *Mothers,*" he admonished himself. "One dad widower (D); one [mother] symp[athetic] with son; one, with father, etc." The bulk of the amplification is given to the last son, who is to be a political radical intimately involved with organized labor.

E, son of prof.[,] grad[uates] from East or U.C.; to newspaper; feels to be real proletariat must work with hands; job shop—Memb[er] Typo[grapher]s

* This estimate was later raised.

> Union—at 29 is young Sec[retar]y of Labor Council of S.F. tho' bucked as Long-Hair—High-Brow. Also is Socialist.

A dozen pages at the end of the notes he then gave to the organizational background of this character as he was able to observe it at two meetings of the Labor Council. He made notes on the meeting place, on the several unions represented there and their delegates, on procedure, on topics under consideration, on speech habits, on dues, and changed the initial conception of E. "E. is probably not secy. of labor council, but just a delegate. Study photo engraving or whatever trade he represents."

The last sentence introduces a major ingredient in the literary method of the mature Lewis, that systematic "research" on which much of his fiction will come to depend. The plan itself suggests what is to become his characteristically schematic structure. While there is no evidence that Lewis proceeded even a little with the actual writing of this work, the attention he gave to the labor movement suggests that here was the beginning of the "labor novel" that he was to think about over so many years and never write. If he did not write at it now, it may be because his notes were too slight, his conception too unspecified to enable him to proceed. In a memorandum to himself, he at one time wrote the following:

> fellow
> A named ________
> man
> A town by the name of ________ in ________: —these are (often unconscious) declarations of inferiority in the subject.

In the final pages of his notes for *The Children's Children,* a crisp summary, he gave his characters first names:

> One quarreled away (Samuel)
> John Wesley led away by friends
> Ross instinctively away & Genegirl
> Irving educated away.

The autobiographical echoes are clear. Lewis's great-grandfather was Lemuel and was born near New Haven; his grandfather's name was John and he moved to Minnesota; his father's name was Edwin, a professional man if not a professor, but one can only speculate on the relation of that name to Ross; Lewis's one friend in Sauk Centre, his "other self," so to speak, was named Irving, and Lewis, "educated away," a would-be socialist, was writing in San Francisco. Struggling as he may have been to make his material concrete in his own mind through the use of his past and his person, his shorter fiction shows him to have been still totally unprepared to launch upon, much less to complete a work with the scope of this project. Disguised by history and geography and profession, it was not only the earliest conception of the "labor novel" but more especially his *Moon-Calf,* never to be born.

One piece of shorter fiction, a story called "Polly" that he wrote either at Carmel or at Benicia, he had sold to *Sunset* magazine in July of 1909, and, probably upon publication in January of 1910, he received for it "$35.00 in transportation." Polly, a young wife, gives a first-person account of the outdoor life she lives with her husband somewhere near Carmel; she tells how they dream of New York and then, when the opportunity to go to New York presents itself, they choose, instead of "the stone streets," "this star world," and remain. The story was the occasion for the publication, in *Sunset* for December, of the first Sinclair Lewis publicity photograph, as large as a postage stamp. It had further consequences in some not very clear arrangement that he made with Charles S. Aiken, the editor of that periodical, in which he was to travel about the state and write for the magazine.

He had taken notes on San Francisco, notes on the city beach and the Cliff House, on Sutro Heights and Fillmore Street, on city night noises, on the fog; and immediately after he left the Associated Press, he utilized many of these in an article called "A San Francisco Pleasure Cure" that *Sunset* accepted on February 23 for "$25 cash & $25 in transportat'n." An account of the recreational possibilities in San Francisco after the great fire, the article argues for the restorative powers of nature and of play. At this point, Sinclair Lewis did the rather unusual thing of acting upon his own advice. After buying a blanket, a knapsack, and outdoor eating utensils, he departed on February 25 for Carmel and, once more, the free life. It lasted three weeks.

With what was the quasi guarantee of *Sunset,* he could free-lance. His father, gratified that the young man would be out of doors again, wrote with more than the usual understanding.

> I suppose since writing is to be your life work it is better to try to make that bring in a revenue and I can easily see how it is impossible to try to do two things at the same time. With nothing else on hand you of course can put in better work and avoid all carelessness and haste in your writings as you would be tempted to do now and I can see that it comes easy if once you can break into the circle and get acceptances coming.

Breaking once more into his own circle, he reduced his fifty-five-dollar debt to the Cookes by forty-one dollars and fifty cents through copy reading, and conceptions came; acceptances, however, did not.

A year and a half later, writing of the origins of what was to be his final contribution to *Nautilus,* he remembered Carmel on an early morning:

> A sunny dawn. . . . Among the pines in the valley, little curls of mist, sun-brightened, drifting from the sea that thundered incessantly on the beach

> beyond the valley. As I lay on my out-o'doors sleeping cot . . . and looked down into the valley, it was to hazy wakening fancies, still inexplicably mingled with memories of dreams; it was all like lying in the berth of an anchored air ship, gazing at sea mists below. And so came the picture of Jarl Nordenhaus, as it appears in the first chapter of *Captains of Peace.*

Interwoven with his visualization were the abstract themes of the novel, and in a few moments, "while I lay there, in the morning air redolent of pine and sea-scent, the novel had assumed a tangible form."

> Then up and to breakfast. Out in Carmel, even so gracious and lofty a poet as George Sterling is not ignorant of the intimate details of breakfast porridge; while Grace MacGowan Cooke—I wish the readers of *Nautilus* could see her, whose work they have so enjoyed, making abalone soup over a picnic fire! After breakfast, Grant Wallace came riding into the yard, on a rangy ranch pony—as though sent by some telepathic message at this necessary time. For Grant Wallace is even greater as an occultist, a metaphysician, than as a war correspondent, or an explorer of the Arizona deserts. Looking quietly from under his great sombrero, Grant heard my suggestion for the new novel; approved, suggested; by his interest put the cachet of finality on the scheme.
>
> But it was not till after months of the closest study of electrical phenomena—electrical ordinances, etc.; aviation; hydroplanes, and so on, that the flesh was given to this idea-spirit.

Flesh, precisely, and a sufficiently firm "idea-spirit," were what his fiction for a long time after *Captains of Peace* was still to be without. His problem was certainly not a want of situations as such. It was rather a lack of imaginative focus and an inability to develop fictional situations either fully or dramatically. When he left St. Cloud he had a file of over a hundred plots. This file must have grown in Waterloo and New York and Carmel and Benicia and San Francisco. Benét recalled his performance in producing impromptu narratives as they tramped along the coast. But the oral inventiveness did not translate itself readily into the written form. Then, in happy coincidence, Jack London came to visit the Sterlings at Carmel, and London's problem was precisely the opposite from his. London found no difficulty in developing situations once he had them, but he had great difficulty in conceiving them. A sensible transaction followed: Lewis would sell plots to London.* Michael Williams, writing in 1928, remembered the trunk that Lewis had brought with him, a trunk packed with notes,

* This curious episode in the history of American letters has several times been discussed in print. The most responsible account is that of Franklin Walker, "Jack London's Use of Sinclair Lewis Plots, Together with a Printing of Three of the Plots," *Huntington Library Quarterly,* Vol. XVII, No. 1 (November 1953), 59–74. The notes in *The Man from Main Street* say that Lewis sold "outlines and ideas to various writers of the day, including Jack London." The London transaction is certain, but Lewis's own detailed records provide no evidence that he had on any occasion before this sold plots or ideas to anyone else.

newspaper clippings, and his plot file; and one night, in George Sterling's cottage, London sat up with him until dawn going through it. The first sales followed.

Under the date of March 10, Lewis entered in his accounts the item, "14 sh. st. pl. sold to Jack London—$70.00." Of these fourteen plots, two became published stories and the third became the beginning of a novel, *The Assassination Bureau,* so fantastic that even Jack London could not finish it. There were two further steps in this relation. Six months after Lewis left Carmel, London wrote to ask if he had any more plots. Lewis promptly sent him twenty-three, and on October 4 London mailed his check for fifty-two dollars and fifty cents to cover the cost of nine of them. Of these we know again that two became published works. The price that Lewis put on his plots was usually five dollars, but for an ambitious plan for a series to be called *The World Police,* he asked forty dollars. London did not accept the idea for *The World Police.* Fully a year later, London bought three of seventeen Lewis plots for fifteen dollars. Whether he used any of these is uncertain, and their relationship, such as it was, drifted on to another basis.

The first sale of seventy dollars nearly covered the railroad fare to the Atlantic seaboard, and in the very week that he made that sale, Lewis itemized the cost of three telegrams. His friend F. K. Noyes had proposed a small position in Washington, D.C. Lewis seized it. Again, one must be impressed by that discrepancy between "idea" and action that had already become so characteristic of the life of Sinclair Lewis.

He was in Carmel, Carmel was free, and *Sunset* provided a certain security without imposing bondage. His father (not entirely informed as to the facts, of course) wrote, "Your prospects just at present seem flattering. Personally the Sunset job would appeal to me more than the Washington innovation. . . ." One of the plots that Jack London was presently to buy contrasted the restrictive East and the expansive West, as another contrasted the effete Academy and the Open Road. Jack London, or at least, Jack London the adventurer, was symbol of all that was admirable:

> The high literary point was watching Jack London read Henry James for the first time.
>
> I hand this study on to the professors who deal with a mystery called Artistic Influences. Jack had quit being a galloping adventurer and had become a country gent, devoted to bridge-playing and pig-breeding. He used to stay with the Sterlings at Carmel, and though the great man was extremely friendly to the skinny, the red-headed, the practically anonymous secretary, it bothered that secretary to find that Jack seemed content now to play bridge all afternoon, all evening.
>
> At a neighboring cabin Jack picked up James's *The Wings of the Dove* and, standing there, short, burly, in soft shirt and black tie, the Master read

> aloud in a bewildered way while Henry James's sliding, slithering, glittering verbiage unwound itself on and on. Jack banged the book down and wailed, "Do any of you know what all this junk is about?"
>
> It was the clash between Main Street and Beacon Street that is eternal in American culture.

The antithesis is not quite exact; one might better say that it is the clash between poles of interest that the work of writers like London and like Lewis has itself established as "East" and "West," or, even more exactly, "Europe" and "America." Where did young Lewis stand?

The plot summary of "Kings While You Wait," one of the projected stories for the *World Police* series, begins,

> It was a very magnificently dressed young man, smoking very magnificent cigars, who rented offices in the sixtieth story of the Assurance Building in New York. He installed thousand dollar rugs and genuine paintings of Childe Hassam—and one typewriter girl at ten plunks a week; and waited.

That was the "East," subject of satire if not of sneer. Later, when Sinclair Lewis had money enough to buy pictures, he bought seven Childe Hassams with their faint, pastelly, pointillist effects. This was not only the "East" in its most enfeebled form of European derivation, it was also his conception of elegance in art, realized at last out of a bare and graceless youth. Where did he stand? He stood in Main Street, midway between the "East" and the frontier, only a little closer to the second than to the first, pulled toward both and free to choose neither. "Culture" against "vigor," refinement against crudity, convention against freedom—how long these polarities, this tension, have disturbed American writers and confused their social insights! As this tension is frequently central to the novels of Sinclair Lewis, so it seemed to be central to his temperament.

On March 18, 1910, he left Carmel for Washington. The choice was not between freedom and bondage, not even between East and West; it was, as it always would be, between the place in which he was and elsewhere, elsewhere!

2

HE WAS NOT, to be sure, either now or for some time to come, to move into a life of elegance and ease. He was to move, in fact, into the dullest position he had yet held and, at fifteen dollars a week, the least well paid. He kept it for just six months.

Unnamed on its masthead, he was a kind of subeditor and general clerk in the offices of a periodical called the *Volta Review*. In a long letter to Gene Baker written almost immediately upon his arrival in Washington, he described its function and his:

> I find that the Volta Review is the new format of a chaste and cute little sheet which bore the caption of "The Association Review of the American Association to Promote the Teaching of Speech to the Deaf." Now, Alexander Graham Bell, inventer of the telephone, and a great teacher, was founder of the Association and chief executive and backer. He decided that the Association Review . . . ought to be broadcast and "popularized". . . .
>
> My classmate Kinney Noyes was dragged down here to edit it; and he has gotten out the April number, the first under the new regime. . . .
>
> I shall be his assistant, chief clerk and most everything from office boy to contributing editor, till we make a little more money. We are going to get right after people, and *try* to boom the circulation tremendously.
>
> Meanwhile, I work night and day; and scarce have time to see this leisurely and beautiful city. But there'll be a good time coming, when things are started, I think.

The magazine did not become what the young men hoped it would. In a few issues F. K. Noyes wrote signed articles on subjects of somewhat more general interest than the teaching of the deaf, but Sinclair Lewis's name never appeared, although his initials were several times set below brief book reviews. Much anonymous technical information was unsigned and may well have represented his galling chore, as the work soon came to seem. He kept from his parents the fact that his descent in salary had been from thirty dollars to twenty-five dollars to—now—fifteen dollars a week, and his father inquired persistently. "I imagine that you have plenty of work ahead of you but you don't say how much salary you are getting," he wrote in mid-April. "That is quite an item with beefsteak at 22 per." Lewis's answer was evasive, and in his next letter his father said, "I infer from what you write that you do not get much for your work. Possibly the experience may make it up but I should not hesitate to change when something better presents." (He went on to laugh at a Dr. Lamb, the new and self-important young practitioner in Sauk Centre whom E. J. Lewis could not tolerate and who "now wears long tailed coats and *smokes* Gee—")

The "experience," Lewis soon learned, could be nothing but restrictive and exasperating as long as Frank W. Booth, the ancient superintendent of the Volta Bureau and General Secretary of the Association, remained at the top of the organization, and as long as Noyes was his superior.

Life in Washington might, even on his wretched wage, have compensated for the grubbiness of his work. With vast indiscretion he bought a suit of evening clothes at forty-three dollars and twenty-five cents (on that day, the item "Gr[ub]" amounted to "$.20") and he attended an occasional opera or play for fifty or seventy-five cents. His poverty did not permit frequent indulgence of this sort, and whole stretches of his Washington life were merely dull. He wrote one very long letter to Gene Baker that was entirely devoted to the heat, and a long paragraph of another was devoted to cataloguing the inhabitants of his boardinghouse, an establishment where he lived and ate for twenty-four dollars a month. He apparently shared a room with Noyes, but Noyes (who "has been doing newspaper work in New York till he has lost most of his sensibilities") proved to be a trial. "I'm afraid there's going to be one merry hell of a time ahead of me, these next weeks," he wrote Gene Baker.

> I decline to express it otherwise. Noyes and I have been on beer-and-gossip every-evening terms, till the last few days, when he has been getting sulky again—as he was for a month or so before he went off for a long absence. That means we shall fight—a diversion for which I am always lamentably eager. And if we fought enough, I'd tell him to get a new sub; and do the old wearisomely familiar stunt of trekking off, nearly penniless, god knows where. I'm capable of going back to Yale to get a Ph.D. in English; or enlisting in the army with a commission in view; or otherwise entering into some prison of the spirit with the view of seeking freedom! But I hope that we shall manage to agree.

To his mother he wrote about sleeping on the roof, where he did not have "to awake in a bedroom filled with foetid indoor air" and where he did not have to tolerate "the sweet tricks of Noyes . . . when he is always deliberately boorish."

His father had urged him to look up one John Boobar, "an old Sauk Centre boy" who "will treat you kindly." This he did, and, such was the general drabness of his life and work, that he found in Boobar and his wife, of all things, "color."

> So tonight, when I met the Man from Home, when we exchanged stories of the By Heck and Waliswan type, he seemed sparkling with the vividest color. He made the old men of Minnesota, great bearded, rough, "decently ignoble" (to quote Gissing); he made them fresh fine virilities.
>
> The Man from Home is the librarian of the House of Representatives. He is building him a bungalow. I went out with him and his parroty, delightful wife—Christian Science equals fancy work with her—to the new house; and we strolled to neighbors of like well-to-do insignificance; sat on the Front Lawn with a Pitcher of Lemonade and Chatted. Minnesota; Lord the very image of those shirt sleeved gatherings in wonderful dusks where the vast harvest moon was but a back ground to interminable tales of politics and crafty business. . . .

The scene presents at least two men "from home," one of them, in his lonely dissatisfactions, wallowing more than the other in nostalgia, even as the "village virus," unbeknownst to that one, was gathering force.

> Lordy. There was all the little Middle Western town in that talk of the Man from Home. Color. Hell yes, buckets, brushes, large trucks and quantities. I could fairly smell the wooden station platform, reeking with oozing sap; the hot rails; the dusty roads; the dust of golden rod as the fall came on; hear the creak of the "buggy" in which Dad goes prairie chicken hunting; taste the well water.
>
> Now, actually, I prefer ice water to well water; prefer a benedictine served by a waiter whose manner hints a title incogged to beer served in a country bar room smelling of farm boots mucked with Mother Earth and things. I prefer insignificant little mutts who hap— to know chamber music to huge bearded farmers. Yet, as I said, in the change was color. I could be a Minnesotan keenly—being in Washington and safe.

He had a special reason, of course, for his discontent in the binding routines of his job. Although he wrote his mother that he "Never got more writing done in my life," he implored Jack London to buy some plots and free him.

> I hope to gawd that you will feel like taking a considerable part of them, because, if you do, it will probably finally give me the chance to get back at the free lancing—nothing but writing—which I haven't done for over a year; can the job and really get at decent work. I've saved up some mun, but not enough yet for a sinking fund. Next spring I shall receive between two and three hundred for a novelette; so that if I get started now I shall be able to hike along nicely, with the novelette money as a safeguard if I don't sell much at first. . . . Gawd I'll be glad to get back at writing; for here what I've done—tho it has been a fair quantity—has been only at the cost of sleep—which is too cheap and instructive an amusement, is sleep, to be wasted.

When his vacation came in August, he abandoned the idea of a tramp through the Virginia mountains, in order to stay in Washington and write with brief freedom and singleness of mind. What he did manage to write is not clear. He was thinking still of *The Children's Children* and probably now of *Our Mr. Wrenn* ("the novel bulks as ponderously and insistently as ever," he wrote Gene Baker) and he bought three curious books that must have represented background studies for the former: *Autobiography of a Pioneer; or, the Nativity, Experience, Travels, and Ministerial Labors of Rev. Jacob Young* (1857), *Autobiography of Rev. James B. Finley, or Pioneer Life in the West* (1853), and *History of Ohio Methodism: A Study in Social Science* (1898). The backgrounds did not find their way into a foreground. He wrote his father that he had finished a novelette called *Milord the Wayfarer* and was working on a story called "The Passion of Father August." These works did not find their way into print. He was working on his novelette for *Nautilus,* but perhaps only in its preliminary stages: he noted having spent seven dollars and ninety cents for "Books (for Capt—Peace)"; and for the purposes of this work, the offices of the Volta Bureau proved useful. *Nautilus* reported:

> Mr. Lewis was allowed to examine invaluable, yet unpublished notes made by Dr. Bell during recent years. . . . It was he who started Glenn Curtiss flying; and before the Wrights were flying, Douglass McCurdy was already in the air at Baddeck, N.S., in a machine designed by Bell. Not only on the practical side, but still more on the theoretical side, was Bell a great pioneer; and his findings, carefully dictated and preserved, were examined in extenso by Mr. Lewis.

One story, "The Dawn," which he had sent to his agent from St. Cloud nearly two years before, appeared in the "Literary Magazine" of the Pittsburgh *Dispatch* for May 1 and brought him twenty-five dollars. It is a sentimental bit about Sophie and Will and takes place on the day that Will returns from the penitentiary. Sophie fears that he may have become a hardened criminal and, not knowing how they can confront the townspeople, she wishes that they had five hundred dollars with which to go away. "We have," says he, and he produces it. She assumes that he has already committed a new robbery. But no; for thirteen months he has been free, working with an electric wiring company in Montana, and now he is its superintendent, and they are going there, free, in their dawn.

To be free! Increasingly, this was his wish, and it drove him at last to a rare, if not quite unique, act in relation to his father; but long before that, the pressure of the wish to be elsewhere was making itself felt in milder ways. Almost at once he longed for California. "I was plumb melancholy," he wrote within a week after his arrival in Washington, "and as homesick for California as tho' I were a boarding school girl away from home for the first time." His longing for Benicia is obliquely suggested in his second absurd Christmas booklet for Benét, "Beautiful Bill of Beniciay," over which he must have spent hours. He maintained some tenuous connection with Charles S. Aiken, the editor of *Sunset,* and did some research for him on the efforts of other cities besides San Francisco to present an exposition in honor of the opening of the Panama Canal. In May his father wrote,

> Hope you can get a good stand in with the "Sunset" as you will probably like that kind of work much better than the kind you are now doing. And the west is better to work in and the east better for loafing and seeing things.

In reply, Lewis wrote his father, "Well, Charles Aiken hasn't come through with anything more definite in regard to a Sunset job." But discussion of the possibility was not shut off—as late as the last day of August, his father wrote again, "I hope your Frisco scheme will go all right. It strikes me you are a sort of man Friday to Noyes where you are." And this (together with his father's final complaint in July, "You have never told us how much you are getting in Washington") gave Lewis the opening for a long, single-spaced, four-and-a-half-page letter, an eloquent, unusual plea. He is, he agrees, no more than a clerk to Noyes and can only be that until the old and incompetent general secretary retires, which will not be soon.

> I'm not overly well pleased with working *under* Noyes—he's too near my own age; too surly; and too fond of the cheaper aspects of life—cheap stories, cheap slang, and cheap women—not clean women at that. He's pretty much of a come down after George Sterling, Bill Benét and Colonel Benét; who, though a practical soldier and commander of men, is a delicately exact scholar and a charmingly witty gentleman of the world.

He will not return to a newspaper office; over that possibility, the present job has

> this advantage—the work, though taking a fair number of hours a day, does not have that tearing, wearing, tissue destroying quality of newspaper work. In any case, I can't do newspaper work; am a less excellent newspaperman every year. The only way I can write a story is to polish; think it out; rewrite. . . . So it was with Jack London; a wonderful short story writer but, they told me in San Francisco, a rotten newspaperman. Never could get him to write a newspaper story as they wanted it—too much interested in aspects of a matter which had no news value. I can always make a living in newspaper work—but that's about all; and it's at the expenditure of tremendous nervous energy.

He could, he suggests, wait it out in Washington for some job that would give him the leisure to write at the same time, but he has been waiting for seven years and he is tired of waiting.

For the waiting game began when I began to send in stuff to the magazines. And by God I'm going to go on working toward the end of getting to be a really great writer; even if gray hairs find me still plugging along. I've met with some recognition from some pretty big people—Jack London, for example; and it's enough to make me believe that I can succeed—and succeed at a game where success is immensely difficult and demands absolute concentration for a life time, in nearly all cases. . . . Lordy; it's funny; I'm just as foolishly determined to try to do something big—something in the writing game which shall be comparable to, say, the work of the Mayos, in the medical game—just as kiddishly determined, unblushingly idealistic, as when I was a Yale Freshman, seven eventful years ago.

Well along in his second page, he says that if his new novelette, *Milord the Wayfarer,* should sell, he would be able to go up to New York and become reacquainted with editors; but if he went without that sale, he would have only fifty-four or fifty-three dollars when he got there. He should go at once, however, since the *Nautilus* has nearly committed itself to the purchase of another novelette, which he has in mind but has not had the time to write, for two hundred and fifty dollars; furthermore the publishing firm of Stokes has expressed some interest in him. "Young Stokes is a very good friend of mine." ("Young Stokes" was heeling the *Lit* when Harry S. Lewis was on the board.) Finally he breaks his silence and admits his salary: "losing $250.00 for the sake of holding on to a job at $15 a week. Yes; that's what I'm getting." He will have to borrow again; and why not? After all, he had repaid the one hundred and twenty dollars [?] he had borrowed from the Cooke ladies.

If you care to lend me a suitable sum, as a business transaction at 7% annual interest annually payable semi annually, repayment to be made (LITERALLY) as soon as possible, I should not only regard it as a tremendous favor—since I have no security; but also regard it as a good business investment for me—giving me the chance to wade into this *Nautilus* novelette; and get reacquainted in New York. . . . I can live on fifty dollars a month in New York, but it would take six months for me to get really well established there. If you care to let me have $300 (in fifty per month payments if you prefer, starting a month after I get there—for I have a little over fifty here, THEN DO IT!

You have said, regarding my last going to Carmel, that you believe that the best thing for a man who wants to write is to get out and write. It is. But he must get in line. Allan Updegraff, who once starved with me, was enabled to get in line through the leisure brought him by his wife's small stock of money. Now, he is supporting himself and her, excellently. In my six months of Carmel and two of Benicia, I had the leisure to work out a style. Now I'm ready to face the editors in New York, and get into the game. You must realize that I don't write to escape from the drudgery of jobs; but because it is the one thing in life which I am born for. You shouldn't have been a reader of Milton, as a young man (I have your copy right here), if you hadn't wanted your son to be a writer! You're one yourself, when you want to be. This is not at all a "jolly." It is simply my working out of the fact that I'm born a writer, and nothing in this broad work-a-day world but a writer. So I'm born; and I've been getting a good bit of experience. It's about time for the clock to strike.

The letter continues by outlining all the advantages ahead of him if he has a little capital on which to base his career. He assures his father that he has "imbibed enough of your spirit to wish not to run into hopeless debt," and that if he were not so very certain of the *Nautilus* sale, he would not propose the loan. He outlines again the method of repayment. And—

I think and hope that it will be a matter of much pride to you to see me a sizable writer; one of whose books everyone must know. And I think that getting into New York now, before October first—when the editors are making up for another season—when they are looking forward to a fall-and-winter's work—may save me about a year in attaining that success as a writer.

Things will be different in New York now from what they were two years earlier. He has learned a good deal and can cope with the situation.

Can you do it? I'm sorry to have dragged in so much about my personal grievances and my young ambitions; but besides percent. on your money, you ought to have some security. And, where it's a matter between father and son, the ambitions, energy, and, most of all, the honor of that son, are security. That's why I have been very frank and rather minute. But, I want to put it as a commercial proposition, and I hope, most eagerly, that you will see it as a safe one.

And even all of that—even the strategic increase of one per cent over the interest rate on his father's mortgage holdings—even all of that left the good flinty doctor unimpressed. He replied promptly, however, as was his habit:

The way it stands I think you will have to plug along as you are. For I have no money on hand except for running expenses all is loaned out on 3 to 5 years time in North Dakota. I confess it seems strange to me that you could throw up a 30 per week job to go to Washington to take 15 and one which requires more hours than you had in Frisco. The only way I can see is to do some writing on the side and keep eyes out for something better.

As to whether you will succeed as a writer you are the best judge. I have no criticism to make, but I know that I am not going to put my self short to make you a loan for I want a lot of it for fun this fall and my many years of hard work entitles me to that.

He concludes with a comment on the hot weather in Minnesota and another on the welfare of the dogs.

For one who has never been and will never be given to the serenities of even temper, the immediate reply from the son comes as an almost beautiful piece of friendly restraint:

> I've been pounding the type-writer keys all day till that set of muscles has about gone up. . . . I'm doing my best to get that Nautilus novelette done.
>
> While, of course, I'm mighty sorry to find you can't conveniently lend me that $300.00 I'm very glad you took the proposition on the strictly commercial basis intended.
>
> Anyway, as it is, when money does come in—whether from the novelette Miss Holly has, or from this Nautilus thing, I shall not then be owing money, & that will be a comfort.
>
> No, I'm not sorry I came to Washington, even for a "merely nominal salary." It gave me a chance to get East & have bread & butter assured.

Then, four days later, with thirty-nine dollars and fifty-five cents between some bread and butter and none whatever, he made a four-day prospecting trip to New York. About September 29 an offer came from the Frederick A. Stokes Company, and without any delay, he went back to New York with his final monthly check for sixty dollars from the *Volta Review*. He was going to a position that would perhaps provide him with more interesting work. His salary, however, was identical, fifteen dollars a week. Or perhaps it was only twelve dollars and fifty cents, as he sometimes remembered. We cannot be certain, since, if he kept accounts during his first seventeen months in New York, they no longer exist. When he began them again eighteen months later, in March 1912, the weekly salary had gone up to twenty-five dollars.

3

"I FIND NEW YORK AWAKENING, after being away for two years. It may prove deadening after a while, but it sure ain't just now. And I hope that one of its results may be some good plots to submit to you." So Sinclair Lewis wrote to Jack London on October 16, 1910, and the remark is telling—New York was awakening him and the plot machine. But intellectual New York was itself on the very eve of an extraordinary awakening. A young writer could not have chosen a more exciting moment in this century to have arrived there, as many young writers coming from the New England colleges, from Chicago, from the small towns of the Midwest, knew or were at once to discover. It was the day of "the Rebellion," of the "Young Intellectuals," the time was theirs. The air was charged with the promise of "emerging greatness," and in art, in literature, in politics, in manners, in thought, all seemed fermentation, effervescence, insouciance. "We are living in the first days of a renascent period"; the "American Risorgimento" was imminent; yes, America was "coming of age" at last! These were the flying verbal banners.

In 1910, aged twenty-five, Sinclair Lewis, it is clear, was conscientiously at work in the offices of the Frederick A. Stokes Company for about $12.50 a week; but it is difficult to locate him in the intellectual life of the time and place. There are glimpses, but glimpses only, and one must conclude that he was more than ever a character on the fringes, outside looking in. But why? He was more familiar than the newcomers with that part of downtown Manhattan that was now coming into its own brief life as Greenwich Village; the rebellion against traditional values of every kind was so inclusive that it gave him more than enough room for the expression of any element at all in his generally dissenting spirit, and there was a variety of groups within which that expression could have found its place, even its leading place. There are perhaps three explanations. One is that nothing he had yet written suggested that he was a writer whom one could take seriously. A second lies in the excesses of his own personality, which would have colored his intellectual no less than his social affiliations. Frances Perkins has written the biographer:

> As I remember it, he was at that time tasting of everything that came along, but he was always an outsider. I remember that a number of the men whom I knew very well, like Arthur Bullard and Howard Brubaker, regarded him as a pest and a nuisance and never took him seriously.... He was... always making an exaggerated statement of any theory that any one of these people might have been interested in—a statement so exaggerated as to make them feel it was ridiculous and, of course, it made them withdraw from any friendship with him.

Tasting of everything and committed to nearly nothing, he is the subject of almost no references in the memoirs of this period. But there is a third explanation, and one that may control the other two. Suppose that, then or later, he had tried to answer the question posed by Eugene Jolas in *transition* in 1928, "What particular vision do you have of yourself in relation to twentieth century reality?" Would he not have had to reply, "My relation finally is to that American 'dream of success'—material success—that I have myself abused but never with my whole heart or even with very much of it"? If "the rebellion" had any central target, it was precisely the harsh materialism of American life.

In a long list, compiled some years later, of the people he said then that he had seen most frequently in the years from 1910 to 1915, Sinclair Lewis included the following: Howard Brubaker, Randolph Bourne, George Cram Cook and Susan Glaspell, Floyd Dell, Francis Hackett, Harry Kemp, Albert J. Nock, John Reed and Louise Bryant, Mary Heaton Vorse, Art Young.*

* Among the many other names is that of Benjamin De Casseres. The general unreliability of the list seems to be indicated by an anecdote, "Portraits en Brochette," by Casseres, that appeared in *The Bookman* for July 1931:

> An anecdote about Lewis when he was still Jude the Obscure. Joel's "Bohemia," about 1912. A Saturday night, about 11 o'clock. The place was so crowded that Host Joel planted me at a table with a lanky, red-haired, gawky-looking fellow. He introduced me. The name Sinclair Lewis meant nothing to me at that time. What I meant to him I do not know; but this strange fellow, after announcing that he was from Sauk Center, Minnesota, said to my astonishment;
>
> "You must be from Philadelphia."
>
> "How do you know that, Mr. Lewis?"
>
> "Because you left your spoon in your coffee-cup."
>
> Atheist and Pantheist thereupon shook hands and proceeded to slip small glasses down the old swivel. The gang grew. At six A.M. Lewis proposed Childs, where he offered to out-butter-cake and out-buckwheat-cake any two men in the crowd, which he did, while the night manager of the restaurant kept punching checks.
>
> This was the only time I ever met Sinclair Lewis, but after eighteen years he remains imbedded in my memory.... Sinclair Lewis has up to date written the only authentic history extant of the twentieth-century American.

With such an estimate of Lewis's achievement, would Casseres not have made as much of the association, rather than so little, as he could have? But what, at the height of his reputation, impelled Lewis to include the name of this *lumpen*-intellectual in a list of people he wished to think of as having been his intimates?

Most of these people have left their memoirs behind them, but Mary Heaton Vorse is nearly alone in remembering Lewis, however casually, in hers. ("A sweet young woman, a friend of all," George Soule recalled.) Harry Kemp, to be sure, attempted to memorialize him as the derided character, Julius "Red" Flatman, in his now forgotten autobiographical novel, *More Miles* (1926). These names forcibly remind us that when Lewis came to New York the literary capital of the United States had indeed shifted from Boston, for some of these names at least are centrally associated with the most active interests of those years.

A good half of them, but most particularly those of Dell, Reed and Young, one connects with *The Masses,* established in the last month of 1912. *The Masses* was the crowded intersection of young literary and artistic endeavor and of the American radical movement—in Walter Rideout's description, "a common ground between artists, writers, the intelligentsia on the one hand and the left-wing labor movement on the other, enabling a significant number from the first group to come in contact, not only with the spirit, but also with the actuality of labor revolt against monopoly capitalism." Nearly every lively young writer of those years, of whatever political stripe, is to be found among the contributors to *The Masses,* but never Sinclair Lewis. And what of the other new periodicals—*New Republic* (November 1914), with which we associate Randolph Bourne together with Van Wyck Brooks, Waldo Frank and Paul Rosenfeld? Or the more purely literary periodicals that were springing up—*Dial, Poetry, Little Review?* Nothing. Waldo Frank remembers declining a story that Lewis submitted to *Seven Arts* (and Lewis's declining a novel of his!).

Much later, Van Wyck Brooks was to find the influence of Randolph Bourne's "transcultural America" in the novels of Sinclair Lewis; but in what Lewis was writing in the years when Bourne was disseminating his happy conception of a national culture and the apostolic role of the young intellectual in creating a national consciousness, we find little trace of these ideas. In 1913, Margaret Anderson came to New York to raise money for her projected *Little Review,* and she remembered meeting Sinclair Lewis and his fiancée, neither of whom shared her enthusiasm for a performance of *Tristan and Isolde* under the baton of Toscanini (the first Mrs. Lewis remembers that they *did* enjoy it), but she did not record her several visits to the offices of Stokes, where, for example, George Soule, who also worked there, gave her money, while Sinclair Lewis gave her none. He had little enough money to give, to be sure; but he seems, too, to have had no interest.

Certain writers of stature whose peer or superior Lewis was ultimately to seem to be, writers like Dreiser, Sinclair and Anderson, whose associations cannot be fixed with any particular group, are yet capable of being placed in a way that Lewis is not. With one group, however, we can assume that his sympathies were ready; these are the journalistic shockers best represented by *Smart Set*. Henry L. Mencken and George Jean Nathan first joined the staff in 1908 and became its editors in 1914, and while Lewis was not to contribute to this magazine under their editorship for some time —his writing was simply not good enough—the tone, Mencken's invective and certain of Mencken's ideas (notably his early campaign for an American language against standard literary English), would have been congenial to Lewis, and indeed certain ambiguities in Mencken's own person were also the ambiguities in his: the uneasy attitude toward Europe vis-à-vis the United States; the antibourgeois fulminations coming from a deepest self that was profoundly bourgeois.

In politics, at this point, there would have been no meeting of their minds, for Lewis was a member of the Socialist Party—Number 12157, Branch One, New York Local—a dues-paying member from January 16, 1911, to April 1912. Six weeks before his membership began, in a letter signed "Yours for the Revolution!" he expressed his zeal to Jack London:

> We're going to bring out a red hot and damned good socialistic novel, "The Chasm," by George Cram Cook. I'd never heard of him before, but he sure can write; and is a good "red." He quotes Jack London in one interesting scene. I'm going to send you a copy when the thing comes out (next Spring, I think).

On the day after his membership began, he wrote to Gene Baker:

> I'm reading Karl Marx—a dusty collection of terms which seem to refer to use, profit and rent and wages and things. His book is a dreadful gook. I'd rather read that antiquated anthology of superstitions, The Bible. . . . But I've joined the Socialist party and my damn New England conscience insists on my knowing something of Socialistic economics.

He tried to convert his old college acquaintance George Soule to the cause, and when Soule resisted, he said, "All right, George. We'll be on different sides of the barricades." Yet it was Soule's conviction that Lewis's political views were not very firmly held, certainly that they did not lead him either into attempts at journalistic participation (in *The Masses,* for example) or into personal participation in catastrophes such as those in the textile mills of Paterson and Lawrence. One may guess that his socialism was, as much as anything else, an effort to form some genuine associations with an intellectual group. Again, to Gene Baker, he wrote as follows:

> You'd like *some* meetings of the Heretics Club—a woman with high cheekbones, intense eyes and a noble columnar neck. Stella Comyn—La Goldman's niece, of whom I spoke, talking to a silver and black haired man, whose chin is always held high, about the respective merits of Toscanini, Gustav Mahler and Walter Damrosch as conductors. Two Socialist newspapermen.

At Christmas in 1910 he attended the Anarchists' Ball, and from a letter to someone—the internal evidence suggests that it was almost certainly to Gene Baker—he preserved a carbon copy of his account of it.

> Emma Goldman has never been married, living openly with the man of her choice. She is so violent a radical that a U.S. soldier was given three years in the military prison at Leavenworth for merely attending one of her lectures and then shaking hands with her. . . . And this bomb-thrower proved to be a stout, plain faced, eye-glassed woman like a Jewish haus-frau with a little education. . . . Just a comfortable, busy, immensely practical and undreamy and anti-violent housewife and engaged in—hear me now, this is literal—standing at a counter selling pies and tarts and ice cream for The Cause! Beside her was her young niece, a tawny smooth cheeked girl, with hair so softly black and fine that it seemed more dusky than black.
>
> Only for a while did Emma leave her radical occupation; when she went up stairs, to the bar room, and had a couple of glasses of Rhine wine at the table where was my crowd. She got into a discussion of the advancement of anarchism, with Theodore Dreiser, author of "Sister Carrie," and about the biggest realist in America—coming right after Frank Nelson [Norris?], I think; in spite of the fact that he's done only the one book, so far. Dreiser, seated next me, waggled his scrawny forefinger, and looked superiority through his heavy, gold rimmed, scholastic eye glasses; but Emma sent back hot shot—speaking as quietly as the haus frau she seemed to be; yet tremendous in her conviction that a complete and immediate emancipation of individuality from all the old bonds of religion and government and prejudice and ignorance is at hand.*
>
> Almost thou persuadest me to be an anarchist, Emma. But first, I think we must fight to have the Socialist economic regime; so that we may educate ourselves and, in a couple of hundred years, be ready for anarchism.
>
> Dreiser was fascinated, apparently, by Dr. Greil, in her close-fitting graceful gown of cerise, and her dark keen face. He, she and I went to a cafe—Joel's—after the ball; and watched the actresses celebrate Xmas at 4 in the morning. . . .

* This was not the first encounter of Sinclair Lewis and Theodore Dreiser. Three years before, in the interim between Helicon Hall and the return to New Haven, Lewis included an account of Dreiser in "Editors Who Write," a two-column article for *Life* (October 10, 1907).

> Theodore Dreiser, whose realistic novel, 'Sister Carrie,' has made a furore, has just left the managing editorship of the *Broadway* to become the editor of the *Delineator*. Mr. Dreiser is a man of surprises. He surprised every one by getting 'Sister Carrie' reissued after the publishing house which first issued it declined to push it—in fact, temporarily killed it—because one member of the firm decided that the book was immoral, strong though it was. Mr. Dreiser's rather attenuated verse surprises one who knows the vitality of his novel. . . . His removal to the *Delineator* is also surprising, for 'Sister Carrie' is not the sort of lady who is readily associated with household recipes and a children's page. Finally, his appearance is surprising. He looks more like a wholesale hardware merchant than a properly hollow-cheeked realist. Mr. Dreiser wears waistcoats, real vescits, and they are well-filled!

> Wish I could tell more of the Anarchist Ball—the sensuous Jewish girls with quick eyed partners; a loose lipped, loose eyed slouching youth who posed all evening; a heavily bearded man in black, with a waistcoat cut like an evening waistcoat yet, also, with a red four in hand which waved melancholily about his shirt front. The only drunk person at the ball was this same bearded anarchist. He was most interesting when talking to Bavard (Bayard?) Bovesen, a faculty-member whom Columbia U. is trying to kick out (to his delight) because of his avowed anarchistic beliefs. Now the bearded man was some what blurred of feature; while Bovesen has bored pale eyes; a Greek nose; lips curving when seen in profile—lips like a less fleshly Oscar Wilde—a proud, fine, unhappy curve those lips had—and he listened to the drunkard with a weary courtesy which said—"Oh, really, what's the difference—a fool drunk or sober?"
>
> People are beastly different anytime or place but there—why, they were as different as the aspects of the Metropolitan Tower—that greater campanile; now milky in a morning mist; now sharp cut across a band of uneasy, uncanny after-sunset green; now all of pasteboard with sharply light-defined windows, and the great clock lighted.

The preserved carbon, the straining prose, the "literary" flourish at the end, the effort throughout to "characterize"—all these suggest that what most concerned the young Lewis was material for fiction, and the social rather than the concretely political occasion. Anarchism, mingled in the general melange of Village political attitudes—left and right socialism and plain progressivism—was only one more idea, along with woman suffrage, birth control, vegetarianism, psychoanalysis, good for discussion at the Liberal Club over Polly Halladay's restaurant in Macdougal Street, or in the restaurant itself (where one might hear Hippolyte Havel, Emma's ex-lover and Polly's cook, expounding it with his ferocious invective), or at a Mabel Dodge "evening," had Sinclair Lewis ever appeared at one. Even though he thought that he remembered that he saw a good deal of Jack Reed, Mrs. Dodge says that she never saw him.*

Frances Perkins tolerated him, at least. She, like many another, was actively engaged in the causes of uplift—settlement houses, civic reform, the Consumer's League, and so on—but to that general atmosphere she now feels that Lewis did not "react at all." In certain well-publicized affairs he did play a part. Miss Perkins thinks that he probably marched in the Woman's Suffrage Parade of 1912. His own report, in a communication to *Nautilus,* is as follows:

* In 1918–1919, the Lewises saw Louise Bryant, who would presently be Jack Reed's widow, in Minnesota, but there is no evidence of intimacy. In the years 1912–1913, when Mabel Dodge's salon in New York was everybody's haunt, Jack Reed was her friend. She did meet Lewis many years later—in February 1930, when he was married to Dorothy Thompson, and Mabel to the imperturbable Tony Luhan. He, too, was there—at a picnic given by Lincoln Steffens in Carmel.

> I couldn't march—I had to be on the job handing out copies of a women's suffrage paper for girls to sell along the line of march. But I watched the parade from a seventeenth story window between whiles. . . . It was a parade of brains expressed through marching feet! It was a great thought of justice, made visible. It was—oh, let a newsboy friend of mine express it. I heard him say, after the parade, to another boy: "Say, gee, dat was some parade—all dose women walked like dey was queens!"

Such group excitement would, of course, have drawn him, and participation was easy. Similarly, Miss Perkins thinks that she remembers "that on one occasion Lewis made a speech at a street meeting that was addressed by Inez Mulholland."

> I am not sure that he made a speech but, at any rate, he held up a banner or a sign at this street meeting and always spoke of it as a great event. However, this was again mostly a conversational and romantic notion of his. . . . He was much more interested in his job and in writing a novel some day. He used to try out a lot of ideas on me and I seemed to have to listen. . . .

But did he purposefully act on ideas? Did he join Mary Heaton Vorse and the others in their excursions to the Lawrence textile mills, or Jack Reed in his efforts with the Paterson Pageant at Madison Square Garden? Did he ever appear at Stieglitz's "291," where all artistic spirits gathered? There is no record that he did. His first wife recalls that they attended the Armory Show, which educated a whole generation of intellectuals in that new painting from abroad—to which, however, Lewis was never to respond—but by and large he seems not to have concerned himself very actively with the general concerns of the Village.

It is strange to observe how impervious he seems to have been to the whole intellectual ferment that marked these years and of which Greenwich Village was the center. He could hardly bring himself to read Marx. He was apparently unsusceptible to the fashion of Nietzsche and Bergson, to the exciting discovery of Freud. To the new music of Bartok and Schönberg he was deaf. The Garnett translations of Dostoievsky, beginning in 1912, marked the new Russian fashion, but Lewis, although he would refer later to Tolstoy and Dostoievsky as giants, did not like them, according to Dorothy Thompson, and could not read them. (*War and Peace* may have been the exception. In 1932 he recorded his having read it as a boy—there is no record of it in the diaries—and in 1943 he read it—or much of it—again and wrote Marcella Powers that he thought "perhaps it *is* the greatest novel ever written.") The clear exception was the fashion of Shaw and Wells; to these, and especially to the latter, he responded with enthusiasm.

In *Intellectual Vagabondage,* Floyd Dell treats Shaw and Wells as the great liberating influences on his generation:

> And suddenly there came into our minds the magnificent and well-nigh incredible conception of Change . . . gigantic, miraculous change, an overwhelming of the old in ruin and an emergence of the new. Into our eternal and changeless world came H. G. Wells prophesying its ending, and the kingdom of heaven come upon earth; the heavens shall be rolled up like a scroll, and all the familiar things of earth pass away utterly—so he seemed to cry out to our astounded ears.

Lewis, who had been reading Wells ever since he was at Yale, was not influenced by the political Wells any more than he was by the pseudo-scientific Wells (when Lewis wrote of airplanes, he tried, with one exception, to write of them as they were, not as they one day would be), but rather by the Wells who satirically observed manners within the class structure and who liked to present as his hero a simple, humdrum person like Mr. Polly.

As Dell found political sanction in Wells, so he found a political motive in the notion of artistic and intellectual vagabondage, "the essentially homeless and childless and migratory life to which capitalism had largely condemned us." Lewis, with his roving restlessness, was already a vagabond, and he inevitably responded to the "cult of vagabondage" without any need to rationalize it or to deceive himself into believing that he was "reunited with the romantic tradition" of Dell's "homeless but happy poets and artists." With Lewis it was not so much a *"zest* for being somewhere else" as, already, it was a compulsion.

The appeal of Provincetown to the artists and writers who in 1910 began to go there in the summers was the appeal of Vagabondia, and it was almost inevitable that Lewis should have spent his vacations in this colony of transported Villagers. Two of them, Susan Glaspell and George Cram Cook, both of whom were Stokes authors, he came to know at least well enough to defend them some years later against Upton Sinclair's denunciation of their drinking habits, and if those of the rest who are alive now have only the faintest recollections of him, it is not surprising. He was a person of no importance among persons of relative literary sophistication, an unknown, quite graceless, indeed, quite irritating young man who was now writing nothing more than an adventure story for boys on a publisher's commission. Such an effort could hardly have interested the others, and even if they had already founded the Provincetown Players, Lewis's stage efforts of this time would have interested them no more. But Vagabondia is a free country, and in it he could even have hoped to find his "Glorious Playfellow."

More important to him than the movement for women's rights in itself was this by-product in social attitudes. Again, it is Floyd Dell who writes of it most enthusiastically.

> We had chafed against the shelter to which the vestigial feudalism of the Home subjected her, and the artificial narrowing of her personality and activities by such an institution. We wanted her as a Companion. We wanted her, no doubt, more as the companion of our play than of our work; but it was truly in learning to work with us that she learned for the first time to play with us. She now played with us, that is to say, upon our own accustomed masculine terms. She became like us, like what the world we worked in had made us, for good or ill—more interested in ideas, more honest, and less finicking. Our Victorian ancestresses would have said that she had become, like us, coarsened. But we liked her.
>
> The difference between the masculine and the feminine idealists of this period is now apparent. We were content with what was happening to woman because what we wanted was something for ourselves—a Glorious Playfellow.

For Lewis, this notion became not only a *modus operandi* but, what was worse, an attempted *modus vivendi*. It became, too, the theme of his poetry, as in a work called "Playmate o' Mine," which reads in part as follows:

Gravely the bearded and great and wise,
  This side of the magic sea,
Bid me earnestly theorize
  And gravely bid you be
A timid decorous chatelaine.
But—playmate, playmate, the murmurous grain
Shivers with gold in the playtime land
Hiding a secret
  Narrow, curious,
    Hiding a *won*-der-ful Sunny path
That we shall take, as a robber band,
Stoutly waving our swords of lath,
Stoutly armored with joy and dreams,
  Playmate o' mine.
Then, to the forest of elfin streams,
And up to the sea cliff, windy and high,
To a grassy crevice where we may lie,
  Lulled by the spell of the kobold pine,
Looking over the endless sea
  Into the smile of the setting sun,
Talking madly of Arcady,
  And watching sharp for a galleon.
Hand in hand, oh playmate divine,
  Hand in hand where the tide waves leave

The wet sand bright, shall we skip when eve
Comes tenderly, playmate o' mine.*

When he found her, she was not one of the Village girls, although he had unsuccessfully addressed himself to many of them. The attitude toward "Red" Flatman in Harry Kemp's *More Miles* suggests the reason for his failure.

> " 'Red' Flatman, though he has his qualities . . . if you're looking for my opinion—just DOESN'T BELONG!—'Life of the Party'—have any of you ever travelled on shipboard?—well, on every ship a moron is sure to pop up, early during the voyage, known as 'Life of the Party'—nuf said."
>
> "That's what 'Red' has tried to be ever since he hit the Village. . . ."
>
> "—Right! He doesn't get us at all—"
>
> "You bet he doesn't—strives so hard to be 'Bohemian' . . . feels it incumbent on himself to try to kiss all the women."

Neither socially nor intellectually did Sinclair Lewis share very intimately in the life of Greenwich Village. He had not yet "learned to be charming." And he was not moved either by the grave Bournesque optimism or by the rather crude Menckenian pessimism derived from Ibsen and Nietzsche. But we must remember two facts. One is suggested by Henry F. May when he points out in *The End of American Innocence* that most American skeptics were not desperate, alienated pessimists. Sinclair Lewis fits into an older American pattern than that of the New York radical—the familiar "small-town scoffer," who "usually read Paine and Voltaire." Professor May continues:

> Though he delighted in raising the hackles of the orthodox, he was seldom really antireligious and never unmoral. His enemies were censorship, prudery, and what he thought of as the lies of the churches. He delighted, in the name of real morality, to expose hypocrisy and to smoke out the sins of the godly. He usually espoused some kind of mild social radicalism, often a type of monetary inflation. His style was violent and deliberately picturesque.

And the second fact is that young Lewis, in New York, was a businessman, employed in the offices of a commercial publisher and himself determined to become a successful commercial writer.† The people whom he saw most frequently in these years were other young men in the publishing

* One must make an effort to tolerate this nonsense. It may help to remember that even D. H. Lawrence, in his 1912 novel, *The Trespasser,* employed the notion and the vocabulary sympathetically.

† When, in the fall of 1912, Sigmund Spaeth came into the literary agency of Dorothy Priestman as a reader, one of her clients was Sinclair Lewis, for whom she had been able to sell nothing. Flora May Holly had been abandoned; after Dorothy Priestman, there would be four other New York literary agents: Brandt and Kirkpatrick, Ann Watkins, Curtis Brown, Ltd., and Marcella Powers.

houses: William Rose Benét, George Soule, Alfred Harcourt, B. W. Huebsch, Harry Maule, Harrison Smith.

With these men and others, Sinclair Lewis met informally at lunch every month to talk about books and business, but even in this congenial atmosphere, B. W. Huebsch remembered, Lewis was noisy, raucous, demanding. Although he did not enjoy dirty stories, he showed a vein of coarseness not in the others, a pruriency that leaked out from his restrictive puritanism and from what was almost certainly a by now festering and troublesome virginity. He talked about "garter snapping," and one is reminded of the second Mrs. Upton Sinclair's account of her first meeting him in 1912. They were sitting side by side at a café table, and his talk was entertaining, but "while it poured out he gently laid his hand on my knee and began to press it. . . . 'Is that the way you make love in New York?' His hand was withdrawn and the conversation was not interrupted." The son of Arthur S. Hoffman, who employed him in 1912, remembers his father telling about a stag dinner at which Lewis persisted in making salacious remarks about a young woman whom everyone in the company except Lewis knew to have recently become engaged to marry one of the men who was present, and the acute embarrassment of all of them.

Yet he had a kind of gawky gallantry, too, that appealed to older women, even against their will. George Soule remembered Frederick A. Stokes as a very proper gentleman with a set of rigid office rules, among them the rule that there be no smoking on the premises. Sinclair Lewis smoked a good deal, and smoked cheap, odorous cigarettes called Home Runs that cost five cents a package. He occupied a cubbyhole of an office next to Mr. Stokes's own, and he kept a little box in his drawer into which he would ditch his butts when anyone approached; when they had passed or gone, he would, in his thrifty way, light up the butt. Mr. Stokes's secretary, a Miss Vera Quinn, middle-aged, efficient and very severe, knew that he was breaking the rules, but she had a real affection for him and never told. She was touched by him, and he was always gracious to her. (Later, in October of 1913, when Soule, Lewis, and Harrison Smith all took rooms uptown at 2469 Broadway in the residence of the elder Soules, Mrs. Soule was warmly fond of him. She was deeply New England, restrained and aloof, but Sinclair Lewis's native gentility, or perhaps gentleness, under the clumsy, explosive exterior, touched her interest and her sympathy.)

Lewis was at Stokes for a little over two years, from October 1, 1910, until October 20, 1912. Beginning as a manuscript reader, he was slowly moved over to publicity and in November of 1911 he boasted to Jack London that he was "planting about as much as any press agent in the country." He was an aggressive and successful young editor. While he chafed under the tyrannical William Morrow, the editorial power in the firm, he yet did his work faithfully and well and with utmost conscientiousness. With George Soule's support, he approached Morrow with the proposal that the house take on both H. G. Wells and Theodore Dreiser, but Morrow refused to consider either on the grounds that Wells was too intellectual to sell and Dreiser too immoral to publish.

He was encouraged, however, in his nearly sly campaign to win Jack London away from Macmillan. An initial inquiry brought a firm refusal from London but also led him to ask for information about the highest royalties that Stokes paid and about magazine rates paid to the best-known authors. Lewis dutifully sent him the results of his researches into these matters, but the question of London's coming to Stokes was dropped for nearly a year; then, in response to another inquiry from Lewis, London suddenly sent him a highly conspiratorial telegram in which he asked what Stokes's top price for a book of connected stories would be. The flurry of interest at Stokes nearly brought London to New York, where Lewis was offering to house him (one wonders how), and then the whole matter died again.

The old plot arrangement had died, too. In August of 1911, London closed a letter with the invitation to send along any plots that he wished to dispose of at any time, and Lewis immediately obliged by sending him seventeen and a price list. When, after six weeks, no reply had come, Lewis sent him a curious inquiry.

> How do you find my plots go, in general? Good investment? I sure hope they are. I've had so much fun reading the stories you have made from them—for instance the capital "Abysmal Brute." Do they prove a good business investment? Some time I'll have to get real tactful and try to find a way to get you to make me a *wedding present* * of some modest per cent. of your profits on 'em. Please tell your pleasant lady, Mme. Charmian, to tell me how to get you to ante up in this cheerful fashion to this youthful and timid partner (or is it local manager?) of yours.

London's ungracious answer came ten days later:

> Dear Lewis:–
>
> In reply to yours of October 10, 1911. Yes, I received the plots some time ago, but have not been home very much. Please find inclosed my check for $15.00 for THE GRIT OF DOCTOR PIBBIN, THE DESERTER, and GREATER LOVE. Several reasons prevent me from taking more of them. In the first place, a number of them are regular O. Henry plots. O. Henry could have handled them, and they'd have been great for his style of handling. And then, since the first of the year I've been working quite steadily on the SMOKE BELLEW takes for THE COSMOPOLITAN, and the SUN TALES in SATURDAY EVENING POST. You see, I haven't been using up any outside short story ideas at all.

* If he was really contemplating marriage, one can only speculate as to the identity of the lady in question. He was not to meet his future wife for more than a year.

How would you suggest a possible play out of THE ABYSMAL BRUTE? I can't possibly see any. Frankly, I don't know whether I'm making money or losing money by working up some of those other short-story ideas I got from you. Take THE ABYSMAL BRUTE, for instance. I got $1200.00 for it. After it had been refused by the first-class magazines. Had the time I devoted to it been devoted to SMOKE BELLEW or SUN TALES, I'd have got $3000 for the same amount of work.

The foregoing is merely in reply to your question. Personally, despite the fact that it did not make a financial killing, I'm darned glad I wrote THE ABYSMAL BRUTE.

Thanks for the tip about the new Hampton Columbian Magazine. Luckily, they do not owe me anything. But you can understand how extremely valuable your tip would have been had they been in my debt. Gee! Any time you get a tip like that, send it along.

Sincerely yours,
Jack London

So much for the "wedding present"!

Lewis survived the blow. "Thanks for the fifteen—it is now a part of a winter overcoat, very much needed in these pleasing N.Y. winds." A final note on this relationship appears in a letter of June 27, 1931, from Lewis to George Sylvester Viereck, in which he gives Viereck permission to publish a letter from Lewis to his bibliographer, Harvey Taylor, and adds, "But it seems to me that it might give a false impression—that Jack London had to have new plots from other people. That was not at all the case. He had plenty of his own but, like most writers, as I now know, he got tired of plots that had been too long with him, and a fresh one always seemed more enticing." The assertion that London had "plenty of his own" may be questioned.

In at least one of his letters to London, Lewis expresses his impatience with his job and his hope that he can leave it soon in order to free-lance. After only a few months at Stokes, he was apparently considering possible employment that would give him greater freedom; in a letter dated January 11 his father wrote him in response to some such suggested possibility, "Your Millionare tutorship would be rather pleasant I imagine in the way of ease and travel but you would be of about as much social standing as the butler." In the early spring, he apparently proposed to his mother that he come back to Sauk Centre and devote himself to writing. She replied:

Of course if you can get three or four weeks vacation and feel you can afford the trip, we shall be glad to see you—but as to staying a long time—do not think it will prove beneficial to you or any of us—You always *were going to write* when home before, but never did—nor in California or elsewhere—Your best things have been written when you had some steady work—& don't you see my boy that you like to be idle, dream, smoke &

> loaf—& think it is genius, but it is not. A young man that can't make good & keep one position for at least two years—will not do good work any where—So my dear Harry look at it sensibly and keep a good thing, as you have many hours for writing as well as office & play—
>
> It is because we want you to do good work and be a manly man & fill your place in the world as one who has your advantages, should—

The good woman then sends him a paragraph of local news and concludes,

> Do not think me harsh—but that we care so much for you, that to see you make the best of yourself & form habits of work—as well as play, is my great desire.
>
> Lovingly,
> *Mother*

That this letter threw the young man into a rage of disappointment is suggested by the fact that the letter was crumpled into a ball before it was smoothed out again and saved. He then wrote two letters, one in reply to his mother, another in explanation to his father. Both were proofread and signed, but apparently, on consideration, neither was mailed, for the originals were saved with the letters from his parents. To his mother he wrote:

> Will you kindly remember that I am not a child. Your letter of the 5th is one of the most highly inadvisable which I, a businessman, accustomed to read many highly inadvisable letters from unsuccessful writers, have had the misfortune of reading.
>
> The fact that I have, hitherto, been almost childishly frank in my letters to you has, I now see, also been exceedingly inadvisable. I shall not continue in the error.
>
> Will you kindly also recall the fact that, actually, you know nothing whatever regarding my ability, the use of my time, my habits, means of writing, or anything else of importance regarding me.
>
> You may be very sure that I shall not plan coming to Minnesota for a stay *with you* of any considerable time. I shall probably come; but not to stay with you—rather to camp, on the lakes, and on my own money. The tone of your letter might easily be construed as exceedingly inhospitable. But I know that it proceeds only from your unfortunate conclusion that you are qualified to advise me in matters of which you know nothing whatever. How much experience have you had with writing that you should regard yourself as qualified to advise me, in the tones of a long-suffering school teacher? Kindly do not repeat the error. It will save my temper. Kindly, also, do not go into hysterics over this letter. It is thoroughly justified by yours; but it will not be necessary for me again to speak thus.

He signed it "Sinclair Lewis." And so he signed the letter to his father, but typing "The Stokes Co." beneath that signature as if to remind the old doctor that he was indeed "a business man."

I regret to learn from Mother's letter of the 5th that she does not wish me to come and stay at her house. I had supposed that I might be a welcome guest. But that is, of course, her business. Any hostess has the right to censor her list of guests. Much though this hurt me, it is as nothing, however, in comparison with the dictatorial advising tone of her letter. I am writing her to the effect that it will not be necessary, hereafter, for her to endeavor to direct my authorial affairs, as I do not regard her as sufficiently experienced in the writer's craft to be qualified to speak to me, an expert, of matters regarding which I am best qualified to judge. I do not expect her to apologize; but I do pray, however, that I may be freed from hysteria regarding this justified rebuke of mine.

And on the back of this letter, in pencil, appear these jottings:

our
M
Mr. Wren, Mr. Wm.
Wren, Sales Club of
the
M Pct
shoo

In his expense account for the last week of that April 1911, he wrote, "No salary—out of office 1 wk. writing—hence $25 less on hand than would be normally." *Nautilus,* later that year, reported that "Sinclair Lewis has been studying more aviation this summer down at Provincetown, Mass., where he has been writing a boy's book, working on his new novel, reading Arnold Bennett, and sticking on the job—as he says in a recent letter."

That summer he took a two-month vacation, apparently on salary, to write a boy's book to order for Stokes. In 1938, replying to an inquiry from Chauncey Tinker, he said,

You're damn right I wrote HIKE AND THE AEROPLANE, for the sole and not very commendable purpose of getting from the firm of Frederick A. Stokes & Company, who paid outright for the book at salary rates, a long vacation to do a few words on my first novel, "OUR MR. WREN." The transaction was deplorable on all sides, and I believe the book is now worth a lot of money.

Under these circumstances, it is curious that the contract, witnessed by George Soule, was not drawn until April 18, 1912. By its terms, Lewis was to be paid two hundred dollars and a three per cent royalty, and two hundred dollars was precisely two months' salary. Again, this meant seeing Mary Heaton Vorse, who was kind to him and for whom, all his life, he felt a rather special affection and loyalty, even though they were never intimately associated. It was in this summer of 1911 that she is supposed to have made that statement about writing that his lifelong quoting was to make famous: "The art of writing is the art of applying the seat of your pants to the seat of your chair." (His variant, in an interview nearly forty years later, ran, "A mighty important thing for all authors to cultivate is this thing Mencken refers to as *'Sitzfleisch.'* ")

Among other Provincetown inhabitants was the critic Edwin Björkman, whom Lewis had first known at Helicon Hall; and Harry Kemp gives us some reason to think that, toward the end of Lewis's second month, Björkman accompanied him on his visit to the Updegraffs at West Becket, Massachusetts—when "about 10,000 sailors and their 'cute' officers especially" dropped anchor in Provincetown harbor. In *More Miles,* the character called Jessie is obviously meant to represent Edith Summers, Updegraff's wife, and Jim is Updegraff.

> Jessie chattered excitedly, nervously: about poetry; about herself; her student days; her subsequent life when she was secretary for Penton Baxter at Halcyon Hall . . . she spoke much about her present days with Jim and about "Red" Flatman, who was one day to be the author of the great book "Commercial Street," satirical of the dullness and stupidity of life in the small town . . . Flatman, aping and japing in the small town manner ever natural to him . . .
>
> Then was brought up in reminiscence of the previous summer, an anecdote of "Red" Flatman's unconscious selfishness . . . when he had been visiting, as I now,—at Hillwood . . .
>
> It was told me how one morning Flatman had nonchalantly dipped his hairbrush into the waterbutt, afterward applying its wet bristles to his mop of unruly hair.
>
> "He's so keen on himself he often doesn't know what he does."
>
> "It made poor Workmann, the Swedish literary critic, retch, from a delicate stomach—

Then, on the second of September, he returned resentfully to the offices of Stokes and his five-dollar room at 10 Van Nest Place. Harry Kemp, together with George Soule and William Rose Benét (then at *Century* magazine), also had rooms in that house. All poor, they lived frugally. In Lewis's accounts, the item "Gr" is some times as little as forty cents a day, although the average is perhaps more nearly seventy-five. On Sunday mornings, the three friends usually went to the Brevoort where they had "brunch," a term that George Soule believed they invented. Harry Kemp, whose personal resentment of Lewis was to become so patent in later years, was not entirely of the group. George Soule remembered that, on one occasion when Kemp boasted that he knew more lyric poems than anyone else, Sinclair Lewis challenged him to a contest. Each then began a long, alternating recitation, lyric poem after lyric poem, one after the other. It went on all through the night, through the dawn, until breakfast time, when they called it off. Benét, in *The Dust Which Is God,* gives us a glimpse of the setting:

The hall-room had a welsbach that popped and glowed
with a red tatter   the trunk and bed and chair
and bureau filled it   the street was a vocal swarm
of brats by day and cats by night   stout people
elbows on pillows in windows   and the "L"
whining around a curve
the landlady had beer
down in the parlor every Saturday night
and a buxom genial bearing
Larry Harris
lived just across the hall . . .

Living in Greenwich Village, not entirely accepted by its leading spirits, Sinclair Lewis had his own reservations, even suspicions, about Bohemia. Very early he developed one of his exasperatingly reiterated terms to describe this world and to express his resentments and his suspicions—Hobohemia. These attitudes, which come to something of a climax in *Main Street* when we are told about Carol Kennicott's experiences with the Bohemians of Chicago, were established before the word was coined, and they were maintained until the end of his life. But still, now, he clung to the fringes of that world.

In the summer of 1912 he went again to Provincetown for the month of July, and there he finished a first draft of *Our Mr. Wrenn.* In *Time and the Town,* Mary Heaton Vorse, while confusing his literary activity of one summer with that of another, gives a tolerant glimpse of him in that mood of japery that so irked most others.

Sinclair Lewis was back, living at the Avellars' wharf. He was prodigious. He would come into the house, roaring that "he had a girl and her name was Daisy, when she sang the cat went crazy, with delirium and epilepsy and all sorts of cataleptics." A stream of fantasies, of stories, of ideas streamed from him. He never stopped. He ate almost as much blueberry pie as Wilbur Steele. . . .

He was never still, his hair flamed, his blue eyes blazed, his long, sensitive hands gesticulated. He got himself sunburned to dull plum color over and over again and peeled. He galloped over the dunes barefoot. He shook sand into the picnic basket. He came in shouting he had an idea, and a flood of nonsense to float Noah's Ark would resound through Kibbe Cook's house.

I would chase him out with a broom. The children would join in. The dog would bark. We would go slamming in and out Kibbe Cook's house doors, with Red leading all of us, looking like one of the earlier Sennett films.

Other women found him entertaining, too. Miss Perkins, wondering why, was among them.

He was queer, he was funny, he was also amusing. He was also appealing. That is, he appealed to one's parental sense, and one felt like protecting

> him and not letting him be hurt by other young men whom one knew, and who tended to make fun of him. . . . I grew to like him very much for no reason that I can now assess. He never was a protective or helpful or romantic young man, or if he was romantic, we thought it was make believe.

Frequently he joined her and her friends in Sunday excursions on Staten Island, sometimes on fine, fair winter days, sometimes in the spring before the season had begun, and they would walk and build a fire on the deserted dunes of South Beach and have a picnic. A few times she went alone with Lewis, and from one of these occasions comes a nice illustration, not single but double, of his naïveté. In the ferry house he observed two girls who were alone and he began to worry about what would happen to them in the wicked city.

> . . . since he at the same time saw the little whitecapped worker from the Florence Crittenton Mission, nothing would satisfy him but that I get as excited as he was, and he asked the Florence Crittenton worker to make sure these girls did not get into trouble. I remember they were quite young and quite pretty. She at first declined but Lewis insisted very dramatically, and I suppose I agreed with him. She actually boarded the ferry with these girls and we all hovered around and Lewis stuck closely by them when we got off the ferry and took them by the arm over to the elevated railway. There one of the girls turned and said to me, "What are you doing to us? What have you got against us, anyway?" Sinclair then tried to explain to her the horrible danger she was running there. She looked at him and said, "What are you doing? I have been on the turf since I was fifteen. You get along now and don't ruin my night's business."
>
> Lewis was crestfallen to think that his judgment was wrong and that these were a pair of professionals. The Crittenton Mission worker had given up earlier. I have never forgotten the look on that poor woman's face as she went back to the ferry. She gave us a look of utter disgust and annoyance at having been led on a wild goose chase. Lewis was all stirred up by this time, however, and on the elevated railway he spotted a young couple. The girl looked ill, and very dopey, I must admit. Lewis' immediate reaction was that here was a wicked man who had been giving dope to this young girl, whom he expected to seduce. They were headed north and he insisted on going with them. We sat opposite them, watching them very closely. They finally went as far as a street in the 130's and we, sticking right with them, got off when they did and followed them down the street of a fashionable and respectable neighborhood. As they turned in, the man turned around and said to us, "I would like to ask why you are following us." "We think that girl is doped and we want to know what you are up to," said Lewis. Then the woman turned and said, "I have got a terrible sick headache and my husband is taking me home." In other words, Lewis had chosen to follow a perfectly respectable young married couple.

Miss Perkins' generous feelings about him survived these occasions, survived even the embarrassing time when he proposed marriage to her "at the top of his lungs on a warm summer evening when all the windows in the apartment building where I was living were open." Similarly, Elizabeth Jordan, writing about him in *Three Rousing Cheers,* recovered from the "annoyance and embarrassment" he caused her one Sunday evening when, riding downtown on a streetcar, he decided to amuse the other passengers by imitating a drunk. The recollections of Sonya Levien (later Mrs. Carl Hovey) were of the same sort. She was studying law in Washington Square when she met him, and she remembered his gawkiness, his wrists always extending out of his sleeves, the color of his rough skin (for which she and a number of others referred to him as "the blue boy"), and his insisting that he was the true poet, that his friend, William Rose Benét, was the prose writer.

Since he seemed to become intoxicated on a single drink and since she did not drink at all, she frequently protested about his drinking, and one night when they were waiting together for a Fifth Avenue bus and she protested again, he said that she was conventional. This she denied and he said that he would prove it, whereupon he knelt on the sidewalk, opened his arms, and at the top of his voice began to recite—to chant—Robert Burns. She fled up the street, he pursued her, and when he stopped her, made her admit that he had proved his point. Still, he amused her and they were frequently together. Once, when it was said in the Village that Hippolyte Havel had been evicted from his room, the two of them raised enough money to pay his rent. The anticlimax came when, having climbed the steps to his place in order to deliver the money, they found him sitting in a hall window reading a Greek text and were brusquely told to go away and not to disturb him with their bourgeois concerns.

Another such relationship was with Edna Ferber, three of whose letters he preserved. In *A Peculiar Treasure* she wrote about him and clarified the strange gibberish of these letters.

> Business was unimportant to me. Sometimes the odd young man who was publicity writer for the Stokes company used to talk to me about it, whenever he managed to talk seriously at all, which was practically never. He was a gangling, red-headed popeyed fellow; shambling, untidy, uproariously funny. Together we would go gesticulating and jabbering along the New York streets, leaving a procession of startled or shocked faces turned toward us as we went. The cuckoo young man's name was Sinclair Lewis, but everyone called him Red. He and I had built up two characters which we always assumed when together. Red was Gus, the janitor of a mythical office building, and I was Tillie, the scrubwoman. We talked in a bad German dialect, faintly Weber-and-Fieldsian, and not very funny except to us.
>
> "Tillie, you vas earning goot money on new chob, ain't?"
>
> "Ja, only for my knees, them new kind stone floors."
>
> This would go on for hours. Red was better than I at it—more outrageous. His linen was the grubbiest, he had no money, he would escort

me to the door of one of those literary parties to which I had been bidden, but nothing could induce him to come in.

"Naw, I'd be trun out of there. They wouldn't want me in there."

In a year or two I, too, learned that literary parties got you nowhere and were very dull stuff indeed.*

The everyday association with Stokes and with Stokes's authors was about to end. After Lewis had returned from Provincetown in August, he wrote to Gene Baker about his plans.

> And now? My dear, I'm going to stick so tight on this job [rewriting *Mr. Wrenn*] that one could scarce, even with infinite pains, insert a bit of gold leaf between me and it, till I get Mr. Wrenn finished and either accepted by a publisher or in a good littery agent's hands; after that, till I've made some money by writing some magazine rot or otherwise; and then I'm going to beat it, *I hope,* and never be on another job again except some fool job I hold down for a month or so to get some copy.

But on October 20, having resigned from Stokes, he became an assistant editor on the pulp magazine *Adventure* at twenty dollars a week. On November 1, his total resources added up to $1.25, and he owed various people $62. In two years, he had not come far on a way littered with disappointments.

Adventure was edited by Arthur Sullivant Hoffman, who had employed Lewis as his only assistant at *Transatlantic Tales* in 1907 and who sought him out now when his associate editor retired. *Adventure* was a Butterick magazine, an addition to the Dreiser trio of *Delineator, Designer* and *Woman's Magazine,* and Dreiser's office was only a few feet away from Lewis's. The old Butterick Building was a huge pile, with presses in the basements and many floors of packaging and mailing rooms. The main lobby of the editorial suite was elaborate with stained glass, leaded panes, dark-wood paneling, and old Mr. Gannon, one of the company officers, is reported often to have remarked that it looked like a "fifty-dollar house," an impression that was heightened by the scores of underpaid young girls who worked there.

In this atmosphere of vulgar opulence, Hoffman and Lewis put together their unlikely magazine dedicated to the pure and pulpy adventures of brave and brawny men, and the office became "a world crossroads for explorers, big-game hunters, prospectors, and ship captains"—or so said *Newsweek* in its account of the twenty-fifth anniversary of the magazine in 1935. Lewis and Hoffman shared the job of reading manuscripts, copy editing, correcting proof, setting up dummies, and every other bit of routine that the publishing of a magazine involves, and the relationship between them was always amicable.

* Copyright 1938, 1939 by Edna Ferber. Copyright © 1960 by Morris L. Ernst, et al., Trustees. All rights reserved.

"Many years afterward," Mr. Hoffman remembered, "he told me a big factor in our friendship was that I had never given him an order." After the unpleasant experience of "Kin." Noyes's self-importance on the *Volta Review* and of William Morrow's martial notions and Frederick Stokes's genteel rigidity, this freedom at *Adventure* was a change that Lewis welcomed. And then there was whimsey besides, that major necessity: between them, Hoffman and Lewis set up a "Society for the Suppression of Useless Giving," known as "Spugs," and planned endless greeting cards for all the gift-giving holidays until their prospective publisher saw that, if he were to pursue their plan, the demand for greeting cards might well vanish along with foolish giving, and then that whimsey evaporated into some other.

Of more real concern to Arthur Hoffman and apparently to Sinclair Lewis was "The Camp-Fire" section at the back of their book. "It is the one place in the world," they announced in their issue of February 1913, "where every adventurer is welcome and where all who love adventure can gather to ask questions or to answer them, to talk over old times or plan new tilts with fate, to make new friends or once more to grasp the hands of old ones." Here they published letters of reminiscence, plans for expeditions, inquiries about expeditions being planned. To this section, in May, they added another, headed "Wanted—Men and Adventures," and in June still another, called "Lost Trails." In "Lost Trails" Lewis himself published an inquiry: "Where is Kenneth, or 'Kid' MacNicoll, last heard of in Carmel, California, and Arizona? Address Tom Graham, care *Adventure.*" It was "Kid" MacNicoll who, with Mike Williams, had invited Lewis to his first "mulligan" at Carmel. *Ubi sunt?*

From "The Camp-Fire" came The Adventurers' Club, an informal dinner club that met as early as December 1912 (Lewis's accounts for December 7 include the item "Adventurers' Club—$4.15") and that held its organizational dinner in February of 1913. Its membership consisted not only of many contributors to the magazine but also of professional explorers who were not writers, and very quickly branches were formed in Chicago and San Francisco, Honolulu and Los Angeles, and elsewhere. Lewis was instrumental in organizing the club and was himself eligible because of his trials and tribulations on cattle boats some years before. His admiration for physically competent men (and boys) goes back to old reveries, and there is no question about his enjoyment of the respectable roustabouts who met at the Adventurers' for dinner. In the August 1913 issue of the magazine, he wrote an extended account in "The Camp-Fire" about Grant Wallace, a correspondent in the Russo-Japanese war and a reporter for the New York *Evening Sun* whom Lewis had known at Carmel, and in this account he reports at length on Wallace's sagacity about the threat of the Japanese to the United States. "Then he used to watch their crafty methods of getting into the United States. By paying enough they can perform this operation as follows: They land in Mexico, get tickets for Canada," etc. "Grant made prophecies . . . as to the large number of Japanese soldiers who are coming and will come to California, well officered and trained; the ease of investing California clear to the Sierra Nevadas and fortifying the passes; and their desire to do so."

An earnest young man, misguided by his earnestness? or an uncommitted young man, playing the publishing "game"? Either way, it is not easy to relate him, as he appears in such writing, with the jape that he also was. James Mitchel Clarke, who came to *Adventure* shortly after Lewis had departed (and he departed in that very August of 1913 in which his notes on the threat of the wily Japanese had been published) remembers Arthur Hoffman's talking about him after he had gone.

> Lewis would come into the office, or into homes of friends, and launch into verbatim reproductions of conversations he had heard. . . . Lewis was gifted—or cursed—with total recall, and these performances would sometimes go on for hours. The duller the conversation, the more pleasure Lewis seemed to take in repeating it. I gathered from Hoffman that listening was rather like being in the same room with a tape recorder which could not be turned off.

This is the earliest account of that habit of imitation that went on for the rest of his life and that could be briefly amusing and very quickly so tiresome. Yet one must remember that he had other qualities, serious convictions if no real commitments, convictions perhaps no less tiresome than his imitations, but capable of being acted upon. He stayed with The Adventurers' Club well into the war years, and the Adventurers, to a man except for Lewis, were enthusiastic about American participation. Lewis was a pacifist, and at his last dinner with the club, when the talk grew warm, he arose in his place, submitted his resignation from the club and announced his intention of sailing with Henry Ford's Peace Ship. (On the same grounds, he quarreled violently with Updegraff in 1915, and their friendship broke off; after that, Updegraff remembers, they saw one another seldom, and with little warmth.) He did not sail, of course, but in resigning from the Adventurers' he had actualized his conviction up to about twenty per cent. The Peace Ship, foolish comedy that it proved to be, would have demanded more than a flourish.

With at least one other group, a looser and much more literary assembly, he also associated during these years. This was the "Bagdad Club," as remembered by Waldo Frank.

> A bunch of us got together either once a week or once a fortnight, in one of the "red-ink" caravansaries . . . I was a newspaper man. The other chaps

were predominantly journalists, workers in advertising agencies, publishers houses. There were no established writers among us; but we all professed a love of literature. (The club's name argues some sort of admiration for O. Henry, or at least for his thesis of New York as a city of magic and wonder.) Lewis was one of us. . . . What did we have in common? Not values or tastes, surely. I recall one chap named Wood who adored Wagner (then at the high-tide) whom I detested. Lewis adored the new English novelists—chiefly Wells, whom I also despised. (Unjustly, somewhat, it now seems to me). But we all loved books, and I'm sure each of us was sure who would be the author of the Great American Novel. My sense of Lewis is that he always had high literary dreams—and tried to laugh them off, finding them uncomfortable to possess—particularly after they had seemed to "come true." . . . My feeling is that Lewis was very much concerned always with literary merit. He also wanted to make money, and he had a hard time, perhaps, fusing these two drives. He did not seem to be sure of himself as a writer—I mean, as a writer of value and stature. Perhaps, therefore, he pretended he was a hard-boiled "commercial." He was at times almost uncomfortably humble, with me—who had done nothing, in those days.

The "high literary dreams" were to remain just that for another twelve months when Lewis accepted employment with the Publishers Newspaper Syndicate on August 30, 1913. W. E. Woodward, later the author of a work called *Bunk,* was in 1912 an employee of the J. Walter Thompson agency, and he had observed that the dullest advertising in all newspapers outside New York was on the book page, and that the book page itself was about the dullest in the paper. It occurred to him that he might syndicate a weekly book review page written by informed New Yorkers and, as part of his service, obtain advertising from publishers.

He contracted with a dozen newspapers throughout the country, employed Edgar van Slyke, advertising solicitor for the book page of the New York *Evening Post,* as his partner, and needed now only an editor who would actually write the reviews. It was Rodman Gilder, the son of the editor of the *Century,* who suggested Sinclair Lewis for that position. "Listen," Woodward in his autobiography, *The Gift of Life,* reported Gilder as having said, "this Lewis chap has been knocked all over the lot by people who think they are his betters. He's had a hard life, and is dog poor, but he has ability. I'm sure he'd be a good man for you. Call him up and see him." At dinner at the Brevoort, Woodward explained the position to him and offered it.

"How much are you going to pay me?"

"Oh," I said hastily, "I'd forgotten. I'm sorry. The job pays sixty dollars a week."

Lewis looked at me across the table in utter surprise. It showed all over his countenance. "Sixty dollars a week!" he exclaimed, and jumped up, almost overturning his chair as he rose. "Sixty dollars! Shake." He reached across the table and seized my hand. "Shake on it. It's a bargain. When do I begin?"

Then Woodward hired a second young man as editorial assistant, George W. Bunn, Jr., newly graduated from Princeton, and to this young man Lewis and modern literature were to owe a peculiar debt. In the preceding spring, George Bunn had written the book for the Triangle Club show, and he talked about it with Lewis because he had some idea of rewriting it in the hope of a Broadway production. Probably neither of them knew that its title had been used earlier for an obscure short sketch by Nathaniel Hawthorne, and Lewis allowed that it would be a good title for a novel. The title was *Main Street.*

With Woodward, Lewis would plan the material that was to go out each week, and then he would go over it with George Bunn—Lewis looking like a country editor in the green eye shade that he now and always afterward wore at work. Between them they wrote the reviews. Lewis's, if written in prose, were usually signed "S.L.," but sometimes he would use a general pseudonym such as "An Army Officer." He signed his initials to a regular column called "The Book of the Week," but his occasional rimed reviews were signed "Tom Graham" or "Max Besont." There were two further columns, the first "The Village Doctor Says," colloquial and chatty, the second "The Tower Window," by "Michael Strong" (who may have been George Bunn), high-brow and literary. Occasional outsiders were invited to write reviews—Simeon Strunsky, Lincoln Steffens, Willa Cather, Booth Tarkington among them—and although the offices of the Syndicate were not very imposing (two inside rooms, one occupied by Woodward, Van Slyke and a stenographer, the other by Lewis, Bunn, and an office boy who kept the scrapbook), the staff fell into the habit of serving tea (or whisky—in teacups to deceive temperate ladies) to visiting authors. He was rubbing elbows frequently with persons whose literary dreams had been realized.

What was he doing to realize his own? Many people remember his supreme self-confidence, his conviction that a great literary career lay ahead of him. Sonya Levien was only one of them. "At this time," she said, "he thought that the world was his; he had an enormous and inexhaustible enthusiasm. He saw everything in a heightened form. If the sun was bright, it was brighter for him; if people were amusing, they were *more* amusing for him." This was no doubt his usual public self, but his disappointments were many and bitter, and his confidence was to flag. In early 1911 he wrote Gene Baker, "I am a persistent young youth. . . . I keep on writing . . . (short stories!)", but he had very little success, and in these years he was "acquiring . . . a conviction that he never would, never could, learn to compose anything more imaginative than advertisements for bad novels." Even after he had managed to publish two novels, their small success discouraged him, and he "who had tried to be a writer of fiction" gave up "that folly forever and wistfully hoped some day to be George Doran's partner (in charge of author-lunching and London-trips)."

Before coming to that conclusion, he was making every kind of literary effort. "There are few people who can hold a job and do creative work on the side," wrote Mary Heaton Vorse, whom Lewis credited with frequently sending him back to his typewriter when he wanted to stop writing. "Sinclair Lewis is one of the few people I have ever known who had the necessary vitality." The fact is, of course, that the work he was doing in these apprentice years when he was also regularly employed is quite unimpressive. When he came to New York at the end of 1910, he had published nearly seventy pieces of one sort or another (and had earned about one thousand dollars), but if we put all this work together, it is impossible to discern any central thematic interest or point of view, or even much to indicate what his characteristic techniques were to become. (A rather labored bit in a 1908 issue of *Puck,* called "Wailing and Fixing of Teeth," is an exception in its attempt at characterization, satirical self-revelation, through colloquial speech.)

Willa Cather once said that "the years from eight to fifteen are the formative period in a writer's life. He may acquire a great many interesting and vivid impressions in his mature years, but his thematic material he acquires under fifteen years of age." She meant, perhaps, not *subjects,* but rather values, basic patterns of conflict, the special attitude of mind, the particular emotional range and *timbre* that would prove to be characteristic of the entire mature work. Thus one might say of her own work that the basic material was "the past," the basic tone "elegiac."

But can one detect any such central focus in the early work of Sinclair Lewis? Only through fleeting hints that do not resolve themselves into considerable statement until the first novel. Then, perhaps, we can say that the basic theme is "The Other Place," or "Elsewhere," and the basic emotion, "Loneliness." Geographically, "The Other Place" was always to prove illusory; temporally, if Van Wyck Brooks is correct, it was the dream of a future America envisioned by Randolph Bourne.

He continued to write his absurd poems—Kiplingesque wishes to wander, baby-talk playhouse nonsense, some jaded Dowsonese, love poems addressed to an obdurate princess in towers with the poet in the role of jester outside and below.

"Lo what is yonder pool
Within the forest shady?"

"Why 'tis the heart's blood of Jacques-Fool
Who dieth for his Lady!"

It is all the more remarkable that he should have nourished such poetic preferences when he himself had already called Whitman "the only American poet," but it is perhaps merely just to point out that the state of poetry in the United States probably had never been so impoverished as in the first decade of this century, and that when Lewis's tastes were being formed, none of the poets who were to make literary history in the century had yet come upon the public scene, their tuning fiddles not yet heard. *Democratic Vistas* might never have been written, and the main body of American poetry had yet to hear Goethe's challenge—

Amerika, du hast es besser
Als unser Kontinent, der alte,
Du hast keine verfallene Schlösser
Und keine Basalte. . . .

Writing in 1911, G. E. Woodberry was quite accurate in observing that "the imaginative life is feeble, and when felt is crude; the poetic pulse is imperceptible." Floyd Dell, in *Intellectual Vagabondage,* serves to remind us that Lewis was hardly alone in his outrageous taste. Dell quotes from a much-admired, now little-known poet named Park Barnitz, "a mixture of Baudelaire, Swinburne, Wilde and Gautier"—

I am a little tired of all things mortal;
I see through half-shut eyelids languorous
The old monotonous
Gold sun set slowly through the western portal,
Where I recline upon my deep divan,
In Ispahan

—and adjures us: "Do not laugh. We of the younger generation all felt very much that way . . . it ill becomes us to sneer at the tawdry and banal and second-hand prettiness and pessimism of these lines. For who can doubt the sincerity of this performance?" Even Lewis's tawdriest lyrics, put beside such lines as these, do not look much worse. "A Canticle of Great Lovers," which appeared in *Ainslee's* in 1912, is a good enough example, but most of his verse he no longer published; increasingly, it was for private eyes alone.

In 1911 he tried his hand at the libretto of a musical comedy. In March of 1912 he told Gene Baker that "The bally musical comedy is still with the first firm of managers to which it went. The reader passed it up to the chief, but he's been sick for six weeks and hasn't read a single Ms." He remembered this work later as *President Poodle*—"never read by any one except SL and an agent," written "with a zealous joy and an ignorance of the stage which I suppose rarely to have been equalled"—but, from the evidence of the third act, which remains in manuscript, it was called *President Pip,* with *Prexy Pip* as the suggested alternate title.*

The comedy is set in a women's college, Gazelle Campus, and is meant to be a satire on woman suffrage, with the leading females named Amazona and Oceana. The old president has somehow been deposed and the new one is a young fellow who is determined to get the aggressive females married. He is also making a fortune in the false-hair market. There is some background in aviation that is not clear, but at the end of the script the author volunteers the following:

> The writer has worked out the mechanical method of handling the two aeroplane scenes—both the fall and landing in Act One, and the flight away from stage, end of Act Two—so that they can be set inexpensively and absolutely practically, either with town or road companies, and give the appearance of real flights.

Of the twenty-one songs that Lewis wrote for this effort, eight are extant. Where now were Randolph Bourne, John Reed, Floyd Dell?

It Makes No Dif, What One You've Won
If the One You've Won Wants You

John Henry was a honest youth,
But John was cross-eyed, very.

* Inaccurate as his recollection may have been, it was not so wildly mistaken as William Rose Benét chose to make his recollection (or optimistic reconstruction) in *The Dust Which Is God:*

In the Village life went on at carefree speed
save that Larry Harris was working hard
on a three-act play He read a little to Raymond
and Raymond thought it monstrous fine . . .

Out of the blue one morning
in the telephone the voice of Larry Harris
with Raymond in his office at the receiver
"I'll buy you a big one! Melvin's taken my play
It opens in October" . . .

Raymond with battering hands
And thumping heart heard the loud fusillade
roll wave after wave . . .

and there was Larry
tall and pale and grinning his wild red hair
a fiery beacon He was pumping hands
and saying "Thanks . . . gee . . . thanks! . . .

"Hats off to Larry Harris!"
"If 'The Moon is Blue' we're not The more balloons
Of national stupidity it punctured
the more it made us laugh."

Same man; different play.

The girls each handed John the hook,
But John kept bright and merry.
John would propose at half past eight,
And when he got rejected,
He'd find another girl by nine,
For that's what John expected.

CHORUS:
It makes no dif, what one you've won
If the one you've won wants you.
If you can't have your steak well done,
Then a piece of rare will do.
If Eyes of Brown should turn you down,
There's many eyes of blue.

Love Is My Aeroplane

For you, dear heart, I dare to fly,
And play at tag with death.
Among the singing stars I wing,
Upon the cyclone's breath.
I cheer the lightning's sudden flare,
The charge of bitter rain.
I risk the gale and dashing hail,
For love's my aeroplane.

REFRAIN:
I soar in heaven's highest blue,
Or roar through ringing rain.
My motor is the thought of you,
And love my aeroplane.

A harmless if perhaps melancholy effort, this comedy maintains the old interest in flying and initiates the lifelong desire to write for the stage.

Airplanes figure prominently too in that long short story for *Nautilus* called *Captains of Peace* that was finished in Washington but not published until the end of 1911 and the beginning of 1912. A hodgepodge of Wellsian "air science" and New Thought, it rested on a certain amount of research done while he was on *Volta Review*. The story was Lewis's most ambitious up to this time, but the truth is that he did not regard it seriously and was embarrassed when he learned that Gene Baker was reading it. Germany is about to destroy England, and Jarl Nordenhaus, a young Danish Nobel prize winner, impressed into the German service, escapes by plane to the United States where, through the money and interest of David Osborne, a billionaire New Thought poet, he organizes the Peace Army. Japan joins Germany, and the United States joins England, but the

Peace Army, with its magnificent new weapons, turns on both in the battle of East Rock, New Haven, and enforces peace at the cost of only a few hundred dead men. David Osborne is killed; Jarl and Colonel Gloria are joined; and a New Thought United Nations is organized with Jarl as President of the World. The New Thought elements are almost entirely limited to the idea of a determined optimism, of willing what you want.

Such optimism must have been in effect during the composition not only of this story but also of the other three stories that Lewis published during these years—one in *The Coming Nation* for April 29, 1911; another in *Short Stories* in August 1912; the third in *Short Stories* in March 1913. The first, "A Promising Young Man," is a feeble account of a stuffy young lawyer who meets a socialist girl and is converted to her cause after he sees her brought into the Night Court for Women for having picketed with some garment workers; he is also converted to her. The other two stories are attempts at satire. "Loki, the Red: The Career of a Near-Nihilist" is concerned with the theatrical career of an explosive Russian immigrant and tries to make a comedy out of current radical politics. "Scented Spring and the G.P." tries to make comedy out of advanced fashions in painting current in Greenwich Village and ends with the Metropolitan Museum buying a forged Monet. It is the old cry out of Philistia: modern painters are without talent and the public, even the expert public, is gullible.

Hike and the Aeroplane, written in three weeks in the summer of 1911, was published in mid-August of 1912. Combining his recollections of Benicia with his new knowledge of the "tetrahedral aeroplane," Lewis wrote what appears to be a perfectly conventional adventure story for boys, in the manner of *Tom Swift.* The story is made up of three separate episodes in each of which a villainous Captain Welch plots against the efforts of the sixteen-year-old hero, Hike, to make virtue prevail. The book was dedicated "To Edwin and Isabel Lewis, the Author's Oldest Friends," and the Yale copy carries the inscription, "To Sinclair Lewis from the author, Tom Graham, his altered ego." He put no great store in it and wrote Gene Baker as follows:

> It's not much of a book; it's all rather thin adventure; tho I've had three aviators—J. A. D. McCurdy, Glenn Curtiss and Captain [Paul W.] Beck of the Army, read it, and they've all praised it—I enclose a copy of the letter McCurdy wrote the firm about it. But that ain't no sign.... Since when were aviators established as the perfect court of literary judgment? Besides, I know all three of them personally.

Two enthusiastic responses from the audience for which the book was intended are extant. Clipping it from a letter, Lewis preserved the following: "Bryce Hapgood is crazy about Hike. His mother couldn't drive him to bed, and he was up at *five* next morning reading it"; and to that he appended this note: "Bryce Hapgood, the son of Hutchins Hapgood and nephew of Norman Hapgood, is a boy of about twelve." From young Stephen Vincent Benét, he had a direct response:

> It's swell, one of the best boys books this year, indeed the best. Are you going to write a sequel? I guess you are for you let the villain escape! Miss Granicle who has been visiting us says she will present a copy to the Benicia library. So you see how famous you are!!

There was no sequel. It was a job that he had taken on in order to have some free time to explore "the shabby little personality of Mr. Wrenn," as he wrote Gene Baker. In March of 1912 he wrote her again:

> For weeks I haven't written anything, but now I shall probably amuse myself with a novelette. I wanted awfly to finish Mr. Wren, but was wise (or unwise?) enough to hand over the 50,000 words I've written of him to a couple of friends, and they warned me that he is very immature; to be laid aside for some years. I've taken their advice, for once.

Frances Perkins remembers that she "read quantities of it in manuscript. He was serious about the novel and anxious to get ahead with it," and perhaps he asked others to read it as well. W. E. Woodward remembered that he took half of it to Mr. Stokes, and that Mr. Stokes returned it, saying that he hated to see a young man waste his time. "You're not cut out for a writer," said he, "and that's all there is to it. It's just not your game, and if I were you, I'd forget all about it." But Lewis did not agree. In August 1912 he wrote Gene Baker again to say that he had finished a first draft and that now he was going to devote himself to revising it; and that was his major effort during the winter that he worked on *Adventure*. His revision was completed well before he left that position. Macmillan, Century, and Holt had all declined it, but on May 6, 1913, Harper & Brothers accepted it. Elizabeth Jordan was his editor.

> I worked with him on the manuscript, and some of the changes I had to ask him to make were the kind that break an author's heart. He took them all with entire good-humor, and he never lost his grin. When he had done all the reconstruction he thought he could endure at one session, he would sit up suddenly and say, "Now, *praise* me!"
>
> The praise he liked best was my repeated prediction that he would develop into one of the great authors of his day.
>
> "Are you sure of that?" he often asked.
>
> "Absolutely," I always said. Then his grin grew wider. He was sure of it, too. Fortunately, we were both right.

Almost simultaneously an event of even greater importance than the acceptance of a first novel had occurred, and the combination left him spinning dizzily with unaccustomed happiness.

He had in these years pursued a dozen girls, fancying himself in love with them, proffering proposals half in earnest, half in jest, not unlike his own character of Cross-eyed Johnny in the song. Sonya Levien, Frances Perkins, Rose Strunsky, Edna Kenton—these are only a few of the Village girls about whom he flung his puppet person. Even Gene Baker ("Princesse Lointaine"), three thousand miles behind him in Oakland, was among them:

> Wives—none in sight, my dear. Of course I ain't heart whole and fancy free; I shouldn't be myself if I were. But I always fall in love with some mean devil like yourself who will none o' me. So I remain safe; and every Friday nite have enough money left over to go to a moving picture show.

His tentative endearments to her were met with a tart irony, and his experience of rejections went so far back in his twenty-seven years that he would no longer risk a serious proposal; but he had, at the same time, no way of subduing his frenetic interest in women. One thing had improved with the years: the hands still dangled from the scrawny wrists, the wrists still dangled from the cheap blue serge, but the hands themselves were thin and fine, the fingers long, and women looked on them with pleasure.

Late in the summer of 1912, Lewis and B. W. Huebsch took two girls, their names now forgotten, to the Lafayette for dinner and then drove to the beach at Port Washington. There, Lewis and his girl wandered off along the shore, and when they came back, the girl was crying, for she had lost her brooch. Ben Huebsch found the brooch and the tears subsided. Very soon after—on September 12, 1912—Sinclair Lewis found a lady, and his tears began. After working hours on that day, he accosted one Grace Hegger in the freight elevator of 443 Fourth Avenue, with the familiar "Haven't we met before?" Two months later he acquired at last his own "veskit," cost five dollars. In January of 1913 he spent twenty dollars on dancing lessons. In February he wrote his father about his wish to marry. The sage of Sauk Centre was as unbending as ever.

> I know of course that you would like a home but the getting together of a couple of people dont always make that a fact as your observation must teach you, and I think it best to look the ground over for ditches before making the jump. Were you getting thirty per here you might make a home but that is a question even here the way things are.
>
> I made such a move as you know but I would not do it again with added knowledge. The handicap is too great . . . Now don't for a moment think that I say all early marriages are wrong. Upty & Bill & a lot of your friends may be happier than kings & queens, but you can name a dozen to one that are not, and thats what you have to decide. There is another side you have not considered. "Adventure" may be a winner this year and go bump next you can't tell, there you are out looking for another job, alone

> thats no matter but with a dear little woman and possibly a kiddy to swing along its different.
>
> Were you in a way and had a royalty from two or three accepted books then all would be well. So my idea is get the foundation first and then take your chances. You can say of course that I won out but it was by such a hard struggle that I doubt you would like to have gone through it and I can and always feel had I waited five years longer *I* might have been a John B. Murphy * for I was much to the good when we were together but instead of sticking I had to go for bread & butter for the *family* had to be supported. Get your position first and then you can better afford to take chances. Now this will close the chapter, do just as you please, I am giving you actual experience from my viewpoint. While your life may be all roses I imagine you will find a lot of thorns mixed up in it like the rest of us.

What stolid advice to force upon the panting Jacques! But it was really irrelevant, for the lady would not yet have Jacques, *bouleversé* as he was.

* Dr. John B. Murphy, whom William J. Mayo called "The surgical genius of his generation," attended Rush Medical College during Dr. Lewis's last year there, but his training was longer and included an internship that Dr. Lewis had to eschew.

4

SINCLAIR LEWIS'S FIRST MARRIAGE is the subject of a twice-told tale, told each time by the same person, Grace Livingstone Hegger. She told it first as fiction in *Half a Loaf* (1931) and then as fact in *With Love from Gracie* (1955). The accounts are substantially the same. These are the only sustained reports on this at first bright, then soon bitter and rapidly deteriorating, relationship; but there are, of course, many more fleeting glimpses into it. "He took on the burden of a family," wrote Waldo Frank in *Time Exposures* (1926), "when he was not smart enough yet to bear the burden of himself." Perhaps we have observed the early evidence in sufficient detail to understand that this was the burden that he would never be able to bear. Because: what *was* the self? More important: *where* was it? And who was less equipped than "the lady" to help him to the answers?

The self-portrait that is evoked by these two books is perhaps more precisely drawn than the portrait of the major subject. She was very pretty and quite vain, spirited, crisply arrogant, proud of an indeterminate English background, could dress smartly on a low budget and valued smartness, was competent at her work, at once sensible about and exasperated by her life, given to airs and an accent. He—gawky, bumbling, unacquainted with elegance or style, unsuccessful in his major ambition, oafishly dressed, at once naïve and yet familiar with a quite tough experience of life and commerce, habituated to poverty, virginal still, restless, rejected, derided, and lonely—he found her everything of which one dreamed, the veritable "Princesse Lointaine"! Had they no sense whatever of fatality?

She perhaps a little more than he, or at least some doubts. He began almost immediately to make his proposals of marriage, but she held him off for a year before she consented and did not marry him until seven more months had passed. He was at once enormously proud of her and, from the beginning, humbled by her. In a most remarkable way, she objectified his own divided being: the very qualities that attracted and impressed the provincial who aspired to worldliness—her chic, her poise, her snobbery, her delight in appearances, her respect for social convention—were the qualities that outraged the easygoing, uncentered dissident. Thus he was eager that she should be displayed to his friends and acquaintances (he even took her to New Haven to meet his old professors), but he warned them first to pay no attention to her manner—and so he did throughout their relationship. When he first dined with her and her mother at their flat at 345 West 70th Street, he was so impressed by the pink-shaded candlelight and the silver that, with country-boy enthusiasm, he reported these details to W. E. Woodward.

At the same time, their opposing values—her aristocratic hankerings, his undefined socialism—were already setting up the first strains in that tension that would grow until it finally pulled their marriage apart. ("Any two people who have spent more than two days together," Lewis wrote in *The Trail of the Hawk,* "have the material for a lifelong feud, in traits which at first were amusing or admirable.") The temperamental contrast suggests that this was another relationship like that between George Sand and Flaubert, but with the roles reversed—the lady now the contemptuous conservative indifferent to public issues and to progress, he the libertarian, optimistically peering down democratic vistas.

Still, even while he lectured her on her mistaken ideas about class, clothes, aristocracy and religion, he called her his "Silver Maid" and cast her in the role of distant princess to his futile fool. But from the very beginning, in spite of her doubts about him as a possible husband, he had called up in her a protective impulse that exercised itself at once and resulted in a considerable transformation of his exterior. Her eye was sharp not only to the general effect of his clothes—waistcoat and new derby—but to their details—the pattern of a tie, the color of his shoes and gloves. Frances Perkins, when they called on her in 1913, observed the alteration:

> My only impression of her was that she was a typical New Yorker, very different from Sinclair; that she knew how to work and would probably be a good influence on him; that she had style, and that was shown by the change in his wardrobe. She bought him strong, thick, good tweeds, and the accessories that would go with them. It was much more becoming to his peculiar style of ugliness than the cheap, ready-made suits of dark blue that never fitted him and made him look like a picked chicken. About that time he began wearing a monocle also, largely for spoofing but then serious affectation. He looked like a distinguished visiting Scottish author, which is exactly what I think he was aiming at. Grace Hegger was all right . . .

She helped him. She worked with him on his flat Midwest speech.* She read the manuscript of *Mr. Wrenn* and made suggestions, especially

* "She taught Carl to say 'dahg' instead of 'dawg' for 'dog'; 'wawta' instead of 'wotter' for 'water.' Whether she was more correct in her pronunciation or not does not matter; New York said 'dahg,' and it amused him just then to be very Eastern."—*The Trail of the Hawk,* p. 382.

about dressmaker details; she urged him to read some French before they went to a performance by Sarah Bernhardt; with her own strain of adventuresomeness, she rose to the role of "Glorious Playfellow" and *played* with him—Patchin Place and Macdougal Alley, Pavlova and the Park, country excursions, tramps, picnics; she responded to his whimseys with her own. When she was ill, he composed a miniature daily newspaper for her, *The Dream Vendor,* by which she was delighted. "Adventuring," in their vocabulary, was "daventuring." They cast themselves in the roles of children and he wrote her poems about eating bread and milk out of little blue bowls; he was Toby in his little dress with a blue sash; she was Issa, Panfish, Dolly and Tobina.

Straining now to imagine the difference in manners in a lost age, we must still conclude that here there were extremities. When the gorge does not rise, the heart bleeds for them: if only they had had a little maturity, their love might have had a chance! But it was adolescent in its indulgences, and cruel in its sentimentality. They began to dream and write of a little white cottage in the country, and she sent him clippings of Nell Brinkley drawings from the newspapers—of a large-coifed girl waiting at a cottage gate with a child in her arms, of a boy and girl lying on the ground on oriental pillows and dreaming of a cottage in the clouds. If she "civilized" him, she also encouraged the silliest strain in him, and something in him froze.* He had already written her of "that beastly humility which does come to me when I think how very wonderful you are, Silver Maid"; and —as she reports the incident in *Half a Loaf*—in their first serious connubial quarrel, brought on by her cold treatment of a raffish friend whom, without warning, he had brought home to dinner, he (as represented by the protagonist, Timothy Hale), says, "I am afraid of you in a time like this, and it is not good for a man to be afraid of the woman he loves." Twenty pages on, after the alarming rejection of a manuscript (*The Innocents*) on the income from which they were counting, we come upon this passage:

> He looked at her with the faith of a child whose mother has promised to mend the wheels on his little red wagon. And she felt as if a shield and spear had been placed in her hands and a voice from the clouds had commanded: "This is your man, and no other's. He is yours to defend, in sickness or in health, in petty failure or in bitter success. He has a great talent

* In *The Trail of the Hawk,* Carl Ericson, a largely autobiographical character, suffers from a six-week attack of typhoid fever shortly after his marriage. "During convalescence Carl was so wearily gentle that she hoped the little boy she loved was coming back to dwell in him. But the Hawk's wings seemed broken. For the first time Carl was afraid of life.... He took to watching her like a solemn baby, when she moved about the room; thus she found the little boy Carl again; laughed full-throated and secretly cried over him, as his sternness passed into a wistful obedience. He was not quite the same impudent boy whose naughtiness she had loved. But the good child who came in his place did trust her so, depend upon her so...." (pp. 388–89)

> which at times will overwhelm him. He is also your child. Cherish him."
> She stood up and held his head tight between her young breasts. She wanted to lift the head, *dismembered from its body,** up to the clouds from which the voice had come and swear eternal loyalty.

Ah, there were complexities, not only prattle!

Amuse her as he did, and tenderly disposed as she may have been, she was not certain that she loved him until the night in September 1913, when he appeared in West 70th Street with the page proofs of *Our Mr. Wrenn: The Romantic Adventures of a Gentle Man,* and showed her the dedication: "To Grace Livingstone Hegger." Their engagement was announced in February of 1914, in the month that *Our Mr. Wrenn* was published, and in her copy he wrote:

> Dear, this is your book, not mine,
> You—to whom it's dedicated—are its mistress and its fate
> And the cause of its design. . . .
> He that makes the garments live
> dares not wear its tender lace.
> No! It is designed for Grace.
> Dear, this is your book, not mine—
> Or will you command it go
> Winnowing for you and me,
> Bringing us the wonder-sea
> And the little bungalow?

Winnowing it went in a mild way, but gleaning is perhaps the more accurate term for the way in which it was written, if the word suggests at all that the novel was largely composed of such straws as Lewis could most readily gather from the harsh fields of his recent past: cattle boat trips to England, rather disappointing tramps in that country, steerage, the grubby life of boarding houses in lower Manhattan, poverty, his uneasy feelings about Bohemia, loneliness, friendlessness. Yet for all the oblique resemblances in character and the direct resemblances in experience, the central figure of the novel is drawn not so much from life as from the fiction of H. G. Wells. The title that comes at once to mind is, of course, *The History of Mr. Polly;* and, more generally, one thinks of H. G. Wells's *Atlantic Monthly* article of January 1912, "The Contemporary Novel," in which, stating his aspirations for fiction, he probably helped Lewis formulate his own. The novel not only was capable of being written as a serious tool of social and moral criticism, but also could be free, expansive, personalized in form and, inferentially, optimistic in attitude.

In 1941 Sinclair Lewis wrote a brief foreword to a new edition of *Mr. Polly,* first published in 1909, and he included characteristically garbled autobiographical detail. He said that in 1909 he "was a cub editor in New

* Italics mine. M.S.

York . . . enamored . . . of a young lady with black eyes" in whose apartment he picked up this novel, which quickly put her charms out of his mind. He was, of course, in the far West in 1909, and it was there that, having read *Mr. Polly,* he conceived *Mr. Wrenn* and wrote its earliest portions.* Gene Baker, on March 17, thanked him for her inscribed copy:

> The "first friend" of Mr. Wrenn perhaps, but not the last, my dear Hal, because you didn't "scamp" the work—and because the Henry James of it has quite disappeared—Your book is very like you, you know—whimsical, mercurially gay and—a little wistful.

There is indeed nothing of Henry James in this novel except for the famous "international theme" itself, and that was not the theme as James conceived it but the expression of Lewis's own restless yearning for "the other place." That yearning, curiously enough, found its sanction in H. G. Wells's liberal individualism, in Mr. Polly's climactic discovery that one need not merely yearn, that one *can be* free, one can break loose. If each of these little men, Mr. Wrenn no less than Mr. Polly, saw himself as "A weakly wilful being struggling to get obdurate things round impossible corners—in that symbol Mr. Polly could recognize himself and all the trouble of humanity,"—each had a further revelation:

> . . . when a man has once broken through the paper walls of everyday circumstances, those unsubstantial walls that hold so many of us securely prisoned from the cradle to the grave, he has made a discovery. If the world does not please you *you can change it.* Determine to alter it at any price, and you can change it altogether. You may change it to something sinister and angry, to something appalling, but it may be you will change it to something brighter, something more agreeable, and at the worst something much more interesting. . . . [Mr. Polly] could, for example, "clear out."

So could Mr. Wrenn. And Sinclair Lewis had at last found his theme.

"Our Mr. Polly," like Mr. Wrenn, is a small clerk, full of whimsey and dreams of adventure, of "delightful impossibilities," who is trapped by his poverty until a relative's death and a small legacy free him to wander; like Mr. Wrenn, he comes close to "romance" in the person of an impossible girl, but settles into the "reality" of a humdrum marriage. After fifteen years, Mr. Polly breaks out again and H. G. Wells lets him achieve a fantasy happiness. Sinclair Lewis lets Mr. Wrenn subside into the demands of the real.

Our Mr. Wrenn is a poor novel, but in many ways it is more suggestive than *Mr. Polly*. The basic conflict of the book is between the appeal, the impossible temptations of the exotic (Europe, Istra Nash, vagabondage)

* Considering his struggle with this book, one must wonder how seriously to take Lewis's inscription in the University of Minnesota library copy: "Naturally, in writing this, my first novel, I had the happiest time of all my writing life."

and the real satisfactions of the ordinary (America, Nelly Croubel, the job). Mr. Wrenn, an expert on travelogues, yearns to experience all the glamour of "this world so wide," but all the time the book asks, What is America? The answer comes from the corrupted American heroine, the fantastically unreal Istra who nevertheless has clearer perceptions than Wrenn and articulates the "values" of the book (an unaffected honesty and individuality) and recognizes the "value" of Wrenn himself, impossible "Mouse" that he may be—his "embryonic imagination," his "virgin soul," his American innocence.

Within this theme another theme plays. If adventure is to be had in the world, loneliness too is to be had. In a world so wide as to be cold and strange, one settles for what company one can get, and company is imperative. A theme that is to be developed in *The Trail of the Hawk* and *Babbitt* and elsewhere is the need of a male friend, and into Wrenn's broken friendship with Mort, a railroad clerk, with all the attendant yearning, idealization and frustration, Lewis flings his own long grief. Wrenn at last decides that what he really wants are two things: "somebody to go home to evenings" and "someone to work with and work for." "He spun his watch around on the table, and listened to its rapid mocking speech, 'Friends, friends; friends, friends.' " These he will not find in Europe. The individual may be free to break out of the routines and the clichés of his existence, but if he is the lonely American there awaits him the attendant discovery of his own emptiness without them. He flees to the security of a home, a stolid wife, a job, and, if now and then the old yearning for something else assails him, he reminds himself—as Wrenn does in the closing lines—of the immediate pleasure of the evening ahead: a game of pinochle, a new way to cook eggs, the potato salad in the container in his hand.

There is no need to point out the weaknesses of *Our Mr. Wrenn* as a novel—they are all too clear to anyone who chooses to read it today—but there is a point in observing its tone, which, like its central conflict, is considerably ambiguous and will plague the author even when he is writing more successful novels. It is a patronizing tone, not quite satirical, that tries at once to make us take Wrenn seriously and at the same time to allow us to be superior to him, a coy sentimentality about *his* sentimentality that seems at once to want both to sanction his choice as the wise, general choice, and to deride him as an unimportant chooser—an eaten-uneaten cake situation that did not disturb contemporary reviewers or readers.

The book was well received, treated even as quite out of the ordinary, original and convincing, both. The New York *Times* found it—in a little over six inches—unusual, at once "wholly of our own day" in story and treatment and at the same time imbued with a "spirit and feeling" derived from Dickens. This was the general observation of reviewers throughout the country—its unusual combination of the lifelike and a whimsical humor then thought of as "Dickensian." Most tellingly, perhaps, the Cleveland *Plain Dealer,* dismissing the "mental confectionery and train robberies" of most American fiction, praised *Our Mr. Wrenn* as being like "nothing that has ever been written" and promised Lewis's readers a "thrill over the reality of his romance." It is the last phrase that is most suggestive of the reason that this book struck readers and reviewers as new. The same words appear in a congratulatory letter to the author from Rupert Hughes, who referred to the "Hybla-fed style . . . that made 'Our Mr. Wrenn' really *our* Mr. Wrenn," and continued (writing now of *The Trail of the Hawk*) by commenting on what he regarded as the particular innovation of Lewis's technique, a method of shifting back and forth from romance to reality "until they are interwoven."

"Lewis had learned," writes William Couch, Jr., "to combine a viewpoint that was at once rebellious and idealistic, with a mode of fictional presentation that was essentially naturalistic . . . this bifurcation, characteristic of his fiction, placed Lewis in interesting relation to the prolonged controversy between 'romance' and 'realism,' and brought him to the attention of the critics." * Mr. Couch is using the terms, "romance" and "realism," in the way that the reviewers themselves used them, as critics have used them since the early writings of Howells. "Romance" suggests qualities that are at least idealistic, optimistic and cheerful, if not downright sentimental; "realism" suggests facts, a reproduction of the world that is, and implies unpleasantness and controversy. ". . . the balance that Lewis maintained between contentious extremes, while he steadily exploited the acceptance of realism in his time," is the balance that Howells's own best work best represents, but perhaps no one after Howells had sought this balance between the contentious extremes, popular fiction maintaining the old line of sentimental romance or melodrama, realism moving into the violent naturalism of Frank Norris and the dismaying pessimism of Theodore Dreiser.

The reviewers of Lewis's novel, even though in no sense recognizing the special place that he was asking to hold in literary history, praised him for his realism—the carefully detailed scenes of ordinary life, the ordinary characters and their colloquial speech, the rather good-natured social satire (one must search for evidence that the author had just recently drifted out of the Socialist Party)—in its combination with a prevailingly optimistic

* "The Emergence, Rise, and Decline of the Reputation of Sinclair Lewis," an unpublished Ph.D. dissertation presented at the University of Chicago in 1954. I am deeply indebted to Mr. Couch's pioneer work.

point of view, an optimism that, while never denying the existence of cruelty and greed and suffering, was yet capable of sentimental nonsense on the one hand and, on the other, of a rather admirable liberal individualism derived from Wells and best summarized in America by Herbert Croly's book *The Promise of American Life,* published in the very year of *Mr. Polly*. Mr. Wrenn was a large part of that promise.

It is precisely this complex of qualities in the novels of Sinclair Lewis that marks him as having been formed before 1914 and sets him off so sharply from the only slightly younger writers who matured during the First World War and were publishing their exciting early books—*The Great Gatsby, The Sun Also Rises, Manhattan Transfer, Soldier's Pay*—simultaneously with Lewis's big ones. The same complex of qualities revealed in the early novels remains in the big books and all through his decline to his last novel in 1951, and beside the work of these younger men, even in the 1920s, even the big books already seemed in some ways curiously old-fashioned. It was an older America than theirs that Lewis loved and praised and chided, and an older vision that supported his effort.

The reviews that must have pleased Sinclair Lewis most came from the several newspapers on which he had served his undistinguished employment. The Sauk Centre *Herald* professed to be pleased that he was "making rapid strides in his chosen literary profession." The editor of the Waterloo *Daily Courier* wrote him a letter and enclosed a kindly clipping that noted the publication of this work by his former "telegraph editor and editorial writer." The reviewer and acting editor in chief of the New Haven *Courier* wrote him, too, wrote him as "dear Sinclair—famous Sinclair now . . . I rejoice in your success and your Wrenn book and and—well I must close." Sinclair Lewis's success had moved the man.

Old friends rallied. Updegraff, not yet having read the book (and when he had, he did not like it), dashed off a note: "Good work, B.F., old horse." The Yale professors not only praised it but read it: J. M. Berdan wrote to say that he believed that Lewis alone "of the Yale fellows" was "on the right track," and he reviewed the novel for the *Alumni Weekly*. William Lyon Phelps was predictably ecstatic.

> . . . I want to tell you right off that I am simply delighted with it. It is an absolutely bully book from the first word to the last. It is full of humor, observation, knowledge of life, human sympathy and charm. I am recommending it to my classes at Yale. . . .

And only a few weeks later:

> If you had been present at the Lit banquet last night and heard the tremendous send-off that I gave you in my opening remarks, you would have been pleased. I am delighted to hear such good reports of the sale of your book.

The sales were in fact not at all remarkable, rather the contrary—Harper published only 3,000 copies; * but, sales or not, just two weeks after the second Phelps letter, Sinclair Lewis made the choice of Mr. Wrenn and took unto himself a wife.

In 1912 William Rose Benét had married his old San Francisco love, Theresa Thompson; and, together with her sister and brother-in-law, Kathleen and Charles Norris, they had taken little houses on the edge of a field in Port Washington, on the north side of Long Island. Shortly before the Lewis marriage, the Norrises gave up their house and the Lewises determined to take it, even though it was brown rather than white. Grace Hegger happily left her desk in the office of *Vogue* magazine, so near the "magic elevator" where they had met, happily gave up the flat in West 70th Street, bundled Ma*ma* up and took her down to Port Washington to help prepare the house, and then, having ensconced her in a nearby boardinghouse, returned with her to New York for the marriage ceremony on April 15, 1914.

Like so many things in her marriage, it fell far short of her dreams. The superstitious would have been warned, and wisely. Rain positively poured out of the sky—more than a threat to the feathers on her hat. There was no bridal veil, no church aisle, no ritual, no lovely, tulle-swathed attendants to the bride, no attendant. She was given in marriage by her brother, Frank, a not conspicuously successful automobile salesman. The place was the Ethical Culture Lecture Room, 2 West 54th Street, with Dr. Henry Newman, head of the Brooklyn Ethical Culture Society, officiating. The groom's best man was George Soule; the ushers were Owen Johnson, Albert Payson Terhune, Harrison Smith, and Edward L. Morrison—a brother of the new Mrs. Lewis's best friend. "Part of the ushers' duty," Terhune remembered in *To the Best of My Memory,* "was to steer wetly arriving guests away from an undertaking establishment that stood with invitingly open portals at the head of the stairs." The Chesapeake honeymoon that followed was hardly more auspicious: the first night in a Baltimore hotel, then a disastrously uncomfortable Pocomoke River trip, a broken-down hotel in Onancock, an overly expensive hotel at Old Point Comfort, the conclusion in a boardinghouse in Salem, Virginia. It was a relief to have it behind them and to settle into the bungalow at Port Washington. The details of the life they lived there are to be found in Grace Hegger's books and, only a little less literally, in the last chapters of *The Trail of the Hawk.*†

* The figures for this and other works are derived directly from the files of the publishers. Harvey Taylor, in the inaccurate bibliography that accompanies Carl Van Doren's *Sinclair Lewis: A Biographical Sketch,* gives much higher figures for which there is no substantiation. The inadequacies of this bibliography are curious in that Taylor had Lewis's cooperation in preparing it.

† An interesting omission from this considerably detailed book is any account of the ceremony that united Carl and Ruth, the heroine, but the reason for the omission is

In midsummer of 1914, with Europe at war and the prospects of the publishing industry in the United States uncertain, W. E. Woodward decided to end his newspaper syndicate, and Sinclair Lewis was out of work. George H. Doran, who published his recollections in *Chronicles of Barabbas* in 1935, admired his "fine qualities of editorial judgment and publicity" and hired him at once, at sixty dollars a week, as editorial assistant and advertising manager.

> The change from Dawson to Lewis was revolutionary. Dawson, calm and serene, wrote out his briefs for or against a manuscript in beautiful Addisonian phrases. Lewis pounded out on a typewriter the crispest of American staccato opinion and criticism, literally reams of publicity stunts. He was a dynamo of energy and freshness of thought. After he had been with me a fortnight he came to me, and in the exuberance of his happiness volunteered that he was so contented that he was settled and located for life if I would have him. I was delighted, for while he was a bit too fast for my mental processes and thoroughly impractical in many ways, he had a commendable sound sense, indefatigable energy, and downright industry, which properly harnessed would go far to the making of a young publishing house.

His salary was raised to seventy-five dollars a week, and "his strident tones and his clattering machine gave an air of intense industry and activity" to what had previously been the "sedate establishment" of the George H. Doran Company. This atmosphere was appropriate to the list of highly respectable British best-selling authors who gave the Doran list its distinction: Bennett, Beresford, Cannan, Mackenzie, Maugham, Onions, Swinnerton, Walpole, and others. For such as these, all of whom Lewis was later to know in England when he had himself become their peer, he was now writing the promotion material.

And he was cementing his own relations in the publishing industry by regular attendance at his informal luncheon club. In 1914 this group, largely made up of men involved in book advertising, agreed that book promotion was becoming more and more meaningless, that readers would like, and deserved to have, plain descriptive accounts rather than adjectives. They decided to publish a monthly pamphlet, to be edited by George Soule, in which every publisher could list two of his books each month with a brief and neutral descriptive account and no praise whatever. (Such countercurrents as this publication may have set up to the rising swell of the American advertising frenzy, Lewis himself did a good deal to reverse, in the schemes that he was to develop for the promotion of his own novels.) In 1915 this group, as an entity, dissolved in a larger if hardly more formal

---

not far to seek. He gave Ruth an aristocratic New York background that would have made mandatory a fashionable cathedral wedding of a kind that he had not experienced and could not easily imagine, whereas the New York ceremony that was his own would have been highly inappropriate in the context he had created.

luncheon club, Christopher Morley's "small fry." Sinclair Lewis was one of its three founding spirits.

Even in 1914, three hundred dollars a month was not a salary on which a young commuting householder could easily live. Mrs. Lewis continued to do some writing for *Vogue,* and in 1915 she engaged to write a beauty column for the trade paper of the Nyal Drug Store chain. Lewis, too, still scurried about for extra dollars. For some time now he had ceased to try to find them by writing short stories of his own, but he could still sell story plots to others. "Another short story on one of my plots sold!! I got a check for $40.00 from Terhune on that account!!" And he did more for that well-known protector of the interests of dogs. Terhune remembered:

> In 1914 Sinclair Lewis helped me out with the plot of my serial, '*Dad*' . . . and he wrote two or three of its chapters. But this was wholly a business arrangement. I gave him 25 per cent of the serial's price and of the subsequent book royalties.

A close reading of *Dad* does not enable one to isolate one man's prose from the other's in the general wash of it.*

In November of 1914 he published an essay in *The Bookman* that represented his more serious thought. Called "The Passing of Capitalism," it was one of a number of pieces that made up a symposium, *Relation of the Novel to the Present Social Unrest.* The article concludes,

> . . . summing them all up, going from real observer to real observer, it may be contended that practically every thoughtful writer of today sees behind the individual dramas of his characters a background of coming struggle which shall threaten the very existence of this status called capitalism. Approve or disapprove—there's the struggle, mirrored in fiction.

The body of the article had discussed a variety of novelists whose work presumably supports this theory, but it had praised in particular Wells, Dreiser, Sinclair, Herrick, and Walpole. Other novelists, like Frank Norris, also demonstrate the thesis, but the implication is that they are not quite serious, since they see capitalism as a step in progress, rather than as a stage that must be reversed. And yet Sinclair Lewis himself did not seem at all clear as to the alternative to capitalism in "this year of international disgrace." Some of these writers point to Socialism, many to other socialisms, and, although his sympathies seem to move toward the left socialist position, he was not so clear that he could be certain, or not so certain that he could be quite clear.

It is impossible to imagine the husband of Grace Hegger in attendance

* But bibliographers may be interested in a copy of *Dad* autographed to one John Stuart Groves and now in the possession of Professor Samuel Allen of Williams College, where Terhune noted that Chapters 21, 22 and 23 were written by Sinclair Lewis.

at meetings of the Socialist Party, and with the lapse of his dues some time before his marriage, we may assume that that brief practice had come to an end. His interests, however, were still on the side of the causes of justice rather than on any other. He made speeches in the neighborhood of Port Washington on behalf of woman suffrage and in this year did march in the Fifth Avenue parade. If his pacifism did not lead him to board the Peace Ship or to take any other public position about American intervention, it led him to contribute a bit of humorous personal pique to F.P.A.'s "Conning Tower" in the New York *Tribune:*

Certain Animadversions on a Brave Poet Urging His
Countrymen, and Other Countrymen, to Go Forth
and Die for Their Countries, Even Though
They Have Cowardly Desires to Go On Living
Without Asking the Poet's Permission

By Our Mr. Wrenn

He sits at home in pearl-gray spats
And kills the Prussians off like rats.
So long as one foul foe may live
He'll risk his last gold adjective,
And shed his every drop of ink
To prove that only cowards shrink
From charging German gats.
He spreads the British Eagle's wings
And mounts a comet's crest and flings
His roaring challenge to the Dutch,
But go himself and fight—not much!

He calls the man who stays at home,
The pup who preaches peace,
A "flea upon a rooster's comb,
Obtuse, obscene, obese,"
And other most insulting names
Until to hide their dwarfish shames,
They rush to dare the German flames.
And has their bard and leader clomb (sic)
The German trench?
Oh, no.
He's home.

So still his clarion voice is heard
At ten to twenty cents a word.
And still his clamor beats the sky,
His fearless summons, bold and high,
Bids every true man go and die—
Well, that is, every *other* guy.

When Upton Sinclair appealed to him on behalf of Bouck White, the minister of the Church of the Social Revolution who was arrested for disorderly conduct after he led his people into the Rockefeller church on behalf of striking Colorado miners, Lewis volunteered to do what he could. What he did is unrecorded, but he pursued the renewed relationship by sending Sinclair three books of a radical cast recently published by Doran. A few years later, when Sinclair began the serialization of his book *The Profits of Religion* in his short-lived, long-titled periodical, *Upton Sinclair's: A Monthly Magazine for a Clean Peace and the Internation,* Lewis wrote him about his old Helicon Hall and Carmel associate Michael Williams and his apostasy in reverse:

> Your quiet, unanswerable, conviction-carrying rebuke to Mike Williams re "A Prophet for Profits" is a *masterpiece*—far better than Stevenson's "Father Damien." I wonder if Mike will ever dare to try to answer it.

He permitted Sinclair to publish this letter, and a second one, of particular interest as having been written by the future author of *Elmer Gantry:*

> I have been exceedingly glad you did "The Profits of Religion," and I hope that it reaches a wide audience, because more and more I believe that conventional religions are among the most active foes of progress. I remember with amusement how ten years ago I used to be told that I'd outgrow all this highly youthful fervor against religiosity, whereas I find myself only the more youthfully indignant against it each year. My objection is not so much the positive evils of the systems as that great negative evil—the turning of young, fresh emotion-charged thought from reality to devotion to symbols, priest-worship, "church-work," listening to shallow sermons and singing damned bad verse, while a whole world of nobility and need waits outside.
>
> You sail in, Lord how you sail in! I hope people read it!

Lewis's relationship with Jack London, already rather strained, jogged to an end in 1915 after London had rebuked him for a real or imagined breach of confidence in some unidentifiable bit that Lewis had presumably published, and in the next year London was dead. In spite of occasional gestures, Lewis was certainly not putting his major energies into social causes. These he reserved for what he now thought of as a full career in publishing, and for his second novel.

He worked zealously for George Doran, and effectively; and he learned so much about the techniques of modern publishing that he was, in later years, to astonish editors who were happy to have him sit in on sales conferences when they discussed the promotion of his own novels. Only one of a number of extraofficial chores that he performed for George Doran was to write an appreciative essay on Hugh Walpole which, together with similar encomia from Arnold Bennett and Mrs. Belloc Lowndes, appeared in 1915 as *Hugh Walpole, Master Novelist,* with the Doran imprint. It is an unimportant little piece, but it had an important consequence; one can hope that Sinclair Lewis did not remember that essay in 1930, when one of the two congratulatory notes on the Nobel award from British writers came from the subject of his fifteen-year-old praise.

Resigned as he now may have been to subsiding into a career in publishing, he had not relinquished his primary ambition, and the thesis of his second novel was in fact to argue that it was unnecessary, indeed deadly, to submit to routine. He was already at work on this novel when *Our Mr. Wrenn* appeared, and he continued to pursue the work with a kind of ferocity whenever his editorial duties gave him the time.

5

IN AN ARTICLE called "How I Wrote a Novel on Trains and Beside the Kitchen Sink," in *The American Magazine* of April 1921, Sinclair Lewis gave his account, at least impressionistically true, of the composition of *The Trail of the Hawk: A Comedy of the Seriousness of Life.* He wrote when he could, in snippets, and after his marriage, that meant that many of these were achieved on commuting trains between Port Washington and the Pennsylvania Station, or early in the morning before he left his house, with breakfast coffee, or on the truncated weekends of a day and a half that businessmen then enjoyed. Much of the book had been written before his marriage, and Harpers had the manuscript early in the next year. Finished copies were ready by September 2, 1915, and it was published on September 27.

The Trail of the Hawk (which Lewis later liked to think of as prophetic of the early career of Charles Lindbergh) is a strange book and interesting to anyone who is charmed by the transformation of fact into fiction and in the power of fantasy to transform fact; it is, therefore, of particular importance to the biography of Sinclair Lewis.

The book has three parts only loosely joined by the single hero and the theme of adventure: The Adventure of Youth, The Adventure of Adventuring, and The Adventure of Love. The necessary ingredient of the first is rebellion; of the second, freedom; of the third, a playmate. The threat to all of them is the compliance with routine; the alternative to the third is loneliness. The terms are those of *Our Mr. Wrenn,* but in this resolution no compromise is made with "rebellious optimism." *

The Trail of the Hawk scrambles back to fields more distant than those of *Our Mr. Wrenn* and, finding those earliest straws, distributes them more parsimoniously and interestingly. The novelist splits himself up among a

* The phrase was Updegraff's, developed from the "optimistic rebels" to whom the book was dedicated—Soule, Smith, Updegraff, Noyes, Harcourt, Huebsch—and used in Updegraff's letter of congratulation, his last letter. (It is 1915: a quarrel; another friend falls by the wayside; but there is now a playmate-wife, willing to begin presently the trek on the highway.)

number of characters. When the book opens, we meet eight-year-old Carl Ericson, the son of Norwegian immigrants in a town called Joralemon, Minnesota, not to be distinguished from Sauk Centre; he is a lonely, imaginative child, escaping from an austere home where only invented pleasantries are possible, playing imaginary games with "Nail People" in the woodshed when he should be piling firewood. The year is 1893, when the author too was eight years old. Carl, like the young Lewis, long habituated to solitary walks, is intimate with the character of railroad ties; but he is also a hunter and swimmer and intrepid woodsman, successful with boys and girls, and he has friends.

Among his friends is one Ben Rusk, a doctor's son who occupies a social position higher than Carl's and whose older brother is going to become a surgeon. But Ben does not enter the plot until both boys are in high school, when Carl, for all his social handicaps, is successful and indifferent to success, while Ben appears exactly as young Harry then was: unsuccessful with the boys, mooning for the girls, incompetent at and uninterested in hunting, reading all the time. Ben, not at all surprisingly, goes off to Oberlin, and he vanishes from the story.

Carl attends Plato College, a grimmer Oberlin, where he is successful with "the gang" and where again he meets another of his counterparts, the real young Harry who might just as well be called Ben Rusk but is now named Eugene ("Genie") Field Linderbeck. Genie helps Carl toward serious thought, and Carl befriends Genie. A summer vacation intervenes, during which Carl, like Harry's brother Claude, strings wires for the telephone company; Carl also reads about airplanes, builds a glider, flies it high, crashes without damage to himself. Returning to Plato, he is persuaded by Genie to enroll in a course offered by a young radical professor who is presently dismissed from the college for his opinions and for lecturing enthusiastically on Wells and Shaw; and Carl, behaving as a young Harry would have behaved had he been active, is likewise dismissed. Then Genie disappears from the story. Carl alone is left to embody both the high dream of flying and the muddy, grounded reality.

Much of the reality comes directly out of the trunk of notes. Carl drifts through a variety of jobs all over the eastern United States. Unemployed, he goes to the Joint Application Bureau for aid, and the Lewis notes from that experience are brought into play. He ships for Panama, and those notes are utilized. He reads and dreams about airplanes, and that research is salvaged. The California experience is highly useful. But then the plot deserts reality and pursues the dream: Carl becomes a daring flyer, is handsome, rather dashing, a worldly success; wins the esteem of a man he admires, one Forrest Haviland, who becomes his true friend, a man with whom he can exchange confidences; and makes a triumphant entry into, of all places, New Haven, when he lands his plane on the Green in a race that he wins, is the hero of the students and the toast of the faculty, and concludes that now he needs only two further things—to read a lot of books and to find "the girl with whom he could play."

And at this point Carl Ericson, insofar as he has been developed as a character, begins to disappear into Sinclair Lewis as he was in 1914. Forrest Haviland, the never-never friend, dies, and Carl sells his monoplane; he reappears, aged twenty-seven, as the designer of the "Touricar" for the VanZile Motor Corporation, of New York City, which might just as well be called Stokes. Now he becomes involved with two young ladies. One of these is a home town girl, Gertie, who has come to New York and whose situation resembles that of the Grace Hegger whom Lewis first knew—mother, brother, West Side flat, et cetera. When Gertie gives a party and Sinclair Lewis for the first time clearly uses the broad satiric techniques that were to make *Main Street* famous, Carl decides that the Joralemon atmosphere is not for him. But he is lonely, lonely! The other girl is the Lewis idealization of Grace Hegger (uptown wealth, aristocratic attitudes, real "class"). When Carl sees her, he pretends to have met her before; and in this, and in most details, he now becomes indistinguishable from badgered, blistered Sinclair Lewis, aged thirty—suffering from defiant feelings of social inferiority, thinking of himself as the "Outsider," trying to make an "Adventure of Business" but chafing for freedom.

The courtship of Ruth Winslow has the character of his own: the whimseys, the adventuring and play, the boy lover, the diminutive talk even to the blue bowls. ". . . I'm the kiddy in patched overalls you used to play with when you kept house in the willows," and so forth. It also follows the same pattern: the class difference, the reluctance and persistence, the sport and the spats, the marriage, the first quarrels and the slammed doors, the reconciliations and the burst into freedom as, in the last pages, Ruth and Carl are off on South American adventures and the prose turns purple in what, at the time of composition, was still an entirely anticipatory experience and was, in reality, to prove to be no resolution at all.*

The novel contains biographical detail beyond the significant revelation that lies in the apparent necessity to make the sexual relationship an infantile thing. It ranges from an extended description of one of Lewis's most well-known imitations, that of a clergyman, which he attributes to Ruth's brother, Ray (and hilarious it was!), to passages that suggest that he was not without self-knowledge:

> Carl . . . knew that both Ruth and he had the instability as well as the initiative of the vagabond. As quickly as they had claimed each other, so quickly could either of them break love's alliance, if bored. Carl himself,

* Lewis's inscription in his wife's copy said, "This is not so much a novel, dear, as a record of our games and talks and thoughts and journeys. Without you, none of it could have been written—if it is good, it is your merit; if bad it is my faulty effort to express us."

> being anything but bored, was as faithfully devoted as the least enterprising of moral young men. . . . But was Ruth so bound? She still refused to admit even that she could fall in love. . . . He knew that even if the rose dream came true, there would be drab spots in it. And now that she was away, with Lennox and polo to absorb her, could the gauche, ignorant Carl Ericson, that he privately knew himself to be, retain her interest?

How complete that self-knowledge was, one must guess. The novel makes plainer than any other the irresistible allure of "the Beyond," the further place; none makes clearer the tenacity with which he would resist every threat to his freedom to discover it; but whether he had any notion of the ruthlessness with which he would push aside such threats, one can only wonder. The importance of male friendship is nowhere urged more eloquently than in the portrait of Forrest Haviland, whose death shatters Carl; but there seems to be no implication that the author would be unable to maintain such friendships, would, indeed, be impatient until they were broken. "Nobody but you can hurt you," prophetically says Bone Stillman, the antisocial anarchist, to Carl Ericson; but, for Sinclair Lewis, the sentence would require another half to complete the prophecy: *but you can deeply hurt others.*

Bone Stillman, the cracker-barrel agnostic, and S. Alcott Wood, President of Plato College and a blind bigot, are two types introduced by this novel that were to become prominent in the Lewis gallery of American characters. Almost accidentally, the novel slips into the kind of satire that was to become the Lewis hallmark, and then just as easily slips out of it into the Lewis sentimentality that marks his forthright aspiration. And here, for the first time, we have extended passages of that characteristic of the Lewis prose that consists of accumulations of detail with adjectival comment on the detail to punctuate it: "*meaningless* scrolls in plaster bas-relief" . . . "The floor was of hardwood in squares, dark and richly polished, highly *self-respecting*" . . . "The drawing-room, to the left, was dark and still and *unsympathetic* and expensive" . . . "Watteau shepherds and shepherdesses, making silken *unreal* love and *scandalously* neglected silky unreal sheep." Reviewers, without benefit of hindsight, did not observe these steps in the development that would lead to the mature novelist.

In more than a hundred periodicals, the praise was nearly unanimous. Hildegarde Hawthorne, in the New York *Times,* thought it an advance over *Our Mr. Wrenn,* maintaining the same congenial qualities but "digging deeper into our American experience . . . vital . . . actual . . . honest . . . straightforward . . . clear . . . good art without a taint of the 'artistic.' " The New York *Evening Post,* the *Globe,* the *Evening World* all praised it, the last naming Lewis as "the foremost member of the younger group of American novelists." New York was echoed in Boston, Philadelphia, Duluth, Chicago, Los Angeles; and in Columbus, Ohio, those portions of the novel that are today well-nigh intolerable were selected for particular comment:

> We can't remember having ever read anything in published fiction quite so beautiful in purpose and unconventional in spirit as Mr. Lewis' chapters on the playmate comradeship of "The Hawk" and Ruth.

Among the more serious journals, *The Masses* applauded it as a book "flushed with youthful liberalism" and called it "Sinclair Lewis's promissory note for a great American novel." *The Nation* was enthusiastic, and George Soule, in *Book News Monthly,* wrote in his friendly way that he had heard people say that the next great American novelist was to be Sinclair Lewis, and, indeed, Franklin P. Adams said in print that he "may someday write the G.A.N." Beside this, what matter if Fanny Butcher in the Chicago *Tribune* deplored the realism of the novel, or that Harold Stearns, in the *New Republic,* welcoming the realism, yet found little significance in the revolt of Carl Ericson because he was without real political and social awareness?

Two books had established Lewis as a serious realistic novelist of American manners, with a palatable satirical touch and an engaging optimism, from whom great work could be expected. But *The Trail of the Hawk* did not sell. Only 6,500 copies were printed, and even if all of them were sold, the royalties from a novel priced at $1.25 would hardly have seemed just compensation for the dedicated work of more than a year. If *The Trail of the Hawk* was a 1915 continuation of the tradition of Horatio Alger, using now the mystique of mechanics, rather than the formula of hard work and brave honesty, as the key to economic success, it did not hand that key to Sinclair Lewis. In the terms of success, he was still almost exactly where he had been before, but chafing.

His friends were enthusiastic even when they made qualifications. Updegraff thought it was great but deplored the title and the handling of certain scenes. Professor Berdan saw its considerable advance over *Our Mr. Wrenn* in technique but felt the absence of any central organizing thought. Rupert Hughes had no complaints, but J. D. Beresford thought it too long and advised him to "Write that 200,000 word book [*The Job*] you are on in 120,000." Nevertheless, it

> has given me a clearer impression of American life than any novel I've read in the past fifteen years. You've got all that into it & got it well. It is true that you have not made me want to live in America, East or West, but that is part of your achievement as a writer. You have convincingly pictured people & conditions & that was your job. You've done it. Did you make Hawk so very virtuous, in fact, as a concession to a Puritan public? or was that true, too. So much of the book rings true & honest that I just wondered why in that one case, I had a doubt.

From a Mr. Charles Gallup, of Coxsackie-on-Hudson, the book brought the first request for an autograph, and from Professor Phelps, the usual enthusiasm—except that he did not much care for the section that recounts Carl's wanderings after he leaves Plato College. That section, contrariwise, was the only part of the book that Upton Sinclair found endurable.

> You seem to me one of the most curiously uneven writers I have ever known. You will write pages and pages of interesting stuff, and then you will write a lot of conversation which is just absolutely waste, without any point or worth-whileness at all; and you don't seem to know the difference.
>
> Everything of yours that I have read is about half and half. In general, it seems to me that wherever you are writing about the underworld, you are at your best, and when you come up to your own social level or higher, you are no good. . . .
>
> The story of the two children (at the beginning) is absolutely common place, also all of your college talk, and all of the society and love talk towards the end of the book; but all thru his hard luck period and his aviator life, your hero is thoroughly interesting and alive.

And he added the postscript, "Don't be cross."

Sinclair Lewis was not cross; or, at any rate, his reply was moderate, more moderate than one might expect when one considers the general exacerbation of his feelings that the reception of the book had brought about. He had, in his capacity of promotion man at Doran, opened a correspondence with the reviewer of the Los Angeles *Times,* Gordon Ray Young, and to him he wrote openly:

> Oh Christ I'm sick and sore of novel writing—not but what I'm going to keep it up, and make 'em all as good and true as I know how, till I'm clean out of the game—and as I'm only thirty now, that means forty or fifty more years of it. But when I think how easily I can make money and praise by magazine stories—I'm selling 'em to the Saturday Evening Post—it makes me sore as hell to read the piddling reviews of The Trail of the Hawk in the New York papers—reviews of a book I worked on like hell for nearly two years, dismissed in a quarter of a column of easy comment, and OF COURSE Mr. A. finding all of the book commendable EXCEPT the wanderjahr of Carl, and the equally laudable Mr. B. finding *only* that part commendable. Hell's bells, at least one doesn't get reviews on magazine stories. . . . But I'm going to write a third book that will make them all sore as hell—all of them except you and Edgett [Boston *Evening Transcript*] and about four others. It will be the office as I know it, the real office of real workers, without any of the romance of the Business Melodramas and Big Deals. And of course the bedamned thing will take me two years and I'll be lucky to get $500 out of it, which the same I could make it in two weeks—and do so make it—writing for magazines. So I shan't be entirely Prrrrrrostituted. But I shall, while I'm still young, reserve the right to curse the goddamned reviewers—again excepting you and the few others.

His exasperation did not lead to apathy about the commercial failure of *The Trail of the Hawk* but rather to an active attempt to make it succeed. At the suggestion of Alfred Harcourt, he wrote a long letter to Harper & Brothers in which he outlined his ideas for a promotion campaign. Booth Tarkington's *The Turmoil* and Ernest Poole's *The Harbor* were current popular successes and had been praised as giving their readers true pictures of the real America; so had *The Trail of the Hawk*. The Lewis notion was that Harper take a large advertising block and begin it as follows:

> THE REAL AMERICA REVEALS ITSELF
>
> They have come! . . . . For years Americans have been crying for a group of young novelists who should express America as it is, today—as Wells and Bennett have expressed England. They have come! Booth Tarkington in "The Turmoil," Ernest Poole in "The Harbor" have made America *real*, and fascinating, and now they are joined by
>
> Sinclair Lewis,
> in
> THE TRAIL OF THE HAWK

Then were to follow a dozen quotations from reviews which Lewis happily supplied.

Harper & Brothers did not act upon this suggestion, but Miss Jordan (his editor there), his wife and others made a countersuggestion: since his novels were making no money, and since he had so many story ideas, why didn't he try once more to write short stories along with *The Job?* For some time, Albert Payson Terhune remembered, he had urged the same course.

> Sinclair Lewis and I used to argue hotly and at much length . . . as to where the big money lay in writing. From my own experience, up to then, I held that it was all in the magazine end of the game—if it were anywhere at all. Lewis believed there was more money in one successful book than in an armful of magazine work. It was his ambition, he said, to write best-seller novels, rather than well-paying magazine yarns, and he was certain that one day he could do it. . . . Lewis had a queerly unswerving faith in his star.

But for the time being he let it swerve.

In July of 1915 the Lewises, on vacation, walked from Buzzard's Bay to Provincetown, the length of Cape Cod. (In an article of 1918 advising women what to wear on such a pilgrimage, Mrs. Lewis helps us picture them: "If a man and wife are vagabonds, one nicely adjusted canvas duffle bag to hang on his shoulders will be enough luggage.") On this excursion, Lewis had an idea that may have been conceived as a jest but was nevertheless motivated by the chief conflict in his life at the moment and was to change the course of his literary life. The idea was to result in his first publication in *The Saturday Evening Post*. Written at Wellfleet, "Nature, Inc." is a humorous story about a health colony on Cape Cod, managed by a quack but including in its company a beautiful and sincere girl with whom a Boston real-estate man is in love and because of whom he lives in the colony until he exposes the quack. In Boston, the routines of business and the dissipations of city living leave them both unhappy, and they return to the Cape, a baby coming, to set up a "nature colony" of their very own. The free life was vindicated, and on August 10 Sinclair Lewis received a check for five hundred dollars from George Horace Lorimer, together with a letter of commendation. Had the tide turned, the cloud shown its lining, fortune smiled, dawn come, oil been struck, the jackpot hit? Perhaps. He was hoping to be free in May. And certainly the pot would boil.

6

BACK IN NEW YORK and Port Washington, Lewis continued to work at *The Job* at the same time that he took up Lorimer's advice to "go ahead and become a household word." In rapid succession he wrote three more stories for the *Post:* "Commutation: $9.17," about suburban snobbery; "The Other Side of the House," about trains and young love; and "If I Were Boss," about progress in business. And Lewis himself was progressing in business: for the fourth story his check was $1,000. With $2,500 he could seize freedom at last, and at the end of November, six months before he had planned, he resigned from George H. Doran Company. Kathleen Norris remembered the day:

> He one day went by the house in an open car with Grace, the picture of propriety, on the front seat and he, with no tie on and his red hair blazing, and he shouted to us, "I'm a free man, I've escaped from bondage. I told Doran what I thought of him today and I'm out."

Ironically, he had just written for Baker and Taylor's *Christmas Bulletin* an essay called "The Home Without Books," in which quiet readers are contrasted with people who "prefer to air their brains by a motor trip," who neglect their minds to "climb in the new car and sing out, 'Where shall we go from here?' " On December 3, 1915, they left Port Washington for their "Research Magnificent." *

Their plans were indefinite. From New York on December 6 he wrote his friend Young in Los Angeles that they were "off to Florida, on a year's hike that will probably take us to California before we get back," and to Hamlin Garland, to whom he had been trying to get a copy of *The Trail of the Hawk,* he wrote on December 14 from Baltimore somewhat differently, "Your kind note suggesting luncheon reached me just as I was leaving for the South for the holidays—perhaps for the entire winter—and

* So, borrowing the title of Wells's novel about a search for the most fulfilling life, they dubbed their "daventuring."

I didn't even have time to telephone you before going." To Garland, in an earlier note, he had acknowledged his indebtedness:

> If I ever succeed in expressing anything of Minnesota and its neighbors, you will be largely responsible, I fancy; for it was in your books that the real romance of that land was first revealed to me. This is a responsibility which you may find it mighty heavy to bear if I learn to write as badly as most of the writers who have chronicled that fabulous land of Titans, the Great West. But it takes years to learn to write as badly as one can, and perhaps you will be spared the onus!

Garland, it was to develop, declined it.

Baltimore, Washington, a boat trip down the Rappahannock to Fredericksburg, Christmas in Charleston, a pause with Irvin S. Cobb in Savannah (Lewis had earlier in the year contributed a eulogy to *Irvin Cobb, His Book*), New Year's with Colonel Benét and his family at the Augusta Arsenal, and finally St. Augustine, where from January 8 to February 18 the Lewises rented a bungalow at North Beach and their first reversals began.

The *Post* accepted one more story, "Honestly if Possible," a moralistic little tale about a Florida land development firm, and then rejected not only the next six stories (most of these written after the Lewises had moved on from Florida), but a serial, *The Innocents,* to which he had devoted two of the precious six St. Augustine weeks. The editorial complaint was that it was sentimental! The *Woman's Home Companion* came to their rescue with a thousand dollars, and all was well again. Published later as a book, *The Innocents* is almost certainly the worst thing that Lewis ever wrote, but interestingly, among those first *Post* rejections is also one of his best stories, "I'm a Stranger Here Myself," which went to four periodicals before it was accepted by *Smart Set* for the dramatic sum of seventy dollars.

"I'm a Stranger Here Myself" is the first sustained work recognizably written by the author of *Main Street.* It is the story of a tour of Florida and the East Coast made by a middle-aged, Middle Western couple who are uncomfortable in the presence of anything or anyone different from that to which they are accustomed, who are happy only when they are with other people exactly like themselves and doing the same things that they do at home. They frequent shiny big drugstores managed by hustling Midwesterners and nothing is quite as splendid as its equivalent in the place they came from. The story is the work of a man who has at last permitted his ear to catch the accents of Midwestern speech and his eye to look without sentiment upon provincial American types.

Among the tourists whom Lewis in fact encountered in St. Augustine were William Dean Howells and his daughter. The occasion is interesting not only because less than fifteen years later the famous Sinclair Lewis was to treat Howells rather unfairly in his remarks about him in the Nobel address, but more particularly because in fact Howells's middle-class liberal optimism was so much like Lewis's own, his social criticism, again like Lewis's, deeply tempered by it. Both, steering a clear line between a surly proletariat and a stuffed plutocracy, wished to assure the middle class that the promise of American life lay in its best values. Savage and boisterous as Lewis's writing was sometimes to be, his reticences about sex and the turmoil of the subjective life were Howells's too. Yet one cannot assume that the meeting in 1916 involved any shock of recognition. Years later Lewis was to remember only—and report it with a chuckle to Daniel Aaron—that Howells kept talking about someone named "Pussy Jones," and that Pussy Jones was Edith Wharton!

At their meeting, Lewis presented a copy of *The Trail of the Hawk* to Howells, and Howells responded by letter.

St. Augustine,
Feb'y 11, 1916.

Dear Mr. Lewis:

I did not like your boy in the beginning; I thought him overdone; and so dropped the book for a while. Today I took it up and read about the flying, from the mob scene in California to the end of the flying at New Haven. It was all good, BETTER, BEST. The go was full of throbs, and the people real and palpable. I am awfully glad of it. Now I shall keep on to the end—I hope.

We expect to go to Palm Beach by boat on Monday; I hear you are going later. We expect to be at the Hotel Saltair, West Palm Beach.

With our best joint regards to Mrs. Lewis and yourself,

Yours cordially,
W. D. Howells

Lewis was not happy with the fortunes of that novel at Harper & Brothers, and when his friend, Alfred Harcourt, still editor at Henry Holt & Company, expressed some interest in getting Lewis's name on the Holt list, Lewis wrote from St. Augustine with the hope that the move could be made.

> I'm making *The Job,* my next novel, just as big as I can, and may not get it finished till the end of the summer, simply shan't think of the element of time, for first of all I want it to be as big, as real, as sincere, as I possibly can.

Then he quoted from a letter that he had written to Miss Jordan at Harper (the only person there that he really cared about) in which he complained that *The Trail of the Hawk* had sold only 3,665 copies up to January 1—"that isn't much of an advance on the first season's sale of *Our Mr. Wrenn* . . . I remember them as somewhat over 2000,"—and mentioned vaguely the interest that both Doran and Holt had expressed in his future work. The letter then returned to Alfred Harcourt with the information that Miss

Jordan herself might be leaving Harper, and if she did, he would "wiggle out" of the option they held on the new book. "If she exits, then it's Harcourt ho! and let's see if we can't give this damn province a real realistic novelist, Gawd and Alfred Harcourt assisting that poor boob, Sinclair Lewis."

The Lewises left North Beach on February 18, and for nearly three weeks they traveled in Florida, and then on March 9 Lewis went alone to Chicago, leaving his wife with the Benéts for three or four days, and for three weeks after that with an Augusta family named Tulliver. Their marriage, during the last months in Port Washington, had not been entirely serene. Lewis was working under very heavy pressure—at the office and on stories and on *The Job*—and he was impatient with his wife and short-tempered. But as soon as he left her for Chicago, his desperate loneliness revealed his profound need of her and the emptiness of his life without her. The letters he wrote her from 2147 Washington Boulevard in that month of March 1916, from which she has published excerpts, are one long, lonely wail, but these lamentations punctuate a period of frenzied work and activity. "Have met Sandberg [sic]," he wrote Harcourt. "Rough but *real.*" He sought out Margaret Anderson and saw her a number of times. She recalled the meeting:

> . . . we did our best to be friends. But we couldn't communicate across the chasms that separated us. He was always attacking my standards for the *Little Review.*
>
> You're too remote from the common herd, you believe in art for art's sake, you ought to be interested in the psychology of the average person as well as that of the exceptional person.
>
> I am always so bored by this argument that I ignore it. I tried to make him talk of himself instead. He is an amusing and ardent person, condemned to perpetual vitality. He wouldn't be sidetracked. He wanted to talk about his barber and prove his theory. He had just come from his barber and told me a story about him on which I found it hard to fix my attention. I insisted that the only interest in the story was Sinclair Lewis' interest in telling it.
>
> No, he said, the barber *is* interesting. It's your limitation that you don't "see" him.
>
> He told me that a certain man was in love with me.
>
> Yes, I said, I knew it.
>
> But you refused him.
>
> Yes, I know that too.
>
> You don't care for him?
>
> No. That's why I refused him.
>
> But—well, I thought I'd like to talk to you about it, if I may, because I know he really cares for you.
>
> Well?

I thought perhaps you didn't know.

Oh yes, I know.

That didn't make you care for him at all?

Should it?

Well, it often does.

It doesn't with me.

But how do you know?

Because it didn't.

But no, be serious with me.

I'm serious but the conversation doesn't seem to me enlightened.

Now just a moment. What I want to say is that perhaps you don't know yourself yet. That's the way it was with my wife and myself. We didn't fall in love at first sight. [He did! *She* didn't.] But when she found I cared for her and I found she cared for me—well, that made all the difference. We discovered that we were in love.

But I'm not like that.

Not like what?

So—long, shall we say, in finding things out.

But I'm telling you we thought we weren't like that either. And you see we were.

But I'm not.

How can you be sure?

Because I've never been.

But . . .

My limitation? Or is life at such levels interesting?

At a quite different literary extreme, Lewis sought out the book reviewers, even that one who had been particularly cold to his books, Miss Fanny Butcher. Burton Rascoe left a curious notation about this meeting.

> . . . a lanky, freckle-faced, sandy-haired, most amiable, most immediately friendly young man, vibrant with nervous energy, had come to the office to see Fanny Butcher, who wrote a column of book news and comment for one of the Sunday sections. Miss Butcher introduced him to me. He was Sinclair Lewis. He acknowledged the greeting with "Hello, Burt!" Soon afterwards I was calling him "Red," whereas Miss Butcher stuck to "Hal." He was in town to get a job in a real-estate office, out of the experience of which he wrote *The Job.*

He may have visited real-estate offices, and certainly he was in Chicago to gather material, but he took no such job. Here, as in every city on the journey west, he began his practice of calling on the editors of newspapers and of lingering in busy city rooms. He was involved in searching out new markets among the periodicals with a rejected story called "The Kidnapped Memorial," which was sent out eighteen times, before, in 1918, it was finally bought by *Pictorial Review.* Almost every short story that he wrote was published in due time. Only one story of this period did he destroy as

"N.G.," no good. That, first called "The City Dutiful," found a new title before he at last gave it up: "Culture in Gopher Prairie." He was on his way back there now.

His wife arrived in Chicago on April 3, and until April 20 they lived at the Brewster on Diversey Parkway. Then they took the train for Sauk Centre. They arrived on April 24 and the town was still covered with snow.

They were good for small headlines in the *Herald:*

Noted Young Writer of American Fiction
Spending Summer as Guest of Parents
and Friends in Sauk Centre

He was now "one of the most compelling young fiction writers in the country," and his parents feted him at a dinner that the first Mrs. Lewis has twice described, along with other problems of adjustment involved in a stay of more than three months in the plain, punctilious residence of Dr. E. J. Lewis.

Sinclair Lewis rented a room above Rowe's Hardware Store on the corner of Main Street and Fourth and went on with *The Job*. He visited his old haunts in the surrounding countryside and he made public appearances. He lectured before the Commercial Club and the Citizens' Club, and, "a forceful, rapid fire talker," he told "the real 'inside' of how the modern literature of today is made" for the benefit of the Bryant Library. He wrote a short piece for the *Herald* to help publicize an announced Homecoming Week:

> It is perfectly obvious that homecoming to Sauk Centre means the rediscovery of lakes and fields and woods, of the natural beauty that so well stands comparison with any place you may wish to name, and perfectly obvious too, that the rediscovery of the Arch, the Bridge, the Crossing, the Indian Mound brings back the Days of Play to those of us who were born here. But I wish to recommend the prescription of Drs. Wallace and Husba: "Take one homecoming week to restore your faith in Mankind," for a reason which should peculiarly appeal to all who have gone from Sauk Centre to some large city—It will give you friends again!
>
> The urbanites who used to live in Sauk Centre will understand what I mean when I say that out of the hundreds or thousands or millions of people in their city, they can have but few friends. The distances, the nervous tension, forbid. When I returned to Sauk Centre the other day after 8 years of absence it was astonishing and delightful to be able to hail every other man on the street by his name; to find the whole world composed of friends; to find that there are plenty of people who remember one's first name! To go down the pleasant streets in the sunshine and be able to say, "Hello, Fay!" "Mornin', Charley!" "How are you, Ed?" without receiving in return the congealed stare of the big city—that alone would make it worth while to come many miles to be present at Homecoming Week.

> The abominable existence of the Great War would seem to indicate that the art of friendship is dead, but a return to Sauk Centre restores one's faith.

But, tired of the nostalgic recreation of small-town life in popular fiction, he was even then taking notes for *Main Street*.

His own recollection in 1937 was that, there in Sauk Centre in 1916, he wrote thirty thousand words of which he used about ten thousand in the final version. One may question the recollection since we know that he was hard at work on and coming near to the end of *The Job*. Notes he was certainly taking, and he was seeing the town again, but seeing it now, as his wife has reported, through her eyes, which were to be Carol Kennicott's.

Besides his work, there were visits back and forth with Claude Lewis and his family. His nephew, Freeman Lewis, then a small boy, observed these city strangers with interest, and he feels that this was perhaps the happiest time in the Lewis marriage. Sinclair Lewis had yet to achieve his first real success, and her success as Mrs. Sinclair Lewis had not yet really turned his young wife's pretty head. (Nor was she indolent in Sauk Centre; she had taken notes for a *Woman's Home Companion* article on the elder Mrs. Lewis's famous project, the Sauk Centre Rest Room, which led the *Herald* to comment that "the rest room is of more value to the transient public than anything else the town can offer.") Freeman Lewis remembers the occasion, twice reported by Mrs. Lewis, when the couple rolled silver dollars down the slight slope toward Main Street in front of old Dr. Lewis's house: they behaved like children, delighted with one another and quite without self-consciousness, to the astonishment of the natives who recognized their difference.

Then they bought the Model-T Ford, of which so much has been made, designed a tent that could be attached to it, invested in camping equipment and set off for a trip through the Iron Range and to Duluth. In Hibbing, Minnesota, Mrs. Lewis was mistaken for a most unlikely person, Elizabeth Gurley Flynn, the I.W.W. agitator, and was stared at by the populace and followed by the police. In Duluth they spent much of their time with the Claude Washburns, and there Lewis finished *The Job*. ("It is the best thing I've written," he was presently to write to Joseph Hergesheimer.) It was sent to Miss Jordan on August 2. Then they drove back to Sauk Centre to say good-by to the old people, stayed one day and on August 7 set out on a four-month hegira to the West. Lewis wore a tweed Norfolk jacket and a cap; Mrs. Lewis says that she was "comfortable, and decorative, in a khaki riding habit of knee-length coat and short divided skirt." *

* Fashion Note. In a 1918 article, "By Foot or Gasolene," for the *Woman's Home Companion,* Mrs. Lewis outlined details of clothing for the edification of other travelers: ". . . blouses of crêpe de chine or boy's shirts of madras with a tie of brilliant hue; a soft wired sports hat of corded tan taffeta, lined with chocolate-colored straw, and with a satin band under my chin to disregard the wind," etc. "The largest bag was really a small trunk for long stops. In it was a blue serge suit, a pair

Over the rutted roads of dusty Dakota and Montana they made their bumpy progress.

> Distances are enormous in the West, and when we saw that we could not make a town by six o'clock, the normal supper hour (a wise precaution if you want a real meal), we would stop on a pretty prairie edge, or beside a lake, or perch on a hilltop, and start the water from the thermos bottle boiling. While my husband smoked and watched the sun setting, I arranged biscuits, jam, tea ball, and the other simple supper accessories.
>
> This was the time we usually had guests—a rancher riding by, spurs jingling, to round up his cattle; a young harvester changing jobs, some "honyockers" or home steaders in a prairie schooner, creeping along contendedly to stake a claim. We did it for good-fellowship, for information's sake, and to propitiate the God of the Open Road.

By August 17, they were in Miles City, Montana, and by September 12, in Seattle, where for a month they stayed in the Hotel Chelsea. Four rejected manuscripts greeted him, but a letter from Harper was enthusiastic about *The Job*. Out went the manuscripts again, and out went Lewis to master this city that he had not seen before. He renewed his acquaintance with Anna Louise Strong, who remembers still his note-taking zeal.

> He knew he intended to be a great American writer, depicting the life of Americans of his day and age. He worked towards it always. . . . When he came to Seattle he showed me notebooks full of descriptions. He went, for instance, to the docks in Seattle and wrote down lists of what he saw . . . the size of packages, what was in them, how they were loaded or unloaded, where they came from, what everything looked like on those docks. . . . He did this everywhere he went, across the country. . . .

Taking new notes, he was utilizing earlier ones for two stories: "The Ghost Patrol," which after several rejections was to appear in *Red Book* in the following June, is set in Chicago and is concerned with an Irish policeman who reconciles the Italian and Jewish parents of young lovers; "The Scarlet Sign," accepted at once by *Metropolitan,* is set in central Minnesota and reminds us of the healing powers of the "sunlit prairies" as against the vice and brutality of most of their inhabitants. Similarly, those earlier stories that were still going the rounds present a double view of life in the small Midwestern town: in "He Loved His Country," the old virtues of neighborliness, tolerance, love of earth are corrupted by wartime hatreds; in "The Kidnapped Memorial," the pioneering spirit has died under the weight of the films, bridge, automobiles, "respectability," and is only momentarily revived. Lewis's general practice was to use his notes to create a

---

of white flannel trousers, a separate dark gray jersey coat, shirts, collars, and extra underwear for my husband. For me, a flossy hat, a taffeta street dress, a white net frock, a sports hat and coat, some pretty blouses, two linen skirts, pumps, white and black, and a few accessories."

setting that reflected his own attitude toward it, and then to impose upon it an invented situation either melodramatic or sentimental. When his notes were shaped up for their own sake, as in "I'm a Stranger Here Myself," he usually produced better stories.

In Seattle, besides writing and exploring, there were parties, lectures by each of the Lewises to the journalism students in the University of Washington, a side trip to Vancouver and Victoria. Then on October 14 they began a slow trip south to San Francisco, and, after two days in Berkeley with Leonard Bacon, Lewis's old Yale admirer ("Len Bacon," he wrote to Tinker presently, "has a pleasant house, a charming wife, an undiminished enthusiasm, in Berkeley"), they arrived in Carmel on October 30 and settled into a simple redwood cottage among the pines for a little more than two months.

The visit was not a success. Some members of the old casual Carmel colony were still there and they did not take to Mrs. Lewis nor to the tweedy Lewis into which she had tamed the wild, unkempt boy they had known, and they thought the general fuss that the Lewises made over their Ford was silly. The impression that the Lewises left on the Carmelites was so strong that, thirty-five years later, one of them, Jean Ritchie, could easily recall it for the Carmel *Pine Cone-Cymbal,* and some of them still remember with amusement that one of the Bohemians expressed his resentment by shoving the famous Ford into a ravine. That automobile had served its purpose well: it was to supply an extraordinary amount of material for publication in the next few years; but when the Lewises left Carmel in early January they sold it and continued their travels by train and boat.

The two Carmel months were fruitful in fiction. Lewis wrote four stories and began a fifth. The first and third of the four returned him to the bountiful rewards of *The Saturday Evening Post.* The other two went to *Metropolitan* and *Hearst's,* which paid him equally well. The fifth, one of his best-known stories, found its way into *Century* and paid a mere two hundred dollars.

"A Story with a Happy Ending" is a footnote to *The Job,* the story of a career woman whose activities threaten her with the loss of her lovableness, but this heroine survives the threat. "The Tamarack Lover" deals with a rougher kind of business woman, the keeper of a hotel and saloon in the northern Midwest; but again, the story demonstrates the womanliness beneath the rough exterior. "The woman behind the business man, the woman who could darn socks and long for a hand in hers, was lonely for him." Two of these stories, "Twenty-four Hours in June" and "The Poinsettia Widow," return to the Florida setting, and both assert the superiority of small-town virtues to urban snobbery. The last, "Young Man Axelbrod," returns to Yale College and the lonely life of an isolated eccentric, and again, the contrast is between honest if naïve aspiration and a ruthless snobbery, the innocent Midwest and the arrogant, corrupt East. Once before, Sinclair Lewis had left California for the East with precisely this double-jointed gesture—one commitment in his writing, another in his conduct.

In December he traveled as far south as San Diego, and at the same time Grace Lewis was in San Francisco to consult an obstetrician and assure herself that she was pregnant. ("I am at once amazed and amused by the situation. Also considerably peeved by the way in which it curtails my activities," she wrote to Elizabeth Jordan.) Proofs for *The Job* had come, and on the last day of the year Lewis wrote to Tinker about it.

> The work has gone well; I shan't have to go back to an office desk; I write glib and ineffective tales apace.
>
> In a couple of months my first real novel, *The Job,* will be published. . . . I'm not at all sure that I shall send you a copy; you prefer your immediate Children to the One Who——
>
> You deserve it not, but I still worship you as, in swaddling days when I tagged yammering after you till you called Jim Donneley [the campus policeman] to send me back to South Middle, I once did.

They left Carmel on January 11 without regrets and with some resentment,* spent a few days in Santa Barbara, a few more in Los Angeles, a few more at the Coronado in San Diego, where the local newspapers observed their arrival, and then traveled east through Arizona, the Grand Canyon, Santa Fe, to the Mexican border, and at last to New Orleans, where for four days they occupied rooms in Rampart Street in the French Quarter. On January 31 they sailed for New York on a Southern Pacific Company steamship, the *Antilles.* They learned on board that the United States had severed diplomatic relations with Germany.

They took an apartment until June 8 at 309 Fifth Avenue, a block and a half away from the old Waldorf-Astoria Hotel in whose gaudy grillroom Lewis had habitually lunched with his publishing friends. And now, with a baby on the way, he wrote slick short stories as if the furies had beset him. Beginning with "Nature, Inc.," he had written sixteen short stories that had been or were to be sold for a total of $7,587—the work of eighteen months. But now, from the time of his arrival in New York until shortly before the publication of *Main Street*—a period of less than four years—he was to publish forty-four stories † at a total of $33,875, exclusive of

* These feelings are manifested by the protagonist of "The Enchanted Hour" (*The Saturday Evening Post,* August 9, 1919), who returns to the New Light Colony of Pasqual, California, with recollections of a glamorous intellectual excitement, only to find everything gross, dirty, shabby and false.

† I have used the word "story" loosely here, since the number forty-four includes two serials, "Free Air" and "Danger—Run Slow," which, when they were combined, made a book-length work, and five articles (three of them on automobile travel). Of these forty-four stories, one, "The Willow Walk," was chosen for inclusion in the O'Brien *Best Short Stories* series.

agents' fees. In addition, in these years, he earned over $4,200 from a play and sales to the films. It would seem that we may doubt the long-circulated story, started by Lewis himself, that upon the completion of *Main Street* he was so poor that he had to borrow five hundred dollars from his father.

This mass of short stories presents a certain problem: they are mechanical, contrived, and sentimental or melodramatic or both, the frankly potboiling effort of a man who was trying to earn his living outside an office, and for these reasons they are hardly worth discussion. Yet they are an important part of that man's literary education and they rest on attitudes that they themselves helped formulate and that likewise inform his serious work, and for this reason they demand discussion.

A group of seven stories about an advertising man named Lancelot Todd, written for *Metropolitan,* together with a single story for *Popular Magazine* called "Gladvertising," satirize in a farcical way the peccadilloes of advertising men. Lancelot Todd, a suave immoralist and, indeed, a swindler, is sometimes brought to heel and is sometimes permitted to escape; but the plots of these stories are of no real interest. Their interest, rather, lies in the fact that here Lewis is investigating the world of George F. Babbitt and Elmer Gantry, the world of high-pressure salesmanship, and he exploits his knowledge of New Thought, Chautauqua, quack religion, woman suffrage, the dressmaking business, the automobile industry, patent medicine, trade publications, poetry for businessmen—the whole world of boosting and commercial razzmatazz and the fast buck, all presented in a raucous tone of satirical exposure.

The same motive and tone characterize an article that he wrote for *Metropolitan* in 1917. His friend Sonya Levien was now the wife of the editor of that periodical and was herself active on it, and when a man whom they had commissioned to do a spiritualist exposé did not wish to go on with the article, they turned to Lewis, who was happy to take over the project. "Spiritualist Vaudeville" appeared in February of 1918 and is chiefly amusing because Lewis asked to see the spirit of H. G. Wells, then at his most robust, a presence that was duly brought forth from the world beyond.

Satire and the spirit of exposure are not the most characteristic marks of the bulk of these forty-four stories. Among the remainder, to be sure, are "Hobohemia" and its sequel, "Joy-Joy," *Post* stories that oppose the false "intellectual" and "artistic" values of Greenwich Village to the down-to-earth honesty of a Midwestern businessman and of a "normal, sensible Northernapolis girl"; "The Shrinking Violet," which amuses itself with little theater groups, avant-garde writing, and literary hostesses; and "The Post-Mortem Murder" and "A Citizen of the Mirage," both of which satirize the follies of scholarship. But by and large these stories, most of which were written for the *Post,* are sweetly sentimental even when they contain a polemical barb.

A common theme is the vindication of the small and insignificant person as against the powerful and prominent, and one is always reminded of that Yale essay, "Unknown Undergraduates." Stories with this theme can find their setting anywhere—among doctors, as in "The Whisperer"; among manicurists, as in "The Hidden People"; among waiters and day laborers, as in "For the Zelda Bunch"; among theatrical troupers, as in "A Rose for Little Eva"; among social secretaries to debutantes, as in "An Invitation to Tea"; among career women, as in "Moths in the Arc Light"; among swindlers in honest small towns, as in "The Watcher Across the Road"; among presumed descendants of the passengers on the *Mayflower,* as in "Speed"; and among debonair automobile salesmen, as in "The Good Sport."

This is almost certainly the controlling situation in most of this short fiction—the superiority of the "real" (the "genuine Amurrican") over the false, the phony—probably an artist; over the Easterner—a snob; over the rich man—a swindler. The diagram of the plot is the unseating of the mighty by the good-humored unknown, of the pretentious by the humble. And generalizing Lewis's theme to this extent, one finds most of the remaining stories falling into the pattern of revelation (of true value against false) even when the plot itself does not give the victory to the "true." Thus, in "Mother-love," the irony is that the mother does not love her son but her scorned sister does; in "The Shadowy Glass" an apparently grim and unloving mother-in-law proves to be the protectress of her daughter-in-law's interests against the irresponsibility of her son; in "The Shrimp-Coloured Blouse" a supposedly knowledgeable New Yorker proves to be gullible in the Midwest; in "The Willow Walk" a slippery bank teller is hoist with his own petard; in "Bronze Bars" an apparently frivolous girl proves to be self-sacrificing and wins a proper love; in "Things," a *nouveau-riche* father burns his house and all his possessions to insure his daughter's happiness among the simplicities; "The Enchanted Hour" re-creates the Bohemian life of the Carmel colony and asserts the importance of individual love over generalized ideals; "A Matter of Business" opposes true craft to crass commerce. And so on.

Perhaps a dozen of these stories elude the formula. "Afterglow" is a rather pleasant little piece about two old Indian fighters who have outlived their time. "The Swept Hearth" distinguishes between fear and fear of fear, only the second of which is cowardice. "The Cat of the Stars" is a tour de force that means to demonstrate the illogicality of consequence: a small boy, pausing to pet a cat, sets up a chain of circumstances that concludes with three thousand dead in a South American war and the collapse of a British fortune. "Habeas Corpus" locates its plot in the atmosphere of anarchist, socialist, I.W.W., and liberal do-good activities, and seems to say only that everyone in the story is dreadful. "The Way I See It" tells us that everyone sees differently from everyone else and that some people don't see at all. An insignificant little man in "Number Seven to Sagapoose," a Mr. Rabbit, given to random and homey chitchat, influences a variety of people to choose the path of good (quite like "The Smile Lady" in Lewis's first New Thought story for *Nautilus*)—including one young man, a faint promise of Martin Arrowsmith, who chooses a relatively low-paid medical research position over the promise of wealth as a surgeon.

Incidental to the major themes but almost always lurking within them are a bundle of familiar motifs and attitudes: the loneliness of human beings in cities, the rewards of honesty and middle-class responsibility, adventure versus routine, hard work versus artiness and glib intellectuality, simple candor versus snobbery, country kindliness and wisdom versus city harshness and pomp. It is perhaps the last that appears most frequently.

Yet one should expect the author of *Main Street* to make an occasional exception to this cliché of American fiction, and there are indeed five of them. "A Woman by Candle-Light" tells of a young small-town salesman who, rather than marry the conventional daughter of the richest man in town, chooses to fall in love with an older woman who has a feeling for the beautiful and a gift for experience. "Detour—Roads Rough" deals with a friendly Philadelphian delayed by a motor accident in a small town whose inhabitants are universally bigoted, suspicious, self-important, deceitful and cruel. And the three articles called "Adventures in Autobumming" are simply a factual extension of the observations in the story, with Sinclair Lewis himself the marooned hero whom the villagers reject, deceive and insult.

He was thirty-five, and at least it was a living. But what did this great mass of fiction do for Lewis besides support him and keep his wife happy? We may conjecture, in the first place, that, whether or not it made "a household word" of his name, it gave him a wide popular audience of a kind that his early novels did not reach. It changed his status from that of amateur to professional. It enabled him, next, to explore and record a hundred social, vocational and geographical areas in American life, to crystallize his observations of them and to set his attitudes, even when they were ambivalent, toward them. More technically, it helped him to construct and control tightly unified fictional situations; and, on the other side of that coin, it encouraged him often to falsify them with a mechanical twist or a patent contrivance that ignored the human materials. More technically still, it developed and fixed his stylistic method: if the early novels showed some slight potentiality for impressionistic nuance and suggestiveness, these now vanish or turn into purple patches. The audience he was addressing demanded the explicit, the demonstrated, the heavily documented, the overdrawn and the broad. The style, like the man, was made.

And most of these qualities we can observe in *The Job: An American Novel,* which was published by Harper on February 23, 1917, in a printing of 5,000 copies. It is a clear advance over its predecessors, its chief fault being that it is much too long and that the logic of its plot is sacrificed in a sickly sweet turn at the end.

With its more concentrated realism, its grayer tone and relative freedom from whimsical interludes, *The Job* was Lewis's first controversial book. Its general subject—a young woman struggling for a place in the ruthless world of business—was in itself still controversial, but more than that were certain ancillary interests with which *The Job* is also concerned: women's rights, divorce, birth control, socialism, realistic and radical fiction. It has been argued that the movement of population from the farms and the small towns to the cities at the end of the last century and the beginning of this was largely a women's movement, part of the whole effort at emancipation from domestic drudgery into self-realization and independence. Dreiser's Carrie Meeber, a "half-equipped little knight . . . venturing to reconnoiter the mysterious city and dreaming wild dreams of some vague, far-off supremacy," is perhaps the first major example—and Edith Wharton's Undine Spragg, so different, the next?—of a whole procession of heroines in American twentieth-century fiction who dramatize this movement of aspiring women, sometimes themselves heartless, into the heartless city. Sinclair Lewis was to build novels around a number of them, but Una Golden in *The Job* is the first, and in 1917 a candid examination of her problem was not yet a cultural commonplace. A glance at C. Wright Mills's account of the white-collar girl in American fiction indicates with what completeness Sinclair Lewis created the image and the pattern of life in Una Golden, to be followed by Alice Adams, Minnie Hutzler, Janey Williams, Kitty Foyle, and all the others, including Ann Vickers.

At twenty-five, in 1905, Una Golden comes to New York with her mother, and in their situation as it is discussed in an extended parenthesis on widowed mothers and young spinster daughters, they are suggestive of Mrs. Frank Hegger and her daughter, Grace; but suggestive in situation only, for Una "was an untrained, ambitious, thoroughly commonplace, small-town girl." She wants two things—a job and "some one to love, to talk with." She sees the city through a haze of glamour, attends a business school, finds no one to love, but finds a copyist's job on the *Motor and Gas Gazette*. She has faith in business and "the theory of efficiency, the ideal of Big Business," and so, as he tells us in another long parenthesis, has Sinclair Lewis. ". . . the vision of an efficiency so broad that it can be kindly and sure, is growing—is discernible at once in the scientific business man and the courageous labor-unionist."

At eight dollars a week, it is not easy to maintain her faith, but the drudgery and the routine are alleviated by the presence of her immediate superior, Walter Babson. He is an erratic, energetic, nervous young editor, slapdash and irresponsible. A Kansas farm boy with literary ambitions, and now "desperately lonely," waiting for "any love, any labor, that should want him enough to seek him and demand that he sacrifice himself," his past is shot through with Sinclair Lewis's own autobiographical recollections. He thinks that he loves Una, but he has no money and no promise of a career, and they seem to have no future together. The treatment of love is somewhat more mature than it was in *The Trail of the Hawk,* or, at any rate, it is true to the characterization. Walter speaks for Lewis:

> ". . . I'm as bad as a nice little Y.M.C.A. boy—I bow to conventions, too. Lordy! the fact that I'm so old-fashioned as even to talk about 'conventions' in this age of Shaw and d'Annunzio shows that I'm still a small-town, district-school radical! I'm really as mid-Victorian as you are, in knowledge. Only I'm modern by instinct, and the combination will always keep me half-baked, I suppose. I don't know what I want from life, and if I did I wouldn't know how to get it. I'm a Middle Western farmer, and yet I regard myself about half the time as an Oxford man with training in Paris."

Abruptly, Walter decides to go west and find himself. Una loses her job in an economy drive and gets a new one with an architect. In 1907 her mother dies and she dedicates herself to Business with renewed fervor.

But she cannot maintain it. Office routine is poisonous and she has nothing else. Her boardinghouse life is so dull and lonely that she moves to The Temperance and Protection Home for working girls, and there she makes friends. But with Walter gone, she feels the need of a man, and when she takes her vacation on a Berkshire farm, she meets a crude middle-aged salesman named Julius "Eddie" Schwirtz, a widower, who is noisily attentive, and as she goes back to the awful office, she assures herself, "But I do like him!"

She goes to work now for a drug firm which is brutally efficient. Eddie Schwirtz pursues her and the office exhausts her, and she gives up the ideal of The Job to marry him. The scenes that follow are the best in the book: the couple has a dreadful honeymoon during which Eddie rather proudly admits that he has no interest in the sexual graces; he reveals that he has exactly one hundred dollars; they take a room in a New York family hotel; disillusioned, she wants still to make a go of her marriage.

For two years they live the dreary life of hotel rooms and Lewis develops the theme of the relationship between physical boor and refined lady. Eddie is unfaithful. Finally he loses his job, and the scene in which he tells her so, and charges her with frigidity, has something of the pathos that characterizes *Death of a Salesman.* He declines into an alcoholic stupor and she goes back to work—in real estate now. She is successful. In 1915 she manages a whole new subdivision on Long Island, and when she returns to the office, she has a new position and $2,500 a year. From this, she very quickly becomes the manager of a hotel chain, and lo! a steadier Walter Babson is the publicity man. She'll divorce Eddie and keep her job—for a while—until Baby comes. . . .

Again, of course, the themes are familiar: the escape from the narrow province into the free world, the loneliness of two misfits, the failure of an ideal but the personal success, the triumph of persistency and of human biology. The tone is less sentimental than in the earlier work, and less satirical, more downright; and in the marriage scenes it achieves a certain brutal directness. The writing is a real development, with a new stylistic authority and firmness that is without the insistent, high-pitched raucousness that marked much of the earlier writing. In structure there is a development, too: covering ten years, the novel is the first to move by the unit of the short, sometimes very short scene, the method that will characterize *Babbitt* and *Main Street.* Finally, there is a development here in the harsh realism which, even though the subject itself is New York City, derives from a frontier tradition that would seem to have developed out of the barrenness of that life itself.

The best of Lewis's novels thus far, it had perhaps the least favorable press. Lewis summarized the unfavorable reviews for Hergesheimer as "a sordid, sex-ridden, blind, cheaply slangy, mufflefooted thing, false in its picture." In number, the reviews went to about four hundred, and the discussion centered on the realism of the novel, which left many reviewers uneasy. Their quarrel was not with the detail as such but with the whole picture of the American business community that emerged. The New York *Herald Tribune,* in a review called "Cheap and Chippy," complained that "as for *The Job* being 'the real thing in literature,' so is a weed patch or a compost heap the 'real thing' in nature. But there are other 'real things,' just as real." The liberal weeklies were enthusiastic. In the *New Republic,* Francis Hackett wrote: "It is extremely seldom that a novelist is sufficiently free from convention and sufficiently interested in life itself to see a new subject firsthand. This Mr. Lewis has done." *The Nation's* reviewer felt that it showed "a keener perception of the problems of modern America than Frank Norris in his novel *The Pit,*" and *The Masses* found in it at least partial payment on that promissory note. The Sauk Centre *Herald* was equanimous in about two hundred and fifty words.

There were, of course, letters of praise—from Joseph Hergesheimer, for example, who later was to be repaid in the dedication to *Main Street;* from faithful friends like Gene Baker in Oakland; from faithful, and proud, professors like William Lyon Phelps:

> *Job* is your best yet. It is a very fine novel, genuine realism in the truest sense, and I'm proud of you and proud of Yale. Yesterday I *lectured* on it as you see per enclosed. I am writing Harpers a recommendation. Great work!

He had prefaced a public lecture on Browning's *Ring and the Book* with an enthusiastic report on *The Job*.*

The Job—of which Lewis, in his inscription to his wife, said that he was "the supposed author" and she "the real author"—is perhaps most remarkable in the alteration of its tone from that of the two novels that had preceded it. These novels were imbued with something of the cheerfulness, exuberance, spontaneity, and bright optimism for the future of American life that were characteristic of that short period of the "rebellion" before the war; from 1914 to 1917, as American intervention became more and more likely, that insouciance was gradually dissipated. Is it stretching a point to suggest that the gray dreariness that distinguishes *The Job* from its predecessors derives from the black shadow that was spreading over American intellectual life in general? Perhaps; for in his personal life the war did not touch Sinclair Lewis.

Holding a vague pacifist position, he had turned his back on the war in 1915 to drive west in a Ford. It was in a way a symbolic gesture. Most of the stories that he was writing for the big periodical markets were informed by that same early "innocence" and easy optimism that is evident in the first novels. He played no part in the formation, in May 1917, of the People's Council of America which had attracted countless liberals and radicals, and in September, the very month when young men like Joseph Freeman

* Lewis must have taken pleasure, however belated, in a three-and-a-half-page letter of August 14, 1918, eighteen months after publication, from Norman Angell, whom he had obviously met at some time. It read, in part:

> I have just finished reading *The Job* and I want to tell you what a fine, honest and able piece of work I think it. I seem to have read a review somewhere which was disparaging, or at least patronising.... It is of the first water... in unpretentious form you have made a great contribution to modern American literature; the kind of contribution which I believe is most needed. [Angell goes on at length to demonstrate how it is also] a contribution to my own subject—politics and internationalism... it helps to correct a fundamental error in political thinking. That error is the assumption that the ultimate problem in politics is concerned with the struggle of rival states for domination and survival; whereas the ultimate problem of politics is the quality of life lead by the men that make up the states.... If we could become deeply interested in the quality of the common life in our states—if that were our main interest—we should see that most of our wars have no bearing thereon.... In a simple way, without pretentious obscurantism or false mysticism, a book like this may help Americans to see that things that they have assumed without question to be good, may be evil, and evil good. I shall hope to see you one day tackle even bigger issues, the moral forces underlying the big struggle in the Labor field that faces America; and America's great Alsace-Lorraine problem—the negro.... I want to congratulate you on your book, and hope that you will continue along that line, and not be dragged too much into "Evening Post" pot boiling; and will one day, have a shot at these other themes. [And he adds a postscript to say that his secretary, "a not undiscerning American girl," found the novel "coarse."]

Interestingly enough, Lewis was to struggle with the first suggestion for years, and finally to write a novel about the second.

and Max Eastman went to the convention of the Council in Chicago to formulate its antiwar program, Sinclair Lewis drove to Minneapolis to look for a place to live. And when the war was over he emerged with that "innocent" optimism largely unimpaired, suffering from none of the disillusionment that assailed the intellectuals and those other writers to whom the war was a trauma. Nevertheless, in that one work, *The Job,* he seemed to have been touched by the shadow.

An earlier work, properly called *The Innocents* (and less appropriately subtitled "A Story for Lovers"), was serialized in the *Woman's Home Companion* in February and March of 1917. In April, Alfred Harcourt proposed that Holt publish it as a book if Harper did not wish to do it, as seemed likely, and his first novel thereafter "about which we talked as entitled *Main Street.*" The terms proposed by Harcourt were, for these years, remarkably good, with royalties beginning at 15 per cent rather than 10 per cent, and with an advertising guarantee tied in with sales and charged in part against the willing author's royalties. Sinclair Lewis would not commit himself to another publisher without exercising some substantial control over the promotion of his books. But Harper, who held an option on the next Lewis novel, did publish *The Innocents,* which Lewis presented as the next novel, on September 14, 1917, in an edition of 4,000 copies, and if the publication served no other purpose, it presumably fulfilled the terms of his contract and freed him.

His worst book, it is also the hardest to come by. In the University of Minnesota copy he wrote, "I don't own a copy of this. (1) I don't much want it. (2) I can't afford it." Later, he rather disclaimed it, but at the time of its publication, he was sufficiently proud of it to dedicate it to a whole group of British writers whom he did not yet know, including H. G. Wells, for whom he confessed his "strident admiration." A short time later, to St. Paul newspapermen, he tried to escape the embarrassment that it was causing him by pretending that it was a satire, a take-off on the "horribly optimistic persons that you'd like to kill."

An extended short story rather than a novel, *The Innocents* presents Mr. and Mrs. Seth Appleby, a pair of cheerful, simple old New York folk who, one summer during their annual vacation on the Cape, decide to leave New York and open a teashop at Grimsby Head. The project, completely mismanaged through their naïveté, fails, and when they return to New York the old man cannot get back his job as shoe clerk. They go to the home of their termagant daughter and her husband, a druggist, in Saserkopee, but the false show of affection and the bullying of the young people is intolerable, and they flee. Once more in New York, they live in Lewis's old haunts on Avenue B, but they cannot find employment and, in desperation, take to the road to beg. For a time they camp with hoboes, and "Mother" Appleby reforms the drunks. In a town in Indiana they are treated kindly, and when they say they wish to live there, the townspeople are delighted. Appleby takes over a shoe store and makes a success of it. He buys a house for his wife. When their daughter reads about them, she writes them an abusive note and sends her husband to bring them home. Seth meets him at the train and pretends meekness. He takes him to his house, and there a great party is going on (all of the best townspeople are celebrating the Applebys' presence), and the son-in-law is routed. When the son-in-law suggests that he would like to open a drugstore there, Appleby tells him that there is no chance of that; and the novel ends with The Innocents chortling away together in the glow of their hearth.

There is nothing of shadow here, nor even much of mind, and the sentimentalization of village life outdoes anything in the *oeuvre* of Meredith Nicholson.

In May, Lewis went alone for a five-day visit at the handsome West Chester, Pennsylvania, place of Joseph Hergesheimer. On June 8 the Lewises gave up their apartment and sublet a house for the summer at Spuyten Duyvil. There on July 12 they bought a new Hupmobile, and in that machine on July 25 Lewis drove his wife to the New York Lying-in Hospital, where on the next day she was delivered by Caesarean of their only child, Wells. There was apparently some debate before the name of Wells was settled upon. To Hergesheimer, Lewis wrote: "I met Carl Van Vechten on the street; he said he had been down to West Chester, and insisted on Geo Moore Lewis, or at least More Lewis as a compromise, but I turned on him a face of granite." Years later, Sinclair Lewis was to write a letter to H. G. Wells, beginning,

> *Dear H.G.*
>
> Some eighteen years ago when I named my eldest son, Wells Lewis, after you, I promised myself that I would never let you see him unless he turned out pretty well. It seems to me that he has!

This is paternal solicitude of a kind that he did not always show. In her recollections, the boy's mother says that Lewis was very thoughtful of and attentive to her during her pregnancy and in the hours of her labor, but that he never seemed to think of the child that was coming, and that after the child was born the father never held him in his arms except when she placed him there to take snapshots of the two.

She now hoped that they could find a house of their own somewhere, and when she indicated as much, Lewis, alarmed by the threat, challenged her with an observation she had earlier made, that a child would make no difference to their adventuring. She submitted.

On September 30, with a Seattle friend, Jack Carrigan, as his companion, he started on another trip to the Middle West. Carrigan stayed with him as far as Columbus, Ohio, and then, near Hebron, Ohio, Lewis's car was in a collision with a Ford and he was detained for several days while it was being repaired. (This is the source of that irritation with village life that found its expression in the "Autobumming" articles and in the story, "Detour—Roads Rough.") His wife and child were following by train and they joined him in Minneapolis.

For two weeks they lived on a poultry farm at Marine on St. Croix, and there they were persuaded by St. Paul friends to try their city for the winter. They rented a considerably lavish house of yellow brick and white scroll work at 516 Summit Avenue and, having made these arrangements, went to Sauk Centre for a week to visit the old ones. From Sauk Centre on October 20, Lewis wrote to Hamlin Garland to decline an invitation to serve on a Committee of the Literary Arts because he would be away from New York for the winter. Then he went on to praise Garland's most recent book, published in 1917:

> It chanced that when your letter came I was thinking of writing to you because I am now reading with delight your *Son of the Middle Border*. It has become obvious to say that nowhere else may be found a more convincing picture of the Middle Border as it was in the making, but I want to add to that obvious chorus; to tell how real and vital seemed so many scenes—the awakening boy, the blizzard round a prairie shack, the venture of the wagon to new horizons, the thrill of the first trip into the mellow and magic East.

He could hardly have written this letter from a more appropriate place, but they left that place as quickly as they decently could, to take up their elegant St. Paul residence on October 25.

Early in November, Lewis wrote to Mrs. Upton Sinclair that

> Now we've come out for the winter and spring—possibly next summer, too—in this middlewestern environment, watching the solid, stolid Real America in its faults and virtues, its stability and reluctances. And there is an easy friendliness here rather pleasant. . . . Also lower rent!

He was a man of some prominence now, and they were well received. In the St. Paul *Pioneer Press* for January 18, 1918, one reads:

> A group of society folk will assemble tomorrow evening at the home of Mr. and Mrs. Sinclair Lewis . . . to hear Danny Reed, producing director of the Little Theater Association, read the dramatization of Mr. Lewis's play, "Hobohemia," which recently appeared in the *Saturday Evening Post.*

Daniel Reed, in fact, helped him compose the unhappy stage adaptation of his story, and apparently they were still working on the play at the time of this reading. In Lewis's accounts he says that he began writing about December 1, 1917. Daniel Reed, who was then twenty-four years old, with ten years' experience of the theater, remembers the association as follows:

I have since thought we were more enamoured of the title for commercial purposes than we were of the material itself. I did try to help and practically lived at the Lewises for the months of that winter. Sinclair and I played a lot more than we worked because he was a most indulgent procrastinator—and so was I. Also I was putting on rather elaborate shows for an ardent little theater group of St. Paul society folk and had my own calendar to face. Sinclair could afford to be more scornful of people—and he was. I must say his attitude toward most of his fellowmen—regardless of caste or status—when he considered them in group formation particularly—was critical and most often scornful.

On January 4, 1918, Lewis wrote to Elizabeth Jordan, "And I—you will shriek with consternation, having been through the grind yourself—am writing a play and actually working on it!" On January 15 he wrote her again to say that "Grace and I have just been skiing—and there's been lots of skating and good parties and work on my play." And on the same day he wrote to Alfred Harcourt at Holt:

Dear Alf:

Naw, ain't writing a novel, writing a play, and when the managers have all turned that down with derision and contumely and the rest of Roget's Thesaurus I'll get some sense and write another novel. I started in gravely to write the Jim Hill novel—actually spent a couple of weeks reading oceans of dope—and for the first time in trying to do a thing like that, turned back baffled—couldn't see my way out.* So the novel when it does come will be either our old friend *Main Street*—of wh[ich] you must be heartily sick by this time—or a novel about a traveling man—a man like Mr. Schwirtz in *The Job*.

All goes well and cheerfully—we've made hundreds of good friends in St. Paul—enough parties, despite the war; skating and skiing; all feel well. Regards to your people and regrets we're not at Spuyten Duyvil to be near you—tho otherwise I'm more 'n happy in Sinpul.

Sever

He finished the play on February 9, 1918, and on that day sent it to his agents, Brandt and Kirkpatrick. It found a producer within twelve months. The play meant a good deal to him and he had (by his own word) worked at it intensively. To Gene Baker (now Mrs. Frank McComas) he wrote:

* One hears little more of this project. James J. Hill, "the empire builder," was a St. Paul man, who had died less than two years before. Interest in the man would have been great at that time, and Lewis's presence in St. Paul would have facilitated his researches. The project may even have been his motive in living that year in St. Paul. Among the several ideas for novels that he carried through his lifetime, one was "a railroad novel," and in 1924, at dinner with Arnold Bennett in London, Lewis referred indirectly to the Jim Hill novel. The talk had turned to old railroading days, to "the careers of the famous Van Hoorn and Jim Hill. Lewis thought of it as an idea for a novel: what I should say it was."—Bennett, *Journals,* Vol. III, p. 21.

> ... most of the time in St. Paul I have been engaging in the unspeakable and paranoiac luxury of writing a play! ... I had a delightful time writing it, worked on it to the verge of prostration, strained and kneaded every word and gesture and situation in it—and now my agent is having anything but a delightful time trying to sell it, which he probably won't do it.

Hobohemia had elevated the Midwest virtues over Bohemian artiness, and as if to prove the point for himself *in extremis,* Lewis, immediately after the completion of his play, went alone to Cass Lake, where he stayed at a lumber camp for five days to experience the great north woods in winter. Impatient and restless as always, he was in 516 Summit Avenue for spurts of story writing and then out again. A vacation with woodsmen on Cass Lake was no doubt a release from steam-heated family concerns in "Sinpul." The wintry delights of "skating and skiing" that he had mentioned in his letter to Harcourt are perhaps more accurately described in *Arrowsmith,* when, in the early war years in Nautilus, Iowa, Martin conducts a gauche winter flirtation with one Orchid Pickerbaugh under the eyes of his wife. The Lewis marriage was not yet four years old; if the marriage boat was already floundering in heavy seas, Lewis's letters do not say so. To Hamlin Garland he wrote on November 12:

> If my handwriting becomes shaky at this point it's because my wife has just caught me defenseless, pounced on me, & is now vigorously rubbing my still-thick hair with some abominable mixture supposed to keep one as fresh-& youthful-looking as a movie-actor or a bond-salesman.

His photographs show that culture had moved into the Age of Sta-comb.

On February 10, 1918, he had written to Young that "in a couple of months, now, we start East—we'll probably have summer on Cape Cod. If it weren't for the baby, tho, we'd motor west again." It was less than "a couple of months" before the St. Paul household began to break up. On March 27 he set out for New York in the Hupmobile, his wife and child following by train on April 14. At the beginning of May they found a cottage at Chatham, on Cape Cod, in which they lived for two weeks, and then, with a nurse for Wells, they moved into another cottage for the remainder of the summer. Already Lewis was planning another move. On May 24 he wrote Hergesheimer:

> Give heed, now. Here's something I want you to arrange to do—motor with me the long and royal way from here to Seattle, next fall—starting some time in August or September. We'd cross the manufacturing eastern Middlewest—Ohio and Indiana; see the pine forests of Minnesota; hit the vast prairies with their sea-like vistas; go over range on range of the Rockies, with valleys of ranches and sagebrush between, and so at last to the Pacific and the sunset! That's the northern route; but we could also go south, to San Francisco, and north from there.... Think about it and plan for it and come—see America!

In the first week of June they motored in the Berkshires and, in an effort to mend a friendship, spent two days with the Updegraffs at Woodstock. Florence Maule, a well-known suffragette, was the new Mrs. Updegraff, and Updegraff himself was writing a novel, which Lewis would presently try to persuade Alfred Harcourt to publish. On June 7 they were on their way back to Chatham. In July Mrs. Hegger and son Frank came to visit, and Sinclair Lewis departed for New York, where, for five and a half weeks, he occupied the William Woodward apartment in West 79th Street. In his letter to Hergesheimer of May 24, Lewis had written, "And now, today, I start the novel, *Main Street,* and go on with it, breaking off now and then for short stories." Woodward's recollection of Lewis in that summer may be accurate:

> I remember that Lewis was writing *Main Street,* but he never showed me a chapter or a page of it as he said he had not made it good enough yet to show anyone.
>
> He seemed much depressed. He would come down to my office and sit there for an hour at a time. When he was there we usually went out to lunch together, and he said frequently that he would like to give up writing, and go into some solid business like banking.

This is plausible. He wrote three short stories in May and then no other short stories, except for one in July, and a serial, "For Sale Cheap," which was repeatedly rejected and then abandoned. It is not clear from his record, however, whether this serial was written in the New York summer (which, had it been, could have been the source of his dejection), in the later part of the summer at Chatham, or in the fall, after he was once more in Minnesota. In July, according to the manuscript record, he wrote four scenarios for Hollywood, and one of these, *Prairie Gold,* was sold to Universal for $750, and filmed, with Mary MacLaren, as *The Unpainted Woman* in 1919. One sale out of four attempts could also have caused dejection. If the fragments called "The Thesis of *Main Street,*" published in *With Love from Gracie,* were written at this time in New York, the cause of dejection is clear enough: they indicate a novelist still groping wordily toward his material, not in the least in charge of it. But the whole matter is confusing, and the fragments of Lewis's extant correspondence from these months do not help to clarify it.

We know that he had made notes for *Main Street,* that he had discussed it and settled on a title with Alfred Harcourt, that he had probably made some plans for it and probably attempted to state its "thesis" in writing. Toward the end of the summer, he returned to Chatham, and two years later, in a letter to Tinker, he referred to this period as "a forlorn time when I was making the first of my several efforts to start *Main Street,*" and in an autobiographical sketch of January 1932, he wrote:

> . . . winter in Minneapolis—1918–19. Here he began definitely to plan *Main Street.* He had once written 20,000 words on it, and thrown them away. The plan advanced during the summer of 1919, while they lived in Mankato, a town in Southern Minnesota, and while he was writing *Free Air.* [It was the continuation of the serialized *Free Air,* called "Danger—Run Slow," that he wrote in Mankato.]

But on September 10, 1918, when he wrote to Miss Ellen Eayrs (Alfred Harcourt's secretary and later his wife) to say that he had registered for the draft at Chatham and had used the Harcourt address in New York (he was classified 4A—married, with dependents),* he said:

> The novel, the great and only presumably-to-be-issued-by-Holt novel, is going strong. I've written eighty thousand words. Looks as though it would be about 130,000 in all. But that probably will be considerably cut.

What novel? About ten days later (we can date this letter approximately because Lewis directs his correspondent, an unidentified "Hans," to read "The Swept Hearth" in the current *Post,* September 21, 1918), he said, "Me, I have done nothing but work on my novel since I got back here, and it approaches an end." Later correspondence suggests that this could not possibly have been *Main Street.* On December 9 of that year he wrote Hergesheimer from Minneapolis:

> I by God *will* write *Main Street.* It's in my mind every day. Last summer I spent about 2 weeks developing plans for it, but I found I needed another (the present) trip out here before I wrote it. I often do that with things—thrash 'em over for several years before I finally write 'em & they're always the better for it.

Was it *Free Air* that he was working on or even the despised *For Sale Cheap?*

To "Hans" he continued as follows:

* His attitude toward the war seems to have undergone a change. In July 1918 the Author's League of America expelled G. S. Viereck because of his pro-German activities, and in August it expelled W. B. Hale, who then announced that he had not known that he was a member. In response to this statement, Sinclair Lewis addressed himself on August 26 to the New York *Times* in part as follows:

> A charming August fancy is the thought of what sort of an organization would satisfy Dr. Hale, would gain the approval of that great man who, as he himself says, has been accustomed to "sending long dispatches at critical moments." Would it have the celebrated Dr. Hale for President? Would it beg Karl Rosner to come over and head the Executive Committee? Or would it include only persons whose names begin with an obscure "von"?

In 1920, he wrote the following for Volume III of *The History of the Class of 1907:*

> His work during the war was publicity writing for the Bureau of Foreign Propaganda of the Committee on Public Information, for the Y.M.C.A., the Liberty Loan, etc.

National Archives in Washington is unable to verify this meager statement.

We have decided to spend the winter in the Middlewest again—Minneapolis, this time. We spent last winter in St. Paul and liked it—had a mild feeling of home such as one does not get in NY. Also I write much of the Northwest, and, if not over done, it doesn't hurt to see something of the territory one chronicles.

Before we go (wife and young travel by train; I drive my car out) I shall be in NY for a few days (probably around October 1st) and I shall see you then. . . .

Harrison Smith drove with him as far as South Bend, Indiana, and from that point he continued alone. In Minneapolis, he rented an office in Harmon Place, a run-down residential district, and by October 21 the family, with Ma*ma,* was established at 1801 James Avenue South.

From this address an exasperatingly vague communication went to Alfred Harcourt. Dated only "Sunday," it says: "Back all right, and on the job. The *Free Air* and *For Sale Cheap* mss. have arrived, and I'll get to work on *Free Air* P.D.Q." George Soule believes that the influence of Alfred Harcourt in turning Lewis from literary failure to success was crucial, and that he exercised that influence by arguing against Lewis's preoccupation with success: Lewis was to abolish from his mind all notions of what he thought the public wanted and write the novel that he really wanted to write, for its own sake alone. One wonders.

Both the current works were planned as magazine serials but presumably Lewis had consulted Harcourt as to their potentialities as books on the Holt list. The "Sunday" communication seems to suggest a meeting with Harcourt, perhaps even the occasion on which he left the manuscripts with him. Such a meeting took place in early February of 1919 when Lewis went to New York for the opening of *Hobohemia* and Harcourt went to the play with him. The implication seems to be that Harcourt encouraged him to do more work on *Free Air* (which the *Post* had already accepted) and advised him to put *For Sale Cheap* aside. This is implication only; the accounts record of *For Sale Cheap* is very unclear as to dates:

FOR SALE CHEAP—*serial*
Rej. by *Everybody's;* rej. by *Hearst's.*
Cosmo rej.
First draft to Red Book, October 30 [1918]. Rej.
Rej. by *Pict. Rev.:* Popular.
To be Dropped or Rewritten

It was dropped, but he wrote and sold three *Post* stories, and by the end of the year he had finished *Free Air,** which the *Post* accepted on January 11, 1919.

*In his accounts he makes the note, "abt. 56,000 wds.," so that this could hardly have been the novel of which he had finished 80,000 words by September 10, and which he projected at 130,000.

The winter passed much as had the winter before. The relief of the war's end was countered by the solemn fact that Prohibition was upon us. Still, one could hold an audience at the Minneapolis Institute of Arts with a lecture on "Contemporary Fiction as an Interpretation of Modern Life." Still, there were parties and excursions. It is at this point that anecdotes about the Lewis marriage begin to accumulate. Mrs. Lewis proved to be irksome to more and more of Lewis's friends, and the Middle Westerners were not to be imposed upon. On one occasion, when the Joseph Warren Beaches were entertaining them at dinner, Lewis arrived with a bottle of whisky and caused a considerable stir. He asked for a towel and, with that over his arm, served it—great impersonation of a waiter. At dinner, Mrs. Beach remembered, Mrs. Lewis complained of the fashion in which he was eating his peas, whereupon he arose from the table in protest, sat on the floor in a corner, finished his meal in his lap. Mrs. Beach always had the impression that Mrs. Lewis remembered that massive ducal stairways swept up out of the great entrance hall of her father's house, with distinguished people flowing up one flight and distinguished people flowing down another, and she, with a languid wave of the hand, saying, "*This* I can give to Hal!"

She did not accompany him to New York for the opening of *Hobohemia* on February 8, 1919. The play, having been read and declined by Cohan & Harris, Charles Hopkins, Arthur Hopkins, Frederick Stanhope, and possibly still others, was at last accepted by Frank Conroy and Harold Meltzer. It was given a considerable production with a good cast, including Helen Westley, in the elegant new Greenwich Village Theater on Sheridan Square. The *Post* story had been more than merely adapted, it had been changed; but the changes did not improve it. The satire was so broad as to be meaningless, the movement was jerky, and it concluded with a high degree of irresolution. The critic for the New York *Times,* John Corbin, was no more severe than the several others who deigned to notice it at all:

> The author's strategy consists in the very simple process of representing the citizens of this burg as howling idiots, and the Mid-Western young lover as a paragon of brains and homely virtue. It is a stand-off between the two lots as to which is the more preposterous. . . . The most successful feature of the production is its title.

Still, it ran for eleven weeks, apparently to an uptown audience. In *Garrets and Pretenders,* Albert Parry wrote:

> The early plays about the Village had their audience among the very same Villagers about whom the plays were written. But it was different now, in the season of 1918–1919. Now, the staid readers of *The Saturday Evening Post* came to see the play with a secret expectation of beholding nude models somewhere around the corner.

And George Jean Nathan, writing after he had become Lewis's friend and admirer, said:

> The fellow was known . . . to me, specifically, as the author of a play called *Hobohemia,* produced the year before down in Greenwich Village and exquisitely—if I may be permitted so critically indelicate a word—epizoötic.

"Epizoötic" or not, it attracted the attention of Harry Bache Smith, a well known librettist who had collaborated with Victor Herbert and Irving Berlin, and who thought for a time of turning *Hobohemia* into a musical. In that form, it might have succeeded, but the "wad" that Lewis anticipated for a time as a result of it did not materialize.

On February 28, after Lewis had returned to Minneapolis, he mailed to Miss Eayrs the signed agreement with Henry Holt to publish *Free Air.* Writing of Alfred Harcourt, he said:

> He, poor patient man, may be glad to know that I'm already making plans for considerable addition to *Free Air*—distinctly NOT padding, but a whole new section, carrying on the story at the end, with the life of Claire and Milt in Seattle. And that before the year is over, I'll probably have written a new novel—a hundred thousand words or more—and, one hopes, more basically important than *Free Air.*

How he could work on two novels, write a whole series of stories at the same time, and not only make his continuous excursions but also plan a long one is difficult to understand. They were thinking of a trip to the Orient with Gene McComas, and it was Mrs. Lewis who was reluctant, because of Wells's health, to pursue the plan.

> The immediate need is a new shelter for the first of May when our present lease is up. Hal's father has begun to slip away from life * and we are going up to see him the last of this week. Then we shall do a little exploring in the north of the state, where we shall be near Canada and Dakota and golden wheat fields and shining lakes.

For a time they thought that they would spend the summer in a town named Fergus Falls, and in the meantime, at the end of March, they planned to motor to New Orleans but then found that they could not get more than ten miles out of the city in any direction because of the Minnesota spring mud. On the day after this plan was abandoned, March 29, Lewis wrote Harcourt that he was working well on the expanded version of *Free Air.*

> And I hope, before the year is over—MAIN STREET! I'm quite flush now, financially, and we're going to spend the summer in a Minnesota town . . . especially and exclusively to finish up my Main Street dope. I'm thinking about the plan of the thing all the time.

This letter was followed by another that suggested that perhaps it would be wise to delay the book publication of *Free Air* until after the publication

* Dr. E. J. Lewis was not one "to slip away from life," his daughter-in-law to the contrary.

of *Main Street,* and in his reply of April 10, Alfred Harcourt agreed. He then went into the Harper tangle:

> I have inquired at Baker and Taylor's as to what sale the books are having. Their sales from the first of last September to the first of April are as follows: *The Innocents,* 4; *The Job,* 1; *Mr. Wrenn,* 1; *The Trail of the Hawk,* 2. It's a crime to let books get as dead as that, and then to think of getting anything like cost out of the plates and stock.

He urged Lewis to check his contract and then to try to buy back the plates at their value as old metal.

Harper asked $1,455 for the plates and sheets of the first two novels, and on the fourteenth of April, Lewis wrote Harcourt again to say, "Here's the dirty lying scut letter I am sending to poor Mr. Hoynes [of Harper] today." He protests that he cannot possibly pay that sum. ". . . when I do get ready to have another novel published, I wouldn't dare to ask the publisher to pay me back the total sum your figures amount to . . . I had a little talk with Holt about taking over my novels, when I was in New York, and though they seemed interested, they were not so much so that they would be likely to pay more than half the amount asked." If Harper cannot propose a lower figure, will they please give him a last call when the time comes to melt the plates? He pretends that at the moment he is interested only in writing short stories and plays. Then, in his letters to Harcourt, he asked if the title *Main Street* can be copyrighted—Harcourt said no—and he suggested changing the title of *The Trail of the Hawk* to either *Hawk* or *This Young Man* when it is reissued by Holt. Harcourt agreed. But in less than three weeks Harcourt himself resigned from Holt.

When their lease expired, the Lewises had found no house in Fergus Falls, and they spent the month of May in the Hotel Maryland, Minneapolis, waiting for June 1 and the beginning of a two-month lease on a comfortable old brick house at 315 Broad Street, Mankato.* For a week in mid-May, Lewis, seeking relief from the concentrated domesticity of hotel rooms, went off alone in his car to explore the prairies, and just after they moved into their Mankato house with Ma*ma* and a nurse and cook, he departed for New York. Alfred Harcourt had had proposals from other publishers; but he was debating the possibility of forming a house of his own, and in a letter he had consulted Lewis, who replied by telegram with the request that Harcourt meet him at Grand Central Station on the following Sunday morning.

> Hell, Alf [Harcourt remembered his saying when they met], I got your letter. I wrote you a letter, I wrote you a long night letter, and then I said to myself, "This is important." I drove a hundred and twenty-five miles to

* One may suppose that the final plans for *Main Street* took their shape here. Carol Kennicott was raised in Mankato, "not a prairie town, but in its garden-sheltered streets and aisles of elm . . . white and green New England reborn."

> Minneapolis, put my car in a garage, bought a railroad ticket and berth, and sent you a telegram to meet me here this morning. What I came on to say is, "Don't be such a damn fool as ever again to go to work for someone else. Start your own business." I'm going to write important books. You can publish these. I've got a little money saved up and you can have some of that. Now let's go out to your house and start making plans.

Among the many problems was the matter of Lewis's release from his newly signed Holt contract. Back in Mankato, he wrote to Roland Holt on June 16 to explain that his coming to Holt was almost entirely because of his personal association with Harcourt and that he would like to follow him. On the nineteenth, Holt replied, pleasantly agreeing to release him, and on the twenty-fifth, Lewis pleasantly thanked him. Thus he became a Harcourt, Brace, & Howe, Inc., author, whose first book for them would be *Main Street.* So they thought, briefly. But the success of the serialized *Free Air* caused them to reverse their plans.

He had that monocle, slaying Mankato, and now he was working on his signature. It became a sweeping contraction that reads, "Slewis." Shades of Harry! of H. Sinclaire Lewys! of Doodle! But Alfred Harcourt went along with the silliness and for a time addressed him as "Dear Slewis." And what he was writing to "Slewis" on June 27 was that a lot of people were talking about the *Post* serialization and that perhaps it should be published as a book before the interest in it died. Lewis, who had had doubts about the wisdom of publishing *Free Air* as a book and even graver doubts about publishing it before *Main Street,* was nevertheless, in the general excitement, game; and he enthusiastically wrote away at the sequel that would make *Free Air* a book-length work. But he held out the movie rights, which Famous Players had already offered to buy for three thousand dollars. He did not want an advance against royalties and he invested two of the three thousand dollars from Famous Players in Harcourt, Brace & Howe, and he was already making suggestions about the promotion of *Free Air.* The sequel, which would fill out the earlier part to "dignified" proportions, would be about 30,000 words long, and these he was writing in the back room of a photographer's "studio" that overlooked the railroad yards of Mankato.

Then, in September of 1919, when Lewis was in Philadelphia, Lorimer, putting aside the precedent that no serial in the *Post* could ever continue after a break, was offering him twenty-five hundred dollars for the sequel. The author accepted. Harcourt was momentarily disturbed but contented himself. He published the two serials as a book, *Free Air,* on October 23, 1919, almost before the sequel had finished its serial run. The documented details of the ten-year association, now beginning, of Sinclair Lewis and Harcourt, Brace & Company (as the firm was presently to become) are available in the book of letters called *From Main Street to Stockholm.*

Before the publication of *Free Air,* the Lewises had, of course, moved again. Two months of Mankato had sufficed; leaving Ma*ma* behind with Wells, to close the house and follow them, the "daventurers" went "daventuring." Harry had more than done his filial duties. In July he drove to Sauk Centre, brought his parents down to Mankato, housed them and then made a pilgrimage with them to Elysian, scene of the aged parent's early Algerian struggles. (How the graveyard there haunted him! More than twenty years later he went back, still searching for tombstone information about his father's fathers.) But enough of Minnesota! On July 31 they were off—down, down to Chicago, into Indiana, into Kentucky, into Tennessee, into Virginia, 1,600 miles to the scene of their honeymoon five years before.

At Rockbridge Alum Springs, a once fashionable but now decayed resort, they spent three days with James Branch Cabell, whom Lewis had known through correspondence since his years at Stokes and for whom he had an inordinate admiration, which was shared, in those years, by many. The last manuscript that he had accepted at Stokes was Cabell's *The Soul of Melicent,* and later, at Doran, he declined the work that was to be called *The Cream of the Jest.* In *Preface to the Past,* Cabell reconstructed Lewis's objections, which rested largely on his impression that the novel contained no attractive characters.

> For, as this hypercritical romanticist went on to explain—prior to subscribing himself "Sincerely yours, Sinclair Lewis,"—the general public simply cannot be induced to buy novels about unattractive and ignoble people, although the future author of *Main Street* and *Elmer Gantry* did go so far as to admit that disagreeable characters might be permissible "as villains in naïve literature which is still unashamed of melodrama."

But after several years, when the book was published, it received a good critical press.

> . . . I had heard again from that stripling Sinclair Lewis who had been the first of this book's many rejectors. The intervening three years had so debased his literary standards that he now quite approved of *The Cream of the Jest;* thus we met before long . . .

The occasion was the summer 1919 visit, when Lewis asked Cabell to read and criticize the considerable portion of *Main Street* that he had finished. Cabell obliged. He had read—and he must have been one of the very few—each of Lewis's preceding four novels and "already possessed inscribed and autographed copies of them"—or so he wrote in *As I Remember It.*

> Well, and the general conception of *Main Street,* which I had heard all about of course from its not unduly taciturn writer when I read the novel's uncompleted typescript at the Rockbridge Alum Springs, and prompted a few changes in it, during the summer of 1919, appeared to me a deal better

than was its final printed expression in 1920. I enjoyed, that is, parts of this book far more than I did a vast quantity of its other parts. I thought the novel too long, and the writing of it straggly.

These recollections were put down in 1955, after Lewis was dead, long after Lewis's person had ceased to give Cabell pleasure. But the 1919 visit was a success.

> . . . we got on together excellently. I found that, for my part, it was not possible to help liking and admiring this Sinclair Lewis, even after the droll and deferential boy whom I first knew had turned out to be a world-famous genius, owing deference to nobody and specializing in drolleries of a nature so caustic as to make his first letter to me of large monetary value.

Early in 1920 Lewis wrote Cabell from Washington to say:

> I have destroyed all but a few pages of the 30,000 words I have written of *Main Street,* in complete dissatisfaction. Have started it again, and for two months have been doing nothing but write it. I think it is much better. Yet it may be rotten. Certainly the former 30,000, which you saw, struck me as incomparably clumsy—and, at times, vulgar when I read it. I was off on the wrong feet. I think now, perhaps, it really will be a book.

From Virginia the Lewises drove to Pennsylvania where, in West Chester, they visited another novelist whom Lewis much admired, Joseph Hergesheimer, but this visit, although long planned, was less successful. When Mrs. Hegger and Wells arrived in Philadelphia, the four settled into the Mansion House at West Chester in the hope of finding a house to rent for the winter. Hergesheimer was patronizing (he asked Lewis to read a set of proofs and when suggestions were forthcoming, Hergesheimer cut them off; in criticism, he cared only for the word of Conrad and of Gosse!), and even before they moved into the house that they had rented, they decided that it was impossible. It cost over seven hundred dollars to break the lease, but they did so and tried New York. New York offered nothing that they felt was both adequate and financially possible, and they tried Washington. There they found "a compromise of a house" at 1814 16th Street, N.W.—pale-green and deep-purple satin upholstery, arty but practical, with a marble tub, a garage, and a cook—and they lived there from September 26 to June 1, 1920.

In less than a month after they had settled in, *Free Air* was published as a book. Harcourt, Brace ordered two prepublication printings which totaled 11,000 copies, and the prepublication sale was over 8,000. But after that initial sale, the book did not do much more.

Free Air is a loosely constructed novel strung along on the events of the Lewis's own automobile trip from Minnesota to Seattle, and the author seems more interested in recounting the relatively unfamiliar experience of driving through the West than in telling his story. The story concerns

Claire Boltwood and her father, wealthy persons of social prominence, from Brooklyn Heights, and Milton Daggett, a garage mechanic from Schoenstrom, Minnesota. The Boltwoods, visiting in Minneapolis, decide to drive west instead of returning home, and on the first day out, when their Gomez-Dep bogs down in mud somewhere between Schoenstrom and Gopher Prairie, they are rescued by Milt, who, when he has seen Claire in Schoenstrom, turns the garage over to his helper and impulsively sets out after them in his Teal. Day after day he rescues them from one near disaster or another, foils the plots of a variety of villains, and is of course falling in love with Claire. His sense of social inferiority is heightened when he learns about Jeff Saxton, her most persistent suitor, who also follows her west, but in the free air of the world of adventure, social differences, like urban conventions in general, are overcome, and Milton's resolve to study French and engineering at the University of Washington assists in the process. When at last Claire says to him, "Make me become real! A real woman!" the journey is over.

The theme is the familiar one of the outsider who gets "in" through the door of adventure, of the free life, but the novelist is even less intent here on facing the problems of class difference than he was in his earlier novels. A secondary and no less familiar theme is the conflict between East and West, but the chief conflict seems to be between the ambiguous attitudes in the author's own mind, between his love of the West's vigorous freedom and his loathing of its drab monotony, between his scorn for the East's effete snobberies and his country hankering for what appeared to him to be its glamorous sophistication. (It might be observed that the distinctions Lewis drew between the cultivated taste of the East and the downright taste of the West were lost on his British readers; when *Free Air* was published in England, Filson Young observed that he and his countrymen could see no real difference between "the humble swain" and "the great lady.") More interesting than either of these themes is the sociology of travel—hotel service, garage service, how to sleep out of doors, mountain scenery. Many reviewers ignored the book, many attacked it as a lapse into triviality from serious realistic work, some praised it mildly as hammock reading. The New York *Times* was rather exceptional in its praise. Not only did it find it as "American as corn on the cob," it also saw it as serious social criticism.

> Mr. Lewis is capable of hitting hard at American faults. He deals the bad food and bad hotels which have earned the curses of travelers these many years all over this broad land some thwacks that should leave a mark. He does not spare comment on the surface bad manners of our young America, but he shows the kindliness and good humor that lie beneath.

Lewis, who thought highly enough of the novel to suggest that Harcourt, Brace & Company submit it to the Pulitzer Prize Committee as fulfilling their lightly regarded terms that the prize novel present "the wholesome atmosphere of American life," nevertheless was worried about its possible influence on the reception of *Main Street,* which was to be published in exactly one year after the publication of *Free Air.* On the one hand, he suggested that the book be advertised with a poster at every gasoline pump in the nation that boasted the then familiar "Free Air" sign; on the other hand, he wrote to Alfred Harcourt that he thought that "one thing we might do is to send a letter to about a dozen reviewers (Francis Hackett, Mencken, Burton Rascoe, etc.) telling them frankly that we know *Free Air* and *Innocents* were light, but in *Main Street* this brilliant young author . . ." and so forth.

It was a winter and spring of exhausting effort. Lewis rented an "office" at 1127 Seventeenth Street, only a few blocks from their rather small house, and worked furiously and long, even as the pace of the family social life accelerated. He was invited to join the Cosmos Club, and there he met many new people—public figures, politicians. He had developed the habit of picking up strangers, whom he would bring home with an enthusiastic introduction—and then let his wife dispose of them. There were new friends —Clarence Darrow, Hendrik Willem Van Loon, the Dean Achesons, the Paul Hannas, Hazel Hankin (a pretty National Woman's Party organizer), the Richard Boeckels, Elinor Wylie. "He must have been one of Elinor's first contacts with literary people," wrote her sister, Nancy Hoyt.

So long before as 1912 Elinor Wylie had published anonymously a small volume of verse in England, and now Lewis was not only encouraging her in the composition of the poems that were to appear as *Nets To Catch the Wind* but also, it has long been rumored, took the volume to New York and pressed for its publication with Alfred Harcourt. This beautiful, self-centered poetess had broken up her husband's marriage, and Washington society spurned her; but she was the daughter of a former Postmaster General, and Grace Lewis was titillated by the connection. The Lewises gave a box party at the old Belasco Theater, and among the guests were Elinor and Horace Wylie, making their first public appearance together. "Isn't it odd," Elinor Wylie asked, "that everyone seems to be looking at us?" To which Horace Wylie replied, "They *are* looking at Elinor and me. They haven't seen us for a long time!" And, it is said, the Wylies did not appear in public again. Presently Elinor left Horace Wylie for Sinclair Lewis's old friend William Rose Benét. Before that liaison developed, Lewis was urging her not to confine herself to verse, but to write prose, too—"a more lucrative employment"—and his enthusiasm for *Jennifer Lorn,* her first fiction, may have stemmed in part from his share in its inception.

When, in January of 1920, the Society for the Suppression of Vice served a summons on Robert M. McBride, the publisher of Cabell's *Jurgen,* and seized all plates, sheets, and copies of the novel, Lewis, at Cabell's request, took time from his work to write a long letter of protest to Guy Holt, an editor in that firm. It was, he argued, a work of high art, a work of noble idealism, and the seizure was incredible. A month later, when the "Emergency Committee Organized to Protest Against the Suppression" was formed and solicited letters from many writers, Lewis not only wrote another but obtained from members of the Washington Press Club signatures to his protest of the suppression of this work "of sheer magic and beauty." His January letter had ended as follows:

> I have read, if I remember, that Hugh Walpole has praised *Jurgen*. That should be impressive testimony to its art and importance. Mr. Walpole is undoubtedly the most brilliant of the younger British literary men, coming now to rank with Bennett, Wells, and Galsworthy; and his praise of the book—precisely because it *does* come from a foreigner and not from an American, who might be prejudiced—indicates the book's extraordinary merit.

This letter led Guy Holt to tell Lewis that Walpole would be in Washington in April, and Lewis promptly addressed himself to him:

> I have known you a good many years—at a distance. As editor and nimble writer for Doran, before I fell by the way and took to novels myself, I wrote that first pamphlet about you which Doran got out some five or six years ago. It was, as I remember it, a fairly bad piece of work, but it represented a real admiration.
>
> I shall be more than glad to do anything I can to divert you while in Washington. If you haven't other plans, I'd be awfully glad to put you up, without advance warning. . . .

Walpole, who was in the United States on a lecture tour, was happy to accept this invitation to be the Lewises' house guest and to meet his American admirer under those circumstances. And in his notebook observed that Lewis was "typical modern American, ugly, harsh-voiced, pushing, but kindly and bursting with enthusiasm." They became friends, of sorts, and in the next year their names were coupled, together with those of three others, in Cabell's intricate and affected system of dedications in *Figures of Earth*. Three years after that, Lewis's name would be joined with four others in the dedication of Walpole's autobiographical work, *The Crystal Box*. Like Lewis, Walpole was a man of quick and high enthusiasms.

Lewis's major enthusiasm and his chief energies were dedicated now to ten- and twelve-hour days of writing *Main Street* in his bleak rented room. And not only *Main Street*. In March of 1920, Mrs. Lewis retired to Pompton Lakes, New Jersey, for a conditioning course, but her husband permitted himself no such respite. The legend is that now he had completely turned his back on hack writing and commercial success, as on society. William Lyon Phelps was only one of many people who disseminated the legend. In 1927, Phelps wrote:

> He gave all this up, withdrew from the world for a year, with the determination to risk everything on one important book. . . . He remained in seclusion a year, and wrote *Main Street.*

The extreme form of the legend has it that he lived in Sauk Centre, supported by his father. A milder version has him borrowing five hundred dollars from the old doctor in order to live. His own version was that he borrowed this sum after the novel was completed.

He was clearly not in retirement, he had not stopped hack writing, and even in the face of the word of his wife (recorded much later, to be sure), one must doubt the loan. It would not have carried them through a month, in the first place. In the second, he could have taken his two thousand dollars out of Harcourt, Brace at any time, or he could have asked for an advance against royalties, as, indeed, he did—$500—just as he was finishing his final draft. The royalties on 9,000 copies of *Free Air* would have been about $2,000. In October the *Post* paid him $900 for a new story called "Bronze Bars"; in late October, $2,500 for the three "Autobumming" articles; in November, $900 for "Habeas Corpus." Again, in November *The American Magazine* paid him $500 for the article called "How I Wrote a Novel." In February, 1920, he wrote an article for the *Post* called "It's So Provincial," but destroyed it after six rejections. In March he sold "The Way I See It" to the *Post* for $900. Immediately after that, he wrote half of a projected serial called "A Woman Who Didn't Know Love"—"planned as 30,000 wd. serial, ½ done, dissatisfied, talked over w[ith] Bessie Beattie, destroyed." In these six months, in short, his accounts show only one month, January, in which he was not writing something besides *Main Street,* and his income during this period was about $8,000. Nor had he come penniless to Washington.

This is not at all to suggest that he was not working fiercely at *Main Street,* but rather to qualify a little the picture of heroic sacrifice for high art. He had finished about 100,000 words of it before Christmas of 1919, and his first draft, well over 200,000, words was finished on February 27, 1920. The spring and early part of the summer were devoted to revision and to cutting. Brigadier General John N. Greely, who had known him at Yale, caught a glimpse of him in the street during that summer.

> I had been envying him his literary success. He said, "It never made me rich and now I can't even sell a short story. I'm obsessed with a novel. I've sent my wife and son out of town. I get my own breakfast and lock myself in a stifling room on the top floor of a rooming house till nine at night to finish the damn thing. Then I probably can't sell it, and if I do it probably won't make a cent."

They had given up their house on June 1, and Mrs. Lewis and Wells and Mrs. Hegger had gone as paying guests to "a run-down plantation in Bluemont, Virginia." Her recollection is that Lewis lived at the Cosmos Club, but he used his "office" address in correspondence. Whether or not he was making his own breakfast, he was working hard—"eight hours a day, seven days in most weeks, though a normal number of daily hours of creative writing is supposed to be about four. . . . I never worked so hard, and never shall work so hard, again."

There was, of course, no question of "sale." Harcourt's promotion plans were made, publication had been announced in the first week of May, a dummy had been set up on the basis of the first ninety pages, the jacket designed. And on July 17, 1920, Lewis delivered the finished manuscript to Alfred Harcourt in the hope that it would sell 10,000 copies. Harcourt was enthusiastic. He thought that it was great, he thought that it would probably sell as many as 20,000 copies before it stopped, and his sales manager believed that they could probably expect a sale of 25,000.* In the first six months of 1921 it sold 180,000 copies. It was finally to go into millions. Did Lewis now abandon the plot file? Just before the publication of *Main Street, The Saturday Evening Post* accepted a new short story, "The Good Sport." Price: $1,000.

* That these figures vary from account to account does not matter; whatever they may have been, the difference between expectation and fact provided one of the most surprising dramas in modern publishing history.

This portrait of Lewis was taken in 1925 by Man Ray, famous avant-garde *photographer and artist.*

Sauk Centre, 1868. "Thirty years before there was nothing here at all . . ."

Harry Sinclair Lewis, 1889. "I eat grass like cows."

Emma Kermott Lewis, 1848–1891. The mother whose features he clearly inherited.

Dr. E. J. Lewis, 1848–1926. "Harry, why can't you do like any other boy ought to do?"

Isabel Warner Lewis. The foster mother. "Will you kindly remember that I am not a child."

The Lewis house, circa 1897. Claude, Dr. Lewis, Fred, Isabel Lewis, Harry.

German House Diners, Oberlin Academy, 1902. Harry Lewis upper left.

"He had . . . one friend – Irving Fisher, and Irving Fisher only."

Sinclair Lewis. "Starched notions of elegance."

Carmel, 1909. Lewis with George Sterling and local belle.

Carmel, 1909 A market fair. Lewis and Opal Heron, the 16-year-old wife of local poet Herbert Heron.

Carmel, 1909. Standing: Sinclair Lewis, Alice MacGowan, William Rose Benét. Seated: Helen Cooke, Grace MacGowan Cooke, Miss Scannell, Kitty Cooke, Arthur Honeywood Vachel.

Grace Hegger Lewis and "small Wells."

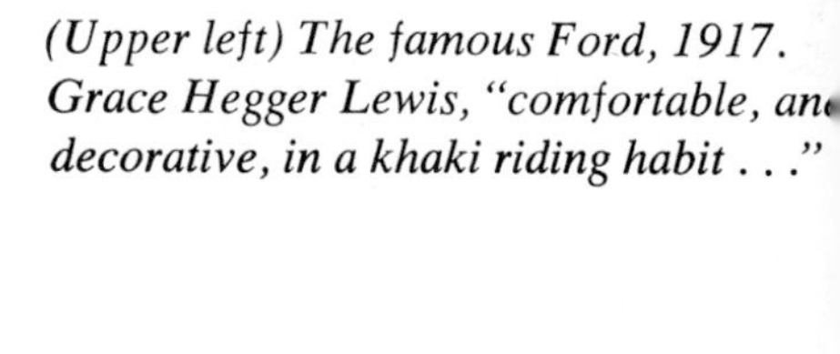

(Upper left) The famous Ford, 1917. Grace Hegger Lewis, "comfortable, and decorative, in a khaki riding habit . . ."

WIDE WORLD PHOTOS

Lewis at Le Val-Changis, *1923. "And for the country, plus fours."*

Grace Hegger Lewis and Telesforo Casanova at Atlantic City, 1927.

"Dorothy Thompson and Sinclair Lewis have the honor to announce their marriage which took place in London, on Monday, May 14th, 1928." (right)

". . . in his hour of awful nakedness in Stockholm." 1930 (below)

CARL VAN VECHTEN

"A kind of distinction." 1938

TRUDE FLEISCHMANN

". . . a small-town editor by nature . . ." 1932

Sinclair and Michael Lewis.
"There was a question of
paternal tolerance."

Sinclair Lewis
by Sinclair Lewis, mid-1930s.

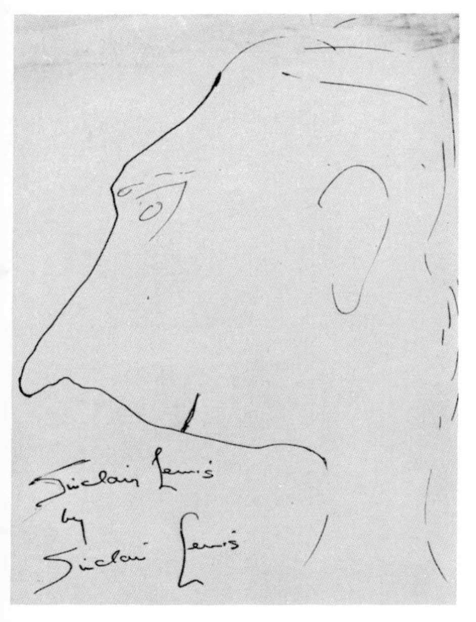

FIRESTONE LIBRARY, PRINCETON UNIVERSITY

Sinclair Lewis and Dorothy Thompson
". . . quiet country satisfactions . . ."

WIDE WORLD PHOTOS

*". . . Darling – come soon
I count the days." 1938*

Lewis in It Can't Happen Here, *Cohasset, 1938.*

(Right) Marcella Powers, Provincetown, 1939.

Lewis and Marcella Powers, Mayflower Hotel, 1939. "Just going South."

Lewis and Marcella Powers in Shadow and Substance, *New Orleans, 1940.*

Sinclair Lewis, 1950.
Villa LaCosta, Florence.

NEW YORK TIMES

Mrs. Katherine Powers, 1948. Italy.
"Una vecchia governante."

(Right) Lewis, ". . . Funny hat and all," with Arthur J. Sloane, managing editor of the New Haven Journal and Courier, *at Yale Reunion, Class of 1907.*

(Left) Michael Lewis. "Dear Hal: This is your son. A handsome devil, as, alas, he himself thinks! Wish you'd occasionally kick him affectionately in the pants. If you don't hurry, you won't dare – Dorothy – Doesn't he look like Wells? You don't guess Gracie had him, do you?"

Sauk Centre, 1948. "He never left home . . ."

Sinclair Lewis and Ernest Hemingway, Key West, 1940. "He ate some birds."

Lt. Wells Lewis, 1917–1944.

Marcella Powers, 1942. ". . . the one distinguished event in my life . . ."

Manhattan Chess Club, 1944.
A lesson from an expert, Frank Marshall, Jr.

Hollywood, 1943. Inscription reads: "To Marcella: with increasing wonder at how you can get along with a guy like Red – Fondest, Dore Schary."

". . . it must be great to be really one of that real Parisian bunch."

FOUR

Success

I

HE HAD NOW, when he wished to exercise them, charm and graciousness. "A Mercutio from the prairies," Clifton Fadiman would one day call him. His talk could be entrancingly and, finally, exhaustingly lively, and his impersonations entertaining and, presently, tiresome. His talk; for he had no conversation: his mind could not stay with an idea any longer than his body could stay in a chair, but leaped from point to point, from sense to extravagance, from the mundane to the earnest to the arch to the whimsical to the fantastic and, at last, to the boring, the irrelevant, the merely demanding. He seldom sat, but often slouched, long thin shanks folding and unfolding, hands always plucking at face—nose, ears, cheek, chin—much jumping up, prancing, slouching again, smoking, smoking. When he was at home alone or with his family, he slouched around in carpet slippers and an old bathrobe or a tattered cardigan; but he also had developed starched notions of elegance that made him conspicuously well dressed when he dressed. He was briefly tolerant of many people and sharply impatient, trigger-tempered, with a few—those closest to him. His wife annoyed him almost all the time; but at this point, although frequent short periods of freedom were essential, he could not yet conceive of living for long without her. His son did not interest him, and when the child required attention that the father thought might better be paid to himself, the little boy was a simple nuisance at least, or an object that aroused a petulant jealousy. He drank, but not yet in excess, or at least not often. He could be as delightful as he was distraught. Except for a few weeks of mild and unnecessary economic anxiety just before and after the publication of *Main Street,* he would never be poor again. He was well-launched at last, the great lover of Thoreau, upon his life of noisy desperation.

The remainder of the summer of 1920, after he had summoned his family back, was spent at an expensive resort on Lake Kennebago, in Maine—hardly a Thoreauvian interlude. He had, before making this pastoral retreat, stayed at Harcourt's house in Mount Vernon to go over his typescript for the last time. It was 200,000 words long, and Harcourt argued that it should be cut; one extended episode of about 20,000 words near the end could surely go. Lewis insisted that it remain. Harcourt bargained with him: would he agree that if its deletion involved him in no more than ten other changes, it was hardly integral? Lewis agreed, and next day he reported that it had required only seven, all but two of them after the episode; and the 20,000 words went into the wastebasket.

Almost at once at Kennebago galley proof began to arrive, and although his wife reports that he was by now bored with *Main Street* and was concerned instead with a new book, he still was sufficiently concerned with *Main Street* to worry Harcourt with letters about its possible reception, urging again, for example, a personal letter to critics that pointed out the difference between *Main Street* and his earlier, lighter novels. Nevertheless, ideas were forming for *Babbitt,* "the story of the Tired Business Man, of the man in the Pullman smoker, of our American ruler, of the man playing golf at the country club at Minneapolis, Omaha, Atlanta, Rochester," a man to be called G. T. Pumphrey, of Monarch City; the book to be called *Pumphrey.*

And toward the end of *Main Street,* Gopher Prairie is indeed reaching toward Zenith. The town launches a "campaign of boosting" under the auspices of the Commercial Club, and a newcomer, "Honest Jim" Blauser, a "Hustler," is its director. His speech at the Commercial Club Banquet not only anticipates Babbitt's speech to the Zenith Real Estate Board, but also initiates Lewis's persistent use of the braying public voice to characterize the social *milieu.* "I want to tell you good people, and it's just as sure as God made little apples, the thing that distinguishes our American commonwealth from the pikers and tinhorns in other countries is our Punch." In the wings, George F. Babbitt is perspiring with anticipation, and Lewis is planning his entrance. He gives himself two years before he will let Babbitt make it.

On September 10, the Lewises returned to New York and settled briefly at the Manhattan Square Hotel. The winter they would spend again in Washington, and Mrs. Lewis went down to find a better house than they had had before. She found one at 1639 Nineteenth Street, N.W., that charmed her, larger and more stylishly furnished, and on October 17 they took possession. In less than a week, on October 23, *Main Street* was published, a kind of explosion that led Robert Littell to remark, two years later, that "if *Main Street* lives, it will probably be not as a novel but as an incident in American life."

It was the most sensational event in twentieth-century American publishing history. Two years after it appeared, John Farrar, who did not like the novel, described the event in *The Bookman:*

> His friends all bought the book, then the cognoscenti, then the literati, then the literate, a paltry thousand or so. Then the sleeping beast turned over,

rubbed its eyes, and woke up. Fifty thousand. It howled in an ecstasy of self-torture. One hundred thousand. His publishers estimate that it has beyond doubt reached two million readers. And people are still buying it and reading it for the first time. . . .

But it was a matter of only a few days before that beast woke up. Harold Loeb, in his little bookshop in Washington, disposed immediately of his prepublication order of ten copies, and with the first reviews, the next fifty copies went and he found himself waiting for a new printing. So it was, all over the East, and almost at once in the West and the Middle West. The printers could not keep up with the orders, and the publishers had for a while to ration out copies to booksellers. William Allen White, wishing to distribute autographed copies of the novel among his friends as a Christmas present, sent Lewis a blank check to be turned over to Harcourt, Brace & Company. Vachel Lindsay organized a campaign to make every resident of Springfield, Illinois, read the book, and he urged Lewis to urge Harcourt to flood the Middle West with review copies. "And why all this, do you say? Well, I am fond of Architecture, and want them to tear down those flats across the street, and build a Taj Mahal." Simply by being coupled with *Main Street* in public comment, other novels were swept into the brackets of the best sellers, notably Floyd Dell's *Moon-Calf*, Zona Gale's *Miss Lulu Bett* and, particularly, Dorothy Canfield Fisher's *The Brimming Cup*.

Hamlin Garland, reading it in January of 1921, found it false and unconvincing, and, in indignation, went to Henry Seidel Canby, who, he thought, had "an editor's power to accept or reject"—Canby had just come from New Haven to edit the *Literary Review* of the New York *Evening Post*—and urged him to take a public position against writers like Lewis, "with their belittling of the descendants of the old frontier." No reader was indifferent to *Main Street:* if it was not the most important revelation of American life ever made, it was the most infamous libel upon it. Whether or not the individual reader saw himself in the book, America in general found that a new image of itself had suddenly been thrust upon it, an image that even so reluctant a reader as Hamlin Garland was almost immediately to accept. Garland was on the committee that was reading for the Pulitzer prizes, and although in March of 1921 he lamented that "All the novels I have read recently are lacking in style, in workmanship. I cannot vote a prize to any of them," he went along with the other members of his committee and voted the prize to *Main Street*. Two years later, in 1923, when he returned to the Middle West on a lecture tour, the dreary countryside and the drab lives lived upon it depressed him more than ever they had Sinclair Lewis, and he wrote in his journal that his "resentment of Lewis' *Main Street* is somewhat softened."

Other readers did see themselves in it—scores of fancied "Carol Kennicotts," many of whom wrote gushingly to the author to tell him that he had discovered their plight, that they were grateful that he "understood," and to ask him desolately, "What now for me?" Of these a poor creature in San Antonio was typical:

> I have been an actress, a Little Theatrite, so to speak. Three years ago I left dear New York, and Washington Square to marry a salesman, and come here to Main Street. . . . Will you please tell me what people are doing and saying in New York? Every day I repeat: 'I must go on.' I have sat on the slippery edge of a bath tub and privately wept, many and many a time. Dear tender treasured longings which cause us who hunger to weep! *

"Main Street, A Fox Trot Song," with lyrics by Vincent M. Sherwood carrying "old home town" sentiments very far from those of the novel from which the song took its title, appeared almost at once, and the name of the old home town itself, Sauk Centre, became archetypal in jokes about small towns told across the country. The residents of Sauk Centre did not weep with the girl in San Antonio, but raged in indignation. For five months, the *Herald* declined to say anything at all. In nearby Alexandria, the book was banned from the public library, and Henry Johnson remembered that, at a Minneapolis reunion of former Sauk Centre residents in 1921, resentment against Lewis was still so high that one "sensitive housewife remarked that he would probably be lynched" if he returned to visit Sauk Centre. But in less than two years he was welcomed back as the town's chief ornament. Very soon, on Main Street, the Gopher Prairie Inn opened its doors, and presently the Main Street Theater would boast a bronze plaque, later stolen, that carried a rather silly message written by Sinclair Lewis: "Here are the portals of imagination. Recover hope all ye who enter here."

The chief ornament of Sauk Centre, he also became through this single book the spokesman for a literary generation, and the year 1920 is in this sense historic. American culture seems always to have had a literary spokesman, a single writer who presented American culture and American attitudes toward its culture, to the world. The last of these had been William Dean Howells, who died in the spring of 1920, ancient and honored. The summer gaped; autumn brought *Main Street*. And no writer since Howells has more nearly approximated his position than Lewis, albeit in much narrower scope, as a national disgrace to chauvinists and an aesthetic delinquent to critics, and hardly for a decade in span. With *Main Street,* he

* Carol Kennicott is not yet dead. Most recently: "I was born in 1921, the year after *Main Street* was published. . . . If it hadn't been for *Main Street,* my mother might never have decided to produce a child. However, that novel made a profound impression on her. She was convinced that it was she who had inspired Mr. Lewis to create Carol Kennicott. True, she had never met him, but, '*He* certainly knows *all* about *me*. He may very well have observed me from afar.' " Et cetera. (Merle Miller, *A Gay and Melancholy Sound*. 1961)

ceased to be only a storyteller and became what Constance Rourke early discovered him to be, "a fabulist," and with that he became different from his contemporaries. He was different, too, as she observed, in this: "With one exception none of those definitive novelists have appeared who make an aspect of contemporary life their own and leave it with the color of their imagination upon it forever afterward. The exception of course is Sinclair Lewis. . . ." He maintained his singularity and his position through five books, and when the Nobel award came to him in 1930, international literary opinion sealed, as it were, the decade of his prominence, just as *Main Street* had opened it. Since 1930, the end of that decade, with the increasing conformity at the surface of American life and the increasing fragmentation at its base, there have been no contenders at all.

Have we enjoyed a cultural irony more absurd than this, that it should have been Sinclair Lewis who emerged to fulfill Walt Whitman's cry for a "literatus"? Whitman had called for a popular prophet, a maker of democratic images that would elevate and amplify the democratic life which was falling short of its promise. Sinclair Lewis emerged, no mystagogical orator of the sort that Whitman had in mind and he himself was, but an image maker certainly, stridently drawing for Americans the picture of their crass, petty, hypocritical, and barren lives. The phenomenal success of *Main Street* demonstrated that American democratic culture had received, at precisely the right point, what American democratic culture above all wanted.

The difference between *Friendship Village,* published in 1908, and *Miss Lulu Bett,* in 1920, represents not only a change in the attitude of an authoress but, somewhat more importantly, a change in the social structure of American life. By 1920, the village as an important unit in capitalist economy had ceased to exist, had become backwash, and, with that life gone from it, its social and moral attitudes had become fixed in the rigidities of its past. The war was necessary to the discovery of what had happened. Thousands of intelligent young people had for two decades been fleeing to the cities; those who could not, the many who were left behind, were frustrated and corrupted in their discontent. For an enormous audience, *Main Street* defined, in the most relentless detail, a situation that it had already experienced or from which it was still suffering. But if there had been only this concurrence, *Main Street* would hardly have been occasion for controversy.

Attitudes die lingering deaths, and the small town, in spite of the change in sociological status that had overcome it, was still conventionally viewed —as by Sinclair Lewis himself in other moods—as the best place after all, the real America, America at the roots, America at its kindest, its friendliest, its human best. Conventional literature for generations had maintained this view, and in 1920 it still did. The clash of this view with the view of the "young realists" was noisy enough to elicit from the stately *Times* an editorial called "Sin and the Small Town," which, citing Booth Tarkington and Meredith Nicholson, suggested that the younger writers "have brought out some unconsidered facts which ought to impose a judicious silence on the writers who argue that God made Hickville Centre and the devil made New York." If the "Friendship Village" view was pervasive in American fiction, its stronghold was in the so-called Hoosier School, and particularly in the writing of Booth Tarkington and Meredith Nicholson. It was Nicholson who, in 1912, made the famous and fatuous remark that

> It's all pretty comfortable and cheerful and busy in Indiana, with lots of old-fashioned human kindness flowing round: and it's getting better all the time. And I guess it's always got to be that way, out here in God's country.

Eight years later, Nicholson was to praise *Main Street* as a novel but protest against any claims for universality. Perhaps Minnesota towns were like that; towns in Indiana were emphatically not. Given his qualification, he found it hard to hold his note in the chorus of praise:

> The trouble with Mr. Lewis's Carol Kennicott was that she really had nothing to offer Gopher Prairie that sensible self-respecting people anywhere would have welcomed. A superficial creature, she was without true vision in any direction. Plenty of men and women vastly her superior in cultivation and blessed with a far finer sensitiveness to the things of the spirit have in countless cases faced rude conditions, squalor even, cheerfully and hopefully, and in time they have succeeded in doing something to make the world a better place to live in. This is not to say that Carol is not true to type; there is the type, but I am not persuaded that its existence proves anything except that there are always fools and foolish people in the world.

Although Sinclair Lewis in 1920 would hardly have accepted this view of Carol, he would very nearly have accepted it later, and we would all accept it today. But in 1920 hundreds of women saw themselves in Carol, and hundreds of small towns saw themselves in Gopher Prairie, and for that reason could, with equal ease, praise or blame the book, and in either case buy it. In 1900 Woodrow Wilson had made the pronouncement that "The history of a nation is only the history of its villages written large." The success of *Main Street* suggests that twenty years later the nation still believed Wilson's utterance was axiomatic.

So did Sinclair Lewis. The book begins, "This is America. . . . Main Street is the continuation of Main Streets everywhere. . . . Main Street is the climax of civilization." Sauk Centre thought differently. When, on March 31, 1921, the *Herald* first noticed the existence of the novel, the editor wrote, "A perusal of the book makes it possible for one to picture in his mind's eye local characters having been injected bodily into the story." A month later Lewis himself seemed to have corroborated the editorial suspicion.

SINCLAIR LEWIS GETS INSPIRATION HERE

Author Says He Knew Many of His Characters of "Main Street" In the Flesh

Sinclair Lewis [says] Sauk Centre to a large extent played a part in his inspiration for *Main Street* according to a statement given out by the author before a club in Detroit, Mich. recently.

Lewis, never a man to stay on a single spot, found it worth his trouble to issue a denial from Cornwall in two letters to the editor, one personal and friendly, the other for publication and rather austere; both appeared in the *Herald* for August 4, 1921, and the second reads:

> It has come to my attention that a certain number of people in Sauk Centre believe that my novel *Main Street* portrays real people and real scenes in Sauk Centre, and that there has been an attempt to identify my fictional characters and scenes with real ones. May I say that this is totally erroneous? Practically all of the characters and scenes in *Main Street* are either composites, combinations of the things and persons I have noted in the scores of American towns I have seen in all parts of the country, or else they are totally imaginary.
>
> In the whole book there is only one character even suggested by a person whom I met in Sauk Centre, and that is one of the younger men in the book. Even in his case, the character was merely suggested by an actual person, and as the story worked out, the character departs sharply and completely from the actual young man—who, by the way, left Sauk Centre years ago.

It is somehow comforting to have this single acknowledgment, fifteen years later, of the existence of that figure of pathos, Charles T. Dorion, who was in fact the genesis of *Main Street,* although one suspects that by now Lewis, like the townspeople, had forgotten his name. Much else of Lewis's experience in Sauk Centre is poured into his novel: his mother's club, the Gradatim, become now the Thanatopsis, and its efforts at uplift; the famous rest room and the anti-fly campaign; his father's country practice and the little professional rivalries; the Bryant library; the amateur theatricals and the traveling performers, the summer cottages and the church affairs—it is a whole scrapbook of his youth. Much, also, both of his experience and of small-town life in general, is necessarily omitted. The most curious omission has not been observed: in Gopher Prairie there is apparently no childhood at all, no boyhood or youth except for a single, revolting boor.

More important than anything else that Lewis's letters to the Sauk Centre *Herald* suggest is the reminder that many small towns had thought themselves the model of Gopher Prairie, that small towns throughout the nation were prepared to seize the mirror that *Main Street* seemed to be and gaze into it with lacerated attention. The book seemed, above all, to be *American,* and that, at a time when most American fiction was imitative of the already faint provincial fiction of Great Britain, was another element in its great success. Many of its readers had never been exposed to a novel that was so uncompromisingly American both in its seeming truth to the native scene and in the language that communicated it. In spite of novelists like London, Norris, Dreiser, Cather and Anderson, American fiction until the war still labored under the shadow of England, and publishers in New York still treated Georgians like Galsworthy, Bennett and Walpole—not to mention such lesser spirits as Onions, Beresford, Cannon and Frankau—as superior to even our most impressive American talent in fiction. If Mencken, through an article in *Smart Set,* established the critical quarrel between American and British fiction that was to run through the 1920s, it was Sinclair Lewis who, during the same period, was to demonstrate most forcibly the position of the positive. Ironically enough, he himself had endless esteem for just these British writers and almost none at all for those few who were really making modern British literature—Joyce, Virginia Woolf, D. H. Lawrence, E. M. Forster. Ironically again, it was the native quality of *Main Street* that appealed to these British writers quite as much—more probably more, since they had no stake in the matter—as to writers in the United States.

Lewis was inundated with letters of praise from his fellows. Not only because of the efforts of Alfred Harcourt, but often independently and always out of genuine enthusiasm, English letters came from, among others, Compton MacKenzie, Hugh Walpole, May Sinclair, J. D. Beresford, W. L. George, John Drinkwater, H. G. Wells, Rebecca West, H. Granville Barker, Wilfred Meynell, John Galsworthy. The Galsworthy letter, written in Denver, was the great surprise and the great coup—". . . remarkable book indeed . . . it seems to me that so wholesome and faithful a satiric attitude of mind has been rather conspicuously absent from American thought and literature. I *think* your book may well start a national mood toward Main Streets and other *odd places* of national life . . . altogether a brilliant piece of work and characterization. . . ." American congratulations came from every quarter: Rupert Hughes, Zona Gale, Hendrik Van Loon, Claude Washburn, Mary Austin, Fannie Hurst, even Hamlin Garland, Waldo Frank, Octavus Roy Cohen, Vachel Lindsay (who had always been charmed by the mention of his name in *Free Air*).

A number of letters have special interest. One of nonliterary source, for example, came from a nearly legendary figure in Pinehurst, North Carolina:

Dear Sir I want to thank you very much for using my name in your wonderful story Main Street—every one here who has read the book say it is wonderful. Just now there is none on sale at news stand so I am loaning mine to friends. Again thank you I am very truly yours

Annie Oakley

One might put this beside the letter, which plays an old game, from Edna Ferber:

> Well Guss I see by the papers how you done a swell piece and I read it and Gus they got right it is swell and I am surprised how somebody as dumb as you can write a swell piece like that well I do not do so good lately I do not know why I guess I run around too much. How is little Olga I guess she must be a big girl now. Well if you come this way drop in and see me I am the same old Tilly and remain,
>
> Rspctfly,
> *Tilly*

A more solemn letter from another young writer, also enjoying his first great success in 1920, is as follows:

> I want to tell you that *Main Street* has displaced *Theron Ware* in my favor as the best American novel. The amount of sheer data in it is amazing! As a writer and a Minnesotan let me swell the chorus—after a third reading.
>
> With the utmost admiration
> *F. Scott Fitzgerald*

It is surprising to discover that Fitzgerald, whose own work was so different from that of both Sinclair Lewis and Harold Frederic, should have held such regard for *The Damnation of Theron Ware,* and interesting that he should have mentioned it, because, in its treatment of village life, it is one of the relatively few novels that we can place in the background of *Main Street,* and, later and for a different reason, in the background of *Elmer Gantry.* It is, of course, a novel that Carol Kennicott knows and mentions in *Main Street.* The reference to their common state almost forces the contrast upon us—Fitzgerald moving with such apparent ease into the life of Princeton, enjoying so immediately his fantastic success, blithe heir to all that glamour that Lewis was never to know, let alone embody, moving so easily into "that real Parisian bunch" that always shut Lewis out, writing two great books of subtle charm and beauty and pathos, and one of them a perfect work of art and socially important as well—how different! Yet Lewis troubled Fitzgerald. In 1925 he wrote John Peale Bishop to ask, "Is Lewis' book [*Arrowsmith*] any good. I imagine that mine [*Gatsby*] is infinitely better . . ." And there is an ironical similarity in the biographical line: the waste of life in alchohol, the disintegration of marriage, the crack-up, the pretty young mistress to be educated, the final isolation and despair. "We do not have great writers," said Hemingway. "Something happens to our good writers at a certain age. . . . You see we make our writers into something very strange. . . . We destroy them in many ways."

> "Tell me first what are the things, the actual, concrete things that harm a writer?" . . .
>
> "Politics, women, drink, money, ambition. And the lack of politics, women, drink, money and ambition," I said profoundly. . . .
>
> "But drink. I do not understand about that. That has always seemed silly to me. I understand it as a weakness."
>
> "It is a way of ending a day. . . ."

But Lewis now, like Fitzgerald, was living in the very blaze of noon, as every letter served to remind him. There were letters, of course, from the faithful professors, Tinker and Phelps. Phelps, whose salutation read "Dear Sin," wrote, "I call you Sin because you are as original as sin," and assured him that *Main Street* was "a novel of high magnitude." Writing from *The Nation,* Carl Van Doren told him that "at Columbia University everybody seems to be reading the book, and one of my colleagues there recently argued with a whole gang of men at luncheon that your book is the most truthful novel ever written." Lewis's own colleagues were not so unstinting in their generosity.

There was the curious business with Floyd Dell. Lewis praised Dell for *Moon-Calf,* which had preceded *Main Street* by several months, and sent Dell a kind of astrological chart that he had drawn. At the top of the sheet he had written, "Hail, Floyd!" Immediately below it he drew two large stars, one labeled "Floyd," the other "Zona." About three inches below and to the right of "Zona," a smaller star is labeled "Sinclair," and three inches below that a tiny star, less than half the size of "Sinclair," is named "Herbert George." The modesty that led Lewis to give precedence to both Floyd Dell and Zona Gale is understandable, if not exactly characteristic, but the impulse that led him to eliminate nearly entirely from the literary firmament his much admired model, H. G. Wells, is totally mysterious. Dell's reply, demoting Zona Gale and elevating Lewis above himself, is signed, "Yours with dignity, as from one Young American Immortal to Another."

He described this letter and its background in his autobiography, *Homecoming.* There he says that *Moon-Calf* was ignored until Heywood Broun reviewed.

> Sinclair Lewis's *Main Street* and Zona Gale's *Miss Lulu Bett* were the best sellers of that year, marking a revulsion of feeling against the mob-hysterics of the war period; and my novel, which was usually referred to in all the reviews along with *Main Street,* was carried along with it to a considerable sale. . . . My book achieved that success by the accident of its coming at the time it did; if I had finished it in any year earlier than 1920, it would have been as much neglected, I believe, as Sherwood Anderson's first novel

> was. It profited by a sudden and rather hysterical fury of popular resentment against business, regimentation and conventional life.

He goes on to say that it was reviewed, like the Lewis and the Gale novels, as though he intended it as an exposé of the Middle West, whereas he had thought of it as an exposé of Felix Fay, as, for a time, he had thought *Main Street* an exposé of Carol Kennicott.

And this is the burden of his letter:

> It only remains for me to discover—which I think is probable—that you wonder if I know what a damn fool my hero is—and the puzzle will be complete. . . . Until I had painfully reflected [upon] all these things, I really believed that my novel was different in significance from yours. . . . I believed you were saying one thing and I another. The conclusion to which I am astonishingly pushed is that we are both saying the same thing (whatever it is!) But I wouldn't have known or guessed that except for the unanimity of opinion (so far as I have heard it) which unites our two books together in praise or blame.
>
> Is it possible that you and I agree? . . . I don't know yet just what it is we agree about—whether it is that Carrie and Felix should be hanged at sunrise, or that they should be elected Chief High Commissars of These Soviet States, or that they should elope with each other and pester each other with their ideals instead of the rest of the world.

To this lengthy epistle, Lewis replied on November 27:

> Don't you think that the difs between M-C and M St are 2, both important. One, Felix is young, unbound, a male—*free to go;* while Carol is (since she *thinks* she is) not free. Second, your Davenport is just enough bigger than G.P.—to be worlds bigger! Give Carol just one Felix Fay (who isn't silly & you know it!) & she would be contented enough to begin to create life about her. . . . Floyd—Floyd—we've done, I think, good books. I pray (to the spirit of Lenin, perhaps) we may do great ones. There's some good writers in these Soviet States now: you & I, perhaps; Hergesheimer, Gale, Anderson, Dreiser, Cather, Charley Norris, Wharton (now that she is back from Francomania). Perhaps we may yet be worthy of the International.

It is almost as if Lewis had not seen the *Tribune* of a month before, October 7, when Dell published his objections to *Main Street,* "not as a work of art but as an argument," and deplored Lewis's misunderstanding of the role of the idealist in America, who need not submit, as Carol does, to the forces of convention and commercialism, or on November 12, when Dell took up the subject again. (Heywood Broun, on that day, observed the oddity that the contributor to *The Saturday Evening Post* should be "far more impatient with American life" than the associate editor of *The Liberator,* and adjudicated: "A little of the sawdust of the trail still clings to Lewis. Dell has been longer on the mourner's bench.") Nor would one suspect that on the next day, November 13, Lewis sent Harcourt an expanded version of the views that he would set down again in his letter to Dell, and urged Harcourt to "plant" it somewhere as coming from someone else. Dell's contribution to the controversy was helping the sales of the book, as Harcourt saw, and a year later, in *The Bookman,* Lewis was to publish his very friendly pen-portrait of him, the "faun on the barricades," written in much the same spirit as his letter, a similar mixture of politics and throbbing sentiment: "slender, young, rather shy, discussing the significance of the Third International with overwhelming knowledge, yet all the while wishing that he could be off to the Isle of Aengus, where they sleep and sing and make verses and make love and haven't yet heard about even the First International."

Sherwood Anderson—he, too, wrote in praise, although later events and records were not to suggest it. His first letter is dated December 1, 1920:

> *My dear Mr. Sinclair Lewis—*
> I am writing to tell you how glad I am that you wrote *Main Street.* Hope it will be read in every town in America. As a matter of fact I suppose it will find most of its readers in the cities. You've sure done a job.
>
> Very truly yours,
> *Sherwood Anderson*

Lewis replied on December 6:

> I am very proud & glad to have a letter from you about *Main St.* . . . I have been a rather ardent booster for *Winesburg,* & I am looking forward to *Poor White.*
>
> Some day—God knows where & when—I wish Floyd Dell, Joe Hergesheimer, James Cabell, Waldo Frank, Ludwig Lewisohn, Dreiser, Masters, Mencken, Hackett, you & I could get together—in a savage place without constabules—have a week together, & fight & roar. Either we'd all be dead at the end or have started something—or, conceivably, all quit writing novels! At least it would be damned interesting!
>
> The other night I picked up *Winesburg* again & found myself re-reading it with even more pleasure than at first. That's an authentic test.

To this characteristically spacious outburst, Anderson sensibly replied as follows:

> Your imagination frightens me. The crowds you propose to put together in a place where no one may hide. May I go to Gopher Prairie instead. Mine is a timid nature.
>
> Just the same I'm glad you liked *Winesburg.* I hope you may find pages or at least paragraphs of beauty in *Poor White* and I hope everyone in every small town in the country reads *Main Street.*

But that final sentiment was apparently soon to change, and one can only suppose that Anderson came to feel an honest outrage that his books were relatively unsuccessful while Lewis's, one after the other, were sensations. Already, in *The Nation,* an unsigned review—written by Ludwig Lewisohn—of *Main Street* and *Poor White,* said of the latter that "compared to *Main Street* it lacks fire and edge, lucidity and fullness." In the next year, Anderson wrote to Hart Crane, "There seems to be a good deal of talk of *Poor White,* but it doesn't really sell much. I suppose *Main Street,* for example, has sold more in one week than *Poor White* altogether." And then to Paul Rosenfeld:

> This has been an amusing year. Neither *Poor White* nor *Winesburg* were selling much until W. L. George and later Sinclair Lewis began talking about me. Now they do sell, not hugely, but surprisingly well for me. In other words, I find people taking these two fellows' word on me as an artist. The gods must be amused.

The note of rancor has appeared, and in the following decade, it could only be expected to grow. So it did, but deviously.

On March 4, 1921, when Lewis was on his first lecture tour, Anderson wrote him very graciously:

> *Dear Sinclair Lewis*
>
> O, you Babe Ruth among boosters. You have ruined my life. Here I was living a quiet obscure life in this fragrant railroad terminal and you come along—make a few speeches and now look at me.
>
> The wife of every fat business man west of Pittsburg has heard you speak. She has told her husband what you said. My life is a wreck.
>
> At that Lewis you are much more generous and fine than I suspect you know.* Don't forget that novel about the Christian Science people.
>
> Sincerely yours,
>
> *Sherwood Anderson*

The final sentence suggests that they had met before this letter was written and the occasion was probably a dinner party at the Chicago home of Burton Rascoe. Rascoe describes the affair but does not exactly date it in *Before I Forget:*

> That evening we called upon Sherwood to tell his famous Mama Geighen story—his best unpublished story and his most hilarious story, published or unpublished. He was in top form about this fantastic binge he went on with George Wharton and about their encounter with the massive and marvelous woman who ran a saloon on the side of the road in Wisconsin, far from town or village. He sent us into gales of laughter, and he smiled modestly in satisfaction that his performance had been good. Lewis left the room. He came back after a minute or so. He had turned his collar and his vest hindpart before, parted his hair severely, powdered his face white. He held his

* Lewis received similar thanks from Waldo Frank, whose recent novel, *The Dark Mother,* he had also been praising in these lectures. "You are a generous person, entirely aside from your amazing powers as an author."

hands before him, tips of fingers to tips of fingers. There was a look of severe piety on his face. He delivered an extempore sermon on the evils of drink and on the evil that women like Mama Geighen do in this world, so realistically that had he delivered it in precisely the same way in a Protestant church where he was not known I am sure it would have been accepted as a very elevating and ennobling sermon indeed. We all paid this manifest genius as an actor, improvisor, orator as well as great novelist the tribute of complete silence until he had concluded. Then there was an uproar of laughter and acclaim. Lewis went into a bedroom to remove the powder and change his collar and vest. Sherwood was sitting beside me on a piano bench. Sherwood was jealous and mad as a wet hen because his performance had been capped. He turned to me and said, "It's a pity. He wants it so bad, and he will never have it." I did not ask Sherwood what he meant by "it." I knew. He meant "genius."

The question of genius apart, the two were of sharply antithetical talent, the antithesis only heightened by the fact that both were concerned with essentially the same subject, the frustrations of hinterland America. To that subject they brought absolutely opposing styles, techniques, methods of composition, structural conceptions; and from it they derived absolutely opposing effects. Lewis admired Anderson for his difference, but Anderson came increasingly to resent Lewis for his. Writing his "Four American Impressions: Gertrude Stein, Paul Rosenfeld, Ring Lardner, Sinclair Lewis," and publishing them in the *New Republic* late in 1922,* Anderson may have detected the chief flaw in Lewis's novels, the quality of the prose, but he was also obliquely praising the quality of his own prose.

> The texture of the prose written by Mr. Lewis gives me but faint joy and I cannot escape the conviction that for some reason Lewis has himself found but little joy, either in life among us or in his own effort to channel his reactions to our life into prose.

Anderson seems to be echoing Henry James in his comment on novelists like Balzac, who, eschewing the "lyrical element," are with "huge feet fairly ploughing the sand of our desert." He goes on to allow that Lewis has, with "his sharp journalistic nose," certainly discovered a great deal about the external lives of Americans, but there are vast areas of American experience, the deepest areas, that he is incapable of registering. These areas a better writer, like Ring Lardner, could perceive.†

* These "Impressions" have been consistently misdated, first by Anderson himself (whether by some devious intention, or whether by a memory gone fuzzy in four years, no one can know) when he reprinted them in his *Notebooks* in 1926. Careless editors since then have perpetuated the error. The "Impressions" appeared first on October 11, 1922.

† Anderson's sketch is probably the first of the many articles that have praised Lardner at Lewis's expense. The contrast must sometimes have become rather painful to Lewis. A writer who did not like him, Morris R. Werner, has told me that at a party once he asked Lewis point-blank if he didn't think that Lardner was the greatest living American writer of fiction, and received for answer only silence and a red

> In America there is something like a dawn that Mr. Lewis has apparently sensed but little, for there is so little sense of it in the texture of his prose. Reading Mr. Sinclair Lewis, one comes inevitably to the conclusion that here is a man writing who, wanting passionately to love the life about him, cannot bring himself to do so . . .

Later, in *No Swank* (1934), Anderson said of these four pieces that he had had, "perhaps for some malicious reason, great delight in grouping them."

> I imagined the four together, say in a cabin on a mountain, in a snowstorm. . . . I saw them in the room, staring at each other. A delicious thought came to me. It was that Paul and Ring would have quickly found a basis for understanding. I can imagine them withdrawing to a corner of the room to talk.
>
> There is no fire in the room. A storm is raging outside. It is bitterly cold.
>
> Gertrude Stein and Sinclair Lewis are left to talk together. It is bitterly cold.

Leap now nearly ten years, to February 1930. Sinclair Lewis was pursuing researches for a labor novel and the fact was well known. His investigations had carried him into Anderson's industrial South and, in 1929, he published in the Scripps-Howard newspapers a series of articles which in November of that year were collected and expanded as a pamphlet, "Cheap and Contented Labor," published by the Women's Trade Union League. It is a good piece of polemical journalism, but Sherwood Anderson did not like it. On February 20, 1930, he wrote to Nelson Antrim Crawford as follows:

> I wrote a long thing recently, called "Labor and Sinclair Lewis" . . . 9,000 to 10,000 words. My New York agent has it. I'd like $1,000.00 for it, if I can get it. I've been laying for that bird ever since he wrote *Main Street.* Now he is on the labor lay, and I wanted to skin him alive. He'll do to the factories what he did to the small towns, the doctors, preachers, etc.

In March he wrote of it, "and it says something pretty definite that I have long wanted to say about the whole school of modern hard-boiled writers," and,

> I think you will find in it what I think is a true criticism, not only of Lewis, but of the whole modern Mencken, hard-boiled attitude. It takes strength to be tender, and these men haven't strength. It is too easy to attack individuals.

He recognized presently that this was precisely what he was doing. *Scribner's* was interested in the article but objected to giving Lewis this publicity and Anderson agreed to rewrite it as "Cotton Mill," "with all the Lewis end of it wiped out entirely." Proper names and explicit refer-

---

glare, and then the hedging retort that he was at the moment saving the word "great" for Samuel Butler and *The Way of All Flesh.*

ences were indeed eliminated, but the genesis and animus of the article are still there. The essay is a rather inchoate attack on Lewis's stereotype of the small town and on what, from the evidence of the unnamed "Cheap and Contented Labor," would be his stereotype of the machine.

When, then, Anderson begins the account of his weary reading of a novel that is obviously meant as *Main Street,* his limp paragraph structure permits him to slide away from the subject in such a fashion as to avoid telling what he did immediately upon completing it, which was to write Lewis the fan letter stating the hope that the novel would be read in every town in America. There is an uneasy strand of disingenuousness in this curious history. Only a few months after the appearance of "Cotton Mill," the air was cleared when Sinclair Lewis, in Stockholm, spoke of his "great colleague Sherwood Anderson," and perhaps only a little befogged again in 1931, when Anderson wrote of a dinner party at which the conversation dwelt on "poor Sinclair Lewis." Lewis, who suffered from many things but not from rancor, could survive both denigration and condescension. If the most sensitive writers and critics thought him overrated and were made as indignant by his success as by his manners, he could content himself with the plethora of praise. Letters kept coming.

There were letters, of course, from the two novelists to whom Lewis had dedicated his book. Cabell was prompt and effusive, Hergesheimer slower and more stately. The wistful, striving faith that Lewis put in dedications was early but inaccurately observed by Waldo Frank in his 1925 *New Yorker* "Time Exposure" of Lewis: "Whenever he wrote a novel that failed to run . . . as they all failed . . . through a meager first edition, he dedicated it to half the authors whom he knew and whose work, in a humble, arrogant American way, he worshiped." He did, unquestionably, admire all sorts of trash, including that of Cabell and Hergesheimer, but he admired success even more than trash, and these two novelists were supported in the early 1920s by much tougher critics than Lewis. (One can never say that Lewis had a formed literary taste, only flighty prejudice, loose catholicity, and an eagerness to be kindly and helpful to newcomers.) Cabell, with his foolishly tenuous allegories, was regarded as controversial and important, and Hergesheimer, treating himself like a man of letters, the squire of West Chester, Pennsylvania, as elegant and important. One writer, Sydnor Harrison, the author of *Queed,* saw Lewis's superiority to both. "Why did he dedicate it," he exclaimed to Alfred Harcourt, "to two men neither of whom is really in his own class!"

To Waldo Frank's implication of literary social climbing, we must add that Lewis's preference in novels at this time—not only for those of Cabell and Hergesheimer, but of Carl Van Vechten and Elinor Wylie and others —was rather like his taste in women, drawn mothlike to that mannered "elegance" that was most alien to himself. The work of Lewis and Cabell bears, to illustrate, an entirely inverse relationship. Apart from such accidents of literary sociology that both were supported by H. L. Mencken, for his own variety of reasons and along with such still different writers as Theodore Dreiser and Willa Cather, Lewis and Cabell have an interesting literary linkage. As Frederick J. Hoffman has pointed out, both were fantasy writers, the difference being that Lewis created his fantasy out of real social fragments, whereas Cabell's was created out of completely unreal materials. Lewis, perhaps, giving all the illusion of completeness, did not tell us enough; but Cabell told us nothing, with ridiculous if persuasive pretentions. And yet, one must say on Lewis's behalf that, even though he seems to have admired Cabell more than that other Virginian, Ellen Glasgow, he did not admire Booth Tarkington—although he deferred to him too—so much as he did Dreiser, a less complacent Hoosier.

From Dreiser there was no word, but from Dreiser's doughty champion, H. L. Mencken, there was; and with that began the most influential literary relationship that Lewis was to experience. Its origins are obscured in anecdotage. Mencken knew at least as much of Lewis's work as he had published in *Smart Set,* the story about Main Streeters called "I'm a Stranger Here Myself," perhaps nothing else, and he had probably met Lewis once. Influential, as his iconoclastic essays had already made him, Mencken loomed large for Lewis. On October 27, Lewis received an enthusiastic letter from John Peter Toohey, a theatrical press agent, who had "written Harry Mencken to go out and grab a copy instanter," and for once, Lewis did not urge Harcourt immediately to follow up this lead for a possible blurb ("Mencken we'd better let alone—he'll be getting touchy"). Before the thirtieth, another letter from Toohey told him that Mencken had already read it with "great joy," and on the thirtieth, "a voluntary letter" came from Mencken himself, calling *Main Street* "the best thing of its sort that has been done so far," and promising to review it in the January *Smart Set,* "the first issue still open."

Lewis replied on the same day:

> It was damn nice of you to take the time and trouble to write about *Main Street.* I needn't tell you how very glad I am to have you like it.
>
> I am again a quasi-neighbor of yours, and shall be till next April. Had hoped to go abroad this fall, but too broke after a year on the novel. If I'm in Baltimore any time, I shall make another effort to get hold of you and —No, honest to God, I'll let you off with one drink. Wenn es neulich geschrieben wäre so würde man jetz singen, "Der Graf von Luxembburg [sic], er hat sein Booze verjuct, juct, juct," or whatever the Buchstabieren is.
>
> Sincerely yours,
> *Sinclair Lewis*
>
> My German is echt-Minnesota!

The suggestion of an alcoholic occasion in the recent past gives some credence to George Jean Nathan's otherwise rather questionable account, presenting, as it does, Lewis at his most dreadful precisely on an occasion when he was courting the opinion for which he most cared. Mencken and Nathan, the story goes, were urged one evening by T. R. Smith, then managing editor of the *Century* magazine, to drop by at his apartment for a drink.

> When we got there, we found with Smith a tall, skinny, paprika-headed stranger to whom we were introduced as one Lewis. . . .
>
> Barely had we taken off our hats and coats . . . when the tall, skinny, paprika-headed stranger simultaneously coiled one long arm around Mencken's neck and the other around mine, well nigh strangling us and putting resistance out of the question, and—yelling at the top of his lungs—began: "So you guys are critics, are you? Well, let me tell you something. I'm the best writer in this here gottdamn country and if you, Georgie, and you, Hank, don't know it now, you'll know it gottdamn soon. Say, I've just finished a book that'll be published in a week or two and it's the gottdamn best book of its kind that this here gottdamn country has had and don't you guys forget it! I worked a year on the gottdamn thing and it's the goods, I'm atelling you! Listen, when it comes to writing a novel, I'm so far ahead of most of the men you two think are good that I'll be gottdamned if it doesn't make me sick to think of it! Just wait till you read the gottdamn thing. You've got a treat coming, Georgie and Hank, and don't you boys make no mistake about *that!*"
>
> Projected from Smith's flat by the self-endorsing uproar—it kept up for fully half an hour longer—Mencken and I jumped into a taxicab, directed the driver to speed us posthaste to a tavern where we might in some peace recover our equilibrium and our ear-drums, and looked at each other. "Of all the idiots I've ever laid eyes on, that fellow is the worst!" groaned Mencken, gasping for breath. Regaining my own breath some moments later, all that I could add was that if any such numskull could ever write anything worth reading, maybe there was something in Christian Science too.
>
> Three days later I got the following letter from Mencken, who had returned to Baltimore:
>
> Dear George: Grab hold of the bar-rail, steady yourself, and prepare yourself for a terrible shock! I've just read the advance sheets of the book of that *Lump* we met at Schmidt's and, by God, he has done the job! It's a genuinely excellent piece of work. Get it as soon as you can and take a look. I begin to believe that perhaps there isn't a God after all. There is no justice in the world. Yours in Xt., M.

Perhaps; or something like it. George Jean Nathan was a notably unreliable witness in matters of detail, but as a general impression, his anecdote can probably be accepted.

If any account of the episode reached Alfred Harcourt's ears, he had genuine reason to warn his new star that, now that success had changed his position as a novelist, he must "stop wearing his heart on his sleeve and play with the cards closer to his belt." Lewis could rage and sulk, plot and scheme, and on occasion hold a cunning silence, but to ask that he develop restraint and a true discretion was to ask for more than he could ever give or wish to.

When Mencken's review appeared in *Smart Set,* the book was, of course, already made. The boom began with three prepublication encomia from F.P.A. in his "Conning Tower," and with Heywood Broun's enthusiastic review in the New York *Tribune* for October 20, which praised the truthfulness of the novel's recreation of the life of an entire community and, more especially, of the dialogue. "He hears even better than he sees. I can't think of anybody who has been so unerringly right in reproducing talk. He is right to a degree that is deeper than phonographic exactness." * Ludwig Lewisohn in *The Nation* and Carl Van Doren in the *Evening Post* took the novel with utmost seriousness, and Van Doren, in a letter to the author, referred to it as "fearfully truthful." Their view that *Main Street* marked the end of American complacency, that it announced a new national mood, was most fully expressed by William Allen White. In his review in the Emporia (Kansas) *Gazette* he said that "Contentment is more wicked than red anarchy," which led Heywood Broun to remark that if ever he had to preach a sermon, this would be his text. White made the novel the subject of an editorial, and he wrote Lewis to tell him that he had done "a noble thing."

> If I were a millionaire, I should buy a thousand of those books and send them to my friends and then I would go and bribe the legislature of Kansas to make *Main Street* compulsory reading in the public schools. No American has done a greater service for his country in any sort of literature than you have done.

If, two days after his first review, Heywood Broun reconsidered, and announced now that Carol Kennicott was "puerile" and that Lewis's method was unselective beyond necessity and the book's best interest, Mencken, when he came to the novel in January, found its virtue in the brilliantly packed accumulation of detail no less than in its verisimilitude of speech, at the same time that he assumed the puerility of Carol. He defended what he took to be the author's conception of the character, assuming, as Dell

* The matter of Sinclair Lewis's famous "ear" is interesting. After his son Michael had seen a performance of the dramatized *It Can't Happen Here,* he said to his mother, Dorothy Thompson, "That isn't Vermont talk. That's Middle Western talk." Some critics challenge the accuracy of even his Middle Western talk, if not in what was then its idiom and its slang, in its rhythms. Lewis himself told Roger Burlingame in the 1930s that, eager for the greatest possible fidelity, he had once rented a number of hotel rooms in the Middle West and arranged a gathering at which he kept a dictaphone running to record the local speech. Then he found that what he got was totally unlike anything that one would put down in fiction. The local speech habits were lost in the "well, ah's," "you know what I mean's," the "uh-uh's" and the "yeah-yeah's" and all the interruptions of every kind that do in fact take place in a group conversation, and nothing at all was sustained.

had assumed on first reading, that Lewis had meant to show that her "superior culture is, after all, chiefly bogus." But Lewis meant no such thing. As he would not believe that Dell had meant to show Felix Fay to be foolish and immature, so he wrote to Harcourt of Carol as "sensitive and articulate." (When the play that was made from *Main Street* was being cast, he wrote to Harriet Ford, codramatist with Harvey O'Higgins, to say that it was important that "the Carol part *does* require some one with brains," and later, when Peggy Wood seemed not entirely suited to the role, he said, "Do you know, there might be some eager quite-unknown youngster playing with some Highbrow Organization of the Provincetown-Theaterguild type who would not merely make a good Carol but would actually *be* Carol.") In his inscription to his wife, he had written, "To Gracie, who is all the good part of Carol"; but Carol was also a large part of him.* The other part was Will Kennicott, the downright. The struggle was between the halves of his divided being, and one passage in the novel nearly tells us so:

> She had fancied that her life might make a story. She knew that there was nothing heroic or obviously dramatic in it, no magic of rare hours, nor valiant challenge, but it seemed to her that she was of some significance because she was commonplaceness, the ordinary life of the age, made articulate and protesting. It had not occurred to her that there was also a story of Will Kennicott, into which she entered only so much as he entered into hers; that he had bewilderments and concealments as intricate as her own, and soft treacherous desires for sympathy.

The two stories together are his, and the combination of these qualities, his, too.

We must reconsider the origins of the book. He had always as a boy been charmed by things different from "the Sauk Centre usual," and after two years at New Haven, in the summer of 1905, when he was twenty years old, he consolidated the animus of those twenty years in the phrase "the village virus." Living through the summer, through the dry exasperating heat, the monotony of one day following upon another precisely like it, the endless locust staccato of small talk and gossip, unable to bring himself to writing as he had hoped, reading, among many books, Hamlin Garland's *Main-Travelled Roads* with its harsh picture of Midwestern rural life, conversing with a mildly radical clergyman and with the disaffected Dorion, he conceived, perhaps, of a novel about Midwestern small-town life as it

* Later, Charles Breasted was to ask him the question direct. "Then I said, 'What about Carol Kennicott—isn't she a portrait of you?' He seemed startled and said that only a very few people had guessed her identity. 'Yes,' he added, 'Carol is "Red" Lewis: always groping for something she isn't capable of attaining, always dissatisfied, always restlessly straining to see what lies just over the horizon, intolerant of her surroundings, yet lacking any clearly defined vision of what she really wants to do or be.' "

would be viewed by such a lawyer. More than ten years later he returned to the town with his wife, saw it again but now "through her eyes," tried now (he said in 1937) to write it, but could not bring it off.

At some time between 1916 and 1919, he changed the original focus of the novel, and Guy Pollock moved into a secondary position while Carol Kennicott moved into the center. Then it became *Main Street: The Story of Carol Kennicott.* It was as if, in 1916, seeing his wife and his father and his brother Claude, together, he had asked himself, "Suppose Grace had married a man like Claude or my father instead of me, and suppose that they didn't get even to St. Cloud, but stayed here?" Even while she exasperated him, he loved and respected her, and he always felt an inordinate admiration for his brother and an excess of respect for his father. His characters would have a nearly equal sanction, with Carol given the edge. Later, when he was in the habit of referring to "that damn' fool Gracie," his view of Carol would change, too, and by that time he would have developed the perspective to draw Fran Dodsworth. The kind of ambiguity that plagued his point of view from *Our Mr. Wrenn* on would make the shift easy enough, and some readers, as we have seen, assumed the later point of view to have been there from the beginning. But, just as he could not see his wife clearly, so, when he wrote *Main Street,* he could not see his character. The question that must have been in his mind all through his final planning and writing was, What would Grace do? And that is what Carol did.

The reading of Hamlin Garland in that summer of 1905 has, of course, a special significance. Although there had been a forty-year history of "debunking" (the word was the invention of Lewis's friend Woodward) in the American novel, no novel had smashed the myth of the friendly village or the shell of middle-class complacency. But just as English literature had had its double view of village life, beginning with those eighteenth-century poems Goldsmith's *Deserted Village* and Crabbe's *The Village,* so in American literature the tradition of sentimental praise for the rural haunt was countered with a long, if less populous, tradition of critical abuse. It begins with Edward Eggleston's *The Hoosier Schoolmaster* of 1871 and picks up force first in E. W. Howe's *The Story of a Country Town* of 1883 and next, in 1887, in Joseph Kirkland's *Zury: The Meanest Man in Town.* Then followed Hamlin Garland: *Main-Travelled Roads* in 1891 and *Rose of Dutcher's Coolly* in 1895 and, sometime after these, the *Middle Border* books. In 1897, Harold Frederic's *The Damnation of Theron Ware* moved the scene to New England, and some of the early short stories of Willa Cather, like "A Sculptor's Funeral" in *The Troll Garden* of 1905, moved it further westward. All these—and one might also include Robert Grant's *Unleavened Bread* of 1900—share in a tradition that pictures the village not as happy but as grubby and dull, where generosity and friendliness become malice and cruelty, blithe work becomes grueling toil and poverty, intelligence becomes smug complacency and selfishness, and neighborliness becomes corrosive loneliness. Sporadically the tradition had found support in the work of W. D. Howells and Mark Twain and Ellen Glasgow, but spread as it by now had been to nearly every section of the country, the heart of the tradition remained the Middle West. In 1915 it burst forth in poetry from Illinois, in Edgar Lee Masters' *Spoon River Anthology,* and in 1916 from Iowa, in Anderson's *Windy McPherson's Son,* this to be followed by *Winesburg, Ohio* and, in the year of *Main Street,* by *Poor White,* together with those novels of Iowa and Wisconsin by Floyd Dell and Zona Gale.

It was a considerable tradition, but somehow one that had made small impression on the popular consciousness. For that, Sinclair Lewis was requisite. One reason is suggested by Robert Benchley, who, comparing Gale and Lewis in the New York *World,* found the former more subtle but the latter more accurate. More accurate, perhaps, *Main Street* was certainly the fullest indictment that had been delivered, the least compromising and the noisiest, a thunderclap that changed the literary atmosphere. In that very year, Mencken's essay "The National Letters" had seen no escape from the "conformity, timorousness, lack of enterprise and audacity," which he believed to be the enemies of great literature, but in fact, with *Main Street,* he was to discover the beginning of a decade of literary revolt that would challenge every accepted value. Beginning with Lewis's assault on the provincialism of backwoods America, the attack would come to include everything that Mencken denounced—"fundamentalism in religion, capitalism in industry, commercialism in education, science, and the arts, chauvinism in international affairs, reactionism in public opinion at large." And Lewis would always seem to be in the vanguard of denunciation, as, in *Main Street* itself, he permits Carol to explicate the difference between the fictional convention and the reality, and thereby to explode the first. The convention:

> In reading popular stories and seeing plays, asserted Carol, she had found only two traditions of the American small town. The first tradition, repeated in scores of magazines every month, is that the American village remains the one sure abode of friendship, honesty, and clean sweet marriageable girls. Therefore all men who succeed in painting in Paris or in finance in New York at last become weary of smart women, return to their native towns, assert that cities are vicious, marry their childhood sweethearts and, presumably, joyously abide in those towns until death.
>
> The other tradition is that the significant features of all villages are whiskers, iron dogs upon lawns, gold bricks, checkers, jars of gilded cattails, and shrewd comic old men who are known as "hicks" and who ejaculate "Waal I swan."

The two are in fact one, both opposed to the reality:

> It is an unimaginatively standardized background, a sluggishness of speech and manners, a rigid ruling of the spirit by the desire to appear respectable. It is . . . the contentment of the quiet dead, who are scornful of the living for their restless walking. It is negation canonized as the one positive virtue. It is the prohibition of happiness. It is slavery self-sought and self-defended. It is dullness made God.
>
> A savorless people, gulping tasteless food, and sitting afterward, coatless and thoughtless, in rocking-chairs prickly with inane decorations, listening to mechanical music, saying mechanical things, about the excellence of Ford automobiles, and viewing themselves as the greatest race in the world.

Lewis's influence may derive, further, from the fact that he shared in another tradition, the tradition of provincial manners as depicted by Midwestern and Western humorists—George Ade, Artemus Ward, Josh Billings, Finley Peter Dunne. With them he shared a gift for the extreme, the overdrawn, the excessive, the grotesquely absurd. This is the strain that turns merely realistic novels into the Lewis fables and makes them large. From them too, but above all from Mark Twain, he derived the gift of the flow of colloquial speech that poured through his novels, here and there in the five early works, but consistently from *Main Street* on. And this is a strain that at once heightens verisimilitude and palliates terror.

Writing of Sinclair Lewis in 1926, Waldo Frank recognized that in those postwar years the American audience wanted above all to be lashed—but not too hard! And he might have observed that the rest of the world was more than merely well-prepared to stand by and applaud the spectacle, and to believe that the lashing was harder than it was.

But *Main Street* introduced still another element that had not been conspicuous in the earlier work, an element that derives not from a literary but from an intellectual tradition, although a short one. Without abandoning his rebellious optimism (his plot is the same: the young person with a vision beyond the environment; the struggle against the environment in the hope of achieving the vision; success or compromise), his Wellsian sense of life as adventure, the positive side of the "Promise of American Life," *Main Street* yet plays all this down and supplements it. One need only compare the Main Streeters with the idealistic version of second-generation Americans like Carl Ericson in *The Trail of the Hawk* to see what has happened; there, a vision of the American future "lifted Carl's chin in wonder," and there,

> It was for him to carry on the American destiny of extending the Western horizon; his to restore the wintry Pilgrim virtues and the exuberant, October, partridge-drumming days of Daniel Boone; then to add, in his own or another generation, new American aspirations for beauty.

One cannot be very certain what this means, but one can recognize the effusiveness of its tone, and Lewis was clear enough in the same novel when he wrote as follows of the immigrants:

> They swiftly master politics, voting for honesty rather than for hand-shakes; they make keen, scrupulously honest business deals; send their children to school; accumulate land—one section, two sections—or move to town to keep shop and ply skilled tools; become Methodists and Congregationalists; are neighborly with Yankee manufacturers and doctors and teachers; and in one generation, or less, are completely American.

But three *books* later, they present themselves quite differently.

Herbert Croly, too, believed in the promise of American life, but he saw the alternative—a nation of grubbing Babbitts, bound by convention, timorous, scornful of all human difference. It was this alternative that was investigated by Van Wyck Brooks in "The Puritan's Will to Power" and by H. L. Mencken in "Puritanism as a Literary Force," both of 1917. By "puritanism" Mencken meant

> the prejudice against beauty as a form of debauchery and corruption—the distrust of all ideas that do not fit readily into certain accepted axioms—the belief in the eternal validity of moral concepts—in brief, the whole mental sluggishness of the lower orders of men,

a state of mind that Mencken could readily develop into that complex that included religious evangelism, a shabby political moralism, and a fierce commercialism, the whole making up his *boobus Americanus* and providing not only Sinclair Lewis but all the writers of the twenties with the platform from which they could take their literary pot shots at American culture. This is the new strain that comes into *Main Street,* provides Lewis with the basis of his satire, and is to dominate his fiction for ten years.

Yet the exact nature of Mencken's influence is beyond determination. In his review of Mencken's *Notes on Democracy* (1926), Edmund Wilson wrote that "Sinclair Lewis's Babbitt and the inhabitants of his Main Street are merely particular incarnations of the great American boob, evidently inspired by Mencken." Mencken's *A Book of Prefaces* (1917) may well have been the specific influence that gave Lewis the focus for Main Street (although literary "influence" does not normally operate in such a tidy way), but Lewis had already hit on his idea for *Babbitt* before Mencken publicly proposed it. Nevertheless, he was prepared to give Mencken credit. In January 1922, he wrote:

> You ask about the new novel—which won't be out till next September. It's curiously associated with yourself. A year ago in a criticism of *Main Street* you said that what ought to be taken up now is the American city—not NY or Chi but the cities of 200,000 to 500,000—the Baltimores and Omahas and Buffaloes and Birminghams, etc. I was startled to read it, because that

was precisely what I WAS then planning, and am now doing. But your piece helped me to decide on this particular one as against one or two others which, at the time, I also wanted to do.

I think you'll like it—I hope to Christ you do. All our friends are in it—the Rotary Club, the popular preacher, the Chamber of Commerce, the new bungalows, the bunch of business men jolliers lunching at the Athletic Club. It ought to be at least 2000% American, as well as forward-looking, right-thinking, optimistic, selling the idea of success, and go-getterish.

The central character is a Solid Citizen, one George F. Babbitt, real estate man, who has a Dutch Colonial house on Floral Heights. . . .

The book is not altogether satire. I've tried like hell to keep the boob Babbitt from being merely burlesque—hard tho that is at times, when he gets to orating before the Boosters' Club lunches. I've tried to make him human and individual, not a type.

Of this I'm sure—if you don't like the book, nobody in the entire Vereinigen will. In certain ways it seems to be different both from The Sheik, and the better works of Ethel M. Dell and Peter B. Kyne.

The facts, as this letter makes clear, hardly justify the claim of Mencken's biographer William Manchester that "Lewis was looking to Mencken for critical tutelage." He was looking for critical approval, which is quite another matter. Certainly he was looking for it in the right quarter, for Mencken's criticism, before and all through the twenties, was and would be tirelessly directed at the two targets that formed the staple of Lewis's satire: the standardization of manners in a business culture and the stultification of morals in middle-class convention. And the two men were, of course, congenial, even though each was too nearly equal to the other in volubility to provide a satisfactory foil; they did not, as a result, see a great deal of each other except in such public shenanigans as are reported in Manchester's *Disturber of the Peace:*

Between them, on Mencken's visits to New York, they gave bar patrons as bizarre a show in the perversion of American mores as even that jaded audience had ever seen, with Mencken quoting from prohibition pamphlets and Lewis delivering a lecture on the merits of Rotary or a sermon on the beauty of the Church of God. . . . Mencken and Lewis became the champions of the insurgent young men, of the Mooney, Billings, and Debs partisans, and the chief targets of the Philistines. Later, in 1922, Lewis formally announced the entente in a press conference, declaring, "If I had the power, I'd make Henry Mencken the Pope of America."

The one profound difference in their views, the temper of the twenties rather served to disguise. Mencken was stubbornly anti-democratic and could see in American life only a gross display of imbecility that promised nothing but self-perpetuation and proliferation; he preached a Nietzschean doctrine of aristocratic supremacy, of the necessary leadership of an intellectual elite. Sinclair Lewis, while without any very clear partisan convictions in politics, was equally stubborn in his democratic faith and, even in his shrillest denunciations of the blemishes in American culture, never yielded up that faith. This was a faith for which the mood of the 1920s had little room. If 1920 marked the opening of a decade of American cynicism, it also marked the end of two decades of an influential liberalism—an era of progressivism equally characterized by its reformist zeal and its democratic hopes. There is symbolic drama in the death, in 1920, of Jack Reed, an event that moved Sinclair Lewis, and in the publication, in 1920, of Randolph Bourne's *History of a Literary Radical,* the book that summarized his views and closed a chapter of cultural history.

This was the tradition in which Sinclair Lewis had matured; but with *Main Street* he, too, seemed—but only seemed—to announce that it was finished. Floyd Dell reports in *Homecoming* that Lewis "was said to have cut out from his *Main Street,* on the advice of Cabell, the one sensible character in the book, through whom his own constructive views were to have been expressed." It is possible that this is the point at which Guy Pollock faded from prominence and was permitted to fall prey, like everyone else, to "the village virus." And Mrs. Doc Kennicott took over.

Suppose such a character, a clear spokesman for the author, had been permitted to remain in the novel, precisely what would his "constructive views" have been? The complaint of *Main Street* is that small-town life is dull, shallow, unbeautiful, and frustrating; its desire is that it become lively, profound, beautiful and fulfilling. One may wonder whether Sinclair Lewis would have held any clearer or more effective program toward that end than Carol. They suffered from a common limitation, a deficient sense of history. History for both seems to have begun about 1850. Nearly everything before that dissipates itself in mythological reveries, and even their notions about pioneer times are largely mythological, an affair of "partridge-drumming" days. "A thousand dreams governed by the fiction she had read, drawn from the pictures she had envied, absorbed her drowsy lake afternoons. . . ." And it was, after all, the adult Lewis who announced that his youthful disappointments arose from the fact that there were no knights in Minnesota—no turrets except siloes, no troubadours except choir singers. When he wishes to find analogies with Carol's situation, or contrasts, he turns to literary myth:

> Thus in the Vale of Arcady nymph and satyr beguiled the hours; precisely thus, and not in honeyed pentameters, discoursed Elaine and the worn Sir Launcelot in the pleached alley.

Her dreams, like his, lack a plausible reference; her "culture" is necessarily "bogus." *

* The same "bogus culture" is permitted to flourish in the story that *Harper's* bought just after the publication of *Main Street*—"A Matter of Business." Here a small town

"... if I could put through all those reforms at once, I'd still want startling, exotic things. Life is comfortable and clean enough here already. And so secure. What it needs is to be less secure, more eager. The civic improvements which I'd like the Thanatopsis to advocate are Strindberg plays, and classic dancers—exquisite legs beneath tulle—and (I can see him so clearly!) a thick, black-bearded, cynical Frenchman who would sit about and drink and sing opera and tell bawdy stories and laugh at our proprieties and quote Rabelais and not be ashamed to kiss my hand!"

What will she find beyond the "blue horizon," what will her child find?

"We're going to find elephants with golden howdahs from which peep young maharanees with necklaces of rubies, and a dawn sea colored like the breast of a dove, and a white and green house filled with books and silver tea-sets."

It is only the old Lewis cry for the nonexistent elsewhere, elsewhere! It is also an old cry in American literature.

Elsewhere life is lived more richly than it can possibly be lived on this thin and sullen historical soil, and elsewhere works of art with deeply reverberative associations and social complexities can be written. We have a past, to be sure, but is it "usable"? A past, but no sense of the past, which, in the view of Henry James, is so major an item in a writer's equipment. James's lament about Hawthorne, "that the flower of art blooms only where the soil is deep, that it takes a great deal of history to produce a little literature, that it needs a complex social machinery to set a writer in motion," echoed a much earlier lament from James Fenimore Cooper about the "poverty of materials" for the writer in America.

There is scarcely an ore which contributes to the wealth of the author, that is found, here, in veins as rich as in Europe. There are no annals for the historian; no follies (beyond the most vulgar and commonplace) for the satirist; no manners for the dramatist; no obscure fictions for the writer of romance; no gross and hardy offences against decorum for the moralist; nor any of the rich artificial auxiliaries of poetry.

As the frontier moved westward from New England and New York and Virginia, and as thousands of new and dreary little towns were spawned on prairie and bluff, history itself, even a brief history, seemed nearly to vanish, and a young man brought up in Sauk Centre could dream of a false medievalism, and a young woman isolated in Gopher Prairie, yearning for an attractive and traditional way of life, could think in the most superficial way of transporting colonial architecture, and an enterprising manufacturer in Michigan could declare that "History is bunk." Henry Ford, crude and emphatic like no one else, was still by no means

---

stationer with the soul of a poet decides to continue selling beautiful handmade French dolls instead of a commercial line of cheaply made dolls in dreadful taste that would make him a thousand a year and satisfy his ambitious wife and daughter; the surprise at the end is that the wife all along wanted him to make this choice.

alone in his views. A statement of editorial policy in the *New Republic* in 1915 by James Harvey Robinson demands, "Why *should* we respect the conclusions of past centuries?" and serves to remind us how prevalent the attitude was in the second decade of the century. Novels, without intending it, could come to exemplify the view, and the novelist himself could tacitly accept it, together with an anti-cultural view of progress. In 1942, Sinclair Lewis wrote in his Minnesota diary,

> Re-reading my *Main Street* for first time since it was published—because I'm to do a radio script for Treasury Dept. on "Main Street Goes to War." It is probably only just to the tight older people but doesn't take enough account of the younger ones, who will carry out all of Carol's aspirations with none of her artiness or ego, and who will build the fine school buildings of today, nor enough of outside forces—the state which will build the armory, the chain-store companies which, however brazen, will do competent merchandizing, the movies, which will become real drama.

This would have satisfied Henry Ford, but Cooper and James would have blushed in dismay.

If the writing of the "genteel tradition" had tried to gloss over the limitations in American life that Cooper saw, the writers of 1914 and the years that immediately followed did not; and this is their difference, that they seized upon these very limitations as their stock in trade. Willa Cather and Ellen Glasgow, and on occasion Edith Wharton, could explore such historical annals as there were; if no dramatist of manners was to appear, Mrs. Wharton and the young Scott Fitzgerald could, in fiction, show them for however shabby or giddy they may have been; obscure fictions were discovered by such writers of romance as Cabell and Hergesheimer; our gross and hardy offenses against decorum were now common enough and suited the talents of Dreiser the moralist; and Anderson could bring into his best fiction something of poetry. As for follies, the most vulgar and commonplace—it is precisely these that made Sinclair Lewis the satirist, and that made him seem both great in his achievement and clear in his indictment. "Sinclair Lewis in *Main Street,*" wrote Orrick Johns, "gave the country the whole inept, frustrated struggle of a period toward imitation culture."

Between them and others, these writers gave to the 1920s the picture of America as hopelessly vulgar, immoral, and dull. And from this picture, as well as from so much of it as was true, they and scores of other writers fled first to the East and then on to Europe.

> The young man or woman had to go east instead of west; in search of freedom (Floyd Dell), a "style" (Glenway Wescott), culture and sophistication (Willa Cather, Carl Van Vechten, Ruth Suckow), or moral maturity (Wescott, Sherwood Anderson).

So writes Frederick J. Hoffman in *The Twenties.* The name of Sinclair Lewis does not appear on this list of illustrations, and probably for two reasons. One is that his residence in the East was sporadic and that he returned frequently to the Midwest and the West, demonstrating that what he called "the clash between Main Street and Beacon Street that is eternal in American culture" was for him not so much a clash as it was a vacillation. The other is the ambiguity of his literary attitudes. The ambition to find in the East what is not available in the Midwest is usually exposed as false and fruitless, as in *Main Street;* and when the East is pushed on to mean Europe, later novels arrive at the same conclusion. His attitude toward the Middle West is as ambiguous as his attitude toward the middle class: both drawn as hopelessly narrow, the first is shown finally as somehow the only sensible place, and the second as somehow the only sensible people.

These are the unsettled attitudes that determine Carol Kennicott's choices, and one can hardly be surprised that the affirmations of the novel at the end evaporate in vagueness.* Carol turns back from the East to Gopher Prairie, settling for "the nobility of good sense," and the conclusion of the novel seems to lie in these reflections:

> And why, she began to ask, did she rage at individuals? Not individuals but institutions are the enemies, and they most afflict the disciples who the most generously serve them. They insinuate their tyranny under a hundred guises and pompous names, such as Polite Society, the Family, the Church, Sound Business, the Party, the Country, the Superior White Race; and the only defense against them, Carol beheld, is unembittered laughter.

This much, at any rate, is clear, but more positive assertions are mere vapors of words:

> Though she should return, she said, she would not be utterly defeated. She was glad of her rebellion. The prairie was no longer empty land in the sun-glare; it was the living tawny beast which she had fought and made beautiful by fighting; and in the village streets were shadows of her desires and the sound of her marching and the seeds of mystery and greatness.

* One ambiguity in the characterization of Carol Kennicott may or may not be relevant here. Mary Austin early raised the question, "One wonders if he was fully aware of how much of Carol Kennicott's failure to find herself in Gopher Prairie was owing to the lack of sex potency, a lack which he records without relating it to any other of her insufficiencies." Nor does he significantly relate it to the drama. That Carol is frigid, Dr. Kennicott, who should know, several times tells her; but the fact does not disturb him or, in itself, impair his happiness. Whether Eddie Schwirtz is an equally reliable witness in the case of Una Golden of *The Job,* where again the fact seems of little importance, one may wonder, but it is nevertheless to be remarked that this apparently gratuitous imposition of frigidity on so many of his heroines is a mark of Sinclair Lewis's fiction. The explanation may lie in biographical researches beyond the scope of the present work.

It is nearly inevitable that the novel should end in an imbalance, with a characteristic juxtaposition of sentiment and fact, protest articulated and emptiness unadmitted:

> "But I have won in this: I've never excused my failures by sneering at my aspirations, by pretending to have gone beyond them. I do not admit that Main Street is as beautiful as it should be! I do not admit that Gopher Prairie is greater or more generous than Europe! I do not admit that dish-washing is enough to satisfy all women! I may not have fought the good fight, but I have kept the faith."
>
> "Sure. You bet you have," said Kennicott. "Well, good night. Sort of feels to me like it might snow tomorrow. Have to be thinking about putting up the storm-windows pretty soon. Say, did you notice whether the girl put that screw-driver back?"

One can only point out—for whatever it may signify—that the last word is Will's.

These are matters that must enter into any final evaluation, but they were not questions that troubled the great mass of the immediate readers of *Main Street*. Before he wrote that novel, Lewis had already written (but not published) the observation that "If you have it in you to produce one thundering good novel, one really big novel, just one, your place in American literature will be safe for the next hundred years." As the dust settled, *Main Street* seemed to stand there as such a book, a major reputation secured. Carol Kennicott would come to be known as "the Madame Bovary of the wheat elevators," and Lewis as the American Flaubert, the American Dickens, the American Balzac, let alone the American Arnold Bennett.

The comparison of *Main Street* with *Madame Bovary* became a commonplace among American as well as French critics. Stuart Sherman in his little pamphlet of 1922, "The Significance of Sinclair Lewis," was perhaps the first critic to work out a systematic comparison of the two novels, and two years later, in *Mammonart,* Upton Sinclair would work out his. Lewis himself, defending the originality of his work, protested that he had not read *Madame Bovary* when he wrote *Main Street,* as, similarly, he protested that he had not read *Spoon River Anthology,* when, in his *Nation* articles on "The Revolt of the Village," Carl Van Doren found the Masters poem the genesis of all the literature of protest against village life that appeared between 1915 and the early 1920s. (Whether Lewis had read him or not, Edgar Lee Masters was among the list of literary folk that he proposed to Anderson that they assemble.) There were many lovely extravagances that told Lewis he was now among the great, but no one was foolish enough to call *Main Street* the American *Middlemarch.**

* Stanton A. Coblentz, in *The Bookman,* invoking both Jane Austen and George Eliot as the supreme (but comparable) delineators of provincial manners, came close.

Perhaps someone should have risked the fatuity, but stressing the epithet, thus suggesting perhaps that, with our famous lack of social and cultural and moral complexity, this was as near as an American novelist could come to such a work, and that what the book seemed to tell Americans, and Europeans, was that all Americans everywhere make their march down the middle of Main Street, and that this is indeed the poverty and the pain of our lives.

2

SINCLAIR LEWIS was beyond poverty and for the time being was feeling no pain. Yet reports vary on his response to his sudden success. Waldo Frank, in 1925, recorded—almost certainly in error—that it disturbed Lewis, that he had hoped only for outrage on all sides; and Gilbert Seldes, that it shook Lewis's faith in *Main Street* as a work of art. A letter to Hergesheimer, written from London in 1922, lends some support to these recollections:

> Me, of course, I am ruined. With the large sale of *Main Street* I am convinced of my essential commonplaceness. (Quite honestly!) Every once in a while some friend indignantly tells me that some bunch of the very young jeunes—say those at the Café Rotonde on the rive gauche—assert that if the damned book has sold so well, I must be rotten. . . . But I agree with them, I belong to their faction! Hell's sweet bells, here is divine comedy! An earnest young man, Yankee of physical type, comic and therefore the more humorless, writes a long book to slap the bourgeois—the bourgeois love it, eat it! It would make an excellent short story.

Dr. Peyton Rous and his wife, who were seeing the Lewises in these years, remember that the success of *Main Street* frightened him. "This will change us. This will change me. This will change *everything!*" they remember as his lamentation. (Later, surely, except for one brief moment, he took his success lightly enough, quite as his due, beyond astonishment.) The most persuasive recollection is Ludwig Lewisohn's, in *Mid-Channel:*

> I was tempted to ask my friends: How do you live from within outward? From what ultimate satisfactions do you derive your poise, your power, your courage in the face of this apparently empty universe, of age, of death? . . . Sinclair Lewis rushed uptown to see me. Fifty thousand copies [of *Main Street*] had been sold. Did I think it would go on? And slightly drunk on both liquor and triumph, he sketched the Babbitt saga. His long pink face was like a torch. He played with his unparalleled mimetic gift as a Japanese juggler plays with ivory balls. I could not put my question. It would have glided from those happily glittering surfaces.

At another extreme are stories of arrogance and a new accession of rudeness. Washington society in that winter of 1920–1921 paid some attention to the Lewises, and one story has it—it is probably apocryphal, almost certainly heightened, but reported by John Marquand as current at that time—that one day Lewis waited on Mrs. Bainbridge Colby, the wife of the new Secretary of State, at a moment when she was being briefed by the protocol man. Lewis, still gauche in many ways, did not particularly put her at ease, and she was already uneasy about the expectations of her conduct, more so in the presence of the protocol man. At last she said, "Mr. Lewis, I think *Main Street* is a very interesting book. You are surely one of the most promising young writers in the United States." He looked at her, laughed at her, and said, "You go to hell." Gasps, stiffnesses, and, "Really, Mr. Lewis . . ." And Mrs. Lewis, too, became the subject of anecdotes. One story has it that on some occasion when she was introduced as Mrs. Lewis, she turned and exclaimed, "Please, Mrs. *Sinclair* Lewis! Even my dentist says, 'Mrs. *Sinclair* Lewis, spit!' " And it is true enough that she sometimes signed her letters "Grace Sinclair Lewis." And Hendrik Van Loon supposedly put a sign on the second floor of his house that read, "It is forbidden to gossip over three minutes about Grace." They had moved into mythology.

And why not? The novel had been published in October, and before the middle of November, Alfred Harcourt had submitted it to the Secretary of Columbia University as a logical aspirant for a Pulitzer prize for 1921. The jury chairman was Robert Morss Lovett, and his fellow members were Stuart Pratt Sherman and Hamlin Garland. So late as March 1921, Hamlin Garland had not read a novel of the previous year that he felt he could endorse, but already in February he had invited Lewis to tea (Lewis was in Cincinnati and could not accept) and he voted with his fellows that the prize should go to *Main Street*. In May the Trustees of Columbia University overruled the jury and awarded the prize to Edith Wharton for *The Age of Innocence*. On June 22 in the *New Republic* appeared the jury's public protest, signed by the chairman and including Sherman's open letter to the trustees. Then Alfred Harcourt—just before the appearance of *Babbitt*—commissioned Stuart Sherman to write his little booklet on Lewis's "Significance," which was to claim that Lewis was the superior of all his contemporaries, Cabell, Hergesheimer, Dreiser, and of such younger writers like Waldo Frank who were the "lunatic fringe." In January of 1921, before some of these events, which were both to cloud the sun and to heighten the excitement, had taken place, Sinclair Lewis was writing Harcourt urgently suggesting that he find Scandinavian translators and publishers for the book, because there was, after all, the Nobel prize, too. . . . Things were moving in many ways.

Did success spoil Doodle? Almost certainly not. It amazed others, however—others who had known him in his unpromising youth. In January came a letter from old Mr. Lucke of the New Haven *Journal-Courier*.

> *My dear Boy,*
> Just think of it! I myself in touch with one of the great writers of our age who receives highest kind of praise. . . . Wow! . . . I think of the old days when you went out to go to the New Haven High School graduation exercises for the Courier. How little did we think we had a literary genius in our midst!

Less impressed was old Colonel Benét, who nevertheless wrote his son, Stephen, perhaps in some astonishment: "*Main Street* seems to be making money and fame for Harry Lewis. William lunched with him last week." And Upton Sinclair, on January 4, was willing to admit him into an older literary tradition than any in which he belonged:

> It is a lovely job of muckraking—&, you know, I *do* know something about that! A fellow has just sent me a letter telling how *Colliers* is trying to get him to prepare an antidote for yr poison!

There were more mundane enthusiasms. Lewis was lunching with William Rose Benét in New York because he had gone there in response to Harcourt's letter of January 4, which announced that the American Play Company wanted the picture rights to *Main Street* and could produce persons interested in the dramatic rights. On January 15, Lewis sent Harcourt a statement that spelled out the publisher's rights in a stage version of *Main Street,* to be written by Harriet Ford and Harvey O'Higgins for the Shubert brothers, and on January 20 Lewis came to New York again to go to work on the play with Miss Ford and O'Higgins. The work was done at O'Higgins's place near Martinsville, New Jersey—Double Duck Farm, from where Lewis wrote Upton Sinclair to thank him for a copy of *100%—The Story of a Patriot* and to comment on Louise Bryant's "Tragic magnificent story of Jack Reed's death" in *The Liberator*. Adapting *Main Street* to the stage—the three had a play script after about two weeks of work in New Jersey—was in part a matter of softening its social criticism. When the play was produced—like the film of 1923, *I Married a Doctor*—it presented a more clement Gopher Prairie than readers of the novel knew.

The change is not wholly surprising. In early February appeared the article called "The Pioneer Myth" in the New York *Evening Post*. Developing materials from the unpublished "Introduction" to *Babbitt,* Lewis complained of the use of the pioneer myth as an excuse for the lack of imaginative achievement in American life, and protested that his complaint was made not from distaste for but from "a love of Main Street, from a belief in Main Street's inherent power, a belief so strong that the writer is not willing, like the Wild West fictioneers, to insult America by believing that we are all so commonplace that we can find romance only by making believe that we are frontier homicides." And when Carl Van Doren, in his "Revolt of the Village" series, suggested that Lewis hated "all dull people, that is, unintelligent people," Lewis protested:

> In *Main Street,* I certainly do love all of the following people, none of whom could be classed as anything but "dull" (using your own sense of dull as meaning lacking in conscious intelligence): Bea, Champ and Mrs. Perry, Sam and Mrs. Clark, Will Kennicott (dull about certain things though not all), Will's mother, and almost all of the farmer patients. And I love Carol who is dull about all the male world that interests Kennicott. And Guy Pollock who is of only a slight and dilettantish intelligence. And these are about the chief characters.

And when William Woodward wrote him about the novel in January and volunteered that he would rather live in Gopher Prairie than in New York, Lewis replied:

> . . . until you've contentedly stayed in G.P. for at least three years, I shan't believe that you really prefer G.P. Mind you, I *like* G.P., all the G.P.'s; I couldn't write about them so ardently if I didn't.

From the outset, he liked George F. Babbitt, too, and liked him well enough to live with him. Once his work on the play was finished, he returned briefly to Washington and then immediately set out on an extended lecture tour of the Middle West. To Hugh Walpole he wrote, "I am meekly & distantly following in your footsteps as a lecturer (& why in hell should any one not a candidate for B.A. desire to listen to a lecture?)" There was, one need not add, nothing meek about these public appearances, and many people crowded into many auditoriums to listen to the strident exhortations of the new celebrity. He established a *pied-à-terre* at the Queen City Club in Cincinnati, Ohio, and here he consolidated his researches for the new novel. The gray notebooks were already fat with observations, and before he left Washington, his conception was quite clearly fixed. There was still to be some discussion with Alfred Harcourt about the best title for the book. So late as July 1921, Lewis was suggesting as possibilities the following: *Population, 300,000; Good Business; A Good Practical Man; A He-Man; The Booster; A Solid Citizen; Zenith.* But the name of the protagonist, Pumphrey, had changed to Fitch, and Fitch had changed to Babbitt, "commonplace yet will be remembered." Once thought of, *Babbitt* seemed inevitable, "and two years from now we'll have them talking of Babbittry." * Thus in December of 1920. Ten days later he wrote in greater detail:

* The name may have derived from conscious or unconscious echoes of his youth, when Lewis must have seen the widespread advertisements of the B. T. Babbitt Company, manufacturers of household cleansers. B. T. Babbitt is commonly regarded as the founder of national brands.

> He is the typical T.B.M., the man you hear drooling in the Pullman smoker; but having once seen him, I want utterly to develop him so that he will seem not just typical but an individual. I want the novel to be the G.A.N. in so far as it crystallizes and makes real the Average Capable American. No one has done it, I think; no one has even *touched* it except Booth Tarkington in *Turmoil* and *Magnificent Ambersons;* and he romanticizes away all bigness. Babbitt is a little like Will Kennicott but bigger, with a bigger field to work on, more sensations, more perceptions. . . . He is all of us Americans at 46, prosperous but worried, wanting—passionately—to seize something more than motor cars and a house *before it's too late.* Yet, utterly unlike Carol, it never even occurs to him that he might live in Europe, might like poetry, might be a senator; he is content to live and work in the city of Zenith, which is, as everybody knows, the best little ole city in the world. But he would like for once the flare of romantic love, the satisfaction of having left a mark on the city, and a let-up in his constant warring on competitors, and when his beloved friend Riesling commits suicide, he suddenly says, "Oh hell, what's the use of the cautious labor to which I've given everything"—only for a little while is he discontented, though. . . . I want to make Babbitt big in his real-ness, in his relation to all of us, not in the least exceptional, yet dramatic, passionate, struggling.

And to Mencken he was to write that Babbitt was not all boob; but even the boob he found lovable.

He kept his Queen City Club connection for more than a month while he darted in and out of Cincinnati to lecture on current fiction, then spent about a week in Chicago with the same darting, then returned to Washington briefly and, on March 29, lectured in Town Hall in New York and a day or two later in Princeton (where he saw his old Yale professor Robert K. Root, inscribed his copy of *Main Street* "with the affection of one Freshman to whom he gave grapefruit with maraschino cherry & with friendliness," and is reported to have ordered all the guests at a dinner party to remove their shoes), then back to the Middle West for another week of lecturing, then on April 13 shot up to Hamilton, Ontario, to appear before the Women's Canadian Club, then down to New York very briefly, and back to Washington. It was the end of April, the lease on their house was expiring, and for a few weeks the family settled into the Forest Hills Inn on Long Island, where it was proposed to leave Ma*ma* while the three Lewises betook themselves to Europe.

The lecture tour combined field work for *Babbitt* with salesmanship for *Main Street.* "Bully time," he wrote Harcourt from Cincinnati, "met lots of people, really getting the feeling of life here. Fine for *Babbitt,*" and, in the other vein, "I've called on several bookshops, including McClurg's, Marshall Field, Kroch, & become chummy. So this field will, I hope, be more favorable than ever." Wherever he lectured, the stock of *Main Street* was depleted in the shops. A few months later, from England, he wrote Norman Foerster of this period as "a criminally long holiday partly spent in mildly raising hell while lecturing 'round in the U.S. and commending Dreiser and Mencken in Presbyterian Churches and cautious colleges." He was selling contemporary American literature as well as himself.

Reviewing Evelyn Scott's *The Narrow House* in the New York *Times Book Review* in March, he pointed out that a novel so fine as this demonstrates that American fiction can stand proudly beside the best fiction from England. And this was the general theme of his lecture tour. In his Town Hall lecture he attacked New Yorkers for their failure to read, and especially to read native writers, for thinking still that British literature was necessarily superior to American. (Ironically, *Main Street,* which was just then, in early March, being published in England, was reviewed by the *Times Literary Supplement* in three or four inches of icy comment as patronizing to American readers as it was to the book.) Then Lewis would praise the achievements of Dreiser and Anderson and others. He made a point of commending the work of writers who were associated with the community in which he happened to be speaking. Thus, in Milwaukee, Wisconsin, he singled out Zona Gale for his tribute; and received from her a grateful letter:

> What a wonderful thing you did for me in Milwaukee of late. My friends tell me, the Milwaukee papers tell me, and the little home town paper tells me first of all. How very generous you were—oh, much more generous than truthful I know, but I cannot be the less grateful for that.

She writes then enthusiastically of *Main Street,* and concludes,

> Well—thank you for everything—book first and Milwaukee speech next. If I do make them see a Wisconsin hill or two, you have helped them to look, perhaps even to try the hill a bit.

In Omaha, he praised Willa Cather, who was living in Toronto but whose home was Nebraska; and she wrote him in gratitude, saying that the esteem of a few good young writers meant more to her than anything else in her literary efforts.* (It pained him, and her, in the following year, when he was unable wholeheartedly to endorse her next book, *One of Ours,* in a review that he had agreed to write for the New York *Evening Post* before he had seen the book.)

In Indianapolis he balanced his praise for Dreiser with praise for the older and more comfortably native son, Booth Tarkington, but he had the bad luck to be misrepresented by the press. This called for a letter from him:

* The terms of Willa Cather's will make it impossible to reproduce her letters. Those to Sinclair Lewis are in the Lewis Collection in the Yale Library.

> *Dear Mr. Tarkington:*
>
> The enclosed gets my goat. I have been talking about some of the young writers in a number of different cities and in every, or almost every, talk I have said the exact opposite of what is here attributed to me. I have hollered, "When you are considering the clever unknown youngsters, don't ever suppose that because he sells so enormously, Booth Tarkington can't write better than any of them." In slamming the Tired Business Man I have slammed equally the T.B.M.'s wife who supposes that financial success must mean lack of "art." Consequently, it makes me more than a little peeved to have this lie appear.... I don't know whether you'll have seen this thing in the News, and I certainly don't imagine that you care a darn about my opinion, but you see, I do care about yours!

Tarkington had just recently finished work on *Alice Adams,* long thought to be his answer to *Main Street,* and in 1922 *Alice Adams* won the Pulitzer prize.

If Cincinnati was the most important city that Lewis visited for the backgrounds of *Babbitt,* his Chicago stay was important for other reasons. He saw his parents, returning to Minnesota from Florida, in a happy encounter at the home of the Wilmette kin, the happier ultimately because it would prove to be the last occasion on which he was to see his stepmother, who was proud of him and content at last with what he had made of himself. In the city, he was in a high and gregarious mood, making friends on all sides. Robert M. Buck, the editor of a labor paper called *The New Majority,* remembers that

> he would not let any companion spend a penny for food, drink, or anything. He said he was making so much money, newly, that he never could spend it unless he were permitted to pick up all the checks. During that 'play' week of his in Chicago he was in great spirits—riding on the top of the world.

Burton Rascoe remembered a party that serves to illustrate:

> ... there was dancing, and wines and spirits for those who cared for them; Lewis got exhilarated and demonstrated his ability as a "human fly" by climbing out the window and making his way around the three sides of the sunroom on a ledge not more than an inch wide, and then climbing cautiously down the wall to the ground, two stories below, oblivious of the frightened screams and supplications of the women that he desist.

G. K. Chesterton and John Drinkwater were both in the city, and, according to a recollection of Earl E. Fisk in *The Bookman* in 1924, the three literary men, in a haze of alcohol, decided to write a play together, the title devised by Lewis: *Marry the Queen of Scotch.* And Lewis told them that he had been flooded with abusive letters about *Main Street* but that there had been few requests for autographs. He hesitated to autograph books at one shop for fear of offending the others, but he did not hesitate to drop in at Schlogl's, Chicago's "coffeehouse of the literati," the haunt of writers like Ben Hecht, Maxwell Bodenheim, Carl Sandburg, Harry Hansen, Burton Rascoe, Gene Markey, Vincent Starrett, and chide them for their sterile aestheticism. He met and liked and was befriended by H. T. Webster, the cartoonist, and his wife, and he, who had not always been befriended, was grateful:

> Back in Washington . . . It's perfect spring here now, & the crop of Hardings in the White House do not keep the magnolias from gleaming in the grounds . . . I want to thank you for your great graciousness, your manifold hospitalities, in Chicago; & to tell you my hope that I shall see you again before too long.

He met and was befriended by another Chicagoan through whom, in another year, Lewis would meet a man very important to his professional life, Paul de Kruif. Dr. Morris Fishbein, the managing editor of the *Journal of the American Medical Association,* beguiled by Lewis's interest in medicine, had reviewed *Main Street* enthusiastically for the Chicago *Daily News.* Lewis sought out this admirer and was invited to be his house guest in the Fishbein apartment, as he was to be on many later occasions. Dr. Fishbein heard him lecture then and often afterward, and reports that Lewis was not a good lecturer on most occasions. He would talk from inadequate notes and not stay with those, would leap from point to point instead of coherently developing a set of logical propositions, his body meantime leaping about the platform in spasmodic accompaniment. The lecture to the Sunday Afternoon Club of the First Presbyterian Church of Evanston would seem to illustrate the point. He began with an attack on the anti-Semitism of Henry Ford, deduced that Ford's phobia showed that he did not read, and concluded that if Henry Ford had read more in the history of the Jewish race, he would not have frightened people into believing that America was in danger of subjugation by New York Jewish millionaires. From rich men who do not read, Lewis went on to discuss their wives, who do not read either and live in lavish, ostentatious houses. And from that, finally, to the importance of Dreiser, Anderson, Cabell, and company.

Dr. Fishbein makes an interesting distinction between Lewis as lecturer and Lewis as mimic. He could throw himself into a role with complete conviction, but it was the dramatic impulse that was carrying him; when an extended analysis was in order, he floundered unless he was reading from a prepared text. The mimicry carried into his personal relationships; he was not a "sincere" man, but could assume any role he wished in any relationship, could calculate, and did. Then again, his own mercurial moods would serve to trip him in his calculations. But in that exuberant spring of 1921 in Chicago, calculations were not very necessary: everybody was lovely, life was lovely, and the world was a lark.

He was in and out of New York in those last weeks before sailing, and irrepressibly in the *Babbitt* mood. Nathan remembered that his second meeting with Lewis took place one night when he and four or five literary friends had gathered at a restaurant (probably Lüchow's) and Lewis, uninvited, joined them. Nathan described Lewis's generally noisy and messy conduct, spilling beer, knocking plates off the table, and so on, until finally he leaped up on a chair and began a long, stupid monologue in a foolish German accent. Then he broke off the dialect and delivered himself of a long, probably twenty-five-minute Rotarian spiel. Finally, exhausted, he dropped into a chair and waited for some approval of his parody, but only a grim silence followed.

> Concluding by this time that there was nothing to be done about it, the assembled literati decided to make the best of things. One got up and raised his seidel "To our distinguished guest, Sinclair Lewisohn." Another, "To Upon Sinclair, author of *Main Street*." A third observed that it was an honor to have Alfred Henry Lewis present, while a fourth ventured to inquire if the guest could by any chance be May Sinclair.
>
> "Well, anyway, what did you guys think of my speech?"
>
> The answer was a volume of inelegant mouth-noises.

And then, of course, they were to discover in *Babbitt* ("one of the sharpest, most biting satirical and best novels ever written by an American," said Nathan) nearly the identical speech.

Not all his friends treated him so roughly. In his *Diary of Our Own Mr. Pepys,* F.P.A. made this entry for March 31, 1921:

> To the office, and Sinclair Lewis the tayle-writer came to luncheon, and a man at the next table told us how that he liked F. Marion Crawford and Mrs. Humphry Ward and Bulwer Lytton, and that last night he tried to read this *Main Street,* but misliked it greatly; whereat we agreed with him cordially, and S. Lewis said he had heard the book had been wrote by some fellow who pretended to know about the West, albeit he never had been west of the Hudson River. And much more. . . .

In Washington, the British sculptress Clare Sheridan lunched with him at the Shoreham, and her diary entry for April 23 was later to be published (in both the *Times* and the *Metropolitan* magazine) as part of her American impressions. "He is a real Bohemian," she wrote, "full of imagination. One of the few Americans I have met who is not submerged by domesticity, although he is married."

The hubbub over *Main Street* was swelling. Parodies were about to appear, books called *Jane Street* and *Ptomaine Street,* and Donald Ogden Stewart's *Parody Outline of History* would contain a burlesque of it. Negotiations over foreign rights and translations were under way, until ultimately it would be published in a dozen languages. The public quarrel over it continued. In May, the *Times,* for example, published a special article by one Catherine B. Ely that deplored the picture of village life, the dullness of the book ("a muddle of sordid tattle"), and the author's clumsiness: "His capacity for minuteness, plus a lumbering style, makes such a reader (who cares for style) feel as if he were watching an elephant with a teacup—you are afraid he will break it and you wish he would, in order to end a nerve-irritating performance." What matter? Later in the same month the same newspaper would publish an extended interview with the author by W. D. Wagstaffe in which Sinclair Lewis quite blithely associated himself with a new, truth-seeking generation in fiction that included Wilbur Daniel Steele, Zona Gale, Evelyn Scott, and Scott Fitzgerald, experimenters in "the chant of industrial romance," and all primarily concerned with style.

> "I talked about *Main Street* for eight years, till my publisher was convinced that I would never write it. . . . I had written seven novels, all of them mediocre successes. I really wrote eight novels, but one of them I buried in manuscript—it was the story of a stupid man, and I never seemed to get started on the right foot with it, and was out-of-step with the chief character all the time—I wanted to sustain his stupidity, and he kept talking too well."

This was the beginning, and for the rest of his life, Lewis always "talked too well" to reporters—too well for judiciousness, and, often, for the facts. But he liked newspapermen, and he was generous.

At the last moment his generosity included Ma*ma* in the journey abroad, and on May 17 the four of them sailed for Liverpool on the *Carmania.* It was fourteen years since he had last made that voyage under rather different circumstances. Now there were no bales of fodder to lug, no bulls' tails to twist, no stew and plum duff to force down the gullet. Now it was Deck A, it was the captain's table, it was the captain's cocktails and the captain's champagne. It was "class."

3

IN LONDON THE LEWISES took rooms at the Cadogan Hotel in Sloane Street, and out went notes to "connections." That of June 5 to Hugh Walpole was characteristic:

> Behold us in London—for a time at this hotel, then for some months to a country cottage yet undiscovered. I hope that some day we shall see you, but as we are quite admirably busy and amused, please *don't* feel under any slightest compulsion to look us up.

Harcourt had arranged with the London firm of Hodder & Stoughton to import sheets of *Main Street* some months before, and while the novel was by no means the success in England that it was in the United States, it was being read with approval and the reputation of Sinclair Lewis as a critic of American provincialism was established. Sir Ernest Hodder-Williams gave Lewis the name of his tailor, and all of Lewis's incipient dandyism was released for the London whirl that now began with a publisher's luncheon and reception. Van Wyck Brooks has written of the cult of literary dandyism that developed in New York during the 1890s and flourished, together with a certain kind of artificial wit, until the war, when the "care for wit and for dress alike vanished." But it did not vanish for Lewis, who only now was able to fulfill a years-old desire not only for monocle and waistcoats but also for spats and silver-headed cane and, for the country, plus fours. The details of this haberdashery—which left him looking like someone not quite happily dressed for an "occasion"—are reported in *With Love from Gracie,* together with a list of occasions and the persons who were present. Less fully, these latter are reported by Lewis in his letters to Alfred Harcourt.

Almost at once Lewis met Jonathan Cape, who was presently to become his British publisher, and very soon, Sydney S. Pawling, a partner in William Heinemann, and through these and others, scores of writers and public figures. W. L. George helped him to an honorary membership in the Savile Club. To his brother Claude, he wrote, "One of the nicest people I met was old Sir Anthony Hope Hawkins—Anthony Hope—whose *Prisoner of Zenda* and *Rupert of Hentzau* you remember." Harold Laski, Margaret Wycherley, Frank Swinnerton ("My God! Is there anything he *does* like?" Lewis once exclaimed of him), William Robertson Nicoll, Berta Ruck, Ruby Ayres, Clement Shorter, Mrs. Belloc Lowndes, Rose Macaulay, Norman Angell, the Duncan Sisters, the Galsworthys (whom they had seen in Washington), Rebecca West—these were among the miscellaneous many.*

Through John Maynard Keynes, another early Harcourt author, there was even a brief and frosty encounter with Bloomsbury. Mrs. Lewis, depending on Osbert Sitwell's recollection, dates the meeting with Virginia Woolf as of this time, but if it did take place now, certain circumstances in the Sitwell account did not develop until another year. In *Laughter in the Next Room,* Sir Osbert writes of Virginia Woolf's kindness, and then adds,

> She would, I am aware, for I have been present, lay traps for the boastful and the blunted, and greatly she enjoyed the snaring of them (I once had great difficulty in rescuing alive a popular American novelist, whose name was at that time written as a sky-sign round the roofs of Cambridge Circus): but they deserved their fate.

None "of his books . . . was appearing as a serial in a daily newspaper" in that year, as Mrs. Lewis remembered; but *Babbitt,* it is commonly said, was later advertised in this fashion.

The elegant Virginia's response to his insistent garrulity was inevitable. It was, perhaps, the chief impression he made upon the British. Rebecca West said of their first meeting that "his talk was wonderful, but after five solid hours of it I ceased to look upon him as a human being. I could think of him only as a great natural force, like the aurora borealis." Other responses were less cosmic. Mrs. Alfred Knopf remembers the Derby Day dinner at the Bath Club on June 19, when the Lewises "came in very, very late, and old Sydney Pawling, who gave the dinner, had refused to wait longer than twenty minutes and further decided he would keep Red from talking, which Red, of course, always did when he could manage it." This ceaseless volubility was to prevent any genuine intimacy with H. G. Wells. Frank Swinnerton in a recent recollection in *The Saturday Review* recalls that Wells hated noise, and Lewis's endless volubility was noise. This serves to explain Lewis's rather wistful question of Arnold Bennett, as Bennett recorded it in his *Journal:* "How is it I can talk to you and I can't talk to Wells?"—but not, perhaps, Bennett's reply: "Because he is too self-conscious."

* It is doubtful that the anticipated meeting with H. G. Wells took place at this time, since in the following January Lewis wrote Harcourt that he has seen Rebecca West "who is to make me 'quainted with H. G. Wells, when he returns, in about six weeks."

The British condescension was part of their very admiration for him, and they did not hesitate to exploit his volubility. In *One American,* Frazier Hunt writes:

> He painted just the sort of picture of the American scene and its crude intolerances that the average Britisher wanted to read. They welcomed him as one of their own kind—superior, a bit snooty, and extremely critical of inferior breeds.
>
> But Red fooled them. He saw through their own sham and hypocrisy as easily as he could see through a freshly polished pane of glass. When great and near-great tried to patronize his own American self-criticism they were met by a stinging rebuff. Certainly he was not showing up the weakness and intolerance of his own land for the benefit of Englishmen.
>
> The famous bohemian Savage Club asked Lewis to talk at one of their Saturday-night entertainments. . . . Club members naturally expected honeyed phrases for English literature and hopes that some day America might catch up. Instead, Lewis charged them like Pancho Villa's irregular cavalry. He explained that he would like to write a *Main Street* about this self-satisfied and behind-the-times land. He had written *Main Street* for the good of America and not to make his country the misunderstood laughing-stock of a people who were so placid and secure in their own ignorance that they seldom traveled or bothered to keep in touch with other people's points of view and accomplishments.
>
> It left the good ale drinkers aghast. They had never heard such impertinence. But Red made them like it.

His enthusiasm for British writing, now that he was meeting British writers, was unquestionably waning. Presently he wrote to Harcourt to say that "tho the Young British Authors of the Walpole-Mackenzie type have been of great importance, . . . I feel that the Britishers are rather settling down to a great smug contentment with their clever selves," and at the end of the year he was to write in a similar vein to H. L. Mencken. Meeting "the million Bright Young Authors . . . in England," he wrote, "has comforted me about the artistic future of America." Mencken, of course, was delighted and urged him to write an article on the "collapse" of literary England. In August, in response to an American reporter's question, "Why don't you write a novel of the English Gopher Prairie?" he described an experience of the previous month:

> Perhaps I shall, perhaps I shall. But the farther I get from America the more I want to write about my own country. It's surprising how love of your native land seizes you. At a seaside hotel we went to an exhibition by a magician. He did the usual trick of pulling flags out of some receptacle. Finally he pulled out the American flag. "The last to get into the war and the first to get out," he said. To my amazement I found myself standing in the room yelling "Take that back." We had a hot and heavy argument in which I was seconded by an old British admiral. The magician apologized

> and his performance was ended for that night. I want to go back to the United States and live there.

To Harcourt, again, Lewis said, "England *does* make good Americans of us—or rather, not England but the thick English." It was his experience of England rather than of contemporary English literature that induced the change in his views, and presently he was to write to Harcourt that, fine as the visit had been, it had convinced him that England was not a country in which he would care to live.

His most intimate associate was the American, Frazier Hunt.* Hunt sought him out as the result of a cable from Ray Long, then a Hearst editor, that asked Hunt to try to get the next Lewis novel for serialization in *Cosmopolitan.* Hunt was Lewis's exact contemporary, a Midwesterner, a bluff, downright newspaper correspondent, and their friendship was instant, and instantly on a first-name basis. "We mixed like Scotch and soda," Hunt remembers all too aptly, for Lewis's drinking was heavier now, and the two of them became the most congenial of drinking companions. They developed a genuine affection for one another and their conversation was a real exchange. Hunt remembered Lewis talking bitterly to him for hours about his early life—his meager childhood, tyrannical father, the bullying town boys, with the only kind word for his stepmother.

> Often in London I would chide him for his eternal fault-finding and his intolerant attitude toward a poor and faltering world. "Don't you understand," he answered me one evening when we were comfortably ensconced before my own fireplace in Portsea Place, "don't you understand that it's my mission in life to be the despised critic, the eternal faultfinder? I must carp and scold until everyone despises me. That's what I was put here for."

When Hunt complained of the picture of the Midwest in *Main Street,* Lewis urged him to write a novel about his side of Main Street. He helped him plot it and together they found the title, *Sycamore Bend,* and when it was finished, Lewis gave it to Harcourt, Brace & Company, which published it. Lewis did everything he possibly could for it, short of actually writing it, and when it appeared he wrote the editor of the Sauk Centre *Herald,* urging Main Streeters to read it, and the letter appeared in the top center of the front page over Asa Wallace's editorial signature. This generosity reminds one of Forster's "It is better to receive than to give" when we put it beside Hunt's further recollection of Lewis as a "strange man, who seemed to spend half his time fighting his own intolerances and shortcomings."

> In many ways he was a spoiled boy. He always had to be the center of the stage. He could brook no other hero. There was a strong streak of the actor

* Foreign correspondent for *Cosmopolitan* and other Hearst periodicals, Frazier ("Spike") Hunt appears in *Half a Loaf* as Solon ("Solo") Richardson, foreign correspondent for *The Circle,* who "dismissed Susan at once as a wife."

in his make-up, too. Times without number I have seen him impersonate a little German professor of philosophy; again, with his head wrapped in a bath towel, he would become an Indian yogi; with a false mustache he would be the villain about to rape the village hired girl. And I shall never forget an evening at the home of the famed literary agent, Curtis Brown, when in blank verse Red improvised a complete saga of the winning of the West: the covered wagon trains, the start from Independence, the fording of the Platte, the Indian attack, the death of the baby, the wagon wheels grinding over the grave, the arrival in the rich lands of Oregon Territory. It was moving and beautiful. No one else in the world could extemporaneously have equaled it in drama and pathos. It was Lewis the artist, the imaginative American, exalted lover of his own land and its history. I was never so proud of him as I was at that moment.

Soon after his arrival in England, he had written to an American very different from Frazier Hunt—Edith Wharton—to congratulate her on winning the Pulitzer prize; and on August 6 she replied.

Your letter touched me very deeply; and I should have told you so sooner if it hadn't gone to America (where I have not been since the war), & then travelled back to me here.

What you say is so kind, so generous, & so unexpected, that I don't know where to begin to answer. It is the first sign I have ever had—literally—that "les jeunes" at home had ever read a word of me. I had long since resigned myself to the idea that I was regarded by you all as the—say the Mrs. Humphry Ward of the Western Hemisphere; though at times I wondered why. Your book & *Susan Lenox* (unexpurgated) have been the only things out of America that have made me cease to despair of the republic—of letters; so you can imagine what a pleasure it is to know that you have read *me,* & cared, & understood. It gives me a "Nunc Dimittis" feeling—or would, if I hadn't still about a hundred subjects to deal with!

As for the Columbia Prize, the kind Appletons have smothered me in newspaper commentary; & when I discovered that I was being rewarded—by one of our leading Universities—for uplifting American morals, I confess I *did* despair.

Subsequently, when I found the prize sh[oul]d really have been yours, but was withdrawn because your book (I quote from memory) had "offended a number of prominent persons in the Middle West," disgust was added to despair.—Hope returns to me, however, with your letter, & with the enclosed article, just received.—Some sort of standard *is* emerging from the welter of cant & sentimentality, & if two or three of us are gathered together, I believe we can still save Fiction in America.

I wish I could talk to you of all this. Is there no chance of your coming to Paris? I'm only half an hour away.—If not, let me at least tell you again how many hopes your book & your letter have waked in me. Believe me yrs. very sincerely

E. Wharton

He would go to Paris presently, and presently he would lunch with her, and there would be more involvement than that, but for the time being, the Lewises were interspersing their activities in London with excursions into the country by train and rented motor in search of a house. Frank V. Morley, then a student, remembers Lewis's arrival at Oxford—sent by his brother, Christopher Morley, and demanding a guided tour. They searched in all directions, and the house that took their fancy was in Kent, in Bearsted, near Maidstone, an early sixteenth-century establishment that would be ready for their occupancy on August 1. At Hugh Walpole's suggestion, they decided to spend July in South Cornwall, and so took rooms in the Poldhu Hotel in Mullion, on the sea.

To Harriet Ford, who was scheduling rehearsals for *Main Street,* he wrote on July 1 about the enchanting air, the glorious view, the dull guests. And of course he was faithfully reporting each week to his parents, unaware for nearly a month that his stepmother had died on June 14.

It did not occur to the thrifty folk in Minnesota to cable him, and it was, in fact, more than a week later that the old doctor wrote a short note:

> *Dear Harry:—*
> The unexpected came on Tuesday the 14th at 3 a.m. Your mother who had been sleeping awakened me at 2:30 a.m. complaining of great distress over her stomach & a dreadful air hunger and begged me to do something to release her. So rapid was dissolution that she was gone in 25 minutes and before I could get anything to act. . . . When we had the last visit in Wilmette I felt sure it was the last for one or both of us. . . . I don't feel much like writing and Claude has promised to give you all the particulars.

That letter reached the Lewises in Cornwall on July 7. Mrs. Lewis wrote next day and expressed her gratitude for all that the doctor's wife "gave to Hal, which has made him so wonderful a husband and friend." Lewis, who had cabled at once to earnestly invite his father to join them in England, wrote him on the next day, too:

> It is as hard for me as it must be for you to realize that Mother is gone. No matter how far away I have been, she has always been there, an eternal fact, to be thought of; a memory weekly renewed, in the hundreds and hundreds of letters we have exchanged since I first went off to school. I do think that her life was a triumph, not only in all the things she did for all of us at home, the incessant influence for fineness she brought to bear, but also in her influence on the town, and indeed on the whole state. I still remember her first quiet but determined influences on everything from the women's club and the Eastern Star to the meat the butchers handed out in the stores—the way in which she wouldn't let them put it over on her. I hope, Lord how I hope, that she had a lot of pleasure, in her last days, out of the *Main Street* success, and saw in it her own teachings. . . . It seems so strange not to be telling mother all the news, too—there will be several

letters etc. coming for her which started after her death—I hope, terribly, that it will not hurt you to have them coming for her.

The doctor replied to the cable with composure:

Cablegram received this noon. Thanks for your invitation to come to you in England but that would not be best for me just now, and I want to have a good time this fall in Canada or Dakotas hunting ducks. I have also to probate will of your Mother and that will take several months. I think I wrote you that the Roterts have moved into our house and are taking fine care of me and it leaves me with my old room all the furniture and things going on just as they have for years.

Three days later, his father wrote him again:

Some people from Ft. Smith Arkansas stopped for an hour and wanted to know all about you and *Main St.* and I gave them the best spice I knew. Am anxious to have you get at work again as I want to see the new one before I get a call and I hope it will go as well as *Main Street.*

The next day Lewis replied. He reported that Grace had gone off to Somerset with her mother to look up any remaining relatives that they might be able to find, and that he was playing nursemaid to Wells and was at work on the planning of his novel. On the same day he wrote Alfred Harcourt:

He's started—*Babbitt*—and I think he's going to be a corker. I've been working on him for a week now, mostly, of course, turning notes into a final plan, but also writing a little, and I find him coming out firm and real.

He was working every morning and a few hours in the afternoon, and the Harcourt letters are full of requests for "research materials" having to do with real estate and advertising. The writing of *Main Street* had been quite different, and it may be conjectured that the difficulties Lewis had in writing it (it by no means "wrote itself") arose from the fact that the "research" for that novel consisted almost entirely of an unsought experience. But with *Babbitt* began the method that was to characterize his composition from now on: full biographies of all the leading characters; a "field"—in this instance, real estate—to master; elaborately detailed maps of the setting, Zenith; floor plans and furnishings of houses; a complete scenario of the action, step by step. When all this preliminary work was done, the novel would, in effect, "write itself." Most of this work was behind him when the Lewises left Cornwall on July 28, and in Kent he would sail breezily into his first draft.

They were to have this house for two months. Called the Bell House ("this utterly charming half-timbered Elizabethan cottage," wrote Lewis), it stood at one end of the common, with the village tavern at the other, a row of houses between the two, and, on a hill behind, a church with portions dating back to the eleventh century. Surrounded by hop fields, magnificent woods and, a few miles away, the softly rising North Downs, Bearsted was, Lewis would presently complain, "almost too peaceful a spot for writing. . . . This is a lazy country. It gets into your blood. Each day you feel less and less inclined to work." But that was after six weeks and 75,000 words.

He wrote at once to his father, giving him a long description of their arrival and of the Bell House; of Mrs. Hegger's plan to return to the United States on August 5 and of the consequent need for a governess (one ad in the London *Times* brought fifty-five responses).

> Miss Pohlman[n] (her family came from Germany to England in 1760) . . . young, crisp, fresh, beautifully casual, the nicest of girls, yet excellently trained, with normal school education, and five straight years of teaching . . . and if she works out as well as we hope, you'll see her when we come back to America. . . .

In a less domestic vein he wrote to Harriet Ford about the progress of the play, which had been successfully tried out by an Indianapolis stock company in support of the principals and was about to move east, and to Alfred Harcourt about his working day, "from about 9 A.M. to 4:30." To Norman Foerster he wrote on July 30, "I shan't dare to stir from here for at least a month." But when, on August 9, Harold Stearns arrived to spend the night, the two decided to go to Paris next day.

> Sinclair said he had been working hard . . . kept on reiterating that he needed a bit of rest. "Fine," I said at length, "why don't you knock off for a few days and take me for a little trip with you over to Paris? I know the ropes; you'll have a good time. And I'll introduce you to some nice people. Probably it will do your work good, too."
>
> Anyway, we did it—Sinclair providing me with a few extra clothes, for I had not brought down anything except overnight things from London. It was the first time he had ever been on the Continent, let alone to Paris, and he was as excited as a young man donning his first pair of long trousers. There was no sleeping either in the train down to the boat, on the boat, or on the French "rapide" that took us swiftly to Paris. Whenever and wherever we could lay hands on a brandy or a whiskey, we did so. We arrived so groggy and sleepy that there was nothing for us to do for the first few hours but go to a hotel—I think it was the "Oxfort et Cambridge," not far from the Rue Royale off the Rue de Rivoli—and get some rest. After a snooze and a cold shower, Sinclair was ready for any great adventure that Paris had to offer. I rang up Lewis Galantière, and asked him to come to my aid and help me pilot Sinclair around—which he graciously did. It was as hectic a five days and nights [to Harcourt, Lewis confessed to only three days on August 16], as I have ever put in; Sinclair was full of vitality. He wanted to go everywhere at once, to see everything, to visit every bar, explore the "Quarter"—and we cut quite a dash in Montparnasse

those few nights, too. How much he saw, or remembered, of historical Paris that first visit might be put into a very small page of a very small notebook. . . .

Yet most things have to come to an end, and Sinclair's vitality was not inexhaustible, though sometimes it seemed so to me during those five days and nights, when even two hours of sleep was the exception. He had to get back to England. . . . But, he pointed out to me, why should I have to go back? He would lend me any money I needed, and I could write for my things and have them sent on or brought over from London. I said that would be great. . . . And so it was arranged.

If neither Harold Stearns nor Sinclair Lewis had any clear recollection of those days and nights, Malcolm Cowley did, and recorded it in Brentano's *Book Chat* a few years later under the title "Garçong! Garçong!" On an August evening Lewis, armed with the silver-headed cane, arrived at the Dôme. He "made his way to our table . . . slumped into a chair," and began to pound the table with the head of the cane.

"Garçong! Come here, you bloody garçong! . . . Garçong! The lazy Frog. Let me tell you, they'd give us better service in Zenith. Gentlemen, have you ever been in the Zenith Athletic Club? Say, that's a swell joint for you." . . . he was acting the part of his principal character: the naivety, philistinism, nasal sing-song and all the rest of it.

Cowley, who had himself been in Paris for only a few months, was amused by him, even though he did not have the clue to his performance.

His eyes were very large and very round, with an expression which might be mistaken for stupidity. They made me think of folklore. Every fairy-book hero has eyes like these; he is taken for an idiot, and mistreated by his elder brothers, and sent bare-handed into the world to seek his fortune, but he proves the wiliest of them all. Invariably, he marries the King's daughter.

That night at the Dôme, Lewis was not wily, but merely drunk and outgoing. A journalist tried to interview him, and every reply was made as if Babbitt were a novelist. Meanwhile, Lewis bought round after round of drinks for the assemblage, and everyone became so thoroughly befuddled that next day no one remembered what had happened after the interview. But an impression had been made on "that real Parisian bunch."

They were curious traveling companions, Stearns and Lewis, for Lewis was in his new pro-American mood and Stearns had just turned in to his publisher that collective indictment called *Civilization in the United States.* "Great time," Lewis wrote Harcourt when he was back in Kent, "pure but wet." And added, as though he were quite in a position to know, "Watched Stearns with care, and he isn't half so shaky and drunken as we said. . . . I think he will have an ever widening future. I'm for him." But not for long.

In the Bearsted house again, "beautifully sure" of what he was doing, he returned with zeal to *Babbitt.* There were few interruptions. Carlton Miles, a friend and the drama critic of the Minneapolis *Journal,* arrived and stayed long enough to collect his impressions of the house, the village, the countryside, and Lewis's work for a newspaper story, and Lewis wrote a letter to John Drinkwater in London, asking him to see Miles. Drinkwater was invited to dinner but could not accept. He arrived one day, however, with Algernon Blackwood and Henry Ainley, the actor, and through him the Lewises were to meet some of the local gentry who responded with mild and pleasantly dull entertainments. The hop-picking season was on and Lewis amused himself by observing the transient workers who had come down from London and thronged over the fields, and he reported the phenomenon in detail to his father. Donald Brace arrived, convalescing from an illness, and they took him to Canterbury on the last day of August. There they met Mary Austin in the street and she proposed that she take them to meet G. B. Shaw who was at Herne Bay, ten miles away. They chatted with him for two hours. A week later, when Lewis went up to London to see Donald Brace there, he sought out a wigmaker and bought a number of props that would enable him to include Shaw and other bearded persons in his repertoire.

Most of these happenings—even a call from the vicar—he faithfully reported to his father in his weekly letters. He was worried that his father was lonely, and a request for his biography from the *National Cyclopedia of American Biography* gave him, he thought, an opportunity to fill his father's idle hours. He asked if his father could send him the "name of the first Lewis who came to America; from what place in Wales he came, when he landed here, just where he landed, what he did, etc." From this he went on:

> All of this (so far as you know it) will only take a little while to write out, but it leads me to an interesting suggestion. Do you realize that IF I go on with other books as with *Main Street,* there are likely to be biographies of me some day, and for that there will be a need of all sorts of ancestral information? And besides myself, out of your lively and enterprisin' descendants, there are likely to be others besides myself who'd like this information? You have plenty of time, and you write well—so why don't you make a brief biography.
>
> Start with the above; give the data about ALL of our ancestors—Kermott as well as Lewis—so far as you know it; with the Johnson and White and other lines—giving definite dates and occupations and residences and the like so far as you know them or can find them out.
>
> Then give a fuller sketch of your father, his father, and his mother's family on both sides; his birthplace, boyhood, education, various occupations, California adventure, etc. etc. right up to his death. Your sisters and what became of them, and their families. Then same with your mother and

> her family, and yr father's brothers & sisters. Then, much more fully, yourself—birth, boyhood, education, and so on; and same with both Emma Kermott (and her father and mother and brothers and sisters) and with Isabel Warner. Then the early life of your 3 sons. Get in all facts in Family Bible.
>
> All of this could be made as full as you desired—and I rather fancy you'd find it interesting to write out, besides the skeleton facts, many anecdotes of your early life, of your father, etc. etc. I can fancy, for an example, your rather enjoying recalling your study with Dr. Flynn [Fluin] at Redwood Falls; and your first school teaching. The fuller the better. But contrariwise, if you get bored, give at least the basic data. . . .
>
> About this biography, remember that I am in some danger of becoming the best-known American writer—I suppose I am now, already, one of the dozen or fifteen best-known of living American writers—and for future uses it will be rather necessary.

It was an ambitious project that Lewis was proposing to an old, nonwriting man, and one that the father was not disposed to pursue. He sent Lewis the skeletal information from the family Bible as copied out by Mrs. Rotert, said that he did not care to look farther back than his grandfather, and added that some day he would tell him why.

In September there was at least one more journey up to London, this time to dine with Harvey O'Higgins and his wife, and to talk about the stage version of *Main Street,* the New York opening of which was imminent. Peggy Wood had been taken out of the play after Indianapolis, but Stuart Walker, whose company had performed it there, had come to New York to stage it at the National Theater, with Alma Tell as Carol and McKay Morris as Kennicott. The New York cast was to open out of town on September 28, and Lewis was in excited correspondence with Harriet Ford, who had remained with the play. She wrote him about the possibility of three companies—the New York company, a Chicago company and a road company—and Lewis was certain that all three would do well. To his father he wrote on the night before they left England, "I'll make somewhere between $0.00 and $200,000.00 on it!!" * And in that same letter of September 29, he announced that they were leaving for Paris on the Folkestone–Boulogne boat at noon next day.

> . . . we shall probably have a stirring time in ancient and sun-gilded Italy . . . Italy! It sounds incredible . . . I remember still, from Vergil, when the

* The play did not thrive. It opened on October 5, and Alexander Woollcott in the *Times* next day found it "a surprisingly good dramatization of a singularly difficult novel, though it did leave unanswered the question as to why they wished to dramatize it at all." His review reverted to the question of how one is supposed to take Carol, and while Woollcott had no doubt that Lewis meant us to take her seriously, the dramatization left no doubt that "Carol Kennicott is the perfect fool." The part was badly played by Alma Tell, but McKay Morris did splendidly as Kennicott. The play ran until December 17.

wandering sailors awakened early and, looking out to sea, perceiving the land that had been hidden by night, cried, "Italia! Italia!"

If Paris had been more gaily receptive of the Lewises than it proved to be, their trek on to Pallanza on Lake Maggiore might have been put off longer than the two weeks that they now gave to France. *Main Street* was not yet known to the French, and the Americans in Montparnasse were not to be impressed—rather the contrary—by Lewis's success and his background of *The Saturday Evening Post.* He was no doubt made more comfortable by the newspapermen who frequented Harry's New York Bar than by the poets and painters at the Dôme and the Select. He found congenial company in Ernest Brace, his publisher's brother, and urged him to come to Italy with his wife. There were few Ernest Braces in Paris, but the Left Bank in this year saw its greatest influx of expatriate Americans. It was the year in which Sherwood Anderson was writing letters of introduction for the Hemingways to Gertrude Stein and Sylvia Beach and others and the Hemingways were to settle in; but the Lewises had no letters. Lewis had written his own letter to Edith Wharton, and they were invited to lunch at the Pavillon Colombe in St.-Brice-sous-Forêt. There was, Mrs. Lewis reports, an encounter with James Joyce and Nora Barnacle throughout which Joyce said not a word. Through George Slocombe, they met Edna St. Vincent Millay and with her enjoyed a dinner that, again according to Mrs. Lewis, was a frosty failure.

But the major fiasco occurred when the disguises provided by the London wig man were pressed into play. This occasion, as reported by William Woodward in his 1934 *New Yorker* profile, was the interview with André Siegfried, the French interpreter of American culture to Frenchmen. The appointment had been made well in advance; Siegfried and a colleague were to wait on Lewis at his hotel on a certain day. The day came and Lewis spent the morning and early afternoon in bars. When he came to his hotel he summoned a friend to come to his assistance, and when the friend arrived, he found Lewis teetering in the middle of the room, telephone still in hand. Announcing that he would be all right after a half hour's nap, he retired to his bedroom and left his friend to receive the French delegation. When it arrived, the friend said that the novelist was resting after a day of arduous artistic labor but would appear very soon. Time passed; Siegfried grew restive; the friend entered the bedroom; Lewis was still sleeping soundly. Further apologies, increasing restiveness, awkwardness, until suddenly the bedroom door opened. Then an old man with a white beard, side whiskers, metal-rimmed spectacles, and a cane, tottered into the room and introduced himself in quavering nasal tones as Dr. E. J. Lewis, who had come to Paris to visit his son. The Frenchmen, having no reason to doubt him, tried to talk to him in his language, until suddenly he leaped up and whipped off his disguise. The guests were not amused and, after a chilly interview, departed.

Immediately after this interview, Lewis Galantière remembers, he arrived to call on Lewis. Lewis was drunk again. Siegfried, he said, had called him the American Flaubert, and with that he launched into a long tirade against American critics. Loudly and bitterly he complained that they underestimated him as an artist; oh yes, certainly, they talked about his "good ear," but they never talked about his *art*. Drunkenly he embraced Galantière, a much shorter man than Lewis, embraced him, clung to his shoulders, would not let go of him as he shouted that he was an artist like Flaubert, hadn't Siegfried said so, hadn't he heard what Siegfried said? He was just as good as Flaubert, he was an artist, an *artist,* and *no* American knew it!

So, on October 15, off to Pallanza! There, waiting, were the familiar, friendly Minnesotan, Claude Washburn, and his Italian wife. And Lewis was to get back to *Babbitt*.

They established themselves in four rooms on the top floor of the Hotel Eden, about a half mile from the town, and on October 18 Lewis wrote to both Harcourt and his father to describe the delights of the place—the incomparable scenery, the boating, the walks and cycling, the food and the service. Four times a week he took an Italian lesson and on November 1 he told his father that he could buy tickets "for the small steamships which serve these lake towns like trolley cars, and I can buy cigarettes and postal cards, but not much else yet! It's coming fast, though, and I enjoy it. . . ." He urged Drinkwater, by post card, to come and join them and "sit & dream & be great," and in a little over two weeks, he wrote 15,000 more words. But there were shadows. In the same letter, of November 5, he told Harcourt that "We're awfully well and happy" and he instructed him to send no more mail to Pallanza since he was about to leave for Rome.

He had been much upset by the appearance of Carl Van Doren's article in *The Nation* which had dismissed his early work as frippery. The most offensive sentence was, "Before *Main Street,* Mr. Lewis had belonged to the smarter set among American novelists, writing much bright, colloquial, amusing chatter to be read by those who travel through books at the brisk pace of vaudeville"; and Lewis wrote Van Doren an interminable letter that challenged him to *read* that early work, including a good many of the *Post* stories.* He also wrote Harcourt, urging him to do something about the matter. "I think he ought to do an entirely new article about me in the *Nation*."

* Van Doren reprinted this letter in *Three Worlds* (1936), and the two men had by then been good friends for a long time. He conceded that Lewis was right and rewrote the article for its appearance in the book, *Contemporary American Novelists: 1910–1920* (1927).

Ward Brown, an architect they had known in Washington, joined the group, and a blond American girl, whose presence upset Mrs. Lewis. When the girl left, "so did Hal—to find a home for the winter, he said." The departure took place on October 12, and he wrote from the Grand Hôtel de Russie, in Rome, to describe the trip to his father:

> I came down here just at the tail end of the four-day strike and street-rioting (seven killed and scores wounded) which followed clashes between the Fascisti and the Communisti. The so-called communisti are workmen, union men, very few of whom are really socialists at all; and the Fascisti are a kind of American Legion, but much more violent—bunch of young men who love a fight and are always picking one in the name of—oh, of anything handy. Ten thousand of them descended on Rome for an alleged convention, and simply raised hell, and the workers retaliated by striking—railroad men, newspaper workers, bakers, taxi drivers, the whole outfit. I got through all right, baggage and all, except that my train from Milan supposedly running thru to Rome was taken off at Florence at three in the morning, and from that hour till 6:30 A.M. I walked the streets, with an occasional cup of coffee in an all-night dive. Mysterious, quite exciting; and when at last I came to the Piazza di Duomo—the cathedral square—and saw Giotto's famous bell-tower thrust up against a paling sky of coming dawn, I wanted to shout. And I went to early morning mass in the Cathedral—first time I've ever done that, and darned likely to be the last.
>
> On another train at 6:30 and got to Rome at noon, breakfasting on sausage sandwiches I bought along the road. Arrived to find the station guarded with soldiers, bayonets out, and not a taxi or carriage in sight, and no one to meet me. So I figured out the streets from my Baedeker and with no trouble at all walked up to the Ward Brown's hotel after checking my bags.
>
> Next day everything was running as usual. . . .

A few days after he had gone, his wife and child and Miss Pohlmann followed him as far south as Florence, where they stayed until he wired them that he had found rooms at the Russie and eagerly anticipated their arrival. He had found rooms, but his were at the opposite side of the hotel from theirs, and the blonde was to cause trouble. The marriage was coming apart.*

So, even while he was writing George Sterling in late December that "It's far lovelier than England, George, this old-new Rome of gardens & secret ways; & far stranger," he was already contemplating a further separation. Lewis's philandering, his frenetic pursuit of pretty young women, was to become a commonplace of literary gossip, but it sprang

* It would require five years of angry spats and stubborn refusals and sudden flingings in and out and remorseful attempts at reunion and again drunken recriminations and further abrupt departures to complete the process. The fictionalized account in *Half a Loaf* is much more detailed and explicit than that in *With Love from Gracie,* if there should be readers who are interested.

not so much from any physical need as from the psychological need for uncritical adulation. His enormous vitality was nervous, not sexual. A few years later when two friends, a man and a woman, were summoned to his apartment to help him, in an impossible state of drunkenness, to the hospital, they looked about for a small bag in which to put his overnight things, and they found a bag of the right size stuffed full of "nostrums" for the increase of sexual prowess. One may look beyond the irony of the exposer of frauds himself succumbing to them, to the pathos of the man who wistfully hopes to live up to his own show.

Young women liked him. After a moment's revulsion, they forgot his ugliness and yielded to his charm; to this phenomenon there are many witnesses. It puzzled Carl Van Vechten, for one; he remembers seeing Lewis in places like the lobby of the Algonquin, surrounded by what seemed to be as many as fifteen or sixteen pretty girls, all fascinated. Van Vechten liked him well enough (and Lewis liked Van Vechten's novels), but he was more aware of his limitations than of his charm. It was difficult to see him alone, he says, because there could be no real conversation: the show-off always tried to take over. It was equally difficult to see him in the company of other people because of his unpredictability: either he would sit morosely in a corner and make everyone uneasy, or he would begin one of his interminable imitations and bore everyone to death. But the "everyone" did not apply to a good many young women.

In his correspondence, in November, he was addressing himself to an older woman, Edith Wharton, with the request to dedicate *Babbitt* to her. She replied:

> I am a little dizzy! No one has ever wanted to dedicate a book to me before—& I'm so particularly glad that now it's happened, the suggestion comes from the author of *Main Street*.
>
> *Yes*—of course!
>
> I'm glad, too, to have your address, for in the throes of leaving St. Brice, I mislaid your letter, & couldn't remember where to send my friend Percy Lubbock's book, *The Craft of Fiction,* which is full of interesting & suggestive things for people of our trade. . . .

This book, which derives its critical dicta from the practice of Henry James, could hardly have been of use to Sinclair Lewis, as his talent had developed. Yet Lewis was not above quite unlikely literary associations. There was his admiration for Edith Wharton herself. There was his present interest in the little magazine called *Broom,* which Harold Loeb had brought to Rome together with Alfred Kreymborg to assist him. Loeb, long thought to be the prototype of Robert Cohn in *The Sun Also Rises* (Lewis was also to find a place in the Hemingway galaxy) and known as "Low-Ebb" to the young Americans in Paris, received an early subscription from Lewis: "*Broom* seems to me not only to have the originality for which we had hoped but also a workmanlike solidity which promises that it will go on, and be significant. . . ." Kreymborg received a challenging call at the palazzo where the office of *Broom* had been set up.

> One of the first to stride straight in was the long-legged, red-headed author of *Main Street,* Sinclair Lewis. The novel was then at the zenith of its popularity, and no one was more flabbergasted at its reception than the man from Minnesota. He had come to Rome with the air of a bewildered conqueror, and finding Krimmie [Kreymborg himself] in his path, walked up to him with the unexpected query: "Hello, what do you mean by attacking *Main Street?"*
>
> It devolved that Lewis had read about an address Krimmie had delivered at The Dutch Treat Club in New York just before his departure for Europe. The topic of his talk for this famous group of journalists had been The Sunny Side of Main Street. Krimmie assured the novelist the speech had been a defense of Main Street itself and not an attack on the book. Lewis could not be convinced that anything good could come from such a street, and the two men, the one from a remote small town, the other from the metropolis of American cities, argued from positions that had become comically juxtaposed. The novelist was a more accomplished dialectician than the poet and delivered himself with so much speed and gusto that the latter resigned the argument—as he usually did anyhow—and parted with the skyrocket on comparatively friendly terms. Lewis had descended on Rome . . . and rented a magnificent suite in that most luxurious of hotels, the De Russie. It was a strange *denouement . . .*

Recently Harold Loeb has recorded, perhaps disingenuously, a recollection of several Lewis evenings in Rome:

> The next time I saw Lewis, I invited him over for cocktails to meet Blaise Cendrars, who was back in Rome with his *petite amie* and wanted to translate *Main Street* into French. I had hoped to do Sinclair a favor, but the party was a flop. Both Cendrars and Lewis insisted on holding forth in loud voices at the same time. Lily [Loeb's friend, Hemingway's "Frances"] found it difficult to get a word in. Foiled in their attempts to drown each other out, the "tom-cats," as Lily called them, drank too much. Then Lewis discovered that Cendrars did not like to speak German. Thenceforth he would speak nothing else, except, from time to time, to sing a verse from "Barnacle Bill the Sailor." Through it all, Blaise's little friend continued to chat with Lily in a ladylike voice about the weather.
>
> Perhaps Lewis felt he had been inconsiderate, for a few days later, when Gracie arrived . . . he invited us to dinner. In evening dress and silver slippers, Gracie exhibited the shining shoulders which Ford Madox Ford, some ten years later, remembered as the most beautiful in the world. . . .
>
> Asked to suggest a good restaurant, I recommended the Ulpia, an ancient grotto near Trajan's Column, which served good food and local red wine. From a row of niches up near the dome portrait busts of the old inhabitants looked down upon the dining parvenus with calm disdain.

> At first I didn't know what was wrong with Red. Instead of being the life of the party, he was subdued, apologetic. And Gracie proceeded to pick on him; she was contemptuous of his Midwestern mannerisms. I thought Lewis would explode, but he didn't. We managed to get dinner ordered. Then Gracie, assuming that Lily came from Greenwich Village, harped on the "cruelty of village intellectuals." Lily tightened her lips and looked hard at the silverware.
>
> Everything went wrong, even the food. The breaded turkey cutlet tasted as if it had been cooked for luncheon. Red did not like the wine although I thought it superior to his favored Chianti. Grace flatly contradicted everything he said.
>
> Thinking a bit of "side" might help, I asked Gracie if she had run into Irene Castle in London. Gracie came back with Edith Wharton and told us about having had tea with her in Paris. Lily couldn't stand it any longer. She opened up with the Prince Yussupov and the Grand Duke Dmitri, Rasputin's murderers, whom we had met in a night club two nights before—they were drinking champagne bottoms-up as if it was vodka. Lily was magnificent. She kept on talking, and the evening ended.
>
> And so, eventually, did the Lewis marriage. That night I wondered how much of Red's contempt for small-town life was due to Gracie. Could it be that Red was blind to the stuffiness of Carol Kennicott because she resembled his own wife?

Perhaps less so, after such a charming evening as this, than once.

On several occasions Lewis saw Edna St. Vincent Millay to talk about her projected novel, for he was really acting as a manuscript scout for Harcourt, Brace & Company. The Ernest Braces arrived from Paris. And Edgar Ansel Mowrer and his wife sought him out. Mrs. Mowrer leaves the recollection:

> "Who are you?" called a loud voice, as Edgar knocked at the door of a room at the Hotel de Russie in December, 1921.
>
> "I am the Middle West, and you are my prophet," shouted Edgar.
>
> "Come in, Middle West," answered Sinclair Lewis. He was working on *Babbitt* that winter, writing steadily from early morning till teatime, as is his custom. He is an indefatigable worker, and Zenith, the scene of his novel, was a real city to him. He had rolls of maps with every section of it planned and drawn to scale. He knew the history of each one of its inhabitants and could have written three books from the material he had prepared for one.

The Mowrers introduced him to the *trattoria* Al Vero Alfredo, which became one of his favorite restaurants and which he put into *Babbitt* as the Roman haunt of that Zenith cosmopolitan, Lucille McKelvey.

This was about the extent of his literary associations in Rome, and he wrote Mencken nostalgically about native American writing and abusively of the expatriates.

> As to the innumerable young Americans who are here now—in London, Paris, Rome—planning to Live in the Mellow Old Atmosphere while yet being Native to the Manure of Michigan—and incidentally to shoot the good drinks that thank God still amiably abound—I find none at all who strike me as doing anything. They sit and talk—GOD—like the old Brevoort. And where they do anything it's for the dinky little magazines of Finer Things. . . .

In a postscript, he proposed to found a Young Men's Atheist Association and wondered whether the Young Men would celebrate Christmas. He celebrated his own Christmas at a studio party "with reasonable amounts of drinks & dancing & nice Americans & Italians." It is at a studio party in *Half a Loaf* that Timothy Hale kisses the blonde within the range of Susan's watchful eye.

In that novel, the character of Andrea Vengo, an archaeologist who takes the Hales on an excursion to Ostia, is apparently drawn after the man they saw most frequently in Rome, Raffaello Piccoli. Lewis wrote his father about a similar excursion on December 17: ". . . perhaps the best day of all our European stay! . . . Gracie and I and Professor Piccoli. . . . He's the professor of English in the University of Pisa. . . . He's only about 36, very amusing, best of companions."

To Eldon James he wrote six weeks later:

> There we veritably walked through Rome of two thousand years ago and afterward we had lunch on a terrace overlooking the Mediterranean and drank at least enough of native wine and fed sphagetti to ten excessively well-bred dogs. (Did you ever feed a dog sphagetti? It is the most delicate and interesting amusement I have ever encountered.)

New Year's Day they spent with Piccoli on the Appian Way, and this excursion led him to tell his father:

> Italy is so lovely, so charged with history while always, too, lively and real with a life of today; and the people, especially the servants and the small shop-keepers, are so friendly, so skilful, and so beautiful!

Piccoli's book on *Croce* was to be published by Harcourt in the coming year, and Lewis asked Harcourt to "give it an extra big boost for me." Most of these letters, of course, are about his own work—past, in progress, and to come.

Main Street has been sold to the movies for forty thousand dollars and Lewis suggests that it now be advertised as "M.D.B." or "most discussed book of the last twenty years—and now looks as though it might be the most discussed book of the next twenty!" Will Harcourt not commission someone to write a biographical and critical pamphlet about Lewis to be published immediately after the first good reviews of *Babbitt* appear? (He has given up his Italian lessons, he wrote his father, because they stole too much of his writing time.) Now *Babbitt* is progressing splendidly: some revisions have already been made in the first seventy thousand words and the first draft is nearly finished by the end of the year. There is talk of the jacket design, of a uniform binding with *Main Street,* and fifty-seven pages of typescript are mailed to New York for a dummy. He is thinking of the next novel. "I think I shall make my next novel after *Babbitt* not satiric at all; rebellious as ever, perhaps, but the central character *heroic.* I'm already getting gleams of it. . . ."

These gleams did not flicker over an imminent *Arrowsmith.* On December 26, Lewis wrote Harcourt, "Look! Please send Gene Debs, in Atlanta Prison, a *Main Street* with a note saying I asked you to send it to him, & that I hope he will like Miles Bjornstam [the village atheist-radical]." He did not know that a letter from Mencken, dated December 24 and then on the way to him, contained the information that "Old Debs has been let out at last. Harding contrived to do the thing like a cad." Perhaps it was not only domestic difficulties, but a desire, now that *Babbitt* was rolling toward completion, to be near the heroic subject that led him to wire Harcourt on January 3, 1922, that after a short stop in England he was returning to America.

In London he found a "most charming little service flat" at 10 Bury Street, in St. James, worked very hard at *Babbitt* and wrote his neglected wife foolish letters, full of longing. For all the hurtful things that she had done to him and for all the apparently final things that he had said to her, he loved her, he announced, and if she was enjoying a romance in Rome, he hoped that it would be a brief one. To his father, as to Harcourt, he explained the separation on the grounds that Rome was too diverting for his work.

On that day, January 7, he had lunch with Drinkwater and tea with Walpole, and only a week later he told Harcourt that, besides those two, he had seen Galsworthy, George Moore, May Sinclair, John Cournos, Beatrice Harraden, William Archer, Rebecca West and Horace Liveright. Then followed George Doran, Charles Breasted, Somerset Maugham (*two* invitations to dinner—". . . seems to fancy me"),* St. John Irvine, Stacy Aumonier, Sir John Foster Fraser, Frazier Hunt, Jonathan Cape, Lytton Strachey, Lady Colefax, A. S. M. Hutchinson, H. G. Wells. It was a gregarious life from teatime on, and there was for some time no settled plan for bringing Mrs. Lewis back into it.

** Feb. 10.*

My dear Lewis

I am expecting you to dinner (dressing jacket or do they call it a dinner jacket—I mean of course a Tuxedo!) next Friday at 8.

Also on Feb 24th: not the 22nd as we arranged the other day.

Yours always

W. S. Maugham

On January 8 he wrote Harcourt that he had at first planned to take the *Aquitania* home on the twenty-eighth, but had changed his mind. Mrs. Lewis and Wells "may come home with me in the spring, she may stay over and me rejoin them in Italy. We haven't decided about that yet." On February 22, his plans were still vague but he thought that he would "have Grace join me in U.S. instead of waiting for her here." In the middle of March it was settled that she would join him in about six weeks, and on the twenty-sixth he had booked their passage for May 13.

Babbitt progressed and at the end of January he sent his wife fifty pages in carbon to read. On the thirty-first, he received the announcement that he had been elected a member of the National Institute of Arts and Letters (he had been proposed by Hamlin Garland, Robert Grant and William Lyon Phelps), and this invitation he "respectfully" declined on February 14. On the day before, he had declined an invitation to join the Authors' Club, in New York, on the grounds that he had no plans for living there for some years. His skin disease was troubling him and he had a number of epitheliomata cauterized, while Wells, in Rome, had contracted chicken pox and was removed to the Anglo-American Nursing Home. So wrote his mother to her father-in-law, saying, too, that nothing about the Italian winter had disappointed her except the Italians, who were reluctant to admit strangers into their homes. Lewis wrote his father of long walks through London at night, of the fact that the road company would open *Main Street* in Chicago on March 5, of an interview for the *Evening Standard* with Sir John Foster Fraser, the result of which he enclosed for reprinting in the *Herald*. He had first met Sir John when that worthy was traveling the Chautauqua circuit, and apparently met him accidentally again in London.

> I first met Sinclair Lewis in Mankato, Minnesota, two years ago. He was then writing a book. But why in Mankato? Because he was writing about the sort of undistinguished people who live in an undistinguished town like Mankato. And at half-past two in the morning we sat on high stools before the counter of an all-night open eating house, ate ham and eggs and talked books. And the other evening, when I was taking my lemonade in the Bohemian part of the Café Royal, there tumbled in a long, thin, sandy-haired, freckled, ordinary man—Sinclair Lewis.
>
> Between Mankato and the Café Royal he had become the widest read novelist in the United States.

The interview includes general information about the success of *Main Street* and the progress of *Babbitt,* specific information about Lewis's trouble in finding shirts that will at once fit his thin neck and his long arms (what? no shirtmaker?) and a miscellany of opinion: "I like England? Sure, I do, England is the nicest part of America"; but the English have many misconceptions about America and Americans, are themselves provincial (especially in their reading habits), and are the victims of stereotypes.

To Mencken he had written rather more directly in January about tiresome literary teas, condescending young writers and "crooked" publishers. Beginning with this letter of January 21, the correspondence between Lewis and Mencken became increasingly an affair of satirizing organized religion.

> Though I read by the papers this morning that H. H. the Pope is sore stricken, I hope that you will be able to keep up a heart and I know you join me in prayers for him. . . . In Rome I heard two young English Catholics, both Oxford graduates, both rich, one of 'em—Evan Morgan—a poet and the son of a peer—arguing like hell as to whether it was better to bust up the saints and distribute the relics around—a knee joint to each of several churches—or to keep the whole saint in one church, because of the concentrated efficacy. . . . I give you this theme to think about at this grievous time of the illness of H. H.

To this Mencken replied frivolously to say that some of his friends were urging him to run for the office but that he believed his theological talents were insufficient for the post.

Lewis warned Mencken, in an April letter, of a British "plot" to embarrass him. J. C. Squire, the editor of the London *Mercury,* thought that Mencken was "a German son of a bitch" and had been delighted to find that there were several mistakes as to British usage in *The American Language,* and he was no less delighted by the plot against Mencken devised by his friend, John Balderston, editor of *The Outlook*. Balderston was an American who pretended, in his correspondence with Mencken, to be an Englishman, and he deliberately made errors of usage in his letters, in the hope that Mencken would cite them in his next edition as proper Anglicisms. "Couldn't you go on pretending to believe him English, and have the fun on *your* side? . . . And if some time you could take Jack Squire's hide off neatly and very completely, I would light for you seven two-bit candles in St. Pat's."

He took more pleasure in the company of the Americans, Frazier Hunt and Charles Breasted, son of the famous archaeologist and historian, than in that of the respectably malicious English writers and "crooked" publishers. Hunt had brought over his Studebaker and occasionally Lewis would take a day off for a drive through the spring countryside. Breasted had met Lewis when the latter was on his first lecture tour, but their friendship began in London in February of 1922, when they met by chance at the American consulate, both there to extend their passports. Breasted remembers some social occasions—they were not literary—that Lewis enjoyed.

> . . . dinners and simple soirées at the homes of old friends in the Holland Park and Campden Hill sections of London, where we met such diverse personalities as George Peabody Gooch, the English historian; Hermann Gollancz, the Semitist; Maxwell Armfield, the sadly crippled yet extraordinarily active artist; Cyril Scott, the composer; Edmund Dulac, the illustrator; and many others. . . . He was greatly impressed with what seemed to him their un-British easy informality, and with the fact that their social gatherings included every age level and that the young people in their teens seemed genuinely to enjoy such association with their elders. He would always compliment his hosts especially on this latter aspect of their social life, which was in such contrast to the separation between generations in the United States. This in turn would lead him to expound upon the foibles and fortes of life in America. If the occasion included games, he was likely to be in the middle of them, usually on the floor; and as often as not he would end up by teaching a group of guests, including the prettiest girl present, the subtleties of poker.

Of the British literary folk, Breasted also remembers, Lewis did admire Rebecca West "as one of the very ablest living writers of either sex, and perhaps the ablest among women." But Hugh Walpole was another matter:

> . . . while he respected Hugh Walpole's craftsmanship (I remember in London his once spending part of an evening analyzing for me the organizational structure of *The Cathedral*), Lewis despised him as a human being because of what he called "his obscene, beefy, thick-thumbed softness."

Poor Hugh! He, as much as Sinclair Lewis, wanted above all to be liked. (Once, to the Leonard Bacons, whose very nuzzling dog was giving him a good deal of attention, Lewis said, "I'm just like this dog. All I want is affection.")

One publisher Lewis certainly did not despise. That was Jonathan Cape, who had begun his business in March of 1921. The arrangements with Hodder & Stoughton had not been happy, and both Harcourt and Lewis wanted to move. Cape proposed that he publish *Babbitt* and that he republish *Main Street* properly, and his proposal was accepted. (When *Babbitt* emerged, it carried not only a glossary of 125 Americanisms for the British audience, but a three-page introduction by the despised Hugh.) Cape's latter-day editor, Robert Knittel, recalled that Lewis went over to Cape only after having said, "But I'll want to see my name in lights"—by which he meant that he would expect a substantial promotion program—and that Cape took him literally and put the name Sinclair Lewis and the title *Babbitt* up in lights in Piccadilly Circus. The Sir Osbert Sitwell story would seem to bear him out. But Cape himself said that he explained to Lewis at the outset that England was not the United States. Lights or not, Cape published Lewis in England until nearly the end of his career.

The first draft of *Babbitt,* according to a letter to Eldon R. James, a distinguished Harvard professor of law then connected with the Siamese government, was finished in the middle of February, and Lewis hoped that the revisions would have been completed by June 1. He had known Eldon James at the Cosmos Club in Washington, and it was apparently James who had urged Cincinnati upon him as the ideal setting for his researches.

> In more than one thing, as you know, I am indebted to you for the material of the book. I am quite sure that none of our friends in Cincinnatti [*sic*] will ever know it—as a matter of fact, there are only two characters in the entire book who are directly drawn from real people, and both of them I knew in Washington—but it was very useful for me to go to Cincinnatti—it gave me a renewed sense of the exact flavor of a large American city of today.

But that was now a very nearly closed chapter; the book was, in effect, finished. There had been enthusiastic letters from both Alfred Harcourt and Donald Brace about as much of it as they had seen. Lewis was urging Harcourt to come to England immediately rather than in the autumn; he could then go over the first draft with him in London and be in New York to work on the book when it was being manufactured and published. Harcourt countered by suggesting that Lewis come home in April and go off with him for a week or two to Atlantic City or some such place to talk it over and lay plans for the promotion campaign. But Lewis lingered. Even as he revised *Babbitt,* he was thinking about that next, "heroic" novel.

> Will you please send me two books: the Harcourt *Short History of the American Labor Movement* by Mary Beard; and the *Life of Debs,* written, I think, by David Karstner [Karsner], and published, I believe, by Liveright? With them you might include the Stearns *Civilization* book. . . .

Then, on March 26, he announced to both Harcourt and his father that "Grace will join me here on May first or second."

She left Rome for Naples with Wells and Miss Pohlmann on April 22 and sailed for Southampton on the twenty-fourth. He met them at the dock and, in greeting his wife, "only succeeded in knocking my hat almost off my head," a very annoying experience, no doubt; but in a Southampton hotel that night, she contentedly read the end of *Babbitt.*

They had about three weeks in England and Lewis persuaded his wife to leave Wells and Miss Pohlmann in London and join him, with the Frazier Hunts and Walter Fuller,* Max Eastman's brother-in-law, in a motor trip

* Immediately upon his return, Lewis wrote a letter of introduction to Hugh Walpole for his new best friend, Walter Fuller, "one of the most charming people I know." Fuller was an Englishman who had just returned from a long period in the United States and hoped to find editorial employment in London.

to Glasgow in the Hunts' Studebaker. It would take about a week, from May 4 through May 9. Hunt was gathering material for an article to be called "Is the World Going Dry?" and for this purpose he wanted to see Scotland. All the way they stopped at inns, trying the ale and the spirits, and at last did arrive in Glasgow. In *One American,* Hunt recalls the experience in this way:

> It was a Saturday afternoon when we reached Glasgow. That night Red and I wandered off to the slums. I had seen Chicago's red-light district and New York's Bowery, and I had watched men have the D.T.'s on the streets of Brisbane, Australia. I had seen opium dens in Shanghai and tequila and *aguardiente* bars in Mexico, but never had I seen anything to compare with this Scotch border town at the hour when the pubs closed for the week end. Men, women, and children were fighting in the dirty streets; gin-drinking charwomen were lying helpless in the gutters and alleys; a quarter of a great city was over-run with hundreds of poor, helpless, drunken wretches whose only sin was poverty, and who for a few hours were finding escape from their everlasting fears and their defeats by the only road they knew.
>
> Finally Red stopped and raised his clenched fists to high heaven. Tears were streaming down his cheeks. "I can't stand it any more," he cried. "I can't stand it!"
>
> All the way back to the hotel he cursed and raved. "God damn the society that will permit such poverty! God damn the religions that stand for such a putrid system! God damn 'em all!"

Was it either the system or the poverty that so disturbed him, or was it the prophetic mirror of horrid human degradation?

The *Aquitania,* sailing for New York, left a considerable wake across Anglo-American literary relations, and Lewis brought all his public utterances about British writers and the English character to a climax upon disembarking. Greeted by newsmen, including a man from the London *Times,* he summarized his complaints. The attack called forth a long letter to the *Times* from Shane Leslie, in which he wondered whether Lewis's bomb was meant to burst in Main Street or in Grub Street, W. C., whether his remarks were meant to repay the debt of a year's hospitality abroad or to create a patriotic sensation among the people who had made him a best seller. He denied Lewis's charge that British writers are "a complacent lot" without "pep" who mingle only with others of their own kind, "too darned literary for any use." Furthermore, literary controversy in England can be conducted without recourse to the vocabulary of "pep" and "darn." Good American writing, finally, was well received in England. Another objection came from an "Anonymous Novelist" in a letter to *The Outlook.* He was, complained this writer, becoming a starving man for the very reason that British publishers were flooding the market with American books, generally poor but widely popular.

In the same periodical, J. C. Squire, in his weekly column signed by "Solomon Eagle," taking up Lewis's remarks about the patronizing attitude of the English ("I have been mothered by young English upstarts till I'm sick of it. It is time for us to stop looking at England for anything at all . . . go our own way and produce the finest literature of our time") said that it was absurd to argue that "every young Englishman, two years out of Oxford, adopts the mother attitude toward writers like Edith Wharton, Joseph Hergesheimer, James Branch Cabell, and Sherwood Anderson." Finally, Filson Young, cited in an editorial in the New York *Times,* argued that the charge of literary insularity was to be hurled rather at writers in New York and Chicago than at those in London; American writers necessarily depend upon themselves because America is without that leisured and cultivated society into which British writers are so easily absorbed—they have only themselves; and the fact is that when British writers do gather in groups, they are rather unfriendly.

It is, of course, a dusty old quarrel, and even then it was a teapot tempest. Yet it reminds us of Lewis's plight as he makes one more exile's return, leaving behind him again the unsatisfactory elsewhere, returning to the inadequate nowhere. They sailed on May 13, with ample staterooms in which Lewis made his last large revisions of *Babbitt,* his trumpet blast at the American middle class, and they arrived in New York on May 19, 1922. He was living out the first stages of that pattern that Malcolm Cowley was to describe when the whole pattern had been completed by many American writers:

> There was the first stage when young writers born at the turn of the century were detached from the native backgrounds and were led to think of themselves as exiles in fact, even when living at home. There was the second stage when they went abroad, many of them with the intention of spending the rest of their lives in Europe. The voyage had an unexpected effect on most of them: it taught them to admire their own country, if only for its picturesque qualities. But they still preferred to admire it from a distance, and many of the younger exiles would have agreed with the opinion that Hawthorne expressed to his publisher in 1858. "To confess the truth," he said in a letter from Italy, "I had rather be a sojourner in any other country than return to my own. The United States are fit for many excellent purposes, but they are certainly not fit to live in." Yet Hawthorne went home to Concord in 1860, whether or not it was a fit place for him to live, and the new generation of exiles came straggling back to New York.
>
> They had entered a third stage of the adventure, one in which the physical exile had ended while they were still exiles in spirit. At home they continued to think of themselves as oppressed by the great colorless mass of American

> society, and they tried to defend their own standards by living apart from society, as if on private islands.

And here Lewis begins to make his variations of that pattern that was more exactly suited to writers ten or fifteen years younger than he: there was his enormous success, the security of his money to shore up the insecure self. But, as Cowley also observes, "In those days writing could be a profitable business, but it was a perilous business, too, and the ordeal by success was fatal to almost as many talents as was the ordeal by failure." But nothing, except possibly his marriage, yet presented itself as an ordeal. To the New York *Evening World* the exile pontificated with perhaps more assurance than coherence:

> Every human being is provincial; wherever a group of provincials are gathered together is Main Street. So I conclude that not only America, not only Europe, but the world is full of Main Streets. We have less excuse for being provincial than any other country—we can change. The Main Street mind, the world over, wishes to see every other mind created in its own image. In Europe the Main Streeters take it out in wishing; here Carry Nation takes the hatchet. England is imitating our worst, not our best—she can't have too much of jazz. Americans are less fond of money than Europeans, but there is more snobbery of family here. America is the one country—except possibly Russia—that is the country of hope.

These observations appeared under a row of eight photographs of his face turned in various directions, as though he were looking for a place to go.

In New York, where had they to go? There was, of course, only one kind of place, a hotel. They chose the Chatham.

Some work remained to be done on *Babbitt* both in verbal details and in laying plans for its publication, and Lewis needed to stay near New York. Mrs. Hegger was again at the Forest Hills Inn on Long Island, and they retired there. But *Babbitt* went to the printers very soon (there were finished copies by July 22) and Lewis was free. On Decoration Day they motored to Vermont with Alfred Harcourt (his ailing wife was abroad) and spent a night with Harcourt's associate, Joel E. Spingarn, at Amenia, New York.

Returning, there was an encounter with Upton Sinclair, who asked Lewis to read the proofs of his new book, *They Call Me Carpenter: A Tale of the Second Coming,* but when the proofs arrived at Forest Hills on June 16, Lewis, no doubt appalled by what the title promised, wrote that he was too busy with *Babbitt* to get at them "for some time." ("As to the danger of the incoming shekels turning me from radicalism—see *Babbitt!*") This is an interesting bit of deceit because on the day before, June 15, he had written Tinker to say that he was coming to New Haven for his class reunion ("for the first time in history") on the eighteenth and hoped to see him.

He had bought a new automobile, a beige Cadillac touring car which they named "Old Growler," and in this he betook himself to New Haven for the fifteenth reunion of his class and permitted himself to be photographed, funny hat and all, with these now more friendly fellows. At the reunion dinner, probably the most famous alumnus of the class, he was called upon to speak. He stood up and studied their faces. "When I was in college, you fellows didn't give a damn about me, and I'm here to say that now I don't give a damn about you." Then, calling out names, he reminded a dozen of them of their special snubs to him. They were uproariously amused. What a wag!

He conducted himself in New Haven quite as in the old days. E. Robert Stevenson, who had also worked on the *Journal and Courier* as a student and was then to become a newspaper editor in Waterbury, Connecticut, remembered the following, and the *Journal-Courier-Times* reported it in 1935 when the play *Dodsworth* was about to open in New Haven:

> Stevenson one evening [during the reunion] stood beneath Lewis' window in the old Vanderbilt dormitory in the court on Chapel Street. In answer to his call Lewis came down in his pyjamas, sat on the court curb and smoked a cigarette. It was 10:30 o'clock, a perfect June night.
>
> Stevenson looked at Lewis' pyjamas, unorthodox street garments, and nonchalantly proposed, "Let's ramble down Chapel Street." There was not even a quiver of hesitation in Lewis. In pyjamas and slippers he went along to the street, through the lobby of the Taft Hotel, to Chapel Street and so to Temple and the newspaper plant of the *Journal-Courier* then located in Temple Street on the site of Mory's old Temple Bar. There a brief visit was paid to Arthur J. Sloane, managing editor, where days of undergraduate reporting were recalled.

In New York again, there was a meeting at some point with Willa Cather. She wrote him on June 27 to tell him how happy she was to have met the Lewises at last and how delighted to have learned that Lewis was going to review *One of Ours* in the New York *Post*. She asked him to telephone her when he was next in town. It may be doubted whether he called her, as she proposed. The book was an embarrassment to him, and presently he would complain to Mencken:

> I am damnably disappointed with Cather's *One of Ours*. It's not merely her thin second-rate account of the war but [has] a certain wobbly indecisiveness throughout. Like a damn fool I'd let myself in for reviewing it for the NY *Evening Post,* hoping to be able to cheer for it. Funny what Greenwich Village does to all these birds [Miss Cather was living in Bank Street]. I

see Sherwood Anderson is living there now. Send him back to Chicago or New Orleans or Prague or somewhere.

He decided to send himself back to the Middle West, to visit his father and to look for a possible winter residence in Madison, Wisconsin, or in Saint Paul. He left in the Cadillac, and Mrs. Lewis, according to a letter to Gene Baker McComas, intended to follow immediately, omitting "the hysteric delights of Sauk Center" but hoping for two weeks on a Wyoming dude ranch before settling down in a Midwest city. These plans did not develop.

He went first to Madison, but left without any great enthusiasm for that city as a winter residence, and drove up to Sauk Centre, where he arrived in the first week of July and, "meekly bored . . . not aggressively," planned to stay for about ten days. He was well received by the villagers and by the *Herald*.

> There seems to be an impression that the people of this vicinity were "frothing at the mouth" so to speak. The usual equilibrium of the community was not disturbed by the arrival of the famous author nor were the dogs of war unchained. . . . [*Main Street*] has proven to be a mighty substantial meal ticket for its author and his friends rejoice with him in his success.

How he filled his days in Sauk Centre is not clear. Although the slight correspondence with Harcourt, Brace & Company at this point does not say so, he may have been correcting the final proof of *Babbitt*. This chore must have occupied him at some point between mid-June and now.* Per-

* The proof correction of this novel was rather careless, and has recently been the subject of discussion in Fredson Bowers's *Textual and Literary Criticism*. "Louis N. Feipel, whose hobby was proof-reading printed books, supplied Harcourt Brace with a list of about a hundred inconsistencies and errors in the first printing of Sinclair Lewis's novel *Babbitt*. To which Lewis commented in awe, 'This man Feipel is a wonder—to catch all these after rather unusually careful proofreading not only by myself and my wife but also by two or three professionals.' Even so, Lewis showed himself uncertain of his meaning of *B* in B.P.O.E. since he twice gave it in error as *Brotherly* and only once correctly as *Benevolent* (*B.P.O.E.* is the abbreviation for an American fraternal society, The Benevolent and Protective Order of Elks). And Lewis's spelling of *Oddfellows* and *Redmen* (two similar orders) as one word instead of two is not quite the way in which these organizations choose to denominate themselves. The mordant satirist of American 'joiners' and their groups did not, on the evidence, always have a keen eye for such details in the objects of his laughter." (page 19).

Mr. Bowers, basing his observations on Matthew J. Bruccoli's "Textual Variants in Sinclair Lewis's *Babbitt*," *Studies in Bibliography*, XI (1958) himself misspells *Babbitt* as *Babbit* when he cites this essay. On pages 26–27, he returns to the problem of the *Babbitt* text: "There should be no complacency about our modern texts. The plates of a book may be altered without notice in any impression, yet the latest printing from altered plates is not necessarily the most correct. For example, Sinclair Lewis's novel *Babbitt* had two sets of plates made in 1922 from the original type-setting after proof-correction. The first set of plates printed the first to the fourth impressions. In the first impression we have two readings corrected in a rare example of modern stop-press alteration of plates. Six more readings were changed in the

haps he now wrote his essay, "Minnesota: The Norse State" (although it was not to appear in *The Nation* until May 30, 1923). The essay contains a certain amount of statistical material that would have necessitated ready reference books, and it mentions Carlton Miles, "just back from a European year spent with such men as Shaw, Drinkwater . . ." It attempts to describe a "civilization" just seventy-five years old—all bustle and progress and industry and complexity—and is as far from the *Babbitt* mood as it is from the mood of Harold Stearns's symposium. It is moderately factual, cool but appreciative, yet with little of that nostalgia that generally invaded Lewis's prose when he wrote reflectively about the home place, and none of that even gentle chiding that informed the little speech he gave in St Cloud during this visit.

Part of his time was spent with his brother. There, "at the opening of the new home of the St. Cloud Country Club," he delivered a fifteen-minute impromptu response to a toast in which he "stated that he was a moralist and more of a preacher than an orator." He praised the English because they do not boast of their civilization, but "we Americans are a very boastful lot, and especially in the West."

Sometime before July 19 he had arrived in St. Paul (on that day he wrote to a Mr. S. C. G. Watkins to say, "Yes, it seems to me that the soldiers bonus bill is unnecessary and unwise. Yes, I believe the crippled should be cared for—but the crippled of the battles of peace, of industry, quite as much as those of the battles of war"), and on the twenty-first he lectured at the University of Chicago and enjoyed a "spiritous" evening with a number of book salesmen.

Next day his wife joined him at the Blackstone Hotel and reported to him the threatened legal difficulties with a Boston man named George F. Babbitt. The flurry of correspondence set in motion by this Mr. Babbitt was resolved when Lewis reminded Harcourt that *our* Mr. Babbitt was a real estate man in the Midwest, not a journalist in New England, and that his middle initial, "F," stood triumphantly for the inimitable "Follansbee." On July 26 or 27 they began the journey back to New York and Fishers Island.

There followed another motor trip in New England. Neither Wisconsin nor Minnesota had made an appeal to Lewis in this year, but Connecticut did, and by mid-August they had found a house that they liked at 25 Belknap Road, Hartford, situated next to the golf course and available

plates for the second impression, and thirteen more in the fourth. However, after 1942 all printings were made from the second set of plates; but these had not been carefully kept up-to-date with the alterations made in the first plates and hence all printings from 1942 to the present day revert in fourteen out of twenty-one cases to the original first-impressions. A critic who uses any other printing of *Babbitt* than the fourth may quote a passage that in some detail does not correspond to certain of Lewis's revised intentions."

on September 1. Hartford seemed to have the advantage of being an independent city, not a suburb of New York, and the house had the advantage of belonging to a lady who had had lessons in batik and had lived in Florence. There was a minstrel gallery, a dry fountain at the base of a curved stairway, a guest room with a canopied bed and a shrine, and a lot of carved mahogany. And almost immediately Lewis was off to Chicago again.

He was in search of his hero. On August 19 he wrote Upton Sinclair from Terre Haute to say that he had "called on Mrs. Debs yesterday. What a lovely woman she is!" He said, too, "I tremendously want to see your education book [*The Goose-step*], but I'm unreachable just now—I'm wandering with no fixed address." He was in fact going quite directly to the Morrison Hotel in Chicago, where he arrived next day, and he wrote his wife ecstatically on August 26 about his meeting with Debs, who was staying in a naturopathic sanitarium near Chicago.

> It's been a great week. . . . I've been Union Laboring hard. Most important, two evenings at Carl Sandburg's house, out [at] Elmhurst, with Gene Debs. . . . Gene really is a Christ spirit. He is infinitely wise, kind, forgiving —yet the devil of a fighter. . . . He has told me of his boyhood (he was an awkward, odd boy who never could swim or dance & who read Voltaire & the encyclopedia) . . .

The working title of the labor novel was *Neighbor*.

Then he saw Dr. Morris Fishbein again. Fishbein called with Sandburg, Harry Hansen, and an influential literary columnist and local wit named Keith Preston, and there was a "spiritous" evening which ended with Lewis's staying in Fishbein's apartment. He was enthusiastic about Fishbein's wide reading and open generosity, but he thought that he could improve on his name. Dr. Fishbein had not yet made the considerable reputation that he was to make, and Lewis told him that he would never get anywhere with a name like that, it was funny, change it; but he didn't want to change it, murmured the doctor. "Well, I'm telling you that you should! What's a *fish-leg?*" (Ten years later, both famous and wealthy, Dr. Fishbein said to Lewis, "Well, I never did change my name and I didn't do so bad, did I? And no one has ever mixed me up with anyone else, the way Sinclair Lewis is always being mixed up with Upton Sinclair.")

An occasion both more alcoholic and more consequential followed in a day or two. Lewis called on Fishbein again, this time at the offices of the American Medical Association, and Fishbein told him that in the building there was a man whom he wanted Lewis to meet—Paul de Kruif. De Kruif was a powerfully built man (he wore a size 18 collar) with great physical vitality and equal appetites; he had taken a Ph.D. in bacteriology at

Michigan, then had become a researcher at the Rockefeller Institute, and was now in the process of becoming "a good bellicose scientific journalist as well." Fishbein had reviewed his book, *Our Medical Men,* which had cost De Kruif his Rockefeller appointment, and this review had started their correspondence. Now De Kruif was about to begin a series of articles on medical subjects and he had come to Chicago to discuss ideas for this series with Fishbein. Fishbein had sent him up to a laboratory to examine a whole collection of alcoholic "tonics" of a sort that, during the Prohibition period, flooded the American market. Fishbein hoped that both could come to dinner at his apartment, and both agreed. And here the printed accounts and Dr. Fishbein's recollection part. Lewis did not write to his wife about the events of this evening, but when he recalled them in his published account in *The Designer and The Woman's Magazine* in June 1924, he wrote:

> The three of us fell to debating. De Kruif and Fishbein hurled ideas about medical education at each other as though they were bricks. We planned to go to dinner together—an early dinner and home at nine—certainly nine, at the latest—lots of work to do.
>
> At two next morning we were still shouting philosophy.
>
> All the while I meditated, "Here's my next novel, now that I've read the proofs on *Babbitt.* What protagonist of fiction could be more interesting, more dramatic, and less hackneyed than a doctor who, starting out as a competent general practitioner, emerges as a real scientist, despising ordinary 'success'?"
>
> From time to time the meek novelist murmured to the raging giants, "I ought to write a novel about a bacteriologist."

Dr. Fishbein remembers that De Kruif had sampled the "tonic" with such enthusiasm that he became ill, but he recovered presently and they did have dinner. The conversation between Fishbein and De Kruif concerned itself largely, De Kruif later told Burton Rascoe, with "experiences in the medical institutions of the country, showing how difficult was the path of the young man in America who wanted to devote himself to pure research. . . ."

> Petty politics, jealousies, faculty rivalries, and all sorts of cheapening influences were at work, they said, to make the weak-willed man shift his devotion from science and push his own personal gain for private profit.

Listening to them, Lewis may very well have said that some day he ought to write a novel about medicine, but now, he told them, he was about to begin a labor novel. To that end he had been seeing Debs, a great man, out in Elmhurst, and why didn't they all get into a cab immediately and drive out there to see him. Agreed. Once in the cab, De Kruif and Lewis fell into a noisy argument about something of no importance except as it seemed to them at the moment. At the intersection of Van Buren, Ashland and Jackson streets, they got out of the cab and broke into a tussle, the huge, burly man and the long, thin one, and Lewis, shoved against the cab, managed both to tear his trousers and to cut his leg. Fishbein knew the pharmacist in a drugstore on that corner, and they went in there, attended to the leg, and continued.

Elmhurst is more than twenty-five miles from the center of Chicago, and as they drove on, a violent summer thunderstorm broke, and it became more and more difficult to drive. Fishbein suggested that they stop at a nearby country speakeasy with which he was familiar. The place was dark —the lights had been blown out by the storm—but by the glimmer of a few candles they could see three or four sinister-looking toughs, probably gangsters, at the bar. To get even with De Kruif, Lewis amiably said to them, "My friend here can lick you." A ruckus followed which demanded all of Fishbein's ingenuity and apologetic explanations to halt and to control. They drank. It was now past midnight, and Lewis telephoned Debs to say that they had been delayed. Debs told them to come along. The storm had subsided, but now another car collided with the cab, smashed a fender and pushed in a door. They continued and the fantasy grew.

Suddenly they saw in the beam of their headlights a line of men walking along the edge of the road through the wet, dark countryside. Lewis shouted, "Stop!" and leaped out of the cab. He approached the nearest man and asked, "Who are you?" The answer was that they were striking streetcar conductors who were walking from Buffalo to St. Louis, where they hoped to find work. Lewis said, "Do you men know where you are? You are just a few miles away from Eugene Debs." Said they, "Who's he?" One of them thought that he had once worn a Debs lapel button when he was "running for something." Their ignorance even of the identity of the great labor leader shocked Lewis, and he turned abruptly to the other two and said, "Give these men some money," and got into the cab without himself giving them anything. They arrived at the sanitarium at about one o'clock.

Debs was waiting for them and he had a bottle of whisky. They drank it. At four he announced that he had to go to bed. The others then went over to Carl Sandburg's house and, not finding him at home, chatted with a drowsy Mrs. Sandburg, whom they had routed out of bed. Then they started the drive back to Chicago, the best of friends.

It was then, Dr. Fishbein remembers, that he asked Lewis if he really wanted to write a novel about labor. Did he have a real story, did he have a point of view, did he even have the necessary enthusiasm? Why not write a novel about medicine? Lewis later recalled that it was not until his second meeting with De Kruif that they agreed to work together on such a novel, but Dr. Fishbein believes that the matter was settled then, in the returning cab, that the notion of a plague in the Caribbean as a part of the novel was developed, and that they agreed to make a research tour together and then continue to Europe and write the novel.

They drove as far as the Bismarck Hotel. The cabdriver had long since abandoned his meter and said that he had had such an entertaining time that he didn't really care how much they paid him, just so the fare would cover the damage to the cab. They settled for fifty dollars and went to breakfast at the Bismarck. Dr. Fishbein adds that while Paul de Kruif was a very heavy drinker, Lewis was, too—that he could tip up a pint of whisky, open his gullet, and let it pour down, like a peasant with a wineskin, until the bottle was empty. Then he would become not drunk, but sleepy, and after a short nap he would have returned to his senses, completely alert. This latter observation has been made by many others, but many others also say that he could drink very little and that he felt the effects of very little almost at once.

A good deal of drinking, certainly, mingled with the "labor unioning"; and the Fishbein account, however outrageous, is given credibility by the fact that between Lewis's letters to his wife of August 26 and of August 29, he had, at least for the time being, lost interest in the labor novel. He had made an effort to interest himself in union activities by attending strike meetings, loitering in union halls, reading labor newspapers and circulars, interviewing workers. He had picked up a waiter in his hotel who hoped to become a garment industry artist and who had subscribed to a correspondence school course that offered to teach the art of Ben Day—the kind of shadow drawing that is commonly used in clothing catalogues. Lewis took Harry Hansen to this waiter's house, where the man was practicing his new art, and Lewis spent the entire evening in putting questions to him about his working conditions. But more and more of his remaining time he spent with Dr. Fishbein.

Hansen remembers a luncheon at which Fishbein told Lewis about the files of the American Medical Association, crammed with records of medical fakes and quacks, available to him if he would write a novel about medicine. On the twenty-ninth he wrote, "I am melancholy—I feel rather lost. I don't believe I shall be able to do the *Neighbor* novel—that is, do it right." It is Hansen's view that had Lewis "been able to visualize a working man, who became a leader by sheer force of personality, and that man's family, I think he would have written his labor novel," but his approach was theoretical, and the experts he later employed to help him talked labor theory to him, and this left him helpless. "Ben Stolberg told me: 'Lewis can't handle ideas.' " The immediate difficulties seemed simpler: labor news bored him, many union men were "plain boobs," the organizational quarrels were tiresome, and even a Debs, "pure spirit" that he might be, disappointed him in the credulity with which he accepted the naturopathic nonsense to which he was then submitting.

And yet, had he settled with Paul de Kruif? "I think I may do my American abroad story, but with very long, detailed study of him at home first. Take a business man, a Zenithite, but NOT a Babbitt; a university man who in college wanted to be a socialist; a lover of books, music . . ." But this figure would develop into Dodsworth. Or "I might do the Glorious Company—the barbers & lunch counters—now. We'll see."

On September 4, the day after Mrs. Lewis was writing to Alfred Harcourt from Hartford to express her satisfaction with the essay on Lewis by Stuart P. Sherman, Lewis left Chicago.

During his absence from New York, on August 20, a characteristic Lewis statement had appeared in the *World,* where, together with seven other prominent writers, he had delivered his views on the activities of John Sumner and the Society for the Suppression of Vice.

> Any committee which sets itself up to judge the morality of any branch of art is on the face of it an absurdity. Art should be, must be and is creative and original. In order to bloom with those qualities it must be unhampered. Any artist who works with the tapeworm of censorship gnawing at his vitals, knowing that some blue-law committee is to sit in judgment on his work, would be stultified from the outset.

He concludes by saying that he would subscribe to a committee of really distinguished people to rule "over each form of human activity," such as William Jennings Bryan for biology, Billy Sunday for morality, Fatty Arbuckle for the theater. But "who is Mr. Sumner?" This is a return to the H. L. Mencken mood, and his correspondence with Mencken would pick up at once again, in Hartford.

And still the idea of a "heroic" novel about the "Christ figure" had not been abandoned. He had earlier made himself known to Debs's biographer, David Karsner, and to him he wrote on September 28, "Thank you for all the material re Gene. I want to have a long talk with you. I'll call you up some time when I'm in N.Y., if I may."

Very early in the Hartford stay, on September 16, the Hartford *Daily Times* published an extended and amusingly inaccurate interview: Mrs. Lewis was English, she had two children, and she had deleted the horrid word "smutty" from the typescript of *Babbitt;* she, and her husband no less, hoped that Hartford would become their permanent residence, and she had not known that there were such hospitable people in the world as the people of Hartford. Lewis expressed an interest in the industrial life of Hartford and in the size of the Italian colony, and a hope that the reporter would sometime soon take him on a tour of the factory district. When he was asked his opinion of Rudyard Kipling's recent statement that America had lost its soul in 1860, he made a comment and then said, "Say, that isn't bad, is it . . . you might copy that down."

> But before it could be copied down, he had rushed off to get a pencil and copy it down himself. Then he produced the following formal statement, the only definite one to which he committed himself in two and a half hours: "Apropos of Mr. Kipling's discovery that America has lost her soul, one has only to note that America has retained enough of her soul to appreciate Mr. Kipling more than any other nation in the world, so perhaps there is still hope for her."

The interest in labor conditions in Hartford suggests his unsettled mind about the next book. Still, in Hartford their most frequent meetings were, significantly, with doctors—Harrison Smith's father, Dr. Oliver Smith, and Dr. Thomas N. Hepburn. And he began to read in bacteriology. But on September 14, before much activity of this sort could have got under way, there was another explosion—the publication of *Babbitt*.

4

THIS TIME, OF COURSE, the excitement for Lewis was less, because it was more expected. The prepublication printing was 80,500 copies as opposed to the 15,000 of *Main Street,* and Harcourt was predicting a sale of 200,000 before Christmas. Sinclair Lewis need hardly hope, because Alfred Harcourt could be counted upon hardly to risk. The newsstands throughout September displayed a *Smart Set* whose cover was a gaudy caricature portrait, in reds, oranges and yellows, of Lewis complete with monocle in eye and cigarette hanging from lips. On August 13 out went a direct greeting from Mencken, on shipboard, enclosing a copy of his review for *Smart Set;* it would appear on publication day as the first part of his monthly omnibus review (which then went on to the still unfortunate *One of Ours* and other books) and give the whole its title: "Portrait of an American Citizen." So Lewis had the assurance, well before publication, that one influential voice would announce to the world, "I know of no American novel that more accurately presents the real America." In the same letter, Mencken told him that he was also writing the review for the Baltimore *Evening Sun* (and he added that he was quite certain that "Babbitt's brother-in-law, Frank J. Thompson, is aboard with his new wife . . . God help us all!").

There were other prepublication auguries. There was, for example, the fact of the Stuart Sherman pamphlet, about to be released, which would, in effect, enshrine the subject with solemn academic sanction. There was the news from the editor of the New York *Times Book Review* that May Sinclair had submitted a most enthusiastic review. "In his hands Babbitt becomes stupendous and significant," it would read; and, commenting that it was a very remarkable achievement to have made such a creature as Babbitt so lovable and so alive, it would conclude that in style, in construction, in technique generally, as in perception, it was a better novel than *Main Street.*

When that review appeared a week after publication, the Harcourt, Brace advertisement of the novel could already present the marshaled praise of Ludwig Lewisohn from *The Nation,* Burton Rascoe from the

Tribune, John Farrar from *The Bookman,* as well as Mencken and F. P. A. —all concurring with the judgment that it was a bigger book than *Main Street.* Friends rallied in an ecstasy: Carl Van Doren, Upton Sinclair in *The Appeal to Reason,* and above all, Owen Johnson, whose *Tribune* review was blown up to poster size and plastered on the sides of the *Tribune*'s distributing trucks. Simultaneous publication in England brought forth the same kind of applause; a relentlessly complete satire on the commercial spirit of American life, it was yet not without pathos and even a nimbus of heroism. The review that seems to have meant most to Lewis was Rebecca West's in the *New Statesman:*

> It has that something extra, over and above, which makes the work of art, and it is signed in every line with the unique personality of the writer.

Quoting from one of Babbitt's public speeches, she continues:

> It is a bonehead Walt Whitman speaking. Stuffed like a Christmas goose as Babbitt is, with silly films, silly newspapers, silly talk, silly oratory, there has yet struck him the majestic creativeness of his own country, its miraculous power to bear and nourish without end countless multitudes of men and women.... There is in these people a vitality so intense that it must eventually bolt with them and land them willy-nilly into the sphere of intelligence; and this immense commercial machine will become the instrument of their aspirations.

That was one way of taking it. But there were also those who argued that the vitality of the novel was only the aimless if "unique" vitality of the author himself, and what a critic like Gilbert Seldes in *The Dial,* even when praising the book, was really saying was that the imaginative vitality of Sinclair Lewis failed to find any satisfactory aesthetic organization. The whole book should have been rewritten, he argued, after Lewis had taken a long look into himself. The implication was—and it was made explicit by others—that the book had no values beyond Babbitt's own, and that satire, comic and critical as it may be, must found itself on positive standards that are clearly there even if they are not stated. To personalize this observation—as Ernest Boyd, always anti-Lewis in an unpleasantly personal way, was the first to do—would be to say that Lewis himself was Babbitt, and to ascribe the success of the novel to the fact that the audience that Lewis satirized recognized in the author not an enemy but an ally, not a teacher but a brother. And, indeed, many of the most loosely enthusiastic reviews that the book received came from the newspapers of those middle-sized Midwestern cities that most resembled Zenith.

The newspapers of five such cities—Cincinnati, Duluth, Kansas City, Milwaukee and Minneapolis—each declared that its city was the model of Zenith. And if Minneapolis, for example, celebrated a "Babbitt Week" so spirited as to embroil it in a civic feud with St. Paul, some spokesmen in this as in other cities and towns throughout the United States would attack Lewis for his malicious distortion of the facts of American life. Edwin F. Edgett of the Boston *Transcript,* who had admired the early, gentler Lewis, flatly denounced the book as "yellow," and as it became the subject matter of pulpits and lecture platforms, one might have concluded that the author had committed an act of treason.

All over the country the novel became the material of newspaper editorials. The New York *Times,* whose editorialists were often to have rather staidly malicious fun at Lewis's expense, approved of *Babbitt.* In a September editorial called "Boosters Truly Pictured," the *Times* found Babbitt "real, alive and recognizable as a known, familiar, and abundant type," and in October, in "Topics of the Times," it tried to comfort the outraged Middle Westerners by assuring them that Babbitts were to be found by the hundreds everywhere and that Lewis had used the Middle West as his setting only because he was most familiar with it.

In the same month, Anne O'Hare McCormick took up Paul Riesling's tripartite division of the Zenith citizenry—the satisfied, the restless, the implacable—as a means of understanding the various response to the book: readers of the first kind liked it; of the second, resented it; of the third, were bored by it because it was so much like that which bored them to begin with. "What makes Zenith so comic," she concluded, "is that it has been sold more equipment for civilization [by Babbitts, the American middlemen] than anyone in the world has ever owned, just at the moment when it is perfectly plain that there is no civilization for the equipment."

Lewis had managed again to put himself at the heart of a national controversy of many voices: on one side there were those who said simply that it was a great book, those who said it was a true picture, those who said it was a necessary corrective; on the other side were those who said that it was a poor novel, those who deplored its distortions, those who denounced its lies. What could have mattered less than the question of which voice was raised? Everyone was buying it. Even the men in the "service" clubs, who hardly ever bought a book and almost never read one, were buying it and reading it as well.

The subject of a dinner address by one Dr. Emanuel Sternheim at a regular meeting of the Cleveland Kiwanis Club was "Babbitt, A Challenge to Men." In Minneapolis, an amiable attorney, C. C. Champine, reviewed the book with amusement in a trade journal called *The Realtor* (this is the exalted term on which Babbitt insists and which *Babbitt* brought into our commercial jargon), and was sharply answered by a real-estate man named Norman F. Emerson, who, in a letter to Champine, asserted that Lewis "had in mind a certain member of our real-estate board." Still amiably, Mr. Champine challenged Mr. Emerson to a public debate upon this subject: Resolved that Sinclair Lewis's novel, *Babbitt,* is not a libel . . . At the other extreme from such comedy is so solemn an opinion as H. S. Canby's, made long after the quarreling was over:

When he came to *Babbitt* he had begun to digest his own education, saw that George was a tragic figure, and with complete fidelity to every mood and gesture brought him to life, letting him buzz down man's long road over concrete and under green lights until he discovers that his experience has been all mileage without a destination.

For Lewis and Harcourt, the public controversy was, of course, a dizzying delight, but there were also quieter satisfactions for the author in many letters from people whose opinion he valued. Everyone wrote again, but among the first was the subject of the novel's dedication:

> There is so much to say about *Babbitt* that I don't know where to begin —unless at the dedication, which gives me an even warmer glow of satisfaction, now that I've read what follows, than when you first announced it to me!—If I've waited as long as this to have a book dedicated to me, Providence was evidently waiting to find just the Right Book. All my thanks for it.
>
> And what next? Oh, do jump on a steamer, & come over & have a talk about it! It kept me reading till one a.m. the other night, & started me again at 5—& at every page I found something to delight in, & something to talk about.—The prevailing impression, when one has finished, is of an extraordinary vitality & vivacity, an ever-bubbling spring of visual and moral sensibility—& this kind of "liveness" is one of the most important qualities in any work of fiction—or of any other art—
>
> I don't think Babbitt as good a novel, in the all-round sense, as *Main Street,* because in the latter you produce a sense of unity & of depth by reflecting Main Street in the consciousness of a woman who suffered from it because she had points of comparison, & was detached enough to situate it in the universe—whereas Babbitt is in and of Zenith up to his chin & over, & Sinclair Lewis is obliged to do the seeing & comparing for him. But then there is much more life & glow & abundance in the new book; you must have felt a stronger hold on it, & a richer flow. I wonder how much of it the American public, to whom irony seems to have become as unintelligible as Chinese, will even remotely feel? To do anything worthwhile, one must resolutely close one's ears & eyes to their conception of the novel; and I admire nothing more in your work than your steady balancing on your tight-rope over the sloppy abyss of sentimentality.
>
> I've only begun to say what I wanted; but the rest must be talk—except for one suggestion, which I venture to make now, that is, that in your next book, you should use slang in dialogue more sparingly. I believe the real art in this respect is to use just enough to *colour* your dialogue, not so much that in a few years it will be almost incomprehensible. It gives more relief to your characters, I'm sure, than to take down their jargon word for word.
>
> Thank you again for associating my name with a book I so warmly admire and applaud, & believe me, with kindest remembrances to Mrs. Lewis,
>
> Yours most sincerely,
>
> *E. Wharton*

Then she proposed to enclose a clipping from an English periodical (presumably the *Times*) because she hoped he would refute it if he had not already done so. "I am convinced [that it] doesn't represent what you feel, or would wish to say, on the subject."

> The way to prove what we are is not to complain of lack of recognition, but to join doing *Babbitts—& Super-Babbitts!* But, as I said, I'm sure this idiotic interview doesn't represent you, & I admire your talents so much that I hope very much you will write a line to the *Times* denying it in substance—or to me, if you prefer, authorizing me to do so in your name.

Her faith in him is rather charming. And her attractive letter makes one wonder just what Lewis's motives in dedicating the book to her were. Friendly, she was clearly not an intimate friend. She was a writer of some, but not of such great prestige that he would have much to gain by associating her name with a book of his. Was it, perhaps, a gesture of *noblesse oblige,* a real or feigned generosity that was to suggest that yes, indeed, it was she, not he, to whom the Pulitzer prize should have gone? Or was it the recognition of a real indebtedness?

He had first read her when he was a college student and he had admired her, and he had tried to imitate her manner when he was a novice writing in California. Gene McComas, praising *Our Mr. Wrenn,* was glad to see that "all the Henry James" of the first attempts at that novel had disappeared; that was probably Henry James as he came to Lewis through Edith Wharton. If no superficial traces of that manner remained in his work, other characteristics of Edith Wharton did. One day Arthur Mizener would refer to Lewis as "the Edith Wharton of the provincial American middle class," not only because he described their manners as she did the manners of her class, but because he, like Edith Wharton, was so profoundly *of* his class even when alienated from it. The New York society that Edith Wharton pictured was as flat and as futile as the society of Zenith, and the "Four Hundred" of that world was as indifferent to art and learning, if not as actively hostile, as the Boosters' Club. And when she looked at life in the Middle West and the West she thought that she saw much that Lewis was indeed seeing and ultimately recorded, and perhaps her distant gaze helped him to see the close-up. For her, according to Van Wyck Brooks,

> the whole vast region was merely a world of banal church-suppers, blackmailers, realtors, drummers and shady deals. It was part of the dim dingy waste in which, for Edith Wharton's mind, the humbler classes carried on their vague existence,—the "fat man with a creased stomach and soft pale lips" and the waitresses with their "pert faces" and "brazen eyes."

When she confronted the materials of provincial manners, she showed, as in the opening of such a relatively early work as *The Custom of the*

Country, a strain of broad satire verging on burlesque that, conceivably stimulated by the example of his novels, came out in later work, *Hudson River Bracketed* (1929), for example, as almost indistinguishable from his:

> She added in a postscript that Mr. Weston had showed the terms of Vance's contract with *The Hour* to the celebrated authoress, Yula Marphy, who was over from Dakin visiting with friends at Euphoria, and Miss Marphy had said, why it looked to her like a downright swindle, for she could get five hundred dollars any day for a story in the big magazines, and she'd never heard of *The Hour* anyhow, and she guessed it was one of those high-brow papers that run at a loss for a year or so, and then fizzle out. And what she advised was for Vance to come straight back West, where he belonged, and take up newspaper work again, and write pure manly stories about young fellows prospecting in the Yukon, or that sort of thing, because the big reading public was fed up with descriptions of corrupt society people, like there was a demand for in the East.

As if to acknowledge their literary association, she introduced into this novel a minor character, a writer named Tristram Fynes who had published an extraordinarily successful book called *The Corner Grocery.*

> Readers all over the country had felt its evident sincerity, and its title had become the proverbial epithet of the small-town atmosphere. It did not fully satisfy Vance; he thought the writer left untouched most of the deeper things the theme implied; if he himself had been able to write such a book he would have written it differently. But it was fearless, honest, preternaturally alive. . . .

Tristram Fynes is hardly characterized at all, but she permitted him one speech. At a party a new young writer is presented to him with the expectation that Fynes will talk about the young man's work, but Fynes assumes that the younger man wants to talk about *The Corner Grocery.*

> Mr. Fynes's compressed lips snapped open. "About *The Corner Grocery,* eh? Well, there's a good deal to be said about it that hasn't been said yet," he rejoined energetically, fixing his eyes on Vance. "You're one of the new reviewers, aren't you? Do 'The Cocoanut Tree' in the *New Hour?* Yes—I believe I saw something of yours the other day. Well, see here; this is no place for a serious talk, but I'd be glad if you'd come round some day and just let me tell you exactly what I want said about *The Corner Grocery.* . . . Much the best way, you know. The book's a big book. . . . Come round tomorrow, will you? I'm going to cut it now. . . ."
>
> He vanished and Vance stood dazed.

Tristram Fynes and Sinclair Lewis have no physical resemblance, but with a certain involuted irony, Edith Wharton makes Fynes the most important member of the awards committee for the Pulsifer Prize, and in just a year she has "The Cocoanut Tree" crowd patronizing him as "Poor old Fynes," and the resemblance in the names is obvious enough. Finis?

This resemblance suggests another and a very concrete indebtedness that Van Wyck Brooks observes in passing. Her proper names, both of places and of persons, remind one, he says, of the names in Dickens and in Sinclair Lewis. They are much more nearly those of Lewis than of Dickens, and one may guess that he learned from her his trick of underlining his satire by combining in a name the grandiose with the short and flat. Is *George Follansbee Babbitt* not quite like her *Claude Walsingham Popple?* His *Mrs. E. Louetta Swanson* and her *Ora Prance Chattle?* His poet, *T. Cholmondeley Frink,* and her "female Milton of America," *Irene Astarte Pratt?* Above all, his *Vergil Gunch* of *Zenith* and her *Undine Spragg* of *Apex City?*

And finally, is not one of the blemishes in her writing also apparent in his, the tendency, again observed by Mr. Brooks, to impose upon her American scene European habits of speech and manners that in the context are only absurd and destroy the illusion that she would create? To repeatedly describe a citizen of Zenith as wearing his hair *en brosse* does not heighten irony, it only reminds us that the author's experience is somewhat more cosmopolitan than that of the brushy one. If, in Edith Wharton, it is chiefly in the dialogue that such disruptions of texture occur, in Lewis it is chiefly in the expository and narrative passages, but in both mentor and pupil—if he was—the effect of milieu violated by point of view is the same.

From another mentor, H. G. Wells, Lewis received even less qualified approval:

> *My dear Lewis*
>
> I want to write praise. *Babbitt* is one of the greatest novels I have read for a long time. He is what we call a "creation" but what we really mean is that he is a completely individualized realization of a hitherto elusive type. He is the common American prosperous business man *got.* You have got him. No one has been anywhere near getting him before. He lives & breathes another atmosphere! He moves about. His baseness, his vile gregariousness, his vulgarity &—what is the hope of America—his suffering & struggling intimations of beauty, are all wonderfully done. You never seem to strain. Your ease is perfect. In every way I think *Babbitt* knocks *Main Street* (which is a very good book you know) into a cocked hat. Reading it fills me with regret that I did not see more of you while you were in England. I salute you with gestures of respect & affection. I wish I could have written *Babbitt. . . .*
>
> I am my Dear Lewis
> Yours completely
> *H. G. Wells*

A gratified Lewis replied at once:

Dear Mr. Wells:

I started another letter to you, & my wife said it was extremly ingenu. Well, damn it, why shouldn't it be? For so many years I have admired you, written about you—I remember reading *Tono Bungay* by a log-fire during a California sou'wester; [*The New*] *Machiavelli* all one summer night on Cape Cod; I remember the sensation of each of your books; & why shouldn't I be a bit ingenu at your flattering praise of *Babbitt?* I am far sorrier than you can be that we did not see more of each other in England, & I devoutly hope that will be remedied when we go abroad again—probably in a year from now. Please accept my wishes for a happy & prosperous autumn, & believe me

Yours sincerely,
Sinclair Lewis

A thank-you letter is as hard to be spontaneous in as a note of condolence—except that one blessedly can say damn!

There was a letter, too, from his new admirer, W. Somerset Maugham. Maugham recorded in *A Writer's Notebook* that, traveling in the United States, he was baffled by the middle class, he simply did not know what it *was,* but reading *Main Street* enabled him suddenly to conceive it. Now, of *Babbitt,* he wrote from Bangkok:

I think in many ways it is a much better book than *Main Street.* It seems to me a more complete and rounded work of art; of course I read it with interest and amusement, but, as you will not be surprised to know, also with horror. I cannot imagine that such a ruthless depiction of a certain type and a certain class has ever been attempted; and the objectivity, so cold and merciless, with which you have written gives one a very curious sensation; except that people never recognize themselves I should say that you must be on the high road to being one of the most disliked men in America. I read *Babbitt* with sweating palms at the thought of how shy all those people would make me if I met them in real life. I thought I knew from *Main Street* what the man was like in his high stiff collar and ready-made suit of clothes whom I saw in the smoking compartment of a Pullman, but now I know that this was only an optimistic sketch of him. After reading *Babbitt* he stands before me in all his fleshiness.

I hope the book will have as great a success as *Main Street;* I am curious to know with what you will follow it up, for it seems to me that you have in *Babbitt* exhausted a vein, and I shall look forward to his successor. You are a very lucky young man. . . .

"Babbitt," Zona Gale wrote him, "is an infinite book. . . . You are as good for life as you are for fiction." Not for Somerset Maugham alone, but for all Americans and for readers everywhere, the novel had brought into focus an image of American culture, partial as it may have been, that

enabled them for the first time to see it, understand it, and criticize it. In 1922 a poem called "Babbitt Jamboree," signed "A Song by Vachel Lindsay for Sinclair Lewis," appeared in the periodical *Pan, Poetry and Youth;* it is a rather heavily ironic commentary on the noble heritage of the American Indian reduced to Babbitt dressed up like an Indian.

In 1923, in *Broom,* appeared Malcolm Cowley's "Portrait by Leyendecker," an impressionistic sketch of C. Wesley Brown, a Babbitt plain and simple, dedicated to Sinclair Lewis. The two together suggest that Lewis had provided a critical focus for the avant-garde no less than for the middle-brows. If *Broom* was also to award Lewis its booby prize of one dollar, that was because he was the Babbitt of art. But could he have created one if he had not been the other? John Farrar, the anonymous author of the "Literary Spotlight" series published by *The Bookman,* had written of him:

> So Main Street, the insulted and injured, had won out after all. It has taken Lewis into its materialistic camp. It has made him worship, against his surface will, perhaps, its own kind of success. He "belongs" now, does Sinclair Lewis. The "Bigger and better" bug has bitten him. Is he strong enough to overcome it, or will Main Street's revenge be lasting?
>
> Meredith has a few lines which apply extremely well to the Sinclair Lewis of to-day, the slayer caught in his own mesh, the tamer tamed:
>
> O Raphael! when men the Fiend do fight,
> They conquer not upon such easy terms.
> Half serpent in the struggle grow these worms . . .
> . . . While mind is mastering clay
> Gross clay invades it.

Still, only mind itself can know that the clay is there. John O'Hara has said that Lewis was born to write *Babbitt,* which is probably to say that he was born Babbitt *in order* to write it, yet with this difference—a supreme difference—that he alone was able to see it.

> Lewis was born to write Babbitt's story. That was enough. It wasn't all, but it was enough. One man out of many thousands of authors and journalists and poets and playwrights was properly equipped in all or nearly all the essential ways, and by the accidental timing of his birth, to be present and able to observe, reject, and finally to create George F. Babbitt. All the commonplaces about the similarities between Babbitt and Lewis himself ignore the factor that made Lewis and Babbitt totally dissimilar: Lewis, the only Lewis, saw Babbitt. All the other novelists and journalists and Babbitt himself were equally blind to Babbitt and Zenith and the United States of America until 1922. Do you know of anyone since Fielding who made such an important discovery-creation, and without a war for a backdrop? *

* John O'Hara in a letter to the author, February 17, 1959.

Babbitt and the United States of America in 1922 seemed nearly coextensive. When Isaac Marcosson interviewed Trotsky, he found him reading the Russian translation of the novel:

> I find *Babbitt* curiously interesting and instructive although it is too bourgeois in character. In the last analysis, however, Babbitt, the man, is no more bourgeois than your John D. Rockefeller, J. P. Morgan and Henry Ford.

In 1931, even one so remote from the United States as George Santayana—I take instances at random—wrote a friend:

> And is America really so helpless and distracted? I don't know whether I have told you that last summer I read *Babbit* [*sic*]—not the Harvard Babbit [*sic*], but the true classic; there the prophetic intention is evident, although no suggestion of the direction appears in which salvation may come.

That America was really so "helpless and distracted" the world happily believed. C. E. M. Joad's bitterly biased account of American civilization in *The Babbitt Warren* (1926) simply translates *Babbitt* itself back into rather bad expository prose. When Sinclair Lewis died, Lewis Gannett reported, a Bogotá newspaper observed that in George F. Babbitt, he had created a character "as representative as Don Quixote, Hamlet, Faust, or Tartarin de Tarascon." Whatever the deficiencies of the novel, George F. Babbitt had moved into the archetypes.

The deficiencies are many, and only the most obvious need be named. When, only a year after the publication of *Babbitt,* Lewis replied to an inquiry from Arthur B. Maurice, literary editor of the New York *Herald,* about the origin of *Babbitt,* he said that all he could remember was that the original name of the protagonist was Pumphrey and that "I planned to make the whole novel 24 hours in his life, from alarm clock to alarm clock. The rest came more or less unconsciously." The name Pumphrey remained in a minor character—"Professor Joseph K. Pumphrey, owner of the Riteway Business College and instructor in Public Speaking, Business English, Scenario Writing, and Commercial Law"—and the original structural conception remains in the first seven chapters. The rest, twenty-seven chapters, one may conjecture, did not come about unconsciously. One does not "exhaust a vein" in this fashion.

These twenty-seven chapters are systematically planned if rather aimlessly assembled set pieces that, taken together, give us the sociology of middle-class life. These pieces have as their topics such matters as Politics, Leisure, Club Life, Trade Association Conventions, Class Structure and Attitudes, Conventional Religion, "Crank" Religion, Labor Relations, Marriage and the Family, and such lesser topics as The Barbershop and The Speakeasy. There is no plot to effectively contain and unite these interests, but their fragmentariness is in part overcome by the fact that Babbitt moves through all of them in the course of his rising discontent, his rebellion, his retreat and resignation. Each of these three moods, in turn, centers in a more or less separate narrative: the first in the imprisonment of Paul Riesling after he shoots his wife; the second in Babbitt's attempt to find sympathy in Tanis Judique and "the Bunch"; the third in the pressures brought on him by the Good Citizens' League and his wife's happily coincidental emergency operation. It is not surprising that the general thematic and narrative movement, like the central figure himself, is sometimes lost to sight in the forest of marshaled mores.

Edith Wharton's gentle observation that the novel seemed to depend on an excess of slang suggests another defect; and this arises from the danger that is inherent in the habit of mimicry. C. P. Snow, discussing Dickens, has pointed out this danger for the novelist:

> The danger is, it is too satisfying; it is too satisfying even when there is no audience: it gives one the slightly inflated feeling that there is nothing left to say. The inflation gets more balloon-like when there is an audience; one forgets about people one can't imitate, one concentrates on the mimicries that come off, and with those one is happy repeating the turn. . . . Dickens was like a mimic in a bar. As Frank O'Connor says in *The Mirror in the Roadway,* there is "a flight to the periphery of the story," where he is happy with the characters which, he knows from trial and error, he can mimic without thought and make his audience respond.

Nowhere does Lewis's pleasure in mimicry threaten to carry him so far beyond the demands of his fiction as in his use of public addresses of one sort or another; yet one might point out, too, that if these more than any other elements in his story tend to carry him to its periphery and only there, they are also a very integral part of his satire. Elocution is an old American institution, and a windy, mindless rhetoric has been of its essence. Lewis's use of elocution adds a swelling note to the already loud *blat-blat* of that public voice that roars and clacks throughout the novels, and if Lewis lets Babbitt admire Chan Mott because he "can make a good talk even when he hasn't got a doggone thing to say," he is also making an observation on the empty and noisy restlessness of American life.

Lewis's irony is sometimes oversimplified in a positively geometric fashion, as when, for example, he immediately juxtaposes the disaster for the Babbitts when the McKelveys condescend to dine with them, and the disaster for the Overbrooks when the Babbitts condescend to dine with them. (This is precisely like the mechanical juxtaposition in *Main Street* of Carol's despairing observation of the town and Bea Sorenson's delighted observation of it.) Gross lapses in tone, when sentiment overcomes irony, is another old weakness. No one need know of Sinclair Lewis's reveries over young Helen Cooke or of his need to reduce the sexual relationship to an infantile diversion to be embarrassed in reading about Babbitt's night and morning dream of his "fairy child."

> He slipped away, ran down the paths of a midnight garden, and at the gate the fairy child was waiting. Her dear and tranquil hand caressed his cheek. He was gallant and wise and well-beloved; warm ivory were her arms; and beyond perilous moors the brave sea glittered.

In this familiar prose, Lewis's satire has lost its focus.

These matters are all obvious, but they are not the matters that troubled those contemporary readers who were left unsatisfied by *Babbitt.* Nor was it Lewis's satiric exposure of American commercial culture in itself that disturbed them, but rather their failure to find in the novel anything beyond this grossness. With Santayana, they saw "no suggestion of the direction . . . in which salvation may come." In Babbitt they saw only the exemplification of Mencken's "boob," who was not capable of being saved, and in the novel at large they saw no one who was, and Sinclair Lewis seemed to them, like Mencken, to be without "spiritual gifts." Lewis's world, necessarily, was a damned world, and T. K. Whipple, for example, eloquently described it as he saw it:

> Life dehumanized by indifference or enmity to all human values—that is the keynote of both Gopher Prairie and Zenith. And nowhere does this animosity show itself more plainly than in hostility to truth and art. The creed of both towns is the philosophy of boosting, a hollow optimism and false cheeriness which leads directly to hypocrisy, as in making believe that business knavery is social service. Toward ideas likely to break this bubble of pretense the people are bitterly opposed; toward new ideas they are lazily contemptuous; toward other ideas they are apathetic . . . intellectually both are cities of the dead, and in both the dead are resolved that no one shall live.

In England, Filson Young had already said that "a world inhabited by Sinclair Lewis's characters would be a nightmare." Maxwell Geismar, later, observed the hellish quality of Zenith: "it is almost a perfectly conceived poetic vision of a perfectly standardized money society; it is our native *Inferno* of the mechanized hinterland." And not, many readers inferred, of the hinterland alone. The spectacle was supposed to be America. The complaint was to say of Lewis, in effect, what Lewis said of Babbitt, that he was "without a canon [of value] which would enable him to speak with authority."

Had the Wellsian optimist vanished in the Menckenian pessimist? The essential narrative pattern had not changed: the individual trapped in an environment, catching glimmerings of something more desirable beyond it, struggling to grasp them, succeeding or failing. Babbitt fails—or nearly does—with the result that the comic-satiric element here is both heightened and broadened over that of the earlier novels. Clifton Fadiman, writing of

Dodsworth, defined this central pattern when he wrote of Dodsworth as a man who "can neither give himself wholly over to the business of *being* a businessman nor give himself wholly over to the more difficult business of being a man. His vacillation between the part and the whole forms the basic theme of all of Sinclair Lewis's finest novels. . . ." Similarly, Frederick Hoffman suggested that there are two Babbitts, one the perfect Menckenese "boob," the other the "doubting Babbitt." A double question follows: Can the doubting Babbitt conceive of the qualities that make a man as well as a businessman, that create a society as well as a mere association of "joiners"; and, can Sinclair Lewis?

The novel makes it easy enough for one to name the values that would save Zenith, and Babbitt with it; they are love and friendship; kindness, tolerance, justice, and integrity; beauty; intellect. For the first two of these Babbitt has a throbbing desire, if no very large capacity. Of the next four he has intimations. The seventh he can approach only in the distortions of his reveries. To the last he is a total stranger. Of Lewis one must say that he was much like Babbitt in the first two, with no greater capacity; that the next four comprise the core of his character and of his demand on life; of the next, that it is too readily softened by sentiment and too easily represented by unsullied native scenery, a Venetian lagoon, tooled Florentine leather, those cafés of Paris, lanes in Kent. When "beauty" is brought into *Babbitt,* a hush may fall, but the prose blurs and deteriorates:

> Sometimes Paul came over in the evening with his violin, and even Zilla was silent as the lonely man who had lost his way and forever crept down unfamiliar roads spun out his dark soul in music.

And of the last quality, one can only say that, on the evidence of the novels, the matter remains enigmatic.

We have omitted from our list the power of observation, which, in its full sense, may depend on all the other qualities taken together and become the highest form of intuition; but in the more limited sense in which we usually use the term in both social intercourse and literary discourse, it is the quality that differentiates Lewis from his creature.

Perhaps it is futile to approach any Lewis novel as a work of art. Certainly, if *Babbitt* cannot be thus approached, none of the other novels can be. And generally speaking, artistic considerations in 1922 were of far less importance than the fact that, once more, Lewis had precisely hit upon a current mood and given it popular definition.

A year before *Babbitt* was published, Harold Stearns had completed his compilation called *Civilization in the United States,* and in his "Preface" he wrote that he had found three major contentions that were basic to all of the essays that his thirty writers had contributed. These contentions are exactly the contentions of *Babbitt.* The first is that in our business civilization we are hypocrites, that there is an appalling gap between our professions and our practice. The second is that we fail in too many quarters to recognize the fact that American civilization is being determined by an enormous variety of national strains, and that until "we begin seriously to appraise and warmly to cherish the elements which make up our life, and to see the common element running through them, we shall . . . remain . . . a polyglot boarding-house." The third is the "most moving and pathetic fact in the social life of America to-day," our "emotional and aesthetic starvation, of which the mania for petty regulation, the driving, regimentating and drilling, the secret society and its grotesque regalia, the firm grasp on the unessentials of material organization of our pleasures and gaieties are all eloquent stigmata." In one novel, Sinclair Lewis had simultaneously dramatized the conclusions of thirty American minds. Thousands of other minds, caught in or fleeing from Commercial Street, as earlier, in and from Main Street, were waiting for this confirmation of their disgust and of their inarticulate dreams.

Perfectly timed to match the national mood, the novel was, furthermore, the first of its kind in two striking ways. American literature had a rich, if brief, tradition of the business novel. James, Howells, Norris, London, Phillips, Herrick, Sinclair, Wharton, Dreiser, Poole, Tarkington—all these writers had been centrally concerned with the businessman; and, after James and Howells, only Tarkington was to find in him any of the old, perdurable American virtues. Business was synonymous with ethical corruption; the world of business was savagely competitive, brutally aggressive, murderous. The motivation of the businessman was power, money, social prestige—in that order. But the businessman in all this fiction was the tycoon, the powerful manufacturer, the vast speculator, the fabulous financier, the monarch of enormous enterprises, the arch-individual responsible only to himself. And his concern was with production.

After the First World War, the tycoon may still have been the most colorful and dramatic figure in the business myth, but he was no longer by any means the characteristic figure, and *Babbitt* discovers the difference. This is the world of the little businessman and, more particularly, of the middleman. If his morals are no better, his defections are anything but spectacular. Not in the least resembling the autocratic individualist, he is the compromising conformist. No producer himself, his success depends on public relations. He does not rule; he "joins" to be safe. He boosts and boasts with his fellows, sings and cheers and prays with the throng, derides all difference, denounces all dissent—and all to climb with the crowd. With the supremacy of *public* relations, he abolishes human relations. All this Sinclair Lewis's novel was the first to give back to a culture that was just becoming aware that it could not tolerate what it had made of itself.

And it did it with a difference. The older novels, generally speaking, were solemn or grandly melodramatic denunciations of monstrous figures of aggressive evil. *Babbitt* was raucously satirical of a crowd of ninnies and buffoons who, if they were malicious and mean, were also ridiculous. And yet, along with all that, *Babbitt* was pathetic. How could it possibly have failed?

Almost daily communications from New York to Hartford assured its author—who was living in the kind of house that the Charles McKelveys had in Zenith and to which the George F. Babbitts aspired—that, once more, his was an extravagant success.* Almost at once there were requests for dramatic rights, and in November Harcourt closed with Warner Brothers for film rights. The reputation of Sinclair Lewis was now so secure that it seemed simply good business for Harcourt to reissue the three early novels, *Our Mr. Wrenn, The Trail of the Hawk* and *The Job,* without any changes and with no apology for their amateurishness. Were these not the workshop out of which America's leading novelist had come? †

America's leading novelist was not very happy in Hartford. He had hardly come there when he began to wonder why he had. To Mencken he wrote on September 13:

> We seem to have settled in this town which has no virtues except that one can live in a lordly manner on not very much money, and that though it's quiet for work, it's also only three hours from NY. I have never yet been able to find where in these beatific Vereinigen I could be content to live for more than a few months. This is another experiment: we have leased a house for a year.

Perhaps it would work out as a permanent residence—with frequent trips and journeys, of course; and to H. G. Wells at the end of September he said that they had no plans then for going abroad. But very soon Hartford came to seem exactly the wrong sort of city for him. Shortly after he arrived, he was entertained at a dinner given by newspapermen and including prominent citizens. They had talked to him so much and so exclusively about the wealth of Hartford, of its great insurance companies and its industry, that he, in his dinner speech, told them that they would do better to forget its wealth and think of its literary tradition, the Hartford of the Connecticut Wits, of Harriet Beecher Stowe and of Mark Twain (he prob-

* On the world at large and ultimately on the United States, *Babbitt* was to make an even stronger impression than *Main Street.* In England, for example, it had much larger sales. But in the United States, the sales of its hard-cover edition were only 253,237 copies, as against the 414,222 copies of *Main Street.* Its reprint sales, however, had gone to 1,278,081 copies by June 30, 1959; those of *Main Street,* to 759,833 copies.

† The books were ready to go out, but Harcourt, waiting for a lull with *Babbitt,* did not release them until the following March.

ably did not know of Wallace Stevens, who was paradoxically right there in the office of an insurance company). The speech suggests the discontents that would grow. He had put himself into the heart of exalted Babbittry—wealthy, conservative, outlying America. His erratic conduct was calculated to offend hostesses for whom a lush propriety was more important than the whims of a not entirely amiable young lion. H. S. Canby wrote of him in this period:

> Too many easy judgments were formed of Lewis in his percussion-powder days. He had a face of boiler plate, but his mental skin was as sensitive as a baby's. If he drank, it was, as with Poe, to quiet his nerves, usually with contrary results. There was a noble independence about the man, to be respected even when he used it to sneer at the genteel age, which was his enemy. I have seen him rise from a dull dinner party, say "I'm tired," go through the nearest door, pop into the most available bed—and emerge two hours later in excellent humor. Once he chose an ambassador's room, which made difficulties with protocol.

Once he chose to swear at the card table of a Hartford hostess whose chilly reproach impelled him to order his wife to follow him out of the house, never to return. The recollection is Mrs. Lewis's.

The popular recollection in and around Hartford is that the Lewises were "frozen" out of that society. Nearly five years after they had gone, when a prominent Hartford broker, the son-in-law of "the social leader of Hartford," was involved in a New York scandal, the Bridgeport *Herald* reported as follows:

> The story of Sinclair Lewis's "throw down" at the home of the Aldriches has never been officially verified but has been told so many times by Lewis's friends that it has become a classic. . . .
>
> They were entertained and they entertained. Mrs. Lewis inaugurated a series of Sunday morning breakfasts that became popular with the young literary set.
>
> Then came the party at the home of Mr. and Mrs. C. Morgan Aldrich, where the pink of Hartford's younger set gathered, including the Lewises. The party became somewhat gay, and Lewis, who is an irreverent fellow, as everybody knows, got to singing a song which has been sung by college fellows more times than a few. The song contained one or two irreligious passages, not obscene but making fun of sacred things. The song was objectionable to Mrs. Aldrich, so the story goes, and Lewis was requested to stop singing it. Lewis, seeing nothing objectionable in his song, was displeased and insisted on singing it or quitting the party. The host and hostess are said to have stood by their original contention that the song was too irreverent to be sung in their home, and the Lewises left the house. Shortly afterwards Lewis . . . went to London to work on a new book while Mrs. Lewis eventually went to New York. The Aldriches had decreed "thumbs

down" on the Lewises and Lewis had become disillusioned about Hartford. . . .*

When that story was published, Mrs. Lewis was within months of obtaining her divorce, and—poor woman!—one can only exclaim for what she had been asked to endure. Small wonder that in February of 1923, left behind there with her mother and her son—Miss Pohlmann had returned to England—she should have written Mrs. McComas to cry out that Hartford was loathsome, the City of Dreadful Day, not Night!

From the beginning, Lewis would break away from Hartford in exasperation and dash to New York, and he soon arranged with his lecture agency to go on a six-week tour. He gave his first lecture in Detroit on October 12, and a few other lectures in the Middle West, but almost immediately, in a week or less, he was back in Hartford in a state of nervous exhaustion. Except for a lecture scheduled to be delivered to the Philadelphia Forum on November 2, he canceled the rest of his tour and then, with his wife, went off on a week's motor trip to collect himself. They drove as far as Quebec. On October 29 he was again in Hartford, writing Mencken to welcome him on his return to the United States. (In England, Mencken had not sought out Lewis's friend, C. E. Bechhofer Roberts, who, in the following year, was to dedicate his *Literary Renaissance in America* to Lewis, "Most Romantic of Realists," but in Berlin, where Mencken was happier, he did find him and they "got stewed.") On the thirtieth he wrote his father in detail about the motor trip, describing the scenery, the architecture, the conditions of the roads, and he told him that he was "glad to have given up the lecturing; it will save both my time and my nerves. Grace and I both feel strong as oxen after our trip."

In Philadelphia, Lewis spoke on a Menckenian theme: bunk. He walked onto the stage of the Academy of Music clutching a sheaf of newspaper advertisements and, after entertaining his audience by reading some of the more outrageous of them, threw them into the air and announced that ours was the "Olympian age of bunk." But trust to the young, the revolutionaries, the clear-eyed who see through the complacent clichés of their moldy old professors, through the claims of the scorned advertisements on the platform floor, through the pretenses of religion; and do not charge them with sacrilege if they are skeptical enough to question the existence of God. "In the gentle art of saying a great deal out of nothing," concluded the *Public Ledger* next morning, "and keeping a house, filled to overflowing, in a state bordering upon hysteria for more than an hour, Mr.

* *With Love from Gracie* contains a similar anecdote, but the setting is England in the next year, the occasion a weekend party at Lord Beaverbrook's country place. After dinner the two Lewises entertained the assembly with an impromptu song, a parody revival hymn. "There was a horrible silence and we saw Tim Healy, devout Catholic, stare at these sacrilegious Americans and leave the room. We were sick with shame."

Lewis may be said to be a particularly apt exponent of the merits of 'bunk, bunk' and more 'bunk.' " This newspaper account led Mark Sullivan, in Washington, to write Lewis a few days later at great length, praising him for having taken up, in *Babbitt* as in his speech, the important matter of our commercial spirit, "the source of what is wrong with America and civilization . . . my hope is you will press on with the theme you have got hold of."

"Yuh, I AM thinking about the next novel—a lot," he wrote to Harcourt on November 22, "it's ripening slowly but I hope it'll be the real big thing when it belooms." (And had Harcourt by any chance thought of a de luxe edition of *Main Street* and *Babbitt* for the Christmas trade?) He had told his father that he had to get back to a lot of writing that he was committed to do, but there is no evidence that he was doing much. An article in the *International Book Review* of the *Literary Digest* for December would seem to be all. Called "A Review of Reviewers," it consists of gentle chiding of the old-fashioned, lady-librarian sort of reviewer and of complaints about the new, "hard-hitting" young newspaper reviewer, tough and insensitive. He was, however, working toward *Arrowsmith.*

The origins of that novel float uncertainly in the alcoholic haze of Chicago. On November 17, Mencken wrote to propose more of the same in New York:

> Nathan and I are planning to pull off a quiet and refined literary dinner in New York some time soon—a sort of lofty answer to the lousy and degraded affairs which now disgrace the town. No more than 12 head of men. No filthy bootleggers' varnish, but genuine goods out of my private cellars on my Maryland estates. We have in mind you, Joe Hergesheimer, Dreiser, Boyd, O'Neill, etc.—no college boys, but all hairy men and experienced pots. Would you come down for it? I surely hope so. Keep it very quiet.

Lewis replied enthusiastically to "Dear Brother":

> Your proposal of a conference of the brethren to consider the state of our missions in Korea comes, it seems to me, from a direct inspiration by the Redeemer. In this hard pastorate, where the vestrymen now examine my correspondence with every choir singer, I see as a light on the distant mount your invitation to foregather with the sanctified and in the innocent company of the realists and other stews to make sweet sounds of hymnody. I should come were I much farther even than Hartford from the kindly precincts of General Theological Seminary.

Such banter fills the rest of the page of his note paper.

On the twenty-third he wrote again to say that he and his wife would be in New York from December 7 to December 15 or 18, that they would be at the Chatham, and would Mencken as soon as possible please settle on some date in that period. The editor of the Harcourt-Lewis letters says that the Lewises arrived in New York on December 5. Perhaps he wished to allow himself two days for more sober business than any meeting with Mencken was likely to permit. At any rate, in that New York visit, two events of some consequence occurred. He saw Paul de Kruif again, whether by accident or appointment, and it was arranged that they would go to Washington immediately after the New Year and sail from New York for the West Indies on January 4. A contract was drawn up for a full collaboration: the Lewis share in royalty would be 75 per cent, the De Kruif, 25 per cent. De Kruif was paid a ten-thousand-dollar advance and went hastily back to Michigan to marry a former student, Rhea Barbarin. The other event was Mencken's party.

One would like to know who was there. The sullen Dreiser? The malicious Boyd? It hardly seems likely. But Carl Van Doren apparently was, and this was probably the beginning of their long if frequently inactive friendship. In a note to Mencken after he had returned to Hartford, written on December 20, which suggests that he had stayed until his outside date, Lewis said, "Das war aber—Christ am I forgetting my patriotism—that was yet a beautiful party I had with you in N.Y. . . . The Rev. Dr. Carl Van Doren is indeed a holy & praying Kerl." In the same note he tells Mencken that if they are to have the "Literary Soiree" in Baltimore that had been discussed, it would have to be between January 1 and 3.

Nathan he certainly saw, and Nathan's continuing recollections, which no doubt extend into later periods in New York, probably take their start in that pre-Christmas holiday.

> I began to meet our friend more frequently. He would stop in at my apartment in the late afternoon for a Florestan cocktail, sometimes so moody that he didn't speak five words and at other times so excited and voluble that he would stand up and, apropos of nothing at all, make speeches at me for an hour on end. These speeches, generally couched in dialect of one species or another, were invariably on one of two subjects: himself—in terms of a facetious self-appraisal predicated upon critics who did not sufficiently appreciate him, and myself—consisting for the most part in deplorings of the unhappy facts that I didn't drink enough, that I didn't have the sense to recognize *Hobohemia* for a swell play [one must doubt that!], that Mencken and I were nice enough fellows all right but that we ought to get married, and that something ought to be done about our recognizing Stuart Sherman anyway.* At other times I would call on him in

* Stuart P. Sherman, once a student of Irving Babbitt's at Harvard, later an English professor at the University of Illinois and literary editor of the *Herald Tribune*, and an apostle of the New Humanism long before that view became a matter of public controversy, was the constant butt of Mencken's criticism. Sherman, an academic defender of the conservative, "puritanical" tradition in American literature, particularly objected to the novels of Theodore Dreiser, works to which Mencken was particularly attracted. It is rather remarkable that Sherman should have made an exception of Sinclair Lewis among the "realists" and found his work so admirable. From about 1922 on, Sherman began to take a less rigid literary attitude.

> whatever hotel room he was occupying that week. He never used a chair in any such room, but always favored a far end of the bed, the rest of the bed usually being taken up by a varying and various assortment of individuals who gave one the impression that he had run down into the street and herded them in indiscriminately a few minutes before. Who most of them were, I never had the faintest idea. Many of them looked like a comic-strip artist's idea of anarchists; they all talked at once about everything under the sun; and they all drank his liquor very proficiently. He called them all by diminutives of their Christian names, always duly announced in introducing each one of them that each was a grand guy, and confidently and enthusiastically predicted to me on each and every occasion that no less than six of those present were virtuosi of one sort or another who one day would take the critics off their feet. None of them—there were at least eighty or ninety he thus eulogized in the period of my visits—has yet been heard of.

In his mood of high exhilaration, and with the knowledge that he would almost at once be free of both Hartford and domestic responsibilities, home and wife and child, he no doubt strode up and down the length of Manhattan with his imitations. And sometimes they were not only spirited but charming and truly inventive. Canby leaves such a recollection:

> Once at my house he rode high on an imaginary conversation between Shakespeare and Ben Jonson. Jonson was the patronizing high-brow; Shakespeare was the popular writer, humble in a dangerous way before Art and Learning. He could give the people what they wanted, since he was not writing for posterity like his learned friends. To this day I see Lewis's quizzical Will and pompous Ben more vividly than in any historian's portrait.

After such exertion, was it not time to prepare for a long and restful ocean journey? Back in Hartford, Lewis made his preparations. Mencken wrote to complain that the idea for the new novel "is the damndest nonsense I have heard for years. Your next one must be a full-length picture of an American college president. De Kruif is in the pay of the Turks." Lewis defended the conception of a novel about "a Civilized Man who happens by profession to be a bacteriologist," and on December 30, beginning with a spate of bacteriological jargon—

> I still think you are unjustified in your assertion that all micrococci possess flagella, and certainly your definite assertion that all large spirilla tend to manifest themselves in serous media as lophotricha is unsubstantiated.

—and, working his way through other nonsense, he concludes by arranging that he and De Kruif will meet Mencken in Baltimore on Tuesday, January 2.

In December of 1921 Mencken had lamented that, although in his cellar were "bottles enough to keep me stewed for 15 years," a prescribed diet had put him on milk, eggs, "zwieback and schmierkäse—a diet for sucklings." Mencken's preparations for Prohibition are legendary and the legend is confirmed by his biographer William Manchester. But Manchester's tale has a sad end: "Steadily, his liquor stock dwindled, until in January, 1922 [January 2, 1923], after a devastating visit by Red Lewis, he had touched bottom." Next day, in New York, Lewis and De Kruif met the Ernest Braces by accident in the Haitian consulate and took them back to their hotel where there was another extended party that night. When they sailed on the *Guiana* on the afternoon of January 4, 1923, Mencken was there to see them off, and he wrote Dr. Fishbein in Chicago to apprise him of the fact that he had "poured them on the boat." Mrs. Lewis, one must infer, was not present to observe the spectacle.

Of Martin Arrowsmith, Lewis was to write, "he found that whisky relieved him from the frenzy of work, from the terror of loneliness—then betrayed him and left him the more weary, the more lonely. He felt suddenly old. . . ." Friendship, for Lewis, was much like drink—a gulping, indiscriminate distraction from himself that was bound to fail, and fail nearly as frequently, the need each time more desperate, the "remedy" each time less able. So spin! spin!

In *Memoirs of a Superfluous Man,* Albert Jay Nock writes of the "desperate generation," and he gives as his example John Reed. ". . . they had frankly given themselves up for lost, and were wretched, dissatisfied, desperate," their desperation "directed only against themselves," obsessed as they were by an almost insane passion for self-destruction. Watching the life of Sinclair Lewis unwind itself, one wonders if Nock had found the most telling example. Perhaps. For Sinclair Lewis differed from the men Nock had in mind in at least two ways: two things that he knew he wanted—money and fame—they did not much care about; and he had many more years than they through which to endure the self-destructive agonies.

5

AND THEN HE HAD that extraordinary capacity, compulsion, for work, work of the most meticulously systematic kind that would sustain itself through many hours, day after day, even under holiday circumstances.

The new novel would be called *The Barbarian.* Struggling up through who knows what throbbing layers of hangover, the two men on shipboard shook themselves into seriousness and clarity, and went to work on it. Without Paul de Kruif or a man like him, this novel would, of course, have been an impossibility; De Kruif was the expert; Lewis's initial equipment to handle this material did not extend beyond an old and long autobiographically rooted feeling for the subject.

> A small boy whose memory is of being awakened by his father's talking to a patient, down at the door; of catching sleepy 3-A.M. phrases: "Where is the pain? Eh? Well, all right, but you ought to have called me earlier. Peritonitis may have set in." A small boy who was permitted to peep at anatomical charts and ponderous medical books in The Office. Then his brother going off to medical school—gossip of classes, of a summer's internship, of surgery versus general practice. And behind father and brother, a grandfather and uncle who were also doctors.
>
> With such a background, the work and ideals of the doctors have always been more familiar to me than any others, and when I began to write novels . . . I thought of some day having a doctor hero. Part of that ambition was satisfied in Dr. Kennicott, of *Main Street,* but he was not the chief character, and furthermore I desired to portray a more significant medico than Kennicott—one who could get beneath routine practice into the scientific foundation of medicine—one who should immensely affect all life.

In New York he had discussed several quickly spun plots with De Kruif and discarded them all, and when they began to work on shipboard, they had only a title for the novel and the general theme of a young medical man who was average in his share of human limitations but remarkable in his dedication, in spite of all impediments and beguilements, to pure research. Their aim, during a sea voyage of two months, was to educate

Lewis in bacteriology and epidemiology and in the methods and spirit of research, to observe conditions in the tropics for a major sequence of scenes, and to work out on paper as complete an outline of the story as possible. They were equipped with a small library of medical textbooks, maps and charts, and any number of letters of introduction to "tropical soldiers, doctors and former pirates and brigands turned respectable."

The boat carried freight to and from the West Indies, and about twenty passengers. Leaving New York, it touched at St. Thomas on January 10 * and proceeded directly south across the Caribbean, paused at a number of small ports in the Lesser Antilles, including that of St. Lucia, and docked at the little extremity of Barbados. There, the chief medical officer of the island was their guide to hospitals, alms houses, a leper asylum. After eleven days of Barbados, they boarded the *Crynssen* † of the Royal Netherlands West India Mail line for a cruise of the Spanish Main. On the last day of the month Lewis wrote his father from Curaçao, where they paused for two days, to say that now they would sail round the horn of Colombia to Puerto Colombia and from there to Colon and the settlements of the Panama Canal Zone.

In Panama they visited the bacteriological laboratory and observed the sanitary work of Dr. Goldthwaite, and on February 10, about to sail again, he wrote his father to tell him how generous a reception the Panama medical men had given them. On February 13, between Puerto Colombia and Curaçao, he wrote an omnibus letter to everyone at Harcourt, Brace & Company, chiefly about De Kruif and their work; another to his father, about a storm between Colón and Puerto Colombia, about their diverse traveling companions, and about his daily salt-water bath; and a third to H. G. Wells:

> With me is Paul deKruif, the bacteriologist, a man whom you would like enormously, a man with a knife-edge mind and an iconoclasm that really means something. Our wives (that sounds somehow polygamic) will join us in England, where we'll probably stay all spring and summer. I hope very much to see you.... Can't DeKruif and I have the pleasure of your dining with us some evening in London—or of lunching—or any other excuse for talk! Let me assure you again of my most affectionate appreciation....

(To this letter, Wells appended a note: "See to this—a week end for both of them.")

Then, after this sobriety, with the afternoon waning, he let himself go, in a fourth letter—to H. L. Mencken. It was headed: "Some damn where in the large and not always quiet Atlantic between Puerto Colombia and

* From St. Thomas went a postcard to Mencken: "Dear Col[onel]—We are comparatively sober. In X [Christ], Paul & Red. XXX G.M.U. [Gott Mitt Uns]."
† "Crynssen" became a county in the novel.

Curacao—some damn time in the afternoon between curacao after lunch and a, as they spell it on the chits, dubble whisky soda before dinner, on the 13th. . . ." The letter reads, in part:

> The book goes grand, Paul De Kruif proves to have as much synthetic fictional imagination as he has scientific knowledge, and that's one hell of a lot. It's going to be my best book—though it isn't just *mine* by a long shot. . . . . We've viewed a lot of dinges and a lot of assorted places, and I must admit that between times we have shot a number of drinks . . .*
>
> Travel notes: On the Guiana we met a Boston florist, aetat 66, a member of the Elks and the Rotary Club, who nevertheless each year goes wandering like the lead in a WJLocke novel, and loves everything exotic—skirts, booze, and grub. . . . . In Panama I saw pinned to the Sam Browne belt of a major who superintends a hospital a Rotary Club button, and I saw a major general who reads Menck, Walpole, Joey Hergesheimer, and SL, and damn well knows what he likes or does not like about em, and why. . . . . In Trinidad I saw a Hindu woman washing clothes beside a stream and wearing, besides absolute rags, about nine thousand dollars worth of silver bangles and coin chains. . . . . Three weeks ago I refused a drink. . . . . On board there is an Englishman who wants US to take over the West Indies and Canada—and then get ready to take over England. . . . . This is a large and occasionally interesting world.

They stopped in at La Guaira, the port of Caracas (to Dr. Fishbein: "We went shooting from La Guaira up to Caracas, a hell of a thrilling drive by motor, among other things"), and then for two days at Port of Spain, Trinidad, and reached Barbados once more on February 20. Next day, still on the *Crynssen,* they sailed for England, and on the twenty-fifth, "four days out from Barbados," crossing the Sargasso Sea, Lewis wrote his father again. (It was ostensibly while they were in the Sargasso Sea that Paul de Kruif wrote his account of what it was like to work on a novel with Sinclair Lewis.) † On March 1 they were passing the Azores, and on March 6 they came in at Plymouth. At the London station, they were greeted by Frazier Hunt, who bore a tray with a cocktail shaker of martinis. These they drank with roistering immediacy. They were a picturesque trio: the two huge, handsome men, rough and tweedy, and the long, thin, grotesque dandy *manqué,* one of whose first errands in London would be a fitting for a black broadcloth opera cape with a purple silk lining.

During the two months at sea, they had worked and drunk with equal enthusiasm ("played" was their gentler and more balanced term for the latter activity). One can feel only an awed admiration that they could have accomplished so much of the first with so little sacrifice of the second. De Kruif, of course, was perfectly equipped to help Lewis in his present

* In his letters, Lewis had a habit of using a string of dots, five, six, or seven of them, to separate his sentences. When, in this text, five dots are used, they are Lewis's, and they do not indicate any omission of material.

† "An Intimate Glimpse of a Great American Novel in the Making," *The Designer and The Woman's Magazine,* June 1924.

task. He had been a teacher of bacteriology in the University of Michigan, where he had been associated with Dr. F. G. Novy and had concentrated his research on immunology. He had served in the Army as a captain in the Sanitary Corps of the Medical Department, worked on the poison and antitoxin of the bacillus of gas gangrene and made the first prophylactic injections of gas gangrene serum. At the Rockefeller Institute he had been an associate in the division of pathology and had been able to observe the person, the character and the work of the great Jacques Loeb, and not only Loeb, but Alexis Carrel, J. H. Northrop and others, all working under the direction of Dr. Simon Flexner. His enthusiasm for the novel was at least as high as Lewis's, and his temperament permitted the most fruitful kind of rapport. Lewis's letters during the voyage and later in London are positive paeans— "... we can work together perfectly ... his totally unusual and fine though fiery brain ... a damn clever man ... the Rock of Ages ... he takes it for granted that he is not to sign the book with me ... when I'm compiling notes into a coherent whole, De Kruif is preparing more data—clear, sound, and just the stuff for dramatic purposes ... De Kruif will be with me in London—thank God!" Thus, over the days, to Harcourt; and to his father as the journey came to an end:

> It's extraordinary how well De Kruif and I work together; we've been together practically twenty four hours a day now for a month and a half, and never a row, never a disagreement—except some extremely interesting ones on an abstract theme.

The arguments were part of the method of "research," and one that Lewis was habitually to use thereafter in getting material from his informants. He would ask De Kruif a question on such a matter as the motivation of a pure-research man, and De Kruif would give an answer; then Lewis would argue, criticize, deride, De Kruif becoming more insistent, more voluble, more informative; and when he thought that he had everything on that issue, Lewis would subside and comfortably allow that De Kruif was probably right. So he learned not only about the materials and the methods of bacteriological research, but about the spirit of the scientist. De Kruif could serve more specific purposes; it was his charge, for example, to work out the complete professional histories of both Arrowsmith and Gottlieb, and to sketch those of lesser characters. From his own various experience in medical science, he could produce prototypes that would suit the conflicts of the developing plot. With Lewis, he would observe the men around them in search of proper physical types; thus they found Arrowsmith himself, "a grave black-haired youngster looking at us across his rum-swizzle glass in the ship's smoking-room." He even found the setting of the plague city:

> A part of the story is laid in a tropical city smitten into tragic silence by a murderous epidemic of bubonic plague. One hot, still Sunday afternoon our

steamer touched for a couple of hours at the island of San Lucia. I wandered ashore while Lewis worked, and came presently into a large square plunged into a deserted Sunday stillness, gloomy under the shade of giant mango-trees. Here was our plague city! I hastened back to the ship, which was to leave in a half-hour, dragged Lewis from his work and hurried him to the square, where he proceeded to conjure up fantastic funeral processions of imaginary plague victims passing by the ominously closed shutters and drawn shades of the balconies of the surrounding houses.

Then back to the ship to set down on the endless yellow sheets of paper the impression of that hot, dark-green, almost sinister, twilight stillness. Of course it wasn't really sinister. It was just a lazy tropical Sunday. But for Lewis it meant a town deserted by panic-crazed people who fled from the creeping death.

Thus the work progressed: maps of towns and cities; floor plans of houses, hospitals, laboratories; time schedules; full biographies of a score of characters; endless notes on yellow sheets—and then all of it systematically fed into the maw of the growing plan. On February 18, Lewis wrote his father, "The book has gone superbly. I've written 25,000 words of plan."

Their working hours were intensive and long. They would "get up at six-thirty, have a sea-water bath in the tub, talk awhile, breakfast, work till lunch. I have a nap and, after some brisk walking round and round the deck, we work again till dinnertime. . . ." And *The Barbarian* was always the subject of their talk. De Kruif draws the picture of two men completely abstracted from the real world, living entirely in the imagined one that they were in the process of creating. Lewis is somewhat more mundane in his accounts and one observes no decline in the habitual gregariousness.

The trip had been jammed with sights and people amusing in themselves and as material useful for this or later books—officers on the two steamers, wandering Americans and English and Germans and Dutch and Spanish, all the curious races of the West Indies and Spanish America—English settled there for ten generations, Negroes with curious dialects, thousands of Hindus in Trinidad, Chinese there and in Panama, feeble little Colombians, sturdy Indians, all kinds. Our intimates have been curious contrasts—on the "Guiana," a roughneck English engineer; in Barbados, a prosy but capable old English doctor; in Panama, Major General Sturgis and his wife; on the "Crynssen," the cheerful first mate and a regular stage Englishman who regards drafts (window ones, not bank drafts!) with indignant astonishment. DeKruif and I today counted 155 separate persons whom we've met since January 4th and whom we seem to know intimately!

One day out from England, he urged his father and Claude to come over for six weeks or two months, if they would. The plan was not yet finished, but he would have more than two months free of his wife—she would sail from New York on May 5—to work on it alone or, when he needed him, with De Kruif.

Lewis settled back in 10 Bury Street; De Kruif, whose wife had joined him, presently found a flat in Chelsea, but until then, they too were in Bury Street. The De Kruifs had arranged that his mother and sister come from Brussels for the Easter weekend, and Lewis, knowing the plan, had arranged to spend the weekend motoring to Bath with the Hunts. But then he decided that he wanted the De Kruifs to come with them. When De Kruif reminded him of the earlier plan, Lewis lost his temper, called him ungrateful, and told him that he was not worthy to work on *Arrowsmith.* Very well, De Kruif agreed, and he withdrew to discuss with his wife their immediate return to the United States. All evening Lewis sent abusive messages to the De Kruif rooms, and at midnight he himself appeared—but now, after all the irrational anger, in apologetic tears, abject. De Kruif stayed.

With his connections, De Kruif found it easy to introduce Lewis to many medical scientists and into laboratories and clinics in and near London. His father had written querulously to ask whether the newspaper reports that he was planning to stay in England for two years were true, and on April 26 Lewis replied reassuringly that they were not true. His plans were indefinite. However,

> The plan of the new novel is finished and the actual writing going ahead promisingly. I've been in a couple of laboratories with DeKruif and, after hearing a lot about the theoretical side of bacteriology, it is interesting to see the actual work, the actual technique—for example, Dr. Inman of the Brompton Tuberculosis Hospital doing blood tests for T.B.—a fixation test, like the Wasserman for syph. I've also had lunch recently with Sir Walter Fletcher, who used to teach physiology at Cambridge and is now head of the governmental Medical Research Fund. He seems to admire Cushing even more than the Mayos.

It was easier to write his father about medicine and *Arrowsmith* than about his social activities. His meeting Bertrand Russell and Lloyd Osborne, his lunching with Hugh Walpole, with John Buchan, his weekend in the country with H. G. Wells, with Ramsay MacDonald and the Duchess of Warwick also present—these matters he did not mention; nor did he describe the motor trip to Bath with Frazier Hunt, Boardman Robinson having taken the place of the De Kruifs, or his new friendship with George S. Kaufman (who also lived at 10 Bury Street) and Marc Connelly, or his proposal to Connelly and Kaufman that they dramatize *Babbitt* and their declining on the grounds that their current play, *To the Ladies,* dealt farcically with a kind of Babbitt, and much else. Some such material he does communicate, his weekend at the house of Sir Philip Gibbs, the war correspondent, for example.

> The Gibbses have quite a small place among soft hills. . . . I much prefer it to the gorgeousness, the luxury, of the great Italian Renaissance palace of Lord Astor, where I spent the week-end before—frightfully nice tho Lord and Lady Astor and the others were.

And he could appeal to his father's country snobbery by telling him about Lord Beaverbrook:

> These Lords! Tuesday evening I dined with H. G. Wells and Lord Beaverbrook. Beaverbrook is a curious person. Born in Canada, his father a poor Presbyterian parson—like the beginnings of the present prime minister, Bonar Law—he was at somewhat over thirty one of the rich men of Canada, and now at about 44 he is a peer of the realm and a power in all of England and so frightfully rich that it makes you ache. He is variously called, by my acquaintances, a scoundrelly rogue and a keen adventurer who is one of the men who will make the new British Empire that is bound to come. Anyway, he is an amusing, gay, baldish, littleish chap, and we got along together capitally. Both he and Phil Gibbs appear to be staunch adherents of *Babbitt.*

Babbitt had been a sensation in England, and it had inevitably extended Sinclair Lewis's social prestige. Its popularity in England is indicated by a letter that it called forth from one T. Owen Jacobsen to the New York *Times,* in which he expressed his admiration for the novel's vivid and incisive Americanism and confessed that he and his friends "compete in working extracts into their everyday conversation." It may be assumed, however, that neither the novel's nor Lewis's present popularity among the English had changed his manner, of which we probably may accept the reflection in George Jean Nathan's recollection of that spring in 1923, once we allow for his characteristic extravagance in remembering the extravagances of others.

> The day I arrived I went to a lunch party, where I found myself seated between John Drinkwater and Philip Guedalla, neither of whom I had previously met. I had not sat down before Guedalla said to me, "You are an American and I have a message for you. If your country doesn't recall Sinclair Lewis at once, there will be war between England and the United States!" It did not take a confidant of the oracles to imagine what had been happening. Our friend Red, as his nickname goes, had all too evidently been living up to his sobriquet, if not [in] its communistic implications, at least in its taurian. It developed that the moment he had set foot on the English shore he had begun to make speeches. These speeches—according to Guedalla amounting up to the hour to a total of something like two or three hundred and delivered in dialect on every conceivable occasion at the rate of a dozen or so daily, or rather nightly—had mainly to do, it appeared, with the shameful failure of the English critics, excepting only Hugh Walpole, to take a proper interest in American literature. Our friend, despite

> the German, French, Italian, Cockney and Way Down East dialects in which he couched his diatribes, may have minced words but certainly not meanings. He not only, while calling loudly for 'arf and 'arf or a spot of whiskey old top, named names, but dates, places and weather conditions. Every now and then, by way of prolonging international amity for a little while longer, it had been necessary for De Kruif, a veritable Sandow of a man, to grab hold of his colleague, pull him down into a chair, and sit on him.

Nathan concludes this portion of his recollections with three anecdotes then current in London: one, that at a dinner party given by a lady of title, Lewis expressed his gratitude for their praise of his work by rushing about the room and "imprinting a very moist buss on the lips of all the female guests"; a second, of his throwing his arms about two elderly men of letters at a gathering of the celebrated and insisting that he be allowed to teach them American dances; and the third, that to a dinner party given by a lady novelist, he brought with him "two strange Germans, a Russian, three Americans whom he had picked up at the American Express Company that afternoon, and two taxicab drivers, both boiled."

Middleton Murry met him in a more reflective mood. They encountered one another on their host's doorstep, Lewis resplendent in his evening cloak.

> He looked and felt hellishly successful. But again the impression he made was strong and satisfying, arousing in me vague and sentimental reminiscence of Abraham Lincoln and the White House. Though one knew that this magnificence was not Lewis's native garb, he bore himself without awkwardness and with ease.

They talked together later of D. H. Lawrence. Lewis had favorably reviewed *Sons and Lovers* years before for Woodward's newspaper syndicate, and afterward he had bought a copy, presumably to reread it. One may be quite certain that he had read no novels of Lawrence's after that—*The Rainbow* or *Women in Love* or *Aaron's Rod*—for he would have choked on that fare. But to Murry he said that he admired Lawrence, at the same time that he confessed his annoyance with a slighting remark that Lawrence had published about him. The only remark about Lewis in Lawrence appears in the essay, "Surgery for the Novel—or a Bomb," which had appeared that spring in the April issue of the *International Book Review,* and which derided "the popular novels—the *Sheiks* and *Babbitts* and Zane Grey novels."

> It was one of Lawrence's most irresponsible dicta; and I did not try to defend it. What chiefly struck me was Sinclair Lewis's frankness in acknowledging that it stung him because it was unjust. "Whatever I may be," said Lewis in effect, though I can no longer vouch for the words, "I deserve something better than that."

Lewis's own literary irresponsibility was almost always on the side of generosity. He had recently urged a novel by his friend Claude Washburn on Harcourt, but the firm felt that it had to decline. Now he was urging with the greatest fervor a novel that his one-time fiancée, Edith Summers [Updegraff] Kelley, had completed and submitted to the firm, even proposing that he would undertake to edit it. This novel, *Weeds,* Harcourt, Brace did publish, and Cape brought it out in England; publicly and privately, Lewis continued to praise it until long after it had died out of print. That spring, his own novels were being reissued—*Our Mr. Wrenn* by Cape in London, with a bit of Anglicizing in the text, and with wall posters in the underground; and three novels by Harcourt. In an omnibus review by Henry L. Stuart, in the New York *Times* in April, the first two of the Harcourt issues were dismissed as hopelessly influenced by the standards of the popular magazines, and the third, *The Job,* was given some praise as representing the gifts of the mature Lewis—". . . Mr. Lewis has flattered, has sought to amuse and distract, has studied his generation. His success, artistic as well as material, dates from the day that he arraigned." To Lewis's repeated requests for information about the sales of these early novels, Harcourt at last wearily replied that they had hardly sold at all. But since Lewis was well into the actual writing of *Arrowsmith,* he could not have cared very much.*

On May 9, in a state of high elation, he wrote Mencken about the progress of the novel.

> Menck, the possibly wild project which Paul de Kruif and I started really has worked. The novel is going. It is harder than hell to do, but there's some 60,000 words of plan—some of it almost the final MS itself—lying here cold and threatening, and now I'm off with the story. I have, Gott sei Dank, a year or more to work on it, and I think I shall get something good, with the correct principles of Presbyterianism in it, and a number of interesting reflections on the value of bacteriophage.
>
> Paul is settled, his wife over here, they two happy. . . The scientific gents here, the real ones who go out more for math than for knighthoods, give him great honor, and he is very happy. . . . . I know no dread details, but the amount of viryle bed-bouncing that goes on in that humble Chelsea flat must be overwhelming to aged critics like you and myself, who have only the thumb still in action. . . . . All through the trip, Paul was wonderful. His greatest pleasure was to be called on for some damn hard problem, in-

* There was endless correspondence with the publishers about the title. Beginning as *The Barbarian,* it threatened to become any of the following: *Barbarian, Courage, Horizon, White Tile, Civilized, Work, Brains, Strange Islands, The Merry Death, The Savage, Martin Arrowsmith, Test Tube, The Stumbler, Martin Arrowsmith, M.D., Dr. Arrowsmith, The Shadow of Max Gottlieb, The Destroyer.* Not until September 21 did plain *Arrowsmith* appear in the lists. For a time, Lewis referred to it as *Martin,* Harcourt as *Martin Arrowsmith.* In its serialized version it appeared as *Dr. Martin Arrowsmith,* and so it appeared in England because of the existence of a publishing firm called Arrowsmith.

> volving not only sheer scientific knowledge but also an imagination, a perception of what was dramatic..... He is quite mad; he will either, when he grows up, do something very beautiful or not a damn thing.
>
> Me—I work and drink and read medicine. Gracie arrives next Sunday...

That was May 13. Perhaps it was high time. Perhaps, too, there was the immediate old irritation with her. At about this point, Lewis tossed off a rather entertaining short piece of fiction called "The Hack Driver," to appear in *The Nation* for August 29 of that summer. The narrator is a distinguished judge who develops the theory that every successful man knows and loves a scoundrel or a scamp who lives the simple life somewhere, whose company he prefers to that of "all the high-falutin' leaders of the city."

> ... perhaps it means that we retain a decent simplicity, no matter how much we are tied to Things, to houses and motors and expensive wives. Or again it may give away the whole game of civilization; may mean that the apparently civilized man is at heart nothing but a hobo who prefers flannel shirts and bristly cheeks and cussing and dirty tin plates to all the trim, hygienic, forward-looking life our womenfolks make us put on for them... the only thing duller than a polite dinner is the conversation afterward...

Except for this and a very casual little piece called "Authors and Interviewing" that Lewis wrote for the June issue of Cape's *Now and Then* (it points out the general absurdity of interviews with writers and concludes with a list of contradictory opinions that the press had attributed to him), his writing had not deviated from the struggles of the dedicated Martin and from his engagement with the simplicity, the directness, the selflessness of his heroine, Leora.

The Lewises had planned to attempt the simplicities at once in a walking trip in Devonshire. There would be free air, adventure, and country inns; no flannel shirts, to be sure, or bristly chins and dirty tin plates. In the meantime, however, there was the problem of Master Wells, who had arrived with his mother on the thirteenth. The problem was quickly disposed of when his parents found an "immensely nice and comfortable boys' school" near Guilford (so Lewis wrote his father), and on the afternoon of the eighteenth, a Friday, they took "the train to Bideford, in Devon, then start off on foot tomorrow for the lovely old town of Clovelly." The plan was to walk for a week, conclude the excursion with the next weekend at H. G. Wells's country establishment, and return to Bury Street for June. The honeymoon, however, was long since over: this time each of them carried a rucksack.

They returned to London on May 25, "in time to go to a big revue... and hear Paul Whiteman's jazz band, which is supposed to be the best American jazz organization and which is quite the sensation of London now, but which I didn't care for—to me it sounds like Noise and nothing much else." Next day, before leaving to spend the night and Sunday with H. G. Wells, Lewis wrote to his father in answer to questions about the sale of *Babbitt,* and he wrote to Harcourt, too, to ask the same questions of him. He had the satisfaction of telling his father (who had once rather tauntingly boasted to the son of his investments in Dakota mortgages) that "by the middle of next year I shall have about $97,000 invested in gilt-edged bonds, permanently, and the income from this will add to my current and movie earnings." But then—a minor note:

> I see that just as Edith Wharton's *Age of Innocence* beat *Main Street* for the Pulitzer prize, so did Cather's *One of Ours* beat *Babbitt.* I'm quite sure I never shall get the Pulitzer—my books are too critical to please polite committees. And I see that some of the New York critics are raising the devil about it. Personally I don't care a hang.

No? *The Age of Innocence, Alice Adams,* and now, of all books, *One of Ours!* In the very air of indifference one can detect a decision in the making.

With Willa Cather, whose hopes for the reception of her novel had now been vindicated, there had been no communication after the appearance of Lewis's review in the *Evening Post.* Had there been, they could not have found much to say to one another, for certainly no two novelists, nearly contemporary, have been less alike in attitude and gift. The contrast between her nostalgic love of the lyric past of America, her imagination haunted by a ghostly history, her religious feeling and her pleasure in the "hand-made," the grave composure of her work, its high degree of selection, her ambition to "unfurnish" the novel—the contrast between all this and his delight in the present, the topical, his infatuation with the new and the efficient, his raucous skepticism, the explosive satirical vein, the mimic fidelity, the naturalistic compulsion to put in everything, the crowded externality—these surely are radical antitheses. One must suspect that his work made her impatient; that he admired much of her work attests again to his catholicity and impersonality. But to try to think of the two together as persons is almost as difficult as to imagine him in Anderson's frosty encounter with Gertrude Stein.

One wonders if Willa Cather's name came into the discussion that presently brought Lewis before the London literary public, as it had come so frequently into his defenses of American writing in the past, and would again. On May 29 he was to debate with the novelist Ian Hay (Major John Hay Beith) in the London School of Economics, for the benefit of London hospitals. Hay had been a highly successful British propagandist in the United States during the war, but he was also one of those gentle English novelists whom Lewis despised, and a year before, Lewis had sent Mencken a clipping that quoted some publicly delivered "tender words of that noble Britisher, Major Beith," in which Beith suggested that if a novelist "found that he gave pleasure to a certain world which included sick persons and children, who did not want to be faced with deep problems, it was a privilege not lightly to be despised."

The subject of their debate was "Main Street and High Street." Hay argued that the English people wished their literary heroes to have aristocratic connections, while Americans wished them to be self-made, an observation that led Lewis to lament the arrogance of the British. He disapproved of the anti-American sentiment that, in the years immediately after the war, was a commonplace of the British press and stage. The English condescended to American writing, were suspicious of freedom and smug in their binding conventions, and above all, they were supercilious. This last quality showed nowhere so much as in the utterances of the English lecturers who toured the United States. If most of these were like the Big Three—Walpole, Gibbs and Major Beith himself—America would be much fonder of Englishmen. "I love England," he concluded. "I hope to be allowed to love England." And while the New York *Times* editorialized on "Our Prophet Abroad" two weeks later, asserting that "Beith buttered Lewis, Lewis buttered Beith," the chairman, Sir William Beveridge, adjudicated by observing that complacency and conceit were probably as strong in Englishmen as in Americans, but the reticence of the English protected them from an insistent public display of these qualities.

That final month in London was largely devoted to social activities which were meant to compensate Mrs. Lewis for her agonizingly dull winter and spring in Hartford. It began with the weekend with Wells, whose other guests were Philip Guedalla and Mark Sullivan. In the next week, they attended the opening of Drinkwater's *Cromwell,* which starred their acquaintance, Henry Ainley. The play was poor but the evening was saved when in an entr'acte Lewis met Arnold Bennett for the first time, and Princess Alice ("I had met the Prince of Wales at Lady Astor's big reception, but this was the first time I met royalty really personally"). After the theater, they brought Henry Nevinson, the old war correspondent, and Mrs. Thomas Lamont up to their flat for a time "and cheerfully damned the show." The next evening they dined at Lord Beaverbrook's house, along with Sir James Dunn, a Canadian banker "much more like Babbitt than like the fictional ideal of a baronet. It is impossible to keep from calling him 'Jimmy' after a couple of hours." On the next afternoon, "Claude's admiration, Stefansson, the artic explorer, came in for tea"; that evening St. Loe Strachey, the editor of *The Spectator,* had them for dinner, and the next evening they dined with E. V. Lucas. The weekend they spent at the house of Mrs. L. Allen Harker, "author of rather romantic tales of pleasant quality but of no great importance," and on Monday, back in London, Lady Maclaren Brown and General C. B. Thomson came to dine with them. It was a whirl.

And it would seem that, up to a point, Lewis enjoyed it quite as much as his wife did. To Mencken he had written in May just before she arrived that he had no plans for coming home.

> I'm sorry, oh king of Babbitts, president of the Central Committee of International Rotary Klubs, but I feel wretchedly little desire to return to the Vereinigen Staaten. I do not discern here in England any future, but after that dear Hartford, Conn., I am so childishly pleased by discovering conversation not only among the intelligentsias but among the well-to-do.

He concluded by quoting an obscene limerick composed by "the Very Rev'd Aloysius Bechhofer" that hardly serves to illustrate his point about the charms of conversation.

Yet he must have been chafing, too, to get back to work, and at the end of his report to his father on June 5, he said that England had been wonderful but that they had had enough of it and "next Monday [June 11] we go over to France for a week or so; we *may,* possibly, spend next summer in some quiet little country house in France, instead of in England, and we're going to explore a little." What they found was hardly, of course, a cottage. It was Le Val-Changis (George Moore had slept there) near Fontainebleau, at Avon, Seine-et-Marne, a large and formal country house of white plaster with an enormous two-story dining room, a garden wing separate enough from the rest to suit the novelist, stables and an overgrown tennis court, the whole set in its own spacious deer park dotted with marble nudes. When the family of three arrived they were to have in attendance a new governess, a new cook and a new maid; and they were traveling with eighteen pieces of luggage.

But that was to happen only after a return to London and another ten days crowded with engagements: lunch with Beatrice and Sidney Webb; dinner with Donald Ogden Stewart; the theater, and afterward, supper at Mrs. Ford Madox Hueffer's (Violet Hunt; Hueffer had by this time changed his name to Ford, abandoned her and established himself in Paris), to whom they brought "one of the nicest men we have met abroad," Marc Connelly; tea next day for Connelly, who brought with him "an amusing little Armenian (tho thoroughly Anglicized)," Michael Arlen; then on to dinner at J. Maynard Keynes's, where were also Lydia Lopokova and Virginia Woolf (did Keynes repeat his folly, or was this in fact the dinner that Sir Osbert Sitwell remembered?); then, on their last Wednesday, up to Oxford for Commemoration Week as the guests of Bevil Rudd, secretary to Lord Birkenhead and Olympic champion in middle-distance running—lunching with undergraduates and recent graduates, punting up the Char for a picnic supper in a meadow, dancing all that night until breakfast ("altho Gracie went to bed at two"), and back to London on Thursday evening in time for a gratefully quiet dinner with the De Kruifs and Donald Brace, who, like Chauncey Tinker, had arrived from the United States;

then on Friday, dinner with Stacy Aumonier; and on Saturday, the thirtieth of June, the climax. With Lady Beaverbrook they motored up to Hendon to attend an aviation meet where they sat in a private box a few feet from the royal enclosure which contained the King, the Queen, Queen Alexandra and her sister, the Dowager Empress of Russia, the Duke and the new Duchess of York, the Duke of Sutherland. Then they motored down to Lord Beaverbrook's establishment, Cherkley, at Leatherhead, Surrey. His guests included His Excellency Timothy Healy, Governor General of Ireland; Sir Edward Hulton, "second most important newspaper proprietor in Great Britain"; Sir William Turner, commander-in-chief of Canadian troops at the beginning of the war; Sir James Dunn, the banker; Sir George Perley, for eight years the Canadian high commissioner in England; Castlerosse, Beaverbrook's Winchell; and others.

> But actually most of them were nothing in God's world but amiable and capable Canadians, perfectly good North Americans, whom to call by a title was almost funny. But we did have a good time, with walking, tennis, a private movie show, a girl who came down from London to sing creole songs, noble food, and a lot of conversation. The real one there was Tim Healy . . .

Healy, who had retired after their ill-judged, impious singing!

Mrs. Lewis wrote to her father-in-law on the heavy, crested letter paper of the household. She was more impressed by this grandeur than that downright ancient would be when he received her information.

On July 5 they arrived at Avon in a pelting rain. Next day Lewis wrote Harcourt to confess that for six weeks he had not "done a lick of work." But "now here . . . I'm settled down again for from three to five months, and damn glad to be . . . already I'm started at work." And he worked intensively then, with the old dedication. On July 31 he wrote his father:

> Almost a month here now . . . and how the work has gone. I've written about fifty thousand words—that, of course is first draft . . . I'm afraid this damned book is going to be as long as *Main Street*. . . . We had thought somewhat of buying a second hand motor here and selling it again, but the prices are too high for very cheap cars, so we have gone back to our early Port Washington days—we have rented bicycles!—and had a lot of fun, a lot of good exercise, out of them.

After London, their life at Avon was quiet and rather pleasant. Every now and then there would be an entertaining guest, usually someone who had his own work to do during the daytime and did not disrupt Lewis's schedule. George E. Slocombe, the engaging British journalist, a friend of Frazier Hunt whom Lewis had met in London but who was now writing out of Paris, was one of the first Fontainebleau guests. They took him, on a Saturday evening, to a notorious establishment that was situated nearly next door to them—the Institute for the Harmonious Development of Man, founded by Georgi Ivanovitch Gurdjieff. Lewis tried to help his father imagine the place:

> ... we went to the dances of the Goudjieff [*sic*] colony, which happens to be about five minutes walk from my place here.... Goudjieff is a Russian, and his chief apostle Ouspensky is a Russian, and between them they run the latest thing in phony High Thought colonies. He has had a rather distinguished list of patrons, including Lady Rothermere (her husband is brother of Lord Northcliffe and manages now the Northcliffe properties), Katharine Mansfield the excellent short-story writer, who died recently, and Orage, former editor of the *New Age,* whom I'd met in London. The people do their own work—everything from cooking to digging rock—learn elaborate symbolic dances, and listen to "esoteric lectures." The dancing is very interesting, some of the dances are imitations of Oriental sacred temple rites, some of them stunts requiring a high degree of muscle control —doing quite different things with the two arms at the same time. But it must be a hell of a place to live—they sleep only four hours a night, and eat almost nothing, with occasional fasts of six or eight or ten days! The place itself is beautiful—a large villa built for Madame de Maintenon, later owned by Dreyfus, with a great sweep of gardens and tree alleys. Here they have built their own "gymnasium," as they call it, though essentially it's a kind of hall for dancing, so hung with Oriental carpets that it looks like a cross between a cabaret and a harem!

Slocombe was considerably taken by Lewis, more tolerant of him than some of his countrymen, and more perceptive, too. He had, Slocombe wrote in his *Memoirs* of 1936, "an extraordinary energy of speech, a very great diversity of ideas, a certain air of frenzy in his look, speech and gait, a frenzy half comic, half melancholy." It is that "frenzy ... half melancholy" that one must keep in mind when Slocombe or anyone else describes Lewis's antics. "He might have been poet or actor, so novel, so wild, so rhetorical were his sudden enthusiasms, his genial affectations, his native power of invention, mimicry and gesture." And Slocombe then recalled a public dinner given in Lewis's honor in London, when, in response to the praise of his hosts, "he chose ... to assume the part of an American Senator," and how, some years later at another such occasion in New York, when he did not wish to talk at all, he finally, because the chairman insisted that he say something, delivered himself of an endless harangue in German. And one night, when he was dining with Slocombe and Walter Duranty in Montmartre, he became a Midwestern traveling man "who met a royal aide-de-camp in a public-house in London and persuaded himself that he had been taken by his chance acquaintance to visit Buckingham Palace and to meet the King," and then returned to his native place—as would Lowell Schmaltz in *The Man Who Knew Coolidge.*

With such displays he protected from view the core of melancholy and, often, that of good sense. But very sensibly he could defend his own quixotic, apparently most unsensible conduct. In that summer of 1923, his father was furious because, after he and Claude had gone to some effort to have Fred's son, Edwin, admitted to West Point, Edwin had changed his mind. Lewis wrote his father:

> It's too bad that Edwin did not appreciate your efforts, but you must remember two things: First, West Point, though a good training physically, is none too wonderful intellectually, and while a good many regular army officers are fine fellows, a lot of them are wasters, loafers, who would be no good at all outside the easy routines of garrison duty. Second, the boy had to decide for himself. He may not know what's best for him—but maybe you don't either. You answer, Well then, he should have made up his mind before we took all that trouble. That's only partly true. Are there *any* of us who decide things right off, before partly going into arrangements? . . . Stop sulking at Edwin, or you'll make him feel guilty and self-conscious, and you have no right to do that. If he's shiftless—ALL RIGHT. . . . Claude and you and even my perfect self are too confoundedly impatient with people who haven't our sort of ambitions. Why should they have? And we have no right to . . . make them feel guilty—a frame of mind in which it's much harder to get on. . . . . Huh? . . . . When you say "I am thru with him for he deceived us"—hang it, the best way to make the poor devil deceive all of you is to be impatient . . . you give him another chance, if you have a chance to give him a chance!

"I'm out of touch with everybody here," he wrote Harcourt, which was not, of course, quite the fact. ". . . and it's been superb—quiet, beautiful, working like hell all day and practically every day . . . and the book has gone tremendously." His bicycle provided all the exercise he needed, and every eight or ten days he and his wife would go off on an excursion to neighboring villages—Barbizon, Troyes—or for a picnic in the fields, with bread and Camembert and wine and fruit. They entertained Edith Wharton at lunch when she drove down with "two delightful men," an English businessman and an American professor of medieval history at Cambridge (Gaillard Lapsey). General Thomson came for several days, and Michael Arlen for ten. During Lewis's few months in Hartford, Hugh Walpole had been their house guest, and in a friendly letter of August 14, Lewis urged him to come now to them; if he really did dislike Walpole, this letter shows him in one of his "insincere" relationships:

> Is there any chance . . . that you can come stay with us—*any* time? Please do, if you can. If not, perhaps we'll see each other in Italy; we'll go there in October, though just where we shall be I don't yet know. There is a possibility of our hunting a flat in Rome.

The Lewises were to spend a day or two with Edith Wharton at the Pavillon Colombe, but it developed that Mrs. Lewis would have to go to

London to have her "very tough and fibrous" tonsil roots removed. This was in the early part of September. Then Stacy Aumonier came to Val-Changis, and on September 5 the two of them went up to Paris to lunch with Edith Wharton and Lewis to seek out his dentist. Back at Avon with Aumonier the next day, Lewis had General Sir Nevil McCready for dinner. He was

> commander in chief of all British forces in Ireland during some of the worst days; he was for a while commander of all the police in London; he has served in Africa and Ceylon and most every place you can think of . . . a charming man, very simple and direct.

Lewis was always much happier in the company of forthright men of action or bluff journalists than he was in that of recherché literary people, and we are compelled again to observe the difference between his literary and his social tastes. In September he wrote to Carl Van Vechten:

> *The Blind Bow Boy* is superb. It is impertinent, subversive, resolutely and completely wicked. I didn't believe any American could do that—I know my own wickedness is so feeble and apologetic—only a little above that of the bright and happy Y.M.C.A. secretary daringly whispering that he doesn't believe the whale swallowed Jonah and that, if it weren't for the bad example to young men who might not underSTAND, he would just love to play one game of poker . . . you slap the tradition that highbrow American novels must be either lugubriously and literally "realistic" (I, of course, am not a realist at all, though you have been one of the few to discover it) or else acrobatically "original" like Waldo Frank and all the others who are deriving from the solemn theology of a Gertrude Stein. (Poor Sherwood: so excitedly shrieking his discovery of the first cod-piece in history!).
>
> I'm off, next week, for a month loafing in Italy, then London for the winter, back to America in the spring. The new book marches.

And not many weeks later he was writing in the same vein to Elinor Wylie of her "delicate extravaganza," a book once again remote from what one might suppose he would like.

> The only thing I want to talk about is *Jennifer Lorn.* I wonder if there has ever been written a more distinguished first novel? I am so interested in it as an American phenomenon that I can scarce think of it in relation to you. If the critics had any sense, if the analysts had any sense, they would see that you, both in your poetry and in *Jennifer,* together with Hergesheimer, Cabell, and Van Vechten make a more important "news item" than all the bellowing of politics and business put together, because you four mean definitely that for the first time America has ceased to be a Colony, has become a Power. . . .

In September he wrote to Mencken to wish him well with *The American Mercury,* which he and Nathan were just starting (presently he would urge him to ask Stuart Sherman to write a piece for the magazine, giving him "complete freedom to slam you & co. as much as he wished. *Spicy*."), and promised to write for the magazine himself, "but not till next summer, as till then I'll be absorbed in the damn book, which goes on forever—and I think goes well." His absorption was extensive, including even thoughts on possible libel suits, and he sent his publisher the names of the twelve most important characters in the book with the request that someone in the office go through *Who's Who* and various medical registers to be certain that none of these names were those of living people. It included, too, thoughts of future novels: he had, he wrote Harcourt, eleven novels that he could write next; *Neighbor* was still on the list, but it had moved down, and more prominent now was a big novel about religion. At the same time he was working furiously on *Arrowsmith,* and by September 24 he had very nearly completed the first draft.

Paul de Kruif arrived from London on that day to spend a week over the manuscript, and at the end of that week Lewis, in a jubilant mood, wrote his father:

> . . . Paul de Kruif has read it all and he is wildly enthusiastic. He says both that the science in it is perfectly natural and accurate and that, in his opinion, it is much the best book I have done. Of course Paul is at once the best and the worst possible critic of the book, because he has been so intimately associated with it. One good thing—he really is honest—never a taffy-monger. Paul has returned to Paris, to get some more material from Pasteur Institute; he sails for America on October 25. I hope perhaps you may meet him and that Claude may. . . .

To his father he then recommended the novel *Weeds,* a copy of which had come to him from Harcourt, and only a few days before, he had been recommending Marcel Proust (because of Edith Wharton's enthusiasm) to Harcourt.

They were about to move on again. A "very fine school-home" for Wells had been found above Lausanne. The first draft of *Arrowsmith* was finished on September 30. "It comes out 748 pages plus a certain number of insert pages—about 245,000 words long." The typescript was full of suggestions for changes made by both De Kruif and Mrs. Lewis, and was sent up to Paris for De Kruif's final attention. On October 4 Lewis wrote his father for the last time from Avon.

> We're off today for Paris . . . and tomorrow I'll have lunch with [Paul] in town and we'll go over that last part. He wrote me a couple of days ago, "Plans for my immediate work are just beginning to return to my brain, from which everything was driven by the overpowering attack of the novel. The more I think of it, the finer it becomes, and no words can express my admiration for the superb thing you have done." So (since Paul really is honest!) *one* person likes the darn thing, anyway!

They left Le Val-Changis at the end of three months, and they were glad to go. For Lewis the time had been a good one, fruitful in work and pleasant in associations. He apparently enjoyed the French people he had encountered. In one letter to his father he had corrected the latter's notion that the French people spoke with much gesticulation—only the Southern Italians do that, said the wise son, and here there were "a surprising number of fine old French women who look rather like New England farmwives." But three months is, after all, a long time to be in one place. Mrs. Lewis had had a less pleasant time. She wrote to her sister-in-law in St. Cloud to complain of the pettiness of her landlord, of her irritation with the continual tipping of service people and postmen and every creature who came near the house with a parcel, of her bewilderment and outrage with the lying, the parsimony, the insults of the natives. French honor, she concluded, bore no relation to English and American honor. Wells, to be sure, had picked up a good deal of French, but nevertheless, they would spend only one day in Paris and then get out of the country.

There had, of course, been excursions to Paris all during those three months by both of them and by Lewis alone, and there would be future times in Paris when Lewis would expose himself to the condescension and the derision of "that real Parisian bunch." Another impression of George Slocombe's:

> There were times when the friends of "Red" Lewis found him in . . . sombre mood. Morbidly sensitive to criticism, he stood it reluctantly from his friends, and angrily from his enemies. The artist in him was hungry for recognition of his work for its art's sake, critical of the overwhelming commercial success that had come to him. His very integrity as a writer made him conscious of his deficiencies in style, sensitiveness to beauty, sensitiveness to change, motives, psychology—all the untold, untellable and largely fictitious distinctions which make or mar a work of art in literature. His sensitiveness as a person made him acutely and morbidly conscious of the envy of superior literary gentlemen. Much of his challenging, boastful, noisy and childish insolence was the mere insolence of the parvenu which he felt himself to be in the circles of the elect. His garrulity, his lapses into a schoolboy obscenity, his fits of temper and defiance, were the rough, awkward and embarrassing clash and jingle of the armour he felt obliged to wear over the sensitive idealism and frustrated creativeness of his own naïve, generous but timid personality.
>
> In such moods he became the hero of unhappy scenes in London and Paris.

George Slocombe's friend, Sisley Huddleston, remembered him in *Paris Salons, Cafés, Studios.*

> He flung himself on a couch and his long loose limbs grew longer and looser. He jumped to his feet, strode across the room, and he was taller and lankier than ever. His face glowed and his hair caught fire.

"His face glowed and his hair caught fire." It sounds rather attractive, but it was not; his sensitiveness about his literary reputation was probably less acute than his sensitiveness about his face. (In a letter to his wife he referred to those pullulations that had to be removed by electric needle or radium as "disgusting.") Montparnasse and Montmartre were harsh places in which to expose those two sensitivities; he could probably have found none harsher, and thus in none would he have behaved more brashly.

Sisley Huddleston remembered his talking about his method of composition, how systematically he prepared to write, and wrote. "I don't care what the critics say. The more they say, the better the book sells. Here's one of them who says my last book is a compound of bunk, ignorance, and lies. Don't they wish they could put over bunk, ignorance, and lies!" But he cared, of course, and his caring drove him into "fits of moody silence." Huddleston remembered one evening shortly after he had come from England when, twirling his monocle, dressed in severely cut black clothes with white spats, and carrying his cane, he was in such a mood—". . . the most American of writers was the most English," but looking, somehow, like "a clergyman who does not possess the habits of Elmer Gantry." Then, on another evening, he "woke up with a vengeance. We were at dinner. He monopolized the conversation."

> He spoke of everybody by their Christian names. I was Sisley for him and he spoke much of Gilbert and of Hugh.
>
> "We are getting fed up with these English novelists who come on lecture tours and get away with good American dollars. I am not saying that for you, Sisley, but I told Hugh himself that it was too thick. Last year there was Bertrand—whom, of course, I like, and he is in a different line. I don't think Gilbert quite went down. A lot of silly women laughed when he poked fun at America, but he certainly overdid it. I am not going to say anything against Philip, but perhaps we've had enough of him. As for James, he is a likeable fellow. No, good luck to them! Only we are rather idiotic to stand for it."

This is mild enough, and, in fact, most newspapermen, who had no reason to envy him his success or to observe his literary deficiencies, "liked him immensely," as Huddleston did; but the literary crowd of American expatriates was another matter.

In his autobiography, *Being Geniuses Together,* Robert McAlmon sees him from that angle. He tells of an evening when Djuna Barnes cut him at the Gypsy and how Lewis "looked wistful and went away"; how, on another occasion, somewhat intoxicated at the Dôme, he stood up and announced that he not only depicted character more sharply than Flaubert, but had the better style, and someone shouted, "Sit down. You're just a best seller," and he was crushed; and how, on still another occasion at the Jockey, a "tough little flapper" shuddered when she saw another woman greet him with a kiss, said something loudly about his ugliness—her phrase was "withered carrot"—that he overheard, and was not impressed when he turned redder than usual, and then quickly pale and trembling, demanding of her, "Do you know you are speaking to a man of international fame?" McAlmon tells, too, a story of Mrs. Lewis, who, on first meeting him one evening at the Stryx, demanded to know if he did not think Lewis America's finest literary artist, and who, when he did not answer her directly, "flew out of the door refusing to drink with me."

Other such stories appear in Samuel Putnam's *Paris Was Our Mistress.*

> Conspicuously seated at the Dôme is a gaunt-looking chap with a shock of reddish hair. . . . We are in the habit of calling this type, as distinguished from the ordinary summer tourist or vacationing college boy, the "big shot from home." Now, there is a curious telepathy, a kind of grapevine, that operates between those terraces, and within a very short while every one on all three of them is aware that the visitor is . . . "Red" Lewis. At the same time . . . no notice whatsoever is to be taken of Mr. Lewis's presence.
>
> It is the slap direct from the Joyce and Stein brigade. . . . It would be hard to say how much, if any, of this Mr. Lewis gets; but, in any event, he very soon makes his exit, and as he does so his face is about the color of his hair. There is an unuttered snort as he stamps out, and a giggle, becoming a laugh, runs around the tables and spreads down the street to the Coupole and across the way to the Select. . . .

These stories are not very funny, they are cruel, and they may not even be true, but they serve to demonstrate the hostility with which the Left Bank received him, and Putnam is no doubt right in thinking that such incidents "may have had something to do with the violent feeling which Mr. Lewis later displayed toward the Parisian variety of aesthete." He had in mind Lewis's article, "Self-Conscious America," which appeared in *The American Mercury* in October of 1925. "Violent" is perhaps too strong a word for the feeling there expressed, but the article does communicate Lewis's own revulsion, compounded both of common sense and of anger and wounded pride. It is chiefly a defense of the writer's prerogative to write in any way that he wishes. The argument is not entirely coherent, and it proceeds by attacking "the geniuses and their disciples who frequent the Café du Dôme at Montparnasse," and, without naming him, one of them in particular—Harold Stearns. Stearns had been a friend of Lewis's, but he had also become the most notorious free-loader in Europe and one of the most intolerant of snobs. While Lewis rather good-humoredly chides Upton Sinclair for his pretensions at social reform through literature, he quite spitefully attacks Stearns as the "very father and seer of the Dôme, who is an authority on living without laboring and who bases his opinions of people's intellectual capacity on the amount of money he can borrow off them." The article caused a great commotion in the Quarter, waiters were reported as describing Lewis as "the biggest hick that ever came from Main Street," and Harold Stearns threatened to go to New York for the sole purpose of "punching his face in." To the press he hotly retorted:

> Mr. Lewis speaks sarcastically about somebody buying a drink, but if Mr. Lewis himself ever was caught buying a drink for anybody, at least 1,000 people would drop dead. Several times when he was raving at the Dôme café he rose and screamed exactly the sums everybody owed him with accrued interest. Naturally, Mr. Lewis spoke about the interest, because gentlemanly loans are unknown in the Minnesota bush, whence Mr. Lewis comes. . . .
>
> I will not join Mr. Lewis in a competition of ignominy. Just because Mr. Lewis, by his malicious personal attack, chooses to expose himself at last in public as a cad and bounder, he cannot expect me, in spite of my great admiration for his salesmanship talents, to imitate him.
>
> Discussing his article objectively, it is chaotic, cheap, inaccurate, and absurd. He missed both the good points and the bad ones of the American Montparnasse colony,—the good points, because he couldn't understand them, and the bad ones, because he so perfectly exemplified them.
>
> The chief point, of course, is that remotely, somehow, somewhere, even the dumbest American expatriates have been touched by the spiritual forces of French life. The realization that there is something in France which he had missed was what finally drove Mr. Lewis back to a country where his publications have a dignity which, to Europeans, is simply incomprehensible.
>
> Many of the eccentricities and absurdities which Mr. Lewis mentions are, of course, quite true. In fairness to the people mentioned, I ought to point out, as one of them, that they are only grouped together by Mr. Lewis's spite.

And, he might more accurately have said, by their initial spite toward Mr. Lewis.

To this spite the Lewises were not now, in October of 1923, further exposing themselves. Friday, the fifth, was spent with Paul de Kruif over the typescript of the novel, and on the sixth the Lewises departed for Switzerland. Wells was left at the Lausanne boarding school and his parents, traveling now with only three bags, continued to Basel. One day they crossed into Germany, and then returned again, and from Basel, on the twelfth, went on to Venice—"the most wonderful day's journey I've ever made: between 7 A.M. and 8 P.M. we came from Basle . . . clear across Switzerland, down into Italy, then (from Milan to Venice) half way across Italy. . . ." This letter was written to his father on the seventeenth, and it continues with a long chatty account of the changing scenery and of Venice. "Every morning at 10:30 we have coffee & rolls (a second & most luxurious & lazy breakfast!) in the sun in front of Florian's Café on Piazza San Marco. . . ." They read E. V. Lucas's *Wanderer in Venice* ("our guide, rich aunt & *cameriere* here") and Lewis wrote the author to say that his "delights as a companion of the bar" were now "o'ergilded" by his "merits as a leader." But after a week, Venice began "to seem too much like over-rich plumcake," and it was something of a relief, he wrote his father, to see "normal citizens at real work" as they went through Padua, Vicenza and Verona on their way to Menaggio on Como. These towns, he said, "were all of them rather dusty, rather dingy, rather sleepy, but all of them had interesting old churches," and then followed what might have been a simple if extended transcription from Baedeker. On the twenty-third, "if it storms, as it threatens," they would leave Como for Milan, Florence, and Siena. In Siena they saw "the procession of the Fascists, the Black Shirts, celebrating the March on Rome of a year ago."

> They're a kind of Ku Klux Klan, but more efficient—grim young men in black shirts, trim military trousers, tasseled black caps (like fezes dented down the center) and automatics on their hips—young men under the secret sway of millionaire steel men and the like who want to keep labor "in its place." Then, when we went on to Florence, we saw the Fascist parade there, too, with Mussolini himself (a flabby faced, hard-jawed, mad-eyed fanatic) rushing through in a procession of motor cars, the line of march guarded by policemen, plain clothes men, Fascists, and soldiers standing shoulder to shoulder, with bayonets fixed.

So to his father. There followed another guidebook account of the beauties of Florence. From Florence they went north again, back to Lausanne, but they found Wells in such good shape that they decided to leave him until they had an establishment in London. Then Paris, the Channel, London.

But for Alfred Harcourt their trail had vanished. He was trying by letter and by cable to communicate with Lewis about the offer of fifty thousand dollars for serial rights to *Arrowsmith* from *The Designer*. Did Lewis want him to accept? When by October 29 Harcourt had had no reply and Sewell Haggard, the editor of *The Designer,* was pressing for an answer, he took it upon himself to close the agreement on Lewis's behalf, and he comforted Lewis—in the event that he would disapprove—by pointing out that "this is the highest bona fide price for magazine serialization that I've ever heard of." Back in London in the first week of November, the messages caught up with Lewis, who cabled his approval if he could be relieved of two quasi-commitments to the Hearst offices and *Red Book*. On the sixth he wrote from the Hotel Curzon to add that he supposed the novel would have to be shortened for the magazine but that "I will not change the thing into a sunny sweet tale nor will I permit him to. DOES HE UNDERSTAND THAT?" And there is a new address: 58 Elm Park Gardens, London, S.W.10—"a rather charming furnished house we've taken for the winter—just on the borders of Kensington and Chelsea—taken it till next June though probably I myself will be coming home considerably before that, leaving Gracie and the kid. . . ."

To his father, next day, he described the house again and told him that its owner was "Sir John Wallis, former chief judge of the province of Madras in India, [who] proved to know all about me and to have read *Main St.* and *Babbitt.*" Now he must get back to hard work—as soon as he could "find some sort of room for an office." Already their social life had begun.

> Last evening we dined with my English publisher, Cape; tonight with Oswald Villard, owner of the American *Nation,* here in Europe for a few weeks; and this afternoon we're going to the big reception given by the American Women's Club to the premiers of all the colonies—ought to be a good show.

In less than a week he had found an "office" off lower Fleet Street—Number One Crown Office Row and Big Tree Court, Inner Temple. He wrote his father:

> I have an office, in which to write, in, of all charming places, the Temple—the old, enclosed part of London (reminding one somewhat of an American college campus set down with its quiet courts and gardens right in the busiest part of London) in which the lawyers have their offices. I'm in a comparatively new building—only two hundred years old—but right near is the round Norman church, built in about 1100, when the Knights Templar, the crusaders, had their houses here. Dr. Johnson, Lamb, Goldsmith and countless other famous authors have lived and written here, and Goldsmith is buried here.

This "office" was, Frazier Hunt remembers, in a small building owned by the wigmaker to London barristers, which is somehow entirely appropriate. He was able to go to work in his "office" even before they moved into Elm Park Gardens on November 14.

He was revising with a vengeance, "raising hell with the first part, which starts rather too slowly," he told Harcourt. At the same time, according to Edward Kemler in *The Irreverent Mr. Mencken,* he "was fertile with proposed contributions [to the new *American Mercury*], among them a critical essay that would condemn all literary schools as damned nonsense and end all literary strife forever; but he was slow to oblige." To Mencken, Lewis explained again that his work on *Arrowsmith* prevented him from writing anything else at that time.

> But it'll be done by May, about, and then I'll fall to. And as a matter of fact then, some months after the great hurray of starting, will be an excellent time for me to rush in brandishing a pious essay.

He was interested in Mencken's suggestion that he join him in covering the national presidential conventions in the summer, and asked whether Mencken could think of a newspaper proprietor who might want to send him. He was anticipating his return to the United States.

I like London, but I begin now, after eleven months abroad, to yearn for the cornpone, the Ku Klux, and the refined intercourse—both kinds—of the homeland, and I think I'll stay around America for a couple of years. I'm more than likely to be living in Washington, neighbor to you, and I hope to be permitted to join you on some of your evenings of Scottish song recitals.

To Harcourt he sent more concrete plans:

I hope to have *Arrowsmith* finished by the end of April or earlier, and to come over to the States with an expectation to stay for a long time. As soon as I've gone out West to see my father, and generally floated around a little, I'll settle down to the next book. This one may be much shorter and more adventurous [an apt description of *Mantrap,* which would be the next book, but of which he did not yet have a conception], and you could probably publish it in the spring of 1926, a year after *Arrowsmith,* with the next, again a long one [*Elmer Gantry*] coming a year and a half after that.

The background of *Mantrap* was to be made possible by a new friend in England, Sir George Maclaren Brown, the general manager of the Canadian Pacific Railroad in Europe. With him the Lewises motored for lunch in mid-November to the fine old country place of the Earl of Stafford.

Both Lady Stafford and her brother, Lord Colebrook, who was also there for lunch (along with Lady Wemyss, and Lord and Lady Queensborough) are great boosters for my books. All these people belong to the best of old English families, but they are as simple and direct and easy as anybody could be. . . . Stafford is the nephew of Lord Byng, now governor general of Canada.

He enjoyed this grandeur, up to a point, and certainly he enjoyed writing his father about it, as he did about the money he was making. He reported the fifty-thousand-dollar sale to *The Designer.*

Now if we get another forty or fifty thousand for the movie rights we'll be able to buy our winter's coal. Golly, I don't know how come I ever made any money. I should say that of all the people I know I'm one of the least likely to do so. But perhaps by continuing to write books to suit myself I may yet contrive to die poor—I hope so—and that being the case I'll probably make a million or so!

Such bits of news were no doubt related to interested persons in the Minnesota village. The letters themselves were always forwarded to Claude and his family in St. Cloud, often with a laconic note attached, such as this: *"Dear Folks*—Harry's last letter. Hope you are not frozen out. Quite a cold spell again. Had to thaw out cistern pump. *Dad."* In November, the Sauk Centre *Herald* carried a strangely belated and inaccurate news item that announced that Sinclair Lewis would take two years to write his next novel, about a doctor, and that he had hired (the publishers to pay the fee) a doctor to live with him for a year and submit to his study. Paul de Kruif was then back in New York, his work for Lewis finished.

At the end of November, Lewis enjoyed an academic weekend when he went up to Cambridge alone. His host was Gaillard Lapsley, who put him up in chambers in the oldest part of Trinity College. On Saturday evening he gave him dinner in his rooms, with Sir Arthur Quiller-Couch and A. E. Housman ("who is really a great man, author of those most gallant poems, *The Shropshire Lad,* but mostly engaged in classical scholarship"), Lascelles Abercrombie, and one or two others. On Sunday morning Lewis attended college chapel, then took a long walk with Lapsley, spent most of the afternoon with J. B. S. Haldane, a great admirer of De Kruif, and "dined in hall," opposite William Archer. Archer, Housman and Haldane had all read and enjoyed *Babbitt.* On Monday, Haldane showed him through the extensive biochemical and physiological laboratories, and they no doubt talked about *Arrowsmith.*

In London, Lewis now was not only revising for the final version but cutting as he went, for the *Designer* version. Yet he found time for public pastimes. The general election was about to take place, and suddenly Sinclair Lewis erupted in British politics. He was a neighbor and friend of Bertrand Russell, who was standing for office, and Lewis took it upon himself to campaign for him. He sat on platforms and made speeches, and the press commented acidly on this interference in British affairs by a Midwestern American. The climax came when, on the eve of the election that was to put in the Liberal party and show the strength of labor, the Lewises dined with Beaverbrook at the Savoy. In January, when the dust had settled, Lewis addressed himself to the *Daily Express* in reply to the criticism to which he had been subjected, and at the same time he took occasion to write an enthusiastic bit of propaganda for his friend, Brigadier General C. B. Thomson, who was to be knighted, become the first Labor M.P., and head the Air Ministry.

The London days were crowded. In a Christmas letter to his father, written on December 15, Lewis again reports on the activities of the week that was ending. Sunday was spent in the country with Henry and Mrs. Ainley, and at supper they met "Lady Rhondda, who's supposed to be one of the richest women in the world, as well as one of the few women in England who are peeresses in their own rights, not just through their husband." On Tuesday they dined with Sir Philip Gibbs, and on Wednesday Lewis lectured before the American Women's Club in its enormous new clubhouse, formerly "the residence of Sir Edgar Speyer, the banker who lost his baronetcy during the war, as a German sympathizer, and went off to America. . . . I suppose Speyer must have had a staff of at least thirty servants." The concern with wealth and rank is perhaps deceptive; what

Lewis does not report to his father are the many nights that he was dining and drinking, without his wife, in less impressive but more convivial company.

In that Christmas letter to his father, he put the annual enclosure for his poor brother Fred—a bank draft for fifty dollars—but to his brother Claude, a few days later, he wrote directly to wish him well. In that letter occurs this passage:

> Do you remember speaking to me, a year and a half ago, about some expedition which goes all through Northern Canada every summer, getting entirely away from civilization, and taking two or three months to make the trip? What is it? Does it occur every year? Would there be any way in which I could go with them—they might be glad to be "written up," * and of course I'd stand my share of the expenses. I live far too sedentary a life, and I'd like to do something of that kind. Can you tell me with whom to get in touch about it? And would there be any possibility of your coming along? Such a long and husky rest would be fine for you.

Claude was interested and explained to him again that the expedition he had spoken of was the annual Treaty Trip made through the Canadian North by agents of the Indian Affairs branch to pay every Indian, man, woman and child, five dollars, in return for what had once been Indian land. Why didn't his brother approach one of those important Canadians he had been meeting? Thereupon, Lewis wrote a note of inquiry to his friend Maclaren Brown; Brown turned it over to the office of the high commissioner; that office forwarded it to Ottawa and the Secretary of the Department of Indian Affairs; and ultimately Sinclair Lewis would find himself in the Saskatchewan wilderness.† In the meantime, there were more comfortable excitements.

Knowing Bertrand Russell was gratifying to Lewis, but knowing Arnold Bennett was a good deal more so. "Recent acquisition, Arnold Bennett—I like him," he wrote Harcourt on December 27. They had dined with Bennett "in his charming house not far from us" on December 20, and next day he told his father about the affair.

* In this notion he was thoroughly mistaken. The Department of Indian Affairs had no wish whatever to publicize the annual Treaty Trips. Quite the contrary. These trips were handled with considerable ceremony and circumspection. The Government was anxious not to expose the Indians to worldly influences and was eager to keep outsiders out. That the Lewises were permitted to make one of these trips was highly exceptional and was brought about only because of the influence of Sinclair Lewis's friends in London and the consequent interest of the Secretary of the Department in Ottawa.

† An account of the backgrounds of this excursion, of Sinclair Lewis's part in the excursion as recounted by a diary kept by Claude Lewis, and of the implicit relations of this diary and Sinclair Lewis's *Mantrap* has been published by the University of Minnesota Press. Edited by Donald Green and George Knox, it is called *Treaty Trip: An abridgment of Dr. Claude Lewis's journal of an expedition made by himself and his brother, Sinclair Lewis, to northern Saskatchewan and Manitoba in 1924* (1959). Dr. Lewis had previously made his diary available to me. *M.S.*

> Several other writers and an editor or two there; Bennett very easy and cordial, and apparently an admirer of my books. He showed me a precious thing—the manuscript, the original MS, of his *The Old Wives' Tale,* one of the greatest novels ever written. It's a strange MS, handwritten, in the most delicate script, legible as typing, with almost no changes in it, and decorated with colored initials by him, so that it's like a monkish scroll.

And on that same day, Bennett himself was writing to his chatty friend Frank Swinnerton:

> I gave a dinner last night to Sinclair Lewis and his wife. You know, I like both of them. I don't say they are great shakes, or in the least educated, or much decruded. But I like them both. They live near here . . . Amazing, how they like *The Cathedral* [Walpole]. I wasn't going to stand for that. However, they all like *Riceyman Steps* [Bennett]. . . .

"Acquisition" was then perhaps too strong a word, but the Lewises did "acquire" him when, in two weeks, they returned his dinner. In his *Journals,* Bennett recorded how he had hurried home from a literary tea in order to arrive promptly at the Lewises'.

> I did not get enough to eat.* Present a young quiet English sort-of-journalist named [Montgomery] Belgion and Sir George Maclaren-Browne (British representative of the C.P.R.) and Lady D.K. These two were fine. . . . Lewis has a habit of breaking into a discussion with long pieces of imaginary conversation between imaginary or real people of the place and period under discussion. Goodish, but too long, with accents, manner, and all complete. He will do this in any discussion; he will drag in a performance, usually full of oaths and blasphemy. A most striking contrast between the dinner and the tea. The latter all bookishness and what is called, I believe, culture. The former all life and scarcely any bookishness or culture at all.
>
> Lewis soon began to call me "Arnold," and, once begun, he called me "Arnold" about 100 times. He has things to learn, but I like him. He showed me the first typescript of his new novel—all blue and red with millions of alterations,—a terrible sight.

The after-dinner conversation, when Lewis was not usurping it with mimicry, was mainly concerned with early railroad days in America, and Lewis wrote Harcourt to say that Bennett had urged him to write a novel about them. "You ought to do that; it's never really been touched; you've scolded enough so you can be romantic for once with a clear conscience." But Lewis was also thinking about a detective story, another collaboration with De Kruif on a novel about a university president, and "the big religious novel." Very soon he would write Harcourt with the request that he send over the chief periodicals of the Methodist and Baptist churches and "a magazine devoted to the business of the evangelists." In the meantime, there was still a good deal of work to be done on *Arrowsmith.*

* This sentence does not appear in the English edition of the *Journals,* only in the American, as though he wished to let Mrs. Lewis know.

Most Sundays were holidays. Lewis had encountered an acquaintance of seventeen years before, the young man named Scott whom he had picked up at Covent Garden in 1906, and now, on a Sunday in December, he met him in the country by arrangement and Scott drove them to his place.

> Since [1906] he has married a Russian baroness—her family was rich then, and lost everything in the revolution—got control of 800,000 acres in Panama, lost it all during the war, and now he runs a pig farm of 1,200 acres—which, in tiny England, is like having 100,000 acres in Texas. They have a big bare old-fashioned house, and live an almost feudal life, with their 150 or so employees scattered about in cottages.

And then there was the interruption of Christmas. On Christmas Eve they did nothing but arrange the presents—Wells was to receive his first toy soldiers—and on Christmas day Wells was left in Elm Park Gardens to play with them while the Lewises went out. They called at the apartment of Helen Augur and her husband, Warren Vinton, where they met Lincoln Steffens (or so, at any rate, wrote Steffens; two years before, he had written Ella Winter to say that he had "never read *Main Street*. . . . For it is, as you say, as dull as Main Street.") But for dinner they went to the house of Curtis Brown, the literary agent. To his father, Lewis described "the chief incident—to me—of the Xmas dinner."

> Almost ten years ago, when Grace and I were on our honeymoon, I once heaved a pine cone at her, and she hid it and announced that I'd get it back when I least expected it. I did—when I'd forgotten it, she put it in a gorgeous box, much wrapped in tissue, at Xmas, and when I opened the gaudy "present" I found it. Once at Port Washington, when Harrison Smith came down for the week-end, and presented a magnificent box of candy to G, opening it she found a handsome assortment of small lumps of coal with the pine cone in the center. Last Spring, I sent it to her, at Hartford, from London, in a jewelers box timed to reach her for our wedding anniversary and she, expecting at least a million dollar pearl necklace, opened to the old pine cone, which she had not seen for a year and had completely forgotten. . . . . Well. . . . . When the beautiful plum pudding came to me at the Curtis Browns' dinner, I was slightly dazed to see, lying among the brownness of the pudding, something that looked strangely like a pine cone. I was rather slow in perception, and while the rest—all of them warned beforehand—watched me and choked in their efforts to look sober, I dug the damn thing out and realized that Gracie had certainly put it over on me. . . . She had brought the thing around a week before and arranged it all with the C Brown's butler. . . . But the joke was they had it all snug in a sweet potato, and there were so many other things to eat that, to the agitation of everybody, I never touched the potato, and the kitchen, after a wild conference, tried it again in my plum pudding—with admirable results.

How very jolly! In the next year he was to write to his young nephew Freeman, to remind him that when Lewis wrote his father, he told him only things that the father would want to hear.* That this was the fact no letter makes clearer than this about the happy Christmas pine cone and its long trail through the disintegrating years. For the record, a generalized account of this marriage, sustained now in collapse, may be found in the concluding glimpse of this London winter as it appears in *With Love from Gracie*. Mrs. Lewis mentions there her husband's "ruthless and quite public abasing of me before others." Lewis's friends seem to remember rather her sharp, public attacks on him. It was no doubt an equal battle, and if not yet a "pitched" one, a pretty continuous and messy squabble, bad for both of them, and remarkable only in that it did not seem to harm their child.

She had suffered, too, from a series of bad colds brought on by a particularly horrid English winter, and presently she would remove herself and the boy from London. But not until the holiday season was over. On New Year's Eve, they dined with Violet Hunt and took her to the theater, a review called *The Beauty Prize,* starring George Grossmith.

> The thing of interest to G. and myself in this somewhat inferior review is that Grossmith in a scene supposed to portray Palm Beach . . . puts on horn-rimmed spectacles and a big cigar and sings "Won't you meet me down on Main Street where the George F. Babbitts grow?" Did you know there was such a song in London? I sent in my card and between acts we went around to Grossmith's big dressing room . . . more than friendly . . . met Charles Dillingham . . . and Guy Bolton, the American playwright.

Then they went on "to a big party given by one Betty Rickets, a very rich Jew, wife of a doctor; huge house with a ballroom."

> Most of the people were in costume—me, I made up as Bernard Shaw; my nose and forehead and general long lankiness are like his, and with red beard, red mustache and heavy eyebrows, I looked like Shaw at forty. . . . But false whiskers are the damndest things to eat and drink and smoke through!

They left at about two-thirty to rest, for H. G. Wells was coming to dine with them that evening, alone ("which was bully because it gave us a real chance to know him—we've always seen him with so many other people about. He seemed to enjoy it and stayed talking till after midnight, though he is an early-to-bed") before his departure, next day, for Portugal. Two nights later was their dinner for Bennett and the Maclaren Browns, and the night after that, dinner for Bertrand Russell and Lincoln Steffens. "AND meantime I've been working consistently, and it goes splendidly."

* "I do hope that you will keep the series of letters from me which your grandfather gave to you entirely to yourself. You must remember that in writing to him I write the sort of things that he would want to see and not necessarily the sort of things that I am most eager to write about. Perhaps some day I will make you destroy these letters and give you in exchange some real letters to you and some from other famous people. We will talk about that when I see you next." The letters to his father passed into the possession of Freeman Lewis's sister, Virginia.

Then he was left alone with the three servants—a butler, now, plus cook and maid—while Mrs. Lewis went to Torquay in Devonshire. The first number of *The American Mercury* had come and he wrote Mencken to congratulate him (and wrote his father to tell him to see to it that the Bryant Library subscribe). To Mencken, he expressed continuing interest in covering the presidential conventions and wondered whether the Chicago *Tribune* might not be a good newspaper to approach. Mencken apparently made the approach, and a month later, on February 11, Lewis was writing him to say that he had had a "bid" from the *Tribune* but that now he doubted whether he could cover the conventions for anyone because he would be exhausted when he had finished his book and should probably "get off to the woods for most of the summer." Or perhaps he would get a press seat from *The Nation* and do a single piece for that journal rather than fifteen hundred words every day for a newspaper.

In the meantime, there was no abatement in his London activities. On January 15 he attended the ceremonial of His Majesty's proceeding to Parliament. He was seeing his new political friends constantly. He became involved in a brief correspondence with a woman named Daisy Adler Hobman, the author of a first novel called *Zion* who wished to dedicate her second novel to him. Chiding her gently for an excess of earnestness ("Don't *explain* your characters—make 'em live!") and protesting that "I so dreadfully lack the measured dignity which one should have to be an Author" of the sort who receives dedications, he nevertheless gave his permission. Every night there were dinners, and at one of them he met the new ambassador from the United States, Frank B. Kellogg, and his wife, the latter more impressive than the former. There was also Lord Birkenhead, too arrogant toward Lewis's friends of the Labor Party wholly to please him, yet it was pleasant that he, like the Kelloggs, knew *Main Street* and *Babbitt*. At a Tuesday lunch in February, Lewis was the guest of honor and the speaker at the English-Speaking Union, and in his introduction, the chairman, St. Loe Strachey, "talked entirely about *Babbitt* and indicated that I was a cross between Jack Dempsey and God Almighty, all of which is as it should be of course."

His wife had returned in time for Beaverbrook's dinner at the Savoy on January 22, but Devonshire had been miserable and her cold had hardly improved. Lewis had been "seeing millions of people," including "Spike" Hunt, had revised nearly 100,000 words of *Arrowsmith,* had passed his thirty-ninth birthday on February 7, and was feeling tired enough by the last weekend of February to leave his desk for Bath, and then, back in London, to decide to take his wife to Spain, where they hoped for sun. They left on March 5.

In Paris they encountered W. E. Woodward and his wife, and from Carcassonne Lewis wrote him on March 10, urging him to come there if he wanted "to forget America complete." Madrid, Toledo, Seville: cold, wind, rain. From Seville, on March 15, Lewis wrote Wells to say that they had considered trying to find him in Portugal but that they would not have time. The sun did come out there and they met the congenial American colony. Whatever the final felicities, they cut the journey short; Mrs. Lewis dropped off at Biarritz "for five or six days" (it was eleven or twelve), and Lewis returned to London alone.

He wrote Harcourt to tell him that the plans for the Treaty Trip into Saskatchewan were definite, and on the same day he wrote his father to warn him that he would have only a few days with him in June because he and Claude would have to be in Prince Albert on June 7 or 8. At the end of the first week in April, when Mrs. Lewis was back in London, he wrote his father again to say that the rest of his letters would be short, he was "working like the devil to finish up," and "We have ahead of us, thank the Lord, not a single date except a probably light dinner with [B. W. F.] Armitage [the Cambridge anatomist] this evening." And he was having his portrait painted by C. R. W. Nevinson, "one of the best painters in England"; fortunately, it was to be done in pastels and would require only two afternoons for sittings. And "the paintings of Nevinson" became one of the topics of an enlightened man's conversation in *Arrowsmith.*

C. R. W. Nevinson, in *Paint and Prejudice,* left an account of these sittings. He did not remember his dates exactly—he thought that *Babbitt* had not yet been written—but he did remember some moderately entertaining anecdotes about Lewis in London. He was an impossible sitter, "restless, clownish, and intense as only Americans can be," and prowled round the studio "while all the time he poured out the most remarkable monologue of love and hate, shrewdness and sentimentality," and left Nevinson finally in a state of exhaustion and elation such as no one had ever produced in him. Lewis, he said, "was obsessed by a dread of the future and of his own in particular, fearing that his creative faculties would dry up," and one must wonder—at this point particularly, when he was finishing what he thought to be his finest book—whether this was not a role that permitted him to play the serious artist. Meanwhile, he would direct his devastating irony at his contemporaries, French, English and American. No man Nevinson ever knew was at once so sensitive and so gifted at gaucherie. He broke "all the snob rules laid down by the mumbo jumbos of English literature" and then infuriated everyone "with a taint of preciosity" of his own. Sometimes he seemed positively possessed; and sometimes he could be beaten at his own game.

Nevinson remembered two such occasions.

> Once we were at dinner with Somerset Maugham, and among those present were Mrs. Maugham, [Edward] Knoblock, [Charles] McEvoy [both playwrights], Osbert Sitwell, and Eddie Marsh. There was nobody in the party

> to whom Sinclair Lewis could take exception; and as for our host, I have always noticed like many others that he is the one man admired by all authors. After dinner, Sinclair Lewis took Eddie Marsh's monocle, stuck it in his own eye, and began parading up and down with Eddie Marsh following like a dog on a string. Then, to amuse himself, he parodied highbrow conversation in the best Oxford manner, at times imitating McEvoy's cracked voice, which was sometimes bass and sometimes treble. All of us were embarrassed, as the parody was grotesquely realistic, and I saw McEvoy pull his hair over his forehead and begin to look like a village idiot, a danger signal in him.
>
> I knew it would come, and sure enough McEvoy suddenly interrupted the parody and inquired if Sinclair Lewis was an American. Sinclair Lewis looked taken aback at the question, but fell right into trouble.
>
> "Yes," he said. "That is what makes me so sick with you condescending Englishmen."
>
> "I don't care if you are sick," replied McEvoy calmly. "In fact I should be rather pleased. But you are just the man to tell me why old Americans are so much nicer than young ones."
>
> Poor Lewis. The eye-glass fell from his eye and he was silent until we left.

The other episode is reminiscent of that occasion at the Jockey bar in Paris.

> I took him on to a night club and he began to regain courage. A little Chelsea girl joined us; and, still sore, he began boasting. I knew this Chelsea girl to be a terror and by no means as innocent as she looked, but in spite of all my efforts to silence him he would talk about himself. With murmurs of disbelief the girl urged him on until he was announcing to the world at large that he was the author of *Main Street,* which had the largest circulation, bar the Bible, of any book in America. The wicked little girl looked at him with wide-open eyes and asked, "Are you a writer?" By now he was in a mood to repeat himself. "Sure I am," he bellowed. "I am telling you I wrote *Main Street,* that has the largest circulation, bar the Bible, throughout America." With a look of complete innocence the girl went on, "You an author? I thought you were an American! But surely you were a publicity agent once?"

And then there was the occasion when, after repeatedly demanding of Beaverbrook, "What do you think, Max?" that worthy wheeled on him and suddenly snapped, "What do you think, Sinc?" Sinc was silenced. And reasserted his Americanism by purchasing Nevinson's painting of the Brooklyn Bridge.

In April, with each of the two versions of *Arrowsmith* so nearly completed, he made his plans for returning to New York. He announced them to Harcourt, to his father and to Mencken, and he told the latter that he would "expect a large party" before he went West. He would sail alone on the *Scythia* on May 10, arrive in New York late on the eighteenth or the nineteenth, stay there until about the twenty-seventh, then go west for a visit with his father and north for the summer. He also told his wife. There was no point in disturbing Wells's schooling nor in curtailing her pleasures; she could spend the summer in France. This was not her notion, and so she wrote Harcourt on April 30: she was sailing with Wells on the *Veendam* at the end of the first week in June. But she changed her plans. She did not linger in London. On May 20, from Paris, she wrote her sister-in-law in St. Cloud (urging her not to send Freeman to a department store, or factory, like the University of Minnesota, and offering to tour the Eastern colleges with him) to say that she was sailing "this Saturday," which would have been May 24. But apparently she delayed. Forlornly perhaps but in considerable style, she followed him as first planned and arrived in New York on the fourteenth of June (Lewis had escaped to the West in good time), went to Ma*ma*'s retreat at Forest Hills, gathered her up, and presently settled with her at Siasconset on Nantucket for the rest of the summer.

Lewis's plans proceeded as he had outlined them. He came into New York on the nineteenth and announced that he had sat up until three that morning finishing *Arrowsmith.* According to the New York *Times,* James G. Dougherty, customs inspector, was the first person to see the new manuscript.

> The author was quite patient while the Inspector poured over chapter after chapter. Finally he said:
>
> "Mr. Inspector, I really must be going."
>
> "Pardon me, sir," replied the Inspector. "I've read your other books, and I wanted to see if this were up to standard."

He confessed to "a million Main Street thrills" at seeing the city skyline again. When shown some of the newspaper clippings on his London controversies, he said, "I am cured. There has been so much alteration of what I may have said, that I'll never talk of any of the peculiarities of England or America again. The English are an admirable people and I like many of them. I don't like all of them as I don't like all Americans." He wondered which was worse, the Prohibition law or the lawlessness of enforcing it.

He went to the Chatham, where began at once two days of violating the law. Whether the party with Mencken was managed is not clear, but on the third night, when Mencken's friend, Philip Goodman, gave a party (Burton Rascoe recalled that it included De Kruif, Mencken, Dreiser, Ernest Boyd, Elmer Rice and W. C. Fields), Lewis was unable to attend— ". . . he was exhausted from the parties in his honor and had to go to bed."

But he appeared in public frequently enough to let his enemies do their field work. Reliable Ernest Boyd composed this "portrait":

Tall, slim and well-barbered; his sandy hair sleeked down on either side of an immaculate parting; his clothes carefully pressed; two inches of shirt cuff showing; his shoes well-shined—Sinclair Lewis looks the personification of conventional elegance, as badly dressed as only the wearer of standardized fashions for men can be, when every trace of individuality, of personal taste, is lost in a resolutely orthodox combination of "what the well-dressed man is wearing." Sartorially he realizes the ideal of the supporters of nationally advertised products, "authentic styles for the better-dressed man," "designed to combat the rigors of hot weather, and in addition, to give that lasting dressy appearance," "suits in the New York manner, smart, cool-looking, and spirited," which "excel in smartness as well as service," and unexcelled "in patterns, styling, and fit." He looks the part of an aggressive, forwardlooking, up-standing citizen, a sales promoter of ability, a key man and live wire, who works entirely on leads and full organization support, 80 per cent of whose annual business consists of repeat orders.

His appearance does not belie his activities, for Sinclair Lewis is the drummer of ideas, the sales executive of the new American literature. . . . He has made the Revolt of the Younger Generation a paying proposition, operating an exclusive territory on a royalty basis, and presenting an unusual household specialty, a burlesque made up to look like satire. . . . It is the genius of Sinclair Lewis that he is able to combine the outlook of Carol Kennicott with the language and technique of his now famous realtor and boom the result as a satire on both. . . . This, then, is "the significance of Sinclair Lewis," that he has burlesqued himself and "gotten away with it." . . . And so, this lithe, neat, well-groomed young American business man, on whose every garment and idea one can see the label that is a guarantee of authenticity, has come into his own, just like the hero of a success magazine story. He has carried the gospel of 100% Americanism into the effete countries of Europe and shown them what a live, two-fisted, literary he-man can do. In return, he has begun to take on a certain flavor of cosmopolitan experience, realizing the sweet uses to which a monocle may be put, and the charms of an established social hierarchy, where men are not merely men, but sometimes gentlemen. He has discovered, like so many of his countrymen, that it pays to advertise . . . Babbitt.

Harcourt, whose first wife had died and who was now married to his secretary, Ellen Eayrs, had hoped that Lewis would spend a good part of his New York time at Mount Vernon with them. Probably there, during this week, *Arrowsmith* had its editor-author going over. At some time, the final portions of the shortened version were delivered to *The Designer*.* And at

* "*Arrowsmith:* Genesis, Development, Versions," by Lyon N. Richardson (*American Literature,* vol. XXVII, no. 2 [May 1955] pp. 225–44) is chiefly concerned with a detailed examination of the difference between the serial and the book version. The changes are extensive but none of them affects "Lewis's remarks on science, medicine, or medical institutions." Many "philosophical" parentheses, satirical thrusts at other than the main subject, and curses were removed. All gratuitous wisecracks at religious

some point early in his stay, Lewis found time to write, for *The Nation* of June 4, a piece called "I Return to America," a rather lively narrative impression of American political apathy, "our fat and cigar-chewing indifference," as compared with European political vitality. He concluded this article with a determination to discover whether the college generation was as smug as the generation of its elders.

Where he was going—and where he seems to have gone before the month of May was out—he would have small opportunity to observe the educated young. He stopped in Chicago to visit Dr. Fishbein, who obliged with a dinner. The guests, besides Lewis, were Ben Hecht, Carl Sandburg, and James Weber Linn, then well known in the community as a professor of English at the University of Chicago. His middle name was pronounced *Weeber,* and the professor insisted on the pronunciation. Linn began to taunt Lewis in a mild way about the commercial motives of his writing. Lewis argued temperately, but always in reply he would begin, "Now Professor James *Webb*er Linn," and repeated the mispronunciation so often that the other man was at last infuriated and began to pound the table, shouting, "*Weeb*er! *Weeb*er, I tell you!" When Lewis gently replied, "Now, Professor James *Webber* Linn, I must insist that I am an acolyte at the altar of literature," the dispute collapsed with the remark of one of the other men, "Ah, yes, indeed—an alcoholite at the altar."

While Lewis was in Chicago in this brief period, Karl E. Harriman, who edited *Red Book* in that city, saw him. *Red Book* had been interested in the possible serialization of *Arrowsmith* but had lost out to *The Designer.* Now the editor proposed that he would pay Lewis the same sum that *The Designer* had paid—$50,000—for his next novel, whatever it might be. Neither knew that it would be *Mantrap.* Lewis agreed that *Red Book* should be the first periodical to see that next novel, if it was to be serialized at all. (And Dr. Fishbein remembers that when *Mantrap* came in, *Red Book* backed away in horror; however, *Collier's* then bought it for $42,500, delighted to have it.)

On June 4, Lewis wrote Harcourt from Sauk Centre. He had visited his father, who was not feeling very well, but Lewis himself was already beginning to feel rested, and he was leaving the next evening for Canada. Mrs. Lewis, in Nantucket, had reason to think that he was spending his time with the "town sports," a clothing store clerk and a garage mechanic, both inebriates, and that now Sauk Centre labeled the novelist a drunkard. Quite possibly. However, he did find a sober moment in which to write

---

practices were cut, the picture of the country doctor was softened, Martin's physical appetites were played down and his fits of neurasthenia removed, and close-up examinations of the details of disease and anatomy were removed or generalized. The result in total effect is that the serial version is more rapidly paced narrative than the book version, and Mr. Richardson is inclined to think that the shorter version may, on the whole, be the better.

his little article for *The Nation* called "Main Street's Been Paved." This purports to be a visit to Gopher Prairie, where, four years after *Main Street,* the author interviews his characters, especially as to their attitudes toward the coming elections. Kennicott is stolidly conservative. Carol has become highly respectable. Guy Pollock is going to vote for Robert M. LaFollette, against Calvin Coolidge. Main Street is more stuffy than ever, even though four blocks of it have now been paved.

Claude Lewis arrived from St. Cloud on June 5, and that evening the brothers set off together by train for Winnipeg. Harry had probably visited Abercrombie & Fitch in New York, with the result that he "had a carrying sack for his stuff" that "would take about two redcaps to lug . . . to say nothing of a portage of three miles." Dr. Lewis does not tell when or how this equipment was reduced to those essentials that Harry could manage once trains were behind them, but presumably this first step in his education as a woodsman took place sometime between their arrival in Winnipeg on the morning of June 6 and their departure from Big River, Saskatchewan, on June 18. These were twelve days of carousal.

At Winnipeg they were met by a newspaper photographer and the secretary of the Kiwanis Club. Reporters arrived at once at their hotel. Liquor was laid in. To the press, the excited Harry was proclaiming:

> It won't be any picnic. The purpose of the party is to pay off the pensions of the Cree Indians, in right of their land grants and such like, and to give them medical or other help. For me it will be a chance to relax and forget all about writing.
>
> We won't have any rest houses to reach at the end of the day's march, mind you, where one can get a hot bath and sleep between sheets. We'll pack our own kits and portage our own canoes. We'll pitch camp where night finds us. It's going to be bully.

The preliminaries, at any rate, were. At noon, at a Kiwanis luncheon, Lewis addressed about four hundred people on the subject of Anglo-American relations and spent the afternoon driving with a bookseller who had disposed of over three thousand copies of *Babbitt.* On their return, the newspapermen were waiting for them. "The Scotch whisky flew fast and furious, and Harry seemed in his element. . . . About eight o'clock, Harry ordered supper, which was served in our room for the whole crowd." Later, at Harry's insistence, the party went to "the home of a doctor" whom none of them seemed to know but who supplied "plenty of hard liquor." At eleven, Dr. Claude "began to holler;" by half past twelve he had won his point and gone to bed.

They loitered in Winnipeg in this fashion, the doctor chafing with "this social stuff," until June 9, when they moved on to Regina, Saskatchewan, in the company of W. R. Graham of the Department of Indian Affairs. At Regina they met William R. Taylor, the Indian agent for Trip Number

Ten. Harry "had to do the reporters," Mr. Graham gave them a luncheon party ("the elite were all there"), and that evening Lewis addressed a combined meeting of the Kiwanis Club and the Men's and Women's Canadian Club. "Harry gave a good spiel," after which a lawyer took them home "for a drop of Scotch. Harry sure has a good nose for it. . . ." At one in the morning Dr. Claude " put up a fight" and got back to their hotel. Tuesday—another club dinner with "witty remarks" by Harry, and another Scotch party. Wednesday—golf with General Quebric ("Harry was the caddy for Quebric"), the Princess Pat jazz band, and the doctor's dour observation that "Prohibition is just a joke up here." On Thursday, the twelfth, they moved on to Saskatoon, where Harry "seemed to fill the bill" at another large luncheon engagement, and then a literary tea with the Saskatoon ladies, one of whom took Dr. Claude to be the author of *Main Street*. "I fainted. . . ."

They left the tea party for Prince Albert. "The town representatives were all there and conducted us in great state to the hotel. Then they all piled into the room and a booze party began." At half past twelve, Dr. Claude began to undress for bed "and the crowd finally had sense enough to go home." Again, on Saturday, "a couple of chaps were here until after ten," when with Harry and Taylor, they went off "for some kind of a party." Next day, Harry was late in rising to meet the mayor, who was taking them to the golf course. On Sunday, a talk to the Rotarians at lunch and another to the Kiwanians at a ladies'-night dinner. "Harry went home as he was tired." Next day, June 17, having been joined by the Trip's doctor, J. W. MacFadyen, and eight Indians, they proceeded to Big River, an abandoned sawmill town on Cowan Lake, in a freight train that took nearly eight hours to cover ninety miles. The hotel was filthy but there was "booze." It was apparently the last place for thirty days in which that commodity would be available, and there is no evidence that Harry stowed any away with his gear. This is the more surprising since Taylor, the leader, during these preliminaries, had been quite as bibulous as he.

But now Taylor had his government business to attend to. They set out in a drizzle at about half past two on the afternoon of June 18. Taylor's canoe, like Dr. Lewis's, was equipped with a motor, and these two towed the other two. Harry's Indians, named Norman and Silas, were hardly ideal companions since they could not speak English and he was not prepared to perform for them in Cree. The rain turned heavier and after twelve miles and an hour and a half, they decided to camp. "We got to bed early and were out at 4 A.M.," says the now contented Claude.

The second day they traveled against the wind and gusts of rain for fourteen hours, but then enjoyed the felicity of dining on wild duck shot by the Indians. "The ground had ceased to jump up and bump one, and I didn't move all night." The doctor snored, however, and Harry, struggling against the earth with which he was seeking reunion, plaintively begged him to "turn over." Next morning, June 20, they were routed out by the now intent Taylor at five minutes to four, and that day even the doctor found rather long.

> I thought Bill would never quit and he did not pull in for camp until 9 P.M. We had a rotten place—all the stuff and the canoes had to be carried up a 15-foot bank, and tent sites had to be chopped out of the brush. We finally finished up supper at 10:40. Some long day—from 4 A.M. to 11 P.M.

Saturday was another tiring day, during which they shot boulder-littered rapids for ten miles, but at the end of that day they arrived at their first community—a Roman Catholic Mission on Lac la Plonge with seven priests, nine nuns, and an Indian school of sixty pupils. That night it rained, and it rained until noon on Sunday, but they stayed on land, which was a blessing, and had supper at the Mission school.

They set forth again on Monday, in gorgeous weather, to maneuver Ile-à-la-Crosse Lake and arrive at the Hudson Bay post on that lake to make their first payments. Indians from the entire area had come in bands and had set up their white wigwams all about the village. Taylor established himself on the porch of the priest's house with the doctor, and as each band approached him, the chief of that band would sit with them. Each chief received $25, each of his three councilors, $15, and everyone else, $5. The brothers Lewis watched these proceedings for a time, then investigated the village and met Constable H. C. Macbeth of the Royal Canadian Mounted Police who, with two young trappers, lived near the encampment.

On June 24, Taylor was to begin a trip to Buffalo Lake and Lake la Loche and then he would return to Ile-à-la-Crosse, and this excursion Harry decided to omit from his itinerary. "Harry thought it would be a fine time to take a rest as this 4 A.M. to 10 P.M. gets on his nerves after a day or two. I don't know what he will do after he leaves here, as it will be one steady grind and no chance to stop off." Surprisingly, Claude decided to stay with him; they made pleasant little excursions during the day and at night there was poker at Macbeth's. This went on for a week, and on the last day, June 30, Harry, rested and still expecting from six to eight weeks ahead of him, wrote his publishers that the trip was going beautifully, that he had not had a drink for eleven days (this is two days less than their travels since Big River had taken; perhaps he did have just a bottle or two of whisky with him at the start), that he had lost his "jumpiness" and his "daily morning feeling-like-hell," and he did not miss liquor in the least.

They left La Crosse in the afternoon of July 1 and floated through forest fire smoke so thick that Claude could not see Harry's canoe behind him, but they had a good night and next day they entered the Churchill

River, ran three rapids, and presently arrived at a Chippewa settlement. The Chippewa are less tidy than the Cree.

> ... they are surely a dirty bunch. And dogs! You never saw so many in your life. About the smallest number each family has is eight and there were about thirty families. The whole place smelled like a hog yard and I am not surprised that Taylor wanted to get away as soon as possible.

The Churchill River connects a whole series of lakes, through which the party passed, and the scenery had become very fine. In the upper reaches of the Churchill, it was necessary to approach Lac la Ronge by a series of seven portages, and on that day it was very hot. Goose Lake, Snake Lake, Trout Lake and Clam Lake, and at last, on July 7, Lac la Ronge. Then back again by way of Nut Portage. "As we left the portage, Taylor got out his flag, and Norman, the bowman in Harry's canoe, put up his blue handkerchief and Harry fired his gun in salute to the great pleasure of the boys." On July 11, they arrived at Stanley, and at Stanley Harry announced that he had had enough.

He would leave the party at its next stop, Pelican Narrows. "Guess he finds this traveling hard work." Claude argued with him—certainly they should both see the beautiful Reindeer Lake country; the trip was doing him immense good, "especially without booze." But Harry was adamant. He would leave with two Indians, one tent, and as much food as he needed; "go by Sturgeon Landing to Cumberland House [three days away on the Saskatchewan River], and then by steamer to Le Pas" in Manitoba, where he could get a train back to Minnesota. Claude, who feared that Taylor would want him to go, too, if his brother went, pointed out that, after all, Harry got in three or four hours of napping while they traveled, whereas he, Claude, had to stay awake to tend his motor; but when he learned that Taylor hoped he would continue with him, Claude subsided and was willing that Harry should depart. There was an exchange of magnanimity: Claude offered to go out with him; Harry said, Certainly not, and really, "his mental irritation would spoil the rest of the journey for them."

On July 14 they started off again, and Harry, glad that he was leaving, "seems very happy." Claude's testiness with him did not diminish because of this prospect. "Harry, with his customary fishing ability, has lost two complete trolling spoons this afternoon." The camping spot that night, among rocks, was "miserable."

> Harry had arranged the beds, but he had made a poor guess, as his rocks could not be surrounded and guess he had a bad night. I had a rock just under the middle of my back, but by turning on my side, the rock could sink into my belly, so that being tired, I slept like a rock . . . Harry looks

> tired to death this morning and guess he'll be very glad to go south at Pelican Narrows.

They came into Pelican Narrows early on Wednesday, July 16, and the worst was over.

They had been out for almost a month, and on part or all of about twenty of those days, Harry had been in the canoe with his noble savages. From here on, things were convivial again, and in ten days he would be back in Winnipeg. He immediately met Arthur Jan, a friendly fur trader who lived in a very tidy house that delighted him, and beer, at least, was available at once, and at that night's poker party, something more. "They must have had a good time as there are a few headaches today." Taylor was once more in the pre-Big River mood, and Harry was preparing for civilization. On Saturday, July 19, the sober doctor wrote as follows:

> The pace that Taylor and Harry have traveled here has been fierce, and Taylor is still about half shot from last night. They have played poker every night and drank booze so that they were all lit up every night. Harry said he quit at 3 A.M. and guess Taylor and Jan kept going until 4 or 4:30. I woke up about 4:30 and found Harry lying on his bed, not a stitch of clothes removed and proceeded to get him to undress and to bed. Taylor did the same thing, but Mac, who sleeps in his tent, never touched him. The two of them didn't come to until about 9 A.M.

At noon, the party got under way again, and next morning, Harry and Arthur Jan and two Indians, Norman and Joe, took off in "the busted canoe" for Sturgeon Landing. "That gives him until Thursday noon to catch the steamer for Le Pas. Three days is plenty of time even without a motor and old Joe has made the trip many times."

Now, with Jan, it was all uproarious. When Dr. Lewis and Taylor arrived at Sturgeon Landing a month later,

> They told us of Harry's arrival with Jan and the big party. All drunk, killed 9 bottles of scotch and played poker until daylight. That's the life for Harry if you add a woman or two at the proper time.

And at the next stop:

> Harry must have had another fierce party at The Pas, as Jan and Dr. Crock went with him that night as far as Hudson Bay Junction, and from what I could hear he was loaded to the gills.

On the twenty-sixth of July, he was sleeping on the train to Winnipeg, and in another day, he was once more in Sauk Centre, the prodigal Thoreau returned again to the thin parental bosom.

This episode in Lewis's biography is even funnier and more pathetic than a similar episode in his *Babbitt,* for in the latter the novelist was able to see the humor of the city man's attempt at natural renewal amid the realities of wilderness life, whereas in his own experience, he was as naïvely expectant of refreshment and as deluded about the realities as Babbitt himself had been. The only tolerable ingredients of the experience in the wilds were those contributions from civilization—drink, cards and gregarious company. But the comedy extends one step further when, in *Mantrap,* Lewis would use the materials of his adventure but so transpose the actualities as to vindicate the gentle city man and show him to be the master of hardship and the match of brutes. But it would be some months before the adventure had receded far enough to permit such a transmutation into splendor of a trying fiasco.

From Le Pas he had wired Harcourt to say that he was again in touch with civilization and Harcourt wrote him at once. Harcourt had no very surprising news—only that they had proof of *Arrowsmith,* were showing it to the motion picture studios but had had no bids, that Warner Brothers reported they had lost money on *Main Street* and were losing money on *Babbitt,* and that this news had circulated and left other studios hesitant about the new book.

Lewis stayed in Sauk Centre for ten days. There, almost certainly, he wrote his enthusiastic review of Van Vechten's *The Tattooed Countess,* which appeared in *The Saturday Review of Literature* for August 30. What else he did in Sauk Centre must remain unknown: perhaps he continued to disport himself with the mechanic and the clerk and thereby led the *Herald* to shield its eyes entirely from his visitation. On August 5 he wrote Mencken to say that he was out of the wilderness after "a good trip, boozeless and not too hard," and that he was on his way East,

> where I shall doubtless, unless Morris Fishbein and his malign company kill me with fusel oil, appear briefly in NY, hoping to behold your beneficent countenance, then on to Nantucket Island, where my wife amiably awaits me.

On that day, too, he left Sauk Centre, and then took three weeks to move sluggishly by way of St. Paul, Chicago, Detroit and New York, to his wife and mother-in-law and son on Nantucket.

In New York he had discussed with Harcourt the possibility of publishing a collection of short stories, and he took away with him a set of proofs for *Arrowsmith.* But these, he reported to Harcourt on September 6, he had not yet looked at because he had "never been more agreeably and profitably lazy than here, in this island of sea breezes and moors." And he is preparing once more to go abroad "for God knows how long." There was no hurry because *The Designer* serialization was causing book publication to be put off until well into 1925, and perhaps he could delay with the proofreading until he was on board ship. In the meantime, he did rouse himself to read Sherwood Anderson's *Story Teller's Story* and to write a generous review of it for the *Herald Tribune.*

> . . . he is a great man, and we see in *A Story Teller's Story* not merely the directing tale of an American voyageur, not only a fine perception of our own land and time, but as well our own stupidity in regarding as somehow a wicked man the possessor of a fine and earthy innocence.

The review was a defense of Anderson against those who reported that he was immoral—and this after Anderson's merciless incarceration of a freezing Lewis with a freezing Gertrude Stein!

He was himself the subject of a newspaper piece called "A Literary Luncheon," written by "Quiz" for the New York *Evening Post Literary Review* and published there on October 18. Those at the luncheon with Lewis were Cosmo Hamilton, William Gropper, and Dr. Joseph Collins the moralist. Lewis defended the rights of skepticism against a kind of automatic faith endorsed by Collins. He also attacked Freud, whom he had not read: "He has been responsible for all sorts of professional charlatans who are doing great harm—men who put their dirty fingers into the delicate machinery of the mind and distort it." The serialization of fiction, he said, made for "an inferior form of the novel," and he announced in conclusion:

> I dislike literary discussions about anything. I dislike the habit of some literary men who want to talk book stuff. The really literary species do not talk about books; they are too busy writing them.

He was almost always eager to be kind. In New York he saw his onetime friend, Allan Updegraff, now employed by *The Literary Digest.* They were no longer close, but Lewis wanted to be of use to him. Updegraff had published two novels—*Second Youth* (1917) and *Strayed Revelers* (1918)—without success, and now he was at work on a third. Updegraff's recollection was that at this point Lewis persuaded Harcourt to take an option on this novel and pay him an advance against royalties, or, in his own words, "to pay me $200 not to finish a certain impossible novel but to begin another." That was probably *Dancers in the Wind,* which was published by Boni & Liveright in 1925.

On September 19, Harcourt wrote Lewis to tell him that Paul de Kruif was leaving New York and had come in to discuss the acknowledgment to be made to him for his work on *Arrowsmith.* He had proposed—modestly enough, it seems, when one remembers Lewis's enthusiastic dependence on him—the phrase, "In collaboration with Paul H. de Kruif," to appear in small type either on the title page or on a page following. Lewis found this excessive, and when he came to New York presently, he proposed instead an extended statement:

> To Dr. Paul H. de Kruif I am indebted not only for most of the bacteriological and medical material in this tale but equally for his suggestions in the planning of the fable itself—for his realization of the characters as living people, for his philosophy as a scientist. With this acknowledgment I want to record our months of companionship while working on the book, in the United States, in the West Indies, in Panama, in London and Fontainebleau. I wish I could reproduce our talks along the way, and the laboratory afternoons, the restaurants at night, and the deck at dawn as we steamed into tropic ports.

When Harcourt discussed this proposal with De Kruif, De Kruif agreed to accept it if the phrase "for his suggestions" were changed to "for his help," and Lewis agreed to the change. Thus the acknowledgment appeared in the book. But the transaction had robbed the collaboration of its luster for Paul de Kruif. Even today he is grateful to Lewis for what, quite incidentally, he had taught him about writing, but he lost interest in the book they had worked out together, and Lewis lost another friend.*

In this interim, too, the Woodwards gave a party that Lewis attended and that Morris R. Werner, the biographer, remembers. Everyone was, of course, drinking Prohibition liquor and Lewis was demanding the stage. Literary ladies "were clustered around Lewis and cooing, 'Oh, Red, imitate Osbert Sitwell!' " Lewis obliged, and Werner, having long since had his fill, "behaved like the Marx brother who sometimes went out of the room slamming the door behind him in disgust." It was on this occasion that Werner asked him tauntingly about Ring Lardner, and learned from the stiff response that Lewis was at present reserving the word "great" for *The Way of All Flesh*—and himself.

There is a small mystery in this interim, too. Lewis left Siasconset about September 20, a few days after Mrs. Lewis, with her entourage, had gone once more to Forest Hills. Then, George Slocombe remembers, he met Mrs. Lewis in Washington after a private showing of the uncensored *Potemkin*. Lewis, on "completing his novel *Arrowsmith* [reading proofs] . . . was living at a house in Georgetown." Slocombe's recollection is that he dined with the Lewises and at their house met Senator Shipstead of Minnesota, "the solitary Farmer-Labor member of the upper house." It is possible and characteristic that they should have taken a house in Georgetown for that time. There were about three weeks to dispose of, and after all, they had to live somewhere. They had no notion where they would live next, but on October 8, four and a half months after their last return, they sailed for England on the *France*. Europe was a reasonably large and various continent. There would be something, and something preferable, surely, to this. . . .

* When several years later the book was bought for the films, Ann Watkins, the agent, turned to De Kruif rather than to Lewis for scenario assistance, which De Kruif generously gave.

6

THEY LEFT NEW YORK as the presidential campaign was coming to its climax, and Lewis's remark to the press as he boarded the *France* was that his only regret in sailing was that he would not be able to vote for Robert M. LaFollette. He had found time before sailing to write for *The Nation* three brief, pro-LaFollette pieces that appeared in the last three October issues of that weekly. Called "Be Brisk with Babbitt," these purport to be interviews with certain inhabitants of Zenith. Babbitt and Vergil Gunch and one Schnaufknabel, a former mechanic now a plant foreman, will all vote for Coolidge. Seneca Doane, the radical lawyer, and Paul Riesling, will vote for LaFollette; so, surprisingly, will Charles McKelvey, the representative of big business. On the train east from Zenith, the interviewer finds that the news butcher will vote for Coolidge but the brakeman will vote for LaFollette. It is characteristic that, for all his published interest in politics, Lewis's personal commitment was not intense enough to have led him to obtain an absentee ballot. In this campaign, as in most political situations, the issues were not of primary interest to him; his motive was, rather, hardly political at all: it was his inability to tolerate the dull that moved him.

During their rapid but uneventful passage, Lewis finished correcting the proof of *Arrowsmith,* and only now, in the proof stage, had that title been settled upon. On October 13, one day out from Plymouth, he wrote at least three letters. To Harcourt he said that he had "had the finest lot of assorted sleep" on board. To his father, after explaining the difference between a French liner and others, he said that he had served as chairman of the ship's concert. To Edith Summers he sent encouragement. She was having trouble with a second novel and had written him in the hope that he might be coming to California, where he could help her with it. He was regretful and suggested that, "if the book begins to drag," she might turn to short stories and send them to Sewell Haggard, to whom he had recommended her work.

In a few hours now the lights of England will twinkle on the port side, and by this time tomorrow evening we'll be having a drink with Spike Hunt in London—or gravely talking philosophy with Monty Belgion—or learning with what girls Bevil Rudd had fallen in love while we have left him alone. . . .

London was not much more interesting than these prospects suggested that it would be. They took a service flat at 45 Park Lane, but this time no "office," since Lewis had no immediate plans for a new book. The Shaws came to tea, and Shaw was not amused by snapshots he was shown of a bearded Lewis as Shaw. Hugh Walpole was their neighbor. There were the expected reunions with people like General Thomson, and the observation of another British election, "discovering with pleasure [this to Mencken] that the election slogans, even as mouthed by such a standard intellectual and Norman-descended gent as Lord Birkenhead, are in no way ahead of Rotary Club slogans in the USA or the murmurs of Dr. Coolidge." There was the usual roistering, perhaps rather accelerated. There seems to have been greater circumspection than in the past in Lewis's public utterances. There was young Wells, approaching the age of eight. They arranged to enroll him in the English Preparatory School at Glion, above Montreux. And on November 11 they gave up their flat to take him there.

"There's a very nice class of boys" in the Swiss school, Lewis wrote his father, "who will give Wells the companionship he needs as an Only Child." Leaving him and most of their bags there, they decided to tramp in the Alps. They spent the first night at Montbavon, the second at Gstaad. "I've worn my thin B.V.D. underwear and nothing else for more than twenty years," Lewis, hard-pressed for news items, wrote his father, "but this time I wore besides them—my pyjamas!" By a combination of foot and rail, they went then to Zweisimmen, Spietz, Interlaken, and Lucerne; then to Zug and Zurich; then by train back to Glion to spend half a day with Wells and pick up their luggage; then back to Paris where, on December 1, they settled into three rooms at the Hotel Élysée-Bellevue, 2 Rue Montaigne, off the Champs Élysée, where they remained fixed for two and a half months, "as far as possible from the Dôme and other haunts of Harold Stearns."

This to H. L. Mencken, to whom, on December 12, Lewis apologized for not yet having sent him anything for the *Mercury*. The writing of *Arrowsmith* had exhausted him and "it's taken till now to feel like writing again . . . but really, one or two or three articles for that instructive journal are positively the next things I'm going to do." And he would presently—but not yet—write "Self-Conscious America," to the outrage of Harold Stearns.

The year rather trailed to an end. Lewis was seeing his dentist, a

Nebraskan. He was taking French lessons from a Berlitz instructor. He was thinking about a novel to be called *The Yearner* and about "the novel about the Methodist preacher which I've planned so long." There were occasional parties, at one of which Eldon R. James, who had in the past tried to interest Lewis in a trip to the Orient, apparently was doing so again, with greater success. Lewis wrote to Claude, "the damnedest correspondent living," who had never told him "a thing about the trip after Pelican except that Bill was cranky," and he wrote him again, on the day after Christmas, with these plans: "I'm thinking, still rather vaguely, about a trip to the Orient late next year. . . . *If* I go, I don't believe I'll take Grace. . . ."

On Christmas day the Lewises lunched together on Montmartre among "all the simple and cheerful and natural French"; Mrs. Lewis reports that she inadvertently learned of a certain "Jane" whom Lewis was seeing; they had dinner alone in their sitting room; and their son was in Switzerland. "A quiet but agreeable Xmas," wrote Lewis. There was a gift from Hugh Walpole—a copy of *The Crystal Box* with Lewis's name included in the fivefold dedication. Lewis thanked him graciously next day and then chided him for his "references to 'realism' as though it was something evil," and for his attack on James Joyce.

> They can co-exist, *The Cathedral* and *Ulysses*. Personally I would rather read the first than the second, but why should you or I dictate to others or even reason with them if they prefer it the other way? And I do not think you make valid your case against Joyce by asserting that he has neither nobility, fine feeling, nor any other restraint. He—or rather his followers, for I understand that he himself says little—could answer, "What do you mean by those words? Are you using them in a sense of a High Church bishop, a Methody missioner, a county baroness, a London chauffeur, or how? Joyce is weary of all those conventions; he says, 'Let us look into life and see if it can not be made interesting as the devil without any of the customary and lying bedizenments with which the romanticists seemingly have to smear their characters to make them tolerable.' " He could answer thus and otherwise. It seems to me the best condemnation of a Joyce, if one wants to condemn him, is a curt "I find him uninteresting and unimportant."

In this letter, Lewis expressed once more his uncertainty about himself. "I envy you so for the eagerness and serenity with which you go on writing novels. I shall go on, always, but it is with so many doubts." At this moment, indeed, nothing much was coming from his typewriter; but he could throw himself into the excitement of the forthcoming *Arrowsmith*.

Prepublication printings of 51,750 copies were ordered. There would be a limited, autographed edition of five hundred copies, to be published simultaneously with the large general printings on March 5, 1925. In the meantime, there was the whole business of promotion. In New York, Paul de Kruif was not communicating with Lewis but he was assisting Harcourt in his preparations. He was helping to assemble lists of the names of bacteriologists, physicians and other scientists to whom advance copies of the book should go, and Lewis added the names of continental scientists. He thought, too, that it would be profitable to get adverse comments from Freud, Jung and Adler, and he enjoined Harcourt not to neglect the critics of major stature, "Brandes, Croce, et al," and "James Joyce in Paris, Gilbert Seldes and Wilson Follett and other highbrows in America." Then, the reviewers—couldn't Harcourt "get after Edith Wharton . . . perhaps cable her with prepaid reply"? He was busy as a bee.

The flyleaves for the limited edition were sent to Paris for Lewis's signature in December, but were delayed until January 27, when Lewis returned them together with his new photograph—the most striking he ever had taken—by Man Ray, and this would presently grace the pages of *Vanity Fair.* Harcourt was busy with sales promotion plans and with corralling reviewers. He was not eager for many reviews from men of science; "I want that crowd to realize that they have gotten into literature and that they should buy and read the book rather than expect to have copies given to them." Publication day had been deliberately chosen as March 5, and a full-page advertisement announced the fact in *Publishers' Weekly,* every week for ten weeks before the date of publication, "so that booksellers will know for dead certain that the day after Calvin Coolidge is inaugurated they will have nothing else to do but sell *Arrowsmith.*"

The prepublication excitement gave an edge to Paris parties with other Americans. The Ernest Braces arrived. Philip Goodman arrived. The William Woodwards arrived. One day, when the Woodwards were lunching at Lapérouse, crowded as always, a sudden commotion attracted their attention, "and above the noise I could hear one strident voice shouting, 'It's Bill Woodward! Sure, it's Bill! He's right over there!' . . . Then I saw approaching, and pushing diners and waiters out of the way, the tall, red-headed figure. . . ." After that, they were together nearly every day, for Woodward, like De Kruif and Hunt, was a big, bluff, hearty man of appetite. There were weekends at George Slocombe's place at Les Andelys in lower Normandy with his hearty fellow journalists; and Mrs. Lewis would sometimes go to Switzerland to visit her son.

Lewis was seeing, he wrote his father in mid-January, Fred Howe (formerly of Harcourt, Brace & Company), the dramatist Louis Shipman, Prince Bibesco, Princess Kropotkin, Bernice Kenyon, Struthers Burt, Mrs. James Hazen Hyde, and—Elsa Maxwell! He was doing "a little writing"—it was little, indeed, in this frenzy. He had given up his Berlitz teacher and found a professor in a *lycée,* a man of about sixty, who was very good, and to whose apartment the pupil went for his lessons. He gave his father a description of a typical concierge—"Of her you inquire the particular floor on which lives the tenant." His English imitation of French syntax was more successful than his French composition, of which one sample is extant. At a café he met a young American professor, Henry R. Brush, who was studying at the Sorbonne. Brush had a letter from Lewis's old Spanish instructor at Yale, Rudolph Schevill, in which Schevill moderately enjoined him to "drink a good glass of wine or beer now and then and think of us." On the reverse of this letter, under the date of January 8, 1925, Lewis scrawled the following:

> M. Schevill:
>
> *J'ai vu que M. le Professeur a eu assez de vin et, a[u] lieu de biere, peutetre un peu de fin et—per m'rappeler les jours d'Espagnol à Yale—j'ai le grand plaisir de vous presenter, cher Monsieur, mes compliments les plus distingués.*
>
> Sinclair Lewis

He passed his fortieth birthday while his wife was in Switzerland. He probably spent most of that day with Philip Goodman. To Harcourt he wrote on January 28 that Goodman was "a hell of a good fellow," and on February 1 he announced that he was "going to write a play." Goodman was a *bon vivant* who had written advertising copy, had worked for a publisher and occasionally produced plays. He was also, Lewis wrote his father, "one of the most entertaining and intelligent men I have ever known," and it was he who persuaded Lewis to try, once more, a play, which Goodman would produce. For a week they worked out their plans for it, and on February 8, the day after his birthday, they retired to the *Bierstuben* of Munich to compose it.

As for many a Babbitt, reaching the age of forty was a painful climax for Lewis, and the occasion of heightened follies. There went youth, somehow unfulfilled; there went more than half of life, somehow, in spite of the vast success, a failure; there was so little time left, and all that running down. So spin, spin, spin in a frenzy! Drown in insensibility the knowledge of failure and the haunting sense of irremediable loss of whatever it was that one never knew. Chase the girls, Georgie Porgie, pinch the girls, kiss the girls and make them cry, paw and maul the girls, when they submit, in your wife's presence as well as in her absence, bounce into bed for a frenetic thrust at anyone who's willing, and be quick to bounce out again, never mind about hurting the pride of a proud and pretentious wife, it can all be patched up again for a week, ten days, then burst out again. But stay free, free, and keep on running! ("Hell making," he had called it, when he was an awkward boy in the chemistry laboratory of the Sauk Centre High School.)

He began to go to pieces, Rebecca West believes, when he ceased to be respectable, and that began in a serious way with the Caribbean journey. Paul de Kruif was not a man with whom Lewis should have sought to compete, nor was Frazier Hunt, nor was William Woodward. Lewis was often a stubborn man, but he was neither a hard nor a strong one. He needed respectability, needed bourgeois support, needed what he could least endure and what was best symbolized by Hartford, Connecticut, needed least what he wanted—the company of a heavy-drinking, high-living man like Philip Goodman in the bibulous atmosphere of a dissolute German city.

The play, needless to say, was not written.* Mrs. Lewis, left behind in Paris, protested in letters to her father-in-law and her sister-in-law that she was enjoying herself and would not join her husband in Munich for several weeks. But her husband apparently had no such plans for her. He was working on the play, listening to spoken German ("nothing could be odder than to see through one of these Gothic arches a bright blue, very modern car come shooting"), trying to speak it himself, spending a good deal of time with his German publisher, Kurt Wolff ("very gay and charming, with a beautiful wife and a charming house") and his associates, in the middle of carnival time, the *Fasching*. Through the Wolffs he was meeting other charming people, notably the Viennese Baron and Baroness Schey ("to whom I took enormously"), and with them he attended several carnival balls, "enormous crowded costume affairs, with plenty of beer but no visible drunkenness." (This to his father.) But in two weeks he was back in Paris.

Writing his father this censored report of the Munich excursion on March 1, he assured him that he would now finish the play in Paris. And so he had written Harcourt on February 28. But he apparently held his letter to his father until March 3, when he appended a note:

> The play is no good. It tends to be cheap—sensational—& rather than have that, I'm chucking it. I'll be off, with Gracie, in four or five days . . . first to Southern France (the Riviera, that golden shore of the Mediterranean) . . .

And on the fourth, he sent the same news to Harcourt.

His thoughts had returned to *The Yearner,* but before he settled down to writing it, they must make a great circuit which might take them as far north as Stockholm. They left for Marseilles on March 7, two days after the publication of *Arrowsmith.* To herald it, Harcourt, Brace & Company had published another little pamphlet about Lewis, full of biographical inaccuracies and critical excesses, by "Oliver Harrison," who was Harrison Smith, Lewis's friend and Harcourt's editor. Rather elegantly bound in Japanese paper, five hundred copies of this work were presented with the compliments of the publisher to the delegates of the American Booksellers

* It was to be called *City Hall.* In 1926 Lewis told Harcourt that it "never got beyond the first act."

Convention in Chicago, and the bulk of the edition was placed on sale in the shops, where it sold. Said Lewis, "It's a corker."

Arrowsmith brought almost entirely new subject matter into American fiction. There had, of course, been novels about doctors, and even novels about doctors who vacillated between lucrative practice and professional integrity—as in Robert Herrick's *The Healer* and *The Web of Life;* and there were, no doubt, others. Martin Arrowsmith, however, once he is on his way, is not primarily a doctor but a research scientist fighting for his different kind of integrity. Except for a minor character in Lewis's own story "Number Seven to Sagapoose" written in late 1920, it is almost impossible to find such a figure in previous fiction. Perhaps H. G. Wells's very minor novel of 1912, *Marriage,* is unique: there a molecular physicist, pressed by his wife's need for comfort and elegant company, deserts the laboratory for business, and then, having made money, deserts business and, with his wife, goes off to Labrador to think things over, and emerges with the resolution to become a critic of society in prose.

Lewis, working in New York when this novel, written by one of his favorite authors and dedicated to another, Arnold Bennett, was published, almost certainly read it, and it may quite possibly have dropped an idea, applied to the science that *he* most respected, into the unrecorded plot file in his mind. His inscription in H. G. Wells's copy of *Arrowsmith*—"To H. G. Wells, this reassurance of the long admiration of Sinclair Lewis"—might even be construed as an acknowledgment of indebtedness to *Marriage;* but one would hesitate to so construe it. At any rate, no one else remembered this unimportant novel in 1925, and Martin Arrowsmith, pursuing in his laboratory what are here presented as his lonely truths, was a new hero, scientific idealism a new subject, and scientific individualism a new (and rather unscientific) perspective. That "crowd" had "gotten into literature" at last, and Lewis, getting them there, was once again in the vanguard.

All this particularized subject matter exists, of course, within the familiar Lewis pattern: the young person who has his glimpse of values beyond the reach of the environment, his struggle to achieve it, his success after sacrifice. But the variations in the pattern made this novel seem almost to present a new Lewis: Arrowsmith *was* a hero, as earlier central figures had not been; the hero, after his human fumbling, acts on a platform of clearly defined affirmation; the hero can both love and give up love; the woman whom the hero loves is a heroine, one whom contemporary readers could themselves love and admire. Leora seemed to Lewis's readers to be a "realized" character, as no woman in his previous fiction had been, and she commanded their nearly universal praise.

Scientific research as a prominent strand in American culture has called up an ambiguously double response. On the one hand, as Max Lerner has pointed out, it is the little understood object of fear, the interest of "queer geniuses" beyond comprehension, and in popular literature this response has long found itself in the notion of the "mad genius," sinister and beyond humanity yet tinkering with human destinies. On the other hand, it has also increasingly become an object of inordinate respect, for men of science are "miracle men," and their work is profoundly involved with the national destiny. Thus, according to Mr. Lerner, "The American makes a cult of science as a tribal symbol, just as he makes a cult of success as a personal symbol." Lewis was the first novelist to exploit science as a tribal symbol; the delightful irony was that he should have done so on behalf of the personal symbol. Attacking materialism, he doubled his bank account.

For *Arrowsmith* was another instant success, and this time without the benefit of much controversy. If, here and there, some doctors muttered in their beards (Joseph Collins, for example) that the novel was only a "caricature" of certain features of the medical profession, their murmurs of dissent were lost in the shouts of praise. Reviewers and critics, English as well as American, were almost unanimous in asserting its superiority to *Main Street* and *Babbitt,* and in basing the claim on aesthetic grounds. The *Atlantic Monthly* announced that Lewis was "no longer the composer of superlative jazz. He has shown himself an artist, sincere, powerful, restrained." Joseph Wood Krutch, in *The Nation,* found it "better" because it was "essentially truer," and T. K. Whipple, in *New Republic,* took the same view; the New York *Times,* in two different reviews, agreed, along with Stuart Sherman in the New York *Herald Tribune,* who none too lucidly found that it was "hot with the authentic fire in which art and science are purified." "The humanity of it outshines the science," declared the *Literary Review.* Other reviewers thought that in its very attention to science, it had performed a tremendous "service." Robert Morss Lovett, in *The Dial,* said that Sinclair Lewis had served "a public cause which gives largeness of view and significance to *Arrowsmith.*" Mencken and Carl Van Doren, Heywood Broun and Burton Rascoe and Grant Overton, Dr. Fishbein and Keith Preston in Chicago—all hosannas.

The novel impelled Wilson Follett, in the New York *Sun,* to write a two-column essay on the thesis that "All criticism is an attempt to find the right superlatives." To Lewis this thesis applies only with a qualification:

> . . . the unique thing about Mr. Lewis is this very difficulty of finding the unique thing about him. He is resistant to classification—and this very fact is what classifies him. His great secret is that he has no secret. He withholds nothing except the fact that he is giving everything—everything he has.

He baffles criticism: "he turns the critic into a pure reader, leaving him at the end with nothing critical in his mind." Most reviewers had to content themselves, like the writer for the Boston *Evening Transcript,* with summarizing the plot and uncritically declaring that the novel was "deeply understanding and unflinchingly honest," or finding in it, with the London *Times Literary Supplement,* "a stirring epic quality."

In Evanston, Illinois, an obscure young English teacher named Bernard De Voto was able to say what the book was not: it was not urbane, sophisticated, ironical, symmetrical, concise. If it was in some ways naïve, so were Hawthorne, Whitman, Mark Twain. And this is what Arrowsmith *is*—America!—in its naïveté no less than in its splendor. And thus, trying to tell us what Sinclair Lewis's quality is, this young critic flounders too. But not the enthusiastic reader:

> It is the most American novel of the generation; and if it is not the best, at least it can never hereafter be out of mind when the few, diverse novels entitled to compete for such an epithet are considered. . . . It goes down to the roots of our day. It is the almost inconceivable pageant of our America. . . . And that will . . . put *Arrowsmith* safely among the permanent accomplishments of its generation—to endure with a few other great novels of America, none of them quite innocent of defect.

The voice grows hoarse; it was, the young De Voto confessed within the review, "the most extravagant praise" he had ever written.

If *Arrowsmith* stilled the critical voice, it also seemed to answer those carping voices that had complained that Lewis failed to comprehend the American experience, that he lacked "spiritual gifts," that he suffered from "inaccessibility to a spiritual idea." The last phrase is that of one Alexander Harvey, who had written a two-column complaint to the *Herald Tribune* Books Section in which he argued that Lewis had no comprehension of the " 'agony' of American life." He used the word, he wrote, in the Greek sense—"the anguish of the discovery that the decisive moment is still ahead, still to endure."

> The agony of American life emerges from an American spiritual ambition that exceeds American spiritual capacity. The average American—one encounters him everywhere except in the pages of the "best sellers"—longs to be a better man than he is ever likely to be. The American woman strives unceasingly for triumph on the spiritual plane. Hence the tension, the irritability, the true source of what is called by people who write novels the "strain" of American life.

However this may be as argument, such dissent was now subdued: not only did *Arrowsmith* rotate on the basis of a "spiritual idea" (selfless dedication to truth seeking), it also permitted its chief characters to realize their "spiritual" ambitions, to transcend the "strain" and the sordid struggle.

If Alfred Harcourt gave Freud, Jung and Adler an opportunity to demur, they apparently declined to accept it. The nearest voice to theirs that reached Lewis's ear was that of Upton Sinclair, who complained that Lewis had neglected to take "mental healing" into account. That, Lewis replied, was because his characters, Dr. Gottlieb and Arrowsmith himself, were not concerned with "mental healing." They were, Lewis's readers were discovering, concerned with something more important: the most splendid idealism; and this was Sinclair Lewis's too, a strain that had always been present in his work but was now shown bright and lambent above the satire. The satire itself, one could now see, was the painful cry of a disappointed idealism, an idealism, still, that would not submit to hypocrisy and pretense and deceit and pomposity, but uncompromisingly exposed them for what they were. Thus, even while the shabby and the shady were denounced, and William Lyon Phelps could say, "Sinclair Lewis resembles Tamburlaine; he is the Scourge of God," the best qualities in American life seemed to have been named and vindicated. The vindication is summarized in Martin's "prayer of the scientist":

> God give me unclouded eyes and freedom from haste. God give me a quiet and relentless anger against all pretense and all pretentious work and all work left slack and unfinished. God give me a restlessness whereby I may neither sleep nor accept praise till my observed results equal my calculated results or in pious glee I discover and assault my error. God give me strength not to trust to God!

The line between the idealism of "rebellious optimism" and that of plain sentimentality is very thin, but if *Arrowsmith* wavered back and forth across this line, few readers were troubled by the fact. Some men of science were. Hans Zinsser, in *Rats, Lice, and History,* deplored what seemed to him the sentimentalization of the heroic medical man, dedicated and self-effacing, as the portrait has so often been presented in fiction, and of Lewis's novel he added, "If an epidemiologist on a plague study talked and behaved in the manner of the hero of *Arrowsmith,* he would not only be useless, but he would be regarded as something of a yellow ass and a nuisance by his associates." That response came some years after the novel was published. A more immediate one was from Dr. William A. Evans, the author of a syndicated health column for the Chicago *Tribune,* who complained of Lewis's ignorance, as it is revealed in some of Martin's procedures, of the best medical practice.

Dr. Evans's criticism was answered by Dr. Morris Fishbein on grounds which appear dubious when we recall Lewis's own determination that the "science" of his book be absolutely foolproof. Dr. Fishbein argued that *Arrowsmith* is a novel, not a medical textbook; that Martin is "portrayed as an idealistic, visionary and somewhat eccentric young man" who "would inevitably choose the dramatic and perhaps less useful procedure." Would this defense have satisfied Lewis's own ambitions in the novel?

Of more concern to the profession than the novel's scientific accuracy was the identity of its scientists, for from the beginning it was regarded as a *roman à clef*. In the planning of their story, the De Kruif-Lewis procedure for the bulk of their characterization had been to use traits of real people whom De Kruif had known and, sometimes combining the traits of several people, change the physical features of the originals and thus disguise them. The buzz of speculation at last led Dr. Malloch, the librarian of the New York Academy of Medicine, in 1929, to consult Miss Sue Biethan, then the medical librarian at Ann Arbor, about her suppositions in the matter. Miss Biethan guessed that the character of Robertshaw was drawn from Dr. Warren P. Lombard, that of Stout from Dr. Rollo E. McCotter, of Silva from Dr. Victor C. Vaughan, of Davison from Dr. D. W. Edmunds, of Geake from Dr. R. Bishop Canfield. She concluded:

> The first part of the book which pictures the worshipful attitude that Arrowsmith has toward the professor of bacteriology is Paul de Kruif's attitude toward Dr. [F. G.] Novy. Dr. Novy, however, is not a German Jew. I have heard that toward the end of the book the characteristics of Jacques Loeb have been combined with those of Dr. Novy, I know that Dr. de Kruif was a great admirer of Dr. Loeb.

Her guesses, as far as they went, were good (she was wrong about Dr. Silva), but she could speak only of De Kruif's Michigan acquaintances, and it was generally known that he had drawn further on his Rockefeller Institute experience for the picture of the McGurk Institute and its personnel. Dr. Malloch then pursued De Kruif himself, and on April 16, 1931, De Kruif sent him a copy of the book and, "as well as I can now remember them," the names of real persons who had suggested characters.*

Don Vickerson	created by Lewis; no prototype
Martin Arrowsmith	R. G. Hussey, now professor of pathology at Yale
Max Gottlieb	F. G. Novy Jacques Loeb
Fatty Pfaff	Theodore Adams, medical student at University of Michigan, circa 1916, now obstetrician
John A. Robertshaw	Warren P. Lombard
Angus Duer	Henry J. Vanden Berg, now prominent surgeon at Grand Rapids, Michigan
T. J. H. Silva	T. G. Huizinga, formerly a practitioner at Zeeland, Michigan
Roscoe Geake	R. Bishop Canfield

* He stipulated that this key be sealed for thirty years, but has generously withdrawn that stipulation so that the material could be used in this book.

A. DeWitt Tubbs	Simon Flexner
Sondelius	created by Lewis; no prototype*
Almus Pickerbaugh	Wm. de Kleine, medical director of Red Cross
Rippleton Holabird	Peyton Rous Rufus Cole
Terry Wickett	T. J. LeBlanc J. H. Northrop

If Terry Wickett was derived from two living medical men, he was also in some ways Lewis's self-portrait: impatient with social forms, without tact or "taste," the source of many unimportant antagonisms and of a few important and hot loyalties, clumsy in his crass humor and dedicated with an almost "surly intentness," given to snorting rages, "red-headed, rough-faced, wiry." Just as clearly, certain of Lewis's traits spilled over into the characterization of Martin Arrowsmith. Martin, too, loved the downright and the direct, hated deceit and was impatient with pretense, felt himself awkward in elegant society and at once alien and drawn to it. Like Lewis, he had an inordinate respect for work as work and had an extraordinary capacity to put everything else aside for it. If he had self-doubts, he did not formulate them; the demands of the subjective self, if it existed at all, were met by alcohol, success, and the comforting arms of a child bride, or they were not met but turned themselves into neurasthenia. Martin was given to strange fears, and so was Lewis—at twenty-one, quaking in a New Haven bed; at fifty-seven, shuddering at imaginary sounds in an empty house in Excelsior, Minnesota. Thus, Martin:

> At night all halls are haunted. Even in the smirkingly new McGurk Building there had been a bookkeeper who committed suicide. As Martin groped he was shakily conscious of feet padding behind him, of shapes which leered from doorways and insolently vanished, of ancient bodiless horrors, and when he found the switch he rejoiced at the blessing and security of sudden light that recreated the world.

In "the madness of overwork," Martin's fears themselves turn into madness, and they are recounted in three extraordinary pages—extraordinary because they seem to have so little to do with the whole characterization of the man, as though they are biographical gratuities. Of his own physical fears, Lewis has left, of course, only the slightest record. But it is known, for example, that he hated to be alone in a room at night, that he would induce servants to sit up with him not for their company but for their

* It is of some interest that Sondelius was Lewis's own invention, since he designated this relatively minor character, in his Nobel Foundation "Self-Portrait," as "the favorite among all my characters."

physical presence. Perhaps this distaste for being alone is the source of the pleasure he took in living in hotels, where the hum of human traffic never quite subsides.

Many minor characters in *Arrowsmith* may be presumed to be without prototypes, but the chief women in the novel, Madeline Fox, Joyce Lanyon, and Leora Tozer, would seem to derive from the wives of the two men at work on the novel. Both Madeline Fox and Joyce Lanyon, at any rate, bear certain biographical resemblances to Mrs. Lewis, and Leora, many people, including Alfred and Mrs. Harcourt, have thought to be "Sinclair Lewis's idea of Paul de Kruif's idea of his wife in the first year of their marriage." It was Leora, the selfless martyr, who drew the highest praise from Lewis's reviewers. Heywood Broun's eulogy of the characterization was so extreme that it brought an angry retort from a female reader who found Leora worthless and unreal, and whose letter, in turn, drew forth an editorial comment in "Topics of the Times."

The identity of the original of Leora was likewise to be disputed—at least by one small voice, that of Edith Summers, who, writing to thank Louis Adamic for his kind words about her novel *Weeds,* said:

> It was rather acute of you to notice beneath all the superficial differences the fundamental resemblance between Judy [her heroine] and Leora. I was an early friend of Sinclair Lewis, in fact I was his "girl" more years ago than I care to dwell upon, and I was his model for Leora. I put a good deal of myself into Judy, so you see the two girls are sisters.

A strange, imaginative clairvoyance, this! Whoever the prototype may have been, it was Leora who softened the hearts of Lewis's readers, including those of certain judges. *Arrowsmith* could hardly have failed to win a prize.

But it would prove not to be the prize that Lewis himself had in mind. In April a Harcourt publicity release announced belatedly that Lewis was planning a walking trip from Marseilles to Cannes to the Italian Riviera; from Genoa to Munich to Vienna to Budapest to Berlin "and possibly Stockholm." They had started out from Paris more than a month before, but this time he was not to arrive in Stockholm. On March 26 he wrote Harcourt, "Any thoughts on pulling wires for *Martin* for Nobel prize?" To this Harcourt quite seriously replied that he had suggested to Stuart Sherman that he try to start things from America, had proposed that Cape do the same from England, and urged Lewis to make the suggestion to Kurt Wolff in Munich. But on June 1, Harcourt, Brace & Company issued another publicity release that announced that Sinclair Lewis "has abandoned his idea of a walking trip through Europe and has returned to the United States."

After a day in Marseilles, they were driven out by the mistral and they took the train for Carcassonne and had three days there; then to Nîmes and

Avignon and a second day in Marseilles. At Hyères they saw Mrs. Wharton briefly (she was in bed with a cold, but did manage tea with them and announced that *Arrowsmith* was the best of his novels) and dined with Struthers Burt "at his villa on the edge of the sea." He began an article for Mencken:

> These damned Americans who live in So. France or Italy—they are so thin-blooded, so introverted, so refined, so Literary. But how the hell could one find 'em in any save a Henry James book—how & why describe a cheese soufflé? In their presence I become so refined myself that any one (except of course a Britisher) would think I was English, & not till the ninth cognac do I permit myself so much as one son-of-a-bitch.

But with effete Americans they were not spending much time. At Cannes they saw J. D. Beresford and W. J. Locke and Sir Edward Hulton. They spent one night with the Ernest Braces at Vence, and then returned to Cannes. An occasional walk was not quite making up a walking trip. The train took them to Monte Carlo and the bus to Nice. They stayed in Monte Carlo for nearly a week, entertained by an aunt of Harrison Smith and dining with Marc Klaw, the New York theatrical manager, and Sir Charles and Lady Sackville-West. Then on to San Remo. "I love Italy!" he burst out to his father. At San Remo they waited on Lincoln Steffens and Ella Winter in their rented villa, and Steffens observed that Lewis was "trying to get into rage enough at Europe to lay a novel somewhere abroad." At Alassio they climbed in the mountains for ten miles before continuing to Genoa. At Nervi they saw Claude Washburn, and with Washburn, Lewis hiked over miles of hills to Portofino, took a boat to Rapallo, and a train back to Nervi. In Genoa, their plans were becoming more definite. On April 5, the day they left for Munich, Lewis wrote Woodward to say that "We'll probably be back in Paris in early May & sail to the States, for the summer, before June."

They paused at Bolzano and were in Munich at the end of the first week in April. They discovered that Kurt Wolff was away, but the Scheys were there, and on the following Monday, the day after Easter, the Lewises followed them to Vienna. The Baron Schey was a successful banker and in a position to fête the Lewises. He presented them to his friends, the Krauses (Krause was a chemist especially interested in dehydrated foods), and the six of them went together to the Tegernsee. In Vienna, the Scheys gave them a number of supper parties. There was time, too, for excursions to Rothenburg and Nuremberg. But after a week they were off to Prague, and after two days there, on to Berlin. Another week for Berlin, and then "a few days among the glorious mountains & lovely valleys of the Bavarian Oberland, & all the gemütlich old villages." They motored to Oberammergau and talked to Anton Lang. By May 9 they were back in Paris, and by May 15 Lewis was once more ensconced—alone—at 10 Bury Street. *Gemütlich* is a word that comes with a shock in the context of this mad tourist race.

Mrs. Lewis and Wells had stayed behind in Paris, but Lewis had come on to London because "I must get some clothes from my tailor before I sail." (What did the old man mutter to himself upon reading that sentence?)

> I have not seen Wells since November, and I think I have never seen a more really beautiful increase in intelligence and good manners in anybody in so short a time. . . . He and I have become the most tremendous friends, and I look forward very greatly to joining them on the steamer.

In London there was time for lunch with Arnold Bennett, time for other renewals, and time to bask in an editorial comment in *Living Age* on the extraordinary popularity of Sinclair Lewis's novels in England.* Then, on May 23, he met the *Albert Ballin,* which had not only Mrs. Lewis and Wells on board, but Mr. and Mrs. Philip Goodman and Mr. and Mrs. Donald Brace. So there was conviviality on the return.

He wanted to write *The Yearner,* he had told his publisher, and the European chase had given him a lot of material—for *The Yearner* was to be *Dodsworth.* But that story could not be written until the author, like his character, had lived through the end of his marriage. So he wrote instead, on his return, *Mantrap*—which is perhaps a thin cut above *The Innocents,* the most deplorable of all his books.

Back in New York at the beginning of June, Mrs. Lewis with her son went once more to her mother on Long Island; Lewis stayed in town. Within two weeks Mrs. Lewis had sublet Loudon Farm at Katonah, in Westchester County, and Lewis departed for the Middle West. Westchester County was as bad as Hartford, or worse—all very well if friends from New York dropped in for an evening of drinking, but polite dinner parties in the houses of the local gentry were intolerable.

The details of his trip to the Middle West that summer are impossible to reconstruct because of the paucity of the records—a single letter to H. L. Mencken, a single reminiscence by Lloyd Lewis, the Chicago journalist. It may be presumed that Sinclair Lewis visited his father and his brother, and he may have seen his nephew Freeman, with whose academic future he was to be much concerned in the following months. The letter to Mencken, written at some undisclosed place in the Middle West, is dated June 13 and says that while the article Lewis had written for the *Mercury* was a

* The fact is that *Arrowsmith,* well received as it was, was less successful in England than *Babbitt* had been. Some reviewers complained of the awkwardness of the style and of the continual eruption of scientific jargon into it. Interestingly, and predictably, the Germans were delighted with the novel, and regarded it not only as Sinclair Lewis's masterpiece but as one of the few masterpieces of twentieth-century fiction in the world. This enthusiasm seemed remarkable enough in England to call forth an editorial in *Living Age,* "Arrowsmith in Germany."

failure, he would write another as soon as he had returned to Katonah. The Lloyd Lewis recollection, called "Last of the Troubadours," is of one of Dr. Fishbein's literary parties in honor of the novelist. The talk at the party was about the baronetcy that had been offered to Lewis in England (an obvious impossibility) and that he had declined. Ben Hecht dubbed him "Sir Red," * there was a good deal of noisy banter, and finally Fishbein asked Carl Sandburg to sing. Sandburg's guitar brought silence, and he sang "The Buffalo Skinners."

> ... it's a great rough song, all about starvation, blood, fleas, hides, entrails, thirst, and Indian-devils, and men being cheated out of their wages and killing their employers to get even—a novel, an epic novel boiled down to simple words and set to queer music that rises and falls like the winds on Western plains. I've heard the discoverer of the song, John Lomax, of Texas, sing it, but never like Carl sang it this night. It was like a funeral song to the pioneer America that has gone, and when Carl was done Sinclair Lewis spoke up, his face streaked with tears, "That's the America I came home to. That's it."

And Keith Preston is supposed then to have nodded his head at Lewis and said, "Kind hearts are more than coronets."

It is as easy to believe in the drunken sentimentality as it is to believe in the drunken rages, cruel and irrational, that characterize that summer as two opposing temperaments came into their final grip. Katonah, fortunately, permitted frequent escapes to New York, and stories, true and false, perpetuate these sporadic visits. On one occasion some days before the close of the Tennessee "evolution trial" in July, Lewis and Clarence Darrow were present at the same luncheon when, on a sudden impulse, Lewis leaped to his feet and made Darrow's closing speech at the trial for him. Once, at a party at F. P. Adams's, he decided to tell a lot of plots from unwritten stories, to the vast boredom of everyone present, until Adams finally left the room, returned with a gigantic bound volume of his "Conning Tower" column, placed it in the center of the room, and announced, "Next!"

Still another story, probably as apocryphal as it is characteristic, has it that at a drinking party, after endless mimicry, Lewis announced that he would telephone Bishop Manning and impersonate the Bishop of Birmingham, a recent arrival in New York. It was about two o'clock in the morning, and the telephone conversation began with a long apology from Lewis for disturbing so eminent a person, but "the Bishop of Birmingham" was in need of advice: he had been asked by an American lady to baptize her

* It is conceivable—but not at all likely—that the Crown or the Government had proposed some lesser honor. Mrs. Lewis has no recollection of the sort. When she had arranged for her presentation at Court, Lewis forbade it as inappropriate for the wife of Sinclair Lewis. It was a severe disappointment: she would have been taught to curtsy, she would have had a veil floating down her back, and she would have worn "th-ree plumes in my lovely blonde hair!"

baby, and he needed advice on that "ecclesiastical point." The conversation went on for some time on this matter, to the delight of the party. Finally Lewis led up to the question that particularly troubled him; he had forgotten, said "the Bishop of Birmingham," which end of the baby one baptizes.

There was much revelry with Mencken and Goodman. An August letter to Mencken concludes:

> I enjoyed the chewing gum we found on the Resolute the other night, even if we did have to risk moral obloquy by smuggling it ashore. But I thought your action in striking the bouncer at the Männerchor somewhat less than gentlemanly, and your attempt to bite the bare limb of the young woman was not what I should have expected from a young editor of such promise as yourself. It was not her fault that it was bare; the truth is that Lily Goodman had stolen her pants; and I hear that the poor victim has since died of pneumonia as a result.

Another letter to Mencken has to do with a liquor bottle label (Mencken collected them): "Enclosed off a schmuggled bottle German liqueur. Grand evening day fore yesterday. Auf bald wiedersehen."

He found time to write a number of fugitive pieces amid the social nonsense and the domestic fury. With twenty-one other well-known European and American writers, he wrote a letter protesting—his was a very mild protest—Russian political persecution, these letters to form the introduction to a volume called *Letters from Russian Prisons. The Nation* for July 1 carried his article, "An American Views the Huns" (later reprinted in an anthology called *The War Guilt*)—a satirical account of the brutal Teutonic character that concludes with a serious account of the gracious people who had recently entertained him in Munich and Vienna. On July 14 he mailed Mencken a satisfactory version of "Self-Conscious America," which appeared in the October *Mercury*. In August, Mark Van Doren, then on *The Nation,* invited Lewis to contribute to a series called "Can an Artist Live in America." "Hell! Of course he can!" Lewis replied, but he was doubtful if he would contribute. However, he did, in a piece that appeared in December. Following on a number of statements that had taken the question seriously, Lewis decided to "kid" it, proving from several lists of writers that the artist could, could not, should, should not, etc., live in America, and concluding that the artist should do as he pleased—if he could! And he wrote one book review for the *Saturday Review of Literature,* an enthusiastic endorsement of *Manhattan Transfer* by John Dos Passos, who is superior to Marcel Proust and "even the great white boar," James Joyce, and all other "Egoists in the novel," egoists being subjective writers.

At Katonah, Lewis worked in the empty chauffeur's quarters, and chiefly he was working on the novel *Mantrap*. This novel required no intensive effort of concentration and almost no research materials. The latter consisted of Claude Lewis's diary of the Saskatchewan journey. On July 22 he reassured his brother:

> Do not be afraid that I'll use any of the stuff in an embarrassing way, because I'm going to be careful not to use any real people as characters in the story. In fact I'm going to invent a whole new region up there—supposed to be laid about where the Churchill River is, but with all the rivers, Hudson Bay posts, lakes, etc. given entirely fictitious names. The story will be about 60,000 words long . . .

And he urged him to plan to come to Japan for three or four or five months, beginning in about November.

The trip to Japan, a letter of the same day to his father makes clear, may be necessary if he is to gather certain material for a book that he is planning. It is possible that "the yearner" was to wander in the Orient as well as Europe, or perhaps it is some wholly different book that Lewis had in mind. Certainly it was not *Mantrap,* for, he tells his father, he is now finishing *Mantrap Lake,* as he apparently first called it. (He did not finish it for several months.)

The letter as a whole is the kind of chatty affair, making everything sound lovely, that he was in the habit of writing his father. Wells has recovered from an attack of poison ivy, they have bought the boy a collie, the three of them spent the weekend at Black Point, Connecticut, at the home of their landlord, Dr. Lewis Conner, a professor of medicine in Cornell University, and on the way home they stopped at Fenwick to spend a night with the Hepburns, their Hartford friends, with whom, because there were so many other children, they had left Wells. Oh—almost as an afterthought—what was best of all: he had earned a very easy $10,000 from Famous Players-Paramount Company for a scenario of a film to be produced in connection with the three-hundredth anniversary of New York City. On the back of this letter his father penciled a notation: "If I could make money as quick as that I would go to Japan & Timbuctoo myself. It is certainly marvelous how such a bundle of nerves can pull in the money."

He showed, in this summer, a strange interest—for the very reason that it did not seem particularly personal—in young Freeman Lewis, and was busy trying to arrange for the entrance of that young man in Phillips Exeter Academy. On July 11 he had written Claude a long letter in which he explained in detail the advantages of a year at Exeter before Freeman entered Harvard, more detailed explanations of the advantages of Harvard itself ("easily the best university in the country"), and still more detailed instructions about filling out the application forms for Exeter. Then came the news that Freeman had been admitted to Harvard directly from his high school and that Exeter would not be necessary.

This put Uncle Harry into a considerable quandary. Should Freeman go to Exeter *now,* he would probably go with the assumption that he did not have to work hard, and he might fall into habits of laziness. The uncle does not know Freeman well enough to be certain that this would happen to him, but "I would ask the same question about myself at seventeen." Of course, there are many things that he could gain at Exeter—he could do a lot of reading for himself, he could start German, he could finish up his Cicero and Vergil, he could take more ancient history and chemistry. What he should definitely *not* do is go off on a proposed student cruise around the world. After his freshman or sophomore year in college, he should ship to Europe on a cattle boat, or go third class, and after college he should go to Europe for a year, with four months in each of three countries—England, France and Germany—but none of this uninformed hopping about in which one sees nothing. Would Claude please arrange to have the boy come East early, say about September 1? Then they would help him meet some Eastern boys, and they would help him buy the proper clothes and furniture for his room, and they would themselves deliver him either to Exeter or to Cambridge, as it should develop.

> There's one unimportant-sounding little thing which he simply *must* do. I don't know whether he now has the western hair-cut—I mean the kind in which the clippers are run in front of the ears, and the hair is clipped short half way up the back of the head. If he has that kind, he must get over it before he comes East—though you see it on the nicest boys in Minneapolis, here it is seen only on toughs. Let him let his hair get even a little too long and shaggy and have it cut in New York, if he can't get just the right kind there, rather than have it too convict-like, for that would make a bad impression on first meeting the other boys, and these first impressions are sometimes dangerously important.

The voice of experience! And it would not be stilled.

A week later he wrote Claude another long, "fussing" letter. Exeter has been settled upon, and Sinclair Lewis is delighted that the thought of the world cruise sponsored by New York University had been abandoned.

> It's typical of the beastly sketchiness and shallowness in most of our American education. We learn so few things thoroughly. I have never been impressed by mere travel, unless it's backed up by study and trained observation, as an educational factor. I've met too many people who've been in scores of countries and know almost nothing.

Then he wrote out a short letter to the director of admissions at Exeter that Claude was to copy and mail, and he added the injunction: "Be sure and address him as G. L. Richardson, Jr., *Esq.*—most of these people like the Esq." He is looking forward to Freeman's early arrival, and he suggests the "prettiest" train route for him. And the haircut: "Tell him I'm serious abt that hair-cut business—you don't speak of it in yr. letter."

Freeman did not arrive early. On August 26, Lewis wrote his brother to say that he had decided that he did not need the Japanese travel material after all, and while he still hoped that Claude would some time go to the Orient with him, it would probably not be in that year. He had nearly finished the first draft of the new serial. And he was expecting Freeman.

> Shall I help him get evening clothes and perhaps some tweeds in N.Y.? Has he golf sticks of his own? Now that he has started the game, he may as well keep it up. It is no longer, thank heaven, simply a rich man's game.

With the first draft of his serial finished, he could conveniently leave his wife. He had had enough of Katonah, and enough, for the time being, of marriage and of family. One night late in August, after who knows what storm of rage and abuse, he took the last train out of Katonah and registered at the Great Northern in New York. And now, having left his wife, he found a secretary—a public stenographer named Louis Florey who served as drinking companion and audience, valet and bootlegger, at least as much as he served as typist. There had to be someone.

On September 5 he wrote to Claude to say that he had had to come down to New York to conduct negotiations on the serialization of the new book and to attend to some revisions of the film he had written. His wife and son were "visiting friends in Connecticut,"—and she was; she had gone to stay with Mrs. Hepburn at Fenwick. André Siegfried had been touring the country, "studying political movements in America," and Lewis was grateful to Claude for having received him. "Lord, you gave him such a happy time and such a view of real sure-enough American life as he could never possibly have had otherwise. . . ."

All very calm. But on the same day, September 5, he wrote the first of three letters to his wife, violent, protesting, disingenuous, naïve, almost intolerably repetitious, of which he kept carbon copies.*

> *Saturday September 5*
> *The Great Northern, NYC*
>
> Gracie, there are so many things to say. I have wanted not to write till I had done some solid thinking. You have been with me day and night since I left on that last train from Katonah. I have been so conscious of you,

* In *With Love from Gracie,* Mrs. Lewis says that in the months of September and October she received fifteen letters from Lewis, and her book in effect ends with her excerpts from these letters, but includes a page or so of excerpts from letters of which there are no carbon copies in the Lewis papers. The excerpts from those that he kept in carbon contain passages that are not in the carbon, and omit much that is for reasons of "discrimination and good taste." Perhaps Lewis rewrote his first drafts and kept no carbon of the letters he finally mailed. At any rate, no letters reveal him more completely than these, and it therefore seems important to include here the documents as he preserved them. Canby, calling him a *genus irritabile,* once said of him that he was "as little restrained by good taste as an angry cat." Since this book is attempting completeness, considerations of "taste" must be put aside.

planning little sprises, of you climbing into bed, so dear and sleepy a child, of all your superb care for me and Wells. Peculiarly have I been conscious of you, and almost called for you, in the happy moments which always I have wanted you to share—when a steamer goes zhhh on the North River, and last night at Walter White's when Roland Hayes' accompanist played and sang some spirituals I did not know . . . . . so incredibly beautiful that in my desire to have you share them I felt like weeping.

But on the other hand—

You have of late become extraordinarily bullying. You give me orders, grimly, as though I were a drunken private and you a colonel. Your theory has been that you *had* to do this, because I was drinking so much that I was no longer dependable; and for that theory you have had vast justification. But actually the fact is that by your assuming this stringent leadership you have deprived me of self-government; actually when I am by myself, given enough time and leisure to realize my problems, I straighten up and take charge of the show quite satisfactorily.

And that is what, just now, I must and will do, for a period which may be only a few weeks, and may be forever. It is immensely too early as yet to know what the period will be, and I think we should be unwise to try to fix it just at present.

The second feature is that more and more you want to have a settled life with intelligent but definitely respectable neighbors, while I want an unsettled life with unrespectable neighbors. You have denied this many times, yet I think that if I had not fought you I would have settled down to being a good little neighbor of people like the Fowlers, the Emmets, Mrs. Marquand (how sad you were that I dared to appear in that aristocrat's presence without a coat or a tie!) With such people you would, I know, like the Carl Van Doren's, and the Fritz Scheys; but essentially they must be people on whom you can depend as regular. And why not—for you. But they are not for me.

Oh this discussion could go on for pages, ever more vainly. I'm really not trying to argue about the matter at all; I'm merely seeking to give one or two of the more clearly defined reasons why I feel (rightly or wrongly) that I must have a time now of going to heaven or hell in my own way, unguided, unbossed, unbullied.

Since I began this letter . . . . . Alf Harcourt has telephoned me from home and told me that you had (very wisely) a talk with him, and that you are going to Fenwick and to Kate Hepburn for some time. I am so glad! I hope that you will make many plans for yourself. I shall of course back them up in every manner in which you may permit me. . . .

Now as to winter, I hope that you find a flat in New York, London, Paris, Vienna, Berlin, Rome, or whatever city best pleases you, and have most decidedly a life absolutely your own. However low your opinion of me at this moment (or it may be high but jeest, think how low it may be soon hereafter!), you must admit that I am glad in every possible way to have you conduct your own life absolutely as you desire, providing only that such conduct of it shall not imply the bossing of my life.

I think it might be wise for us not to see each other for some weeks, till we have done a little thinking . . . . . and I don't think you need worry about my leading too gross a life of crime. . . .

So much to say to you! That I really do love you better than anybody else in the world, but that not even by you can I any longer be bullied. That I understand rather well how often I have been a blinkin' little pest to you. That I feel—honestly!—that this hiatus will be as good for you as for me. That I think you are unwise to hate me. That I hope that for at least three months we can manage never for a moment to see each other and so fall into all our old absurdities of interminable discussion, but that at the same time we may write to each other, and often.

Your [hand]writing came to me on the letters forwarded from my father, my brother, and Dorans (who had the bright idee that they could endure my saying some sweet things about Elinor's new book) and in the letter with enclosures from Monty [Montgomery Belgion, now at Harcourt, Brace & Company] et al I longed to have more of it, the actual sound of your voice as sometimes I do get it from your writing. But you were wise not to write yet.

Dear Lamb, may God bless and keep you and make you happy. May he give you your own place, your own friends, your own purposes, unpolluted by mine. And I do love Wells—

Friday, September 11

Your letter this morning. I had awaited it eagerly; I was glad to have it. I had imagined, only too poignantly, all that you tell me of loneliness; particularly imagined how gray and desolate the evenings after Wells is asleep. And all week I have been cursed by having almost everything remind me of you, and of things we have done together. For one example from hundreds: I went with Menck, Phil, and Ernest Boyd (whom I have come to like immensely!) to that marvelous German Bierhalle in Union Hill—it really *is* Germany, tout complet, with admirable dark beer. First I thought of how you would have enjoyed the place, the company, and the particularly good talk—and possibly even the beer. Then, when the orchestra played Wo Hast du Deine Shoene Blaue Augen Her, I could have wept, so completely did it seem bound up with you; and when they played Trovatore, I thought of how we heard Verdi together in Venice, how we came out into that little square where the scoffer with the white beard was laughing at the whole opera, how we went on then to the Piazza San Marco, and probably met Scott Moncrieff. . . . So goes everything, reminding me of you.

And because of this, it does not seem possible that we shall break permanently. . . . . The other evening, alone here, waiting for Phil, standing by the window, when it came suddenly to me that perhaps I should never have you again to work for and aspire for, life seemed grotesquely empty. For so many years—years before our marriage—I have, perhaps more than you know, sought everything, from money to views, to show them to you, and without you to behold them, they all seemed purposeless.

BUT I am convinced as ever that it must be a long while before we even see each other. This resolution may break down, but I hold it firmly now, for the reason that once we are together, it becomes impossible to think independently, plan boldly. We'll be bullying each other, and talking—God how we do discuss!

Two things I wish: That you would absolutely chuck the Conner place, because it exposes you to loneliness on the one hand and the curiosity of the good neighbors on the other, and always to reminders of the very happy times we have had there. Hang the cost—it would be like that insane-seeming yet very wise time in West Chester (another Westchester!) when we paid to get out of our lease and fled to Washington; it would not be a loss but an investment. Only, because of Wells, I wouldn't come to New York *yet.* Try Fisher's Island or Sconset. Or, if it's too late for these places, *have at least two people come to stay with you at Katonah.* Get Kate Hepburn to come and stay a week—she might enjoy a moment sans family. . . .

Now the second: I wonder if you are wise in planning to spend all winter in NY: partly because I shall *have* to be about the place, partly because I don't really think you will like it very much. Whom is there you much like? Wouldn't you be happier in London? Aside from the fact that where here you can get only a mangy flat for $300 a month, and there a mansion; here it costs $100 for one servant per month, and there $60 for three; you are essentially English, and settled there for a year, independent of me, staying with people like Lady Barrington, Beatrice Hackett, Rebecca West, Marion Ryan, any friends of Allan—what's his name: our friend of the Carmania and Berlin? [Allan Graves was a casual English acquaintance] and so on; tother hand freed of Spike and M. Bechhofer-Roberts and so on; you would make a career and a happy life of your own. And Wells would be rather happier than in NY. . . . You would have a *home,* not just a resting-place in a town where you can't cross the street.

But that's up to you.

I think I see this future, a rather happy one, for us: A complete and resolute separation, cost what it may, for several months. But never a divorce, never a loss of that Toby and Issa affection which means so tragically much to both of us. After these months, joyous friendship but, then and forever, separate establishments except for occasional vacations when we elope together—to Sharon or to China. To see each other exactly as I see a Paul or a Spike or an Alf—eagerly, loyally, but with no vexing *claims.* But meantime, complete independence; each to live where and as (within financial limits) she or he pleases; each to have precisely such friends, loves, drinks, theories, clothes, hours, travels, as she or he pleases, absolutely without dominance from the other. A sort of Fanny Hurst dual menage without its publicity and fuss; and the thing understood among all our friends, so that we lose none of them.

I do not think that either of us, after these years of peculiarly intimate adventure, can contemplate divorce or any other ugly break. But I do know now damned well that unless the two Hawks, you and I, are left free to fly *absolutely* as we desire, without even explanations one to the other, there will be such a break.

This future as friends seems to me desirable, to be contemplated with happiness. But if it is to be accomplished, it must be with resolution—particularly resolution to the matter of staying apart for a while of thinking clearly, and of determining to let each other rule himself.

In this, it must be you particularly who must be resolute, for the reason that it's so much easier for a man to call up somebody and propose a party when he feels distraught with loneliness. You must be prepared for some months of isolation, and you must resolutely plan your own life without being overwhelmed by its at first apparent desolation..... Thank God you have Wells!

Complete independence. I must no longer lie, shift, ask permission, resent orders, await your plans. I must run my life and at any cost—to me as well as to you—I will! If you can face this sternly taking our lives and with a "to hell with you" to other people as well as to ourselves remodeling them to an independence-cum-friendship, then we can win through to a happiness not less but greater than in these recent years of getting on each other's nerves. If I fall in love with some girl, it must be my business. And, as you know, I shall come back to you..... providing you still want me.

There has, it seems to me and to Phil, been a definite change in me since I made this break. Actually, here in this little flat with all I want to drink right at hand, with the chance to get as drunk as I want and nobody to criticize, I have been drinking incomparably less. It's I, now, who am the boss, who am therefore responsible, who therefore cannot take any chances on things going wrong. All my life, whether in relation to my father, my university, my bosses on jobs, or to you, I have functioned better, more surely and resolutely, when I have been in charge, not bullied by some one else. I look better, feel better, am working more keenly and interestedly. And by God I'm not going to lose that. And I believe that the same will be true of you; and, with you in charge of you, you will in every way run things more serenely and surely. This is no general rule for "couples"; it just happens to apply to lone wolves like us.

So much for general proposals. Now some details:

When I say that we ought not, for some time, to meet at all, of course I know that we are more than likely to encounter each other by accident. In that case—let's just (while others look on with itching curiosity) just laugh and be pleasant on the surface. It's in letters that we can really talk. ..... One advantage of letters is that the other devil can't interrupt you and so spoil one of your very best denunciations!

When I say completely independent, I mean just that. I mean that you or I are to decide without asking the other to go to Europe, and go. As to money, there is going to be much more now than before because, now that I no longer slavishly feel that I must ask your permission to do this or that, I'm going to make a hell of a lot more than I ever did before. We are to have any friends, ways of living, hours of arising, loves, vices, grim virtues, that we want.

As to writing: I have got to write Pieces like the devil. I doubt if I shall write to you oftener than once a week—or once a fortnight. Nor shall I any longer feel (as all these years, in all these vacations, I have felt, however estranged and distant we were) that I must explain what I did last Wednesday evening, lest you think I was out with a girl . . . . . which I probably was. (The joke now is that after taking this resolution and having ceased to give you a calendar, I should not all this week so much as have spoken to a single girl, but have led my evil life entirely with such desperate characters as Rabbi Browne, Dr. George Dorsey, Alfred Harcourt, and Phil!)

No, we'll write just as I should write to Hal or Paul—only much oftener—that is, without any feeling or compulsion to report to the boss, which compulsion, subconsciously, I imagine you have felt as I most certainly have.

Now as to the official attitude toward our present and future separation: It is evident from your letter that with all the sweet and generous attitude in it, you are still committing one of your old crimes—you are worrying as to what the neighbors think! Christ God Almighty, what do you care what even such nice people as the Ramsay Hunts think? All your life you have been arranging things to placate the nice Ramsay Hunts of the world—and what is more important to me, you have been trying to arrange *me* to suit them, which is one of the reasons why I am now here alone, and damn well intend to stay alone. You say "I am left with explanations and lies—I who like honesty." In the first place, what else could have been done? It would hardly have been practical to ask you to get out and leave me in Katonah, with or without Wells, would it? And in the second place, why lie? Simply *laugh.* Tell 'em both that I'm busy here and that you rather suspect that after a year together, I'm enjoying my vacation. They'll talk—but talk less unpleasantly than if they were to see us together with me obviously going slightly crazy under the horror of being just your slave. Say that I'm off on trips connected with my next novel. Or say nothing. This is the beginning of the probably damned lonely and unpleasant process (as it has been lonely and unpleasant to me, I conclude it has been and *will be* to you) whereby, alone, we may make it possible to go on being friends . . . . . such dear and gallant friends . . . . . providing we leave each other alone and completely free.

I have with some (not much) resolution determined to do what I want. You must do the same. Do you want to spend the winter in New York—London—Paris—Munich (a damn good idea, with Fritz and Annie [Schey] for simply divine guides)? Do it! We can't be insane about money, but there will be enough for any of those things. You must not bind me by not seeing what you want to do, and doing it. . . .

You say that no longer is there a little voice in your heart that says "Toby loves you." Doesn't this letter and the other say that he does—only that we must not let love be any longer a typical [tyrannical?] scourge?

Dear, dear, don't in this letter become irritated in the supposition that I assume that you are a poor fish needing my affection! I could change almost every "you" to "I" in this letter. We need each other's affection, respect, and play, I think . . .

Let yourself be free. You have your chance!

The Shelton
Friday, September 18

[No salutation]

I have felt sort of happy, somehow, today, and I think that a huge part of it comes from a feeling that you are beginning to find a life, make friends, begin activities, for yourself. I have worried so frightfully; I have been so obsessed by the thought of you alone and lonely. I hear hints, without details, of your going out with Phil and Hal, and I rejoice that you do.

I think the very first and most important thing to do is to give up the house at Katonah at the very first possible moment when you can move into New York; not determine to wait to October 15 or any other arbitrary date. Gooosh, financially it would be of value; I've wasted much more than a thousand dollars' worth of time in worry over you disbarred from life out there. The autumn colors are all very well, but not worth exile.

You have your chance of freedom. It will, if you have resolution, mean at least as much as it does to me. Be patient. And act! . . .

I read an article yesterday by Katherine Hinkle, the psychologist. She spoke of the amazingly large number of women today who, when their husbands make some sort of a break for themselves, were at first completely boulversees [*sic*] and lonely bewildered, then began to find their own lives, to keep their own souls, and suddenly—after the first grayness—found everything incomparably more real and stirring. . . . . I think it may often be so.

And I begin to feel real and strong and determined again. . . .

And next spring—Germany, the beloved Fritz, you and I?

Toby

The documents speak for themselves—of him, of her, of the now doomed condition, which they still did not entirely recognize, of their marriage. There were to be further attempts to make it work out. These do not enter into Mrs. Lewis's narrative, but the remaining page of excerpts from Lewis's October letters provides some information: he is working on the scenario for the New York tricentennial and is outraged by a *Daily News* "Most Beautiful Girl for S. L. pageant" program; he is listening to the Rev. John Roach Straton preach and plans to gather material for the next novel, *Brass* [*Elmer Gantry*]; before that, he will write a play; and "tomorrow evening" (these letters are not dated) will see *Mantrap* completed, with the revising novelist racing just ahead of the secretary, who is typing four copies to go out for bids from four magazines.

Freeman came, and, with dinner jacket, never to be worn at Exeter, went. On September 29 Lewis wrote him, pleased with the boy's report of having settled in, and enclosed a reading list consisting of about seventy novels, mostly French and English, and a list of thirty classic American names through which are scattered those of Dreiser, Anderson, Cather, Hergesheimer, Mencken, Nathan, and John B. Watson, the behaviorist professor.

All this sounds calm and busy, but in fact Lewis was restless and unhappy, and there were the usual moments of outrage and wounded vanity. One day Lewis was to lunch with Harrison Smith, and they had arranged to meet at the desk of the Great Northern. Lewis arrived with a parcel which he asked the clerk to get to his room. "What is your name, sir?" asked the clerk innocently enough, whereupon Lewis exploded in a rage, and then demanded, "Do you realize that you are talking to a fifty-thousand-dollar-a-year man?"

During these months, his name was not neglected. In July, Carl Van Doren published in *Century* magazine his article called "Sinclair Lewis and Sherwood Anderson: A Study of Two Moralists," in which he pointed out that for all their differences, both held to a constant theme—"the conflict between aspiring individuals and the complacent societies which oppress them." The Rotarians declined to be part of the complacent oppression: in August, the New York *Times* reported a radio speech by Charles E. Keck, president of the New York Rotary Club, which, in its delightful rhetoric, defeated its own purpose:

> I am going to take a fall out of Sinclair Lewis. . . . He's due for it. If he were a big enough man to tell the story straight, he would be all right. But he fixes up a little city of Zenith, or whatever you call it, and has a little Rotary Club, and tells everybody that a Rotary Club is a bunch of great, big, bumptious small-town boosters. Of course there is in every Rotary Club a spirit of good fellowship and a lively interest in any proposition that is for the common good. But that is distinctly not the basis of Rotary. The basis is the need of something to bring businessmen in a big city together in a way that no other organization can, to enable them to work for the good of the community. . . . Lewis is just a little bit off his trolley.

Rotarians were not annoyed with Sinclair Lewis; they just laughed at him. They laughed with him, too, and for good reason. In September, Lewis persuaded the editor of the Sauk Centre *Herald* to sign his name to a defense of the values of Main Street, written by Lewis, and publish it on his front page:

> A lot of us like to live in small towns, but lately the authors have been worrying about us. They pity our hard luck in not knowing gunmen, burlesque girls, bootleggers, and gum-chewing stenographers of the cities. We have stood it meekly, but sort of hoped some one would come along and take a shot at some of these fellows.
>
> It's been done. A book that really gets the small town has just appeared —*Sycamore Bend* by Frazier Hunt, who has been a famous war correspondent but who came from the corn-belt and for three years ran a country weekly in Illinois.
>
> It's a story about real folks—the doctor, the editor, the furniture dealer, the town policeman who was scared of burglars. Mr. Hunt loves them all,

> and he makes you love them; he sees their humor; and makes you laugh with him; he sees their pathos; and makes you cry.
>
> Sauk Centre is proud of Sinclair Lewis, but we've felt that in *Main Street* he only told one side of the story, missed the fun of the small town. Hunt hasn't missed anything, and it's our guess that the whole country will get over the *Main Street Blues* and enjoy itself with *Sycamore Bend.*

And one may guess, too, that Sauk Centre's esteem for the literary quality of Sinclair Lewis's work, rose, along with that of President Keck, when they read his serial, *Mantrap,* presently to be issued by *Collier's* magazine, the book to be dedicated to Frazier Hunt.

Sinclair Lewis enjoined his brother to subscribe to the periodical, to miss no part of it.

> You will recognize some of the characters in the far North—although all of them are changed a good deal—but there is no one in the least like yourself, Bill Taylor, or Dr. McFayden.

He suggested that Claude write to these two men and give them this assurance.

This letter was written on October 24. On that evening he entertained at dinner at the Shelton. His guest of honor was Brigadier General the Right Honorable Lord Thomson, P.C., D.S.O., C.B.E. His other guests were Alfred Harcourt, Harrison Smith, and Montgomery Belgion; Philip Goodman and Walter Lippmann; Edgar G. Sisson, the fiction editor of *Red Book,* and George A. Dorsey, the journalist and anthropologist; C. M. Thomas, a banker, and Dr. Stuart P. Sherman. Frazier Hunt was unavoidably detained at the last moment and missed the brave revelry.

Two days later, on October 26, Mrs. Lewis records, her husband telephoned her with pleas that she join him in a journey to California. His urgency persuaded her and she agreed—"daventuring" again!—but after she had put down the receiver she thought better of the proposal. Four days later, on October 30, Lewis was writing to his brother again—giving him the important bulletin that *Collier's* would begin the serialization of *Mantrap* on February 13, 1926—with this news:

> In order to have a little more quiet to do the play on which I have now started, I am leaving for Bermuda tomorrow, to be gone three or four weeks. . . . . Then I'll return to New York and be here till about February, then go West, at which time I shall probably see you.

The letters from Bermuda come from the Hotel Frascati. On November 4 he wrote to his brother to say that he had not yet started his play, had spent all his time thus far in bicycling around this gorgeous island; he had brought his secretary, Mr. Florey, who was taking the dictation of this letter and was highly inefficient (as he was: he dated the letter October 4);

that Gracie and Wells were settled in a charming New York apartment at 157 East 75th Street belonging to the actor George Arliss. (He does not say that on September 20 Mrs. Lewis had met a charming Spaniard named Telesforo Casanova at Katonah, and was seeing him with pleasure.) He regrets a little being away from them and having to go west immediately upon his return. "But then maybe a vacation from me will not be too bad a thing for her—she must get a little sick of hearing me talk all the time!" Wells is in splendid shape, "going to a school with an English head master. It is at once thoroughly modern and devoid of the softness and sentimentality and general artiness which characterizes so many of the schools which try to be modern." Would Claude not like to invite Brigadier General Lord Thomson to St. Cloud? He would deliver a public lecture for $350 or $400, and the Lewises could probaby "have the fun of entertaining him."

On November 10 he wrote Harcourt that he was "now into the play with all four feet" and said that he saw no reason why *Mantrap* should not be published as a book (Harcourt had earlier suggested that Lewis might wish to think twice about this matter). He also wrote his wife, asking her to join him in Bermuda (out of sight, in mind—that had always been the pattern), but she declined—she was settled, she was content. On the fifteenth he wrote his father that he had nearly finished two of the three acts, and on December 5 he wrote him again to say that he had finished a first draft of the play, had thrown most of it away and written another version, but whether it was good or not he did not know. The films would probably buy *Mantrap* for $50,000. "That will mean $89,000 since coming back from Europe." After a long discussion with his wife, he acknowledged, they had agreed that it would be silly for her to take a large apartment in New York since he would have to be away from New York most of the winter; therefore he would take a room at the Shelton and have his meals with her. He had already written Harcourt to say that he was leaving Bermuda on December 12, that he hoped Harcourt had called his wife and perhaps had had lunch with her, that he himself certainly meant to "have Christmas with her and I hope for any number of agreeable teas and that sort of thing without impairing either her independence or mine."

Almost at once on Lewis's return, H. L. Mencken's mother, to whom Mencken was devoted, died, and Lewis, who did not know her, wrote him a gracious note of condolence; but there would be no parties in that quarter. On the same day—December 21—he wrote Van Vechten to congratulate him on *Excavations,* on his knowledge of "the byways of literature," of which Lewis himself, he protested, was so ignorant. On December 23 he wrote to William Woodward, who he had heard was in New York. "I hope to Christ that you will call me up." On December 25, one may suspect, there was no Christmas pine cone.

In that year, Bernard Shaw was awarded the Nobel prize in literature.

He accepted the prize but not the money. That, he decreed, should be used as a fund for the promotion of better literary relations between Sweden and England through the Anglo-Swedish Literary Foundation, which devoted itself then to subsidizing the publication of a series of good translations into English of modern and classical Swedish works.

"I hope to Christ that you will call me up."

7

NOTHING IN *MANTRAP* SUGGESTS that its author was worthy of any prize, even the booby prize of *Broom*. The novel was serialized in *Collier's* from February through May of 1926, and published by Harcourt, Brace & Company in June. In that year, too, Robert Herrick published *Chimes;* in that novel of disillusionment with the Wellsian vision of an engineered Utopia, one of the characters says to another, "I suspect . . . that all your life you have been searching for something lost, inside, something that would release you and let you live." *Arrowsmith,* like most of Lewis's novels, is a novel of search, and, even though in the novelist himself the search may have been "for something lost, inside," in the novels, as in the novelist's life, the search is always made through things *outside*. Among these are the glories of untrammeled nature.

At the end of *Arrowsmith,* in a remote quarter of Vermont, Martin had achieved, most implausibly, ideal circumstances for medical research and natural freedom for himself. Gone were all women, wise and silly; gone the foolish social round of dinner parties and receptions; gone all the nonsense of "culture" and the empty distractions of prestige and "success." Now at last life was simple and bare and honest and manly, with one best friend and co-worker to share it.

> . . . He hurled out hypotheses like sparks. He began, incredulously, to comprehend his freedom. He would yet determine the essential nature of phage; and as he became stronger and surer—and no doubt less human—he saw ahead of him innumerous inquiries into chemotherapy and immunity; enough adventures to keep him busy for decades.
>
> It seemed to him that this was the first spring he had ever seen and tasted. He learned to dive into the lake, though the first plunge was an agony of fiery cold. They fished before breakfast, they supped at a table under the oaks, they tramped twenty miles on end, they had bluejays and squirrels for interested neighbors; and when they had worked all night, they came to find serene dawn lifting across the sleeping lake.
>
> Martin felt sun-soaked and deep of chest, and always he hummed.

If the diction of *supped* and *tramped* and *lifting dawns,* and the structure of such a sentence as the last, do not assure us that the idyl is false, the inversion of the grubby Saskatchewan reality into triumphant melodrama in *Mantrap* more than does.

It has generally been asserted that Lewis knew exactly what he was doing when he was hack writing. Cabell said that Lewis referred to his periodical writing as "whoring," and that he thought that a writer could "whore" and then return with purity and impunity to his serious work. George Jean Nathan, writing specifically of *Mantrap* in his *Intimate Notebooks,* said: "Always forthright and completely honest with himself, he made no bones of what he was doing, but frankly announced to anyone who would listen that he was, to use his own locution, turning out a swell piece of cheese to grab off some easy gravy." Two points might be made: one is that the most "gravy" came from the work that he did not regard as "cheese," and the other is that the same attitudes that are present in the "cheese" are present in the serious work. Among these is that toward noble nature and nature's noblemen.

In *Mantrap,* Sinclair Lewis appears in the person of a mild, unmarried New York lawyer named Ralph Prescott, on the verge of nervous collapse, and in spite of occasional touches of satire, Prescott becomes the wilderness hero. The competent Claude is transformed into Ralph's bullying, Babbitty companion, E. Wesson Woodbury, whose boorishness makes it impossible for Prescott to continue the trip. Then, at the point at which, in reality, Harry deserted with Arthur Jan, Lewis introduces Jan's counterpart in the true woodsman, Joe Easter. Easter compels the obnoxious Woodbury to continue by himself and takes Ralph, recognized as the gentleman he is, away for comradely fishing and camping. Thus the novelist took his revenge on the facts. The remainder of the novel, except for a fragmentation of details, deserts the facts and becomes adventure fantasy.

Ralph Prescott, the fantasy assures us, is a man with no great taste for whisky. Drunken poker parties are not for him. Joe Easter has a wife, Alverna, who flings herself at Ralph, and he struggles between his attraction to her and his friendship for Joe. When guilty feelings drive him to leave Joe's house at Mantrap Landing to backtrack and search for the abandoned Woodbury, Alverna complicates matters by pursuing him. Then he demonstrates his manhood along with his woodsmanship as they meet ordeals far more taxing (and sexually colorful) than those that Harry, with Brother Claude, had been asked to meet. With the greatest of ease, when they are nearly starving, Ralph catches "a ten-pound muskalonge more beautiful than the silver doe of heaven," and now "his mouth had an angry steadiness. It no longer drooped and twisted in the duress of vain philosophizing." Easter pursues them—not in revenge, it seems, but in order to save Ralph, his new best friend, from forest fires and Alverna's. Manly friendship proves stronger than woman's wiles. The mantrap is unsprung, and Ralph, confident as he had never been before, returns to New York.

And a scenario had been achieved—the book was published on June 3, the film was released in New York on July 7—that did not severely tax the talents of Ernest Torrence and Clara Bow. The reviewers, in the meantime, had not been harsh about the novel. Mr. Lewis in a light vein, said most of them, and tried to forget it. A few were more solemn. Harry Hansen in the New York *World* found it, on the whole, less interesting than Stewart Edward White's memorable *The Silent Places* of 1904; Joseph Wood Krutch in *The Nation* thought it a minor work with a worthy message—all good men were not necessarily as powerful as Tarzan, and the Babbitt cult of the outdoors that Lewis castigated in Woodbury was, if no great threat, a social nuisance. The English liked it. The *New Statesman,* its critical stays undone, was more than kind: "It is better worth reading than any novel we have seen this year—which is what we are entitled to expect, at the very least, of Mr. Lewis."

Lewis, long before, was trolling for other fish. In an interview in early January of 1926 he said to Malcolm Cowley, "I'm going west. I'll buy a secondhand automobile and go touring through the desert. For the last five years I've been seeing people. Now I'm tired, and I'm going to take a rest." He did not buy a secondhand automobile, and the rest was brief.

On January 10, a Sunday, Mrs. Lewis wrote to her sister-in-law that in the next week her husband would be off to discover the Southwest, and that if he found it to his liking he would send for her in March. He did not wait for the next week. On January 13, Harcourt, Brace & Company issued a publicity release that announced Lewis's departure for Kansas City, where he planned to spend ten days with "the Rev. William L. Stidger, the prominent minister," and then, after a tour of Arizona and New Mexico, settle in southern California to work on his new novel. He stayed in Kansas City at this point for two weeks.

Lewis had known William Stidger, the pastor of the Linwood Boulevard Methodist Episcopal Church, from earlier encounters, and he went to Kansas City because of him. Their first encounter had been in Terre Haute in August of 1922. Stidger was then preaching in Detroit and was at the moment lecturing in Chautauqua. When he saw Sinclair Lewis's name in the register of the hotel where he was staying, he asked to see him, and at lunch he quarreled with him amiably about his portrait of Dr. Drew, the preacher in *Babbitt.* Stidger urged him to write a novel about clergymen as they really are, and Lewis, who had contemplated a novel about the church, was interested. He asked if he could come to Detroit and live in Stidger's house and learn about clergymen as they really are, and Stidger urged him to come by all means. In less than two months, Lewis did come to Detroit, but he was not yet ready to turn to this novel. When at last, late in 1925, he thought that he was, he remembered Stidger and wrote him once more in Detroit. By that time, Stidger had moved to Kansas City, and he persuaded Lewis that Kansas City was an ideal "research" field for the book, a kind of crossroads of American religious practices where he would find everything.

Stidger was a flamboyant man who in many ways resembled Elmer Gantry. Built like a prize fighter, he brought to his pulpit the methods of vigorous salesmanship, not to say vaudeville, decorated his churches with revolving illuminated crosses, and published books on church methods with such titles as *Standing Room Only*. Unaware of the kind of novel that *Elmer Gantry* was to be, he went about Kansas City from the outset boasting that the central character was to be modeled after himself, and this indiscretion he would live to regret, as Lewis would live to regret his friendship. Why he should have used Stidger is clear enough, but why he should have liked him is not. During his two-week visit, at any rate, Lewis was enthusiastic about this new friend—"a corker (& his book sermons are excellent)," he wrote to Harcourt; and to Mencken,

> I had two weeks there, staying with a Methodist padre who is a hell of a good fellow. I am going to fight bitterly with you about the intelligence of some of the more liberal Methodists, Baptists and Presbyterians, even—or especially—in the cornbelt. I met a dozen preachers in Kansas City who form a liberal preacher-group and are as vehemently opposed to fundamentalism as you. It is true that most of them are for prohibition and reforming in general; it is equally true that they have kidded themselves into a belief in Jesus as a Christ; and it is true that they have become sentimental about the value of the communion of souls in a church meeting. But on the whole I found them no more filled with bunk than any group of writers, doctors, or editors that I know. . . .
>
> With this bunch as a start, I am going back to Kansas City for a couple of months to plan the book. I am getting a kick out of viewing America again after too much Europe.

Through Stidger he met a group of Methodist ministers who were among the trustees of the proposed Lincoln and Lee University, a Methodist institution. At their meeting, the discussion was concerned chiefly with appropriate college yells, and Lewis, who contributed to a fund for a rose window in what was planned to be the Chapel of Higher Education, assured them, perhaps remembering that his own earliest attempts at verse were made in the form of high-school yells, that their yells were "rotten" and that they would be wiser if they gave their attention to recruiting a faculty. (In the same mood, he told the city fathers that their two-million-dollar memorial to soldiers of the World War was a "perfect type of teutonic architecture" that "would look well in Munich.")

With Stidger, Lewis spent two days as the house guest of William Allen

White in Emporia, where he was told that he was White's favorite novelist. Through Stidger, too, he was invited to attend a monthly luncheon meeting of Kansas City's liberal ministers, among them the Reverend L. M. Birkhead, a Unitarian and an agnostic. Stidger was jealous of his lion and had no desire to see him get off alone with another minister, but at an early meeting with Birkhead, Lewis is said to have whispered, "Can't we get rid of Bill?" They did, and drove off in Birkhead's car, and parked and had a long talk about Birkhead's career and about religion in Kansas City; and at the end of it Lewis said, "I've found my man!" It was to Birkhead rather than to Stidger that, a few months later, he was to return.

Birkhead described himself as "an immoralist" who "wouldn't try to reform him," and he had a wide Protestant experience that could be of real use to the novelist. Born in a Baptist family, he underwent an adolescent conversion at a Methodist revival meeting, was licensed to preach at eighteen, attended a small Methodist college and conducted revival meetings; then his fundamentalist faith gradually failed him, he enrolled at Union Theological Seminary, became an agnostic even while still preaching Methodism, and at last slipped over to Unitarianism in 1915. When Lewis met him he was pastor of the All Souls' Unitarian Church, and before Lewis left Kansas City on January 28, it was agreed that they would work together upon his return.

He left for Santa Fe by way of Fort Worth, Texas, where he wanted to observe a well-known preacher, J. Frank Norris, conduct a service in the First Baptist Church. He had never, he reported, seen so many people in a church. In Santa Fe, where he met Mary Austin, his researches had to do with an Indian buffalo dance rather than with Christianity, and "a damned good spectacle it was." But Santa Fe was cold, and on February 4 he left for Los Angeles, where he stayed for several days, and arrived in San Francisco on about the tenth. There he bought a Buick touring car, employed a young secretary, looked up his old high-school football idol, Jim Irsfield, now a San Franciscan, and saw a good deal of George Sterling who, like Lewis himself since the old Carmel days, had become a considerable drunkard. "George will drive with [Bernard] Simon (the new secretary) and me part or all of the way to Los Angeles, stopping for a day or two at Carmel and Pebble Beach," he wrote his father. When he arrived at Pebble Beach, about February 16, he drove up to the Del Monte Lodge, a luxury hotel owned by another former football player, a dazzling Yale classmate who had not known him then, S. F. B. Morse.

If Lewis's circumstances had changed considerably over fifteen years, so had those of Carmel.

> Here I am [he wrote his father], a mile from my old haunts at Carmel. Gosh how the whole place has changed. Carmel is about three times as big as it used to be, and where once the main street had just simple ordinary grocery

> stores and so on, now it has arty shops selling English pottery and French lamp shades and that sort of junk; where once every one was poor and simple and walked, wearing corduroy trousers and flannel shirts and sneakers, now they *ride,* in fairly expensive cars, and wear smart English tweeds; where once we went picknicking on the rocks, carrying our grub in baskets, now they go over to the Del Monte Grill to dine and dance . . . . . and those same once wild rocky shores, so free and uninhabited then, are covered with expensive houses. All in fifteen years!

In Pebble Beach he saw again his old friend Gene Baker McComas, but he saw more frequently Gouverneur Morris and his house guests, Pola Negri and Rudolph Valentino, with both of whom he was much taken—he, "manly and likeable . . . she charming AND with a sense of humor." Pola Negri had written her memoirs, and in the interest of this manuscript, Lewis telephoned Harcourt in New York. He was also urging Harcourt to arrange for a book of San Francisco literary reminiscences by George Sterling, and Harcourt was interested in both projects. But Sterling, in that same year, was to die in suicidal despair just before he was to have met Mencken, who had been publishing the essays that had suggested a book to Lewis, and from that curiously pathetic source no more work would come.

George Sterling and Pola Negri, H. G. Wells and Freeman J. Lewis—the names suggest that there were no limits to his literary altruism. To Wells he wrote from Pebble Beach with concern over a controversy in which Wells was embroiled with Poultney Bigelow, and with advice about a libel suit that Bigelow had threatened to bring. Freeman Lewis, at the same time, was brooding about the work that he was planning to submit to the *Harvard Monthly* when he arrived in Cambridge, fearful that it was commonplace rather than literary. "The writing of most ambitious youngsters," pronounced his uncle, "suffers from being too 'literary' "—strange advice from the author of such a sentence as this in *Arrowsmith:* "Misty mountains they saw, and on their flanks the palm-crowned fortifications built of old time against the pirates." But his intentions were always kindly, and so, now, were his most intimately personal feelings. On February 20 he wrote his wife in the hope that she would meet him at Tucson for two or three weeks of adventuring.

He left Pebble Beach with his secretary on February 21 to drive to Los Angeles by way of the Imperial Valley. During the two days there, he saw film people, "especially the very nice Florence Vidor, who played Carol in the film version of *Main Street.*" Then Palm Springs, Calexico (with dinner in Mexico), Yuma and Chandler, Arizona (dinner with George Barr McCutcheon), and Tucson on March 1. "Here Gracie is to meet me, next Saturday, coming on from New York."

In Tucson, Lewis was interviewed in connection with a long account of the discovery by Dr. Aleš Hrdlicka, the anthropologist, of an emergent "new American type." Lewis took occasion to speculate on the portliness of the ruling American types, the businessman and his wife, as opposed to the slimness of the young American envisaged by Dr. Hrdlicka, and to speculate further on America as a business aristocracy in which democracy was only apparent. He believed, he said, in the value to American life of the mixture of national strains, and he believed that the melting pot was really beginning to melt.

So, it seemed, when Mrs. Lewis arrived, was the marriage pot. He cried in her lap and assured her that no one in the world but she understood him, no one in the world but he understood her, and that, whatever faults they might have, they felt secure with no others. "Neither Gracie nor myself has ever had quite so joyous a hike as we are now enjoying," he wrote Harcourt presently; "And G. and I have never been so serene." And so he wrote his father. He told him, too, of meeting in Tucson a man who would later prove to be of importance as a friend—Ramon Guthrie, a young poet and novelist—and of spending an afternoon at the ranch of Harold Bell Wright.

> Wright is a damned bad writer, and I expected to find him a pompous, sermonizing, moralistic rustic, four-flushing about his knowledge of the West. I found a most charming and intelligent man, with a sense of humor; one who really belonged to the ranches and cactus plains of which he writes; and I liked him so much better than most of the men who write so much better.

It was probably the return to the companionship of his wife that led him in Tucson to dispense with the services of his new secretary, although to his father he said that he did not have enough work to keep the young man on, and to Harcourt that the young man was "too damned collegian to be efficient yet." Perhaps all these were reasons, plus the additional one that even without a secretary, their entourage was sizable. They had rented a "Wonderbus," a de luxe and fully equipped house-car, and attached to that was a supply wagon, and they were driving the Buick, so there were the two of them, a trained Arizona guide ("a real cow-puncher, yet a bully motor driver"), a Japanese cook, and a mechanic who drove the supply wagon. "Yes, it's a yacht, that's what it is, a desert yacht . . ."

> We motor by ourselves, in my own car, top down, all day; then at evening we have waiting for us, in the motor caravan, a perfect dinner . . . . . and sleep in the bunks on the side of the car, outdoors in the soft yet rousing desert air, and wake in the morning, miles from any house, to look across cactus and sagebrush to huge rock mountains bright in the morning sun . . .

They set out in this fashion on March 11. On March 13 they arrived at the Bar O Ranch near Tombstone, Arizona, where they stayed until Monday. He mounted a horse for the first time—and probably the last ever—since he had stayed with the Benéts at Benicia in 1909. Then, after lunch on the fifteenth, they proceeded for a week in a slow swing up to Lordsburg, New Mexico, and back to Phoenix. En route he wrote Mencken of the charms of tequila and of Harold Bell Wright, and he concluded, "Oh Christ to have lived to find Geo Moore a rotten apple, Wells a dull fellow, and Harold Bell Wright a sound fellow. It is only that I have paid in advance for this caravan till the 24th that keeps me from committing suicide till then."

They were back in Phoenix, however, by the twenty-first and returned the caravan to its owners. Everything had gone "very happily," and they were feeling superb. One irritating item spoiled the Phoenix pleasures, an anecdote in the Washington, D.C., *Kiwanis Magazine*. Very rudely, Lewis felt, it referred to him by his first name and attributed to him an accident that had in fact befallen Claude, and all because he was mistakenly presumed to have attacked the Kiwanis Clubs in *Babbitt*. To Claude he wrote:

> ... it was you, not I, who got the busted skull—and that by a kick, not a dive.... The joke is that they gently suggest that I am crazy, as a result of that dive-kick; whereas it is you, of course, who are thereby rendered crazy —so crazy as to join the Kiwanians!

Next day, March 23, they were driving on to Santa Fe, and from there back to Kansas City.

For some time Lewis had thought of *Sounding Brass* as the title for his next novel, but in Santa Fe he discovered that in England Ethel Mannin had just announced a work with that title. What did Harcourt think of Elmer Bloor as the name of his central character, and *Rev. Bloor* as the title? In Santa Fe, too, he discovered that from there to Kansas City they could expect nothing but mud by way of roads, and he arranged to have his car driven for him, while they would take the train. So he informed his nephew. And brooding still about that young man's introduction into the great world, he added:

> Why don't you consider dropping the J. from your name? Freeman Lewis is a thoroughly distinctive name—and the more so without a middle initial. Middle initials belong to the insurance office and the corn belt.

On the next day, March 30, they themselves started back for the corn belt, and on that day Alfred Harcourt was writing in New York to say that everything indicated that *Arrowsmith* would win the Pulitzer prize. For this delightful contingency, Lewis could not make his preparations until, early in April, he was once more in Kansas City. There, Mrs. Lewis helped him establish himself for the several months of residence that he planned. He took a two-room suite in the Hotel Ambassador, and when he discovered that it had formerly been occupied by Morris Gest, author of a controversial religious play called *The Miracle* that he had disliked, Lewis exclaimed to the press, "My God, I hope that isn't symbolical!" One of the two rooms was rearranged to serve as study and sitting room, Mrs. Lewis found a Negro woman to come in and cook for him, and on April 5 she left for New York. All was peaceable. She thought that she might go to Germany in June and, his book finished, he might join her there in about October. "The trip has been a great success," and only served to indicate to him that everything could be made to work out yet, so long as one was not asked to submit to those absurd daily demands that so many dull folk seemed to regard as being among the indispensable conditions of marriage.

On the day before his wife's departure, he addressed Alfred Harcourt confidentially on the looming matter of the Pulitzer prize.

> I hope they do award me the Pulitzer prize on *Arrowsmith*—but you know, don't you, that ever since the *Main Street* burglary, I have planned that if they ever did award it to me, I would refuse it, with a polite but firm letter which I shall let the press have, and which ought to make it impossible for any one ever to accept the novel prize (not the play or history prize) thereafter without acknowledging themselves as willing to sell out. There are three chief reasons—the *Main Street* and possibly the *Babbitt* matters, the fact that a number of publishers advertise Pulitzer Prize novels not, as the award states, as "best portraying the highest standards of American morals and manners" or whatever it is but as *the* in every-way "best novel of the year," and third the whole general matter of any body arrogating to itself the right to choose a best novel.

The matter could hardly be clearer, and it makes almost entirely irrelevant the issues posed by the controversy of a month later—whether Lewis was sincerely acting on principle, or whether he was obtaining enormous publicity for a mere one-thousand-dollar sacrifice. Obviously, he would have accepted the prize for *Main Street;* probably he would have accepted it for *Babbitt;* but the double neglect could only be construed as an insult. His motive was personal indignation, or hurt vanity; his intention was retaliation. The general principles that he then invoked, whatever their merit may have been, were secondary and in other circumstances would almost certainly not have been raised at all. But at this point, just as obviously, motive and intent must both be buried under the arguments that would substantiate principle, and to that end Lewis asked Harcourt to send him certain materials that would enable him to draw up his document of refusal well in advance of any announcement. "I'll be ready for them."

The Pulitzer possibilities gave the month of April 1926 an undercurrent of unusual titillation but they in no way impeded progress on the main task. Returning to Kansas City, Lewis already had his general story pretty clearly in mind and, according to Birkhead, had started work on his outline. Birkhead was prepared to assist him and this time there was no ambiguity as to the assistant's status: "it is distinctly understood that he is temporary assistant—in no sense a collaborator." Almost immediately Lewis began to make pulpit appearances in the churches "to give me a real feeling of the church from the inside." He had already spoken in Stidger's church, and on April 11 he spoke in Birkhead's church on the subject, "Some Rebels I Have Known," and was to speak in pulpits all over the city (not to say before the Rotary Clubs, the Ad Club, the Chamber of Commerce, and a variety of literary groups). But the climax to these appearances came early—on April 18, in the pulpit of Burris Jenkins in the Linwood Boulevard Christian (Campbellite) Church, where he presumably gave God fifteen minutes in which to strike him dead as an infidel and thereby prove His existence.

Although Lewis himself later referred to the occasion as that on which he "spoke up to papa God," the demonstration was not quite so childish as an exhilarated national press and an outraged clergy made it appear to be. Lewis was not delivering a sermon; he was addressing a Sunday evening forum regularly conducted by Jenkins's assistant, the Reverend Earl Blackman. As usual, the talk was informal. It began with a defense of "flaming youth," and moved from that to an attack on the fundamentalist conception of a personally vindictive God. It was a commonplace in fundamentalist circles to speak of the death of Luther Burbank as divine vengeance upon an infidel. Why, then, reasoned Lewis, did William Jennings Bryan, a fundamentalist, die at an age fifteen years younger than Burbank? God would have made matters clearer by striking Burbank down at the time that he was making his atheistic avowals rather than years later. And with that Lewis pulled out his watch and announced an experiment. He would give this fundamentalist God, if He existed, fifteen minutes—and so forth—and he continued to talk: the trouble with most preachers was only that they were so unspeakably dull, et cetera. "Is there no joy, no greatness in living? Is it the fear of hell that makes us good? If this theory is part of the Christian religion, then damn your Christian religion"—et cetera. The fifteen minutes were over and Lewis stepped aside.

This is the substance of the story as the Associated Press delivered it to the New York *Times,* and it probably put an undue emphasis on the act of defiance, on the "dare." Burris Jenkins denied the published accounts, and only so recently as 1953 one Ruth Mary Weeks, who was on the platform with Lewis, tried to correct them in a communication to the Kansas City *Times.* Reading a newspaper letter about God's dispatch of Burbank to the flames of hell, Lewis went on to say, according to Miss Weeks, that

> "God is not like that . . . modern man does not so picture Him. If there were such a deity as this letter writer imagines, he would certainly strike me dead for what I am about to say in the next fifteen minutes." . . .
>
> After a bit, Lewis paused and remarked: "Well, the fifteen minutes are up. I am still alive, and the writer is wrong. God is not as he pictures Him."

The matter is a quibble, and one prefers the later version chiefly because it suggests that Lewis was not without an awareness of anticlimax: a well-known anecdote about Shaw had him giving God only *three* minutes to strike him down because, said Shaw, he was a busy man. And when questions came from Lewis's audience, they had to do not with God's wrath or His reticence, but with "flaming youth." How did Lewis propose to stem its "tide of growing folly?" "Who of you are wise enough to lead them?" was the evasive reply. Did Mr. Lewis not believe that the harnessing of the wild horse of the plains, while it interfered with his glorious freedom, was best in the end? "It might be best for me to have the horse to plow my garden, but if so I wouldn't have the infernal nerve to tell the horse that I did it on his behalf."

Whatever the exact nature of Lewis's utterances, he had provided material for half the pulpits throughout the country and for every one in Kansas City, and the derision and denunciation went on all through that spring. The appraiser of the Port of New York, at a Masonic ceremony, suggested that only one of the "many Christians with strong fists in the world" could render the proper rebuke. More moderately, a New York *Times* editorialist suggested that Sinclair Lewis read Jonathan Swift's verses on the Day of Judgment, wherein Swift (according to the *Times* man's faulty text) quoted God as saying, "I damn such fools? Go, go your bit." But with his own group of fifteen or eighteen friendly clergymen in Kansas City, the core of his "research," Lewis lost no favor.

He not only preached to get the "real feeling," but investigated the practices of all the churches in the city. (When he left, Earl Blackman believes, he knew more about the private life as well as the public reputation of every preacher in town than, most of all, the preachers themselves.) He attended two or three church services on every Sunday that he was there, and he took advantage of every possible tangential experience in the religious community. He turned his hotel room study into a religious reference library (scores of these titles were reproduced by L. M. Birkhead in his pamphlet, "Is *Elmer Gantry* True?") and to Earl Blackman Lewis showed a bibliography of over two hundred titles—works on the philosophy of religion, the history of Christianity, religion in America, sectarianism, et cetera—that he had already read before he came to Kansas City. His most useful "research," however, came from what he called—and was widely publicized as—"Sinclair Lewis's Sunday School Class."

The group consisted of Birkhead, Stidger, Jenkins, Blackman and eleven others, including a Roman Catholic priest, the most distinguished rabbi in the city, and the head of the Rationalist Society who, like Birkhead, was an agnostic. They met in Lewis's apartment on Thursday noons for luncheon (each man was expected to pay for his own food), and at each meeting a topic would be announced for the next meeting. During the intervening week, Lewis would read about the topic and arm himself with challenges, and the session would consist of rapid interrogation about loose terms, sloppy conceptions of faith, plain ignorance. One session was about "The Holy Spirit," another about "Denominational Contributions to American Civilization." When he came to the latter, he knew about the social efforts of every denomination in the city, and as he went round the circle he was able to puncture the pretenses of every speaker. He saved the Catholic priest for the last, and when he came to him, he launched upon a satirical tirade. "Here we come now to the great Mother Church, the great imperial Roman Church, the Church Universal"—and so forth—and finally wheeled on the priest and cried, "Well, Father, what actually has your great Church done?" The priest laughed softly and replied that he could only be reminded of the story of the ant that stood next to the elephant and demanded, "Move over and give me some room." Guffaws from everyone, including Lewis, brought an end to that session.

One of the ministers, a liberal Presbyterian named Samuel Harkness, published his recollections of the class in *Christian Century* that summer.

> Soul-shaking moments come when Lewis speaks with the passion of an Old Testament prophet, demanding, "What sacrifices do you make? What risks will you take to end these paralyzing influences which you tell me are creeping over your church? Who will give up his wife and children, house and bank account? Who will literally follow Jesus into loneliness, ridicule, and death?" Lewis had been reading the New Testament and its iron and flame have gotten into his blood. "Why do you men stay in pulpits and use terms that mean nothing to you, and repeat creeds you have denied to me?" . . .
>
> There is a sophistry in the ministerial attitude that he scorns, and to which he attributes the fading distinction between the church and the world. "Why don't you tell your congregations that you are agnostics?" he storms. "The conventional Christ is sheer myth. Your Jesus is the hatrack on which men have hung their prejudices through the ages. Do you not realize that organized Christianity has had two thousand years to conquer the mind—and has failed? What other idea has ever had a like chance? Don't you see that no man can be a successful preacher unless he is a Fundamentalist, because dogmatic denunciation is the intellectual gait of the people in your pews?" So he flings verbal grenades into the theological dug-outs. There is nothing flippant about him now, and there is an uneasy hush. Instantly he feels that his words have given pain: "I am sorry for you—you are caught in a dilemma, but you must face it like Luthers and Wesleys."

Mrs. Birkhead remembers that every now and then he would begin to preach in all sincerity, and then he would pause and say, "I have to stop this! I *could* have been a preacher." And one is indeed forced to wonder who was teaching whom.

An unlikely source of reminiscence on these occasions comes from the

Memories of Ethel Barrymore. On a long vaudeville tour with *The Twelve Pound Look,* she too was at the Ambassador while Lewis was there.

> On the way to my apartment I would have to pass the open door of his. It was always crowded with ministers of every denomination whom he was bullying, in the hope, I suppose, of extracting something for his book. He would stride around the room, pointing a finger at one of them after another and saying, "You know you don't believe in God."
>
> They all seemed transfixed except one little Catholic priest who said, "Sit down, my son, and don't blaspheme."
>
> That silenced Red for a moment. Then he said, "Will you have a drink, Father?"
>
> "I will," said the priest.
>
> Sometimes he would ask me in for a few minutes. . . .

That little priest, one suspects, was as impervious to liquor as he was to the Lewis form of logic, but the mention of drink suggests Lewis's own statement to Markham Harris, made in 1933, "that part of his research into the person of Elmer Gantry had been in the form of taking evangelical parsons out and getting them drunk enough to tell the truth about themselves."

There were social occasions, of course, that had nothing to do with "research." When Gilbert Frankau arrived from England, Lewis entertained him. When Clarence Darrow and his wife arrived, Lewis entertained them. There was the Sage of Emporia. There were the usual interruptions by people in search of help—no young regional writers with manuscripts, apparently, but at least one young minister with a hard-luck story who wanted to give up his church to become a writer. Lewis was interested, lent him a pair of pajamas, and let him spend the night, but next morning he changed his mind about him and sent him on his way, and the preacher told the newspapers that all that came of his effort was this dubious privilege of sleeping in the Lewis nightclothes. There were drinking parties with the local newspapermen, dinner parties with the secular Babbittry. At one of these, uninvited, arrived the medical columnist, Dr. Logan Clendening, very drunk, pounding on the door, demanding entrance, shouting, *"I'm* Babbitt. I have to meet that man"—and he was admitted. Lewis's own drinking was not now excessive, according to Mrs. Birkhead. He was working very hard, putting down his data. (While the character of Elmer Gantry was certainly a composite, Mrs. Birkhead says, everything that Elmer did was done by one minister or another known to them, and it was such data that were being compiled.)

By the time he left Kansas City in May, he had laid out a full scenario of 20,000 words, with complete biographies of twenty-four of his seventy-odd characters, and a copy of this precious outline was deposited in the vault of a Kansas City department store for safe keeping. Elmer himself did not yet have his name. Elmer Bloor, Elmer Skaggs, Elmer Flaugh—these, and Myron Melish, were among the possibilities; but it was not until June 12, when the writing of the novel itself was well under way, that he became Elmer Gantry.

In the meantime, Lewis's own name had appeared in every newspaper in America and in most of those throughout the world. No one before him had ever refused the Pulitzer prize: here was one of the truly great man-bites-dog stories, overshadowing not only Lewis's own earlier exploits but those of others as well, including those of his friend Mencken. The postal ban of the April *American Mercury* when it published Herbert Asbury's story "Hatrack" had caused a newspaper tempest, to which Lewis had contributed in a statement to the Kansas City press:

> Yes, indeed, I am very glad to hear that Mr. Mencken—or Apollo as we usually call him at the Algonquin—is being properly dealt with by Frank T. Chase, the Postal Department, the smart set of Farmington, Missouri, and like authorities on art and good manners. This fellow Mencken has been going around insisting that all of us know what all of us know, and if such a doctrine were to be accepted, the Church and Calvin Coolidge would be ruined.

That excitement died with the furor brought on by Lewis's supposed defiance of God, but no one except Harcourt and Lewis himself expected him to cap his own sensation with a greater one, and within only two weeks.*

The calculations that preceded Lewis's gesture are recorded in the Lewis-Harcourt correspondence, yet even he was not wholly prepared for the event. Mrs. Birkhead remembers him, a little dazed, walking into her room on April 25 and saying, "Sister, I have been offered the Pulitzer prize," and to Harcourt he wrote next day, beginning, "Well doggone it, it's happened. . . ." He had "been spending about as much time" in the preceding twenty-four hours "in refusing this thousand dollars as ordinarily I'd spend in earning it." He was zealous for Harcourt's comments on the draft of his refusal, and also for those of Donald Brace and Joel Spingarn. Harcourt treated this document with all the care of a conscientious schoolmaster correcting a prize essay by a star pupil. He outlined Lewis's arguments for him, questioned matters of tone, deliberated about word choice, and suggested that Lewis explicitly mention (to show his consistency) the fact that he had declined membership in the National Institute of Arts and Letters some years before. Harcourt assumed that the Associated Press would wish to release the statement under a Kansas City dateline, but when he consulted with friends at the Associated Press in New York, he learned that the New York

* Mencken's biographers are overzealous in his behalf. Two of them—William Manchester and Charles Angoff—credit him with persuading Lewis to decline the Pulitzer, whereas in fact he only applauded him for having done so. A third—Edgar Kemler—asserts that Mencken recommended L. M. Birkhead to him as his consultant.

office wished to release it. "It is late because we have been standing on our heads to do a prompt and careful job on your statement," he wrote Lewis on May 4. "You have done a perfect job and I am proud of you." Harcourt, Brace & Company mailed out a thousand copies.

The final document, polished, historic, and disingenuous, read as follows:

SINCLAIR LEWIS REFUSES PULITZER PRIZE
(For Release Thursday, May 6th, 1926)

The Hotel Ambassador
Kansas City, Mo.

To the Pulitzer Prize Committee,
Courtesy of Mr. Frank D. Fackenthal, Secretary,
Columbia University
New York City.
Sirs:—

I wish to acknowledge your choice of my novel *Arrowsmith* for the Pulitzer Prize. That prize I must refuse, and my refusal would be meaningless unless I explained the reasons.

All prizes, like all titles, are dangerous. The seekers for prizes tend to labor not for inherent excellence but for alien rewards; they tend to write this, or timorously to avoid writing that, in order to tickle the prejudices of a haphazard committee. And the Pulitzer Prize for Novels is peculiarly objectionable because the terms of it have been constantly and grievously misrepresented.

Those terms are that the prize shall be given "for the American novel published during the year which shall best present the wholesome atmosphere of American life, and the highest standard of American manners and manhood." This phrase, if it means anything whatsoever, would appear to mean that the appraisal of the novels shall be made not according to their actual literary merit but in obedience to whatever code of Good Form may chance to be popular at the moment.

That there is such a limitation of the award is little understood. Because of the condensed manner in which the announcement is usually reported, and because certain publishers have trumpeted that any novel which has received the Pulitzer Prize has thus been established without qualification as *the best* novel, the public has come to believe that the prize is the highest honor which an American novelist can receive.

The Pulitzer Prize for Novels signifies, already, much more than a convenient thousand dollars to be accepted even by such writers as smile secretly at the actual wording of the terms. It is tending to become a sanctified tradition. There is a general belief that the administrators of the prize are a pontifical body with the discernment and the power to grant the prize as the ultimate proof of merit. It is believed that they are always guided by a committee of responsible critics, though in the case both of this and other Pulitzer Prizes, the administrators can, and sometimes do, quite arbitrarily reject the recommendations of their supposed advisers.

If already the Pulitzer Prize is so important, it is not absurd to suggest that in another generation it may, with the actual terms of the award ignored, become the one thing for which any ambitious novelist will strive; and the administrators of the prize may become a supreme court, a college of cardinals, so rooted and so sacred that to challenge them will be to commit blasphemy. Such is the French Academy, and we have had the spectacle of even an Anatole France intriguing for election.

Only by regularly refusing the Pulitzer Prize can novelists keep such a power from being permanently set up over them.

Between the Pulitzer Prizes, the American Academy of Arts and Letters, amateur boards of censorship, and the inquisition of earnest literary ladies, every compulsion is put upon writers to become safe, polite, obedient, and sterile. In protest, I declined election to the National Institute of Arts and Letters some years ago, and now I must decline the Pulitzer Prize.

I invite other writers to consider the fact that by accepting the prizes and approval of these vague institutions, we are admitting their authority, publicly confirming them as the final judges of literary excellence, and I inquire whether any prize is worth that subservience.

I am, sirs,

Yours sincerely,
Sinclair Lewis

It was like battle news: a summary report at 4:01 P.M. on Wednesday, May 5; the complete statement at 4:07; the stiff reply at 7:35 of Ralph Pulitzer, son of the founder and one of the eleven-man Advisory Board; a day story for May 6 at 1:45 A.M. And then the flood of stories across front pages all over the world, and up and down their editorial columns. When Bernard Shaw was asked whether he agreed with Sinclair Lewis's action, he, with his own show running, replied snappishly, "I don't agree with anything."

Most newspapers attacked Lewis for having refused the prize on the grounds that he gave, and imputed to him instead the motive of publicity seeking. A few writers came publicly to his defense—Agnes Repplier, Zona Gale, Carl Van Doren. Members of the Pulitzer Advisory Board argued that no man would write a novel with a prize in mind and protested that they themselves did not take seriously those terms of the Pulitzer will that specified as the prize novel's content "the wholesome atmosphere of American life." William Allen White, who dined with Lewis at the Ambassador on May 12 (he attended the last meeting of the Sunday School Class on May 13) insisted on Lewis's sincerity. Mencken was delighted, of course, and praised him in the columns of the Baltimore *Evening Sun* and in a note. Michael Williams, a friend from an earlier time, was later led to reflect that the great exposer of hypocrisies had "himself, through the action of the very social forces and mechanisms which he has become famous by satirizing," become "a primary example of those forces!" If any reader in the world had not already known that Sinclair Lewis was in Kansas City, working up the material for his next, sensational novel, he knew it now.

On May 14, Kansas City celebrated Straw Hat Day, and one haberdasher had decorated his window with a giant straw hat, size 207⅝. A humorous jeweler named L. J. Ryer bought this object for $27.50 and hired a truck. He wrote a note: "To Mr. Lewis—Since recent developments indicate that the brain-children, Dr. Kennicott, Babbitt, Arrowsmith and Elmer Flaugh may occupy enlarged quarters, here is an adequate roof for the 'superstructure.' From a Reader." This missive a bellboy delivered to Lewis at his apartment, and the boy was immediately followed by two truck drivers who had turned the hat on edge to get it through the doorway.

> "What is it?" asked the author. "It might be a bathtub." He walked around the affair, eyeing it from various angles. "I wish my little boy was here to see it," was his comment. "Children like things awfully big or awfully little."
>
> He refused to have his picture taken standing under the hat, and asked that it be removed from his apartment. The big sailor occupied about all of the small room which the author uses as his study.
>
> "Have you any snappy comeback in reply to the note?" he was asked.
>
> "No, I guess not," he said after a long pause.

In the street below, a large crowd had gathered under the impression that, in a ceremony either solemn or hilarious, Sinclair Lewis was about to be crowned King of the May. Next day he left that town in his Buick with Earl Blackman.

At the last meeting of his Sunday School Class, he announced: "Boys, I'm going up to Minnesota, and write a novel about you. I'm going to give you hell, but I love every one of you," and as each man left the room, he embraced him and said, "Good-by, old man; God bless you!"

He did not know exactly where he was going, but for some weeks he had planned that it should be to a quiet Minnesota retreat. He had written Claude on April 24:

> If you happen to hear of any good cottages in northern Minnesota (on some lake considerably wilder than, say, Birch Lake or Fairy Lake) you might make a note of it so I can talk it over with you when I get there. I shall want two cottages because some friends will be with me and at least one of these cottages should be fairly well equipped with kitchen and so on. The other, in which I shall work, ought not to be too near to other cottages. I could not possibly work among a bunch of cottages closely jammed together as are the cottages at, say, Sauk Lake.

The friends were, of course, Dr. and Mrs. Birkhead and their young son, Kenneth, and the Birkheads were to follow as soon as he and Blackman had found a place to bring them, and on May 14 he wrote Claude again to tell him about Blackman and of their probable arrival at St. Cloud on the twentieth or the twenty-first of May.

In the meantime, he had continued his little admonitory notes to Claude's son. Freeman had written an unfavorable essay on *Manhattan Transfer,* the Dos Passos novel that Lewis had praised so enthusiastically that its publishers had turned his review into a pamphlet for promotion purposes. This pamphlet he sent to Freeman with the observation that "ten years from now you will like [the novel] a lot better." And then suddenly Freeman thought that he should reconsider the decision to go to Harvard. Did not Yale have a better English department? Perhaps, his uncle allowed, "but even if it were true the difference would be so little as to be unimportant and in general the atmosphere of Harvard is unquestionably much better than that of Yale." With his new companion, Earl Blackman, who had been an American Legion chaplain (and, because he was also a boxer, had been known as "The Fighting Chaplain"), Lewis had removed himself about as far from the atmosphere of Yale as was possible.

They planned to drive north by way of Omaha, Nebraska, but before they had left the business area of Kansas City, Lewis suddenly said, "Earl, what do you say we drive east on Highway 40, spend tonight in St. Louis, and drive on tomorrow to Terre Haute, Indiana, and call on Eugene Debs?" Blackman, a conservative Republican who had long thought of Debs as the arch-enemy of all things American and good, could only simulate enthusiasm for this change of plan. Lewis talked then of his ambition to write a novel about labor with Debs as his hero, about his deep love for Debs, about Debs's Christlike quality. Blackman listened and Lewis dropped the subject.

Then Lewis decided that they should play a game—they were always playing games—when they stopped presently for coffee. They would enter the restaurant in "one hell of an argument," Blackman pretending to be a grocery salesman and Lewis pretending to be a shoe salesman, each furious with the other and each furiously defending the superiority of his wares. They began to shout at one another as they left their car, entered the restaurant in what appeared to be nearly uncontrollable rage, beat on the counter with their fists, did not once let the argument subside while they drank their coffee, stomped to the cashier's stand where each stiffly paid his own check, kept up their loud squabble as they marched out and into their car, and left behind them the astonished faces of a few customers and their waitress. Only after they had driven out of the town did they slow down their automobile and collapse in an explosion of laughter.

There were other forms of boyish fun, some more useful to Lewis than this. Blackman had been an evangelical singer in his youth, and Lewis would keep insisting that he sing the old revival hymns that he knew, and would enjoy listening to them. Or he would say, "Now, Earl, we're going to have a little play. In my novel I have this character, Reverend Frank Shallard, a liberal, tolerant preacher who wants to make Christianity an active force for social good. Now, then, Earl, you talk the way Frank Shallard would talk, and I'll talk the way Elmer would talk, and we'll have a conversation." So they enacted many roles in the novel—a variation on Lewis's own old workshop habit of mimicry.

He talked much about the novel, as he had not done in Kansas City. He told Blackman that the clergy there would not receive it favorably when it appeared, and promised that, if Burris Jenkins should discharge him because of his close association with Lewis, Blackman was to telegraph him, wherever he might be, and he would take care of him. He would take Blackman and his wife and young daughters to Paris, leave the latter there to study music, and he and Blackman would go around the world together. He told Blackman that the novel would contain a portrait of the ideal preacher, Andrew Pengilly, and he added, "But mark my words, when the book comes out, not one reviewer will mention the fact that this good preacher is in it."

Arriving in Terre Haute on Tuesday, the eighteenth, they drove directly to Debs's house and were greeted by Debs himself, who embraced Lewis in an affectionate display. Then they sat down and began to chat as though this were simply a neighborly call rather than the climax of a four-hundred-mile drive. Debs asked Lewis about himself, but Lewis turned the questions back to Debs, and very modestly Debs obliged and talked about himself. It was the only occasion in his experience that Blackman saw Lewis as the listener rather than the talker, and he listened with intense interest and respect. Debs talked about his prison experiences but brushed aside the suggestion that he had been courageous in Atlanta; it would require a certain kind of courage *not* to be true to the God within oneself, he said, but to be true to that God is not courage at all. Lewis's eyes grew moist, and then, when Debs recounted a particular prison experience, the tears spilled over. He had heard of an especially difficult prisoner, an enormous and reputedly maniacal Negro, and he had asked to be allowed to talk to him; when the warden's protests were overcome and the Negro was brought to Debs's cell, Debs simply said to him, "Brother, I want to help you." And this completely changed the character of the man, who had never been called brother by anyone; he became Debs's friend, and as long as Debs was there, at least, never again caused any difficulty.

Debs and his wife took the two men to dinner at the Pennsylvania Railroad Station, and after they had said good-by, Lewis proposed a further change of itinerary. Lewis would take the eight-o'clock train to New York to say good-by to his wife, who was sailing for Europe presently, and Blackman would take the Buick and drive to Kendallville in the northeast corner of the state, where his parents lived. He had not, Lewis knew, seen them for a long time. Then he and Blackman would meet again at the La Salle

Street station in Chicago on Friday afternoon and continue from there to Minnesota.

They met again in Chicago as planned and continued their tour on Saturday. Most of that morning they spent in Zion City, north of Chicago —a former center of revivalist religious activity that had quickly disintegrated when its leader had been exposed as a fraud. In Wisconsin they spent the night at Lake Placid and arrived in Sauk Centre late in the afternoon of May 23. Blackman observed with interest the formal meeting of father and son.

> "Well, Hal, how are you? You're looking well."
> "How are you, Dad? You're looking well yourself."
> "Well, you know where the rooms are upstairs, and the bathroom. Supper will be ready at six."

After supper they sat briefly at the table and chatted, but the old man, always impatient with such loitering after a meal was over, arose very soon and Lewis suggested that he and Blackman drive down to Main Street, where they stopped at the chief garage.

They were greeted boisterously by the garage owner who immediately took to the telephone and in less than half an hour had assembled the town marshal, the district game warden, the county sheriff, the wealthiest man in town, and several others. Everyone greeted Lewis enthusiastically and presently they crowded into three cars and drove out of town to a farm house—a country speakeasy characteristic of the Middle West in those years. They sat around a big table in the kitchen and the farmer produced a gallon jug of "moonshine." Lewis, always interested in processes, questioned him closely: how did he distill his liquor, where did he conceal it, how did he manage his business, and so on. The party went on until about two in the morning. Then, as Lewis and Blackman approached the old doctor's house, Lewis said that they would have to be very quiet—in fact, they would remove their shoes and try to reach their room without making a sound. And so they entered.

Next morning, Dr. Lewis routed them out at six o'clock and his housekeeper produced the kind of breakfast least calculated to ease the disordered stomach. The doctor peered at his son over his glasses and said, "Hal, you were a little late getting home last night, weren't you?" "Oh, not so late, Dad. We just had a nice visit with some of the fellows downtown." "I heard you," said Dr. Lewis. "I knew when you came in." Lewis asked questions about relatives and neighbors, but the conversation was not lively, and presently the doctor—who was in semiretirement now but still kept precisely the old office hours—arose and excused himself. His son announced that they would be leaving shortly to call on Claude and his family in St. Cloud but would try to stop in Sauk Centre again on their return.

The night before, he had been "one of the boys," but on the way out of Sauk Centre he stopped the car at the Arch, the old swimming hole, and told Blackman about his youth, when he was not, and remembered the tauntings, the clothes tied up in knots, the attempted compensations in books and reverie.

From St. Cloud they drove directly north along the Mississippi and on May 26 they were lunching at Breezy Point Lodge on Big Pelican Lake, near Pequot. It was an expensive hotel, patronized by Twin City Babbitts and their wives, and owned by the Minneapolis publisher, Captain "Billy" Fawcett of *Whiz Bang* fame. When Lewis asked Mrs. Fawcett if she knew of any places nearby that he might rent, she was quick to see that to have Sinclair Lewis in the area would be a considerable attraction for her guests, and she urged the man in charge of the casino in the basement of the lodge, one R. B. Hamilton, to rent Lewis his cottage, which was about five miles up the shore. The transaction was completed: the Birkheads would occupy the cottage and, about a hundred yards away, two tents would be erected—one a commodious affair to be used as Lewis's study and sleeping quarters, the other for the Hawaiian boy who was to be their cook. Pictures were taken, one of which would appear in the Minneapolis *Tribune* for June 6 ("Sinclair Lewis, Nature's Own, Roughs It . . ."), and Lewis promised to be back, ready to settle in, within a week.

They drove back toward Sauk Centre on Friday, June 28, and it was Blackman's plan to take a bus to Minneapolis on the way south and a night train from Minneapolis that would get him into Kansas City early on Saturday morning, in time to prepare for his Sunday services. But Lewis urged him to spend that night in Sauk Centre and to plan to arrive in Kansas City on Saturday evening. When Blackman protested that he had to compose a prayer for Sunday morning and that he could not do these things easily, Lewis said, "Hell, I'll write you a prayer," and Blackman agreed. Once more, then, he had an opportunity to observe Lewis's behavior in the presence of his father—as deferential, indeed, as submissive, as a well-mannered school boy in the presence of his principal. In the brief time, thirty or forty minutes, between their arrival and the evening meal, Lewis sat by a sitting-room window with pen and a writing pad, and when the housekeeper called them to supper, he arose from his chair and handed Blackman three pages upon which he had written "My Prayer."

> . . . Deliver us—let us deliver ourselves—from worn-out babbling and from all wordiness—from all phrases that do not intensely bear a burden of passion for righteousness, a passion for the well-being of every living thing. Teach us simplicity in prayer. Let us not think that thou hearest us alone, that to hear us, in this hour, thou hast given up the governance of a million other swinging worlds. Let us have so high a vision of thee that we will comprehend we are but tiny and graceless in thy vast plan. Smite our egotism and quicken our imagination until we perceive that we are but a

few out of the numberless multitudes who at this moment seek to lift their spirits by this effort toward communion with thee. . . .

Did he not hear the groan that went up from Baltimore?

By June 3, Lewis was established at Pequot and a week later the Birkheads arrived. The Claude Lewises arrived for a visit almost on the heels of the Birkheads. In the meantime, on June 9, Mrs. Lewis had sailed with Wells on the *Mauretania* to spend the summer near her friends the Fabers in St. Gilgen, Austria (at Salzburg she was to meet the brilliant young American journalist Dorothy Thompson), and the present plan was that either Lewis would join her there in the fall or she would return to the United States and, somewhere, open another house.

He liked the place where he was. To Hugh Walpole, praising *The Man with Red Hair,* he wrote that it was "a delightful place; rather ragged and uncivilized woods shutting off the world on one side and a lake opening almost like an arm of the sea on the other with a sand beach like that of the ocean." He seldom ventured from the place. Once he was persuaded to go into the village to see the film of *Mantrap* in the local movie house, and when the manager announced that he was in the audience, he made a brief speech in which he said that he was glad to have read the book for he would not have recognized it from the movie.

Once he drove the twenty-five miles to the town of Crosby. This is the strange reminiscence of Mrs. Frank E. Taylor, then a little girl in that town. She was playing in the garden of the house of a friend when they heard music coming from the living room. They peered in through the open French doors and saw a Catholic priest at the piano, playing *St. Louis Blues,* and next to the piano, a purple-faced man, Sinclair Lewis, who nearly screamed at them, "Little girls, go away!" Perhaps this musical cleric was one of the two priests who, Mrs. Birkhead remembers, arrived at the cottage one morning with a half case of communion wine. They encountered young Kenneth Birkhead, then about twelve, and told him to get Lewis out of his tent. "Tell him Upton Sinclair is here." Bewildered, Lewis appeared, but recovered quickly enough; they drank the wine and grew raucous under the trees.

Generally speaking, it was the world that came to him in Pequot. Mrs. Birkhead, again, remembers that the people from the lodge would arrive in carloads. Lewis himself was not buying liquor in this summer, but the local sheriff was an obliging bootlegger, whose best customers were the guests at the lodge, and when these people arrived, they were armed with liquor and Lewis did not hesitate to join them. Lewis's friend William McNally, writing in *The Nation* a year later, described this procession of invading Babbitts. "Poles asunder though they be in outlook on life, in temperament they are blood brothers. . . . The oddity of Lewis is that he would open his doors to all his characters as readily as he opens his pages to them. He is as incapable of intellectual snobbery as he is of social, and as incapable of moral snobbery as he is of intellectual."

Among other visitors in that summer was a young violinist from Minneapolis named Karl Andrist. He reminded Lewis of Louis Dodd in Margaret Kennedy's recently published *The Constant Nymph,* and against the advice of all his Minneapolis acquaintances who knew anything about music, he decided that Andrist was a neglected genius. According to William McNally, he let Andrist have his car for a time and he discouraged him from accepting a proffered academic appointment that could only interfere with his art. Then he announced that he was giving him five thousand dollars and sending him to Europe to study. Andrist came on to New York and presently continued to Paris. To Mencken, Lewis wrote:

> I am giving a letter of introduction to you to Karl Andrist, the violinist. He is a superb and authentic musician, and personally he is a man whom, I think, you will love as much as anyone you have ever met. I can see him sitting down with papa Beethoven—and what is more, I can see him sitting down with you over innumerous seidels.

These enthusiasms did not hamper the progress of *Elmer Gantry,* even though certain historic events made it necessary to change a portion of the plot. Sharon Falconer, the lady evangelist, is often thought to have been drawn from Aimee Semple McPherson, and while Miss Aimee's well-publicized antics (together with those of that other persuasive lady, the "child evangelist," Uldine Utley) almost certainly colored Lewis's characterization, perhaps even largely formed it, he would not allow the resemblance. To Mrs. Birkhead he said that the idea for the character and her fate was entirely his own, that it derived from a dream he had of a female evangelist who drowns, and so he had planned the lady's fate in his outline.

He had earlier sought an interview with Aimee Semple McPherson but without success, and Mrs. Birkhead does not think that he ever heard her preach. They went to a variety of revival meetings, but she does not remember that any of them were conducted by women. (Earl Blackman remembers an evangelistic tent meeting at which Lewis was quietly observing the proceedings when one of the women workers stopped at his bench and asked him if he were saved. He said that he did not know. She asked, "Well, don't you want to be?" He said that he did not know that either. Did he not want his sins forgiven? And then he said, no, he did not want his sins forgiven, he loved his sins; and the worker had no answer.) At any rate, Aimee Semple McPherson disappeared and was thought to have drowned, and when the Birkheads arrived at Pequot, nearly the first questions that Lewis asked were about her—what was the latest news, had her body been found? He said, "We'll have to change that whole section of the book or everyone will think that Sharon is Aimee." Even though Aimee made her miraculous reappearance in the Mexican desert on June 23, Sharon's fate was changed from death by water to death by fire.

While he was working at one novel, a new one was forming in his mind. One day on the porch of the cottage, Birkhead read aloud from a newspaper the story of a Middle Westerner who had met President Coolidge, and when he came home, at a meeting of his "service" club, he was asked to stand at the door and let every member shake the hand that shook the hand, et cetera. Lewis then broke into an extended improvisation, the monologue of the proud and happy citizen. Later, from Europe, he wrote the Birkheads to tell them that he had written the book that began there on the Pequot porch.

June 26: ". . . getting into my novel about the preachers with both hands and feet. It will either be a handsome opus or the dullest book ever written." July 22: ". . . and the Reverend Dr. Gantry progresses in holiness." August 24: "The preacher book goes apace, and I think you'll like it." But August 24 marked an interruption in the work, for on that day he wrote, too, "I'm at a house party on the Canadian border. . . . . . A keg of beer rests on the porch . . . . . . real beer . . . . . . God has not, as what the fundamentalists vainly call Nitchy alleged, yet died."

He was at International Falls, on one of the innumerable islands in Rainy Lake, this owned by a wealthy Chicago family (the money was in mines) named Dahlberg. As guests at the lodge, they had met Lewis, and they came back to Pequot to pick him up and lead him to Rainy Lake. He planned to stay for a week, and he met there, among the other guests, his friend Charles Breasted. The holiday was interrupted when, at midnight on August 29, old Dr. E. J. Lewis died, not quite seventy-eight years old.

For several days before his death, as his condition grew weaker, efforts had been made to reach the famous son, according to the Sauk Centre *Herald,* but it was only on the morning after his father had died that Lewis was found. On August 31, the New York *Times* reported the activities on the preceding day of "motorboat parties" searching out "remote streams" for him. But the news, according to Charles Breasted, did not come to him as a total surprise.

On the night of the twenty-ninth Lewis had an intuition that word of his father's death was to come next morning. He could not sleep and he woke Breasted and asked that he sit up with him. Smoking incessantly, he talked:

> My father has never forgiven me for *Main Street*. . . . When I saw him a few weeks ago, we shook hands—but he can't comprehend the book, much less grasp that it's the greatest tribute I knew how to pay him. He felt that I should have served an honored profession by becoming a doctor

myself, instead of derogating and besmirching it in a book libeling my own birthplace. *Main Street* condemned me in his eyes as a traitor to my heritage —whereas the truth is, I shall never shed the little, indelible 'Sauk-centricities' that enabled me to write it—that made the unbridgeable difference between me and my son Wells!

This is rather pretentious talk, perhaps only a little more exact than the report of the New York *Times* that "Credit is given [E. J. Lewis] by friends for having been a strong influence on his son's leaning toward literature." But Lewis enjoyed such improvisation, and we may take Mr. Breasted's word for it as he continues:

> Suddenly he rose, went to a mirror, and, turning his head from side to side, studied his face for some time. Then he said quietly: "You know, as the fire dies down inside of me and I grow old, I shall resemble somewhat a dignified old gentleman of the old school, but actually I shan't be. It takes three generations, and I'm only the second. My son Wells is the third. I think he *is* a gentleman, and perhaps he may create literature—as I have not. I've already done my best work, and of that *Babbitt* will probably be rated my best book—though my own favorite will always be *Arrowsmith.* . . . Oh, in the future a book of mine will probably always be good for a sale of fifty thousand—but neither the critics nor the author will be fooled. The best of what I'll ever have produced will bear the same relation to true literary achievement that a jacket blurb does to the text of a really great book."

Then next morning a motorboat brought the news in a telegram and the same boat took Lewis to the mainland, where he got into his Buick and drove back to Pequot. He drove all through that night, and next day, with the Birkheads, continued to Sauk Centre, where he arrived early on Wednesday, the day of the funeral.

They took rooms in a Main Street hotel. Birkhead went to the barber shop and, not revealing his identity, was told by the barber that Sinclair Lewis, in his view, had not written those books, his wife wrote them. Lewis, rather drunk, came out of the hotel in midmorning and met Ben DuBois in the street. "When are they going to plant the old man?" Lewis asked. They planted him that afternoon at two o'clock.

After the funeral, in his old home, he went to the bathroom and presently called Mrs. Birkhead to show her the rumpled rug on the floor. For years he had been annoyed by the fact that when the bathroom door was opened, it shoved aside this rug, and it was one of his father's fixed passions that the little rug must always be straightened out. Earlier that summer, when his father had wired him and, as always, referred to him as Hal, Lewis replied in an inordinately long telegram in which he explained that his name was Sinclair, and then he chortled to the Birkheads over the picture in his mind of his father counting all those unnecessary words and totaling the expense. One of his favorite imitations was based on his boyhood recollection of his father ordering the household about—his wife, his sons, the hired girl—fanatically concerned with a multiplicity of minute details, each to be precisely observed. Yet among the several characteristics that Lewis himself had acquired from his father, none was more prominent than, when he was not being positively sloppy, this same, nearly compulsive attention to the details of neatness, order, precision, promptness, and, when he was not throwing his money about, the same penny-pinching and suspicious thrift.

Ever since his wife's death, Dr. Lewis had been taken care of by a couple who lived with him, the Roterts, and before Lewis left again with the Birkheads, he gave the Roterts a check (Cyril Clemens says that it was for one thousand dollars), saying that he had no doubt that his father had left them some money, but whatever the amount, he could be certain that it was not as large as it should have been. Cyril Clemens reports, too, that at this point he gave his Buick to his brother Fred. Fred, as a matter of fact, was now in better circumstances than he had ever been: each of the sons had inherited eighteen thousand dollars.

Dr. E. J. Lewis was dead, but the son was not and never would be free of him. He had had no affection for his father but he had an appalling regard for him, and his regard fought with his resentment against him and all that he represented. Such conflicts, left without an arbiter, rage on endlessly. Harry, the brave boy runaway, and Harry, the guilty boy failure, had grown up uneasily into Sinclair Lewis, the raucous rebel against convention, and Sinclair Lewis, the Babbitt—Lewis, the amoral, heavy-drinking dandy, and Lewis, the prig and puritan. The one admonition to which he could never shut his ears was, "Harry, why can't you do like any other boy ought to do!" Whether in revulsion from it or in submission to it, his conduct, like his work, vacillated between the extremities that the charge implies.

If the death of Dr. Lewis brought nothing important to an end, it did end the summer of 1926. Back in Pequot, Lewis prepared immediately to leave for the East. Lewis's relations with his wife when she sailed and during that summer had been pleasant and affectionate. He had suggested that she join him in Pequot, and then he proposed that he himself come to Europe, bringing Birkhead with him. She had discouraged both proposals. But now it was settled that in mid-September she was to return to the United States where she would find a school for Wells, and a house for the two of them in Washington ("Dearest Hal," she wrote, "I want so much to be your very good and loving wife. Do help me to be."), where he would finish *Elmer Gantry* in domestic peace.

About half of the first draft had been written at Pequot and was now being packed. He planned to spend a day in Minneapolis and a few days in

Chicago. In Chicago he again encountered Charles Breasted, who found him in a curiously subdued mood. "Just as on the island on that last night, he spoke of his best work as already accomplished, and he seemed unimpressed by the prospect of whatever he might produce during his remaining years."

He could, it is true, hardly have gone beyond the success that he had already enjoyed. In that year, the London *Mercury* declared that "His name is probably better known abroad than that of almost any other transatlantic writer. In a sense one might say that he overshadows almost all of his contemporaries," and it declared further that *Babbitt* was in many ways "the finest novel that has come out of America in this century." At nearly the same time Mary Colum published in *Scribner's* a very different estimate that, nevertheless, in its own curious way likewise observed the phenomenon of his power. Lamenting the absence in contemporary American literature of what she called "significant mind," she wrote:

> Sinclair Lewis . . . has . . . seriously damaged for other artists the material he uses instead of adding to its significance by the power of a transforming imagination, and has actually somewhat exhausted it for other writers: *Babbitt* and *Main Street* have become docketed, and ticketed and placed in pigeon-holes; they are labeled and do not walk the world as free ideas. Sinclair Lewis has not treated them with a free creative imagination, but has, to use a phrase of Paine's, written like a citizen for fellow citizens. We have in his work a perfect example of what happens to significant material passed through a mind that is not significant. He labels the material instead of transforming it.*

As if to illustrate her point, the businessmen of Richmond, Virginia, on the day that Lewis arrived in Chicago, requested the city fathers to change the name of Main Street, which, after Lewis's novel, was a commercial liability: it "exercises a depressing effect on the retail business." Other cities, with Buffalo, New York, among them, followed the example of Richmond.†

* The resentment in this observation is not unlike that of Sherwood Anderson in *Hello Towns!* (1929): "He [Anderson himself, the small-town editor] drives his car down to the town and parks it on Main Street. Since Sinclair Lewis wrote his book he has been hating the words, 'Main Street.' 'I will call it something else,' he says to himself. He hates all expressions that become, as is said, 'a part of the language.' He is to hate later the name 'Elmer Gantry,' as representing preachers and 'Babbitt,' as representing the business man of the American small town. 'The names are lies in themselves,' he is saying to himself. 'They are too easy. There is too much malice in them.' "

They were not lies, merely half-truths, and one may speculate as to whose aesthetic ambition was the more mistaken—Lewis's satiric-restrictive treatment of his material, or Anderson's lyric-expansive treatment that aspired to assimilate the "whole truth" and was almost necessarily swamped by it.

† But history closes its cycles. In 1960, "The Sinclair Lewis Year," the city fathers of Sauk Centre, Minnesota, acting on the advice of the Chamber of Commerce, renamed their Main Street: it became The Original Main Street.

He arrived in New York on September 10, and a week later, in the *World,* Harry Hansen reported that he was met at Grand Central station by Alfred Harcourt, to whom he handed a heavy black bag. " 'What is it?' asked the astute publisher. 'Dynamite,' declared America's greatest realist, in a hoarse whisper." The most libelous label of them all, it was the half-finished manuscript of *Elmer Gantry,* and Lewis now went once more to the Shelton Hotel to continue work on it.

On the day after his father's funeral he wrote to Mencken and, without mentioning his father's death, proposed an early meeting at dinner. In New York, according to George Jean Nathan, he telephoned the two of them to fix the engagement, and when they arrived at the Shelton, they found him in bed, ill, running a temperature. They rebuked him for having got them out when he could not come with them, whereupon he jumped out of bed in his "short, white old-fashioned nightgown," and began to harangue them as if he were a Methodist minister exhorting them on the beauties of heavenly love. This went on much too long, until, his temperature apparently having shot up, "he let out a loud whoop, informed us that we were both low infidels bent for Hell, fell back into bed, and, exhausted, was sound asleep a few minutes later." The harangue, like so many before it, would appear in almost identical form in the current novel, the last 30,000 words of which, Mencken later wrote him, were composed in a state of drunkenness. It is possible. Certainly the next four months were to be among the roughest that he had yet lived through.

Morris R. Werner remembers that Lewis telephoned Harcourt, Brace on one occasion from the Shelton with the announcement that he was about to jump out of the window. The publishers hurried over to prevent the catastrophe only to find when they arrived that he had abandoned his plans for it. It was at this point, too, Mr. Werner remembers, that members of the firm began their periodic headshakings and ominous mutterings, "Red is finished." But, of course, he still had a number of surprises for them, and, after *Elmer Gantry,* an extended decrescendo of a dozen novels. And whatever his excesses at this point in September of 1926, he himself was in no consistent despair.

His wife returned in the middle of the month, Wells was sent off to the Eaglebrook School in Deerfield, Massachusetts, and Mrs. Lewis found a commodious Washington house at 3028 Q Street, N.W., at six hundred dollars a month. Three servants would come to a little more than two hundred dollars. On the twentieth of September, Lewis wrote Van Vechten to say that he was "going off to Washington for the winter but I shall be coming up to New York from time to time and I hope that we shall have a party before the winter is over." They moved into the house in early October, and everything seemed secure; to the Woodwards he wrote that they would be there "for all winter," and on the same day, October 7, he wrote Mencken that, except for a possible "two weeks' jaunt to Bermuda or something of the sort," he would be there all through the spring. He rented an "office" on the ninth floor of the Hotel Lafayette where he plunged ahead with *Elmer Gantry,* and already the designers at Harcourt, Brace were working on its jacket. On October 12 he assured Freeman Lewis that they were "thoroughly well settled," and he was "very hard at work." Ten days later, plans were under way for the Christmas holidays: Wells would come home, of course, and Freeman would come down from Harvard, and others would be there as well. There were many guest rooms in the handsome house, and everything would be very gala. But already on November 11, according to the diary notes in W. E. Woodward's *The Gift of Life,* the happy state was in jeopardy: "Gracie Lewis—the former Miss Hagger [*sic*]—came in during the forenoon to tell Helen of her troubles with 'Red' Lewis. . . . It appears that she and Lewis are about to separate." Sinclair Lewis managed to endure this final attempt at a marriage until November 22, when he fled once more to the Shelton in New York. There Charles Breasted found him "in a bleak, gray tower room, in a state of abysmal depression and near-collapse. After a final flare-up, he had rushed away from Washington with virtually nothing save his current manuscript. The only other personal effects I noted were three brandy bottles, two of them empty." Breasted invited him to share his bachelor apartment at the Grosvenor on lower Fifth Avenue and from that address, on November 29, Lewis wrote to Gene McComas about the death of their friend George Sterling:

> Yes, George's death was a shock to me—but a shock of the imagination entirely, because it was nothing unexpected of him. But it did make one remember his thousand splendors. I am most touched by remembering him as the King of Carmel, living serenely (at least apparently) with Carrie, looking over his Cup of Jade from his front porch, sitting with all us brats by his splendid fire of pitch-pine. God, what a tragic place Carmel is. . . .

Carmel? In Washington, by the end of November, Mrs. Hegger was once more living with her daughter, and her daughter was packing her husband's trunks. Although he was now living in New York, they were going to maintain a decent front through Christmas in order to make that a happy time for Freeman and Wells and Mrs. Hegger. Lewis would finish all of the original composition of *Elmer Gantry* before December 24 and then come back to Washington for the Christmas week. Already the clergy were whispering about the impending publication of that novel, and since it was bound to raise a public scandal, personal scandal, for the book's sake, must be smothered. Many holiday invitations had been received and one was to the most important party of the season, Mrs. McLean's dinner dance on New Year's Eve.

So Lewis, at the Grosvenor, wrote furiously at the final pages of *Elmer Gantry,* but by no means in retirement. He went to a party, for example, where very few of the guests knew him well, only by reputation as a considerable iconoclast, and on the way he decided to present himself as if he were a Calvin Coolidge, whom he then proceeded to imitate perfectly, in voice and manner as well as in the taciturnity and the extreme conservatism of opinion. Without ever having dropped the role, he left the party, and left the guests amazed at this reversal of their expectations. On December 5, by way of further example, at six o'clock in the evening, he called the Woodwards to ask them for dinner at once. "We went over there and had dinner with him and six or seven people, none of whom I had ever met before. From the conversation I judge that Lewis himself had not known any of them longer than a month. He is always surrounded by new acquaintances." A few days later, when Woodward lunched with him, Lewis told him about the novel, did imitations from it, and said that it was finished and that he was now revising. Ten days later, on December 17, he wrote Harcourt to say that the manuscript would be in, "ready to start setting," within a week. The manuscript was delivered as promised, and on December 24 Lewis returned to Washington.

It was quite a throng that gathered there in Q Street. An exhausted, haggard Lewis. His meek, long-appended mother-in-law, to whom he had always been kind. His nine-year-old schoolboy son, an incredibly beautiful child with bright, dubious blue eyes and a mass of red-gold curls, who had sat for his portrait, not long before, to a Viennese "society" painter, Leo Katz, who had shown him looking wary, defensive, and so, surely, he now had every reason to look. ("He was as much like his mother, and as unlike his father, as any small boy could be," wrote Elizabeth Jordan of an occasion only a few weeks later.) There was Claude's amiable boy, about to turn nineteen, observing. Karl Andrist, the musical protégé on his way abroad and of whom the whimsical Maecenas was already wearying. A harried wife intent on gaiety. Her admirer, Casanova, the handsome, gallant and indigent Spaniard of distinguished lineage, whose attentions to the lady were encouraged by the husband who was about to flee forever.

Immediately there was a fashionable dinner party to attend. When the time to leave had come, Mrs. Lewis, splendid in satin, found her husband sitting dully on the edge of his bed, scrawny, clad only in his B.V.D.'s. "I won't go," was all that he would say. She took Casanova in his place, and the lady who sat next to him observed, "I did not know that Sinclair Lewis looked like you." Then, at dinner at home on December 27, Mrs. Lewis appeared, crisply gay, laughing, handsomely garbed as always, only to confront a sloppily dressed, soddenly drunken husband. It was, understandably, too much! In the presence of everyone she upbraided him sharply and bitterly about his appearance and his conduct. He said nothing. He looked at her as she spoke, then got up as she was speaking still, and, simply and wordlessly, walked out. And that was the end. Or nearly.

He went to the Hotel Mayflower and telegraphed Mencken. Would he meet him in Baltimore in Drawing Room A, Car Three on the train leaving Washington at nine o'clock next morning? They would go to New York together, where parties would be piled on weariness and on misery. But not for long. Both Alfred Harcourt and Donald Brace had written him enthusiastic praise of *Elmer Gantry* (any changes could be made in proof, which was already coming from the printer) and they had ordered 140,000 copies—the largest first printing of any book in history. But none of this could soothe the exacerbated nerves. On New Year's Eve, Alfred Harcourt drove him up the Hudson to Bill Brown's Training Camp, a well-known establishment for the speedy if temporary rehabilitation of drunkards who could no longer help themselves. But, in departing, Lewis begged Breasted that there be no liquor in the apartment at the Grosvenor on his return, and he took with him the first thirty galleys of *Elmer Gantry*.

On January 4, with the boys back at school and college, Mrs. Lewis wrote Harcourt to say that she was "thro, quite thro."

> This whole Washington venture was my last gesture, and it has failed. Physically as well as mentally I have reached the limit of my endurance. My last gift to him is complete silence until the book is out and the first heated discussion dies down. For him to divorce God and wife simultaneously would be bad publicity. I am really ill at the present moment, and I will go to some sort of a sanitarium to normalize myself.

And she withdrew then to Cromwell Hall, in Cromwell, Connecticut.

Harcourt replied: "I do really hope you can achieve serenity in the course of time. Of course I hope Hal can also, but those hopes are much more faint."

8

ON JANUARY 8, 1927, he returned to the Grosvenor in high spirits, and looking fit. He had been, he wrote Mencken at once, "in the country," a euphemism for an experience that had not greatly changed him. Charles Breasted remembers that, before unpacking his bag, he telephoned his bootlegger with a generous order, and almost at once "the familiar procession of people began milling through our living room at any hour between two P.M. and three A.M." They were strays of every kind—university students and journalists, Village hangers-on and barflies, taxi drivers and editors and unknown poets, as well as friends like Elinor Wylie and William Rose Benét, the Van Dorens and Nathan, Rebecca West and Hugh Walpole and Osbert Sitwell, Laurence Stallings, Lewis Browne, William Seabrook, Arthur Hopkins, the Woodwards. When he came home from his office at the end of the afternoon, Breasted never knew what gathering he should expect to find, but there almost always was one.

He did not neglect his wife in Cromwell Hall, but telephoned her and wrote her with assurances of his continuing interest and of his wish to "stand behind" her in their separation and of his hope that there would be no bitterness between them. She was occupying herself in an attempt to write an article about the variety of houses that they had rented abroad. He was of unsettled mind as to whether he should go abroad when the *Gantry* galleys were finished. For a time, urging Breasted to give up his public relations work and take up writing instead, he hoped to persuade him to become his assistant in research for the labor novel; if Breasted agreed, they would get a car and tour the country, visiting every kind of industrial center. When Breasted insisted that this was impossible for him, Lewis decided to go abroad.

He telephoned L. M. Birkhead and asked him and his wife to come to Europe as his guests, but Birkhead declined on the grounds that one of them must be in the United States when *Elmer Gantry* was published. Lewis was spending his mornings, with the help of two secretaries, on the galleys of that long novel, making considerable revisions, and the combination of hard work and hard frivolity exhausted him once more, so that he was compelled to spend three days in the Harbor Sanatorium in the last week of January. Before he made that retreat, he telephoned Earl Blackman in Kansas City and asked him to come to Europe with him. Blackman was to be in New York by February 2, because they were sailing at 12:01 next morning. Lewis told him what clothes he should bring along, and enjoined him not to buy anything that he did not already own, they would do that in New York. Blackman arrived a day or two early, and Lewis took him to a department store immediately and outfitted him, luggage and all, and then he took him to a party at the Woodwards that went on until four in the morning.*

On the evening that they were to sail, Lewis himself gave a party, but he was too indisposed to appear at it. Woodward took occasion to warn Blackman about Lewis's drinking and urged him to "try to keep him sober." After a dinner party for which she had come down to New York, Mrs. Lewis and Casanova arrived to see them off, and Elinor Wylie made tart observations that indicated that Lewis had been less discreet than he had promised to be about the real nature of their separation. Nevertheless, Mrs. Lewis was still solicitous of his condition: let him do as he wished, let him sleep with chambermaids if he must, but, she begged Blackman, try to keep him from drinking a great deal and bring him back in good health. As they stood at the first-class rail, waving down to his wife and Casanova below, Lewis said, "Earl, there is Gracie's future husband." And when questioned by ship's reporters about the separation, she said, "I adore him, and he adores me."

Blackman had brought news from Kansas City. Before his departure, a group of his friends, the Reverend Stidger among them, had given him a luncheon, and Stidger had seen advance sheets of *Elmer Gantry*. He was outraged by the book and announced that he had discovered fifty technical errors in its account of church practices. L. M. Birkhead challenged him to name one and he was silent. But his rancor did not cease, and presently, on March 13, when he preached a sermon on the text, "And Ben-hadad Was Drunk," he told his congregation how disappointed he was in Mr. Lewis, how he regretted having had him in his house, and how he should have been warned by the fact that the novelist was drunk all the time that he was working on the book.† But that sermon, like those of hundreds of other ministers, was yet to be delivered.

* In his book, *The Gift of Life*, Woodward misdates this party as "February 9," the day that Lewis and Blackman arrived in England.

† In January of 1930, writing from the Copley Methodist Episcopal Church in Boston, where he was then employed, Stidger was contemplating a number of talks in Kansas City, and he planned at that time to make a public retraction of these remarks. To this end, he wrote Lewis a letter of apology for his falsehoods. In a long and bitter reply, Lewis declined to accept his apology. To L. M. Birkhead he sent a carbon of his reply and the original of Stidger's letter, and when Stidger came to

In London Lewis took the usual suite in Bury Street. To the newspapers he talked about his unquiet life, about his wish to be a newspaperman once more, about the prevalence of American slang in British speech, about the loquacity of the English and the impossibility of finding quiet in a railway carriage, about his plans to wander for two years "unless stopped and made to write another book." The *Manchester Guardian* wondered how anyone in a railway carriage would have an opportunity to talk to Mr. Lewis, since it was well known that Mr. Lewis always did all of the talking. His English friends, it said, had gone into training to keep up with him vocally and with his "allegro movements around the luncheon table." The New York *Times* editorialist wondered just who would stop Mr. Lewis and make him write a book.

Lewis's remarks about his marriage were suggestive enough to induce American reporters to invade the offices of Harcourt, Brace & Company for information, to pursue Mrs. Lewis to Cromwell Hall, and, after she had returned to New York, to ferret her out at the Stanhope on upper Fifth Avenue where she had taken an apartment. There, to the *Evening Post,* she emphatically denied the divorce rumors and explained that she had stayed behind because of the schooling of their son, which henceforth would be strictly American. These rumors of permanent separation started up a whole crop of stories about her. One had it that a friend, protesting her snobbery, said, "But, Gracie, you are an American, aren't you?" and she replied, "I was born in America, *but* I was *conceived* in *Vienna."* Lewis himself furthered these tales. He is said to have reported that once, when she went to a hospital to call on a friend after a serious operation, and the friend protested that it had been "nothing," she replied, "Well, it was your healthy American peasant blood that pulled you through." With these and similar tales he was entertaining his English friends, all of whom he was seeing when he was not showing Blackman the sights of London and its environs.

At once upon his arrival, he telephoned Lady Sybil Colefax who invited them to tea, and then Lewis decided to give a party as a quick way of rounding up his friends. He invited Lady Sybil, Lord Thomson, Bechhofer Roberts, and a half dozen others. It was a dinner party, Lewis had been drinking during the afternoon, and long before the party really got under way, he was quite drunk, with the result that the party broke up even before dinner was over. Lewis, at the head of the table, would leap up and move around behind the chairs of his guests making remarks that, when not highly offensive, were at least highly inappropriate, and then presently he collapsed and was put to bed.

Kansas City in March, Birkhead released the correspondence to the Kansas City *Times.* After that publication, Stidger fled to a hospital with an acute tooth problem and then vanished from Kansas City forever. He died in West Newton, Massachusetts, in 1949. The correspondence is in the possession of Mrs. Birkhead.

When Blackman emerged from the bedroom, everyone was gone except the tolerant Lord Thomson, who stayed and chatted with him for half an hour, and then Blackman lay awake most of that night, despairing of what he must expect on the Continent. Finally, at dawn, he fell asleep, and when he awoke and came into the living room, he found Lewis in his pajamas before the fire, smoking a cigarette. Blackman said that he wanted to apologize for not having prevented Lewis from making that horrible spectacle of himself, that he should have seized him by the neck at once and forcibly hauled him into his bedroom. Lewis warned him never to lay a hand on him, and then Blackman asked for his fare back to the United States. Lewis looked at him and began to cry, and then, saying that he was going to make a promise, he asked Blackman to call the porter and to tell him to take out all the liquor that he did not want. "And from now on, for the rest of this trip, I will only drink what you agree that I should drink." Blackman called the porter and had him remove everything but one bottle of brandy, and after that they would have a cocktail or two before dinner, or, on one of their walking trips, beer, or, in France and Italy, wine in moderation.

Lewis gave him a guidebook tour of London and, motoring and walking, took him to Stratford, but the London stay was for only ten days, and on the twentieth they took the train for Southampton, where they spent the night for an early morning Channel crossing. Near Southampton, in a considerable establishment, lived Homer Vachell, a well-known pulp writer, and his brother, Horace—both friends of Lewis's. He suggested that they call on these brothers, who received them pleasantly. Then they returned to their hotel and got ready for bed. It was late, and Blackman was ready to go to sleep, but Lewis was not. He said, "We had a good time tonight, didn't we, Earl?" Earl agreed, and Lewis said that it would have been very different if his wife had been with him. Then he kept Blackman awake for more than an hour while he did an imaginary dialogue between his wife and himself in which, discussing the evening, he was continually berated. He began the dialogue by having his wife announce that one does not invade people's homes without warning them that one is coming, and went on from that with the entire catalogue of his social gaucheries. He ended at last by telling Blackman, rather inaccurately, that after the first two weeks, his marriage had been "no good."

In Paris they were met by Karl Andrist, the musical protégé who was about to lose his patronage. In a café with a number of others, Andrist, no doubt in an effort to amuse the humorous master, began to sing the Doxology and to parody it. Lewis was outraged and ordered him to stop. (The logic of excuses never disturbed him when he was ready to sever a relationship.) Andrist dutifully stopped, the entire table was ordered to sing the

Doxology solemnly and sincerely, which they did, and no more is to be heard of the unhappy parodist, who presently returned to the United States.

In Paris, Lewis looked up a few friends—Ramon Guthrie, Marc Connelly, Allan Updegraff—and again showed Blackman the expected sights—Notre Dame, the Louvre, the Eiffel Tower, Montmartre—and then left "for a regular hustling American Tourist trip" to Zurich, Lake Maggiore, Milan, Venice and Florence. They were back in Paris in ten days, and now Blackman was edified with the spectacle of a nude Josephine Baker descending on a tinseled paper moon to the stage of the Folies Bergère. He sailed for the United States from Cherbourg on March 10, the publication day of *Elmer Gantry.*

The American public did not await his obscure entry into New York Harbor to set up its clamor, and the clamor this time was a good deal noisier, if perhaps less important, than it had been over *Main Street.* Harcourt, Brace & Company, of course, did everything in its power to encourage the clamor. For weeks before the publication of the novel, the press was teased with secretive hints of the impending explosion, and the clergy was steeled for the blast. Then the Book-of-the-Month Club named it as its March selection. Announcing the novel as a work of art, the publishers then put nearly their full emphasis on the size and the sensation of the event. An early publicity release was headed "What it Means to Manufacture the First Edition of *Elmer Gantry,*" and it provided statistics on amounts of paper, thread, glue, board, cloth, and ink, both black and orange—black for the text, orange for the cover. (The approach was not inappropriate, since, as Lewis tells us in the novel, "Elmer was ever a lover of quantity.") The novel was advertised on five enormous billboards of the General Outdoor Advertising Company in New York, and in May of the following year, when the General Conference of the Methodist Church assembled in Kansas City, on forty-nine billboards including, in the center of the city, thirteen that were illuminated.

The book, to the great advantage of its sales, was immediately banned in Boston, and the ban brought to something of a climax in a fanfare of newspaper stories across the country, the entire Boston censorship folly; and bans of one kind or another—from the simple refusal of public librarians to put it on their shelves, to announcements by booksellers that they would not sell it, to wholesale municipal bans—extended from Kansas City to Camden, from Boston to Glasgow. Every ban provided the publishers with the least expensive form of promotion.

News stories of every kind developed out of the publication of the book and the character of the author. The Boston *Transcript* announced that "it is neither wrong nor unjust to accuse Lewis of being one of the greatest egoists in the world today"; he was invited to a lynching party in Virginia;

one cleric suggested that a prison sentence of five years was clearly in order. Letters of abuse cluttered his mail. Some were signed, others were nameless. An example of the nameless is as follows:

> Some of us who try to live clean lives and hope to leave behind us footprints on the sands of time not to our discredit—consider your book the nastiest—vilest—most immoral piece of writing put before modern civilization. We think that the author and publishers who will put such a book into the hands of the general public deserve the fate or worse! of the preacher Shallard described in the book.

An example of the signed variety is more terse: "Have just read your *Elmer Gantry,* it's rotten. I think you are entitled to the chair ahead of Judd Gray."

In April, in a resolution supporting the Anti-Saloon League of New York State, the Rev. Dr. Otho F. Bartholow declared at the annual session of the New York East Conference, "The Methodist Church is cordially hated, not only by the class represented by Mr. Sinclair Lewis and the rum organizations, but also by every evil organization of every kind whatsoever," while, two weeks later, the graduating class of New York University voted Sinclair Lewis its favorite author. An item in an Ohio newspaper (reprinted as a publicity release) ran as follows:

> Trouble in the home of Leo Roberts, general manager of the Roberts Coal and Supply Company, began when his wife brought home a copy of *Elmer Gantry* and he burned it as undesirable reading matter, according to Mrs. Roberts at a hearing Wednesday before Judge Bostwick of Probate Court, when Roberts was ordered to a private sanitarium for a short rest, after his wife, Mrs. Margaret Roberts, 1671 Franklin Park South, charged him with lunacy.

Very soon ministers' wives were seeking divorces on the grounds that their husbands were Elmer Gantrys, i.e., adulterers; and ministers themselves were demanding that colleagues too attentive to their choir singers be investigated. In less than six weeks, over 175,000 copies had been sold,* and by that time even the least literate of churchgoers had heard the novel discussed from the pulpit of his church.

Never has a profession cooperated so zealously with a publisher as the clergy, of all denominations and faiths, in 1927. Generally, of course, the novel was the subject of denunciation: "slime, pure slime," "sordid and cowardly," "venomous," "unprincipled," "an insult," "filthy"—these were the terms of abuse. The evangelist Billy Sunday called Lewis "Satan's cohort" and shouted that he "would have soaked Mr. Lewis so hard there would have been nothing left for the devil to levy on." Lewis was not only

* The sales of *Elmer Gantry* in its hard-cover form reached 257,146 copies, about 4,000 more than *Babbitt;* but its total sale of 616,303 copies is nearly 1,000,000 less than *Babbitt,* about 500,000 less than *Main Street,* and about 100,000 less than *Arrowsmith.* (June 30, 1959.)

"Mencken's minion," he was Judas. Yet here and there, quieter clerical voices suggested that, while Elmer Gantry was a monster, the novel itself was a useful tonic. In Kansas City, Reverend L. M. Birkhead defended the book even while a number of members of his congregation were detaching themselves in indignation. The Reverend Sparks, pastor of the Congregational Church in Sauk Centre, deplored the book and announced that the town was ashamed of its famous son. The Reverend Percy Ladd, in Denver, said, "I met him in Denver last summer and he appeared to me as being religious and sincere," but the novel was a betrayal of those clergymen whom he had come to their city to interview. Lewis had been in nearly every city in the United States, but Denver, Colorado, happened to be one of the few which he had never seen.

The pulpit fury raged for a year and was not only dutifully reported by the press but frequently supplemented in editorial columns. Very early the New York *Times* amused itself by coupling the fact of Mencken's several ecstatic reviews of the novel with that other fact that the novel was dedicated to him—a hilarious instance of "back-scratching." The most famous and widely quoted editorial comment came from William Allen White, a lost friend:

> Sinclair Lewis stood in the pulpit of a Kansas City church last spring and defied God to strike him dead. So far as Sinclair Lewis, the artist, is concerned in the book *Elmer Gantry,* God took him at his word.*

To these observations, Clarence Darrow remarked, "Just wait and see. Dead, huh!"

A letter to the New York *Times,* widely reprinted, came from Will Rogers:

> When I am playing in a town and it looks like there is not going to be much of a house, I announce through the papers that that night I will read passages from *Elmer Gantry,* the Baptist sheik, and the house will be packed with Methodist and Presbyterian women. Old Elmer sure had it.
>
> Yours,
> *Will*

In the meantime, in a widely syndicated newspaper article called "The New American People" that was itself the cause of a good deal of editorial comment, H. G. Wells based his observations of American culture on the novels of Sinclair Lewis, including *Elmer Gantry,* as though they were the most reliable of social documents.

Not all reviewers of the novel agreed, but most of those who were

* There is no indication that White and Lewis ever met again, but in 1930, White wrote Harcourt as follows: "Remember me affectionately to Red Lewis, who is the best all-around, single-handed, catch-as-catch-can, no-holds-barred, Greco-Roman writing man that the American Continent has produced, willing to meet all comers. *Elmer Gantry* fouled him but he knocked out all the rest, God bless him."

favorably impressed with it praised it for the accuracy and the fullness of its reporting. Elmer Davis, H. L. Mencken, W. E. Woodward, Carl Van Doren, Joseph Wood Krutch, T. K. Whipple all praised it in major reviews. Most of these men were, to be sure, Lewis's friends; but some friends, old friends, among them William Lyon Phelps and Rebecca West, deplored the book. Other major reviewers who did not like it included Robert Littell and Heywood Broun. The New York *Evening Post,* which published the Woodward review, published in the same issue another review, by the famous evangelical preacher Reverend John Roach Straton, who denounced the book as the product of a "disordered . . . imagination," and declared flatly that "there never was such a man as Elmer Gantry." In response to this declaration, Paxton Hibben devoted his review in the *New Masses* to a list of known debaucheries by clergymen whom he named, the first of them being Henry Ward Beecher. English reviewers, while astonished by the book, were almost unanimously enthusiastic, but the sharply divided opinion of New York reviewers was reflected in the provincial American reviews. If Dorothy F. Gilman in Boston found the novel grossly distorted, Fanny Butcher in Chicago called it Sinclair Lewis's best novel, and Bernard DeVoto, still in Evanston, believed that it marked an advance in Lewis's fictional art. *Time* magazine amused itself as follows:

> Author Sinclair Lewis . . . has made another large roundup of grunting, whining, roaring, mewing, driveling, snouting creatures—of fiction—which, like an infuriated swineherd, he can beat, goad, tweak, tail-twist, eye-jab, belly-thwack, spatter with sty-filth and consign to perdition.

Enthusiasts invoked a whole new pantheon of literary ancestors for Lewis, as his comparable predecessors became Boccaccio, Rabelais, Voltaire, Swift, Samuel Butler, and Anatole France. In all the uproar, there was almost nothing that one can call criticism, and there has been very little since. It is perhaps for this reason that one thinks of *Elmer Gantry* as until recently Lewis's most neglected novel.

The novel brings to its extreme the satiric method that began in *Main Street* as that early strain of youthful, idealistic optimism vanishes almost completely from the stated text. In *Elmer Gantry,* any drama exists in the immediate victory of the worst over the weakest (who are the best), or in the conflict of the bad to survive among the worst: all is corrupt. In this extraordinarily full account of every form of religious decay, nothing is missing except all religion and all humanity. As there are no impediments to Elmer's barbarous rise from country boob to influential preacher, so there are no qualifications of the image of barbarity. On the very fringes of the narrative, among his scores of characters, Lewis permits a few shadowy figures of good to appear—Bruno Zechlin and Jim Lefferts, the amiable skeptics who are routed before they are permitted to enter the action; Andrew Pengilly, a humane preacher who asks the most striking question in the novel ("Mr. Gantry, why don't you believe in God?") but who himself no more enters the conflict than his question enters the intellectual context; and finally, Frank Shallard, who does come and go in the story, an honest human being, but one so weak that he presents no challenge to Elmer, serves only to illustrate the ruthlessness of Elmer's power.

The action of *Elmer Gantry* is an entirely one-way affair. Like most of Lewis's novels, it is a loosely episodic chronicle that breaks down into three large parts, each nearly independent of the others. In each part, Elmer's progress is colored and in two of them threatened by his relation with a woman, but from each, Elmer emerges triumphant. The first part takes us through his Baptist education, his ordination, his first pulpit and his escape from Lulu; the second takes us through his career as an evangelist with the fantastic Sharon Falconer; the third takes us through his experience of New Thought * and his rise in Methodism, together with the decline of his marriage to Cleo and his escape from Hettie, who threatens to bring him to public ruin but who is herself routed as, in the final sentence, Elmer promises that "We shall yet make these United States a moral nation."

It should not be supposed that the frank prominence in *Elmer Gantry* of sexual appetite—a rare enough element in a Lewis novel—or the fact that it several times seems to threaten Elmer's otherwise unimpeded success, in any way provides the kind of dramatized counterpoint on the absence of which we are remarking, or that it in any way serves to introduce an element of human tenderness that qualifies Elmer's brutal nakedness. On the contrary, it is an integral part of his inhumanity and an integral part of the inhumanity of the religious environment within which he exists. Indeed, of all the forms of relationship that the novel presents, the sexual relation is most undilutedly brutish, and it is perhaps the chief element in that animus of revulsion that motivates the creation of this cloacal world. Finally, its identification with the quality of Elmer's religious activity is made explicit in the climactically phantasmagoric scene in which Sharon capitulates to Elmer before an altar where she associates herself, in a ritual invocation, with all goddesses of fertility. The extravagant absurdity of this scene is underlined by the absence in it of any candid recognition of human need or of human fulfillment. The travesty that it makes of both the sexual and the religious experience is of course to be associated with the temper of orgiastic evangelism with which the book is full. Dramatically, however, it must be associated with such an earlier scene, as homely as this one is horrendous, in which a deaf old retired preacher and his wife

* His old editor on *Nautilus*, Mrs. Elizabeth Towne, announced to the press that she was not disturbed by the probability that Lewis had modeled his New Thought female after her.

are going to bed after twenty-seven years of marriage, and the whole of that experience of twenty-seven years is equated with the recollection of an "old hoss." The two scenes, the extravagantly repulsive and the devastatingly barren, supplement one another; they represent the extremes of the nightmare image of a world that, totally empty of human value, monstrously, and without relief, parodies the reality.

If the narrative method of loose chronicle, without sustained dramatic conflict, is the primary means to this end, certain orders of technical detail contribute their part. It has been complained, for example, that there is a coarsening of Lewis's style in this novel, and that his view of the hinterland threatens to fall into a kind of cracker-barrel stereotype. Both charges are true, but it can be argued that both qualities make possible the kind of effect we are trying to describe. *Elmer Gantry* is the noisiest novel in American literature, the most *braying, guffawing, belching* novel that we have, and it is its prose that sets this uproar going; if we are to have a novel filled with jackasses and jackals, let them, by all means, bray and guffaw. On the same grounds, one may defend the "By crackee, by jimminy" crudities of the physical environment within which this noise goes on, this imbecilic articulateness, only pointing out in addition that Lewis's old ability to invoke a concrete world—the smell of Pullman car dust, the food at a church picnic, the contents of the library of a small Methodist bishop —is still sufficiently in force to cram full the outlines of his stereotypes.

One can go further. At each of his three climaxes, Lewis abdicates such sense of the dramatic scene as he may have had and retreats into melodrama: once to an inversion of the farmer's daughter situation, once to a catastrophic fire, finally to a cops-and-robbers treatment of some petty criminals who have attempted to play the badger game on old Elmer. In each situation, through bad timing, through a refusal to develop even a suggestion of suspense, any potential human elements in the situation are sacrificed to the melodramatic stereotype. And yet, out of this very weakness, cumulatively, arises again the whole impression of bare brutality which is, after all, the essential social observation. As the drama is only half realized, so the social observation is only half true, but in its partiality resides such force as it has.

Most novels operate through a conflict, dramatized in a plot, of social and individual interest, and the more sustained the pressures of the plot, the more likely is the individual to be forced into a position of new self-awareness, which prominently contains an awareness of his relation to his society. A certain dynamic interchange has been at work, and the result is that the historical forces which contain the individual's experience have been personalized in his awareness. What is most characteristic of the novels of Sinclair Lewis, and above all of *Elmer Gantry,* is that there are no such dynamics of social action, that we are presented with a static, unpersonalized image—and that *there* lies its horror.

A character so open to self-deception as Elmer is not in a position to estimate the forces that have made him so: to him, society is given, accepted, used. Elmer Gantry was raised in an important if stultifying American tradition: the Protestantism of the hinterland; and Sinclair Lewis gives us a complete and devastating account of it that extends over four pages.

> The church and Sunday School at Elmer's village . . . had nurtured in him a fear of religious machinery which he could never lose. . . . That small pasty-white Baptist church had been the center of all his emotions, aside from hell-raising, hunger, sleepiness and love. And even these emotions were represented in the House of the Lord . . . the arts and the sentiments and the sentimentalities—they were for Elmer perpetually associated only with the church . . . all the music which the boy Elmer had ever heard was in church. The church provided all his painting and sculpture. . . . From the church came all his profounder philosophy . . . literary inspiration . . . here too the church had guided him. In Bible stories, in the words of the great hymns, in the anecdotes which the various preachers quoted, he had his only knowledge of literature. . . . The church, the Sunday School, the evangelistic orgy, choir-practice, raising the mortgage, the delights of funerals, the snickers in back pews or in the other room at weddings—they were . . . a mold of manners to Elmer . . . Sunday School text cards . . . they gave him a taste for gaudy robes, for marble columns and the purple-broidered palaces of kings, which was later to be of value in quickly habituating himself to the more decorative homes of vice. . . . And always the three chairs that stood behind the pulpit, intimidating stiff chairs of yellow plush and carved oak borders, which, he was uneasily sure, were waiting for the Father, the Son, and the Holy Ghost. He had, in fact, got everything from the church and Sunday School, except, perhaps, any longing whatever for decency and kindness and reason.

And having neither decency nor kindness nor reason (as the novel contains no animated examples of these humane virtues), Elmer is necessarily unaware of the history in which he is involved.

That history, perhaps no larger than it is beautiful in our tradition, is nevertheless considerable, and Sinclair Lewis was aware of it even if, because he had no alternatives, he could not let his characters become so. The whole brutally accurate conception of R. H. Tawney, which coupled business success and salvation, and then, in popular culture, began to pay dividends on the "saved" soul; the obvious connection between the puritan repressions (in Mencken's sense) and the orgiastic outbursts of middle-border evangelism; the Gospel of Service (made in Zenith) becoming the equivalent of the Gospels—all this is in the author's mind as he creates his characters, but the very nature of his creation prohibits it from in any way sharing his knowledge. The result is that the Lewis character cannot separate itself from the Lewis society; and this, in the dynamics of fiction, means that the Lewis character *has* no character apart from the society in which he is embedded, and that therefore the Lewis society is not a society at all, but a machine, or a parody, or a poetic-satiric vision.

That vision, however impressive or outrageous one may find it, is static, since it lacks a certain reverberating largeness that would animate the concretely conceived situations, a largeness that characterizes all great art, including great satiric art. This quality even a partisan could not claim that Sinclair Lewis had. Quite justly, Robert Cantwell described him as one "who thought of his writing not in terms of its momentary inspirations and the pressure of living that played through him and upon him, but in terms of the accomplishment of a foreknown task"; and quite plausibly, Maxwell Geismar wrote that "Just as there is really no sense of vice in Lewis's literary world, there is no true sense of virtue. Just as there is practically no sense of human love in the whole range of Lewis's psychological values, and no sense of real hatred—there is no genuine sense of human freedom." Most of this indictment one may allow, but if we are speaking specifically of *Elmer Gantry,* we would wish to insist on two of the items that these descriptions deny him: "the pressure of living that played through him and upon him," and the "hatred."

Elmer Gantry is a work of almost pure revulsion. It seems to shudder and to shake with loathing of that which it describes. The very fact that the novelist must create the image of the thing he loathes, in order to express his loathing, points to the peculiar imaginative animus that motivates this novel. We can speculate about its sources: Lewis's own early evangelistic impulse, his dedication to the missionary field now turning in upon itself; the lonely, goofy boy at Oberlin, himself pushing the handles of a handcar (as Elmer Gantry does) to get to a rural Sunday school where, without conspicuous success, he doled out Bible stories; the poor fool of the hinterland at New Haven, who had never been given more by the hinterland than the dubious gift of deriding it, and therefore of having to love it. Perhaps such speculations are not much to the point. The point is only that in no novel does Sinclair Lewis more clearly announce his loathing of the social environment with which he is concerned, and in no novel does he make it more mandatory that we remain within the terrifying limits of that environment.

Sinclair Lewis is not unlike Elmer Gantry. The vicious circle in this picture exists, of course, in the fact that Elmer remakes society in precisely the terms that society has already made him. No one can break out; everyone, including the novelist, spins more madly in the mechanical orbit.

The novelist trapped in his own hallucination of the world as a trap: this seems to be the final observation that we can make. But it is not quite final. Finally, we are left with the hallucination of the novels themselves, with their monstrous images of what we both are and are not, their nearly fabulous counter-icons in our culture.

"The book I wrote," Sinclair Lewis told a reporter in Paris on the day after its publication, "is what I saw." It is useless to argue that he did not see enough. He saw and listened and heard, and from the whole mass of data he selected only those details that would serve to create the half-truth at which he aimed. From what he saw and heard came the composite character of Elmer himself, a composite made up in large part of traits observed in the Reverend Stidger and in the career and performance of Reverend John Roach Straton in New York (the very accents of his pulpit style come over into Elmer's rant). What he did not observe was any literary tradition: once more he had created an "original."

All through the nineteenth century, in both England and America, there had been novels about ministers, many of them written by women. Winston Churchill's *Inside of the Cup* and Mrs. Humphry Ward's *Robert Elsmere* are characteristic: stories of sincere believers whose struggle is between conventionally literal and socially liberal interpretations of the Gospels. In the novels of "Mark Rutherford" in England and Harold Frederic (*The Damnation of Theron Ware*) in America, the process of liberation goes further, into a loss of faith and the relinquishment of the priestly role. The Frederic novel Lewis knew well, but nothing of its complex ironies and nothing of the naïve character of its hero came over into *Elmer Gantry,* which, from the outset, exposes a cheating, calculating brute who is as incapable of faith as he is of thought. One scene, with its atmosphere of aesthetic sensuosity, may have suggested to Lewis his scene of ritualistic adultery, but nothing more.

The background of *Elmer Gantry* is the real religious activity of America in evangelistic circles and the attitude of the nineteen twenties toward it. That the religious life in the United States had fallen into a condition of lassitudinous (and enthusiastic) decay is apparent. Harold Stearns could find no one to write the chapter on religion that he had planned for *Civilization in the United States.*

> ... it was really difficult to get them to talk about it at all. Almost unanimously, when I did manage to procure an opinion from them, they said that real religious feeling in America had disappeared, that the church had become a purely social and political institution, that the country is in the grip of what Anatole France has aptly called Protestant clericalism, and that, finally, they weren't interested in the topic.

And one is reminded that Tocqueville, almost a hundred years before, searching for the strength of America in her material resources, found it, rather, in her churches, and that his conclusion was that when America ceased to be good, she would cease to be strong. What the Lewis novel pictures, in part, is the confusion of these two interests, and the corruption of both, that Tocqueville named in *Democracy in America.*

Ever since their first encounter, Lewis had been playing Mencken's game with him: the derision of the clergy. In June of 1924, in his "Clinical Notes," Mencken belabored the young clergyman who entered the church not because of religious conviction but because this "spiritual" alliance with American commercial ambitions was shrewd. An advertisement of 1925, announcing "Salvation and Five Per Cent," was the subject of an article by Gilbert Seldes, and it represented the gross extremity in American thinking that Mencken liked to pillory in the "Americana" section of the *Mercury,* a portion of that periodical that Lewis enjoyed as wholeheartedly as thousands of undergraduates. Mencken's indictment extended far beyond American religious life to American culture in general. In 1926, writing of Ring Lardner, he said:

> His baseball players and fifth-rate pugilists, beginning in his first stories as harmless jackasses, gradually convert themselves into loathsome scoundrels. The same change shows itself in Sinclair Lewis; it is difficult, even for an American, to contemplate the American without yielding to something hard to distinguish from moral indignation.

In the same series of *Prejudices,* even while Lewis was at work on his book, Mencken put forth his call for such a book:

> Worse and more incredible still, [contemporary novels] neglect the most American of all Americans, the very *Ur-Amerikaner*—to wit, the malignant moralist, the Christian turned cannibal, the snouting and preposterous Puritan. Where is there the American novel in which he is even half limned? There are, to be sure, glimpses of him in *The Song of the Lark,* by Willa Cather, and in *Babbitt* . . . though the Puritan Father lies embalmed magnificently in the pages of Hawthorne, his heir and assign of the present day, the high-powered uplifter, the prophet of harsh and unenforceable laws, the incurable reformer and nuisance—this sweet fellow yet awaits his anatomist.
>
> What a novel is in him! Indeed, what a shelf of novels! For he has as many forms as there are varieties of human delusion. Sometimes he is a hireling of the Anti-Saloon League, sworn to Law Enforcement. Sometimes he is a strict Sabbatarian, bawling for the police whenever he detects his neighbor washing bottles or varnishing the Ford on Sunday morning. Again he is a vice crusader, chasing the scarlet lady with fierce Christian shouts. Yet again he is a Comstock, wearing out his eyes in the quest for smut. He may even be a female. . . . Whatever his form, he is tremendously grotesque and tremendously amusing—and always he drips with national juices, always he is as thoroughly American as a bootlegger or a college yell. If he exists at all in other lands, it is only in rudimentary and aberrant forms. Try to imagine a French Wayne B. Wheeler, or a Spanish Billy Sunday, or a

German William Jennings Bryan. It is as impossible as imagining a Coolidge in the Rome of Julius.

Elmer Gantry more than answered this call. And Mencken, who was to write that Calvin Coolidge, if he was remembered at all, would be remembered only as a footnote to the fancy of Sinclair Lewis, was enchanted. *"Voltaire! Not since Voltaire . . . !"* he exclaimed, and Lewis had, in a way and momentarily, become "Mencken's minion." But only apparently. When, in September of 1927, *The Nation* tried to characterize Lewis, the very antitheses in the description implied the continuing difference:

> Nature as a novelist was never in a more paradoxical mood than when she invented the torrid, rich, and variegated character of Sinclair Lewis, proletarian plutocrat, bourgeois gypsy, patriotic expatriate, unmannerly critic of manners, and loud-speaking champion of the subdued voice.

The patriotic expatriate, lonely in France without his Kansan preacher, spent a week wandering about Touraine contemplating châteaux while the sales of his novel, pouring out its American juices, mounted and mounted. No novel had ever sold in such quantities in Kansas, and Sinclair Lewis, with nothing else to do, drifted aimlessly back to alien Paris.

9

"HE IS CONSTANTLY making plans that never materialize," wrote Charles Shaw in *Vanity Fair* for November 1927. In mid-March a number of such plans were in the making. He was writing to his friends that he would stay in Europe for the winter, that he would spend the summer quietly in the Tyrol or in the Pyrenees, to neither of which he was to go. Then he hired a car and a driver and invited Ramon Guthrie to motor to Spain with him, and when Guthrie agreed they drove instead to Venice, where they remained until April 10. In Venice, amid the comforts of the Danielli, Lewis talked to Guthrie about a projected novel to be called *The Man Who Sought God,* the "labor novel" that was never to materialize. Its hero was still a man like Eugene Debs, who lived by "the God within" him and was persecuted accordingly by the forces of economic reaction. And Lewis would talk about the Sacco-Vanzetti case which, in that year, commanded the attention of the world, and in which Lewis, while taking no active part, saw an analogous persecution. Later, he would solicit Guthrie's help with the labor novel project.

But now Guthrie felt that he had to get back to his own writing in France, and they parted. Alone again, Lewis turned south and east, and stayed for a week at the Grand Hotel Imperial in Dubrovnik, Yugoslavia. He wrote his publishers and his friends that he was feeling "fine," more "serene" than he had felt for two years, that he had completely recovered from the exhausting effort of writing *Elmer Gantry.* From Dubrovnik, too, he wrote to H. G. Wells to thank him for his support of the novel, and he conjectured that, although "Rebecca roasted the book," with Wells's "imprimatur & Arnold Bennett's . . . I shall struggle on." In the meantime, Harcourt kept him informed by cable and letter of the novel's progress. There had been a good deal of interest in dramatic rights, first from Laurence Stallings with Arthur Hopkins as producer, but then, definitely, and the contract drawn, from Bayard Veiller with Robert Milton as producer. A Denver correspondent named Henry Chisholm assured him that the district attorney should incarcerate him either in the penitentiary or in a madhouse. Indifferent, Lewis went on to Corfu and then to Athens to look at ruins, and then back to Vienna and to Munich and, by May 30, once more to Paris. Charles A. Lindbergh had arrived there in "The Spirit of St. Louis" on May 21, and Lewis cabled Harcourt, "Why dont Grosset [the reprint firm] start intensive campaign Trail Hawk which is really story Lindbergh. Can hook up with fact we born forty miles apart." *Elmer Gantry* had passed the 200,000 mark.

Now what? He telephoned Ramon Guthrie in a distant village in Dordogne and told him that, while "a specialist in Vienna had warned him that he was facing a complete collapse unless he entered a hospital immediately," what he really wanted to do was to have Guthrie come to Paris and set off on a ten-day walking trip in Alsace with him. Guthrie obliged, they entrained for Strasbourg, then rode and walked to Basel, entrained for Freiburg and walked in the Schwarzwald. Lewis carried a rucksack that, except for a toilet kit, contained only a Bible, an *Imitation of Christ,* and a copy of *The Bookman* which he presently discarded. On the train, he had armed himself with a whole stack of Tauchnitz editions of novels by E. Phillips Oppenheimer, and, glancing swiftly through these, he had tossed them one after the other out of the train window. Reduced to more essential fare, he substituted beer for cognac and seemed, for ten days, happy.*

They talked more of the labor novel, which would take as its text "Blessed are they which are persecuted for righteousness' sake." There was to be a lawyer, modeled after Clarence Darrow, who would defend the persecuted hero, and an "international waiter" (waiters, like hotels, were nearly obsessive concerns with Lewis, and his earliest "researches" on the labor novel had involved long talks with a Morrison Hotel waiter in Chicago) whose cynicism would serve as a foil to the simple idealism of the hero.

> "God is the *lacrimae rerum,*" he said, "the eternal tears of things." . . . the hero of the labor novel was to be a workingman who came to social and political awareness flounderingly, in the course of his search for what he himself would perhaps never know to be God. Inevitably he was to run afoul of Church and State on the charge that "he stirreth up the people." But the final crisis of the story was to be his inner struggle against an insidious messiah complex that threatened to destroy his humility and integrity.

* The walking trips with Ramon Guthrie in this summer are reflected in *Dodsworth* in the walking trip that Sam takes in the Bernese Oberland with Ross Ireland, although Ross Ireland seems to be modeled on Frazier Hunt rather than on Guthrie. This trip takes place just before Sam meets Edith Cortright in Venice, just as the last trip with Guthrie took place immediately before Lewis's meeting with Dorothy Thompson in Berlin.

Then, before mid-June, they were back in Paris.

What now?

> Oh, he was lonely, this big friendly man, Sam Dodsworth, and he wanted a man to whom he could talk and boast and lie, he wanted a woman with whom he could be childish and hurt and comforted, and so successful and rich was he that he had neither, and he sought them, helpless, his raw nerves exposed. So searching, he strolled after dinner to the Select . . .

So Lewis wandered about the cafés, encountering Americans. He met the Stephen Vincent Benéts, who reported that one night "we drank a great deal of Vouvray and sang spirituals—or rather a red-bearded gentleman named George Slocombe sang and the rest of us howled. . . ." He met the William Lyon Phelpses and took them to dinner in Montmartre. Ramon Guthrie remembers this occasion as illustrative of his great capacity for patience with bores if they were not pretentious, and Mrs. Phelps was an unpretentious bore. Lewis listened politely to her endless and tiresome small talk and finally announced that he had recently been bitten by a rabbit. Mrs. Phelps was incredulous, but he said, "Oh yes, you can be bitten by a rabbit. I have been bitten by a rabbit," and so on, entering rather than ending the stream of trivia. He met the Ludwig Lewisohns, who reported,

> He was in flight from himself; he tried to compensate by his immense vaudeville talent. Why? He had written *Babbitt* and *Arrowsmith* and I agreed with him with all my heart that the sharp youngsters who sniffed at him as a mere superjournalist succeeded in making asses only of themselves. He seemed to have no inner certainty, no balance, no serenity, nothing between heaven and earth to which he could withdraw for quietude or healing. He did and said things that, as I well knew, outraged his true self. . . . Sinclair Lewis at the height of his powers, wealthy, world-famous and still young depressed us . . .

He frequently wrote his wife. Divorce or no divorce?—he could not make up his mind. Never before had he been at such loose ends, so undone in himself. What now?

In mid-June he persuaded the mistress of a London friend to set up an establishment with him in the Rue de Varize at Auteuil, and to Mencken and others he wrote that he had taken the flat for three months. He invited the Lewisohns to a house-warming party on the twenty-third of June. His companion, of Irish-French blood, was known no less for the voraciousness of her sexual appetites than for her desire to obtain such prestige as an association with Sinclair Lewis could give her. It was impossible! Before the end of June he had detached himself from her embraces, fled back to the Guthries, begging them to go to Munich with him, and they left together on July 1.

On July 2 he suddenly wrote his wife that he was returning to the United States and would she join him on Nantucket. On July 4 he wrote his publisher with the same news: "I go from here to Dresden & Berlin, return to Paris, & sail on I don't yet know which boat." On July 6 the Munich party broke up. "When he saw us off for Paris, he seemed so forlorn . . . , so in need of help and companionship, that only the necessity of my earning a living kept us from changing our minds about leaving him." But his train left almost immediately after the Guthries had gone, and on July 8 he met Dorothy Thompson in Berlin. On July 24 he cabled his publishers, "Staying Europe several months more. Please inform Grace." He stayed for thirteen months, and came back with his second wife.

Dorothy Thompson was handsome and brilliant, the most popular newswoman in Europe, and the least adequately photographed. Her beauty was of her self rather than of her face alone, a shining expression of her warmth and vitality and intelligence. She had candid, hazel eyes, was fair and of imposing presence, with nothing petite or mincing in her gait, impulsive and generous, of a relaxed self-confidence that held no shred of self-importance. She was perfectly at ease with men, and with men of power who were no more than her equals, and she enjoyed their company. Her laughter was irrepressible, as were her opinions, which were as multitudinous as they were firm. She enjoyed the waltzes of *Der Rosenkavalier* and good food, was contemptuous of most newspapers, liked to cook, and did not readily tolerate fools, or, in the catalogue of her friend Dale Warren, "cant, hypocrisy, sloth, shiftlessness, willful stupidity, resignation, and whatsoever is cheap, shoddy, and meretricious."

Her tastes had been Europeanized, but she was proud of her background, which was American in a plain and spare way. The daughter of an upstate New York Methodist minister, she had been educated at Syracuse University, then had taken a job with the Buffalo headquarters of the Woman's Suffrage Party and become one of its most effective (and disputatious) speakers. She needed to earn more money to help her younger brother and sister through college, and went to New York to write publicity. In 1920 she acted on a long-held desire to go to Europe to become a newspaper correspondent, and although she had only $150 after paying for her passage, and although she knew very little about journalism, her pluck, her forthrightness, her gift for making friends, her ability to manage the language, and a series of fortunate "breaks" found her successfully filling one assignment after another until, when she met Sinclair Lewis, after four years in Vienna and four more in Berlin, she was well-known through Central Europe, the Berlin correspondent to the Philadelphia *Public Ledger* and the New York *Evening Post,* and Chief of the Central European Service in Berlin.

A number of newspaper people have claimed credit for the introduction, but no one argues as to the place. The German Foreign Minister, Gustav Stresemann, was in the habit of holding a weekly press conference and tea party for foreign correspondents, and Dorothy Thompson's own recollection was that R. H. Knickerbocker, the New York *Times* man in Berlin, brought Sinclair Lewis to such an affair at the Foreign Ministry on July 8, 1927, and presented him to her. The next day was her thirty-third birthday and she was planning a party, to which she invited Sinclair Lewis. He amused her. And she cabled Philadelphia about his arrival. He came, her story runs, with a Rotary button in his lapel, and carrying a rucksack containing a heavily annotated Bible. He had hoped to remain incognito, had signed the Ministry register as S. Lewis, correspondent of the *Volta Review,* and he was writing a new novel on the churches. When the Foreign Minister was unable to appear, Lewis volunteered to take his place if questions were limited to Franco-German relations. "Lewis tries to remain incognito because, as he says, he does not want to be interrupted in his work by being feted in a land where his works outsell most German books." He had, it would appear, recovered his good spirits.

If she found him amusing, he found her enchanting. Only a day or two before, she had received from Budapest a decree that ended her unhappy, four-year marriage to an irresponsible if fascinating young Hungarian intellectual, Josef Bard, and her party was therefore a double celebration. Later she was to write him about that first occasion in her apartment.

> I will never forget how you looked, or how I felt, that first night. I felt a terrific indignation. I thought, "My God, how he suffers." I had suffered pretty brutally myself, and was still suffering pretty brutally, but suddenly I wanted to say: Let's stop suffering. Suddenly I felt oddly gay.

Sinclair Lewis proposed marriage to her that night, and to her laughter he said, "I am going to propose to you every time I see you from now on, in public and in private." Two days later Lewis's present Berlin publisher, Ernst Rowohlt, gave him a party which he insisted that she attend. When he was called upon for a speech, he arose and, ignoring everyone else, looked at her and said, "Dorothy, will you marry me?" That was the totality of his speech.

He was as good as his word. They met constantly and he constantly proposed. Fortunately, his wife, with Casanova's prospects looking up, had already determined on a divorce. On August 7, Lewis was to write her with the request that she divorce him, but before his letter reached her, she had already written him to make the same request. (When her next letter arrived, signed Grace Hegger, he unjustly appended the note, "dramatic and foolish as ever.") In the meantime, there had, of course, been no attempt at that incognito role that he had initially announced. On July 16 he spoke at the Berlin-American Club in emphatic denunciation of the "judicial unjustice" meted out to Sacco and Vanzetti by the American courts and incidentally gave out the news that he would spend most of the winter in Berlin.

On July 18, when workers' riots broke out in Vienna, Dorothy Thompson decided abruptly to fly there, and when Lewis heard that she was going, he leaped into a taxi and followed her to the airport. He had grave doubts about flying and had never flown, but now he got in beside her and said once more, "Dorothy, marry me, will you?" Frances Gunther, the wife of John Gunther, who had come to see her off, was pressed into service as a chaperone, and the plane took off with Lewis grimly holding onto the arm rests, saying, "Dorothy, will you . . . ?" In Vienna she said that she would begin to take his proposals seriously if he would write his impressions of the riots for the *Public Ledger* syndicate, and although the revolution had been abortive—nothing remained but to bury the dead—he agreed. The first of his stories was about the flight itself, the second about the mass funeral. These dispatches caused a considerable sensation in journalistic circles, and while there was no revolution to report, some excitement had developed when Lewis, charged by a dishonest news photographer with giving him a bad check, had a brief skirmish with the police.

In some ways, the Vienna excursion seems to have determined matters, for on August 7 they went to England for a walking trip of four weeks in Shropshire and Cornwall. Lewis had been doing no writing, presumably because all his intention was centered on the pursuit. Dorothy Thompson enjoyed him. Like many other women, she soon forgot his ugliness and was made to feel that charm which arose in part from his clowning, in part from the incandescence of his mind, in largest part from the sense that he could give a woman of his own utter helplessness without her, the sense that only she could save him from despair and give his life direction. Yet she had doubts about him. She did not particularly want to marry him. Very early in the relationship her letters to him echo with phrases such as these: "To love you is like trying to love Undine, something slippery about you" . . . "To try to love you is like trying to love mercury, but I think the astrologists are right in saying that Mercury is a beneficent god" . . . "But you are a creature of air." But she did love him, and now for nearly six weeks they vanish together from the documents.

After four weeks in England, they continued walking—now in the Rhineland with the Guthries, whom they had summoned to meet them at Cologne. At Mainz, Dorothy Thompson decided that she must return to Berlin, and she left Guthrie and Lewis to wander about in the Rhineland for a few days more. There was renewed talk about the labor novel; and in their plans for it, its disconnected episodes began to take on a certain coherence. It was, Lewis felt, going to be superior to *Arrowsmith,* but he expressed doubts about his readiness to do it yet and thought that he should delay it until he had written another, quite different novel. They returned to Berlin and on September 14 Lewis wrote W. E. Woodward from the Hotel Atlantic to say that he was looking for a flat where he could settle down for the winter. He chose an establishment called Herkules-Haus.

He had for some time been promising and half-promising Mencken a story for the *Mercury* about a Babbitt who is a college classmate of President Coolidge. Now, in September, at the urging of Dorothy Thompson and Ramon Guthrie—who pointed out that all he needed to do was to write down what was already one of the interminable monologues—he wrote it in about fifteen thousand words, and having done that, he went seriously to work at a novel that he variously called *Blind Giant* or *Sunset* or *Exile,* but which would ultimately be called *Dodsworth. Neighbor,* or *The Man Who Sought God,* he would put off until he was once more in America, he told Harcourt, and would Harcourt be so good as to send copies of *Our Mr. Wrenn, The Trail of the Hawk, The Job, Free Air,* and *Main Street* to Mrs. Dorothy Thompson, 8 Händelstra., Tiergarten, Berlin? Love was not, apparently, to be without its labors for her. On October 1 he went to Paris to meet his New York attorney, Melville Cane, to discuss the possibilities of a Parisian divorce.

It was appropriate that at this point, which seemed to mark an end and a beginning, he should have attempted a summary statement of his life and at least a partial self-assessment. The particular occasion of his "Self-Portrait (Berlin, August, 1927)" was Rowohlt's request for promotion materials and the whole or parts of the sketch appeared in German newspapers. The original document, in English, found among his papers after his death, is less inaccurate than several other autobiographical accounts, but it is also less concrete. He recognizes some of his follies but none of the important ones. He attributes to himself qualities that he did not conspicuously possess, notably a steady loyalty to friends, and he neglects qualities that he conspicuously had, notably an uncritical gregariousness and concomitant loneliness. If he does not suggest that he lived under peculiar stress or even that he knew he did, he acknowledges his rootless wanderings. And when he ends, "A dull fellow, and probably unimaginative. Otherwise he would stay home and be inspired by his own vision instead of having to be aroused by new streets, new hills, new faces," he seems to be echoing the complaint of Rebecca West, made only a few months before:

> If he would sit still so that life could make any deep impression on him, if he would attach himself to the human tradition by occasionally reading a book which would set him a standard of profundity, he could give his genius a chance.

But the "Self-Portrait" makes it clear enough that "standards of profundity" were not the goals of his search.

He saw, now and then, in Berlin, people of some profundity. There was Lion Feuchtwanger, for example, who enjoyed his company and wished to dedicate a book to him. There were Thomas and Heinrich Mann. Young Erika and Klaus Mann, whose picture of the United States, where they wished now to go, was formed largely by Lewis's novels, met him, and he urged them not to go to the United States because of Prohibition. "Why should you exile yourself, voluntarily, into that dry inferno?" But most of the time he spent with journalists, Dorothy Thompson's colleagues—the Knickerbockers, the Edgar Ansel Mowrers, George Seldes, Frederic Kuh (who, when he saw him performing with his false mustache, detected "a terrific streak of adolescence"), Louis P. Lochner (who decided that Lewis was "outright stingy . . . a penny pincher" when Lewis inaccurately told him, "I never give a free copy to anybody. If anybody wants to have my books, let him buy them"). Harold Nicolson was there, and the impression remains with him that Lewis was not entirely at ease with Dorothy Thompson's newspaper friends, or with more serious intellectuals such as he, that he wandered about among them in a lost way. But he was never really "at ease" anywhere, and he was always rather "lost." The evidence seems to suggest that he was less lost in Berlin in 1927 and 1928 than he had been for a long time.

Lord Beaverbrook arrived from London with his entourage and gave a dinner party at the Adlon, the bar of which was the favorite Berlin meeting place of all the foreign correspondents. At his dinner was his Sunday columnist, Viscount Castlerosse (who said of Oscar Wilde that he was every other inch a gentleman), Lady Diana Manners, two other knighted Canadians, George Seldes, Sinclair Lewis, and Arnold Bennett. (In September, Bennett wrote to H. G. Wells of this Berlin jaunt as "a mad 4 days.") Castlerosse, writing about his Berlin encounters with Lewis several weeks later in the *Sunday Express,* said that Lewis "revered" Bennett, and George Seldes's recollection of the Adlon party bears him out. Someone asked Bennett why he had never been knighted, and Lewis demanded, "Yes, why? From now on I will call you 'Sir.' " But he changed the term to "Maestro," even as he began to take Bennett to task for writing potboilers.

> "But I am writing very decent books. No one ever complains of my work as of Lawrence's," replied Bennett.
>
> "I mean good books," said Lewis. "I mean *The Old Wives' Tale,* which is a classic—the books for which you will live forever. Some of your new books are trash in comparison, you will pardon me for saying, Maestro."

Bennett then explained that he had always wanted a yacht and when he discovered that a yacht cost thirty thousand pounds, he wrote a book that he could be sure would bring him thirty thousand pounds. And he bought the yacht. But then he found that it required another thirty thousand pounds to outfit her, and he necessarily had to write another book of the same sort. Then he discovered finally that it would require thirty thousand pounds every year to keep her afloat, and he was committed to writing one such book every year.

"Berlin sometimes reminded me of a huge railway station," Mrs. Mowrer wrote later, recalling another evening in September when much the same group assembled in Dorothy Thompson's studio. Bennett and Castlerosse and Lady Diana, trying to find Lewis after dinner ("perhaps all of us might go and see night life," Bennett recorded) were invited to the Thompson flat, and the Mowrers, who lived below, came up, too, and others. Lewis, Mrs. Mowrer recalls, did an extended hell-and-damnation sermon with reversed collar, and when Lady Diana began to sing "soldiers' ditties," "Pastor" Lewis ordered Mrs. Mowrer to play hymns at the piano and "led the choir with 'Onward Christian Soldiers.' " (His Berlin "Self-Portrait" says "that he would far rather chant the hymns of his boyhood evangelicism than the best drinking song in the world. . . .") Bennett was morose and slightly drunk, but Castlerosse was lively and urged everyone to go on to a night club. "I want to be lewd," he kept repeating. "You can be as lewd as you like," said Dorothy with amiability and determination, "but not in my flat."

Perhaps it was the same occasion, perhaps later, when Dorothy Thompson remembered that Arnold Bennett and Vincent Sheean were present. Sheean, like Dorothy Thompson, was leaving soon for Moscow for the celebration of the tenth anniversary of the Bolshevik Revolution, and he was insisting that everyone must be in Moscow for the seventh of November. Then suddenly Lewis "burst forth"—

> "Oh, you must come to Moscow for the seventh of November," he chanted, giving the sentence the obvious contour of a line by Vachel Lindsay—all about what was going to happen in Moscow on the momentous day (with a boom, boom, boom!) and how it was imperatively necessary for everybody to go there to see it. When we had recovered from this he went on and did the same thing in three other styles: Longfellow, Swinburne, Tennyson. The rhymes and metres were perfect, the parodies so keen that even the Germans did not need to be told what they were. The Tennyson parody was a triumph of ingenuity and wit, for it is always more difficult to hit off a good poet than a bad one. I have never heard anything like those improvisations; even Red could never do them so well again.

Dorothy Thompson's list of poets is a little different but her recollection is essentially the same. "We all sat with our jaws dropped. No one had ever witnessed such a tour de force, or likely ever will again. Lewis threw away, on his friends or casual companions, enough talent to have made another writer."

Theodore Dreiser was in Berlin on his way to Moscow, ill at the Adlon, and Dorothy Thompson, a warmhearted young woman, helped to take care of him. B. W. Huebsch, Lewis's old friend, had crossed on the *Mauretania* with Dreiser, and on October 28 Lewis and Huebsch sat together at his bedside, chatting and smoking. According to Helen Dreiser, it was Lewis who now found a third doctor for Dreiser when Dreiser refused to act on the advice of two others that he delay his entrance into Russia because of his respiratory infection. He waited until November 2, when Dorothy Thompson was already in Moscow. For a time Lewis had planned to accompany her, but he was "up to [his] ears in the new book" and decided to stay behind.

There were other reasons. Melville Cane had advised against a Paris divorce and later against a Berlin divorce, and in the meantime, Mrs. Lewis, who had in August agreed to go to Reno, was vacillating in New York. Suddenly Lewis decided to go to Nevada himself "and get the thing really done." He cabled Harcourt on October 22 to say that he was sailing at once; but a few days later he sent another cable to say that he was remaining in Berlin. A generous cable had come, between these two, from Mrs. Lewis in which she urged him not to interrupt his work and agreed to establish residence in Nevada in mid-January, directly Wells's holidays were over and he was back at school. Lewis unpacked his trunks and went back to work "till I get *Exile* done—remain an exile myself till then!" It had occurred to him, however, to interrupt that work and make a small book from "The Man Who Knew Coolidge" by adding five similar "drools" to the *Mercury* piece. He would wait to make that decision until he heard from Mencken. In the meantime, he had not "for years felt so serene, well, secure," and he informed Harcourt further that, because of Dorothy Thompson, he had had nothing to drink except wine and beer "for a long time now."

Dorothy Thompson left for Moscow at the end of October and they exchanged almost daily letters. She was fascinated by what she was seeing and wrote him urgently, This is extraordinary, you *should* come! you *must* come! He had conjured up for her an image of a Vermont farm that, once she married him, would be their permanent *pied-à-terre,* a pastoral paradise that would always be theirs whenever they tired of the busy world, and the picture had its charms for her. Now she wrote him occasionally of that unlikely house and told him how she had been buying linen for it. For companionship in Berlin, he had Ramon Guthrie again, for before she left, Dorothy Thompson had written him in Paris and asked him to come to Berlin during her absence—he could have her apartment—to keep Lewis company. And although he was working on *Dodsworth,* they talked more about the labor novel than about the work in progress. But even a letter (coming in a few weeks) from J. B. McNamara, a political prisoner in San Quentin who had heard of Lewis's project and urged him to pursue it, did not deflect Lewis from *Dodsworth* to write what was to be that major work. A more trivial project did.

Mencken and Nathan were both immensely amused with "The Man

Who Knew Coolidge" in its 15,000-word form, and when Alfred Harcourt and Donald Brace read it, they were equally entertained, and Lewis wanted now to expand it quickly to a work of about 60,000 words. ("Can write this stuff incredible speed and have whole mailed in four weeks. . . .") In the meantime, however, he had been upset by a change in plans for the dramatization of *Elmer Gantry*. Bayard Veiller suddenly announced that he had completed his stage adaptation and then destroyed it "because the uproar that it would cause would do the theater harm." Newspapers generally questioned his motives and wondered why it had taken him six months to discover that the novel itself had caused an uproar. Harcourt suggested to Lewis that the real motive was the fact that Veiller's tremendously successful play, *The Trial of Mary Dugan,* had been threatened by the district attorney in New York and "that some of the church people have used this as a club to scare him off *Elmer Gantry*." At any rate, when no play was forthcoming, the contract with Veiller was scrapped and a new one drawn with Patrick Kearney. Lewis, who had first wished to bring suit against Veiller, was placated.

When, on November 29, he had finished 50,000 words of the first draft of *Dodsworth,* he decided to pursue Dorothy Thompson to Moscow, and he left Berlin on that day. News of his flight had preceded him and he was greeted at the Moscow station by representatives of the Soviet Society for Cultural Relations, by a number of Russian writers, and by a brass band. The chairman of the society delivered an address of welcome and then, perhaps in the hope of eliciting praise on the occasion of the Bolshevik anniversary, asked Lewis why he had come to Moscow. "To see Dorothy," he replied. Bewildered, the chairman repeated the question. "Dorothy," he explained, "just Dorothy." It is probable that the Russians never did understand the quixotic Lewis, and equally probable that he had no great interest in understanding them, or, if he did, not at this time.

He was entertained at a dinner that evening given at the Grand Hotel by members of the American colony, which included Walter Duranty and Anna Louise Strong. He was entertained in succeeding days by official cultural groups and by the literary organizations, and he discovered that even the least of his works was available in Russian. So recently as the past July, Soviet officials had reprimanded the *Gosizdat,* the state publishing trust, for flooding the Soviet market with translations of foreign works while ignoring young Russian writers, and had pointed out that the sale of certain American writers—O. Henry, Upton Sinclair, Sinclair Lewis and Jack London—exceeded the sale of contemporary Soviet authors.*

* On November 9, Dorothy Thompson had written him: "They have jolly well pirated everything. . . . You and O. Henry are, I am told, the most popular Americans at present. Upton is falling off. People are getting bored with politics. I regret to tell you that *Mantrap* appears to be rather more popular than *Babbitt.* And it is quite true—*The Green Hat* is a serious competitor, and so is *So Big* and Fannie Hurst in her lighter moments."

Nevertheless, officials of *Gosizdat* now spontaneously asked Lewis to see them and then suggested that they would be agreeable to paying royalties on eight of his novels. Lewis, with a generosity that was not rare in him, replied that his works in themselves were of no importance. "Give their royalties to all and I'll take mine." To his surprise, the officials declared that they would be quite willing to pay royalties on all the translations from the United States that they published, but that they had no publishers' convention which would make that possible. Informally, then, they drew up the draft of such a convention, and it was agreed that the *Gosizdat* and Lewis would communicate with leading American publishers in order to fix such a convention.* In the meantime, Lewis took no royalties.

He refused to be interviewed on his impressions of Russia. In reply to the question, "What do you think of American movies from an artistic standpoint?", asked by a writer for the *Soviet Movie Gazette,* he gave the bewildering reply, "How long is a piece of string?" He would say no more than that he had enjoyed his visit in Russia, found it a most interesting country, and had spent a weekend at Troitsky Monastery, forty miles from Moscow. He had visited clubs and factories and farms, often in the company of his old friend Anna Louise Strong. Miss Strong later wrote:

> I showed him and Dorothy around Moscow, and—in fact—gave to Dorothy the data which led to the famous fight between Red and Dreiser. . . . It was a lot of hastily compiled notes which I gave to both Dreiser and Dorothy, and which both of them used in undigested form. . . . Hence the charge of plagiarism on both sides. . . . In those days people like Walter Duranty and myself, living in Moscow, got lots of stuff we couldn't sell . . . and made it available to travelling VIPs . . . who, doing books in a hurry, did not always bother to rewrite in their own words . . . but incorporated paragraphs as their own without change.

"Hastily compiled notes" kept in duplicate? It hardly seems likely; but Miss Strong, a zealot, may well have had at her disposal many copies of useful Soviet pamphlets in translation. She was seeing both Dorothy Thompson and Theodore Dreiser, and Dorothy Thompson herself was seeing Dreiser. He was still ill when he arrived in Moscow, and once more she had helped him, even to the point of arranging that he have a better room than the one to which he had been assigned in the hotel where both were staying. Later, Dreiser let his biographer, Robert Elias, believe that Sinclair Lewis, when he arrived, was jealous of him, but Lewis himself, without any reason for guile in his correspondence with W. E. Woodward, wrote as follows:

> I saw Dreiser there, and didn't think he was particularly happy—impatient at the still universal inefficiency of a nation which has had to make some-

* On his return to Berlin, Lewis immediately took up the matter with Alfred Harcourt and opened correspondence with the Russian officials, but in the end, of course, nothing came of the project.

thing out of nothing. But I've never liked him so much—he was really charming.

Anna Louise Strong was undoubtedly a vigorous and instructive guide, and Lewis followed with indefatigable good humor, but Dorothy Thompson had the assistance of Russians and other European press people. Lewis's last words, as his train left Moscow, were, "Well, anyway, I shall sleep until I get to Berlin." He returned on December 10 and in two weeks wrote Harcourt to say that in a few days he would be sending all of *The Man Who Knew Coolidge*. On the same day he wrote Mencken, wishing that he could be with them in Berlin for their happy Christmas, and saying that he had added about 35,000 words "of complete obscene imbecility" to the original story of Lowell Schmaltz. Alfred Harcourt had shown good sense about this project: he had at first suggested that he publish only the original piece, and when Lewis insisted on the 50,000-word version, he urged him not to "force the new material to 50,000 words if it doesn't come naturally." It came to Lewis, of course, almost as naturally as his breath, or as his expectations: the book, he assured Harcourt, might sell 200,000 copies. Harcourt knew better.

Dorothy Thompson had returned to Berlin, too, and was working hard at her Russian articles for the *Evening Post* and the *Ledger,* and Lewis told Harcourt that he would send him nearly the entire manuscript of the book they would form immediately after Christmas. Finished, she wrote a Christmas sonnet to Sinclair Lewis and to that house in the Vermont hills to which they expected to go. Then (if one can trust a single clause in a letter of December 23: "after a week's vacation in the mountains") they made another of those charming disappearances from the documents and from Berlin, and the year came to an end as tidily as it did happily.

But the next year, 1928, opened with both a whimper and a bang. George Seldes met Lewis, who had been reading Upton Sinclair's *Money Writes!*

> "I love Upton," he said, almost weeping. . . . "But look what he writes about me. He says I am one of those writers spoiled by money. He says, 'Sinclair Lewis has a million dollars.' I give you my word, George, I haven't got more than $600,000 and he calls me a millionaire."

That was the rather amusing whimper; the bang came on January 3 in a long, outraged letter to Sinclair himself.

> *Dear Upton:*
>
> I am thoroughly dissatisfied with what little I have as yet been able to read of *Money Writes!* . . . I would advise you to withdraw it from the market, and to pray for humor and, still more, for accuracy.
>
> Your insults to Joseph Hergesheimer are intolerable. . . . To say that Mr. Cabell by his reference to sex in *Jurgen* has "thus caused many thousands of

lads to suffer atrocious torments from gonorrheal infection, and many thousands of young women to have their ovaries cut out"—this, that you call "a notion false or true" is perhaps the most ridiculous statement that I have ever seen in my life. There never was a book less aphrodisiac than *Jurgen.* Believe me that I mean it quite literally and coolly when I say that the various scenes of sexual intercourse in your *Oil* are decidedly more aphrodisiac than anything in *Jurgen,* because they are so much more detailed & because they belong so much more to a non-fantastic world; and if Mr. Cabell really has thus affected the ovaries of thousands of young women, you will have affected the same organs of tens of thousands.

I greatly admire and like your wife, but it was very unkind to her for you to compare her verse to that of Amy Lowell. . . . If I were your wife, I should be very cross indeed.

Now to come to myself. You are much kinder to me . . . and . . . thoroughly and outrageously inaccurate. You, pretending to give inside information, simply and calmly make up what, unfortunately, most of Europe and some of America will regard as "facts."

Let me point out a few of these inaccuracies:

(1): The talkative radical in *Main Street* is *not* a "wobbly." He is a self-taught, loveable, but indolent crank. Therefore I am not guilty of the crime of "camouflaging my knowledge" and "elaborately keeping [the reader] from knowing anything so dreadful."

(2): I am *not* "close to a millionaire," or if I am, I don't know who the devil the millionaire may be. I suppose, however, that you mean that I am close to being a millionaire. You are only about $900,000—about 90%—wrong, which is rather a good grade for a man who is advertised as able to give the public all the real inside facts. And to say of a man who has dared to write *Elmer Gantry,* knowing the fury, the threats of lynching, that it would arouse, that he "might *venture* to tell the whole truth" is damned impertinence.

(3): I did *not* make Max Gottlieb out of Jacques Loeb by "performing a major surgical operation, cutting out Loeb's Socialism, and throwing it into the garbage can." That's the sort of reasonable-seeming and totally false statement which, on the part of others, you so joy in damning in *Brass Check.* In the first place, I never in my life saw Jacques Loeb except for about one half hour, during which we never mentioned social problems, Socialism, or anything of the kind. In the second place, though it is quite true that I often thought of him, and often asked Paul de Kruif about him while I was planning *Arrowsmith,* yet in the concept of Gottlieb there is as much of half a dozen other men—for example the head of the Pasteur Institute in Paris—as there is of Loeb. In the third place, I very carefully related Martin Arrowsmith's own crusade to the social crusade—I very carefully explained why he was not more social-minded—by saying that because he found his own researches so fascinating, he never could understand or sympathize with the workers who, doomed to uninteresting tasks, could never have his own indifference to long hours and low wages. In the fourth place, I had more than enough to write about without going into

Socialism and the Labor movement. I'll do that job when I get ready—and if anything keeps me from it, it will be your urging me to do it, because I shall, if you urge me enough, be afraid of being as inaccurate and egotistic as you are in dealing with it.

(4): Your criticisms of *Elmer Gantry* are so inaccurate that I wonder if you have read the book at all. . . .

. . . .

I did not want to say these unpleasant things, but you have written to me, asking my opinion, and I give it to you, flat. If you would get over two ideas—first that any one who criticizes you is an evil and capitalist-controlled spy, and second that you have only to spend a few weeks on any subject to become a master of it—you might yet regain your now totally lost position as the leader of American socialistic journalism. I could make this letter rather long. I could point out that the two times you quote me in *Goose Step* you quote me with such inaccuracy that I sound in your book like a liar. But I think I have said enough. You will, of course, regard this only as the wrath of a millionaire best-seller, and go on being the only authority on all known subjects—including diet, and therapeutics as illustrated by the Abrams method; go on shamefully dragging your wife into your books and even your advertisements—simultaneously with criticizing Mr. Hergesheimer for mentioning his wife, so delicately and beautifully.

My God, Upton, go and pray for forgiveness, honesty, and humility!

I have, before closing this letter, re-read the earlier pages. It seems to me cruel, and I hate cruelty. Yet I can do no other in answer to the sadism—and not only sadism but *smug* sadism—of your book. If you will re-read your own beastly words about George Cram Cook, you may, if you can possibly accomplish the near-miracle of detaching yourself from your own papal grandeur, understand a little why any decent man, Socialist or Tory, must so resent this volume of mental paresis.

Sincerely yours,
Sinclair Lewis

He was, it is quite true, in no mood to be cruel or even angry. To W. E. Woodward he wrote on January 12,

> I really have managed the miraculous come-back which, a year ago, I didn't think I could possibly achieve. I feel better, more peaceful, more like working, than I have for three or four years. I'm going to stay over here till—probably—next August; then home.

Their plans were made. Dorothy Thompson would marry him in London as soon as Mrs. Lewis obtained her divorce, and for the next few months they could only wait for that event.

In February Lewis received a shock in a note from Telesforo Casanova. Casanova was a broker, and his letter told Lewis that he had very sad news to convey, he had lost fifty thousand dollars for Mrs. Lewis, whom he hoped to marry "to toil with me." There is no evidence to indicate that Lewis, in his euphoric relationship with Dorothy Thompson, was much upset. They thought that they would take a villa in Sicily for the time that remained until he was divorced, and at the end of February, after Dorothy Thompson had resigned her position and closed her apartment, she went to Naples, Lewis following. They found seclusion as the guests of Mrs. Janet Hepburt Dagata in the *dependenza* of the handsome old Villa Galletti on Cape Posillipo, the establishment in which Maxim Gorky had hidden out for a number of years. With Vesuvius in view and the city glimmering across the bay, with lovely gardens in which to walk and lunch, the Villa Galletti provided a suitably idyllic interlude of rest and quiet and beauty between hectic, wintry Berlin and a summer of touring England. Lewis was not drinking, he was making fine progress on *Dodsworth* (now sometimes called *Home* and *A Man Alone*), and there were excursions to Capri and Pompeii and Sorrento and into the tortured, colorful alleys of Naples. The whole idyl is recreated in the closing scenes of *Dodsworth,* which also give us this impression of Lewis's state of mind:

> He sat for hours with Edith, or alone by the bay, staring at the miraculously involved branches of a cypress, discovering the myriad skyscrapers in a patch of moss. And he began to desire to have—with Edith—a farm at home, and not a gentleman's show-place, to increase social credit, but an authentic farm, smelling of horses and cattle and chickens, with cornfields baking at noon. . . . This simple-hearted ambition stirred him more, gave him more feeling that he had something secret and exciting to live for, than any of the business plans which were rousing him again to self-respect. . . . But it must be with Edith. . . . He smiled a little to think of himself, this bucolic lump, drawn back to earth by her thin unearthen hands. Edith!

Yet even at Posillipo they were not quite obscure. Mrs. Lewis's presence in Reno became public knowledge on March 13, and on March 15 the New York *American* announced that Lewis was planning to marry Dorothy Thompson. On March 17, in a telegram to the Associated Press in Rome, Lewis denied the rumors. "As I am married and as my wife is not suing me nor I her for divorce, any rumor of my engagement is ridiculous and even libelous." Suing him on grounds of incompatibility and desertion, Mrs. Lewis was granted her divorce on April 16, fourteen years and one day after her wedding. The settlement was generous: a $50,000 trust fund was established for Wells Lewis, and Mrs. Lewis was to receive $1,000 a month as long as she remained unmarried and as long as his annual income was at least $48,000; should his income fall below that sum, the total of her annual alimony would be reduced to one fourth of his income.

News of the Lewis divorce brought forth a flurry of not entirely pleasant comment throughout the American press; characteristic was the Columbus (Ohio) *Journal*'s humor:

> Well, Mrs. Sinclair Lewis has got her divorce and we knew she couldn't stand him much longer after we noticed a few weeks ago that he has reached the point where he deliberately had his picture taken with his chin resting on his hand in an attitude of alleged deep thought.

It was as well that he was far away, where his content could not be punctured.

In Rome on April 23, when Lewis was on his way to England to establish the short residence necessary to marriage there, he announced his engagement to Dorothy Thompson. In the meantime, in New York, Henry Holt & Company had announced that they would publish her book, *The New Russia,* in the autumn, and Harcourt, Brace & Company, on April 5, had published *The Man Who Knew Coolidge: Being the Soul of Lowell Schmaltz, Constructive and Nordic Citizen.**

"This is a dismal creation," began a Chicago notice of the book, and the same judgment was to be made by any number of reviewers. A few of the major reviews were favorable (notably those by Canby and Hansen) and some of them were long. The New York *Times Book Review* gave it the front page, most of which the writer used to express the hope that this book had relieved Sinclair Lewis of an obsession with Babbittry. This book did not anger its readers, it merely bored them. "The dullest writing ever to come from a first-class writing man," said Heywood Broun; and F.P.A., in his *Diary of Our Own Mr. Pepys,* reflected that the entire book might have been written in six sketches of two thousand words each. When, some years later, Lewis was autographing his novels in the collection of the University of Minnesota, he chose with strange irony to write in this book, "Edith Wharton said this was my best novel . . . I hugely admire Edith Wharton." No such letter from Mrs. Wharton is extant, but if she did indeed write him in praise of these six maniacal monologues by a Babbitt without any of Babbitt's humanity, of what was she thinking? Lewis had at last succumbed to a threat that had always been present in his work—the disappearance of his own mind in the mindless swamp of his subject; and without the resources of the techniques of plot, he had no means by which to highlight his satire through ironically contrasting action or the observations of other characters on the main one. It was all Lowell Schmaltz, and only that.

Gilbert Seldes has pointed out, perhaps a little ingeniously, that the initials of Lowell Schmaltz are the author's initials in reverse, and that the difference between the two is perhaps not as great as one would suppose. Lewis was no Schmaltz, but he could be almost as exasperatingly garrulous, and he had written Mencken to say that he loved "the imbecile,"

* A study of the differences between the *Mercury* story and the book can be found in Lyon N. Richardson's "Revision in Sinclair Lewis's *The Man Who Knew Coolidge,*" *American Literature,* vol. XXV, no. 3 (November 1953), pp. 326–33.

and, in another letter, from Naples, that he had "become so phlegmatic that some times at dinner I let other people talk for a minute at a time." It is Lowell Schmaltz's first characteristic that he has no notion whatever that his insane garrulity keeps everyone else from talking at all. Still, in a *Nation* article called "Mr. Lorimer and Me" that Lewis was writing at about this time for a series "in which various persons describe the world they would like to live in," Lewis declared his fondness for the American middle-class world as it is, the world of Lowell Schmaltz. "I like the Babbitts, the Dr. Pickerbaughs, the Will Kennicotts, and even the Elmer Gantrys rather better than any one else on earth. They are good fellows. They laugh—really laugh." Not many readers laughed. The sales of the book, for a work of his, were minute.

In London, at the Savoy, he wrote to Dorothy Thompson to say that he was making the arrangements for their wedding. She must arrive in London not later than May 10 for an appearance at the Registry Office. He met Noel Coward (who "says *Elmer* is the greatest book of the century") and was much taken with him. He continued work on *Dodsworth,* which was nearly finished in the first draft. He toyed with the idea of writing an introduction to *This Side Idolatry,* a book about Dickens by his friend Bechhofer Roberts, and did not do it, but used the promise as a reason for declining to write an introduction to *You Can't Print That!* by his friend George Seldes. He completed negotiations for the purchase of a two-thousand-dollar trailer which, attached to an automobile, would make up the widely publicized "caravan" in which he and his bride would spend their summer honeymoon. He drew up a guest list and busied himself writing many notes of invitation to his wedding.

He saw newspapermen, one of whom, C. F. Crandall, remembered a dinner party with Lewis and two other journalists at which, when Crandall mentioned Ford Madox Ford's ability to compose a coherent sonnet in two and a half minutes from any set of end rhymes given him (Tietjens performs this feat in *No More Parades*), Lewis said, "Anything that fat slob can do, I can do. Want to bet?" The bet was made for a pound, but then Lewis asked that he be given four minutes since he had not written a poem for twenty years. He composed his sonnet in three minutes and fifty seconds, and it is neither better nor worse than most of the rhymes he had written in his youth.* After this, he asked his friends to name any current news topic and any poets, and he would versify the topic in their several styles. Kipling and Milton were suggested, and the news topic was a current scandal about a well-known M.P. and international lawyer who had been arrested for committing improprieties with a girl in Hyde Park. On this subject, Lewis began enthusiastically to reel off his lines and con-

* This work can be consulted in the New York *Herald Tribune* Books Section for September 2, 1951.

tinued until his friends begged him to stop. When Dorothy Thompson arrived in London, they dined with Arnold Bennett, and Bennett noted sourly in his *Journal* that "Sinclair did too many imitations."

They were married at noon on Monday, May 14, in a civil ceremony, witnessed by Jonathan Cape and his wife, at St. Martin's Registry Office in Henrietta Street, where a dozen news photographers awaited them. Immediately after, in another ceremony at the Savoy Chapel, they repeated their vows before the Reverend Hugh B. Chapman, who, after what was not so much a sermon as a talk to the bride and groom in which he enjoined the novelist to write books that men will "go to for strength when they are in despair," read the Benediction in the Church of England service. Among the guests here, and at the luncheon that followed at the Savoy, were Anita Loos, Hugh Walpole, Gilbert Frankau, Mercedes de Acosta,* Mrs. Bertrand Russell, Mr. and Mrs. Pethick Lawrence, Lord Thomson, Crosby Gaige, Ferdinand Reyher, Rebecca West, and Sir Thomas and Lady Cunningham. At lunch there were toasts, of course, and Dorothy Thompson's most vivid recollection was of Lewis's response to one of them: he took a piece of paper from his vest pocket, put on his glasses, and pretended to read a speech on the jute industry, covering the entire British Empire, to a convention of jute dealers.

What did the groom look like? A few years later, Peggy Bacon was to accompany her cartoon of him with this sketch in *Off With Their Heads:*

> Pinkish, red-head, hair smooth and flattened in front, neglected, dishevelled and bunched in brief strands behind. Irritable brow. Long, flat plane from temple to collar. Flesh like canned tomatoes with the seed in it, changing abruptly to cream-colored forehead. Pale blue, clever, bulgy eyes glaring dizzily at something in the offing, possibly ant-hill. Sandy eyelashes, invisible eyebrows, lips gathered on a draw-string with puzzled purse like old lady-esque reticule. Nose of a grocer adding up slips. Freckled hands with an elegant shape, sensitively caressing cigarette. Face wiggles formlessly into collar, long seamy neck to rear. Gold-rimmed spectacles, mal-fitting collar, hunched shoulders. Looks overheated, corrugated, modest and oafish. A country-store type.

Even now, in his Savile Row clothes—pin-striped blue serge suit, wing collar, pearl-gray hat, cane, yellow flower in lapel—the impression tallies

* Mrs. Acosta reports that, meeting the Lewises at a dinner party in Greenwich Village in the early twenties, she found Lewis not helping her into her chair but pulling it out from under her, as she crashed to the floor with a nasty bang to her head. She recovered good-humoredly and remarked on the salubrity of a sturdy shake-up before a fine meal. There were no further encounters between the two until, very late on the night before his London wedding, he telephoned her to say that he wanted her to attend, that he had always admired her for her charming behavior so long ago, when he had behaved so badly. There were no meetings thereafter.

with the photographs. But he did not look like that to his bride, whose "eyes were other."

Their wedding announcement read:

Dorothy Thompson
and
Sinclair Lewis
have the honour to announce
their marriage
which took place in London,
on Monday, May 14th 1928.

Guarranty Trust Company
50, Pall Mall
London, S.W.

Why did she marry him? For the obvious reason that most women marry the men they choose to marry: she loved him. "Why else should I have married him, considering my own position when we met, except because of that pull of his genius and my faith in his almost agonized protestations, at times, that he *needed* me?" His unexamined, inarticulate suffering was another source of his attractiveness, and when he met her in Berlin this had reached a point of intensity he had not known before. If it was this same suffering that would presently make her see "him destroying himself, as a man, a husband, a father, and even as an artist," the spectacle did not obtrude on the present, which was bright with promise that gilded the future and glossed the ugly along with the willful.

On May 19, two days before they set out on their caravan trip, Lewis wrote Mencken facetiously to say that "Dorothy married me only on my promise that I avoid you and all your friends"—nonsense, of course; and yet, given a little prescience, she might well have made that condition, for she would learn soon enough that Mencken and Nathan and Goodman and most of Lewis's gay companions saw him not as a man, as she must see him, but as a literary and social phenomenon. More seriously Lewis wrote him—as he had been doing for the past weeks—about possible country areas that they might fruitfully search for a house on their return to the United States. They had been thinking of Maryland—along with Vermont and California and now New Hampshire—as the scene of the *pied-à-terre,* and Mencken was suggesting Pennsylvania, especially "Hergesheimer's country," the loveliness of which, Lewis confessed, he well knew. Was he wondering about the whereabouts of his ex-wife, remembering perhaps the fiasco of the West Chester house? On the very day that the Lewises set out in their caravan from Oxford, the first Mrs. Lewis was writing Mencken to say that she had just returned to New York, would look about on Long Island for a place to live, and was greatly relieved by and happy with all recent developments.

In Oxford, the new Mrs. Lewis, preparing her caravan larder, showed a butcher how to cut an American steak; she would do the cooking, both would drive, and both would write. They had two typewriters, all the necessary writing supplies, a library of forty books, and no radio. Lewis had agreed to write a series of articles to be called "Main Streets and Babbitts of Britain"—nearly one a week through all that summer—for the New York *Herald Tribune,* most of them to be syndicated by the United Press. The articles begin at once, ten miles out of Oxford: "This is England, this flat field." And they follow the caravanners into Surrey and Kent, to the south coast and the Cinque Ports, then down and west through Sussex to Salisbury, where they paused for a week while Lewis finished the first draft of *Dodsworth* and began his revisions; on into Dorset, Devon and Cornwall, back to Salisbury for several days, and on to Wales; then up through the Midlands and the West Riding, through Cumberland, and as far north as Edinburgh, then back to London. Sometimes they turned the caravan over to a driver and made quick trips by train; sometimes they left the trailer in a field and went off for an excursion in the car alone; and sometimes they abandoned both trailer and car, and tramped. There were pauses along the way to visit friends, like Hugh Walpole, in the country. Altogether, in less than three months, they had driven a leisurely four thousand miles, no pressures pushing.

Lewis's articles are relaxed and expansive and familiar in subject. They reflect on the restful taproom of a British inn and the noisy American saloon—"the security of tradition"; on the influence of American business methods and the Babbitts of Britain; on the joys of caravanning, which satisfies the gypsy impulse with all the civilized advantages; on poor hotel service and the limitations of British cooking; on the vulgarities of Margate Sands and the shabby contentment of the low; on the hospitality of the country folk; on England as "a nation of villagers"; on Main Street versus High Street (the English villager loves his village and does not wish to leave it or to change it); and on the insularity of the English versus the internationalism of the Germans. One article is given over to American tourists and complains of the attitude of the British press toward Americans, especially toward their speech, and quotes from a number of periodicals to make the point. In one of these quotations, an American, highly illiterate, is represented as having been graduated from Yale, and this causes Lewis to write as follows:

> The Yale College in which this Typical American Tourist learned his remarkable Babu English is a recent frontier institution only 225 years old—and in tradition, since its founders and its first dons were themselves English university men, quite as old as Oxford. Among its professors are A. S.

> Cooke, one of the half dozen authorities on Old English in the world, and Chauncey Brewster Tinker, whose books about Samuel Johnson and his circle are as much read in England as in America. Taft, between his term as President of the United States and his appointment as Chief Justice of the Supreme Court of America, was well content to serve as a professor of law in Yale. And it was thar, under such rough frontiersmen, that our hero larned his extraordinary dialect.

And then there are final reflections on the alert inhabitants of the ugly northern cities, on the spirit of progress in England, on the process of automatization.

Lewis amused himself in the familiar ways, and his new wife was content to play his games. Once, when they were hiking, each shouldering a pack, they approached the inn of a secluded village. Lewis proposed that his wife carry both packs and follow him meekly into the inn. The innkeeper responded with predictable astonishment and contempt. "Is it customary, sir, for men in America to allow their wives to carry the luggage?" Lewis replied, "Certainly. That's why we marry." After lunch, they left in the same way, with the wife trudging behind the striding husband, carrying the packs.

The three months of driving and walking and camping about were pleasant and did not indicate that, indeed, in the next few years, it was to be she who would bear the burdens. It was clear enough already, to be certain, that this marriage would be amusing rather than ardent, that what one would hope for would be an easy and lively and working companionship, that this would entail an endless stream of conversation and monologue, much of it entertaining, many people coming and going and many parties, and japery that could be diverting. Very well—such a relationship was not to be despised. . . .

The last of Lewis's articles was written in London in mid-August.

> And so, finishing this last article, in the friendly city of London, I look out on the Thames and feel reluctant to leave the old wisdoms of England. And yet I am glad that I am going to Paris tomorrow, glad that I shall run back to eager Berlin before I sail, if I can squeeze in the time, and gladdest of all that I am going to the dynamo of America, into the radiance of the American autumn. Is the wanderer like myself homeless—or does he merely have more homes than most people?

On that day, meeting C. F. Crandall, he asked him if he would be so good as to buy him all the books of P. G. Wodehouse for the voyage home, and from Paris, on August 17, he cabled Harcourt that he would probably want four months more to finish *Dodsworth.* In Paris with the Guthries, he asked them to read his manuscript and check it for facts—place names, the names of streets and cafés—and with the nearly finished book they sailed for America on the *Hamburg* on August 22. Disembarking, Lewis had a new experience: the ship's reporters were as interested in his wife as they were in him, for she, after all, had had the longer and the more intense experience of Europe; when questions were asked that either might have answered, she did not hesitate to give the answers. On one matter, both spoke: they shared an equal dread, they professed, of living under Prohibition.

10

THEY WENT DIRECTLY to the offices of Harcourt, Brace & Company, and looking down into the swarming channel of Madison Avenue, Sinclair Lewis, in a sibylline mood, pronounced, "Within a year this country will have a terrible financial panic." Why did he think so? "I don't think. I know. Can't you *see* it, *smell* it? I can *see* people jumping out of windows on this very street." Vincent Sheean was later to write that the real curiosity of 1928 was the failure of educated people to consider the spectacle of Wall Street, that while thousands must have known that a speculative boom of such dimensions could only be followed by a crash, except for "Dorothy and Red Lewis, I cannot remember a single acquaintance of mine in America who perceived the shallowness of the 'prosperity' and the inevitability of the crash." Yet, when, fourteen months later, Lewis was reminded of his prediction of August 28, 1928, he could not recall it.

Lesser crashes had occurred. The August newspapers had announced the opening of Patrick Kearney's dramatization of *Elmer Gantry* at The Playhouse on the seventh, and when the Lewises disembarked, they confessed that they knew nothing about the recent history of the stage plans for that novel. The play had had an appropriately noisy history. It had been tried out for an unexciting month in Cleveland, and then for more than another month recasting and script problems had been worked over in New York. Then, just before it was to open on Broadway, a "doctor," Thompson Buchanan, had been called in to do the last, desperate work. Two days before the scheduled opening, the newspapers were reporting quarrels between the director, Lumsden Hare, and the producer, William A. Brady, on one side, and Patrick Kearney on the other, about whose lines were to be used; and on the day that the play was to open, both director and producer announced their retirement from the project.

The opening was delayed while replacements were found, and on August 9, when it took place, the audience was greeted with a curbstone invocation—a fanfare of trumpets, invitations to salvation by a throng of evangelists, and pious words from a grave, sermonizing cleric under the marquee. During the second act, while a revivalist scene was being enacted, supers came down the aisles of the theater, exhorting the audience to be saved; and among them was the press agent for the production, one Robert Edgar Long, who was shouting with the others, but shouting, "I love Jesus more than William A. Brady," and after this throng had trouped up on to the stage, he continued his obbligato, "William A. Brady has ruined me!" Next day, when Brooks Atkinson reported some of these antics in the *Times,* he concluded that the first two acts were Kearney's, the third, Buchanan's, and the whole, "flat and disorderly."

By the end of the month (the play closed on September 15), the noise had probably quieted down, and the house had thinned out, and the Lewises, for whom this was the first theatrical experience on their return to New York, were depressed. Mencken was in town, however, and his "medical convention," as Lewis called it, supplied some cheer. One could also take cheer from the fact that the *Times* of August 26 had included in its columns the information that, together with Upton Sinclair, Sinclair Lewis was the most popular American writer in Sweden. Rumors began to drift about that when the Swedish Academy at last looked to the United States for a recipient worthy of the Nobel prize in literature, its glance would rest on Sinclair Lewis. And "*Dodsworth* ought to go to my Swede publishers as soon as possible," Lewis instructed Harcourt when finished copies of that work were available.

With Alfred Harcourt the Lewises went to Riverside, Connecticut, where they were to be his house guests for as long as they liked. Lewis had the accumulated affairs of eighteen months to disentangle and settle in New York, there was an automobile to be bought, and excursions in search of a house were to be made into the Connecticut countryside, and then farther afield in New Hampshire and Vermont. At one point during this stay with the Harcourts, Harrison Smith had a weekend house party at his Connecticut place, and there Lewis reencountered Morris Werner, another Harcourt author whom he had first met some years before, when Werner had made it clear that he found him trying. Now he tried to placate Werner; for all his flaunting of himself, he had an almost wistful sensitivity to personal criticism, a gnawing need to feel that he was liked, a "good guy." He flattered Werner: "It was really you who started the biography wave with your *Barnum,* wasn't it?" Werner protested that Lytton Strachey had come before him and was much better. Had Lewis met Strachey in London? "A very difficult man to get to know," Lewis said, and indicated that Bloomsbury was hardly *worth* knowing. William Seabrook, another Harcourt author, was also there, and Lewis, who got on well with him, was presently suggesting that the two of them collaborate on a novel about labor in the United States.

He was also telling everyone that he was going to show America to "little Dorothy," who for so long had been away from that "dynamo." She took almost no part in the talk, let the buzz of conversation swirl round her while, on a chaise longue, she read Keyserling's *Travel Diary of a Philosopher*. She could hardly have chosen a more appropriate title for her ruminations. Later, on Sunday, after Harcourt had arrived to pick up the Lewises, Werner passed the room in which Lewis was packing his bag. Lewis beckoned him to come in, took his hand, and said, "Morrie, the first time we met, you didn't like me, I know. Look, if I ever do anything you don't like, *please* come and tell me!" Werner, in his embarrassment, could only mutter, shufflingly, "Certainly, Red, certainly. . . ."

There were always compensations. Harcourt had read the first draft of *Dodsworth* and was telling everyone that it was the best novel that Sinclair Lewis had ever written, and Lewis was happily repeating that judgment to his friends—Mencken, Woodward, Edith Summers—everyone with whom his many letters were reestablishing American connections. And then there was the happy adventure of house hunting. They had already taken an apartment at 37 West Tenth Street, in New York, and they could have that on November 1, but in the interim they hoped to find the country place for which they had planned in Europe. On September 12 they found themselves in Plymouth, Vermont, the birthplace of President Coolidge, and this obviously indicated a post card to H. L. Mencken. "Stopping in this idyllic spot today we bared our heads and in your behalf as well as our own, sent up a prayer for the welfare of our Pres. and the success of the party." Plymouth is in the neighborhood of Woodstock, and in this handsome part of Vermont, in less than a week, they found the place that they wanted, half way between the little villages of Barnard and Pomfret.

There were two houses on three hundred acres, a farmhouse of 1796 and a larger house, and they knew at once that this was the property that they must have. The owner, their New York landlord, was still occupying the farmhouse. He asked them to stay for dinner, and the papers for the exchange of ownership were signed that night. When the owner obligingly offered to remove himself at once, the Lewises took possession. It was the first house that Sinclair Lewis, aged forty-three, had ever owned. And when the whole establishment was developed into what would be called Twin Farms, it was—although he would rent and buy and sell other houses in the future—to prove to be the only real home he would ever have had.

That first autumn was an enormous success. Everything was easy. They found servants in nearby Woodstock and proceeded with their work as though they had been in the house all summer. Plans were made for the remodeling of the larger house. Men were hired to clear out weeds and brush and to plant new gardens. Wells Lewis, now aged eleven, came for a weekend. He approved of his father's new wife (he was in due course to become devoted to her)* and he enjoyed the two cats named Mencken and Nathan. The leaves turned in the spectacular Vermont October, and Manhattan saw nothing of the Lewises. Occasionally guests arrived. One of the first was Vincent Sheean who, having his own work to pursue, found the simple pattern of their life there much to his taste. All three worked during the day, meeting only at mealtime and in the evening for talk and nonsense and laughter. They managed, he reported, to shut New York out of their lives more completely than anyone else he knew, and this impressed him, but, a young writer, he was even more impressed with Lewis's method of work.

> His ruthlessness with his own work was a part of the phenomenon: he thought nothing of throwing away a hundred thousand words, cutting out more than he left in, or abandoning a novel altogether when it did not please him. The spectacle of such volcanic energy under the control of a first-rate artistic conscience was one of the most impressive that could have been offered a lazy youth, and it should have done me far more good than it did. . . . He could make up ten short stories at breakfast and invent a novel before lunch. The fertility of his imagination never failed to amaze me; it was so curbed and subjected to the observed realities in his books that it came as a surprise to learn that he was actually as inventive, in the easy, effortless story-telling way, as Ouida or Marion Crawford. Occasionally he made up a short story and presented it to me. The first short story of a more or less professional cast that I ever wrote was one of his, concocted, in the midst of general laughter, at the breakfast table.

Lewis was engaged in the detailed and drastic revisions of *Dodsworth,* revisions that took him longer than he had planned, and he was still working on them when, at the very end of October, the first snows came and drove them back to New York. For a week they stayed at the Brevoort while the apartment in West Tenth Street was made ready.

That apartment was as attractive in its way as the farmhouse was. The new Mrs. Lewis's household gift was for a rich ease and informality. She brought the accumulated loot of her eight years in Europe out of storage and made the Village duplex—in Lewis's phrase—"surprisingly charming." On the second floor was a large studio that became her place of work; Lewis, in his accustomed and preferred fashion, rented a hotel room nearby as an "office." The German couple who had been her servants in Berlin were brought to New York. There was much German conversation. All was *gemütlichkeit.*

Until the Dreiser ruckus. The *Evening Post* articles, which had appeared nearly a year before, had been revised and supplemented and published

* The present biographer's first acquaintance with any member of the Lewis family came ten years later when he was an instructor in Harvard College. At a party of literary undergraduates he heard Wells Lewis spiritedly defend Dorothy Thompson's political views at a time when it was considered smart in many circles to attack them.

in early October as *The New Russia.* Then, in November, came *Dreiser Looks at Russia.* Readers at once observed the verbal similarity and even identity of many passages. On November 13, F.P.A. wrote in his *Diary of Our Own Mr. Pepys:*

> So home to read Dorothy Thompson's *The New Russia* and T. Dreiser's *Dreiser Looks at Russia,* and saw many points of verbal similarity between them, which was odd, forasmuch as Miss Thompson's words were printed first. And I thought there might be a pamphlet written called "Dorothy Looks Askance at Theodore."

She herself later observed to an interviewer that his book might better have been called *Dreiser Looks at the "Evening Post."*

Lewis was even more indignant than she and they went precipitantly to his attorney, who filed a complaint with Dreiser's lawyers asking that his book be withdrawn. They replied that they were prepared to have her bring suit if she was so disposed. Dreiser said nothing, except to insist that there had been no plagiarism and to make innuendoes about "gallantry." Later, he let his biographer believe that it was really his material in the first place, that he had given it to her in Moscow, and that he had seen no reason for not using it himself. This is a less likely explanation than that they had used common source material and on occasion used it "raw." At any rate, legal proceedings were dropped and the stories died out of the newspapers.

The Lewises were busy people. Sinclair Lewis, proud of her reputation as a journalist, was eager that Dorothy Thompson continue her career. Thomas Costain, then an editor of *The Saturday Evening Post,* remembers encountering Lewis and suggesting that, since he had not written for the *Post* for so many years (but was still referring most amiably to "Uncle Lorimer"), he should consider writing some stories for the magazine. Lewis was interested but was even more interested in persuading Costain that the *Post* should have some articles about Europe by Dorothy Thompson. Costain arranged a luncheon in Philadelphia with Lorimer and the Lewises to talk over the possibilities, and the result was that Dorothy Thompson did a series of successful articles.* He took her to the offices of New York editors whom he knew, in the expectation of further increasing her American markets. She had continued to write for the newspapers with which she was already associated, and from the moment of their return from Europe, she had been in demand by clubs and colleges as a lecturer. With the publication of her book, the demands were more

* Costain remembers arranging another luncheon in Philadelphia to discuss a possible Lewis work. Costain's idea was that Lewis should write at least the first volume of an autobiography—*A Midwest Boyhood*—for the *Post.* The Lewises came down with the DeVotos, all very high, and Lewis enthusiastic about the Costain proposal. Nothing came of it. Could he have faced it?

frequent, and with Lewis's encouragement, she tried to meet them. He, meantime, was in one of those crescendos of final effort on a book that kept him at his desk for hours on end and shut nearly everything except the book from his mind. When an appeal for his aid came from the Mooney Defense Committee in California, he wrote Mooney as a brother ("Dear Tom") and said:

> I am coming in as far as I can on the Tom Mooney Committee but I can do nothing, really, for another six months. After that I hope that at least I shall be able to start a novel which will tell something about the actual situation of labor and what it is actually facing. If I seem lukewarm now it is only because I must finish a book in hand. Bless you!

As in the past, the effort on the "book in hand" exhausted him. He turned in the completed manuscript on December 15, and on the sixteenth they left New York for two weeks in Hot Springs, Virginia. From The Homestead there, on the day after Christmas, he wrote William Rose Benét to commiserate with him on the startling death of Elinor Wylie, and he concluded:

> I have not seen you since my return to New York from Vermont—indeed I have seen almost no one—because I have been driven & tired out night & day by finishing the new—& long—book. But now it is over, & after the quiet & fresh air of these hills, I shall come back to New York half-human again.

They returned on December 29. He had been reading and continued now to read a good deal of contemporary fiction at the same time that he corrected the proof of *Dodsworth.* In January he wrote to his nephew:

> Are you and your young fellow geniuses watching the work of Morley Callaghan, Josephine Herbst and John Herrmann . . . along with that of Ernest Hemmingway [*sic*]? I should think that these may be the children who will kick me off my chair of honor in a few more years. Callaghan seems to me particularly to have a really authentic power of making his impressions of life—mad life or lugubriously sane life—completely vivid.

This reading would provide the basis of his reflections on current fiction when he put them together in an article for the *Herald Tribune* Books Section in April. "The American Scene in Fiction" urges the importance to the novel of fully realized setting, of the novelist's using only such settings as he knows intimately, and it catalogues various areas of American life that might well be looked into by novelists in search of a scene since they had not yet been adequately treated in fiction. He was himself responding to the American scene with some querulousness. In March, "Publicity Gone Mad" appeared in *The Nation*—a blast against the paid testimonial and the mechanics of advertising in general that hardly suggests its author was a man whom one could not call reticent in the promotion of his own work. In February, he wrote an angry letter about the Broadway theater to the New York *Times:* "I am sick and tired of wearing myself out getting to and from a Broadway theatre, irritated at having to pay prices out of all proportion to the enjoyment which I receive, tired of seeing vast sums expended to produce trash, weary of stars instead of performances," et cetera. That letter appeared on February 17, a day or two after the Lewises had withdrawn from the New York scene again for six weeks in Florida.

They went first to Homosassa on the Gulf of Mexico, where they stayed for two weeks, and then by motor to St. Petersburg and Tampa, Winter Haven, Mountain Lake, Avon Park, Okeechobee, Palm Beach, and Miami. On March 14, Mrs. Lewis left her husband to keep a lecture engagement in Pittsburgh and to return to New York, but Lewis went up to St. Augustine and stayed on there until nearly the end of the month, although he was immediately lonely. ("It's too absurd—you've been gone only four days, and yet I am so lonely for you that I could howl. Owwwwwwwww! I am coming back in just a few days.") He wired W. E. Woodward in Charleston, hoping to persuade him to join him in Florida and motor back to Charleston, but Woodward was away. In January he had agreed with Ray Long to write a series of stories for *Cosmopolitan,* and these he had begun before leaving New York and continued to turn out during the Florida trip, and, if nothing else, they served to take his mind away from himself in his solitude.

There were, finally, thirteen of these stories, and beginning in May of 1929, they appeared month after month in *Cosmopolitan* and had not run their full course until July of 1931. In 1931, too, four more such stories appeared in *Redbook* and *The Saturday Evening Post.*

They make a strange and random miscellany. Half a dozen of them fall into the old pattern of turning the situation against amorous or complacent or foolish or dishonest persons who had previously enjoyed success. Seven or eight of them are broad satires: of Prohibition, of misguided parents, of Hollywood values, of correspondence courses in fiction writing, of persons who think the neighboring pasture greener, of materialistic Europeans who berate Americans for their materialism. One is a fantasy about a lonely little bear; another, a farce about a man who leaves a train in his pajamas. Some of these stories utilize Lewis's European experience, and some develop as themes the mixed attitudes that he had himself developed toward Europe; a few give expression to his feeling about Vermont; but what is nevertheless most remarkable about these stories is the absence of any important feeling (except, occasionally, loneliness) that had touched him deeply. There is perhaps one exception in the work called "He Had a Brother," which is about drunkenness.

It begins:

> It was the familiar morning guilt, the old-fashioned evangelical American sense of guilt, which oppressed Haddon even more than the anguish beating in his temples, the rancid taste in his mouth, the dryness of his hands. He could not escape; he had to admit that on the evening before he had again played the fool. But as long as possible he protected his aching mind from reviewing the especial sorts of idiocy he had committed, while he tried to protect his body—curious racked body that once had lived so peacefully and sweetly with him—from the tortures of every light-ray, every yammer of the street.

Charles Haddon is a successful Manhattan attorney who is rapidly going to pieces. In an effort to save himself, he decides to return to the simple pleasures of his native village, Glen Western, but the dour suspicions of his brother and sister-in-law, rigid, narrow people, impel him to continuous drinking, and here the story duplicates Lewis's liquor bouts with the men of Sauk Centre and his experience of the farm speakeasy. Haddon returns to New York, where his drinking pal, Micky McShea, reveals that his doctor has warned him that he must stop drinking or die, and that he has decided to go out in a blaze. Haddon then devotes himself for two weeks to keeping McShea away from liquor, an effort that necessarily keeps him from it as well; and at the end of that time, cured, he discovers that McShea had been feigning in order to keep Haddon from drink. Thus, he discovers, he *does* have a brother in this one true friend. What begins as a candid use of his own felt experience (if without any attempt to examine motives) is twisted at the end to the double demands of plot and sentiment.

Some of these stories are perfectly respectable commercial products but some of them are considerably embarrassing in their excesses. Lewis was jealous of his reputation, and one can only be surprised that he felt that he could be so free with it. When, in the next year, his publisher in France proposed a collection of stories, Lewis told Harcourt that he thought it would be a mistake. "The same applies to our publishing here a volume of [my collected] short stories. The critics laying for me would have too good a chance." He thought that out of all his stories, he might be able to winnow one volume of good ones, and was presently writing to Harcourt, "*Re* short stories, see 2 of the best I've ever written—"Noble Experiment" in August and "Bongo" in September *Cosmopolitan.* I really think we mite do a volume of these. . . ." They are among the worst he ever wrote. When, that spring, *The Golden Book Magazine* wished to reprint his sentimental story about dolls, "A Matter of Business," he was happy to see the story reappear for one hundred dollars. However, when Groff Conklin wrote to ask for the right to reprint in an anthology some *Smart Set* verse of 1907 and the good story, "I'm a Stranger Here Myself," of 1916, Lewis replied:

> Indeed I should very much object to having reprinted, in book-form or otherwise, the verse of mine which was published in *Smart Set*—22 years

> ago, when I was a very young man. Nor is there any reason why it should be published. It is not only youthful verse but also plain bad verse—imitative, banal, watery—and while I neither disclaim nor am particularly ashamed of these crimes of my youth, I should regard any effort to drag them out of the blessed darkness as viciously unfriendly.
>
> As to the story . . . it is not quite so bad, but neither is it good enough to republish, and I do not wish to have it republished.

At Conklin's urging, he allowed the story to be reprinted. Certainly none of the 1929 stories was as good. But they kept him busy in the absence of a larger project.

While Lewis was in Florida, *Dodsworth* was published. Before that event, and, indeed, before the Florida journey, brother Claude and his wife had visited briefly in New York and then gone up to Cambridge to see their son. To him, from Florida, Lewis had written:

> I was extremely interested in your account of your father & mother in Boston. It's a good thing he *is* determinedly midwestern; it gives him a solidity, an integrity, likely to be lacking in those of us who always want to be some place where we ain't. . . .

And this passage he might appropriately have used as an epigraph to the new novel. For Sam Dodsworth is like Claude Lewis, if one can imagine the latter with a New Haven background that touched him hardly at all, and as a successful manufacturer of motor cars instead of a surgeon in a city smaller than Zenith. *Dodsworth* is *Main Street* in reverse. Whereas in earlier novels he had satirized the stuffy Midwestern citizenry, with its smugness, materialism, and aggressive provinciality, and approved of the "outsiders," Carol and Paul Riesling and Martin and Shallard (who was lynched, to be sure), now he satirizes Fran Dodsworth, the poor specimen of critics of Babbittry that he chooses to give the reader, and approves the unstuffed Midwestern citizenry in the person of Dodsworth, who has more money than Babbitt and needs, therefore, to think less about it, but who is hardly less aggressive in his own kind of provincialism. The terms are the same, and the pattern is the same—of the man who glimpses a dream beyond the actualities and the habits of his life, and who, now, can make it real. Only the emphasis has been shifted, and the object of satire drastically reversed. This time it is as if Lewis had asked himself, "What if a man like Claude had married a woman like Gracie?"

For the first time in his major novels he was handling material that was by no means new—for generations there had been novels about Americans in Europe; but what he was doing, or so it seemed, was new to him: approving the substantial middle-class, Middle Western virtues, the best of Babbitt. He had, of course, been doing this all the time and very explicitly in the early, little-read books; but after *Elmer Gantry* and *The Man Who*

Knew Coolidge, it seemed a sharp reversal, and in Chicago, for example, Fanny Butcher announced "a new personality" in Sinclair Lewis. Critics generally observed the difference and approved it, and even when they did not, there was no fanfare, no denunciation, no controversy. Mencken, predictably, was not happy about the change and published a review in the *Mercury* half in praise, half in blame, but argued "that his work will probably endure, at all events as long as any other fiction of the Coolidge *Aufklärung* endures." William Lyon Phelps, quite as predictably, was delighted, and said so at length in *Scribner's.* There were further favorable reviews from Harry Hansen, R. L. Duffus, Herbert Gorman, H. S. Canby. In the *Times,* Louis Kronenberger lamented the absence of art but approved the substance. Isabel Paterson in the *Herald Tribune* and T. S. Matthews in *New Republic* were not enthusiastic, but friendly Carl Van Doren, in *The Nation,* found "a hundred years of American reflection upon 'Europe' . . . summed up in *Dodsworth,* in a crackle of comedy." The most remarkable review came from Ford Madox Ford in *The Bookman:*

> . . . the title might just as well have been *Europa, an Epic.* For Mr. Lewis presents to you practically all of Europe that counts in our civilization, including New York which isn't America. He also poetizes these places . . . *Dodsworth* is a poem. . . .

E. M. Forster was led to write for *Life and Letters* an essay, "A Camera Man," which was reprinted by the *Herald Tribune* Books Section. ". . . I persist in exclaiming, for what Mr. Lewis has done for myself and thousands of others, is to lodge a piece of a continent in our imagination." His photographic method, as practiced in *Main Street* and *Babbitt,* served him superbly; but then, first in *Elmer Gantry* and remarkably in *Dodsworth,* from which Forster quotes, there was a falling off.

> What has happened? What has changed the Greek Confectionary Parlour at Gopher Prairie, where every decaying banana matters, to this spiritless general catalogue? The explanation is all too plain: photography is a pursuit for the young. So long as a writer has the freshness of youth on him he can work the snapshot method, but when it passes he has nothing to fall back upon. It is here that he differs from the artist. The artist has the power of retaining and digesting experiences, which, years later, he may bring forth in a different form; to the end of life he is accompanied by a secret store.

No reviewers observed the larger significance of *Dodsworth* in the career of Sinclair Lewis and to modern American writing. Between the end of the war and the beginning of the Depression, a revolution had overtaken American life in manners and morals and all intellectual assumptions, and *Main Street, Babbitt, Arrowsmith* and *Elmer Gantry,* whatever their aesthetic limitations, had played a major part, probably the major literary part, in the transformation. At the end of the decade, writers were left either in the situation of Scott Fitzgerald, trying "to hold in balance the sense of futility of effort and the sense of the necessity to struggle," or in the situation of young radicals who tried to turn their writing into social action on behalf of a hypothetical "proletariat." Only extremes of attitude presented themselves as possible: the jaded "aristocratic" attitude implied in the work of Scott Fitzgerald (and explicit in such a school of criticism as the New Humanism, however far this school may have been from him) and the enthusiastic espousal of the revolutionary "working class" attitude exemplified by *New Masses* and any number of "proletarian" writers. In *Dodsworth,* Lewis refused the extremes and turned back to a reassertion of those very middle-class, middle-brow, and Middle Western values that the decade of the twenties seemed to have destroyed forever, and that it had most emphatically modified at least; and with these values, he, who would henceforth seem to be the most old-fashioned of modern American novelists, would henceforth abide.

Only one reviewer, Henry Hazlitt, observed the more concrete element that chiefly troubles a reader today—the blurred characterization of the hero, which itself reflects the anachronistic situation in which the novelist now found himself. Giving Sam Dodsworth some of the attributes of an S. F. B. Morse—a popular athlete and a club man at Yale, then an enormously successful businessman who would have at least a patina of social grace, who reads some Proust and listens to Beethoven—Lewis tries to mix these with the manners and the blunt perceptions of a Claude Lewis, whose favorite expression is "By golly." He deprives Sam Dodsworth, however, of his brother's rugged self-confidence, and he attributes to him instead his own capacity for suffering from the most humiliating fits of inferiority, usually as the result of his wife's barbs, her silvery scorn and tinkling snobberies.

The sharper portrait is of her, Fran Dodsworth. Clifton Fadiman has described her:

> . . . Fran, the babied adult, the well-groomed female American monster, with no business on which to exercise her prehensility, a "success"—that is to say, a sulky-eyed, sulky-mouthed emotional virgin, immature in the home, the salon, the bed. You may see ten thousand Frans on Park Avenue in New York City any day of the year.

The model for this portrait is obvious enough, and the characterization in general is accurate enough, but one should observe the inaccuracies: how Lewis transfers to Fran his own restlessness and rootlessness, his own preference for hotel suites to a home, his own sexual infidelities; and how, identifying himself with Dodsworth, the stable old home-loving, bumbling sentimentalist, he in effect denies all his faults and, making several jibes at the original Casanova, justifies his part in the disastrous history of his recently ended marriage.

The novel is, of course, a summary of the Lewis experience of Europe through the interlude at Posillipo, and as such it is more complete than it is interesting, threatens often to become a fictionalized guidebook, and often, a fictionalized debate on Europe versus America. But the novel raises a more interesting problem than that of the old "International Theme," and one that Lewis had not hitherto directly confronted—the character of the American sexual experience. In *The Opinions of Oliver Allston,* Van Wyck Brooks wrote as follows:

> "In America, men are belittled and cramped by the competition of business, from which women are or ought to be, free." So says Francis Parkman in one of his notebooks, and I agree with him heartily. Is not this the reason why Henry Adams said, "The American man is a failure"? Adams was right in feeling that American women are, on the whole, superior to American men. There is a spaciousness in certain types of American women that has no counterpart in the other sex; * and the whole observing world has shared this feeling since the Civil War. Our men are less developed than our women, precisely for the reason that Parkman gives, because competitive business belittles and cramps them.
>
> * If Allston had read Sinclair Lewis's *Dodsworth,*—which recalled a well-known type of American man,—he might have felt differently here. (V.W.B.)

Fran Dodsworth is the antithesis of the type of noble American woman that Allston has in mind.† Sam Dodsworth, however, is the "cramped" man, but he emerges from his business world to make a series of discoveries that will free him.

> Look at him [wrote Clifton Fadiman] discovering that leisure is not synonymous with "a vacation"; that leisure is something within which you rise, whereas a vacation is something into which you sink. Watch him concluding that mere command over one's environment does not mean maturity. See him finding out that "culture" is not buyable, that "freedom" is bigger than a mere release from the office. Look at him learning that play is more than being entertained, that conversation can be an *action,* not a time-waster. Look at him finally, aghast, desperate, exalted before the face of love. Watch him coming to an agonizing conclusion that marriage must be more than an adjustment to maladjustment, that a true woman must be neither a possession nor a possessor.

Making these discoveries, Sam marries Edith Cortright, such a "spacious" woman as Allston writes of, however faintly she may have been drawn by Lewis.

† In its treatment of the American wife, *Dodsworth* is in a number of ways suggestive of David Graham Phillips's *The Husband's Story* (1910), but for his novel, Lewis needed no literary hints from others and needed to do no research outside his own experience; and, of course, the Phillips novel was largely forgotten.

These discoveries were likewise those of Sinclair Lewis, and the pathos of the remainder of his life was that he would be unable to cope with his discoveries, to utilize them. He, too, had married a woman of "spaciousness," and that marriage would have only half the life of his first. Generosity and amplitude of spirit may be more difficult to endure than the cramped and little.

Returning from Florida, he took his new wife one day to the editorial offices of *Pictorial Review* where they fell into a friendly argument about the position of women in the United States. Lewis insisted that America was a veritable paradise for women, and Mrs. Lewis replied that she would debate that issue with him whenever he wished. The editor suggested that they write out their debate for publication. The result was a double article called "Is America a Paradise for Women?," which appeared in *Pictorial Review* for June and in which he argued that it was, and she, that it was not. Discussing this article with an interviewer, she said that Lewis's argument was the more interesting but hers was the sounder. One of Lewis's arguments was that professional possibilities for women in the United States were unlimited, and he gave as an example "Miss Frances Perkins, recently appointed State Commissioner of Labor in New York . . . a position considerably weightier than that of the King of Norway or Sweden or the President of the Irish Free State."

This was one of his old acquaintanceships that had now been renewed. "He made a very considerable comeback for a few years," Miss Perkins remembered. "I had dinner at their apartment several times and they dined with us. Actually, Dorothy was more interesting than he was at the time." This was a matter that their friends were all busily discussing and settling in accordance with their own temperaments, and the Lewis marriage was itself almost at once the source of speculation and surmise. William McNally, arriving that year from St. Paul, found Lewis working in his hotel room, and found him ecstatic about his wife—she was a marvelous woman, vastly talented, et cetera. Then, in the middle of a convivial lunch, Mrs. Lewis arrived and, McNally feels, "cut" him, but next day, "under orders," she telephoned with a dinner invitation and was entirely the gracious hostess. Who is the master in West Tenth Street? their friends were asking, rather prematurely, for their life together (when they were together) was happy, and their arguments amiable. Speaking of their published "debate," Mrs. Lewis observed mundanely, "There's nothing like getting paid for a marital argument."

Early in April Mrs. Lewis went to Canada for nearly a month to lecture and to gather material for a series of articles on the liquor situation there. Immediately, Lewis was lonely again. He urged his nephew to come down from Cambridge and visit him in her absence (he had earlier instructed that young man not to "do a thesis on me—it would be prejudiced, pro or con, by the relationship.") The once despised Sir John Squire arrived in New York from London and, only in part because he had given *Dodsworth* higher praise than any other English critic, Lewis saw a good deal of him. At a luncheon given by Sir John, all the guests—C. Hartley Grattan, Clarence Darrow, and others—were known to him except one, Granville Hicks, a new young writer. Lewis gave all his attention to Hicks, trying to break down the barrier of unfamiliarity—in the sociologists' lingo, making that old sad effort "to relate." There were the narcotics of writing short stories and of liquor, but he pined for the return of his wife. On May 10, almost at once after her return, they went to Vermont for the summer.

Now they looked to the big house that adjoined their farm. They remodeled it by adding an enormous barn as a studio–living-room, and an ample bedroom-study for Lewis, but they did not begin—as Dodsworth had dreamed—actively to farm it.* "Are you coming? Are you coming? The place is beautiful now, and salubrious . . ." he was writing to his friends. To Harcourt, who received such a summons, he wrote:

> I feel about one million per cent better up here than in New York. Curiously, I don't get in the least lonely. Evenings we read and sneak off to bed at 11, instead of one or two. And now I'm going out and chop some wood—well, not *much* wood!

But he was also feeling rather poor. He urged Harcourt to do something about the reprint editions of his novels, which should go on selling much better than they were. *Dodsworth* was selling steadily (American sales were at 85,000 by July 10), but he wished that someone would propose play and film purchases. At the end of May the New York *Times* announced that E. Ray Goetz had acquired these rights, but the report was in error. Samson Raphaelson expressed interest in making the dramatic adaptation, and Lewis referred him to Ann Watkins, the agent who was handling the matter, but nothing came of this. Harcourt could do nothing more than she, and some time would pass before negotiations for dramatic rights were at last closed.

In that summer, lightning struck the Lewis house, but it was not by the will of a Kansas god: it also struck the steeple of the Methodist Church in Barnard. Trying to think out the idea of a "god within," Lewis was brooding about the labor novel with no results.

In July he decided that he needed expert help with it, and when the Guthries, returned from Europe, arrived in Barnard for a visit early in August, they found Ben Stolberg, a well-known young labor journalist and a very entertaining raconteur, in residence with one or two other, now nameless authorities.

* In 1939, after Lewis had abandoned her, his wife took to farming the place.

Everybody except Red was buckled down to the job of writing the book. Red himself seemed rather baffled and disconcerted by the invasion. He would take naps, go for walks, read detective stories, get quietly and purposefully drunk, turn out pot-boilers for [*Cosmopolitan*], while the board of experts sat in solemn conclave laying out the novel.

Ben Stolberg was a Marxian theorist, and his approach to the novel was both theoretical and radical, an approach hardly suited to Lewis's talent. He had persuaded Lewis that the original concept of the story was naïve, that "Debs was an insignificant dreamer of no possible interest to any serious student of labor," and that Lewis was too ignorant of European economic thought to write a novel about labor. Lewis himself protested that he did not want to write the kind of novel that his experts wanted him to write. And the matter died out once more, and the experts went back to New York.

Then Lewis went alone to the Bread Loaf Writers' Conference at Middlebury College. He had been invited to give two special lectures to the general session, which consisted of an audience of the aspiring and idealistic young and of spinster schoolteachers, with Robert Gay, Edith Merrilies, and Grant Overton in charge. Lewis was fantastically drunk. He smoked on the platform, swore, and made faces at his tumbler of water. He assured his listeners that they were wasting their time, that it was impossible to teach "creative writing," and that writers generally were a bastard lot of human beings. His major theme, however, was that too much attention had been given to Colonel Lindbergh and not enough to Willa Cather, and presently he was talking about the admirable work of Colonel Cather. When he finished, there was no applause whatever. He had been invited to a party afterward at Robert Gay's cottage, but he wisely chose to disappear for an hour and nap. Then he turned up. How to get rid of him? everyone wondered. But he was now quite sober and he completely charmed them. He was not, however, held to his second engagement, but made a hurried trip to New York, where he arranged with Harcourt, Brace & Company that they contract for the novels of his newest young protégé, a Barnard neighbor named Fred Rothermell, author of two novels called *Superman* and *Fifth Avenue* that Lewis thought promised greatness.

In New York, he continued his revelry. At one party he met Dr. Walter M. Simpson, chief of the Kettering Research Institute, and he made an excuse to draw Simpson aside. They retired to the library, and after some hedging, Lewis asked Dr. Simpson how much danger was involved to a woman in her thirties having her first baby. The doctor suggested that the danger was not great if she was not very close to forty. "Well," Lewis is reported to have said, "it looks like I'll have to get on my bicycle and peddle." On his return to Vermont, he had a letter from Harcourt that said,

"More power to your elbow, which I hope had enough pleasant exercise to justify your visit," and Lewis replied, with a small boy's fib, "I enjoyed my brief bat in New York—my only one in three months."

He made one more public appearance in September when he addressed the Rutland, Vermont, Rotary Club on ladies' night. The Rutland *Daily Herald* account of this talk was later published in an anthology called *Vermont Prose.* When the editor of this volume asked Lewis's permission to reprint the piece, he gave it, and wrote a rather engaging letter in which he regretted its clichés and other stylistic flaws, and a kind of boasting cosmopolitanism.

> This is all deplorable but as it might be of some value in the study of rhetoric, as an example of how not to speak, you are welcome to publish it if you do so wish, and this letter of mine as an introduction—as my apology for not having better expressed an authentic feeling.

The "authentic feeling" was for the natural beauties of Vermont and his belief that it was the obligation and the privilege of the citizenry to preserve those beauties and prevent Vermont from being transformed into another Cape Cod or Florida.

In a more sober mood than that at Bread Loaf and a more serious one than that at Rutland, he wrote—together with many other liberal notables—a letter to the August issue of a Boston periodical called *Lantern,* which was commemorating the second anniversary of the execution of Sacco and Vanzetti. He named the complacency of Americans as their "most terrifying" quality.

> Sacco and Vanzetti were martyrs but, since they were not altogether unwilling to be martyrs, the tragedy does not lie in that. But if they shall have been martyrs in vain, if their agony shall have been lost in a flood of greasy indifference, then will this land prove itself but a blind smug monster.

And he hoped that the anniversary meetings would serve to "ruffle our smugness and remind us that we have not been so just, so free, so honest, nor even so efficient as we like to think."

The mood was too diffuse to help him write the labor novel, and he felt that he needed more practical experience of his subject. In spite of his love of Vermont, he left it at its most spectacular time, early in October. Mrs. Lewis was off on an extended lecture tour, and Lewis decided suddenly to go to Marion, North Carolina, to study the conditions of the textile mill strikers there, and to report them for the Scripps-Howard newspapers. These dispatches were then revised, extended, collected, and published as the pamphlet called "Cheap and Contented Labor." There were six dispatches, and Lewis was probably in Marion for no more than three or four days to gather his impressions of this appalling situation of police brutality and economic slavery. With a tone that varies from the melodramatic to the rather heavily satirical, his account of working and living conditions is nevertheless effective journalism of the kind that it was meant to be, and the Depression seems already to be there in the bald prose that would characterize so much writing about workers in the 1930s.

October, 1929, the month of the stock market crash, was an appropriate time for Lewis to make his most serious efforts to get into his labor novel. He had been "reading innumerable books on the labor movement in the United States," and, back at Twin Farms by October 15, he was planning to leave that day for Toronto where he would attend, for the United Press, the convention of the American Federation of Labor. At the press table of the Royal York Hotel, he met Carl Haessler, the reporter for Federated Press, a labor news service. Ramsay MacDonald, who had already betrayed British Labor, was in Toronto, and Haessler and Lewis were both dismayed by the irony of witnessing the A.F.L. men turned out of their convention hall while MacDonald addressed a large group of Toronto businessmen, and then, in turn, of hearing William Green, the A.F.L. president, invite MacDonald to address his group, which greeted him with equal applause. It was becoming clear to Lewis that organized labor in the United States was in a confused state.

He invited Haessler to his room late that afternoon, and before a considerable party, Lewis, in a raincoat and false mustache, took off MacDonald's speech. He invited Haessler back that evening. Perhaps Haessler, with his more practical experience of labor, could help him as Stolberg, amusing as he was, had not. He returned to his original conception and told Haessler about his plan for a novel with Eugene Debs as the hero, about his need for expert assistance, and about his hope that Haessler would undertake the task.

> He proposed a week or so at his summer home, . . . a week in and around New York, then striking into the field, especially the Pittsburgh and Gary areas and also taking in various meetings and conferences of labor origin or significance. We would be gathering material and color, elaborating the skeleton he already had in vague outline, working out single episodes or chapters, and finally settle down in Bermuda or Nassau where he would hammer out half a million or more words, to be reduced later to normal novel length.

Haessler was interested, and there, on Royal York stationery, Lewis typed out an agreement, which both signed, whereby Haessler was to receive $150 a week and expenses for one month, and if, at the end of that month, "it is agreed to continue," Haessler would receive the same fee together with five per cent of the American royalties on the projected novel. Lewis then gave him the inscribed holograph of his dispatch to the United Press and scribbled on it, "the first baby."

Haessler lived in Ravinia, near Chicago, and he returned to his home now to transfer his business to a friend and to prepare for an extended absence. Lewis returned to Twin Farms, to say good-by once more to his wife, who left for another lecture tour on October 23. On October 26 he wrote to Harcourt about Haessler:

> I'm keener about this novel than anything since *Arrowsmith.* And at the A F of L convention I met exactly the right man for the De Kruif-Birkhead of my novel—Carl Haessler of the Federated Press; college man, Rhodes scholar at Oxford, imprisoned as conscientious obj[ector] during the war, ever since up to his ears in the labor movement; sense of humor; delightful to work with; eager to do the job. He is to join me here, and we'll go snooping about the country together.

Fred Rothermell and his wife were about to move in with him and keep the farmhouse open for the winter, and he was himself planning to stay on "until the roads get bad, making plans for the novel" with Haessler, "so we won't waste motion when we start out." He hoped to have the book finished in a year. On October 30, he wrote his wife:

> I was pretty ba-a-a-d today; I sat reading most of the day, it being very gray and cold out. But I have finished 62 million letters, and I am ready for Carl Haessler's coming this evening. Two weeks—and I'll see you! My little love!

Snow was falling when Haessler arrived, and the nights were cold now, but they stayed on at Twin Farms for about ten days, accomplishing very little but coming to know one another. A request came from an agricultural journal for an article on Russian farms, and Haessler told Lewis what he knew of collective farming, and Lewis wrote the article, for which he received $100. Then a book for review came from *The Nation*—James Myers's *Religion Lends a Hand.* Both found its patronizing attitude toward labor offensive, and when Haessler urged Lewis to review it scoffingly, Lewis told Haessler to write the review and he would sign it. This was done, the review was published, and Lewis endorsed the ten-dollar check to Haessler. They walked in the woods, exchanged reminiscences, and told moldy sexual jokes. Sometimes they talked about the novel. Once, walking through the fields, they amused themselves by compiling a list of surnames for characters, and discussing the kind of characters who would suit the names. On another occasion, Lewis paused on the brow of a hill and looked down the valley below.

> A faraway expression came over his face as he straightened his tall lank figure. He looked solemn and began monologuing about wanting to serve humanity and never betraying his trust. It was some minutes before I realized that he was as it were chanting the beginning of the labor novel about Debs, poetically transfigured by Lewis in this scene as an earnest youth in the mountains looking down into a partly industrialized valley and dedi-

cating himself to the cause of the people. He asked me what I thought of it. Privately I considered it overly sentimental but I told him it might be a good beginning if the softish tone were not carried too far into the book.

For a time, apparently, his plans for the "research" journey with Haessler remained uncertain. On November 3 he had written to Mencken to tell him that he had not a word that he could contribute to the *Mercury,* and concluded:

I remain here in sulky solitude for another couple of weeks, then New York for a week, . . . then out West. Why West? God knows. It is a curse put upon my family, ever since my grandfather was hanged for nameless vices.

They left for Boston on November 7. On the train, Lewis, looking out at the industrial towns of the Merrimac Valley, suggested that they might come back into that area later. In Boston they visited factories, and in a speakeasy, Lewis confessed to Gardner Jackson that his one hope in life was to win the Nobel prize. In New York, Haessler stayed with Lewis on West Tenth Street until Mrs. Lewis returned in the middle of November, but they continued to have daily meetings and excursions after he had moved to the apartment of an academic aunt. They went one evening to a bazaar of the International Labor Defense, a left-wing organization that provided legal assistance to workers, and Lewis joked brightly with the girls in their booths. They went to Paterson, New Jersey, where a textile strike was in progress, and mingled with the strikers. Once they went to the Brookwood Labor College, an independent labor school at Katonah. After these occasions, there was always an analytical session between Lewis and Haessler in which they would discuss motives, personalities, relationships, and Lewis would be eager for Haessler's correction of his impressions.

Alfred Harcourt gave a literary farewell party for them, celebrating the future rather than the immediate past. With the stock market crash, the sales of *Dodsworth,* at about 100,000, had come to a sharp end, but Harcourt told Haessler that he thought Lewis had "a great idea for a successful book." He enjoined him to try to "keep him on the wagon," and it is Haessler's recollection that he drank nothing during those several weeks that they toured Pennsylvania. As they left for Reading on December 1, Dorothy Thompson left on another lecture series that would keep her busy until nearly Christmas, and Lewis did not plan to return to New York until she did.

In Reading they called on James Hudson Maurer, who had been a vice-presidential candidate on the Socialist ticket and head of the Pennsylvania State Federation of Labor. Maurer took them to Harrisburg and regaled them with tales of political and industrial corruption. From Harrisburg, they moved on through western Pennsylvania industrial towns until they came to Pittsburgh, where they paused. For almost ten days, Pittsburgh was their headquarters while they made excursions to nearby coal and steel communities. They went, for example, with a group of National Miners Union men (a small, left-wing rival of the United Mine Workers) to an open meeting of unemployed workers in the steel town of Ambridge. Police followed them in and out of the town, pistols in hand. At the meeting, after the speeches were finished, a collection was taken that totaled $21.95. Twenty dollars had come from Lewis and one from Haessler; the ninety-five cents in nickels and pennies eloquently represented the state of the unemployed.

Their immediate reason for being in Pittsburgh was to attend the sensational trial of Salvatore Accorsi, a coal miner who was accused of killing a state trooper when the police had broken up a Sacco-Vanzetti memorial meeting. The state did not hesitate to bring in fraudulent evidence against Accorsi, who had in fact been clubbed and arrested when the actual killer had escaped. It was a dramatic trial in which the defendant, on December 13, was finally vindicated, to Lewis's great joy. That afternoon, Lewis spoke in exhilaration to about twenty-five hundred students at the University of Pittsburgh. That evening the defense lawyer gave a party at a Pittsburgh club that "provided rich material for Lewis's quest, both in speeches and in table conversation. There was liquor but he did not touch it." He found himself in a congenial atmosphere, and the rank-and-file workers with whom he was talking—and having up to his rooms for dinner on occasion—delighted in his informality and his eagerness for material from their lives. In Pittsburgh, Lewis's social zeal led him to write a letter to the New York *Times* urging Senator Borah to act on American interference in the Nicaraguan elections, and a similar letter appeared in *The Nation* for December 18, called "Devil Dog Rule," and again attacking United States Marine control of Haitian and Nicaraguan politics.

After the Accorsi trial, Lewis spent a few more days in Pittsburgh, now in the company of Ben Stolberg, whose tales he enjoyed, as well as in that of Carl Haessler. With Stolberg he inspected mines and the Westinghouse plants; but on December 16, he left with Haessler for Washington to attend a Southern organizing conference of the American Federation of Labor. With the recent demonstrations of police brutality in textile and tobacco communities like Marion and Gastonia, Lewis and Haessler were hoping for some genuine consolidation of and consequent assistance from the Federation. Urgent young labor men from the South would present their situations to the conference and ask for the help that had brought them there, only to be told, over and over, in William Green's "ponderously hollow tones that the A.F.L. itself was but a federation of international unions, without power or funds of consequence." The workers' hopes, like Lewis's, were dashed. There did not seem to *be* a labor movement! (And it was, of course, another half-dozen years, when John L. Lewis founded the Committee for Industrial Organization, before American labor became an effective operation.)

During the two days of the conference, Lewis's rooms were crowded in every interim with the more progressive of the delegates whom he had encountered. A long table had been set up to accommodate them with food and drink, and on one occasion, after a particularly disappointing session, with everyone in an agitated hubbub, the waiter stood for a long time in front of Lewis, waiting for him to select the menu. At last Lewis threw up his hands, looked mournful, and wailed, "Honest, I'd like to help you, but I'm just a little shit like Willie Green. You'll have to ask somebody else." There were roars of appreciative laughter.

It was at this point that Lewis's interest in Negroes and the Negro situation began to develop. It is Carl Van Vechten's impression that he took them up with a kind of religious fervor rather than out of any human feeling for the individual Negro. But if this fervor grew, the labor fervor, or at least the fervor for the labor novel, began again to subside. What Lewis had seen of organized labor had not encouraged him, and he had been counting on organizational efforts somehow to give his subject shape. Haessler urged that he end the novel with Debs's release from the federal penitentiary by President Harding, but he wanted to end it on a note of triumph or at least of promise, and United States economic history in the early twenties, with the imminent defeat of Robert M. LaFollette in the presidential campaign, did not seem to provide such material. Perhaps his problem was a good deal simpler than he recognized. The working class, in whatever state of organization or disorganization, and whatever its aspirations, was not the middle class. Perhaps the life of Eugene Debs could no longer be relevantly seen in the framework of feeling provided by the idealistic humanitarianism of the years before 1914. The world had turned, and the return of Lewis and Haessler to New York was accordingly gloomy. Lewis's own threatened income, about which he was brooding, did not help matters.

In New York, Haessler urged him and Stolberg to accept an invitation from his aunt to attend a concert at the Women's University Club. In the club dining room, Miss Haessler was understandably offended when Lewis impatiently exclaimed, "My God, I've never seen so much chastity in one place!" The concert itself bored him and Stolberg, and they left at the intermission.

Haessler was returning to Chicago for the Christmas holidays, but it was understood that he and Lewis were to meet in Gary, Indiana, soon after the New Year to continue their field work in the steel mills. But Haessler never saw him again. On January 11, Lewis wrote him as follows:

> I've had a hell of a time these last three weeks trying to decide what I want to do. I've been seeing that our plan of hammering the novel right through will result in its being thin, sketchy, journalistic; I've been seeing

> that I must take perhaps a year of fasting and prayer before I can even begin. But if I do that, I can't possibly afford to have you with me. And in the end I may decide not to do the thing at all. At no matter what cost of derision because I haven't carried out my plans, I won't do the thing unless I can do it in a way that satisfies me.
>
> Loafing around here, meditating, I see more than ever how complicated the whole situation is. And it can't be cleared up just by a few weeks of seeing more people and plants and conventions.
>
> Also the last few days I have been in a rage at the Communists and all their sympathizers for the way in which they have, so far as they could, ruined Karolyi's arrival and his first meeting.* They have lied to him unscrupulously about the Rand School and liberal sympathizers; under pretense of helping him, they have led the poor man into a swamp of confusion. Which same rage is another thing to be digested.
>
> With all affection for you, and all admiration for the splendid help you have given me, I can't see anything for it save to call off our arrangement, at least for a while . . .

He paid him scrupulously and returned a brown sweater that Haessler had left behind, and Haessler went back to his proper work.

It was the beginning of 1930. He was at loose ends. He dashed off little notes such as this to George Seldes, who had visited them in the summer:

> Dear Geo just got book will read it in coupla days and see if I can say Nice Things about it we both love you cummon back quick Yr Accomodations engaged Vermont Dorothy sends love give love Ramon and Marguerite [Guthrie]; send us Tidings your wanderings. Dr. Red Lewis

And there was, of course, the distraught activity of parties.

Mrs. Lemuel Parton remembers entertaining the Lewises at dinner at her Charles Street apartment on January 13. Her other guests were the Woodwards, Mr. and Mrs. E. B. White, and Jack Black, a former burglar and author of *You Can't Win.* Lewis was already considerably intoxicated when he arrived with his wife, and a few more cocktails put him in charge of the party. Making a running commentary on the prospective food, American customs, and a variety of other matters, he began to reseat the guests. Mrs. Parton was about to serve a large roast, perfectly cooked, and she grew increasingly anxious as Lewis continued to reshuffle the seating arrangements. Finally, however, everyone was seated to his satisfaction, the first course was concluded, the roast was produced, carved, and served.

* Karolyi, a Hungarian revolutionary exile, had at last been admitted to the United States for a lecture tour as a result of liberal pressure on the State Department, and a committee of liberals, including Lewis, had arranged for him to speak at the Rand School. Karolyi, however, was persuaded that the Rand School was controlled by "fascists," and he broke his engagement. The committee disbanded, but when Karolyi spoke at Carnegie Hall on January 8, Lewis was in the audience, and after the lecture, strode to the platform and demanded of Karolyi whether he was speaking under Communist auspices. Karolyi replied that he was speaking under private management.

At that point Lewis leaped to his feet with his plate and carried it over to a corner table where the Partons' high-school daughter was dining by herself. "I'd rather talk to you," he said. "You and I aren't civilized—we are cave folk." Whereupon he sat down at her feet, his shoulders partly under the table, the plate of roast beef balanced, neglected and congealing, on his knees, while he discoursed on the subject of cats. Everyone tried to pretend that nothing unusual was happening, and Dorothy Thompson talked about Europe. When dessert was served, Lewis returned to the table but ate nothing.

Then suddenly he leaped up again and announced that he had to telephone the *Daily News*, and from the next room they heard him ask for the City Editor. Lemuel Parton, a newspaperman, was alarmed, and followed him. At his elbow, he overheard Lewis, in a piping Oxford accent, announce that he was Bishop Manning's secretary. "I say, the Bishop is hoping rather badly that you will overlook that little incident . . . What? . . . Oh, that little incident involving the actress . . . What? . . . Oh, just a chorus girl, you know . . . Well, the Bishop feels the whole matter has been quite misunderstood . . . What? . . . Well, really very unfortunate but quite unimportant you understand. . . ." The editor's voice was clamorous for details, but Lewis very gently put the telephone in its cradle. "Now Washington," he said briskly. "The State Department ought to know about the latest international scandal." When this was discouraged, he suggested Hollywood, but the telephone was taken from him, and his wife took him home. The Parton child, who had never before observed intoxication, remarked, "What a nervous man Mr. Lewis is!"

Mrs. Parton remembers two other occasions of this time. One was a lunch at the old Murray Hill Hotel with Clarence Darrow. A band, leading a procession with banners, marched down the street. As if on springs, Lewis leaped to the window, flung it open, and leaned out. Clapping, waving, stamping his feet to the music, he called down to the marchers, "Hurray! Hurray!" Then he turned to Darrow and laughingly said, "Always keep step with a crowd, Darrow. Follow the band! Never gets you into trouble, marching with the crowd." For Darrow, the defender of unpopular causes, there were never any marching bands. Lewis looked at him fondly and said, "Great guy! I love you."

On another occasion the Partons came to his hotel "office" to keep an engagement, and as they were all about to leave, he stopped abruptly and said, "Wait a minute. The tap's running." He called his secretary into the room and began a stream of dictation—scene, persons, events poured out in a cascade, never a pause. Then suddenly he turned off the tap, and they went out.

He was dictating material for the labor novel all the time, but it was not adding up to a novel. He had read enough to write a four-volume history of the labor movement in the United States, but he had no novel. He had no other project into which he wished to fling himself. The rumors that he was a Nobel candidate had died away as mysteriously as they had begun. Thomas Mann had just received the award in literature for 1929. Now what? He announced to his wife that they were going at once to California.

II

MRS. LEWIS had no great desire to see California at this point, nor to travel, and she had several reasons. Among others, she was pregnant and expecting her baby in five months. But Lewis had at least one good reason for wishing to go west, at any rate as far as Reno, and she agreed. On January 18, writing to L. M. Birkhead about his correspondence with Stidger, he concluded:

> I leave Monday for Reno, Nev., then on to California for 6 weeks. . . . I must be in Reno on the 25th. . . . My ex-wife and I have some questions about alimony to settle, and I have to be there for the hearing—as Grace got the divorce there, the Reno court still has jurisdiction. Dorothy will join me there after about three days, and she and I will go on to California for about six weeks. We hadn't expected to go for a couple of weeks, but this hearing thing makes us start off suddenly.

He left New York on January 20, and on January 22 he successfully petitioned the Reno court to reduce his alimony payments to $200 a month on the grounds that he had suffered reverses, that his 1930 income would be no more than $10,000. He was on the witness stand through the whole day and into the evening, but the judge was sympathetic. Mrs. Hegger Lewis, however, was understandably not sympathetic and delayed matters by challenging the claim, with the argument that Lewis's income in 1929 had been $100,000. Within a few weeks, her challenge was denied, and the alimony was reduced—for a time—to $200.

Mrs. Lewis had joined him and they continued west to San Francisco and then to the Carmel area to hunt for a house. In Monterey, less "arty" than Carmel, they found a charming old adobe house with a walled garden, very near the more lavish establishment of Lewis's friends the Gouverneur Morrises. There was a writing room for Lewis, and the garden was lovely, with blooming acacias and quince, roses, forget-me-nots, narcissuses, and, once established, Dorothy Lewis was content.

Gouverneur Morris, the author of flighty "society" novels, was an entertaining man, and his wife was delightful, and the Morrises introduced them to the rich, fashionable, and dull Pebble Beach crowd. Very different from these were Lincoln Steffens and Ella Winter, who lived in Carmel, and whom they also saw. "Sinclair Lewis is here now," Steffens wrote early in February. "He wants to do a Labor novel." Later, Steffens remembered a bit more:

> Once upon a time he called upon me saying he wanted to write a novel on Labor. He pumped me and opposed everything I told him until I lost my temper and roasted him. He danced with joy and when I ceased suddenly from insulting him, he pleaded with me to go on with my interpretation. "Oh, don't stop. Go on and get mad. I can't do a novel unless I can get in a rage and that's what I came here for. I thought you would make me mad." I failed him. . . .

If Steffens said nothing further, that was probably because there was nothing further to be said. Lewis was "loafing."

Yet the book nagged at him and he was impelled to make some effort on its behalf. They had bought a secondhand automobile on their arrival, and early in March they drove to San Francisco, where they stayed for a week. Lewis's chief purpose was to talk to the political prisoners Tom Mooney, J. B. McNamara and Matthew Schmidt (whose name he misspelled) in San Quentin, and he saw them on March 6. His interest in the Mooney-Billings case led Mary E. Gallagher, active in the defense organization, to give the newspapers Lewis's Monterey address, where reporters found him. On March 12, his opinions on the long-delayed pardon were made public.

Upton Sinclair, who lived in Pasadena, suddenly wrote him. He hoped that Lewis was no longer angry about *Money Writes!* and offered his assistance with the labor novel. Lewis replied that he was no longer angry but that he still found the book as "false, unjust, and terribly egotistical" as he had two years before.

> It was generous of you to offer to talk over the labor novel with me, but it would be mistaken. I have talked a lot to such people as Norman Thomas, Jim Maurer, Oscar Ameringer, Tom Mooney, Schmitt and McNamara, and such opposition figures as Green and Matty Woll of the A. F. of L. But two novelists discussing it would see it in too literary a way; and each of us would later be afraid to use certain ideas—though ab initio we might each of us have them in common—for fear we had taken them from the other.

His circumspection was so great that when, presently, he drove his wife to Los Angeles, he did not attempt to see Sinclair.

Helpful as Mooney may have been to the novel, Lewis did not see him again, although he had hoped to. When Mary E. Gallagher urged him to protest publicly a *Collier's* article on the Mooney case (which Mooney himself presently answered) Lewis declined on the grounds that the article was too "ephemeral" to be of any importance. However, Lewis did trouble to interest an influential San Franciscan broker in the case, Jesse Lilienthal, "son of the Lilienthal who was President of the San Francisco Street Railway when Tom was sent to prison. He is an extremely nice chap and remarkably fair-minded. I actually got him to promise to go with me to call on Tom if I should be able to go to San Quentin again." But he did not go back, and at this point, did nothing more for Tom Mooney.

He did not get on with the novel, but he enjoyed Monterey and the company it provided. His wife, however, was growing increasingly restless, bored with the Pebble Beach people and, nearly thirty-six now, anxious about her pregnancy and eager to be near her doctor. "This country," she wrote impatiently to Mencken on March 28, "is full of cypresses, polo ponies, and morons. We shake its dust from our feet in a few days." Hollywood had shown some interest in the three-part *Cosmopolitan* serial, "Let's Play King," and there was renewed interest in the dramatic and film rights to *Dodsworth* ("I'd be glad to get 50,000, but I'd take less"), and the Woodwards were in Los Angeles, urging the Lewises to visit them. They decided to make their return by way of Santa Barbara and Hollywood.

They were the Woodwards' house guests. Woodward was ghostwriting the autobiography of William Gibbs McAdoo, *Crowded Years,* and when McAdoo and his wife, Woodrow Wilson's daughter, heard that Sinclair Lewis was with them, they asked to meet him. Woodward recalled that whenever Lewis was to meet strangers, especially distinguished strangers, he made a point of being drunk, but on this occasion he was sober and delightful. Next day, however, when Louis Bromfield arrived to meet him, followed by a number of newspapermen for an interview, Lewis could not at first be found, and when he was found at last, it was in a hammock on the lawn, asleep and snoring, with a nearly empty bottle of Scotch and a glass on a little table beside him. They could not waken him. Bromfield stayed until seven o'clock, hoping that Lewis would get up, but he slept on and at last Bromfield went away. Later in that visit, they did meet, and discussed the horrors of writing for the films, Bromfield's present occupation.

Mrs. Lewis's impatience did not decrease. When Mrs. Woodward announced that she was to go to the hospital for several days for a tonsillectomy, Mrs. Lewis "declared that she could not cope with the confusion and excitement of the situation." She wanted to go home and said so again to Lewis. He said, "Yes, you go. I'll follow." And she went off by herself. She paused for a few days with her friend Rose Wilder Lane in the Ozarks, and then continued to New York. She was deeply hurt, and looking back, she thought that this was the point at which she knew that her marriage was not going to be a marriage after all, that she must protect herself in preparation for its collapse.

On the day that Mrs. Woodward entered the hospital, Lewis went to a cocktail party at the house of Samson Raphaelson. Woodward was too busy to go with him, but it was understood that Lewis was to bring a half dozen of the guests back for dinner. Long past the dinner hour he had not come back, and when Raphaelson called at last, it was to say that as soon as Lewis arrived at the party, he lay down on a couch and went to sleep. They had been trying ever since, without success, to rouse him. Woodward volunteered to get him, and after a good deal of effort, managed to push him into a taxi, and on the drive home he revived "wonderfully." At dinner, as a joke, Woodward said that he now knew who had written "Ten Nights in a Barroom," and when asked who it was, he pointed to Lewis. Lewis arose from the table, announced that he had been insulted, left the room and was seen no more that evening. When Woodward went to bed, he looked into his room and saw that he was asleep.

> Around two in the morning he came into my room and sat on the edge of the bed. "Bill," he said, "I love you, but I must go. I don't fit in here. I want to hire a chauffeur for my car. I don't trust myself in driving. Can you let me have Robert for a few days?"
>
> I said I could not spare Robert, and I told him that he could get a chauffeur in the morning by calling up an agency.
>
> Next morning I went down to breakfast at eight o'clock and there was "Red," sitting at the table and eating his oatmeal. He looked as lively and pleasant as one could wish. . . . Outside, in the street, his car was throbbing with a chauffeur at the wheel. He said good-by cordially, and we parted on good terms.*

He drove back to Monterey, sold his car and on April 10, a Thursday, wired the Birkheads in Kansas City to tell them to expect him on the following Tuesday. "Don't tell anyone coming." But on the day of his arrival, the Kansas City *Star* found him. The Stidger correspondence had been published, and the reporters were eager to know whether Sinclair Lewis wished to add anything to his letter. Replied Lewis, and was so quoted: "I feel that by himself the Reverend Mr. Stidger has already been able to obtain sufficient publicity out of his slight acquaintanceship with me, and I am disinclined to give him any more." He stayed for a few days, but on April 20 he was writing Mencken from his New York address: "I have just returned to Christian lands. . . . I spend my days in arduous and godly labor in a room at the Hotel Lafayette."

Lewis was expecting a daughter. Writing to his nephew about their summer plans, he said, "I don't know whether I have told you, but you will have a new cousin, Miss Dorothy Sinclair Lewis." Their plans were to go to Vermont at once, get the house in order, and return to New York

* But the friendship was over. The end was sealed when, four years later, Woodward published his *New Yorker* profile, "The World and Sauk Centre."

until the baby was born. They left on April 23, and Mrs. Lewis stayed at Twin Farms until May 5, when she returned to New York alone. He was drinking heavily and feeling very miserable, and before she left him, Mrs. Lewis called Ramon Guthrie in Hanover to say that she was afraid to leave him there alone and would Guthrie come and keep him company. Presently Lewis received a letter from Ray Everett, a young editor in the Harcourt office. Paul Morand had published a short article about Lewis in France, and Lewis had suggested that it be translated and offered to the *Saturday Review of Literature* or the *Times Book Review*. Harcourt had obliged, and Everett's letter, which began "Dear Red," told him that the piece had been shown around but that "nobody had fallen for it."

The phrase, "fallen for it," outraged his pride, and he seized upon the impertinence of the salutation to fly into a rage. Who was a little unknown clerk in Alf Harcourt's office to take such liberties with him? Was Lewis's name not big enough to merit Harcourt's exalted attention? The rage grew as the day faded, and at about nine o'clock that night, Lewis began to telephone. He called Harcourt's house in Riverside and got Mrs. Harcourt. Alf was at a movie in New York. "Well, have him paged. This is important! I've got to talk to him tonight!" He was in the city all right, but he was not at any *movie,* Lewis stormed. Then he called Donald Brace's house and got no answer. Now he was reminded that Harcourt had not done anything about getting out a collected edition of his novels, and that was really too much to endure. His mind snapped with a decision: Guthrie was to telephone George Doran of Doubleday, Doran and Company at once! This was curious, since Lewis had disliked Doran ever since he had worked for him, and no less so since he liked to make his own telephone calls. His reluctance to make the call himself may have been the small voice of good sense as it opened the way for Guthrie to persuade him not to do it.

Guthrie suggested that he would be in a much better position if he had a book at least well under way before he began to look for another publisher, and he pointed out too that it would be much more in keeping with Lewis's position to let Doran come to *him.* The second was a persuasive argument, and Lewis subsided; but he continued to brood over his grievances. When Guthrie was next in New York, Harcourt got in touch with him chiefly to discover whether he thought that the firm had let Lewis down and whether Lewis really thought so. Lewis did think so, and, in spite of an occasional thaw, there was a new coolness between him and his publishers. The old, flourishing correspondence between Lewis and Harcourt dwindled to matter-of-fact notes on routine matters.

In about a week, Lewis followed his wife to New York. There were nearly six weeks of the city to endure.

At the end of *Exile's Return,* Malcolm Cowley gives an account of the swirling madness that characterized literary New York in 1930, the crazily drunken irresponsibility, the cracking relationships, the breakdowns, the suicides—as if the decade that had ended were pulling itself together in a last, shrill concentrated crescendo of self-laceration and disgust. Lewis —trying to settle down, feeling gentler about the United States than he ever had, about to become a father for a second time, but nursing resentments and fancied injuries too—could only have been encouraged in his own follies by this atmosphere, especially since he had no real project to which he could devote his "arduous and godly labors." Mrs. Lewis was doing what she could to keep him from drinking, but she had small success. He had his ready ruses. One evening when the Harrison Smiths were coming for dinner with some others, he asked Smith to bring a bottle of gin and leave it in his coat pocket in the hall closet, and during the evening, ostensibly not drinking with the others, he would surreptitiously retire to his coat. The secrecy of the act lent to it a thrill of guiltiness. When the baby was a little late in arriving, Lewis insisted that they give a prenatal celebratory party. At that party, Mrs. Lewis's labor pains began. For him the revelry was over as he took her to the Woman's Hospital far uptown and, while the party went on, awaited the baby's birth.

Michael Lewis was born on June 20. "I crave the honor of helping you, at the first convenient time, to celebrate the auspicious event. I suggest naming the boy Irving Babbitt Lewis." * (Lewis was presently to be quoted in the newspapers as saying that he hoped the boy would grow up a Babbitt of his own kind. "What's wrong with them?") Mencken sent the child a toy and Beethoven's Ninth Symphony, and helped the father celebrate. George Jean Nathan remembered an invitation to dinner at West Tenth Street delivered suddenly and mysteriously late in the afternoon. Three other men had been summoned: "one a writer, one a labor leader, . . . and one an intermittent producer of theatre plays"—Mencken, Stolberg and Goodman. In the middle of dinner, Lewis announced that his surgeon was arriving to treat his face and the guests were to observe his performance with the electric needle. "Protests being of no avail, we had to entertain Lewis while the surgical performance was in progress. 'Looking at you guys gives me such a pain,' he observed, 'that the other one in comparison won't seem so bad.' " Such japery was hardly calculated to comfort or compliment his wife in her confinement. He called on her each day, having first set the time, and then invariably arrived hours late and almost always intoxicated, in a haze of boozy affection.

As soon as she was able, she returned to the relative calm of Vermont. Thanking Mencken for his attentions, she wrote, "The Michael whom you

* On May 4, writing to commend Mencken for his book *Treatise on the Gods*, Lewis had written: "I am therefore all the gladder that you have done so superior an opus just before May 9th, when Irving Babbitt will bury you, Cabell, Dreiser, and me with brief and bitter obsequies." Babbitt, on that day, was to debate publicly with Carl Van Doren and others on the New Humanism.

hail is red-headed, has a mighty nose, a quivering nostril, a prodigious frown, a tremendous yell, and a charming grin. There is no question of his legitimacy." If there was no question of paternity, there was a question of paternal tolerance. Lewis, puttering at his novel, found the nursery atmosphere and the child's noise, uncongenial, and it was arranged that little Michael and his nurse should be established in separate residence in the smaller house, the farm. Guests, and there were many in that summer, would stay at the farm, too, or, if necessary, spill over into the big house.

Lewis's writing was not progressing. He wrote a letter to the *New Masses:*

> Listen, Comrade! I met Mike Gold the other night and I think he is a grand guy. But when he said that Walter Pater wrote like a fairy for a fairy, it seemed to me that he was merely doing the Humanist idiocy from the opposite angle. No matter. I am sending $1.50 for a year's subscription to the *New Masses.*

But he was in no political danger, as is made evident by his chilly letter to the *Gosizdat* in Moscow, which had asked, under a misconception, for advance proofs of his next novel.

> The Gosizdat is in error in understanding that I am writing about the class-struggle of California textile workers. In the first place, there are no textile workers in California; in the second place I am not writing about either California or textile workers. As a matter of fact I do not know just exactly what I shall next write about. But when I finish my next novel, I shall be glad to have my publishers send you proofs well in advance of publication here, and I understand that I shall then be paid royalties.

He reminded the State Publishing House of his efforts on behalf of a publishing convention with the United States, but now he added, "I should be glad to receive royalties on the already published novels." In August, the credit in his royalty account at Harcourt, Brace & Company was only $866.

Jonathan Cape had issued a uniform, five-shilling edition of his novels in England, and Lewis had been urging Harcourt to do the same in New York, with the difference that each novel would carry an introduction by a distinguished writer, most of them Europeans. His wife, with her many connections, would make the arrangements. Harcourt was proceeding with this plan when, early in August, Lewis announced that, after consideration, he felt that the novels deserved "a really fine edition—say $3.00 or $3.50 a volume . . . on *paper that will last.*" Harcourt pointed out the economic impossibility of this proposal and offered again to proceed with the inexpensive reprint.

Wells Lewis, who was about to enter Phillips Academy at Andover, spent the entire summer at Twin Farms, and Mrs. Lewis gave much of her time to "trying to keep him from getting on his father's nerves—& failing." She was happy with her baby, but she was also brooding about her future. For her own work she should have several months abroad, and it was at first planned that in October they would take the child to Europe for the winter. In August, Lewis wrote H. G. Wells to ask whether he would be in England between October 15 and November 15, when he expected to be in London. The stream of house guests continued through the summer. H. L. Mencken, belatedly married, brought his new bride to Barnard as part of their honeymoon.* Late in the summer, F. P. Adams and his wife appeared for a weekend, and by now the Lewises' plans for Europe were wavering. When it developed that the Adamses' house in Westport was free for rental, the Lewises, who did not want to spend the winter in Manhattan, decided to postpone the European journey and take the Westport place, and in the new year, Mrs. Lewis might go to Europe alone for a month or six weeks.

They would stay on at Twin Farms until mid-October. Lewis's writing had settled down to a series of efforts for *The Saturday Evening Post.* For *The Nation,* he wrote an enthusiastic review of Mary Heaton Vorse's *Strike!,* a novel "of the horrors of the Southern textile mills," but his own novel about labor had once more been put aside. In September he announced to Ramon Guthrie that he was going to write a novel about a businesswoman. Did Guthrie know anything about businesswomen? Neither, said Lewis, did he. But that novel, too, which would prove to be *Ann Vickers,* would be a long time in coming. In the meantime, he had discovered a new literary enthusiasm—Thomas Wolfe's first novel, *Look Homeward, Angel,* which had been published a year before, and he wrote Wolfe in praise. "There is, you needn't be told, authentic greatness in it." In New York, Wolfe found his candor hard to accept. To Cornelius Traeger, Mrs. Lewis's doctor, he kept repeating the question, "What does Mr. Lewis want?" A suspicious man, Wolfe found it hard to believe that a famous writer, quite simply, admired him.

The letter to Wolfe was written after Mrs. Lewis had gone down to Westport but not before she herself had written a long letter to the Woodwards in which storm signals are evident:

> . . . *my* brain has gone *phut* but that's due to domesticity—(which is unavoidable. Show me a woman married to an artist who can succeed in her

* Congratulating him, Lewis wrote with prophetic facetiousness: "Don't let Phil Goodman persuade you that the lady will be unable to tolerate you for more than seven weeks. Think! In over two years of marriage, Dorothy has left me forever not more than five times, and she is still with me—unless, possibly, what she asserts to be a shopping trip to Woodstock shall prove to have been only a sly method of escaping. I believe, then, that if the lady is a good cook and of remarkable patience, and if you will but give up creme de menthe before breakfast, your union will endure."

> marriage without making a full-time profession out of it. Oh, Jesus God!) ... a couple of months by myself seems necessary and desirable—a couple of months away from my very little boy—ten or twelve days journey away —seems brutal. Brutal, I mean, to me. He is the most lovely thing that ever happened to me.

Again Lewis had let her go ahead without him. He was lingering on for two weeks in Vermont, closing that house while she opened the other. Then, early in November, with no clear literary purpose in mind, he followed her. She was preparing to settle down to journalistic activity and, indeed, on the morning of November 5 was in Manhattan. On that morning Lewis got up very late and was lounging about in his pajamas when the telephone rang and an excited voice with a Swedish accent announced to him that he had been awarded the Nobel prize in literature. The voice was that of a Swedish newspaper correspondent in New York who had managed to track Lewis down for the Swedish Embassy, but Lewis thought that it was the voice of his friend, Ferd Reyher, who liked to do imitations and play jokes. "Oh yeah?" he replied. "You don't say! Listen, Ferd, I can say that better than you. Your Swedish accent's no good. I'll repeat it to you." And he repeated it, "You haf de Nobel Brize," and more. The bewildered Swede protested in vain and finally called an American to the telephone to confirm the news. Lewis fell into a chair.

In a few moments the telephone rang again. It was Thomas Costain at *The Saturday Evening Post.* Lewis had sent him a story that was rather longer than his usual contributions and Costain wanted to propose an adjustment of his payment. Costain could not seem to make him understand; his voice was faint and blurred. At last he said, "Tom, I have won the Nobel prize. No one knows. I've just been sitting here." He was most amiable about the adjustment of his word rate.

Then he telephoned his wife. "Dorothy," he said, breathing heavily, still dazed, "Oh, Dorothy!" She thought that he was ill and asked in quick alarm, "What's the matter?" "Dorothy, I've got the Nobel prize." "Oh, have you!" she said briskly. "How nice for you! Well, I have the Order of the Garter!"

"... I today counted 155 separate persons whom we've met since January 4th and whom we seem to know intimately!"

FIVE

Decline

I

FROM THE PEAK, one looks down a long, descending road. "This is the end of me," Lillian Gish heard him say. "This is fatal. I cannot live up to it."

He said nothing of the sort on that first day. The telephone kept ringing, but Lewis managed to dress himself at last and get to New York, where Harcourt, Brace & Company had arranged a press conference for that afternoon. He managed, too, to prepare a statement to be distributed at that conference, a statement that answered the two questions that he had been persistently asked on the telephone that morning: what was he going to do with the money; and why was he going to accept this prize when he had not felt, four years earlier, that he could accept the Pulitzer? The answer to the first question was that he would "use it to support a well-known young American author and his family, and to enable him to continue writing." (This reply was widely interpreted, especially by the Germans, to mean that he was going to give the money away to some worthy young writing fellow, and it was hailed as an act of extraordinary magnanimity.)

The answer to the second question was more complicated: the Nobel had no strings attached to it, since the Swedish Academy interpreted the clause in the Nobel will, "the most distinguished work of an idealistic tendency," to mean only that it was not merely commercial work (he did not observe that the clause had been advanced as an argument against a number of candidates, including Ibsen and Hardy), whereas the comparable clause in the Pulitzer will indicates a nonliterary standard of merit. (To demonstrate his point, Lewis listed five American novels, of high distinction in his view, that had not won the Pulitzer; he did not suggest that a large number of Nobel winners, from the first, Sully Prudhomme, on, were of small literary consequence.) A further difference lay in the fact that the Nobel went to a man for his *oeuvre,* whereas the Pulitzer went to a single novel, and in any one year, there might be a number of equally fine novels, all but one of which would not be honored. (The Swedish Academy made it clear that the prize to Lewis was determined by the single novel, *Babbitt.*)

Most reporters and editorialists found these arguments disingenuous, and many—particularly Ernest Boyd in *The New Freeman*—did not hesitate to suggest that Lewis was hoist with his own petard. And from the outset, even before these utterances began to rumble through the press, Lewis was discomfited. The press conference on November 5 was not a vast success. Harcourt, Brace & Company had filled an office with folding chairs rented from a funeral parlor. When Lewis entered the room and sat down at a desk that faced the room, a reporter from International News Service, Croswell Bowen, more brash than the rest, seized his chair, placed it at the desk, and, with his back to the crowd, said, "I'm Bowen of the I.N.S. Congratulations," and, his face thrust within two feet of Lewis's, stared intently at him. (The account is H. Allen Smith's.) Lewis stood up. "Perhaps you'd like to sit in my chair," he said stiffly.

> "Ha!" cried Bowen of the I.N.S. "That's a good one! No, I'll stay right where I am. How does it feel?"
>
> "How does *what* feel?" asked Lewis. . . .
>
> "To win this prize," said Bowen. . . .
>
> "Well . . ." said Lewis, trying to make the best of an uncomfortable situation, knowing the rest of us were sitting there watching the little drama, realizing that he had to handle himself carefully or run the risk of making an ass of himself. "Well . . ."
>
> "Listen," [Bowen] said, leaning even closer to Lewis. "What're you gonna expose next?"
>
> Lewis glanced appealingly over the room.
>
> "What do you mean, what am I gonna expose next?"
>
> "I mean," persisted Bowen, . . . "what're you gonna expose next?"
>
> "What have I exposed already?" challenged Lewis.
>
> "Babbitt," snapped Bowen. . . . "You exposed Babbitt and all the others, and now I wanna know what's next on the list."
>
> Lewis was patently irritated.
>
> "Young man," he said, "I'm not, as you have it, gonna expose nothin' next. I'm not in the exposin' business. I'm—"
>
> "Oh yes, you are. . . . I want a yarn out of this about what's next. Now, come on. What'll it be next?"
>
> "God damn it," said Lewis, "I told you I'm not in the business of exposing things. I'm a novelist. I write novels. I don't go around—"
>
> "A-h-h-h!" said Bowen . . . and, turning to face the rest of us, grinned knowingly and winked, letting us know he was in control of this situation. Then he turned back to the furious winner of the Nobel Prize. "Let's have it," he insisted. "What're you gonna expose next?"
>
> Sinclair Lewis sat and looked at Bowen of the I.N.S. for a long time. Then he got up from his chair, walked around the desk and faced the rest of us.

Someone drew Bowen aside, and the others took over. "It was pretty dull, too, after Bowen dropped out." But Lewis was irked. To one question, he named the American novelists who, "beside myself," he considered great; it was the usual list—Dreiser, Cabell, Hergesheimer, Cather, Wharton, with Thomas Wolfe now added. To another question he snapped, "I don't know *what* the hell this country needs."

Before that conference was over, the office of Harcourt, Brace & Company was being flooded with congratulatory telegrams. Word came from his former wife: "The one thing that you wanted I cried with happiness when I heard." (In the next week, she petitioned the court that her alimony be returned to a thousand dollars per month.) There were wires from friends, of course, from publishers, and from reviewers; but the interesting list is made up of the writers who were impelled to congratulate: from France, only Paul Morand; from Germany, only Lion Feuchtwanger; from the United States, Louis Bromfield, Lynn Montross and Owen Johnson (Barnard neighbors), Vincent Sheean, Carl Van Vechten, W. E. Woodward, Wallace Irwin, William Seabrook (all friends), Eugene O'Neill, René Fülöp-Miller (a Westport neighbor); from England, none. There followed, of course, letters of congratulation, some from unknown persons, many from friends, the prominent among these—Frank B. Kellogg, William G. McAdoo, John Haynes Holmes, Frances Perkins, William Green, Sidney Hillman. There was a moving letter from a Viennese doctor, a friend of Dorothy Thompson: *"Ich fange an, an die Welt zu glauben,"* and wishing that young Michael *"hatte ein so heisses Herz, einen so starken Verstand und ein so bewegliches Mundwerk wie sein Vater."* There was a charming letter from the infirmary of Phillips Academy at Andover:

> *Dear Father,*
> I couldn't write yesterday because I had both eyes closed with poison ivy. Its wonderful wonderful wonderful about the Nobel prize. The only one you wanted. Oh how proud and happy I am.
> Eeeeeee!
> Love and love and love and lots of love
> from *Wells*

But the interesting list is made up again of the names of writers who chose to praise him: Cabell and Sinclair and Hergesheimer; Waldo Frank; Willa Cather, who, while she could not honestly say that she was happy that he rather than she had won the prize, would, she said, rather see him win it than anyone else; Morley Callaghan; and William Lyon Phelps ("It's too gorgeous for words").* Only two British writers chose to tell him of their pleasure: Hugh Walpole, predictably, and E. M. Forster, most engagingly:

* In thanking Phelps, Lewis wrote, "It is, by the way, absolutely the only word I have had as yet from Yale." Within a week, however, he had official greetings from the secretary of his class ("The fellows were awfully pleased"); this letter contained the jolly admonition that Lewis must not again let himself appear in the newsreels.

> I want to add one letter more to the thousands that are encumbering your desk, and to tell you how delighted I am about the Nobel award. It was a splendid decision—they have done themselves proud—and I hope that you two are pleased about it, and realize that, through you, many a fellow writer of yours feels that he has himself been honoured.

The Lewis desk was not encumbered with thousands of letters, and it had been made all too clear to him that few writers felt themselves honored through the international glamour that had been thrown upon him.

Rebecca West, looking back, says that most British writers were outraged by the award, but the British press in general viewed the choice of the Swedish Academy with approval. The *New Statesman* was rather exceptional in its harsh view that "previously none of the awards has been noticeably ridiculous." Critics and commentators on the Continent were, in general, satisfied, and most were enthusiastic. But in the United States, "something very like a groan went up," said Ludwig Lewisohn, from most writers and critics. The mood that Lewis had briefly exemplified more emphatically than anyone else was over, and Lewis was generally thought of as finished.

The aggressively enlightened had, of course, almost never taken him seriously. The experimentalists and the expatriates thought of him as a commercial hack. The academic critics, whether simple literary historians like Fred L. Pattee, or dogmatic authoritarians like Professor Babbitt and his followers in the New Humanism, or old-fashioned conservatives like Henry Van Dyke in the American Academy—they were united in their displeasure. "Nothing [Lewis] can write can matter much now," Professor Pattee had just pontificated in *The New American Literature,* and the brilliant young liberal critic, T. K. Whipple, had just published his damaging estimate (one of the few genuinely critical appraisals of Lewis up to that time, and up to this) in *Spokesmen.* Young radicals found Lewis politically illiterate. Older writers of no particular allegiance, like Sherwood Anderson, spoke out against him on the grounds of art. A younger writer, Ernest Hemingway, writing to a friend, called the award a filthy business whose only merit was that it had eliminated the Dreiser menace. Dreiser sulked in his tent.

It is possible that in 1930 Sinclair Lewis despaired of ever winning the prize he coveted, but Alfred Harcourt knew that in Sweden it was common knowledge that an American was to be chosen, and that the choice lay between Lewis and Dreiser. (Harcourt did everything he could to keep this knowledge from Lewis, who, in some rash statement, might so well have ruined everything.) Shortly before the announcement of the awards, the Stockholm newspaper *Dagens Nyheter* published a series of articles by a close friend of Erik Axel Karlfeldt, the chairman of the Nobel committee in that year, on these two novelists, and prefaced them with another article on the background of American writing up to the point at which they had begun to publish. Dreiser, this estimate concluded, was in some ways mightier, but Lewis, with his humor, was more attractive.

Lewis was nominated by the late Henrik Schück, member of the Swedish Academy and eminent Uppsala professor of the history of art and literature. He proposed the name with the utmost brevity, without the special argument that usually accompanies nominations. It was the first time that Sinclair Lewis had been nominated for the prize. When the special three-man committee of the Academy came to vote, Anders Österling moved for Dreiser, but Per Hallström, with Karlfeldt, chose Lewis, and the simple majority ruled. Österling himself was later to write that the "gay virtuosity and flashing satire" of the latter was preferable, in the committee's view, to the more substantial qualities of "the ponderous and solemn" Dreiser, and the Academy wished "to recognize a vigorous trend in modern literature —high-class American humor, the best traditions of which had been continued with such marked success by Sinclair Lewis." *

In the United States, Dreiser's friends were bitterly disappointed. Madeleine Boyd wrote him and expressed her regret. For a long time, Dreiser too had looked with longing toward this award. So early as 1911 he had shared his hope with Mencken, in the further hope that Mencken would nominate him—a procedural impossibility. In 1920, writing again to Mencken, he was like Lewis in his indifference to election to the National Institute but allowed that he would "take the Nobel Prize or any other cash prize or cash. . . ." He repeated the hope in 1921. It could only have grown after the publication of *An American Tragedy* in 1925, and, with the current of gossip in 1930, could only have come to its climax. Yet to Madeleine Boyd he expressed indifference and did not mention the name of Sinclair Lewis; he only regretted that his friends had occasion to feel regret.

Lewis could hardly have been unaware of this giant nursing his wounds; the fact was one more barb, repeatedly thrown by the press, to prick his pleasure, and there could have been little balm in such an immediate request, for example, as that of Vrest Orton, founder of the *Colophon* and a publisher and fine printer in Vermont, that he be allowed to compile his bibliography. Vacillating between humility and arrogance, between graciousness to his fellow writers and snappish irritation with reporters, holding at last all that he had wanted but deprived somehow of all its deepest satisfactions, Sinclair Lewis was not a triumphant man. W. E. Woodward later

* For some of this material I am indebted to Carl R. Anderson, *The Swedish Acceptance of American Literature* (1957) and to Anders Österling's essay, "The Literary Prizes," in *Nobel: The Man and his Prizes,* ed. H. Shück (1950). A more recent account is Sheldon Grebstein's "Sinclair Lewis and the Nobel Prize," *Western Humanities Review,* vol. XIII, no. 2 (Spring 1959).

said that the Nobel prize had cured him of his feelings of inferiority; he could hardly have been more mistaken. More accurately, Ludwig Lewisohn observed in understatement that he "did not bear the glory that had come to him with equanimity or ease."

There were three weeks, in this charged air, to make preparations and to celebrate, and there was much of celebration. Preparations did not include arrangements for sailing on the *Drottningholm* on the twenty-ninth, all of which were attended to by the Swedish embassy. They did lead Sinclair Lewis to seek out a new skin doctor, Dr. Paul Gross, whom he first saw on November 12. Lewis was sensitive to pain, and Dr. Gross remembers that he would manage to have had a good number of numbing drinks before coming to face the pricks of the electric needle that removed the precancerous growths on his face. But, in at least one recollection, Lewis stayed quite sober during this period of celebration, while his friends, who were speculating on his conduct at the court of King Gustav, which they assumed would in one way or another be hilariously malapropos, carried on.

A letter of congratulation came from Laurence Todd, a Washington labor reporter, urging him not to "forget that your labor audience is waiting for the publication of your best book," which would now be "tenfold more effective with the gents who stand on the workers' necks and talk about golf"; and another came from Carl Haessler, to whom Lewis replied:

> I still may do the labor novel some day, but I think it will probably be in very different form from that in which I was planning it. It is not a question of its being more or less radical. It is a question of its being more a novel of character and less one of ideas and propaganda, because the novel of character is really the only one I can do with any success.

It may be conjectured that he was now not very much concerned with the labor novel. Another letter, less of hope than of gratitude, came from Thomas Wolfe, thanking Lewis for his kindness and for his having mentioned his work at the press conference on November 5; and Lewis, in reply, eagerly proposed a meeting in London in January.

On November 25, the P.E.N. gave a dinner in Lewis's honor at the Commodore Hotel. Wallace Irwin presided, and about one hundred and fifty writers and publishers attended to hear William Lyon Phelps praise Sinclair Lewis as an "idealistic man of letters." * Another dinner was go-

* The dinner in Lewis's honor was a gracious gesture, but he himself must have been impressed by those who were absent. The New York *Times* listed the names of the persons who seemed to its writer most distinguished: Dr. and Mrs. Harry Elmer Barnes, Silas Bent, Mr. and Mrs. D. C. Brace, Dr. and Mrs. Henry Seidel Canby, Mrs. William Brown Meloney, Irita Van Doren, Charles Caldwell Dobie, of San Francisco; Mr. and Mrs. D. A. Doran, Phyllis Duganne, Will Durant, John Farrar, Clayton Hamilton, Alfred Harcourt, Roland Holt, Fannie Hurst, Inez Haynes

ing on simultaneously for Rabindranath Tagore, the only other non-European to have won the Nobel prize in literature, at the Biltmore, and Lewis and Tagore had earlier been brought together at the home of Henry Morgenthau. No Indian serenity infused Lewis's remarks at his dinner: if American authors and artists would begin to take their work and themselves seriously, they might come to enjoy some of the esteem that the public squanders upon carburetor manufacturers, politicians, golf champions, football coaches, and home-run hitters. And find, he might have asked, that Europe, too, would praise them?

He was a moderately harried man, hastily leaving the United States and groping toward the Swedish court. On November 26 came a telegram from an agent of a South American periodical called *Critica,* attempting to fix arrangements for an interview that the publicity man at Harcourt, Brace & Company had "made every possible effort to make impossible." On this telegram, Lewis scribbled a variety of notes that were to remind him of things to do. There were matters of insurance, Michael's guardianship, the forwarding of mail, roses to be sent to someone, and so on. There were also the names "of Queen & princes & princesses" to be memorized (there was no Queen of Sweden just then), and those of "Other Nobel winners." There was an adjuration not to forget the Swedish writers, "Ostenso—Rohlvaag." There was a list of writers who had not won the Nobel prize: Galsworthy, Croce, D'Annunzio, Wells, Joyce, Feuchtwanger, Hemingway. And there was a curious bit of arithmetic:

$$\begin{array}{r} 48000 \\ \underline{16200} \\ 31800 \end{array}$$

The first sum represents the approximate amount of the prize; the second might be the total of his former wife's increased alimony, his son's tuition, and perhaps the cost of staying on in Europe for a time and the passage back. Whatever the angry, the injured, the jealous, the vindictive were saying, Sinclair Lewis would presently have thirty thousand dollars net.

Two days later, speaking to the Germantown (Pennsylvania) Business Men's Luncheon Club, Dr. Henry Van Dyke, the Princeton cleric and academician, commented unfavorably on the award of the Nobel prize to Lewis. (Justice Holmes wrote of Van Dyke that he was a man who could strut when he was sitting down.) Whether he said that the award was "an insult to America," as the press and, in his Nobel address, Sinclair Lewis reported, or whether he said that "it was a backhanded compliment" to America, as he himself claimed when he clarified his remarks to the press,

Irwin, Wallace Irwin, Dr. Henry Goddard Leach, Mrs. Alice Duer Miller, Mrs. Elinor Mordaunt, Mrs. Corinne Roosevelt Robinson, Fortunat Strowski, and Carl Van Doren.

hardly matters. His observation, made on the eve of Lewis's departure, renewed the controversy and could only have hurt and angered Lewis more.* He rallied, however, when they sailed next day. Asked to comment on Van Dyke's remarks, his face clouded, he hesitated, and then replied, "What can I say? Nothing. If I were to say what I think it would burn up the paper. . . . I am honored no less that American colleagues have attacked my work, and I am particularly honored that the attack came from where it did." Carrying a book called *Swedish in Ten Lessons,* a volume of Swedish short stories in translation, and a book about Alfred Nobel called *Dynamite and Peace,* he told reporters further that "he had been expecting [the prize] for years."

> Naturally I felt that some day I would get this recognition, but I did not know when. I should be just as glad if Eugene O'Neill had received it. . . . I'd have felt the same way about Ernest Hemingway. He'll get it some day, but I suppose he hasn't written enough yet. I think Hemingway will get the award in ten years.† Then there is Willa Cather . . .

Their crossing of the wintry north Atlantic was rough, and Mrs. Lewis was seasick most of the time, a warning of further illness to come. They arrived in Stockholm on a midafternoon train on December 9 and were met by the car of the United States legation officer Edward Savage Crocker, with a formal invitation, in confirmation of an earlier cable, to dine that evening at the legation; and they proceeded to their apartment at the Grand Royal Hotel. Lewis's address, to be delivered on the twelfth, was finished, and he cabled Harcourt at length about the urgency of his having the exact text for the press since it was certain to "cause repercussions."

It was the season of the festival of Santa Lucia, when lovely girls crown their heads with seven burning candles and wander about offering coffee to

* On Van Dyke's death, the following verses, almost certainly addressed to Lewis, were found in his desk:

To Thersites

You seem to hate me. Well, what does it matter?
I do not have to read your peppery patter,
Nor you my books! Let's take our ways apart,
And follow each the guidance of his heart.
You say God's dead, and life's a bawdy tale;
I think God lives and goodness will prevail.
You mock mankind with lewd ungainly mirth:
I find a lot of folks to love on earth.
On prejudice you feed and nurse your spleen:
I'd rather have more wholesome food, and clean.
You write a language hitherto unknown;
To Shakespeare's tongue and faith, I fealty own.
So ride your road, Smart Aleck, gaily ride;
I keep my path; the future will decide.

† O'Neill won it six years later, the second American; Hemingway, the fifth, won it at last in 1954.

strangers, and it is said in Stockholm still that on the first night that Lewis was in his hotel, such a creature appeared in his room and, with her mythological appearance, terrified him into screaming. But the festival lent gaiety and fantasy to the more solemn occasions of the Nobel awards. These began on the afternoon of the tenth, when the Lewises and the three other award winners gathered with the royal family and certain members of the Swedish Academy at the Concert House. A distinguished international crowd of about two thousand people awaited them when, with a flourish of trumpets, they entered the auditorium and the orchestra broke into the royal march. The royal family took seats in the front row while the laureates, each with his conductor from the Academy, stepped up onto a platform and sat down to be inspected by the King and the crowd. It was a ceremony of nearly two hours, and Lewis, who was the last of the four to be presented, grew fidgety and ruddier of hue as the speeches and presentations dragged on. "The noted author from Sauk Centre, Minnesota, appeared to be enduring a sort of celestial Minnesota high-school graduation exercises," observed the United Press.

At last his turn came. Erik Karlfeldt, a poet, secretary of the Academy, presented him in a long review of his five major novels. Mrs. Lewis was fearful that he would trip as he came jerkily down the red carpet to King Gustav. He did not, but he stopped too far from him and bowed more deeply than was necessary, and the King had to motion to him to come closer to shake his hand. Then he received the portfolio with his certificate, gold medal and bank draft, and students at the back of the platform dipped the American flag.

After the ceremonies, all the great, the honored, and many of the audience proceeded to the City Hall, where, in the immense Golden Hall, the traditional banquet took place. It began with a toast to the King, who in turn toasted the memory of Alfred Nobel (he had died on this day in 1896), and after an elaborate dinner each of the prize winners gave a short speech of gratitude. Then the King led the laureates to a balcony overlooking the Blue Room, where the university students had been enjoying their own banquet. The students saluted and serenaded the King and his fellows, dancing began, liquor flowed, and the party went on for hours.

On the afternoon of the next day, the officers of the American legation presented the Lewises to the full Swedish Cabinet at a tea, a reception that was preliminary to the state dinner in the royal palace. They arrived in a flood of rain at half past seven. When the guests were assembled, the silver trumpet sounded again and the King entered. All the ladies of the Court were dressed in black, for the Queen of Sweden had been dead only since April 4. The long table at which the eighty-eight guests were seated was almost buried in roses, and the dinner service was of gold. This time there were no speeches. When the King prepared to smoke, Lewis pulled a cigarette out of his pocket, and when he was told that only the King might smoke, his face showed his democratic disgruntlement. But on the whole he conducted himself with utmost punctilio, to the disappointment of friends like George Jean Nathan, who had expected him to rush about bussing the little princesses.

On the afternoon of the next day, December 12, in the Stock Exchange, Lewis delivered his famous speech before the members of the Academy and their guests. He had already proved to be the most interesting of the prize winners to his several audiences, and now he won them completely. He had been "as nervous as a college freshman" before he entered the hall, the newspapers said, pacing up and down the corridor, "pressing his chin against his stiff shirt front, fidgeting with his tie and showing all the symptoms of acute stage fright." But once on the stage, humming Mendelssohn's "Wedding March" under his breath as he walked, according to his wife, and then, hearing Erik Karlfeldt again present him, he relaxed. He spoke naturally and easily, with much gesticulation, and his material ranged from broad and insulting satire and witty innuendoes which brought forth great rumbles of laughter, to an obviously patriotic exaltation that deeply impressed his audience, and when he had finished he received what was perhaps the most extended applause that he had ever known.

The speech had all the air of being historic, and from the uproar that it caused in the United States ("Mr. Lewis in his hour of awful nakedness in Stockholm," said the *Herald Tribune*) one might well have thought it so, but in fact it was historic only in the sense that it forced the American Academy of Arts and Letters into silence and no doubt helped to rout its most conservative forces and to make way within it for livelier writers and a livelier conception of literature. Dr. Henry Van Dyke had been of greater service to Lewis than he could have anticipated, for the speech took off from Van Dyke's observation on the award to him.

Van Dyke, Lewis asserted, stood for all that remnant of atrophied gentility in American literary values that was also represented by the Academy and that was utterly antithetic to (hence anachronistic in) the revolutionary character of the United States in its hundred and fifty years of history. It demonstrated the divorce between the intellectual life in America and any real literary standards, between the theories of the New Humanism and the actualities of American experience, between academic values and those actualities. "Our American professors like their literature clear and cold and pure and very dead," and the Academy "does not represent literary America of today—it represents only Henry Wadsworth Longfellow." The fault lies in the prestige of William Dean Howells, Lewis argued—forgetting that Howells had praised Ibsen, Zola and Hardy, and had risked his own reputation in defense of American writers like Frank Norris and Stephen Crane. (Similarly, to dismiss Emerson as one of our "sentimental reflections of Europe" was to forget that, years before Lewis had made this plea for a vital native literature, Emerson had made his in "The American Scholar.")

Whatever the preferences of "official" custodians of American culture, Lewis's own fantastically successful books in the past decade seemed to demonstrate that American readers in general were eager for such stronger fare. Yet his account of the status of the artist in the United States has much to commend it, and his argument that our material culture has far outstripped our intellectual culture is axiomatic. Naming our major writers in the United States—with his enemies, Dreiser and Anderson, at their forefront—and some of the best younger writers who were just emerging for European audiences, he did call attention to the fact that America had indeed come of age.

In the United States, dudgeon was high, and it was not mollified by the remark of Calvin Coolidge, in one of the great English sentences, that "No necessity exists for becoming excited." It was the assumption of most critics that Lewis's work, like his speech, found favor abroad because both gave back to a jealous Europe the dismal picture of American life in which it wanted to believe. And in an oblique and secondary sense, the assumption had validity. For many years in Sweden the authoritative account of American culture, and especially of American literary culture, had been found in Knut Hamsun's highly derogatory *The Cultural Life of Modern America,* and when Lewis enjoyed his first great Swedish success in *Main Street,* it was because this novel seemed, in an amazing mood of self-criticism, to confirm that account. Other American novelists who were popular in Sweden—Jack London, Upton Sinclair, Edith Wharton, Theodore Dreiser, Sherwood Anderson—were read in much the same spirit, as social critics of the same materialism and chauvinistic complacency, and with no important aesthetic discriminations to be made between them.

Under these circumstances, it is not surprising that Lewis, who was the sharpest and the most detailed critic and who yet wrote out of what seemed to be love of his country, should have come to seem the leader. He had come to seem the leader, however, of a body of literature that was in itself as exciting as any in the world, and a body of literature that, in its very criticism of American culture, demonstrated that American literature was no longer what Hamsun had thought it, and that American culture therefore could not for very long be. If Sinclair Lewis's reception of the Nobel prize was the historic event—and his spokesmanlike acceptance of it only the marker of the event—its historic import was not merely in its putting American literature on a par with any other literature in the world, but also in its acknowledging that in the world America was a power that, twenty years before, it had not been, and that, until now, Europe had been reluctant to concede it was. In December 1930 Sinclair

Lewis was bigger than America knew; proud as he may have been—and he was proud, above all, because he was regarded as of equal importance with three eminent scientists—he was bigger than even he himself knew, or would ever know. Or should one say that he was a smaller writer than he thought and a larger symbol?

He was bigger than some Swedes knew. The New Humanists in the United States had put great energy into backing Paul Elmer More for the prize that Lewis won, and their efforts had not been without some impact. Immediately after the awards had been made, the Swedish newspaper *Nya Dagligt Allehanda* published a long article on More that was very critical of the award to Lewis and declared, "Sinclair Lewis is a noisy savage." But most Swedish newspapers, like newspapers all over Europe, were delighted with his address, and on December 13, the New York *Times* correspondent cabled, "Sinclair Lewis became the hero of all Stockholm today."

The day, Santa Lucia's day, began with the telephone: Sweden's beauty queen, newly named and the very Lucia herself, was in the lobby, lighted candles on head, wishing to serve the Lewises their coffee. They declined. Then began a whole round of visits to their rooms, luncheon with Academy people, and in the afternoon, a series of receptions. That evening they had invitations to five balls and tried to go to several; one was an entrancing affair staged by the United Societies—Swedish-American and Swedish-Austrian. (These groups, under the joint names of their chairmen, sent an ambiguous cable to Secretary of State Stimson in Washington, announcing their loyalty to him in spite of their celebration for Lewis.) It snowed that night, and on Sunday Lewis was able to see Stockholm as he had hoped, covered with white. On Monday they were to be entertained at a Foreign Press Association dinner, with the entire diplomatic corps in attendance. Mrs. Lewis was in bed with a temperature. At dinner, asked to speak, Lewis, taking cognizance of the unfavorable reception of his speech in the United States, said: "I say the hundred-per-cent Americans are the highest form of human beings, the most pure and most cultured. Having thus cleared myself in the eyes of America, I may sit down calmly." After dinner he found a string of dancing partners waiting for him, but he seized his hat and coat and fled to Dorothy.

Every day there were small, private affairs arranged by Academy members, and on Tuesday he interspersed these with a radio address in which he talked about his life as a Minnesota country boy and his wish that he might have met and come to know some of the country people of Sweden, and, in the evening, with a dinner in his honor given by his Swedish publisher, Thorsten Laurin. Wednesday he saw a little more of Stockholm and spent the afternoon at the villa of Prince Eugene, looking at his collection of pictures. Thursday he left for Gothenburg, where he had agreed to speak before the Anglo-Swedish Society, stayed there through Friday, and returned to Stockholm on Saturday. On Sunday, December 21, they left for Berlin and arrived there next day, only to become the center of a whole new round of festivities arranged by their eager newspaper friends—the Knickerbockers, the Mowrers, and others. They were to stay in Berlin through New Year's Day and then leave for Copenhagen, where Lewis had promised to speak on January 3. Then Mrs. Lewis was going to Russia and Lewis to London, to wait for her.

On Christmas night, the Knickerbockers were giving a very gay dinner for ten people, including the Lewises, at their house in the suburbs. Hilarity mounted. Lewis did an impersonation of a Nobel prize winner accepting the honor in Norwegian. They worked out her Russian itinerary for Mrs. Lewis and almost decided that they would all get on a train for Vienna at once. That plan subsided, and at midnight, when taxicabs arrived to take the guests back into the city, Mrs. Lewis complained of a stomach-ache. At the Adlon, the house physician was called, Mrs. Lewis asked for her doctor, he summoned an ambulance, and at three o'clock, Mrs. Lewis was taken to Mommsen Sanatorium with a ruptured appendix. Lewis was frantic. In midmorning he got a few minutes' sleep and then dashed back to the hospital, and he was dashing in and out all day until, finally, late that night he went to bed. She was in satisfactory condition next day. He canceled his Copenhagen engagement and some less important ones. Mrs. Lewis was to be in the hospital for ten days. On the morning of January 1, 1931, she received a telegram signed by twenty-eight persons—friends at a celebration—and the twenty-eighth name was that of Sinclair Lewis. More reassuring cables and letters were coming from Westport, Connecticut, where Rose Wilder Lane was in charge of young Michael. There had been a slight accident to the Ford on an icy road, but the boy was well, and he had seen his first snow.

It was the depth of winter in Berlin when Mrs. Lewis came out of the hospital. Her husband wanted her to rest comfortably (and he was in need of rest as well as she),* and they went for ten days to the Thuringian mountains, away from telephones and newspapers, where he pretended to ski. They had reorganized their plans. Mrs. Lewis would not go to Russia; there was a good deal of material for a newspaperwoman in the Germany of 1931. Back in Berlin, Lewis said over the wireless that, in spite of all the ties that bound him to Europe, he felt himself to be one-hundred-percent American. And then he went off to England.

* He was being badgered as well as feted. A few weeks later, in London, he told a New York *Times* reporter about his problems:

"I'm still getting letters, and they all want money. I tell them I'm poor, too, but it doesn't do any good.

"There was a gypsy sent me a letter in Berlin, asking me to pay off the mortgage on his old homestead, and when I said I couldn't do it, he sent me five postal cards calling me some names I never heard of, and saying he was praying every day at his mother's grave that something terrible would happen to me and my wife."

He would like next, he said, to write a life of Clarence Darrow. "He's one of the finest fellows in the United States."

In London, he took his old Bury Street rooms in St. James. His best friend, Lord Thomson, had been killed in an airplane accident some months before, and his absence left a melancholy gap. Melancholy, too, was the break that Lewis had made with Harcourt, Brace & Company just before he left Berlin. For a long time, he wrote Harcourt, he had felt that the firm had lost real interest in his books, and the failure of the firm to rise to the occasion of the Nobel prize made its indifference all too clear. With proper advertising, all the novels would have leaped into soaring sales figures again. Worse than that, Harcourt had done nothing, even though he had the whole European press at his disposal, to counteract the supercilious and denigrating remarks about Lewis in the American press. "If you haven't used this opportunity to push my books energetically and to support my prestige intelligently, you never will do so, because I can never give you again such a moment." Harcourt had promised to bring out a Nobel prize edition of all the novels and had failed to do so. And he added, absurdly, that Harcourt's "lack of confidence is most important, because it is keeping me from starting work on a new novel."

Harcourt's reply came to him in London. It did not trouble to answer Lewis's charges. It did not even trouble to point out that the Nobel prize edition of the novels had been published on January 28. It was civil and friendly and moderately regretful, and it returned the canceled contracts for two unwritten books that Lewis had requested. "If I've lost an author, you haven't lost either a friend or a devoted reader." But it was the end of another friendship, in fact, and this time, probably, of the most important friendship in Lewis's life.

Through no real fault of Harcourt's and with his best intentions, an unfortunate event occurred between the date of Lewis's letter and the arrival of Harcourt's. The firm had rushed into print, in pamphlet form, Lewis's award speech and Erik Karlfeldt's survey of his novels at the presentation ceremonies, and they had used as their text the New York *Times* version, which had been dispatched to the newspaper in cablese. The result was that Dr. Karlfeldt was purported to have said that American streets stank because there were no sewers, and much of Lewis's text made no sense at all. Lewis cabled Harcourt in indignation and demanded that as many copies of the pamphlet as had not been distributed be destroyed, and Harcourt obliged. Of the three thousand copies that had been printed, two thousand were destroyed, and a corrected version was published in a printing of two thousand, with a footnote by Lewis appended to the unhappy Karlfeldt error. Lewis made a multitude of not very important changes in his own text, and it is this form that is now generally available.*

* It is reprinted under the title, "The American Fear of Literature," and in *The Man From Main Street* it is described as "revised." His corrected first version is in the Library of Congress, the gift of Mr. & Mrs. Jean Hersholt.

When Lewis saw Harcourt in New York in March, he said, "Alf, why—if my books did mean anything to you—why didn't you get on a boat and come to London and ask me to stay?" Apart from the fact that such a gesture was not in the character of Alfred Harcourt, he may very well have felt that the separation came at a logical time. The decade through which Harcourt, Brace & Company had helped to make Sinclair Lewis an international reputation, and in the course of which Lewis's novels had helped to make of Harcourt, Brace & Company a substantial firm, was over. Throughout that decade Lewis had promulgated his version of the American reality, and his effort had been brought to a climax with a great honor. But the decade was over, and Lewis's sense of reality was no longer central to American history. He would never be able to change that sense, but history had already changed and would continue to change in his time, leaving him uneasily behind. His own discomfited sense of the change and of his inability to cope with current history as confidently as he had coped with the past may very well have been the major ingredient in his dissatisfaction with his publishers. His novels would continue to make money, but they would never again bring distinction to a publisher's list as, in a succession of five smashing titles, they had brought to Harcourt, Brace & Company.

When Lewis had Harcourt's reply, he wrote to his wife in Germany:

> So I can't go back on the Europa with you. I have been thinking a lot of doing so. I don't merely miss you: I feel downright lonely without [you]. Perhaps I wouldn't have felt SO lonely if I had been working hard, but I have been rather loafing—looking at myself to see what I'm like. . . . . Moods. But I am coming out of them now, beginning to work. I would like to go with you. But I had better not, with Publixes coming. But I will work. But I'll get out of London and see some new places—not too far, so can return for Publixes. But I adore you.

"Publixes" were the representatives of American publishers with whom Lewis was expecting to discuss new contractual arrangements, but he did not make such arrangements in England, and he did not leave London.

His writing consisted of a story or two for *The Saturday Evening Post.* When an interviewer for *Everyman* asked him if he had an idea for a new novel, he said, "I've got the idea in my head very clearly. I wish I could run away from it. It means too much work." It was the labor novel, still, but it had grown in its historical dimensions. He gave a hint of it in the "Self-Portrait" he had written for the Nobel Foundation:

> The next novel, yet unnamed, will concern idealism in America through three generations, from 1818 till 1930—an idealism which the outlanders who call Americans "dollar-chasers" do not understand. It will presumably be published in the autumn of 1932, and the author's chief difficulty in

composing it is that after having received the Nobel Prize, he longs to write better than he can!

That there were graver difficulties is clear from Carl Van Doren's more complete account of Lewis's present plan:

> The American labor movement seemed to him . . . a chaos and tangle of politics full of the conflict of antagonisms which came from Europe. He decided to make his novel perfectly native, the story of three generations of American liberals: a circuit rider on the frontier, a sentimental, heroic socialist, a scientific social engineer. This, Lewis thought, would be his history of a hundred American years. . . . He drew a magnificent genealogical chart of the family of his first hero, Aaron Gadd. But the story would not take shape in his imagination. More than half of it must run its course in a world of which he could know nothing at first hand. He might by reading find out enough about it for a historian, but not enough for the kind of novelist he was.

But in London he could not do even the reading that such a book required, let alone the writing, and he let the idea float in his mind in the midst of increasing restlessness and boredom. He was bored even with his Nobel publicity. Whole packets of newspaper stories that came to him from his clipping bureau were not even opened there, or in his lifetime. One series of events broke the mood.

On February 5, Thomas Wolfe wrote in his diary, "Red Lewis—Georgian House—I've seen him." And in *You Can't Go Home Again,* he expands the entry in the person of George Webber:

> Then, for the first time, I saw [Fame]. I met Mr. Lloyd McHarg. That curious experience should have taught me something. And in a way I suppose it did. For in Lloyd McHarg I met a truly great and honest man who had aspired to Fame and won her, and I saw that it had been an empty victory. He had her more completely than I could ever hope to have her, yet it was apparent that, for him, Fame was not enough. He needed something more, and he had not found it.

Wolfe had been overwhelmed by Lewis's public praise of his novel, and his gratitude is evident in the account of the meeting of Webber and McHarg. There are modifications in minor facts to disguise the prototype of McHarg, but they are transparent, and the general account, nearly a hundred pages long, is substantially literal. The physical portrait of Lewis is perfect and no less is the representation of his behavior. His restlessness, his drinking, his compulsive informality, his generosity, his sweetness and his willfulness, his suffering, his dissatisfaction, his fits of exhaustion and sudden recovery, his imitations, his meaningless companionships—they are all here. A telephone call in one scene makes it clear that the rupture with Harcourt was already known in New York, but this is quite incidental to the major episode which follows on McHarg's sudden decision that George is to go with him to visit a friend in the country as the first stage of a tour of English cathedral towns, and immediately, without any preparation whatever. The friend was, in fact, A. S. Frere, Wolfe's editor at William Heinemann, Ltd., and an old friend of Lewis's, and after their wild drive through the English night, they arrived in a state of equal intoxication and both had to be helped into the house.

Wolfe changed these facts and presented Webber as a good deal more earnest than he himself was, and Lewis, not as drunk but as utterly exhausted. From the portrait of Webber, one would not gather that, according to Charles Breasted, Wolfe arrived at Lewis's apartment at two o'clock one morning after overturning and crashing every dustbin in Bury Street and presumably halfway across London. Wolfe himself told Robert Forsythe that one night after he and Lewis had been dining and Wolfe had returned to his lodgings several hours after midnight and was on his way to bed, Lewis telephoned to say that he must return to Bury Street immediately, it was a matter of the greatest urgency. Wolfe pulled his clothes back on and returned to find Lewis in the company of another man. When he entered, Lewis cried in triumph, "You see! Didn't I tell you he was a big bastard?" The episode characterizes the inconsequence of the relationship, a brief, roistering rapport that ended as abruptly as it began.

London was neither more nor less dull than ever, but even at its best for him—a dinner at the Savoy, given by the American newspapers' Correspondents' Association—left him listless. He spoke wittily about his employment by the Associated Press years before, about the torture of appearing before distinguished gatherings, about his grueling pangs of homesickness, and said that he preferred newspapermen who without fuss would call him "Red" to literary types who were as self-conscious as they were formal.

There was, of course, no tour of the cathedral towns with Thomas Wolfe. All plans always changed, and at the end of February, he rejoined his wife on the *Europa* and sailed for the United States. They arrived in New York on March 4. The usual shipboard interview was more entertaining than many. Lewis indicated that he was irritated and hurt by the American reception of his Nobel speech. To a question about his plans for changing publishers, he said, "That's a personal question, a matter of personal business"; but Ann Watkins, his agent, who had come to meet the boat, said, "He is going to change."

J. B. Priestley had been lecturing in the United States and was reported as having said, after being in this country only twelve minutes, that New York had the noisiest streets in the world, and only the night before, it was reported, he had said that Lewis, the novelist, was finished. Lewis replied: "New York may have the noisiest streets, but London has the noisiest lecturers." ("And the noisiest come from America," added *John Bull.*) "He says my day is done. Well, I suppose that means that at least I've had a day. That's more than I would say about some others. I wish he would take over all the writing there is to be done. Writing novels is the dreariest and greasiest job I know of. If Priestley would take the job over there wouldn't be any more criticism. I'd much rather read his books than mine anyway. I've read some of his books. I really enjoyed them." Two days later, Alfred A. Knopf, whom Lewis had approached as a possible new publisher for his books, wrote H. L. Mencken to say that he did not think that he would pursue the matter—it was three years since Lewis had turned in the manuscript of a novel, he had none in hand now, and the Nobel prize had had a most unfortunate effect on him.

In every part of the United States, and in every kind of periodical, Lewis and his reputation were being reassessed during this year. Lewis Mumford had led off in December with an article in *Current History,* which, after surveying Lewis's work and gliding over the work of others, begrudgingly allowed that Lewis was a writer who, certainly, should have at least been considered along with ten or twelve others, as worthy of the prize. *Elmer Gantry,* of course, was unspeakable, but *Dodsworth* was splendid. "Not since Henry James had anyone so well portrayed the dilemmas of the untutored American in Europe, exposed to that irresponsive but quickening scene." But on the whole, the Lewis satire was partial and predictable, and the award was, at best, a "subtle disparagement." Robert Frost's America, probably unknown to the Swedish Academy, more nearly represents "what is most precious and significant in contemporary American literature."

At Yale, the short-lived if elegant undergraduate periodical called *The Harkness Hoot* gave a prize to an essay on Lewis by one E. V. Rostow, who found him vastly overrated; an answer in spirited defense of Lewis was written by an editor of the magazine named Selden Rodman. At Columbia University, three undergraduates debated with three Smith College girls on whether he should have won the prize; the boys took the positive, the girls the negative, and the negative won. V. F. Calverton, taking the left position in the *New Review,* argued that Lewis's shallow, bourgeois characters sapped the author himself of that creative energy necessary to real art, and found it a "hopeful sign" that the "next novel is to deal with Eugene Debs and the life of a more energy-giving class." *Vanity Fair* republished from the German fashion magazine, *Die Dame,* a photograph of Lewis wearing false whiskers, and to this the reliable Ernest Boyd appended the following observations:

> There is something symbolic in a photograph of Sinclair Lewis in false-face, taken in Berlin during his recent literary vaudeville tour, when the "gate" was $46,000—the Nobel Prize for literature of an "idealistic" tendency. . . .

> His false whiskers present a curious analogy with that false sense of values which enabled him to cite as examples of great artists, suffering from the neglect of the American public, a few of the most popular, best-selling authors in America. His face is no more disguised than his real sentiments in literature, which are those measured in terms of advertising and royalty checks. Truly, Sinclair Lewis in false-face is a symbol.

It was as if all of America were determined to badger him, and one wonders how much comfort he could take in the figures he received from Harcourt at about this time on the foreign rights to his novels: eight contracts pending, thirty-two under consideration, and seventy in effect.

They went directly to Westport, and next morning, during an interview with the Boston *Evening Transcript,* Lewis was calm and wistful. Still in his pajamas and dressing gown, he said nothing outrageous. The mail was brought in and it included a letter of congratulation from Edith Wharton. "That's what I was waiting for," he said. He was asked if the prize medal could be seen, and he went upstairs to get it and his certificate, and these were inspected. Presently he announced that he was going back to bed, made an amiable farewell and retired. The opened mail was left on the sofa where he had dropped it, and the gold medal lay forgotten on a table at the end of the sofa, among cigarettes and matches and a book or two and papers. It had meant everything and it had brought him almost nothing.

The rupture with Harcourt became public knowledge, and in quick succession that spring three more widely publicized disasters took place. The first was of a sort to which the American public was accustomed: Lewis was to speak in Constitution Hall in Washington on March 24, but on March 12 the Daughters of the American Revolution, who owned the building, announced that they would not permit him to appear in their honored abode. The lecture was accordingly moved to Central High School. Before he could deliver it, he became embroiled in one of the best-known episodes of his life—the public fracas with Theodore Dreiser.

In the afternoon of March 19, Lewis delivered his lecture "American Literature Comes of Age," at Town Hall, in New York, and, as usual when he spoke on this subject, he praised the novels of Theodore Dreiser above all others. That evening Ray Long was entertaining about two dozen writers and journalists at dinner in the Metropolitan Club in honor of the Russian novelist Boris Pilnyak. Dreiser, who was confused about the street address, was very late in arriving, but the party waited for him through a much extended cocktail period that no doubt contributed to the events that followed. In the recollection of William G. Lengel (as reported to Dreiser's biographer, Robert H. Elias), Dreiser approached Lewis and said, "Congratulations, Lewis," but Lewis only sneered at the extended hand. At dinner, according to J. Donald Adams, who was sitting next to Lewis, Lewis swung a bottle under the table while he muttered threats about breaking it over Dreiser's head.

Still, all went well enough until brandy and cigars, when Long called on his guests for speeches. Lewis, invited to speak first, arose slowly, bowed and said in a lackadaisical fashion, "I am very happy to welcome Mr. Pilnyak to this country. But I do not care to speak in the presence of a man who has stolen three thousand words from my wife's book, and before two sage critics who have lamented the action of the Nobel prize committee in selecting me as America's representative writer." With that, he sat down and picked up his cigarette. Everyone looked at Dreiser, who fidgeted in his place with reddening neck but said nothing, and then, thinking of the reference to the "two sage critics," the astonished guests began to look at one another, for there were many present to whom Lewis might have been referring (he probably had in mind Heywood Broun and Arthur Brisbane, who had been among the most vociferous). Quickly, Long called on Irvin S. Cobb, who obliged with anecdotes that broke the tension and started the men laughing. Later Dreiser spoke in defense of communism in Russia and without reference to Lewis. When Pilnyak responded to the speeches, he ignored Lewis but referred repeatedly to "Père Dreiser" with the greatest deference.

If Lewis's nerves were frayed and his pride suffering, Dreiser's own temper in that year was at its most intransigent. He was being pushed toward the Left somewhat against his will, he had had a bitter quarrel with his publisher about motion picture royalties on *An American Tragedy*, and he had, of course, not won the Nobel prize. When the meal was over, Dreiser went around to Lewis at once, said, "Hello, how are ya?" and asked him if he would like to step aside and speak to him. "You made a statement about my taking stuff from your wife's book," Dreiser reported himself as having said. "I know you're an ignoramus, but you're crazy. You don't know what you're talking about." Then he asked Lewis to make the statement again or take it back. Lewis made it again. "So I smacked him. And I asked him if he wanted to say it again. He said it again. So I smacked him again. And I said, 'Do you want to say it again?'" Then William Lengel rushed to them and heard Lewis say, "Theodore, you are a liar and a thief." Lengel seized Lewis, but his arms were completely limp. Lengel suggested that Dreiser go, and Lewis repeated, "I still say you are a liar and a thief." "Do you want me to hit you again?" "If you do, I'll turn the other cheek." "Aw Lewis, you shit!" But by now Lengel was urging Dreiser out, and Dreiser was shouting, "I'll meet you any time anywhere. This thing isn't settled." Lewis followed them, mumbling, and Dreiser flung back, "Lewis, why don't you peddle your papers somewhere else?" and left. Later Lewis asked Lengel, "Why didn't you let him hit me again?"

Next morning, of course, the story was in every newspaper in the country. Jimmie Johnston, the fight promoter, wired Dreiser an invitation to a fifteen-round bout to a decision at Ebbets Field on June 3, offering the writers 50 per cent of the gate and movie receipts. Dreiser's first public comment on the affair was only, "Rash and unwarranted insults were rewarded with two slaps upon the face," but on March 24, arriving in Los Angeles, he said that there was no armistice, that on a similar occasion he would use his other hand, and that, after all, he had been asked to write *Arrowsmith* before Lewis was. Reporters found Lewis in Washington, where he was about to speak to the League for Political Education, and when they told him of Dreiser's fantastic claim, he was left "speechless." " 'Did he really say that?' Mr. Lewis managed to gasp after two full minutes." Then he telephoned the De Kruif residence, got Mrs. De Kruif, and obtained a ready denial from her. Earlier, he had been quoted variously about the incident: "It was an outrageous, scandalous affair," and "I'm just a country hick living on a farm, and every time I leave it I get into trouble." Less than twenty hours later, he was in Toledo's Town Hall, talking about the emancipation of American literature, praising Theodore Dreiser as one of America's greatest writers and apologizing for not appearing in a more "ferocious mood."

Presently rotogravure pictures of young Michael, looking hefty and happy, would appear with captions like "Say 'Dreiser' to this young man and he'll punch you on the nose." But on the whole, the press was sympathetic to Dreiser. Typical was the Philadelphia *Public Ledger* for March 21, which said:

> Mr. Lewis, it appears, hasn't improved his public manners since the famous occasion in Stockholm, when he openly bewailed the intellectual and artistic shortcomings of his own country. . . . If Mr. Lewis lingers about in Mr. Dreiser's neighborhood his manners may at last be improved and even polished.

Most astonishing was the demonstration of virulence against Lewis made by the mass of congratulatory mail that Dreiser received and saved. "I am much obliged to you for slapping Sinclair Lewis's face—but why didn't you use your closed fist?" "Thank you for slapping Sinclair Lewis. You did just what many thousands of Americans would like to do. Thank you." "No face ever deserved it more than his." "Congratulations! You should have stab[b]ed the dirty dog!" "Why only two slaps? As many more as would assure us he had been slapped out of the good old U.S.A." "Many, many thanks, Mr. Dreiser, for that *slap*. Might one call it the proxy slap of many of us Americans?" "You should have knocked him sensible—he is senseless now. . . ." And so on. A man in Vancouver was impelled to write a poem entitled "The Slap Heard Round the World."

Nothing had satisfied the public so completely since Rudy Vallee had been struck in the face with a grapefruit.

When Lewis returned to New York he went to the Biltmore and immediately reporters tried to reach him, but he was in a new mood of reticence. A. S. Frere was in town and very late on the night of March 22, when Frere was preparing to go to bed, Lewis telephoned and demanded that he pack a bag at once and meet him at the Grand Central entrance of the Biltmore, they were going to Washington. When Frere arrived, Lewis said, "The reporters are after me. Come on!" "Where?" "Do you know the shuttle? We'll shuttle." And so from Grand Central they found their way to Pennsylvania Station in time for a late train to Washington, where, early on the morning of the twenty-third, they settled in a small hotel.

Then began thirty-six hours of drinking and very little sleep, with Lewis occasionally wondering about the speech he was to make on the night of the twenty-fourth, and for which he had brought no text or even notes. At some point in this debauch, it became imperative that Frere have an official tour of the White House to increase his respect for American traditions and institutions. Lewis had a friend in the Hoover secretariat and he telephoned him, demanding the tour for his British friend, variously described as a colonel and a major (Frere had been a captain in the Royal Flying Corps), or as a little runt of an Englishman who had to be taught something. Very elated, Lewis propelled Frere into the White House, where they had their tour, and then, behind the President's desk, pounding his fist, Lewis announced to Frere (who by this time was "you lousy little Limey") the emancipation of American literature. Back at their hotel, he collapsed in utter coma.

Frere served as valet. In due time he got him up, got him into the shower, got him dressed, got him into a taxi, and all but propelled him onto the stage. Lewis had simulated notes out of scraps of paper and newspaper clippings, and as he moved across the stage, before an enormous audience, like a man in a trance, these drifted to the floor from his limp hand. He faced his audience, and, in a long silence, gaped out into the space before him as if he were trying to remember why he was there. Then suddenly the words poured out.

He began with an attack on "the British publisher" who was sitting in the front row, and every now and then he would return to the attack, but between these sallies, he discoursed with perfect coherence and even with brilliance on the native tradition in American writing that had at last manifested itself in a whole series of splendid writers, Dreiser at their head. Were there would-be writers in the audience, looking for subject matter? America was *stuffed* with unexplored material—the proletariat, the garage mechanic who laughs at the stupidity of you and me, the authentic Westerners who are the descendants of the pioneers, the New England farmers who struggle with their rocky soil to compete with the Midwestern farmers on their fat earth, the great financiers and industrialists, men, like J. P. Morgan, who met their first duke at the age of six and are so rich that money means nothing to them. Money!

After the lecture, he was once more in a state of high elation. Had Frere ever been in Baltimore, a great American port and the home of H. L. Mencken? He had not? Then they must go instantly. They found an automobile rental agency and set out, and found themselves at last in "the cluttered mystery of a port at night—metal rails, brick walls, masts and funnels black against starlight." Lewis began to make speeches. "Look at that! All this shipping . . . American industry, production, wealth. . . ." His enthusiasm settled on a particular ship—"There's America, Frere, there it is!"—and he was determined to board her. Frere was unwilling to follow him as Lewis climbed up the unguarded gangway. Minutes passed and Frere became apprehensive, and then suddenly Lewis came off the ship as if propelled—and roughed up, his face bruised, his hair tousled. It was a Czechoslovakian vessel.

He was not daunted. Now they must call on Mencken! They drove to the house in Cathedral Street where Mencken lived with his new wife and, in the early dawn, routed him out of bed. While Mencken and Lewis talked and Lewis drank, Frere managed to doze on a living-room sofa, but suddenly Lewis was shaking him awake. They must go at once!

Now it was to Annapolis, where there was better Queen Anne architecture than anything in England. Through a high official whom Lewis knew, they were admitted to the Naval Academy where Frere was now introduced as a general of the Royal Flying Corps, and Lewis commandeered a full cadet review. When they were presented to the most honored cadet in the graduating class, Lewis begged him to explain something of American naval traditions to this unfortunate little Englishman who was in fact a bastard. And then Lewis himself delivered an eloquent lecture on American marine history.

For how many hours had Lewis been talking? The whole venture was incredible to the now nearly exhausted Frere. They drove back to Washington, and the talk continued to flow with the drink. At their hotel they discovered that reporters were again on their heels, and they scuttled about on back stairs and fire escapes until they reached their rooms. They locked the doors behind them only to discover a pretty female reporter in the bathroom, and her honest face roused Lewis to new animation. She must dine with them! He summoned a waiter and ordered an enormous meal, and even as the completely expended Frere fell asleep over a vast bowl of clams, Lewis began to dictate to the girl a perfectly calculated interview, amusing and face-saving. But Frere was beyond listening, as he was beyond dining. Next day they dragged themselves back to New York.

The third episode occurred in May when Lewis and Harrison Smith were driving to Vermont to open Twin Farms. Lewis had his medal with him, and on a sudden impulse, in New Haven, he decided to present it to the library of his alma mater. Both men were shabbily dressed for country work and in high, holiday mood. They sought out Lewis's young defender, Selden Rodman, to whose periodical, *The Harkness Hoot,* Lewis had contributed a short inquiry, "Are Colleges Obsolete?", the month before. This article suggested that the whole system of college education was outmoded and should probably be scrapped; but obviously this change would not come about overnight, and in the meantime, Yale seemed the proper place for the Nobel medal.

Young Rodman guided the two men to the library and to the librarian's office, but the librarian was unfortunately away from New Haven and had left in his place a not very alert young assistant named Rush. The men introduced themselves and flaunted the large gold object, more plaque than medal. Not surprisingly, the young man, Rush, was impressed rather by the rough appearance of the two men in those genteel surroundings than by the object that the more extraordinary of the two swung like a pendulum, and he was probably most dubious of their identity. At any rate, his reply was, "What is it that you want? You wish to see our collection of medals?" Lewis flew into an abrupt and wild rage of denunciation and abuse, and the two men stalked from the library, fled down the stairs, and for the next fifty miles, Lewis drove in furious silence.

The newspapers had the story immediately. The *Yale Daily News* said, "We think he has, or had, hardly a leg to stand on. Provided he remembered on the following morning what had happened. . . ." Rush, in interviews in New York, made it plain that intoxication was the cause of the fracas. Lewis's own old paper, the New Haven *Journal-Courier,* was most persistent in its attacks on him. Lewis himself, so much later as October, was still outraged. In a letter to the secretary of his class, he complained that none of Rush's superiors had ever asked for his side of the story. "They are not interested. This does not greatly disturb me, but it does prevent my ever again having anything to do with any Yale activity."

When the secretary suggested that they meet and discuss the matter, Lewis replied:

> What is there to discuss? If you had come to my house—if a servant had been intolerably rude to you—if I had learned thoroughly of the incident from its being reported in the newspapers—if then I had paid no attention to the matter, had not even taken the trouble to write asking you what had really happened—would you care to have anything more to do with me? I am not blaming the servant in this case. He is just that kind of little man. I am blaming his superiors. No, I am not blaming them; I am not working up a controversy; I'm just finished.
>
> Incidentally, not only did no member of the Yale faculty and officers

show any interest, but also no member of the Class of 1907 showed any. That is quite all right, but I don't just see why I should pretend to have any interest in an institution now devoted only to athletics and the cadging of money to build architectural monstrosities.

These documents were referred to President Angell, and there was no doubt a diplomatic attempt to soothe the ruffled feathers, and that was presently accomplished. In the meantime, on July 24, through the efforts of Vrest Orton, Lewis's would-be bibliographer, the medal went—on loan—to the Vermont Historical Society, in Montpelier.

In the country, things quieted down. While Lewis had no book, and was not writing one, he did have a new publisher. When the news of Lewis's leaving Harcourt had broken, many publishers expressed interest in taking over his work. The United States was in the depth of the Depression and the book business had nearly come to a halt, with almost every publisher losing money. A made name such as that of Sinclair Lewis would almost certainly assure any publisher of some profits.

Through the influence of A. S. Frere, Doubleday, Doran & Company was an early and strong contender. An energetic young promotions man in the firm, Daniel Longwell, was determined to get at least his section of Doubleday out of the red, and he persuaded Nelson Doubleday to invite Lewis to lunch at Garden City, Long Island, where the firm's offices then were. Lewis accepted and Longwell prepared a full "presentation," as Madison Avenue now calls the layout of a promotion program: this is what they would do for the still nonexistent next novel. What they would do for Lewis more specifically was to give him a $25,000 advance against unearned royalties, a contract with a $25,000 advertising guarantee, and royalty rates beginning at 15 per cent. Longwell planned to print 60,000 copies of whatever book came in from Lewis, and if they sold them, they would more than break even. On the drive back to Manhattan from Garden City with Frere, Lewis decided that he would go with Doubleday, and he had the car stopped and telephoned back to say so and to ask that the proposed contract be drawn up. "I like you," he is reported to have said. "You're so God-damned *commercial!*"

The news was announced in *Publishers' Weekly* on April 4. In the same month began the serialization of *Half a Loaf,* Mrs. Hegger Lewis's *roman à clef*. There is no record from Lewis of his response to this work, but the author herself wrote to Gene McComas to say that she had heard that he was furious and that an "official" cable from him to England had prevented its publication there, that six publishers had wanted it but that all of them feared the strict English libel laws and had ultimately declined.

A more attractive account of Sinclair Lewis than that presented by his first wife was about to be written by Dean Christian Gauss of Princeton University for a series of articles, appearing in *The Saturday Evening Post,* on distinguished men and their education. Gauss began to correspond with Lewis about materials early in May, and in late July he came to Barnard with his wife to interview his subject. This visit resulted in a full-page spread in the rotogravure section of the Boston *Herald,* pictures that suggest a peaceful summer life, all composed of quiet country satisfactions. The photographs deceive. Sometimes when he came to his wife in the night, drunk and demanding, Lewis exuded an odor, she remembered, that was—she paused in the recollection as she sought for the exact analogy—that was like rotting weeds.

Yet some satisfactions there were. *Arrowsmith* had been sold to Samuel Goldwyn for a substantial sum, Ronald Colman and Helen Hayes to star. Dean Gauss's article was most satisfying: "It is a swell piece I am flattered," said the subject's telegram.

Henry Hazlitt, on the staff of *The Nation,* had proposed that he write an entire book for Doubleday on Sinclair Lewis. Harry Maule, of Doubleday, was enthusiastic, and Sinclair Lewis wrote Hazlitt approvingly from Barnard, and thoughtfully offered a short bibliography of already published writings about himself that included a German dissertation and Walter Lippmann's coolly balanced if damaging essay from *Men of Destiny*. "In this is, I am told (I have never read it) a very nasty and well-done showing up of myself." As for his plans, he would be going to Europe on about October 20. Vrest Orton, the bibliographer, had yielded priority in that matter to Harvey Taylor, and Lewis was happily if not very accurately collaborating with him on the project. The Hazlitt book was not to materialize. Instead, Doubleday turned to Carl Van Doren for such a work, and to this, Taylor's bibliography became a supplement. To Frere, Lewis wrote on June 21:

> I'm enormously enjoying being in the country, and the place is, with the growth of the gardens, more beautiful than last year. Menck and Mrs Menck and the Phil Goodmans are coming up for early July; otherwise we shall see few people this summer other than Dan Longwell (whom I like and respect immensely). He's been here once and is coming a couple more times. I'm just now finishing up some stories . . . . . with them done, I do nothing whatever but the new novel. I'm really ready for it.

The Menckens and Goodmans came as promised, and as a thank-you present, Mencken sent Mrs. Lewis a shipment of malt, hops and corn sugar, a bag of caps, a capping machine and a syphon, and elaborate instructions for the making of home brew. Wells Lewis came for his usual long visit. There were many pleasant neighbors, none too close for comfort. And Lewis, calmer, seemed less sensitive to criticism than he had been in the spring. Once, dining with George Seldes, he met Seldes' brother, Gilbert, who had written some moderately unfavorable reviews of the big Lewis novels in *The Dial*. Lewis said, "How do you stand now, Seldes—

for or against me?" and he seemed very blithe about the whole matter. Robert Hillyer, the poet and then professor at Harvard, called, and when the talk turned to poetry, which Mrs. Lewis enjoyed but which Lewis no longer read, he buried himself in a newspaper. Hillyer was trying to recall a complex seventeenth-century poem, Donne's "The Canonization" or something of the sort, and when he could not get on with it, Lewis suddenly put down his paper, quoted the entire poem without faltering, and then returned without comment to his reading.

But under the easy surface of the summer, there were rumblings, too. Once, when the Seldeses came to the Lewises', they arrived before any of the other guests, and Lewis, excited about a new automobile that he had acquired, wanted to take them for a drive at once. They returned a little late, after everyone had arrived, and Mrs. Lewis was annoyed. The whole evening turned difficult. Four people spoke no English, and after dinner, Lewis, taking over, ordered all the English-speaking people to one side of the room and talked to them, and indicated that all the non-English-speaking people were to sit on another side of the room where Mrs. Lewis would preside. Ultimately, they would use separate sitting rooms, each with his own audience.

The new stories finished for the *Post,* there was still no novel. Lewis was a sponsor of the National Mooney-Billings Committee, and he had recently sent out a plea to many influential acquaintances for signatures to a telegram addressed to the new governor of California, urging a pardon. At Mencken's request, he cabled Maxim Gorky in Moscow to urge him to exert his influence in obtaining a reprieve for the ailing, imprisoned mother of Albert Parry, an American writer. Pursuing another kind of justice, in his view, he wrote the Swedish Academy to nominate H. G. Wells for the next Nobel prize (it was only in 1949 that nominations from previous winners of the prize were accepted by the Academy), and sent Wells a carbon of his letter. Injustice troubled him, but somehow not powerfully enough to irritate his imagination into a fully conceived novel on the theme. Radical politics, in and out of labor, troubled him, too.

To Carl Haessler, thanking him for some newspaper clippings, he speculated that the Communists had done far more harm than good in the case of the Scottsboro boys, who had been sentenced for rape. This letter was written at the end of June, and he said in it, "I'm starting the new novel. It will get pretty far away from any plans we discussed—it will not, indeed, be called a 'labor novel,' at all, though one of the characters will still be based more or less on Gene Debs." All that summer, he *hoped* to start it, and again made arrangements for "research" assistance.

In New York on April 1, immediately after the drunken expedition with Frere, he had met Louis Adamic at dinner with a group that called itself the Literary Rotary, and he was much taken with him. Adamic was a Yugoslavian immigrant in his early thirties, a warmhearted, rather sentimental fellow who had had a considerably rough experience of the underside of American life, and who was the author of a book called *Dynamite: The Story of Class Violence in America,* just published. Ben Stolberg, a friend of Adamic's, brought Lewis to the Literary Rotary, which was assembled for dinner at Scheffel Hall, a German beer place, and most of the diners Lewis knew—Harry Hansen, Henry Hazlitt, Lewis Gannett, Walter White, V. F. Calverton, Harry Elmer Barnes, among them. To Adamic he exclaimed directly upon meeting him, "Christ, Louis, you wrote a grand book!—*Dynamite*—just read it—jeez, a grand book!" *

He was cold and haughty to everyone present except Stolberg and Adamic, to whom he devoted himself. The atmosphere was stiff with embarrassment. He attacked Calverton angrily for his piece on him in the *New Review,* and he turned on Hansen, an old and friendly acquaintance, crying, "You lied about me in your column!" (Hansen had simply observed in print what everyone knew in literary gossip—that Lewis had left Harcourt, Brace & Company because he felt that they did not give his novels adequate promotion.) He said that Americans behaved as though the country were ashamed that he had won the Nobel prize. Stolberg, who had his arm around Lewis's shoulders, would try to calm him down, telling him not to be a damned fool. Drunk when he arrived, he drank a seidel of beer and did not touch his food, but over the noise of the German orchestra, he immediately began to shout invitations to Adamic to start off with him in the next week on a tour of the industrial Middle West. He had asked Stolberg to come, he said, "but he's a high-brow—doesn't want to come." When even his shouts could not be heard over the general din, he lapsed into silence and stared moodily at Adamic, winking at him whenever their eyes met, and to Stolberg he said that he didn't like this crowd, they were all high-brows except Louis, the only proletarian among them.

When the dinner broke up presently and the group was preparing to move on to Calverton's apartment, Lewis asked Adamic to come with him. "I don't like this crowd. High-brows!" he kept repeating. Reluctantly, Adamic went with him. They walked up Third Avenue, and Lewis kept urging the trip to Detroit, Chicago, and Gary, Indiana. Adamic was noncommittal, and presently Lewis said, "Wait a minute," and went into a cigar store. When he came out with a package of cigarettes, they walked on, but now it was as if Lewis were entirely unaware of Adamic beside him. He paused to pet a cat on an ash can, and Adamic asked him if he

* There are two accounts of this dinner, substantially the same. One is a letter at Princeton from Adamic to Carey McWilliams, and the other, developed from that letter, is in Adamic's *My America* (1938). Harry Hansen remembers the occasion.

liked cats, and there was more silence. Then suddenly Lewis stopped, put out his hand, told Adamic to go back to his party, and said good-by, walking off into the darkness alone.

Adamic married, and in the autumn, living at Yaddo in Saratoga Springs, he wrote Lewis to ask if he would support his application for a Guggenheim fellowship. Lewis was prompt and agreeable in his reply. Then, a few days later, a long-distance telephone call came from Mrs. Lewis, speaking for her husband. He, she said, was leaving for Vienna in about two weeks and would like Adamic to join him there after New Year's to work with him on his novel about labor. Adamic, with a new wife in California, hesitated, and Mrs. Lewis then persuaded him to come to Twin Farms and talk the matter over. He went. The Lewises were charming to him and Sinclair Lewis was persuasive. He would pay the passage to and from Europe for both Adamic and his wife, and he would pay Louis Adamic fifty dollars a week for as long as need be—"two or three months, possibly longer"—just to be near him if he needed information or advice. Adamic was honored and excited. Stolberg advised him to go but warned him that he would have problems—Lewis was a *verrücktes Genie*. Excitedly, Adamic wrote his wife to tell her to prepare for the trip.

Then, two days after he was back at Yaddo, he received a wire from Lewis that told him the plan had been changed. "Do nothing till you hear from me again." A few days later a letter explained that Lewis had decided he should do the book in America, and would Adamic, in a few months, work with him in New York instead? Mrs. Lewis was going down that day to find an apartment. Adamic suggested that they make some fixed agreement so that he could settle his affairs, but Lewis found that impossible since his plans might change at any time, and the matter was left with the understanding that if Adamic were living in or near New York, he would be glad to make himself available.

In November Adamic heard (he thought from Stolberg) that Lewis had given up the labor novel and had turned instead to a story about a feminist. In the following years, however, they "exchanged several letters and notes. He seemed to want to keep in touch with me; I thought he might have some sort of unconscious idea of wanting to use me sometime. I was willing to be used. But—"

He came down from Vermont in time for a luncheon at the Railroad Club given by Oswald Garrison Villard for H. G. Wells, at which Wells and Lewis argued about British lecturers in America and American lecturers in Britain. The new apartment, with its double sitting rooms, was at 21 East 90th Street, and having found it, Mrs. Lewis, early in November, left for Europe. (It was in that month that she managed her famous interview with Hitler.) Lewis's last *Post* stories had appeared and he had gone to work on *Ann Vickers*. The year had brought very little else from his typewriter—an outraged letter to *The Nation* complaining of a review of *Vermonters: A Book of Biographies,* and the sentimental little piece, "The Long Arm of the Small Town," for the fiftieth-anniversary issue of his high-school annual, the *O-Sa-Ge*. He permitted the republication in *The Home Magazine,* a Woolworth throwaway, of one of his worst stories, "The Tamarack Lover," of 1918, under the title "Warrior Woman"—a story about an enormous Norwegian woman who more or less mauls a pretty young minister, slight and small, into marriage. He was feeling rather mauled himself, and the feeling would grow.

In December, he came to a cocktail party at the apartment of Carl and Carol Brandt with his Doubleday editor. They were on their way to the première of the film of *Arrowsmith,* and when they arrived neither was in need of further drink. John Marquand was present, and Lewis met him for the first time. He asked Mrs. Brandt for Scotch, and when she gave it to him, he cried, "Do you call that a drink? Please let me make my own," and he poured himself a tumbler full. With Marquand, the first-name basis was peremptorily established—John and Red. Although he had come with his editor, Lewis was in an anti-publisher, anti-agent, nearly an anti-public mood. Everyone exploited the writer, said he, and, with a great deal of profanity, he wanted to ally himself with Marquand against the room. "Come on, John, I want to talk to you, let's get away from these lousy bloodsuckers, these goddamn hucksters, these fucking exploiters."

This went on and on, and every now and then his editor would intervene and protest that they had to get to their film, but Lewis would push him aside and say, "Let me alone, let me alone, I want to talk to John here. John and I understand each other, we know what a writer is. Keep these goddamn bloodsuckers away from me, will you?" And then, "Come on, John, I want to talk to you, I want to talk to you about your writing, John. Listen, come to Detroit with me! We'll disguise ourselves as waiters and get jobs in some joint. Will you, John? What do you say? Detroit! Waiters! How about it? Let's get away from these. . . ." And when, finally, they did separate themselves from the group, presumably for a conversation, Lewis sang Methodist hymns to Marquand for fifteen or twenty minutes. His editor's continuing interruptions had been persistently brushed aside, but at last they left together. They saw enough of *Arrowsmith* to enable Lewis, who was delighted with it, to praise the maturity of the movie industry to the New York *Times* next day.

2

HIS WIFE RETURNED for Christmas to find him, as she would for some years more, impatient for her return and then almost immediately impatient with her. She found him, too, working hard at *Ann Vickers.* Having failed to persuade Marquand to go incognito to Detroit, he urged Ben Stolberg to come to Barnard with him in January. It was a very cold and stormy winter, but he thought that Twin Farms would be good for his writing. Stolberg agreed to go but he found himself terrified by the country silence, the vast snows, the cracking sounds of the house in the cold, the bare trees squeaking and moaning when the wind rose. He fled back to the city he knew, and Lewis, who liked to tell this story afterward, stayed on through most of January, for a time with his wife. He was writing from four to six thousand words a day. At the same time, he also wrote the longest autobiographical account that he was ever to produce—some twenty-two typewritten pages for the use of Carl Van Doren, who had been commissioned by Doubleday to produce his adulatory biocritical essay, to be published simultaneously with *Ann Vickers* in a year.

Returning to New York, he continued to work at his long book, but he was restless and distraught. When his wife entertained at dinner—even when she was entertaining his friends—he would disappear for hours, then reappear and suggest that they all go out for chop suey or scrambled eggs. In a February interview, she reported that "he has very little liking for writers, for literary people in general. He is very easily irritated by them," and she added,

> Sometimes he walks up to his small son, hardly more than a baby, and takes him by the shoulder. "Don't you be a writer," he tells the child. "Writing is an escape from something. You be a scientist."

She was frequently away from New York, lecturing here and there, and in March she once more had to go abroad. Lewis, left alone in the city that so easily undid him, increased his drinking.

One evening Daniel Longwell found him well along on a solitary spree, and he decided that this was one of those occasions when he had to be put in the hands of friends who would take care of him. He asked him where he would like to be driven, and Lewis said that he would like to go to Wallace Irwin's house. On the way, Lewis rambled on at length about his marriage, telling Longwell how much it meant to him and of his complete fidelity to his wife, and he vowed that he would stop drinking. The Irwins took him to their country place at East Setauket, and there, even after they left him, he stayed with his book. To Carl Van Doren he wrote:

> I'm out here at Wallace Irwin's house (him and Tish being in town) for a few weeks, working righteously. I don't know yet just when I'll return to town, to stay a little while before going up to the country about May 1st. Work in Progress progresses greatly.

When he returned to New York, he decided to follow his wife to Europe, and he arranged that Philip Goodman would sail with him on the *Dresden* on April 15. For ship-news reporters he played what was now an old game with Mencken, in which each would lament the "reform" and new abstemiousness of the other, and he praised the writing of Hemingway, Wolfe and Dos Passos as "more than swell. It makes me feel old and tired and what's the use of writing? They know how." And then he chose to praise, of all novelists, Jane Austen! He was in Europe for just a month. Surrounded in his hotel by a miscellany of people including a Roman Catholic priest from Iowa, he met his wife in Paris, and since they had arrived separately, there were, for the first time, rumors of an impending divorce. These were stifled when he brought her back on the *Europa* on May 26.

When he returned, the negotiations with Sidney Howard to dramatize *Dodsworth* for Gilbert Miller had been announced. Howard had written the scenario of *Arrowsmith,* and his satisfaction with the result and Lewis's pleasure in it encouraged him to consider *Dodsworth* as a possibility for the stage. He met Lewis in a speakeasy with a list of typewritten scenes, and their discussion led him then to follow the Lewises to New England, where he took a New Hampshire house about twenty miles from Twin Farms on the theory that there would be considerable interchange about the dramatization. Howard did come to Twin Farms a half-dozen times, but they talked little about the play; chiefly, he recalled later, they drank beer and gossiped as they studied the view down the valley.

Again, the summer was calmer than the winter had been. It began auspiciously with a Yale *rapprochement.* The librarian made a handsome recovery when he proposed a Yale exhibition of Sinclair Lewis's work, and presently the medal came to its proper rest. Lewis himself came to his twenty-fifth reunion—the great guest—and this, Professor Tinker remembered later, was his surrender. At dinner with Tinker and the librarian, he wanted to know which of his novels they thought his best, and, now that *Ann Vickers* was nearly finished, what profession or group should he examine next? The law? The Jewish problem? He wanted to write a "beautiful" book, he asserted.

His work, of course, almost always began with a general subject rather than with a conception of character, and this is not surprising in one who was himself by no means a sound judge of people, or even of his own talent. His miscalculations were sometimes amusing. Dorothy Thompson remembered that at about this time he decided that Murphy, the yokel who was their Vermont hired man, possessed a refined and sensitive spirit under the rough and taciturn exterior, "the soul of a poet," and Lewis would bring Murphy into the house and make him listen to recordings of classical music by the hour, until Murphy finally quit his job in desperate boredom.

When he had returned from Europe in May, he told reporters that he had finished his new novel, 170,000 words long, at sea. He had probably finished the first draft, and during most of that summer he continued to work on revisions. Daniel Longwell came for a weekend to find everything in the household revolving around the manuscript. Lewis was eager for praise. "I have just written this. What do you think?" he would ask, thrusting some pages of typescript into Longwell's hands. "Read these pages," he would insist, and so on. On the eighth of August, when the novel was finished, he came to New York and rented two rooms in an apartment hotel at 66 Park Avenue, and there, under his watchful eye, Louis Florey, the professional stenographer and Lewis's occasional secretary, typed the manuscript.* Mrs. Lewis came down four or five days later, and they gave a party in this "office," where the manuscript was isolated on a table. Again, it is Longwell's recollection that Lewis spent the whole time rushing from one guest to another saying, "Here, read these pages," and "Here, tell me what you think of this."

It does not sound very professional, but the fact was that Doubleday found in him their dream of a writer. He had a perfect understanding of the publisher's problems and never caused any difficulty. He was in no way a prima donna, his ideas for promotion were many and almost all

* Louis Florey, whose association with Lewis was at once more sporadic and longer than that of most of his companion-secretaries, was the son of an illiterate French-Canadian blacksmith whose name was L'Heureux. A United States customs official misunderstood his accent and wrote the name as "Florey" on his first application papers for citizenship. Since he could not read, he could only assent, when asked, that what was written was the correct spelling of his name; and Florey his son became. Or so Lewis later wrote Mencken in commenting on the corruption of proper names as a topic for *The American Language.*

good, and he was realistic about advertising. The publishers were as pleased with the novel as they were with its author, and now arrangements for its serialization were completed with *Redbook.*

The Lewises were planning to sail on the *Europa,* this time taking Michael with them, on August 24, and Sidney Howard was working desperately against that deadline. He finished a first draft and then they worked together for two sweltering days, from early one Saturday morning until early on the Monday following, with Louis Florey retyping in the next room "as we staggered on" through scene after scene.

> I remember one Lewis slogan from those two days—he spoke it so often it became a slogan. "What's the idea in this lousy speech?" he would say, and indignantly, too. "It came out of the book," I would answer. "Take it out of the play," he would answer me back. "It's no good in the play." When we had finished there was scarcely a line of the book left. Now and then he retired for a nap. When those forty-eight hours were over we both retired for some days of napping, he at sea, I back in New Hampshire.

He could not sail, of course, without a comment for the press, and now he chose to declare that the current presidential campaign, Hoover versus Roosevelt, was a struggle without principle between one "fat head" and another. Next day the *Times* editorialized without naming him: since the poor man had been doomed to citizenship in a country inhabited by such wretches, it was only kind not to mention his name. Sailing for Cherbourg, he was not struck by this barb.

His wife went directly to Austria, where, in Semmering, two hours from Vienna, they had leased the Villa Sauerbrunn for the winter. Lewis went to Germany. He rejoined her in the second week of September and wrote Frere enthusiastically about the villa, "a cuckoo-clock house in aspect, with Ritz comfort in beds and bathroom and kitchens and chairs and lights," and set in an ample garden. They looked down a deep valley and then to a pastoral upland and the slopes of the Rax and Schneeberg mountains. Already they were planning a Christmas house party, and already there were guests, the Adolphe Menjous among them. But happy as everything seemed, on September 17 they were off for three weeks in the Tyrol and Italy, and Lewis was photographed with the Menjous in the Alps.

They came back and almost immediately Lewis left again, to return to Italy. His wife wrote him:

> . . . It's probably just as well I didn't go. You were cross with me and whenever I was with you I was lonely. Sometimes I think you don't see me at all, but somebody you have made up, a piece of fiction, like Ann Vickers, so terribly lifelike that you almost convince me that's me, until suddenly my heart is crying outside a locked gate with the other "me" inside. I looking in on the false one, with you. Anyhow, I was tired in my heart and needed rest, and the rest has done me good.

The role that he saw her in was not only the public figure of growing prestige that he wanted her to be. Toward the end of 1932, Oswald Garrison Villard wished to step down from the editorship of *The Nation,* and the magazine approached Dorothy Thompson as a possible successor. She was not interested in taking on such a regular professional commitment, but Lewis urged her to do so. "How *can* I take the *Nation?"* she wrote him. "What about Vermont? Europe? You? I *see* you staying home and minding the baby!! *Du."* No, the role was rather of the aggressive domestic figure who wished to rule him—when she only wished to help him—and to rival him—when she had no such ambition whatever. The rivalry was in his mind alone. "I love Dorothy," he told Paul C. Smith at this time, "but I get so God-damned tired of 'This Situation!' " He is reputed to have said that if he ever divorced her, he would name Hitler as corespondent.

In Europe, of course, she was as it were at home in a way that he was not. She was the familiar of influential Europeans and met them on equal terms, as he could not. In the United States they sought her out, not him. She had, besides, her American and English newspaper friends, hers before they were his. Daniel Longwell and others have speculated on the strange world that Lewis had moved into upon his marriage—political experts, diplomats, foreign correspondents, high-powered international politicians. He was lost with them, lost to their intense interest in large world affairs, and lost in spite of his personal friendship with a few of them such as Sheean and Gunther. And he was always withdrawing in a pet. Now he had disappeared alone into Italy, wandering once more like Dodsworth. It may have been at this time that—in Mrs. Mowrer's account—he wandered back to his old Roman haunt, Alfredo's. The place had changed a great deal, had become fashionable and crowded.

> He sat in a corner, eyeing a little wistfully the elegant crowd, and toying with the menu, on which the passage from *Babbitt* was proudly quoted. You could order other dishes there, but *fettucini al burro* was what the waiters expected you to take. . . . So Sinclair Lewis ordered some. . . . As he lingered over the meal and the restaurant emptied, the proprietor came to chat with the tall stranger who sat alone. He referred casually to the number of Americans who always visited him, boasted of having been written about by one of the most famous novelists in the world, and tried to impress the visitor.

Alfredo produced then his guest book, crowded with the names of celebrities.

> "Perhaps the Signore would also like to put his name among the famous ones?" It was a kindly gesture to a lonely stranger. Sinclair Lewis drew out his fountain pen, signed, wished the man good night and went out. He had written "John Smith."

Or perhaps that was later, for he was to wander about Italy and sit alone in Rome on many another occasion. But until the last time, he always drifted back "home," and for a long time to his wife.

He drifted back to Semmering toward the end of November. There were new resolves about drinking, *his* resolves. He took a small apartment in Vienna to which he could commute for work, but he was not writing much of anything. He had an American car and could drive about, and he had a radio in his flat over which he spent a good deal of time. He sought out a psychoanalyst and had one session with him, and then determined to have no more of that. News would reach him about *Ann Vickers,* which was being serialized. Early in December came a letter from a Michigan man named Rose, who, "having absolutely nothing else to do the other evening," read the November installment, and "I have yet to read anything as rotten, as stinking and filthy as that story."

> Why you dirty low down smelly nasty disgusting, obscene, maggot filled manure minded, skunkassociating sap, of just what value do you think a story of that kind would be to the world or to the readers. They [*sic*] may have been rottener stories written, but I never read one, I thought Joseph Hergesheimer, Rupert Hughes and Somerset Vaughn [*sic*] took the toilet paper for dirtiness, but you have them beat. I never read one of your ramblings before, to call it a story is to insult every amatuer [*sic*] writer that ever scratched a pen and I never will read another one, and I hope you never thrust another one on the public.

He concluded by wishing that "Dreiser had hit a few more times and all of them harder."

Lewis, posing as a secretary, addressed his correspondent as "Mr. Ross," and replied:

> Mr. Sinclair Lewis directs me to thank you for your friendly letter, and to extend to you the compliments of the Season.
>
> As you have shown so kindly an interest in his new book, *Ann Vickers,* as it has appeared serially in the *Redbook,* Mr. Lewis hopes that you will read it further in book form, which will appear under the auspices of Doubleday, Doran & Co. on January 25, this year, and that you will then write to him again, and in greater detail, as he is always glad to hear from his admirers.

He heard, in the meantime, from Daniel Longwell about the plans for the book. Doubleday had made a small first edition of 2,350 copies, and had stipulated to booksellers that one copy of the first edition might be had with every order for twenty-five copies of the regular printing, a scheme that aroused both considerable irritation and great prepublication interest. Doubleday was hoping to dispose of 100,000 copies in the first year.

Such news heightened holiday cheer, and the Christmas party ran nearly its entire course of ten days with the greatest success. The guests included the Mowrers, the Gunthers, Christa Winsloe (author of *Mädchen in Uniform,* and an old friend of Mrs. Lewis), and Frere and his future wife, the daughter of Edgar Wallace. With Michael, there were five children, and the Lewises rented the entire *dépendance* of the Semmering hotel to house the party. There they set up a private bar and employed a little orchestra for dancing. There was an enormous Christmas tree, and swimming in the hotel pool, and sleigh rides to mountain inns for lunch, and singing, and snow; and at the end, the entire party, except Sinclair Lewis, went off to Budapest. Lewis, after a quarrel, left Semmering, alone, and his wife wrote him in dejected humility, begging him to return.

He returned in time to give an enormous dinner for the Goodmans at Schöner's, where, for six people, he ordered seven bottles of wine, five of which he drank. ("I suspect Red," Goodman wrote Mencken, "of liking to receive deep bows from servants.") They dined a little later with W. C. Bullitt and were questioned afterward by reporters who wished to confirm the rumors that Bullitt was a secret emissary of President-elect Roosevelt. There were rumors, too, that Sinclair Lewis had been selected for a "special post" under Roosevelt, and in response to this news item, he replied, "Unfortunately, it wasn't kind enough to let me know what post, leaving me timorous as to whether it may be the embassy in Peking or a cell at Atlanta." He was reported to be ill, which was not true. He was reported to be buying a house in Austria, which was not true. He was reported to be at work on a new book, and this was true—he was blocking out and planning the "beautiful" novel that would be *Work of Art,* and this effort, he told Longwell, was "the *real* work" on a novel, rather than the writing itself, which was nothing once the plan was in hand.

Longwell and Harry Maule, at the same time, were giving him the details of their promotion plans. They referred to their campaign as a "circus" and hoped that they were not overdoing it; and they were not—as the advance orders, which were splendid, indicated. The novel would appear simultaneously in thirteen languages in sixteen countries. It was, after all, his first novel since Lewis had won the Nobel prize.

But all this gave him small comfort or confidence. On February 3, Philip Goodman wrote Mencken again:

> Darthy is leaving Wredde. Yesterday was the pay-off when they came to blows that were actual and not rhetorical. Her charges will be simply that he's a dirty son-of-a-bitch. She wishes no alimony, but only to be rid of him. Say what you will, the woman is all decency and dignity. Her stories are long, it is true, and that she is a lady journalist (worse, a lady foreign correspondent who is always privy to wars that are being secretly made between countries whose names she is unfortunately not at liberty at present to divulge) is also true. But she's not without steel in her character, and

her inner self stands erect and rather proudly. As against Wredde, I'm all for her. He speaks of hiring a plane ($700) and going to London, and also of renting the Sir Percy Lubbock house in the charming English village of Somewhere-on-Something at a cost of $1000 per month. Yesterday he sent a limousine to my door, to be at my disposal for whatever use I wished. Lily told the chauffeur that I regrettably had other engagements. Poor Wredde! I fear it will be said of him that he couldn't remain a celebrity, but had to become a mere notoriety. But of Darthy you must revise many of your prejudices. She has her own ego, and it goes marching down the street behind a brass band at times, and she is an energetic money-maker; but she is honest and not cheap, and she hates all of Wredde's vermin friends. More: she tells him so. Her plan is to earn enough to support herself and her baby, and to give Wredde the rest of the earth in which to get drunk and make a public damn fool of himself. At least, all this was the earful Lily and I got last night. For all I know, as I write this they may be in one another's arms.

They were not. Sinclair Lewis was in London, once more in Georgian House, Bury Street, and presently his wife would go to Munich and then to Portofino. In the meantime, *Ann Vickers* had been published. In the United States, Ellen Glasgow, at the end of January, wrote despairingly to Allen Tate:

. . . we must live down the literary oligarchy of the Middle West, and that isn't easy, with all my friends the Van Dorens writing about one another—and about Mr. Sinclair Lewis. Have you read *Ann Vickers,* a whole mob of a book? And, still worse—oh, far worse, have you read Carl Van Doren's *Sinclair Lewis?* "Mr. Lewis," remarks Mr. Van Doren, "is America writing."

The popular reviewers, or most of them, heralded the book as if this were indeed the fact. Burton Rascoe, J. Donald Adams, Lewis Gannett, William Soskin, Sterling North—all praised it in large areas of print as Lewis at his best. Bernard DeVoto found it the equal of *Arrowsmith,* by "the finest American novelist of his period," but deplored Carl Van Doren's critical excesses. Malcolm Cowley in the *New Republic* thought less well of it, and Mencken's disappointment was apparent. A New York *Times* editorial, commenting on this novel and Wells's most recent work, *The Bulpington of Blup,* found both extremely dull, productive only of an overpowering weariness with a method as unselective as a speech by a filibustering senator. In London, the *New Statesman and Nation* likewise compared Wells and Lewis, but with pleasure: both were publicists, both reformists, both were without the taint of aestheticism. "They have the interest and point of view of the common man, with an added lucidity beyond his reach. They remain commonplace with a tenacity that amounts to genius, completely ordinary in an extraordinary degree." And most of the major newspaper reviews in Great Britain were enthusiastic, at least one of them going so far as to call the novel "permanent." In the United States again, a Roman Catholic periodical, *America,* regarded the book as obscene—it gives its approval to sexual freedom and abortion, and Ann's last lover is a Catholic—and Michael Williams, in *Commonweal,* satirically treated the book as a possible remedy for the Depression.

The enormous sales of the novel were remarkable in 1933, and it had been observed that the whole publishing industry was grateful to Sinclair Lewis for this priming of the publishing pumps. "Why stop there?" Williams asked.

> Surely if readers begin to buy mass production novels once more, they will have to buy food to keep them going, and houses to live in while they read, and automobiles to reach the bookstores and rental libraries. Meanwhile the flood of advertising and reviewing will speed up the paper mills, which mean freight for the railroads, which in turn will send up the price of stocks, which in turn—but here we reach dangerous ground and I had better stop.

He then deplored the novel as "sentimental romance, seasoned with 'hot-cha.' "

> The literary historian will marvel that in any age such a weak, wild, cheap, raw, crude lump of inane and crapulous balderdash could have been bally-hooed into popular favor.

Ann Vickers is neither so bad as Michael Williams found it nor so good as some others did. In Lewis's own work, it marks a falling away from the point of highest interest. Taking off, as *Ann Vickers* may have, from Wells's *Ann Veronica,* the references to Wells are probably just. Certainly, like Wells's prewar novels, *Ann Vickers* is something of a *Bildungsroman* that, through a large part of the life of a single character, tries to sketch in the chief interests in a whole period of social history. For this history, Lewis drew largely on the background of his wife's life, partly on that of his own—prewar Christian Socialism, feminism and settlement house work, charity organization, liberal and radical thought, prison reform, sexual emancipation, the Depression, careers for women, equal rights. Through it all is the recurrent theme of a woman who is trying to find herself as a woman as well as a Great Woman, just as *Dodsworth* was the story of a man trying to find himself as a man as well as a Business Man.

Perhaps more interesting than either the major theme or the main subject matter are the many hints of transmuted autobiography—a small child defying God, a reference to the New Haven *Journal-Courier,* a college like Oberlin, the degeneracy of expatriate Paris, and so on. There is, and more and more intensely as the novel approaches its end, the obvious ambiguity in the feeling of the author toward his heroine: his uneasy approval of her dedication to "do-good" principles; his resentment of "liberal" and "radical" causes that his own characterization of her commits him to approve; the sporadic but sprawling satiric touches, settling on her, on him, on *them,* but never pulling these together into real satire at all. Most interesting is the portrait of Ann's husband, a feeble fellow who is jealous of her expansiveness and prestige; it is a portrait not without its share of self-criticism.

> He decidedly wanted her to be Big enough to hold an office which would make them both socially important; he did not mind her paying the rent and grocery bills; he was irritated when she did not show off properly at public dinners and when she fell into clichés. . . . Only, privately, she had to be a Little Woman—otherwise how, standing beside her, could he be Big Mans? (He had told her of a girl who used to call him "Big Mans." But even in her tenderest moments, when he had brought her Viennese chocolates and been funny, she'd be hanged if she would ever be as littlewomanish as that.)

And:

> Ann was, with plain tale and flourish of figures, maintaining that not one in ten of the prisoners, men or women, who are supposed to have a trade has really mastered it. The company seemed interested. Probably she was pontificating a little; probably she was forgetting that she was a wife, and taking herself as seriously as a male golf player. But it did hurt—not merely infuriated but hurt, deep in her heart where dwelt her loyalty, when Russell publicly drawled:
>
> "Well, now you've settled that for us, dearie, just explain Russia, and tell 'em about bio-physics!"

And:

> Russell Spaulding (a man who was, Ann amazedly recalled, related to her by marriage) talked always in his lighter amorous moments of "playing" at things, of "making believe," and he engaged in these diversions so hysterically that he was as embarrassing to Ann as the spectacle of a fat man dancing at a nudist colony.

And:

> He flared, "Being married to you is like sleeping with the Taxation Problem!"
>
> She was instantly remorseful.

Ann Vickers is rescued from Russell Spaulding by a man with red hair, but he bears almost no other resemblance to Sinclair Lewis—he is burly, with a beard, earthy, tender, sexually competent and at ease, full of easy appetites—a kind of dream figure; while Sinclair Lewis, in London, writing and cabling his wife in the hope of altering her resolve to leave him, at the same time sulked that he might just as well be married to the "Taxation

Problem." He sulked, too, when he saw a New York *Times* advertisement of James Gould Cozzens's novel, *The Last Adam,* published by Harcourt, Brace & Company at nearly the same time that Doubleday had published *Ann Vickers.* The advertisement quoted a reviewer as saying, "Here is a youngster in his twenties who can write rings around the old maestro and can teach him a lot he doesn't know about small towns." This advertisement Sinclair Lewis sent to his wife with the penciled note, "Alfred getting back."

He had with him for a time in London his new publisher, Nelson Doubleday. Doubleday was, of course, very happy about his new author. The directors of "March of Time" had almost at once found his novel to have so much public interest that they made a dramatization from it for the newsreels, and this production had been so successful that the RCA-Victor people wished to make a recording of it. *The Saturday Evening Post,* which had not for years run a book advertisement, was advertising *Ann Vickers.* The New York Public Library had ordered 150 copies and had then canceled the order because 150 copies would not fill the demand (or because the librarian did not care for the abortion scene). It was difficult to keep the bookstores supplied. The first trade sales were mounting toward 90,000 copies, and in all editions, the novel would finally go to 133, 849 copies. Daniel Longwell's section of Doubleday was out of the red.

One day Longwell's telephone rang—it was his first transatlantic call. The voice was Nelson Doubleday's in London. "I have a friend here who wants to talk to you," he said, and then another voice came on, saying, "Hi, Dan, this is Red. What time is it there?" Uncomprehending, Longwell told him what time it was, and Lewis replied, "That's what's wrong with you God-damned Americans—you're always five hours behind the time. It's nine over here," and the receiver was slammed down. Almost at once the telephone rang again and it was Lewis again, with his serious message: he wanted to tell him how delighted he was with the sale of *Ann Vickers* and with everything that Longwell had done for that book. He had just passed his forty-eighth birthday.

In a somewhat more bemused condition, he wrote his wife on February 18.

> I am staying here in England sort of vaguely. . . . . I am staying here partly because I hate to go farther from you. You seem to me in my mad life my one refuge and security. You see I don't care a damn—not any more at least—for fame and all those amiable experiences, but only (and this is a not-too-easy contradiction) for you and Mickey on the one hand, and Freedom (whatever that empty thing may be) on the other. But I think I shall go in just a few days. . . . . And I love you; I hate to be so far from you and I see Vermont and a vision—with us in it.
>
> *Jacques*

A week later he sailed—incognito at first—on a small ship, the *American Farmer,* carrying only seventeen passengers. He wanted to get away from people, he declared, and not even the steamship company knew that he was to be aboard since he had had an agent book his passage anonymously. His sailing might have been completely unnoticed had he not, at the last moment, revealed it to Bruce Lockhart, a gossip writer. Politically infected, he darkly predicted to Lockhart a world war within a year, starting between France and the Little Entente, and Germany, Italy, Austria and Hungary—with Russia drawn in later. He believed that the United States and Britain would have "enough sense to keep out." Just before disembarking he wrote his wife, and his letter ended:

> We're due off Nantucket lightship. Home! I like home. Europes are nice, but I prefer Vermont. I long to be there with you. It is true, isn't it, that there will be apple trees, and flaming lilies, and the moon over the low mountains, and you and me, after dinner, sitting smoking on the terrace, and inside when it becomes chilly, the fireplace and lamplight and lots of books? Love me, so we can go home.

On shipboard, he had found the kind of "bunch" that he enjoyed, and he arrived in first-rate humor, "swinging his malacca stick like a boulevardier." He introduced his "Smoking Room Cabinet"—Gus Yorke, the Potash of *Potash and Perlmutter,* returning from a London revival of the old play in which he played the same role that he had created in 1914; Bob Anderson, whose performing horse, Dixie, was ill in the hold after weeks of British vaudeville; Dermot Darby, an Irish newspaperman; and Captain William B. Oakley, "the finest skipper ever." Yorke: "And on the boat, I been his bodyguard, in charge of seeing he don't get to bed too early." Lewis: The trouble with the Depression was that there was too much debt and that there were too few vice-presidents. The new vice-presidents were to be Ed Wynn, Will Rogers, H. L. Mencken, and Bishop James Cannon, Jr. Women were now nearly equal to men but men still had them licked. There would be a war in Europe within two years.

Did he know that *Ann Vickers* was the nation's top best seller? "Please, don't be so commercial-minded. After all, you are talking to an artist and money is a secondary matter. Does anyone know how many of the books have sold?" He finds that writing has become easier for him . . . he enjoys planning a novel . . . the new novel has elaborate plans . . . Shaw is the only writer capable of being witty in an interview. . . . Did he know that the President had just declared a moratorium on the banks? He did not. He had only eighty-five dollars in his pocket. However, on that day his alimony payments ceased, for on that day Mrs. Hegger Lewis married Telesforo Casanova de Ojea in a civil ceremony in New York and sailed with him for Havana.

Lewis wrote his wife to tell her that he was staying for a time at the Hotel New Yorker (in "a cavernous apartment," Longwell remembers), gathering material for *Work of Art,* and his plan was to take "a weekend at some different good inn within 75 miles of here each week." She replied on March 25 from Portofino:

> I had no emotional strength with which to try to pull it off. Your going back to drinking spirits is part of it. You yourself had said, you know, "If I go back now on my own decision it will be very serious." It seemed to me that our life together was falling into exactly the pattern of your life with Grace; that it would move in the same direction and to the same denouement, and that nothing I could do would help you stop it. Then, your own letters were curiously remote and cold. They did not bring you to me; rather the contrary. These two which came this morning . . . they're sweet . . . and you might have written them to anyone. I thought: I must save myself. I must really, now, save myself. I really tried hard not to love you; I confess it. I have been too hurt in my life, Hal, before, to dare even to think of being hurt in the same way again. Only it wouldn't be the same way now, but much, much worse. . . .

She plunged into her work. She returned to Germany to gather material for a series of articles on the treatment of the Jews, and she was planning an anti-Nazi play.

Through most of March, Lewis was working and "playing" with Louis Florey in and out of the Hotel New Yorker, where he continued to plan his novel about hotels. Less than a week after Lewis's return, the New York *Times* interviewed Florey on Lewis's methods of work, and Florey told the reporter how Lewis would dictate notes at a rate of about two hundred words a minute and Florey would take these words down in something resembling outline form. In those notes, characters were born and named and described, cities and towns named, population figures recorded, homes and rooms and furniture described. On his maps, Lewis would name not only the streets but the kinds of trees that grew on them and the color of the dogs that crossed them. Florey did not neglect Lewis's personal habits: how he would sleep for long periods in his clothes; how he could sleep anywhere as he could write anywhere; how he would fall asleep in the middle of a conversation or in the middle of lunch and then wake up thoroughly refreshed; how he would get up at any time at all during the night and go to work for five minutes or five hours; and how he would sometimes go on working for days and nights on end without any sleep at all.

Once his plan was set down—in this account it does not seem so much a plan as notes for a plan—Lewis himself took over the typewriter and, from the plan, typed out a twenty- or thirty-page summary of the novel, and if this remained too vague to satisfy him, he rewrote it in forty or fifty pages. When he began to write the novel itself, he deliberately overwrote, and when he was finished, he cut it down once, perhaps twice, perhaps a third time before he turned it over to the typist for a clean copy which might again be revised. Nor did his blue pencil ever come to rest until the last page proofs had gone to his publisher for the last time.

Lewis found Florey a congenial spirit, and presently, toward the end of March, abandoning his plan for gentle little visits to nearby inns and starting out instead for the West Coast, he took Florey with him. The change in plan was, as usual, sudden. One evening he went to Sidney Howard's play *The Late Christopher Bean* and afterward went backstage to wait on Pauline Lord, the star. He had made an engagement for lunch with Miss Lord and arranged for two interviews, one in which he would tell the world how wonderful New York hotels were and another in which he would tell the world how wonderful his wife was. But these arrangements were forgotten when, next morning, he abruptly took off for California.

Setting out, he announced once more that he had abandoned his plans for a labor novel—he saw no solution of American problems in labor, and "the doctrinaire and foolish young Communists" were only compounding the confusion; but he was enthusiastic about the Roosevelt Administration and delighted with the appointment of Frances Perkins to the Cabinet. Traveling west, they paused along the way—Chicago, Kansas City, Santa Fe—to study the machinery of hotels. In a Chicago restaurant, Dr. Fishbein was dining with Lloyd Lewis and his wife, and when he saw Sinclair Lewis at another table he persuaded him to join them. Since Lewis had read Lloyd Lewis's Civil War writings, the talk turned to that subject, and presently to the Kansas jayhawkers. Lewis was fascinated, and when Lloyd Lewis came to his office next morning, he found messages saying that Sinclair Lewis had been telephoning him from the Stevens Hotel since eight o'clock. Lloyd Lewis called back, and Sinclair Lewis asked if he would collaborate with him on a play about the jayhawkers after *Work of Art* was finished. Lloyd Lewis agreed, and Sinclair Lewis promised to keep in touch with him, and went on west with Florey, coming at last to settle once more at Del Monte Lodge, near Carmel. There they stayed for about three weeks.

An enterprising young newspaperman in Carmel, Herbert Cerwin, presently to become the public relations man for the Del Monte Properties, approached Lewis for an interview and, in the following weeks, saw a good deal of him. When he first saw him, his hands were shaking so badly that he could not lift his glass to his mouth without assistance, and to this end he had invented a very effective device. He would unfurl his napkin and put it around his neck, and holding one end of it in his right hand, he would also take the glass in that hand and then, pulling down on the other end of the napkin with his left hand, elevate his drink. When Cerwin asked him how he could both write so much and drink so heavily, Lewis replied that his drinking was much exaggerated. And he was indeed writing on *Work of Art* every morning. His researches in the purlieus of the Lodge were assiduous, and he would turn up everywhere—in the kitchens, in the cellars, in the housekeeper's quarters—gathering his exact and detailed information. And he hunted up a number of those old Carmel acquaintances who were still living in that altered part of the West.

Among these was a pulp writer named Stephen Allen Reynolds, who said to Cerwin that now that Lewis was famous and he, Reynolds, was only a hack, Lewis would not want to see him. Cerwin, who had found Lewis warmly engaging, could not believe this and urged Reynolds to telephone him—which Reynolds did. Of course, Lewis would like to see him, he would come over to his Carmel cottage at four o'clock. Reynolds, who had not seen Lewis for a good twenty years, was excited about the meeting and laid in some whisky to celebrate appropriately. When, at about five o'clock, Lewis still had not appeared, Reynolds despaired and, with Cerwin watching, emptied his bottle of whisky. Then presently a big black Cadillac drove up, and Louis Florey stepped out to assist his highly incapacitated employer into the Reynolds cottage. He just managed to fall into a chair with the greeting, "Hello, Steve," and Reynolds just managed to return the greeting with, "Hello, Red," and then the two old friends sat in sodden silence for half an hour. Finally Florey said to Cerwin that, since obviously nothing more would happen, they might as well take Lewis away, and thus the reunion ended.

He was back at Twin Farms by April 30, awaiting his wife, who was arriving on the *Rex* on May 11 with her friend Christa Winsloe and would come home to Vermont on about May 15. To the United Press, Lewis denied as "a deliberate lie" a published report that he was contemplating divorce. He continued the writing of *Work of Art* (to Mencken: "I am writing mightily upon my new novel, which deals with the life of Cardinal Newman," et cetera) and paced the woods, impatient for his wife's return. He was not drinking hard liquor, the work went swiftly, and the reunion was amiable. When, in June, a letter came to him from an infatuated girl, Mrs. Lewis good-humoredly answered it. To Frere, Lewis wrote:

> This is a very quiet summer of nothing much but work and loafing under the trees. I have about two-thirds of the new novel done [July 7] and the rest is going smoothly—probably so smoothly that it will be rotten!

In midsummer Mrs. Lewis sailed for Europe with Christa Winsloe on a very brief trip, and Miss Winsloe wrote Lewis a humorous account of his wife's activities in nonpolitical areas:

> Dotty is doing a lot of shops. I . . . did not always join her because it was too much for me. Dotty has the strength and perseverance of six men, and I mean I have not. One day I promised to join her later. I found the young man who had taken her around, under a heap of curtains, he had fainted. The lady who had taken his place screamed with hysteria and just got carried off by the firebrigade. The boss of the shop was on his knees before her, imploring her . . .

On August 17: "The first draft of the new novel is about seven-eighths done, so I begin to have hopes!" His wife returned. The spirited Christa Winsloe came for a long visit, Wells Lewis came as usual, Philip Goodman and his wife came, the DeVotos came on their way to Bread Loaf, others came and went.

DeVoto, in the recollection of Gorham Munson, persuaded Lewis to come to the final session of the Bread Loaf Writers' Conference, trustful because Lewis now was drinking only beer. Lewis agreed to serve as leader at the last afternoon round-table discussion and to attend the closing banquet, and he arrived at Bread Loaf with a large bottle of whisky, which he at once passed around. The discussion was not very lively because the students were in awe of the visitor and some of them, conceivably, remembered an earlier, disastrous occasion. At one point Lewis tried to provoke them into discussion by a fiery demand that they speak up, without conspicuous success. In the evening his spirits were even higher. At a considerable distance from the speakers' table, he indulged in mimicry of Arnold Bennett and other English writers, and he improvised at intervals a free-verse poem on "Bennie DeVoto from the Wasatch Mountains," a Sandburgian bit. DeVoto was writing his novel, *We Accept with Pleasure,* and he could not resist creating a character, Frank Archer, "a great novelist," in the image of Sinclair Lewis.

> It took her some moments to realize that Frank Archer wasn't drunk, that this appalling restlessness, this St. Vitus, this inundation of talk was his normal pressure . . . he was a kind of electrical disturbance. He wasn't actually spinning like a top or hanging by his toes from the ceiling but you had a dizzy impression that he must be.

The alteration of physical characteristics—short and round, black and gray-haired, bushy-browed—is no disguise, nor is the anticipation of a still unenacted item in his matrimonial history.

> Two women had divorced Archer. In the purest self-protection, as one would flee from a falling cliff. . . . He had the mind of a cheer leader. Ploughboy gaping at the eternal dawn. Diurnal wonder of the tremendous platitude. Periodical discovery of the utterly apparent.

The appraisal, like the portrait, is nearly just; it is also cool.

It was time for Sinclair Lewis to think of his new best friend, Lloyd

Lewis, and the play that they were going to do. Writing him on August 24, he said that the novel was finished but that he was too tired from that effort to go to work on the play at once—he "wouldn't be any good." He would rest for a few weeks and then, if Lloyd Lewis wanted it that way, he could come to Chicago in secret and take rooms in some out-of-the-way hotel. "And do you know a good stenographer—male, so we can work at night—who can take down dialogue fast if we want to dictate it?" Marc Connelly, who was a casual friend of Sinclair Lewis, was a close friend of Lloyd Lewis, and when the latter had asked his advice about the project, he was concerned about the effect that Sinclair Lewis's drinking would have on any collaboration, but their common enthusiasm led him to bless the union. Now the two Lewises were thinking about bringing Connelly into the collaboration if he would consent. But would it not be a good idea, Sinclair Lewis asked, if only two of them wrote the first draft? "I really wouldn't care whether you and I, or you and he, did the first work together."

As matters worked out, the three of them arranged to meet in New York at the New Weston, where Lloyd Lewis would come for a brief stay, and there they were to have a three-way discussion of the play's outline.

> I remember Lloyd's graceful concealment of the distress he must have felt [Marc Connelly wrote recently] when Red arrived, drunk. I suppose Red's condition was due to inner panic. Like many novelists Red was unable to approach dramatic writing with the same care and skill with which he could plan a novel. The theater fascinated him, but I do not think he ever had any comprehension of its technical demands. Some of his suggestions for the new play were frivolous and extravagant. However, a theme was decided upon and, in subsequent sessions, Red, sober and earnest, gave all he could to the work.

Mrs. Lewis, writing her own play, employed a new nurse for Michael, Emily Walker, a young Scotswoman newly arrived in America. She first met Lewis on Labor Day. Never having heard of him, she was nevertheless "scared to death" when she met him—so tall, glowering, tweedy, leaning over her, saying only, "You're little. Have you met my son?" "Not yet." "You will!" She was taken to the farm house and did not see Lewis again for nearly a week, but after a few days, Louis Florey, who was in attendance for the typing of *Work of Art,* came over and reported that Lewis approved of her. "She's little, but she keeps that brat of mine quiet." After that, he no longer alarmed her, and she discovered his gentleness, his kindness, his boyishness.

But where was the family to be housed for the winter? Mrs. Lewis preferred an apartment in town, but Lewis was insistent on the suburbs; and, without considering her wishes, he bought an enormous house at 17 Wood End Lane, in Bronxville. As Arnold Bennett found it necessary to write faster and faster to maintain his yacht, Lewis had to write faster and faster, more and more willing himself into manufacturing novels regularly, in order to maintain large establishments and the standard of living that they necessitated. The actual writing of *Work of Art* had taken less than four months. Then, on September 18, he turned the house over to his wife for furnishing and decorating, turned over his typescript to Doubleday (who called it "his most likable book"), and with Florey, took rooms in the Sherry Hotel, Chicago, near the Lloyd Lewis apartment.

Lloyd Lewis, who was the Chicago *News* drama critic, knew something about stage techniques, and as the author of *Myths after Lincoln* and *Sherman,* was a master of the subject matter from which their play was to be drawn. First called *The Skedaddler,* and then *Brother Burdette,* and finally *Jayhawker,* it was to deal with the Kansas-Missouri border raids before and during the Civil War; with the emergence, through oratorical bombast, of the first United States Senator from Kansas, a wily roisterer not quite a criminal; with a scheme to end the Civil War through the seizure, by both parties, of Mexico; and with a love story. Farce, satire, sentiment, and the spirit of the Gettysburg Address were all somehow to be fused into a dramatic unity.

How were the two men to fuse their talents? First, having blocked out their dramatis personae and the general movement of the play, they took it up scene by scene. They would discuss a scene thoroughly, improvising speeches as they went, making notes, and then each man would write out his version of the whole. They would exchange manuscripts, each would criticize the other's, and then they would knock out a combination of the two. Lloyd Lewis, in the end, was responsible for the substance of the historical scenes, Sinclair Lewis for the love story, and Sinclair Lewis passed finally on all dialogue.

He was drinking. Once when they all went down to the Lloyd Lewis farm on the Michigan dunes, he got very drunk and, in the middle of a conversation on the porch, collapsed. Florey got him up to his room and the Lloyd Lewises sat on the porch and thought about him. An hour later he reappeared, perfectly sober, and he picked up the very phrase that he had dropped as he had passed out. It was not even at the beginning of a sentence, but in the middle, where he resumed and then finished his interrupted remarks. And nothing was said by anyone about the interruption.

By the end of October, when Lewis returned to New York, a first draft was well along toward completion. Lloyd Lewis now came east and they continued the process. In the middle of November, Sinclair Lewis once more joined his collaborator in Chicago. By the end of the month they had a script that they thought they could show around. Marc Connelly, who had not in fact worked on the play, was interested in producing it, and on December 7, Lewis wrote Frere to say that Connelly had it under consideration. But the play was by no means ready for production.

Mrs. Lewis's anti-Nazi play also failed to find a producer. In that autumn, Lewis's anti-Nazi sentiments, publicly muted as they may at this point have been, gave him occasion for a public gesture. Klaus Mann had included his name in a list of *Mitarbeiter* on the masthead of his anti-Nazi periodical, *Die Sammlung,* and its presence there had led a number of German booksellers to decline to handle his novels. Lewis wrote Ernst Rowohlt, in answer to a seven-page single-spaced letter that had explained the situation, to tell him that Mann had used his name without his permission. Nevertheless . . .

> Suppose I *did* most heartily agree with Klaus in everything. What would that have to do with the desirability of such entirely non-political books as *Arrowsmith?* The book is good, and worth handling, in itself, or else it isn't, and its merits have nothing to do with my political ideas, athletic records, or private morals. Did these booksellers wait to see whether I would write for Klaus and what I would write? They did not! Because of the inclusion of my name in a long and obviously unofficial list of names, they began to refuse to handle my books.
>
> Very well, if they have done so, there will be, even if this *Sammlung* incident is forgotten, some other like attempt to censor me. So we might just as well start in right now and agree that under the present regime, none of my books can any longer be published or sold in Germany and, agreeing to that unfortunate fact, part as friends.

Rowohlt cabled at length in German with complete approval: "I will inform the German book trade of [your decision] in order to let them see that there are still men among writers."

It was a splendid gesture, and it should have brought Lewis public sympathy in the United States. If it did, he lost it again late in December at a dinner of many distinguished people held at the Hotel Roosevelt in honor of living Nobel winners and of Alfred Nobel on the centennial of his birth. He was seated on a dais between Anne Morgan and Albert Einstein, and when photographers began to take photographs of the notables (thus delaying the dinner), Lewis snapped to a fellow guest, "I haven't attended a public banquet in five years and I don't see why the hell I should be photographed." With that, he stalked from the banquet hall and went up to his room on the tenth floor. The other guests were astonished and bewildered, dinner waited, and the photographers were induced to go to Lewis's room and apologize to him. He would not admit them. Mlle. Alma Clayburgh, the opera singer, and Estelle M. Sternberger, director of World Peaceways, tried next, and after a further delay of about twenty minutes, they induced him to return, and dinner proceeded. Einstein spoke in praise of Nobel as an idealist, and Frank B. Kellogg spoke of the chances of keeping peace in the world, and Lewis said that he was glad that this was one dinner that was not given to celebrate the repeal of Prohibition. Next day the New York *Times* editorialized: "Sinclair Lewis paid tribute to the memory of the inventor of dynamite by exploding in his honor."

It was a dispirited, even a petulant and sulking performance for the man who had only a few years before written his friend George Jean Nathan, "After all Messrs. Nathan, Mencken and Lewis exist as public figures largely because they have given so much offense to so many people." The *élan* had gone, the style, even the absurdity. But it was a way of ending a year.

3

NINETEEN THIRTY-FOUR heard the hum and buzz of a considerable household there in Bronxville: the three Lewises, with Wells a frequent visitor on holiday from Andover and presently from Harvard, a German cook, a French maid, the Scottish nurse, a butler named André, and the secretary-companion Florey there much of the time. The establishment was organized with an efficiency that made possible the continuous peregrinations of its proprietors. Dorothy Lewis's attentiveness to the imperious routines of her spouse is perhaps evidenced by this excerpt from her typewritten instructions to André:

> Put half a dozen boxes of matches in Mr. Lewis's study and in his bedroom, in the drawer of his night table, and see that there are always half a dozen there. Set this up when you make his room every day. Also, please see that he is always a carton of cigarettes ahead—keep that many in reserve in the butler's pantry.

Lewis's relations with the servants were not of the best. He was very much the grand signor; and still he was liked by them. Emily Walker remembered that, for all his boyishness, he was also the Master, and she could not imagine ever addressing him, however intimate or disgraceful the circumstances became, without saying "sir"; and this was also true of the other servants. But he was capricious with them. Every now and then when Mrs. Lewis came home from the city, she would find that he had dismissed an excellent maid. The only reason he would give was that he was tired of seeing her face around, and Mrs. Lewis would deal with the nuisance of persuading the girl to come back or of interviewing new girls. One cook they had who refused to be dismissed: "No, Mr. Lewis," said she, "Mrs. Lewis hired me and if I am to go, Mrs. Lewis will send me." She stayed—and Lewis was amused.

He was often thoughtful of them, too. In the country, he bought a Model-A Ford so that Emily Walker could take "the girls" out for drives. When he decided that he was going to devote himself to serious music (until then his favorite composition was Brahms's *Waltz in A Major*), he bought an expensive Victrola, and he ordered Emily to bring the cook into the drawing room to admire it. He was drunk, and the cook needed a new stove; she refused to look at the Victrola. Emily reported as much to him. And then, although it was very late in the afternoon, he telephoned the electric company and demanded that a new stove be installed immediately. During the installation, he retired, and when he roused himself sometime later and walked into the kitchen, he demanded of the cook where she had acquired that stove. She reminded him, and he said, "Yes, and you wouldn't look at my Victrola."

Sometimes, after they had worked hard with weekend guests or after a big party, he would go away for a week or more, advising them to rest while he was gone. He depended on Emily Walker in a curious way. Once, when Mrs. Lewis had given her a week off, he was annoyed that she was going, and when she asked how she would get back to Twin Farms from Rutland on her return, he snapped, "If you want to go, go; I'm not going to worry about you; go on, go on, get out, get along with you," et cetera. But when she was due to return, he had practically the entire establishment waiting for the arrival of her bus in Rutland.

He depended on her for company. "He was terribly afraid to be alone," she remembered. When Mrs. Lewis was away, she would often have to sit up with him in the living room until two or three o'clock in the morning. He did not talk to her; he would sit there thinking, or reading, or listening to music, but she had to be on her hassock near him. There were several servants elsewhere in the house, but he wanted someone in the room. (Commenting to James Thurber two years later about one of Thurber's stories, Lewis said, "All of us are afraid to be alone in a country house at night, but you are the first one brave enough to admit it in print.") When she sat with him, she was expected to keep his glass filled, and after he had had three or four highballs, she would begin to water them more and more, until he said, "You're a rotten bartender!" and she replied, "Perhaps you're losing the taste of the liquor, sir."

They respected him, even felt affection for him, and they were glad to wear their feet out in executing his orders as literally as he expected them to. He was particularly tyrannical about his breakfast. He demanded that no menu be repeated within any one week—he would have kidneys on one morning, finnan haddie in a milk sauce on the next, scrambled eggs on the third, and so on. When the cook made the error of repeating one of these, he would take down the breakfast menu that he had written out for that week, show her the error, and await another breakfast.

Emily Walker, like Mrs. Lewis, did not approve of Louis Florey, who in their view encouraged his drinking for reasons of self-interest. (Mrs. Lewis remembers that one of their great quarrels was about Florey's "using" Lewis, an observation that infuriated him. "You can permit no authority but your own!" he raged, and stamped out of the house.) Once, when Florey brought him in very drunk and got him down on a sofa, only to see him roll off onto the floor, Florey walked out, saying to Emily, "There, Scottie, do what you want with him." When Lewis recovered from such a condition, he wanted only two things—Louis Sherry chocolates and buttermilk.

Mrs. Lewis would do what she could. Daniel Longwell remembers that at one point they were trying out a scheme of rationing: he could have only one pint of whisky in a given evening, and this had to do not only for himself but for any casual guests that he might have. Longwell remembers how torn with mixed feelings Lewis would be, what a visible struggle went on in him between the desire to have a drink himself and the necessity of offering a friend a drink that would mean one less for himself later. Finally, quite grudgingly, he would mutter, "Want a drink?" But when things became really difficult, Mrs. Lewis would have no liquor in the house at all. In one such period, when Christa Winsloe had arrived with a bottle of splendid London gin and Lewis was in town, the two women settled down happily to some leisurely Bronx cocktails. They saw a cab draw up outside, and Miss Winsloe hastily piled everything on the tray and fled with it into the passage to the butler's pantry. That passage was one step up from the living-room floor, and she tripped, fell, sprawled, spilled everything with a great crash. At that moment, Lewis entered the room, saw what had happened, and, amiably drunk, laughed, while general hysteria broke out among the assembled servants.

But so often he was not at all amiable. When, years later, Dorothy Thompson encouraged Emily to talk about her life with them and asked her whether she thought that he really cared for her or for anyone else, Emily said, "He worshiped the ground you walked on. When he heard you were coming home from a trip, he would send for the barber to shave him, insist that all his clothes be in apple-pie order, dress as though he were going to court. And then, often you'd hardly be in the house, when he'd start a quarrel, and then, as likely as not, he'd call the car and leave. You don't know how often I'd go to my room and cry. I never understood why he acted so." Often, during one of these apparently unmotivated rages, Mrs. Lewis would simply leave him and go up and sit on Emily's bed, or in the nursery if Emily was already sitting on her own bed. When Lewis, having dashed his own expectations and flung out of the house, would reappear in a day, two days, a week, he would be as meek as a guilty boy.

His problems were no doubt multiple, but chief among them was his need for adulation that cost him nothing in responsibility. His desire to be a free man of the world, however, conflicted with what was a profound and provincial puritanism. His puritanism showed itself in trivial as well as major ways—his compulsive and spinsterish neatness in personal possessions, whether they were writing materials, household keys, or clothing; and in his attitude toward such matters as charge accounts. Mrs. Lewis disliked shopping and bought her wardrobe twice a year and then paid off her bills in installments over a period of months. This habit more than merely offended Lewis, it outraged him; it was, he insisted, the same as stealing. And when Mrs. Lewis pointed out that department stores and expensive shops were organized to deal with exactly such arrangements, he refused to be persuaded.

These traits may be dismissed as crotchets, but at least one more important manifestation of his puritanism cannot be. That was his incapacity for tenderness. He could be generous, he could be sentimental, but to tenderness he was a stranger. He did not like the body, his own or others'. Early in their marriage, he had said to his wife, half whimsically, half apologetically, "I exist mostly above the neck," and he was always telling her that the erotic relation between people did not really matter at all. The erotic relation is not the whole of tenderness, to be sure, but it is almost certainly its base, and its dearth infects the rest of life. Sinclair Lewis would make love to his wife on occasion and then arise from her embrace only to deliver cruel and vindictive charges, suddenly invent some reason for verbally abusing her, as though the erotic experience called up nothing in him but guilt and malice. This she endured, with much else. "I was too conventional for him," she lamented, "too conventional!"—and meant that she expected an ordinary decency, both ways.

Both liquor and work were flights from guilt; and, in general, he alternated between them. Friendship, likewise, was largely a distraction from the guilty self, and that was why it could be utterly indiscriminate. In January of 1934 he discovered a new distraction when *Dodsworth* went into rehearsal: the group activity of the theater. Since the play was continually being rewritten, Lewis took a vigorous part in these rehearsals, and he wrote Tinker of the pleasure of working in the theater after the "lonely task of novel writing." In the next year Lewis said that he had been responsible for "about 6.7 per cent of the dramatization."

Walter Huston was playing Dodsworth, and he did the part superbly. Fay Bainter was playing Fran, and gossip still has it that during rehearsals, Lewis repeatedly misspoke her name and would call out to her, "Come on, Gracie, you can be much bitchier than that!" Carl Van Doren said later that the best scene from that play was never shown on the stage; it was heard by only a few people in the Bronxville house. Fay Bainter was among the guests, and suddenly, without premeditation, she and Lewis slipped into character as Fran and Sam Dodsworth, began an argument on some trivial issue, let the argument work into a quarrel, and the theme rose to "comic frenzy" amidst shrieks and laughter. The play was tried out in Philadelphia in early February, and on February 24 it came to the Shubert in New York, where it was a great success. In the meantime, John Henry Hammond had undertaken the production of *Jayhawker,* which Lewis was once more rewriting.

In the meantime, too, Doubleday, Doran & Company were hoping that they had another *Ann Vickers* in *Work of Art,* and they were doing everything to persuade booksellers that they did have. For them, they published an elaborate "Idea Book"—a large, twelve-page folder full of suggestions for bookstore advertising of the novel. They invited Lewis to their promotion meetings—an extraordinary gesture—and profited from his endless fecundity in this area of publishing. They prepared a dozen different posters and a variety of other sales devices, and they commissioned a well-known painter, Ernest Fiene, who had never before designed a book jacket, to do an elaborate and much-publicized wrapper for the book.

It was the first of Lewis's "serious" novels since *Main Street* to be completely without distinction. H. S. Canby and William Lyon Phelps and J. Donald Adams were able to praise it; John Chamberlain found that it was "not a boring book"; Elmer Davis, T. S. Matthews, Maxwell Geismar all deplored it; Granville Hicks in the *New Masses,* finding here the ultimate capitulation to the status quo, concluded that "Sinclair Lewis couldn't write a labor novel without revealing himself as a double-crossing apologist for the existing order." And Lewis, inscribing a copy for the University of Minnesota, wrote: "This is the only novel of mine that did not get the credit it deserved."

Work of Art brings to its climax Lewis's lifelong and obsessive interest in hotel-keeping, beginning with his boyhood experience as a substitute night clerk in the Palmer House, Sauk Centre, and it brings to a climax no less his uneasy suspicion of intellect and art, and his deep respect for middle-class virtue. The novel opens in a hotel such as the Palmer House, and in a town like Sauk Centre, although located in Connecticut. The owner of the American House has two sons, Myron and Ora Weagle. Myron is steady and reliable and, even as a boy, dreams of someday owning a perfect hotel. Ora is "literary" and spends his good-for-nothing days mooning over princesses in Poictesme and in writing verse of much the same sort that Sinclair Lewis wrote as a boy, and this portrait—a fantastic caricature—is Lewis's belated act of exorcism.

Ora grows up to be a commercial success and a hack, always self-deluded and scornful of his downright brother. But Myron is the true artist, and Lewis makes nearly his every effort analogous to an act of artistic creation. Ultimately, he even keeps a notebook, "what must, in exactness, be called 'The Notebook of a Poet,' " in which he jots down ideas for improving hotel management and reflections upon his experience as a hotel-keeper. Myron, too, has great success, then through the chicanery of others falls to low estate, and recovers when he concludes that no hotel can be perfect but that he can still make a "work of art" of a tourist camp in Kansas. If one wishes to learn about hotel management, the novel is no doubt an admirable handbook, and no duller than a handbook; if one wishes to learn anything about art, there is nothing here at all. *Work of Art* is the fantasy of the perfect Rotarian.

Rotarians, unfortunately, are not much given to reading novels, and after the initial spurt of about 50,000 copies, *Work of Art* stopped selling entirely.* Doubleday had given Lewis a contract identical with that for *Ann Vickers,* and when the sales stopped, a good remnant of the advertising budget remained to be spent. Longwell suggested that they discuss the matter with Lewis himself. He came to meet them and they showed him exactly how everything had gone from prepublication sales to that day. "There's this much money left to spend on advertising. What would you do?" He said immediately, "I'd stop advertising." Then they all went out for a drink.

This was the season in which *Anthony Adverse* had mushroomed into its success, and suddenly Lewis began an improvisation of *Work of Art* in the manner of *Anthony Adverse.* He would rewrite his novel in that way and be successful yet, and for half an hour or more, then and there, he rewrote it accordingly, to the great entertainment of his fellows. Longwell found it an impressive as well as an entertaining display, for it showed Lewis's detachment from his work in a degree almost impossible to any other "big" writer. Detachment of this sort would not be difficult for a man who had Lewis's other kind of detachment—the absence of any genuine imaginative commitment to his material even when, as in this novel, its animus was in a sense self-directed; and from this lack almost everything else that he would write was to suffer. In *Green Hills of Africa,* published in the next year, the character called Kadinsky says, "Tell me what is Joyce like? I have not the money to buy it. Sinclair Lewis is nothing. I bought it. No. No. Tell me tomorrow. . . ."

He did not wait for the brilliantly successful opening of *Dodsworth* but went, in mid-February, to Bermuda, where, at the St. George Hotel, he rewrote *Jayhawker* yet again. He was joined by his wife and son at the beginning of March, and they stayed until nearly the end of the month. In the course of that month, he wrote a long letter protesting the possibility of legalizing motor traffic on the island and gave this to Ronald Williams for publication in his magazine, *The Bermudian.* Of Lewis, Williams later wrote: ". . . a strident, vivid man who would rather astonish you than impress you."

* But with reprints of various kinds, even this novel had sold 118,000 copies by the end of 1959.

Home again, he wrote Frere that he was rewriting the play "completely" and that rehearsals would begin in August. Then there was the seasonal business of moving the household from one establishment to another, and early in the summer, as soon as Twin Farms was once more resettled, Mrs. Lewis left for New York and Europe—England, Austria, Germany. Immediately Lewis was writing her, bitterly lamenting her absence, telling of his loneliness, complaining of the barn-empty rooms of the big house. In July, the situation became intolerable for him and he decided to take Louis Florey to the Middle West. On July 25 he wrote his wife from a boat called the *Octorara* as it passed through a narrow channel in the northern peninsula of Michigan. The letter ends:

> Next January, the play on, your lectures done, Christmas done, we're going on the Rex, we two very strictly alone, for a month in Italy. Just ambling. I think I have written that before recently. Well, sweet, I shall again. For that profound notion I make propaganda..... I'll get up a petition to you about it, to be signed by Roger Baldwin, Oswald Garrison Villard, Al Einstein—darling.

They drove to St. Cloud to visit Claude, and twice Lewis went on to Sauk Centre—once to show the town to Florey, and once with Claude, "sans Lou." So he wrote his wife on July 30.

> ... and it was a wringing experience in recalled memories. We found the Stone Arch—over a little creek, beneath railroad tracks—which was the holy of holies in the way of playground when we were kids ... and found there, boldly carved and still fresh, initials Claude had cut into the stone forty-five or so years ago..... Did not make one feel too young. That was exciting but tragic, for this country is drying up—conceivably for keeps, this once the richest of farming lands but now becoming arid through too much industrious slashing off of trees. The really lovely creek that once flowed through that arch is absolutely gone—just a dirty dry channel....
>
> The people I used to know in Sauk Centre—the garage man from whom I bought my very first car ..... the brothers in the Gentses' Clothing Store—the postmaster—they were so sweet and friendly that I enjoyed it ..... for one day: a week would be a strain.

So they had a country dinner at noon with Brother Fred and left again, and Lewis took Florey back to Vermont. In *Work of Art* he had written, "It is only in fiction that busy young men far from home spend much time in longing to view the dear, bright, vacant faces of childhood friends and every loved spot that their infancy knew."

Carl Van Doren came to stay with him and one day they drove to Plymouth to look at the Coolidges on their front porch, and while they did not see the Coolidges, they mingled with other sightseers who had come to the village on a touring bus. (Van Doren told this story as an example of Lewis's "creative" relation to strangers.) Lewis struck up a conversation with "a pleasant, weathered old man, a farmer from Ohio," and after learning a good deal about him, he pretended that he was the editor of a country newspaper on his way to New York to buy new type, and presented Van Doren as his cousin, a country doctor. A whole fantasy was then developed in which the Ohioan took an interested and solemn part. Lewis "liked losing himself in a cheerful game," to be, not himself, but, for example, "a country editor on a vacation with his cousin."

Once when they were having lunch they amused themselves with a plan to write an entire novel in twenty-four hours. They would get four secretaries—no, six—and, taking turns, dictate the whole thing without stopping. Then, without the secretaries, they began at once. Van Doren started, and presently Lewis took over,

> grabbed the story, which he had never heard or thought of before, and swept onward in a state of improvisation. Characters sprang into it as if by a magic seed planted in magic soil. Incidents came in crowds. . . . Yet the main line of the story was never for an instant lost in the tumult of detail. It moved like a steeple-chase.

When some interruption in the next room brought the game to a halt, "Lewis was as hard to check as a runaway horse. . . . Storytelling is a process of his whole nature. He could no more stop telling stories than he could stop his hair growing."

In August he went to New York and took an apartment at the Berkshire, where he stayed through the period that *Jayhawker* was in rehearsal. Fred Stone, a popular comedian in musical shows, had been cast as the lead, Ace Burdette; and Stone's daughter Paula was playing Burdette's daughter Nettie. This casting, together with the reputation of the collaborators and the fact that it was the young and fashionable John Hammond's first production, aroused a good deal of interest in the play. Any current activities of Lewis, however, were abruptly overshadowed by headlines about his wife, who, on August 25, became the first American journalist to be expelled from Hitler's Germany.

She had registered at the Adlon in Berlin as a representative of *The Saturday Evening Post,* but her book *I Saw Hitler,* published in 1932, had been a generally derogatory report, containing such statements as, "He is a little man . . . his countenance is a caricature of a drummer-boy risen too high," and was hardy calculated to please the authorities. Within a few hours after her arrival she received official orders that she be out of the country within twenty-four hours. She repacked her bags and at the railroad station found nearly every foreign correspondent in Berlin, who filled her arms with great sheaves of American Beauty roses. In New York, Lewis announced that he was not perturbed, and when asked to comment on the political situation in Germany, he said rather testily, "Miss Thompson is the political expert. I am not."

His apparent indifference is the more surprising since only a few weeks before, in the recollection of Daniel Longwell, he had shown great concern for her. His wife was at sea, and Longwell and Lewis were alone at the farm, when news came of the first great Hitler purges. Lewis had been drinking only a little, but the news agitated him extremely and he became nearly hysterical in his fear that her life was in danger, in his helplessness somehow to arrange for her protection. It required the whole evening to calm him.

Many weekends at summer's end and in the early autumn he spent in Vermont where, among other books, he read H. S. Canby's *The Age of Confidence* for the *Saturday Review of Literature,* and *Appointment in Samarra,* John O'Hara's first novel. Canby had reviewed that novel most unfavorably, arguing that there was no excuse for "making art out of plumbing," and Lewis, in his review of the Canby book, took gratuitous occasion to support Canby's view of the novel as consisting of little but infantile erotic visions of a hobbledehoy behind the barn. This was a very unusual position for Lewis to take since, when he could not praise a young writer, he almost always said nothing. It is possible that he was irritated by John Chamberlain's review of the novel, which compared the O'Hara book with *Babbitt* but concluded that O'Hara had passed his *Babbitt* stage and was already at his *Dodsworth* stage, which was to say that he was aesthetically mature. And then, too, O'Hara was the brightest new writer on the list of Alfred Harcourt.

There were comic consequences. Some time later O'Hara found himself standing beside Lewis in the men's room at "21." They had never met, and now O'Hara said, "Well, Red, I've always wanted to tell you off, and this seems the right place for it. I'm John O'Hara." "I know you are," said Lewis and, hastily finishing his business, scampered out before O'Hara could say more. "21" was among several places in which Lewis had developed the reputation of a nuisance drunk. There was the occasion in 1932 when, with an intoxicated friend, he was not admitted, and he sat on the curb in 52nd Street and lamented, "What's the use of winning the Nobel prize if it doesn't even get you into speakeasies?" In 1935, when O'Hara published *Butterfield 8,* he had included a reference to Harry S. Lewis, a novelist, who was getting the "drunk treatment" at "21"—a simulated telephone call that brought the objectionable guest near the entrance, out of which he was then firmly eased. This reference Harcourt asked O'Hara to remove, and he obliged by changing the name to "Henry White, the writer."

On at least one occasion Lewis removed himself (if briefly) from "21."

He was with Vincent Sheean and Louis Florey, and suddenly he determined that they would get a taxi and drive at once to Vermont. He could be inflexibly willful in his whimseys, and his friends were not permitted to demur, so out into the street they tumbled, seized a taxi, and were off to Vermont. Lewis at once fell asleep. On Riverside Drive, when they were at about Grant's Tomb, he awoke as suddenly. "Where are we going?" he demanded. "Vermont." "Ridiculous! Driver, back to '21'!"

Not every leisure occasion was sodden. There was a party, for example, at which, when dinner had been served, Lewis organized the entire group as an assemblage of small-town men at which each was to speak in character. (The recollection is again Carl Van Doren's.) Lewis as chairman called on the speakers: one was a visiting cleric, one a retired Army officer, one a delegate of the Ku Klux Klan, one the local Casanova, and so on. If the persons he called upon could not respond, he spoke for them, and if they did speak, he made the speech again and improved upon it. "Impresario and virtuoso, he set his stage and filled it, while the audience demanded more and more."

Van Doren makes the interesting point that, unlike Mark Twain, for example, Lewis almost never relied on autobiography in his improvisations. "He prefers to work out large projects for what ought to happen," as on the occasion when he developed a fantasy about an academy of illiterates, a kind of burlesque of the American Academy—a fantasy complete in every organizational detail. Improvisation, too, was distraction.

Such diversions did not interrupt the progress of *Jayhawker,* which was being directed by Joe Losey. The play opened in Washington on October 15 before a fashionable, largely political audience, who found the play amusing—possibly because Fred Stone's lines seemed often to comment on current affairs and to reflect the activities of contemporary politicians like Senator Bilbo and Governor Huey Long rather than to evoke the atmosphere of the Civil War. The Washington reviews were encouraging. But when the play went on to Philadelphia, a good deal of rewriting, especially of the third act, seemed necessary. This was done chiefly by Sinclair Lewis and Joe Losey, and Lloyd Lewis thought that it was for the worse. Both he and his wife tired of the project, and of the collaborator too, and one night they tried to lose him and disappeared. However, he traced them to the hotel where they were and arrived, immaculately dressed and quite sober, to announce that "This is a hell of a business for two family men to be in." The New York *Times* announced that Sidney Howard had been called in to help, and that the play, which had everything but a last act, where it crumbled, was worth saving.

But when it opened at the Cort in New York on November 5, the reviews, even when they praised the acting and the first half of the play, were listless. Robert Benchley was alone in finding it "a good job from start to finish." On November 18, in response to Elmer Rice's recently expressed objections to Broadway critics, Sinclair Lewis made a series of statements under the title "Last Word" that the New York *Times* published in a black-bordered box.

> The critics have been much kinder to me than I deserve, both with my novels and with my plays. I have no complaint against the critics. I wish that the critics would go on getting rid of rubbish in the theater—whether it's my rubbish, or Mr. Elmer Rice's rubbish, or anybody else's rubbish.
>
> There are many plays which might go on if the critics weren't so clear-minded.
>
> I have no complaint.
>
> I have done two plays, five or six movies, ten or twelve novels.
>
> I have no complaint against the critics.
>
> I have been roasted. I have had the hell roasted out of me. I have been praised, but I have no complaints.
>
> In regard to Mr. Elmer Rice's complaint that the theater is commercial, I do not see how it could be otherwise than commercial. I do not see how a man can put $50,000 into a play and not desire to get it back.
>
> I have no complaint.

The play closed on November 24 after a run of less than three weeks. Sinclair Lewis had no complaint when Doubleday proposed that they publish it as a book. In a copy for the Minnesota library, he wrote: "Much more Lloyd than Sinclair, alas." The book sold 1,076 copies.

Winter had come, the Barnard house was closed, they were once more in Bronxville. Twice during that autumn when Dale Warren called, he found Lewis drinking only milk. The third time was another matter. When he arrived, an overnight guest, neither of the Lewises was at home. Then presently Lewis stumbled in with a taxi driver named Oscar, into whose care he had given himself instead of meeting his wife at Grand Central Station as they had agreed. When he saw his wife coming up the path, he fled to his room, and she, depressed, retired, too. Other guests arrived for dinner, but Lewis did not reappear. Long after midnight, about an hour after Warren had gone to bed, Lewis came into his room and asked him to come downstairs for a chat, and Lewis produced milk and sandwiches for the two of them and talked until dawn. Then he proposed that they take a car and drive to the Catskills, an excursion that Warren's appointments for the day did not permit, and he escaped by an early commuters' train.

Late in November Mrs. Lewis was on a lecture tour, and she wrote him a long letter from a train. After sympathizing with him for the failure of his play, she addressed herself to the problem that was on her mind.

> I hear from home that you have been ill again and had to have Jerry [Ziegler, his doctor] out and the news depresses me. Darling when if ever,

will you do something about your health and something about your pathological drinking? I do not blame you for it any more than I would blame you for having nephritis or diabetes, but I suffer intensely from it as everyone about you does, because when you are drunk you act exactly like an insane person. You are cut off from so much . . . more and more your life becomes nothing at all except work and drinking and—recovering from drinking. I don't blame you, as I have said, but what I do blame you for and often very bitterly, is that you refuse to face it and take no steps whatever to deal with it. And no one is permitted to mention it . . . we all must treat you when you are ill as one treats a most exacting patient . . . you yourself insist then that you shall be treated as a victim of an illness which he cannot help—but when you are clear-headed and could take measures, then you (and I) are expected to act as though everything were all right. What I blame you for is that you show no disposition to want to be cured, as I believe you could be if you wanted to. It is probably a combination of physical and neurotic mal-adjustment but there are very brilliant men in the world who have dealt with this sort of thing. . . . It is not going to do you the least bit of good to force your will on the matter and to go on the waggon and all that; what you have to get over is the obsession with it. And of course if you don't, I shudder to think not only of your future but of mine and above all Micky's. As far as I am concerned, I feel able to deal with the situations that your illness creates, although it has taken me several years to learn to do so, and often now—as during that night in Philadelphia —I feel quite incapable, and as though your drinking had become my phobia, a mania under which I will eventually crack. But the future of the child worries me to distraction. I don't need to go into this because you have sufficient imagination yourself. Often often often I think that I ought to take him away now, now while he is still very young. I think of Wells and although I know that with us circumstances are different, still I have seen too much with Wells and know how this has complicated his life. I happen to love you very very dearly and in the good moments to be happier with you than ever with anyone in my life, and the child loves you, too, and would suffer in all probability more (or as much) from separation from his father than from the pain to which he will be exposed if things go on as they are.

I write all this with great difficulty but I feel that I must. If we are to be truly close together then you must let me talk about something which is right in the middle of both our lives. And I simply cannot understand your unwillingness to do anything about it. Lord, if you had T.B. you would comb the country to find doctors and spas where you could get well but with this you won't give anybody half a break and go on talking about "taking a rest" and "getting some exercise."

Now I feel sad because I fear you will be angry with me, but whether you are or not I have got to say this.

Michael Lewis was four and a half years old, more of a stranger to his father even than Wells had been. These sons Lewis was presently describing in a letter to Edith Summers:

> My Wells—Grace's boy—is now seventeen and in his first year at Harvard, after doing well at Andover. He is, somewhat unexpectedly—because I was afraid he would catch her disease of pseudo-smartness—definitely scholarly and hard-working, with a slant toward history. And Dorothy's and my Michael is four and a half, a husky brat, and apparently intelligent—rather a bruiser but affectionate; a complete extrovert, where Wells is rather introvert.

When Lewis Gannett asked a number of well-known writers about their children's reading for his column in the *Herald Tribune* during Children's Book Week, Lewis interested himself enough to write a note saying that, being so young, Michael did not read beyond the alphabet but enjoyed being read to, especially about animals. Then he turned his attention to the more important matter of a four-part serial called "Seven Million Dollars," for *This Week,* a syndicated newspaper supplement. This is an absurd farce about a bankrupt rustic named "Cordwood" McCash, who, surprisingly acquiring seven million dollars, manages to spend it only by taking the entire community of Jackrabbit Creek to Paris.

In the mood for writing short fiction again, he wrote three more stories that would presently appear in *Cosmopolitan, The Saturday Evening Post* and *Scribner's.* The first, "The Hippocratic Oath," has slightly autobiographical overtones: a doctor, who has often wondered whether in certain crises he might break his oath, is repeatedly called upon to rescue a drunkard, and, thinking himself in love with the drunkard's serene and patient wife, he contemplates helping the patient out of his misery in a final way; but when the lovely wife herself suggests as much, and the doctor sees that she is really an aggressive, hypercritical woman, he makes every possible effort to save the drunkard's life and does so. The second, "Proper Gander" (a pun), is a foolish satire on senatorial ambitions in Washington. The third, "Onward, Sons of Ingersoll," is about the children of militantly Bohemian atheists who make Sinclair Lewis's choice of the middle-class proprieties.

With *Work of Art* and stories such as these behind him, and with his own reconciliation with Yale complete, there were hardly any grounds for declining a second invitation to come into the National Institute of Arts and Letters. When, proposed by the entire Council of the Academy, the governing body, the president of which was Lewis's friend Wilbur L. Cross, such an invitation did come on January 16, 1935, Lewis reported himself "delighted to accept." (One year later, he was proposed for membership in the Academy by Cross, Phelps, Owen Wister, Sidney Howard, Robert Grant, Walter Damrosch and Eugene O'Neill, but he was not elected; in the next year, 1937, when the same group proposed his name again, he was elected, and he accepted membership, and for the rest of his life he was active in the Academy's affairs.)

He now prepared a selection of his short stories for publication in June,* and in his introductory note he himself observed with some surprise that the stories were "so optimistic, so laudatory."

> But I wonder if this American optimism, this hope and courage, so submerged now, are not authentic parts of American life. They are good things to have. Dialectics—clarity—yes, but without a quite primitive courage these are feeble.

He was nearly at his fiftieth birthday, a season of stock-taking. Writing "This Golden Half-Century, 1885–1935" in January, he reviewed the background of his life: all the mechanical, material, intellectual and, vaguely, moral changes that had come about in those fifty years. It is all impersonal. And nearly as impersonal is the New York *Times* birthday interview, wherein he would talk rather about changes in Babbitt and changes on Main Street than about changes in himself. When asked if his acceptance of the Institute was a sign that he was growing old, he replied:

> Perhaps I am kidding myself. . . . Perhaps I am getting to be a fossil and do not realize it. But it seems to me that the Institute, like Main Street, has changed. It has opened its eyes to what's going on in the rest of the world and taken in as members a lot of young men with new ideas. Like the rest of the nation, it has become sophisticated.

And of himself he only said that "it's hard for me to believe that I have grown up."

He had not. His birthday the Lewises spent in Boston, where they dined with Dale Warren and Wells Lewis, and the two, father and son, "were very serious together, both ill at ease." His difficulty with his sons was almost certainly the product of his immaturity, a condition that he was presently to display most vividly during a journey on which he and his wife were immediately to embark. On February 10, they were in Bermuda, and from Bermuda they went on to Falmouth, Jamaica, where they planned to stay through March. There he entered into one of his irrational moods. He said unpleasant things about his wife to other people in their hotel, and he said unpleasant things to her—that she did not really love him and stayed with him only for economic reasons (a patent absurdity), that she was a burden and yet not enough of a burden, too much of a wife and no wife, a weight and yet too independent, that he was an artist and that she choked his art. He took up his old habit of public flirtations and made a *sotto voce* assignation with a lady doctor—but not so *sotto voce* that it was inaudible to an entire roomful of people—and snarled at his wife, "Can't you mind your own business?" Then he banged out of their hotel in a rage, announcing that it was forever. And a few days later he

* This volume, *Selected Short Stories,* caused little comment and in its hard-cover edition sold only 3,308 copies.

wired his wife and asked her to join him at Constant Spring. Patiently, she replied, "I am not feeling well and do not want to undertake the trip across the island in any case for a few days."

When he wrote her, then, she replied to say that they were as happily married as either of them could possibly be to anyone else. "Why not accept it, and be happy in it? Why tear at each other, why make each other miserable?" With a good deal of hurt forbearance but without bitterness or reproach, she surveyed his recent conduct. Then:

> When you walk out like that, as you did on Sunday, all the reasons you give seem so convincing. . . . You convince me. I cast myself in the role you design for me . . . I too must shoulder my burden . . . must walk off . . . must free you. I picture my home dissolved . . . our home . . . I speculate what to do with Micky . . . I work myself into a state of anxiety approaching hysteria. I lose all touch with reality . . . what is real and what is imagined. I do not after seven years know what of your feelings are real and what are imagined. I have no security with you . . . no inner security. What can a woman do under conditions like these except to try with all her will to make herself *innerly* independent, innerly free? Tell me, if you know the answer. Do you think that being innerly free means that you don't love another person? On the contrary. It is only then that you know what love really is . . . love that doesn't clutch and demand but really understands, is tender and gay. I just can't get myself all tied up in emotional knots about you because unless you work me into a role in your drama, real or imagined, I don't have any emotional knots about you. I feel that you are part of my life, as close to me and as part of me as my own hands and feet, and as indispensable, the person in the world with whom I feel myself most free, most fulfilled. I feel naturally as easy with you as though you were a sort of twin brother. I take you very much for granted. True. But isn't that what one *wants* in marriage, what one wants more than anything else—taking someone for granted. . . . Oh, Hal—you and I were made for each other—I feel that, and I think you feel it . . . God damn soul mates. And then suddenly this feeling which seemed so solid is blown into atoms. And I sit in the dark.

She could not resist some injunctions about his drinking, because it was only when he was drinking that his rages came upon him.

> . . . why do you think you have got to go on surpassing yourself? And mourning your lost youth? It is a grand thing to be grown up . . . it has its own pleasures . . . I don't think I am so hot. I am not such a damned attractive woman. Arrogant, and self-willed, and stubborn, and prejudiced. And terribly impatient. But did you ever think that considering the kind of person I am, I have a great deal of patience with you? Haven't you noticed that? Then you aren't a very good noticer, and your worst enemy wouldn't say that of you.

She urged him, then, to come back to Falmouth.

I had been trying to adjust myself to a life without you, since I have a very bad habit of taking what you say seriously. You gave me a damned bad time. At present the mere thought of taking up another temporary residence is more than I can bear. Nor am I at all sure that you really want me to come, or will when I get there.

He came back, of course. There were new resolutions about liquor and another reconciliation. And after they returned to Bronxville, he conceived the idea of a novel about the threat of fascism in the United States, and he began to make his "plan"; and then, in that summer, he hurled himself into an almost inconceivable effort of dedicated concentration. First attacked in May, the idea was a finished novel before the middle of August. And, as usual, a long one.

It Can't Happen Here would never have been written if Sinclair Lewis had not been married to Dorothy Thompson, if he had not absorbed a good deal more than he often pretended from those excited discussions, in which she was the center, of the situation in Europe (which Lewis would scornfully refer to as "It," while protesting his weariness), especially in Hitler's Germany, and of its reflection in the political situation in the United States. The long tradition of irrational demagoguery in American politics seemed to have come to a climax in the threatening power of a figure like Huey Long, and in the proliferation during the 1930s of dozens of fanatical political groups, each giving its fealty to its own crackpot leader. With the example of the imprisonment of Tom Mooney, of the execution of Sacco and Vanzetti, of the verdict delivered to the Scottsboro Boys, and of a thousand less publicized examples of tyranny, the vociferous rhetoricians of the Communist Party were insisting that fascism could and was happening here. Liberals, "rational" men who were equally troubled by these disgraceful travesties of political justice, were yet nearly as reluctant to accept the demagogues of the Left as they were to accept those of the Right, and they wondered what was to happen to them. The fate of Doremus Jessup and of others in *It Can't Happen Here* was one conjecture so magnificently timed that, again, the novel was inevitably a success and its publication a *cause célèbre.*

No distractions in that summer were permitted to interrupt the work. When Christian Gauss suggested that he and his wife come for a visit, Mrs. Lewis replied that her husband was "working nine hours a day on a novel which he is writing all in one flood with great enthusiasm and to the exclusion of everything else"; however, he did pause for meals. One distraction, young Wells Lewis, was not on the scene that summer but traveling abroad, with letters to his father's friends, including one to the man after whom he had been named. When Lewis did see friends that summer, especially neighbors like George Seldes who had had some political experience, he pumped them eagerly for information; and his wife was there, with her experience of Germany and her strong views of American politics, bubbling with information and prophecies. It was easy for Lewis, given this subject, to keep his mind absolutely on his book, seven days and nights a week. His first draft was finished by the middle of July, and this time his revisions were swift. When the book was finished early in August, Lewis rushed with it to New York and his happy publishers rushed it to the printers.

Then followed one of those characteristic descents into relaxation. Freeman Lewis, who was now in publishing in New York, remembers that during the period when his uncle was to read the galley proof, he was quite incapable of managing the task. He would telephone Freeman Lewis at his office and ask him to help, and when the younger Lewis would stop in at the uncle's hotel rooms after work, he would find the place a madhouse, since Lewis had also asked half his New York acquaintanceship to come in and be of service. Freeman Lewis, in fact, read most of that proof; and, he adds, if he was never thanked for his assistance, that was only because Sinclair Lewis did not remember his presence. In this condition of exhaustion and perpetual inebriation, one drink would send him spinning. His wife came to New York and took him to Europe on the *Ile de France* on August 31, and the presses began to clatter.

They were abroad for six weeks and returned separately in time for the publication of the novel on October 21. In the interim, Huey Long had been assassinated and, since his name appeared frequently in the novel, Lewis sent a long cable to his publishers directing them to change any such references to "the late Huey Long." The result in the published text was not entirely consistent, but this was a minor matter that disturbed no one. The book was a "shock," a "blow," and its readers, like its critics, did not trouble with details. In general, reviewers did not argue that it was an artistic achievement, but they applauded it as a major political act. Even so austere a critic as Richard P. Blackmur, accepting Lewis as "a publicist" in fiction rather than as a novelist, treated the book rather kindly as "a weapon of intellect." Ben Stolberg, however, complained that Lewis was helpless to give his characters any genuine ideological support. Lincoln Steffens said that "we call him a novelist because he's a prophet and habitually beats the news and gets it wrong in detail, like now." A few thought that it was a good novel, and at least one found it the very climax of Lewis's career as a novelist.

When there were complaints on political grounds, they were usually to the effect that Lewis had been content to impose the outlines of the history of National Socialism in Germany on American traditions, and that the two were incongruous. Nevertheless, the novel related readers of conflicting political views in a common anti-Fascist sympathy. It was severe with the Communist Party in the United States, but even some

Communists found it good. While neither Doremus Jessup, its hero, nor the book itself took any very clear political position but stayed safely somewhere near the middle of the road, liberals applauded its general point of view and, like Dorothy Thompson in the next year, cited such passages as this in defense of that point of view:

> "More and more, as I think about history," he pondered, "I am convinced that everything that is worth while in the world has been accomplished by the free, inquiring, critical spirit, and that the preservation of this spirit is more important than any social system whatsoever. But the men of ritual and the men of barbarism are capable of shutting up the men of science and of silencing them forever."

This is a basically conservative brand of liberalism, and if, boarding the *Ile de France,* Lewis could announce again his enthusiasm for Franklin D. Roosevelt, it was his conservatism that, later, was to lead him to the borders, at least, of the America First movement.

Reading *It Can't Happen Here* today, one is impressed by its qualities as a tour de force. It is an example of the extraordinarily detailed kind of fantasy that Lewis liked to spin orally, and this is why it was possible for him to write it so quickly. Great areas of the novel are taken up with the details of reorganizing the political structure of the United States, with documenting the transformation of traditional political and social customs into their opposites. It is the *game* that matters rather than the plot or the characters or the political animus, and one wonders why readers in 1935 found it an "angry" book. Much of it is, in fact, comic. Doremus Jessup himself is *au fond* a character out of American comic folklore. His sullen hired man, Shad Larue, who is meant to be the American equivalent of European riffraff rising with the fascist tide to sinister and brutal power, never ceases to be a simple-minded, ill-mannered lout:

> He had thought, when he was a hired man, that there was a lot more fun in being rich and famous. He didn't feel one bit different than he had then! Funny!

Considered as a whole work, *It Can't Happen Here* differs from other examples of its genre in having neither the intellectual coherence of Aldous Huxley nor the persuasive vision of a nightmare future of George Orwell. But in 1935 readers in the United States, like readers in Britain and in France (*Impossible ici!*), were sensitive to their immediate history, and it was to the immediate possibility of that history that Lewis's novel shook their attention. In the United States alone, the trade sales went to more than 94,000 copies, and the total sales, to more than 320,000 copies. It was another sensation. And it encouraged the radicals in its demonstration that even if Sinclair Lewis was against *them,* he was not *for* Hitler.

It encouraged them to provide later times with one of the comic episodes in the literary history of that lugubrious decade. On November 7, this letter went out over the signatures of Genevieve Taggard, Henry Hart and Malcolm Cowley:

> You are invited to attend a small dinner in honor of Mr. and Mrs. Sinclair Lewis on Wednesday, November 13th, at seven o'clock. The dinner, arranged by a few members of the League of American Writers, will be held at John's Restaurant, 302 East 12th Street. We will discuss the subject of Lewis's novel, *It Can't Happen Here*. We hope that you will wish to take part in the discussion.
>
> We are limiting the group to twenty-five invited guests. Your dinner will cost you $1.00, wine extra. For the sake of informality, we wish to guarantee our guests no publicity, no uninvited persons, real talk for mutual benefit.

John's Restaurant ran a regular advertisement in the *New Masses* during the 1930s that read, "A place with atmosphere where all radicals meet," and the naïve ambition of the Lewises' hosts positively glares from that apparently opaque clause, "real talk for mutual benefit." ("It's an old trick of the Communists, and a good one," he wrote two years later, "to coax an illustrious innocent to serve as show-window dummy.") The occasion was well-planned: limited attendance, friendly faces, informality, and such a kindly nonpolitical figure as Carl Van Doren persuaded to act as the chief speaker. Horace Gregory, who was himself drifting away from the activities of the League but who was curious to see Lewis, came in from Sarah Lawrence College with Genevieve Taggard, and it is his recollection that after Lewis had listened to half a dozen speeches praising his book as a great anti-Fascist novel, he stood at his honored place and said, "Boys, I love you all, and a writer loves to have his latest book praised. But let me tell you, it isn't a very good book—I've done better books—and furthermore, I don't believe any of you have *read* the book; if you had, you would have seen I was telling all of you to go to hell. Now, boys, join arms; let's all of us stand up and sing, 'Stand Up, Stand Up, for Jesus.' " And as Cowley and Gregory hastily left the room, they saw everyone else obeying Lewis's order, standing with joined arms, solemnly singing, "Stand Up, Stand Up, for Jesus." "From then onward," says Horace Gregory today, "Lewis had my admiration."

Lewis did not, in fact, place a very high value on his novel. To Daniel Longwell, who had by this time left Doubleday, he said, "It's a bad book, but at least it gives Doubleday a chance finally to make some money on me." A few days after the hymn-singing dinner, he inscribed a copy of it to H. G. Wells—"with the gratitude of one who has learned from him all that he knows." It was Wells who, at a tremendous party given in his honor in that winter by the Lewises in their Bronxville house, pontificated that the trouble with Americans was that they were "under the influence of that second-rate, shall I say third-rate mind, Karl Marx." There were American Marxists at that party, but Lewis was temperamentally much closer to the independent Wells than he was to them. And he would not permit them to use him.

He was impervious not only to all ideology but even to any real political commitment. At nearby Dartmouth College in those years of the mid-thirties, as in colleges all over the country, bright young students were fervently exploring the mazes of Marxism, and when one of them, named Budd Schulberg, learned from his professor, Ramon Guthrie, that the author of *It Can't Happen Here* lived in the neighborhood, he went eagerly if with some trepidation to call on him. Schulberg found Lewis alone at Twin Farms and in a generously expansive mood. They had a first drink together, and another, and more, and the visit extended itself through the afternoon, through dinner, through the evening, overnight, and through all of the next day. Instead of treating the fascist threat with any seriousness, Lewis did imitations of Father Coughlin, Huey Long, and others on the lunatic political fringe as though they were great clowns and nothing more.

Schulberg was rather dismayed, and yet he thought that it would be a *coup* for the students on the Left if he could persuade Lewis to come to Dartmouth to talk. Lewis was happy to oblige, and when he came he performed for them precisely as he had for Schulberg, and then sat down. The earnest young radicals began to ask him their ponderously Marxian questions, and at first he good-humoredly parried them; but when the theoretical questions turned into obvious baiting, his answers grew more and more curt, and at last, with reddened face, he leaped to his feet and shouted, "You young sons o' bitches can all go to hell!" and stamped from the platform. Later, he stormed and blasphemed for hours at the house of Ramon Guthrie; now he knew the truth about those little pipsqueaks, he raged. And he was to take his "revenge" upon them in his next novel, *The Prodigal Parents*.

A painful and protracted strike was under way in the marble quarries near Rutland, Vermont. Strikebreakers had been brought in by the owners and armed with clubs, state deputies flooded the five little mining communities, there was talk of armed, ruffianly "minutemen" keeping "order," and the striking miners were suffering bitterly in the New England winter. Lewis's friend, Ramon Guthrie, was among the many liberal sympathizers with the strikers, and Budd Schulberg had started a movement that made the quarry strike a nationally known affair.

Lewis was persuaded to go to Rutland and investigate conditions. He saw what was going on, talked to a newspaper editor, talked to a writer for the *New Masses* named "Jack Wilgus," and was quoted by the Rutland

Herald as having said that he had "soured on the strike" and that it was just "an ordinary strike." He qualified these statements in a telegram that asserted his sympathy with the strikers and explained that all his remark had meant was "that I had found nothing that I myself wanted to write about." Nevertheless, he became the butt of an angry *New Masses* article by "Jack Wilgus" called "Sinclair Lewis Visits a Strike"; and Ramon Guthrie remembers young Budd Schulberg saying of him, "A marvelous mind never used for thought." In December, shortly before the article was published, he did the *New Masses* a favor and himself a literary disservice when he let it publish this prayer:

> Oh, dear Lord our God, Thou Jesus of Palestine, a Jew, I wonder what Thou thinkest of Christmas, Thy birthday, today.
>
> Thou hast found that in Germany today Thy people are slaves.
>
> And Thou, who art a Jew, Thou who didst give us the ideal of peace on earth, good-will to men, Thou seest that the troops of Italy are conquering Ethiopia, the oldest Christian nation in the world.
>
> Oh, my dear Lord God, Thou who art a Jew, I can hope for no great happiness for Thee, nor for us, this Christmas.

One might suppose that he was drunk again.

But no. He had had little to drink since October, when too much drinking on the *Berengaria* coming back from Europe had put him into the hospital. Dr. Cornelius Traeger had attended him and they had become good friends. Candy and music now were his substitutes for liquor, and he contemplated the half century of his past with dismay. He saw the pattern in which he had imprisoned himself—complete immolation and isolation in the writing of a book, and then gregarious bouts that finally blacked out everything, including sex—and he began to feel again, as he had at forty, that he had not "lived."

Now and then events occurred that reminded him that he had lived, however he might feel about the matter. A young editor of the Yale *Lit* named Brendan Gill arrived in Bronxville in December to ask for a contribution to the centennial number to appear early in the next year. Lewis was alone, in charge of Michael. He talked almost exclusively of his wife, proud of her work and pleased with her reputation. He was fascinated with the powers of the telephone company and assured Gill that he had only to say to the operator, "Get me Dorothy Thompson," and they would promptly "get" her, although she might be hundreds of miles away. Michael was being a nuisance, and after a half-dozen sweet attempts to restrain him, Lewis suddenly slapped his face and set him howling. The interview ended, but he would write something for the *Lit*. Good old Yale —Yale remembered!

On December 16, he could have read this letter in *Time* magazine:

> Sinclair Lewis will be remembered when most everyone now living is forgotten. He is one of the important men of our time. He has written the most important book of our time. I nominate him for at least *Time*'s man of the year.—GEORGE SELDES.

Good old George—if only he had written that blurb for his book!

Metro-Goldwyn-Mayer had bought the film rights to *It Can't Happen Here* from a typescript copy, and now good old Sidney Howard had done an admirable script and in Hollywood they were about to begin to shoot.

Even the Nobel prize had not been forgotten. Three or four days before the end of the year, the New York *Times* reported that the Abbé Ernest Dimnet had announced that he would have preferred that Edith Wharton or Willa Cather should have had it in 1930, that Lewis distorted the truth, that he did not represent America; *he* had lived, but perhaps the America that he could picture no longer did.

4

WHEN, ON JANUARY 18, 1936, Sinclair Lewis heard that Rudyard Kipling was dead, he wept. "It was not mere sentimentality; something had gone out of existence for him that he would have liked to see endure." He wept easily, drunk or sober, and on this occasion, at dinner with Malcolm Johnson, of Doubleday, he was probably sober; Kipling was one of his earliest loves, and by and large, 1936 was a sober year. It was not as sober as has been said or as Lewis himself led his associates to believe. In April, Ramon Guthrie believed that Lewis had touched no liquor for six months; but other testimony reveals a sustained debauch in Bermuda during March. In December, Wells Lewis believed that his father had been totally abstemious for eleven months, and he so reported to his mother; but there had been other interludes than that of March that were unknown to the young man. Yet, the fact is that in that year Sinclair Lewis was making at least a considerably successful effort.

A number of events occurred in the first two months of the year that provided another kind of stimulation. The first was an invitation to Mrs. Lewis to write a thrice-weekly syndicated column for the *Herald Tribune*. With Lewis's proud urging, she agreed, and when "On the Record" began to appear in March, she became the first woman to publish regularly on international affairs. She had just completed a lecture tour of more than forty cities, and now, for about six weeks, they lived in Washington, "getting 'atmosphere,' she for her column, and he for a new novel." There they saw multitudes of people, including Senator and Mrs. Arthur H. Vandenberg (Lewis and Vandenberg developed a great admiration for one another), Heywood Broun, Herbert Agar.

It was in Washington that they received the news, on February 15, that Metro-Goldwyn-Mayer had decided to abandon the film of *It Can't Happen Here*. The first news releases announced that Will Hays of the Film Production Code Administration had banned the film for fear of international complications and the displeasure of the Republican Party. The Hays office denied any ban and a Metro-Goldwyn-Mayer spokesman announced that the Howard script would have involved production costs greater than the studio could undertake. Samuel Goldwyn said that the film had been halted because of casting difficulties. Sidney Howard announced that he had seen a lengthy memorandum from Joseph I. Breen, director of the Production Code Administration, pointing out the "dangerous material" in the film and suggesting a drastic revision of the script, and that the decision to stop production had been made at a joint conference of Hays and Breen and Metro representatives. Bulletins from both Germany and Italy approved the decision of the studio and the German Film Chamber in Berlin called Lewis "a full-blooded Communist." Lewis himself made lengthy statements to the press in which he pointed out that he had no further financial interest in the matter but that he was shocked by such a blow as this to the right of free expression. Whether or not Metro-Goldwyn-Mayer had acted on the advice or the orders of the Hays office, the motive for stopping the film was probably less political than economic. Not only would this film have been banned in Germany and Italy and other foreign markets, but probably all Metro films would henceforth have been kept out of Germany and Italy.

The novel was at the top of the best-seller list, and the controversy over the film helped to keep it there. A group called the Legion of Freedom, organized by a Vassar student, a Yale student, and a young dramatist named Norman Burnstine, began a post card campaign to bring pressure on the studio to put the film into production, and so much later as September, the Typographical Union of the American Federation of Labor resolved to petition the Hays office to lift its ban. The film was never made, but by November another dramatization of the novel was causing other excitement.

In February, too, but without fanfare, appeared the centennial issue of the *Yale Literary Magazine* with Lewis's little contribution, "Random Thoughts on Literature as a Business." He advised young writers to find some trade (not advertising, journalism or teaching) to support themselves, for the great days of making much money from books were over. The essay contained, too, some incidental criticism of Hemingway's book *Green Hills of Africa,* which had not been kind to Lewis, and he appended these verses:

Mister Ernest Hemingway
Halts his slaughter of the kudu
To remind you that you may
Risk his sacerdotal hoodoo
If you go on, day by day,
Talking priggishly as you do.
Speak up, man! Be bravely heard
Bawling the four-letter word!

And wear your mind décolleté
Like Mr. Ernest Hemingway.

It is unlikely that Hemingway's later vituperative feelings were in any way aroused by these lines, which he probably never saw. The article had pleasant consequences, however, in the repeated calls at Bronxville that the young Yale editor, Brendan Gill, now made. At the first, they talked, among other matters, of *The New Yorker,* the periodical with which Gill was later to be associated and which Lewis at this point described as "provincial." Lewis told him, too, that he had had a letter from an obscure college in the West inviting him to accept an honorary degree, and was it not an interesting fact that no such proposal had ever come from the dignitaries at Yale? Back in New Haven, Gill reported the conversation to William Lyon Phelps, and Phelps carried it to Carl Lohmann, secretary of the university, and the next time that Gill went to Bronxville, he arrived in West End Lane as an unofficial emissary of the secretary to discover whether Lewis would accept such an invitation were it forthcoming. The people at New Haven had felt that he would not; he made it clear to Gill that he would be delighted to accept. Presently a formal invitation arrived, and Lewis wrote Phelps:

> I'm very pleased to accept the Litt. D. degree, and I'm so writing Secretary Lohmann today. And triply pleased that it's you who are to present it. I suspect how many foul and secret plots you and that agent of the Yale O.G.P.U., Brendan Gill, have undertaken to accomplish this. . . .

In Washington it had been gossip that he was working at or toward a new novel, but the fact was that he wanted now to write a play. It was to be called *Undiscovered Country* and it would be about anti-Semitism in New York medical schools and hospitals. In the city, he had been using his medical friends in getting information and in arranging for tours of hospitals. But if he was going to write a play, the obvious thing to do was suddenly to leave for Bermuda with Louis Florey, and without informing his wife. They sailed on March 1, and at sea he wrote her to say what he was doing and to abuse her about their unsatisfactory life together in New York. The letter was mailed from Bermuda. She replied:

> . . . if I ever pulled anything on you like that I would never hear the last of it. You've heard the last of it with this note. I shan't bring the matter up again, but that's only a smug demonstration of my really superior nature. . . . Your letter about New York which was really vituperative, all about I shouldn't interfere in your life, and let you alone, etc., rather hurt my feelings. I thought it unjust. . . . You are so terrible, so terrifying when you are angry. . . . When you are like that you freeze something in me. Then I simply try to sink myself in work & forget it. I think it is too bad. We could care very much for each other. I do care very much for you in a frustrated

& rather hopeless way. At least so it seems to me tonight. I wish you were here.

He was, for the time being, content where he was, and James Thurber, who was also there, remembers that "you couldn't always tell at seven in the morning whether he was having his first drink of the day or his last one of the night." Nothing came of the play about anti-Semitism. They were staying at the Elbow Beach Hotel, and when Lewis took his ambling walks along the paths of Smith's Parish, he would engage a Negro minstrel to precede him, strumming his guitar. Once, Ronald Williams came to his room only to find him sitting on the edge of his bed, the tears flowing down his cheeks as he listened to a young couple sing old songs like "The Keeper" and "Sweet Molly Malone." "They just don't *write* songs like that any more," he sobbed, having had a piano hauled up from below in order to indulge this sweet pain. And he told Williams that the two men in the world he most wanted to meet were on the island—Senator Bronson Cutting and James Thurber—and would Williams arrange it? Cutting had made his reputation as a liberal when he proposed the deletion from the Tariff Act of the provision against obscene books and had won a partial victory against Senator Smoot in the result.

Williams arranged the meeting with Cutting and when next he saw Thurber he told him of Lewis's eagerness. The result was a dinner invitation from Lewis to both the Williamses and the Thurbers. They were greeted by Louis Florey who warned them of the Master's condition, and when they came to Lewis's room, he was hurling unexplained invective at two departing guests, Hugh Baillie, president of United Press, and his aged father. Seeing his new guests, he stopped, smiled amiably, put out his hand, and called Thurber "Jim." As they drank, Lewis recited, almost word for word, Thurber's story of 1928 (which Thurber himself had nearly forgotten) called "Mr. Monroe Holds the Fort."

When they were about to go down to dinner, he instructed Florey to bring along a stack of *Herald Tribunes*. Dorothy Thompson's column, "On the Record," was now appearing, and he was going to read every one of them aloud to the company at table. Florey managed to take his mind from that subject and they descended. Lewis had engaged the entire grillroom for his party, and an orchestra, but he was annoyed that the bass fiddler was not present. The first course was served, Lewis tried to eat an oyster, could not, stumbled to his feet, excused himself for a fifteen-minute nap, and did not reappear. His guests found him in his room after dinner, quite sober, and full of vividly entertaining talk.

He was less entertaining when, having been invited to lunch at the Williamses' house, he neglected to leave for three days. Several times each night his hosts would be aroused to quench his thirst, and he seemed never to go to bed in a proper fashion. He would drink until his talk stopped, retire for his fifteen-minute stupor, and reappear refreshed and ready to continue the revelry, each burst of which would be a little shorter than its predecessor.

Back in New York, there were new resolves. He would go to Vermont, he would go back to the labor novel, summoning Ramon Guthrie to aid him, and he would learn to do without the services of Louis Florey.

Guthrie was a teacher at Dartmouth now, and would not be free for field work until after final examinations in June, but in the meantime he was free to come frequently to Twin Farms to discuss their plans and make more notes. The story had returned to its original shape and scheme. Now the hero was to be called Roy Blodgett, "an artist among mechanics" —a Debs-like figure who, "groping for a God who is at once the tears and the meaning of things . . . was to become a radical and to suffer the penalty for his convictions." * He was also in some ways, a Lewis-like figure, with stolid parents like Lewis's own. Again, as in *Work of Art,* the hero was to have a brother whose defects in virtue were to contrast with the hero's splendor. Skeletal biographies of these and many other characters were prepared, and Lewis had supplied himself with "a small library of machinists' manuals." Guthrie, in his youth, had worked as a semi-skilled mechanic in Connecticut factories and was quite able to familiarize Lewis with machine-shop technicalities. For such information now he was avid.

And yet there were interludes that it was necessary to keep from his collaborator if the latter was to believe in the seriousness of his purpose. On April 18, 1936, George Seldes, Lewis's neighbor, made a memorandum that said that the night before Lewis had arrived at his house, intoxicated, and in pajamas. He was boasting about Dorothy Thompson, but broke off suddenly to announce that he had married a senator, and, "George, you don't know anyone around here who is looking for a job as mistress, at least part-time mistress, do you?" He wrote down for Seldes a Jewish joke that amused him; it is meant to represent a dialogue between a customer and a waiter in a restaurant:

F U N E X
S V F X
F U N E M
S V F M
M N X

* Ramon Guthrie's detailed account of his part in this project, "Sinclair Lewis and the 'Labor Novel,'" appears in *Proceedings* (Second Series, Number Two), American Academy of Arts and Letters (New York, 1952), pp. 68–82. A shorter version of this essay appeared in the *Herald Tribune* Books Section for February 10, 1952. The correspondence and notes for the project that were left in his possession are the property of the Baker Library, Dartmouth College.

The memorandum ends: "lonely old man . . . drinking. . . ."

There were other occasions of the same sort before his son Wells came up from Cambridge to spend the summer with him. One weekend he was to be with Roger Burlingame and his wife, Ann Watkins (who was Lewis's agent), at their house in Redding, Connecticut. He arrived, being driven, waving a bottle of Scotch out of the window as the car came up the driveway. His first words were, "Soda, Roger! Soda, Ann!" This was the prelude to the by now familiar drinking pattern: he would have a drink, excuse himself and sleep briefly in his room, reappear, burst into brilliant talk for a time, slowly blur, retire again, and so on and on in this extraordinary repetition which continued without alteration for twenty-four hours. Sleep did not always come so readily. Guthrie has a story, which may be of an earlier year, about an occasion when he arrived at Twin Farms to find Lewis on the verge of delirium tremens. Lewis begged him to call a Woodstock doctor; he needed a dose of chloral hydrate, a hypnotic that would, with one application, prevent the seizure and put the patient to sleep. Three doses were necessary before Lewis at last fell asleep. Very early the next morning he was up and rushing about as usual.

He had done a little fugitive writing in that spring—an essay about Vermont for the *Forum,* and two pieces for *The New Yorker,* the autobiographical "My First Day in New York," and a profile, called "Vamp in Violet," of an imaginary shoe manufacturer, Madame Effie Kayshus. He was corresponding with Carl Van Doren and gave him permission to reprint in his forthcoming autobiography, *Three Worlds,* the early letters in which Lewis protested that he was a serious writer before *Main Street.* Later he would review that book by his friend under the title, "Pre-War, Post-War, Post-Crash America," with unqualified enthusiasm. In May he returned to Bronxville, partly to see his dentist, more especially to address the American Booksellers Association on the subject, "Enemies of the Book." The enemies of the book are films, radio, automobiles, night clubs, bridge, cheap magazines—every distraction that diverts attention from the lonely act of reading. Back in Vermont, he was himself reading little but his reference works and an endless stream of detective stories.

In June Mrs. Lewis joined him for the honors at New Haven. They were the house guests of President and Mrs. Angell, and during the ceremonies, Mrs. Lewis wept a little and said to Mrs. Angell that the presentation of the honorary degree from Yale meant more to Lewis than anything else that had happened in his life. The citation was read by William Lyon Phelps, and in the course of it he said contentedly that Lewis's nickname, "Red," had outlived its applicability. The Angells were planning to leave New Haven immediately after the ceremonies, but Lewis wanted to meet Dr. Harvey Cushing—the only person he did wish to meet—and Cushing was summoned. It was he who helped Lewis close his bag, and he took the Lewises away with him.

The meeting with Cushing had an echo later in the year. Gilbert Seldes was conducting a radio program called *You,* and for a part of the series he had sent out a questionnaire to a number of well-known people. One question was, "If you have to live your life over again, *exactly* as it was, would you do it if the alternative was to drop dead instantly?" Lewis put a large "YES!" beside the question. A second question was, "Do you think that the more sensitive a person is, the more likely he or she is to choose instant death?" To that he said, "No." And he added a footnote: "What is commonly called 'sensitivity' is often only apprehensitive [*sic*] and insecure *vanity.* A Harvey Cushing or an H. G. Wells is more authentically 'sensitive' than 99% of suicidal poetasters." Was he thinking of Harry Crosby, of Hart Crane?

Mrs. Lewis was preparing to attend the national political conventions and did not go back to Vermont with her husband, but Wells Lewis came for the summer, and Ramon Guthrie was ready to cover the Naugatuck and Connecticut River valleys with Lewis "to gather documentation."

> The program of a typical day was a morning of conferring, getting notes in order, reading local newspapers for names, activities and interests; lunch with a factory owner or executive; an afternoon spent inspecting a factory or two and a CCC camp; dinner in a beer garden with a group of workmen; a post-midnight snack and a prowl through some of the more obscure quarters of town with a police reporter.

The trip lasted for about two weeks and all seemed to go well. The workers they met, who did not know who Sinclair Lewis was, responded warmly to him, and a good deal of material piled up in the notebooks. The discussions of this material between the two men were friendly and fruitful. Then suddenly, just before the Fourth of July, Lewis proposed a fantastic trip to Barnard by way of Provincetown, Massachusetts, and when he was dissuaded, left his car with Guthrie (who was expecting his wife in Connecticut), hired a second car and a driver, and left for the Berkshires. Departing, he spoke with enthusiasm of their work, and then added the mysterious remark, "And now I am sorry I have to go home and be a fascist." He did not explain the remark. Perhaps he was thinking about the next novel that he would in fact write, the anti-Communist *Prodigal Parents,* but he was not writing it now. Nothing was said about abandoning the labor novel; indeed, they had a few more sessions over it in the months that followed, but the project was, in fact, abandoned once again at that point.

There were rumors that Dorothy Thompson was to campaign for United States Senator from Vermont. The idea had been proposed to her by Herbert Agar, but in a letter to Dean Gauss, who had offered her his support, she treated the suggestion as an absurdity. During the preconvention period, there was even gossip to the effect that her friends were proposing her as a presidential candidate, and Lewis, upon hearing this, is supposed to have said, "Fine. Then I can write *'My Day.'*" She would herself have liked to see Robert M. Hutchins present himself as a presidential candidate. During this entire decade, Hutchins and Lewis and his wife had a friendly, relaxed relationship. Hutchins enjoyed Lewis's eagerness, curiosity, enthusiasm and anger, especially his anger about academic conventions, which he shared. Lewis shared his wife's enthusiasm for the idea of Hutchins as presidential material, and in the first of Dorothy Thompson's "Grouse for Breakfast" columns, it is the "Grouse" who characterizes Hutchins as the perfect man for that office.*

If Lewis could be flippant in public about Dorothy Thompson's great success, he was less and less flippant about it in private. Indeed, he now used it as his chief instrument of abuse. To a letter charging her with neglect of her proper duties, she replied:

> Hal, darling, I don't *like* to do what I'm doing. A whole lot of my nature is in rebellion against it. I am telling you the truth when I say I don't like to be in the public eye. I would rather have love, personal love, dominating my life. I resent the time work has taken from you, from Michael. . . . When you get angry at my work I feel that there is more than ordinary injustice in it, because I feel that you *made* me do it. You never would let me settle down into domesticity, first because you yourself rebelled against it and made it futile, and second because you kept egging me on. Frank Adams was right when he said no normally articulate human being could live with you and not become a writer. That's what you are. You aren't a husband or a lover or a father but a person of expression, a man of words, who positively presses words into and out of anyone who feels you closely. I sometimes laugh to read a piece of mine that you might have written—your style which is vigorous with verbs, your preference for the adverb to the adjective. I can't help it. I feel that there is *sense* in our relationship—in our caring for each other—that we make sense to each other. . . .

They rejoined one another at Twin Farms and, since Lewis was not drinking, the summer proceeded amiably. For the first time, Wells and his

* The first of these columns appeared on October 9, 1936, and others followed sporadically through the next year. The earliest examples did arise from conversations with Lewis, who makes a mordantly apolitical, often very witty foil for the columnist. "But actually the grouse was usually myself," Dorothy Thompson later wrote; "he would appear when I had not seen Sinclair Lewis for days or even weeks, [but] eventually he became lame, I thought, and disappeared from the newspaper column." The suggestion made by George Jean Nathan and others that Lewis's observations were responsible for her success as a columnist is without basis in fact. The "Grouse" began as Lewis but almost at once became a useful convention in the expression of the columnist's own attitudes and observations.

father managed to maintain an easy relationship. Guests came and went. The idea of a play about anti-Semitism had been transformed into an idea for a novel about anti-Semitism. On their way to Montreal, Mr. and Mrs. Louis Untermeyer spent a night with the Lewises. They sat up until long past midnight, "and no less than five unwritten novels seemed to be brewing in the vat of 'Red's' imagination." They had hoped to get an early start next morning, but at breakfast, Lewis began to tell them about still another unwritten novel, this one to be about Jews. "What are they, what makes them what they are?" he asked. "Is it their warmth, their capacity for excitement, some kind of sublimated sensuality?" He talked on and on about this book, and the Untermeyers did not get away until after lunch.

But he seems actually not to have written anything in July except a brief essay called "Literary Felonies" for the *Saturday Review of Literature,* which was now being edited by his friend Bernard DeVoto. The essay consists of a series of parodies of what Lewis regarded as crimes in current writing. One is "Kidnapping of Plot" by the essayistic impulse; another is "First Person Singularism," with its subjective trivialities; another is "Obtaining Game under False Pretensions," which attacked Hemingway's anti-intellectualism; another is directed at gossip columnists; the last two take off oratorical inflations and hackneyed figures of speech.

The apathy of the summer came to an abrupt end when the directors of the Federal Theater of the Works Progress Administration in Washington proposed to produce a play version of *It Can't Happen Here* in fifteen cities across the nation, the first curtains to rise simultaneously on October 20.* The dramatization was to be made in collaboration with J. C. Moffitt, a Paramount screenwriter, but Lewis would make the preliminary draft alone. On August 7 he wrote Carl Van Doren to say that he had been "working night and day on the play" and that by August 12, when he would be coming to New York, he would have "two acts done, and the third nearly enough done so that it will be ready to turn in" on the fourteenth. In New York, he took an apartment at Essex House, where Moffitt lived. There they worked together for a time, and when Lewis returned to Vermont, Moffitt went with him. Back at Essex House on September 8, the collaborators began to quarrel, Moffitt became indignant at Lewis's constant changes, and finally, according to Mrs. Flanagan, they were not speaking but communicating through notes delivered to her.

The newspapers were giving the project enormous publicity both favorable and unfavorable, and managed to devote 78,000 lines of comment to it even before the opening. Directors throughout the country were clamoring for a final script to give their companies. Vincent Sherman,

* A full account of this enterprise appears in "States United: It Can't Happen Here," a chapter of Hallie Flanagan's book, *Arena* (New York: Duell, Sloan & Pearce, 1940).

the director of the chief New York production, took over and worked on the Lewis-Moffitt script.* Political considerations caused the cancellation of productions in New Orleans and in Missouri, but there would be four productions in the New York area (one of them in Yiddish), a Spanish production in Tampa, and a Negro production in Seattle. The major New York production was at the Adelphi.

Lewis, who had been writing and rewriting for days and nights on end, made this production his special project and selected its entire cast and rehearsed it as well. The final number of cities, not including all those where it played on tour, was eighteen; of productions, twenty-three. And in spite of a hurly-burly of difficulties, the play opened simultaneously in those eighteen cities on October 27. Everywhere there were capacity or overflow audiences. At the Adelphi hundreds of people stood at the back of the house. After innumerable curtain calls, Lewis appeared and in response to audience demands for a speech, said, "I have been making a speech since eight forty-five."

That night the Lewises were giving a party at the Plaza for the company and for many others. It was a brilliant party, Roger Burlingame remembers, with many brilliant people, not the least of them being Sinclair Lewis himself. He was not drinking, was at the very top of his form, exhilarated by his success as congratulatory telegrams poured in from all over the country. He announced that his next play, a work about Jews now to be called *For Us the Living,* would be written in collaboration with Vincent Sherman, who also would direct it. "Whatever the papers say tomorrow," he said, "I think it's a great show." Then someone urged a drink upon him and he took it. Very quickly he began to deteriorate. Dorothy Thompson stood there looking at him and her eyes filled with tears as he became more and more frightful, and as he fell off the wagon and the party fell to pieces, she said nothing about the debacle to her departing guests. "I have to smoke so many Murads," she once said to him, referring to a then well-known advertisement about cigarettes and nonchalance. For the next six months, she needed a large supply of Murads indeed.

The reviews next morning and on the days that followed were less enthusiastic than the first-night audiences had been. Most of them agreed with Brooks Atkinson that, while the play had indubitable value as political shock, it was "careless, slipshod theater work" and, on reflection, not very convincing. George Jean Nathan speculated that if Lewis gave to dramatic technique "half the serious preliminary effort that he gave to even his worst novels, he would probably write very good plays indeed."

* On a script marked "Stage Version" in the Lewis papers at New Haven he is given author credit. In the published script (*Federal Theatre Playscript #1*), he is not given credit, nor does his name appear on the final acting version.

But the deficiencies of the play as play did not bring it to an end, as they might have, had it been given a standard Broadway production. With its twenty-one companies performing in their variety of ways, it played a total of 260 weeks, or the equivalent of five years' showing of a single production. The Adelphi version ran for 95 performances before 110,518 people, and it showed no sign of demise when it had to be moved to another house because of Adelphi commitments to another play. But Sinclair Lewis did not want it moved. Mrs. Flanagan reproduces his telephone call of December 20 as follows:

> Well, Hallie, it's all over—I'm sorry but it's all over. Now don't say a word—I know it's not your fault, but you told me a week ago that I could have my own cast at the Adelphi; you know that I gave the better part of my life to that cast; I trained them myself; I sat there day after day going without food, going without sleep . . . I suffered, I tell you—nobody knows what I suffered. Why, I made that play out of my life's blood, and you know it's the only good play that the Federal Theater ever did . . . and here it is, playing to packed houses, turning people away by the hundreds—and that, mind you, in spite of the fact that there's not a word in the papers about it—everybody in a conspiracy to keep anybody from knowing that a play of mine is on Broadway. And now you close it—you move it into a back alley somewhere—you take all my beautiful actors that I have trained with my own hands and put them in some other play . . .

And so on and on, before he at last conceded that there was a good reason for moving the play to another theater, where it continued its run.

This is a period in which tales about him proliferate again. Dorothy and Lillian Gish remember a dinner party at their mother's house at which, while Mrs. Lewis was talking, Sinclair Lewis was sitting on the floor in the corner, singing under his breath, "Dog, dog, more faithful than man." Sometimes he did not sing but mumbled pages from his own work. But with the reelection of Franklin Delano Roosevelt, Dorothy Thompson's column stopped abruptly for two months, while she removed herself from such spectacles under the necessity of going to Europe to gather new material. The Gish sisters remember another dinner party when Lewis appeared alone, splendid in tails, top hat and white tie, at a Park Avenue apartment where, entering the foyer, he promptly crumpled to the floor and was put to bed.

Someone had told him that he should get into shape at a well-known and luxurious establishment in the Catskills known as "Dr. Ford's," and it was after such an occasion as the last that he decided he would go there. Dr. Ford's establishment had been a vast estate and was now a rest home for exhausted urbanites and mildly nervous ladies, not a place that tried to cure alcoholics. It was popular with certain writers associated with *The*

New Yorker, including Wolcott Gibbs, and in his sketch, "Eden, with Serpents," * Gibbs has left a fictionalized account of Sinclair Lewis's arrival there, dressed in evening clothes and drunk, in a New York cab. "The tall man, getting up in sections," is asked to leave by the proprietor, a Dr. Hardy, and he does, but shouting at the genteel guests as he goes, "The hell with you! You drunkards!" So, in actuality, Lewis did go back to Bronxville where he sobered up, found a copy of Renan's *Life of Christ* that as an undergraduate he had borrowed from Tinker, mailed it back to him after "something like a generation," and returned to Dr. Ford, who took him in.

In that year, 1936, the *Colophon* conducted a poll among its readers: "What ten American authors now living do you think have the best chances of being considered 'classics' by the reading public in the year 2000, ranked in the order of their chances of permanence?" Sinclair Lewis easily led the list. †

* *Bed of Neuroses,* New York: Henry Holt & Company, 1937.

† In 1948, when *Colophon* repeated its question, he was still high on the list, only two votes behind the leader, Eugene O'Neill.

5

HE SURROUNDED HIMSELF with theatrical people and tried to write his play about anti-Semitism. He cultivated S. N. Behrman, whose play *Rain from Heaven,* also concerned with anti-Semitism, had recently had its Broadway run. Rather missing the point of that play, Lewis chided Behrman for his timidity in making his leading character only one-eighth Jewish (there would be no such hedging in *his* play about anti-Semitism), and yet he quizzed him endlessly about the techniques of the stage. His questions were curiously naïve: he asked him, for example, how long a first act should be, and when Behrman good-naturedly assured him that there was no easy answer to that question, he counted the words in the first act of *Rain from Heaven,* and, thinking that he had found the answer for himself, proudly told Behrman of his count. He cultivated the producer Jed Harris, who, like Lewis himself, was a man of quick enthusiasms for new friends. He was accepted by Lawrence Langner, head of the Theater Guild, who a few years before had been among those who congratulated Dreiser for his slaps. Mr. Langner himself remembers one dinner party at his house when both Lewis and Carl Van Vechten were present.

> Sinclair was very over-stimulated and monopolized the conversation at dinner to such an extent that Carl, in order to bring the proceedings to a stop, started to laugh hysterically. His hysterics grew louder and louder until finally Sinclair Lewis was completely subdued, after which the conversation became normal.

And at another Langner party, Lewis, arriving a little early, decided that he would pretend to be the butler. As the other guests began to appear, some did not recognize him, others did not let on that they knew, and the joke rather turned on him as, with no one laughing, he had to continue his pretense until everyone had arrived and then say, "Hey, I'm Red. . . ."

Early in this year he met Diana Forbes-Robertson Sheean, newly come from England, and she still remembers a party at which he would interrupt his monologues only to wag his finger at his wife and say, "Dottie, stop lecturing!" After ten years he met again Klaus and Erika Mann, and now he did not reproach them for having come to the United States. "He knew what we had lost, for he had lost something, too." *It Can't Happen Here* had been translated, almost unbelievably, into German as *Das ist bei uns nicht möglich* and been promptly banned. Later in the year, when the German producer who held the Central European stage rights to *Dodsworth* wrote to say that he would need evidence of the dramatists' Aryan descent if the Reich Theater Chamber was to allow a production of the play, Howard and Lewis, in a joint letter, protested that they could not provide that evidence.

> . . . Who knows what ancestors we may have had in the last few hundred years? We really are as ignorant of them as even Hitler of his.
>
> In answering please use our proper legal names: Sidney Horowitz, Sinclair Levy.
>
> Yours sincerely,
> *Sidney Howard* and *Sinclair Lewis.*

In what was probably a mood of gentle deceit, Lewis had written his brother Claude on February 1 as follows:

> I had a touch of the flu and spent a few days in Doctors' Hospital, not so much because I was sick but because I wanted to get into good shape, with massage, colonic irrigations and that sort of thing, and I now feel magnificent.
>
> I am busy writing a new play on which I have been working for three months and which may take me another three, four or five months. Then, in Vermont, I shall start a new novel.

Nothing came of the play and he probably gave his attention at about this point to *The Prodigal Parents*. The only piece of writing that he certainly completed to his satisfaction was his inaccurate reminiscence, "Breaking into Print," which he gave happily to the *Colophon* in return for its gratifying poll. Nor were his plans for himself, with the usual summer in Vermont, carried out any more successfully than his plans for his writing.

When his wife had returned from Europe and resumed her column and her other activities, the disintegration of their marriage began to accelerate. His reproaches were more frequent, more irrational, more violent, piling up one upon the other—and because they were always made in liquor, she endured them. She endured them, too, because he had often demanded of her a pledge: returning to her from his abrupt and maddened departures, he had on many of these occasions, sober, made her promise that she would keep him as her husband, that, no matter what he in his compulsive throes might insist upon, she would never divorce him. She always promised. And then, finally, "quite cold and quite possessed," he told her that her work had ruined their marriage, that she had robbed him of his creative powers, and he walked out of the house in Bronxville for the last time on April 28, 1937.

She did not pursue him. She waited. She wrote him many letters that she did not—could not—mail: she did know where to address them. (One of them, the longest, she sent him nearly a year later.) These letters were cool and thoughtful, rational attempts to explore an irrational situation. They went back to the beginning, to the first meeting in Berlin. "Then I had the feeling, 'This is the man I have been looking for all my life.' "

> There was never face so pleased my *mind*. I loved the shape of that face, the tall and narrow skull, the thin, silky red-blond hair, the long, adventurous hands, the narrow feet, the almost absent thighs. I loved the mercurial moods, the darkness and light, the hilarity and the agony. Then I loved them, and I love them now. All sorts of men have crossed my life. . . . But you were my man. . . . I am, therefore, in a not very classic way, the very picture of Penelope.

She had married him, she wrote now, not because she expected to be happy, but because he made her feel alive; but everyone must have rest, an anodyne—his was drink, hers work. But when he was drunk—

> This restless, dynamic, overcharged, demanding personality which is you, becomes intensified to the point of madness. It is energy completely explosive and completely off the track. In our early marriage it dragged me with it, until I vomited from revolt that I couldn't control. I tried to stop you. We had crazy fights about liquor . . . I saw it destroying something—however temporarily—which I loved with all my heart and all my mind.

Work alone saved her, and then he made of her work the straw man that must suffer his abuse. Was it not possible that his own fear of creative exhaustion lay behind both his drinking and his resentments, so that he behaved "like an animal in heat and impotent. It's a brutal phrase, but it's the most brutal thing I have ever seen. And the awful, terrible thing for one who loves you is that one can't do anything about it."

It was her belief, she wrote, that he would recover from this phase, but she did not want to be battered by it, and she would wait for him.

> This business that you have built up now in your mind about me and you, about being the husband of Dorothy Thompson, a tail to an ascending comet, and what not, is only because you are, for the moment, stymied, and you have been that many times before.

She was superior, she told him, in only one thing:

> a really superior capacity for love. . . . Go away for six months, or three months, or six years, or three years. I shall sit at home, in our home, and be there when you come back to it.

But he did not come back. He removed her power of attorney, and he began to make arrangements for a trust fund for their son. And he went about telling his friends that he was through, and telling them of the occasion on which he knew that he was through. It was one Sunday morning in bed. The telephone on the night table beside his bed rang. He lifted the receiver. The White House was calling Dorothy Thompson. He passed the instrument across his body to her. The wire stretched taut across his neck. For half an hour she advised the President of the United States, while he lay imprisoned and helpless. The very intimacy of the sleeping arrangements demonstrates apocrypha.

His son, not quite seven years old, said, or had said, or would soon say, "I hate my father and when I grow up I'll kill him."

Many years later Mrs. Lewis said reflectively,

> In this story, as it involves Lewis's personal life and relations, *there are no heroes or heroines.* I was inadequate to a relationship I undertook in fairly alert awareness. It required a far more sacrificial soul than mine. Intellectually, and rationally, I *think* that that would not have worked, either. But nobody *knows* this. All I do know is that I have too strong a sense of self-preservation (perhaps, even of self-worth) to have immolated myself on the altar of his genius.
>
> Yet, there was no time during our long separation and divorce when I would not have gone to him if he had called me. . . .

She was called upon almost at once.

From New York, a friend telephoned to say that Lewis had disappeared; with Louis Florey, the rumor went, he had started off for Connecticut, but no one knew more precisely where or why. A practiced instinct told her that he was in real difficulties. Somehow she managed to find a list of Connecticut inns and, quite systematically, she began to telephone down the list until, remarkably, she located him at last. He was in Old Lyme, and Florey told her that he was in a bad way, that he had suffered a fall. She hired a car and drove to Old Lyme where she found him raving, in the grip of delirium tremens. Florey, who had once watched him slide off a sofa, told her that he had fallen out of bed. She telephoned Dr. Traeger who recommended that she take him to the Austen Riggs Center, a reputable sanitarium in Stockbridge, Massachusetts. They set out. It was "an incredible, tragic drive," because Lewis thought that they were together again and began making plans for an immediate jaunt to Europe; they would "go places" again. Riggs did not take alcoholic cases but they could hardly turn him away, especially when they discovered that he had three broken ribs. They strapped him up and put him to bed, and his wife stayed on for several days. But when he was sober once more he did not want her with him, and she returned to New York.

Now again he abandoned liquor and promptly recovered—or, shall one say, recovered as much of himself as remained to be recovered. Then he rented a house near the sanitarium and stayed on in Stockbridge for the summer. Yet he could not, of course, stay on alone. Under the renewed conditions of sobriety, Louis Florey would be impossible, and he really wanted, as secretary and driver and companion, a young literary person. His wife now was in a Manhattan hospital for a minor operation, and Lewis returned to New York, in part on her account, chiefly to look for a secretary.

A young man named John Hersey, recently graduated from Yale and returned from a year of study in England, learned from a friend at the *Herald Tribune* of Lewis's need and applied for the position. Three interviews followed. The first was generally confined to Hersey's application, but at the next two, Lewis did all the talking—about Yale, England, the American Legion, lady columnists. During the third of these, another young man who was applying for the position called up from the lobby of the hotel where Lewis was staying, and the only means that Lewis took to acquaint Hersey with the fact that he was hired was to tell him now that he had to shave and change his clothes to go out, and would Hersey be so good as to interview the applicant for him? He gave him a month to take a quick course in shorthand and to learn the touch system at the typewriter, and then, at the beginning of July, Hersey joined him in Stockbridge to assume his duties, which consisted chiefly of taking letters, driving, buying chocolates, and typing manuscript. Of chocolates (no nougats or nuts) he ate a pound each day. And he developed his surprising little paunch, a kind of melon protuberance that popped out as tidily and as abruptly as it popped back in.

When Hersey arrived, Lewis had finished *The Prodigal Parents* by a rigorous effort of will. Sometimes, he said, he had worked from five o'clock in the morning until six o'clock in the evening, but since the novel, not very long and presenting no special problems of subject matter, was a flimsy affair in the *Saturday Evening Post* manner, this accomplishment is not as remarkable as it might at first appear. Once that summer, on a drive, he said that he thought that he could write more of those big novels of his if he wanted to take out a couple of years to do the research; but the prospect bored him, he wanted to do something new—a play. And yet he suffered from long fits of despondency that seemed to arise from his sense of the failure of his powers.

His emotional situation was precisely that of ten years before, when, having abandoned his first wife and yet not quite abandoned her, he had wandered, distraught and lonely, about Europe, searching for new moorings. Then he was forty-two years old; now he was fifty-two. Then he had put an ocean between his wife and himself; now he hovered in his wife's neighborhood, at once disaffected and still dependent. Occasionally he would drive to Barnard, and occasionally she would come to Stockbridge. He wanted to be with her and he could not abide her. Her concern with politics exasperated him, who never had and had not now any real concern with public issues. Once he burst out, "God damn it, if I hear anything more about 'conditions' and 'situations,' I'll shoot myself." He would visibly seethe, mutely rage, while she talked through an evening, and would try to hold in his fury until she had gone. But one morning at breakfast he exploded; he told her that she had been all wrong in what she had argued the night before, that the matter was not that way at all, but this way. She listened to him, and later, when he thought that he saw his views reflected in her column, he was furious all over again.

In one September, when they were both in New York again, they were watching an American Legion parade from the windows of his apartment over Central Park South and she was led to reflect on the possibilities of American fascism. He groaned. "Oh, Dorothy, let those men have a little fun! Some of them haven't had a chance to get away from their wives for years. Let 'em have their fun, for God's sake!" And yet, in the summer of 1937 when he was planning an autumn trip abroad, he had urged her to come to England with him, quite as, ten years before, he had suddenly proposed to his alienated wife that she join him on Nantucket. The difference was that she did not believe their marriage was over, and for nearly five years, both in friendship and in animosity, it hung suspended.

He saw a variety of people who were summering in and near Stockbridge—the journalist Joseph Alsop, Alexander Woollcott, Owen Johnson, John Marquand. He would gather such people at his house on a summer evening and try to amuse them with the sort of paper and pencil games that amused him; John Marquand remembered an entire evening given to projects like "Who can write down the names of the most rivers beginning with M?" Or they would pour over telephone directories to see who could come up with a list of the most outrageous proper names. But his chief diversion lay in the Berkshire Theater, in Stockbridge, where he loitered during much of his leisure, "looking on," as he later said, "with moonstruck envy." He was fascinated by the young actors and actresses who made up the company, and they, liking him, were in and out of his house all summer while he agonized over his impossible play about the ravages of Communism in an imaginary Central European country called Kronland. On August 27, the New York *Times* announced that this play, *Publish Glad Tidings,* was finished and being read by Guthrie McClintic in New York and by Max Gordon in California.

In September his wife closed the Bronxville house "without regret" and took an apartment in New York, where she put Michael in school. Lewis, too, decided to take an apartment in New York and asked for linen from the Bronxville house. His wife wrote him of her apartment, "There is a bedroom for you, very quiet and comfortable, should you care to live there," and complained that she found it almost impossible to learn the language of their new relationship. When he declined her invitation, she helped establish him in his own apartment at the Wyndham, 42 West 58th Street, where he began work on a new play.

They continued to meet. She came to his parties now and then, he occasionally to hers. Irita Van Doren remembers an evening—the evening on which she met Wendell Willkie—when they encountered Dorothy Thompson, who urged them to come with her and one or two others to Lewis's apartment. He was not responsive to their presence, but his wife took over, made them drinks and kept the conversation going. One lady of the group wandered into Lewis's study, where some half-finished sheet was in his typewriter; Lewis followed her, removed the paper, put it in his desk drawer, locked the drawer and left the room without a word. Then he went out and sat on the terrace, where he stayed until everyone had gone. He preferred the company of theatrical people, and when he went to his wife's apartment, he would bring not newspaperwomen but ladies like Ina Claire, Mady Christians, Kitty Carlisle, and fancied himself in love with the latter two. In the meantime, his play was having no success with producers, and the new play was not going well. Sometimes he despaired of it; at other times he was exhilarated by it. One morning when Hersey arrived for work he found Lewis at his desk, happily writing. Jed Harris had been with him until five o'clock that morning and had shown him what to do with the material, and now he felt wonderful, like a boy, and everything was clear sailing.

Such moments could not sustain themselves, and, feeling poor, he began to arrange for a lecture tour that would extend from late October to late February of the next year. It was a form both of self-indulgence and of self-punishment, for, according to John Hersey, he hated lecturing. He felt only contempt for his audiences, and in a chapter on lecture tours in his later novel *Gideon Planish,* he exactly expressed his own feelings about them. At the same time, he agreed to write a weekly column on books for *Newsweek,* to be called "Book Week," which began on October 4, and continued through April 18, 1938.

A few of the "Book Week" essays have some special interest. An early one attacked Hemingway's *To Have and Have Not* as "Glorious Dirt" and begged Hemingway to save himself and let Spain alone. Lewis was one of several critics who had deplored that novel and who were deplored in turn by Eliot Paul in a *Saturday Review of Literature* article of several weeks later where it was asserted that Hemingway at his weakest could write rings around Lewis at his best. (Hemingway himself waited fourteen years, until *Across the River and into the Trees,* to take his revenge on Lewis.) Another of the columns, "Seeing Red," was an attack on Communist writing, and it appeared just a day before an article by Robert Forsythe in *New Masses* attacked Lewis for the "plague on both your houses" attitude to which he was giving expression on his lecture tour. The Communists had decided that he was beyond use.

The material of his *Newsweek* writing spilled over into his lectures, and his lecture material spilled over into *Newsweek.* Giving twenty-two lectures in twenty cities, he offered his sponsors their choice of one of four topics. "Main Street Revisited" was probably an extension of his recently composed introduction to the Limited Editions Club reprint of *Main Street,* an essay that considerably confuses the true history of the composition of that work. The other topics were "The Novelist as Prophet," "Propaganda and Poppycock," and "It Has Happened Here." The first two of these three contained much of the material of the third, but it was under the third title that he appeared in the majority of these lectures. The "It" of his title refers to "an intellectual softness so advanced 'that, unless we wake up pretty soon, perhaps the barbarians won't even want to come in and take over the country.' " We are slaves to the concept and the practice of salesmanship; indeed, the salesman is the equivalent in the United States of the dictator in fascist countries. (The *Times* editorialist demurred.) Our choice is not between Communism and Fascism, but between dictatorship and the "free, inquiring critical spirit" that will give us a genuine democracy. He often varied his lectures by including impromptu topical or local material—an attack on censorship that started off from a recently published list of plays that Cardinal Hayes had denounced; a list of national heroes that linked Charlie McCarthy and Clark Gable, Mickey Mouse and John L. Lewis, Dale Carnegie ("the Bard of Babbittry") and Father Divine.

He began in New York, then jumped to Cedar Rapids, Iowa, and from there went to Oklahoma, to Texas, to Kansas. He did not lecture in Kansas City, but he was entertained at luncheon there, his host being Dr. Logan Clendening, something of a wit and presently a highly theatrical suicide. Lewis was late in arriving, and Clendening held his guests at the bar for half an hour. Then, complaining that he was a busy man, he ushered them into the dining room where luncheon was served. Lewis arrived in the midst of the first course, explained that he had been detained by the press, apologized, and declined a drink. The irritated Clendening began to jibe at him as he took his place, and was not to be distracted by his unhappy guests as the verbal sparring, neither friendly nor tactful, continued. Lewis held his temper until Clendening brought up Dorothy Thompson, whose support of Zionism, he asserted, was motivated not by conviction but by money. Then Lewis stood up. "The first time I met you, I thought you were an ass. Later, I found you amusing, even brilliant, and I tried to be friendly. Today proves that my first impression was correct." And with that he stalked from the room.

Later, when Thomas Hart Benton and Clarence Decker found him in an uptown hotel, he said only, "I can't stand intolerance—against my wife or anyone else," and, his composure restored, he spent the afternoon in conversation with the two men who had sought him out. Now and in the future he permitted himself to satirize his wife, to parody her "pontificating," as he called it ("Now I am Dorothy Thompson," he would say. "Ask me anything."), and to imitate her domestic managerial qualities, as he saw them, but always, if another person attempted to criticize her in his presence, he rose hotly to her defense.

From Kansas City, he went to Milwaukee, then to Philadelphia and back to New York, where he lectured at the Brooklyn Academy of Music, at Town Hall and, on December 16, at Columbia University. Then he paused until January 12 to celebrate a sober and a lonely Christmas.

He filled his time by struggling with his new play, this to be a comedy called first *Queenie* and later *Queenie and the Jopes,* and he was to struggle with that work, writing and rewriting and reconceiving, all through the late winter and spring of 1938. Early in that year, *The Prodigal Parents* was published. Although Lewis Gannett announced that this novel might be Lewis's most important, Lewis did not wait for its publication before setting out on his lecture tour again. On January 13 he lectured in Chicago, on the seventeenth in Albuquerque, and the book appeared simultaneously with his arrival in Los Angeles on the nineteenth.

On the twentieth he lectured there on "Propaganda and Poppycock." Upton Sinclair was in the audience, delighted with the many references to himself as the propagandist from Pasadena, but he did not make his presence known. He had just finished reading *The Prodigal Parents* and pointed out presently in a review that the novel was "a blazing piece of propaganda in defense of the American businessman and the world he has created, and against all those groups in our society who ridicule and criticize the capitalist system." With this book, Lewis had become the apologist for "the United States Chamber of Commerce and the American Liberty League." Other old friends, the Ludwig Lewisohns, now "found Babbitt to be merely the man with whom Lewis is in love." This novel marked, in fact, no new development in Sinclair Lewis, and one can only wonder why it came as a surprise to so many.

A few reviewers found it amusing in a vague way, but most of them pointed out that it was shockingly bad. "He has never been less an artist," observed Lloyd Morris, and Malcolm Cowley, "flat, obvious, and full of horse-play that wouldn't raise a laugh at an Elks' convention." Louis Kronenberger wrote that it was "not just reactionary in its political implications; it is equally anti-intellectual in its whole view of life." *Time* magazine, reminding its readers of the dinner at John's Restaurant, thought it quite a joke on the Communist Party, which only so recently had tried to make a hero of the novelist. And the Communist press, between sneers and rage, denounced it as a crime against humanity.

This story of Fred Cornplow and his wife, Hazel, in revolt from their foolishly radical and irresponsible children, brings to a sad end, no doubt, Lewis's ambition to write a novel about political idealism.* Radical politics are parodied in the figure of a comic-strip Communist and through the vagaries of undergraduates whose absurd concern with labor is apparently the net result of Lewis's experience of liberal student attitudes at Dartmouth. Against these feeble antagonists is set the good American, Cornplow, a stodgy bundle of received opinions, the stereotype approved. At the same time, in his lectures and in interviews, Lewis was pleading for individualism and independent judgment and struggle against the conformist barrage of press agents, salesmen, radio and motion pictures, every kind of propagandist organization, including organizations to fight propaganda.

Engaged in "that most pretentious form of acting, lecturing," he was confident on the platform; but when his opinions were sought in interviews, he was edgy. Asked by one reporter whether the poverty in the world did not annoy him, he spat out the word, "Annoy!" and leaped to his feet to say, "Don't you try to make a damn fool out of me, young man. God did that already, and you don't need to try to help Him." He finished his lecture tour, which had earned him about eighteen thousand dollars, on February 24 in Washington, and he was ready to accept Seat Seventeen in the American Academy, untroubled now by the lingering presence of all its once despised shades. He returned to the Wyndham and his play.

The play *Queenie,* Lewis announced to the New York *Times* on February 9, was finished, and Sam Harris was reading it in Florida on a thirty-day option. This earliest version was about a woman of the world and her confrontation with a small town, and it was this version that Lewis first sent to Helen Hayes to read. When neither Harris nor Miss Hayes expressed enthusiasm, the dramatist plunged into a revision which was completed in May. Now the first act had been moved to a college campus. The hero is a doctor who is in love with Queenie, but her career is more important to her than his love. This version was not satisfactory either, and Lewis began to make notes, which extended well into the autumn of 1938, for still another version that would be set entirely on a college campus.

> . . . the central theme of the play: the character of a clever, forceful, and attractive woman, who can successfully settle all the emotional problems of others but who herself, when she falls in love, is as helpless as any of her dependents—the physician cannot heal herself . . .

He had notions about other actresses—Ina Claire, Fay Bainter, Gertrude Lawrence—who might play this character suggested to him by his wife, but none of these ladies nor any other was ever to grace the stage in the role. Although in his notes he adjured himself that his characters must

* Sad or not, the novel enjoyed hard-cover sales of nearly 50,000 copies, and with book club and subscription and reprint sales, nearly 100,000.

not be presented as eccentrics, the play gives, in fact, a Hollywood version of a campus in which there is no sense whatever of the real tensions in academic life and which, to avoid merely endless talk, falls constantly into farce and melodrama. His fascination with the stage had not created a dramatist.

Long before he gave up *Queenie and the Jopes,* however, he had an invitation to satisfy that fascination in another manner. It was the year of *Our Town,* and Lewis had been in correspondence with Thornton Wilder, who had been pleased by what Lewis had written of the play in *Newsweek* in a review of recently published plays (he dealt at length with the character of Canon Skerritt in *Shadow and Substance,* a role that he would presently attempt.) In New Haven in the meantime, Alexander Dean, who with his wife, Virginia, directed the South Shore Players in Cohasset, Massachusetts, in the summers, was trying to persuade Wilder to come to Cohasset to play Doremus Jessup in a projected production of *It Can't Happen Here.* Wilder declined, but he urged Dean to approach Lewis himself. There was the coincidence then, on the night of the day on which this letter had come from Wilder in Tucson, of a telephone call from Dean's agent in New York, urging Dean to come to New York to talk to Lewis about acting. Dean sought him out in mid-April, Lewis said that he was eager to act but not in *It Can't Happen Here,* and then at last agreed. He would, however, rewrite the Federal Theater Project version before rehearsals began. And now, once more, life seemed to have a point.

It had, until then, been a rather gloomy and disappointing spring. To the American Booksellers Association late in March he had defended the ivory tower, declaring that "A proper writer should stay home—where it's quiet—and write"—precisely what he could hardly bear to do. Sober, with a downright, businesslike woman as his new secretary, writing plays that found no audience, he had been depressed and irritable. Carol Brandt remembers asking him to dine early that spring with Harry Hopkins and others, and while Hopkins was animated and charming, Lewis sat in a sulk throughout the entire evening, and rather ruined it for everyone else.

But after the Cohasset prospect had opened, he himself gave a party that began with lunch and lasted all through the afternoon until six o'clock, an occasion that Molly Costain, then a young literary agent, remembers still as "the golden afternoon," when everything was perfect. Edith Haggard, Lewis's agent in the Curtis Brown office and a close friend, brought Nunnally Johnson, and Lewis and Johnson established instant rapport, and everyone seemed at his absolute best, inordinately witty and lovely, the whole one of those rare, euphoric successes that were almost entirely unknown to Sinclair Lewis but which he himself, in top form, had now achieved. If no particular friendship with Nunnally Johnson was to develop, and if Lewis was later to indulge in a violent denunciation of Miss Costain over almost nothing, what matter? There had been that long afternoon, with its bright benignity. The mood grew. When in April the editor of his early novels, Elizabeth Jordan, published her reminiscences, he wrote her graciously and nostalgically:

> Good Lord! it began twenty-four years ago—when for a while we were so happily associated. I think that at that time you and Charley Towne and Grace (but of course Grace was herself only an amateur then and not sure of her own judgment) along with Mary Heaton Vorse, gave me more encouragement as well as hard practical advice than everybody else in the world put together. To three of these four I owe something that can not be repaid except in lasting affection.

In this mood, he presented the manuscript of *Work of Art* to the American Academy. A year before he had given the manuscript of *It Can't Happen Here* in the novel form to Yale, where Alexander Dean was a professor of drama. Now he wished to do more, and in mid-May, President Seymour announced that Sinclair Lewis had presented all his manuscripts to Yale, some titles involving everything from notebooks through early drafts, final draft, galley proof, page proof, finished book; and a large collection of letters as well. In the meantime, the struggle with the recalcitrant *Queenie* material had its complement in the revision of the already relatively successful *It Can't Happen Here*. The new version, somewhat shorter and a little tighter, was finished by May 31, just as it was time to move to Cohasset, where he took a house on Sandy Cove for the summer.

His wife, in Barnard, hoped that he would come there. "This place seems senseless without you," she wrote in a letter sending him bulletins about Twin Farms.

> I wish you weren't going to act. You know that, and I know that my wishing it won't make any difference in what you do. . . . I can appreciate the lark . . . but my instinct is that you shouldn't do it. Why not get a good understudy, get all the fun there is out of rehearsal, and then admit that you're scared? Not that you are . . . well, I would be . . . Darling—come soon—I count the days.

The advice was wasted, and he did not come. She supplied him with Greta and Josef, an able couple they had once shared, and he employed a local driver.

The theater was an exciting release for him. The young girls in summer stock, the whole youthful atmosphere, gave him a lift as he himself was sagging into his old age. The excitement of collaboration with others, the social business of the theater, relieved his loneliness, and although he had aged far beyond his years (he was only fifty-three, and although he was not drinking, his hands shook as with the ague), his restless energy, undiminished, was temporarily satisfied in all the business and excitement of the theater. Something else was not satisfied: frantically he pursued all the young women, but he was a failure and a joke with them. One by one they would wander off with him, and the others would wait for the one to return and report, to their amusement and derision. Dr. Traeger was his house guest much of the time, and Wells was with him, at work on a first novel, and when Lewis returned to the house with a girl, he would send them off, to the worldly young Wells's somewhat amused disgust.

If, in his relations with these young women, he was at his worst, he had occasion that summer to demonstrate what was best in him. In Barnard, his other son, Michael, fell seriously ill, and Lewis hastened there—his one visit—and was all selfless concern and devotion, and he remained until the eight-year-old boy had passed the crisis of pneumonia. There was something admirable, too, in his determination to master the actor's art. He had no great illusions about his natural talents in that direction. Earlier in the year, in Los Angeles, he had recalled for the press his experience with amateur theatricals in St. Paul in the winter of 1917 and 1918. No critic mentioned his work there, but, said he, a friend chided him with the remark, "For some time there has been a discussion as to who is the world's worst actor. The discussion is now closed." He is reported to have said to Alexander Woollcott, "I am a better actor than you are," and when Woollcott began his tour in *The Man Who Came to Dinner,* he wired Lewis, "From one elderly exhibitionist to another."

But it may be conjectured that Lewis's fling on the stage was not so much a matter of exhibitionism as it was his attempt to get the "feel" of the theater from the inside and to learn at first hand the techniques of play-writing. He worked very hard and with intense interest. Actors in this summer and in the next year became his constant associates, and Dean Jagger, for example, remembers that he would sit quietly for hours, asking questions, testing theories, and listening intently to every hint or suggestion that an actor could give him. Fay Wray was at Cohasset in that summer, and he spent a good deal of time with her in such discussions. In the following summer, they were to play opposite one another, and she remembers that for all his earnestness in learning, he remained very difficult to play opposite. He had no natural grace, and if he played a shambling character, he was not really acting at all. His lack of discipline made him difficult, since she would never know where he would be on the stage as he went through a loose, sprawling, lanky performance in which he too often sloughed and swallowed his lines.

It Can't Happen Here, in John Wildberg's production, was the fifth of eight plays at the South Shore that summer, and it opened on August 22. The opening was a sellout, crowded with notables from New York. In his first performance as Doremus Jessup, Lewis was good. He was a small-town editor by nature, says Dr. Traeger, and, when without self-consciousness about the part, he played it well; but when he became aware of himself as an actor in a role, which happened within twenty-four hours, he was poor. On that first night, he did not miss a cue or a line in two hours and forty minutes, and the audience gave him seven curtain calls. At last he made a speech in which he earnestly pleaded that fascism not be allowed to happen here, and he gave his novel and his play some credit for the fact that thus far it had not.

Afterward Raoul de Roussy de Sales gave a great party, and Dorothy Thompson, who had come down from Barnard, protested to the *Herald Tribune* that Lewis would not act in other plays, as was already being said. "He's too good a writer for that." To the *Times,* Brooks Atkinson wrote that he was "a man of valor" and "adequate" as an actor, and to *Newsweek,* George Jean Nathan reported that if he was not "a fine actor," he was certainly "a fine performer." He was at least a curiosity: the house sold out for the entire first week and popular demand caused the Deans to postpone the next play, by James M. Cain, and hold over the Lewis play for another week.

Then the excitement died, and as Lewis ceased to be the center of interest in Cohasset, he began to sulk. He was suspicious, now, of the Deans, and he delivered a diatribe against Alexander Dean to James M. Cain, who was Dean's good friend. When Cain did not join him, Lewis's manner cooled toward Cain, and that friendship, which had been pleasant if casual for fifteen years, was concluded. At the end of the season, the Players gave a routine closing party. Both of the Deans were ill in bed, and somehow Lewis had not been invited to the party. He telephoned their house that night, roused Mrs. Dean from bed, stormed on and on about the insult to him, and finally, with a scream of rage, hung up. The Deans did not see him again in Cohasset, but six weeks later, from New York, an inscribed copy of his Cohasset version of the play appeared in their mail, and then, at an opening some months later, they met in an intermission and Lewis wrapped his long, thin arms around Mrs. Dean in a forgiving embrace.

On September 1 his wife wrote him a full, chatty letter from Barnard. Wells was there now, near to the end of his novel. She had given him a dance. She was sorry that his father hadn't "found time to come for a few days." She had been happy to see him surrounded by so many admiring friends at Cohasset, but "the talk about divorce upset me . . . to understate the matter. . . . I mind that our child must also grow up, like Wells, without a father." She feels that he no longer *likes* her, that his image of her is fixed, and that what he had once found attractive in her as "eagerness" has been converted in his mind to the dismal business of "holding forth." What were his plans?

He was on his way back to New York, where he took rooms at the Plaza. There, with Fay Wray, he began work on a new play that they had planned together in the summer—*Angela Is Twenty-Two.* He knew that he lacked a sense of visually dramatic effects and even a feeling for the development of dramatic scene, and for this he had decided that he needed professional aid. Miss Wray helped him by talking through the play with him. Actually, she did no writing, and he did not always listen to her suggestions, but he nevertheless insisted that she have equal credit as author with him. They worked on this first version throughout September, and when she returned to Hollywood they continued the "collaboration" in correspondence.

In the meantime, Wells Lewis, on the way back to Harvard for his senior year, arrived with the completed manuscript of his novel, a mildly comic affair about a young man continually frustrated in his determination to be free of his virginal condition. His father had had nothing to do with the planning or the writing of this novel, but now the son sought his opinion. Lewis called Miss Costain and asked her to dine with them at the Plaza and then go over the novel with him. After dinner Wells paced about uneasily until his father sent him away, and then, with Miss Costain, Lewis settled down to the manuscript. It was not a long novel, and they read it rapidly and enthusiastically, and when Wells reappeared they had finished it and were able to assure him that it was splendid ("an enormously clever piece of work," he rather exaggerated in a letter to his brother). His father praised him and gave him the title: *They Still Say No.* It was probably the happiest moment in their lives as father and son, and a rare one. (There was to be at least one such moment with his son Michael as well, when, after having seen him perform creditably in a bit part, Lewis praised him as having succeeded where he had failed.) Then Miss Costain took Wells off to a party in the Village, and she remembers him as in a happy daze through the rest of that night.*

At the beginning of October, Lewis moved into an apartment at the Lombardy, in East 56th Street, and continued to work at *Angela,* and by the end of that month he had a finished version to show John Wildberg, who agreed to produce it. Flora Campbell, whom Lewis had come to know at Cohasset, was cast as Angela, and Lewis himself would play opposite her. Both Wildberg and Miss Campbell worked on the play now, and by November 19, a second version was finished and ready to go into rehearsal. And Sinclair Lewis was in fine spirits.

He took the trouble to issue a protest, sponsored by the Federal

* *They Still Say No* was published by Farrar & Rinehart in 1939. A rather touching note is introduced when we are told of Crane Stewart, the hero, that "His parents . . . had been married long and charmingly." The work suggests that the young man had closely followed his father's work. As in many of his novels, there is no real plot, and the devices of style are much like the older man's, especially in the curiously dated diction, i.e., "He grew almost pompous with contentment. . . . He stretched, relaxing gorgeously."

Council of Churches, against the Jewish persecution in Germany. He joined Actors Equity, sponsored by Helen Hayes, and was kissed by her for the photographers. He presided at a P.E.N. dinner at the Algonquin in honor of Pearl Buck, the new Nobel prize novelist, and not only praised her generously for bringing a fresh awareness of the Orient to her readers, but, observing Ford Madox Ford in the audience, also took occasion to praise him for general excellence. Ford, a considerably neglected man of great distinction, was moved by this recognition.

> *My dear Lewis:*
>
> I was so struck all of a heap by your reference to me the other night that, not to mention the omission of all tribute to Miss Pearl Buck—to whom I had prepared a quite nice little one!—I omitted any thanks to yourself or expression of admiration for your work—for which the merest decency would have called!
>
> The fact is: I first fell wondering who could be the phoenix you were lauding and then concluded that Thomas Mann must be somewhere in the audience and that you were talking of him. So when you dropped out my name I clean forgot everything I had prepared. I am not, you see, modest but you went so far beyond any praise I could allot to myself that I clean forgot all my manners!

And Lewis replied:

> Any tribute that I have paid to you was merely the most plain statement of fact, and if there are people who do not recognise your dukedom in English letters, the joke is on them and not on those of us who have so admired and profited from your books. I have often thought that your story of collaboration with Conrad was the one great book on the technique of writing a novel that I have ever read.

That letter was written one day after Lewis had excitedly written his brother, Claude, about his current venture:

> The worst has happened! A member of the medical Lewises has actually gone on the stage! I don't know whether the family will ever recover, but the fact is that I star in my own play, *Angela Is Twenty-Two,* which we shall open in Columbus, Ohio, on December 30th. We shall appear in Minneapolis on January 19, 20 and 21, and I have written the dread news to Fred and made a lot of trouble for you by suggesting that maybe Mary and you might take him and Winnie down to see the show there. If you do plan to go, you'd better order tickets right away for the thing will have some chance, at least, of being sold out. And if you're smart, you'll go to the St. Paul opening instead on January 17 and 18. I would certainly send you tickets myself, but I have no way of getting them.

When *The New Yorker*, in mid-December, sent a man to observe a rehearsal at the Vanderbilt Theater, they found the cast, Lewis among them, still most uncertain of its lines, but he was trying conscientiously, studying his script when he was not on the stage, taking directions affably, letting his "rural" voice go nasal whenever he made a dramatic speech, having great difficulty with his arms and legs, and, when he was making a speech sitting down, winding and unwinding himself and forgetting to keep his head up. There were continuing difficulties with the script, which was in constant process of revision now and for some time to come, but Sinclair Lewis was in a condition of euphoria.

On an evening just before the play was to go on the road, S. N. Behrman came into "21" for dinner and saw Lewis happily ensconced beside his lovely leading lady, Flora Campbell, in the midst of six or eight members of the company. He was elated, triumphant in an excited happiness, and he came bounding over to greet Behrman at his table. Behrman had never before that winter read *Babbitt,* and, having just read it, thought it great, and this impression he communicated to Lewis. But he also knew that Lewis's career in the theater was doomed, and he asked him why a man who could write such a novel was spending his time on the stage. Lewis looked back at his table of actors as though he were beholding a banquet of spirited gods and goddesses. Then he said that writing novels was the solitary business of lonely Vermont and that he at last preferred living. Behrman, who had often thought of telling Lewis most seriously that his theatrical efforts were a waste of his time and that he should abandon them, saw in this moment that it would be useless advice, and he let Lewis, aging specter of a man in boyish high spirits, go eagerly back to join the bright company of life.

The play opened as scheduled on December 30 before a packed house in Columbus, Ohio. There were ten curtain calls for Sinclair Lewis, who, rather carried away by his success, announced at last that "the American theater is coming into the grandest renaissance of all times."

Angela Is Twenty-Two was generally well received because Sinclair Lewis was acting in it. As a play, it is loose in conception and cloudy in motivation, and it is of interest now only because in it Lewis seemed to pose to himself the question of what would happen if one of those young women that he was so busily pursuing would not only have him but marry him. Set in 1936 in its opening act, the play's hero, Dr. Hilary Jarrett, Professor of Medicine, is exactly the age of Sinclair Lewis in that year—fifty-one, the widower of a heckling wife who had been dead for twelve years. At a country inn he meets young Angela Quayle * and falls in love with her. She is also admired by a gruff young medical scientist named Ellis Plum

* Lewis was so desperately in pursuit of such young women that, while he could no doubt quite seriously find them all angels, he could hardly have intended a pun on the word *quail,* which in the vernacular of the time indicated a special type of young female, nonangelic. Or perhaps he could have.

and by a jaded playboy named Ross Cromer, who is married to a rich dipsomaniac. Impervious to their charms and taken by Hilary's, Angela, at the end of the first act, agrees to marry him. Acts Two and Three dramatize in diffuse and wavering scenes her growing discontents, but never with sufficient force or point to persuade an audience that in the very last moment of the play she would decide to go away with Ross, who is divorcing his wife for the sake of his work, and to leave poor Hilary to the bluff ministrations of his old best friend, an attorney named Price Dixon. A play's a play, Sinclair Lewis must have concluded, and declined to learn from the experience he had created for his contemporary, Hilary Jarrett.

The play toured over twenty cities in the Midwest for about two months. The details of that tour were to provide the background for the novel *Bethel Merriday,* but early in the tour, learning about the provincial theater as he went, Lewis announced that he would soon leave his role in favor of Philip Merivale, who was already traveling with the company. Angela was twenty-two, but he had discovered that he was nearly fifty-four, and directing the company as well as acting in it was exhausting him. He had lost ten pounds within a few months, and he was sleeping only four or five hours a night. His hands shook so violently that a scene in which he was to fit a gun together had to be removed from the play. In Madison, Wisconsin, on January 16 he announced that he would write a commentator's role for himself—"a prologue and epilogue, a Greek chorus, a living newspaper, our portable Walter Winchell." But he continued in the lead role through the Minnesota performances. In Minneapolis he interviewed Governor Stassen and announced that he would begin a one-man campaign for Stassen as President of the United States. Invited to address the Minnesota legislature, he struck out at provincialism after one legislator had attempted to bar his appearance in the mistaken belief that the speaker was to be John L. Lewis. He was the guest of honor at a reception given by the Community Club of Sauk Centre, where all was at peace.

Still revising the script of his play, he found time to write an appreciation of William Lyon Phelps for the *Saturday Review of Literature.* He dropped the central role in Davenport, Iowa, on January 23 and thereafter gave informal little speeches before the first curtain and after the last, and he finally achieved the script he wanted in Detroit on February 20. From Detroit, the play went to Toronto, and then, for a week, to Pittsburgh. It did not, however, go on to New York, but moved west again to Chicago for three weeks. There Lewis lectured at least once, when he was introduced by the novelist Margaret Ayer Barnes. To that audience he said that he and the novelist's husband, a Chicago attorney named Cecil B. Barnes, were "in the same boat. I also am married to a very distinguished woman. She disappeared into the NBC building ten years ago." He left the play for Hollywood before it closed on April 1—it had cost him thus far, he told S. N. Behrman, $125,000—and wrote his wife with the request that she divorce him.

He stayed at the Beverly Hills Hotel for about a month, and there he worked on a screen version of the play for Lester Cowan. He employed a young woman named Miriam McGrail as his secretary and to her he dictated much of the script. He would sit with his face covered for a time, then suddenly put down his hands and burst out in a stream, acting as the words came. Hollywood conventions made him impatient, and once, when it was decided that he should change the word *fairy* to *nance,* he exclaimed, "Oh, throw the God-damned thing out of the window." But he finished the script, and, somewhat rested, returned to the Lombardy early in May. He had started work, in the meantime, on a new novel that was to be about the theater.

He had had, for the moment, enough of public appearances, and when Chauncey Tinker wrote him with an invitation to speak at an exhibition of his manuscripts to be held at Yale in June, he declined; yet, when Ernst Toller committed suicide late in May, Lewis appeared at the funeral services (alarming the Communist sponsors) to speak on behalf of Toller's ideals in a world succumbing to slavery. And he was planning his entire summer around further engagements in the theater. Not included in his plans was a letter from his first wife, in desperate straits in Dallas, Texas, which arrived late in June. To her he replied:

> It is nearly two years since I have had a novel published, & I can ill—indeed can *not*—afford to, but I am herewith sending you $500. Luck, Hal.

Of this note he kept a carbon copy.

His present wife had declined to seek a divorce: there were her promises to him, and how could she know that this is what he really wanted? She hoped still that she had a marriage and that presently he would come "home." And now indeed, in this summer, he did return to Twin Farms for two weeks, where his friends, Diana and Vincent Sheean, had rented the smaller of the two houses and served as a convenient buffer in the stalemated truce between man and wife. But he left in July for Ogunquit, Maine, where he was to play the stage manager in Thornton Wilder's *Our Town* from August 7 to August 12, and where he settled down to continue work on *Bethel Merriday*. Here he rented a cottage and wrote his wife:

> I have worked like the devil; written over 15,000 new words on the novel. I have been all over the theater's technical equipment and seen quite a little—not too much—of the actors, especially the young ones, and all this has been both pleasantly relieving of loneliness and useful as a review of the theater and its young aspirants, for the novel.

He could not have known, of course, that within a very short time he would meet one such "young aspirant" whom he would come to know with that degree of intimacy for which he had long and frenziedly yearned.

On August 13 he left Ogunquit for Provincetown, where, at the Wharf Theater, he was to play the role of Nat Miller in Eugene O'Neill's *Ah, Wilderness!* On August 14 he met a young apprentice to the Provincetown Players, Rosemary Marcella Powers, and he remembered her later, with "all your clothes in one funny big old bag, with a broken strap, that you tugged pluckily along."

In 1938, at seventeen, Marcella Powers was graduated from a South Orange, New Jersey, high school, and for the next twelve months she worked in a series of stock companies in New Jersey. Her father had been dead since she was nine years old, and her mother managed by taking in boarders. She was now eighteen, wearing saddle shoes and white ankle socks, very pretty, very small, and, she says, quite ignorant. At the moment she was enjoying her first serious flirtation with a young man of twenty who was also in the company and in whom the directress, somewhat older than he, was likewise interested. It was obvious that Lewis would need someone to "cue" him while he learned his lines, and knowing something of his proclivities, the directress assigned Miss Powers to the cuing job in the expectation that this association would conclude her romance with the younger man. And so it did. They were together constantly, hours on end every day for the week that he learned his part—and fascinated her. Fatherless since childhood, she was not ill-disposed to older men; but on his part, she believes, it could have been any other girl.

Perhaps; but hardly another so congenial. She fell at once into his penchant for games and private jokes. At once they developed their fantasy that they were under the constant scrutiny of invisible little people, called Small Size Spies, who were watching them everywhere, and nine years later he was to dedicate a novel to her under the opaque rubric, "S.S.S." She was called Peggie Powers, and had always been, because her mother did not like to hear people abbreviate Rosemary to Rosie. But Lewis thought that Peggie suggested a housemaid's name, and he urged her to use her middle name, which, fortunately, she liked, and so she became Marcella Powers, and her nickname, Mark.

In nostalgic mood, he offered to pay $150 for a book called *Reminiscences of Provincetown, 1911,* the year that he first went there to write *Hike and the Aeroplane*. He had gone far since then, and gone far back, too. He had no success in finding the book, and that was perhaps as well, for he was finding new pleasures that must have suggested to him that he close his eyes to his long and battered past.

These first pleasures were short-lived, for Lewis was scheduled in the next week to play in *Our Town* again, now in Clinton, Connecticut, while Miss Powers remained in Provincetown, ironically enough to play a housemaid's part in *Angela Is Twenty-Two*. But after a week's separation, they met in Boston for a weekend at the Ritz, and then went on together to Skowhegan, Maine, where Fay Wray had been in summer stock and with whom (she somewhat reluctantly) he was to play in *Angela* in the oldest, and then the largest, summer theater. Miss Powers lived in a luxurious cabin and, since she had been surviving all summer on the starvation diet of a scholarship apprentice, for the first time in months had enough to eat.

But September was well upon them now, a dark September: in the week that he was playing in Provincetown, Europe had been plunged into war. Summer was gone. The theaters were closing all over New England, the leaves were about to turn and to fall. They hurried back to New York together on the first day of autumn. And he had, one might say, put his hand on Pandora's box.

"When are they going to plant the old man?"

SIX

Fall

I

HE HAD DONE now what he should first have done twenty-seven years before, or, that failing, twelve years. He had found a young woman of almost no experience who could admire him and to whom he could be of use, a young woman without the background or the inclination to be critical of him, a young woman who would consent to his whims without challenging his freedom and his freedom from responsibility to her. She could cosset him, make him feel appreciated, knowledgeable and worldly and so amusing. She was a young woman with a great deal to learn, much of which he would be able to teach her; and a young woman, finally, for whom he needed to create no role or image in which he would then insist on casting her, because now at last he could in effect create the woman herself. But alas, having found such a woman, he was at least twelve years too late, and probably twenty-seven. Companionship proved more essential than the scanty hymeneal pleasures of the aging man: his expectations were more insistent than his energies, and the bed was not for very long important to the relationship.

He introduced her to all his friends, usually as his "niece," a device which even she thought absurd under the circumstances, but tolerated. To his old Minneapolis friend William McNally he said that she "missed being my granddaughter by just about three weeks." He expected everyone to accept her without questioning him or patronizing her, and, in fact, while there were those who thought it a miserable comedy or resented her for her use of him and pitied him for his folly, at least as many of his friends thought it a good relationship in which each was helpful to the other. At first she was kind to him, a cuddling, kittenish companion who saved him from loneliness. Marriage was not in her mind, and if it was in his at this point, it was as a desired but improbable fantasy; nevertheless, when he introduced her to his son Wells, it was as the boy's "future stepmother," and he asked his friends to treat her as his "wife." Now he urged her to permit him to send her to college, but her interests were in the theater and she did not encourage this notion.

He returned to his apartment at the Lombardy and set up Miss Powers on the eleventh floor. He was working hard, finishing *Bethel Merriday,* and he was eager to start work on a play. There was a month of excited attendance at the theater for both of them as the new season opened. Leonard Sillman was producing the New York Drama Festival, reviving once successful plays like *Journey's End* and *They Knew What They Wanted,* and one night after a performance of the latter, Lewis came flying backstage, demanding to meet Sillman. Miss Powers was with him, a still unformed young woman, Sillman remembers ("something out of a novel by Wassermann," very different from what she was to be when he met her again four years later, elegant and poised). Lewis was tremendously excited by Sillman's experiment in reviving those "great plays," and he wanted to do something for him. Did Sillman know Winchell? No? Well, then they must go at once to the Stork Club to meet him.

At the opening of *Skylark* by his friend Samson Raphaelson, he took Miss Powers backstage to meet the playwright and the competent but hardly remarkable actor, Donald Cook, who was playing the part of Tony Kenyon. In his dressing room they encountered S. N. Behrman, who was duly presented to the young woman. Behrman looked politely ironical, and Lewis drew him aside. "I want to tell you, Sam, about a typical day in the life of Dorothy Thompson. She is in Washington. Before breakfast, she has a long telephone conversation with Senator Vandenberg. Then she has breakfast with the Secretary of State. In the morning, she is busy with Harold Ickes and Bernard Baruch. For lunch, the White House. In the afternoon, the Chief Justice of the Supreme Court. Tea with Senator Taft, cocktails with Frances Perkins, dinner with the Right Honorable Philip Henry Kerr, Marquess of Lothian, and a nightcap with Harry Hopkins. Then she writes her column. Before going to bed, she reads a book about the refugee situation." He paused. Then, "Now take little Marcella there—she thinks *I'm* great, because I can bring her backstage and introduce her to Donald Cook!"

Everywhere the two, Lewis and the wise, observing child, appeared together, but then, when *Bethel Merriday* was finished and turned in, they decided to disappear. On October 22 they took a train to Washington and next day Lewis said to the Washington *Post,* "I don't know where I'm going. Just going South. Want to keep moving." They moved on to Jacksonville, Florida, and there Lewis bought a Buick convertible, paying for it, to his young companion's unforgettable astonishment, with $1,350 in new bills. They drove on to St. Augustine, where many years before, with his first wife, Lewis had conversed with Howells; and then on to the Gulf coast, where, ten years before, he had taken his second wife; to Sarasota, where for a few weeks he rented a cabin on Long Boat Key; and then, finally, on to New Orleans. At best he was an erratic driver, but their approach to New Orleans, made in a tremendous rainstorm, was positively hair-raising; nevertheless, he managed to draw up before the St. Charles, where they took rooms for a few days, and then he rented an apartment at 1536 Nashville Avenue for four months. And kept it for two. Nothing was very different.

Immediately—this was almost always the routine when he came to a new town or city—he telephoned the major newspaper to say, "This is Red Lewis. I'm here." Then he took the second step in that routine, which was to tour the churches, large and small. His interest in domestic church architecture was inexhaustible, as was his interest in organized religious activities. On Monday mornings, no matter what the headline news, he would turn first to the reviews of sermons delivered on the day before, and with the New York *Times* religious page he could entertain himself for hours.

Almost immediately upon their arrival, Lewis was invited to dine with the editor of the *Times-Picayune* and his wife, who was the daughter of the Southern politician Champ Clark. The other guest was Mrs. Alice Longworth. He said, as he always would, that he assumed the invitation included his niece, and the two went together. The atmosphere of the party was not easy. Lewis took quick resentment at what he felt was a patronizing air, especially in his hostess, and in a sudden characteristic rage, he berated them both, while Miss Powers and Mrs. Longworth, embarrassed, fell into a long conversation about Ethel Barrymore. Mrs. Longworth was kind to the younger woman, who was experiencing for the first time a situation with which, in the next few years, she would become all too familiar, when he, angry at someone, usually a woman, blew up a storm and left her to converse stiffly with a stranger, usually grand, on an elegant occasion.

The apartment that Lewis rented was owned by a relative of Hodding Carter on whose newspaper, the *Delta Democrat-Times,* in nearby Greenville, Mississippi, Wells Lewis was employed. There was talk of his father's coming to visit him, but he never came. Wells had been offered his position as a result of the efforts of David L. Cohn, a friend of Carter as well as of Dorothy and Sinclair Lewis, and Lewis was busy now repaying Cohn by writing a foreword for his book, *The Good Old Days.** In this brief essay, he argued that the superiority of fiction over history lies in its concern with the concrete details of everyday life, with *things;* that readers prefer to know about living rather than about Life. He had simplified the concrete details of his own life by employing a Negro servant, Joseph Hardrick, who would function as valet, driver, butler and cook, and would remain with him, the faithful retainer, for some years.

If there were any Christmas communications between father and son,

* In 1947, on page 258 of *Kingsblood Royal,* Lewis was to deride Cohn as "that aristocratic old planter . . . who in the obliging *Atlantic Monthly*" warned any reformers against attempting "to break down segregation in the South by Federal fiat."

the son did not mention them to Hodding Carter. He had, however, received one invitation, from Dorothy Lewis, to come north for his holidays, his expenses to be paid by her; and Carter, who was very fond of him, offered to let him have all the time off that he wanted. After deliberating for a day or two, he decided to spend Christmas with the Carters instead. He had always been fascinated by toy soldiers, and now he gave as his reason for staying in Mississippi the fact that he had bought a lot of lead soldiers and had built a fort for the Carters' oldest son, who was then four. And he and his employer spent most of Christmas Day maneuvering toy troops on the living-room floor.

Because of the boy's interest in lead soldiers, Lewis had become something of an expert on the market for them. It was one of his hobbies to discover little enterprises that, if properly handled, could make a fortune. When John Hersey was with him, Lewis had chosen the toy-soldier industry for Hersey and in fact had sent him around to shops to investigate lead-soldier manufacturers and outlets and generally to learn what he could. "You go into that," he advised him, "and you'll make a million." With his own sons, he rarely showed such playful interest, nor the more serious kind that he was in the habit of lavishing on other young men. Ken McCormick, who later became editor-in-chief at Doubleday, was young and new to the company when Lewis brought his books there, but he remembers still the extraordinary interest that Lewis showed in his future, in his ideas, his problems, his plans for himself. And yet, friend and adviser as he so easily was with so many casually encountered young people, father he declined to be.

Sinclair Lewis, too, had declined an invitation to go north. On February 5, Yale University was opening the Sinclair Lewis collection, and a number of his friends there were urging that he be present. To Tinker he wrote:

> I've taken a flat here for all winter, with the notion of writing a play in comparative quiet, and No, I couldn't by any magic be coaxed to New Haven for the fatal day . . . You are to make a speech in which you refer to me, aetat 19, as a silent youth with black locks and a surprising taste in Mosel and incunabula, inscrutable above the chess board. And for that, ah, it would be a far, far better thing that I would do to stay away.

At once upon their arrival in New Orleans, Lewis had written Samson Raphaelson to praise the city, lamenting only the absence of any real theater; in the next few months, there would be nothing but four little-theater plays. Those were to be the performances at Le Petit Theatre du Vieux Carré, and very soon Lewis presented himself to Bernard Szold, the director. Szold knew of Lewis's efforts on the stage and proposed that he do some acting for the Little Theater. Lewis said that only one role interested him, that of Canon Skerritt in *Shadow and Substance,* played by Sir Cedric Hardwicke on Broadway. When the Paul Vincent Carroll play had finished its Broadway run, Eddie Dowling, who owned the rights, had given the first amateur rights to his friend Father Edward F. Murphy, a priest in Xavier University, of New Orleans, and Szold knew that he held them. Accordingly, he asked Father Murphy if he would give the production rights to the Little Theater, thus accommodating Sinclair Lewis, and himself join the company as technical adviser for the production. Father Murphy was happy to consent, and *Shadow and Substance* became the fifth item in that season's repertoire.

Meeting Lewis, Father Murphy observed in his face

> a wistfulness which somehow suggested that of a little boy kept indoors for his behavior and peeking out a window. Too, the face seemed a parchment on which many things had been written, erased, and re-written; and I began to wonder whether any past God-challenging upon the part of this celebrity had been only a perverse form of truth seeking.

And he began to wonder, too, if there was any possibility of converting him to the faith. An easy friendship developed between the two, but when, finally, Father Murphy was emboldened by the recent conversion of Heywood Broun under the ministrations of Fulton Sheen to ask "with affected casualness, 'Why don't you do a Heywood Broun?' " Lewis wheeled on him and inquired, "Why don't you do an Elmer Gantry?"

Marcella Powers was cast in the role of Brigid, the servant who identifies herself with a saint. As always, Lewis energetically devoted himself to his work, was the first to know his lines, the first to arrive for rehearsals and the last to leave, the first to arrive for performance and again the last to leave. There were a few explosions: once, when he thought that a young woman was laughing at his acting, he ordered her out of the theater and the company; again, exasperated by the glare of the spotlight, he shouted that his vision meant more to him than any play, and stamped off the stage to his dressing room—only to let Father Murphy believe that he had been acting and that he thought *that* would convince the skeptics in the company of his ability; and finally, more mildly, when he was adamant with Father Murphy that his cassock be lined and piped with red, suitable for a monsignor, rather than with white, correct for a canon.

He could not learn to make a proper sign of the cross. After a special première for the clergy of the city, Father Murphy's fellows twitted him for failing to teach his actor how to bless himself; but then, at another special performance for nuns, he mastered the symbolic gesture at last and announced that he had played to "an audience of angels." The play opened to the secular public on January 15, 1940. The local press, which treated the activities of Le Petit Theatre as social rather than aesthetic events and therefore offered nothing resembling reviews, was content with the splendid audience, if silent as to the splendors of Sinclair Lewis's performance; but the New Orleans *Item* felt that in the work of Marcella Powers, the audience had witnessed the debut of a young woman whose imminent command of the American stage was obvious.

The play was to run for four nights, but because Mardi Gras that year was early and, busy with carnival balls, not everyone who had wanted to see a performance had been able to, it was held over for an extra performance and closed on January 20. Lewis, who was apparently already thinking of writing a novel to be concerned with Negroes, spent some time at Xavier University, a Negro institution, where he consulted with members of the staff; he had met and talked with Roark Bradford, the well-known author of fiction about Negroes, and now he saw Mrs. Bradford frequently, and he managed to while away some time in the Basement Book Shop, the center of New Orleans's sluggish literary activity.

But he was soon impatient to be gone. Local gossip has it still that, because he had introduced his young friend as his niece, she had received and accepted invitations to several carnival balls from young Orleanians, and that Lewis was jealous. At any rate, immediately after the *Shadow and Substance* experience, the apartment lease only half-expired, Joseph was suddenly ordered to pack them and to drive the Buick to El Paso, where they, taking the train, would meet him. Then they drove to Tucson, to Phoenix, to San Diego, and on January 30 arrived in Los Angeles, where Lewis at once rented the Elsie Janis house at 724 North Linden Drive in Beverly Hills—a great Hollywood-Spanish pile that seemed always to be available for rent and that had among its few virtues a pleasant patio and a swimming pool, curved, of course.

In New Orleans he had written a single short story, "Carry Your Own Suitcase," which appeared in *This Week* on February 25—a story about the theater, with one Matt Carnival as its hero, which, employing the old formula of true versus false, pits the real hard-working troupers against the glamorous but egotistic fake, and puts the latter down—but he had also been working on a play, first called *The Talking Woman,* finally to be called *Felicia Speaking,* and it was to this play that he chiefly devoted himself during the next few months in Hollywood.

It is appropriate to the quality of *Bethel Merriday* that Lewis should have been living in Hollywood when that novel was published on March 22, 1940. Less embarrassing than *The Prodigal Parents,* it is hardly more important as fiction. Taking as his heroine a young girl who aspires to be an actress, Lewis was able to include, through her education in summer stock and touring companies, everything that he had learned about the theater; attached to, rather than incorporated in, this handbook material is a pale romance. Learning as much as one does of the theater, one learns nothing of the impulses that drive an actor or of the kind of satisfactions that an actor finds in his profession; and while the novel at one point glances at a "May and December" relationship, one learns no more of Sinclair Lewis's passion for young women than for the stage.

"The results of months of touring with my own play *Angela Is Twenty-Two,"* he wrote in a copy of the book; "anyway, my acting was better than the play." And he might have added, "Or the novel." Yet it was received in a friendly fashion by most reviewers, who thought it kindly, exact and informative, and it was the rare reviewer like Peter Munro Jack who found it "full of figures and empty of life." If most serious reviewers of fiction were no longer attending to Sinclair Lewis at all, some old friends—Ludwig Lewisohn, for example—whose fiction had not enjoyed the kind of success that Lewis's "shallowness and adolescent pseudo-verve" still brought him, took bitter consolation in his decline.

One must wonder what Lewis himself thought of a novel such as this. Was it only more of the old "whoring," or was it in his view "serious"; or had he meant it as serious only to discover that he had in fact been whoring? It is hard to know. There is plenty of evidence to suggest that for at least a decade he had been exacerbated by the knowledge, half-secret or half-recognized, that he could no longer write novels of the kind that he had produced in the 1920s, the knowledge even that he too was only another writer who had fallen into that pattern so familiar to most American novelists—the decline of power in the prime of life. It was a phenomenon of which he was quite aware, and a subject that he had discussed at length with William L. Shirer in Vienna in the exasperating winter of 1932 and 1933, when he was putting the blame on his wife for what had happened to him. And yet in that same winter he was also telling Shirer that he was about to write his greatest novel, which was to be nothing less than a history of America. He must have had in mind the projected, three-generation labor novel, but what he was in fact involved with then was the plan for *Work of Art.* That novel, if he could not regard it as a history of America, he did take seriously. But *Bethel Merriday?* A note to the librarian of Yale University, written from New Orleans, suggests that this, too, in his mind, was important work:

> . . . I shall add to [the collection] the MS of my new novel, *Bethel Merriday,* . . . along with every single note and page of revision used and discarded during the writing of the novel—a dismaying mass of scribbling such as I have never kept before in writing any novel.

For a Lewis novel, it was a relative commercial failure; with its hard-cover sales going only to a little over 33,000 copies, it had the smallest sale of any of his novels since *Free Air,* and the 50,000 additional copies that were sold through book-club selection and reprint editions did not bring it up to *The Prodigal Parents.* Certain dubious compensations, however, were to develop in Hollywood. Much of the novel was concerned with a tour of *Romeo and Juliet,* and when Laurence Olivier and Vivien Leigh took their production of *Romeo and Juliet* on the road, Alexander Korda developed the notion that they would be the perfect stars for a film of *Bethel Merriday.* William Dozier, who was handling Curtis Brown authors in Hollywood, persuaded Korda to offer Lewis $50,000 for screen rights. Then, unfortunately, the Olivier stage venture proved to be unsuccessful, and with that debacle, the very *raison d'être* of the screen play evaporated and the film was abandoned. Korda then suggested that he be released from his agreement, but under legal pressure he finally paid the full sum. At this very point Lewis was engaged in a lawsuit over another of his theatrical enterprises, *Angela Is Twenty-Two,* whose producer he had brought into court over what he took to be inaccurate accounting.

William Dozier's recollection of Lewis in Hollywood in that spring is not of a man who had achieved even temporary serenity. He had not been drinking for nearly a year, and his nerves were on constant edge. His nervousness, the unremitting agitation, the insistence of his fierce and frothy energy, the endless pacing up and down, up and down, left others as nervous as himself. He always needed company, and reached far for it. Mrs. Powers came for a ten-day visit with her daughter, her expenses paid—the first of many excursions which that until then untraveled woman was to make under the Lewis dispensation. Dr. Traeger was summoned for a visit from New York, his expenses paid; and he obliged.

Lewis always tried to quell his restlessness by moving, and with Dr. Traeger and Miss Powers, he now impulsively dashed to San Francisco and to Berkeley, where he wanted to talk to Dr. Herbert Evans, the distinguished experimental biologist, whom he knew in only the most casual way, and Dr. Evans arranged that they should meet Dr. E. O. Lawrence, the physicist, in his laboratory. Dr. Lawrence had just received the huge Rockefeller Foundation grant that would enable him to build the large cyclotron at the University of California, and he had written on his blackboard,

$1,150,000.00
Whew!

Below this, Lewis fastened a dime with Scotch tape, and wrote,

and 10 ¢.

Then they dashed back to Beverly Hills.

When he could not move, he gave expression to his fits of restlessness, as often as not, in fits of cruelty. He would lash out in a quite vicious way at some innocent who had irked him or who, he thought, would tolerate his invective, or at a friend in whom some harmless mannerism had suddenly become an outrage. Marcella Powers was spared such abuse. He treated her, with his older friends, as one would treat a child—patient, tolerant, amused; and yet every now and then he would make a considerable show of wanting to hear her point of view on a subject and would encourage her to chatter and chirp. He seemed, his Hollywood friends felt, intent on proving something to Dorothy Thompson, with whom he was still in some way smitten, the only intellectual equal who was ever close to him and whom—the efforts of his anecdotage and the subject of his current attempt at a play to the contrary—he could not dispose of and whose name and career he seemed to bring, however irrelevantly, into every conversation.

Nor could she quite dispose of him. They had, after all, a young son, aged ten, and she had her tolerant affection. On the day that *Bethel Merriday* was published, as she was about to depart for England, she wrote him about the boy, who was coming to California with his nurse to visit his father:

> Be a sweet man and do not introduce Marcella to Mickey—if she is still with you—, as his future Ma. He would not like it, and he is sensitive, aggressive, difficult, jealous, and very, very nice. Please take the foregoing statement at its face value. I know about Marcella. Whatever resentment I felt—and I did—has evaporated. I cannot begrudge you a single hour of happiness, but be kind and considerate of the child . . . that is reasonable and wise. You will understand what I mean. . . . An amusing boy . . . antisocial and individualist, and I wonder what and where he gets it from.

Lewis was not making many new friends in the film colony, but he did make a new friend. He had met Stephen Longstreet in the offices of Random House, and when Longstreet submitted a novel called *And So Dedicated* (by "Thomas Burton") to Harrison Smith, Lewis offered, out of friendly feelings, to write a reader's report on the manuscript. This he did, and dated the report March 24, 1940. It was an enthusiastic report on a young writer in whom Lewis found "real power, vitality, observation; authenticity with beauty," but who had still to learn about the architecture of the novel, about selectivity, about diction, and above all, about how to resist the influence of Ernest Hemingway. In revising his manuscript, Longstreet attended to Lewis's criticism, but he did not delete the bullfight scene that Lewis had particularly deplored, and when the novel was published, Lewis annotated that scene with the words, "Bull, Booze, Fine, Hemingway, Balls." In Hollywood, the men became friends.

Longstreet was a painter, and Lewis told him that he had long wished to write a novel to be called *The Artist,* but that his lack of experience with painters had prevented his doing it, and now he hoped that Longstreet would provide that background. They met frequently to sketch out the plot, individual scenes, bits of dialogue. The story that they worked out was to center in a conflict between a Babbitt-Dodsworth tycoon and his son, a painter, an original genius, for the affections of the heroine; the father would prove to be the better man and would win the girl—the triumph of "the poetry of materialism" over the degenerate aestheticism of the son, who would deteriorate into a Bohemian tramp.

This novel was not written then, nor was it ever to be written by Lewis, but the discussions about it brought out much about him. He had no taste in painting and disliked all modern art, as he disliked all experimental modern writing. He defended O. Henry and he greatly admired *Huckleberry Finn:* "take out Tom Sawyer and it's the greatest book ever written." He was apolitical, politicians were "Yahoos in silk hats." He confessed that "Perhaps my eye has aged." His literary tastes, however, had apparently not changed, and Dickens, whom he could quote at length, commanded still his greatest admiration. On one occasion, when Longstreet told him of a letter that Justice Holmes had written Milt Gross about his book, *Nize Baby,* Lewis expressed interest in seeing the letter, and they started to drive to Gross's house; but on the way, Lewis began to recite from Pickwick's trial, and Longstreet stopped the car at Rodeo Drive and Olympic Boulevard and parked, while Lewis recited for an hour without pause. They did not get to Gross's. Ernest Hemingway was much on his mind; he spoke contemptuously of Hemingway's women as "dream lays," and deplored his influence on the young. He was particularly tired of young people in stories who, having had a drink, announced that they felt very "fine," and then found it expressive of their condition repeatedly to use the word "balls."

Intermittently the two men would return to their discussions of *The Artist,* and not only now in 1940, but in the next year and the next, when Lewis was again in Hollywood. Finally, in 1943, Longstreet urged Lewis to go ahead and write the novel, but Lewis said that he had lost interest and why didn't Longstreet write it instead? Utilizing the material that they had developed together, much of it Lewis's own, but reversing the original plan to let Philistia triumph, Longstreet wrote the novel, graciously dedicated it to Lewis "In Memory of Many Meetings," and published it as *The Lion at Morning* in 1954.

By the end of April, Lewis had finished what then appeared to him to be a possible version of his play, and it was shipped off to New York to make the rounds of the producers. Arrangements had been settled for his appearance with Marcella Powers in a half-dozen summer theaters ("The new Sothern and Marlowe, or maybe Bill Fields and Mae West," he wrote Raphaelson), and in the middle of May they began a leisurely drive back to the East. In Chicago, they saw his friend Lillian Gish, who was playing in *Life with Father.* Like Miss Gish, he was at that time vigorously opposed to American intervention in the European war and was quite cool toward Franklin D. Roosevelt, his sympathies with the America First people. To Miss Gish he said, "If Dorothy comes out for war, I'll take Madison Square Garden and come out against war." Shortly after that, back at the Lombardy in New York, he was writing his son Wells in this mood: "Your job in a world at war, one that few can do, is to go on writing and thus help to preserve sanity," an observation that echoes one of the closing sentiments of *Bethel Merriday:*

> My only propaganda is against these apologetic actors who say that their work seems insignificant compared with the big events abroad. Now's just the time when every artist has got to take even his tiniest job more seriously than ever, so that civilization may have a chance to go on.

In that novel, too, he had declared that "acting is heightened life," and of course it was this, rather than the more exalted motive, that led him now to prepare for a summer of theatrical activity on the straw hat circuit. He would do two plays, *Ah,Wilderness!* and *Shadow and Substance,* opening as the guest star in the first of these, again in the role of Nat Miller, in Cheryl Crawford's Maplewood, New Jersey, theater on June 24, Marcella Powers playing Muriel McComber. Robert Van Gelder observed him at the rehearsal hall in West 46th Street, working diligently and earnestly, showing a humble eagerness to be taught. His play script was covered with markings in a variety of colors to guide him in gesture and inflection, and some of the print had been rubbed away with use. While other members of the company were still rehearsing with their scripts, Lewis's was in his pocket; he knew the entire play.

With Van Gelder, he chatted about the pleasures of acting, made again the observation that writing was "a lonely business," told how difficult it was for an early riser such as he to adjust his hours to those of actors, habitual late risers, and kept nervously pulling out his watch to see if it was not yet time to go to rehearsal. He brought up Thomas Wolfe, who was now dead, and whose posthumous novel, *You Can't Go Home Again,* in which Lewis appears as the drunken Lloyd "Knuckles" McHarg, had recently been published. He objected mildly to the nickname that Wolfe had given him and, putting his hand beside Van Gelder's, showed that his knuckles were not in the least large. Mildly, too, he objected to the twenty-three-hours-a-day drinking in which Wolfe had him indulge. But he showed no bitterness. Indeed, when Edward Aswell, editing the novel at Harper, had asked him to read proof of it before publication lest he object to the portrait after publication, he said, "Go ahead. If that's the way Tom said it was, go ahead." And to Van Gelder, on that morning before a rehearsal, he added only, "Writers kid themselves—about themselves and other people."

Ah, Wilderness! ran its week at Maplewood. There was a week's rest and further rehearsals, and then they opened in *Shadow and Substance* at Stony Creek, Connecticut, on July 8; another week's rest, and *Ah, Wilder-*

ness! again, now at Clinton in the week of July 22; without any pause, then, *Shadow and Substance* again, now with the Guy Palmerton Players at the Lake Whalom Theater outside Fitchburg, Massachusetts; then, three days in mid-August with *Ah, Wilderness!* and three more with *Shadow and Substance* at Woodstock, New York; and, finally, *Ah, Wilderness!* once more during the first week of September at Ogunquit.

To Stony Creek came a letter from Booth Tarkington, on whose American Academy Committee for the Howells Medal Lewis had asked to serve, and now he was asked in turn to submit the names of a few writers "whose work would not be repugnant to Mr. Howells." An odd academic intrusion into "heightened life"! Even more academic and hardly less surprising was his encounter at Saybrook, while Lewis was at nearby Clinton, with Norman Foerster, the professor of American literature at the State University of Iowa. Joseph, wearing blue serge and a chauffeur's cap, drove the Master to Saybrook in a limousine one day. Foerster later recalled the episode:

> . . . we sat on the veranda of The Riversea while he drank plain soda water —he explained that he had been on the water wagon for several years. I told him I much wanted him to come to the University of Iowa to help our graduate students in creative writing.

And Lewis, surprisingly, was interested. From Woodstock he accepted Foerster's tentative invitation enthusiastically, and immediately took up the mundane problems. Could Foerster find a large house in Iowa City with four bedrooms (four "master bedrooms," he always said) and another for his "chauffeur-handyman" at not more than two hundred and fifty dollars a month?

> I think I would have no other requests—oh yes, one: some suave and crafty person to convey the really shaking news that though I love watching others drink, I myself have been a complete tee-totaller for three years, so that I have barred myself from all the really rarefied hobohemian circles.

Foerster reported the matter to his dean, George D. Stoddard, who was delighted, but the acting president of the university, C. A. Phillips, objected on the grounds of Lewis's reputation as a drunkard and turned the matter over to the Iowa State Board of Education, which denied the appointment, and Lewis, back in New York by then, was outraged.

There was a pleasant encounter with his old friend Allan Updegraff, whom he had not seen in years, in Woodstock, where Updegraff lived in the summers, and while he did not take to Lewis's young companion, he enjoyed the renewed friendship with Lewis when he had the two to dinner. It was to prove to be their last meeting. A few years later, from Duluth, Lewis sent Updegraff a newspaper clipping in which he reminisced about their life together in New York in 1907, telling how Updegraff had gone off "to the breadfruit islands to eat the breadfruit that fell into his lap."

This angered Updegraff, even after all that stretch of time, and he wrote sharply to Lewis, saying that he knew damned well how it had really been, how Updegraff had been sick with malaria, without a penny, and how the girl, presently jilted by Lewis, gave him twenty dollars so that he could leave New York, and how he returned then to marry her. In the wrong, Lewis "clammed up," as he always did when he was in the wrong, especially, Updegraff remembered, with him. And a little later, sorry that he had let such a dusty trifle disturb their new harmony, Updegraff wrote Lewis to tell him so, but he had no reply, then or ever.*

Back in New York, Lewis wrote Norman Foerster in indignation, and on September 12 he decided to be indignant with his publishers as well. To Nelson Doubleday went an angry letter severing their relations:

> ... you have not the slightest interest in me, nor in my novels as anything more than items on your sales list. All this past year I have felt as though I had no publisher at all.

The fact was that Harry Maule, Lewis's editor and old friend, had gone to Random House, and he was taking Lewis with him. Before the month was out, a news release from his new publishers announced that he had come to them with a novel tentatively called *The Quiet Mind* (a few notes and an idea only) and that the novelist's play, *Felicia Speaking,* was being "readied" for Broadway. The play had been shown to a number of producers, and in mid-July the New York *Times* had announced that it was being read by "two feminine stars" ("There is a minor role the author could play should he so desire"), but it was clear by September that it would have no takers in its present form.

He had, in the meantime, published a story, "Is This a Dagger—So What?" in *This Week* that combined his old interest in the theater and his new interest in the academic life. Another Matt Carnival story, it is a farcical affair in which Matt, unemployed, takes over the part of Macbeth in a troupe of amateurs playing in P. J. Bowthorpe College. His acting so impresses the authorities that they offer him a professorship for a semester, during which he will present Shakespeare's plays. He accepts in the belief that anyone can be a professor, but when he is given some inkling of the kind of learning he is presumed to have, he flees from the place and takes a more suitable job as a comic in burlesque. The flight of Matt Carnival from Bowthorpe College was to prove in some ways prophetic.

Before this prophecy was to be enacted, he wrote three more stories —two of them still concerned with the stage. One, called "Fellow Trouper,"

* This is the recollection of Allan Updegraff himself as he reported it to me in Paris in 1953. The evidence of Lewis's engagement book for 1942 suggests that there was at least one more meeting: on February 1, the entry reads simply "Updegraffs"; on February 7, "Call Updegraff"; on February 8, "Updegraff?" and on February 15, "Allan—Dora." Dora Miller was Mrs. Updegraff.

also to be published in *This Week,* is another Matt and Millie Carnival story, concerned again with the difference between the dedicated and modest professional and the pretentious and arrogant amateur. The story may well reflect Lewis's annoyance with the intrusion in New Orleans of frivolous "society" people into what he rather too solemnly regarded as his professional domain. The same feeling underlies the other of these two stories, "They Had Magic Then," which appeared in *Liberty* in the next September and is about the return to the stage of a great old actress, one Lily Layton, who shows the young people in a summer theater a thing or two about acting and trouping.

The third story, "The Man Who Cheated Time," written for the March *Good Housekeeping,* is quite different from these anecdotal bits about the theater and is rather better. A man with an extraordinarily exact sense of time observes that the hands of the time clock in a football stadium move backward as they mark the minutes and the seconds up to the end of the game. He has a vision, then, of such a clock, but with six hands—one for the month, another for the week, another for the day, the hour, the minute, the second—all moving backward, and he is convinced that when all those hands come together in exactly two months, eight weeks, and a certain number of days, hours, minutes, and seconds, he will die. When he lives through the predicted moment, he finds himself free of time, and therefore free.

> I know now that I don't know what's going to happen, or when the end will come; so I have all of eternity to do whatever I want to. I have all of eternity, every day. That's all I know—that's all I want to know.

Whatever the virtues of this story, it is nearly as contrived as the Carnival stories. He could write these things almost without effort, and he had written so many of them over the years that it may be assumed that it would have been almost as easy for him to tell ambitious young writers how to perform these tricks. The curious fact is that he was not interested in teaching this sort of thing; but he was interested in teaching.

He had been more than merely tempted by Norman Foerster's proposal that he teach and he had been challenged by the Iowa administrators' refusal of his talent. On September 14 Leonard Lyons reported that Lewis was returning to the Midwest, and, indeed, bundling up his play, he left New York on about that day in search of a teaching position that would prove to Iowa that it was wrong.

He drove first to Olivet, Michigan. The president of Olivet College was Joseph Brewer, whom Lewis had known casually in London some years before, and Brewer had established Ford Madox Ford as writer-in-residence at Olivet. But Ford had died in 1939, and Brewer had written

Lewis with the suggestion that he take his place, and now Lewis remembered. He spent a night with Brewer and next morning met a group of students with literary ambitions whom Brewer had hastily assembled. That afternoon he decided not to come to Olivet; he felt that he was "too high-powered" for the students, that their problems were still too elementary for his patience, and that what he could help them with—the last stages of amateur standing—they were not yet ready for. But there was the University of Minnesota, larger, with graduate students— He drove on.

He drove to Madison, Wisconsin, where he arrived on September 23, and he called his old acquaintance the scholar-poet William Ellery Leonard. Leonard arranged a lunch next day with members of the department of English in the University of Wisconsin, and dinner that evening with the president, Clarence A. Dykstra, and presently Lewis was offering his services as "professorial lecturer in English" without salary, to be in residence three or four months in the year. On the following day, the chairman of the English department arranged that a graduate student named Reginald Watters and his wife take Lewis on a tour of the campus. They showed him through the University Theater, which had been designed by Lee Simonson, and to the press he announced that it was "the most beautiful in the world." He predicted fascism in the United States if we became involved in the war and probably if we voted a program of conscription. He asked the Watterses if they could gather some students whom he could take to dinner, and after dinner they all went to the Watterses' apartment and played one of his games—it is supposed that all the participants have entered a lecture late and do not know the subject, and the test is to see how long the speaker can talk in coherent platitudes before anyone can guess what he is talking about. Lewis gave a brilliant and extended performance, liked the group very much and left early next day for Minnesota.

When his friends in the University of Minnesota discovered his new academic interest, he was invited to come there, but the size of Minneapolis discouraged him and he was determined to go to Wisconsin. He visited his brother in Saint Cloud and drove on for a day in Sauk Centre—"very kind and affectionate, but I couldn't remember more than one out of three of now-wrinkled people who came up to me on Main Street and said, 'I bet you don't remember me, Harry!' And all around, prairies like tumbling ocean . . ." So he wrote Miss Powers in New York; and, returning to Madison, he wrote again:

> . . . and a general feeling that it would be dandy to have Uncle Harry come to teach the boys and girls to be novelists. Madison a sweet town—60,000; big enough to buy records, small enough to make country quiet available within a mile; the dome of the State Capitol at one end of town and the University's towers at the other end, and all this on a green peninsula

between two large, blue, bluff-rimmed lakes, and nice keen youngsters, along with older shepherds, in the English Department. I was tempted. (And—later bulletin—I have since done fell, hurray!)

The Board of Regents had approved the appointment "with no pay, no tenure, and no official rank."

This phraseology, unnecessarily blunt, perhaps, offended Lewis, and he was tempted to abandon the plan. To university authorities he complained that the language made him feel that he "wasn't wanted," but after a four-hour conference with the president, the head of the English department, and several other professors, he was persuaded to remain.

On September 30 he rented the largest house that he could find in Madison:

> Already today I have found a house—nearly as good as our Beverly Hills castle minus patio and pool, and just as large, at one third the rent. It's on a curving hillside road, very near the sprawling giant beehive of the university . . . . . but I shan't be able to get into it for two-three days, maybe a week. My real university work doesn't start for over a week, so tomorrow I really settle down to work on a new act. . . .

And from 1712 Summit Avenue, on October 2, he wrote his agent to say that "the above will be my address, till spring . . ."

Joseph, who was in attendance, hired a housekeeper, and Mrs. Watters * became the new secretary after a tryout—she was given several folders of unanswered letters arranged in two groups—those that she was to answer in her own person and sign, and those that she was to answer for him and that he would sign, in either case working out her reply from the notes that he had scribbled on the margins. Having managed this, she was employed. Lewis had, over the years, grown increasingly fond of cats, and the first task of the new secretary was to establish a kitten in residence. Mrs. Watters was to appear at the Summit Avenue house every morning, stay for lunch, and leave in the afternoon whenever the day's work was finished, Lewis in the meantime having had his habitual postluncheon nap. Once she ignored the "Do Not Disturb" sign on his door when a call from New York came just after lunch, and the "haggard apparition in an old dressing gown" who angrily opened the door told her that the sign meant what it said. But this was the only unpleasantness between them. Although he often referred with a kind of longing to John Hersey ("He was so wise, so gentle"), he liked Mrs. Watters too, made her feel that they were friends, and turned their daily lunch into a gala occasion.

The university community was considerably excited. Why was Sinclair Lewis there? It could only be because he planned to write a novel about

* Now Mrs. Lawrence Billwiller, of San Francisco.

academic life with the Wisconsin faculty serving as his guinea pigs. But if he wanted to observe them, then why had he announced that he did not wish to become involved in any extensive social activities? He was, in fact, quite blameless of any ulterior motives, as a letter of October 7 to Miss Powers makes plain enough:

> I have got only a little acquainted with any of the people here . . . . . but the bulk of all the people I like, and I think I shall have some good friendships among them. And after a year and a half of actors, so charming but so unaware of everything in the living world of action or the immortal world of learning, it's pleasant—and just as intimidating—to be again among a surging of teachers . . . . . whose business it is to know and in a casual way to discuss everything in the world!

If then and in the course of his stay he saw little of his academic colleagues or of Madison society, he did, in a moderate way, cultivate a number of persons of artistic bent in the community and established pleasant relationships with them. Among these was John Steuart Curry, the regional painter who was artist-in-residence in the university. There was Gunnar Johansen, occasional pianist with the Pro Arte Quartet and a considerable virtuoso, from whom Lewis decided to take piano lessons. He rented a Steinway, and once a week Johansen came to Summit Avenue to teach him scales and simple exercises, and while he found no talent for the piano in Lewis's agitated, ill-coordinated hands, he grew fond of him, and Lewis of Johansen, to whom he inscribed a novel as follows: "To Gunnar Johansen who has superbly been the Max Gottlieb to my clumsy musical Martin—with much gratitude."

And then there was Samuel Rogers, a professor of French, a good pianist too, and a novelist rather in the James tradition. Lewis took public occasion to praise Rogers's *Dusk at the Grove,* which had won an *Atlantic Monthly* prize; and he brooded about his later novel, *Lucifer in Pine Lake.* "He said he thought it was a good story and wondered why it had not sold better; he had come to the conclusion that it was because of the involved style. . . ." And he went through about twenty pages of the novel, chosen at random, and, with a pencil, made deletions of material, especially of phrases and subordinate clauses, that seemed to him extraneous; and then he wrote in the inside cover of the book, "To Sam Rogers, this copy inscribed by the author-in-reverse." "He did the whole thing so kindly," Mr. Rogers remembered, "that one could not take offense."

If his presence had made some of the faculty uneasy, it excited the literary students, and there was a crush to get into his class. He had announced that he would like the enrollment to be limited to fifteen students and that these would be admitted only after he had read a sample of the writing of each and had conducted an interview, but, under the pressure not only of students but also of eager faculty wives and of aspiring townswomen, he admitted, at last, twenty-two. The class was closed to auditors and to newspaper people, and he directed his students to say nothing to reporters about what went on behind his classroom doors. "This is a workshop, not a circus." The class was to meet for a period of two hours each week when he would lecture on writing and discuss their work in general, and informally on Tuesday evenings at his house, when he would confer with individuals about particular writings, and the group would drink ginger ale and eat cookies.

Each student was either to plan out a novel and begin to write it, or to write a short story of no less than six thousand words. The class discussions were given over largely to the planning of a hypothetical novel never to be written by anyone, a kind of *Mantrap* in plot and locale. These discussions were to serve as the means of bringing to the students' attention, in concrete form, the many real problems that any working novelist must solve. Most of Lewis's advice on writing in general arose from these discussions of the particular. Most of it is familiar advice: the importance of a working title and of names for the characters; the importance of observation, of detail, of a knowledge of one's characters outside the action in which one was showing them; the usefulness of maps and charts; the indispensability of a working schedule; the deplorable tendency of beginners to imitate Hemingway. Some of the advice, however, comes as a surprise: if you want to write for the pulps, study them, but don't try to do any hack writing here, because with that I can't help you; write only to the highest standards, because without nobility, writing is worthless. He brought into his advice his knowledge of New York—the machinery of editorial offices, the uses of a literary agent, the connections between New York and Hollywood. And the students found him always intensely stimulating, almost always helpful.

Everything apparently proceeded satisfactorily. On October 18, he wrote Carl Van Doren about a proposal that he lecture at the University of Hawaii.

> I'd be delighted . . . if or when I do go to Hawaii. I'm here at least till the end of January—end of the first semester—with a rather tenuous connection with the University; once a week I talk to a class or seminar of 22 of the best student writers here, and I read their (rather surprisingly good) efforts at fiction, with no "themes." . . .
>
> Between lectures, I'm rewriting Act III of the play I wrote last winter—it may be produced this year, but it seems a little like backwater to me now—and I have to write one short story, and then into a NEW NOVEL, which I'm planning all this while. And I'm actually taking piano lessons—an old ambition, often thwarted. . . . All this is better than the tearing hours a day of an actor, and almost as new-blood-infusing, for an aged novelist, as the rackets of the theater.

What novel he had been "planning all this while" is not clear, but it was more probably the Negro novel than any other. No novel called *The Quiet Mind* was ever published. The elaborate research for what would in fact be the next novel, *Gideon Planish,* had not yet been started, and "Grand Republic," the site of the novel after that, *Cass Timberlane,* had not yet been discovered. Mrs. Watters's father was a geneticist in the University of Toronto, and Lewis asked her to find out from him whether a man and woman who thought they were white could produce an unmistakably Negro baby. Her father said no and wrote out an account of the principles of genetics that were involved. Lewis, reading this reply, looked unhappy, because there, presumably, went a real crisis in a projected plot.

The letter to Van Doren continues:

> My purpose in being in this particular slice of the country, of course, is to renew my knowledge of the Middle West.... But I'm not sure that I like academic life. I *feel* caution in the air..... and a certain jealousy of old barroom-haunting wastrels like you and me.

The letter concludes with a brief account of the activities of Marcella Powers. She had taken a one-room apartment at the Middletowne on East 48th Street and remained in New York in the hope of finding a part in a play. When, toward the middle of October, she had still had no success, she came to Madison for two weeks to stay with Lewis. The sudden presence of a niece caused some eyebrows to lift, but there was no excitement except among a small group of student actors when Lewis persuaded the director of the University Theater to recast his production of *Stage Door* to the extent of giving Miss Powers the part of Bernice Niemeyer. The play ran for four nights, from October 23 through October 26, and immediately after it closed, she returned to New York. Lewis hoped that Mrs. Carl Van Doren would telephone her. "It's a lonely job, being a 19-year-old Bethel Merriday in NY."

To his secretary he said that come November, he would vote for Wendell Willkie. He had met both Willkie and Franklin Roosevelt, and, while both were "stuffed shirts," the country needed a change. When Mrs. Watters argued with him, he listened to her, but he did not then change his mind. However, when, toward the end of the month, Dorothy Thompson telephoned from New York to ask him to speak on the radio on a country-wide roundup for Roosevelt, he said that he would. He wrote a speech, and he had Mrs. Watters clock him while he rehearsed it over and over. On October 28 he publicly announced his position, and in his radio speech on November 1 he confirmed the announcement, arguing that no man in the world wanted less to be a dictator than Franklin D. Roosevelt. Two days before, he had denied Walter Winchell's report that he had been to Reno "to get a melting from Dorothy Thompson."

There was, however, a sudden divorce from the University of Wisconsin. On November 6, at the fifth of his class meetings, he announced without warning that he was leaving. He had told the class everything that he knew; anything more would be repetition. A day or two before, he had told Samuel Rogers his reasons: he found it hard to concentrate in Madison; he could not settle down; the English department was pretty dull, after all; and he had finished his play. To the press he said only that he was expected in New York to help with its production. And immediately, on November 7, he left Madison, left his enormous house to be occupied rent-free by Mrs. Watters and her husband, and left the administration of the department of English to deal as best it could with the mess that he had made of twenty-two student schedules.

Although Erwin Piscator had wired to express his interest in the play, *Felicia Speaking* found, finally, no producer; and that is not surprising. Apparently taking off from the abandoned *Queenie and the Jopes,* it is "backwater" indeed. The heroine again is an educated, highly effective, and highly articulate woman, this time an archeologist in Yucatan, and her assistant is hopelessly in love with her—hopelessly, because in her busy life there is no room for love. The scene shifts to Zenith, where she is concluding a brilliant lecture tour and where she marries Webster Grout, a local newspaperman. At a dinner party, she lectures her guests throughout, and the second act ends with her leaving Grout (after four months) when he accuses her of being an incurable "boss." In the last act, they iron things out: he is going to run for the governorship of the state; she is going off on another expedition and will do so every six months. This, they agree, is the only way in which two such powerful people as they can manage to live together even part of the time.

In New York, he took the penthouse apartment in the Middletowne, high above his protégée. Here Robert Hutchins saw him in that late autumn for the last time, with Marcella Powers present, smiling a Mona Lisa smile throughout their conversation, adding nothing to it. Really, after this date, Lewis was to have no important relationship other than that with her; he continued, of course, to make and break his endless new and casual connections, but never again would he enjoy sustained rapport with a man of Hutchins's stature.

He had said that he might, before the year was out, return to Madison for a week to see how those novels were coming along, but he did not return. After stanchly refusing to come to the University of Iowa for four days in December, he was prevailed upon by the personal appeal of Grant Wood and Dean Stoddard, and he made the long trip in order once more to read and criticize student manuscripts and to join in their discussions. And once, in May of the following year, he went to Bennington College to address the entire student body on the subject, "How Not to Write Popular

Stories," an important item of advice being to avoid names like Michael and Peter, and to take over William Troy's class, even though Troy, who had other standards than his, was not enthusiastic about this intrusion. In New York, there was constant playgoing with Miss Powers, even as his own play was dying on its rounds, and night clubs afterward. But he was not drinking.

In Wisconsin he had found a certain yeast treatment for his skin, and he had written his doctor, Paul Gross, to say that "Never has my face been so smooth and sound," yet he had also developed a nervous habit that gave the appearance that he was washing his face with his hands, or that he was hiding it. Sonya Levien said that in these later years his very ugliness had become a kind of distinction, and a caricature-portrait by Boardman Robinson which had portrayed him with much exaggerated weakness of chin and bulge of brow, rather bears her out. And yet, only fifty-five years old, he could also look like death itself. Daniel Longwell, who was now an editor on *Life,* was at this time involved in a picture story about "21." When the photographs were developed, the entire group was sent to the owners of "21" for their approval. Among them was a picture of Lewis, looking like an absolute corpse, dining with Marcella Powers, and it was one of the two that the owners of the restaurant said that they would rather not see in print. Longwell then sent that picture to Lewis himself and asked him what he thought of it. He responded rather as he had to Wolfe's literary portrait: "Go ahead. That's the way I look, why not run it?" And the picture was published. He had a quick and angry pride but no real vanity, and yet his face distressed him because he knew that it repelled and shocked others. Like a high-school boy, he was always combing his hair, thinning and faded though it was; and, since Miss Powers had complained of his bad breath, he was always disappearing into bathrooms to gargle with mouthwash.

On December 16 they left New York to spend the holidays in Cuba. The departure was well timed, for they thereby missed the opening, three nights later, of a new play by Edward Chodorov and H. S. Kraft called *Cue for Passion.* Gossip about the play was warning enough: "The characters are said to have been suggested by several persons in the public eye, including a feminine columnist, a novelist with an interest in the theater. . . ." The leading female character is the editor of an influential weekly journal of opinion and is presented in the opening act as highly condescending and patronizing to the celebrated novelist who is her husband and is about to make his debut as an actor. Although he is quite as objectionable as she, the critics found the first act believable. But at the opening of the second act, the husband is murdered, and the play degenerates into a conventional mystery play. Its life on Broadway was short.

In Key West, Lewis and Miss Powers met Ernest Hemingway and his wife, Martha Gellhorn. Each of the men had felt and expressed enough irritation with and even malice toward the other that an amiable first meeting was hardly to be predicted, yet the four of them enjoyed one another's company, and the Hemingways went along to Cuba with Lewis and his companion.

On the ferry to Havana, Hemingway remarked that he and Lewis were not like the cautious dull folk who worry about missing planes and trains and have to get to them early; they arrive dashingly at the last moment. Lewis palely agreed. But he repeated this story many times afterwards; it amused both him and Miss Powers, because it was she who got to trains with only a minute to spare while he would be there an hour early, often before the train had been made up. When Miss Powers was traveling with him, she submitted to his caution, and often found herself waiting for a half hour or more on a cold platform while the porters finished preparing the cars. As for planes—he never took them: they frightened him.

They stayed at the Sevilla-Biltmore, met the dictator Battista, and spent a day at Finca Vigia, the Hemingway establishment at San Francisco de Paulo. Hemingway, dressed in a red turtleneck sweater and white shorts, was boisterously amiable, and Lewis, rather overimpressed by his vigor, was deferential throughout the day. The big event was a game dinner, when any number of woodcock and snipe, all shot by Hemingway's young sons, were served on a platter as large as a coffee table. The sight of the dead little birds in their sauce, all with their legs in the air, revolted Lewis, but in this household he was not disposed to make a scene. He ate some birds.

Late in the next year, Hemingway was to send Lewis a long letter in which he asserted that they understood each other well when they talked, as on that Cuba trip, and that having been with him there had made him feel good for a long time afterward. With that brief encounter, the year came to a happy end, and with the opening of 1941, Lewis and Miss Powers returned to New York.

2

IN MIAMI they had made arrangements that Gant Gaither's stock company there would present *Angela Is Twenty-Two* with Lewis and Miss Powers, that Gaither might try out *Felicia Speaking,* and that Miss Powers would play with his company throughout the season. They returned to New York only to reorganize themselves for this new venture and then, on January 10, began the drive back to Florida. In Miami, their companions were wealthy, vacationing Midwesterners; and, staying first at the Sea Isle Hotel and then at the Lord Tarleton, there was at least as much play as work, although for Lewis play no longer included alcohol. *Felicia Speaking* did not get its tryout, but *Angela* ran through the week of January 20. On the day of its closing, Lewis announced that he would act no more: he was planning a new novel.

The relationship with Marcella Powers was now over a year old and in that time she had come to know her powers in the relationship—his pathetic need of her. It was to be expected that, young as she was, she would look beyond him, who was first a kind of father and then a kind of older brother, for romantic diversion; but what was natural enough for her did not appear so to him, and in Florida, after *Angela* closed and *Felicia* was not to open, he exploded in a rage and abruptly left the company, left Miami, left her. He drove to St. Augustine, where after many years he encountered James Branch Cabell, and Cabell, in *As I Remember It,* recounted the episode:

> . . . Hal Lewis of a sudden appeared in St. Augustine, and . . . among the cluttered and gaudy eighteen-eightyish splendors of the Hotel Ponce de Leon, I passed a far more than saddening evening with him . . . he could talk about nothing whatever consecutively except to tell me over and over again the unhandsome details of how very badly he had been treated by some young actress or another upon whom, throughout the last several months at least, he had centered his affections. She but that week had discarded him, as I remember matters, in Miami; and I found him, in the most kindly terms which I can now think of offhand, to be maudlin over the young so-and-so's ungratefulness after all he had done for and had spent upon her.

It was Cabell's further recollection that Lewis drove on to Jacksonville, that there he addressed the congregation in the Jewish temple, bitterly denouncing American aid to Great Britain, and that later in the day, "he declared he had been swindled out of $160 by a chance acquaintance first encountered there in a wayside tavern, in, as it happened, the barroom. Lewis had the man arrested, and then, overnight, continued his way north without appearing in court against the accused."

The suggestion is that in his bitterness he returned to liquor. Once back in New York, he called Dr. Traeger and told him that he was going to South America and that, never having really known how to drink wine, he wanted to learn now. Dr. Traeger urged him not to, but two days later he was summoned by the management of the Middletowne to say that they were about to put him out of the hotel, that he was smashing the furniture in his apartment. Traeger called Dorothy Lewis, and the two went together to find him very drunk and getting worse, his apartment a shambles, even the treasured Capehart in splintered ruins. Dr. Traeger did what he could —administered paraldehyde, summoned two male nurses to hold him in his wild struggles, finally called an ambulance, got him into a strait jacket, and hauled him off to Doctors Hospital.

The sight of his wife, when he recognized her, enraged him, and in an extraordinary fit he suddenly began to talk to her as though she were he and as though he were she, as he imagined her: "You've ruined your life, you're ruining mine! You've ruined your sons, you miserable creature! You're sick, sick. . . . Can't you take hold of yourself? What's wrong with you anyway? Hal, be your old self, *be* something! Hal, listen please, this is Dorothy! *Hear?*" So screamed Hal, the parodyist, and then insistently demanded a divorce.

In Miami, Marcella Powers presently lost her job and came back to New York. Among the men in New York who paid her their attentions was one of Lewis's few close friends, as old as he and hardly more handsome, but Dr. Traeger believes that later Lewis was somehow led to believe that it was he who had made overtures to her. At any rate, Lewis forgave her for the Miami defection and resumed his protectorship, and for a time the three of them were frequently together, until abruptly Lewis broke with Traeger, and the doctor heard nothing more from him until 1947, when, without mentioning the hiatus, he resumed their friendship. Now, in 1941, he began to attempt an accommodation of Miss Powers's youth: he would urge her to make engagements with young men more nearly her age than his (and, with lonely precision, note in his engagement book that she was occupied), among them, for example, his son Wells, but Wells complained to his mother that he did not want to take her out, that she bored him.*

* Miss Powers and Lewis's first wife met once, at dinner in Peterboro, New Hampshire. When Miss Powers entered the room, Mrs. Casanova walked directly across

And he began to give what he called "children's parties" for her, embarrassing affairs at which he would try to mix with his contemporaries younger people, not only some who were in their late twenties, like Diana Sheean and Molly Costain, but others who were barely twenty, for her. And the young people would sit together and wonder when the endless conversations between their tiresome elders would terminate.

The Sheeans had rented the Lewises' Bronxville house and during a night in the second week of February that house burst into flames. The tenants, with their two small children, escaped being burned to death by leaping from windows, but they did not escape injuries, and the stone house burned to a shell. Gone was the house, as, later that year, the Lewis marriage itself would finally go.

Lewis's importunate demands upon Dorothy Thompson took an odd turn in March, when, possibly moved by his own "A Note on Book Collecting," in which he dilates for the Limited Editions Club upon the pleasures of owning books, he announced to her that he wanted his books. She protested that they did not own things separately, any more than they owned Michael separately, and would he please consider the idea of making up a library list that she would buy for him. He answered coldly and, as he said, "rationally," but her letter, he complained, "was written in a tone of complex self-pity which is impossible to answer. I can only make some suggestions"—and he then listed six points, the fifth of which was as follows:

> I am touched by your picture of spending lonely evenings with [the books]. Yet I am not too much touched, remembering the lonely evenings that *I* spent with them, in Bronxville and on East 90th Street, while you were out, building up a career, and remembering the many solitary times since then when I have wanted to have them.

The matter was dropped and the library remained intact, but the larger matter was not dropped. Early in July Lewis renewed his demands for a divorce:

> Two and a half years ago, in Beverly Hills, I told you that I wanted a divorce. I now want it even more than I did then.
>
> We have not lived together for four and a half years, and there is no chance that we shall ever live together again. I know that it is impossible for me, and I imagine that it is impossible for you, to compose any sort of normal and decent life so long as we are held in this bondage.
>
> As a resident of Vermont, you can get a divorce there, on the grounds of desertion, mental cruelty, or what you please, with speed, ease, and little or no publicity.
>
> You are now the most prominent advocate in the whole country not

---

the room to her and, offering her hand, said, "I understand that you know my son, Wells."

only of Freedom but of generosity to those who differ with us. Are you going to deny your entire faith by holding an unwilling ex-associate?

As for Michael, it will be very much better for him to have a father who, no longer resentful at being deprived of all normal freedom, can begin to associate with him on unstrained and natural terms.

I would like you to do this this summer. We have already had four and a half years to think it over.

He signed that letter "Ever yours"—thoughtlessly, perhaps; but there was an irony here that he could not recognize, the fact that, while she submitted to his clamor at last, he was indeed in some ways to remain ever hers.

She replied at once but not yet in capitulation.

I cannot recall that you ever asked me what I would like, even in the years that we lived together. But what I do not like is a divorce, and I am not going to get one. I know the divorce laws of Vermont, for at one time, I confess, I thought of getting a divorce. It was because of the brutally inconsiderate manner of your treatment of our relationship in your affair with Marcella, even going so far as to introduce her to Wells as his future "stepmother." That filled me with blind rage, and I thought I should spare myself any future insults of this kind. But the very basis of my relationship to you is that I cannot cherish any grudge or feel even normal resentment against you that endures, or that changes my feelings. "This is the way he is," is the only answer I can find. . . .

Hundreds of times, Hal, you made me promise that I would never leave you and never divorce you. I made the promise, because I meant it, and felt so, also. Why should I believe that you meant that and mean this, or that you did not know your own mind then and do know it now? I have never been able to repudiate our marriage, even to myself. Now you ask me to do it publicly. Such a step would be an unbearable self-violation. . . . In a curious way you are asking me to make something between us mutual again—to make common an aversion as once you besought me to make common a love. But I cannot. It is *not* common. The whole case would be an unmitigated fraud. It would not make me free. I shall live with you, in one sense, to the end of my life. . . . Don't you see, Hal, that you are asking *me* to banish *your* resentment? And you ask me, by attempting to blackmail me through the child, knowing how deeply I wish him to have a father. But your relationship to Michael depends upon your feelings for Michael, and nothing *I* do will influence those feelings. Only what you do will influence them. Either you care for him, or you don't. My getting a divorce will not awaken a love in your heart for our child, if it is not there. . . . I still live every day in the crazy illusion that the door will open and you will come back—as though from Bermuda. I know with my merciless intellect that you will not come home, but there are realms outside intelligence and outside logic.

His reply attempts first to shame her into concurrence, then implores:

I shall not continue repeatedly writing to you. Your letter of July 6th makes it obvious that, as usual, you refuse to listen to anyone else. You have become the Supreme Being, and you alone can decide what is right and just.

I had hoped that you really had something of the noble generosity of which you publicly write with such deceptive skill. I had thought you might take some satisfaction in generosity for its own sake. And I still do think so, if you will but see how earnest I am—and have been, these four and a half years.

You say that your highest desire was that "our marriage should be productive—creative." Well, to my powers of creation, it has been disastrous. That is why I want it broken, before it is too tragically late. Do you relish the notion of keeping me lonely and disfranchised, year on year on year, until I die? I'm sure you don't.

I hear you are writing a book about your father. He was gentle, generous, thinking more of how his actions might benefit others than of any satisfaction in being a dictator. But Eliza, your step-mother, was vindictive, self-righteous, certain that whatever she might do was divinely right both for herself and for others, and given to accusing people who differed from her of lacking her superior piety and insight.

Dorothy, you're like him, aren't you, not like Eliza? Come off it, Dorothy. Be the generous, realistic girl you usually are! Forget the very reverend Frank Kingdon's praise of you as a prophetess and be the girl for whom I did every damn thing it was in my power to do. If you get a divorce, life will be a hell of a lot saner for Micky, for me, for you.

I shan't write much. You're too excellent a dialectician for any novelist to argue with. But if you'll listen for it, you'[ll] hear me saying this, earnestly, without rancor, wherever you are ..... whatever you may be writing. Dorothy! Be generous!

Replying on the night before she was flying to England, she refused to be impressed by his fear of her dialectic, and she repeated that while she has always accepted any action that he took, she herself will not take this action.

I shall continue to give you your way. If you wish to divorce me, I shall not contest the suit. I shall keep still. . . . I will not go into court and make a case out against you. I would fight through all courts and through all eternity for the exclusive custody of Michael. That is my only condition.

But I still think that you should come home, under whatever conditions you care to make. I think that out of my knowledge of you. I think you could be happy, if you would get over an attitude that you have built up in your mind. Our marriage was *not* disastrous to your work. On the record, your work has suffered since we separated. I am not suggesting that our marriage was a help to your work. I think your work is independent of anyone else—independent of happiness or misery. You were wretched with Grace and very productive. You have been happy and unproductive, and

> happy and productive. Sometimes one produces out of tension and sometimes out of despair, sometimes wonderfully and sometimes not at all, but you must get over blaming other people, Hal, for your own difficulties. It is unfair and unkind to them, and only complicates your own relations with people.

And, she might have added, "With your real self, which you will never be able to see."

To her "dialectic" he was, of course, impervious, as he was to her common sense, and, at last, recognizing the fact that this would always be the situation, and hoping for that better relationship between the father and his son that the father promised, she capitulated abruptly just four months later.

Lewis, in the meantime, had gone back to work. He had hired a young man named James S. Hart, a former secretary to Governor William H. Vanderbilt of Rhode Island, to collect all manner of materials on philanthropic organizations and on the many propaganda and antipropaganda organizations that, on the eve of entry into the Second World War, flourished in the United States. He renewed his friendship with the Reverend L. M. Birkhead, who was in New York now as the director of one such organization, called Friends of Democracy, Inc., and who gave Lewis useful information about the operations of such groups even while Lewis teased him as a "windmill tilter." (Friends of Democracy, Inc., had been set up in 1936 to study and report on antidemocratic propaganda in the United States.) The frequent visits with Birkhead were to continue until two years later, when this field work, along with a mass of other "research" by both Lewis and Hart, would be consolidated in the novel *Gideon Planish.*

In the meantime, however, Lewis had been thinking of a very different kind of novel and had written a first rough sketch of it. To be called *The Quiet Mind,* the story of a contemplative man, "The complete & continuing Rationalist," who was to be concerned with native "roots," and with the development of a new New England that reasserted Thoreauvian values. Had Lewis been able to write this book, it would have been quite different from any of his others and most strikingly different from the recent novels, with their plea for the dullest values of the American middle class.

The friendship and the correspondence with Mencken had flagged as Lewis brought out one of these "bourgeois" novels after another (Philip Goodman, in some way hurt by both of them, had well before this time disappeared from the company of either), but now it was somewhat haltingly renewed. In March, writing still from the Middletowne, and finished (as he thought) with acting, Lewis told Mencken about the new novel:

> . . . now I am a new man, whitened and purified, and I am just settling down to writing a new novel in which the chief persons to be roasted will

be Great Leaders who stand up on platforms and lead noble causes—any damned kind of causes. (I never realized what amiable fellows and easy to handle were Bruce Barton and Dale Carnegie until the new crop of Saviours of Democracy came along.)

The project was, of course, precisely the sort that would, at that point in history, have most delighted Mencken:

> The news of the new book is swell news indeed, and I needn't tell you that my prayers follow it. . . . God knows the quacks who now afflict this great Republic deserve to be embalmed. No more impudent scoundrels have ever been seen on earth. We must sit down at some time in the near future and discuss the sorrows of the world. Like most other sorrows, they seem to be rather amusing to a man who does not share them. I am in the happy position of not caring a damn what happens.

In some ways, Lewis shared Mencken's mood of "not caring a damn," and in that mood he could parody without discrimination all organized efforts on behalf of the public welfare and, indeed, public-spiritedness itself. In his mean gallery he would ungratefully include a lampoon of his second wife under the rubric of "the Talking Woman." But in other ways he did care what happened. If in 1941 Dorothy Thompson had become one of the most vocal supporters of American aid to Great Britain, Lewis himself became a member of the America First Committee. Like many another misguided pacifist (although few responsible people were left in the movement at this late date) he saw America First as a means to the preservation of peace for the United States and to the shortening of the war in Europe. As the subject or even the background of a novel, war never interested him; "pure culture," he told Dr. Paul Gross, must go on in spite of war.

It was not on behalf of pure culture, one may presume, that in this spring he joined in a project developed by George Macy called the Readers Club, a book selection club with four judges—Clifton Fadiman, Carl Van Doren, Alexander Woollcott, and Lewis—who were responsible for the publication, each month, of some worthy book that had not in its first publication had the reception it deserved. The judges held monthly meetings at which they discussed these choices and farmed out the prefaces among themselves. In his two years with the club, Lewis was to write such prefaces for eight books and, after Woollcott's death, to make his contribution to the anthology called *The Three Readers*.

While Van Doren and Fadiman chose a wide variety of short selections for their sections of this book, Lewis included finally two novelettes—Eleanor Green's *The Hill* and Ruth Suckow's *Country People*. His choice of these works is characteristic of his choices in general—he was always quite personal, always urging selections by writers whom he wanted to help. Thus, for example, he urged the republication of Ramon Guthrie's *Marca-*

bran, and he repeatedly brought to the attention of his fellows the now forgotten novel by Edith Summers Kelley called *Weeds.* When another judge urged *The Counterfeiters,* he wrote that he found it "a complete mess; a distasteful stew of homosexualism, pretentious psychology, Oscar Wilde, and perverted Balzac. No." When a scheme was developed to add Somerset Maugham, André Maurois and Thomas Mann to the panel for the selection of one hundred "best books," he opposed it.

> Maugham by himself might be fine, if he could ever be pinned down to actual choices, but Thomas Mann has become such a Messiah that you might as well try to invite in the Trinity (or even Dorothy Thompson, Harry Luce, and Ralph Ingersoll, if you feel the Trinity is now a little old-fashioned.)

It is not surprising, even though he had only recently held such a dim view of Hemingway, that he should now have spoken vigorously in his behalf; for in the interim, there had been that pleasant personal encounter. Of *The Sun Also Rises* he wrote:

> This was the first of the three great novels which have—along with his minor yet still magnificent work—revealed Hemingway as one of the few truly important and almost savagely individual authors living.

To John Marquand, Lewis said in this year that Hemingway was permanently immature, a man who really did not know what the world was like (together, Lewis and Miss Powers called him "everybody's little boy"), but he recognized his powerful fictional talent.

Later in that year, when the directors of the Limited Editions Club asked Lewis to serve on a jury with Clifton Fadiman and Sterling North to name the novel most deserving of a gold medal that it wished to award, Lewis was instrumental in obtaining the medal for Hemingway and his novel of 1940, *For Whom the Bell Tolls.* The medal was to be presented at a special luncheon in November, and Lewis wrote Hemingway to tell him of the award and to invite him to New York for the luncheon. Hemingway replied graciously but declined to come to New York on the grounds that he had promised a trip to the Southwest to his wife, without whom he could not have written the novel at all, and Martha Gellhorn likewise wrote to thank him. Maxwell Perkins, Hemingway's publisher, accepted the medal in his place, and Lewis made the presentation address. Hemingway, he said, ranked with the half-dozen greatest living novelists, with "that foggy giant, Dreiser, with Cather, that cool, gray genius, with Maugham, Wells and Jules Romains." When, in the following year, the Limited Editions Club published a special edition of Hemingway's novel, Lewis rewrote his luncheon observations as an introduction to it, and now he found that Hemingway was "a lone scarred tree, for the lightning of living has hit him."

For an older friend than Hemingway, Lewis tried to do a different kind of favor in the spring of 1941. William Rose Benét's publishers asked him to read the galleys of *The Dust Which Is God,* that curious document written in a kind of bastard poetry and recording among much else impressions of Larry Harris, Sinclair Lewis in his gawky young manhood. In his reader's report to Dodd, Mead & Company, he urged a good deal of cutting because so much of it was not poetry at all, and he put a section of one galley into prose to show that it was not. "Do beg Bill to make more cuts—perhaps with the aid of suggestions from some critic of the standing of Van Wyck Brooks or Edmund Wilson or Mark Van Doren."

Brooks was on his mind because he had just read *New England: Indian Summer;* and, having read it, he told Brooks that it had impelled him to seek his "roots" in Connecticut, home of his forebears. He was always urging young writers to remain where their roots were, and his sporadic returns to the Middle West were always made half in the expectation of reestablishing himself there. But somehow the Middle West was never quite what it should have been; perhaps Connecticut would prove more congenial. In March and early April he made excursions into Connecticut in search of a house, and in April he found a place at Lakeville, in the northwest corner of the state. On May 8, a day after a luncheon at the American Academy, of which he was an earnest member, he moved to Lakeville for the summer, and to Connecticut, hopefully, for good.

That was on a Thursday, and immediately, on the following Saturday, came the first of a whole stream of house guests: Dr. Traeger and Miss Powers. Miss Powers, suffering from a throat infection, remained briefly in the hospital to recover from a tonsillectomy, but on the following weekend nevertheless arrived Edith Haggard and Harrison Smith. In the middle of the next week, Miss Powers brought her mother, and in a few days Dr. Traeger returned to join the party. There were frequent motor trips into the countryside and, when Wells Lewis arrived in June, a considerable excursion. Leonard Lyons reported that Lewis was looking for a farm, and quoted him as having said, "Everyone ought to have a home to get away from." (In *The Prodigal Parents,* Fred Cornplow reflected, "It seems to me now that it isn't going where you want to that is freedom, but knowing that you can go.")

Early in the summer he wrote another of his autobiographical sketches, this in the form of his own obituary, called "The Death of Arrowsmith," published in *Coronet* in July, but having, in fact, to do with Lewis's own search for "roots" rather than with Arrowsmith. Ostensibly writing in 1971, he shows himself as, for many years, settled in a "small country-place in Northwestern Connecticut" such as he was now occupying at Lakeville.

> It was natural . . . that he should have settled in Connecticut, being weary of travel and of what he himself once called . . . "the chronic wanderer's

discovery that he is everywhere such an Outsider that no one will listen to him even when he kicks about the taxes and the beer. . . ."

Briefly, the quiet country life seemed to be what he wanted, and he wrote a story called "Manhattan Madness" (it appeared in *The American Magazine* in September) that deplored the coldness and the cruelty and the grim snobbery of café society. He enjoyed a few of his country neighbors —Julian Street, the novelist; Gerald Cornell, an actor who had been with the play *Abe Lincoln of Illinois* during its long Broadway run; and one or two others—but he found no farm to buy and his Manhattan friends (including George Jean Nathan and Julie Haydon) continued to punctuate his quiet.

Miss Powers was acting with the Stony Creek Players on the Connecticut shore and, still early in the summer, Lewis let himself be persuaded to join the company for a week in the John Barrymore role in the Turney and Horwin play, *My Dear Children*. The week of July 14 he spent in rehearsals at Stony Creek, and in the following week he acted again. But this, he announced through Leonard Lyons, was "his farewell appearance. . . . Anything beyond this would be anticlimactic. I will have done what Barrymore did—while John has yet to write a book." And yet he did not stay at Lakeville for long. In late August he returned to Stony Creek to supervise a production of *Angela Is Twenty-Two* and at the same time to undertake the direction of a new play, Jack T. Levin's *The Good Neighbor*—"with a grand part for Marcella in it." That play ran for the week beginning September 2, and when the play closed he returned to Lakeville only to move out of his house. ". . . it is the End of Summer," he wrote Dale Warren, "and I soon head back for Sardi's." At the Warwick, tentatively and briefly, he unpacked his belongings.

In the spring he had arranged with his old acquaintance Rabbi Lewis Browne to make an extended tour on which the two would debate informally on a number of topics; but before this excursion was to take place, a headier experience lay before him. He decided to back as well as direct a Broadway production of *The Good Neighbor*. Not only did the play have the substantial part of Hildie for Miss Powers, it also was written around a theme that interested Lewis—the undemocratic treatment of racial minority groups within a democracy. The play had its tryout at Ford's Theater, in Baltimore, in mid-October, and Mencken was presented to the young actress. On Sunday, October 19, Lewis prefaced the Broadway opening with an article in the New York *Times* called "Novelist Bites Art"—on "the joys of directing," and the play opened at the Windsor Theater on October 21. And closed. Father Edward F. Murphy from New Orleans was in town, and Lewis persuaded him to come to the performance and then to a party at his hotel afterwards, where the priest met Sylvia Sidney, Luther Adler, Dudley Digges, Samson Raphaelson, Dr. Traeger, and others—all very gay until a bellhop brought in the early edition of the morning newspapers. The critics were unanimous in finding the play "immensely dull."

> I was with him the following night and wished that I wasn't. We walked on Broadway, and as we approached the theater of *The Good Neighbor,* so alive only twenty minutes before, we saw comparative death. The foyer did not have a single light on, and not a customer was standing at the box office. We turned into the stage alley, which smelled of decay, and the members of the cast were hovering there like ghosts. Thanking them for having tried to make something out of nothing, he paid them off, his hand trembling a little. He had had far more success than most men of his time, but wasn't this now only making failure the harder to bear? I looked up at the stars over Broadway, all the bigger and brighter to me for the dreary well of an alley which served as a kind of telescope, and hoped that he would look up too. But he did not.

Of the critics, Lewis was quoted as saying, "They were right. When you get that universally, there is no use fighting it." The failure had cost him $26,227.79.

Lewis's lecture agency had let it be known so early as mid-summer that one of the topics of the Browne-Lewis debates would be "Has the Modern Woman Made Good?" and on this topic Lewis was to argue the negative. On November 12, his wife "made good" to the extent of acting against her better judgment and filing suit for the divorce that he had so long wanted. To his son Wells he wrote that the break had been made only after "five years of the closest and most worried contemplation of this step," and, in answer to an obvious question, said that he did not think that he would marry again.

Other topics that Browne would debate with Lewis were "The Country [Lewis] versus the City [Browne]," "Machines [Browne] versus No Machines [Lewis]," and "Can Fascism Happen Here?"—Lewis: no; Browne: yes. On November 17, they debated in Newark; on November 18, in Syracuse; and on November 19, on the subject of Modern Woman, in Town Hall, in New York. Almost the only area in which modern women were successful, Lewis argued, was writing, and, with Willa Cather, Ellen Glasgow, Edith Wharton, Claire Booth and Anne Lindbergh, he included Dorothy Thompson as an example of feminine triumph.

On November 25 they left New York for two months. There were debates in Canton, Ann Arbor, Dayton and Olivet, where he stayed for three days. To Miss Powers he wrote, "I don't think I could stand *any* college. The faculty is always so pint-sized and barnyard-minded. . . ." In Cincinnati, where he remained for a week, he wrote an introduction to Bruno Frank's *Days of the King* for the Readers Club, caught up on some back reading for that organization, and began "to plan THE play, the preacher and granddaughter play." From Cincinnati he went to Texas, and from Texas to Los

Angeles, and by the end of the year he was established in the Beverly Hills Hotel where he planned to remain until January 8, when he would go north to Portland and then east again to Minneapolis. In the meantime, Pearl Harbor had been bombarded and the United States was at war. Blackouts on the Pacific Coast deprived the residents of both San Diego and San Francisco, where the debates were canceled, of the Browne-Lewis platform wisdom, and Lewis wrote to his old California friend, Benét, "Here I am in California so much more plush-lined than ours was . . . reading *The Dust Which Is God.* . . . It has such great beauty & life, Bill; I'm proud to be in it. . . ."

On January 2, Dorothy Thompson obtained her divorce decree. Dr. Traeger, the only witness in the courtroom of Woodstock, Vermont, testified that on several occasions he had heard Mr. Lewis say that he did not want to live with his wife. The court observed that provision for the support of Michael Lewis through trustees had been arranged, and ordered that Mr. Lewis was not to remarry within the next two years. Twin Farms and the custody of their son were hers. Freedom was his. He had ended his letter to Benét by saying, "I have no address but my agent's. . . ."

The first day of the new year he spent with Lewis Browne in attending various church services, "winding up just before midnight at Amy McPherson's, where that gay and lovely evangelical nun, in white with a scarlet stole and a crimson cross on her somewhat secular breast, greeted the New Year first with a hell of a sales talk to God, and then tooting a red horn!" For a week he lounged about Hollywood, seeing, among others, Sir Cedric Hardwicke, Burgess Meredith, Stella Adler, and, on his last day, January 8, lunching with Charles Chaplin.

> . . . agreeable, easy, gay, friendly, almost boyishly excited about the highbrow realm that he'd like to belong to. His hair is very gray, but thick, and his face doesn't seem over thirty-five or forty, though he must surely be near to sixty. . . . He looked much more inconspicuous than Charlie Chaplin could possibly be—he was far more delightful than a man so famous for so long could ever possibly be.

That evening, with Browne, he took the train for Portland, and there, on January 11, they held their last debate of the tour. Next day he set out for Minneapolis, where he remained for about ten days. He took over a story-writing class in the University of Minnesota for three two-hour sessions, and one day he spent with his brother, who had come down from St. Cloud. "In the meantime I have been meeting a lot of Minnesota faculty —I like them better than the University of Wisconsin bunch by far, worldlier, though equally instructed. . . ." This feeling would lead him presently to attempt once more his compromise with the academic routines.

He was in New York again by the beginning of February and, taking rooms at the Dorset, stayed there until April 6. There was much playgoing with Miss Powers (from the end of 1941 until early 1946, he saved forty-three playbills marked "With M.") but generally these were two uneventful months. In February he visited the New York State Legislature in Albany to absorb "atmosphere" for his new novel (where no such atmosphere appears), and he spent two days in the Harkness Pavilion, where he underwent a "face operation" at the end of March. Dorothy Thompson wrote him, chiding him a little for his neglect of their son.

> You know, my dear, you baited me to get the divorce with the suggestion that once that was over and our separation clear, we might reestablish a friendly relation and a normal one between you and Mikey. How about starting it?

She resents the unnatural air of repudiation that exists between them, their friends' embarrassment at mentioning him, his total absence from their lives. Will he not come in a normal and natural way and be a father? She cannot explain his perpetual absence to the boy. The result was an afternoon between father and son, and an invitation from the father: Michael was to visit him in Minnesota in July or August.

His brief visit in Minneapolis had renewed the perennial notion that he could put down "roots" in his home state, and early in April the gossip columnists were once more announcing that Sinclair Lewis had left for the Middle West to complete his novel there. His secretary and his wife, together with Joseph, followed him by motor. It was to be another establishment. He would prove that indeed you could go home again, and he conducted the experiment intermittently until March 21, 1946, when at last he gave it up as impossible.

With his new resolve he returned to an old habit, the keeping of a journal—"this Minnesota diary," he called it. The journal is a day-by-day account, often very sparse, of his activities. Hardly more subjective than anything else he had ever written, it is largely factual, crammed with accounts of his many motor trips all over the state, with a meticulous record of the weather, with guest lists, with transcriptions of roadside Burma Shave jingles and religious slogans and of inscriptions copied from tombstones, with observations on hotel service, local speech habits, clothing, and manners generally. The journal does not begin auspiciously:

> Arrived from New York at seven A.M. . . . At first sight, Minneapolis is so ugly. Parking lots like scabs. Most buildings are narrow, drab, dirty, flimsy, irregular in relationship to one another—a set of bad teeth. Window frames either bleak or vice versa, over-ornamented. But modern Star-Journal-Trib and Farmers and Mechanics Bank, gray stone and sleek, yet strong, seem suited to a modern city such as Minneapolis should be.
>
> No planning in a public mind—no "soul," such as a mediaeval city—or Litchfield *—or New York has—no style.

* It is said that in the past summer he had found a place in Litchfield that he wished to buy, but that the established residents of that lovely and quiet old Connecticut community in effect blackballed him.

He was not, however, planning to spend the summer in the city, and immediately after consulting with real-estate agents, he began to make excursions into the country—to St. Cloud, to Marine on St. Croix, to Northfield and Faribault, and to Lake Minnetonka, nearer to the Twin Cities than any of these, and there, outside the village of Excelsior, he found the house he liked.

> It is an oldish house, both roomy and comfortable, with a vast porch, on which I'll dine, against the hot weather. It's on the water, and I'll be popping into the lake often—which one does if he doesn't have to jump into the car and go somewhere. I already know, from old days, quite a lot of people on the lake, which is so huge, and has such irregular outlines that it is supposed to have over 300 miles of shore-line. I'll meet as many new people as I want.

From this point he made many motor trips, in all directions, and kept his journal filled with notations on the details of the face of this land, as if he hoped to memorize it. He lectured to the students at Hamline University, in Saint Paul, on "Environments Don't Make Writers," arguing that writers create the environments that they observe, as, to his class, later, he would argue that writers create history. When, at a party, he was asked directly the question about which everyone was wondering— Why, after such a long absence, had he returned?—he tried to explain about roots, and as if somehow to make this notion a reality, he went next day to the cemetery at Elysian and searched out the "humble and hard to find" graves of his paternal grandparents and copied out the inscriptions on their headstones. He was moved by and copied out other inscriptions too. And he conjectured that H. L. Mencken, Lucius Beebe and *The New Yorker* "would find this all very funny."

Touring about among Minnesota towns, he let his mind move into the old Carol Kennicott habits:

> No one has, so far [as] I know, ever tried to make a prairie village which would be secure, beautiful, convenient. It would not have all straight streets, but curved; it would be walled, almost like a mediaeval village, with trees and shrubs—evergreens that would protect it in winter. It would not be ridiculous to think of tunnels, carrying communal heating pipes, connecting houses to schools and arcaded charming shops.

Yet when, on May 17, he returned to Sauk Centre, he seemed to feel none of Carol's old animus. He was returning to give a speech at a church supper on the occasion of the seventy-fifth anniversary of the First Congregational Church, and to Miss Powers he wrote,

> Sauk Centre was a great success; my speech was pretty good and it was pleasant to see a lot of old friends. And let me tell you that they are no

longer the primitive, inhibited, insular people that their fathers were. They have heard all about it.

The matter of "friends" had become something of a problem for him. In his engagement books he began to make lists of his friends in the several communities in which he settled, and presently, when they dropped away, he would put beside their names the proofreader's sign for *delete,* the Greek letter delta. Not long before, in New York, he had complained to Carl Van Doren about the inconstancy of his friends, and Van Doren remarked that it is more blessed to pay calls than to receive them, adding to that observation, another: "One thing you may not know about friendship, Red, is that you have to work at it. . . ." But his gift was not for that kind of "work." On May 26, 1942, he recorded the following:

> At lake, 9 AM, 66, but *seems* chilly, so coldly gray is the lake now, then alternate rain and mist, in which again the lake stretches out without farther shore—a sea. It is one of those damp, warm, suicidal mornings when nobody loves you, when everybody has done you wrong, when you want to go—away.

That evening he went as far away as the campus of the University of Minnesota where he addressed a ladies' literary society on the subject, "Stay West, Young Woman." In the meantime, he was rereading his own novel, *Main Street,* for the first time since its publication, as preparation for a radio script that he had promised to write for the War Savings Staff of the Treasury Department—a script to be called "Main Street Goes to War," an account of a mobilized Gopher Prairie in 1942.*

On June 3 arrived Miss Powers (who had just completed a course in shorthand), bringing her mother. For nearly ten days they relieved his loneliness and were presented to those of the local gentry whom Lewis was seeing—his old friend William McNally, the publisher John Cowles, Pillsburys and Heffelfingers, the Addison Lewises, Alfred Wilson and his wife, Fefe, and Lewis's niece, Virginia, and her friend, Dorothy Bennett, who, like Miss Powers, were "children." The Powers ladies left again on June 12, for Marcella Powers was to play in summer stock at Peterborough, and on that day Lewis wrote to Carl Van Doren to say, "I hope you're safely settled among the pastures, as I am." And he decided presently to stay among them beyond the summer.

On June 23 he began his hunt for a winter house in Minneapolis "after deciding to, not to, to, not to, and *to* stay in Minnesota till Xmas and teach at University." The decision was made in spite of his discontent with the grubby towns, the ugly city, the silly and aggressive women he met at coun-

* The fortunes of this script are a mystery. In the following March, Lewis wrote Washington to inquire whether it had ever been produced; the only answer he had was that the Treasury Department had no record of such a radio script. The carbon of the typescript is among the papers at Yale.

try club parties, the provinciality. "A state like this needs more eccentrics and more Jews," he declared. At the same time, he was being shown the most elegant and expensive and monstrous houses on Minneapolis's most fashionable streets, where, as he observed, the houses were built from fortunes in railroad signals, Moline tractors, Cream of Wheat, and Lavoris.

> Excellent! Can't get the Harris house—he has an offer to rent it two years unfurnished. May take the Wheeler house, 1800 Dupont—not like it so well but save about $1200 in eight months. This can be put down as a typical example of forethought—not being *able* to get more expensive, I don't.

What he found, finally, was the enormous establishment at 1500 Mount Curve Avenue.

Long before he left Lake Minnetonka, he had completed the planning of and the tentative thrusts into *Gideon Planish* and was writing that novel. His secretary had been very helpful in the collection of materials and in the planning stages of the book, but now Lewis became impatient with him and irritated about the amount of money that he had agreed to pay him for a year. He tried to persuade his friend Cowles to take him on his newspaper, but the transfer did not interest the secretary, who held Lewis to his agreement and disappears from the engagement book. The writing of the novel was, of course, Lewis's own and solitary job. On July 9 he wrote:

> . . . day so damp and breathless that it feels like ninety-five; requires resolution to sit at typewriter—though Gid just meeting Peony. But one gets interested in the writing just from going on with it. Till now, I have really just been planning *Planish* and experimenting—with more interest in exploring Minnesota.

If, at the beginning of July he had hardly started writing, by the beginning of August he had nearly completed a first draft:

> I am a novelist again, and rather enjoying it, now that I have laid down no less than 251 lovely pages. In a certain loneliness of being off by oneself writing novels, I do miss the theater and its associations—pleasant or scrappy—like hell. And I do hope to write another play before next year is over; maybe with all the Queenies and Felicias not quite out of my system, and all feeling that I have to rush gone, I'll write a good one.

This period of relatively concentrated work was interrupted by the arrival of his son Michael on August 5. The boy's father had already arranged with friends that their son, David Shiras, was to join the Lewis party on a camping trip.

> *August 9, 1942. . . .* At 5:30 to Gateway Lodge on Hungry Jack Lake, about three miles from Canadian border. Cottage for two boys and Joseph, who seem friendly; small one for me, of which I become fond—so simple, concentrated.
>
> I am badly trained as a parent; conversation of both Micky and David

> wears me out. It is incessant, as we drive or eat. David asks unanswerable questions—when will we get to Gateway, will we like it, will there be fish, if we have a guide, will he be white or Indian, what time will supper be, what will we have to eat, where will we go next.
>
> No questions for Mick: he is too exhibitionist, proud, show-off—and also intelligent and dominant. He lectures without stop on How Indians blaze trails, How much Chinese coolies are paid, How tiresome it is to see Coca-Cola signs along the road (this with a Lucius Beebe sneer), How Marlene Dietrich gets her effects. He is twelve, just a year older than David, and twice as big. Joseph and I in front seat of station wagon bent mutely to the verbal storm. Mick talks as much as either his father or mother, which Christ knows is twice too much.

At Gateway Lodge, where the party remained for about a week, Lewis wrote a story called "All Wives Are Angels" for *Cosmopolitan,* where it would appear in the following February, the first of five works, two of them quite long, for that periodical. It is the first, too, of a series of stories that take a sharply hostile attitude toward women that would find its fullest statement in the novel of 1945, *Cass Timberlane.* The burden of the first of these is that all wives, as demonstrated by one wife and her daughter-in-law, are by nature termagants, but that a knowing husband can deceive them into a pliable grace.

> The old Lyddy had one last scream left in her: "I know it! That's what gripes me! Winnie, you don't realize what sweetness you'll be tricked into. A man like that—to know perfectly well when you're bad, but never play fair and lose his temper. What chance have we got? Come on!"

On the drive back to Excelsior, he developed an idea for another story: "A study of when children make a couple old; when, as the tradition has it, 'keeps them young.' " The articulate Michael had been a considerable trial to his father, as for many years had been the different, more reticent Wells. It is curious that it was only with his own children that Lewis should have felt such uneasiness and irritation. With the children of his friends he was quite different, having, as Dr. Gross thought, a very "sure" feeling for them, and making always what seemed to children themselves—Dr. Gross's, for example, when a few years before he had brought his family to visit Lewis at Ogunquit—a completely genuine expression of interest in their concerns, of sympathy with their problems, of any amount of patience when it was not required. With his own, this was almost never the situation; but, trial that Michael's visit may have been for the father, it was successful for the boy. He had a few more days on Lake Minnetonka, while his father "hurled out," at the urging of his agent, "a 6000 word piece for a motion picture magazine on Hollywood." * Then, on August 21, putting Michael on the train for Chicago, Albany and Vermont, he returned to his novel.

Dorothy Thompson wrote with gratitude:

* "Sinclair Lewis Defends Hollywood," *Motion Picture,* December 1942.

Michael got back looking wonderful and full of talk about all his adventures... and you. He told me at great length about your way of life: that you have coffee at dawn prepared the night before, that you work, lunch, and sleep after lunch, in fact do little except work and rest, all of which, coming from him as a great illumination to me, caused me considerable inward amusement... thanks for all your great kindness. When I scold Mikey, he reminds me that I do it only for my own pleasure and he is remiss only in order to afford me that pleasure. Unquote. Source: His pop.

The "way of life," as, in the last days of August, Lewis drove nearer to the finish of his first draft of *Gideon Planish,* took its toll:

August 27, 1942.... Late evening, ¾ old moon, sharp tree shadows, lites across lake. Mosquitos terrible. Strain from work, hard to go to sleep—hear burglars, dragons, characters.

There was the business, too, of packing for a trip east, of closing one house and arranging that another be opened, of leaving Minnetonka, and then, on August 30, Minneapolis, for Chicago. There, in his new parental mood, he found time briefly to visit his son Wells, a second lieutenant in the United States Army, stationed at Camp Sheridan, before proceeding to Peterborough. New Hampshire, where Marcella Powers was playing in a work called *Quiet Wedding.* That play closing, they returned together to New York, Lewis once more taking rooms at the Dorset. The crowded two weeks that followed included further research among the "philanthrobbers," especially Birkhead and Frank Kingdon, a certain amount of literary business with his publishers and his agents, and evenings with Miss Powers. Then, on September 20, he was packing again, was on the train on the twenty-first, settling in at the Mount Curve house in Minneapolis on the twenty-second, stocking supplies on the twenty-third, "seeing students for writing class" in his office in Folwell Hall on the twenty-fourth, and, at a faculty tea, meeting, among others, Robert Penn Warren, and, at 7:30 that night, entertaining eight friends at dinner.

Warren had just come to Minnesota. Red-haired, too, but twenty years younger than Sinclair Lewis, not yet the author of the novels that were to make his name widely known, he was fresh from the *Southern Review* and possessed a considerable reputation among the *cognoscenti.* Lewis was uncomfortably aware of him among his colleagues.

...four to six, tea for the English Faculty at the "Institute for Continuation Studies." God how I hate desultory crowds. Miss Jackson, poetry teacher. Scotty of the Minneapolis Book Store. Robert Penn Warren, pal with Allen Tate and John Peale Bishop, who don't like me, as ever posed over his pipe, eyes down, listening and nodding as one who quietly knows better.

Since both were teaching writing, since both had even the same nickname, the failure in rapport must have given rise to awkward moments, but they had almost entirely different sets of friends and kept their wary distance, and then warily became friends of a sort themselves.

Among students and the general public, Lewis's name was, of course, the better known, and the fact that he was teaching a class in the university drew even more attention than it had at Wisconsin.

> With weak good nature I have let in too many middle-aged women "Special Adult" students, so I have fifty-two students instead of the twenty or less I should have. But some of the youngsters look good.*

Only the "youngsters" submitted their work to him, and some of them doubted that he actually read it, since their papers were always returned without any editorial suggestions and without observations even on sudden and radical shifts in method and genre.

The weekly class meetings were almost exclusively lectures by Lewis, and their content was not essentially different from that of the talks that he had given in Madison, but there were more of them. The students were almost entirely female in sex (there was, to be sure, a "Mr. Dodge the unwelcome who wanted to talk about phallic symbology") and the account of one of the young women, then named Eva Holmquist,† is characteristic of their response to him. Excerpts from her diary read as follows:

> *October 14, 1942*. . . . He is a most astonishing man, extremely ugly, with his very high and broad forehead tapering down to narrow face to a sharp chin—red scarred complexion—ugly buck teeth, many filled and missing—ugly eyes peering out from over the top of his glasses. He talks like a machinegun, very rapidly, his voice low and harsh, and often breaking into a squeak like a 15 year old boy's. He's a cynic—but definitely—and violent against rules. . . . I haven't enjoyed myself so much for ages. It was superb—funny cynicism—just a riot—and valuable. It's wonderful. . . .
>
> *October 21, 1942*. . . . His face is really terribly scarred, big blotchy red welts all over it. His eyes are a pretty bright blue, but the light lashes don't enhance them any. I noticed several grins today—when he grins he doesn't look ugly any more, in spite of the fact that his teeth are jagged and hang down over his lower lip, or seem to, so that his grin looks a little fiendish. It looks angelic too, though. His mouth is very ugly, too—the upper lip seems almost deformed—it's too short or something. I am beginning to like the guy, however.
>
> *November 4, 1942*. . . . I could have rushed up and hugged him. . . . He's really awfully loveable—because of his wit and because he's so loving himself—in spite of the exterior gruffness, he's simply reeking with love for

* The number of students in his class was at first uncertain. To Carl Van Doren, on October 23, he referred to "my class . . . in which I have to glance at the MSS of 54 students." When he turned in his grades on December 8, there were 29 bona fide students (7 A's, 8 B's, 12 C's, and 2 D's) and 16 "adult special students," a total of 45.

† Now Mrs. Eva H. Smith, of Livermore, California.

that class of his, and for all struggling young writers, and for humanity in general. Even when he's raving wildly about some idiotic rule, or about a stupid question someone has asked him—he still isn't frightening. He's caustic but he's not mean; he's sarcastic and cynical, but he's not vile about it. He's super. I love him.

November 17, 1942. . . . I wish I could adequately describe the loveable impishness of the man.—He calls us his children, and begs us to ask him questions, because in a few weeks more we will have forever lost the opportunity of finding these things out. . . . How can any one man be so extremely ugly, and go so far out of his way to be caustic and say mean things, and still be so downright sweet? It's amazing.

Another of these young women, Edna Louise Larson,* responded, too, to the "sweetness," the spontaneity, and the running wit, yet astutely glimpsed the face within the face.

To me Sinclair Lewis had essentially a cold rather than a warm personality. I think he would have liked to have a warm personality, and went to some trouble to appear to have as evidenced by his apparent desire to inculcate "informalness" among his students and an "informal" atmosphere at his Sunday parties. But . . . there was not much warmth in Sinclair Lewis in spite of his spontaneous wit and frequent acts of generosity.

He was probably the only one who said anything worth remembering at his parties—and he talked only too little—but nevertheless I wondered about the seeming emptiness in him. . . .

Probably many guesses have been made and will continue to be made about the hidden depths of Sinclair Lewis. I don't think they were there. Or if they were, they were hidden from Mr. Lewis too, as well as from the rest of us. . . . I had the impression that he was putting on an "act" for his class; he was always something of an actor even when he was acting at his most natural. Perhaps even his "natural" self was part of the character he presented to the world. Who, then, was Sinclair Lewis? Did he know himself who he was? Or what he stood for?

Every Sunday he was at home to the bona fide members of his class. His "at homes," he announced, would be from five to two o'clock rather than from two to five o'clock. Joseph, in butler's uniform, was in attendance to admit the students and later to serve the cookies and the ginger ale that, now that Lewis himself was again not drinking, were the standard fare. He would use these occasions to take individual students off to his study to discuss their work when he had something to say about it, but generally they were social evenings, with the young women vying for his attention and rather flaunting their charms, the few young men huddled sheepishly together in an uneasy corner. (One of these young women remembers that he would sometimes take her for walks, fumble at her waist and squeeze

* Now Mrs. Edna L. Cunningham of Sacramento, California.

her hand, and that, before he left, he asked her to come back to New York with him as his secretary; she was otherwise engaged.) Music came from the Victrola, Chopin and Beethoven, and everyone talked about Dimitri Mitropoulos, the new conductor of the Minneapolis Symphony. Sometimes there were games, and sometimes Lewis idly toyed with the dial of his radio, switching from station to station. Once when he happened to tune in on a broadcast of Dorothy Thompson's, he said, "Dorothy Thompson is a woman I used to know in New York."

She came to St. Paul to lecture on the evening of October 28, and in the afternoon of that day F. P. Adams was lecturing in the same hall. Grace Flandrau, the St. Paul writer, invited the two lecturers and Lewis to dinner.

> All most friendly and chatty. You would have thought D and I had always been good, warm acquaintances, and certainly never anything more.... She was terribly nice—except just once, just at the end of dinner, when she started to lecture, and her voice rose and rose, and I had a vision of past irritation.

Momentary irritation did not prevent his hearing her more formal lecture after dinner, delivered to an audience of 11,000, nor his putting her on her train after that.

He himself gave occasional public lectures in and near the Twin Cities. He attended the Symphony, watched Rachmaninoff conduct and heard Marian Anderson sing. He lunched once with Governor Stassen at his desk in the state capitol ("a big young chap—thirty-five—who may some day be President"), he loitered about the city room of the Minneapolis *Tribune,* he saw his faculty friends and his wealthy friends—more and more frequently John and Mary Baxter (Baxter was in the insurance business and a Mount Curve neighbor)—and he tried without great success to mix the two (such a mixture, he told his class, was necessary to the cultural health of the community). He worked hard on a condensation of *Bleak House* for the Readers Club in an attempt to extract coherently those portions of it that deal with Inspector Bucket, "the first English fictional detective," and wrote his introduction, only to discover that a similar operation on the novel had been performed and published in the year before.

On November 4 he wrote Miss Powers:

> The pleasantest thing lately was a Sauk Centre party; three couples, all about my age, the wives all SC girls, now living here, complete with amiable business-man husbands. They were smarter than I'd have expected, in good black with white trim; and all smoking cigarettes like sunaguns, and all quite nice. The hostess—her name was Lily, and another was Hildred and a third Kit—brought out some old photographs, and there was me at graduation from high school, fat-faced, eager, supercilious—very much like Mickey now. You wanted to give the lad one small beating, but you were sure he would do well in dentistry or the pulpit.

But pleasant as the occasion may have been, under their names in his engagement book he wrote the word *"Fin."*

He had a Negro housekeeper named Lillian and, with her assistance and Joseph's, he entertained at occasional large parties. To one of these came not only his niece, Virginia Lewis, but also, visiting from St. Cloud, her parents, and a curious thing happened after this party. Everyone had gone but the Lewises, and Mrs. Lewis observed, among all the empty and half-empty bottles that stood on a sideboard, several opened bottles of rum. She had long had an old recipe that called for rum but had never had any rum in her house, and now she asked Lewis whether she could have these remnants. "Take them," he said. She was not a little surprised, after returning to St. Cloud, to receive a bill for the rum.

Virginia Lewis has no memory of her uncle's ever having given her family, even the children, a present. He, who was repeatedly taken in by near strangers, was highly suspicious of being used by those who were close to him. And in the most trivial matters he could be almost compulsively niggardly. John Hersey remembers that when people wrote him, asking if they could send a book for an autograph, he would reply, yes, if they sent along a self-addressed and stamped wrapper for the book's return. If this injunction was not observed, he simply kept the book. When he and Hersey took their country drives, they would stop at roadside places for coffee, which would cost ten cents for the two; but once, in New York, when they stopped in at a Longchamps for coffee, the check was over a dollar, and Hersey observed how outraged Lewis was. He did nothing overt, however, but tipped the waiter and was polite to him; then, on the way out, as they passed a tray of mints, he scooped up an enormous handful and dumped them into his topcoat pocket. This revenge satisfied him.

Yet we must put beside his parsimonious impulses his almost eccentric lack of interest in money. Alfred Harcourt remembered that he would let enormous funds from royalties collect in his account, until (Lewis himself being no businessman) Harcourt would draw up a list of stocks and bonds, give Lewis the money, and send him over to the Guaranty Trust Company to buy what was listed. When Harcourt lamented the fifty thousand dollars that Grace Lewis and Telesforo Casanova had lost for him in 1928, he shrugged. "After all, I haven't been very good to Grace, and after all, all she lost was money. Let's forget it." And when Harcourt every now and then proposed better contractual terms to him, since he was bringing so much money into the firm, he would turn them down on the grounds that he was not interested in scrounging off the firm. If the lavish circumstances in which he liked to live represented small-town ambitions, the broken leases, the quick resales, the expensive moves came from his indifference to money.

In the Mount Curve house, his major energies went not into parties but into his novel. On October 12 he wrote:

Saturday I finished the first draft of my novel. One always feels so much safer so, once it is *caught* and there is no danger of one of those black moments when the story just won't go on.

On October 16, when his class had been going for only a little over three weeks, he wrote Miss Powers again. Plans were changing.

I am sure I shan't stay here so late as Christmas. I am wonderfully comfortable; I like my class and the kids in it. . . .

But I do feel homesick for home—which is, for me, always, I suppose, New York. I *like* a lot of people here, but I swear there isn't one . . . to whom I can really talk as Me. . . . Some day someone is going to ride up on horseback and whisper through his crepe beard that Minneapolis is PROVINCIAL.

If I don't go to New York, I'll go to California. If I don't go to California, I'll stay in Minnesota. If I stay in Minnesota, I won't stay in Minnesota, I'll go to New York, and if I go to California—

I wish you would give me wisdom on this not-too-new topic.

In his journal for November 22 he wrote, "I'll be finished by the end of this week and three weeks from day-before-yesterday . . . I'll be HOME in New York."

The completion of his manuscript coincided with the end of the academic quarter. He met his last class on December 9 in a somewhat less flippant mood than the one that his students had come to regard as characteristic, was rather solemn, "turned," in the phrase of one of the young women, "almost dramatic." His last words to the class were, "In writing as in life, righteousness is permissible. Thank you." And with damp eyes he departed from the classroom, and he departed next day from the city and returned on December 11 to the Dorset and Miss Powers—and to Carl and Harry, Edie and Alan, Saxe and Bennett, Connie and Mel, Irita and Molly and Dinah and Jimmy, Raeph and Dorshka, Hal and Johnny and Kip and all the others, and to the Readers Club and the American Academy of Arts and Letters, to *The Skin of Our Teeth* and a Christmas matinee of *Rosalinda* with Marcella Powers, all with a promise to himself to return to Minnesota in February of the next year.

3

HE DELIVERED his manuscript to Random House before the end of the year, and then he returned to the writing of short stories. Two of these were for *Cosmopolitan* (July and September), and, like "All Wives Are Angels," used a Minneapolis setting (he called it Cornucopia) and its "Agency Hill" set. The first, "Nobody to Write About," characterized a pretentious woman who wants to write. When she is advised to drop the historical romance that she has in mind and to concern herself instead with the people on her own block, she fails to see their worth as people or the drama in their quiet lives. "And those two buzzards. Why, nobody but this Upton Sinclair that wrote *Main Street* and is such a savage satirist could do anything with such folks." The story ends when the husband she finds so dull impulsively boards an early morning train and leaves her.

The second story is a novelette. Called "Green Eyes: A Handbook of Jealousy," it was sold to the films for Ann Sheridan, and has, indeed, a neatly moralistic end that Hollywood found convenient. A young wife is jealous of her husband, chiefly because she has nothing to do, and her jealousy destroys her marriage. She refuses to give her husband the divorce he wants on the grounds that it would "wrong the real you." She goes off to Florida and contemplates marriage to a wealthy Chicagoan until she discovers with horror *his* jealousy of her. Then she returns to her husband with the resolve that she will always henceforth devote herself to some work that will utilize her energies.

A third story, another novelette published in *Good Housekeeping* in August and September, is called "Harri." We cannot be certain how much of this story is Lewis's, since Herbert Mayes found it unpublishable as it was submitted, and ordered someone else to change it.

> It was so incredibly bad that I had it completely rewritten—and not by Lewis; and I went on the theory that if he wanted to sue me for tampering so materially with his work, that any jury would sustain my course of action.

One is safe in supposing that Lewis never reread the story to discover the difference from what he had written; but whatever the difference, the plot unquestionably remains Lewis's. It is the story of an aggressive woman whose impulse to dominate others brings havoc into every life but her own, and it ends with her son and his stepfather resolving to live together in Nevada as they send her off alone to find new worlds to ruin. It is one more preparatory sketch for the rampant wife-badgered male theme that would provide the substance of *Cass Timberlane,* a novel that, coming out of a crisis in Lewis's own life, would prove to be so different from *Gideon Planish.*

The major publishing event of Lewis's life in 1943 was the appearance of *Gideon Planish* on April 19. Written in something like the mood of *Elmer Gantry* if with none of the solidity of that novel, *Gideon Planish* is intended as a satirical exposé of a charlatan and of a host of charlatans who touch his life in the world of organized opinion, many of them then thought to be derived from public figures.*

Whether such conjectures have any worth is a matter not now to be determined, and in general the characters of this novel were observed to be remarkable for their lack of life rather than for their resemblance to persons in life. The protagonist himself, certainly, was an invention, or, like Elmer Gantry, a composite of traits drawn from many persons. More boob than charlatan, Gideon, in his progress from student to professor to dean to lecturer to editor to "organizator," is nevertheless made to carry much of Lewis's own recent experience in the academy, in the theater, on the lecture platform. From this evidence one must conclude that he had developed small sense of the realities of the first. He had already demonstrated his technical knowledge of the second. On the third, and "the sickness of fluency," he is rather eloquent. But before the novel is half finished, the satire has deteriorated into farce, and as new persons are introduced into the narrative, the characterization grows more and more perfunctory, thinner and thinner.

Winifred Homeward, "the Talking Woman," is something less than a cartoon, and not at all funny. This character is only the most obvious of the many personal intrusions made upon the material. On pages 346–348 appear double-column lists of the clichés of public speaking, presented so

* A letter to Lewis from Cuthbert Wright, of Assumption College, Worcester, suggests that the novel is a *roman à clef* and ventures the following identifications of some of the lesser figures:

General Gong, U.S.A.	General [Robert E.] Wood
Leopold Altzeit	Otto Kahn
Otis Cary	Archibald MacLeish
H. Sanderson Sanderson-Smith	[George Sylvester] Viereck
Winifred Homeward	?[Dorothy Thompson]
Monsignor Fish	Monsignor Sheen
Milo Samphire	Vincent Sheean, William L. Shirer, possibly, but probably George Seldes, a "scholar" in his book on the Vatican

abundantly that it is easy enough to understand why Lewis would always win that game he liked to play of the lecturer who for the longest time can conceal his subject by his language. The novel opens with train whistles, closes with ferryboat whistles—traveling, traveling. . . . Elmer Gantry appears as a minor character. In all this gratuitous welter, one is struck by what may well be the best single sentence that Lewis ever wrote: "Somewhere near by she lay in earth, alone."

Some reviewers found the book amusing (the *Manchester Guardian* suggested that the British would find it funnier than would Americans) but most thought it a tired and perfunctory effort. Both Howard M. Jones and George Mayberry remarked on its being "out of date," and Mayberry observed specifically of the colloquial language that it was outmoded by ten years.* *The Atlantic* suggested that "the blame may lie with a world that has moved faster than Mr. Lewis," and a fellow Minnesotan, James Gray, spoke of Lewis as "a groggy old fighter, fumbling his way with a kind of bewildered ferocity through a struggle the basic rules of which he had forgotten." In *The Nation,* Diana Trilling made a shrewd and kindly point:

> There is something personally endearing about Sinclair Lewis as a writer that checks a completely objective estimate of his recent work—a sweetness of temper, perhaps, that comes through everything he writes, or his boyish idealism of which he is so boyishly ashamed.

The best comment, perhaps, came not in a review but in a letter from Lieutenant Wells Lewis, on duty in Tunisia. He had read *Gideon Planish* at one sitting in his jeep,

> and laughed often, loud & maliciously. As a book, it's undoubtedly your best since *Elmer Gantry,* excepting *It Can't Happen Here,* which I still like as well as any. . . . As a social document, I was less happy about it, if only because you didn't include just one decent organization, as contrast & as a representative for the number of honest & productive ones that do exist, or build up Hatch Hewitt or Milo Samphire as people who could have opinions and speak their minds with some sincerity of purpose. Damning anyone who speaks in the Market Place, Patrick Henry, Lincoln, Wilson & Lincoln Steffens apparently included—as the book tacitly seems to do—you rather align yourself with the late Senator Lodge & the Harding "normalcy" group. Also, the attack on Dorothy was unfair, one-sided & pretty damned unkind, even worse than Fran Dodsworth.

The father, running out of ideas for inscriptions, perhaps, as he autographed all his works for the University of Minnesota, wrote: "My most

* The matter of language is especially interesting at this time, because now Lewis was making a considerable point of having to *hear* his prose. His editor at Random House was that man famed among publishers and writers for his kindness, Saxe Commins, and Lewis now demanded that Commins read his manuscripts aloud to him; when his ear told him that something was not phrased correctly, he would then change it.

serious book—therefore, naturally, not taken too seriously." * In the correspondence columns of the *Saturday Review,* a little controversy played for a few brief weeks, a sad reminder of the dead years when a Lewis novel could be calculated to cause an uproar throughout the national and even the international press. This small flurry began with a three-column letter from Adela Rogers St. John, a Hollywood friend, who assured the editor that she had never heard of Howard Mumford Jones and was not interested in his impertinent opinions; more seriously and at equal length, Harry Elmer Barnes defended the novel against Jones's charge that Lewis was outmoded in technique as in thought. Other correspondents came to the reviewer's defense and a number provided the uninformed Mrs. St. John with the Jones biography. Sinclair Lewis was mute.

Several months before the publication of *Gideon Planish* he had decided once more that it was not easy to put down roots and that New York had compelling splendors. He telephoned a rental agency and announced that he wanted an apartment with a view of all the New York bridges and a living room sixty feet long and twenty feet high. The agency had precisely that, a white elephant, the duplex penthouse at 300 Central Park West. Lewis was enchanted with the opulence of the place, with its terraces, its views. He could, to be sure, be flippant about it. On January 26 he wrote to his Minneapolis friend Mary Baxter:

> Addison will tell you that I have taken a gaudy flat, a cross between Elizabeth Arden's Beauty Salon and the horse-stables at Ringling Circus Winter Headquarters: 29 floors up in the air, and commanding a fair view of the Orkney Isles on the East, of Girard Avenue South on the North & West.

With Miss Powers, he called it "Big Intolerable," or "Intolerable Towers," and her more modest apartment in West 54th Street they called "Little Intolerable," and in their correspondence, they used initials to designate these several establishments: B.I., I.T., L.I. The furnishing of Intolerable Towers was, however, a matter of real importance. Now all of Lewis's belongings came out of the storage warehouse, and now morning after morning was devoted to shopping with Miss Powers. The walls were pale gray, the floors of terra-cotta tile, the upholstery mostly dull green, beige, yellow, the woodwork bleached. The drapes were generally rather flamboyant, giant sprays of mimosa against light-gray backgrounds. On the upper floor, the living room, dining room, and a small sitting room with fireplace flowed together without constricting partitions. Below were the bedrooms and the study. Lewis's bedroom, *House Beautiful* reported, "has a corner on simplicity that comes close to being Spartan, and that makes us suspect that he is just naturally one of those rare neat men." In the living room were walls

* It was taken seriously to this extent: the trade edition sold over 50,000 copies, and the reprint edition nearly twice as many.

of glass and great walls of books, but the whole, in spite of his care and Miss Powers's interest,* had about it the uninhabited look that was to characterize his establishments for the rest of his life. "Even hundreds of books can't keep [it] from looking like a stage set," one observer remarked. He had only one servant, a Japanese houseboy, with no secretary living in, and he exulted, he told *Time* magazine in the next year, in this freedom. But,

> Asked how he enjoyed being a bachelor, he said, "I don't really enjoy it. Of course, it has its advantages but nobody really cares what happens to you. . . . Your friends aren't really interested in your troubles. And you know this is a pretty big apartment. It gets lonely sometimes."

It was now that he took up chess as a way of keeping at least one person with him over a long period of time. He was boyishly eager about learning but was slow to learn and never became very good because he was highly unobservant of his opponent's moves. The failure really to observe was his weakness both as a man and as a writer. Yet chess now, like writing for many years, became a compulsion. He would insist that his friends play with him. Miss Powers was only one of the many to spend endless evenings over his chessboard. Thomas Costain was another, and he, like others, remembers how much Lewis hated to lose the game and yet that one could hardly let him win without showing him what move he must make.

The quiet of chess could be supplemented with the noise of parties, and the new apartment was a fine place for parties, Miss Powers presiding. Even at parties he did not drink. Molly Costain heard George Jean Nathan badger him on the matter. "You're not interesting any more, Red, you're dull, you're damn' dull!" he jibed, without effect. Molly Costain came frequently to these affairs. She was employed in the office of Curtis Brown, Lewis's agent, and he was fascinated by her "career"—by the fact that she could live rather charmingly on twenty-five dollars a week, dress attractively, give little dinner parties. He would question her closely on how she budgeted herself, looking, perhaps, for a model for his young protégée; and at Christmas, when he launched on a very unusual bout of rather lavish gift giving to his friends—champagne, fine leather, sports jewelry—he gave Miss Costain the most imaginative gift of all: a case of canned goods. He was apparently acting for the moment on Van Doren's advice as he understood it—"working" at friendship.

Even before he was established in 300 Central Park West, he felt the pull of Minnesota again; and, once he was established, he sent his unlisted telephone number to all his Minnesota friends. When they came to New

* The project of furnishing the apartment was Miss Powers's, and went on for some months. In August, the cost—not including works of art, books, et cetera—was $9,996.96. For her efforts, Miss Powers was ultimately to be given a mink coat, but this was not forthcoming without reminders.

York, they came to 300 Central Park West. The Minnesota painter Adolph Dehn was frequently there. When Lewis met Howard Haycraft, who was about to marry Molly Costain, he glowered at him for a long time until, discovering that he was a Minnesotan, he swept him into his embrace. He challenged him to name the counties of Minnesota, which are arranged in rather symmetrical tiers; Haycraft managed to get through the southernmost tier, but then both he and Lewis stumbled on the second, and Lewis tore him peremptorily away from the dinner party they were attending and sped with him to his apartment where they studied an atlas until both of them had the names in mind, and then they spent a long time examining an enormous map of the state that dominated the study in that place.* The map figures again in an interview held that spring with Oliver Pilat of the New York *Post.* He took Pilat into the study to see the map and he showed him where Sauk Centre was, and then he talked once more about his hatred and his admiration for his father ("... he was completely grim. Nothing had value unless it could be proved. His attitude was almost pure negation. I reacted against everything my father stood for. He never had any fun in life.") and his affection for his stepmother, "a very gentle person."

Just before moving into the new apartment, he decided that he would like to write a piece about Governor Stassen, and in order to work up his materials he went to St. Paul for about a week at the end of February. There he saw all his friends of the year before, spent a good deal of time in and about the state capital and in the State Historical Society chambers, explored St. Paul, and arranged to give a party for Stassen when he would be in New York in March. To this party, which was probably the first formal affair in the new apartment, he invited people experienced in foreign affairs (or so John Gunther remembered), but on Lewis's own guest list appears also the name of Mary Roberts Rinehart, whose qualifications were of another sort.

The connection had been made through Lewis's current interest in radio. The Martin Jones agency had persuaded Lewis to undertake a project that would be called *Sinclair Lewis's American Playhouse*—a thirteen-week series of dramatized short stories, the first of which was to be Mrs. Rinehart's "23½ Hours' Leave." These were, the agency announced, to be stories about the activities of ordinary Americans in a world at war—"Something new in wartime entertainment . . . for wartime American listeners!" The preliminary plans had been made, the stories selected, a sample dramatized, but the project found no sponsor and was not produced.

Other radio projects were more successful. Mrs. Frank E. Taylor—Nan Taylor—was producing radio programs for the Council on Books in

* Judge Timberlane, trying to stay awake in a sleepy courtroom, "plunged into the Counties of Minnesota, all eighty-seven of them, with their several county-seats."

Wartime. Hitler's book-burning had agitated the liberal world and Mrs. Taylor wanted to base a program on that theme. She had not seen Sinclair Lewis since she was a little girl in Crosby, Minnesota, in 1926, but she telephoned him and asked him if he would do it. He shouted "No" over the telephone and asked her what her real name was. She said that her real name was Nan. He said that this was a very important matter—was it her legal name? Yes. Then he replied, "There aren't enough Nells and Nans any more. I *will* do it!"

He made an appointment with her for a day or two later, and when she arrived, she told him about her recollection of him from her childhood. He said, "I was in kind of a fog—that time," and then, reminiscently, "I shouldn't have come to New York ever." They went over the prepared script that she had brought, and he changed it and improved it. It was evening, the servant had apparently gone, the enormous place seemed empty of all but the two of them. He turned out the lights and took her down the winding stair to the lower level while he talked about going back to Minnesota to live. Then he said good night and retreated into the darkness and solitude. In his engagement book he had several times in this spring made the notation, "Cancel lease?" only to strike it out with his pencil.

There were other radio appearances in that spring, once to make an appeal on a war bond drive, twice on *Information Please,* and once on *Invitation to Learning,* when the discussion dealt with Rolvaag's novel *Giants in the Earth.* Clifton Fadiman was much impressed with Lewis's talk at the monthly meetings for the Readers Club.

> Remembering Lewis, one always felt, after we parted, that there had been a dozen men in the room. Behind everything he uttered, whether a mad pun or a long monologue that could have been inserted into one of his better novels, there worked a pressure of personality to which neither Alec nor Carl could lay claim.

Fadiman had developed an idea for a radio program to be called *Conversation* and, acting on his impression of Lewis's verbal energy, invited him to appear on the pilot program; but it was a disaster, since Lewis did not converse, only glanced at this topic or that, or acted, and did not with either technique permit conversation in others; again, no sponsor was forthcoming.

He turned from the mechanics of mass communication to the wisdom of Thoreau. On May 4 he saw John Marquand for the last time and he told him that he was feeling out of touch with all American realities. Was it that his very fame was insulating him from life as it was being lived? He would return to Minnesota and live simply and, in effect, anonymously, and try to reestablish some sort of relationship with the world. His mood was strangely reflective, but there was no self-pity in it, and no egotism, as his talk turned then to admiration for Marquand's novels. His generosity to young writers (and he was very busy in this spring praising on all sides the first novel of Maritta Wolff, whom he did not know, and of a fellow Minnesota writer, Ann Chidester, whom he knew but slightly)—his generosity extended to writers who were established and nearly his contemporaries. He told Marquand that he had reread his three novels, *The Late George Apley, Wickford Point* and *H. M. Pulham, Esq.*, and that he would very much like to write an introduction to a one-volume edition of the three, to be published as a trilogy under the title *North of Grand Central.**

Then Lewis turned the discussion to his dictionary of names for characters in fiction, an enormous list diligently collected over years. He defended the importance of such a catalogue for a novelist, and the importance of a novelist's finding the perfect name for every character. Marquand argued that he could call a character John or Henry or William and that it did not make much difference to what was really in the character; Lewis argued that the name was in some ways everything. But now it was not a personal but a place name that he was looking for, an address that would give him peace. It was not, clearly, 300 Central Park West.

On May 1 he had written Mary Baxter the news that he was coming to Minnesota for two or three months of wandering and exploring, "with plenty of time in Minneapolis." He proposed to arrive "some time before May 20th." With Joseph to drive him, he was impatient to be gone, and, "Bolstered by the complete works of Henry David Thoreau, newly bought," he left New York on May 11. (To a reporter he said that "a reading of Thoreau would explain all.") On May 13, he was enthusiastically telephoning all his Minneapolis friends from the Hotel Nicollet, but on May 14 he was writing Miss Powers,

> I don't just now think I'll stay more than a month. The people here seem all right, but a little thin, a little simple, a little too easily penetrated. . . . My Eerie in Intolerable Towers has *already* spoiled me for the cloying delights of small hotel suites and Lithuanian maids who are putters-away-of-slippers and bounding convention-attenders.

His engagement book for May 20, a Thursday, carries the entry, "To Winona? or planned tour Mpls—St. Paul & Win[ona] on Friday." The next few days are blank in the book, but the journal shows that the drive to Winona and southern Minnesota was made, Thoreau and all, for Winona was on the way to Chicago, and Chicago on the way to New York, and the entry for May 26 reads starkly, "Ret NY."

For about ten days. Then he was off to New England. On June 9 he appeared at the Williams Inn in Williamstown, Massachusetts, and some ladies of the college ventured to speak to him. They told him that a Wil-

* Marquand's publishers were at that point not interested in the project, but the book was indeed published, and published under Lewis's title, later—without an introduction by Lewis.

liamstown resident was a collector of Sinclair Lewis first editions, and Lewis proposed a call on him, Professor Samuel E. Allen. When Lewis saw Allen's collection of his novels, he suggested that he autograph some of them to increase their value. Next day, when Allen came to call on him at the inn, Lewis said that he had not done justice to those books the night before and why did they not go back to Allen's house and autograph some more of them. This they did. Lewis said that he thought the scenery from the Hoosic River north to Bennington the most beautiful in the world, that he would like to buy a farm in the neighborhood, and would Allen walk at least part of the route with him next day. Allen was otherwise engaged, but at the inn Lewis struck up an acquaintance with the Harvard professor of the history of religion, Arthur Darby Nock, more than Lewis's equal in the world of "characters," and these two went off together. That was on June 11, when Lewis was returning to New York, but before leaving he told Allen that he would soon be back.

The engagement book for June 12 holds a single initial: M—the usual designation of Marcella Powers. The next is blank, but it was not blank in the history of these lives: on that day Dorothy Thompson announced her engagement to the painter Maxim Kopf and had at last entered upon an alliance that would bring her happiness twice-earned. Perhaps on the next day, June 14, certainly early in that week, came a long-distance call from Dore Schary in Hollywood, and on June 20, Lewis was giving himself a farewell party for sixteen people. On June 22, Professor Allen received this note:

> Indeed I have been looking forward to returning to Williamstown, and to staying with you, but quite suddenly, rather absurdly, I'm called out to Hollywood for 10 weeks in the movies. But—next year, I hope . . . I enjoyed myself immensely in Williamstown.

On the next day he wrote to his son Wells and to Mary Baxter with the same news of going to work in Hollywood, "in the galley—just a little golden slave!" And on the next day, June 23, with two bags and a trunk packed, he was off. Whether this luggage contained the complete works of Henry David Thoreau is a question.

He had a number of projects in Hollywood, where, after a brief stay at the Ambassador, he established himself at Chateau Marmont, on Sunset Boulevard. He knew William Fadiman, the story editor at Metro-Goldwyn-Mayer, and he was going to try to persuade him that there were kernels for films in three of his recent stories, "Feathers," * "Nobody to Write About" and "Harri." More important, *Gideon Planish* would surely yield up a fascinating scenario, and to that end he prepared for Fadiman a set of

* I have been unable to identify this story, and there is no correspondence about it in the files of Lewis's agent, Curtis Brown, Ltd.

detailed suggestions for a screenplay. These Lewis projects failed, but the major project was Dore Schary's. Schary was writing under contract to Metro, and he was trying to develop an original screenplay which, in the convention of the Western film, would allegorize the events leading up to and into the Second World War. It was to be called *Storm in the West,* it had occurred to him that Sinclair Lewis might be interested in such an idea, and the credit line would read "Screenplay by Sinclair Lewis and Dore Schary, from an original story by Dore Schary." His telephone call had been an invitation to Lewis to come to California to talk over the possibility; Lewis stayed until the work was finished.

He appeared every day at the Schary house, first for discussions, then for writing. He was delighted with Schary, "a charming, literate, & responsible man" who seemed to deny every preconception about the gross Hollywood mogul; and he was pleased with his working conditions, so casual, so relaxed. ("But—I still can't take the movies seriously!" he wrote to Ramon Guthrie.) The story was set in the period of lawless land-grabbing in the old West. They drew a map of the country that vaguely resembled the map of Europe. They established their cast of cattlemen with names analogous to those of Hitler, Mussolini, Goebbels, Goering, Churchill, Stalin, Uncle Sam and his daughter, Pearl [Harbor], and still other characters to represent pre-Hitler Germany, the old Junker class of professional soldiers, France, Czechoslovakia free and Czechoslovakia enslaved, Poland, the dispossessed Church, both Protestant and Catholic, *und so weiter.* Lewis was much concerned with the names of these figures. When Schary suggested Hiller, Lewis was unsatisfied and after a good deal of thought, came up with Hygatt as much nastier in its effect.

Lewis worked with dedication. He arrived promptly at ten o'clock every morning. He was not drinking alcohol, but he drank endless glasses of iced coffee; the only interruption in his working hours were his consequent and constant marches to the toilet. The method of collaboration was somewhat different from that with Lloyd Lewis on *Jayhawker.* Now they would lay out the content and the development of each scene; then Schary would dictate the form, and Lewis would go off and write out the dialogue; then Schary would put his dialogue into script form. Now and then the novelist in Lewis would interfere and the scene would slow down in narration, but he was quick to see the flaw when Schary pointed it out and quick to revise. In a curious way, the play they worked out predicted the actual circumstances of the death of Mussolini and of Hitler: the film representative of the first hung by his boots (from stirrups, to be sure), of the second, consumed in a burning village.

The temperaments of the two men permitted a smooth collaboration, even though Lewis was sometimes irritated by the conditions of film writing.

...I dislike the whole business, and shall probably never write a film again. It is, for me, and I think for most novelists, both too mechanical and too cooperative.... What really bothers me is the taboos—and among them, not the fact that, say, a couple of gunmen couldn't say anything so vile as "damn," but that all really stirring issues, political, racial, biological, must be sidestepped or not even approached.

When the *Herald Tribune* sent Thornton Delehanty to interview Lewis in Schary's presence, Lewis delivered an extended diatribe against Hollywood, apparently in the hope of rousing Schary's ire, but when he refused to take the bait, Lewis reversed himself and held forth at length on the general improvement of the films over those of past years.

The working day was not so long or so strenuous that Lewis was unable to cultivate a flock of new friends. "I do know the most incredible number of nice people," he wrote to Mary Baxter halfway through his Hollywood stay, and his encounters with these "nice people" make up the main substance of his letters to Marcella Powers. Some of them he had already known—the Raphaelsons, Nunnally Johnson, Cedric Hardwicke, Leonard Sillman, Dorothy and Lillian Gish. Katharine Hepburn he had known as a young girl in Hartford twenty years before when he was a friend of her father, but matters were different now and he saw her repeatedly with Spencer Tracy, "who is becoming a very good friend of mine." Among executives were Edgar Selwyn, Ernst Lubitsch, George Cukor. There was Jean Hersholt, another Lewis collector, and Orson Welles, Humphrey Bogart, Bruno Walter, Franz Werfel, John Garfield, Charles Laughton, Hedy Lamarr, John Erskine, Wallace Beery, Anita Loos, Louis Calhern, Richard Whorf, Thomas Mitchell. At a Lubitsch party he met Greta Garbo, and, once he had completed his extended double-take, he entertained her with approximations of the lingo of Swedish immigrants in Minnesota; she listened. At Mary Pickford's he met Hedda Hopper and Lady Mendl.

But the prize of prizes was Miss Pickford's portrait, painted years ago by some wop artist who is great on pearls and silk but pretty thin on human expressions and noses: it was the izzliest art of America.... And it was stuck in a DARKENED room, lighted by a baby spot, and everybody, even including the now respectable Mike Romanoff and Lillian [Gish], who at least has Traveled, came and said, "Oo, isn't it wunnerful!" If my butcher had sent it to me on a calendar, I would have changed butchers.

Shortly after the first evening he spent with Clifford Odets, Odets was to visit Dreiser. "He will say, 'I met Red Lewis—not a bad fellow.' Wednesday morning you will read of a dead playwright." * At a luncheon of George

* Sinclair Lewis would have been astonished had he seen a letter from Dreiser to his publisher, written on May Day, 1942, about the most likely author for a pamphlet on Dreiser's work to be published together with a collected edition:

In regard to the critics who might prepare a booklet, I notice that you mention

Cukor's was the "red hot, yelling like a parrot, witty and intolerably dogmatic, funny and indecent and idiotic, wicked and curiously lovable, just returned to Hollywood like the Second Coming, the one and only TALLULAH" who "spoke of her successor, Miriam Hopkins, with all the long, slow, cloying affection of Mussolini for FDR." But he did not limit his attentions to the famous. He was kind to and interested in a young, unknown free-lance writer named Peter Ruric and others like him. And there were, of course, young women—bit players, extras, stock girls. He treated them with a degree of courtesy and deference to which most of them were not accustomed. Dore Schary observed them and him: their first open horror at his corroded face and palsied person; his easy, outgoing charm and his expressed interest in their problems, as though they were both unique and fascinating; their softening to him until he had won them over as his relaxed companions—the old story. . . .

Still, in spite of the busy days and the gaiety at night, he looked forward from the beginning to his having done with Hollywood. In the next June he was to write as follows:

> It is amazing how much happier I am here [Duluth] than in Hollywood, a year ago, with all its Kate Hepburns and Cedric Hardwickes and Romanoff Restaurants. It's because really working on the novel, I feel justified, tinily triumphant, in life; out there, doing the piffling work on the childish scenario, I felt guilty and irritably bored.

His letters to Marcella Powers are punctuated with reminders to himself and to her that on September 4 he would be finished and that on September 7 he would be back in New York. And he had the comfort of knowing that he would be held in New York for not quite one month: before he had gone to Hollywood, he had arranged with his lecture agent and with Lewis Browne for another two months of debating on tour.

From New York he wrote Dore Schary to inquire about the fate of their scenario, and Schary was able to tell him that because of the studio's political timidity (although the expressed argument was that audiences were tired of the fascist theme) Metro had decided that it could not produce it, that Schary had resigned and had already gone to Selznick, that he had tried

---

> Carl Van Doren and Harry Hansen. I have always thought of Van Doren as a little literary and rather disturbed by rough and tumble life such as we see about us. As for Harry Hansen, I have never thought of him as a really arresting critic. Names that stick in my mind for a job like this are John Steinbeck and Pearl Buck. Burton Rascoe is much too fanciful and likely to remember things that never occurred. Ernest Boyd, if he stopped drinking long enough, would be excellent, for he certainly knows books and life. What's the matter with Sinclair Lewis? The booklet would certainly be read.
>
> I note in connection with the plates of my books that *Tragic America* and *Dreiser Looks at Russia* are left out in the cold. . . .

One cannot fail to remark the juxtaposition of the once offensive name of Lewis and the once offending title in this implausible context.

to buy the script from Metro and take it there, that Metro would not sell it. It was a painful anticlimax. Perhaps the next three weeks in New York, crowded with pleasure and business and preparation for further travels, helped him to forget it.

Thus on October 4 he was off again for the now familiar debates in towns and cities all over the Far and Middle West: Salt Lake, Spokane, Seattle, St. Louis, Kansas City, Dallas, New Orleans, San Antonio, Houston, Iowa City, Minneapolis solely for a party, Eau Claire, Wisconsin—on and on, until November 26, when he was back in New York for two performances at Town Hall on December 2, another in New Rochelle on the next night, and then, from December 7 to December 10, in Endicott, New York, and Toronto, Canada, and the tour was over, and presently he was back in New York and "the still beatitude of 300 Central Park West," where he suffered an attack of influenza.

He had carried on the many trains *Walden, War and Peace* and *The Brothers Karamazov,* the first for his debates in defense of "rusticity," the others as background for his introduction to Turgenev's *Fathers and Sons,* his last piece for the Readers Club, in which he remarks that while parental tyranny has often been the subject of fiction, "there is more drama and pity in the less-often recounted case of the parents' longing to keep their children's friendship and affection." In December he saw his son Michael twice. His son Wells had in the autumn won the Silver Star for "an incident in the Sicilian Campaign," as he had modestly written his father. On Christmas Day, the father wrote to that son, and in the next year, that son was dead in battle.

4

TWICE IN THE YEAR of 1944, once at its beginning and once at its end, he made impressively modest demonstrations of his generosity and of his inability to nurse grudges. Every fifth year the American Academy presents a special award to a distinguished American novelist, and 1944 was such a fifth year. Not only did Sinclair Lewis argue passionately that the award must go to Theodore Dreiser but on January 3 he himself drew up a draft of the letter that offered it to him. In part it read:

> This year, the directors of the Academy have chosen you, not only for the distinction of such books as *The American Tragedy, Sister Carrie, Twelve Men,* and a long line of other volumes, but also for your courage and integrity in breaking trail as a pioneer in the presentation in fiction of real human beings and a real America.

Almost without any change, this letter went to Dreiser over the signature of Walter Damrosch, the president of the Academy. The final letter added a postscript to inform Dreiser that the presentation would be made at the annual ceremonial on May 19, and that it was hoped that he could attend. Well before that date, Lewis had been made vice-president of the National Institute, and he was serving on the awards committee of the American Academy. Persons of such official prestige would normally appear at the annual ceremonies, but Lewis, having won his campaign for Dreiser, was not inclined to risk an appearance at a second banquet with him. By May 19 he was a thousand miles from New York.

Since Lewis's literary judgments were always so whimsical, it is perhaps of no great importance that, having mistaken many a pygmy for a giant he also knew a giant when he saw one; it is of some importance to know that unhappy personal relations did not make *him* a smaller person. His hatreds could be violent—so violent that the very excess suggested their unimportance to him except in some symbolic way, or suggested, even, his deep, inverted affections or desired appeasements. If his hatreds did not very soon wash entirely out of his feelings (as, by the end of this year, an angry outburst at Bernard DeVoto would have) they become a formal part of his "act," an impersonalized bit of recent social or literary history to entertain his friends and anyone else who would listen—as the Dreiser affair had become—something that he would rehearse to himself and try to perfect in his anecdotal repertoire, and something that he could, with or without request, presently perform for anyone, and with an actor's simulation of the original feelings, long gone, and with an actor's pleasure in the simulation.

Time and again, in a pique or a rage, he brought on a social disaster; but he never planned a disaster, and on other occasions than the Dreiser ceremonial dinner at the Academy on May 19, 1944, he did his best to prevent one. The fact is that even in January he was once more dreaming of Minnesota as his true home, and he had written the Baxters to expect him in the spring or summer. He had written, too, to Margaret Culkin Banning, the Duluth novelist whom he knew casually, to ask that she telephone him when she was next in New York. When she came in January, she found him studying books about her city and maps of the Duluth region. On February 8 she came to dinner in Central Park West with the Canbys and Deems Taylor and Marcella Powers, and in spite of a momentary rumpus when she laughed at a little silver carpet sweeper that the maid used to pick up crumbs from the table, a gadget of which he was very proud (it was a gift from Mrs. Powers), the evening went well, with enthusiastic talk about Duluth.

At the end of February, he was writing his Minneapolis friends, "But I warn you that I expect to stay in Duluth," and on March 3, at the suggestion of Mrs. Banning, a Duluth real-estate agent, Kenneth Cant, wrote him, proposing to find him "housing accommodations" for "some three to five people." When Lewis replied he stated his needs: he wanted a large house with a splendid view of Lake Superior and with land around it, a house with three or four "masters' bedrooms, two masters' baths, two servants bedrooms and bath," and he hoped that when he arrived in the middle of May, Cant would have drawn up a list of possibilities.

He was thinking about his next novel, which would be set somewhere near Duluth, but his writing at the end of 1943 and in the early months of 1944 was still confined to finger exercises for that work. "You Seem to Forget," a story for the January 1944 *Cosmopolitan,* is the painfully exaggerated monologue of a pretty, vain and treacherous wife who belabors her kindly husband and betrays his professional confidences. "Midnight Alley," a longer work that took up space in *Cosmopolitan* for both July and August, is the story of a Yale man who tries to escape from an elegant girl who does not like to be kissed in warm weather. He manages a happily anonymous time as a porter in a cheap hotel in a small town (suggesting Lewis's drunken dream that he and John Marquand could disappear into Detroit as waiters in a cheap restaurant), finds that even an old Yale professor whom he encounters can make the same choice of the Open Road, has a flirtation with a waitress in the coffee shop of the hotel, and is overtaken finally by his relentless Park Avenue girl and brought to heel.

Reading through the magazine fiction that Sinclair Lewis was writing, one is impressed again by the almost dogged way in which the impossible dreams become the material for the dream factory, by his unwitting tangling of his own confused feelings about hopes for what is not, with hurts from what is. This fiction, like *Cass Timberlane,* is painful not because it is dull but because of those things in it that are not recognized by the writer. That is why the third magazine piece for 1944, "There's No Excuse for Lateness," an article published by *Good Housekeeping* in May, is a relief: it comes directly from the top of Lewis's mind, from the self-observed surface of his life. The title of the article summarizes its content: to be tardy for an appointment is selfish and arrogant, and important and busy people (Mencken, Adela Rogers St. John, Carl Van Doren, really gifted actors and actresses, Henry David Thoreau, Sinclair Lewis) are always on time. Punctuality was another of his compulsions. His doctors remember how surprising it was to find him always in the outer office at exactly the moment that he was supposed to be there; and expecting that they would be ready for him, at exactly that moment. Shades of the punctilious, sternly gray father! It is a trait that must be associated with Lewis's compulsive neatness.

Dr. Paul Gross was fascinated by the medicine cabinets in Lewis's establishments, every vial and *flacon* and toenail clipper in its proper place; no less tidy were his book shelves (in new books he always inserted the back of the jacket, with the author's biography and face), his collection of phonograph records, his board of house keys, labeled precisely by himself, and, of course, his study, his desk, its drawers. Having thrown away five hundred dollars on drunken friends and new acquaintances in a night club, he could next morning give his attention to the most trivial minutiae of personal possessions. Thomas Costain remembers calling on him in an apartment that he was about to leave, while a menial was making an inventory, and Lewis was considering a small package of rubber bands which became the subject of a long discussion: "Did we bring these? Are these ours? Did you write them down?" He was, in many ways and moods, a housekeeper exacting to the point of insanity.

The editor of *Good Housekeeping* was then Herbert R. Mayes, and Mayes was at this time giving a course of lectures at the Columbia Graduate School of Journalism. On one occasion he took Bennett Cerf and Lewis with him, Cerf to discuss the problems of handling an author like Lewis, Lewis present to dramatize those problems. At one point Lewis made a remark which Cerf followed by saying, "Now what Mr. Lewis means is this—," whereupon Lewis leaped up and quite roughly said, "I don't need

Bennett Cerf or anybody else to explain what I meant. I said what I meant to say, and what I meant I said." It was an alarming moment for Mayes, who knew Lewis's sudden, flying rages (only recently, at the Stork Club, Mayes had witnessed him smash a goblet with a knife over some fancied slight and splatter the table and the company with glass splinters and a shower). At Columbia, however, the audience thought that he was being waggish and laughed appreciatively, and Cerf was able to turn the fit of pique into humorous badinage.

Miss Powers had given up her ambitions for the stage and Lewis's influence with Herbert Mayes enabled her to obtain a small editorial position on *Good Housekeeping*. The item, "M out," occurs with more and more frequency in the engagement book, and, not writing much, he filled his time with reading current novels when he could not find a chess partner. ("I'm mildly insane about it," he wrote to Mrs. Baxter of chess.) His reading proved of use at a dinner meeting of the National Institute on March 13, when he addressed that body on "What the Young Writers Are Up To," and praised the work of Eudora Welty, Jerome Weidman, Walter van Tilburg Clark, Maritta Wolff, Budd Schulberg, George R. Stewart, Charles Jackson, and Marcus Goodrich. With such a diversity of high talent, contemporary literary culture was quite clearly in splendid shape, more than maintaining the great American tradition of critical realism that had flowered after the First World War and through the twenties and thirties. Within only a few weeks, Bernard DeVoto, with shrill rudeness, was to take quite a different position.

The Literary Fallacy, the revised text of six lectures that DeVoto had delivered at the University of Indiana a year before, was a slashing attack, wild and war-inspired, on the irresponsible writing of the 1920s—the critics (notably Van Wyck Brooks), the novelists, the poets. Among the novelists, Sinclair Lewis was made a prominent example (and *Arrowsmith,* which a younger DeVoto had found so great precisely because it *was* so American, the chief specific instance) of the thesis that "Never in any country or any age had writers so misrepresented their culture, never had they been so unanimously wrong." The *Saturday Review* had published the final lecture as a preview to the book, and on April 15 it published Lewis's reply, "Fools, Liars and Mr. DeVoto." Hardly less angry than DeVoto, hardly less shrill, and a good deal more personal, Lewis came to Brooks's defense and assailed DeVoto for his glib generalizing, for his superficiality, and for his own irresponsibility in writing trashy fiction under a hack's pseudonym, "John August." The attack pleased many, for over the years DeVoto's clumsy critical bludgeon had displeased many, and Van Wyck Brooks was not alone in writing Lewis his praise.

> You put that poor devil through such a wringer that you have squeezed tears out of me. It is simply a masterpiece of demolition,—I don't see how he can appear in print again.

Brooks's letter concludes with an appeal to Lewis to help in a concerted effort to draw really first-rate writers into the National Institute and, to that end, to attend a meeting on April 17. He did attend the meeting, but on the same day he reminded himself to "Start Transportatn" arrangements. His mind was elsewhere. Already he had written to Miss Powers, brooding about his duplex: if he is to be in New York at all, he wants to be further downtown; he should probably put his furniture into storage, because he is about to leave for Minnesota and, having lost interest in his apartment, he does not want to return to 300 Central Park West. He did not act on these reflections. Instead of storing his belongings he found in some old file a copy of his long-dead play, *Hobohemia,* and on several days wrote the title into his engagement book, once, "*Hobohemia* to [Alan] Collins," director of the Curtis Brown office. *Angela Is Twenty-Two* had just been released as a film (called *This Is the Life,* it was, according to the *Times,* "a nice winsome, unpretentious show") and perhaps he thought that dusty old *Hobohemia* could be refurbished for the screen. But it sinks out of sight again in the packed files.

On May 5 he left for Minneapolis once more and went again to the Hotel Nicollet. In ten days there he saw all those of his friends whom he wished to see and actively began his research for *Cass Timberlane.* On May 9 he wrote Miss Powers:

> In three days here I have talked to lawyers, two judges, an obstetrician, an Episcopal minister, a banker, the head of the Northwest district of the Federal Reserve Bank, two manufacturers, a newspaper owner. . . . Next week, two days Winona, then Duluth.

And on May 12 he told her that

> All this week I have been hanging around courts, getting really intimate with not only a couple of judges but also bailiffs, shorthand reporters, and lawyers; watching a couple of cases as though they were my own (my hero in new book a judge), and making notes on silly things like: where does the judge keep his rubbers.

He took a bus to Winona on May 15, returned on the next day and, on the day after that, arrived in Duluth where, for a week, he stayed at the Hotel Duluth while he began to look for a house with Kenneth Cant, the first man he telephoned. And now began the cultivation of an entire new set of friends. Two days after he arrived the name of Mark Nolan appears for the first time in the engagement book. Nolan was a circuit judge who was to be of great help to the novelist, and a bluff, convivial fellow besides. Before the week was out, Lewis had found another judge, eighty-eight years old, with whom to play chess. Every morning at ten Lewis made his ritual appearance at Judge Nolan's court. LeRoy Salsich, a wealthy mine owner who was wooing Mrs. Banning, entertained him at his club. Lewis, in turn, entertained Victor Ridder, the owner of the Duluth newspaper, at his hotel—and found another chess partner in his son, one he could, in fact, beat. On May 20, the day that he found a house, he also found a taxi driver, one Asa ("Ace") Lyons, Jr., who was to be his most constant companion, and three days later he met the train of the summoned Lillian, the Negro woman who had been his housekeeper in Minneapolis the year before, and turned his new house over to her to make his rooms, study and bedroom, habitable at once, and find a cook.

It was known as the "old John G. Williams house" and was located at 2601 East Second Street on four landscaped, if now rather overgrown, city lots. It was a "vainglorious" house, Mrs. Banning says, a house in which no one had ever been very happy. When John G. Williams finished building it, he was too old to enjoy it, and his widow and daughter dreaded the kind of social life for which it was designed. The house was sold to a doctor named Webber who presently died. His widow moved away, his son went off to wartime Washington, and the house was left uninhabited, for sale cheap. Roy Salsich was thinking of buying it, and Mrs. Banning told him that if he bought it she would not marry him—a story that did not amuse Lewis when he heard it. For he himself was pleased with the house and in that first summer told Mrs. Banning that he thought he would buy it.

> I remember that we were out on the long terrace, and everything was rundown and shabby, and I protested. I asked, "But why do you want this house?" He said, laughing, "It's the Sauk Centre in me."

To Miss Powers he wrote on May 20:

> This is my proud new address. . . . It is a kind of English manor house; brick; enter a little courtyard; big drawing room, panelled library, furniture rather shabby but most comfortable; five master bedrooms and three baths; couple servants' rooms; in the basement, a jolly foolish miniature bowling alley, and a game room opening right out through French doors on the secluded lawn—wonderful for a summertime buffet supper. There is a fine terrace with a view on one side of the great open lake and on the other out to piney hills to the east (Duluth runs east and west, not north and south, as it somehow should). It's all so quiet, with enough ground to walk about it. . . . On third story, an unfinished vast attic which is the "ballroom" of the newspaper story enclosed. . . . And outside it, a balcony begging to be sunbathed in. . . . I think I shall love my manorial splendor.

He loved Duluth no less, and the extraordinary variations of its weather. On bright days there is an open radiance about this city that seems to emanate as much from the great blue expanse of its fresh-water harbor as from the blue dome of sky shining above its hilltop pines. In and out of the uncluttered port ride great, beautiful freighters loaded with or emptied of grain or ore or coal, and behind them rises the whole blue swell of Lake Superior. There is a curious coalescence here of modern industry and commerce with the untrafficked freedom of the frontier North. Its business streets are as pock-marked and as junky as those of any town in the United States, but in its good residential sections, handsome houses stand with proud elegance on great lawns, under great trees. It is a small city, almost totally without the anonymous feel of a city, and yet it breathes out a greatness that is beyond the merely urban. It is called the Zenith City, and Sinclair Lewis, contrasting his life here with his life in Hollywood a year before, thought that he could be happy in it, with all its forthright, genuine, warm and unaffected people, of which he was at once meeting so many. But when the sun is not shining, in a winter sleet or an autumn drizzle, Duluth becomes one of the most bleakly gray cities in the world, and its openness is a desolation.

Because of wartime gas rationing, Lewis's car was in storage in New York, and his driver, Joseph Hardrick, was now a corporal in the United States Army. Lewis needed to follow Judge Nolan on his circuit, and he wanted to explore the countryside, and he needed someone to run his errands. Ace Lyons, who was fifty years old, the son of a pioneer Duluth liveryman and known to everyone as familiarly as the city and the country were known to him, solved the problem. He owned a small fleet of taxicabs and was a friendly man with a complacent wife named Thelma. Lewis liked him; and Lyons was tolerant of Lewis's sudden whims and irregular demands, and was always available. He helped with the multiple chores involved in settling the house, and he drove him everywhere, chiefly, for a time, on the trail of the traveling judge. An important murder case was in progress in Carlton County, and this case Lewis followed intently every day for two weeks, familiarizing himself with the lingo of law. Of Judge Nolan he became genuinely fond. Nolan was up for reelection, and when the Minneapolis *Tribune* came to take a photograph of Lewis, he held up the newspapermen for two hours while he searched the city for the judge; he wanted him to be in the picture because the publicity would help his cause. Judge Nolan was, in many ways, that "perfect friend" for whom Lewis had always been looking, and was still looking:

> Mark is a big Irish Catholic, mildly leonine black hair and blue eyes that could be choleric, fond of liquor and women, called by his first name by almost every one from clerk of court to the man running the beer truck up the North Shore, yet a learned and good judge, graduate of Notre Dame and taught Government there for a year after graduation; from the Iron Range and so looked at doubtfully by some of Duluth's more refined; witty, blasphemous, frightfully on to everything; completely a Good Fellow and, I rather suspect, completely honest and rigidly just. . . . He handsomely wears dark double-breasted coat and black tie with fine white stripe when he is on the bench (here, unlike Mpls, the judges do not don silk robes) but off it he prefers sports jacket—or just shirt sleeves, with suspenders festively showing—while he finishes his sixth highball—which, next morning, is incredibly NOT going to produce any hangover at all! . . .

> He is . . . almost a fictional Irishman, lovable, a fighter, a dreamer, a hell-raiser—but with it all a stark streak of Anglo-Saxon strictness in his duties as judge.

"The good gay judge," he called him, and with him "one *is* able to live in a romantic novel for a day or two, now and then!" For several days in June they went off together on an excursion to the north shore of Lake Superior, "a great two days" in and around Two Harbors.

> . . . it is the greatest luck to become so well acquainted with Mark. My man's character will be as different from his as can be, but I do get backstage; come to know how a judge can, or does, drink, read, garden, make love, go fishing, talk. . . . I now really know something about judges with the make-up off. . . .

It was in the opposite direction from Two Harbors and Grand Marais that Lewis discovered the site of his new fictional city, Grand Republic. He was driving with Lyons and when they came to Arthyde, about sixty miles southwest of Duluth, where Lyons saw only a post office, a store, and a Soo Line boxcar serving as a depot, Lewis exclaimed ecstatically, "There's Grand Republic! Look, isn't it beautiful? See that house there—over the hillside! That's where Cass Timberlane lives! Isn't it beautiful? Well, say something! Isn't it?" Blinking at nothing, Lyons said, "Sure, it's beautiful." And working hard, now—always at least from six o'clock to ten in the morning—on *Cass Timberlane,* he was happy. To Carl Van Doren he wrote:

> I don't yet know whether I shall return to NY, for the winter, about September 1st or October 1st. As always, I'm fascinated by the Middlewest, and learning again what people eat and wear and think in America, but I do miss you and a few other people—not so terribly many. But, again, September will be wonderful here, with fine crisp air and turning trees. . . . I've met a lot of people—as many as I've wanted. . . .

In late May, immediately upon his arrival, Mrs. Banning had given him a party at the country club because she was going away for a month and wanted him to meet a variety of people, all of whom she asked to do something for him in her absence.

> He was unmanageable, of course, wanting to meet everyone conventionally and then investigating them with embarrassing questions. That was always the difficulty socially. Everyone was ready to treat him as a genius who could say or do anything he wanted. But that he wouldn't have. He wanted to be treated like anyone else, but God help anyone who did it! *

* As in nearly everything else, Lewis was unpredictable in his social conduct. It was determined at the moment by the persons involved, and *their* conduct. John Hersey remembers him as totally without self-importance, as having no wish whatever for deference, but rather, for the contrary—camaraderie—more likely to be found with

When she returned, he told her inexplicably that no one had looked him up and that he was lonely, but the fact is that he had had many invitations and had accepted many, and that he had himself entertained at both small and rather ambitious dinners and evening parties. His was by no means a gourmet cook, and a number of his guests have complained not only about the quality of the food he offered them, but of its scantness. When he had people in for cocktails, both food and drink were likely to exhaust themselves long before the guests had. He commented in *Cass Timberlane* on the excessive drinking of the residents of Grand Republic. Not drinking himself, he exaggerated in his mind the intake of others and was not inclined to indulge them. It was in this year that he was being quoted on the jacket of Charles Jackson's novel, *The Lost Weekend,* where he spoke as an expert no less on the subject than on the form:

> I think this is the only unflinching story of an alcoholic that I have ever read, and it is as terrifying, yet as absorbing, as the real thing.

Early in July he asked Mrs. Banning to dine with him alone, and after one of his dreary dinners, he told her that Mrs. Powers was coming with her daughter for a visit. He was eager that they enjoy their visit and, his engagement book ready in his hand, he asked Mrs. Banning to introduce them to Duluth. Mrs. Banning, a forthright woman, said, "I want to get this straight first. How do you and Marcella stand? Do you want to marry her?"

"I want to marry her more than anything on earth," he said, and then, "Isn't it astonishing, that's the first time anyone has asked me that. Why didn't someone ask me in Minneapolis last year?"

He talked about her then, about her beauty and her great talents. He was, Mrs. Banning remembers, like a boy who is certain that his girl has every admirable quality, and she found this disarming at first, if, later, "very pitiable." He was as devoid of skepticism, let alone of his habitual cynicism, in this matter, as he is in his description of Jinny Marshland early in *Cass Timberlane:*

> The new witness was a half-tamed hawk of a girl, twenty-three or -four, not tall, smiling, lively of eye. The light edged gently the clarity of her cheeks, but there was something daring in her delicate Roman nose, her fierce black hair.

At this time, he had done nothing much to refurbish his house except to put a theatrical photograph of Miss Powers in nearly every room, and the description of Jinny Marshland suits these professional photographs, with the characteristic pose of head and hair thrown back, neck arching.

---

anonymous males or young females than with women of presence. If, many years before, the young man who hoped above all to be acceptable to elegance, suddenly pulled Mercedes de Acosta's chair out from under her, it was because at the moment Sauk Centre found female elegance intolerable, outrageous.

For several months now he had been legally free to remarry, and in the course of five years the balance in his relationship with Miss Powers had shifted.

> There was no doubt now, [Cass] decided, that he was utterly in love with her, that her small dim presence was a vast blazing temple. She was not something that he had imagined in his loneliness. She was life.

But now it was she who showed a wise and, from some points of view, a generous reluctance.

The ladies arrived on July 22, and Mrs. Banning entertained for them on the next day at a cocktail party throughout most of which the young woman sat at the Master's feet. He was intensely happy but the best of Duluth was rather chilled, and Mrs. Banning's daughter, who was Miss Powers's contemporary, was "disgusted." Nevertheless, Mrs. Banning's guests were cordial and invitations were forthcoming; for these Lewis, if no less rude than usual, was grateful. His first plan, however, was to show the ladies the country, and on the day after Mrs. Banning's party, they set off with Ace Lyons to drive as far as Gateway Lodge on Hungry Jack Lake, that fishing resort on the Canadian border to which, two years before, he had taken his son Michael. The excursion was extended beyond their initial plans, with the result that Lewis and his guests neglected to appear at one of the parties for which Mrs. Banning had been responsible, and since their hostess had gone to a good deal of trouble and expense, Mrs. Banning was properly indignant. A woman of strong will and opinion, she told Lewis that she thought his behavior inexcusable. This was the first of a series not of quarrels precisely, but of temperamental irritations. On this occasion, however, she forgave him, and he, one assumes, made some placating explanation to his affronted hostess.

Most of the people in this Duluth set had camps on the Brule River, and to these the Lewis party was invited on a number of occasions for picnics. Mrs. Banning observed that

> Mrs. Powers was not a rustic type. I remember sitting with her on a bridge looking down at the river, while she told me all about the branches of New York shops in East Orange. . . . Lewis never saw a flaw in her. He would tell you how wonderful she was. She seemed to be able to give him comfort, or maybe a sense of security.

For some time now he had been, in fact, contributing to her support.

Lewis himself gave a dinner party for about twenty people, and after dinner he took his guests to the basement and he, all legs and arms at one end of the alley, set up pins for some of them while they bowled. Others were content to drink their highballs, and Mrs. Banning took offense at Judge Nolan who, in her view, had drunk too much, and she told him in no uncertain terms that a man in his position should conduct himself with greater dignity. This gave Sinclair Lewis his opportunity for fury: it was not her place to judge his guests; if she did not approve of Mark Nolan's conduct, she need not expose herself to it. She departed. But again, the little fracas left no serious scars.

The single real unpleasantness came when he took Mrs. Powers and her daughter to call on the Victor Ridders, who had become Lewis's very good friends, on a Sunday afternoon. The occasion was a trifle stiff, as calls on Sunday afternoon can well be, but as they left, Lewis decided that the Ridders had been insultingly condescending to his guests, and as the three made their way home, his rage mounted. Once inside his own door, he rushed to the telephone and called them and, without giving them a chance to speak, roundly berated them. And that was the end of that friendship, and the name of Ridder does not appear again in the little red engagement books. The journal bleakly reads, "Ev[e]n[i]ng, last of the Ridders."

The Duluth reception of his friends, warm as it generally was on the social surface, began, however slightly, to alter his enthusiasm for the city. On July 31, three days before Miss Powers and her mother departed, he wrote to Samson Raphaelson that "This is rather a tight-minded little city, rather New England in esprit as it was in origin." The scenery, at any rate, was "gorgeous." However, "I begin now to think about New York again. Perhaps I'll see you again in a month or less. . . ." It was to be a few days "less."

And still, the place had charms for him. In mid-August he wrote to Mary Baxter to say that Duluth had been a great success—

> . . . sensationally lovely in its physical background, full of pleasant people and, for working, wonderfully cool all summer, so that my book has gone swimming on. I wouldn't mind really living here . . . . . or in Minneapolis . . . . . just provided, of course, that I could skip off to China or Mozambique on a day's notice.

He had, before the summer was over, begun to reach out and find friends for himself, and he felt free, after his nap, or after his nearly daily drive with Lyons, or after his dinner, if it was solitary, to drop in at their houses unannounced. Among these were two women in particular, Elsa Anneke and Jean Peyton, both widowed, both beautiful, with pretty daughters of about Marcella Powers's age, Mrs. Anneke an accomplished musician who could help him cultivate his rather recent interest in the great composers. He enjoyed, too, the company of Ruth Dancer, the perspicacious wife of a man somewhat older than she who served as Lewis's Duluth attorney. He liked his real-estate agent and his business friends at the Athletic Club, and he made an effort to cultivate an entity that he called "the little people." (When Mrs. Banning asked him what he meant by that term, he gave as an example the faculty at the local teachers' college, and he was briskly assured that the faculty people did not in the least consider themselves "little.") He began to fuss about racial snobbery in Duluth. Why didn't people like Mrs. Banning entertain Jews? She sometimes did. She thought that he was trying to establish a situation that did not exist in order to knock it down.

If he found certain elements in the social life of Duluth a bit trying, he never tired of the clime:

> *The* perfect day so far this summer. . . . Early AM, blaze of sun glory on shadowy woods, purple sea. The air delicious and alive, softly cool and brisk, and a radiance on leaves, grass, stones, tree-trunks, even the dull blue spruce and balsam shining. . . . By noon, the lake for once a deep true blue, with purple streaks and small white caps. Later, lake a flawed blue-gray. . . . Steamer smoke on far horizon somehow poignant—people sailing to strange ports, even on these lakes.

His journal then goes on to describe a Duluth dinner party of that evening, in a house where electronic controls, changing the dining-room lights from pale yellow to pink, announcing the entrance or departure of a guest, flashing green when two bodies settled together on a bed, flashing on signs reading MEN DRINKING at the bar, left him weary and ready for bed himself, and happily alone.

Marcella Powers had brought the news of a serious eye operation undergone by Carl Van Doren, and on the last day of July Lewis wrote him to wish him well and to say that he "might be there any time." He stayed in Duluth, however, for nearly another month, and was now seriously discussing with Kenneth Cant the possibility of buying his house and a number of adjacent lots, but he had done nothing conclusive about the matter when he left for New York and his duplex on August 28.

For the first two weeks in New York the initial "M" does not appear in the engagement book, and shortly after it reappears, an entry reads, "7:30: M, seen Hal?" The name of Harrison Smith has disappeared entirely, but most of the other familiar names reappear. Immediately upon his arrival he called Carl Van Doren, only to learn that he was once more hospitalized with high blood pressure and a near-stroke, and Lewis at once took over—went to the hospital, stayed there, brought his own doctor to see his friend, dealt with Van Doren's lawyer on an important matter, and in every way was, in the words of Mark Van Doren, "Wonderfully useful . . . there could have been no kinder man than he, or one who thought less of his own concerns. He was pure, simple, blazing goodness and affection."

"Blazing goodness and affection"—it is a felicitous description, and almost entirely because of the epithet. Blazing! He had affections, certainly, and he wanted to be good to the people whom, in his way, he loved. Often he was. Once, during those years, when he was in a distant city, he heard that Dorothy Gish was ill in the Presbyterian Hospital, and he telephoned over and over from his far place in order to learn how she was. It was for Miss Gish a touching display of fidelity. And yet, when one remembers the people who had been really close to him and about whose trials he was not at all concerned, one must wonder to what degree his affections were moved by an impulse of will or of sentimental caprice, or simply by the charms of "long distance" and the telephone.

In all that vast and shifting acquaintanceship of his, Carl Van Doren did hold a rather special place; it was one friendship that was not marred by quarrels, one that was never broken. When, in the next year, Viking Press gave a dinner for Van Doren on his sixtieth birthday, Clifton Fadiman, a former student of his, lauded him in terms of the great Americans about some of whom he had written—Franklin, Jefferson, Lincoln. Such mythologizing Lewis would not allow, and when he spoke, he "reduced the god to human dimensions to everybody's amusement and satisfaction and to nobody's hurt." And yet the chief source of his regard for Van Doren lay in his feeling that he was a sage, that he was nobly wise, wise as Lewis felt himself not to be.

Immediately he was longing for Duluth and his friends there.

> I remember those last few days in Duluth so gratefully. Coming back to New York, it seems far too big, too much of a senseless and jungle-like proliferation of buildings and people, and all the people seem too busy; to get to see an old friend, you first write to the Governor and he sends you an application and by the time you get to your old friend, he has died of delirium tremens two months before, and his family hasn't yet buried him—they've all been too busy—standing in line for tickets for *Oklahoma* for November 1945.

He was promising them that he would soon return to their peaceful city. In the meantime, however, he was attending the theater and making public appearances of his own. On September 22, he was one of eight distinguished people who appeared with Vice-President Wallace at a Roosevelt rally in Madison Square Garden where he declared that "as a writer of occasional nonsense" he was in a position to recognize the nonsense uttered by the Republicans and "especially the silver-tongued Mr. Tom Dewey." On November 1 he delivered a brief radio address in behalf of Roosevelt and described Dewey as "a bright young junior partner." And he was arranging with his lecture agency to make one more round of debates with Lewis Browne.

On October 9, however, he made the trip to Williamstown that he had planned to make in the preceding June. With Samuel Allen and Luther Mansfield, a young instructor of American literature in the college, he drove to the top of the Taconic Trail and was for a long time silent as he studied the immense view. He worked in the mornings, walked in the afternoons, and found a professor of philosophy with whom to play chess in the evenings. On the street, he picked up the cat of another professor and brought it back to the Williams Inn, where in the lounge he sat talking to it as Cass Timberlane talks to his cat, Cleo, in the novel. He had written about 100,000 words of that novel, and, on November 11, leaving his manuscript with Random House, he set out for Chicago with Browne.

On that day, too, in his engagement book, he put down his last injunction to "Write Wells." Wells had been dead since October 29, when he was killed instantly by a sniper's bullet. He was the aide-de-camp of Major General John E. Dahlquist, who on October 31 wrote Lewis of his son's death:

> I was near enough to him to catch his body as it fell. He was dead before I laid him on the ground. . . . I was present for the services, and it was as though my own son was being buried. I had known Wells only since July of this year, but in that short period he had endeared himself to me as a real man. His constant good nature, his keen mind, and his everlasting willingness to perform every task given him marked him as a soldier. He was dependable and courageous.

The news had come to the young man's mother on November 13, and she had tried to reach his father in Chicago, but on that day, Lewis was debating in Kankakee, Illinois, and he did not arrive in Chicago until eleven-thirty the next morning, when Miss Powers's telegram came to him at the Palmer House. If he had read a morning newspaper, he already knew. His friends the Lloyd Lewises had seen the story, which included the detail that the father could not be located. Then their telephone rang: it was Sinclair Lewis, asking them to dine with him that evening at the Palmer House. When they came to the hotel, Mrs. Lewis found herself standing beside Lewis Browne at the house phones. He said that the whole day had passed without a mention of Wells Lewis's death, and the three determined then that they would say nothing until Lewis did.

In his rooms, Lewis greeted them with pleasant affection, and other people arrived: Fanny Butcher, and Dorothy Thompson's sister and her husband, and one or two more. It was Dorothy Thompson's brother-in-law who broke the unnatural silence about Wells when he offered Lewis his sympathy. Then Lewis went into a violently ironical act. "Oh, *good* for you, *you're* the one who got to tell it! All day everybody has been trying to tell me—the newsboy, the bootblack, the cigar counter man, the desk clerk, everybody's been trying to tell me. But great, great! *you're* the one who got to tell it!" No one could bring himself to look at any one else. Then the tirade subsided, and Lewis settled down and spoke quietly and soberly about a German father, a Japanese father, fathers all over the world in many different countries to whom such news must be broken.

Someone suggested that he should call the boy's mother. He did, but under these circumstances his voice was more than she could endure and she collapsed in hysterical abuse of him, her shrill, grief-torn voice ringing into the room as she reproached him for his unforgivable irresponsibility as a father. He took the storm mutely, and next day Telesforo Casanova wrote him a note in which he apologized for her, her grief unbearable, and in her bold, strong hand she appended a single sentence that regretted her having sullied the memory of the boy. Next day he was debating in Temple Sholom, Chicago, and the next day in Elgin, and the next in Lafayette. On November 19 he was back in New York, noting "M at mother's." On the next day, "M here."

It has been said that Lewis did not reply to any of the many letters of sympathy that came to him. This is not quite the fact. At least three such letters of reply are extant. They are, to be sure, nearly mute on the major matter and hurry on to trivia. To Mary Baxter he concluded a note about her coming baby with what is in effect a postscript—"Thank you for your note about Wells." To H. L. Mencken, who had written in a most kindly way, he said only, "Bless you for your note," and urged that they meet soon in New York. To Gene McComas he did not even mention the name —"It was sweet to see your handwriting again . . ."—and wrote of Bill Benét and his own work in progress. He did not record the temperature for that day in his journal, wrote only, "Kankakee Wells, Oct. 29."

The death of one son did not make him more solicitous about the other. The yearly income from Michael Lewis's trust fund was about $475, and his immediate expenses, which included a high tuition at the Valley Forge School, were more than $3,500 a year. His mother asked for an opportunity not so much to discuss this matter with his father as to introduce him to Maxim Kopf, about to become Michael's stepfather, and an appointment was arranged at 300 Central Park West. When they arrived, they found that Miss Powers was present and did not mean to withdraw. They had, then, only a stiff "social" visit. Yet when the boy came to New York for his Christmas holiday, his father did not ignore him. He was fourteen years old now, as tall as his father, strong, red-haired, handsome, and opinionated. They met several times—for an uneasy lunch and an awkward, late-afternoon conversation or two.

Before that, on December 16, Lewis delivered a radio address of eight minutes in the Metropolitan Opera House—the third in an Opera Victory Rally Series. Called "The Artist, the Scientist, and the Peace," it asked for the active engagement of writers and scientists in the war and in the construction of the peace and a democratic world organization to sustain it. Reversing the position that he had taken so long before as *Arrowsmith* and so recently as the beginning of the war, he deplored the "old-fashioned type of artist-scientist—the Pasteurs and Whistlers and Walter Paters" who felt that they and their work were superior to the human struggle, and argued that the artist-scientist must join that struggle on the side that fought tyranny. The address, later published in *American Scholar,* was indistinguishable from any liberal cry at the end of 1944 or the beginning of 1945, and no one chose to quarrel with its generalizing sentiments.

Another reversal is perhaps more impressive in that it generously ended a quarrel. When, late in November of that year, Bernard DeVoto's name was proposed for membership in the National Institute, Sinclair Lewis made the seconding speech, a fervent plea in support of the nomination. And when the two men met on the street, they exchanged friendly, casual greetings. It was the season of love, and Lewis kept jotting down the reminder to buy a Christmas tree.

5

LARGER PURCHASES loomed ahead. In September Kenneth Cant had written to Lewis that he could buy the Williams house in Duluth for only $15,000, including almost all of its miscellaneous furniture, and a 1941 Studebaker President sedan for an additional $1,100. He also could buy the adjoining woodsy lot for very little. On January 1 he bought the house, the lot next door, and two more lots across the street to protect his view. The structure had cost $100,000 twenty years before, and in 1945 it would have cost $165,000, but it was much too large to have attracted many buyers and threatened to become an expensive burden on the hands of the Webber heirs. It was perhaps the only good real-estate investment that Lewis ever made—or would have been, had he been content to remain, as, in New York in January, he thought that he certainly would.

Once he had resolved to move again, he was excited by the prospect, and he wrote his friends in Minneapolis and in Duluth to tell them to expect him as a permanent resident early in April. He was working very hard on his novel, he explained, and had at least another month of work ahead; and then there was the whole problem of decorating and furnishing the house, now that he owned it. At the American Academy he bought his seven Childe Hassam landscapes. He was making an inventory of his belongings in 300 Central Park West—for all of this was to be moved—and he had found a decorator.

He had always admired the warmly comfortable and yet stylish effects that Molly Haycraft achieved in her apartments in New York, and he was impressed with her knowledge of New York shops. He persuaded her to go to Duluth in early February to look over the house and make her plans for it; then she was to return for several weeks in early April with Mrs. Powers, receive all the furnishings from the New York apartment, and "finally arrange the house" for his occupancy late in April. Before her first arrival, Lewis had written endless notes to Kenneth Cant about two large rugs that he had bought from the Webber estate; unlike the other furnishings, these were in storage, and his notes, fussy as a spinster's, kept insisting that these must be laid by the time of Mrs. Haycraft's arrival or she would be helpless to proceed. Cant managed to get the rugs down on time and he found a Duluth decorator, William Lindholm,* to assist Mrs. Haycraft. Because of the furniture that Lewis was planning to ship out from New York, Mrs. Haycraft decided that all the dark woodwork should be bleached and that the deep-red damask wall covering in the drawing room should be replaced by grass cloth. These were only a few of the multiple details that were then left to Lindholm for execution before her return and Lewis's arrival.

He had finished *Cass Timberlane* and was spending many hours with Saxe Commins over the manuscript. He was spending as many hours as she would give to him with Miss Powers, but there were empty stretches when he turned to people whom he hardly knew—the young Hollywood script-writer Peter Ruric, for example, who was now writing a novel in New York, and whom Lewis invited to his apartment with his fiancée, and to whom he said that he could not work in New York, that he was returning as soon as possible to his home ground. One afternoon he had this couple to a cocktail party with some other young people, including Miss Powers, and presently he sent the whole party out to dinner, promising to join them later. He made reservations for them at an 86th Street *Brauhaus,* to which they proceeded, and where they dined, danced and waited for him; but he never came. His guests spoke of him with faint scorn, a hopeless case, and Miss Powers, although defensive of him, despaired, too.

In February he was sixty years old and often in despair of himself, sunk in fits of melancholy that even a birthday dinner *à deux* with Miss Powers at the Chambord could not for very long dispel. In his relations with people, now as in the past, it is hard to say what proportion of emphasis to lay on his loneliness, on his desire for an audience, on his genuine interest in others. He would suffer long spells of moody restlessness, and occasionally, with people, he would suddenly become exuberant again, full of animation, begin his mimicry, seem to feel on top of everything. Then abruptly he could not tolerate the people who had just before been necessary to him, would grow heavy with boredom, would want only to be rid of them. Did he see his life as a waste, his present writing as tawdry repetition and decline? Dr. Gross thinks that he was without self-deception, that he could see himself for what he was, and that "this was hard on him toward the end." In the month that he was sixty, he arranged with *Esquire,* "the magazine for young men," to contribute a regular commentary on literary matters, the first to appear in June.

The *Esquire* articles ran for seven successive issues. Written in much the spirit of his *Newsweek* articles of a few years earlier, they are brisk,

* I have invented this name in order to respect the wish of the man in question that his own name should not appear in the episodes that follow.

opinionated, sometimes amusing. Since he was already reading for his next novel, *Kingsblood Royal,* it is not surprising that he should have started with a review of a number of books having to do with the Negro problem. The next takes up the double bugaboo, obscenity (four letter words) and obscurity in literature. A third advises the GI who plans to write about the war how to write about it. The fourth is concerned with a miscellany of twenty recent novels. The most entertaining is the fifth, "The Boxers of M. Voltaire," a satirical treatment of that "Hollywood hack," Louis Bromfield, who had tried in *Pleasant Valley* to write a *Walden* of café society about his Ohio farm called Malabar—entertaining because Bromfield's effort was in fact not very different from Lewis's next attempt at an establishment outside Williamstown. The sixth article praises the efforts of two youngish Midwestern writers, August Derleth and Wallace Stegner, and the last, those of that favorite duo, Maritta Wolff and Ann Chidester. He closed the last of these articles by announcing that he was now turning his attention to a novel of his own.

When the New York *Times* announced his *Esquire* commitment, there were editorial predictions of "turmoil" to come from this old hand at "critical polemics" and "straight verbal alley fighting," but there was none. The public prankishness of even his late middle years was subsiding. On the day of Franklin D. Roosevelt's death—which was also Miss Powers's birthday—he stood with Diana Sheean, looking down at the trees of Central Park under a deep April sky. Lewis, who had once irresponsibly called both Hoover and Roosevelt "fatheads," who had once told Budd Schulberg that the two greatest men he had ever met were Eugene Debs and Herbert Hoover, who had said that Roosevelt, like Wendell Willkie, was a "stuffed shirt," and who was in shrill if not very deep opposition to Roosevelt's policy in the early years of the war, took a very different tone on this occasion. He talked about Roosevelt with what seemed to be real feeling and communicated to Mrs. Sheean so powerfully and quietly his sense of a great man's passage from the world that the experience moved her and remains with her. He was an older and lonelier and quieter man than he had sometimes been, even as he left the terrace to be jolly at still another "children's party."

The affairs of the Academy and the Institute filled some of his time. Eager that worthy age should invigorate itself at the sacred fount of youthful energy, he was one of a few democratic spirits in the Academy who were arguing that the old distinction between the two bodies be abolished. When, in that spring, the Academy was to honor W. H. Auden, Lewis persuaded his young friend Luther Mansfield—who was teaching then at Swarthmore, where a production of the Auden-Isherwood play, *Ascent of F-6,* was under way with a newly written final scene by Auden—to bring the Swarthmore company to New York for a few special performances under the auspices of the Academy. Lewis was enthusiastic about the new material, but the drama coach at Swarthmore put the estimate of costs so high that the Academy was unable to undertake the venture. (Later, when Auden was teaching at Bennington and Lewis was living in nearby Williamstown, each repeatedly expressed the greatest interest in meeting the other; but whenever Mansfield proposed an occasion, one or the other, not really surprisingly, managed to shy away, and they never met.)

There was other business, too, including the whole enterprise of setting up Marcella Powers as a literary agent, which was presently accomplished. There were regular sessions with a teacher of chess. There were the communications with Ace Lyons, who was to come to New York in order to drive Lewis to Duluth in a Lewis automobile, and all the arrangements with the Office of Price Administration about an adequate gasoline ration. There was the proof of *Cass Timberlane* to correct, and the business of subsidiary rights to discuss and conclude. (Before that book was published, Lewis had made nearly $500,000 from it: $50,000 for serialization in *Cosmopolitan;* $75,000 as a Book-of-the-Month Club selection; $250,000 for the film sale to Metro-Goldwyn-Mayer; $90,000 from advance royalties not connected with book club distribution; further cash for foreign rights.) There was the problem of the dedication of that novel: in his engagement book he scrambled Miss Powers's initials in various combinations until he hit upon P. M. R. (Peggie Marcella Rosemary) which is how the dedication was to appear. And then there were travel arrangements to be made for Mrs. Powers and Molly Haycraft, who were once more off for Duluth.

On April 16, Mrs. George Macy gave him a farewell party with the dinner menu printed in red on a white ground and with each course somewhat unappetizingly having "red" in it. There was another farewell dinner party on April 18 with Mencken:

> . . . you and I and Marcella Powers, and possibly George [Jean Nathan], no one else. I think you will greatly esteem Marcella; you met her for a moment four years ago, then a pretty actress; she has become an editor, merry and perceptive. The evening will mean much to me not only because of seeing you again, but also as a farewell to New York. Two days after it I shall leave for Minnesota for a time much longer than most of my friends in NY consider likely.

There was then, on the nineteenth, a final farewell dinner party with Marcella Powers alone at "21," and next morning he set off with his companion, the cabman. The vans had gone, and the vast rooms in 300 Central Park West stood empty as caverns. The New York *Times* had observed, "If it is still legal to quote odds, the betting in reasonably informed quarters is about 8 to 5 that his stay in that cultural center, Duluth, won't be quite so permanent as he now thinks it will be."

The plan was that Lewis and Lyons would make a leisurely tour of New England and then, visiting first in Minneapolis, arrive in Duluth in about three weeks, well after the moving vans had come and gone and the house was in complete order. The plan was, naturally, ignored. Only three days after he had left New York and four or five days before the vans arrived, Lewis telephoned from Ironwood, Michigan, to say that he would be in Duluth in about three hours. All the major changes in the house had been accomplished, but a good many details remained; nothing could be done about these before Lewis walked in, but in the next few hours, his three minions scrambled madly to give the place an appearance of cleanliness and order. When Lewis arrived, he strode up to Lindholm, called him by his first name, said "I've heard so much about you!", and expressed his pleasure at what had been accomplished.

It had been impossible to find servants in Duluth, and next day Lewis drove on to Minneapolis to see a friend or two and to persuade his old Lillian to come back. He returned in time to greet the movers, and with thousands of dollars on his person to pay them, he persuaded Lindholm to bring his bulldog and spend the night to protect all that cash. It was wartime and labor was scarce, with the result that Lindholm, who was charmed by Lewis's informality, did a lot of hard work to which he was not accustomed, including the unloading of hundreds of crates of books and all the New York furniture. He came to the house all day of every day, and he tolerated the taste of Mrs. Powers, which she sometimes exercised over his judgment. When Molly Haycraft left for New York again on May 11, Lewis asked Lindholm to stay on the job and finish the final details in the bowling alley and the ballroom, and he asked him if he would join him in a motor trip to Canada when his son came to visit him. Lindholm was delighted, and later in the day he told Mrs. Powers of the invitation—a mistake, he believes.

That was on a Friday. Lewis suggested that on this weekend they all rest. And on this weekend everything changed. He decided, or was persuaded, that his decorators were incompetent. To Molly Haycraft went what is perhaps the most abusive letter he ever wrote, a letter brutally boiling over spinsterish trivia in which he charged her with a waste of materials and his money and of generally having botched the job; and when Lindholm reappeared on Monday, Lewis was so violently ill-tempered, bickering, badgering, demanding all day long, that almost no work was accomplished and the decorator went home in a state of nervous exhaustion. Next morning he was running a temperature and did not go to work; Lewis telephoned and demanded that he appear; Lindholm's wife, a vigorous registered nurse, told Lewis that he could not and would not come that day, and Lewis announced that then he need not come again. And he did not. When Lindholm submitted his final bill, Lewis paid for the materials in question but he did not pay the decorator's commission on the grounds that he had left the job unfinished.

The ironic conclusion came when *Time* magazine, reviewing *Cass Timberlane* in a Lewis cover issue of October, reported that his handsome Duluth house had been redecorated by Marcella Powers. Miss Powers had at that point not yet seen the refurbished establishment that Mrs. Haycraft, William Lindholm, and, in some objectionable details, her mother, had achieved. She was not even responsible, as local gossip holds, for a peculiarly ugly set of dining-room furniture that Lewis had bought at Wanamacy's—an imitation Tudor table with ponderous chairs covered in imitation leather held by great nailheads —which made the gentle Lindholm shudder.

A cat was installed, and there were the photographs of Miss Powers and in Lewis's bedroom a photograph of Wells, but otherwise the great house, for all its new grass-cloth walls and Kleerflax carpeting and waxed black-and-white parquet in the foyer, was as impersonal as a well-kept hotel. In this atmosphere he was to make the experiments in social brotherhood that astonished Duluth. These began as research projects for *Kingsblood Royal* and ended as nothing less than botched attempts to reform the social structure of the city. He started by inviting in for an evening's discussion two Negro couples and asked his housekeeper to join them. One of these couples was Edward Nichols and his wife, superior people, their sons educated in the university, Nichols himself the local head of the N.A.A.C.P. Nichols was employed as a valet in a fashionable Duluth club and often as bartender in fashionable homes, and the initial meetings, when Lewis was trying to learn from the source what it is like to be a Negro in a segregated society, were not offensive; but when Lewis became more ambitious and on more formal occasions asked the Nicholses to mingle with his wealthy friends, the situation was absurdly artificial, and neither Nichols nor his wife had any wish to go to dinner with the people who employed them.

Such reticence did not give Lewis pause as his impulse to scramble society grew to a kind of mania. Now he extended his guest lists to include ministers of various denominations, Jews, and gentiles white and black. We can credit him, if not with social imagination, with an honest indignation over any intolerance (years before, when his secretary Louis Florey took rooms for them in the best hotel in Bermuda, known to discriminate against Jews, Lewis said, "I won't stay there," and did not), and there is something touching about his fumbling attempts to correct it. He badgered his fashionable friends, not only Mrs. Banning, but those, like Mrs. Anneke, of whom he was genuinely fond: Why don't you have Jews at your parties? Have you ever had a Negro in your house? Why not?

To Miss Powers he wrote,

To begin to begin to know something about Negroes, I had five of them here with one liberal clergyman, Reverend Bert of the Methodists, the other evening—so comely and well-bred, the Negro women, and scarce darker than you, yet ranking with Zulu savages in the minds of most Americans.

Mrs. Powers had an opportunity to observe these occasions. She remembered that Lewis would invite his group of five or six Negroes on something of a schedule—about once a week. He would ask them to sit around the dining table, serve them sandwiches and ginger ale, ask questions about their conception of their future, and give them extended individual advice. The career of one young woman, who was being trained as a nurse in Duluth, especially fascinated him. She was a brilliant girl, and, according to one participant, she sometimes rather vexed Lewis with the sharp precision of her retorts. They played "verbal tennis, and he didn't like it when she could volley as long as he could."

From these first discussions the more ambitious gatherings—a return to the Sunday-school technique of the *Elmer Gantry* research—grew.

Nervously wolfing chocolates, Lewis would usually start the discussion. "We have interracial problems," he would begin, "because we don't know each other. For instance, we don't know Negroes. Why? Because we don't make it a point to know them."

Asking the guests directly, he would say: "Have you ever made it a point to be in a Negro's home? You ask how do we go about going into a Negro's home? Have you ever invited Negroes into your own home first and allowed them to reciprocate?"

Thus launched, the meeting would evolve into complex discussions of economic and political as well as social aspects of the problem. Then Lewis would quietly withdraw to a neutral corner and take voluminous notes. Later, when *Kingsblood Royal* was published, the discussion participants fancied themselves or their fellow guests in various characters in the novelist's story. . . .

The search for interracial materials led him beyond such discussions and personal interviews into the activities of the little St. Mark's African Methodist Church in Duluth and of a Negro Elks Club in Minneapolis and of the affairs of the N.A.A.C.P. in both cities and later in New York. It was to lead him presently into a month's tour of the South, an excursion that may conceivably have arisen from his discussions with a young woman named Betty Stevens, who had been employed by a Southern C.I.O. newspaper.

Miss Stevens had met Lewis casually when he was teaching at the university, and after hearing him lecture in Duluth, where she was visiting, she approached him. He asked her to come to see him in a day or two at five o'clock, and when she came, he took her into the dining room and offered her a drink after showing her his liquor cabinet. ("'I keep this for friends, never drink at all. Used to be a drunk, you know,' he added, matter-of-factly.") He talked about radicalism—how he had no objections to a Communist as such, there were good and bad Communists; how most Midwest radicals were not Communists even when they thought that they were, but were, rather, "agrarian radicals" in the old Populist tradition; that he wanted to write a novel about labor and hoped to get to know the people in the Farmer-Labor Party of Minnesota (it had merged with the Democratic Party in the year before); that he did not really understand labor leaders, hard as he had tried, while he understood perfectly the little old ladies who came to his lectures; that he could not endure "parlor pinks." Then he came to his immediate interest, her experience of the condition of Negroes in the South. "He asked how and where the Negro people lived, exactly how Jim Crow operated in that town, about the streetcars, restaurants and schools." And he told her about his plot for *Kingsblood Royal,* how a man who had always thought that he was white discovered that, far back, he had a Negro ancestor, and was driven out of the white community.

Miss Stevens indicated her doubts about the likelihood of his hero's behavior, as, later, reviewers would have doubts about both that and the community's conduct after his revelation. The present community, Duluth, or at any rate that section of Duluth that had thought he was to be its lion, grew smaller. He announced at the opening of a lecture that if anyone could not understand what he was saying, it was probably because of his "brand-new store teeth." A toothless lion, insisting that the jungle situation must be changed, can be rather tiresome; and so a number of people began to find him, at least when he was insisting on a reorganization of their habitual lives. They were happier when he talked about the importance of redesigning the Duluth harbor, demolishing the drab warehouses, building down there superb riviera hotels, making this the great beauty spot of all America—his hope that, as Cass Timberlane hoped for "Grand Republic," he could "help in setting up a few stones in what may be a new Athens." Such ambitions were harmless, and talk about such ambitions after a dinner party—of wealthy gentile community leaders—could be diverting, even rather beguiling—coming, as it did, from that mad man who, when he wanted to, could be so genuinely if naïvely interested in Duluth, and even rather nice. . . .

In New York, Marcella Powers, for some months, had been seeing a young writer named Michael Amrine, once of New Orleans, and his name began to appear casually in her letters, and sometimes—"a wonderful boy" —not quite so casually. In Duluth, Sinclair Lewis had her mother as housekeeper to remind him of her daughter. She was the very *plainest* of women;

even though her gray hair was tinted orange, there was nothing in the least frivolous about her, nothing that was not stolid and flatly practical, downright, rather dour, and almost extraordinarily ordinary. Her position as housekeeper was uneasy in that she was in a sense responsible for the management of a kind of household with which she herself was unfamiliar, in charge of servants and still not in charge of them, never having had a servant of her own, and in the curiously ambiguous position of companion to Sinclair Lewis himself, her most important role.

After the relationship with her daughter, the relationship with the mother was probably the most satisfying that he could have had. There was nothing in her to be formed, to be sure, but there was also nothing to make any demands upon him. She was completely submissive to his will and his whims, and, difficult as it may be to imagine her as the companion of the aging Mercutio, she was essential to him. He was always kind to her, and aggressively protective, aggressively insistent that she was his peer and the peer of anyone who wished to be his friend. Whenever he received an invitation and she was not explicitly included, his response was, "I take it the invitation includes Mrs. Powers," and most people always said, "Of course." Once he made this response to a bearish old banker and regent of the university, Richard L. Griggs, who replied, "No, it doesn't," and Lewis replied in turn, "Very well, then we can't come."

She attended to his rigorous routines. Her last duty at night was to ascertain that his thermos of coffee, his ash tray, and his cigarettes were on the dining table. His rising hour was earlier than it had ever been. He would get up at four or half past four in the morning, go quietly downstairs in slippers and bathrobe, and drink the coffee that waited for him and work in the dining room until the servants were ready to serve breakfast. Then, at exactly eight o'clock, that first meal was served in the breakfast room. After breakfast he went up to his study and continued to work, intermittently napping. Lunch was served at exactly twelve o'clock. Then, with absolute regularity, he had his nap. At about four o'clock he would appear again, punctiliously dressed now in shirt, tie, jacket, and he would chat with guests if he had them, or walk a bit under the trees in his now carefully tended gardens, or drive into the country with Ace Lyons, who was nearly as faithful in attendance as Mrs. Powers. Well before seven o'clock he would be in the house again, impatient for dinner, which was served with military precision at seven. After dinner he would read and play records while he did so, and he insisted that Mrs. Powers be in the large room with him, he in one chair, she in another, her hands in her lap. And then, ordinarily at ten o'clock or even earlier, like an old country couple, they would go off to their beds for the night. *Hoc pater meus dixit!*

She could not stay beyond the end of June, when responsibilities in East Orange called her home. To her daughter Lewis wrote:

> While she was here, I was never lonely, because there was always some shadow of you in the place, but with her gone, I miss you terribly. I want to go so many places, to do so many things, with you.

He had already delivered the commencement address, "The Excitement of Learning," at the State Teachers College, in Duluth, and after that, had promised to give a series of summer lectures under the title "The Craft of Writing (and the Art of Reading)" which would run from June 20 through July 24. The commitment tied him to Duluth, but he could anticipate flight at once after his last lecture; accordingly, immediately after his first, he wrote Miss Powers with the request that she reserve a suite at the Dorset for him beginning on July 27.

Betty Stevens, who heard the first of these lectures, said that "his body looked gaunt and lonely as a winter tree," and his hands trembled as he clutched the microphone. These lectures at the college were of his usual sort—based on a minimum of notes, free-wheeling, glancing at his current reading, at the writer's problems, at the local cultural situation. He apparently became interested in the development of the Teachers College (it was presently converted to a campus of the University of Minnesota), even though his audience consisted of at least as many Duluth housewives curious to look at a celebrity as of students eager to learn from him. He lectured elsewhere, too, in that summer—at another teachers' college in Bemidji (where his ideal poet, Arthur Upson, had drowned so many years before), and at Carleton College. Such engagements simply punctuated his continuing and wide-ranging excursions into the countryside. Once he had Lyons drive him as far as Sauk Centre ("very earnest with old friends and getting the hell out of there as soon as polite"), and during one of these absences a strange young woman arrived at the Duluth house to be received by Mrs. Powers.

Lewis was not, like so many writers, the frequent object of pursuit by infatuated females, but one such poor creature, living in South Dakota, once heard him lecture and was determined to know him. She wrote him a number of desperate love letters that went unanswered, and then, having heard that he was planning to leave Duluth again, impulsively took a bus from South Dakota to Duluth on the theory that a personal confrontation would melt his heart. Mrs. Powers dealt firmly with the young woman, who, after fainting or pretending to faint at the door, was turned stonily away; and when Lewis received another letter from her, telling him of her cold reception and her frenzied sorrow, and sounding, it is true, quite mad, he grew panicky at the prospect of suicide and scandal and called his attorney, Herbert Dancer. Dancer and his partners composed a letter which, in the chilliest language, threatened legal procedures if the young woman's harassment did not come to an end. It did.

He preferred to choose his own company, and among that which he particularly enjoyed in Duluth was the Babbittry. With a group of businessmen, for example, he had made a tour of the Duluth-Superior Harbor in a motor cruiser, and wrote of it at length in his journal.

> We made our way into Pokegama Bay, on the shore of which, and East for a hundred miles, there is almost nothing but unbroken second-growth woods, gone back into wilderness since the lumbermen were here. We had supper, and a good one—cold roast beef, salad, Lucullan huckleberry pie, while The Boys had a great many Bourbon and sodas and poor Mr. Lewis drank ginger ale, and everybody told informative anecdotes about travelling men and sexual intercourse. A little storm came up—you could see it travelling from the hills behind Duluth, miles away, with long lances of rain—but when it hit us, the anchored boat just rocked comfortably, and Charlie Liscomb said, "Say, have you heard the one about the boy that wrote his father if he would send him $500, he knew a fellow that would teach their dog to talk?" . . .
>
> Said Boys were seven men all from 40 to 55—Kenneth Cant, the real estate man who got me this house, big and kindly and somehow touching and lonely, Lou Castle, the banker, Fred Buck and John Hoff and Winton Brown, all real estate—the first always running charity drives and war loan drives and getting out of it for himself nothing but satisfaction. Arthur Miller, the banker, Charlie Liscomb, the insurance broker. . . . They are all prosperous, they all have wives and children, sons in the war, they are all good members of a Protestant Church and of the Chamber of Commerce, they all hate Roosevelt (and especially Eleanor Roosevelt) and the Farmers' Co-operatives, they all love golf a little and duck-hunting passionately, most of them are college graduates, none of them are dull, really, but they do repeat over and over the same little family-like jokes . . . not very good jokes—not MUCH better, really, than one of Geo. Macy's. . . .
>
> These men are halfway between a Babbitt and a Dodsworth: not so drearily illiterate as Babbitt, not so executive and powerful as Dodsworth. . . . They are Upper Middle Class America, and I think that if one lived among them ten years, one would like them rather better than all our War Correspondents.
>
> They love their sons in the war. . . . They have illusions about their sexual prowess when they go to Minneapolis, they try to pick up what they call, generically, Blondes. . . . They are proud of their city. . . . They are good outdoor men. . . . I think they are peculiar to America, and in Babbitt I just *began* to paint them. . . . In the rich possession of these Babbitworths, [Duluth is] really *far* more interesting than that.

In the rich possession of such relaxed company, he was almost more comfortable than in that of any other—more comfortable, we may be sure, than he was with young Michael when that fifteen-year-old arrived late in June for five days of a duty visit. A more entertaining visit, for Lewis, was that of John Gunther, who was traveling in preparation for his book *Inside U.S.A.* Lewis had complained to Mrs. Banning and to others that he did not really like Gunther, that he was a "brain-picker." This is the same complaint that he regularly made about Dorothy Thompson, whose name he brought into nearly every conversation; on the evening of Hiroshima he said, "Well, Dorothy'll have to get a whole new lot of experts whose brains she can pick." And to Miss Powers he had written of "your buddies Johnny and Jay and Quenty and Franky, the hairy-chested hero-correspondents, who intrepidly cover the Invasion lands from the perilous heights of Radio City."

But in Duluth, Gunther pleased him. To Miss Powers he wrote:

> John Gunther has been here, along with his book, and I take back everything I have ever said about his pomposity or other evil quality, and almost everything about the impossibility of his doing TVB [The Very Big] book. Seeing him, not gasping in an alcoholized salon of logrollers, but really at work, he was wonderful: keen, persistent, informed, easy, pleasant. For our sins we had to sit through three hours of a dinner party at the Salsiches; Margaret was drunk and a monster of babbling inapposites; but John was still amiable through it all and I admire him for it all over again. AND, talking to people who really had something—Judge Nolan and a radical lawyer, Henry Paull—John was a marvel of perception, memory, efficiency.

As Mrs. Banning (she was now Mrs. Salsich) tells the story, Lewis had importuned her to give the big Duluth dinner party for Gunther, had, indeed, given her the names of the people he wanted her to ask, including that of a local attorney and his wife. "I was trying to be pliant but not liking it very much." However, she obliged. The attorney and his wife had an engagement but promised to come in shortly after dinner. "When they came in, Sinclair got up immediately and said, 'Well, we have to go now.' " Even the extremely amiable Roy Salsich was offended by Lewis's behavior and broke an engagement with him for a day at the Brule; nevertheless, they hoped that the tension would subside and that they could all be friends again, but they were leaving Duluth for a time, and when they returned, Lewis was gone.

This conduct is not surprising in Lewis, who more than twenty years before had, on leaving a Hartford dinner party, thanked his hostess for a very dull evening; and yet it is surprising in that he hoped to make Duluth his home. Or perhaps he already knew, in that summer, that his plan would not work out. On August 30, his lectures finished and Gunther gone, he wrote Miss Powers again to remind her that he would presently be leaving Duluth for New York with Ace Lyons:

> It's time for me to leave Duluth. The house is lovely, and so comfortable and practical; the weather is good and the view gorgeous; I get small snatches of chess; I see a variety of people and the planning of the next novel marches on steadily, so that the coming here for four or five months at a

time has been valuable. But have been thinking of the East as home and have been restless to Start Home.

While he had been in Duluth, the war in Europe had ended (the German capitulation came during those strenuous weeks of redecorating at 2601 East Second Street, and Lewis had turned off the radio when, for the third time, he heard President Truman thank God), the first atomic bombs had been dropped on Japan, and the war in the Pacific had ended, too. (In a prisoner-of-war camp, General Homma, commander of the first Japanese invasion forces in the Philippines, was seen squatting cross-legged on his bunk, reading *It Can't Happen Here* in English.) At the same time, Mrs. Banning had been considerably officious, and chess partners had not multiplied; gasoline, however, was not so hard to come by as it had been, and so, on September 4, Lewis set off on a leisurely ten-day drive with Asa Lyons and his wife, and, traveling by way of Canada, arrived in New York City on September 13, checked in at the Algonquin, went at once to the hospital for another "face operation," and dined next evening with M.

The two months in New York were not very eventful. Animated now by his consolidating plans for *Kingsblood Royal,* Lewis sought out the Negroes he already knew and cultivated others. Walter White was an old acquaintance, and he now generously made available to Lewis the files of the National Association for the Advancement of Colored People. Langston Hughes, the poet, was interested and helpful, and he supplied the novelist with letters to other Negroes. There were trips to Harlem. There were two brief trips away from New York—one to Bethlehem, Pennsylvania in the cause of research, the other to Washington for a lecture, which, once more, he was prevented from delivering in Constitution Hall. This prohibition, he announced, was "an honor."

He was writing his final pieces for *Esquire*. In one of these, he had written kind words about Richard Brooks's *The Brick Foxhole*. Brooks was about to be court-martialed by the Marine Corps for not having submitted the manuscript of his novel for official approval. His editor, Edward Aswell, asked Lewis, with a number of other prominent writers, to come to Brooks's defense, but the ire of the Marine Corps abated and nothing happened. In the meantime, however, it had been arranged that Brooks and Lewis should meet, which they did—in a bar, where Brooks did the drinking and Lewis most of the talking. Brooks was an admirer of *Elmer Gantry* and he told Lewis that he thought it would make a splendid motion picture. Lewis was skeptical about the possibilities, but he told Brooks that if he ever thought of making a screenplay of the novel, he should hunt up its outraged reviews first. He confessed that he really loved Elmer, the big bum, and hated only what he stood for; but halfway through the novel he had been carried away, had turned on his character and demolished him. "It was a helluva good pamphlet, but not such a good novel," Lewis said—or so Brooks remembered when, fifteen years later, the climate of opinion in Hollywood had at last permitted him to make an interesting if eviscerated film of *Elmer Gantry.*

Cass Timberlane presented no such problems as did that earlier novel: it was being serialized in *Cosmopolitan;* the films had seized upon it as a perfect vehicle for Spencer Tracy and Lana Turner, the "sweater girl"; even before publication, John O'Hara had gone to work on the scenario. Publication day was October 3. Then the familiar Lewis face appeared once more on the covers of periodicals. The *Saturday Review,* in a kindly mood, had asked Frances O'Brien Garfield to glamorize a little her original sketch, which was accurate and "school-teacherish"—and Lewis was pleased with the softened result. During his sitting at the Algonquin, surrounded by photographs of Miss Powers, he had talked at length about the loss of a great newspaperwoman when Dorothy Thompson took to the soapbox. In *Cass Timberlane,* he had himself stepped down from the soapbox: it is a "love story."

It is his own thinly veiled love story, or rather, an extrapolation of such little love story as he had; and from this situation arise his chief novelistic difficulties. Cass Timberlane is presented as forty-one years old, in love with a girl of twenty-three; but he behaves in some ways like a man of sixty, in others, like a fumbling boy of sixteen. If Lewis had learned, as he told Miss Powers, how judges "make love," this knowledge does not seem to have been applied to Cass, who makes love like Sinclair Lewis—which is to say, when not apologetically, uncertainly, and timidly, then with clumsy coyness. Cass's most remarkable quality—which goes unremarked—is his sexual naïveté, and when Jinny Marshland leaves him and enjoys an adulterous affair with his contemporary and best friend, it is not, the reader must assume, his age that has been his problem. As the picture of Jinny Marshland moving ambiguously into the society of Grand Republic is an extension of Lewis's impression of Miss Powers's reception in Duluth, so all the mooning affection (at least as fatherly as it is husbandly) that Cass feels for Jinny, and all the dumb loneliness that he suffers without her, are Lewis's, too. Writing most of his novel in Duluth, in a room on one wall of which he had tacked an enormously detailed map of his imaginary city not so very different from Duluth, more important than any novelistic considerations of verisimilitude were the personal considerations of whether Miss Powers would come to him and on what terms she could be persuaded to stay.

A number of reviewers were quick to observe a basic similarity in pattern between this novel and *Main Street:* a young woman comes into a strange town, marries a rather stolid citizen of that place, leaves him for jollier companions, returns to her husband in disillusioned defeat, and is accepted by him. There are important variations: if Carol came home because she was pregnant, Jinny comes home because Cass goes to her and rescues her from a nearly fatal attack of diabetes; if Carol's return represented the triumph of Kennicott, on whose terms she would now perforce live, Jinny's return represents the defeat of Cass Timberlane and his acceptance of her will and of her rule.

> Then, for her and his love for her, he gave up his vested right to be tragic, gave up pride and triumph and all the luxury of submerged resentment, and smiled at her with the simplicity of a baby.

If, at the end of *Main Street,* it was Doc Kennicott who was wondering about storm windows, at the end of *Cass Timberlane* that masculine consideration has become the business of Jinny Marshland, "the best storm-window fixer in this town."

This end troubled, among others, Philip Wylie, the expert on "momism," who wondered what prompted Lewis to contrive a " 'happy ending' out of a silly woman's unintentional victimization of her husband—a husband's acceptance of inward cravenness." Was Lewis himself an unwitting victim of America's matriarchal complex, or did he really believe that passionate love of woman involves male abandonment of dignity, integrity, emotional balance and honor?

> It is in a third possibility that I rest my guess. The possibility that *Cass Timberlane* is the most sinister of all the Lewis books. If I am right, its subtlety is equal to its sting. If I am right, the author who has beheaded so many hypocritical liars, who has shouted out the defilement of so many villages and cities, and who has nailed the right names on such a variety of institutions and faiths, is now using a delicate and quieter instrument to make a lethal hole in America's love nest. For, in the "happy" ending of *Cass Timberlane*—by the author's own definition—the couple is not glorified but doomed. Doomed to more suspicion and frustration, despair and detestation, disapproval and misunderstanding, quarrel and provocation. . . .

The prognostication seems sound enough, but not the attribution of intent. The story of Cass and Jinny is treated with a kind of sentimental affection, with only the faintest overtones of irony, and its treatment marks it off very sharply from the treatment of marriage in a whole group of surrounding sketches which the novel presents under the heading of "An Assemblage of Husbands and Wives." In these often brutally conceived accounts of female willfulness, tyranny and lechery, the recognition of the American matriarchy is as clear as the method is uncompromisingly satirical. It is as if the novelist is trying to say two things at once, that all these are American marriages in general, including his own two marriages, but that this one at the center is another matter, the marriage that he would now make if he could. With the slightest change of method—that is to say, with the slightest shift in perspective on his own situation—that central marriage would become only another in the degraded assemblage of marriages at large. But one must remember that even Lewis's best novels were not notable for their clarity of point of view or for their power of self-evaluation. Should one expect these of him at sixty, infatuated?

The novel, understandably enough, irritated certain ladies. Mary Colum announced that she now understood "why the position of women in America is really the worst in any Western country, and . . . why there is practically no love poetry in American literature." Diana Trilling, seeing Lewis as "the victim of his own divided heart," observed the difference between this and some of the earlier work:

> Whereas in books like *Main Street* and *Babbitt* it was Mr. Lewis's special gift to be able to explore the social value of habitual manners and attitudes of which we had hitherto been scarcely aware, in *Cass Timberlane* he deals almost entirely in observations that have been part of our cliché-thinking about love and marriage for many a year.

Marjorie Farber, writing in the *New Republic,* found the "male archness stuffy, if not downright corny," and was, in her brief notice, as impatient with the book as the most severe of the male reviewers, A. C. Spectorsky, with his flat dismissal of it as among Lewis's worst. One or two male reviewers—rather surprisingly, both Edmund Wilson and Edward Weeks—did not think at all badly of the novel. And for Lewis himself, there were, besides these few favorable opinions, other compensations. When the novel became a Book-of-the-Month Club choice, his film contract called for another $50,000; and when the sales of the novel passed the 400,000 mark, still another $50,000 was due him.*

He was too old and too rich and too involved in other matters to worry about the ultimate implications of his reviews. Was not the essence of such a comment as this—

> The author of the Main Street series never seems to be aware that what is the matter with his people is that they are adolescents and always will be and that their lack of cultivation, of sensitivity, their sophistication about material things, the filial attitude of the men to their wives, all are simply an ugly juvenility

—was not the essence, really, the problem in Sinclair Lewis's own life, simply the fact that he was, at the center of himself, beneath the gilded trappings and the expansive gestures, no larger, no more mature, no more human than these characters, forever trapped in a coarse and starved and empty youth?

H. L. Mencken had glimmers of the situation, and tried to let them gleam through a long letter full of banter.

* In all editions, the total sales of this novel were to reach 1,140,000 copies—nearly a million more than *Gideon Planish.*

Dear Red:—

I am not going to tell you that *Cass Timberlane* is comparable to *Babbitt* or *Elmer Gantry* (all except the last 30,000 words, which you wrote in a state of liquor), but it seems to me to be the best thing you have done, and by long odds, since *Dodsworth*. It has the same defect that *Dodsworth* had: the woman is such a bitch that it is hard to imagine a sensible man falling for her. But you have a right to set your own story, and in *Cass Timberlane* you have managed admirably. There is not a trace of the banality that I howled against in *Ann Vickers*. There is none of the patriotic fustian that made me sick in *It Can't Happen Here*. There is no going to pieces toward the end, as in *Gideon Planish*. In brief, a well-planned and well-executed book, with a fine surface. . . .

The country swarms with subjects for your future researches. You did the vermin of the Coolidge era, but those of the Roosevelt and post-Roosevelt eras are still open—the rich radical, the bogus expert, the numskull newspaper proprietor (or editor), the career job-holder, the lady publicist, the crooked (or, more usually, idiotic) labor leader, the press-agent, and so on. This, I believe, is your job, and you have been neglecting it long enough. There are plenty of writers of love stories and Freudian documents, though not many as good at it as you are, but there is only one real anatomist of the American Kultur. I think it stinks, but whether it stinks or not is immaterial. It deserves to be done as *you* alone can do it.

Please don't let the fact that you are approaching bliss eternal stay you. You have done a better book at 60 than you were doing at 50. I myself have printed five since 60, and all of them have sold better than those done 20 years ago. Moreover, I have yielded nothing in them to the current hooey: in all of them I stick to my guns. You are, of course, further gone in sin than I am, but you have just proved that you are still very much alive, so I renew my old urgings and solicitations, and curst be he who first cries "Hold! Enough!" You have no duty to humanity, to be sure: to hell with humanity. But you owe something to Red Lewis, the poor immigrant boy from Poland.

Seeing you on the water-wagon affects me like seeing you on your knees. It is intolerably obscene. But if it is necessary, then let us forget it. At any moment the quacks may order me to join you. If so, I shall thank them for their advice—and retire to a brewery.

This letter is too long, but it is now too late for you to do anything about it. . . .

In the course of it, Mencken had said that he felt that Lewis put too much emphasis on sexual intercourse, that it is less important in marriage than conversation. And he expressed the hope that in his next novel he would show his hero asserting his superiority and his masculine independence over his heroine's efforts at domination.

I hope that *Cass* is selling well, and that you are not laying out all your lucre on ice-cream sodas. If you had any fixed place of abode, like a decent

Christian, and it were near to Baltimore, we might meet now and then and think up nasty names for our enemies. But God seems determined to keep us apart. Maybe we will meet in Heaven. I surely hope not.

Yours,

HLM

There is buried advice, both literary and personal, in this letter, but Lewis was probably not concerned to dig it out; what concerned him at the moment, the early weeks of November 1945, were road maps. He had had plans for investigating Ohio and Michigan, but he was hoping to write a novel about Negroes and he had at his service a willing and companionable driver, a man of the people who could take him to the heart of the people with whom he was concerned. They would tour the South! Mrs. Lyons could return to Duluth by train. Mrs. Powers could follow her and get the house in order. He would tour for a month and return in time for Christmas and a visit from Mrs. Powers's daughter. On November 15 they set out.

The first pause of any length was at Columbia, South Carolina, where on November 18 Lewis sought out a friend in the state university, recently of Duluth, named John B. McConaughy. McConaughy arranged a meeting with a group of students who were interested in founding a literary magazine, and for two hours Lewis gave them his advice. That evening he was entertained at a large stag dinner attended by the governor of the state and the president of the university and twenty-odd professors, and he tried to draw these people out on the subject of racial segregation. After dinner he told McConaughy that he wanted to meet a really violent segregationist, and McConaughy produced one Professor Grubb, who solemnly cited Biblical sanctions for segregation while Lewis appeared solemnly to listen.

Next morning he addressed a large student audience on the new maturity of Americans and chatted informally about writing in general and his experience in particular. In the afternoon, he pressed McConaughy into further service when they made an expedition into the Negro section of the town and knocked at random doors only to ask the startled householder what he most wanted in life. One woman said that what she most wanted was that her son be educated at the best college in the United States, which seemed to be South Carolina State College for Negroes, at Orangeburg. To McConaughy, Lewis said that he thought the students at South Carolina were the best he had ever encountered, and he said that if the university would find him a house, he would like to stay there to teach. The prospect caused a flurry of excitement in the university, but after Lewis spoke next day at Benedict College, a Negro Baptist institution in Columbia, the matter was dropped, and he went on to Orangeburg, to tell the Negro students there about the literary accomplishments of their fellow, Richard Wright.

They drove across Alabama and Georgia, to Oxford, Mississippi, in the expectation of waiting on William Faulkner, and while they found his "Ole

Plantation," they did not find him. Then they turned south, Lewis asking his questions and making his notes as they went. In one backwoods Mississippi hamlet, after Lewis had talked to a group of Negroes, Asa Lyons remembered, the townspeople pressed angrily around the car of the "nosy Northerners," and as Lewis and Lyons drove away in haste, "two pistol slugs whistled an ugly farewell over the cartop." Frightened if not injured, they proceeded to Meridian, to Biloxi and to New Orleans, always for the briefest stops, and then north again to Piney Woods and the Country Life School of Dr. Laurence C. Jones. There they stayed for about a week—ten days in the recollection of Dr. Jones, a remarkable Negro with whom Lewis spent hours in discussion and in observing the operation of his school and the living conditions and attitudes of Negroes in the surrounding country. From Piney Woods, one day, he telephoned Hodding Carter at Greenville, to the west and north, and asked if he could come there next day to talk about his son Wells. Carter was hospitable, but Lewis neither came nor explained. Instead, he went to the west and south, to Natchez, and then, by way of Alexandria and Shreveport, north again, and back to Duluth, where he arrived on December 9 to be greeted by Mrs. Powers.

Her daughter arrived for a Christmas visit on December 20 and left again on December 29. The year came to an end and so, presently, did the experimental attempt to put down roots in Duluth. Miss Powers did not wish to stay. What was there, then, really, except a very bitter winter? "A whole landscape *fuzzy* with fallen snow. . . . Snow on ground *drags* at feet when walk."

Duluth had been exhausted as a research field in the problems of the Negro, and on January 9 Lewis went to Minneapolis to work in the offices of the Urban League and in the State Historical Library, in Negro churches and Negro newspaper offices and Negro saloons, to dine with his friends, and to invite the young writers Ann Chidester and Feike Feikema to visit him when he returned to Duluth. Before he returned to Duluth, however, he was called to Sauk Centre for the funeral of his brother Fred. It was the bleakest time of year in that bleak prairie, "the great gray plain with snow flying." Roots? Poor Fred had never left Sauk Centre! Two days later Lewis returned to Duluth. So recently as the beginning of that January of 1946, he had been taking further options on surrounding property to protect what he called his ivory tower, but immediately on his return, he sold his house and land for $20,000 and decided to stay on as the tenant of the bank president who was its new owner only until his return from Florida in March. To the city editor of the Duluth *News-Tribune* came a telegram from the St. Paul *Pioneer Press:* "Reported here Sinclair Lewis moving away from Duluth. Also some Democrats here would like to see him run for senator against Shipstead. Can you get any dope?" To Miss Powers, Lewis wrote:

. . . aside from Marvin Oreck, and Ace, there is really no one here whom I shall much miss. I have my Grand Republic well founded, and the first story of it built, and it's time to see some more of the world, and maybe—maybe—have a house in some part of the world to which maybe—maybe—I can get you to come for a weekend once every three months or three years or something. . . . I will spend the summer somewhere in New England. . . .

Lewis had dispensed with the services of Lillian at the end of the year, and Joseph Hardrick, returned from the Army, had been put in her place as cook. At first Lewis was delighted with him. "He has grown, with Army grub; he seems very nice, and I thought the chief change in him was, from his Army experience, more and more articulate resentment about Negro segregation." House guests had not been common in Duluth, but now, with Joseph in the kitchen, Lewis welcomed the two young Minnesota writers whose books he had admired, and Feikema's wife.* They arrived on Thursday afternoon and stayed through Sunday morning, and Lewis enjoy their visit. Immediately, at tea, he told them about his novel and presented them with three possible names for his hero, asking them to choose the best; they chose Kingsblood, and he had his title. At dinner, they talked about racial intolerance and the problems of the Negro, then listened to a little Delius, and went to bed. Next day, the talk was about writers whom Lewis had known, and as they watched night close down over the lake, Lewis ruminated for a long time on how a writer reaches his peak and then declines. He told them that he was selling such furniture as he would not want to take east, and occasionally during that weekend a secondhand dealer would arrive, and Lewis would haggle with him and grow triumphant when he managed to raise an offer by a dollar or two.

That evening he had the Nolans and a few others in after dinner, and when someone mentioned a speech that Dorothy Thompson had recently made, he praised her at first, until he remembered how "bossy" she was, and then he went into a wholly inapposite burlesque of the life of Maxim Kopf as he conceived it, under what he assumed to be her stern dictatorship, and his guests, who could not know that the Kopf marriage was near to ideal, were much amused. This led Lewis into a tirade against American women in general and American marriages, and when one of his guests, a lady, said that he exaggerated, he flared at her:

What d'you mean, "exaggerated"? Of course it's not exaggerated. American women are like that. Killers of talent. Unless it's talent which helps them obtain power. But the minute it's talent that they can't control or understand, why, stab stab stab, they've got to prick the balloon. The . . . the . . . of course they're like that.

* Frederick Feikema Manfred, who formerly wrote under the name of Feike Feikema, published his detailed narrative of this visit in *American Scholar* for spring 1954. He deleted the account of the parody of Dorothy Thompson to which I here refer.

When his guest protested mildly again, he kicked back his chair and flung from the room to his study. Ace Lyons advised the embarrassed assembly to go on talking as if nothing had happened, and after much audible pacing above their heads, the host at last returned and apologized, but added that there were some wounds that did not heal. The party recovered.

The next day he explained his methods of composition to Manfred and insisted that the young man must change his publishers. He advised him, too, on certain details of manner and dress. He praised his wife, who was a quiet woman. And next day, just before the party was to leave for Minneapolis, he asked Manfred if his great bulk was an embarrassment to him, and from that he was led to point to his own face and to say that once he had been certain that anyone who professed to love him was a liar.

"Work. Work. Work," had been his final advice to Manfred, and on the day after his guests departed, January 28, he settled down to the writing out of his plan for *Kingsblood Royal,* a task that would fervently engross him for nearly two months. Joseph turned out to be something less than satisfactory as a cook, and briefly Lewis thought of employing Ace full time and Thelma, his wife, as cook in Joseph's place. Miss Powers wisely suggested to him that since the Lyonses were now his friends, they would hardly work out as servants, and Lewis agreed with her; nevertheless, they would drive him east and help him settle into whatever establishment he next found. In the meantime, Ace could take charge of crating pictures and packing books and generally preparing the move that would be made as soon as the plan for *Kingsblood Royal* was finished. The prospect of moving again gave impetus to that work and he ground through ten hours a day, seven days a week. "I am working like a fiend; I shall arrive in the east with 50 or 60,000 words of plan—plan only; not a word of MS. . . ."

As the vision of the East grew brighter, the reality of Duluth grew dingier. "Superior St now seems meagre, ill-constructed and -assorted; a small town—the First Natl Bank's proud bldg just a huddle of assorted brick boxes." On March 14 he closed the diary which had been intended as the record of his discovery at last of home and self: ". . . it is time to wander again. . . . I look for a house in New England for the summer. Then: buy a house there?—England, Ireland, Italy, Africa? Or California? Or the Root River Valley in Southern Minnesota?"

Mrs. Powers was put on the train. Then, on March 21, with Ace and Mrs. Lyons as his companions, he set out, Joseph to follow. Once in the East again, he was reported to have said that "Duluth is Margaret Banning's town." Mrs. Banning had for some time been shut out of his life. So had others who had at first been friends. Now all of Duluth was put aside. Whether or not he said that it was Mrs. Banning's town, it was clear to him that, like every other place, Duluth was not his town.

6

MADISON, TOLEDO, JAMESTOWN, Auburn, Williamstown, Pittsfield, Providence, Provincetown, New Haven, Williamstown again. Ten days, and Williamstown it was to be. The place was called Thorvale Farm, four and a half miles south of Williamstown on Oblong Road—a fine and spacious house set on 750 acres of field and wood and mountain, and commanding, from its front terraces, a splendid view of Mt. Greylock. The house had seven bedrooms, five baths, and was furnished. One cottage made excellent servants' quarters. There was a guest cottage as well, and a tennis court, and, in a glen of birches, a swimming pool. There were barns, a sugar-maple grove of three thousand trees, and a house for a farmer. Briefly, Lewis debated between this establishment and another across the Vermont border, but when, having driven him back and forth between the two places a number of times, Joseph said, "This is the house for you, Mr. Lewis," Mr. Lewis decided that it was. He rented it for five months, from New York, where in the early days of April he was staying at the Algonquin, and, having arranged with Asa Lyons in Duluth to ship his belongings east and to follow them himself, he retired to the Williams Inn on April 15. There, on April 20, he began to write his novel *Kingsblood Royal,* and on April 22 he moved into Thorvale Farm. Almost at once he decided to buy the property. His belongings arrived. Joseph persuaded friends in New Orleans, Alma and Wilson Perkins, to come to Williamstown as Lewis's servants. The place was glorious. This must be home at last!

On June 18, Lewis completed the purchase at $45,000. He had employed a contractor and now spent over $70,000 on repairs and improvements. A family named Bishop was established in the farmhouse, a fine dairy herd in the barns and fields; he bought the best farming equipment and ordered that a new reservoir be dug in the hills; and up went what was undoubtedly the finest henhouse in all New England. He was to be the squire of Oblong Road.

He was beset by a notion of manorial splendor: his house, his farmers, his pool, his tennis court, his view, his hills, his attendants—it was his home at last, and he would make it all as perfect as his image of it. And so, in the externals, he did. When a guest remarked on the acoustics of the dining room, the contractor was summoned and instantly arrangements were made for new ceilings throughout all the main rooms. When the roof showed need of moderate repair, the contractor was summoned, the old shingles were removed, and an entire new roof went on. The swimming pool was rebuilt and attractive new lounging furniture arranged at its sides. He was never known to use the pool. To Abercrombie went orders for the finest sporting equipment: a great archery set, its target hardly ever to be pierced; superb fishing and hunting equipment; a whole closetful of tennis materials, nets and racquets and balls and chalkers never used except by an occasional guest. Lewis's own sporting activities were limited still to rambling walks, and to this end paths were laid out in various directions into the hills, and at any point where the prospect was very good, a bench was set up for rest and gazing and reflective Thoreauvian satisfactions.

Then there was Williamstown itself, one of the most attractive of New England towns, with its pretty colonial architecture, great elm trees arching its streets, its settled society, the college. Already Lewis had friends in the town and he would soon have more; but somehow he made very few new friends, was seldom seen in the streets, and it was Joseph rather than he who became the familiar of the townspeople. On his arrival, Lewis asked Luther Mansfield to give him a party, just a small party to meet some of Mansfield's friends. Mansfield explained the social difficulties of a small party for a lion in an academic community, that unless he asked at least twenty-five people, the bitterness of the uninvited would make his own life intolerable. He showed him a tentative guest list and Lewis began to ask questions about the people on the list; Mansfield gave him a little bio-bibliographical tag for each name, and these Lewis jotted down on the back of an envelope. On reconsideration of his problem, Mansfield decided that there were five more people whom he would really have to invite, but he decided to say nothing about them to Lewis, who would hardly know the difference.

At the party, Lewis was a positive model of gracious comportment, and, putting names to faces, he began to converse personally with each of the original twenty-five, until he discovered that something was wrong. In a hallway, he clutched Mansfield's arm—who were those others, he had no knowledge of them! Mansfield explained and supplied supplementary information; then Lewis returned to the party, continued his charming conduct, and left thirty marveling guests. They began at once to invite him to their houses in the usual manner, with about a week's notice; but Lewis hated to commit himself for even so short a time ahead, and he would either say that he could not be certain but would come if he could and then would not come, or he would decline. Almost without entering it, he dropped out of Williamstown life, and he began to resent the town and would grow furious that there were no more invitations to decline.

At the outset, too, he had hopes that he could play some part in the college. Very early he asked his friend Samuel Allen to introduce him to the president, James Phinney Baxter. Since Baxter many years before had been a student of Allen's, Allen felt quite free to make an appointment, but he was almost as astonished as the president when, arriving at his office, Lewis without any preparation announced that he wanted to teach at Williams. Baxter was so surprised that he could not respond at all except with embarrassed noises, and the resulting conversation was stiff and painful. Nor was his proposal ever pursued. The only faintly official invitation that he received from the college came from the Garfield Club, a kind of social catch-all for nonfraternity men with whom, on one occasion, he dined. Shades of youth and New Haven!

Through Joseph Hardrick he met a number of Negro families and at least once he went to a Pittsfield social gathering of Negroes, where he led the discussion on the topic that at this point interested him most, anti-Negro prejudice. (He had finished his first draft of *Kingsblood Royal* five weeks after beginning it, and was spending the remainder of the summer in revision.) At quite another social extreme, he became friendly in a casual way with his nearest neighbor, a successful young attorney named O. Dixon Marshall, and with still other neighbors, the former Governor of Rhode Island, William H. Vanderbilt, and his wife. In the college, his only close friendship developed with Max Flowers, the director of the student theater, and his wife, and these people, in the next year, when they were suffering academic misfortunes, Lewis put up in his guest house.

But chiefly he depended on his friends in New York and was continually urging them to visit him. Miss Powers came for ten days in May, and for at least a weekend in each of the next four months. Jane White, an actress, the daughter of Walter White, came with her once. George Jean Nathan came for five days, and the Cerfs for four. Louis Untermeyer and a lady-friend came, and Alan Collins together with Mrs. Powers, and the Harry Maules, and Carl Van Doren. ("Let's not lose each other," Lewis begged early in May, and wrote him all through that summer, promising him all the country pleasures, until, at last, in September, Van Doren managed his visit.) Late in September, Saxe Commins came, too, for a week—to go over *Kingsblood Royal* line by line. On September 28, Lewis followed Commins to New York, and on that day his new novel went to the printers.

One who might well have been, but was not, asked to come was Michael Lewis from nearby Barnard, Vermont, for Michael was a problem that his father, in a perversely stubborn way, did not intend to confront. In August of the year before, the boy's mother had suggested that they discuss together the immediate problem of Michael's expenses and the larger matter of his economic future. That letter was never answered. At the end of March in 1946, when Lewis was spending his $70,000 refurbishing his $45,000 property, she wrote again, this time not about money but about affection.

Michael had done badly in his academic subjects at his military school, Valley Forge, although he had become a good cadet. She had thought of sending him to school in Switzerland, where, *faute de mieux,* he would learn some languages, but his extreme pleasure at the thought had given her pause about his whole attitude toward school as indicated in a letter that she enclosed for the boy's father.

> Hal, I wish you would pay some attention to him. He needs you. You do not, as he thinks, like him. He is not resentful of you but attributes it to some inferiority in himself. You are a famous man, and his schoolmates ask him about you, and he makes up stories rather than admit that he may not see or hear from you for a year on end. . . . He will be sixteen on June 20th and we are going to have a party. Why don't you come for it—that would be the best present you could give him . . . just to take note of the fact that he was born.

And she begs for advice as to his education.

On June 20 Lewis was giving a poolside picnic for Max Flowers and his wife. In the meantime, he had responded to the enclosure from Michael, which had made it quite plain that he detested school.

> I am a romantic soul. To me the idea of exploring, etc. is the height of a man's ambition. I am hideously tired of sitting in a stuffy classroom, listening to a sonorous voice drone on interminably. . . . You're right. I wish to go to Switzerland to see the country, not the school; were the school in Abyssinia I would give it the same enthusiasm, probably more . . .

And the letter continued by saying that if he could choose, he would go to work on a farm until he had saved enough money to travel. To this the father suggested briefly that the boy's mother take him at his word. She replied:

> *Dear Hal:* Thank you for your letter. I asked for the opportunity to talk with you about Michael, not for a snap judgment. If you do not wish to come to Vermont, may I come to speak with you in Williamstown?

There was no reply.

Toward the end of June she wrote again. She did not feel that she could let Michael go to work since his whole impulse was really to "escape all restrictions." She suggests the need of a father's attention by recounting Michael's adventures in New York on the way home from school, when he brought drunken schoolfellows and cheap women into her empty apartment and appeared at Twin Farms thereafter a good deal the worse for wear. The experience has made it clear that she must keep him near her, even tutor him at home, if necessary, in the following year. Once more she appeals to Lewis for moral support, and now, again, for financial support of the boy as well. Could he not so supplement the trust fund that Michael could count on two thousand dollars a year?

> I cannot understand your attitude, for normally speaking you have a strong sense of responsibility and duty. I can only think that some psychological quirk impels you to hit at me through him. But I say strongly to that, that, first, it is difficult to understand why that feeling should continue, and apparently have become augmented through years when I have certainly never injured you in any conceivable way whatever my errors may have been in the past, and whatever hurts I may have inflicted; and, secondly, to hurt one's own child because of resentment against his mother, is not worthy of you or anyone else. I am asking you to help Michael and to help me to help Michael, and I do not think what I ask is unreasonable or unjustified.

In a postscript, she begs him to talk to "someone who likes you and who knows Michael. For instance, with John Gunther."

Gunther did make a July visit to Thorvale Farm, but that was after this exchange had come to a stony end, and one may assume that parental obligations to a rather alarmingly wayward son did not take up any part of their conversation.

The correspondence, at this point, ended abruptly. On the weekend that Lewis was entertaining Miss Powers and Miss Jane White, he wrote:

> About once every year and a half, we go thru the same correspondence. You allege that you have been supporting Michael entirely, and I answer that this is untrue.
>
> When we were divorced, I turned over to you the two houses, whose total value was and is something over $100,000—a sum on which even so low a rate of return as 2% would bring $2000 a year.
>
> In return, you were to contribute all of Michael's support above this $2000.00.
>
> That was the agreement; that is the agreement; I see no merit in the annual re-explanation of it.

This was, of course, a bewildering reply, and his divorced wife pointed out its absurdity. The Bronxville house was given to her at the time of purchase; it had burned before their divorce; she collected $20,000 insurance plus $3,000 for the ground, and interest on that sum, she said, would be about $560 a year. Furthermore, there never was an agreement between them. He had offered her $10,000 a year, which she had declined; he had offered $2,500 a year for Michael's support, which she had also declined because at that time it seemed unnecessary, but certainly she had declined only with the understanding that Lewis would help whenever the boy had unusual expenses. To place the marketable value of Twin Farms at $70,000 was ridiculous; and as a part of Michael's inheritance, it was imperative that it not be sold. Finally, the imputation that she had begged for Michael for years was false—not until the year before had she asked for any increased financial support. The fate of one's own child was at stake, but she would not write him again.

That letter was received at Williamstown while Nathan was visiting

Lewis, and Lewis was planning another picnic. He enjoyed entertaining beside the swimming pool, where he had set up a barbecue grill. This convenience was contributing much to the jollity of the summer. In his house was a grandfather's clock, and he kept reminding himself, in his engagement book, to "Wind Clock." Time *was* passing. . . . And, thinking about his novel on the subject of Negroes, he took slow walks over his acres, accompanied by his black cat named William Makepeace Thackeray Shakespeare, an animal that Joseph Hardrick could not endure.

When he had finished his novel and was waiting for Commins to arrive, he wrote two brief articles. One was an encomium of H. G. Wells, who had recently died, with a humorous recollection of his visit to Wells's country place more than two decades before, and of Wells's forcing the inept Lewis into tennis and handball. This is amusing only because in this very summer, a proud country squire himself now, he treated his guests in precisely the same way except that he did not join them. When the Cerfs arrived, he showed them the tennis court and insisted that they play. They demurred; he was adamant. At last they yielded and got into tennis clothes. Bennett Cerf struggled to get up the net, which had apparently never been put up, and they began their game, but they had just started to play when Lewis charged out of the house and announced that it was time for them to come for a walk. Again, they protested, but to no avail; so once more they changed their clothes and went for the walk with him.

The second essay, on "Fiction Writing," where a similar disparity appears, was written for a popular encyclopedia. Having just completed a novel that was almost perversely mechanical, he tried to warn young writers against "standardized junk turned out on an assembly line—ill made and selling cheap." His novel, to be certain, had a "shocking" rather than a conventional subject matter, but the very disparity between the seriousness of his theme and its factitious presentation draws attention to the machinery. Writing, he pointed out further, is chiefly a matter of "work." So, in a recent interview with Robert Van Gelder, he had said, "Writing is just work—there's no secret. If you dictate or use your toes—it is still just work." That is really the only important advice that an older writer can give to a younger. (He might have added that, if you worked as hard as he did and could use only two fingers at the typewriter, it was a help to bind up those two fingers in adhesive tape before approaching the typewriter, as he did.) In this mood, and at the time, he wrote to a young woman at the University of Wisconsin who had asked for a piece on writing for the student paper:

> Why so much advice from old hacks to your young writers, who seem to be doing very well on their own? Advice is the cast-off clothing of the philanthropic exhibitionist.

In New York he stayed at the Algonquin for about ten days, shopped around for terrace furniture, saw his agent and his attorney and Miss

Powers and his publishers, and returned to Williamstown for a series of sessions with his dentist that would result in spare dentures. He continued the repairs of his house, getting it ready for winter and completing the furnishings. (It was a curious fact about that house that the only double bed was in his room and that in the other rooms there was only one single bed, so that even husbands and wives were compelled to separate under his roof.) He fussed endlessly with the details of "M's room" and bath, and he enjoyed two weekends, one in October and another in November, with that young woman. Michael Amrine, whom she had first met in New Orleans when her association with Lewis was new, had proposed marriage to her, and she was determined to end her drifting. One evening they were sitting on the long sofa in Lewis's living room, he reading Dickens and she pasting stamps into a new album. Sad but determined, she announced her intention to marry. Lewis paled, put down his book, and left the room, but presently he returned and said that if marriage to Amrine was what she wanted, very well, but if it did not work out she was to come back to him without any question, and would she please remember that? And about marriage they said no more.

He tried to think about a new novel. Almost inevitably, his mind turned once more to the "labor novel"; because of it he visited the factory town of Waterbury, Connecticut, for three or four days in December and, in the same month, briefly cultivated the acquaintance of the radical economist at Williams College, Professor Frederick L. Schuman. Schuman, a theoretical Marxist like so many of Lewis's advisers before him, could not have been of much help in furthering his novelistic ideas, and he was more frequently playing chess with his neighbor Dixon Marshall, or chatting about books and plays with Luther Mansfield and Max Flowers.

Mansfield was a young unmarried man who could be summoned without prearrangement or who would himself drop in casually at Thorvale Farm, late in the afternoon, without announcement. Lewis was at ease with him and talked freely with him. He told him, for example, that he had at first blamed Dorothy Thompson for the failure of their marriage, but when he heard her tell Churchill how to run the war, he knew that she needed a bigger man than he was. It was a variant on an old story, but he told it amusingly; he was never malicious about her, harsh as his letters to her could be, but rather merry, which they never were. He was similarly relaxed with Flowers, and with him he could talk shop about the theater. More than this, Flowers had become something of a cause. President Baxter had let him know that he would not be reappointed to the Williams faculty, and this outrage endeared him to Lewis. Indignantly, he spoke to others of the waste of this great theatrical talent, and in early December, he sent him to a friend in a theatrical agency in New York in the hope that there would be someone there who "will talk with him about the possibilities of directing and kindred magic arts in Hollywood."

When Christmas approached, he decided that he would have a festive holiday dinner for Mansfield and the Flowerses and their young boy, Jonathan. Joseph had set up a great Christmas tree for the boy's pleasure, and when the guests arrived at about noon, Lewis devoted himself to Jonathan for at least an hour before they dined. Full of apparent interest in him, he regaled him with stories, and he presented him with a little Christmas book with the inscription, "For Jonathan, from that ugly, red-faced man who asked you to Thorvale Farm on Christmas, 1946." There were two enormous turkeys, and wine, and all was jolly, but by the time that dinner was over, Lewis had had enough of Jonathan. "Why don't you go up and take a nap now?" he asked, and to the boy's parents, "Jonathan's not sleepy. Why doesn't he go out now and play?" On New Year's Eve, the Flowerses were once more with Lewis, but without Jonathan. Lewis's plan, so late as December 22, had been to "wander off South till not later than the middle of April," but between then and the end of the year, a telephone call had come from Hollywood that had changed this plan. And it was now Lewis, not his friend Flowers, who was once more packing trunks for California. He left for New York with Joseph on January 4, 1947.

In New York the good news was that *Kingsblood Royal* was a Literary Guild selection, and there was just enough time for Lewis to write a little essay on the novel for the Guild publication, *Wings,* in which he anticipated some of the objections that would be made to his book. Then, on January 8, the New York *Times* announced that Sinclair Lewis would arrive in Hollywood that week to write a photoplay for Leo McCarey under the title, *Adam and Eve*—a satire. St. Clair McKelway had begun the project and had abandoned it. It had been planned for Ingrid Bergman and James Stewart, but they had withdrawn. Now Sinclair Lewis was to rewrite the script completely and save it from ruin for McCarey's direction.

He left New York in mid-January and *Time* magazine reported that, two days after his arrival, at a party of Hedda Hopper's, Lewis was talking "like a native."

> "The movies are no more commercial," declared Lewis, "than any other form of art. . . . There is no reason to suppose that a poor man starving in a garret writes better than a rich man living in a mansion. . . . Human beings are one hundred percent commercial as hell. . . . Rembrandt was one of the most commercial bastards that ever lived."

The brash accents are familiar, but to some, at least, the person was less so. In his nervous shattered state, shaking and twitching, he attracted the attention of Meta Ries, who became his Hollywood agent chiefly because she felt that he needed someone who would be gentle with him. His charm and warmth and goodness were always apparent, and yet he seemed really abstracted from any individual involvement, had yielded to a deep withdrawal in the midst of the social clatter that superficially he still sought.

There were engagements every night: the names that appear in the engagement book are those of Nunnally, Cedric, Bogie, Hersholt, Nathan, Browne, Lubitsch, Kate, Mankiewicz, Hornblow, Dore, Cukor, Kit and so on, sprinkled with those of young females who might as well be anonymous —Valerie and Darleen and Eve, and the places are Chasen's and Romanoff's and LaRue. Stephen Longstreet remembers a large party given by Robert Nathan for writers to meet Thomas Mann and Sinclair Lewis. Mann, at one end of the room, was surrounded by a covey of refugees; Lewis, at the other, by a lot of American hacks: the two groups did not mingle, and Nathan spent his time scurrying back and forth between them, trying to bridge the gap. To Longstreet, Lewis at last said, "Let's get drunk," and they left for the bar of the Beverly Wilshire, where they did get drunk; and presently Lewis did an imitation of Thomas Mann receiving the Nobel prize—to the befuddled amusement of about four other drunks in the nearly empty bar.

But such lapses were rare for Lewis, and he was working hard in the daytime. As usual, he at first found his employer attractive. "A sweet person, and very quick," he wrote; "we work not in the mill of a big studio but in his own extensive offices; altogether the two weeks have been pleasant." But in two more weeks there had been a row with McCarey and Lewis was finished with his work on the script.

> ... I am back to the play. I'll stay around here until February 25 or so, then north to see if I can get a cottage for four weeks, near Monterey, before returning to Williamstown. ...
>
> Bennett and Phyllis [Cerf] are here, very sweet and eager, and I like them. And Joseph is enjoying it—we got a good rented car, very necessary, as out here I am about ten miles from Beverly Hills, twenty from the heart of L.A.

He was writing Miss Powers from the Ambassador Beach Club, at Santa Monica. It was there that he was interviewed at breakfast on his sixty-second birthday and said that he had not changed his mind about George F. Babbitt, that he had not been unkind to him in the first place.

His birthday party was dinner at the Hersholts' house on Rodeo Drive, where he inscribed a copy of *Cass Timberlane,* "To Jean Hersholt, bless him! On my 62nd birthday—damn it!" It was now, too, with the Cerfs, that he heard the unhappy news that Miss Powers was definitely to marry Michael Amrine. His response was to rage, and to pronounce in deliberate but strangled tones, over and over, "I—won't—let—her—go!"

Yet he did nothing to prevent the fulfillment of her plans. Perhaps he recognized some inevitability in the tidy pattern of numbers that marked the end of his major attachments: he was forty-two when he left his first wife, fifty-two when he left his second, and sixty-two when this girl, with a kind of honor, had determined on a marriage of her own and left him. And he must have had premonitions enough, or at least some hindsight. Summarizing the year 1946, probably now or later in 1947, he wrote: "1946 quite a yr! Wrote Kb, plan Responsible, sold Duluth, bought & repaired & refurnished Thorvale." Then he made one of his balance sheets of his personal relations. After the relentless symbol for deletion appears first of all the initial "M," and after that, "Mrs. Malick & Nolan," his best friends in Duluth, then "Ace & Thelma," who had somehow not worked out after all, and then the name of the young man in Williamstown whom, for a time, he had fancied as a research assistant and secretary, Russell Lembke. Following these losses, he lists his gains: "Found Hooper, Dick Marshall, Flowers, Cook, Mary Parrish, Chet Syms, Reynolds & Denton, Davy Deans, 2 Stans, Oley." Most of these names are those of workmen who had helped him refurbish his house and grounds.

The blow did not interrupt his work. The New York *Times* announced that he was writing his play, *The Responsible Man,* and that Cheryl Crawford would have the first look at it for possible fall production. Every morning at ten his secretary would come to his rooms and he would appear in pajamas and, having had his first coffee hours before, order a lavish breakfast for the two of them. After they had eaten it they would work for two hours, at which point he would ordinarily nap, and then they would work again until late in the afternoon. Nor had the blow destroyed his humor. When Hemingway, Dos Passos and Lewis were invited by the government of Czechoslovakia, through State Department channels, to visit the country and report on economic and political conditions to the United States, Lewis declined in a letter of February 22, saying, "Biting journalists should allow no hand to feed them." Nor had it changed his habits: on February 25 he left for Carmel and got as far as Santa Barbara, where he took a house on Anacapa Street for six weeks.

A letter of March 1 to Miss Powers suggests that he refused to admit to his knowledge:

> This is a lovely town between great mountains and great sea. . . . I have found an excellent house which I have taken for six weeks—till April 12—which means I'll be in New York before April 20, then to our Simple Rural Home. . . . I am making hard on the play, now named *Responsible,* and perfect for Cedric.*

But a week later he wrote her once more, now in resignation; he had heard from others that her marriage was to take place that month:

> I send you every most affectionate, admiring and earnest hope for your great happiness, and my strong feeling that Mike and you will find it. You are a great person, both wise and amiably mad; to have known you has been the one distinguished event of my life. . . .

* The penultimate attempt to deal with his labor materials, this play came to nothing although he wrote it through to the end. Williard Hardhack, president of a machine tool company, is "the responsible man" who fights the foolish idealism of his father and daughter on the one hand and the machinations of a crooked C.I.O. organizer on the other.

7

HE HAD BEEN in Santa Barbara for over two weeks before he decided to "find" Alfred Harcourt again. Harcourt had retired from the firm that he had helped to found and was living with his wife in Santa Barbara, and if Lewis's engagement book is to be trusted, they met four times in as many weeks. In his *Recollections,* published after Lewis's death, Harcourt did not remember these occasions specifically nor even the year—they seemed to him to have taken place two years nearer the time of writing than they in fact had—but in a conversation later he recalled their last meeting, when they dined together on the pier at Santa Barbara on a warm spring evening (it was April 4), and enjoyed the most satisfactory talk of their entire acquaintanceship, easy, on every possible subject, rich in reminiscence, deep and personal. As Lewis's life approached its end, more and more of his relationships broke off in shattered, jagged points; all the more satisfying, then, that this one, among his oldest, should have healed itself and been rounded out in a warm serenity. Whether it reduced or heightened his loneliness—the knowledge that such experiences need not be rare in human life—one can hardly say.

On the day after he first met Harcourt again, he began a promising new attachment with a much younger man. Fresh from Yale and Spain, Barnaby Conrad was a Santa Barbara boy who wanted to be a painter and a writer of fiction and a bullfighter and a number of other fine things, and Miss Powers, having taken him on as a client, suggested that he look up Lewis during his stay. A week after their first meeting, Lewis saw him again, and Conrad asked him if he would read the opening seventy-five pages of a novel that he was writing. Lewis agreed. When Conrad returned on the next day, Lewis told him to throw away the first seventy-three pages, keep the last two, where the story really began, and let him see the next seventy-five. Late that night he called to say that these were fine, and over the telephone he proposed that Conrad come to Williamstown at forty-five dollars a week and his expenses. The arrangements concluded, he wrote to Miss Powers:

And thanks to you, Barnaby Conrad came to see me—extremely nice youngster, highly talented—in fact just the sort of chap for whom I was vaguely looking as secretary-fellow-loafer for Thorvale, and I have asked him to spend the summer there, and he has accepted with fervor—will be along about May 15. . . . He will really have no duties except an occasional bit of research, and he can spend all day writing, and be around for a walk now and then . . . and chess. Yes, he is . . . learning it(?)

Lewis's passion for chess did not blind him to his own ineptitude at the game or to the humor of his acting as teacher; nevertheless, even in his brief Santa Barbara stay, he found a frequent partner, someone named Ryon. Five times he met with Santa Barbara's literary luminary, the aging poet Alfred Noyes, and, besides him, saw Wright Ludington and his collection of pictures, and the local museum, a few people on the Santa Barbara campus of the university, McKinley Helm and his friend Wallace Stegner, whose writing Lewis admired, and one or two others—all once or twice at the most. If these encounters were meaningless, he yet had the satisfaction of having found once more an old friend (whom he would never see again) and of anticipating the arrival in Williamstown of a new one (who would survive for not quite four months).

In Los Angeles again on April 7, Lewis saw his agent a number of times, and H. S. Kraft, coauthor of the play *Cue for Passion,* to whom they had given the option for the dramatization of *Kingsblood Royal.* (Actually, Lewis paid Kraft for this attempt, and through the rest of the year the engagement book lists a monthly check of one thousand dollars to "Kraft," until November 19, when the entry reads: "Kraft: final 1000." In April, when this project, which would come to nothing, was new, there was the more advanced problem of the film version of *Cass Timberlane.* Arthur Hornblow, Jr., who was making the film for Metro, tells the story. He had taken John O'Hara off the script when he decided that O'Hara's intention was to show Lewis, through the film, how the novel of *Cass Timberlane* should have been conceived in the first place. Donald Ogden Stewart replaced him, but Stewart was better at lines than at scene construction, and after he finished, Lewis's old friend Sonya Levien was put on the job to patch up Stewart's work. When Lewis saw the script, he was most unsatisfied.

In the meantime, Spencer Tracy was making the protests that were usual with him in the final stages of script preparation, and Hornblow felt that if he did not keep Tracy and Lewis apart, Metro might well lose the half-million dollars that had already gone into the production. On Lewis's last day in Hollywood, Hornblow took him to lunch to talk over the problem. He knew that if he did not take him to a well-known place, Lewis would think it strange, so he took him to Romanoff's, but not before having arranged for a rear table. There Lewis began to tell him how the script should be written, and soared off into flights of foolish fancy that had no relation at all either to what he had written in the novel or to the script as it stood. When Lewis interrupted himself to ask about the well-being of Mrs. Hornblow, Hornblow said that she was at their apartment and was very eager to see him. "Fine. We'll go out there and say hello and then I have to see Tracy."

At the Hornblow apartment, he discovered a collection of all his novels in their first edition, and knowing that few people collected him, he was touched to discover that Mrs. Hornblow had been collecting him over the years. He insisted that he autograph them all, each with a special sentiment, and this project, interspersed with reminiscent chatter, took several hours. When he was finished, his train time had nearly come, he had forgotten about Spencer Tracy, and he left them happily. Next day Tracy said, "I hear Lewis was in town. Why didn't he look me up?" "He didn't have any suggestions that we could use. Don't worry, we'll straighten it out." Tracy subsided as the shooting of the film began, and while it turned out to be not as good a film as *Arrowsmith,* it was much more successful.

Lewis was in New York for five days, during which he twice saw Miss Powers; but that relationship was over, and older friends reappeared: dinner with Harrison Smith, a meeting with Dr. Traeger, dinner with Harry Maule, dinner with the Cerfs. Then back to Williamstown where, in his engagement book, he adjured himself, "Start guest letters." But before any guests arrived, *Kingsblood Royal* was published, in the first week of May.

Lewis had not been without warning as to what the reception of this novel might be. When Jonathan Cape had read the manuscript in London he wrote Lewis to say that he found the conduct of the central character completely unbelievable, but that he would go ahead with publication if Lewis insisted. He had no reply from Lewis. Random House, with its Literary Guild assurances of more than 750,000 copies,* expressed none of Cape's doubts. Advance publicity promised a Lewis novel in the great manner of the 1920s even as it maintained a tantalizingly portentous silence about the subject of the new work. When the book appeared, the black jacket said nothing beyond the title and the author's name except, "A blazing story with a theme that will jolt the nation."

Kingsblood Royal is the story of a respected young banker in Grand Republic who, together with his family, becomes the savage butt of community vengeance when he reveals that he has discovered himself to be 3.125 per cent Negro. Reviewers asked two main questions: would Neil Kingsblood have risked his ruin and the ruin of his family by unnecessarily revealing his remote ancestry? And would a community like Grand Republic, in northeastern Minnesota, have cared in the least? The answers,

* Random House trade sales amounted to 115,223 copies; total sales were nearly 1,500,000 copies.

generally, were no, and even while reviewers were sympathetic to the book's "powerful" intention and some felt that its "anger" might accomplish social good, nearly all found it an oversimplified "sociological tract" and a total failure as a work of art.

The promotion people at Random House, taking advantage of the newspaper hullabaloo, mailed a copy to Senator Bilbo, the noisiest segregationist in Washington, for his comment, but received in reply only a polite, formal note. The trouble with people who do not follow the news, they suggested to the New York *Times,* is that you cannot provoke them. Generally speaking, Southern reviewers were temperate and even thoughtful about the book's theme while agreeing with Northern reviewers that the work was no masterpiece of craftsmanship. Less sober, on the one hand, were the scores of indignant and abusive letter writers who addressed themselves directly to the author; and, on the other hand, no less a functionary than Howard Fast in the *New Masses,* who, offering Lewis shelter with the Communist Party once more, found it "the most vigorous and positive thing he has ever turned out," and contrasted him, with all his vigor, to "the young hopefuls of the Thirties—Steinbeck and Dos Passos and Saroyan and Farrell and so many others" who "have rotted into a spongy and frightful literary hopelessness."

Kingsblood Royal is probably one of those good bad books that, for the wrong reasons, continue to have a certain fascination. Here everything is somehow out of focus even within its own polemical perspective. The concentration on a single social problem makes an arid absurdity of the society within which it exists. The people of Grand Republic almost never talk of anything except the inadequacies of their Negro servants, or, if they do not have servants, of the inferiority of Negroes in general. The book has a hysteria of its own that is real (if unintended) in a way that the hysteria of the townspeople is not real at all. The reports of the failing Lewis "ear" contribute to this effect:

> That wounded Curtiss's ever-present pride of gentility, and he observed, "Bad enough for you to have a manure-shoveler for a father and a chippy like Shirley for a cousin, without having her work as a hash-hustler right next door to us—for the son of a tooth-jerker!"

Through the dialogue at all points show the bones of Lewis's research. One can see him carefully varying the possibilities from his long list of terms of abuse, ranging from "ape" to "zig," that some white men substitute for "Negro"—and all set down in his notebook, which he habitually referred to now as "Ebenezer." Similarly, into the novel comes the information that Lewis had gathered in Madison from the father of his secretary:

> Neil had asked Ash Davis for the exact genetic facts, and learned, as definite, that with the union of a "colored" and a "white" person, the children will

not have one chance in ten thousand of being darker than the darker parent. But he was to find that the universal folk belief, among such peasants as college-presidents and sewing-machine salesmen and popular lecturers . . .

There are less impersonal reminiscences: his animus toward Margaret Banning appearing in the characterization of the matron Diantha Marl; his impression of the dilemma of the Duluth valet, Nichols, personalized in Dexter Greenshaw, the headwaiter at the Fiesole Room. As with *It Can't Happen Here,* there seems to be less of real anger in *Kingsblood Royal* than of sociological schematization. It is even fair to say that the only valid emotion is Kingsblood's yearning to be accepted and loved: the Negro issue is all "work," emotionally meaningless except as it represents an "out" group into which Neil, who has no real "in" with any group, wistfully hopes to associate himself. This returns us to the lonely novelist himself.

He could take comfort in a note from the always generous John Hersey, a note that could hardly have been easy to write, and comfort the greater now that Lewis had a less grave young man in his employ. He was equally perturbed by the silence of Walter White. Clarence Decker, who was White's intimate friend, remembers his disappointment with the novel and with Lewis for his reductive treatment of the complex situation that engrossed White's whole life. It was only well after all the reviews were published that White spoke. In their dismissal of the novel as unimportant as such, the general effect of the reviews could well have been to reduce the importance of its problem. This may have been the motive behind White's statement (in the *Herald Tribune* of August 17) taking note of the critics' "rage" and defending the plausibility of Lewis's account. While the friendship between these two men was over, other Negroes were grateful to Lewis, and at the end of the year, the novel won an award from the magazine *Ebony* as the book that had done most to promote interracial understanding in 1947.

On his return from California, Lewis himself decided that perhaps it was time to promote better familial understanding. Michael's mother had consulted a lawyer about the boy's legal rights, and in response Lewis wrote her to say not only that Michael was provided for in his will but also that he was renegotiating present financial arrangements so that Michael would have two thousand dollars a year. He began, too, to send the boy a monthly check of forty dollars, perhaps because the boy, having been transferred to the Collegiate School, in New York, had been doing better in all subjects and very well in those that interested him, and perhaps, too, because entirely on his own Michael had sold two poems to *This Week.* These happy auguries did not sustain themselves through the summer, at the end of which his mother wrote Lewis again to tell him of her problems with the seventeen-year-old who had taken to driving a car like mad, not to say to drinking and wenching, and then had failed at a Woodstock tutoring school because of late hours and little work.

> He admires you immensely and in some ways tries to imitate what he thinks you are—a man who always does as he pleases and whom the world admires. I have told him over and over that you are a man of prodigious industry whose work comes before everything else, but that rolls off him.

She begs for advice, but even more, and more fervently than in the past, for fatherly companionship for the boy.

This was perhaps asking for too much, and Lewis avoided the issue by writing that Barnard afforded many more opportunities for companionship for a boy than a lonely farm outside Williamstown. "It was *your* companionship I craved for him," she replied, "and that he craves for, too, as I *well* know. I'm afraid I make everything more strained by harping." And once more the correspondence broke off.

In that spring and summer, Thorvale Farm was not a lonely place. Max Flowers and his wife and son moved into the guest house and, when Flowers himself was not in New York looking for employment, they were always available as company. Lewis had not attempted to broaden his Williamstown acquaintanceship much beyond them, but he had made himself known to the Reverend George E. Beilby, Jr., of the First Congregational Church, and through him learned what he could about Williamstown religious activity. He met at Beilby's church with a group of about eighty men to discuss the formation of a men's club, and after holding forth informally on the similarities between Communism and Catholicism, the two great forces in the modern world, both hierarchical totalitarian structures with ultimate power vested in a single individual, he lamented the divided character of Protestantism. He believed in church union, and a men's club might well serve the purpose of promoting understanding between denominations.

When the group began to elect officers, he interrupted to say, "If you are going to have a men's club, why don't you just come together without all the fuss and organization? Now I take my leave, and you can talk about me all you want." With that, he departed, and was never again seen in the First Congregational Church. Nevertheless, he had given Beilby the impression of a genuine interest in religion, and this impression was furthered when he drove with Beilby to nearby Blackinton, where the villagers were trying to revive the Union Church, which had fallen into desuetude, and where Lewis showed real concern for the people and their rededication service. Later he asked Beilby to bring a few of his friends out to Thorvale "to discuss religion."

That evening was a disaster. Lewis greeted his guests with a long tirade against Catholicism, suggested that everyone probably needed a new religion, and declared that Christianity was overburdened with theology. When he subsided, no one said anything, and he suggested that they all go into the dining room and sit around the table. Joseph provided beer for the guests and water for the Master. Beilby, trying to open a conversation, asked Lewis to what power he attributed his creative efforts, and added that W. H. Auden had told him that he thought of himself as the mother of his poems, their father being elsewhere. Lewis swung on him in a rage.

> "Don't talk to me about religion," he shouted. "Don't think I'm one of your snivelling congregation who swallows everything you say. Why, I know more about religion than you'll ever know. I've read more books on religion than you'll ever read. I have a library with all the best religious books of every generation in it. And you talk to me about W. H. Auden!"

Sneering then at Auden's personal life, he burst into a final assertion that his works were his own, and subsided, trembling and panting, staring at his guests. Conversation was now impossible, and the embarrassed group straggled awkwardly out and home.

What Beilby had hoped to hear from him was only whether or not he believed in God. He had another answer when he approached Lewis for a contribution to his church and Lewis regretted that with his heavy expenses he could not afford to make a contribution. That summer, a form letter went out from a Williamstown service club asking for contributions to a projected war memorial. One Sunday afternoon, Lewis had asked Beilby to come to Thorvale to meet Horace R. Cayton,* the Negro writer whom he had cited in *Kingsblood Royal* and who was then at Yaddo in Saratoga Springs. During the conversation, the subject of the war memorial was brought up, and once more Lewis broke into a rage.

> "I'd like to know what right a bunch of snivelling shopkeepers has to ask money for a war memorial for our dead soldiers," he burst out. "Were they over there fighting? Did they have to crawl on their bellies over barbed wire with one hand holding their guts in? I suppose they think this is their way of paying their debt. I wouldn't give them a nickel. They can't talk to me about sacrifices. They don't know what it is to sacrifice. I lost a boy in that war, and they want me to remember him, and pay my respects by erecting a stone in Field Park! I wouldn't give them a nickel."

Nor did he.

He enjoyed making a contribution of a different sort. His generosity to young writers was colored by the need for respectful companionship and by a hankering for the status of patron. Barnaby Conrad's tenure, as things worked out, was to run from May 19 to September 2. His work, as Lewis had explained it to Conrad and Conrad later reported to Norman

* Mr. Cayton has written a telling, still unpublished account of his visit to Thorvale that is especially concerned with Lewis's relations with his Negro servants. Most of the time he was stiff with them, but there were also lapses, embarrassing for them, into casual familiarity. On July 4 he gave a picnic for Joseph Hardrick, who managed the barbecue, and for Alma and Wilson Perkins, who were supposed to relax with the Master on this one occasion in the year, Independence Day. The occasion was rigid with discomfort, and afterward Lewis admitted to Cayton that it had not been a success. Then he made the extraordinary remark, "But you see why I need a Negro mammy, don't you?"

Holmes Pearson, was to get up at five-thirty every morning and write at his novel until noon; to take his meals with Lewis and listen when Lewis wanted to talk and not to talk himself when Lewis didn't want to listen; and, finally, to play a game of chess with Lewis before dinner and another after dinner. Conrad, with his boyishness, his eagerness, the naïveté of his ambitions, pleased Lewis at first, and the arrangement worked out well for both of them. Conrad did finish his novel * during that summer, and Lewis had his chess and his company and the satisfaction, important to him now, of knowing that he was working *with* someone rather than over someone.

As with Hersey, his literary tutelage at any serious level was negligible, but there were certain mechanical matters, and, more important, certain personal habits, that had worked well for him and that he could urge upon the young and aspiring. He was indebted to Barnaby Conrad, too, for introducing him to another companion who was to be of real comfort to him before he abandoned Williamstown—a young woman named Ida Kay who clerked in the college bookstore—pretty, sprightly, literate, free to be called upon at any time, full of chatter and gossip and sufficient deference to the mighty to prove highly satisfactory.

Yet it was not very long before Conrad began to irritate him. His lack of interest in a rigid discipline and routine, his *dégagé* quality, probably his whole flavor of a leisure-class background, proved irksome, and very soon in the engagement books appears the stern rebuke, "Barney rm order," several times repeated. It is not hard to see him, as rigid in his ways now as a spinster and as fixed as his father in his notion of what was proper to his household, peering into his new tenant's bedroom, a young man's litter of rumpled bed and opened books turned face down on the floor, of castoff shirts and socks and sneakers and even the horror of a sweaty jock strap tossed on what should have been a taut and pristine candlewick spread. How often did he have to tell him that there was a fixed arrangement for the poolside chairs and that one was not to be casual in such matters! Barnaby Conrad's successor would be a more earnest person.

He was working still on his play, but already thinking seriously about his next novel, to be called *Neighbor,* for which he would have to go to Minnesota for research, and he rigorously maintained his routine, which the stream of house guests was not permitted to interrupt, fervent as he was for their presence. It was Carl Van Doren whom he particularly urged to come, and to stay for a week if he could—a rare enough invitation, since he tired of his friends almost immediately upon their arrival. Van Doren had once more to delay his visit, but Harrison Smith and Edith Haggard came early in May, and Marvin Oreck from Duluth before the end of it, and John Gunther at the beginning of June. Then Lewis himself went to

* *The Innocent Villa* (Random House, 1948).

New Haven for four days, bearing new manuscript for the Lewis Collection in the Yale Library and joining in those festivities of the fortieth reunion of his class that were nonalcoholic. His own best reunion was with Tinker, whom he urged to come to visit him at Thorvale Farm. For the new *History of the Class of 1907* he wrote:

> My chief idiocy and pleasure during these fifteen years has been venturing into the humbler slums and ghettoes of the professional theater . . . going on a road tour with an extraordinarily bad play of my own; and acting or directing. . . . Directing I have found nearer to the labors of the Creator than anything else I have known, but acting is intolerable, and out of it I got chiefly an admiration for the courage and endurance of professional actors, grimly going on being funny or romantic before the goggling and fatuous. . . .
>
> As to general status, my teeth, hair, and ability to sit up after midnight are about as completely shot to hell as those of the rest of the Class, but I still, with all the youthful violence I had in 1907, dislike all the pompous heads of all institutions—political,* financial, literary, ecclesiastical, educational, social, and Social, and I scream just as in the old days when some one drones, "That's all right in theory, BUT—."

Returning to Williamstown, he received in rapid succession George Jean Nathan and Julie Haydon; Dr. Traeger; the young woman he had met once in Duluth, Betty Stevens, who had written him from New York to say that she was now writing advertising copy; his niece, Virginia Lewis, and her mother. Betty Stevens, who came for nearly five days, observed a number of things: he disapproved of guests who did not bring their own cigarettes; he thought that Henry Wallace had a "Messiah complex" and he disliked people who signed petitions and made speeches in Madison Square Garden; he did not think that the "fleshy side" was one of "the really important things about marriage," like deciding early on whether the bedroom window was to be open or closed; he had known two men, Charlie Chaplin and Bertrand Russell, with whom all women instantly fell in love; he wrote a letter at the behest of the Joint Anti-Fascist Refugee Committee in defense of Howard Fast, an officer in that organization threatened with a jail sentence. He told her about his play:

> There's this factory. And there's this young radical whipper-snapper of a labor organizer who's going to organize the workers. The owner's daughter is working in the factory for the summer, and she falls in love with the organizer. So they try to get the workers to join the union, but the workers won't vote for it. But the owner is a real American, a Dodsworth type of

* In correspondence, he had been urging Senator Arthur Vandenberg to run for the Presidency in 1948. Vandenberg told him that he regarded Lewis's enthusiasm as "a far greater tribute to 'friendship' than to 'judgment.'"

businessman who really believes in unions. So, in the third act, he gets up and makes a speech, telling the workers to join the union. And they do.*

As soon as Miss Stevens left for New York, he wrote Van Doren again, more urgently: "When are you coming? The place needs you!" Before Van Doren arrived, Horace Cayton came again, and John Gunther, and the Cerfs. Bennett Cerf was to give a lecture at Williams, and he asked Lewis if he planned to attend. Hell, no! He'd been at Williamstown for over a year and the college had never made the slightest overture to him. He was making a point of *not* going to the college. Nevertheless, he did go, and he took over the lecture, heckling Cerf throughout to the vast amusement, the lecturer remembers, of the audience.

There were quieter pleasures with Carl Van Doren during the early week in August that he spent with Lewis, who was now deep in his reading in religion and Minnesota history for his next novel. They could discuss these researches together, but, basking in this real and rare friendship, Lewis was seeing beyond both his projected trip to Minnesota (he was writing Asa Lyons about driving arrangements) and the novel itself, to a trip to Italy with Van Doren, who, at this point, did not say positively no. In his engagement book he was writing "Barney lv" and finally, on September 2, "Barney go," but in the meantime he had persuaded Van Doren to telephone his lecture agent in New York about the possibility of arranging public appearances for Conrad. The day after the young man left Williamstown, Lewis himself left for a little more than a week in New York.

In New York he saw the same people who had come to see him at Thorvale, and, in addition, Mrs. Powers and his skin doctor, and on September 12 he left for Chicago. There Asa Lyons met him—Joseph was to have a month's vacation—and Lyons drove him up through Wisconsin and into Minnesota to Minneapolis, where he settled for two months. He worked hard during the daytime at the library of the State Historical Society in St. Paul, and in the evenings he saw those of his Twin City friends whom he could still see with pleasure. Joseph arrived early in October and drove him to Sauk Centre, where he addressed a banquet of the Chamber of Commerce, which was honoring five "old timers" who had completed fifty years in business. That was to be Lewis's last visit on the native heath, which he himself had first abandoned not quite fifty years before.

His reading in Minnesota history had, he found, to be wide and random if he was to acquire the kind of information—about manners as well as events of a hundred years before—that his new novel would demand, and for much of this, he decided, he could depend upon an assistant. He was

* Miss Stevens published her recollections of Lewis in Duluth and Williamstown in the magazine *Venture,* vol. II, nos. 2 and 3 (1957). Her general picture is persuasive even though some of her details are inaccurately remembered.

in the right part of the United States to find someone quite different from the worldly young Barnaby. Through the department of English in the university he discovered James Roers, a GI who had just begun work on his Master degree in American civilization. A native of Minnesota, earnest and disciplined, with no "style" whatever, he seemed to be the perfect man, and for the opportunity of working with Lewis, reading up on the details of costume, military history, home furnishings, domestic routines, communal gatherings, and so on, in the pioneering years of Minnesota, a light and agreeable chore, Roers was happy to abandon his graduate studies. By the time that Lewis left again on November 12 for New York, it was settled that Roers would follow him to Williamstown within a month.

The plans for Thorvale were undergoing expected revision. In his engagement book he reminded himself that in New York he should discuss with his attorneys his decision to abandon his attempt to farm his place, and when James Roers arrived, on December 9, only a few cows and pigs remained, and the chickens. Soon these went, too, and with them the Bishops, and the farm was sold. The Bishops were, in effect, forced upon the dole, and their plight troubled Lewis to this extent, that for months he felt the need to justify himself: "Why should I have a farm if I don't want one?" he would demand of his friends, tiresomely and repetitiously. "Why should I be forced to have a farm?"

Young James Roers was much impressed with his new situation and two days after his arrival wrote a friend about the opulence of the establishment.

> I haven't done much work for him as yet, except draw the curtains and empty a few ash trays. He says he just wants me to read generally on Minnesota history from his library here (which is considerable) and at the library at the college. Then some day he'll ask me what kind of a dress Mrs. Ramsey would wear at the hod-carrier's ball, and I'd better be able to answer. . . . I spoke highly of the New York public library so I hope that he sends me up there in the not too distant future.

He was to go there at once.

From the outset, Roers himself felt that his function as research assistant was of almost no importance to Lewis, that he had brought him to Williamstown, at $250 a month and his living, as a chess partner and a companion in the lonely evenings. Sober and scholarly, Roers was also something of a rustic still, with none of Conrad's gregariousness and social grace, uncertain about little matters of decorum, much too easy a victim at chess for serious sport, and, in the observation of Ida Kay,* these qualities irritated Lewis even more quickly than Conrad's had. He had arrived on a Tuesday. On his first Friday, Lewis asked him to go in to the college library for a number of historical works that he needed. Roers did so, but the

* Now Mrs. Charles D. Compton, still of Williamstown.

head librarian was away, it was already late in the afternoon, and the assistant librarian said that while he was sure that there would be no difficulty in Mr. Lewis's drawing out any books that he needed, the matter would have to wait until Monday.

Roers returned without the books, and that evening at dinner, when Lewis asked about them, he explained what had happened. Lewis was first incredulous and then quickly furious. The idea that the assistant of Sinclair Lewis should not be permitted to take out books at his will, he shouted, was outrageous! Roers explained that the librarian's point was perfectly reasonable, that Lewis had no connection with the college, that the little delay was not important, after all. But the longer Lewis contemplated the matter, the more angry he became, and suddenly he rushed from the table to the telephone and called President Baxter. Into that ear he poured his mounting tirade, in the course of which he seized a heavy crystal ash tray that was beside him and hurled it to the floor where it was loudly smashed. At poor Baxter he shouted over the wire that because Williams was so uncooperative, he would now have to send his assistant to New York immediately in order to draw those books from the Public Library there, and with that he slammed down the instrument.

With Roers and Joseph creeping about picking up broken glass, calm returned, but having made his threat, he had to live up to it, and immediately, even though the books were of no consequence. Roers was told to repack his bags and early next morning was driven to the railroad station, caught a train, and arrived that afternoon in New York without any notion whatever of what he should do there. Lewis's last words were, "Oh, don't bother to do any work for me. Forget about those books. Just have a good time and find yourself in New York." A few days later Lewis wrote him:

> Don't worry about doing any specific research at all unless I send you a problem. I seem to have all I need right here—even the soldiers' uniforms. You will have checks coming on Jan, Feb & March 10th. Spend your time in exploring New York & seeing if you can make a connection so that you can stay there.

For nearly four months, hardly able to contemplate the folly of the situation, Roers lived on in New York at Lewis's expense, enjoying himself, and in March determined to return to his graduate studies at Minnesota.

In *Cass Timberlane,* the hero tries to persuade his housekeeper, Mrs. Higbee, to play chess with him in his lonely evenings during the period of Jinny's defection, but Mrs. Higbee could not learn. So now, alone again in Williamstown, Lewis tried to teach Wilson and Alma Perkins, and to no more avail. In New York, the film of that novel, which was to win the "Box Office Blue Ribbon Award" of the National Screen Council, had opened, and Carl Van Doren had undergone an operation. Lonely wintry thoughts of one true friend! Lewis interrupted work on the plan for his historical novel and wrote an appreciative essay about his friend and put it away among his papers. Kindly and affectionate, its sole barb is directed against college presidents, "that separate, depressing breed." On December 19 he telephoned Mrs. Powers in New Jersey. The page for Christmas Day in the engagement book is blank. The last day of the year holds only a notation about income tax. January 1 is blank. On January 4 he left abruptly for New York to persuade Mrs. Powers to come to Williamstown and keep him company.

She obliged, and much of the remainder of that winter, much of the spring, and the entire summer she spent with him. When in May he went to Maine for five days, he took her with him, and when in June he went to Quebec for another five days, he took her again. These were brief respites from the major occupation of that year, the planning and the writing of the novel he called *Neighbor* and published under the title *The God-Seeker*. For this work, he wrote a plan of 206 single-spaced pages, a document of something over 110,000 words, itself the length of a substantial novel. He worked out his plot scene by scene, with suggestive details and fragments of conversation. Besides this, he compiled a complete catalogue of character sketches to guide him, and lists of names, male and female, first and last, together with a breakdown by nationality. When he converted this mass of material into the novel proper, his first typewritten version was 623 double-spaced pages, the final version, 535 double-spaced pages. He had probably never worked so hard, certainly never to such little point.

With Mrs. Powers present, his need for house guests was not so urgent. Carl Van Doren could not come that summer, but Lewis was hoping to persuade him to go to Italy with him once the novel was finished. He was also urging Dr. Traeger to come, and Harrison Smith, and Marvin Oreck, and Gerald Cornell, the actor, and, finally, Kenneth Cant, the real-estate man in Duluth. His summer excursions with Mrs. Powers persuaded him that she, who had seen so little of the world, was an admirable traveling companion, at once placid and interested, and completely submissive to his demands. Each day, if he had no one else, he would make her take a walk with him, which she agreeably did. And when everyone else failed him, it was she whom he took to Europe in the autumn.

Others who walked with him in that summer were F. P. Adams and his wife, Bennett and Phyllis Cerf again, Edith Haggard again. Sometimes strangers, curious or admiring, waited upon him—Daniel Aaron, from Smith College, to whom he reminisced about Eugene Debs, talked fiercely about anti-Negro discrimination and denounced Sherwood Anderson and Walt Whitman as "fakes"; and Allen Austin, who was writing an M.A. thesis about him at Columbia, and to whom he talked still of writing a labor novel. "I want a hard-boiled labor leader and a hard-boiled factory president. You see, the new manager gets tough with labor, and a young radical in the labor movement keeps trying to stir up trouble. Finally, the president and the old labor leader get together and settle their difficulties." Then he added: "It sounds boring." On the same occasion, he said that he preferred socialism to capitalism, but not the Norman Thomas brand of socialism. He talked of Thoreau as the major influence on his writing—Thoreau, whose radicalism was genuine, while Emerson's was respectable.* Then came, too, Granville Hicks and Newton Arvin, hoping that he would lend his name to a "Writers for Truman" roster. He was kind, cordial, modest, even deferential, and very gently declined to lend his support to their project as he indicated that he was completely skeptical about the usefulness of American writers in public life or politics.

Norman Mailer, who had published *The Naked and the Dead,* was invited to drop by should he find himself in the neighborhood of Williamstown. When he arrived with his wife, he found Lewis waiting for him on the terrace. Rather ignoring Mrs. Mailer, he greeted her husband warmly and led him into the house for conversation that consisted chiefly of the repeated injunction that now that Mailer was a success, he must make a point of never being rude to people—while the affronted Mrs. Mailer, neglected outside on the terrace, quite properly fumed.

There was a reunion with his former agent Ann Watkins and her husband, Roger Burlingame. They were driving by slow stages to Maine and telephoned to ask if they could stay with him for a night. He seemed overjoyed. "I love you, Ann. Forget everything that ever happened! You have got to come! Please come, right away. I love you, Ann!" He met them eagerly, running out to greet them, as though he had been watching for their machine through the great, wall-sized window of his living room. He showed them his house and then insisted on what was to them an exhausting tramp all over his acres (Ann Watkins loathed walking, but no matter), and returned them to his house. There was never a mention of a drink. As dinner approached, the Burlingames, who were accustomed to three good, cold martinis, were lectured instead on the horrors of alcohol. "I can't understand these drinking people, putting themselves through those awful hangovers," he declared, and then he illustrated his sermon with a series of case histories. "I knew a man who . . ." he would begin, and in the fashion of Upton Sinclair, who had so often made Sinclair Lewis the chief actor in his *exempla* on the same subject, would recount his horrid end, entirely because of liquor. All this was presented without a trace of irony or a hint of self-recognition. Finally, just before dinner was served at exactly seven o'clock, Joseph produced one weak, warm martini.

* Daniel Aaron's recollections appeared in *The Reporter* (August 4, 1953) as "The Proud Prejudices of Sinclair Lewis," and Allen Austin's in the *University of Kansas City Review* (Spring 1958) as "An Interview with Sinclair Lewis."

The afternoon walk had tired Mrs. Burlingame and she went to bed very soon after dinner. For a time, Lewis and Burlingame played a game about which publishers could read and which could not, the general theory being that most could not read at all. Alfred Knopf, it was conceded, could read, and Alfred Harcourt, "with his lips moving." This game went on until about ten o'clock, and in all that time, no brandy, no highball. Then Lewis proposed chess, about which Burlingame knew almost nothing. He conceded the first game long before its end, and hoped that that would be all, but Lewis was relentless, and there followed a whole series of games, either conceded by Burlingame or quickly lost by him. Every room in the house contained at least one box of chocolates, which Lewis ate throughout the evening, but still no offer of a drink to his guest. Finally, when it was time to go to bed, Lewis led him into the butler's pantry and grudgingly produced a single, partly empty bottle of whisky. "Want a drink?" he asked. But now Burlingame declined, and the bottle was returned to its shelf.

There was one encounter with his son Michael, but not at Thorvale Farm. The boy had done much better in school during that winter, and his mother proposed that for his eighteenth birthday she and Lewis divide the cost of a car for him. This he declined to do on the grounds that he could not afford it. She submitted gracefully enough and suggested that he invite Michael to Williamstown for a weekend. Michael had become fascinated by the theater, and his father might well have had some advice for him; but neither that nor an invitation was forthcoming. In April, Michael signed up to work with the Peterborough Players for the summer, which was some consolation to his mother for his failure, because of deficiencies in mathematics and language, to graduate from Collegiate. When he made his first stage appearance early in August, Lewis did drive to Peterborough, and he expressed great pleasure in seeing him. He was full of eager questions. Did he learn his lines easily? Did he know how to put on his make-up? And he seemed much impressed with the boy. After the final curtain, he appeared backstage in what seemed to Michael a nearly deferential mood. It was the first time that he had ever seen his father in this way, and it was the first time, too, that Lewis had given the boy his full approval and a real "lift."

In that autumn he redrew his will and left half of his estate to his son, in trust until he reached the age of twenty-five. Should he die before that age and leave no heirs, this half of the estate was to be divided between the National Association for the Advancement of Colored People and the National Urban League. One fourth of the estate was to be divided among Marcella Powers Amrine, Edith Haggard, Carl Van Doren, or their survivors, and Joseph Hardrick, "my faithful driver . . . provided that he either be in my service or under some form of retainer or pension from me at the time of my death." If these circumstances did not prevail, the Hardrick portion was to be equally divided among the three aforementioned persons. Finally, the income from the remaining fourth of the estate was to be paid to "my friend," Mrs. Powers, until the time of her death, when the principal was to be equally distributed among Mrs. Amrine, Mrs. Haggard, and Carl Van Doren.

He was thinking of a new novel, to be called either *Tired Warrior* or *Lonely Warrior,* and was making notes for it. It was a theme appropriate to these autumn days in which he was contemplating Italy with Mrs. Powers and drawing up his last will. In the dozen-odd pages of notes that he jotted down appear the following:

> Not Tired Radical—that implies cafe journalist opinionation & retreat
> List of ignorances—mis-education—
> Bitterness of ingratitude—treachery—loss of friends—conquers How down to last friend—or enemy—lonely & ignored
> What became of:

Max Eastman	2 Seldeses
Art Young	Ezra Pound
John Spargo	Norman Thomas
Wm English	MacAllister
Walling	Mary Vorse
Rose Strunsky	Hutch Hapgood
Bill He[y]wood	Bayard Boyesen
Floyd Dell	J. G. Phelps Stokes
Walter Lippmann	Sidney Howard
3 LaFollet[t]es	
Haldeman-Julius	

Most of these people were not Lewis's friends, but some of them had been, and the list, while appropriate to the biography of an old American liberal, nevertheless suggests the personal situation in which Lewis was suffering and foreshadows a more directly personal story, to be called *Friends,* that he was yet to conceive, and into which *Tired Warrior* would probably have evolved. The notes continue:

> In Lonely W the important thesis, "not 10 yrs older than 50 but blessedly & promisingly 10 yrs younger than 70"
> Rebirth—be[comes] new man
> C[oul]d start as with a letter to Stolberg, from old acquaintance: "You have bec. so testy, intolerant, pontifical that rather not see you again." This shakes & starts remold him—w[ith] thought "Why sh[oul]d I never have any fun."
> G[rea]t celeb[rity] needs simple kindness from people—e.g., corner druggist—as much as any humble person does.
> The Old Warrior (a title)—& this hard for young to understand—sometimes not compromising, not lazy, not greedy, but just *tired*—TIRED
> Tendency to be liberal cramped by nuts, by fanatics, by sentimentalists,

esp. women, even by campaigners w[ith] sound ideas, when they are too urgent. . . .

Been governor, seems retired. Sudden: "What waiting for now—I who always had so many exciting things to wait for. For Death & no! I'll do something to live. . . .

For 30 years S[alem] V[olk] been hearing of self "He's finished"

The 2 contradictory ambitions: to *do* things, esp. work, & to get places personally—office & praise

Sometimes the 2 mingle. . . .

A little of a struggle to keep, in boredom w[ith] continuing followers, from turning vs just the y[oung] radicalisms he once espoused.

If the emotion that these notes imply arises directly from Lewis's own lonely life, the situation suggests the last years of Thorstein Veblen, dispirited, tired, and rootless, and suggests further that in some ways the major contribution of Lewis's novels was their continuation (or, at least, popularization) of certain leading ideas of Veblen, especially as to the leisure class and business enterprise. Looking back again at *Babbitt* from this point of view, we can see it as a dramatization of the divorce between industry and business, of the disappearance in a transitional America of independence and individuality in the machinelike processes of a mass culture. Lewis's own respect for the agents and the products of mass culture in his writing and his illustration of "conspicuous consumption" in his personal life—these are the paradoxical antitheses to his nostalgia, in the notes for this novel and in many other places, for that earlier radicalism in American life out of which Veblen himself had come and which was the background of Lewis's clearest attitudes. One is reminded of that background by his directions to the printer, written at the top of the first page of the final manuscript of *The God-Seeker:*

PRINTER: . . . Follow capitalization of MS. Do not cap pronouns referring to divinity, or heaven or hell, except when capped in MS. Example: God's in his heaven. *SL.*

If the projected work had explored this background it might have been an interesting novel, but, however immediately its situation reflected his own, he decided to delay it until after his European trip. Among the memoranda at the back of his 1948 engagement book appears this item:

"Mid 1949 Lone Warrior tech. adviser."

In the meantime he developed another idea for a novel that would not involve any technical advice. His Italian journey would give him all the background that he needed for it. To be called *Over the Body of Lucy Jade,* it would be the story of an American girl in Italy and the corruptions of expatriate Americans. He discussed the idea with Harry Maule, who liked it, and on the day before he sailed Lewis signed a contract for this novel.

In mid-September he went to New York for five days with his manuscript of *The God-Seeker* and the usual sessions with Saxe Commins and then returned for nearly a month to Williamstown, where he studied Italian by Linguaphone and read Italian history. There was a farewell visit from his brother and sister-in-law; and Claude Lewis, who had not seen Thorvale Farm, was given the usual proud survey. "And there, Claude, is the swimming pool!" The impassive Claude looked at it and asked, "How many cubic feet of water does it hold?" Sinclair Lewis, put down once more by this brother whom he could not impress, reluctantly said, "I don't know."

In New York again, he spent his last night in America with the Cerfs. After dinner, as they were chatting, the telephone rang. Unannounced, William Faulkner had arrived in New York and was suggesting that he come to call. Cerf asked him to wait a moment and then, with considerable excitement, asked Lewis if he would like to see Faulkner. Lewis looked dour and quite icily demanded, "How long have you been a publisher?" Cerf told him. "Well, haven't you learned yet that you don't bring two big authors together?" Cerf then returned to the telephone and told Faulkner that he would see him next day. Presently Lewis went up to bed, and the Cerfs, still sitting below, were suddenly alarmed when from the upper floor Lewis shouted, "Bennett! Bennett!" "What, Red?" A pause. Then, "I just wanted to be sure that you hadn't sneaked out to see Faulkner. Good night."

Next day, October 19, Joseph was on hand to help the Master and his lady aboard the *Saturnia.* He was in charge of their bags, which he was to get up to their staterooms and distribute properly. In the meantime Lewis gave reporters an interview on board: he announced that he planned to write a series of nonpolitical articles for the Bell Syndicate on Italy, where he had not been for fifteen years, and he predicted the election of Thomas E. Dewey to the Presidency in November. When sailing time came and Joseph was already gone, two of Mrs. Powers's bags were missing. Lewis was furious. Every now and then he had decided that Joseph was growing slack, and he had discharged him once, only to take him back immediately. Now it seemed to him, as it did to Mrs. Powers, that he had real grounds for discharging him. From Italy, he wrote to give Joseph that news, even though the bags had been duly recovered. Joseph wrote and begged to be retained. Lewis replied with the single word, "Fired," which meant, too, that Joseph was "fired" from the Lewis will. Only a very few people had anything to gain from the unfortunate Joseph's loss.

For *Cosmopolitan,* which had contracted to publish *Lucy Jade,* Lewis had just written a Christmas meditation in which he asserted his wish to discover what he was, and what he was in relation to other people everywhere, his wish to be rid of the "sneaking daily notion" that he was wiser than other people, his wish, further, for peace and good will and love on earth between men of all colors and sizes, "not slyness and hardness and the loose grin of knowingness. . . ."

8

ON SHIPBOARD he met and liked enormously Dr. Benjamin Camp, an American with a medical practice in Rome, and after a week in Naples, showing Mrs. Powers that city and Pompeii and Capri and the towns on the Amalfi drive, they went on to Rome where for several days they were the house guests of Dr. Camp. Then Lewis took a suite of rooms in the Ambassador Hotel, where they lived until the middle of December, but Camp continued to be his closest associate and they saw him three or four times a week. When both Lewis and Mrs. Powers came down with influenza, Dr. Camp attended them.

Lewis had a car and a driver, and nearly every day there were Baedeker-directed excursions in and out of the city. He maintained, at the same time, the approximate routine that he followed at home: up early, some work in the morning, a drive, lunch and the two o'clock nap, another drive or a Via Veneto café, dinner, an early retirement. In Rome he began to write the first of his ten promised newspaper articles, but he did not finish them until after December 15, when they settled into the Excelsior in Florence for a little more than two months.

Immediately upon his arrival, Americans in Florence were buzzing with tales. It was said that on the train up from Rome he and Mrs. Powers had shared a compartment with two Florentine ladies, one of them a *marchesa* in the house of Antinori. Lewis was buried in his Baedeker and lecturing Mrs. Powers about the towns they passed through, reading aloud from his guidebook about them, while the two haughty ladies sniffed at the vulgarity of the American tourists, and when these vulgarians produced their box lunches and graciously offered to share them, they received a chilly refusal. Then, in Florence, a newspaper account of Lewis's arrival helped the horrified *marchesa* to realize that it had been he on the train, and she telephoned him—she had had no idea who he was, she protested, and she was most eager to see him in Florence. He reported himself as having replied, "We bumped knees all the way from Rome, and that was enough!"

In Florence he became a familiar figure in the seedy Anglo-American colony that had reestablished itself there immediately after the war, and in that atmosphere he returned to drinking hard liquor and became an habitué of Leland's. Everywhere he went he took Mrs. Powers, who, among his articulate and opinionated friends, sat silently or ventured her opinions on the weather. At luncheon with Harold Acton at his great villa, very early in their stay, they met Mrs. Sturges Riddle, the dashing and fashionable wife of the rector, at that time, of the St. James American Episcopal Church. Mrs. Riddle persuaded them to come to church on the following Sunday and to lunch thereafter, and Lewis and Riddle (who was "Sturge" at once) became instant friends, even as the Riddles observed the curiously abrupt way in which his immediate outgoing quality with people he liked came to a stop, like a barrier between gregariousness and friendship. Riddle took them to I Tatti, and Berenson delighted in him even as he failed to comprehend what struck him as the enigma of Mrs. Powers.

At least once each week during their Florence residence, the two would appear at the splendid house on the Settignano hill, for lunch or tea, and while the gracious Signora Mariano would attempt to put Mrs. Powers at her ease, Lewis would perform endless imitations for the delectation of the ancient B.B. To help her, Lewis bought for her a copy of Berenson's *Italian Painters of the Renaissance,* but there was little talk about painting between Berenson and Lewis, even though Lewis, with his old passion for thoroughness, was making a doggedly systematic attempt to inform himself of all the treasures of art and architecture in and near the city. Instead, they played word games of the sort that Lewis as an undergraduate had played with Tinker, games that Berenson enjoyed as much as Lewis, producing mongrel words like *metafuzzical* and *patridiot.*

Lewis was not too old to indulge in some of his waggeries. With his aged mother, a new vice-consul arrived in Florence, a Southerner of the old striped-trouser, teacup diplomacy, a tremendous snob fresh from Luxembourg and disappointed in his assignment to Florence because Florence was without a royal court. Lewis had suggested to Riddle that a group of American men join together in a dinner of welcome, but when Lewis met him at their dinner he was immediately affronted by his pomposity. The guest of honor was asked to say a few words. He responded with a kind of warning: "Gentlemen, there are two things that I never permit. One is to be called by my first name, which only my mother and Winston Churchill use. The other is profanity." Whereupon Lewis jumped to his feet, seized his wine glass, and shouted, "To George, a God-damned old son of a bitch!"

The vice-consul presumably survived this toast, for on another occasion, when Lewis was at a cocktail party in the same apartment building where he lived, Lewis sent a servant to call him down, saying that it was absolutely imperative that he see him. The vice-consul dressed with all his habitual punctilio and appeared, only to hear Lewis shout at him over the din, "George, where the hell is the john in this place?"

His drinking again complicated Mrs. Powers's duties as his companion, and on a number of occasions he made things very difficult indeed for her; but she never attempted to correct him or to persuade him to be more moderate, and struggled simply to assist him, socially and physically, as best she could. If one searches for an immediate reason for his return to liquor, one possibility presents itself in Jonathan Cape's response to the typescript of *The God-Seeker,* when he wrote Lewis some very severe strictures on that dull work. This letter brought forth an epistolary blast.

> When you wrote me about *Kingsblood Royal,* I didn't say anything, I just said to myself, "That's only Jonathan." But now you have gone too far, and I wouldn't let you have this novel if you wanted it.

Cape was at once relieved and disturbed, and Mrs. Cape flew to Italy to try to undo the damage to their old friendship, if not to their publishing relationship. She found Lewis quite drunk and felt that there was nothing at all that she could do. Lewis told her that Cape had been one of his oldest friends but that he would never again be able to trust him, either as a man or as a literary judge, and he turned then to another old friend, A. S. Frere, at Heinemann, where, without any great enthusiasm, his last two novels were published. To Frere he complained of Cape's "condescending jocularity . . . regarding my new book . . . *God-Seeker* may be the best book I have ever written. It is certainly the most serious."

His miscalculations about his own work are part of his miscalculations about everything, including Italy and Europe. The poet William Jay Smith gives perhaps the fullest account of these latter. Lewis met Smith and his wife, Barbara Howes, and they invited him and Mrs. Powers to lunch at their villa, Il Fortino, high up on the Via del Pian' dei Giullari. He showed, they felt, a rather embarrassing sentimentality about Italy, and talked of the universal friendliness of the humble people, as if he felt that he were loved by everyone and that he could love everyone in turn.* There was a good deal of talk about the "soul" of Europe, and the enrichment to Americans who could seize upon it. He himself discovered the embodiment of the "soul" of Europe that winter in a rather battered German blonde of indeterminate background and age who had been lurking about Florence for years and was known to nearly everyone as a tiresome cadger of drinks and meals. Entering a restaurant, willowy and apparently languid, her sharp eyes would sweep the place to discover the most likely touch, but, with her pretense to scholarship and her carefully managed mispronunciation of the

* *Readers Digest* commissioned an article, called "Why I Love the Italians," which Lewis wrote; it was never published. In it, he gave a variant on the *marchesa*-on-the-train anecdote and also, more extendedly, wrote of his love for the loving and lovable Italian people. The rejected typescript is among the Lewis papers at New Haven.

right English words, she was for Lewis the vision of Europe, and he eagerly sought the enriching experience of buying her food and drink. He spoke excitedly of her to the Smiths, at the same time that he threw at them his characteristically blunt questions and admonitions: Why are you here? How long have you been here? Are you working? Don't stay too long!

After that lunch, at which he admired their house and their view, he asked whether there were empty villas in the neighborhood. The establishment immediately below them, Villa La Costa, was available, as it usually was, since it had become a kind of joke among Americans in Florence, being at once so ostentatious and impractical. Lewis expressed a wish to see it, and on the way back to Florence they stopped, found the caretaker and were shown around. Lewis thought it was lovely, but he said nothing more. In another year he would rent it, his last house, another embodiment of the "soul" of Italy for him, and as false, in fact, as the aging, begging blonde.

He was, happily, enjoying himself, as in another year he would not. To Carl Van Doren he wrote in elation after nearly two months of Florence:

> You should, I think, have come to Italy, though you probably would have done no work all winter. In the three months I've been here (with a week in Naples, 6 weeks in Rome, 6 here now and 3 more to come before going off to Umbria) I've done nothing at all except 10 brief articles for the Bell Syndicate, my first such loaf in years, and I've gloried in my shame . . . solemnly coursed through churches and palazzi and galleries, found small restaurants, and read sweetly in the pallid, pure and lyric pages of Baedeker, the greatest of the wandering troubadours. And feel wonderful! And Mrs. Powers takes it all as though she were born to it, and is known to the assorted and friendly society of Florence as Donna Caterina.

The "friendly society of Florence" did not include a reporter for *La Nazione* who referred to Mrs. Powers as *"una vecchia governante."* The governess was about to accompany her charge on a tour of Tuscany, Umbria, the Marches, Veneto, and the northern lakes, before a mid-May sailing.

When the letter to Van Doren was written, Lewis's syndicated articles were already appearing in the United States, and they suggest how little came from that coursing through *palazzi* and churches and galleries. The first describes the generally attractive conditions in Rome for tourists; the next is a friendly portrait of a Pennsylvania matron abroad; a third reports on the triumph (which Lewis and Mrs. Powers had witnessed) of the American girl Ann Kullmer as conductor of the Naples Symphony Orchestra in the San Carlo Opera House. There is then an open letter to F. P. Adams, telling him of a trip to Horace's farm. Two more argue about the necessity of learning the language of the country in which one is traveling. Two portraits follow: one is of a shabby expatriate couple who live by the charity of the tourists they deride; the other is of a simple American couple who have made a contented adjustment to Europe. The final piece offers general advice to prospective tourists of Italy and ends on a characteristic note of patriotic eulogy:

> Now, having praised Italy and the ways of living here, I admit that I would rather build a tar-paper shack in any American cut-over wilderness than live in the Colonna Palace in Rome, in the dead breath of men dead these 400 years; would rather have the cold and exquisite steeple of a Yankee church than even Giotto's tower.*

Farewell, then, to Giotto's tower! The Umbrian tour and the progress northward lasted three weeks, and the old restlessness overtook him once more. They would arrive in a town or a city with their chauffeur, usually late in the afternoon, and find their hotel or pensione. Mrs. Powers would laboriously unpack her things, hang up her dresses and set out her cosmetics and baubles and bibelots, while Lewis would take a quick walk in the town. They would usually get through dinner and sometimes even the entire evening before Lewis would ask, "How soon can you pack?" Submissive to his whimsicalities, she always replied, "In an hour." She would dutifully repack, and when she came down behind a porter, Lewis would be impatiently waiting for her, the chauffeur would be waiting beside the open door of the machine, her bags would be tucked into the back, and they would start off for the next place, where, more than likely, they would reenact the same fitful ritual.

They paused in Assisi, and there, on March 3, the day before the publication in New York of *The God-Seeker,* Lewis began the writing of *Over the Body of Lucy Jade*. For this novel he had written a "plan," or summary, of only twenty-one pages, which ends as follows:

> Lucy: "Yes dear, of course. . . . Oh waitress, this gentleman will eventually remember he wants to buy me some breakfast, but meantime you might bring me a large pot of coffee, with cream, and three slices of buttered toast, just lightly browned, and some honey and marmalade and two boiled eggs—two minutes—and oh, maybe a slice of bacon, quite thin and crisp, will you? Thank you."

And then appears the admonition, "But cf. last [paragraph] of *Our Mr. Wrenn."* That novel had ended, too, with thoughts of food, and the fact that Lewis remembered it so many years later is suggestive, for his final novel, *World So Wide,* which would ultimately emerge from the ill-fated *Lucy Jade,* has many, and rather important, similarities to that first novel.

* Much of the material in these articles forms the early substance of a 130-page fragment of a novel, *The Enchantment of Elaine Kent,* the story of an American girl who marries a Roman and tries to help him adjust to life in the United States. The typescript is in the Yale collection.

In the meantime appeared *The God-Seeker,* quite different from anything else he had written or was to write, duller, and lacking even in that slick literary carpentry that, until now, he had managed to maintain. Intended as an historical novel of the wilderness of Minnesota in the 1840s, it is written as though the year were 1920.

> The Reverend Mr. Chippler, who had organized the revival which would wind up this afternoon, was a leaping little man, fuller of friendliness, optimism, go, zip, imagination, ingenuity, cheeriness and oratory than the nobler and slower animals.

The historical elements are all in the externals, "research," and these externals, while they hardly add up to an imaginative reconstruction, are nevertheless more "real" than any of the characters, and this in spite of the blurb that Lewis himself prepared for the novel but which his publishers did not use. It reads:

> One of the few historical novels in which the people are *real,* with indigestion and irritation as well as love and glory, with political opinions and religious fears as well as screams of patriotism, with more of fried pork and frozen toes and of youth's magnificent gift for making a fool of itself than of swords and ribbons and gadzookses and Hail, Milord the King. They were a very human lot on the Housatonic and Minnesota Rivers in 1848, Yankees and Canucks and Indians, and in this novel we see them as human, not as stuffed historical-costumes. Yet it is also a relief that all the fighting that Aaron and Hulda and Serene shared was free of psychoanalysis and the Bomb.

The characters may very well have seemed real to Lewis, even though he could not make them so, for they had been in his mind for many years. *The God-Seeker* is the final product of all the schemes for a novel about labor, going all the way back to *The Children's Children* project of his San Francisco youth, schemes that had at last resolved themselves into a trilogy which was to be a veritable history of the United States, and of which one working title had for so long been *The Man Who Sought God.* The first volume was to be about a circuit rider on the frontier. Aaron Gadd is not a circuit rider, but a young man who hopes to become a missionary to the Indians. Religion loses its hold on him and he becomes instead a successful contractor in a growing St. Paul, and at its end the book turns away from religious matters to early problems of labor organization. It seems to look forward to the other volumes of the projected trilogy, and the evidence of Lewis's notebooks suggests that the long-planned novel about railroads might have become the second volume, and *Tired Warrior* the third. They were, of course, not to be written, and it is as well. The reviews of *The God-Seeker,* when they were not bruisingly unfavorable, were lukewarm, and the novel sold only a little over 30,000 copies, fewer than any Lewis novel since *Free Air,* and no book clubs, no serialization, no reprints.

A few days after the publication of *The God-Seeker,* an interview with John P. Marquand, published by *Time* magazine, pointed out certain similarities between Lewis and Marquand as satirists. Marquand was reported as most gracious: "I would hesitate to rank myself with Lewis; I don't think I have nearly the same stature. But I am working in his vineyard." This was not the vineyard of *The God-Seeker* or of *Lucy Jade;* the satirical Lewis, at least, *was* finished.

Settled in at the Gritti Palace in March, Lewis was writing at his new novel when a less gentle confrere than Marquand, Ernest Hemingway, arrived in Venice with his new wife. Hemingway invited Lewis and Mrs. Powers to dinner, but Lewis said that they were engaged. Mrs. Powers and Mrs. Hemingway did some shopping together, and there were a few meetings of the four of them. At one of these, Lewis said to Mrs. Hemingway that he gave her marriage one year, and Mrs. Powers remembered Mrs. Hemingway's reply, "Don't you worry, I'll stick to him." Hemingway was at work on *Across the River and into the Trees,* and when that novel was published, it was widely assumed that Lewis had found a considerably gratuitous place in the dramatis personae as a certain anonymous "son of a bitch" or "jerk" observed by Captain Cantwell in Harry's Bar.

> They looked at the man at the third table. He had a strange face like an over-enlarged, disappointed weasel or ferret. It looked as pock-marked and as blemished as the mountains of the moon seen through a cheap telescope and, the Colonel thought, it looked like Goebbels' face, if Herr Goebbels had ever been in a plane that burned, and not been able to bail out before the fire reached him.
>
> Above this face, which was ceaselessly peering, as though the answer might be found by enough well directed glances and queries—

The book version of the novel then goes on to describe black hair that looks like a wig, but in the magazine version, published earlier, it is "hair of a color no Indian would have kept as a scalp, the Colonel thought, it would have spooked them." Both versions continue:

> A little spit ran out of the corner of his mouth as he spoke, peeringly, with the elderly, wholesome looking woman who was with him. She looks like anybody's mother in an illustration in *The Ladies' Home Journal,* the Colonel thought. . . .
>
> But who do you suppose that character is? He looks like a caricature of an American who has been run one half way through a meat chopper and then been boiled, slightly, in oil.

They inquire of Ettore who he is, but Ettore does not know.

"My colleague who works at his hotel, says that he drinks three or four highballs, and then writes vastly and fluently far into the night."

"I dare say that makes marvelous reading."

But in the magazine version, Ettore does know. "You mean the American writer sitting with the mother of his lost mistress?" and Colonel Cantwell later asks, "Do you think the pock-marked jerk is really here with the mother of his former mistress?"

In the book version, after the question, "Do you think that pock-marked jerk is really a writer?" the strange little digression trails off into a discussion of the meaning of *jerk*.

It is doubtful that Lewis ever read this work. When it appeared in *Cosmopolitan* in February of 1950, he was living in Florence again, where that periodical was not likely to reach him. (Had it, the bitterness would have come in a double dose, for *Cosmopolitan* had, just six months before, declined to publish *Lucy Jade* as it would presently decline *World So Wide*.) But if he did see the magazine, or if he saw the book later, a reading of either might well have had to do with what seems to have been, in that last year in Europe, a sudden sharp increase of self-consciousness about his ugliness and an increasing reluctance to let himself be seen by others, especially his friends.

In Venice in 1949 no such development had taken place. His Minneapolis friends Mr. and Mrs. F. Peavey Heffelfinger and their daughter were in Venice, and it was they (at Mr. Heffelfinger's urging), rather than Lewis, who were hoping to avoid a meeting. But one noon in a restaurant when Mrs. Heffelfinger mistakenly wandered into the men's room, Lewis was there and, seeing her in the place marked *Signori,* roared with laughter, insisted that they join him, and then canceled their orders and reordered for them according to his lights. He amused Mrs. Heffelfinger and her daughter as much as ever, but Mr. Heffelfinger was not amused when, leaving the restaurant, it was he who was coupled with Mrs. Powers, who seldom said more than yes and no. Lewis insisted that they all dine together that evening, and at dinner he attacked both Mrs. Banning and Harold Stassen in loud, abusive language, and this amused none of the Heffelfingers.

This was, however, Sinclair Lewis as of old, and so again, after a brief tour of the Italian Riviera late in April, on board ship, when, always rather inebriated, he pursued all the ladies and mistakenly called most of them Dorothy.

He parted from Mrs. Powers in New York, set out at once for Williamstown, and made notes on a changed United States, in which the later part of *Lucy Jade,* still to be written, was to take place.

chewing gum
universal use of "Okay"
Kinsey Report—but Reinhold Niebuhr
television, esp in bars
pansies in NY—ever before?
communists, Wallaceites
delight in big NY drug stores, and curiously not object to quick meals for a *while*—ate too much in Italy
more colored sweaters, ties, scarfs on men
moccasin shoes on even elderly men
overwhelming number of cars; few bicycles and motor cycles, as in Italy

At Thorvale Farm again, he began at once to work such material as this into his story, but it could not fill his lonely evenings, and within a few days he began to telephone Mrs. Powers in East Orange, insistent that she come back to Williamstown. She did, and fortunately, for almost at once he collapsed in a serious siege of pneumonia, which would prove to be the real beginning of his end.

The events of this summer cannot be reconstructed with entire certainty because the accounts of the major witnesses conflict in details of dates and personalities, and Lewis's own engagement book was not very fully maintained. It was Mrs. Powers's recollection that she spent the entire summer at Thorvale Farm, but it is Ida Kay's recollection that at one point, at least, she alone was in charge of the household. It is her remembrance, and Bennett Cerf's, that there was a considerable ruckus over the Random House response to *Lucy Jade,* but it is Harry Maule's recollection that Lewis was all sweet reasonableness. These and other differences are of no vast moment, and one can draw in the major outlines, at least, with some certainty.

During the siege of pneumonia, Lewis's brother Claude arrived, and Lewis tried to persuade him to go to Italy with him in the autumn. He was also urging a return journey on Mrs. Powers; and Ida Kay says that it was she who was invited to come—as Mrs. Sinclair Lewis, if Miss Kay would. Certainly, he was determined to go, and as soon as his convalescence permitted he began to study Italian systematically through three or four weekly sessions with a professor in the college and even took occasional little quizzes on such matters as verb forms. At night he would insist that Mrs. Powers study Italian with him, even when he was still confined to his bed, but at her age she found it difficult to learn an unfamiliar language. It was easier for her to attend to his medicines and his physical needs. His hair had thinned a good deal, and on the top of his head his scalp shone through the remaining wisps of pinkish gray, very little to brush, but every morning when she entered his room, he would point at his bureau and say, "Please give me that hairbrush," and then he would assiduously brush and smooth down what hair he had.

In his bedroom he had a rack of about two hundred ties, many of them Italian ties that he had bought in the winter, and as people came to see him —his doctor, his few friends—he would ask that the tie rack be displayed and admired. When someone said, "This is a handsome tie," he would say, "Yes, isn't it? That one's for you." He kept giving his ties away all summer.

A larger property had grown burdensome. At the end of May, when he had recovered, he went to New York with Claude, who was returning to Minnesota, and just after Lewis himself was back at Thorvale Farm, the New York *Times* announced that the place was up for sale for $75,000, but that Mr. Lewis said that this certainly did not mean that he was planning to remain abroad permanently when, in the autumn, "like 5,000 others" he would take "another trip to Europe."

Back at Williamstown, he finished *Lucy Jade* in about a month. The engagement book shows one visit from Harry Maule on July 11 and another from Bennett Cerf on either July 13 or 14. Harry Maule's recollection is that he wrote Lewis on August 10 with Random House suggestions for changes but with the offer to publish the novel as it was if Lewis wished. But Bennett Cerf remembers reading the manuscript at Williamstown. Lewis kept sitting with him and staring at him, his face cupped in his hands, as Cerf tried to read, and he kept protesting, begging that he be left alone, that he could not read in front of the author, and Lewis finally left him alone to finish it. Cerf knew that it was a bad book, and Ida Kay believes that at this point, left alone, he telephoned her to come to Thorvale, on the theory that if she read it, too, they could all have a friendly conversation about it that would lead to the obvious and desired conclusion. Lewis was at first unwilling to have her read it, but then agreed, she arrived, began to read, dined with the men, and, under considerable pressure, finished her reading after dinner. Lewis came down from his study and began to ask her questions about the novel, and these opened the way for Cerf to suggest, in the most cautious way, some of his objections. But it took very little criticism to send Lewis into a rage: Random House was *not* the only publisher, he knew half a dozen publishers in New York who would seize upon the book and publish it without a changed comma, who was Bennett Cerf to criticize *his* novel, he was, after all, Sinclair Lewis! And with that Sinclair Lewis stalked off to bed.

Next morning, Bennett Cerf remembered, Lewis was calm, and he said that some of the points that Cerf had made were just. He would wait for the opinion of Herbert Mayes at *Cosmopolitan,* and if Mayes agreed with Cerf, Lewis would scrap this version and try another one. Miss Kay says that daily, after Cerf's departure, he would denounce Random House, Cerf, publishers in general; and, as the summer passed, his despair grew deeper and deeper. Herbert Mayes recently recalled that he "didn't have anything to do with *Lucy Jade,* except to reject it." Sometime before July 28, when

Edith Haggard wrote Lewis from the office of Curtis Brown, Ltd., she reported that Mayes did not feel that the novel would hold up as a serial, that "the first part, in Italy, [is] wonderful, but it falls apart after that." For magazine needs it would have to be cut drastically. By August 9, Mayes had decided that, with such drastic editing and cutting, it might be made to do as a two-part serial. By this time, Lewis had himself decided to put the *Lucy Jade* version aside, and Mayes in his turn decided to wait for the rewritten novel. In the meantime, two payments had been made under the earlier *Lucy Jade* agreement.

The details of this episode are not as important as its conclusion, which is that Lewis once more took to the bottle with zeal, and finally, when he was deep in delirium tremens, Miss Kay was summoned to help. She telephoned Dr. Traeger in New York, who in turn telephoned Lewis's doctor in Williamstown and gave him directions about sedatives and intravenous injections. In his delirium, Lewis raved about his greatness and about the stupidity of publishers. When he finally pulled out of this condition, exhausted but alive, he said feebly that he wanted to go away, he wanted to go to Europe. He had already written all his friends in Florence to tell them that he was coming back, and from Berenson he had a warm reply of welcome that expressed the hope that "I shall see you once a week at least."

At Twin Farms, Vincent Sheean had heard of Lewis's illness, and although he himself was suffering from a broken leg which was now in an enormous cast, he suggested to Michael that the two of them drive to Williamstown. Michael, who had been studying dramatic art in London during the previous winter, had grown a forked beard, and on his arrival at Thorvale, Lewis's first words were, "Shave that off—you look like an English fairy." Michael did not shave it off, and the two older men began immediately to drink Scotch. This was, for Sheean, a considerable improvement over earlier calls on dry occasions, when he, like others, had been subjected to lectures on the evils of drink. The drinking was fairly steady for the two days of the visit, and Michael saw his father go through that old routine of drinking himself tipsy, disappearing, reappearing, drinking some more, disappearing again, reappearing, drinking; but through it all he stayed in good humor. As the visit wore away, he became less and less resentful of Michael's beard. At some middle point he said, "You look good in that beard. I like that beard. You look real distinguished." And as the boy was leaving on the afternoon of the second day, his father embraced him, shouting, "My Renaissance son! Never shave it off!"

As the summer drew to an end, no bids were made to purchase the enormous house, but the plans for Europe became clear—Miss Kay would not go, Mrs. Powers would not go, but brother Claude would—and the Italian lessons continued regularly. Then, on September 6, Lewis went down to New York to meet his brother, and they spent the night at the

Weylin. Lewis made one last call at the American Academy of Arts and Letters. His hope that the distinction between the Academy and the Institute be abolished had come to nothing, and when he said good-by to Felicia Geffen, the curator and chief organizing spirit of the Academy, he said, "Felicia, it is now up to you. I charge you with the task. You must pull the two together."

They sailed on the *Nieuw Amsterdam* on September 7. To newspapermen Lewis described himself as "the guide for a party of one." The voyage, he said inaccurately, marked his fiftieth anniversary as a writer; for, just fifty years before, *Harper's* had rejected his first poem. Rejection, dejection. Not yet quite alone, he embarked on his last Atlantic passage.

9

ON SHIPBOARD his new best friends were Professor Perry Miller, of Harvard University, and his wife. A learned literary historian, Miller is also a bluff and downright man of robust appetites, a Chicagoan, not in the least the genteel academician of the sort that Lewis could not endure.* It was a brief but lively relationship, and it went, like so many others, on the assumption that the Millers, these genial strangers whom he had just now met (he did know one of Perry Miller's most distinguished books), were his oldest and his dearest friends. Miller had no doubt that he was dying. His ravaged face and palsied hands were the outward signs. He was suffering from the beginnings of polyneuritis which had attacked his legs, so that he walked with a shuffling gait, pulled his knees stiffly up and threw his feet out to the side, his shoulders hunched and pinched, his head thrown back. Yet he talked animatedly. Jokingly, but seriously too, he elaborated the details of the education in art and architecture that he was about to give his brother. He talked about his own work, about the influence of Dickens and Wells upon it. He ruminated over his past. And he agreed that he would come to Leyden, whither the Millers were bound.

First, however, he must show Great Britain to his brother, and this introduction to Europe was to occupy a little more than two weeks, after which they followed the Millers to Holland, where Professor Miller was lecturing at the University of Leyden. He persuaded Lewis to address his class. The only unpleasantness between Miller and Lewis came about at the dinner table of the rector of the university and his wife on the night before the lecture. When Miller suggested to the rector that Claude Lewis would rather be shown through the faculty of medicine next day than listen once more to his brother talk, Sinclair Lewis exploded, denounced everyone present and said that there would be no lecture next day. He subsided, of course, and the dinner party, like so many before it, limped to its awkward end. Later, in his hotel, Lewis told Miller that when he said that his brother did not want to hear his lecture, Miller had released all the resentments that

* Professor Miller's recollections of Lewis were published in his article "The Incorruptible Sinclair Lewis," *The Atlantic,* April 1951.

Lewis had felt for as long as he could remember. The lecture, then, was a defense of American culture, which rested on all of Europe, and of the conduct of Americans in Europe, which, when it was objectionable, was so only because Europeans goaded Americans into behaving according to the stereotype that Europeans had themselves set up. The student audience was bewildered.

What more the Lewises saw of the Netherlands was largely through the courtesy of the Millers, who drove them to Delft, Haarlem, Alkmaar, Antwerp, and Brussels, where they parted. Then the Lewises went on to Italy—to Bellagio on Como, to Venice and Ravenna, Assisi, Siena and, finally, Florence. They were not always together. At Assisi, for instance, Sinclair Lewis was alone, alone and drinking alone. In his hotel one evening he observed a stranger, a clerk in the office of Thomas Cook & Son, who also was alone, and he asked the manager of the hotel to invite the stranger to have a drink with him. His name was Alexander Manson, and for the last year of Lewis's life, he was to be his constant attendant.*

At that first meeting, Lewis consumed a bottle of brandy and no food, but whatever his state of inebriation, he observed, at least, that Manson was at home in Europe, familiar with its monuments and some of its history, adept at some of its languages. He at once asked that he be addressed as Red, and Manson was Alec, who called himself Major and told Lewis that he was only recently released from the British Army. Next day Lewis offered to drive him to Siena, and before leaving him asked him to look him up in Florence. After two meetings in Florence, he offered him the position of secretary-companion, and then at once sent him off to guide his brother on a tour of the Riviera.

He wanted to stay in Florence, and this time in a house. Remembering the splendors of Villa La Costa, and looking perhaps for the friendly but now departed young William Jay Smiths, he returned to the Pian' dei Giullari and rented the house, the most extraordinary house he had yet occupied, and somehow the final, absurd summary of them all. The Via del Pian' dei Giullari is a narrow road on the southern edge of Florence that winds up and up between high gray stone walls and heavy closed gates and

* Alexander Manson is one of the few people who declined to talk to me in the long course of writing this book, and the only person who declined when I was working on Lewis in Italy. On the telephone in Rome, where he lived when I last heard of him, he said that any material that he had he wished to use himself. What "material" there may be beyond the substance of an article he had already published, first in *The Saturday Evening Post* for March 31, 1951 ("The Last Days of Sinclair Lewis," as told to Helen Camp) and then in a shorter form in *l'Europeo* for August 5, 1951 (*"Gli ultimi giorni di* Sinclair Lewis"), I have no way of knowing. I cannot, therefore, give a firsthand impression of Manson but must depend on the conflicting observations of others, and for the facts of his relationship with Lewis I must depend chiefly on his own account and on a long letter that he wrote to Mrs. Dorothy Thompson Kopf after Lewis's death.

then abruptly opens into a little country square, the Plain of the Jesters. Here, in the Renaissance and before, troops of traveling buffoons and jongleurs camped at night, for the ground levels out and the square lies at the center of a group of great ancient houses where employment for fools was certain. Just beyond it, and still higher up, in a very different kind of house, our latter-day jester lived out until nearly its end his jittery, despairing life.

Number 124, Villa La Costa, stands, like the others, behind its wall and closed gate, and presents not so much a formidable as a blank front, a glare of yellow plaster in the sunlight with eight or ten windows that seem small in such a long expanse, and an enormous arched oak door that the builder had appropriated, like a number of others in the house, from the storerooms of that great national monument in the city, the Palazzo Strozzi. Behind that door, the sight is assaulted by a glitter of marble, gilt, dead-white paint, glass, mirrors, crystal. In a foyer as large as a moderate-sized living room, dark-brown letters of marble laid in the beige marble of the floor spell out, at opposite ends of the area, two messages: *Pax et Bonum* and *Cor Tibi Pandit*. On both sides are expanses of glass, double sets of French doors set in heavy granite arches lined with oak arches. These doors, like all the windows in the house, consist of small leaded panes tinted in light pastel shades—blue, orchid, pink, amber—and in the arch over each appears a crest of no significance in the history of Florence. This house was built in 1939, on the foundations of a modest but ancient villa, by a small Fascist official, and in its showy, shell-like opulence (the walls, under the burden of gilt, are very thin, so that the house rattles with human sounds) it shares with many another Italian monument of those years the atmosphere of minor and ephemeral officialdom on the loose. Peace and well-being.

The doors to the right open into a drawing room that, while it contains an elegant Strozzi mantelpiece, was nevertheless dominated by a flat and perfectly enormous modern portrait, perhaps five by six feet, of a lady associated with the owner's family, in ballroom dress. Under this portrait, less than two years after Lewis's death, stood a small old servant dressed in musty brown, a servant who had been attached to the house before Lewis took over. On the subject which was most commonplace in the world outside, his drinking, she was engagingly reticent, offering a few gently sad reflections that did not at all share the brutal tone of the obituary notices which the Florentine newspapers were to publish with such energetic conviction. (*"Quando Arrivò a Firenze,"* the headline in *La Nazione,* a quite respectable journal, would read, *"Era Già un Uomo Finito,"* and then would quote in its opening paragraph an anonymous friend who purportedly announced eighteen months before his death that "Lewis *è già morto*"—Lewis is already dead. The obituary itself would be not so much the recognition of the passing of a distinguished man as a diatribe on the evils of drink—*"il vizio di bere"*—which, the world would be assured, had destroyed each of Lewis's "three" marriages!)

The old servant preferred another tone, and repeated over and over again that he was *gentillissimo, gentillissimo,* and *malatissimo, malatissimo.* Most ill! At La Costa, she said, he saw very few people, but often he worked for long hours, on the terrace, in the tower, and he lived, she thought, in some great fear. In the management of the household he had small interest; she took her orders from the secretary. Remembering Lewis's detailed interest in the management of his earlier houses, one feels the difference in the drift of his life.

Beyond the drawing room is a commodious library that held such books as Lewis was traveling with. These were glossaries, thesauruses, dictionaries; histories of Italian art and architecture, of the Reformation and of church ritual; seven volumes in the Loeb Classical Library; two novels—*I Promessi Sposi* and Malaparte's *La Pelle;* and histories of and guides to Florence. (Did he, one wonders, remember Number 48 in the small library of an eager Minnesota boy, *aetat.* fifteen—Mrs. Oliphant's *Makers of Florence?*) At one end of the library is an enormous fireplace so badly designed that a fire on the hearth merely pours smoke into the room; to use it at all, a small firebox on metal legs four or five feet high had been placed inside the great opening, to bring the fire near the draft.

One can contemplate again the genius Lewis had for choosing to live in houses that were quite beyond the possibility of being shaken down into homes, or that, at any rate, resisted his possibilities in that direction. (When the banker who had bought his Duluth house resold it, it went to an order of nuns, and when Thorvale Farm was sold after his death, it went to an order of friars. The irony is double: great houses in which Sinclair Lewis was never at home, and Sinclair Lewis's homes sheltering, finally, religious communities.) His were always houses that, for all their richness, were characterized by a cold impersonality; and at La Costa there were not even those touches of his own taste, like his Childe Hassam paintings and his Adolph Dehns, but badly painted portraits of ladies he did not know at all who were ready for a hypothetical dance with someone else. And a staff of strangers. In this hard glitter, what heart had opened to him? Alexander Manson's? Perhaps. Or that of Tina Lazzerini, the young woman Manson presently introduced into the household as his wife? Perhaps.

However that may be, this was less a home than any. He could, after all, only *wish* to be at home. His first novel, like his last, is concerned with a hero who desires "the land of elsewhere," and then cannot abide it. His last hero goes to the American Episcopal Church in Florence and longs for Colorado.

> He knew then that he was unalterably an American; he knew what a special and mystical experience it is, for the American never really emigrates but only travels; perhaps travels for two or three generations but at the end is still marked with the gaunt image of Tecumseh.

He was not the first American writer to wander in this way, but he was the first to wander so relentlessly, with such a bitter demon at his back. And certainly this gaudy villa, so near the Pian' dei Giullari, was only another camp, although for the darkest night.

Across the foyer was a sitting room about the size of the drawing room, with more white-enamel walls and ornamental gilt embossments, a crystal chandelier large enough for a theater lobby, a white-enameled grand piano that required a ten-piece orchestra in white tuxedos and a singer like Ella Fitzgerald to complete it, another even larger portrait of a lady in yards and yards of extravagant chiffon gown, and, at one end of the room, most remarkable, a stairway that winds up to the higher floors. Its balustrade is made of Venetian spun glass in blue and milky white, and the stairs themselves are of that same slippery beige marble of which the floors are made. Small wonder that Lewis, with his bad coordination and his developing nervous disorder, once came plummeting feet first down these stairs and that thereafter the owner boxed his precious balustrade in wood, and that at the bottom, Lewis's servants spread out rugs in the event of another fall. Throughout the house, rubber pads were placed under the treacherous rugs.

Beyond the blinding salon is a soberer, shadowed writing room, and then a pleasantly spacious dining room that opens out onto a capacious loggia overlooking the terraced, somber garden. The dining room witnessed some melancholy meals. Among the few members of the Anglo-American community that Lewis still sought out in this last Florentine year was Lady Una Troubridge, a remarkable woman in her dinner jacket, the purported prototype of the ingénue heroine of Radcliffe Hall's *The Well of Loneliness,* a novel that, in 1929, Lewis had defended as "almost lugubriously moral" when John S. Sumner had seized it and arrested its publisher in New York. Lewis met Lady Troubridge at a cocktail party just before he took La Costa, and on this occasion he devoted himself entirely to her; then, as soon as he had moved into his house, he telephoned to say that he wanted her to be his first dinner guest. She was a new acquaintance whom, like the Millers, he tried to treat as though she were his oldest, dearest friend; and out of her respect for him and great pity, she played his make-believe.

With her he took many drives into the country in the black Studebaker that he had bought (this was his favorite relaxation—to drive out to some isolated *trattoria* in Maiano or Pratolino or Fiesole and, to understate, sample the wines), and with her he planned innumerable fascinating journeys abroad, with detailed itineraries, to be pursued as soon as he had recovered his health. Beginning in a kind of feverish exaltation, assisted by the still inexhaustible gift of verbal improvisation, he would build what she called "fantastic paper castles." They would go here, there, and then on to that place; while North Africa and Egypt loomed large in these plans, there were many other places as well, and all planned for with the same mounting excitement. They would have the most marvelous time! But he believed none of it, and at the pitch of his excitement, the paper castle suddenly fell apart in the air before him, and then he fell in upon himself, the long meager body collapsing in a hump on the table as he groaned, "Oh God, no man has ever been so miserable!"

His gloom was not usually so articulate. There is the testimony of Father Fosco Martinelli, for example, whose church, Santa Margherita a Montici, is just a few steps up beyond Villa La Costa. It is one of the oldest churches in the environs of the city and stands at the highest point of the hills that fall down to the valley of the Arno on one side, the valley of the Ema on the other. On the Arno side the slopes are covered with guidebook gardens cut out sharply by walls and hedges from scraggly olive groves; on the Ema side, the small, highly cultivated fields step down to the river and then rise up from it again, precisely, thriftily, as carefully tended as flower beds, and as different as it is agriculturally possible to be from the wanton spread of Minnesota wheat, "a golden sea for miles about," of which Lewis liked to sing.

Father Martinelli was a gravely handsome young man whose study was a rude plastered cell. Behind the work table, a few years ago, hung a *certifica al patriota,* signed by Marshal Montgomery, that attested to his partisan activities, and later he published a small novel for youngsters about boys in the partisan movement—*I romani siamo noi.* Propped up on top of a wardrobe was an unframed expressionist painting in oil that had been given to Lewis and that Lewis gave to him on the occasion when Father Martinelli was invited to dine at La Costa. It was one of those frequent, half-hearted gestures Lewis made in an attempt to come to know Italians, and like most, a failure. There was a little preliminary conversation in which Lewis ambiguously said that to be an artist, one really needed to learn to think in Italian. At the table, they talked of his work habits and of Italian writers, but Lewis was remote from the conversation, abstracted in gloom. After dinner he gave the priest the picture—Christ before the Sanhedrin—"as a remembrance of this evening," and sank into a chair. When Father Martinelli left shortly after, since they seemed more and more deeply entombed in silence, Lewis said, "Friend, friend, we will see each other often." They never saw each other again. Lewis had shown no interest either in Father Martinelli's religious activities or in his political views. "That evening he was interested in nothing. An inspiration was upon him." *

One would have to search for a better example of the cultural barrier,

* The engaging Father Martinelli published his recollection of this evening in *Il bollettino dell' Instituto Tecnico Industriale "Leonardo da Vinci" di Firenze* (September–October, 1951) as "Invito di Sinclair Lewis."

for of inspiration there was unhappily very little at La Costa, but of drudgery, once Lewis set himself to it, much. Once more, the gap that hard liquor, presently forbidden, and acquaintances, presently undesired, could not fill, work might. On fine days in the spring of 1950, much of that work was done on the loggia off the dining room. This is on the north side of the house and lies entirely in deep shadow. In the garden, with its seven cypresses and struggling box hedges, a gardener later reported, was where Lewis always walked, alone, in the shadows, back and forth, never on the sunny side of the house. One is reminded of a prophetic passage in *Our Mr. Wrenn* of thirty-five years before:

> . . . his loneliness shadowed him. Of that loneliness one could make many books; how it sat down with him; how he crouched in his chair, bespelled by it, till he violently rose and fled, with loneliness for companion in his flight. He was lonely. He sighed he was "lonely as fits." Lonely—the word obsessed him. Doubtless he was a bit mad, as are all isolated men who sit in distant lands longing for the voice of friendship.

He fled once more into work. His secretary has written that he worked from nine to ten hours every day, and he told Father Martinelli that he got up at five and worked until seven, then had breakfast; at eight he was back at his desk and worked until eleven; at four in the afternoon he returned to it and worked until eight; and then, during the night, he would wake up and write some more. It was an old fury, and it would seem that, toward the end, work itself, more than drink or any other *vizio,* had become the most vigorous of all forms of dissipation, if by dissipation one means any drugging activity that helps us to forget the intolerable. Even he knew this, having confessed to "Ebenezer" about "work as escape," and hence no cause for praise.

From the terrace fell the view. Lewis professed to have three major demands of a house: a place to work, decent servants' quarters, and the view. The view that lay beyond the falling hill was of the new, industrialized area of Florence, with none of the monuments that a Florentine would expect in a "view" except, at the extreme left, a section of the cupola of the Duomo; and yet, hideous as it is close up, the new Florence was adequately distant from Villa La Costa to look quite pretty, with its white and yellow planes in the sunlight. The best thing in the immediate view was that Torre del Gallo near which John Milton held his colloquy with Galileo ("the sad Tuscan, who with Optic glass, Exalted, saw the Constellations pass"), and where Lewis in that last novel he was writing located the villa of Sam Dodsworth, as if to have an old friend near him while he suffered in the higher splendor of La Costa. Father Martinelli says of their moment in the loggia, "To the left appeared the city lights; above, the stars." The observation seems important, as the stars above a Broadway alley once seemed important to Father Murphy.

On bad days, Lewis worked in the tower at the top of the house. At the head of the marble stairs, going up from a large open hallway where a huge mirror in a floreated gilt frame doubled the vengeance on the eye of white and gold and crystal-dripping chandelier, further stairs lead up to the square tower that juts from the middle of the roof. A room of about fifteen by fifteen feet, it contained only a large work table and a few straight chairs, and was entirely enclosed in long casement windows made up of hundreds of those tinted, leaded panes. Here, in full visual command of all his ancient surroundings, Lewis finished his novel about Americans from a town called Newlife, uneasily attempting to make something of the old.

He could look, if he wished, straight north to Settignano, and on clear days, with ordinary field glasses, would probably have been able to pick out the clock tower among the cypresses of I Tatti, where, during this last residence in Florence, he almost never went. He appeared there, in fact, only twice; although Elizabetta Mariano repeatedly telephoned to urge invitations upon him and he accepted, at the last moment would come a call from Alexander Manson to say that he was indisposed. Why, after the bright, *simpatico* beginning of the year before, Lewis let that friendship lapse, along with so many others, is not clear, nor was it so to Berenson. But Berenson was suspicious of Manson and reported that on one of those two occasions he challenged him, "Are you really English?" Manson, he said, hesitated and then replied, "My father was English, my mother is a Pole." To which Berenson commented later—but Berenson, one should add, made his share of errors in human judgment—"I know a Central European adventurer when I see one. He was a minor Central European adventurer."

The situation is not made clearer when we observe that in *World So Wide* Lewis attributed to one of his shabbiest characters, an old fake of a connoisseur, a remark that, according to the secretary, caused Lewis to lose his temper at luncheon on one of those two occasions at I Tatti; the remark was that civilization ended with the fall of the Bastille. Berenson, who in conversation at least once defined *decadence* as "the disappearance of an upper class," probably made that remark. If he did, knowing Lewis's democratic prejudices and humble origins ("What kind of manure pile did he come out of?" he once ungraciously asked), he must have made it in the expectation of some such irritated response, but he probably did not expect the second response, when Lewis attributed it to a fraudulent dilettante and omitted mention of his own anger.

Such manipulation of biographical event has biographical significance. Through Berenson, Lewis had met a distinguished Florentine journalist and essayist (and manufacturer of hats) named Arturo Loria, and Loria later reported with a certain humorous horror that after their first meeting, Lewis called him Art. In *World So Wide* it is the shabbiest and grossest American of them all who says, "This is . . . Mrs. Baccio . . . married to a fine young Italian businessman, friend of mine, Art Baccio." It could be Elmer Gantry or Verg Gunch with whom Lewis was identifying his own social manner.

It was Loria who, in 1953, published in *Il Corriere della Sera,* to which he regularly made literary contributions, a gently ironical reminiscence of Lewis in Florence. He remembered Lewis at a party of Europeans in Bellosguardo, where he appeared to be more at ease than he usually was, but one suspects that this was a 1949 rather than a 1950 party. A lovely young American girl was at this affair, and to her Lewis devoted himself. He made her play a game with him that involved him in a whole new cast of impersonations and that commanded the attention of the entire assembly. He was a dangerous young Italian in pursuit of her; a museum guard freed from his lonely boredom upon her arrival in his gallery; an old sacristan, squint-eyed and rude in expressing his suspicions of bare female arms and legs before the naked damned of a fourteenth-century fresco; a cyclist, insisting on escorting her across the street. The girl responded until he challenged her with betraying her puritan heritage in coming abroad to seek out nobility and cosmopolites such as these.

In the midst of all this spouting garrulity, a French woman next to Loria tried to picture Lewis, with all his great reputation, as a member of the French Academy, and a German woman seated at his other side pressed her eyes shut in an effort to recall the reticences of her friend Stefan George, his utterances *"come gocce d'oro."* And the company was aware that the two Americans felt themselves set apart, enjoying themselves in some oblique way at the expense of the Europeans, and that, pleasant as they were, they would laugh at the rest after they had gone. Of Lewis's imitations, Loria, like so many others, was impressed above all by their compulsive quality, until one yearned for *"una sosta, un riposo suo e nostro."* Rest for him and oneself!

Parties such as this, or cocktails with the Anglo-Americans, did not interest him very much any more, as, alone in his house, he slumped into a long bout of reckless solitary drinking. Then finally, on one wild, stormy December night, a telephone call came from Lady Una Troubridge to Dr. Vincenzo Lapiccirella, a distinguished and cultivated Florentine diagnostician and cardiologist. He must come at once to Villa La Costa! The wind roared in the cypresses, rain tumbled from the black skies in torrents, the doctor lost his way and found it again, came finally to the great door and pounded on it only to have it opened and slammed in his face by a servant who did not know that he had been called. A dog came bounding round the corner of the house and added its barking to the tumult. The doctor pounded again, this time to be admitted and to meet Alexander Manson, who took him to the upper floor. Past the two bathrooms out of Hollywood (one apple-green, one orchid, the two separated by a wall consisting chiefly of an illuminated aquarium in which huge goldfish lazily swam back and forth) he entered the master bedroom, a large chamber that, with all its new green-and-gold furniture in heavy Renaissance imitation, seemed crowded. Here there was no respite from the gilt: on the doors, on the ceiling, on the fireplace, on the wide headboard of the bed where lay this incredibly ugly man, red-faced and drunk. He had suffered his first heart attack.*

Dr. Lapiccirella knew who it was that he was to attend, but he was not prepared either for the appearance of his patient or for the circumstances of his life. What he immediately discovered was that the bedside decanter was filled not with water but with whisky, and Manson said that he was drinking a quart of it every night. The doctor listened to the unsteady heartbeat and took his blood pressure, which was over two hundred. He did what he could and vowed to make it his personal business to rehabilitate the great Sinclair Lewis, an effort doomed to be a losing game.

When he was up again, Lewis came regularly to Lapiccirella's office, but he was still drinking. He was much troubled by the condition of his face, and spoke often of how people could take no pleasure in seeing him. He declined invitations on this account (to Lapiccirella's house, for example), and still every day he came down to the Via Tornabuoni, where Dr. Lapiccirella's offices were located, quite near Leland's, and it was to Leland's, where the lights are bright enough, that Lewis went.

As he continued to drink, the doctor decided to talk to him in a *manière forte,* and one day he told him bluntly: he would die, and he would die in the worst way if he drank any more; he would simply go down a hole. What was wrong with him that he drove himself to death in this mad way? Lewis glared at him, but finally he said very well, he would stop, he had done it before. It was arranged then that he should come to the office every day instead of dropping into a bar. He came for five days, but by the end of that time he was raging with nervousness. The doctor invited him to his house for lunch again, and he accepted. They had an *apéritif,* and it was agreed that they would have only one; unfortunately, the doctor was called to the telephone, and his wife could not refuse Lewis's hungry insistence on more. When the doctor returned, Lewis was besotted on four or five of them, and at the table he alternated between moody dejection in which he said nothing, and sudden, rather wild animation, with much waving of hands, about nothing. And then he was drinking again.

Dr. Lapiccirella, who had seen some lepers, feared that it was leprosy

* Dr. Lapiccirella's recollection differs from Alexander Manson's published account in a number of details. Manson says that when he returned to Florence on December 9 (Claude was apparently lingering behind somewhere) and found Lewis in a state of "alcoholic exhaustion," he told him that unless he promised to give up whisky at once, he would not work for him, and that thereafter Lewis "drank nothing but wine, and, except on a few occasions, only in reasonable quantities." Manson dated the first heart attack in July 1950, and placed it in Zurich, but he does refer to a doctor's attention in December, and the prescription of "an extensive vitamin diet."

that afflicted Lewis, and he took him to Dr. Marcello Comel, one of the finest dermatologists in Europe, who was then in the medical school at Pisa. Dr. Comel diagnosed the immediate difficulty as *acne necrotica seborrhoeica,* and he prescribed a treatment that was temporarily effective. Then Lewis did stop drinking. This must have been in a period during the first four months of 1950, when Lewis finished *World So Wide,* and returned to the writing of poetry. With a new flare-up of his skin ailment and his book nearly finished, he once more took to drink, and once more Dr. Lapiccirella gave him a talking to. This was on an occasion when Lewis came drunk to his office, barely manipulating the stairs, waving his arms like a windmill. After the lecture, Lewis wept a little, spoke of his unhappy marriages and all the betrayed friendships in his life, of his sons, one of them dead, of the ruin that his life was. The doctor mentioned his greatness, and Lewis looked at him in such a way as to communicate his knowledge that greatness was long behind him. He left once more, and did not return. "They drew a circle around Sinclair," Dr. Lapiccirella somewhat ominously said. In late May he learned that he—and "they"—had gone from Florence.

The talk of his greatness is suggestive of a recollection of Harold Acton's, of an occasion when he and Evelyn Waugh were having lunch at Villa La Costa. Waugh had just been visiting the Sitwells at their establishment outside Siena, and he was full of talk about them when Lewis suddenly grew furious, denounced the Sitwells as "phonies" and delivered himself of a tirade on British snobbery. Later, in the library, he began to talk in a way that had not been characteristic of him, about his own books, how he was among the very few writers who had contributed words and terms to the vocabulary of English; others were Shakespeare, Bunyan, Irving, Dickens, Thackeray and Harriet Beecher Stowe; but then he suddenly broke off and launched on an extended and rather moving tribute to America, and especially to the landscape of the Middle West.

Dr. Claude Lewis returned from his travels in time for Christmas, and Michael Lewis arrived from London for a Christmas visit. Both bear out Dr. Lapiccirella that at this point Lewis was still drinking whisky, and, in Michael's hearing, Dr. Claude said, "Hal, you go on this way, and I give you one year to live." Early in January, Dr. Claude was to leave, and his brother arranged with his American acquaintance, James Campbell ("Jimmy" to nearly everyone, including Michael, who described him as "that worn-out old expatriate, shabby friend of shabby contessas and marchesas") that he accompany Claude and Michael on the trip to Genoa. At Genoa, Claude Lewis took ship for America by way of Australia, and Michael, returning briefly to Florence on his way to Rome and London, found his father drinking only wine. It must have been at some time in the months before that Lewis, having heard that his old friend Frances Perkins was in Florence, telephoned her, "but he was so ill, so confused, that I realized sadly that he was gone."

Not quite. He had one more novel to write and twelve more months to live. On January 24 he wrote his publisher in London about the winter and La Costa:

> And here I am starting the new novel, now. It should be done by summer, but it will presumably be serialized in America and not ready for publication till very early 1951. It will probably be called *World So Wide,* and deal with the Anglo-American Colony here, especially with an American who is lured from the sensible security of money-making into the sick-sweet perils of scholarship . . . & love story.

After Lewis had finished *Dodsworth,* he wrote Paul Morand to say that "I shall never write another novel in a European setting," but with the conception of *Lucy Jade* and its resolution in *World So Wide,* that decision was reversed. In an interview with the New York *Times,* published for his sixty-fifth birthday, he was quoted as saying, "I am the diagnostician. I don't know what to do about anything. I am not a reformer. I really don't care." To Lewis, the diagnostician of America, Europe had always been a necessary point of reference, even as it had always been an irritant to him, from first novel to last.

Shuffling about the materials of *Lucy Jade,* he produced a somewhat better book in *World So Wide,* but its interest is not so much in its quality as in its resemblance to the first novel, *Our Mr. Wrenn.* Toward the end of that novel we come across the phrase, echoed from Kipling, that supplies the title of the last, in which Kipling is acknowledged: "this world so wide." "My girl . . . My mother . . . must 'ave gone with all the rest"—

> With all the rest which I 'ave seen
> an' found an' known an' met along.
> I cannot say the things I feel,
> And so I sing my evenin' song.
> *For to admire an' for to see,*
> *For to be'old this world so wide—*
> *It never done no good to me,*
> *But I can't drop it if I tried!*

Both novels take that theme, traditionally favored by our novelists, of the American innocent abroad, and while the two heroes are in some ways very different (one a nearly illiterate clerk, the other a successful architect), they are, in some more basic ways than these, alike, and therefore the pattern of their experience is almost identical. There is something compulsive in this theme for Sinclair Lewis, and the pattern, which is resolved by a vindication of our innocence, is no doubt now, as it was a hundred years ago, a portion of our folklore.

In each case, an accident frees the hero from the routines that give structure to his life, and he eagerly seeks the long-desired European experience. Each, without the embracing clichés of "the job," finds himself freed only to his own lonely emptiness—". . . he was desolatingly free to wander in a world too bleakly, too intimidatingly wide," the first hero discovers; and the last, "In Newlife [Colorado] . . . I was as lonely as I am here [Florence]—only busier there." The earlier hero, more desperately, "had no friends in all the hostile world" of London. However, each encounters a girl who seems at home in this hostile world, an American sophisticate—the first, a Bohemian painter; the second, a scholar of the Renaissance. These women, familiar with Europe, are also half corrupted by it, easily seduced by the false values that they associate with it. After a period in which the innocence of these heroes has been exposed to the dubious experience of these heroines, each hero turns to a sounder heroine, the undiluted American Miss with no intellectual or artistic nonsense about her. These fresher ladies are, again, basically alike, in spite of the superficial differences between the incredibly modest, hard-working girl employed by Wanamacy in 1914 and the incredibly brash career woman of 1950 who has a heart of modest gold under the layers of professional lacquer, a seeing eye under the mascara.

These are poor novels but it would be a mistake to call them simple. Each contains unresolved complexities that are probably not so peculiar to Lewis as they are to the American imagination itself. Europe is as fascinating to these heroes as it is insistent that they prove it to be false. The yearning for a deeper experience than America offers is as strong in them as the loneliness that overcomes them when they are freed to that experience which they are then unable, in their wholesome naïveté, to utilize. There is in these novels an undercurrent of fear, fear of Europe itself: in *World So Wide,* Sam Dodsworth lectures the young hero at some length on the importance of not staying abroad too long lest he succumb to Europe; and in both novels Lewis, like Henry James, has his Osmonds and his Madame Merles, those Americans who have yielded up their native inheritance only to be vitiated by an alien tradition that they cannot make their own.

Yet, curiously, it is the "Europeanized" women—silly Istra Nash of *Our Mr. Wrenn* and cool Dr. Olivia Lomond of *World So Wide*—the women whom the heroes must reject, who, nevertheless, communicate such higher values, intellectual and spiritual, as are implied by the total situation in each novel. The result is that when Mr. Wrenn turns to his simple American, Nelly Croubel, Lewis must necessarily shift his novel into a satire on the limits of suburbia; and when Hayden Chart, in the last novel, turns to Roxanna Eldritch, Lewis must necessarily force his plot into sentimental melodrama to bring about the turn at all. These endings are hardly what one could call clear vindications of American values. We are left with the large, staring question: what *was* America to Sinclair Lewis?

Shortly before his death, according to the New York *Times Book Review,* Lewis had reached a decision: "America is too big for the Great American Novel. America's impossible to grasp." It was not Lewis's failure to "grasp" America that depressed if it did not exasperate readers of *World So Wide* when that novel appeared in the *Woman's Home Companion* (*Cosmopolitan* had declined it and retrieved the money that it had paid in advance) or in book form shortly after Lewis's death. It was rather that he no longer dealt with America at all, even when he thought that he was writing about it. His work, always flirting with social parody, had since 1930 been tending more and more toward self-parody, and here the self-parody at last was complete. As Malcolm Cowley wrote:

> Sinclair Lewis's characters in *World So Wide* talk almost exactly like those in *Main Street* and *Babbitt.* The result is that they sound like survivors from a vanished world, like people just emerging from orphanages and prisons where they had been for thirty years conducting tape recordings of Lewis novels.

He finished that book in April 1950, and it was on April 20 that he gave his last public address, to the Unione Fiorentina in the Palazzo Strozzi. Having been persuaded not to attempt Italian, he spoke in English, but in a manner most unusual for him, in *"lente frasi più legate a intima meditazione"*—slow sentences more suitable to an intimate meditation than to a public lecture.* He praised the beauties of Florence, the atmosphere of its daily life, and hoped that it would not become infected by that disease of "Chicagoism" that he already felt so powerfully present in Rome. He put himself in the company of Nathaniel Hawthorne and Henry James, as one with them in his knowledge of and admiration for Florence, and indeed, he confessed, he was their active companion in that he was finishing a novel in which Florence would be the temporary residence of his American characters, where they would find themselves in a kind of probative confrontation with its historical and artistic ambience and the pleasant rituals of its daily life.

As he worked at his novel with mounting fury in March and April, he avoided any probative confrontations for himself by drinking wine almost continuously. When the Millers arrived for a visit in April, "he generally succeeded in knocking himself out by afternoon." He took them to a restaurant where he "commanded the orchestra to play the sentimental tunes of his earlier escapades" and threw his money about like a madman. Manson tells how he tried to keep him from drinking in such excess, and

* Arturo Loria summarized this lecture for *Il trecento* (Florence: Sansoni, 1953), the documentary record of the proceedings of the Unione Fiorentina for *La libera cattedra di storia della civiltà fiorentina.*

how he tried in vain to restrain his wild extravagances, but in New York, Harry Maule was made uneasy by letters that came from Manson, asking for more money to keep Lewis going in the way that he had decreed. It was some ailment more killing than "Chicagoism" that had settled on him. And if he had been gracious in his speech about the amenities of Italian life, the Italians were under no delusion that he was anything but a deranged American. In the illustrated magazine, *Settimana Incom,* appeared an article on the Anglo-Americans in Florence, called "Byron Is Not Their Model," in which he was described as a man who had made millions of dollars from poor Hollywood films derived from bad novels and had now come to Europe to spend them, and to die because alcohol had been forbidden him.

This article, according to Lady Una Troubridge, outraged him, and he went to the American consulate with the intention of bringing suit against the magazine. That passion spent itself, too, like all others. From New York in early May came word that his old friend William Rose Benét was dead of a heart attack; and in July would come further word that another old friend—his very best—Carl Van Doren was dead of a heart attack. Resolving in mid-May to take to the road again and to keep moving, he initiated the final stage of his life, which was a six months' chase toward his own death.

Down through Tuscany and into the heart of Umbria and then abruptly north again and up into the Dolomites for a pause at Gardone. On Lake Garda Lewis had planned to spend two weeks, but after five days he was ordering the bags to be packed again and now they were off for France. Genoa, San Remo, five days at Nice, then Marseilles and Montpellier and Carcassonne, and up through the valley of the Loire to Versailles, and a pause there for another five days. They made a few excursions into Paris, but in less than a week Lewis was tired of France and proposed that they drive into Switzerland; and there he managed to remain at Grindelwald for nearly two weeks before driving on to Zurich, where he was to spend most of July and part of August.

He occupied himself by mastering his Baedeker on every town and city in which they paused, and by the writing of verse. The return to verse had been made in March, when, still in Florence, he wrote a long poem called "Prophets in a Wood," an imaginary dialogue between Milton and Galileo in which each tells the other of the kind of heavenly sights he has beheld. Then the poet contrasts the ancient Florence that they knew with the modern Florence of night clubs, tourists, and Vespas, a Florence that they could hardly have foreseen in their predictions that the world was steadily moving toward greater and greater freedom.

> The world, grown swift and mad now, has never understood
> What prophet said to prophet in the Vallombrosa wood.

In Florence, too, he had begun a long poem called "To All Men," at which he worked all through the circle that they took from Florence to Garda. It consists of a series of satirical dramatic monologues delivered by persons who had been associated with Christ in his lifetime, each to demonstrate the immediate failure of Christ's sacrifice. Flippant and heavily ironical, these have all the air—if not the metrical skill—of poems published in *Smart Set* thirty-five years before or in the early *American Mercury*.

More interesting, perhaps, is a screed written in May, called "Hermit on a Florence Hill," in which the poet pictures himself as retired from the world, from women and folly, living complacently in the atmosphere of ancient learning and art.

Here, strengthened by their scholarly care,
I ponder on the Heavenly sphere
Where once, most miserable of lives,
I thought of my three horrible wives.

My first wife longed for social place
She thrashed about with scarlet face
To get the chance to meet a prince.
My second made me shake and wince
By violence, by blasts and blares,
As she managed other folks' affairs.
My third was winsome, playful, kind,
But often difficult to find,
For it was hard to keep in mind
In what man's bed she now reclined. . . .

Fiendesses now all stalked about
To bully me, to scold and shout—
And very sound professional stuff,
For I had liked my women rough,
Glad to accept whate'er they said—
The way to vote, the right cravat,
The diet to put on more fat,
And the times for attendance on their bed.

I was besieged by beckoning swarms,
Numberless visionary forms:
Coaxing little female devils
Professing virtue, shocked by evils,
In fact, like women on the whole,
They merely longed to seize my soul.
Some praised my intellectual powers—
Oh, they could listen to me for hours!
Some yearned to pet and mother me
And some my dear little babes to be.

Some cried that we would roam together,
Fearlessly singing, any weather,
Some longed to share my weighty work,
An unpaid copyist and clerk.
But all held firm and feminine goal—
To dominate a masculine soul,
My soul to steal, my soul to sell,
Frayed and second-hand in Hell. . . .

A favorite in the neighborhood,
I find my hermitage is good.
Here in my innocence I stay
And fast and softly sing and pray
That women now will keep away—
Away!
Away!
Away!

At these works the misguided poet labored, according to his secretary, hard and earnestly. "Poetry," he announced quite seriously, "is greater than prose," and for five days in the village of Souillac, for example, he did not stir from his poetic efforts. What concerned him there was the completion of a work that he had started in San Remo, "The Happy Man." This is a long narrative poem about an American businessman, a supersalesman for the Cosmic Oil Company, who manipulates a swindle in Arabia, then goes to Italy to rest and overcome his guilt. He meets a gorgeous young Italian girl, one Bianca, both worldly and innocent, the "soul" of his Italy, and falls in love.

In Italy they do not wear as label
That patronizing word Democracy,
Which means you generously say Good-morning
To men with smaller incomes than your own.
Italians keep their hearts well warmed and lighted
As a meeting place for all conditions of men.
A prince can meet and greet a contadino,
A contadino praise the prince's golf.

The story ends when the hero takes a job as a filling-station attendant at one fiftieth of his former salary and, marrying Bianca, becomes "the happy man," fulfilled in domestic obscurity.

In Versailles he wrote a "Prayer to Escape Notice":

Lord, let Thy quiet servant be
Sinful and ambitionless,
From lust and itching hair-shirt free.
Sainthood murder saintliness.

Versifying came to an end in Zurich, where he suffered two heart attacks—the first, at lunch, with a Swiss publisher; the second, five days later in a restaurant. Even when he had reduced his consumption of liquor, he refused to reduce the number of cigarettes that he smoked, and when his Zurich physician said that he must do so, and that he must remain under close medical scrutiny and give up his furious peregrinations, he told Manson (says Manson) that he would rather live briefly as he wished than longer as an invalid, and he made Manson promise not to tell anyone about his heart condition. (He was suffering, in fact, from sclerotic myocarditis.) Then he projected a whole new itinerary—south to Taormina and Sicily for a time, then into North Africa, then Spain and Portugal, then Scandinavia, then Scotland, Wales, England.

In the meantime, Ida Kay came to Zurich on a European tour. She was astonished when Manson's wife happily displayed her wardrobe of couturier frocks, her jewels, everything that Manson had given her, and dismayed by the physical deterioration so evident in Lewis. He seldom left the hotel in which they were staying, but with his usual thoughtfulness, remembering her pleasure in golf, he arranged even then that she should have the equipment and the place to enjoy it. He asked her to try to sell his Williamstown house, to sell it for as little as fifty thousand dollars if she could. He would never go back there, he vowed, and then there were extended fulminations—almost as if he were planning a novel—about an exclusive college like Williams vis-à-vis a great man living in its neighborhood, ignored. Then he said, finally, that not only was he not going back to Williamstown, he was never going back to the United States. "Europe is home to me now." "What was there to return to?" Arturo Loria, who called him a "prodigal son," wisely asked, as he concluded his recollection with the sentence, "The prodigal son, tired and ill, does not return to his house if he does not have a father who awaits him." When, presently, the Millers arrived in Zurich, he told them repeatedly that he loved America but did not like it. He was then drinking only beer, but he should not have been drinking even that. Then he said good-by, and once more was off with his entourage, back to Italy.

> I have returned to Italy and shall spend a couple of weeks in Turin, but I shall be wandering in so unscheduled a way that mail is likely to miss me and so just send me c/o American Express, Florence. . . . I have been wandering round France and Switzerland and shall probably spend the late autumn and early winter in Sicily. I have been making a lot of notes for a new book but don't know when I shall start really writing it.

He had been making notes, but not really very many, for a work to be called *Friends* or *Friendship*. Among these are the following passages:

> *Friends* How X longs to make, to keep them, thinks he lives for them, yet (selfish, opinionated, ambitious, too prone to "resent" "rudeness" or

"indifference") little talent for it, & hence has but few. . . . Does any ambitious man have many?

There can be an insatiable sick *disease* of friendship—like love—always demanding more, so always lonely

Rem[ember] losing wife, partner, doctor, sec[retar]y, valet—all but enemy

Friends can have no fault

What faults one finds w[ith] all friends, in sudden irritable mood—how we dislike them *all.* G's teasing banter & his flattery of women. Co's lying. Ca's dependence on drunk wife. Ha's tardiness *

The theme is set down clearly:

Horror to disc[over] that he who thinks he loves people doesn't really—wants to shake 'em off bosom even more than he did to clasp 'em.
Looking for flaws. [James S.] Hart, Molly [Costain Haycraft] Danger of irritably *testing* friends w[ith] "Let's see if he will remember—"

The identity of "X" is no mystery. One page begins:

FRIENDS
How lose: Paul Hilsdale, Irving Fisher, Soule, Hal Smith, Updegraff, Noyes, Tinker, Billy Fay, Bill Collins, Bob Pfeiffer, Hal Smith, Connie, DeKruif, Grace, Woodward, Dorothy, Harcourt, Brace, Benets, Gunther, Florey, Birkhead, Molly, Edith Summers, Upton Sinclair, Mary Vorse, Fay, Bevil Rudd, H. G. Wells, Banning, Mrs. Malick, Mrs. Nolan, Ben Huebsch, Geo Macy, C N Thomas

Deleted! The list cuts across his entire sixty-five years, and it could have been almost indefinitely extended: Leonard Bacon, Anna Louise Strong, Michael Williams, Grace MacGowan Cooke, George Sterling, Arthur S. Hoffman, Albert Payson Terhune, Charles Norris, Charles Hanson Towne, Philip Goodman, Hugh Walpole, Frazier Hunt, Charles Breasted, Lloyd Lewis—on and on, down to Dr. Benjamin Camp, James Roers, Sturges Riddle, down even to "Hooper, Dick Marshall, Flowers, Cook, Mary Parrish, Chet Syms, Reynolds & Denton, Davy Deans, 2 Stans, Oley," and we would still not have named half of the lost, not even a tenth. No list could name them all, but any list, like his own, could point to a primary problem, as he was pointing now. Deleted, all deleted! Through no choice of his own, he was left untutored in friendship as a boy and as a young man, found in his middle years that he himself could not endure it, and found in his age that he had no friends, only these two strangers with whom he tumbled about in an indifferent Europe. Never a master in the difficult realm of self-recognition, no Scott Fitzgerald to write out his "Crack-up" with clear sight and even a brave *élan,* he had yet come this far in the discovery of what he was, even though he would not live to say so.

* These abbreviations could represent Gunther, Connie, Carl and Hal.

Nearly all that remains to be said must be derived from the report of Alexander Manson. In Turin, Lewis responded well to medical treatment, and they decided to move slowly toward Taormina. The Turin physician said that he must eliminate all alcohol and reduce smoking to a minimum, and Lewis agreed to drink as little wine as possible. And so they went. Yet by the time they reached Naples, Lewis was in such a condition of exhaustion that Manson persuaded him to give up the plans for Sicily and North Africa and turn back to Rome, where adequate medical services would be available. They arrived in Rome on September 24, and Lewis, suffering with bronchial pneumonia, hoped to stay for only a few days before returning to Florence; but Manson quickly found a lavish glass-walled apartment in a building erected in the Fascist years, on the northern edge of the city, overlooking the Tiber, and within two days had ensconced the now listless Lewis there. He became docile to suggestions from his doctor, Manson reports, and eliminated all alcohol and reduced his cigarettes to fifteen or sixteen a day. One wonders why his doctor was a stranger, why Lewis did not call or have Manson call Dr. Camp, to whom he had written before coming back to Italy that he hoped soon to see him. Dr. Camp did not know that he was in Rome until he read in the newspapers that he was there, dead.

One friend from the embassy, Mrs. Elizabeth Deegan, was permitted to see him, and she found him so dazed that she could only conclude that he was under the influence of narcotics; later, she was denied access to him on the grounds that he was too weak to see her. In November or early in December, Alan C. Collins, president of the Curtis Brown agency, arrived in Rome and sought him out. He was obviously very ill, and he explained to Collins that he was completely dependent on Manson in every respect and that Collins was to clear any business matters through him. He insisted that Manson show him the sights of Rome, and a date was made when Manson would come to Collins's hotel with Lewis's car and take him on this excursion. Subsequently, Manson called to cancel the engagement, and when Collins said that he wanted to see Lewis again, he was put off and, in fact, was never able to see him again. What troubled Collins most was that Lewis told him that an Italian doctor was giving him almost daily treatments on which he had also become dependent. Collins remembers that Lewis became more and more upset as time moved on toward six-thirty and the doctor, who had been expected at six, had not yet arrived. That dependence likewise was complete.

Manson himself tells of Lewis's increasing nervousness in November, and his fear of being alone at night. For two weeks, he said, he sat up with him in his bedroom, and then Lewis consented to his employing a night nurse to perform this duty.

At Christmastime Michael arrived from London. He was supposed to arrive promptly at seven for Christmas dinner, but he had been enjoying Rome during the afternoon and arrived about forty-five minutes late. (This is Michael Lewis's account.) He was met at the door by Manson, who, shaken with apprehension, reported that Michael's father was outraged and was insisting that he return immediately to London, the visit was over. Michael did get in to say good-by to him, but he remembers him as "stiff and cold," saying only, "Good-by." That was the last time that they were to see one another.

Manson's report to Michael's mother includes a few more details. When the boy's father told him to return to London, where he could do as he liked and need not take into consideration the feelings of other people, Michael said that he did not want to go directly to London and could he not have a check to take him to Paris. Lewis said that if he wanted a trip to Paris, he should have behaved differently in Rome, and agreed to pay only for a second-class railway ticket from Rome to London, with twenty dollars for traveling expenses. Under these conditions, the boy left Rome on the evening of December 26.

The late notebooks show no evidence that Lewis, during these months in Rome, was working consistently or on anything substantial, but Manson recalls that he was working as hard as ever.*

> On December thirty-first, he worked from six to eight A.M., and then had his usual big breakfast of porridge, honey, bread and butter, and sat in the living room. Suddenly he staggered to the door of my room and said, "Alec, something terrible is happening. I am going to die." I led him to a big chair, and there he buried his head in my arms like a frightened child. Those were his last fully conscious words.

All that day he was feverish and delirious, but he could not be made to stay in bed. He wandered about searching for the stairway of a vanished house. He sat in a chair and muttered incoherently to himself. He thought that Manson's wife was Carl Van Doren. He would call for Manson and, not recognizing him, order him out as though he were an intruding stranger. When the doctor came, Lewis called him "father." The diagnosis was acute delirium tremens, and the doctor explained that, given a certain toxic state of the human organism, such attacks can occur even after the patient has led an exemplary life for a considerable period of time. At five o'clock, when he grew more violent, an ambulance was summoned and he was taken to the Clinica Electra on Monte Mario at the edge of Rome, an establishment that specialized in psychiatric disorders and nervous collapse. He had, it is said, no further wholly rational moments.

* The New York *Times* a few weeks later quoted Lewis as saying that he was working on a novel about the middle class, the prisoner of modern life; and William Couch, Jr., says that he was working on a novel to be called *Courage.*

10

THUS HE WAS SPARED the necessity of any final contemplation of his fall. But suppose that, through the next ten days, his whereabouts in effect unknown, he had rested there in full and lucid consciousness—what, then, would he have known? He could not, of course, have known some of the absurdities that were to follow—how, for example, he would be eulogized in *The Rotarian* as, really, one of themselves who had made Rotary better; or how, ten years later, the inhabitants of Sauk Centre would in a hot summer enact a pageant of his life and rename the street on which he was born Sinclair Lewis Avenue; or how, when his officially sealed effects arrived in New York from Rome and his doctor was asked to examine the case of medicines, he found a wild array of nostrums, one calculated to cancel out another; or how, immediately after his death, Alexander Manson, claiming to be his heir, would write the Lewis executors, who, in turn, would give his claim short shrift. Or might he have wondered why he was where he was, why he had not been taken to the American Hospital rather than to this establishment, known to no one whom he knew? Or, so sensitive to the effect of his face on others, could he have conceived the final indignity—stretched out on a bed in the clinic, his jaws held together by a bandage, for public viewing? The American consul excluded photographers. Few others were curious.

When Mario Praz arrived at seven in the evening, he was the first to come, and to him Lewis looked not sixty-six but eighty, "so thin and wasted is he." A few other journalists came to take their notes for their news stories, and the body was put in a plain coffin next day and was held in the Protestant Cemetery until word came from Dr. Claude Lewis that it was to be cremated, the ashes to be sent to Minnesota.* Two floral offer-

* It has been a pleasant sentimentality to say that Lewis left instructions that his body be cremated and returned to Sauk Centre. One newspaper, *Il Mattino,* reported that in Florence, Sinclair Lewis said to his brother, "I like it here, I want to stay here, even afterward. . . ." If there was any authority for this remark, it could only have been Alexander Manson, yet Manson himself, making a good deal of Lewis's love of America, says that the instructions for the disposition of his remains were in

ings came: one from the chambers of Ambassador Dunn, the other from the offices of Mondadori, Lewis's Italian publisher, with a large maroon streamer that carried in gold letters the firm's name, l'Editore Arnoldo Mondadori. At the cremation, only Manson and his wife and the superintendent of the cemetery were present. The ashes, together with Mondadori's banner, were delivered to the consulate, and six days later they were put on an airplane for the United States. When they arrived in Sauk Centre on January 21, no one knew what the Mondadori "stole" was, or whether the language was Latin or Italian, or what it said or meant. The urn was polished by the village undertaker and deposited in the vault of the First National Bank until January 28.

No one could have conceived the events of that day with more exact detail and livelier humor than he, had he now been able to foresee it.* At two-thirty in the afternoon, the doors of the high-school auditorium were opened. The organist was playing a composition called "Olden Days," a Viennese waltz. An ancient tailor of eighty-three who had made Sinclair Lewis's high-school graduation suit was among the first to enter. The dentist who now occupied old Dr. Lewis's office over the corner drugstore arrived. The ladies of the Gradatim Club came in a body and rustlingly sat down together. Some high-school students straggled in wearing ear muffs and blue jeans. Harry Maule came with Ida Kay. The family came and settled itself in the first row of chairs: Michael; Fred's widow and two sons; Dr. Claude and his wife and daughter and son-in-law. The lectern was draped with Mondadori's cloth. A single basket of flowers, from Michael, stood beside it. The organist played *Finlandia.*

Laurel Kells read a brief biography. Dr. J. F. DuBois read Lewis's sentimental reminiscence from the fiftieth-anniversary issue of the high-school annual about Sauk Centre as "a good place, and a good preparation for life." Then Kells introduced Frederick Manfred as one of the innumerable young writers whom Lewis had encouraged and helped, and Manfred read a long and solemn and considerably murky eulogy that dubbed the subject "greatheart" and ended with Horatio's farewell to Hamlet, the name "Sinclair" substituting for "sweet prince," and improved upon the model by changing the final line, "Why does the drum come hither?" to "Good night, Sinclair, good night, good night." It probably sounded like Shakespeare. A trio of ladies arose and sang "I Heard a Forest Praying," and finally Laurel Kells invited everyone to come to the cemetery.

It was an iron-gray day and bitterly cold, twenty-two degrees below

---

his will. The will, which Manson could not have seen, contains no instructions of this kind at all, only the conventional direction that his executors pay all funeral expenses.

* For the details of this day, I am chiefly indebted to an unpublished article, " 'Red' Lewis Comes Home," by Norman Katkov, who went to Sauk Centre to cover the services and most generously arranged to let me read his account. I am also indebted to the news story in the Sauk Centre *Herald* for February 1, 1951.

zero in midafternoon. A path had been chiseled out of the frozen snow between the cemetery gate and the Lewis family plot, where an opening of about two square feet had been dug and framed in artificial grass to receive the urn. But the thrifty Dr. Claude saw no reason for putting the handsome urn in the ground when it might serve as a memorial to his brother in the Bryant Library. With about a hundred people huddled behind him in the piercing cold, a little snow sifting from the leaden sky—the scene must have been very much like that at Fred's funeral five Januarys before—Dr. Lewis cut the sealed wire of the urn, peered into it, knelt and slowly let the ashes slide out. A gust of wind came up and scattered some of them on the artificial grass, blew some into the air. ("Red Lewis scattered over eighty acres of Stearns County," someone irreverently said.) Dr. Lewis arose and asked the company to repeat with him the Lord's Prayer, which they accordingly did, and then they hurried back to their automobiles, in which the motors had all the time been running lest the radiators freeze. To Michael, Dr. Claude Lewis, not cold to his dead brother but proud of his own precision, said, "Remember what I told him in Florence? I missed it by just two weeks!"

One hears some cosmic laughter. Sinclair Lewis could have imagined the absurd Shakespearean analogy and howled with mirth, for no one knew better than he that he was no Prince Hamlet, and was not meant to be. With introspective brooding he was as impatient as he was with hypocrisy, affectation and pomp. Would he, during those last ten days, had he been conscious, have tried at last to define, then, what he really was? He had come somewhat closer to self-knowledge than when he wrote his whimsical obituary in "The Death of Arrowsmith," and yet he seemed always to shy away from it or at least from any genuine articulation of it.

He was, of course, the kind of artist who is temperamentally unable to objectify his anxieties or even draw upon them except in the most superficial way in his own art, and the artist, after all, is not different from the man who contains him. For all his remarkable resemblance to his beloved Charles Dickens in biographical and temperamental traits as well as in the nature of the artistic effort, he differed sharply in the first in that he lacked Dickens's habit of self-searching, and in the second in the consequent depth and density of his novels. He could, of course, be amusing at his own expense (how often he told the story of seeing the lady impatiently drop her copy of *Elmer Gantry* over the side of a ship!) and up to a point he could be objective about himself. And yet. . . . Sir Harold Nicolson says that Dorothy Thompson once remarked of her husband, "He does not know what knowledge is." Be that as it may, the final evidence suggests that he did not know what self-knowledge is.

Perhaps there was too much, and too much in conflict, to have made self-knowledge possible. Not many men are doomed to live with such a mixture of warring qualities as he was. Consider him at any level of conduct —his domestic habits, his social behavior, his character, his thought, his art—always there is the same extraordinary contradiction. Sloppy and compulsively tidy, absurdly gregarious and lonely, quick in enthusiasms and swiftly bored, extravagant and parsimonious, a dude and a bumpkin, a wit and a bore, given to extremities of gaiety and gloom, equally possessed of a talent for the most intensive concentration and for the maddest dishevelment of energies; sweet of temper and virulent, tolerant and abruptly intolerant, generous and selfish, kind and cruel, a great patron and a small tyrant, disliking women even when he thought he most loved them, profane and a puritan, libertine and prude, plagued by self-doubt as he was eaten by arrogance; rebel and conservative, polemicist and escapist, respectful of intellect and suspicious of intellectual pursuits, loving novelty and hating experiment, pathetically trusting in "culture" and narrowly deriding "art"; cosmopolitan and chauvinist, sentimentalist and satirist, romanticist and realist, blessed—or damned—with an extraordinary verbal skill and no style; Carol Kennicott and Doc, her husband; Paul Riesling and George F. Babbitt; Harry Lewis and Dr. E. J. Lewis or Dr. Claude B. Lewis; Harry Lewis and even Fred the miller, who never left home.

One might list these conflicting qualities in opposite columns and suggest that there were two selves in Sinclair Lewis; but all these qualities existed together and simultaneously in him, and in their infinite, interacting combinations there must have been not two but six or eight or ten or two hundred selves and, because they could never be one, a large hole in the center. When he peered into that, what could we expect him to see?

More probably, had he been clear in his mind during the ten days that he lay there, he would have wondered why he was lying outside Roman walls instead of within the "fortress of reality," a term he once applied to the raw town of St. Paul. His twenty-two novels, after all, had been a long procession all directed toward one discovery, the "reality" of America. This aim was his inheritance as a novelist who was formed in the second decade of this century, when the discovery of the "real" America, an America beyond chauvinistic nonsense and a merely sentimental optimism, became the aim of nearly every writer who took himself seriously—as Willard Thorpe, most recently among critics, has reminded us. It was the era of Herbert Croly, an era that trusted in the promise of American life. For Sinclair Lewis, America was always promises, and that was why, in 1950, he could say that he loved it but did not like it, for it was still only promises, and promises that nearly everyone else had long ago given up.

Promises of what? Promises of a society that from his beginning would have not only tolerated but also treasured *him*. That is the personal basis. Generalized, it becomes an idealization of an older America, the America of the mid-nineteenth century, an America vast and formless but overflowing with the potentialities for and the constant expression of a wide, casually human freedom, the individual life lived in honest and perhaps eccentric effort (all the better), the social life lived in a spirit that first of all tolerates variety. It was the ideal America of Thoreau, of Whitman, of the early Mark Twain, of the cracker barrel and the village atheist. Like Thoreau, Whitman, Twain, Lewis too could see the difference between the idealization and the actuality. It was Thoreau who wrote:

> With respect to true culture and manhood, we are essentially provincial still, not metropolitan—mere Jonathans. We are provincial, because we do not find at home our standards; because we are warped and narrowed by an exclusive devotion to trade and commerce and manufacture and agriculture and the like, which are but the means, and not the ends.

When Sinclair Lewis claimed Thoreau as the major influence on his work, it could only have been this basic element in his own thought, the Thoreauvian ideal of individual freedom, that he had in mind. Of Thoreau, R. W. B. Lewis has written,

> Probably nobody of his generation had a richer sense of the potentiality for a fresh, free, and uncluttered existence; certainly no one projected the need for a ritual burning of the past in more varied and captivating metaphors. This is what *Walden* is about; it is the most searching contemporary account of the desire for a new kind of life . . . the total renunciation of the traditional, the conventional, the socially acceptable, the well-worn paths of conduct, and the total immersion in nature.

How all of this, item by item, even to the last (there was the lonely walker, and the woodsman *manqué!*), appealed to Lewis, how it formed, even, the positive element in his largely negative presentation of American life, should be clear. Into that idealism it was not hard to weave the more diluted optimism that he found in H. G. Wells, that happy belief that the little man, the obscure man, the middle-class man could break into such freedom as Thoreau envisaged. Happiness can be pursued and achieved by an effort of the individual will! No trait, Gerald W. Johnson has pointed out, is more profoundly American, or more central to the novels of Sinclair Lewis; and no other American ambition is perhaps so mistaken. *Ecco* Sinclair Lewis, *morente a Roma!*

The source of Lewis's satire lies in the American defection from the American potentiality for individual freedom. When he scolded America it was because Americans would not be free, and he attacked all the sources by means of which they betrayed themselves: economic system, intellectual rigidity, theological dogma, legal repression, class convention, materialism, social timidity, hypocrisy, affectation, complacency and pomposity. These two, the individual impulse to freedom and the social impulse to restrict it, provide the bases of his plots in novel after novel after novel. Even when he used Europe as his counter, the conflict was not so much between America and Europe as between the true America as Lewis saw it—that is, individual Americans true to themselves—and the false America, or Americans who submit to values not their own or to values less expansive than their own should be. The result in the novels is often an apparent praise of provincialism, even of gross Philistinism, but in its impulse the praise is of something much larger.

How often, nevertheless, in his own sentimentality and Philistinism, he settled for the very stolidity in American life that he castigated! "Sinclair Lewis is the most successful critic of American society," T. K. Whipple said, "because he is himself the best proof that his charges are just." If he was the village intellectual, the village atheist, the rebel, the nonconformist crank for whom the dialect, the cracker barrel and the false whiskers served as counterpoise to the stuffed shirt in his defense of what Lloyd Morris called "the old, free, democratic, individualistic career of the middle class," he was at the same time the pontifical village banker, the loud-mouthed village booster, the successful manufacturer of automobiles, the conservative, the very middle of the middle. His trust in "culture" was equaled by his trust in "things." His respect for science was certainly greater than his respect for art. Brought up in an environment that deplored art and adored success, he managed, in that America, to make a success of "art." Often and increasingly it was bad art, and the success was in many ways vicious and corrosive. In his novels, he loved what he deplored; in his life, he was happiest with the kind of people who might have been the models for his own caricatures.

Dying, would he have wondered, could he have, whether his work would live? He knew—and had said so ten years before—that he had "affected but little the work of younger writers of fiction," that his style and his conception of the novel had in no perceptible way turned the current of the American literary tradition. He did not know, one suspects, how increasingly old-fashioned he came to sound (the penalty of always striving to be "new"), or that the generation immediately following upon his own—Fitzgerald, Hemingway, Faulkner—had nothing to learn from him, that he spoke for an older American experience than theirs. But in a larger sense than is suggested by the words *style* and *structure,* he was an extraordinary influence, the major figure, probably, in what is called the liberation of modern American literature. For writers just a little younger than the Hemingway group, he served as a kind of model of what the literary man can be. James Farrell and Richard Wright have both written of him as a novelist who helped to liberate them as novelists. An older novelist, John Dos Passos, has called him "a sort of folk hero of the time." *

Like his master, Dickens, he created a gallery of characters who have

* John Dos Passos in a letter to the author, February 18, 1959.

independent life outside the novels, with all their obvious limitations, characters that live now in the American tradition itself. If they are not as numerous or as rich as Dickens's, they are nevertheless of the same breed—gigantic, nearly mythological figures that embody (I do not say duplicate) the major traits of their class. His novels, as a result, are perhaps the last important American novels that are primarily concerned with social class. If they often depended on the report of social minutiae and the American lingo and too often failed to realize that material imaginatively, they nevertheless—as Joseph Wood Krutch has said—"reported a range of grotesque vulgarity which but for him would have left no record of itself because no one else could have adequately reported it."

He performed a function that has nearly gone out of our fiction, and fiction is the thinner for the loss. He could tell us little or nothing about the subjective life, he had no sense of the tragic nature of human experience, he was incapable, apparently, of either feeling or giving expression to sensuous ecstasy or lyric joy. But he could give us shuddering glimpses into a kind of frightening reality of which perhaps he was himself quite unaware. As Alfred Kazin put it,

> There is indeed more significant terror of a kind in Lewis's novels than in a writer like Faulkner or the hard-boiled novelists, for it is the terror immanent in the commonplace, the terror that arises out of the repressions, the meanness, the hard jokes of the world Lewis had soaked into his pores.

With that America "soaked into his pores," he could document for an enormous audience the character of a people and a class, and, without repudiating either, criticize and laugh at both. Today this function has passed to popularizing sociologists, and if we have no Babbitts or Elmer Gantrys or Fran Dodsworths, we have status seekers and other-directed faces in the crowd and organizational men, all thinner and more abstract than Lewis's enduring fictional creatures.

He was one of the worst writers in modern American literature, but without his writing one cannot imagine modern American literature. That is because, without his writing, we can hardly imagine ourselves. In at least five solid works—*Main Street, Babbitt, Arrowsmith, Elmer Gantry,* and *Dodsworth*—the endurable core that followed upon his slow start and preceded his long decline, he gave us a vigorous, perhaps a unique thrust into the imagination of ourselves.

Could he have consoled himself with this knowledge, had it been his, and he aware?

II

IN ROME it had been raining for weeks. In the Clinica Electra, the patient, whose condition had gradually improved through eight days, on one occasion sighed and said, or so said one of the newspapers, "At least let the sun come back!" * He slept peacefully, and when he was awake, even though he did not know where he was or who the people who attended him were, he seemed content enough. Manson and his wife came every day, and after a week, Manson said, they were thinking again of taking him back to his apartment. The American consul paid his respects, and a functionary from the embassy, who was not admitted. Sinclair Lewis recognized no one. On January 9 he suffered another heart attack, but he seemed to rally, and he is said to have struggled to smile and to have murmured, "I am happy. May God bless you," to the nun in attendance. On the morning of January 10 he is said to have turned his nearly extinguished eyes to the window and murmured, "There, the sun!" as dawn broke and his eyes seemed to light up a little. Then, at seven-forty the final blow came.

No need to labor the irony. He died among strangers, without even Manson, attended by an anonymous Franciscan nun and having been attended by two physicians little known to their colleagues, in a strange clinic not in, but on the outskirts of Rome. *Città imperiale,* full of ruins! All of the ancient history of the West lay around him. And in the ruin on the bed lay another West, Sauk Centre, Minnesota. He had never left home either. The records of the Clinica Electra read: *"Paralisi cardiaca."* Paralysis of the heart.

* For the details of this death, one can turn from Manson to the Italian newspapers. How reliable these accounts are is anyone's guess. Mario Praz in *Il Messaggiero* can be trusted, but the other writers are anonymous, and the unidentified author of the piece in *Il Mattino* (who says, among other things, that Sinclair Lewis spent Christmas in Florence a year before with a Polish doctor, a friend of his youth) is obviously less reliable. The account here tries to piece out a consistent statement, leaning a little too far, perhaps, in the *Il Mattino* direction, which wanted to believe *"Roma gli fece quest'ultimo dono,"* the sun. It may still have been raining on January 10, 1951. Roman weather reports, even on outlying districts like Monte Mario, are no doubt available to anyone who wishes to continue these researches. *Per me ho finito.*

A Sinclair Lewis Checklist*

Symbols: N, novel; SS, short story; P, poem; R, review; E, editorial; F, fiction; NF, non-fiction.

1902

"Forth into the World," Sauk Centre *Herald,* June 5, NF.
"Odds and Ends," Sauk Centre *Herald,* June 5, NF.

1903

Unsigned news stories in Sauk Centre *Avalanche,* August 19 to September 5.
Unsigned news stories in New Haven *Journal and Courier,* December 18, 1903 to October 1906.

1904

"Launcelot," *Yale Literary Magazine,* March, P.
"A Song of Prince Hal," *Yale Courant,* May 21, P.
"Student Lied," *Yale Courant,* June 4, P.
"Puck to Queen Mab," *Yale Courant,* June 4, P.
"A May Time Carol," *Yale Courant,* June 18, P.
"The Coward Minstrel," *Yale Courant,* June 18, SS.
"Odysseus at Ogygia," *Yale Literary Magazine,* October, P.
"Hallowe'en," *Yale Courant,* October 15, P.
"Father Ambrosial," *Yale Courant,* October 15, SS.
"Um Ein und Zwanzig," *Yale Courant,* October 29, P.
"The Third Estate," *Yale Literary Magazine,* December, P.
"The Seventh Troop," *Yale Courant,* December 10, P.
"The Royal Glamour," *Yale Courant,* December 10, SS.
"The Fireflies," *Yale Courant,* December 24, P.
"When Viziers Speak," *Yale Courant,* December 24, P.

1905

"Behind the Arras, a Christmas Masque," *Yale Literary Magazine,* February, P.
"A Ne'er-do-well," *Yale Courant,* February 11, P.
"Concerning Psychology," *Yale Courant,* February 11, SS.
"A Miracle, Forsooth," *Yale Courant,* March 25, SS.
"The Yellow Streak," *Yale Literary Magazine,* April, SS.
"A Summer's Tale," *Yale Courant,* April 8, P.
"Did Mrs. Thurston Get the Idea of 'The Masqueraders' from Mr. Zangwill," *The Critic,* June, NF.
"An Elementary Course in Erotics," *Yale Courant,* October 12, SS.
"The Loneliness of Theodore," *Yale Literary Magazine,* November, SS.
"Father Kileen," *Yale Courant,* November 24, P.
"Matsu-No-Kata: A Romance of Old Japan," *Pacific Monthly,* December, SS.

* It has been impossible to locate exactly a few of the many fugitive pieces that Lewis published during the first years of his literary career.

1906

"The Heart of Pope Innocent," *Yale Literary Magazine,* January, SS.
"Saint Hubert," *Yale Courant,* March 3, P.
"A Theory of Values," *Yale Monthly Magazine,* April, SS.
"Editor's Table," *Yale Literary Magazine,* April, E.
"At Lightening Time," *The Housekeeper,* April, P.
"Editor's Table," *Yale Literary Magazine,* May, E.
"Unknown Undergraduates," *Yale Literary Magazine,* June, NF.
"Editor's Table," *Yale Literary Magazine,* June, E.
"A Crooning Lullaby," *The Housekeeper,* June, P.
"Editor's Table," *Yale Literary Magazine,* November, E.
"Exit Homo," *Yale Courant,* November, P.
"The Wash-Tub Sea," *Youth,* November, P.
"In Praise of South Middle," *Yale Literary Magazine,* December, NF.
"Editor's Table," *Yale Literary Magazine,* December, E.
"January Nights," *Woman's Home Companion,* December, P.
"December Maying," *Reader Magazine,* December, P.
"Two Yale Men in Utopia," New York *Sun,* December 16, NF.

1907

"Sleepy Head Top," *Mayflower,* P.
"City Loneliness," New Orleans *Times-Democrat,* P.
"Mr. Hopper Frog," *The Housekeeper,* P.
"July in January," *Peoples Magazine,* P.
"Editor's Table," *Yale Literary Magazine,* January, E.
"The Alarm Clock," *Woman's Home Companion,* January, P.
"Faeries o' the Lake," *The Outer's Book,* February, P.
"Editor's Table," *Yale Literary Magazine,* February, E.
"Curly Tailed Pup and Me," *The Outer's Book,* March, P.
"The Gas Stove Beast," *The Housekeeper,* March, P.
"A Rondeau of Farewell," *Yale Literary Magazine,* March, P.
"Canned Poetry," *Puck,* March 27, P.
"The Complete Dialect-Writer," *Puck,* April 3, P.
"May Afield," *The Outer's Book,* May, P.
"A Passage in Isaiah," *The Blue Mule,* May, SS.
"A Rondeau of Sorrow," *Puck,* May 9, P.
"The Celtic Revival," in "Literary Zoo," *Life,* May 23, NF.
"Down Here," translation of poem by Sully Prudhomme, *Transatlantic Tales,* June.
"Art and the Woman," *The Gray Goose,* June, SS.
"A Raking of the Rakers," in "Literary Zoo," *Life,* June 6, NF.
"The Ultra-Modern," *Smart Set,* July, P.
"The Good Ship 'Teeter Board,' " *The Housekeeper,* July, P.
"Nimrod, Junior," *The Outer's Book,* July, P.
"The Quatrain," *New England Magazine,* July, P.
"The Passing Pantomime," *New England Magazine,* July, P.
"Ecstasy," translation of poem by Victor Hugo, *Transatlantic Tales,* July.
"Maecenas Welches," in "Literary Zoo," *Life,* July 4, NF.

"Extracts from a Club-Woman's Diary," *Puck,* July 24, F.
"Dim Hours of Dusk," *Smart Set,* August, P.
"American Kiplings," in "Literary Zoo," *Life,* August 1, NF.
"Forbidden Delights," *Advance,* August 22, P.
"At 'Fessing Time," *Advance,* August 29, P.
"The Song of the King's Jester," translation of poem by Stuart Merril, *Transatlantic Tales,* September.
"Ballade from the City," *The Outer's Book,* September, P.
"The Outer's Song," *The Outer's Book,* September, P.
"Flocki, Remarkable Dog," translation of short story by Rudolph Presber, *Transatlantic Tales,* September.
"To William Butler Yeats," *The Book News Monthly,* September, P.
"City Cows," *National Home Journal,* September 21, P.
"The Sea of Cities," translation of poem by Detlev von Liliencron, *Transatlantic Tales,* October.
"Little Drummer of the Blues," translation of short story by Charles Foley, *Transatlantic Tales,* October.
"Cherries of Provence," translation of short story by Leo Larguier, *Transatlantic Tales,* October.
"A Gambler of a Night," translation of short story by Paul Bourget, *Transatlantic Tales,* October.
"A Dood Boy," *Mayflower,* October, P.
"October Thrift," *Western Field,* October, P.
"Editors Who Write," in "Literary Zoo," *Life,* October 10, NF.
"The Shore," translation of poem by Theodore Storm, *Transatlantic Tales,* November.
"Hippopotamus," *The Circle,* November, P.
"Cradle Song," translation of poem by Detlev von Liliencron, *Transatlantic Tales,* November.
"The Struggle," *Pacific Monthly,* November, P.
"The Affinings of an Affinitist," *Puck,* November 6, SS.
"Moon of Night," translation of poem by Martin Gries, *Transatlantic Tales,* December.
"The Snare," translation of short story by Paul Bourget, *Transatlantic Tales,* December.
"Disillusion," *Smart Set,* December, P.
"Week before Christmas," *Youth's Companion,* December 19, P.

1908

"On Wash Bowl Sea," *New Idea,* P.
"The Man of the Roads," New Orleans *Times-Democrat,* P.
"Derelict," translation of short story by Jean Reibrach, *Transatlantic Tales,* January.
"My California Lady," *Overland Monthly,* January, P.
"Gold in Umber," *Overland Monthly,* January, P.
"Big Brother the Wise," *The Housekeeper,* February, P.
"The Fountain Spirit," *The New Age,* March, P.
"The City Fountain," *The New Age,* March, P.
"The May Baskets," *The Housekeeper,* May, P.
"The Awful Jungle," *Woman's Home Companion,* May, P.
"Makin' Faces," *Holland's Magazine,* May, P.
"On the Window Seat," *Advance,* May, P.
"Wailing and Fixing of Teeth," *Puck,* May 13, F.

"My Big Brother," *Advance,* July, P.
Editorials in Waterloo *Daily Courier,* August 3 to September 14.
"The Mystery," *The New Age,* August, P.
"My Lady's Maid," *Century Magazine,* September, P.
"The Spirit's Call," *The Open Court,* September, P.
"The Clergyman Who Fishes," *The Outer's Book,* September, E.
"Tether Ball," *The Outer's Book,* October, E.
"Queen Moon," *Advance,* October 8, P.
"The Butt," *Puck,* October 28, SS.
"The Death-a-cold," *The Delineator,* November, P.

1909

"Where Fireflies Grow," *The Designer,* January, P.
"That Human Interest Story," *Puck,* January 13, SS.
"Summer in Winter," *Peoples Magazine,* February, P.
"They that Take the Sword," *The Red Book,* May, SS.
"My Policeman," *The Designer,* June, P.
"The Smile Lady," *The Nautilus,* August, SS.
25 articles in San Francisco *Bulletin,* September 21 to November 27, including:
"Talks with a Typist," with by-line, F.
" 'Irish Chink' Frightens Off a Burglar and Saves Block," September 21.
"Transport's Mate Tries to Shoot His Wife," September 21.
Review of light opera at the Princess Theatre, September 21.
"The Masque of Gaspar's Passing," October 23, P.
"The City Shadow," *The Nautilus,* October 1909 through May 1910, SS.

1910

"Polly," *Sunset,* January, SS.
"A San Francisco Pleasure Cure, Being Echoes of the New City's Laughter," *Sunset,* April, NF.
"The Dawn," *Literary Magazine* of the Pittsburgh *Dispatch,* May 1, SS.
"The Outlook for the Blind," *Volta Review,* July, R.
"Books for the Class Room," *Volta Review,* October, R.
"Protoplasm and the Soul," *Volta Review,* October, R.
"Two Writing Manuels," *Volta Review,* October, R.
"Zenata," *Volta Review,* October, R.

1911

"The Singing Men," *The Housekeeper,* P.
"A Promising Young Man," *The Coming Nation,* April 29, SS.
"A Course in Heroism," *Puck,* May 10, NF.
"The Way to Rome," *The Bellman,* May 13, SS.
"Captains of Peace," *The Nautilus,* October 1911 through June 1912, SS.

1912

"A Canticle of Great Lovers," *Ainslee's Magazine,* P.
"John Ames Mitchell, Novelist, Editor and Artist," *The Book News Monthly,* March, NF.
HIKE AND THE AEROPLANE, August, N.

"Loki, The Red: The Career of a Near-Nihilist," *Short Stories,* August, SS.

1913

Letter in *History of the Class of 1907, Yale College.*

"Scented Spring and the G.P.," *Short Stories,* March, SS.

Note on Grant Wallace, *Adventure,* May, NF.

Reviews for Publishers Newspaper Syndicate, August 30, 1913, to mid-summer 1914.

1914

Chapters 21, 22, 23 of *'Dad,'* Albert P. Terhune; N.

OUR MR. WRENN: The Romantic Adventures of a Gentle Man, February, N.

"The Passing of Capitalism," *The Bookman,* October, NF.

1915

"Who Is Hugh Walpole and Why Should You Read Him?" *Hugh Walpole, Master Novelist,* NF.

"Certain Animadversions . . . ," New York *Tribune,* January 6, P.

"C-o-b-b . . . ," *Irvin Cobb: His Book,* April 25, NF.

THE TRAIL OF THE HAWK: A Comedy of the Seriousness of Life, September, N.

"Nature, Inc.," *Saturday Evening Post,* October 2, SS.

"Commutation: $9.17," *Saturday Evening Post,* October 30, SS.

"The Other Side of the House," *Saturday Evening Post,* November 27, SS.

"The Home without Books," Baker & Taylor's *Christmas Bulletin,* NF.

1916

"If I Were Boss," *Saturday Evening Post,* January 1, SS.

Article on Homecoming, Sauk Centre *Herald,* May 4, NF.

"I'm a Stranger Here Myself," *Smart Set,* August, SS.

"He Loved His Country," *Everybody's Magazine,* October, SS.

"Honestly If Possible," *Saturday Evening Post,* October 14, SS.

1917

THE JOB: An American Novel, February, N.

THE INNOCENTS, serialized in *Woman's Home Companion,* February, March, N.

"Twenty-Four Hours in June," *Saturday Evening Post,* February 17, SS.

"The Poinsettia Widow," *Metropolitan Magazine,* March 17, SS.

"A Story with a Happy Ending," *Saturday Evening Post,* March 17, SS.

"Hobohemia," *Saturday Evening Post,* April 7, SS.

"Young Man Axelbrod," *Century Magazine,* June, SS.

"The Ghost Patrol," *The Red Book,* June, SS.

"The Scarlet Sign," *Metropolitan Magazine,* June, SS.

"The Violets," *The Red Book,* June, SS.

"Mother-Love," *Hearst's Magazine,* July, SS.

"A Woman by Candle-Light," *Saturday Evening Post,* July 28, SS.

THE INNOCENTS: A Story for Lovers, September, N.

"The Hidden People," *Good Housekeeping,* September, SS.

"Snappy Display," *Metropolitan Magazine,* August, ss.
"The Whisperer," *Saturday Evening Post,* August 11, ss.
"Black Snow and Orange Sky," *Metropolitan Magazine,* October, ss.
"For the Zelda Bunch," *McClure's Magazine,* October, ss.
"Joy-Joy" (sequel to "Hobohemia"), *Saturday Evening Post,* October 20, ss.

1918

"Afterglow," *Collier's Weekly,* January 19, ss.
"The Tamarack Lover," *Hearst's Magazine,* February, ss. Reprinted as "Warrior Woman," *Home Magazine,* November, December, 1931.
"Spiritualist Vaudeville," *Metropolitan Magazine,* February, NF.
"A Rose for Little Eva," *McClure's Magazine,* February, ss.
"Slip It to 'Em," *Metropolitan Magazine,* March, ss.
"Detour—Roads Rough," *Every Week,* March 30, ss.
"An Invitation to Tea," *Every Week,* June 1, ss.
"The Shadowy Glass," *Saturday Evening Post,* June 22, ss.
"A Widower for a While," *Ladies' Home Journal,* July, ss.
"The Willow Walk," *Saturday Evening Post,* August 10, ss.
"Getting His Bit," *Metropolitan Magazine,* September, ss.
Letter to editor, New York *Times,* September 1.
"The Swept Hearth," *Saturday Evening Post,* September 21, ss.
"Jazz," *Metropolitan Magazine,* October, ss.
"Gladvertising," *Popular Magazine,* October 7, ss.

1919

Letter in Upton Sinclair's: *A Monthly Magazine for a Clean Peace and the Internation,* January.
"Moths in the Arc Light," *Saturday Evening Post,* January 11, ss.
"The Shrinking Violet," *Saturday Evening Post,* February 15, ss.
"Things," *Saturday Evening Post,* February 22, ss.
"The Cat of the Stars," *Saturday Evening Post,* April 19, ss.
"The Watcher across the Road," *Saturday Evening Post,* May 24, ss.
FREE AIR, serialized in *Saturday Evening Post,* May 31 through June 21, N.
"Might and Millions," *Metropolitan Magazine,* June, ss.
"The Kidnapped Memorial," *Pictorial Review,* June, ss.
"Speed," *The Red Book,* June, ss.
"The Shrimp-Coloured Blouse," *The Red Book,* August, ss.
"The Enchanted Hour," *Saturday Evening Post,* August 9, ss.
"Danger—Run Slow," continuation of *FREE AIR, Saturday Evening Post,* October 18, 25, N.
"Six Times One Equals Six," *American Magazine,* October 19, NF.
FREE AIR, October, N.
"Bronze Bars," *Saturday Evening Post,* December 13, ss.
"Adventures in Automobumming," *Saturday Evening Post,* December 20, 27, 1919, January 3, 1920, NF.

1920

"Habeas Corpus," *Saturday Evening Post,* January 24, ss.
Letter in *Jurgen and the Censor,* February 18.

"The Way I See It," *Saturday Evening Post,* May 29, ss.

MAIN STREET: The Story of Carol Kennicott, October, N.

"The Good Sport," *Saturday Evening Post,* December 11, ss.

1921

Letter in *My Maiden Effort, Being the Personal Confessions of Well-known American Authors as to Their Literary Beginnings,* ed. Gelett Burgess.

"The Pioneer Myth," *Literary Review* of New York *Evening Post,* February 5, NF.

"A Matter of Business," *Harper's Magazine,* March, ss.

Review of Evelyn Scott's *The Narrow House,* New York *Times Book Review,* March 13.

"How I Wrote a Novel on Trains and Beside the Kitchen Sink," *American Magazine,* April, NF.

"Floyd Dell," *The Bookman,* May, NF.

"Number Seven to Sagapoose," *American Magazine,* May, ss.

"The Post-Mortem Murder," *Century Magazine,* May, ss.

"A Citizen of the Mirage," *The Red Book,* May, ss.

Two letters in Sauk Centre *Herald,* August 4.

1922

Letter to New York *World,* August 20.

BABBITT, September, N.

"A Hamlet of the Plains," review of Willa Cather's *One of Ours, Literary Review* of New York *Evening Post,* September 22.

"A Review of Reviewers," *Literary Digest, International Book Review,* December, NF

1923

"Minnesota, the Norse State," *The Nation,* May 30, NF.

"Authors and Interviewing," *Now and Then,* June, NF.

"The Hack Driver," *The Nation,* August 29, ss.

1924

Letter in London *Daily Express,* January 24.

Introduction to De Kruif's report, *The Designer and the Woman's Magazine,* June, NF.

ARROWSMITH, serialized in *The Designer and the Woman's Magazine,* June 1924 through April 1925, N.

"I Return to America," *The Nation,* June 4, NF.

"Ioway and the Countess," review of Carl Van Vechten's *The Tattooed Countess, Saturday Review of Literature,* August 30.

"Main Street's Been Paved!" *The Nation,* September 10, NF.

"Be Brisk with Babbitt," *The Nation,* October 15, 22, 29, NF.

"A Pilgrim's Progress," review of Sherwood Anderson's *A Story Teller's Story,* New York *Herald Tribune,* November 9.

1925

Letter in introduction to *Letters from Russian Prisons.*

ARROWSMITH, March, N.

Introduction to Charles E. Benton's *Four Days on the Webutuck River,* July.

"An American Views the Huns," *The Nation,* July 1, NF.

"Self-Conscious America," *American Mercury,* October, NF.

"Manhattan at Last," *Saturday Review of Literature,* December 5; published as pamphlet, *John Dos Passos' Manhattan Transfer,* 1926, R.

"Can an Artist Live in America?" *The Nation,* December 9, NF.

1926

MANTRAP, serialized in *Collier's Weekly,* February 13 through May 8, N.

Abstract of letter refusing Pulitzer Prize, released May 6; complete letter published in *The Man from Main Street,* 1953.

MANTRAP, June, N.

Review of Isaac Goldberg's *The Theatre of George Jean Nathan,* New York *Herald Tribune Books,* December 12.

1927

ELMER GANTRY, March, N.

"Sinclair Lewis Finds Vienna Laughs Again," New York *Evening Post,* July 19, NF.

"Novelist 'Reports' Vienna Revolution," New York *Evening Post,* July 20, NF.

"Lewis Sees Vienna Bury Worker Dead," New York *Evening Post,* July 21, NF.

1928

THE MAN WHO KNEW COOLIDGE: Being the Soul of Lowell Schmaltz, Constructive and Nordic Citizen, April, N.

"The Man Who Knew Coolidge," *American Mercury,* January, SS.

"Mr. Lorimer and Me," *The Nation,* July 25, NF.

"Main Streets of Britain," New York *Herald Tribune,* July 29, August 5, 12, 19, 26, September 9, 16, 23, 30, NF. (First and second published in Minneapolis *Journal,* July 15 and 22, and telescoped into the first in New York *Herald Tribune.*)

Review of E. S. Bates' *The Friend of Jesus,* New York *Herald Tribune Books,* October 7.

1929

Autobiographical note in *On Parade: Caricatures by Eva Herrmann.*

Letter to New York *Times,* in "From the Dramatic Mail Bag," February 17.

DODSWORTH, March, N.

"Publicity Gone Mad," *The Nation,* March 6, NF.

"The American Scene in Fiction," New York *Herald Tribune Books,* April 14, NF.

"He Had a Brother," *The Cosmopolitan,* May, SS.

"Sinclair Lewis Looks at Advertising," *Advertising and Selling,* May 15, NF.

"There Was a Prince," *The Cosmopolitan,* June, SS.

"Is America a Paradise for Women?" *Pictorial Review,* June, NF.

"Elizabeth, Kitty and Jane," *The Cosmopolitan,* July, SS.

Letter on Sacco-Vanzetti in *Lantern* (Boston), August.

"Dear Editor," *The Cosmopolitan,* August, SS.

"What a Man!" *The Cosmopolitan,* September, SS.

Address before the Rutland Rotary Club, Rutland *Daily Herald,* September 24.

"Keep Out of the Kitchen," *The Cosmopolitan,* October, SS.

Cheap and Contented Labor: The Picture of a Southern Mill Town in 1929, October, NF.
"A Letter from the Queen," *The Cosmopolitan,* December, SS.
Letter to New York *Times,* December 7.
"Devil Dog Rule," *The Nation,* December 18, NF.

1930

Letter to William Stidger published in Kansas City *Star,* January 27.
"Youth," *The Cosmopolitan,* February, SS.
Letter to *New Masses,* July.
"A Noble Experiment," *The Cosmopolitan,* August, SS.
"Bongo," *The Cosmopolitan,* September, SS.
"A Novel for Mr. Hoover," review of Mary H. Vorse's *Strike!, The Nation,* October 29.
"Young Man, Go East," *The Cosmopolitan,* December, SS.

1931

"The Long Arm of the Small Town," *The O-Sa-Ge* (Sauk Centre), NF.
Letter in *Opinions on the Amenities of Book-Collecting as Expressed by a Group of Seasoned Bibliophiles on the Occasion of the Printing of Catalogue One Hundred.*
"Let's Play King," *The Cosmopolitan,* January, February, March, SS.
"Pajamas," *The Red Book,* April, SS.
"Are Colleges Obsolete?" Yale *Harkness Hoot,* April, NF.
"American Fear of Literature" (Nobel Prize Address, revised edition), May, NF.
"Ring Around a Rosy," *Saturday Evening Post,* June 6, SS.
"City of Mercy," *The Cosmopolitan,* July, SS.
"Land," *Saturday Evening Post,* September 12, SS.
"A Letter to Critics," *The Nation,* September 16.
"Dollar Chasers," *Saturday Evening Post,* October 17, 24, SS.

1932

"A Letter on Style," in Warner Taylor's *Types and Times in the Essay.*
Letter in *On the Meaning of Life,* ed. Will Durant.
Letter of introduction to "Address before Rutland Rotary Club," *Vermont Prose, a Miscellany.*
ANN VICKERS, serialized in *Redbook Magazine,* August, September, October, N.

1933

"The Art of Dramatization," *Sinclair Lewis's Dodsworth,* Dramatized by Sidney Howard, NF.
ANN VICKERS, January, N.

1934

WORK OF ART, January, N.
"In the Workshop of a Nobel Prize Novelist," *Saturday Review of Literature,* February 10, NF.
Letter in *The Bermudian,* March.
List of Books in "Good Books That Almost Nobody Has Read," *The New Republic,* April 18.
Review of Albert Halper's *The Foundry,* New York *Herald Tribune Books,* September 9.
Review of Henry S. Canby's *Age of Confidence, Saturday Review of Literature,* October 6.
"Last Word," New York *Times,* November 18, NF.

1935

Jayhawker, Play.
Introduction to *Selected Short Stories.*
"Seven Million Dollars," *This Week* (New York *Herald Tribune*), February 24, March 3, 10, 17, ss.
"This Golden Half-Century, 1885–1935," *Good Housekeeping,* May, NF.
"The Hippocratic Oath," *The Cosmopolitan,* June, ss.
"Proper Gander," *Saturday Evening Post,* July 13, ss.
"Onward, Sons of Ingersoll," *Scribner's Magazine,* August, ss.
IT CAN'T HAPPEN HERE, October, N.
"Christmas," *New Masses,* December 17, P.

1936

"Rambling Thoughts on Literature as a Business," *Yale Literary Magazine,* Centennial Number, February, NF.
"Back to Vermont," *Forum,* April, NF.
"Enemies of the Book," *Publisher's Weekly,* May 23, NF.
"Double Life for Writers," *Readers Digest,* October, NF.
"Pre-War, Post-War, Post-Crash America," review of Carl Van Doren's *Three Worlds,* New York *Herald Tribune Books,* September 20.
"Literary Felonies," *Saturday Review of Literature,* October 3, NF.

1937

Introduction to *MAIN STREET* (Limited Editions Club).
"That Was New York And That Was Me," *The New Yorker,* January 2, NF.
"Vamp in Violet," *The New Yorker,* January 16, (Profile).
Reviews in *Newsweek* under title "Book Week," October 4, 11, 18, 25, November 8, 15, 22, 29, December 6, 13, 20, 27.
"Breaking Into Print," *Colophon,* Winter, NF.

1938

It Can't Happen Here, Play.
PRODIGAL PARENTS, January, N.
Reviews in *Newsweek* under title of "Book Week," January 3 through April 18.
PRODIGAL PARENTS, condensed version, *Ladies' Home Journal,* September, N.

1939

"William Lyon Phelps," *Saturday Review of Literature,* April 1, NF.

1940

Foreword to David Cohn's *The Good Old Days.*
"Carry Your Own Suitcase," *This Week* (New York *Herald Tribune*), February 25, ss.
BETHEL MERRIDAY, March, N.
"Is This a Dagger—So What?" *This Week* (New York *Herald Tribune*), August 18, ss.

1941

"A Note on Book Collecting," *Samples* (Limited Editions Club), NF.
Footnote to *A Book of Prefaces* (Limited Editions Club), NF.
Preface to H. G. Wells's *The History of Mr. Polly* (Readers Club).
Preface to H. H. Richardson's *Fortunes of Richard Mahoney* (Readers Club).

"Fellow Trouper," *This Week* (New York *Herald Tribune*), February 2, SS.
"The Man Who Cheated Time," *Good Housekeeping,* March, SS.
"The Death of Arrowsmith," *Coronet,* July, NF.
"Manhattan Madness," *American Magazine,* September, SS.
"They Had Magic Then," *Liberty,* September 6, SS.
"Novelist Bites Art," New York *Times,* October 19, NF.
"My Most Important Decisions," *The Cosmopolitan,* November, NF.

1942

Preface to Bruno Frank's *The Days of the King* (Readers Club).
Preface to Paxton Hibben's *Henry Ward Beecher: An American Portrait* (Readers Club).
Preface to J. B. Priestley's *Angel Pavement* (Readers Club).
Introduction to *For Whom the Bell Tolls* (Limited Editions Club), November.
"Sinclair Lewis Defends Hollywood," *Motion Picture Magazine,* December, NF.

1943

Letter in Preface to *The Three Readers.* "Introductory Remarks" to Section II, *The Three Readers.*
Preface to Ivan Turgenev's *Fathers and Sons* (Readers Club).
Preface to E. H. Davis's *Giant Killer* (Readers Club).
Preface to Joseph Shearing's *The Golden Violet* (Readers Club).
"All Wives Are Angels," *The Cosmopolitan,* February, SS.
GIDEON PLANISH, April, N.
"Nobody to Write About," *The Cosmopolitan,* July, SS.
"Harri," *Good Housekeeping,* August, September, SS.
"Green Eyes: A Handbook of Jealousy," *The Cosmopolitan,* September, SS.

1944

"You Seem to Forget," *The Cosmopolitan,* January, SS.
"Fools, Liars and Mr. DeVoto," *Saturday Review of Literature,* April 15, NF.
"There's No Excuse for Lateness," *Good Housekeeping,* May, SS.
"Midnight Alley," *The Cosmopolitan,* July, August, SS.

1945

CASS TIMBERLANE, serialized in *The Cosmopolitan,* May through October, N.
Reviews in *Esquire,* June through December.
"The Artist, the Scientist, and the Peace," *American Scholar,* Summer, NF.
CASS TIMBERLANE, October, N.

1946

"Our Friend, H.G.," New York *Herald Tribune Books,* October 20, NF.

1947

Biographical Sketch for *History of the Class of 1907, Yale College.*
"I'm an Old Newspaper Man Myself," *The Cosmopolitan,* April, May, NF.
KINGSBLOOD ROYAL, May, N.
"A Note about *Kingsblood Royal,*" *Wings* (Literary Guild Review), June, NF.

1948

"No Flight to Olympus," *American People's Encyclopedia,* NF.
"Christmas Message," *The Cosmopolitan,* December, NF.

1949

Articles in New York *Journal American,* NF:
"Sinclair Lewis Finds Italy Tourist Haven," January 2.
"Sinclair Lewis Writes of His Travels in Italy," January 9.
"Sinclair Lewis Sees U.S. Girl's Triumph in Italy," January 16.
"Sinclair Lewis Warns against Travel Lingo," January 20.
"Sinclair Lewis Tours Farm of Horace," January 23.
"Sinclair Lewis Finds Italy Cramming English," February 6.
"Sinclair Lewis Finds Italy's Inns a Model for U.S. Hotels," February 13.
"Lewis Spots Left Bank Pair in Italy—Sponging," February 20.
"Two of Lewis' Friends Find Italy Like Home," February 27.
"U.S. Shack Life Better Than Palace in Rome," March 6.
THE GOD-SEEKER, March, N.
"Mr. Blethering," *Holiday,* May, SS.

1951

WORLD SO WIDE, serialized in *Woman's Home Companion,* January, February, N.
WORLD SO WIDE, March, N.

1952

New letters in *From Main Street to Stockholm: Letters of Sinclair Lewis, 1919–1930,* ed. Harrison Smith.

1953

The following Lewis material appeared in print for the first time in *The Man from Main Street,* ed. Harry Maule and Melville Cane:
"Suckling and Lovelace," written January 28, 1908, NF.
"The World Police," story plot, written 1910.
"Unpublished Introduction to *BABBITT,*" written 1920 or 1921.
"Self-Portrait," written August 1927.
"Self-Portrait," written for Nobel Foundation, 1930.
"My First Day in New York," written 1936; (unedited version of "That Was New York And That Was Me."
"Early Publishing Days," written October 23, 1946; condensed version appeared in Doubleday *Book News,* 1947.
"The Great Recorder: An Impression of Carl Van Doren," written 1947.
Three story plots in "Jack London's Use of Sinclair Lewis Plots, Together with a Printing of Three of the Plots," Franklin Walker, *Huntington Library Quarterly,* November.

1954

Excerpts from "And Lo It Came to Pass," Yale *Gazette,* July, written December 25, 1909, Christmas booklet for the Benéts.

1955

New letters in *With Love from Gracie,* Grace Hegger Lewis.

Index

About the Author

Mark Schorer was born in Wisconsin in 1908. Educated at the University of Wisconsin and Harvard, he has been writing and teaching simultaneously for more than twenty-five years. He is the author of three novels, *A House Too Old* (1935), *The Hermit Place* (1941), and *The Wars of Love* (1954), and has published well over fifty short stories in *The New Yorker* and other magazines, thirty-two of which were collected under the title *The State of Mind* (1947). He has also published a long critical study called *William Blake: The Politics of Vision,* various anthologies and text-books, and has written many critical essays and reviews. He has held three Guggenheim Fellowships, a Fulbright Grant to Italy, a Bollingen Fellowship, an American Philosophical Society grant, a grant from the American Council of Learned Societies, and a Fellowship at the Center for Advanced Studies at Stanford, California. Many of these fellowships were awarded to enable the author to complete *Sinclair Lewis: An American Life.* Mr. Schorer has taught at the University of Wisconsin, Dartmouth, and Harvard, and is currently chairman of the English Department at the University of California, Berkeley, where he has taught since 1945. By arrangement with the estate of Sinclair Lewis, all of Lewis's journals, letters, manuscripts, and records of every kind were made available to Mr. Schorer for his exclusive use in connection with this biography. The publication of *Sinclair Lewis: An American Life* is the culmination of nine years of research and writing by Mark Schorer.